WHAT IS THE INDIE BIBLE?

The Indie Bible is a valuable promotional tool for Independent Musicians and Songwriters that lists:

- 4200 publications that will REVIEW your music!
- 3400 radio stations that will PLAY your songs!
- 600 services that will help you to SELL your music!
- 350 sites where you can upload your band's MP3s or videos!
- ...and 52 articles that will help your music career to SUCCEED!

ALL styles of music are covered!

Pop, Rock, Hip Hop, Folk, Blues, Classical, Jazz, Punk, ALL Metals, Latin, Indie Rock, Electronic, Experimental, Christian, Dance, World Music, Soul, R&B, Women in Music, Country, Rap, Roots, Bluegrass, Reggae, Ska, Rockabilly, Ambient, emo, Gothic, Industrial, Progressive Rock, Alternative, Americana, oi, Jam Band, Hardcore, Garage, House, Trip Hop, Celtic, EBM, Sacred, Gospel, Space Rock, Noise, Alt Country, Children's, New Age, Singer/Songwriter.

The Indie Bible also provides you with 52 insightful articles that will help you to succeed!

Articles Include

- **How to Submit Your Music for Review**
- **How to Get Radio Airplay**
- **Getting Your Music into Film**
- **How to Market Your Music**
- **Why You Need an Entertainment Lawyer**
- **Band and Press Kit Essentials**
- **How Royalties Work**
- **How to Copyright Your Music**

and MANY more!

NOW – reduced pricing... EVEN MORE Radio & XM Satellite exposure, free website and a NO-OBLIGATION FREE CD just for inquiring!

You've probably already heard about the best place to manufacture your disc

So c'mon—give us a call!

You've more than likely already heard—from your fellow musicians, the BBB, and independent reviewers—that Oasis offers the most reliable and innovative CD and DVD manufacturing and marketing services.

So isn't it time for you to give us a call?

We think it is—if you've put your heart and soul into your project. And you want the discs and packaging you send out into the world to truly reflect (or even improve upon) your original vision. And you need help with the crucial task of getting people out there to actually <u>hear</u> your music.

Because if that describes your situation, may we suggest what it calls for?

It calls for Oasis.

CD MANUFACTURING

web oasisCD.com
tel (888) 296-2747, (540) 987-8810
email info@oasisCD.com

Oasis is the only national disc manufacturing company certified by both The Better Business Bureau and BBBonline.

FREE MONEY-MAKING CD:
"How to Have a Successful CD Release Party...Without Breaking the Bank!"

Just call **(888)296-2747** or visit oasisCD.com/freeCD and enter code **IB**
(And if you want a free full-color catalog we'll throw that in too!)

Yes, your free disc will be a real CD, it just looks like a classic vinyl record! It uses black polycarbonate and actual grooved surfacing technology!

INCLUDED WITH YOUR CD or DVD PROJECT—THE OASIS TOP™ TOOLS OF PROMOTION:

| Your Music on an OasisSampler™ Distributed to Radio Nationwide | XM Satellite Radio Airplay | Galaris/Oasis CD-ROM with 14,000+ Music Industry Contacts | Distribution for your CD/DVD: iTunes Music Store, amazon.com, cdbaby.com, TOWER.COM, BORDERS.com, Waldenbooks.com | A **Full Year** of Electronic Press Kit® Service and Exclusive Live Performance Opportunities: | SoundScan®, Music-Career Software, Retail Cases, Barcodes | **FREE** Website with the features musicians need! |

6 months free, no obligation!

What people are saying about The Indie Bible...

"My press kit is full of positive press from around the WORLD because of The Indie Bible."
— **Terry Christopher, Award Winning Singer/Songwriter**

"All the artists I work with personally are required to have a copy."
— **Tim Sweeney, author of "Tim Sweeney's Guide To Releasing Independent Records"**

"The Indie Bible provides a great service for artists and radio programmers"
— **Kate Borger, WYEP Radio**

"I can't thank you enough for this amazing summary of all your hard work and dedication. My heartfelt appreciation."
— **David Culiner, LovethisLife**

"It's great! The articles alone are worth the price."
— **Beau Wadsworth, Recording Artist**

"I bought the Indie Bible, and am still overwhelmed by it!"
— **Michael Grady, The Strange Angels**

"Thanks for bringing us such a great guide ...over and over again!"
— **Joe Colburn, GotBlack.com**

"This book is stuffed FULL of amazing tips and articles!"
— **Naomi DeBruyn, Linear Reflections**

"Just got the Indie Bible...AWESOME!!"
— **Dax Wadley, The Soul Elephant**

MAJOR LEAGUE REPLICATION

Little League Prices

Media Services, your one stop shop for CD / DVD replication, printing and packaging. Bring your next CD or DVD project into the BIG LEAGUES with our top of the line pressing and printing services. At Media Services, our reps will make sure your project is the CLEAN UP HITTER in any lineup.

Services we offer since 1997:

CD's, DVD's, CDR's, Tapes, Graphic Design, Posters, Low Prices, Major Label Quality, 1x Speed Glass Available, Free Barcodes

Don't forget our distribution partnerships with CD Baby and Bathtub Music *(free to you when you run your 1,000 piece project with us)!!*

Contact us today at:

1-888-891-9091 or sales@mediaomaha.com. Mention this code **(IB2005)** to receive over $100 in promotional items for your band.

www.mediaomaha.com

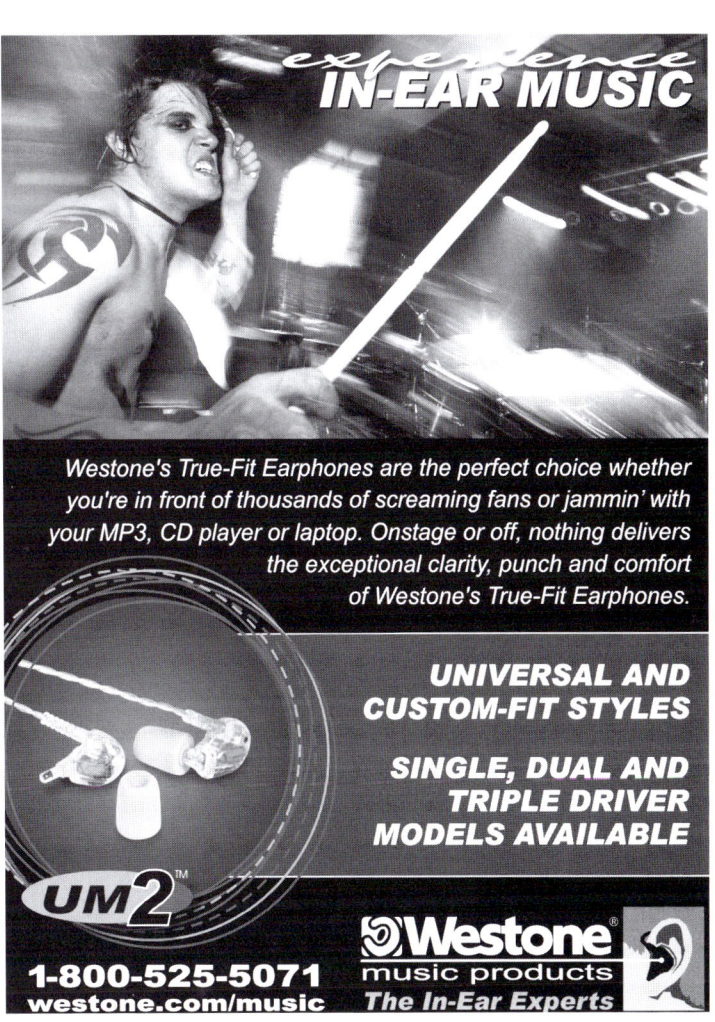

TABLE OF CONTENTS

SECTION ONE: REVIEWERS OF INDEPENDENT MUSIC

Mainstream Publications 1
- North America 1
- South America 13
- Europe 13
- Australia 17
- Asia 17

Blues 17
- North America 17
- Europe 17
- Asia 18

Children's 18

Christian 18
- North America 18
- Europe 19

Classical 19
- North America 19
- Europe 20
- Australia 21
- Asia 21

Country 21
- North America 21
- Europe 22
- Australia 23

Dance 23
- North America 23
- Europe 24
- Australia 25

Experimental 25
- North America 25
- Europe 26

Folk 27
- North America 27
- Europe 28
- Australia 29

GLBT 29

Goth 29
- North America 29
- Europe 30

Hip Hop 32
- North America 32
- Europe 34
- Australia 34
- Africa 34

Jam Band 35

Jazz 35
- North America 35
- Europe 36
- Asia 36

Latin 36

Metal 37
- North America 37
- South America 40
- Europe 41
- Australia 46
- Asia 46

New Age 46

Progressive Rock 46
- North America 46
- South America 47
- Europe 47

Punk 48
- North America 48
- Europe 51
- Africa 52

Reggae 53

Soul / R&B 53

Women in Music 54

World Music 55

SECTION TWO: "REGIONAL" PUBLICATIONS AND RESOURCES

- North America 57
- Europe 117
- Australia 121

SECTION THREE: RADIO STATIONS AND SHOWS THAT ARE WILLING TO PLAY INDEPENDENT MUSIC

Promotional Services 125

Stations that Play a Variety of Genres 127
- North America 127
- South America 146
- Europe 146
- Australia 152
- Asia 153

Internet Radio, Syndicated Shows and Podcasts 153

Blues Radio 158

Children's Radio 159

Christian Radio 160

Classical Radio 163
- North America 163
- Europe 166
- Australia 167

Country Radio 167
- North America 167
- Europe 172
- Australia 173

Dance Radio 173
- North America 173
- Europe 175
- Australia 176

Experimental Radio 176
- North America 176
- Europe 177
- Australia 177

Folk Radio 178
- North America 178
- Europe 184
- Australia 185

GLBT Radio 185

Goth Radio 186
- North America 186
- Europe 187
- Australia 188

Hip Hop Radio 188
- North America 188
- Europe 190
- Africa 190

Jam Band Radio 190

Jazz Radio 190
- North America 190
- Europe 196
- Australia 197

Latin Radio 197

Metal Radio 198
- North America 198
- Europe 200
- Australia 200

New Age Radio 201

Progressive Rock Radio 203
- North America 203
- Europe 204

Punk Radio 204
- North America 204
- Europe 205

Reggae Radio 206

Soul / R&B Radio 207

Women in Music Radio 208
- North America 208
- Europe 212
- Australia 212

World Radio 212

Radio Shows that Spotlight Local Musicians 214
- North America 214
- Europe 225
- Australia 226

continued on page viii

Stop drooling. Start playing!
You need the whole system? You can have it all NOW!

Apply today * and buy with Special Financing!
Visit www.musiciansfriend.com/plat to apply.

SOURCE CODE: BBEYGE

No Need to Wait!

With your Platinum Card you can put together that dream studio right now and pay for it in low minimum, easy monthly payments. Your purchases require no hefty down payment—just make the minimum monthly payment or any additional amount you choose.

You can begin using your Platinum Membership immediately upon approval. Apply online today at www.musiciansfriend.com/plat.

- Online applications may be made between 4:00am and 10:30pm PST.
- Offer valid in continental U.S., Alaska, and Hawaii only.
- Must be 18 or older to apply.

FREE Catalog! 1-800-436-7157

* Subject to Credit Approval by GE Money Bank.

SECTION FOUR: SERVICES THAT WILL HELP YOU TO SELL YOUR MUSIC

Promotional Services 229
Vendors & Labels 234
    North America 234
    Europe 246
    Australia 248
    Africa 248
    Asia 248
Blues 248
Children's 248
Christian 249
Classical 250
    North America 250
    Europe 251
    Asia 251
Country 251
Dance 252
Experimental 253
Film and TV 253
Folk 254
GLBT 255
Goth 255
Hip Hop 255
Jamband 257
Jazz 258
Latin 258
Metal 258
New Age 259
Progressive Rock 260
Punk 260
Reggae 261
Soul/R&B 261
Women In Music 262
World 263

SECTION FIVE: SITES THAT WILL ALLOW YOU TO UPLOAD YOUR MUSIC OR VIDEO FILES

All Styles 264
    North America 264
    South America 273
    Europe 273
    Australia 274
    Asia 275
Blues 275
Christian 275
Classical 275
Country 275
Dance 275
Experimental 276
Folk 276
GLBT 276
Goth 276
Hip Hop 276
Jam Band 277
Jazz 277
Latin 277
Metal 277
New Age 278
Punk 278
Reggae 278
Soul / R&B 278
Women In Music 278
World 278

SECTION SIX: HELPFUL RESOURCES FOR MUSICIANS AND SONGWRITERS

General Resources 279
Databases 287
Equipment, Merch & Software 288
Legal Resources 291
Organizations 291
Songwriting Resources 293
Blues 293
Children's 294
Christian 294
Classical 294
    North America 294
    Europe 296
Country 296
Dance 297
Experimental 297
Film and TV 297
Folk 297
GLBT 298
Goth 298
Hip Hop 298
Jam Band 298
Jazz 299
Latin 299
Metal 299
New Age 299
Progressive Rock 299
Punk 299
Reggae 299
Soul / R&B 300
Women in Music 300
World Music 301

SECTION SEVEN: HELPFUL ARTICLES 304

overview

STAYING AHEAD OF THE CURVE: MOLDING YOUR MUSIC CAREER FOR MAXIMUM IMPACT
by Peter Spellman 304

CREATING AN INDIE BUZZ
by Daylle Deanna Schwartz 306

radio airplay

GETTING RADIO AIRPLAY
by Lord Litter 306

RADIO AIRPLAY 101 - COMMERCIAL AIRPLAY MYTHS
by Bryan Farrish 307

INDEPENDENT RADIO PROMOTER CHECKLIST
by Bryan Farrish 307

INTERNET RADIO: THE AFFORDABLE ALTERNATIVE
by Nathan Fisher 308

ALTERNATIVE RADIO TRENDS AND WHAT THEY MEAN TO YOU
by Liz Koch 309

KNOWING THE DIFFERENCE BETWEEN GOOD PR AND BAD PR
by John Foxworthy 309

getting your music reviewed

HOW TO SUBMIT MUSIC FOR REVIEW
by Jodi Krangle 311

INSIDE THE HEAD OF A MUSIC REVIEWER
by Suzanne Glass 312

WHY MOST DEMO RECORDINGS ARE REJECTED
by Christopher Knab 314

tools

WHAT ARE PERFORMANCE RIGHTS ORGANIZATIONS?
by Jer Olsen 314

UPC & BARCODES FOR PENNIES AND SENSE
by Lygia Ferra 315

SO, WHAT'S THE SCOOP WITH ELECTRONIC PRESS KITS?
by Panos Panay 315

continued on page x

WRITING A BAND BIO
by Suzanne Glass..................................316

WHY MAILING LISTS ARE SO IMPORTANT
by Vivek J. Tiwary................................317

DESIGNING YOUR CD COVER
by Valerie Michele Hoskins 318

THE IMPORTANCE OF MERCHANDISING
by Bronson Herrmuth 319

LEARN THE IMPORTANT SKILLS
by Derek Sivers 319

WEBSITE BASICS FOR THE SINGER/SONGWRITER
by Valerie DeLaCruz 320

BUILDING A MUSIC SITE THAT SELLS: PROMOTE YOUR CD, NOT YOURSELF
by Mihkel Raud....................................320

MUSIC VIDEOS FOR INDEPENDENT ARTISTS AND LABELS
by Allen M. Gottfried...........................321

technical

STREAMING YOUR MP3 FILES
by Luke Sales......................................322

PREPARING YOUR DEMO TO MAKE IT BIG
by Garrett Haines 322

HOW TO CREATE AND MANUFACTURE YOUR MUSIC
by Hadas 324

legal

HOW TO COPYRIGHT YOUR MUSIC
by Nancy Falkow 325

HOW TO TRADEMARK YOUR BAND NAME
by Derek Sivers 325

TRADEMARKING YOUR LOGO
by Vivek J. Tiwary and Gary L. Kaplan........325

ENTERTAINMENT INDUSTRY LAWYERS: WHO, WHERE AND HOW MUCH?!
by Wallace Collins 326

ROYALTIES IN THE MUSIC BUSINESS
by Joyce Sydnee Dollinger 327

ARTIST-MANAGEMENT CONTRACTS
by Richard P. Dieguez.........................327

THE WRITTEN AGREEMENT AMONGST BAND MEMBERS
by John Tormey III...............................328

marketing and promotion

THE 10 RULES OF SUCCESSFUL INDEPENDENT MUSICIANS
by Nyree Belleville..............................329

HOW TO BE YOUR OWN PUBLICIST
by Ariel Hyatt.......................................330

SELLING YOUR MUSIC ONLINE - A REALITY CHECK
by David Nevue...................................331

FOUR WAYS TO ATTRACT MORE MUSIC FANS FASTER
by Bob Baker.......................................333

MUSIC MARKETING STRATEGIES
by Derek Sivers 334

THE BASICS OF BOOKING YOUR OWN TOURS
by Jay Flanzbaum 335

distribution

PREPARING FOR DISTRIBUTION
by Daylle Deanna Schwartz................337

25 THINGS TO REMEMBER ABOUT RECORD DISTRIBUTION
by Christopher Knab 337

WHY AND WHEN IS CONSIGNMENT BETTER THAN DISTRIBUTION?
by Tim Sweeney..................................338

SUCCEEDING WITHOUT A LABEL
by Bernard Baur..................................338

the music business

WHAT IS A BUSINESS PLAN AND WHY DO YOU NEED ONE
by John Stiernberg 340

10 KEY BUSINESS PRINCIPLES
by Diane Rapaport 341

LOOKING FOR AN AGENT
by Jeri Goldstein..................................342

FINDING A SPONSOR
by Bronson Herrmuth 342

getting your music into film and television

GETTING YOUR MUSIC INTO FILM
by Scooter Johnson 343

USING INDEPENDENT FILM AS A TECHNIQUE FOR MORE EXPOSURE
by Ryan Vinson 344

motivational articles

DEALING WITH REJECTION IN THE MUSIC BUSINESS
by Suzanne Glass 345

THE PROCESS AND POWER OF PERSISTENCE
by Brian Austin Whitney 345

BABY STEPS AND THE ROAD TO SUCCESS
by Chris Standring...............................346

SO HOW DO WE MAKE OUR DREAM BECOME REALITY?
by Janet Fisher 348

Sign up for *The Indie Contact Newsletter!*

Every month you will receive a new list of places to send your music for review, radio play etc.

Sennheiser is donating an **E835** microphone and a pair of HD280Pro headphones for our monthly draw.

To sign up visit www.indiebible.com or send an e-mail to indiebible@rogers.com with the word "draw" in the Subject field.

Helping musicians gain exposure and sell more CDs since 1997. Join us!

www.PlanetCD.com

Thirsty Melon Music Tour 2005
PRESENTS
5th Annual Six Flags Kentucky Kingdom Music Festival & Conference

June 22-25, 2006
Six Flags Kentucky Kingdom
& Various Locations around Louisville

Tomorrow's Bands for Today's Fans

Thirsty Melon Music Tour is for music fans whose minds are free enough to choose their own music from cutting edge artists who dare to be different.

*4 Days
*Over 10 Stages
*Over 200 Cutting Edge Artists
*Over 30,000 Fans

FREE YOUR MIND
AND
YOU'LL FREE
THE MUSIC!

Visit www.ThirstyMelon.com for details

ALL MUSICAL INSTRUMENTS
THE NATION'S LARGEST SELECTION AT THE NATION'S GUARANTEED LOWEST PRICES!

NEW YORK CITY, NY	(212) 719-2299	CLEVELAND (LYNDHURST), OH	(440) 446-0850
HUNTINGTON STA, NY	(631) 421-9333	SPRINGDALE, OH	(513) 671-4500
FOREST HILLS, NY	(718) 793-7983	WESTMINSTER, CA	(714) 899-2122
WHITE PLAINS, NY	(914) 949-8448	ONTARIO MILLS, CA	(909) 484-3550
BROOKLYN, NY	(718) 951-3888	CERRITOS, CA	(562) 468-1107
CARLE PLACE, NY	(516) 333-8700	CANOGA PARK, CA	(818) 709-5650
PARAMUS, NJ	(201) 843-0119	WEST HOLLYWOOD, CA	(323) 654-4922
EDISON, NJ	(732) 572-5595	HOLLYWOOD, CA	(323) 850-1050
CHERRY HILL, NJ	(856) 667-6696	CITY OF INDUSTRY, CA	(626) 839-8177
SPRINGFIELD, NJ	(973) 376-5161	TORRANCE, CA	(310) 214-0340
MIAMI LAKES, FL	(305) 628-3510	NEW HAVEN, CT	(203) 389-0500
MIAMI, FL	(786) 331-9688	BURBANK, IL	(708) 499-3485
MARGATE, FL	(954) 975-3390	BUFFALO GROVE, IL	(847) 253-3151
TAMPA, FL	(813) 908-5556	LOMBARD, IL	(630) 424-0767
SARASOTA, FL	(941) 351-7793	NASHVILLE (MADISON), TN	(615) 860-7475
CLEARWATER, FL	(727) 725-8062	LAS VEGAS, NV	(702) 734-0007
ORLANDO, FL	(407) 599-1222	CHARLOTTE, NC	(704) 522-9253
ORLANDO (COLONIAL MALL), FL	(407) 896-5508	RALEIGH, NC	(919) 855-9581
PHILADELPHIA, PA	(215) 612-1339	RICHMOND, VA	(804) 967-0707
KING OF PRUSSIA, PA	(610) 265-6444	INDIANAPOLIS (CASTLETON), IN	(317) 577-3006
COLUMBUS, OH	(614) 436-3919	SAN ANTONIO, TX	(210) 530-9777

www.samashmusic.com — Over 45 Stores NATIONWIDE!

GUITARS • AMPS • PRO AUDIO • DJ GEAR • DIGITAL KEYBOARDS • DRUMS • PERCUSSION
MUSIC SOFTWARE • BRASS & WOODWINDS • SHEET MUSIC • RENTALS • REPAIRS & MORE!

If your website SUCKS
...we didn't do it.

Update your own content!
on the road... day or night... no designer fees...
if you can type, you can do it.

✓ user-updatable pages
✓ one-of-a-kind designs
✓ first class hosting
✓ musician-friendly prices

MENTION INDIE BIBLE AND GET 10% OFF!

RockAndRollDesign.com
-sites that kick ass.

Hear what we have to offer...

ALANNA RECORDS

www.alannarecords.com

SAY IT WITH YOUR MUSIC.   pro·mark

promark.com

COVER DESIGN
Warrior Girl Music www.warriorgirlmusic.com based on acrylic painting "the color hole" by gilli moon

ARTISTS PICTURED
(From top left to right)
i94 www.i94music.com Photo by: Bernard Baur
breech (lead singer Missy Gibson) www.breech.net Photo by: jcsproductions.com
Dina Gathe www.dinagathe.com Photo unknown

(Centre) Jennifer Corday www.corday.net Photo by Ed Spyra

(Bottom left to right)
gilli moon www.gillimoon.com Left Photo by Penelope Torribio. Second to left by Bernard Baur
Deborah Bishop www.deborahbishop.net Photo by Bill Shotland
gilli moon - photo 2nd to right by Penelope Torribio
Gordie Germaine (gilli moon band) - photo by Bernard Baur

CONTACTS ONLY. (not credits. see above for credits)
i94 management@i94music.com   www.i94music.com   Photographer: Bernard Baur EqxManLtd@aol.com
Deborah Bishop debroar@comast.net   www.deborahbishop.net Photographer: Bill Shotland
breech c/o Danny Hughes dorgelo48@yahoo.com www.breech.net.. Photographer: jcsproductions.com
Jennifer Corday corday@envyrecords.com   www.corday.net   Photographer Ed Spyra ed@deltamusic.com
Dina Gathe dina@soundstruck.com   www.dinagathe.com
gilli moon info@warriorgirlmusic.com www.gillimoon.com Photographers: Bernard Baur EqxManLtd@aol.com, Penelope Torribio mythra@earthlink.net

Copyright © 2005 by Big Meteor Publishing

This edition published 2005 by Schirmer Trade Books,
an imprint for the Music Sales Publishing Group

All rights reserved. No part of this book may be reproduced
in any form or by any electronic or mechanical means, including
information storage and retrieval systems, without permission
in writing from the publisher.

Order No. BM 70000
ISBN 0-9686214-5-7

Exclusive Distributors
Music Sales Corporation
257 Park Avenue South, New York, NY 10010 USA
Music Sales Limited
8/9 Frith Street, London W1D 3JB England
Music Sales Pty. Limited
120 Rothschild Street, Rosebery, Sydney NSW 2018 Australia

Printed in Canada by Bradda Printing Services Inc.

CDs in 10 days. Any questions?

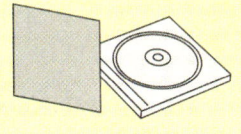

Price includes CDs in jewel boxes with full-color, one-page inserts and tray cards, three-color on-disc printing, and poly wrap.

1,000 CDs IN JEWEL BOXES JUST $1,290!

You can have top quality, retail-ready CDs in just 10 business days. Start to finish. It's just one of the benefits of working with the only company that manufactures and prints all their CDs in their own factory. All our packages are complete, with no hidden charges, and include our exclusive promotional tools, like six months' free web hosting, free online distribution, a free UPC barcode, a review from TAXI, and much more. So while it may have taken you 10 weeks (or 10 months) to record your album, isn't it reassuring to know that the industry's best-looking and sounding CDs are only 10 days away?

DISC MAKERS®
CD AND DVD MANUFACTURING MADE EASY.

Call 1-866-490-7928 or visit www.discmakers.com/indiebible to get your FREE catalog.

TIPS ON USING THE INDIE BIBLE

How the listings are sorted

a) **TYPE OF SERVICE** (Publications, Radio Stations, CD Vendors etc.)
  b) **Genre of Music**
    c) **Geographic Location**

The listings are set up this way so that you can quickly find a *specific* service in a *specific* area for a *specific* style of music. *ie:* Finding a **Hip Hop** magazine in **England** that will **review** your music.

How the various styles of resources are sorted

1. If a publication welcomes submissions from MANY genres, that publication will be listed in the **Mainstream** section. Publications in the Mainstream section welcome a *wide variety* of music, but usually nothing too extreme. Common genres in this section are Pop, Rock, Indie Rock etc.

2. There is an unavoidable amount of *Genre Overflow* from section to section. For instance, if you are in a Punk band, you will not only find sites that will review your music in the **Punk** Section, but you will also find several sites that welcome your style of music in the **Metal** and **Goth** Sections.

Most publications review more than one style of music. The sites listed in the Indie Bible are placed in their respective sections based on the musical style that publication lists as their preference. For instance, if a publication states that they welcome **Folk, Blues and Jazz** music, that publication would be listed in the **Folk Music** section, because "Folk" was the first genre mentioned.

3. Quiz: Where would you find a listing for a magazine that reviews the music of **Christian Women New Age** artists that live in the **Chicago** area? Would you find it in the

  a. Christian Music section?
  b. New Age Music section?
  c. Women in Music section?
  d. The Local Music section under "Chicago"?

The answer is "d", the **Local Music** section. I'm using this example to point out that the Local Music section overrides all other characteristics of any given resource. If it is a resource that provides a service for a *specific* area (country, city, town, state, province) then that resource is listed in the Local Music section (ie: a resource for Country Music bands based in Montana).

The Indie Bible is arranged this way so that you can look at the listings in your area to find out what kind of help is available for you locally. Please make sure to check out the Local Music section for your area. You will be surprised at how many resources there are in your community that are willing to help you out.

4. The majority of the stations listed in the **Mainstream Radio** section are College or University stations that have a weekly show catering to EVERY style of music, both mild and extreme (Country, Pop, Hip Hop, Death Metal, Goth, Classical etc), so make sure that you CHECK THEM ALL.

About the articles

Before you start contacting the various resources listed in the Indie Bible, I *STRONGLY RECOMMEND* that you read the articles in **SECTION 7** to better understand how to submit your music for review, radio airplay etc. These articles are written by industry professionals who have a *wealth* of experience. They know what works, what doesn't work – and why. Reading the articles in SECTION 7 will save you an ENORMOUS amount of time and money, and will help your career to move in a positive direction. In other words, you won't have to make the same mistakes that I and many others have made while trying to survive in the music business. Please take the time to read these articles. You will be glad that you did!

PLEASE READ THIS!!

I have received several complaints from music reviewers and radio hosts about high number of e-mails they are receiving **that have nothing to do with the style of music that their publication or radio show promotes.** PLEASE DO NOT SEND OUT MASS E-MAILINGS to the sites listed in this book telling them about your new product or upcoming shows etc.

Also, do not send out your CD to **everyone** listed in the book. Instead of sending your CDs out to everyone on the planet, take the time to read through The Indie Bible to find out who is looking *specifically* for the style of music that you play.

Put yourself in the position of a Magazine Editor. Let's say, for example, you are the Editor of a magazine that deals with **Folk Music**. How irritating would it be getting continually blasted with e-mails from artists in **Metal** and **Punk** bands asking you to review their CD? How would you feel each day as you grab the armful of CDs from your PO Box and find that about 1 in 30 are actually Folk CDs? Marketing this way is a waste of their time, and a waste of your money.

Note that there are **52** articles in this edition. You will not find in ANY of the **52** articles, a Radio Host or Magazine Editor saying that a *good* way for an artist to make initial contact is by sending out *mass e-mailings*. They all say the same thing, which is "take the time to do some research, and THEN contact the various services personally". These are human beings you're dealing with. The recipient of your personal e-mail will respect the time you have put in to find out about them, and most often will get back to you quickly. On the other hand, a mass mailing request is an insult to him/her, and that e-mail will be deleted immediately. The CDs you send in that do not fit their style will be angrily tossed away into the garbage.

The extra time you put in to do a bit of research, and to personalize your first contact, will pay off for you in a big way in the end!

Final notes

Please contact me with information on any broken links, outdated sites or mistakes of any kind. They will be addressed right away. Also, feel free to send your comments and suggestions to me. ALL suggestions will be taken into consideration. Thanks to your input, the Indie Bible continues to grow with each new edition.

I hope by utilizing the many contacts found in this book that you make some solid progress with your career. If you feel that you made a worthwhile investment by purchasing the Indie Bible, please tell your friends about it.

I wish you the very best with your music!

David Wimble
Editor, The Indie Bible
www.indiebible.com
Phone: 800-306-8167
indiebible@rogers.com

The Healthy Way to Good Promotion!!
It's Vinyl Stickers!

While no vinyl sticker can prevent disease, they can help to get your band, business, club or event noticed. Stickers are cost effective and should be a part of a good promotion or advertising package. Here are some sample prices of just a few of the types of vinyl stickers we offer online at www.123stickers.com

BLACK & WHITE STICKERS

	125	250	500	1000
4.25" X 1.38"	$14	$23	$46	$92
4.25" X 2.75"	$18	$32	$64	$128
4.25" X 4.25"	$34	$61	$122	$189
2.75" X 2.75"	$15	$23	$46	$92
5.5" X 1.75"	$17	$30	$60	$120
3.5" X 2"	$15	$25	$50	$100
7.5" X 2"	$27	$52	$104	$208
8.5" X 2.75"	$34	$61	$122	$144

Black ink screenprinted on 3.25 mil white vinyl. Black background / full bleed OK. Price includes film/setup; shipping additional.

RED & BLACK STICKERS

	250	500	1000
4.25" X 1.38"	$31	$53	$106
4.25" X 2.75"	$34	$61	$122
4.25" X 5.5"	$84	$160	$295
2.75" X 2.75"	$36	$62	$124
5.5"X 1.75"	$42	$68	$136
5.5" X 2.75"	$59	$105	$210
8.5" X 1.38"	$48	$84	$168

Red and Black ink screenprinted on 3.25 mil white vinyl. Full bleed images & backgrounds OK. Price includes film and setup; shipping additional.

It's Great Fun!

ORDER STICKERS.

OPEN PACKAGE.

PEEL AND STICK.

CUSTOM 1 AND 2 COLOR STICKERS

	250	500	1000
4.25" X 1.38" 1C	$86	$89	$124
4.25" X 1.38" 2C	$128	$132	$185
4.25" X 2.75" 1C	$138	$144	$162
4.25" X 2.75" 2C	$206	$214	$241
4.25" X 4.25" 1C	$152	$162	$243
4.25" X 4.25" 2C	$226	$241	$361
2.75" X 2.75" 1C	$115	$118	$138
2.75" X 2.75" 2C	$171	$175	$205
5.5" X 1.75" 1C	$127	$134	$149
5.5" X 1.75" 2C	$188	$199	$222

Standard ink colors printed on 3.25 mil white vinyl. PMS color match $45 ea. Additional ink colors and vinyls available. Price includes film and setup; shipping is additional.

We've got lots more sizes and styles of stickers online at www.123stickers.com including die-cut stickers, full-color digital stickers, bass drum logos, cut vinyl decals, even full-color banners and backdrops!

Judas Rockin' Priest!! These new stickers saved my death metal band from total obscurity!

Start your day right with custom vinyl stickers. A good part of a well balanced and nutritious promotional program.

123stickers.com
Toll Free 877-778-4253 sales@123stickers.com

You made it to the gig. Too bad your guitar didn't.

MusicPro INSURANCE® FOR Music Pros

MusicPro Insurance provides very affordable and convenient coverage for all your insurance needs.

Supported and endorsed by virtually every music organization.

**FOR A FREE PERSONALIZED QUOTE VISIT OUR WEBSITE:
WWW.MUSICPROINSURANCE.COM
OR CALL 800-605-3187.**

MUSICPRO INSURANCE IS A SERVICE MARK OF MUSICPRO INSURANCE AGENCY LLC, A LICENSED AGENT AND BROKER. COVERAGE AVAILABLE WHERE LICENSED. FOR A FULL LIST OF COVERAGE AREAS SEE OUR WEBSITE.

SECTION ONE: REVIEWERS OF INDEPENDENT MUSIC

"What impresses me most about an artist is the quality of their music. A very close second is their professionalism and follow through."- Erik Deckers, Music Reviewer for Indie-Music.com

Mainstream Publications

Just to clarify, when I say mainstream, I'm not talking about Perry Como music. Mainstream is any sort of music that isn't too far "out there". That's not to say that publications in this section won't listen to all types of music, but they are more likely to enjoy Rock, Pop, Indie Rock etc. They are less likely to go for the Death Metal, Industrial, Hardcore etc….although some will accept those styles.

North America

United States

1340mag.com
PO Box 1347, Fairmont, WV 26555-1347
mark@1340mag.com
www.1340mag.com
We listen to and consider everything received.

20th Century Guitar
PH: 800-291-9687 FX: 631-434-9057
tcguitar@tcguitar.com
www.tcguitar.com
CD reviews and features.

30music.com
PO Box 3908, Minneapolis, MN 55403-9998
staff@30music.com
www.30music.com
We do our best to review everything received.

75 or Less
23 Laurel Ln. Warren, RI 02885
75orLess@slatch.com
www.75orless.com
Will review anything in less than 75 words.

ADDreviews
PO Box 650113, Sterling, VA 20165-0113
crew@addreviews.com
www.addreviews.com
All music reviews are 20 words or less. It's about brevity. Terseness. Conciseness. You get the idea.

Agouti Music
PO Box 4233, Hayward, CA 94540-4233
info@agoutimusic.com
www.agoutimusic.com
We listen to ALL submissions.

alt.culture.guide
826 Old Charlotte Pike E. Franklin, TN 37064
Rev. Keith A. Gordon reverendk@mondogordo.com
www.mondogordo.com
Promotes Indie artists and labels.

Alternative Addiction
400 E. 77th, 2L, New York, NY 10021
PH: 917-991-2756 FX: 336-778-0170
Dru Rajacich dru@alternativeaddiction.com
www.alternativeaddiction.com
Features spotlights unsigned bands by offering both CD reviews and the possibility to have your song listed in our Top 10.

Alternative Press
1305 W. 80th St. #2F, Cleveland, OH 44102-1996
PH: 216-631-1510 FX: 216-631-1016
Jonah Bayer editorial@altpress.com
www.altpress.com
News, reviews, new releases etc.

American Songwriter
50 Music Sq. W. #604, Nashville, TN 37203-3227
PH: 615-321-6096
info@americansongwriter.com
www.americansongwriter.com
Interviews, writing tips, industry news, reviews, lyric contests and more.

Amplifier
5 Calista Ter. Westford, MA 01886
PH: 978-846-1177
Joe Joyce JoeJ@AmplifierMagazine.com
www.amplifiermagazine.com
Focuses on Pop, Melodic Rock and Roots Rock.

audiogrid.com
Steve Ekblad c/o Omega Sales,
513 N. Wolf Rd. Wheeling, IL 60090
PH: 847-808-9200
FX: 847-808-9209
Steve Ekblad
se@audiogrid.com
www.audiogrid.com/music
I am an independent music reviewer that maintains a music enthusiast site with comprehensive music reviews.

Aural Minority
PO Box 6681,
Oceanside, CA 92052
PH: 714-914-6498
Jeremiah Griffey
jeremiahgriffey@gmail.com
www.auralminority.com
We are a weekly online magazine looking to promote innovative and intriguing new artists.

Auralgasms.com
Scott Zumberg
szumberg@auralgasms.com
www.auralgasms.com
Reviews, sound samples, bios, discographies, tour dates and links.

Aversion.com
PO Box 271556, Fort Collins, CO 80527-1556
PH: 970-493-0585
info@aversion.com
www.aversion.com
Submit your press kits and demos.

Babysue
PO Box 3360, Cleveland, TN 37320-3360
lmnop@babysue.com
www.babysue.com
Accepts recordings from major and Indie labels.

Bassics
21143 Hawthorne Blvd. #508, Torrance, CA 90503
PH: 310-782-8111
bassicsrg@aol.com
www.bassics.com
Each issue includes tracks from featured artists. All styles of music are covered.

BB Gun Magazine
PO Box 5074, Hoboken, NJ 07030
bbgunmagazine@aol.com
www.bbgun.org
Alternative literary digest featuring interviews with independent musicians.

BettaWreckonize
the_dogg@bettawreckonize.com
www.bettawreckonize.com
Contact us to send about sending in your CD for review.

Better Propaganda
539 Bryant St. #402, San Francisco, CA 94107
contact@betterpropaganda.com
www.betterpropaganda.com
Showcasing truly unique music.

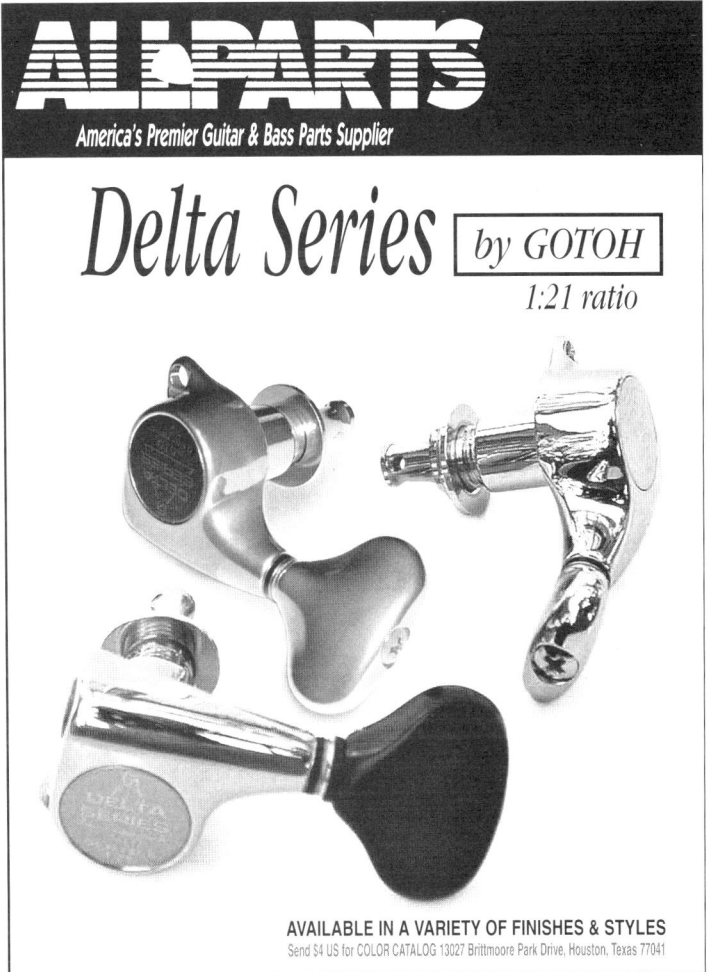

THERE'S A WORLD-WIDE MARKET FOR YOUR MUSIC !

Receive constant, up to date, info on labels, managers, publishers, and licensors that are in the market for all kinds of material, in the USA, England and World-wide!
Intro subscription deal - First 2 issues free on sign up

REQUEST YOUR FREE SAMPLE COPY OF THE

A&R Newsletter
Published for over 17 years

Email bandit.icb@aweber.com or Surf to www.banditnewsletter.com

---

ELECTRIC HEAD
MUSIC VIDEOS ★ COMMERCIALS ★ LIVE DVD'S ★ DUPLICATION ★ EPK'S

Award Winning Productions ... At Affordable Rates

Call Us Today To Discuss Your Next Project
(732) 901-8693
PO BOX 7 - HOWELL, NJ 07731
www.electricheadonline.com

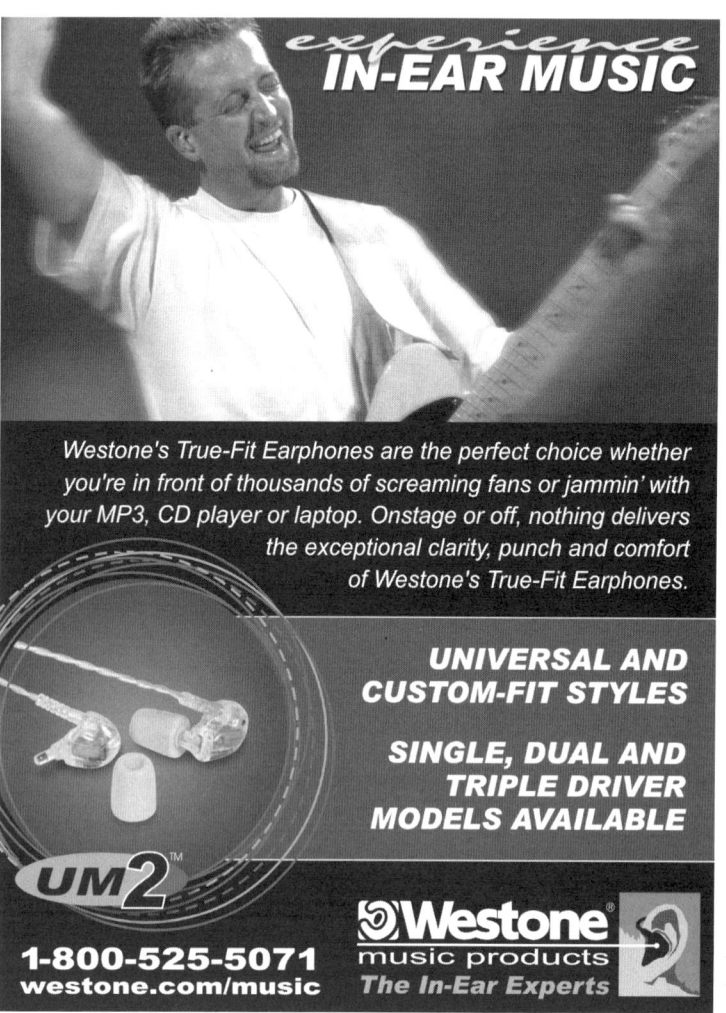

experience IN-EAR MUSIC

Westone's True-Fit Earphones are the perfect choice whether you're in front of thousands of screaming fans or jammin' with your MP3, CD player or laptop. Onstage or off, nothing delivers the exceptional clarity, punch and comfort of Westone's True-Fit Earphones.

UNIVERSAL AND CUSTOM-FIT STYLES

SINGLE, DUAL AND TRIPLE DRIVER MODELS AVAILABLE

UM2
1-800-525-5071
westone.com/music
Westone music products
The In-Ear Experts

Big Takeover
249 Eldridge St. #14,
New York, NY
10002-1345
PH: 212-533-6057
Jack Rabid
sexton@slf.com
www.bigtakeover.com
100 pages of Indie music reviews.

Billboard
770 Broadway,
New York, NY 10003
PH: 646-654-5549
Jonathan Cohen
jacohen@billboard.com
www.billboard.com
International newsweekly of music.

Blink Magazine
PO Box 104,
Oak Park, IL 60303
PH: 877-735-6885
FX: 877-735-6885
Tanya Lewis
tanya.lewis@blinkmag.com
www.blinkmag.com
Your online source for Entertainment. Life. Culture.

blue coupe
Linda Richards
editor@bluecoupe.com
www.bluecoupe.com
Open to interviewing you about your music.

Bornbackwards.com
2355 NW 95th Ter.
Coral Springs, FL 33065
submissions@bornbackwards.com
www.bornbackwards.com
We'll review just about anything.

Buddyhead
PO Box 1268,
Hollywood, CA 90078
FX: 801-684-1387
Travis Keller
travis@buddyhead.com
www.buddyhead.com
Can't even be defined at this point in the game.

buhdge
Alan Haber
alan@buhdge.com
www.buhdge.com
A pop culture juggernaut, raging fiercely through the tangled media net to get to the bottom of that which we hold dear: our favorite new and old music.

Burning Angel
chummy@Burningangel.net
www.burningangel.com
Labels, send your newest releases.

Buzzine.com
PO Box 18857, Encino, CA 91416-8857
PH: 818-995-6161 FX: 818-995-6136
www.buzzine.com
Interviews, concert reviews and up-to-date news.

CD Babel
Jeff Einowski cdbabel@cdbabel.com
www.cdbabel.com
We will review anyones CD so long as it is on CD Baby. That is our only criteria.

cdreviews.com
2929 NW Scenic Dr. Albany, OR 97321
PH: 877-576-0706
Seth Steiling editor@cdreviews.com
www.cdreviews.com
Are you in a band? Do you have a CD out? If so let us know.

The Cheers
thecheers@thecheers.org
www.thecheers.org
Entertainment, opinion, politics, extreme sports.

Circle Magazine
173 Grandview Rd. Wernersville, PA 19565
Penny Talbert circlemag@aol.com
www.circlemagazine.com
Artists can share, learn, grow and find something to connect with.

Cityzen Entertainment
Backoffice Box #230, 345 East 18th St.,
New York, NY 10003
PH: 212-260-0086 FX: 212-780-0579
Craig Cook Submissions@Cityzen.tv
www.cityzen.tv
We're always looking for new and exciting things to cover. If you are an artist, in a band, make films, take pictures, or have an event to tell us about, we want to know whats going down in your part of town.

CMJ New Music Report
151 W. 25th St. 12th Fl. New York, NY 10001
PH: 917-606-1908
www.cmj.com
All styles of music are welcome!

CoffeeHouseTour.com
3615-B St Johns Ct. Wilmington, NC 28403
Attn: CHT Review
PH: 910-793-1507
Annette Warner awarner@coffeehousetour.com
www.coffeehousetour.com
If you are a Coffee House Musician and would like for us to review your CD please forward it to the above address. You must be an act that will actually perform in coffee shops.

Cokemachineglow.com
Scott Reid sreid@cokemachineglow.com
www.cokemachineglow.com
Submit your stuff for review.

The Consensus
Andy Chapman admin@c0nsensus.com
www.c0nsensus.com
We provide brutally honest music reviews for all genres. Each song gets listened to by five different reviewers. The service is free.

concertlivewire.com
PO Box 5, Lake Geneva, WI 53147
PH: 262-949-8852
Tony Bonyata tonyb@concertlivewire.com
www.concertlivewire.com
Brutally honest CD reviews from new artists.

Copper Press
info@copperpress.com
www.copperpress.com
News, reviews, tours etc.

Cosmik Debris Magazine
editors@cosmik.com
www.cosmik.com
Hundreds of reviews of every kind of music.

Creative Line
PO Box 8496, La Crescenta, CA 91224
PH: 818-212-8219
info@artistshelpingartists.org
www.thecreativeline.us
www.artistshelpingartists.org
Send your CDs for review. Also sponsors the Call to Arts! Song & Music Competition.

CreatorsWeb Internet Publishing
Ken Mowery ken@creatorsweb.com
www.creatorsweb.com
Reviews independent musicians.

Creem Magazine
BrianJBowe@CreemMagazine.com
creemmedia.com
News, reviews, interviews and more.

Crud Music
editor@crudmusic.com
www.2-4-7-music.com
All solicited material mailed through to Crud will be reviewed and scheduled for inclusion on a ASAP basis

Crush Music Magazine
Jason Schleweis
jason.schleweis@crushmusicmag.com
www.crushmusicmag.com
News, reviews, interviews. To be considered for "Supporting the Scene" visit our website for submission details.

CTG Music Community
www.ctgmusic.com
Write reviews to get your songs listed.

The Cutting Edge
tkscutedge@aol.com
www.thecutting-edge.net
Rock's finest web magazine!

Dagger Zine
PO Box 820102, Portland, OR 97282-1102
daggerboy@prodigy.net
www.indiepages.com/dagger
Interviews, articles and hundreds of reviews.

Daily Vault
Jason Warburg jasonburg@aol.com
www.dailyvault.com
Reviewing music of all genres.

Daily Sentinel Web Blog Reviews
734 S. 7th St., Grand Junction, CO 81501
PH: 970-256-4269 FX: 970-244-8578
Beverly Durfee bdurfee@usa-navi.com
www.gjsentinel.com
Music reviews of both Indie and major label CDs. We review almost everything. No Christian, no Gangsta.

Deep Water Acres
315 Cindy Ct.
San Ramon, CA 94583
www.dwacres.com
News, reviews, interviews and rants.

Defy Magazine
631 N. Stephanie St. #136,
Henderson, NV 89014
PH: 702-265-9441
peter@defymagazine.com
www.defymagazine.com
Promoting today's bands, tomorrow's stars.

demo diaries
Gary Savelson
gary@demodiaries.com
www.demodiaries.com
A newsletter that critiques several artists each issue.

Demo Universe
c/o Jim Santo, PO Box 4218,
Sunnyside, NY 11104
www.demouniverse.com
Send your recording and whatever else.

demorama
300 Broadway #608,
St. Paul, MN 55101
Deneen Gannon
Demorama@visi.com
www.demorama.com
We review all genres. We also do online reviews.

Devil in the Woods
PO Box 579168,
Modesto, CA 95357
Mike Cloward
mc1@devilinthewoods.com
www.devilinthewoods.com
Independent thought on Independent music.

Dig This Real
244 5th Ave. #29037,
New York, NY 10001-7604
info@digthisreal.com
www.digthisreal.com
Accepts unsolicited material for review.

Dimestore Productions
PO Box 214, Madison, OH 44057
bands@dimestoreproductions.com
www.dimestoreproductions.com
We will review your music and post your MP3s.

Dirty Children dot US
becca@dirtychildren.us
www.dirtychildren.us
A youth oriented website for Underground music.

DiscoveringArtists.com
52 Rogers Ave. 2nd Fl. Manasquan, NJ 08736
dan@discoveringartists.com
www.discoveringartists.com
Giving emerging artists a place to get heard..

Drawer B
PO Box 11726, Columbia, SC 29211-1726
www.drawerb.com
Unsolicited submissions are accepted.

ElOzine.com
PH: 559-798-1281
Guyo Katich entertain@eiozine.com
www.eiozine.com
E-zine with news, reviews, interviews etc.

E.O.M Entertainment
1221 E.20th St. #302, Oakland, CA 94606
Maurice Edwards info@eomentertainment.com
eomentertainment.com
Interested in submitting a cd to E.O.M for review and possible submission? If so, please send a copy of the cd along with a brief artist bio and contact information to the above address.

Do You Make Music?

Visit our Web Site

www.midi-classics.com
Call 800-787-6434 NOW!

Save BIG on the latest Software, Pro Audio, Sound Cards, Converters, Cables, Interfaces, Sample Libraries, Controllers
- LOW Price$ - We Beat Em!
- Unbeatable Selection - 20,000+ items
- Fast Shipping Worldwide
- Thoughtful Service
- Over Ten Years in Business

MIDI Classics
Dept. IB, Box 311, Weatogue, CT 06089 • Intl 860-651-1349

Equal Music
PO Box 456, Marlboro, NJ 07746
PH: 732-580-2537
Danielle Moskowitz danielle@equalmusic.com
www.equalmusic.com
Interviews/reviews etc. Covers all genres. The bands on Equal Music are hand picked. They exude elements of originality and passion and possess something that can't be explained—something that sets them apart.

Erasing Clouds
415 S. 46th St. Apt. A, Philadelphia, PA 19143
Dave Heaton erasingclouds@gmail.com
www.erasingclouds.com
Where regular people write about the music.

Exploit Boston!
343 Medford St. #2A, Somerville, MA 02145
PH: 781-420-9660
Susan Kaup contact@exploitboston.com
www.exploitboston.com
Boston's independent guide to art, culture and entertainment. Featuring a curated event calendar, experience reviews and an internet radio station.

Fader
71 W. 23rd St. #903, New York, NY 10010
PH: 212-741-7100 FX: 212-741-4747
info@thefader.com
www.thefader.com
Digging into the factual experiences of music.

fakejazz
PO Box 9325, New Haven, CT 06533-0325
info@fakejazz.com
www.fakejazz.com
Submit material for review in our publication.

Fallenstars Magazine
editor@fallenstars.com
www.fallenstars.com
Submit your music for review.

Figgle
PO Box 1170, Maplewood, NJ 07040-2706
info@figgle.com
www.figgle.com
Album reviews and interviews with artists.

Filter Magazine
5514 Wilshire Blvd. 4th Fl. Los Angeles, CA 90036
info@filtermmm.com
www.filter-mag.com
Exposure for credible artists.

Firesideometer
823 N. Lesley Ave. Indianapolis, IN 46219
comments@firesideometer.com
www.firesideometer.com
Covering Indie bands that make great music.

First Coast News/Smitten
1783 Van Wert Ave. Jacksonville, FL 32205
PH: 904-633-5568
Paul Zimmerman pzimmerman@firstcoastnews.com
www.firstcoastnews.com/entertainment/musicreviews
Music reviews, interviews, on Firstcoastnews.com. DJ/club promotions via Smitten.

Foundmusic.com
customerservice@foundmusic.com
www.foundmusic.com
We review shows, bands and new releases.

foxy digitalis
PO Box 700965, Tulsa, OK 74170
foxyd@digitalisindustries.com
www.digitalisindustries.com/foxyd
Everything received will be reviewed.

Front Row Fanz Magazine
webmaster@frontrowfanz.com
www.frontrowfanz.com
Interview magazine that will interview indie artists.

fufkin.com
PO Box 7420, Fort Lauderdale, FL 33338-7420
david_fufkin@fufkin.com
www.fufkin.com
Send your CDs to the above address.

Full Value Review
26489 Ynez Rd. C113, Temecula, CA 92591
PH: 909-318-0686
Bill Gould fullvalue@hotmail.com
www.fullvaluereview.com
Our focus is on reviewing food, music, hotels etc. Please send us your CD. We are more than happy to review all genres of music.

GhettoBlaster
392 Central Park W. #5T, New York, NY 10025
info@ghettoblastermagazine.com
www.ghettoblastermagazine.com
Pop culture news, interviews, reviews and MP3s.

Glide Magazine
Reviews Dept. PO Box 570, Bellmore, NY 11710
reviews@glidemagazine.com
www.glidemagazine.com
Submit materials for possible review or feature consideration to the above address.

Grapevine Culture
1398 Courtyard Dr. San Jose, CA 95118-1933
PH: 408-859-5736 FX: 408-850 0465
www.grapevineculture.com
Discover high-quality emerging artists regardless of style. Through a global staff of experienced, professional music writers who uncover the best talent in their home cities — worldwide. We have reviews of CDs, live performances from Beijing to Boston.

Groove Machine Magazine
730 Porchtown Rd. Franklinville, NJ 08322
PH: 856-694-0224 FX: 856-694-0224
Jim Santora coverage@groovemachinemag.com
www.groovemachinemag.com
We do feature interviews, as well as show and CD reviews. Interested artists should e-mail us for more info.

Groovevolt.com
Chauncy Jackson press@groovevolt.com
www.groovevolt.com
Features Indie and upcoming artists.

Groupeez Magazine
PO Box 220017, Chicago, IL 60622
Mike Matray editor@groupeez.com
www.groupeez.com
Submissions are accepted for review, primarily in the area of Rock. Other genres such as Jazz and Hip Hop are also encouraged.

Harp Magazine
8737 Colesville Rd. 9th Fl.
Silver Spring, MD 20910-3921
PH: 301-588-4114 FX: 301-588-5531
scott@harpmagazine.com
www.harpmagazine.com
In-depth features and reviews.

Hear/Say
11012 Aurora Hudson Rd. Streetsboro, OH 44241
PH: 330-528-0410 FX: 330-528-0423
mark.watt@hearsay.cc
www.hearsay.cc
A free music publication for students.

Here and There
19237 Silver Springs Dr. #101,
Northville, MI 48167
Michael@thehereandthere.net
www.thehereandthere.net
We review everything that comes our way.

High Bias
2200 Willow Creek Dr. #312, Austin, TX 78741
PH: 512-440-1513
editor@highbias.com
www.highbias.com
Listening with extreme prejudice.

HITCH Magazine
PO Box 23621, Oklahoma City, OK 73123-2621
R. Lott rodlott@sbcglobal.net
www.hitchmagazine.com
The Journal of Pop Culture Absurdity. We try to review every CD, video, zine, whathaveyou we receive.

HitClick Independent Music Network
138 W. 14th St., Tucson, AZ 85701
PH: 520-867-6686 FX: 216-929-1049
Avallon Julian Rai avallon.pm-div@hitclick.net
www.hitclick.net
Would you like a review of your CD or MP3? Check out our site for submission details.

HitSession.com
6453 Pretti Rd. Corunna, MI 48817
dougc@hitsession.com
www.hitsession.com
Small donation to get your music reviewed.

Direct traffic to your website -
www.indielinkexchange.com/ile

Hot Indie News
269 12th St. #1, Brooklyn, NY 11215-3919
PH: 917-865-2591 FX: 917-591-4846
James Lane HotIndieNews@yahoo.com
www.HotIndieNews.com
Helping independent artists increase their worldwide exposure. Send your CDs and press kits to the address listed above for consideration on our site.

HYBRID Magazine
PO Box 9250, Denver, CO 80209
music@hybridmagazine.com
www.hybridmagazine.com
We listen to every CD we receive.

I Ate Your Microphone.com
chris@iateyourmicrophone.com
www.iateyourmicrophone.com
Introduces original sounds to your ears.

Ice Magazine
PO Box 3043, Santa Monica, CA 90408
PH: 310-829-1291 FX: 310-829-2979
info@icemagazine.com
www.icemagazine.com
Providing release dates for the music industry.

ICON Magazine
PH: 775-363-6821 FX: 425-799-0546
help@icon-magazine.com
www.icon-magazine.com
Monthly e-zine featuring the best independent artists/bands. Please contact via phone, fax, or email for press consideration.

Iconoclast Entertainment Group
PO Box 2366, Orange, CA 92859
Attn: CD Reviews
Keavin Wiggins keavin@rocknworld.com
www.ieginc.com
Profiles exciting Indie bands. CD's for reviews and press packs can be sent to the above address.

Idolize Magazine
Interviews@IdolizeMag.com
idolizemag.com
Your choice to what's known, not known, and up n coming! E-mail me if you would like to book an interview.

Impact Press
PO Box 361, 10151 U. Blvd. Orlando, FL 32817
PH: 407-263-5504
Craig editor@impactpress.com
www.impactpress.com
Send your new releases for review.

In Music We Trust
1530 SE Bevington Ave. Portland, OR 97267-3355
PH: 503-557-9661 FX: 503-650-8365
alex@inmusicwetrust.com
www.inmusicwetrust.com
Exposes talented artists to a larger audience.

Independent Songwriter
PO Box 112, Camden, NY 13316
Jan Best jan@independentsongwriter.com
www.independentsongwriter.com
CD reviews, internet radio and much more.

Indie Artist Station
PO Box 212293, Chula Vista, CA 91921
info@indieartiststation.com
www.indieartiststation.com
Where musicians and industry professionals talk about the business of making music.

Indie Music Explosion
www.IndieMusicExplosion.com
Getting the voice of Indie Music heard!

Indie Pages
757 N. 65th St., Seattle, WA 98103
chris@indiepages.com
www.indiepages.com
Info about your favorite Indie bands and labels.

IndieFan
www.indiefan.com
Bringing Indie to the masses!

Indie-Music.com
PO Box 3339, Cary, NC 27519-3339
Jennifer Layton writers@indie-music.com
www.indie-music.com/reviewpolicy.php
We use a cooperative of independent freelance writers to review indie CDs. You can request a certain writer, or you can simply submit your package and it will be distributed among our current pool of active and new reviewers. Jennifer Layton is our Review Editor/Coordinator.

IndiePerformer.com
PO Box 3721, Brentwood, TN 37024
Carla Archuletta info@indieperformer.com
www.IndiePerformer.com
Enables artists to be recognized and to be heard in a venue for worldwide exposure.

indieworkshop
1978 NW 92nd Ct. Ste.1, Clive, IA 50325
Jake info@indieworkshop.com
www.indieworkshop.com
E-mail before submitting items for review.

Indulged
www.indulged.com
Exposing the latest unsigned musical artists. Check our list of reviewers to see which one fits your style.

Ink 19
1161 Sanddune Ln. #306, Melbourne, FL 32935
Rob Walsh walsh@ink19.com
www.ink19.com
Accepts CDs and artist bio's for review.

Inquisitor Zine
PO Box 132, New York, NY 10024
www.inquisitor.com
A no-hype rag for the media-saturated masses.

Inside Connection
1919 Middle Country Rd. #205, Centereach, NY 11720
PH: 631-981-8231 FX: 631-981-8424
editor@insidecx.com
www.insidecx.com
New releases from independent bands.

Interlude Magazine
Attn: I Rock, You Roll,
PO Box 261693, San Diego, CA 92196-1693
PH: 601-214-0589
Arlan Hamilton arlanhamilton@hotmail.com
www.interlude-magazine.com
Interviews, exclusive performances and more!

InterMixx Magazine
PO Box 287, 304 Main Ave. Norwalk, CT 06851
PH: 203-483-1798
Noel Ramos MixxMag@InterMixx.com
www.intermixx.com
We help Indies market themselves to consumers!

International Online Music Magazine
info@rcatcommunications.com
www.dgmpublishing.com/IOM
A promotional resource for digitally distributed music and the artists that make it. We have an average of over 45,000 visitors to the magazine each month. We are always looking for CDs to review.

Issues Magazine
editors@issues-mag.com
www.issues-mag.com
Reviews any music good enough for radio! Please contact us before sending your CD.

Johari Review
PO Box 45887, Omaha, NE 68145
PH/FX: 866-733-7255
Journey Johari christle@alltel.net
www.JohariEntertainment.com
We offer reviews of all material (except fictional literature), with various levels of exposure and options. We also act as a liaison between artists and film companies on occasion.

Junk Media
Ben Sterling ben@junkmedia.org
www.junkmedia.org
We strive to highlight music and musicians who have been overlooked by the mainstream music press, as well as provide alternative viewpoints and opinions on the "popular" artists of today.

Keyboard Magazine
2800 Campus Dr. San Mateo, CA 94403
PH: 650-513-4300 FX: 650-513-4642
Carl Lumma clumma@cmpinformation.com
www.keyboardmag.com
We are always interested in reviewing music by independent artists and producers.

Kingblind
Martin Lee info@kingblind.com
www.kingblind.com
Online music magazine. Bands get exposure NOW.

Kludge Magazine
8640 Gulana Ave. #J1014,
Playa Del Rey, CA 90293
PH: 310-710-8831
Arturo Perez ksm@ekmag.com
www.kludgemagazine.com
Features local and up and coming bands.

Kriselen Traxx
PO Box 158, Rialto, CA 92376
Kristine Capalla Kris@kriselen.com
www.kriselentraxx.com
Provides interviews, reviews, news, show dates, and profiles on the indie music scene.

Kweevak Music Magazine
38 Oliver Pl. Ringwood, NJ 07456
PH: 973-556-5400
Rich Lynch info@kweevak.com
www.kweevak.com
Music promotion, CD reviews, musc news, artist database, syndicated radio show & more!

Lab Productions
2350 E. Contour, Baton Rouge, LA 70809
PH: 985-974-0792
albums@labproductions.com
www.labproductions.com
Send your demo to get reviewed/featured.

Lexicon
info@lexiconmagazine.com
www.lexiconmagazine.com
New Wave to Modern Synthpop and everything in between.

Lightword Publishing Company
309A National Bank Bldg. 525 S. Main Ave.
Del Rio, TX 78840
Bernie lllightword@lightwordreviews.com
www.lightwordreviews.com/Indie.html
Submit an uplifting CD for review.

Luminous Flux Records
8 Forest Ave. Glen Cove, NY 11542
webmonkey@fluxnet.com
www.fluxnet.com/submiss.html
Reviews new music from new bands.

Magnet
1218 Chestnut St. #508, Philadelphia, PA 19107
PH: 215-413-8570 FX: 215-413-8569
magnetmag@aol.com
www.magnetmagazine.com
Gives attention to Indie musicians.

Mantis Magazine
PO Box 9566, Silver Spring, MD 20916
PH: 301-980-4777
Mark M. Chou submissions@mantismagazine.com
www.mantismagazine.com
A web magazine reviewing primarily Rock, Alt, Hip Hop, Emo-type acts. We also feature artist profiles / interviews and photography.

Masstransfer
PO Box 903, Lincoln Park, MI 48146
editor@masstransfer.net
www.masstransfer.net
Articles, reviews, upcoming releases etc.

Mean Street Magazine
6747-A Greenleaf Ave. Whittier, CA 90601
PH: 562-789-9455 FX: 562-789-9925
hello@meanstreet.com
www.meanstreet.com
Covers the independent music scene.

Metacritic
1223 Wilshire Blvd. #1240,
Santa Monica, CA 90403-5400
www.metacritic.com/music
Reviews your music by assigning it a score.

Minor 7th
PO Box 468, Manistee, MI 49660-0468
alan@minor7th.com
www.minor7th.com
Reviews guitar based CDs.

Modern Drummer
12 Old Bridge Rd. Cedar Grove, NJ 07009-1288
PH: 973-239-4140 FX: 973-239-7139
mdinfo@moderndrummer.com
www.moderndrummer.com
Magazine focusing specifically on drummers.

Modern Fix
3368 Governor Dr. #318, San Diego, CA 92122
PH: 858-650-6885
extra@modernfix.com
www.modernfix.com
Reviews and covers all genres. 20,000 issues a month!

ModaMag.com
editor@modamag.com
www.modamag.com
Will interview up and coming bands.

Moe Magazine
PO Box 320753, Tampa, FL 33679
PH: 813-835-8792
www.moemagazine.com
Reports from the underground world.

Moving In Stereo
213 Dickinson Ave. East Northport, NY 11731
Darren Paltrowitz darren.paltrowitz@gmail.com
launch.groups.yahoo.com/group/movinginstereo
An internationally-syndicated monthly column covering albums, concerts, movies, comedy and books.

Mundanesounds.com
PO Box 720, Carthage, TX 75633
joseph@mundanesounds.com
www.mundanesounds.com
Listens to anything that you send in.

The Music Appraisal
matt@themusicappraisal.com
www.themusicappraisal.com
Want your band's CD reviewed? Want to have an interview? We'd love to hear from you!

Music Box
PO Box 3911, Oak Park, IL 60303-3911
editor@musicbox-online.com
www.musicbox-online.com
Concert and album reviews.

Music Connection
16130 Ventura Blvd. #540, Encino, CA 91436
PH: 818-995-0101 FX: 818-995-9235
contactmc@musicconnection.com
www.musicconnection.com
Interviews, reviews, critiques and more!

Music for Unicorns
Niki Selken unicornrock@gmail.com
www.unicornrock.com
I post MP3s and review them. I also do album reviews and interviews.

Music Head
43 Columbine Cir. #102 Newtown, PA 18940
musichead@musichead.org
www.musichead.org
Information about the artists making up the realm of today's music.

Music Korner
PO Box 58095, Charleston, WV 25358
Geoff musccorn@aol.com
members.aol.com/musccorn
Covers virtually all styles of music.

Music Dish Reviews
editor@musicdish.com
www.musicdish.com
Showcases developments in the online music industry. We have several reviewers. Check our site to find out who best suits your style of music.

Music Morsels
PO Box 2760, Acworth, GA 30102
PH: 678-445-0006 FX: 678-494-9269
Sandy Serge sergeent@aol.com
www.serge.org
E-zine with independent CD reviews, unsigned band spotlights and an industry profile.

The Music Review
CD Reviews, PO Box 41635, Nashville, TN 37204
www.musreview.com
Review site, and music search engine.

Musical Taste
jonny@delicado.org
www.musicaltaste.com
A user-driven community with a focus on individual track recommendations.

musicmisfits.com
musicmis@musicmisfits.com
Cary Christopher cary@musicmisfits.com
www.musicmisfits.com
We ask that you send a query e-mail first. In the e-mail let us know where you are from and what type of music you play. We try to assign the reviews to our writers by geographic location. We generally take submissions of all styles of music.

MuzikReviews.com
PO Box 476, Adams, MA 01220
Keith "MuzikMan" Hannaleck
khannaleck@yahoo.com
www.muzikreviews.com
$50 fee. Keep in mind that your review will be on the MANY sites I post content on.

MuzikReviewz.com
cdreviews@muzikreviewz.com
www.muzikreviewz.com
CD and demo reviews, interviews, press releases etc.

Nada Mucho
6200 6th Ave. NW #8, Seattle, WA 98107
Matt editor@nadamucho.com
www.nadamucho.com
Entertaining and educating the MTV generation.

National Noise
3100 Main #105, Dallas, TX 75226
PH: 214-823-2188
Jason Hadfield jason.hadfield@nationalnoise.com
www.nationalnoise.com
Interviews with the newest faces in Rock music.

Naughty Secretary Club
PO Box 161702, Austin, TX 78716
naughtysecretaryclub@yahoo.com
www.naughtysecretaryclub.com
Music reviews, interviews, recipes and more!

neumu
contact@neumu.net
www.neumu.net
A new Alternative Pop culture site.

New Artist Radio CD Reviews
17121 Berlin Ln. Huntington Beach, CA 92649
www.newartistradio.net
Available to New Artist Radio members. If you want me to put more emphasis on your lyrics, then please provide me with lyric sheets in addition to your band bio.

New Directions Cello Association
501 Linn St., Ithaca, NY 14850
PH: 607- 277-1686
ndca@clarityconnect.com
www.newdirectionscello.com
A network for Alternative or Non Classical cello.

NewBeats
David newbeats@newbeats.com
www.newbeats.com
A music magazine that covers all types of music...the more eclectic the better.

The Night Owl
2804 Woodbridge Estates Dr. St. Louis, MO 63129
PH: 314-846-7551 FX: 314-846-7551
editor@thenightowl.com
www.thenightowl.com
Music reviews covering from Rock to Jazz.

Night Times
PO Box 1747, Maryland Hts, MO 63043
PH: 314-542-9995
Julia Gordon-Bramer wordgirl@nighttimes.com
www.nighttimes.com
The premier St. Louis music magazine offering CD reviews,show previews and artist interviews. We support local, regional, national and international musicians.

Norman Famous Rants and Reviews
PO Box 6218, Albany, CA 94706
Norman Famous norman@normanfamous.com
www.normanfamous.com
In my continuing efforts to expose the world to good music by deserving musicians, I offer online reviews of independent cd releases along with my customary barbed witticisms and wry social comment.

NowOnTour.com
6300 N. Sagewood Dr. #H-533,
Park City, UT 84098
Tyler Champley reviews@nowontour.com
www.NowOnTour.com
Tour and show listings, record reviews of Indie bands and more.

Nude as the News
Tallboy67@aol.com
www.nudeasthenews.com
Focusing on the expansive current state of Rock.

one times one
Jennifer Hall jennifer@onetimesone.com
www.onetimesone.com
Online magazine featuring quality independent music, film, photography and more.

ONE WAY Magazine
311 N. Robertson Blvd. #208,
Beverly Hills, CA 90211
PH: 310-275-5141 FX: 310-765-4765
www.onewaymagazine.com
Showcases new music by developing artists.

OnlineRock
2033 Ralston Ave. #50 Belmont, CA 94002
PH: 650-649-2304
Steve Beck steve@onlinerock.com
www.onlinerock.com
We offer CD reviews which are perfect for your press kit and website. All types of music accepted.

OpeningBands
700 W. Illinois, Urbana, IL 61801
Will Zeiger reviews@openingbands.com
www.openingbands.com/reviews/guidelines.race
To get your CD reviewed - mail two copies (so we can have two people review it) and other press info to the above address. Our address changes almost every year, so please check before sending your CD.

Outer Shell
outershel@aol.com
members.aol.com/outershel
Reviews artists in each issue.

OUtlET Magazine
181 Market St, Lowell, MA 01852
PH: 978-618-1781
Jeff Lail reviews@outletzine.org
www.outletzine.org
An independent performance magazine. We accept submissions for review.

Pathetic Caverns
411A Highland Ave. #404, Somerville, MA 02144
cavernsp@pathetic-caverns.com
www.pathetic-caverns.com
Opinionated and eclectic reviews of music. Please read over our submission guidelines.

Pause & Play
gerry@pauseandplay.com
www.pauseandplay.com
Weekly Pop/Rock artist interview column.

Perfect Sound Forever
editor@perfectsoundforever.com
www.perfectsoundforever.com
Home of musical underdogs of all styles. We respond to every inquiry we get.

Performing Songwriter
PO Box 40931, Nashville, TN 37204
PH: 615-385-7796 FX: 615-385-5637
Mare Wakefield mare@performingsongwriter.com
www.performingsongwriter.com
Interviews, reviews, release spotlights and more. Please be patient and continue to send us your new releases. We do listen to all submissions for DIY consideration.

Pitchfork
3147 W. Logan Blvd. #5E, Chicago, IL 60647
mail@pitchforkmedia.com
www.pitchforkmedia.com
Covers all styles and genres of music.

Plug In music
PO Box 4206, Elwyn, PA 19063-4206
Corinne corinne@pluginmusic.com
www.pluginmusic.com
Band profiles, reviews, interviews and more. Check our site for submission details.

Pop Culture Press
PO Box 4990, Austin, TX 78765-4990
Luke editor@popculturepress.com
www.popculturepress.com
Pop and the rest of the musical spectrum.

PopMatters
1555 Sherman Ave. #324, Evanston, IL 60201
Sarah editor@popmatters.com
www.popmatters.com
CD/concert reviews, artist interview and profiles.

POPsmear
232 N. Almont Dr. Beverly Hills, CA 90211
FX: 310-247-9588
www.popsmear.com
Send us your stuff for review or ridicule.

PopStardom
caiti@popstardom.net
popstardom.net
Features interviews with established and up and coming artists of all genres.

PopZine
8793 Plata Ln. #11, Atascadero, CA 93422
questions@popzineonline.com
www.popzineonline.com
Reviews, interviews, features and more. Please do not e-mail us electronic press kits!

Prefix Magazine
PO Box 21654, Brooklyn, NY 11202-1654
www.prefixmag.com
We will review CDs and concerts.

Prick
PO Box 381, Tucker, GA 30085
PH: 770-723-9824
music@prickmag.net
www.prickmag.net
Reviews on regional and national bands.

pucknation dot com
4421 Shelbyville Rd. #7, Louisville, KY 40207
pucknation@hotmail.com
www.pucknation.com
Send your demo, CD or comic to review.

RAD Cyberzine
1809 E. 3990 St., Salt Lake City, UT 84124-1653
jeff@radcyberzine.com
www.radcyberzine.com
We provide CDs to review, concerts to attend and photo passes with bands.

Radiant Star Entertainment
radiantstarentertainment.com
Focused on helping new, up-and-coming artists by getting their names, music, and messages out to all of our readers.

Resonance Magazine
PO Box 95620, Seattle, WA 98145-2620
PH: 206-633-3500
info@resonancemag.com
www.resonancemag.com
Featuring innovative artists from Indie Rock to the Avant-garde.

RetroRadar.com
4230 Fairway Dr. #6210, Carrolton, TX 75010
PH: 972-939-5417
Leslie J. Thompson leslie@retroradar.com
RetroRadar.com
We are interested in writing reviews for new releases in the following genres: Swing, Rockabilly, Surf, Lounge, Exotica, '50s Rock-and-Roll, Roots/R&B, Blues & Jazz standards. Artists should send two copies of their album and any supporting press.

Review You
question@reviewyou.com
www.ReviewYou.com
Have your album reviewed by a professional music journalist. This is a pay to get reviewed service.

Riff Magazine
PO Box 687, Cudahy, WI 53110
PH: 414-481-3959 FX: 414-481-1524
Paul Barry lulurec@execpc.com
my.execpc.com/~lulurec
We review Pop (with a 50's 60's feel), Roots Rock, Zydeco, Surf and Instrumental Rock, Rockabilly (sorry, no psychobilly) and Do-wop

Rikks Revues
Rikk Matheson rikk@rikksrevues.com
rikksrevues.com
A free music revue site focusing on Indie artists.

Rising Stars Magazine
PO Box 780934, Orlando, FL 32828-0934
risingstarsinc.com
Targeting aspiring & indie musicians, featuring all genres, internationally.

The Rock and Roll Report
rockandrollreport@hotmail.com
www.rockandrollreport.com
If you're not sure if your music fits, send me a couple of MP3s using Dropload. I can have a few listens and then let you know if I would be interested in receiving the whole enchilada.

Rock Music Review
1009 W. North St., Muncie, IN 47303
PH: 317-345-5986
Jack Shepler indiebible@rockmusicreview.com
www.rockmusicreview.com
Honest independent CD and concert reviews.

Rock Reviews
Jason Carter
rockeditor@hotmail.com
rock-reviews.net
Does your band have a CD you would like reviewed? Contact us for information on how to submit your album for review.

Rocket Fuel Online
PO Box 4613,
Austin, TX 78765
Monika Bustamante
monika@rocket-fuel.com
www.rocket-fuel.com
Strict submission guidelines to get reviewed.

Rockpile Magazine
PO Box 63967,
Philadelphia, PA 19147
PH: 877-708-7625
FX: 215-592-0591
rockpile@rockpile.net
www.rockpile.net
Your source for new music!

RockReviews.net
PO Box 151,
Hartland, MI 48353
Shelly Towne
shelly@rockreviews.net
www.rockreviews.net
Specializing in professional Rock, Indie Pop, and various other genres of reviews.

Rocktober Magazine
1507 E. 53rd St. #617, Chicago, IL 60615
editor@roctober.com
www.roctober.com
Articles on obscure musicians in all genres of popular music.

ROCKZONE.COM
60 Soundview Ave. White Plains, NY 10606
Attn: Reviews
Jason Cipriano jasonc@rockzone.com
www.rockzone.com
We review CDs, live shows and do interviews.

Scoot! Quarterly
PO Box 9605, San Jose, CA 95157
PH: 888-337-2668
www.scootquarterly.com
Music and video reviews in each issue.

Scram
PO Box 31227, Los Angeles, CA 90031
amscray@gmail.com
www.scrammagazine.com
Unpopular culture, beatniks, Garage Rock, novelty acts and anything offbeat.

Shmat's Reviews
PO Box 1191, Alhambra, CA 91802
shmat@shmat.com
www.shmat.com
Focus on unknown or on smaller Indie labels.

Shortbus Megazine
PO Box 189634, Sacramento, CA 95818
Mia Baxter mia@shortbusmag.com
www.shortbusmag.com
Send in your music related material for review.

Shotgun Reviews
Troy Brownfield psikotyk@aol.com
www.shotgunreviews.com
Special emphasis on Hip Hop, Britpop, Electronica, and traditional Alternative.

The Shred Zone
Nick webmaster@TheShredZone.com
www.theshredzone.com
Guitar resource with CD, demo and product reviews.

Sing4life.com
464 Rock Glen Dr. Wynnewood, PA 19096
PH: 610-896-3656 FX: 610-896-6255
Darrell B. Gilbert dbg786@net-bizz.com
www.Sing4life.com
Music reviews & sales. Songs from the heart for the heart. A place for the spirit to sing out loud!

Singer Magazine
PO Box 1288, Harrisburg, VA 22803
Greg Tutwiler SingerMagazine@aol.com
www.singermagazine.com
Inspiring vocal performers and independent recording artists.

The Singing Songwriter
112-C Winding Way, Covington, KY 41011
Kenny Hart writer@kennyhart.com
singing-songwriter.kennyhart.com
Tips, techniques, news, reviews, and resources for performing songwriters and others interested in songwriting and performance. Send your CD and bio or press kit. Syndicated feed reaches millions of potential readers.

Slant Magazine
Sal Cinquemani sal@slantmagazine.com
www.slantmagazine.com
Featuring reviews, editorials, and critiques of a wide array of new and classic music and film.

Slender
webmaster@slendermusic.com
www.slendermusic.com
A nice place to find out about great music!

SLIPCUE
Joe Sixpack joesixpack@slipcue.com
www.slipcue.com
Focusing on Indie Pop, Cuban, Brazilian and hick music.

Smother.Net
c/o Demo Submission, 9237 Berkshire St.,
Manassas, VA 20110
J-Sin editor@smother.net
www.smother.net
Covers and reviews all genres of music.

SongExpert.com
expert@songexpert.com
www.songexpert.com
Get your songs reviewed by top industry professionals.

Songsalive!
289 S. Robertson Blvd. #200,
Beverly Hills, CA 90211
PH: 818-442-9294
usa@songsalive.org
www.songsalive.org
We review CDs, but you MUST be a Songsalive! member.

Sign up for The Indie Contact Newsletter
www.indiebible.com

Sound the Sirens
editor@soundthesirens.com
www.soundthesirens.com
Send your CD in for review.

Soundclash Music Webzine
3900 Oxford St., Napa, CA 94558
PH: 818-251-0846
Matt Armstrong shutterbox@gmail.com
www.soundclashmusic.tk
A website focusing on reviews and interviews of small label and unsigned bands.

Soundgenerator
mail@soundgenerator.com
www.soundgenerator.com
Bringing you coverage on many of the best new album, single & DVD releases from every genre.

South Of Mainstream
2775 N. Northwoods Dr. Macon, GA 31204
Mallie Dein reviews@southofmainstream.com
www.southofmainstream.com
Reviews virtually every genre of music.

Southbound Beat
4001 Inglewood Ave. #101-252,
Redondo Beach, CA 90278
PH: 310-366-7526 FX: 310-366-7432
Ray Carver southboundbeat@yahoo.com
www.southboundbeat.com
CD reviews, interviews, columns & more.

sparkplugg.com
PO Box 5125, Richmond, VA 23220
info@sparkplugg.com
sparkplugg.com
Please send all promotional materials to the above address. I will be changing content bi-weekly across the board in order to keep the website as fresh as possible.

SPIN Magazine
205 Lexington Ave. New York, NY 10016
PH: 212-231-7400 FX: 212-231-7312
spin.com
Bringing you the absolute most in infotainment.

Splendid
1202 Curtiss St. 2nd Fl. Downers Grove, IL 60515
G. Zahora splendid@splendidezine.com
www.splendidezine.com
We review everything we receive.

Spotlight Entertainment Magazine
spotlight-entertainment.org
Will do reviews with independent artists.

Spunout Central
4174 N. Newhall St., Shorewood, WI 53211
PH: 414-962-8269 FX: 414-393-6860
Adam Mico admin@spunoutcentral.com
www.spunoutcentral.com
If your act is full-on brilliant, intriguing and / or God awful, send your CD (at least five tracks) for feature consideration to a fully exposed, popular music review site.

Skuawk!
1133 Broadway #706, New York, NY 10010
FX: 212-465-2516
Marcos Bernal marcos@skuawk.com
www.skuawk.com
A webzine where artists are creatively loud.

Stanky Groove
26 Alma Ave. 1st Fl. Belmont, MA 02478
Alan Haworth stankygroove@hotmail.com
www.stankygroove.com
We attempt to review all CDs that are sent to our office.

Stinkweeds Online
1250 E Apache Blvd. Tempe, AZ 85281-5870
PH: 480-968-9490 FX: 480-968-2131
kimber@stinkweeds.com
www.stinkweeds.com
Reviews of new music added weekly. You'll stay on top of everything Indie.

Stomp and Stammer
PO Box 55233, Atlanta, GA 30308
www.stompandstammer.com
We cover a wide range of popular and not-so-popular music.

Stylinzine
editor@stylinzine.com
stylinzine.com
For those who are stylin by heart and soul, the individuals who scratch below the superficial surface and embrace the essence of reality. Will do interviews with independent artists.

Stylus Magazine
120 Brainerd Rd. Apt #1, Allston, MA 02134
c/o Michael F. Gill promos@stylusmagazine.com
www.stylusmagazine.com
Reviews a variety of genres of music.

SugarBuzz
Lucky lucky@sugarbuzzmagazine.com
sugarbuzzmagazine.com
Looking in on today's up and coming Rock 'n Roll artists.

The Synthesis
210 W. 6th St., Chico, CA 95928
PH: 530-899-7708
bill@synthesis.net
www.thesynthesis.com
Thousands of pages of content, ranging from feature articles, concert critiques and CD and product reviews, to MP3 downloads.

talkbass.com
admin@talkbass.com
www.talkbass.com
Interviews for bass players with new releases.

Tangerine Magazine
4821 Maryland Ave. Birmingham, AL 35205
PH: 205-563-9914
Andy acb@tangerinemagazine.com
www.tangerinemagazine.com
For review submission or interview requests contact us.

Tiny Mix Tapes
submissions@tinymixtapes.com
www.tinymixtapes.com
For instructions on how and where to send materials, please e-mail us with a subject that reads "Interested in Submitting."

The Toilet
submit@thetoiletonline.com
www.thetoiletonline.com
We welcome bands from all musical genres.

Trampoline House
info@trampolinehouse.com
www.trampolinehouse.com
Art, music and literature from the underground.

Twee Kitten
PO Box 213, 1547 Palos Verdes Mall,
Walnut Creek, CA 94597
PH: 925-947-2842
goldfish@tweekitten.com
www.tweekitten.com
We focus on music possessing beauty, melody, charm etc.

Under the Radar
238 S. Tower Dr. #204, Beverly Hills, CA 90211
PH: 323-653-8705 FX: 323-658-5738
submissions@undertheradarmag.com
www.undertheradarmag.com
Arguably America's best independent music magazine. We're known for our in-depth and intelligent interviews, and for our sharp photo shoots.

UnEarthed.Com
brian@unearthed.com
www.unearthed.com
We get the music that we like heard by the masses.

United Global Artists
FX: 801-659-9406
Leigh Silberg uga@email.com
www.u-g-a.com
International Indie music reviews.

UNSIGNED Music Mag
Ken Hamlett artists@unsignedmusicmag.com
www.unsignedmusicmag.com
Our mission is to give unsigned musicians, singers, bands, producers, writers and other musical talent a venue to let the music buyers of the world know they create, perform and write great music.

Upstage Magazine
PO Box 140, Spring Lake, NJ 07762
PH: 732-682-5798
Gary Wien info@upstagemagazine.com
www.upstagemagazine.com
Monthly print publication and online publication dealing with all of the arts but especially music. Frequently features and reviews unsigned/independent artists.

usounds
Erich Redson eredson@usounds.com
www.usounds.com
We embrace the experience of music as well as the music itself.

Varla Magazine
PO Box 291478, Los Angeles, CA 90029
PH: 213-484-6128
www.varla.com
We cover everything. We will review your CDs.

Direct traffic to your website
The Indie Link Exchange
A new, free and easy way to promote your website
www.indielinkexchange.com/ile

VibeRate
134 Connor Dr. Royersford, PA 19468
Kristy editor@Vibe-Rate.com
www.vibe-rate.com
We offer CD and performance reviews, music news, band info, gigs, links and more!

Vintage Guitar
PO Box 7301, Bismarck, ND 58507
PH: 701-255-1197 FX: 701-255-0250
vguitar@vguitar.com
www.vintageguitar.com
Will review guitar oriented independent CDs.

WAV Magazine
www.wavmag.com
Since its inception, WAV's mission has been to expose subversive culture and showcase underground sensations.

The Welkin: Online Music Reviews
contact@thewelkin.net
www.thewelkin.net
Reviews covering a variety of genres such as Alternative Rock, Metal, Jazz and Indie, with a particular emphasis on lesser-known groups.

West Coast Rockers
Leigh Davis leigh@westcoastrockers.com
www.westcoastrockers.com
We help "indie" artists by posting links, pictures, reviews, interviews, news etc. & finding and promoting gigs. Come join our family!

Wild Violet
PO Box 39706, Philadelphia, PA 19106-9706
wildvioletmagazine@yahoo.com
www.wildviolet.net
An online quarterly literary magazine, trying to bridge the gap between academia and pop culture. Publishes interviews with Independent artists. Check site for submission details.

Canada

Being There Magazine
220 Viceroy Rd, #13 Concord, ON L4K 3C2
PH: 647-881-8884 FX: 905-764-8367
Cari Crosby cari@beingtheremag.com
www.beingtheremag.com
An online music & film magazine for the literary minded. We include interviews, features, and reviews.

Broken Pencil
PO Box 203, Stn P, Toronto, ON M5S 2S7
editor@brokenpencil.com
www.brokenpencil.com
We cover zines, books, music, film/video and art produced with an Indie attitude.

the GATE
editor@thegate.ca
www.thegate.ca
Reviews, interviews etc.

Guitar Noise
3832 Henri-Julien, Montreal, QC H2W 2K2
A-J Charron gnoisereviews@hotmail.com
www.guitarnoise.com
We review anything guitar related. Check our site for submission guidelines
www.guitarnoise.com/faq.php?id=139

Indieville
PO Box 91017, 2901 Bayview Ave.
Toronto, ON M2K 1H0
Matt Shimmer mattshimmer@gmail.com
www.indieville.com
Dedicated to independent music of all sorts. We review everything!

Mote MGZN
PO Box 65026 N. Hill Stn. Calgary, AB T2N 4T6
PH: 403-241-5453
motemgzn@moteinteractive.com
www.moregoatthangoose.com
Reviews, interviews, live reviews etc.

Soundline
111 4th Ave. RPO 28, PO Box 30022,
St. Catharines, ON L2S 4A1
Krys Grandmond bands@soundline.ca
www.soundline.ca
We accept submissions from bands and artists around the world. Send your CDs for a thorough review from someone on our review board.

Soul Shine
20 Gilroy Dr. Scarborough, ON M1P 1Z9
PH: 416-751-3884
Paul Whitfield webmaster@soulshine.ca
www.soulshine.ca
News, features, reviews, gig listings and Indie radio.

Space Junkies Magazine
205 - 3 Iroquois St., Brantford, ON N3S 6N8
Wednesday Elektra wednesday@spacejunkies.net
www.spacejunkies.net
Supporting and promoting independent music of all genres from around the world for free. Please contact us before you send any music.

South America

Radio MuyModerna
radio@muymoderna.com.ar
www.muymoderna.com.ar
Música para oídos independientes!

Super 45
Los Leones 1315 depto 62, Providencia, Chile
www.super45.cl
Música independiente desde 1996.

Velvet Rockmine
correo@velvetrockmine.com.ar
www.velvetrockmine.com.ar
Revista Virtual de música, cine, arte, moda, teatro y etcéteras (mp3s, videos y especiales muy completos).

Europe

Belgium

Keys & Chords
Hoofdredacteur, Zandkapelweg 18, BE 2200
Noorderwijk, Belgium
PH: +32-14-724961 FX: +32-14-724961
Alfons Maes Alfons.Maes@keysandchords.com
www.keysandchords.com
Lots of reviews every issue. Covering Rock, Blues, Soul and Modern Jazz.

France

Attica
info@atticawebzine.com
atticawebzine.com
News, reviews, interviews...

Bokson
44 rue des Pyrénées, 75020 Paris, France
contact@bokson.net
www.bokson.net
Magazine des musiques Rock, Hip Hop Electro, World. Interviews, chroniques, news.

bubblegum perfume
6 rue André Antoine, 75018 Paris, France
Violaine Schütz violaine.schutz@noos.fr
www.bubblegumperfume.ht.st
Fanzine in French about Twee Pop.

Critic Instinct
webmaster@critic-instinct.com
www.critic-instinct.com
Covers Indie music.

Dangerhouse
3 rue Thimonnier, 69001 Lyon, France
PH: 33-0-4-78-27-15-64 FX: 33-0-4-78-39-26-47
dangerhouse@numericable.fr
dangerhouse.free.fr
Comprehensive zine from a record store in France.

Dig It!
32, rue Pharaon, 31000 Toulouse, France
FX: 05-61-14-06-28
digitfanzine@chez.com
www.chez.com/digitfanzine
Rawk 'n' Roll French fanzine!!!

Grandrock
c/o Emmanuel Gathellier, 325 rue de Charenton,
75012 Paris, France
www.grandrock.net
Webzine Rock Indé.

Inrockuptibles
144, rue de Rivoli, 75001 Paris, France
PH: 01-42-44-16-16 FX: 01-42-44-16-00
www.lesinrocks.com
Online music and arts magazine.

Liability Webzine
79, rue Saint Martin, 75004 Paris, France
Dorian Dumont dorian@liabilitywebzine.com
www.liabilitywebzine.com
Pop::Rock::Indé. Nous écoutons 90% des disques que nous recevons. Si vous voulez avoir votre chronique dans nos pages, envoyez nous vos CDs à cette adresse.

Melodick
31 Cours de Vincennes, 75020 Paris, France
PH: 33-0-609-072-588
Emmanuel Guinot manu@melodick.com
www.melodick.com
Le webzine indépendant!

Nova Planet
33, rue du Faubourg Saint Antoine,
75011 Paris, France
PH: 01-53-33-33-32
novamag@novamag.tm.fr
www.novaplanet.com
Consortium quotidien de culture underground.

POPnews
c/o Guillaume Sautereau, 8 rue Rosenwald,
75015 Paris, France
www.popnews.com
We are very keen on discovering new talents.

positiverage
51, rue Paul Vaillant Couturier,
92240 Malakoff, France
Mathieu Gelézeau positiverage@hotmail.com
www.positiverage.com
Extensive coverage of Indie music.

Premonition
www.premonition.fr
Our purpose is to give everyone the opportunity to hear Independent bands express themselves and, above all, to present the greatest possible number of reviews in every new issue.

sefronia
info@sefronia.com
www.sefronia.com
CD review free e-mail magazine.

Speedvibes
PH: 06-88-96-49-63 FX: 04-42-44-63-27
speedvibes@speedvibes.com
www.speedvibes.com
Bands from everywhere are welcome to submit.

zicline.com
zicline@zicline.com
www.zicline.com
Each week all music info from Jazz to Heavy Metal.

Germany

CD-KRITIK.DE
Dreibergen 79, 27572 Bremerhaven, Germany
PH: 0471-9-31-34-25 FX: 0471-3-00-61-88
Michael Frost redaktion@cd-kritik.de
www.cd-kritik.de
Wir beschreiben Ihnen die CDs, aber die Wahl haben Sie.

Discover
Vennerstraße 27, 53177 Bonn, Germany
PH: 49-228-1801653
andre@discover.de
www.discover.de
CDs, stories, interviews...

Guitars Galore
c/o Mike Korbik, Postfach 41 03 11,
12113 Berlin, Germany
Mike mail@twang-tone.de
www.twang-tone.de/gg.html
A flyer zine and monthly radio show as well.

indiepoprock.net
wqw@indiepoprock.net
www.indiepoprock.net
Chroniques, interviews, live reports, labels etc.

Kinda Muzik You Like
redactie@kindamuzik.net
www.kindamuzik.net
Giving Underground music the attention it deserves.

Plattentests Online
Bismarckstraße 29, 73084 Salach, Germany
PH: 0176-24432675
Armin Linder armin@plattentests.de
www.plattentests.de
Das Beste aus Rock und Independent!

PNG *(Persona Non Grata)*
Postfach 30 14 38, 04254 Leipzig, Germany
cms.png-online.de
News, reviews, interviews and more.

realmusic.de
Wilhelm-Busch-Strasse 12, 27753 Delmenhorst, Germany
PH/FX: 49 (0) 700-732568742
Dirk Scheuer ich@dirkscheuer.com
www.realmusic.de
Review and entertainment magazine.

VISIONS.de
Arneckestr. 82-84, 44139 Dortmund, Germany
PH: (0231) 557131-10 FX: (0231) 557131-31
info@visions.de
www.visions.de
Musikmagazin für alternative Musik

Greece

Scream Magazine
Saradaporou 45, 26223 Patra, Hellas, Greece
PH: 2610-422801
Spiros scream_zine@yahoo.com
www.scream.gr
Covers Rock, Jazz and Blues.

Italy

Rockit
Giulio Pons pons@rockit.it
www.rockit.it
Tutta roba Italiana.

Onda Rock
info@ondarock.it
www.ondarock.it
News and reviews.

Sodapop
sodapop@sodapop.it
www.sodapop.it
News, reviews, demos etc.

Three Monkeys
Via Tagliapietre 14, Bologna 40123, Italy
Andy Lawless info@threemonkeysonline.com
www.threemonkeysonline.com
Current affairs/music magazine with interviews and reviews.

ViceVersa Magazine
viceversa@landscape.it
www.landscape.it/viceversa
Submit promo package for review, possible interview, possible airplay.

The Netherlands

HEAVEN
bladmanager@heaven.be
www.heaven.be
Popmagazine voor volwassenen.

MusicRemedy.com
Vermeerhof 2, 3862 ZR, Nijkerk, The Netherlands
www.musicremedy.com
Send in your music so we can review it.

OOR
Antwoordnummer 14044, 5126 ZS, Glize, The Netherlands
PH: 0161-459533 FX: 0161-452913
oor@betapress.audax.nl
www.oor.nl
News, reviews, events calendar and more.

think small
thinksmall@thinksmall.nl
www.thinksmall.nl
News, reviews and articles written in Dutch.

Norway

Luna Kafe
PO Box 2175, Grunerlokka, 0505 Oslo, Norway
luna@fuzzlogic.com
www.fuzzlogic.com/lunakafe
Record reviews, concert reviews, interviews and more.

Spain

BuscaMusica.org
PO Box 440 - Jaen 23080, Spain
Juanma Cantos redaccion@buscamusica.org
www.buscamusica.org
Electronic magazine, band promotion and new indie label. Upload your music!

.espacio3.com
Nena Casas 42, 1 2 / 08007 - Barcelona, Spain
PH: 34932051363
Gustavo "Bambino" Zapico contacto@espacio3.com
www.espacio3.com
Online music & arts magazine focused in Alternative artists and genres.

eternoViajero.com
info@eternoviajero.com
www.eternoviajero.com
Noticas, fotos, mp3s, cronicas etc.

La Ganzua, Radio Obradoiro
Preguntoiro, 29. 15702, Santiago de Compostela,
A Coruña, Spain
PH: 981-543766-64
laganzua@laganzua.net
www.laganzua.net
E-zine de música independiente con noticias, conciertos, festivales, crónicas, entrevistas, mp3, discos, maquetas...

gruposMadrid.com
www.gruposmadrid.com
Groups, music, information…

Indy Rock
Polígono de Asegra c/Cádiz s/n, 18210 Peligros, Granada, Spain
PH: 958-809809
info@indyrock.es
www.indyrock.es

Manerasdevivir.com
discos@manerasdevivir.com
www.manerasdevivir.com
Punto de ecuentro de todos los amantes del rocanrol. Noticias muy actualizadas, mp3, conciertos, foros...

Music in a Net
Apdo. de correos 4233, 35080 Las Palmas de G.C.
Las Palmas (Canary Islands), Spain
Héctor Noble Fernández info@music-in-a.net
www.music-in-a.net
We do reviews of absolutely every kind of music (from the most Extreme Noise to gentle Classical Music). However, it is always best that you contact us before sending anything and tell us what sort of music you would like to send to us.

Muzikalia.com
A/At. Sergio Picón/Núria Ferré, C/Torrent de l´Olla 123, 2º2ª, 08012 Barcelona, Spain
PH: 93-415-29-47 or 615-44-81-66
info@muzikalia.com
www.muzikalia.com
Completísima web de música independiente.

El Planeta Amarillo
C/ Carlos III, 38 - 4º C, 30203 Cartagena (Murcia) Spain
Rafa Skam rafaskam@wanadoo.es
www.yellowmelodies.com/e-zine/Menu.html
Online and print Pop zine with lots of reviews.

RIFF Fanzine
Apartado de Correos 23.114, 08080 Barcelona, Spain
Pablo Campoy info@riff-fanzine.com
www.riff-fanzine.com
Artículos, Discos etc.

Space Rock Heaters
spacerockheaters@hotmail.com
spacerockheaters.com
Webzine creado en Cáceres con las últimas noticias sobre conciertos, grupos y festivales.

thebellemusic.com
contacto@thebellemusic.com
www.thebellemusic.com
Revista musical Independiente: crónicas de conciertos, cometarios de discos, novedades, noticias, entrevistas y mucho más.

Sweden

melodic.net
Johan Wippsson wippsson@melodic.net
www.melodic.net
Reviews, interviews and "Artist of the Week".

Passagen
www.passagen.se
Forum for Indie artists.

Revolver
Postfack 180, 116 74 Stockholm, Sweden
farid@revolver.nu
www.revolver.nu
E-zine for Indie artists. Submit your stuff.

United Kingdom

Alternative Music Links
4. Osborne House, St. Mary's Ter.
London, W2 1SG UK
reviews@alternative-links.co.uk
www.alternative-links.co.uk
Contact us regarding possible gig or album reviews.

Atomic Duster
www.atomicduster.com
Music, news, reviews, interviews and competitions.

between planets
www.betweenplanets.co.uk
Music news and review site where bands can also publicize themselves.

BIRDpages Record Review
14 Heddington Way, W. Knighton,
Leicester, ULE2 6HF UK
PH: 44-0-116-288-5788 FX: 44-0-116-288-7549
info@birdpages.co.uk
www.birdpages.co.uk

UK record shops, dealers and collecting.

BonaFideStudio
Burbage House, 83-85 Curtain Rd.
London, EC2A 3BS UK
PH: 020-7684-5350
Deanna info@bonafidestudio.co.uk
www.bonafidestudio.co.uk
We offer reviews, artist pages, notice board, sound tutorial etc.

CLUAS
Eoghan O'Neill webmaster@cluas.com
www.cluas.com
Lending an ear to the Irish music scene.

Comes with a Smile
69 St. Mary's Grove, Chiswick,
London, W4 3LW UK
PH: 0794-1010250
cwas.hinah.com
News, interviews, reviews and more.

DirtyZine
dirtyzine@dirtyzine.co.uk
www.feed-back.tk
An Alternative Rock zine. Reviews, interviews, downloads of the month.

Diskant
Stuart Fowkes newbands@diskant.net
www.diskant.net
A network of websites by independent fanzines, bands and record labels.

Do Something Pretty
dosomethingpretty@hotmail.com
dosomethingpretty.com
Building connections in independent music.

Drowned in Sound
61B Pall Mall Deposit, 124-128 Barlby Rd.
London, W10 6BL UK
sean.adams@drownedinsound.com
www.drownedinsound.com
Reviews, gigs, downloads, features and more.

Excellent Online.com
eadmin@odc.net
www.excellentonline.com
The home for North American fans of UK Music.

Fast 'n' Bulbous
savand@fastnbulbous.com
www.fastnbulbous.com
I maintain an editorial policy of publishing mainly positive reviews, with the idea that people should be turned on to the best music.

Funky Mofo
Jo Whitby contact@funkymofo.net
www.funkymofo.net
Online record shop covering Indie music.

get ready to ROCK!
Neston, Cheshire, CH64 0TD UK
PH/FX: +44-0-845-1665853
helpdesk@getreadytorock.com
www.getreadytorock.com
Classic and Progressive Rock music news, reviews and interviews.

Gigs Unlimited
17 Cromford Ave. Stretford,
Manchester, England M32 9RQ
info@gigs-unlimited.co.uk
www.gigs-unlimited.co.uk
Dedicated to promoting fresh new talent to give them the push they need to be the "Next Big Thing".

Glasswerk
340A Pinner Rd. Harrow, London, HA1 4LB UK
Jack Cook london@glasswerk.co.uk
www.glasswerk.co.uk
Promoting the best new music at all levels, locally and nationally. We'll let you know when your review is up.

God Is In The TV Fanzine
Bill godisinthetv2003@yahoo.co.uk
www.godisinthetvzine.co.uk
An indie music and culture zine. Features, reviews and forum.

Hot Press
13 Trinity St., Dublin 2, UK
feedback@hotpress.com
www.hotpress.com
The essential guide to Rock, Pop, Dance and Contemporary music.

ilikemusic.com *Soundstage*
Unit 5 Belbins Business Park, Cupernham Lane, Romsey, Hampshire, SO51 7JF UK
PH: +44 (0) 845-430-8651
Cheryl Rickman cheryl@ilikemusic.com
www.ilikemusic.com
Reviews of unsigned talent, music promotion articles, tips and links galore.

Indigo Flow
www.indigoflow.co.uk
Covers all genres of music.

is this music?
PO Box 13516, Linlithgow, EH49 6AS UK
Stuart McHugh editor@isthismusic.com
www.isthismusic.com
A Scottish music monthly that covers Indie music.

The Joanne Davy Show *Radio Six International*
PO Box 600, Glasgow, G41 5SH, Scotland
www.radiosix.com
Designed to promote up-and-coming unsigned artists from all over the world. From Country to Pop.

Leonard's Lair
leonards.lair@ntlworld.com
www.leonardslair.co.uk
We're particularly fond of Electronica, Post-Punk, Post-Rock, Dreampop. It's best to point me out to a link where I can listen to your music to see if it fits.

LOGO Magazine
Mede House, Salisbury St.,
Southampton, SO15 2TZ UK
info@logo-magazine.com
www.logo-magazine.com
Can help you to be seen and heard.

Loudorama
Mojo info@loudorama.co.uk
loudorama.co.uk
Online Indie zine.

Manilla
PO Box 82, Middlesbrough, TS6 6TD UK
info@manillame.com
www.manillame.com
Free mag which promotes unsigned acts.

The Mind's Construction
PO Box 49111, Wimbledon,
London, SW19 2XP UK
Neil Scott themindsconstruction@yahoo.co.uk
www.themindsconstruction.co.uk
We review and interview new, unsigned and upcoming bands.

Music Maker Magazine
28 Grafton Terr. London, NW5 4JJ UK
PH: 020-7424-0027
Brian Healey tradmusic@btinternet.com
www.musicmaker-web.co.uk
www.tradmusic.net
Dedicated to the promotion of independent record labels, songwriters & performers. If you have a CD you would like to see reviewed in the magazines or played on the website then send a copy to the Editor.

Music Press
20 Ward Rd. Salhouse, Norwich,
Norfolk, NR13 6RG UK
PH: +44(0)1603-722149
Matthew Holland info@musicpress.co.uk
www.musicpress.co.uk
A community based news project for both signed and unsigned bands.

music week
ajax@musicweek.com
www.musicweek.com
Music, news, charts, reviews, analysis, features.

MusicOMH.com
Michael Hubbard MichaelAway@musicOMH.com
www.musicomh.com
Established reviews and interviews site. Contact us before you send your music!

Musicmen.co.uk
PH: 0709-23-999-60
info@musicmen.co.uk
www.musicmen.co.uk
Get your name in lights, by submitting your own review.

MusicShopper
11 Trout Road, Haslemere,
Surrey, England GU27 1RD
PH: 44-1428-656878
Stephen Reynolds info@musicshopper.info
www.musicshopper.info
We review and allow you to promote your music on our site.

New Music Express
news@nme.com
www.nme.com
Reviews, interviews, quotes...

No Ordinary Music
talent@no-ordinarymusic.com
www.no-ordinarymusic.com
The UK's best Alternative webzine, brought to you by lovers of all things musical.

No Ripcord
76 Heavygate Rd. Sheffield, S10 1PF UK
PH: 44-0114-234-2622
mail@noripcord.com
www.noripcord.co.uk
Reviews and features of Indie/Alternative bands.

Nunuworld
nunununa@nunuworldmusic.co.uk
www.nunuworldmusic.co.uk
Covers Indie music with reviews, photos, etc.

pennyblackmusic.com
rich@pennyblackmusic.com
www.pennyblackmusic.com
Contact to get your promo reviewed in the magazine.

PHASE9 Entertainment
FX: 44-0-845-280-1708
Nigel M. editorial@phase9.net
www.phase9.tv
Independent site for reviews and information on music and movies in the UK and USA.

PLAYLOUDER
8-10 Rhoda St., London, E2 7EF UK
site@playlouder.com
www.playlouder.com
Bringing you the very best in new music.

Popjustice
Unit 31, Chelsea Wharf, 15 Lots Rd.
London, SW10 0QJ UK
mail@popjustice.co.uk
www.popjustice.co.uk
The lipstick mark on Pop's coffee cup.

Radio Six International
PO Box 600, Glasgow, G41 5SH Scotland
Music@radiosix.com
www.radiosix.com

rawkstar.net
Bob bob@rawkstar.net
www.rawkstar.net
Reviews of new releases, demos, live gigs, interviews etc.

Record Scout
374 Victoria Ave. Southend on Sea,
Essex, SS2 6NA UK
music@recordscout.com
www.recordscout.com
We write music reviews for many magazines around the country and the bands we review will instantly receive national publicity.

Review Centre *Indie Music*
www.reviewcentre.com/products1684.html
A comprehensive guide to Indie Music. Read about Indie albums and contribute your comments or reviews, to help others discover new music.

reviewed4u.com
PO Box 9749, Birmingham, B28 0WB UK
theteam@reviewed4u.com
www.reviewed4u.com
Music, DVD, gig reviews and music news.

Robot Fist
30 Countess Gr. Killarney, Co. Kerry, Ireland
PH: 011-353-86-174-4212
mail@robotfist.com
www.robotfist.com
A pop culture review website.

ROCK SOUND
Unit 22, Jack's Pl. 6 Corbet Pl. Spitalfields,
London, E1 6NN UK
Darren darren.taylor@rock-sound.net
www.rock-sound.net
Bringing you all the best new music from around the world.

Rock's Backpages
63 Pont St., London, SW1X 0BD UK
Barney Hoskyns barney@rocksbackpages.com
www.rocksbackpages.com
News, reviews and interviews of new artists.

rockcity.co.uk
8 Talbot St., Nottingham, NG1 5GG UK
PH: 0115-9412544 FX: 0115-9418438
boxoffice@rock-city.co.uk
www.rock-city.co.uk
Reviews of both signed and unsigned recorded material and live shows.

RockFeedback.com
PO Box 704, High Wycombe, HP15 7GL UK
press@rockfeedback.com
www.rockfeedback.com
Contact us to get featured on the site.

Russell's Reviews
Russell Barker russ@russellsreviews.co.uk
www.russellsreviews.co.uk
CD, demo and gig reviews from reviewer based in Oxford, UK.

Shindig
64 North View Rd. London, N8 7LL UK
Jon 'Mojo' Mills info@shindig-magazine.com
www.shindig-magazine.com
Reviews Psych and Garage. No plain ole Indie/Alt-Rock.

soundsxp
30 Somerville Rd. London, SE20 7NA UK
submissions@soundsxp.com
www.soundsxp.com
Push your product. Indie, Punk and Electronica.

Sorted
PO Box 6804, Dublin 7, Ireland UK
Donnacha DeLong editor@sortedmagazine.com
sortedmagazine.com
Interviews, album, single and concert reviews.

state51
Rhoda St., London, E2 7EF UK
PH: 44-207-729-4343
intouch@state51.co.uk
www.state51.co.uk
Showcasing the best new music in all genres.

StereoHead
chris@stereohead.co.uk
www.stereohead.co.uk
Contact us to find out where to send your CD.

Tangents Online
PO Box 102, Exeter, EX2 4YL UK
editor@tangents.co.uk
www.tangents.co.uk
The home of Un-Popular culture on the web.

Tastyzine
info@tastyfanzine.org.uk
www.tastyfanzine.org.uk
Recommending the soundtrack for the revolution.

TweeNet
c/o Peter Hahndorf at Saltmine Atelier House,
64 Pratt St., London, NW1 0LF UK
PH: 44-7930-283774
www.twee.net
Submit your music and a press release to us.

UKMusic.com
Doug Cooper info@ukmusic.com
www.ukmusic.com
We have the perfect mix of music news, features, interviews and reviews from all your favourite UK artists!

Uncut Magazine
c/o IPC Media, 25th Fl., King's Reach Tower,
Stamford St., London, SE1 9LS UK
PH: 020-7261-6992 FX: 020-7261-5573
www.uncut.co.uk/music
Reviews CDs of major and independent artists.

unsignedcentral
54 Crayford Way, Crayford, Kent, DA1 4LQ UK
sales@unsignedcentral.co.uk
www.unsignedcentral.co.uk
There is a void in the UK music industry. Its where Rock & Roll used to live.

Whisperin & Hollerin
Cosheen, Schull, Co Cork, Republic of Ireland
Tim Peacock tim@whisperinandhollerin.com
www.whisperinandhollerin.com
Music reviews and interviews with an Alternative bias - covers a huge range of genres.

Zeitgeist
PO Box 13499, Edinburgh, EH6 8YL UK
info@the-rocker.co.uk
the-rocker.freeservers.com
Reflecting the underground through music.

Australia

Alternate Music Press
PO Box 2286, Ringwood North, VIC 3134 Australia
www.alternatemusicpress.com
Reviews, interviews, article and music news. Please DO NOT send Rock, Alternative, or Pop music. There are hundreds of other magazines online, and elsewhere, which cover these genres. We will review Folk, Jazz, Blues, New Age, Ambient and Classical.

Blunt Review
emily@bluntreview.com
www.bluntreview.com
We review Indie music and interview musicians.

Buzz Magazine
PO Box 55, Dromana, VIC 3936 Australia
PH: 61-3-59812979 FX: 61-3-59861449
psutton@r150.aone.net.au
www.buzzmagazine.com.au
Features interviews with Australian and international artists, reviews and columns.

Gods of Music
nycran@godsofmusic.com
www.godsofmusic.com
Honest reviews for all bands/artists.

Long Gone Loser
PO Box 18, Modbury North, SA 5092 Australia
damo@longgoneloser.com
www.longgoneloser.com
Feel free to send anything for review.

Mediasearch
PO Box 132 Melbourne, VIC 3001 Australia
PH: 61-3-9282-4841
info@mediasearch.com.au
www.mediasearch.com.au
Entertainment news on music, film and fashion.

Secrets of Home Theater and High Fidelity
staff@hometheaterhifi.com
www.hometheaterhifi.com
Music, movie and product reviews.

Undercover
11-15 Buckhurst St., South Melbourne,
VIC 3205 Australia
PH: +61-3-9686-4800
Tim Cashmere tim@undercover.com.au
www.undercover.net.au
News, reviews, interviews and more!

Asia

BigO
PO Box 784, Marine Parade, Singapore 914410
PH: 63484007 FX: 63480362
singbigo@singnet.com.sg
www.bigo.com.sg
Features more than 150 reviews each issue.

Indie Culture
1217 Leyson St., Talamban, Cebu City, Philippines
PH: 6332-4160333 FX: 6332-4160409
Ian Zafra ian@indiecultureonline.com
www.indiecultureonline.com
Support and nurtures indie musicians, as they are the authors of music that is timeless and transcends pop trends and cultures.

Blues

North America

United States

Blues Blowtorch
RR 2, Box 5, Clinton, IL 61727-9802
PH: 217-935-8603
Frank deltafrank@bluesblowtorch.com
www.bluesblowtorch.com
Promoting the Blues in all its forms.

Blues Music Now!
Jeff Stevens editor@bluesmusicnow.com
www.bluesmusicnow.com
Contact to send your CD for review.

Blues On Stage
PO Box 582983, Minneapolis, MN 55458-2983
Ray Stiles mnblues@aol.com
www.mnblues.com
Send 2 copies of CDs for reviews.

Blues Revue
Route 1, Box 75, Salem, WV 26426-9604
PH: 304-782-1971 FX: 304-782-1993
info@bluesrevue.com
www.bluesrevue.com
Artist profiles, interviews, reviews and more.

Blues Bytes
Bruce Coen information@bluenight.com
www.bluenight.com/BluesBytes
A monthly Blues CD review magazine.

Bluesrockers
Tom Branson tom@bluesrockers.ws
www.bluesrockers.ws
Information and reviews on the best artists and recordings available.

Blueswax.com
www.blueswax.com
Reviews, industry news, interviews and MP3s.

Cross Harp Chronicles
PO Box 6283, Jackson, MI 49204
PH: 517-569-2615 FX: 517-569-8664
Dave King dking@crossharpchronicles.com
crossharpchronicles.com
Interviews with harmonica/Blues movers and shakers, concert news, CD reviews etc. We encourage independent Blues artists worldwide to drop us a line!

Electric Blues
PO Box 1370, Riverview, FL 33568-1370
herm@electricblues.com
www.electricblues.com
CD reviews, news and more.

Living Blues Magazine
PO Box 1848, 301 Hill Hall, University, MS 38677
PH: 800-390-3527 FX: 662-915-7842
lblues@olemiss.edu
www.livingblues.com
A bimonthly magazine for the Blues.

NothinButDaBlues.com
PO Box 13363, Las Vegas, NV 89112-3363
PH: 702-456-8776 FX: 702-456-8776
mail@nothinbutdablues.com
www.nothinbutdablues.com
Introduces you to lesser known artists.

Europe

Austria

BluesArtStudio
PO Box 54, Vienna, Austria
bluesart@bluesartstudio.at
www.bluesartstudio.at
Supporting and promoting the Blues.

Belgium

Back to the Roots
Knollestraat 1, 8210 Zedelgem, Belgium
PH: 32-0-478-306-325 FX: 32-0-50-27-58-87
backtotheroots.franky@pi.be
www.backtotheroots.be
Is een nederlandstalig magazine voor Blues en aanverwante muziekstijlen.

Germany

Blues News Magazine
Verlag Dirk Föhrs, Freiherr-vom-Stein-Str. 28,
D-58762 Altena, Germany
PH: 0-23-52-21-68-0
Redaktion@Blues-Germany.de
www.blues-germany.de
News, reviews, events etc.

Italy

Blues and Blues
info@bluesandblues.it
www.bluesandblues.it
The Italian Blues website.

The Netherlands

Blue Ears
E. Samsonstraat 5, 1103 MR Amsterdam Z-O,
The Netherlands
info@BlueEars.com
www.blueEars.com
Independent radio station for adventurous Blues (y) music.

Sweden

Jefferson
c/o Ingemar Karlsson, Järpegatan 1 C,
SE-664 31 Grums, Sweden
records@jeffersonbluesmag.com
jeffersonbluesmag.com
Administered by the Scandinavian Blues Association.

United Kingdom

Blues In Britain
10, Messaline Ave. London, W3 6JX UK
PH: 44-0-20-8723-7376 FX: 44-0-20-8723 7380
Jon Taylor info@bluesinbritain.org
www.blueprint-blues.co.uk
Blues news, reviews and interviews and a four page gig guide to blues events in the UK.

Blues Matters!
PO Box 18, Bridgend, CF33 6YW UK
PH: 44-0-1656-743406
Alan 'D' Pearce editor@bluesmatters.com
www.bluesmatters.com
Old, New, Traditional, Nu and any other type of Blues.

Blues Freepress
18 Louis St., HU3 1LY UK
info@bluesfreepress.org
www.bluesfreepress.org
Mark your package with "Promo Material - Not For Resale". Send two copies of each item.

Juke Blues
PO Box 1654, Yatton, Bristol, BS49 4FD UK
juke@jukeblues.com
www.bluesworld.com/JukeBlues.html
Interviews, news reviews, gig guide and more.

Asia

Japan

Tokyo-Blues
www.tokyo-blues.com
All over the Blues scene in Japan like kudzu in Georgia.

Children's

Boopadoo
Box 5173, Norwell, MA 02061
Kimberly Robasky editor@boopadoo.net
www.boopadoo.net
Resources supporting the children's music industry. There's a reviews section, a place to link your own music (downloads). Send products, CDs, permission letters, and any other materials for review, to the above address.

Edutaining Kids *Guide to Children's Music*
submissions@edutainingkids.com
www.edutainingkids.com/music.html
Articles, spotlights, reviews etc.

John Wood Revue
john@kidzmusic.com
www.kidzmusic.com
A great place to find some of the best Children's music.

Christian

North America

United States

Balaam's Miracle's Gothic and Industrial Pages
balaamsmiracle.cjb.net
Dedicated to Alternative music, such as Gothic and Industrial, made by artists with Christian beliefs.

BlackChristian.com
PH: 978-590-4609
www.blackchristian.com
Several resources including music reviews.

CatholicMusicNetwork.com
webmaster@catholicmusicnetwork.com
www.catholicmusicnetwork.com
Source for music by today's top Catholic artists.

The Christian Rapper
PO Box 1752, Carrollton, GA 30117
thechristianrapper@yahoo.com
www.thechristianrapper.com
Please send all materials.

Christianity Today
465 Gunderson Dr. Carol Stream, IL 60188
PH: 630-260-6200 FX: 630-260-0114
music@christianitytoday.com
christianmusictoday.com
News, interviews and reviews. We only review the best of what we receive.

Contemporary Christian Magazine
104 Woodmont Blvd. #300, Nashville, TN 37205
www.ccmcom.com
Supporting Indie Christian bands.

Cornerstone Magazine Music
939 W. Wilson Ave. Chicago, IL 60640
Christopher Wiitala cwiitala@cornerstonemag.com
www.cornerstonemag.com
Reviews, interviews and more.

Godcore.com
12271 Magnolia Way, Brighton, CO 80602
PH: 877-778-4016
jason@godcore.com
www.godcore.com
Helps Christian Rockers gain worldwide exposure.

Gospel Crib
Kenny G. gospelcrib2001@yahoo.com
gospelcrib.8m.com
Showcasing choirs, groups and soloists.

Gospel Synergy Magazine
PO Box 286261, Chicago, IL 60628
PH: 708-272-6640
Andre Carter alcarter@gospelsynergy.com
www.gospelsynergy.com
Articles about God's word and Gospel music.

Gospel Today
286 Hwy 314, #C, Fayetteville, GA 30214
PH: 770-719-4825 FX: 770-716-2660
gospeltodaymag@aol.com
www.gospeltoday.com
New Gospel CDs, record sales charts, etc.

The Gospel Zone
PO Box 5211, Oakland, CA 94605
PH: 510-472-0177
Curtis Jermany info@urbangospelalliance.com
www.thegospelzone.com
Reviews, news, message boards and upcoming events.

GospelFlava.com
info@gospelflava.com
www.gospelflava.com
Reviews new CD and video Gospel releases.

Hammonline.com
4445-B Breton Rd. SE #196,
Kentwood, MI 49508-8411
Tim Hamm tim@hammsterwheel.com
www.hammonline.com
All submissions should include a press kit, or at least a fact sheet pertaining to the release.

Hip Hop For The Soul
caleb@hiphopforthesoul.com
hiphopforthesoul.com
To have your album considered for review, contact me.

HM Magazine
6307 Cele Rd. #573, Pflugerville, TX 78660
PH: 512-989-7309 x101 FX: 512-670-2764
Doug Van Pelt dvanpelt@hmmagazine.com
www.hmmagazine.com
Features interviews, news and reviews of Hard Music. Send 2 copies (if possible), because that will allow us to send one copy out to a freelance writer.

IntenseRadio.com
PO Box 1477, Mt. Juliet, TN 37121-1477
PH: 615-773-2587
www.intenseradio.com
Promotes the Christian Metal sound.

Jamsline.com
jamsline@jamsline.com
www.jamsline.com
Weekly single reviews.

Jesusfreakhideout.com
PO Box 559, Bethlehem, PA 18016-0559
email@jesusfreakhideout.com
www.jesusfreakhideout.com
Send in your CD to be reviewed.

Kay 3 Music
3 Bryn Mawr Ave. Worcester, MA 01605
PH: 978-984-3106
info@kay3music.com
www.kay3music.com
Our mission is to help artists gain support.

Metal for Jesus
Johannes Jonsson johannes@metalforjesus.org
www.metalforjesus.org
If you play in a Christian Metal band and want me to review your CD/demo, I'll gladly review it.

NeuFutur
308 S. Maple St., Lancaster, OH 43130
editor@neufutur.com
www.neufutur.com
Covers anything from Christian praise to Death Metal. Fight on, little ones.

nuthinbutgospel.com
c/o Louis Williams, PO Box 34653,
Washington, DC 20043-4653
www.nuthinbutgospel.com
Send your music in for review.

Onward Warriors
onwardwarriors.filternet.nl
Christian Progressive Metal.

Opus' Album Reviews
www.opuszine.com
If you'd like to send ins a demo, please contact me. Also, a brief bio about your band, influences, etc. would be helpful.

Phantom Tollboth
PO Box 11934, Chicago, IL 60611
PH: 773-274-6413
feedback@tollbooth.org
tollbooth.org
Album, concert and movie reviews, interviews, features and resource links.

Power Source
PO Box 101336 Nashville, TN 37224
PH: 615-742-9210 FX: 615-248-8505
Vickie Gardner vickie@powersourcemagazine.com
www.powersourcemusic.com
Country Christian and Gospel music magazine. Official publication of theChristian Country Music Association.

PraiseTV.com
PO Box 428, Safety Harbor, FL 34695
PH: 877-296-7744
www.praisetv.com
Christian artist profiles, features, reviews and more!

Servant's Heart
PO Box 34064, Bethesda, MD 20827
PH: 240-994-8340
www.servantsheart.net
We're currently serving Christian artists and bands only (or family friendly artists with a positive message) but we'll be happy to help all artists with other free services such as photography, videography, recording, booking, distribution.

Singing News Magazine
PO Box 2810, 330 University Hall Dr.
Boone, NC 28607
PH: 828-264-3700 FX: 828-264-4621
www.singingnews.com
Concerts, new recordings and the latest chart action.

SouthernGospelNews.com
220 Indian Park Dr. #1501,
Murfreesboro, TN 37128 Attn: Reviews
webmaster@sogospelnews.com
sogospelnews.com
News, information, artist interviews, CD reviews and more!

Sphere of Hip Hop
sphereo@sphereofhiphop.com
www.sphereofhiphop.com
Featured items: MP3, reviews, charts, email list, articles and more!

Tastyfresh
www.tastyfresh.com
Christ centered DJ culture.

Virtuosity
423 Cedar St., Ketchikan, AK 99901
Dave Taylor virtuosity@att.net
home.att.net/~virtuosity
Spiritual Progressive Rock reviews. We play songs from the albums we review on the radio show "Holy Tsunami" on KRBD.

Wendy V's Christian/Gospel CD spotlight
2136 Ford Pkwy #206, St. Paul, MN 55116
Wendy Vickers wendyv2941@aol.com
www.wendyv.com
E-mail me and tell me about your CD before you send it in!

What's the Word Magazine
200 Rhode Island Ave. NE #401,
Washington, DC 20002
PH: 202-635-8222
wtwmagazine@hotmail.com
www.wtwmagazine.com
New, reviews, interviews, a chat room and message boards.

Canada

FEED
Box 96, Kingsville, ON N9Y 2E8
PH: 647-722-4306 FX: 866-871-1914
editorial@feedstop.com
www.feedstop.com
Your source for the best in beats, rhymes & light.

GospelCity.com
1410 Stanley, #1020, Montreal, QC H3A 1P8
PH: 514-868-1600 FX: 514-868-1067
michelle@agmediagrp.com
gospelcity.com
News, reviews, articles, radio and more!

Europe

Germany

CCMPlanet
www.ccmplanet.com
Daily news, artist information, concert information, album reviews and more!

The Netherlands

soundmission.tk
soundmission@hotmail.com
www.soundmission.tk
Christian Prog and Metal resource.

United Kingdom

Cross Rhythms Magazine
PO Box 1110, Stoke on Trent, ST1 1XR UK
PH: 44-8700-118008 FX: 44-8700-117002
admin@crossrhythms.co.uk
www.crossrhythms.com
Articles, features and a HUGE review section.

Halcyon Sounds
4 Newark Green, Worcester, WR4 0TB UK
PH: 07830-119190
Mike Deal mike@halcyonsounds.co.uk
www.halcyonsounds.co.uk
Christian band promotion and listings.

talkGospel.com
PO Box 13000, London, SW1P 4XP UK
PH: 020-7316-1300 FX: 020-7233-6706
enquiries@talkGospel.com
www.talkgospel.com
Supports the Gospel music scene, particularly British artists.

United by ONE
PO Box 3093, South Croydon, CR2 0YB UK
PH: 44-0-208 405-2291
info@unitedbyone.co.uk
www.unitedbyone.co.uk
Urban Gospel site from the UK to the world.

Classical

North America

United States

Bass World
13140 Coit Rd. #320, LB 120,
Dallas, TX 75240-5737
PH: 972-233-9107 x204 FX: 972-490-4219
info@isbworldoffice.com
www.isbworldoffice.com
Reviews recordings and music internationally.

Chamber Music Magazine
305 7th Ave. 5th Fl. New York, NY 10001
PH: 212-242-2022 FX: 212-242-7955
info@chamber-music.org
www.chamber-music.org
Send new CDs and books, as well as press releases by mail.

Classical CD Review
bob@classicalcdreview.com
www.classicalcdreview.com
We review CDs we feel are of particular interest to us and to our readers.

Classicalist.com
info@classicalist.com
www.classicalist.com
Add your review to Classicalist.

Classics Today
David Hurwitz dhurwitz@classicstoday.com
www.classicstoday.com
Five feature reviews per day.

Early Music America
2366 Eastlake Ave. E. #429, Seattle, WA 98102
PH: 206-720-6270 FX: 206-720-6290
info@earlymusic.org
earlymusic.org
Artist profiles, interview and record reviews.

Early Music NEWS
PO Box 544, Pacific Palisades, CA 90272-0544
PH: 310-358-5967
info@earlymusicla.org
www.earlymusicla.org
Features reviews of early music CD recordings.

La Folia
86 Church St., Belfast, ME 04915
PH/FX: 207-338-5585
Mike Silverton editor@lafolia.com
www.lafolia.com
We do review Independent CDs. They MUST be Classical, Old and New, or Jazz other than mainstream.

Guitarra Magazine
226 S. Michigan Ave. Chicago, IL 60604
PH: 312-427-5611
guitar@guitarramagazine.com
guitarramagazine.com
Articles and interviews with top Classical guitar players.

Guitart
guitart@guitart.net
www.guitart.net
Classical guitar magazine blending art and music with a European aesthetic.

The Horn Call
School of Music, W. Michigan U.
Kalamazoo, MI 49008
PH: 269-387-4692 FX: 269-387-1113
editor@hornsociety.org
www.hornsociety.org
News, feature articles, clinics, music and reviews.

International Trumpet Guild
cdreviews@trumpetguild.org
www.trumpetguild.org
Improves communications among trumpet players around the world.

MUSIC & VISION
www.mvdaily.com
Encouraging and educating young writers about serious music.

New Music Connoisseur
Barry L. Cohen publisher@newmusicon.org
www.newmusicon.org
Focusing on the work of the composers of our time, with added coverage of rare, neglected Classical music from national and ethnic sources. We are open to the new "crossover" music and to a lot of what is known as New Age.

NewMusicBox
30 W. 26th St. #1001, New York, NY 10010
editor@newmusicbox.org
www.newmusicbox.org
Features any new CD that includes repertoire by American composers.

Online Trombone Journal
PO Box 1758, Starkville, MS 39760
PH: 662-325-8021
www.trombone.org
Provides trombonists a place to share information about trombone pedagogy and performance.

Renaissance Magazine
1144 Rte 12A, Surry, NH 03431
Kim Guarnaccia editor@renaissancemagazine.com
renaissancemagazine.com
We accept music from the Middle Ages and Renaissance time periods for review.

Sequenza21
340 W. 57th St. 12B, New York, NY 10019
Jerry sequenza21@gmail.com
www.sequenza21.com
News, interviews and featured composers.

Strings Magazine
PO Box 767, San Anselmo, CA 94979
PH: 415-485-6946 FX: 415-485-0831
st@pcspublink.com
www.stringsmagazine.com
For the violin, viola, cello, bass or fiddle.

Turok's Choice
PO Box 202, Old Chelsea Stn.
New York, NY 10113-0202
tchoice@concentric.net
www.concentric.net/~Tchoice
Monthly newsletter reviewing new Classical CDs.

USOperaweb.com
www.usoperaweb.com
Online magazine devoted to American Opera.

Violinist.com
www.violinist.com
News, reviews and resources. Feel free to promote your upcoming concerts or CD releases.

Web Concert Hall
webconcerthall@usa.com
www.webconcerthall.com
Providing artist with a chance to gain exposure.

World Guitarist
PO Box 1660, Claremont, CA 91711
Gunnar Eisel geisel@worldguitarist.com
www.worldguitarist.com
Daily news coverage for the world Classical Guitar community.

Canada

La Scena Musicale
5409 Waverly, Montréal, QC H2T 2X8
PH: 514-948-2520 FX: 514-274-9456
Lucie@scena.org
www.scena.org
Publishes reviews from independent artists.

Europe

Czech Republic

Harmonie
Jana Vondráková, Novákovych 8, 180 00 Praha 8, Czech Republic
PH: 266-311-701 FX: 284-820-127
info@muzikus.cz
casopisy.muzikus.cz/harmonie
Classical music and Jazz magazine.

His Voice
Besedni 3 118 00 Praha 1, Czech Republic
PH: 420-257-312-422 FX: 420-257-317-424
redakce@hisvoice.cz
www.hisvoice.cz
Festivals and reviews of contemporary music.

France

Avant-Scène Opéra
15, rue Tiquetonne, 75002 Paris, France
PH: 33-1-42-33-51-51 FX: 33-1-42-33-80-91
premieres.loges@wanadoo.fr
www.asopera.com
Publication for professionals and music-lovers.

naïve classique - andante.com
148, rue du Faubourg Poissonnière,
75010 Paris, France
infos@andante.com
andante.com
News, reviews, concert reviews, essays and more.

Paris Transatlantic.com
www.paristransatlantic.com
Global coverage of New, Classical and Avant-Garde music.

Germany

Crescendo
Senefelderstraße 14, 80336 München, Germany
PH: 49-0-89-74-15-09-0 FX: 49-0-89-74-15-09-11
crescendo@portmedia.de
www.crescendo-online.de
Deutschlands Klassik Magazin

klassik.com
Dillenburger Strasse 93, D-51105 Köln, Germany
PH: 49-221-240-3856 FX: 49-221-240-4147
redaktion@klassik.com
www.klassik.com
Klassik-portal mit umfangreichen Informationen zur Klassischen musik

Klassik-Heute.com
Jägerstraße 17, Hörgertshausen, 85413, Germany
PH: 49-0-8764-92-09-42 FX: 49-0-8764-92-09-43
info@klassik-treff.de
www.klassik-heute.com
Musik, Festival, Konzert, Oper, Künstler, CD, Komponist.

Online Muzik Magazin
Westkotter Str. 166, 42277 Wuppertal, Germany
PH: 49-0-202-50-63-22 FX: 49-0-202-50-13-23
www.omm.de
Das erste deutschsprachige Musikmagazin im Internet.

Oper&Tanz
Brienner Straße 52, 80333 München, Germany
PH: 0941-94-593-12 FX: 0941-94-593-50
redaktion@operundtanz.de
www.operundtanz.de
Zeitschrift für Opernchor und Bühnentanz.

Das Opernglas
Grelckstraße 36, 22529 Hamburg, Germany
PH: 040-58-55-01 FX: 040-58-55-05
opernglas@compuserve.com
www.opernglas.de
Reviews and information.

Italy

Audio Review
tommolini@tommolini.com
c/o TechniPress S.r.l., Via della Bufalotta, 374, 00139 Rome, Italy
www.audioreview.it

Hortus Musicus
Piazza di Porta Ravegnana 1 - 40126 Bologna, Italy
PH: 051-239295 FX: 051-239295
info@hortusmusicus.com
www.hortusmusicus.com
Italian Early Music magazine.

PromArt
36100 Vicenza, contrà san Pietro 21, Italy
PH: 0444-304992 FX: 0444-314320
promart@promart.it
www.promart.it
News, reviews and an artist database.

The Netherlands

Het ORGEL
c/o Dr. Hans Fidom, Zwarteweg 5, NL 9973 PM Houwerzijl, The Netherlands
PH: 31-595-57-18-85 FX: 31-595-57-22-61
fidom@bart.nl
www.hetorgel.nl
Europe's oldest magazine on Organ Art.

Spain

FILOMUSICA Classical music and Opera
Daniel Mateos filomusica@terra.es
www.filomusica.com
We review all kinds of Classical music, including independent.

Goldberg
Poligono Talluntxen, Calle A, Nave 24, 31110
Noain, Navarra, Spain
PH: 34-948-250-372 FX: 34-948-196-276
info@goldberg-magazine.com
www.goldberg-magazine.com
We review only CDs of early music before 1750.

Mundo Clasico
admin@mundoclasico.com
www.mundoclasico.com
Articles, interviews, reviews and news.

Ritmo
10 (Oficina95)-28050, Madrid, Spain
PH: 913588774 FX: 91-3588944
correo@revistaritmo.com
www.ritmo.es
Disfrute del mundo de la música clásica desde Internet.

Sweden

Musik Dramatik
Box 4038, 102 61 Stockholm, Sweden
PH: 08-643-95-44 FX: 08-442-11-33
info@tidskriftenopera.nu
md.partitur.se
Sweden's foremost Opera Magazine!

Switzerland

Cosmopolis Musikarchiv
feedback@cosmopolis.ch
www.cosmopolis.ch/musik.htm
We review music by major labels and independent artists.

HarpEvents Magazine
Dorneckstr. 105, CH-4143 Dornach, Switzerland
PH: 41-61-701-88-58
office@harpa.com
www.harpa.com
News, announcements, CDs and articles.

Musik & Theater
Postfach 1680, CH-8040 Zürich, Switzerland
PH: 41-1-491-71-88 FX: 41-1-493-11-76
musikundtheater@bluewin.ch
www.musikundtheater.ch
CD-Besprechungen, Musik, Theater, Oper, Interviews...

United Kingdom

BBC Music Magazine
BBC Radio 3, London, W1N 4DJ UK
PH: 087-00-100-100
radio3.website@bbc.co.uk
www.bbc.co.uk/music/classical
www.bbc.co.uk/radio3/classical
CD reviews, interviews, features, news etc.

Brass Band World
PH: 44-0-1298-812816 FX: 44-0-1298-815220
editor@brassbandworld.com
www.brassbandworld.com
An Independent monthly magazine for bands.

Classical Guitar Magazine
1 & 2 Vance Ct. Trans Britannia Enterprise Park,
Blaydon on Tyne, NE21 5NH UK
PH: 44-0-191-414-9000 FX: 44-0-191-414-9001
classicalguitar@ashleymark.co.uk
www.classicalguitarmagazine.com
Features, interviews, news and reviews.

Classical Source
31 Great Queen St., London, WC2B 5AE UK
editor@classicalsource.com
www.classicalsource.com
Providing news and reviews.

ClassicalLink *MusicWeb*
Regent House, 24-25 Nutford Pl.
London, W1H 5YN UK
PH: 44-20-7569-3194 FX: 44-20-7725-7024
Len@musicweb.uk.net
www.classicall.net
We post about 12 new reviews a day. We also have areas of the site dealing with live Classical concerts, Film Music and Jazz.

Double Bassist
c/o Orpheus Publications, 2nd Fl. 30 Cannon St.,
London, EC4M 6YJ UK
PH: 020-7618-3456, FX: 020-7618-3483
www.doublebassist.com
The music magazine for double bass teachers, students, players and makers.

Horn Magazine
CAF Admin Service (6206) Kings Hill,
West Malling, Kent, ME19 4TA UK
mike@british-horn.org
www.british-horn.org
News, views, reviews and the Hornascope.

International Record Review
1 Haven Green, London, W5 2UU UK
PH: 44-0-20-8810-9050 FX: 44-0-20-8810-9081
info@recordreview.co.uk
www.recordreview.co.uk
Actively seeks out CDs for review.

International Trombone Association Journal
1 Broomfield Rd. Coventry, CV5 6JW UK
www.ita-web.org
Trombone news, gigs and record reviews.

New Notes
4th Fl. St Margaret's House, 18-20 Southwark St.,
London, SE1 1TJ UK
PH: 020-7407-1640
spnm@spnm.org.uk
www.spnm.org.uk
Promoting New Music!

Opera Magazine
36 Black Lion Ln. London, W6 9BE UK
editor@operamag.clara.co.uk
www.opera.co.uk
News, letters, interviews, reviews and more.

Seen and Heard
SeenandHeard@BTOpenworld.com
www.musicweb.uk.net/SandH
The largest live music review site on the web.

The Strad
PO Box 935, Finchingfield, Braintree,
Essex, CM74LN UK
PH: 44-01371-810433 FX: 44-01371-811065
Peter Quantrill pquantrill@orpheuspublications.com
www.thestrad.com
We review CDs of string music and string musicians.

The Trombonist
1 Broomfield Rd. Coventry, CV5 6JW UK
FX: 44-24-7671-2550
www.trombone-society.org.uk
The magazine of the British Trombone society.

Australia

Opera~Opera
PO Box R-361, Royal Exchange,
NSW 1225 Australia
PH: 61-2-92472264 FX: 61-2-92472269
deg@opera-opera.com.au
www.opera-opera.com.au
We certainly have no qualms about reviewing releases emanating from independent quarters.

New Zealand

The Opera Critic
PO Box 99826, Newmarket, Auckland, NZ
PH: 64-9-525-3996
michael@theoperacritic.com
theoperacritic.com
Reviews, articles and news about opera worldwide.

Asia

CLASSICA JAPAN
iio@tka.att.ne.jp
www.classicajapan.com
Classical music news and links.

Country

Country, C&W, Americana, Bluegrass, Roots, Alt-Country and Rockabilly

North America

United States

3rd COAST MUSIC
237 W. Mandalay Dr. San Antonio, TX 78212
PH: 210-820-3748
John Conquest john@3rdcoastmusic.com
3rdcm.austinamericana.com
I ONLY review indie releases!

alternativecountry.com
alt_staff@alternativecountry.com
www.alternativecountry.com
We review music and include news and information.

AngryCountry.com
Thomas Rhodes angry@angrycountry.com
www.angrycountry.com
Openly reviews Indie projects. All Country music related genres are covered, including Bluegrass, Texas country, and Christian Country.

Blue Suede News
Box 25, Duvall, WA 98019-0025
PH: 425-788-2776
shakinboss@aol.com
www.bluesuedenews.com
We cover the entire spectrum of American Roots music.

Bluegrass Music Profiles
PO Box 850, Nicholasville, KY 40340-0850
PH: 859-333-6465
info@bluegrassmusicprofiles.com
www.bluegrassmusicprofiles.com
Personal interviews with Bluegrass artists.

bluegrass now
PO Box 2020, Rolla, MO 65402
PH: 573-341-7336 FX: 573-341-7352
kumr@umr.edu
www.bluegrassnow.com
Reviews, interviews, profiles and more!

Bluegrass Rules
Gary Cook, RR 1, PO Box 112E,
Lebanon, VA 24266
www.bluegrassrules.com
Submit your new release for review.

Bluegrass Unlimited
PO Box 771, Warrenton, VA 20188-0771
PH: 540-349-8181 FX: 540-341-0011
editor@bluegrassmusic.com
www.bluegrassmusic.com
Promotes Bluegrass and Old-time Country musicians.

Bluegrass Works
31 Oakdale Ave. Weston, MA 02493
admin@bluegrassworks.com
www.bluegrassworks.com
Supports the musicians and other fans who help make the music.

BluegrassAmericana.com
PO Box 5202, Concord, NC 28027-5202
PH: 704-788-6789
info@GoAmericana.com
www.AmericanaConnect.com
We invite you to send your CDs for review.

Country Interviews Online
PO Box 558, Smyrna, TN 37167
PH: 815-361-3172 FX: 309-273-3965
L. Megan countryinterviewsonline@comcast.net
www.CountryInterviewsOnline.net
Reviews & interviews with major & Indie label artists.

Country Legends Association
CLA Review, Box 7171, Duluth, MN 55807-7171
Frank Dell reviews@clalonestar.com
www.clalonestar.com
Send in your Country, Gospel and Bluegrass. We also have radio shows.

Country Line Magazine
16150 S. IH-35, Buda, TX 78610
PH: 512-295-8400 FX: 512-295-8600
T.J. Greaney tj@countrylinemagazine.com
www.countrylinemagazine.com
We are about Country music, born in Texas or raised in Nashville.

Country Standard Time
54 Ballard St., Newton Ctr., MA 02459-1251
PH: 617-969-0331
Jeffrey B. Remz countryst@aol.com
countrystandardtime.com
Your guide to Roadhouse, Roots and Rockabilly.

CountryReview.com
George Peden george@countryreview.com
www.countryreview.com
We're always happy to consider reviewing new music.

Cybergrass
520 Carved Ter. Colorado Springs, CO 80919
www.cybergrass.com
News about Bluegrass music, artists and the music business. Promote your shows!

Flatpicking Guitar
PO Box 2160, Pulaski, VA 24301
PH: 540-980-0338 FX: 540-980-0557
info@flatpick.com
www.flatpick.com
Presenting the art of flat picking the Acoustic guitar.

Freight Train Boogie
PO Box 4262, Santa Rosa, CA 95402
Bill Frater frater@freighttrainboogie.com
www.freighttrainboogie.com
News and reviews of Roots music.

Hillbilly-Music.com
PO Box 18127, San Jose, CA 95158
Dave webmaster@hillbilly-music.com
www.hillbilly-music.com
We can't promise we'll review everything, but we'll try at least to let you the fans know the things that left us with a good impression along the way.

iBluegrass
203 Passage Gate Way, Wilmington, NC 28412
PH: 910-221-9474
Skip Ogden cwo@ibest.net
www.ibluegrass.com
We will accept unsolicited material for review and submission for publication. Check our site for submission details.

Mandolin Magazine
PO Box 13537, Salem, OR 97309
PH: 503-364-2100 FX: 503-588-7707
www.mandolinmagazine.com
We review CDs, books, videos and instruments.

My Kind of Country
100 Sherri Ln. Powhatan Point, OH 44001
Marlene Slater marli@mkoc.com
www.mkoc.com
Country music at its finest.

No Depression
2 Morse Cir. Durham, NC 27713
Peter Blackstock peter@nodepression.net
www.nodepression.net
Covers Alternative-Country music (whatever that is).

Old-Time Herald Online
PO Box 994, Carrboro, NC 27510
PH: 919-967-7727 FX: 919-967-7727
info@oldtimeherald.org
www.oldtimeherald.org
Celebrates the love of Old-Time music.

The Rockabilly Hall of Fame
PO Box 639, Burns, TN 37029
PH: 615-740-7625 FX: 615-740-8181
Bob Timmers bob@rockabillyhall.com
www.rockabillyhall.com
Great Rockabilly compilations and artists.

Rockabilly Magazine
PO Box 19712, Austin, TX 78760
PH: 888-516-0707 FX: 512-385-4300
Orlando orios@rockabillymagazine.com
www.rockabillymagazing.com
The Ultimate Source for Rockabilly info.

Rockzillaworld
PO Box 154329, Irving, TX 75015
Attn: Music Reviews
reviews@rockzilla.net
www.rockzilla.net
Our primary focus is Americana music.

Roots Music Report
107 Blue Oak Ln. Wimberley, TX 78676
PH/FX: 512-847-8346
rmr@rootsmusicreport.com
Robert Bartosh rmr@rootsmusicreport.com
www.rootsmusicreport.com
Reviews and articles on Roots music and artists.

Take Country Back
info@takecountryback.com
www.takecountryback.com
CD reviews, artist features and news.

TwangCast
PO Box 1726, Fredericksburg, VA 22402
R.W. Shamy Jr. twangradio@twangcast.com
www.twangcast.com
Articles and reviews on Twang music.

Western Beat
PO Box 128105, Nashville, TN 37212
PH: 615-248-5026 FX: 615-248-3067
billy@westernbeat.com
www.westernbeat.com
A place where musical integrity rules.

Canada

Country Music News
Box 7323, Vanier Stn. Ottawa, ON K1L 8E4
PH: 613-745-6006 FX: 613-745-0576
Larry Delaney larry@countrymusicnews.ca
www.countrymusicnews.ca
Canada's national Country music publication. Now in its 26th year!!

Fiddler Magazine
PO Box 101, N. Sydney, NS B2A 3M1
PH: 902-794-2558
info@fiddle.com
www.fiddle.com
Feature articles, regular columns and more.

Take Country Back
Box 904, Cranbrook, BC V1C 6W4
PH: 250-417-0085
Laurie Joulie laurie@takecountryback.com
www.takecountryback.com
Online webzine, webcast and quarterly print publication. We're very indie friendly! Americana; Traditional, Classic and Alt-Country, Bluegrass, Honkytonk etc...

Europe

Belgium

Rootstime
Generaal De Wittestraat 11, 3545 Halen, Belgium
Freddy Celis rootstime@mail.com
www.rootstime.be
We promote Blues & Roots, Singer/Songwriters, Rootsrock, Americana, Country, Rockabilly, Cajun & Zydeco-music.

France

Country Music France
63, rue Victor Hugo, BP 30, 94701 Maisons Alfort, Cedex, France
pierre@countryfr.com
country-music-france.com
French directory about Bluegrass, Old-Time, Traditional and New Country.

Germany

Country Jukebox
Th. Dombart - Str. 5, 80805 München, Germany
Max W. Achatz info@countryjukebox.de
www.countryjukebox.de
Published monthly in Germany's Country Circle magazine as well as on the web.

CountryHome
Maiselsberger Str. 5, D-84416 Taufkirchen/Vils, Germany
PH: 08084-9166 FX: 08084-9165
iwde@iwde.de
www.countryhome.de
Das online magazin freier fachjournalisten.

Editor & Journalist for Country Music Christian Lamitschka
An der Pfingstweide 28, D-61118 Bad Vilbel, Germany
PH: +49-0-6101-544613 FX: +49-0-6101-544622
Christian Lamitschka Ch.Lamitschka@t-online.de
www.iwde.de
If you are a Country artist, I can write an article about you for German and European magazines. Do you have a current CD that you would like reviewed? Then please, send it to me.

Insurgent Country
Sachsenring 16 App 40, 35041 Marburg, Germany
Hans Settler settler@mailer.uni-marburg.de
www.insurgentcountry.com
News, bios, reviews etc.

The Netherlands

Alt Country NL
dutchtwang@yahoo.com
www.altcountry.nl
Er voor liefhebbers van Americana en Rootsmuziek.

United Kingdom

Americana UK
29 Avonmore Ave. Liverpool, L18 8AL UK
feedback@americana-uk.com
www.americana-uk.com
UK home for Americana, Alt-Country and "No Depression" music. CDs only please. No CDRs or demos.

Country Music People
1-3 Love Ln. London, SE18 6QT UK
PH: 44-020-8854-7217 FX: 44-020-8855-6370
info@countrymusicpeople.com
www.countrymusicpeople.com
Reviews of latest CDs, features and interviews.

Country Music Roundup
PO Box 111, Waltham, Grimsby, DN37 OYN UK
PH: 01522-750150 FX: 01472-821808
editor@cmru.co.uk
www.cmru.co.uk
Keep up-to-date on the British Country music scene.

Fiddle On
4 Lee Close, Kidlington, Oxford, OX5 2XZ UK
PH: 01865-374624
Jed Mugford jed@fiddleon.co.uk
www.fiddleon.co.uk
A publication for the UK fiddle players.

JigTime International
info@jigtime.com
www.jigtime.com
Slices of life, Bluegrass, Americana and Irish Traditional Music from Ireland and the USA.

Maverick
24 Bray Gardens, Maidstone, Kent, ME15 9TR UK
editor@maverick-country.com
www.maverick-country.com
Changing how Country music is perceived in the UK.

Metro Country
Ray Grundy, 444 Manchester Rd., Astley, Tyldesley, Manchester, M29 7BT UK
ray@metrocountry.co.uk
www.metrocountry.co.uk
Contact to get your CD reviewed and featured.

roots-and-branches.com
brumbeat@blueyonder.co.uk
www.roots-and-branches.com
Contact us with news, views, gig dates etc.

Australia

Country Goss
goss@ihug.com.au
www.countrygoss.com.au
Country music and dance E-zine.

Dance

North America

United States

DeepRhythms
392 6th Ave. #2, Brooklyn, NY 11215
David Wolf david@deeprhythms.com
www.deeprhythms.com
Hear the deepest Underground House sound around. If you want to have your record reviewed here and appear on our mixes, contact us.

DJ Times
25 Willowdale Ave. Port Washington, NY 11050
PH: 516-767-2500 FX: 516-767-9335
djtimes@testa.com
www.djtimes.com
Considered the "bible of the industry" for the professional DJ.

djsinbox.com
5611 S. Sherwood Ave. #6, Tampa, FL 33611
PH: 813-679-4422
Mark Kovach djsinbox@hotmail.com
djsinbox.com
The latest on today's cutting edge music.

Electrocore
www.electrocore.com
Your avenue for up to date information on everything Electroclash / Disko Punk / Electro...

Faize
info@faizemusic.com
www.faizemusic.com
House and Garage music magazine.

Igloo Magazine!
PO Box 307, Corona, CA 92878
editor@igloomag.com
www.igloomag.com
Online source for Electronic music coverage.

Iron Feather Journal
PO Box 1905, Boulder, CO 80306
stevyn@ironfeather.com
www.ironfeather.com
A wicked mega magazine about the subversive HI-TEK underground, Techno + Jungle scenes, smuggling, pirate radio, phreaking, etc. etc.

Jive Magazine
PO Box 2635, Lilburn, GA 30048
www.jivemagazine.com
Extensive review section, events and more! Check our site for submission details.

Lunar Magazine
PO Box 889084, Atlanta, GA 30356
PH: 404-846-8991
www.lunarmagazine.com
Uniting Electronic Dance music.

Pax Acidus
312 Harvard Ave. E. #105, Seattle, WA 90102
PH: 206-349-1514
www.paxacidus.com
Website for the underground arts of sight and sound.

Progressive Sounds
126 N. Charlotte St., Lancaster, PA 17603
www.progressive-sounds.com
Bringing you the latest in Progressive Trance.

Raves.com
Jennifer Warner jennifer@raves.com
www.raves.com
News, reviews, profiles, shows etc.

Sonic Curiosity
PO Box 28325, Philadelphia, PA 19149
Matt Howarth matt@soniccuriosity.com
www.soniccuriosity.com
Alternative/Electronic music review site.

Technotica.com
electrons@technotica.com
www.technotica.com
Our format is Electronic Underground.

URB
6300 Wilshire Blvd. #1750, Los Angeles, CA 90048
PH: 323-315-1700
marketing@urb.com
www.urb.com
Future music culture!

Canada

Klublife Magazine
439 King St. W. 4th Fl. Toronto, ON M5V 1K4
PH: 416-644-8680 FX: 416-644-8684
Nicola Gregory nicola@klublife.com
www.klublife.com
Up to date music reviews and articles.

Tribe Magazine
PO Box 65053, 358 Danforth Ave.
Toronto, ON M4K 3Z2
PH: 416-778-4115
Alex Dordevic editor@tribe.ca
www.tribemagazine.com
Inspired by the people who go out after dark.

Europe

Belgium

Beyondjazz
Lange Boomgaardstraat 114a, B-9000 Gent, Belgium
Lennart Schoors office@beyondjazz.net
www.beyondjazz.net
A Future Jazz community, focusing on the exciting sounds of Broken Beats, Future Jazz and Space Funk.

PLaST IKS
Durletstraal 2, 2018 Antwerpen, Belgium
PH/FX: 32 (0) 3-248-74-24
plastiks@pandora.be
www.plastiks.be
Magazine that covers the best of underground Dance Music. A lot of indepth articles, interviews, reviews etc. Just covering all the good stuff from today!

Estonia

Club Arena
www.clubarena.com
Promos will be reverberated.

Finland

Findance
antti.niemela@findance.com
www.findance.com
Enimmäkseen muuta kuin kotimaista konemusiikkia.

Music Mission
music.mission@mission.fi
www.kauhajoki.fi/musicmission

France

Atome
atome@atome.com
www.atome.com
Send us your charts, promo-copies, demos, news, presents.

IN DA MIX WORLDWIDE
98, rue de Paris, F-94220 Charenton, France
Frederic 'MFSB' Messent
mfsb@indamixworldwide.com
www.indamixworldwide.com
Send your material (test pressings, vinyl, 12", LP, CD, CDR) to the above address.

Novaplanet.com
33, rue du Faubourg Saint Antoine, 75011 Paris, France
PH: 01-53-33-33-00
redaction@novaplanet.com
www.novaplanet.com
News and reviews.

Yet Another Electro-Webzine?
www.yaew.com
Electronic music news, reviews and interviews.

Germany

Couchsurfer.de
Lipowskystr. 4, 81373 Munich, Germany
Michael Kienzler mk@couchsurfer.de
www.couchsurfer.de
A clubculture portal. Send us your Promos & Mix-CDs for review.

Groove
Choriner Straße 82, 10119 Berlin, Germany
PH: 030-44-31-20 22 FX: 030-44-31-20-70
Thilo Schneider thilo@groove.de
www.groove.de
Reviews Electronica, Techno, House etc.

Motor
webmaster@motor.de
www.motor.de
News, releases, tours, reviews etc.

Samplepoolz
Hollenweg 48, 41515 Grevenbroich, Germany
PH: 0211-58004781
Marc s.ample@samplepoolz.de
www.samplepoolz.de
News & Review Magazin. Join up and submit your reviews (don't send in your CD - we don't have the manpower to write extra reviews).

Techno Online
Strasse 133, 21a, 13055 Berlin, Germany
PH: 0172-3110328
Mirko Seifert info@techno.de
www.techno.de
News, reviews, charts, interviews etc.

Italy

Clubbity.com - The Safe Club Culture Site
Jazzimo jazzimo@clubbity.com
www.clubbity.com
News, Reviews, Interviews, Features... Most of the music we promote is by independent artists and labels.

Disco ID
PH: 39-0541-307333 FX: 39-0541-307335
info@discoid.it
www.discoid.it
Reviews, regular columns, charts etc.

Norway

i:Vibes
Stream stream@ivibes.nu
www.ivibes.nu
Reviews of all the latest Trance and Electronica tunes. Interviews with the biggest DJs.

Russia

jungle.ru
info@jungle.ru
www.jungle.ru
News, reviews, artist bio, streaming radio and more.

Sweden

trance.nu
Macman ralf@staff.trance.nu
trance.nu
The biggest Trance community on Earth!

United Kingdom

Blackout Audio
Mark EG info@blackoutaudio.co.uk
www.blackoutaudio.co.uk
Reviews and interviews of new sounds.

| deephousenetwork |
27 Arasain Na Mara, Lower Salthill, Galway, Ireland
www.deephousenetwork.com
Download, mixes, reviews, tracks, charts, community.

DJmag
Highbury Lifestyle, Jordan House, 47 Brunswick Pl. London, N1 6EB UK
PH: 44-0-20-7331-1148 FX: 44-0-20-7331-1115
Helene Stokes editors@djmag.com
www.djmag.com/reviewers.php
Up-front coverage of the Dance music scene.

DogsOnAcid
16 Belle Vue Rd. Old Town, Swindon, SN1 3HQ UK
Jeryl news@dogsonacid.com
www.dogsonacid.com
The world's largest Drum & Bass and Jungle message board and forum with news, reviews, dubplates, audio, video, mixes etc. Please send any tunes (preferably vinyl) that you would like to see added to the DOA promo page. Where possible please include a press release...

Drum n' Bass Arena
Brincliffe House, 861 Ecclesall Rd.
Sheffield, S11 7AE UK
PH: 44-0-114-281-4470 FX: 44-0-114-292-3020
info@lists.breakbeat.co.uk
www.breakbeat.co.uk
The latest info on everything to do with D'nB.

Epidemik
PO Box 5180, Chelmsford, Essex, CM3 3QF UK
PH: 07966-491554
Grant Epidemik grant@epidemik.com
www.epidemik.net
Then let them come to you by promoting yourself!

i:Vibes
kevin@ivibes.nu
www.ivibes.nu
News about Electronic music of all kinds.

Jon Freer *(Freelance Reviewer)*
14 Flaggwood Ave, Marple, Stockport, Cheshire, England, SK6 6HP UK
jon.freer@wrongsteps.com
www.mosoul.co.uk
I write reviews for magazines such as Blues & Soul, XLR8R, City Life, Inner Loop, littleplanet.net, pitchadjust.com, beyondjazz.net, deephousenetwork.com and skansen.no. I review everything 'Dance' based apart from Hard house/trance. Apart from that I'll review all guitar based music except Metal or Punk.I don't really review Classical music. Just about anything else goes, including 'World' type music etc.

M8 Magazine
Trojan House, Phoenix Business Pk.
Paisley, PA1 2BH UK
PH: 0141-840-5980 FX: 0141-840-5995
jill@m8magazine.com
www.m8magazine.com
The latest music reviews and news.

Ministry of Sound
103 Gaunt St., London, SE1 8DP UK
arnie@ministryofsound.com
www.ministryofsound.com
Streaming radio, news, reviews and much more.

mixmag
Mappin House, 4 Winsley St., London, W1 England
PH: 0207-182-8000 FX: 0207-182-8977
mixmag@emap.com
www.mixmag.net
The world's biggest selling clubbing magazine.

Nubreaks.com
DJ Iytal djiytal@yahoo.co.uk
www.nubreaks.com
Helps you get your DJ mix online.

off its face
Neil Roberts webmaster@offitsface.com
www.offitsface.com
Contact to get your music reviewed.

Planetdnb
2nd Fl. 207 Cranbrook Rd. Ilford,
Essex, LG1 4TD UK
PH: 44-0-20-8554-4043 FX: 44-0-20-8554-4043
Andy Rayner mail@planetdnb.com
www.planetdnb.com
One of the leading Drum 'n Bass resource sites.

Soulfelt
info@soulfelt.co.uk
www.soulfelt.co.uk
Promoting talented creative people in the Northwest, covering a wide spectrum of creative disciplines from Musicians, DJs and visual artists.

Tunes.co.uk
Unit 3E, Oslo House, West Wing, Felstead St.,
London, E9 5LG UK
PH: +44(0)20 8985 8700 FX: +44(0)20 8985 2333
www.tunes.co.uk
Dance Music from Soul & Funk to House & Breaks: reviews, real audio & worldwide mail order.

Australia

12AM.com.au
PO Box 1212, Windsor, VIC 3181 Australia
PH: 03-95338255
Marius Jones marius@12am.com.au
www.12am.com.au
DJ and club e-zine for VIC and NSW.

Resident Advisor
www.residentadvisor.com.au
Australian/Global Dance news, interviews and reviews.

Spraci
PH: ++61-(0) 402-605-188 FX: ++1-603-691-5915
support@spraci.com
spraci.cia.com.au
A leading Internet site for information on parties, clubs, drtists, djs, and pretty much anything to do with dance music and the industry that revolves around it.

TransZfusion
derrick@tranzfusion.net
www.tranzfusion.net
Trusted voice in Electronica.

Experimental

Experimental, Electronic, Ambient, Avant Garde, Noise etc.

North America

United States

ambience for the masses
1032 Irving St. PO Box 318,
San Francisco, CA 94122-2200
dfoley@sleepbot.com
www.sleepbot.com/ambience
Archive of artist profiles and reviews.

Ambient.us
PO Box 5, Sealston, VA 22547-0005
Dodds Wiley dodds@ambient.us
www.ambient.us
A positive energy Ambient music guide. Contact me by e-mail if you would like a review.

aural innovations
1364 W. 7th Ave. Apt. B, Columbus, OH 43212
Jerry Kranitz jkranitz@aural-innovations.com
aural-innovations.com
Includes Psychedelia and related Electronic music.

The Circular Cosmic Spot
Art Grauer rpt1700@gmail.com
www.sdriver.com/spot
Electronic/Experimental music reviews and news I will also accept MP3s for review.

disquiet.com
marc@disquiet.com
www.disquiet.com
Interviews Ambient/Electronic musicians.

Dream Magazine
PO Box 2027, Nevada City, CA 95959-1941
George Parsons geo@gv.net
www.dreamgeo.com
Psychedelic (old and new), Experimental, Pop, Jazz, Folk and more.

Electro-music.com
944 Flexer Ave. Allentown, PA 18103
admin@electro-music.com
electro-music.com
Experimental, Electro-Acoustic and Electronic music.

electronicmusic.com
core@electronicmusic.com
www.electronicmusic.com
Send a CD, biography, contact information and a little about the musical equipment used to us.

Fever Pitch
432 Main St. #B, Oshkosh, WI 54901
Joe Stone joe@feverpitchfever.com
www.feverpitchfever.com
Hard to find fresh and innovative music.

Free City Media
90 North Ave. #2C, San Rafael, CA 94903
Heidi@FreeCityMedia.com
www.freecitymedia.com
Psychedelic music and fresh perspectives.

Get Underground
Shlomo Sher sher@getunderground.com
www.getunderground.com
Writings and arts related to personal impressions and Experimental visions.

Grooves Magazine
18 Eastwood Dr. Voorhees, NJ 08043
PH: 866-717-3804
sean@groovesmag.com
www.groovesmag.com
Experimental Electronic music magazine.

Innerviews
PO Box 192966, San Francisco, CA 94119-2966
Anil Prasad feedback@innerviews.org
www.innerviews.org
Music without borders.

Leonardo Music Journal
211 Sutter St. #800, San Francisco, CA 94108
FX: 415-391-1110
isast@leonardo.info
mitpress.mit.edu/Leonardo
Aesthetic and technical issues in contemporary music and sonic arts.

Modsquare
www.modsquare.com
An online magazine in the form of an arts journal covering the most influential and innovative developments within Electronic music and its culture. Covers IDM, Braindance, Mindgroove or simply Experimental Electronica.

MusicEmissions.com
info@musicemissions.com
www.musicemissions.com
A music review site that focuses on non-mainstream music.

Neumu
PO Box 1948, Sonoma, CA 95476
contact@neumu.net
neumu.net
Find the work of artists following their creative vision.

Ptolemaic Terrascope
PO Box 18841, Oakland, CA 94619-8841
Pat Thomas normalsf@earthlink.net
www.terrascope.org
Unearthing Psychedelic/Folk nuggets.

SIGNAL to NOISE
PO Box 585, Winooski, VT 05404
Pete Gershon
operations@signaltonoisemagazine.org
www.signaltonoisemagazine.org
The journal of Improvised and Experimental music.

Squid's Ear
160 Bennett Ave. #6K, New York, NY 10040
Kurt Gottschalk kurt@squidco.com
www.squidsear.com
Experimental, Improvisation, Avante-Garde and unusual musical styles.

Synthmuseum.com
28 Grenville Rd. Watertown, MA 02472
PH: 617-926-2298
jay@synthmuseum.com
www.synthmuseum.com
Our magazine features reviews of Synth music.

Technotica Times
electrons@technotica.com
www.technotica.com
Upcoming shows, reviews, mixes and much more!

(((Thump))) Radio
FX: 415-439-1203
info@thumpradio.com
www.thump-radio.com
Exposing local talent around the world.

XLR8R
1388 Haight St. #105, San Francisco, CA 94117
PH: 415-861-7583 FX: 415-861-7584
Tomas Palermo redwine@xlr8r.com
www.xlr8r.com
Over 100 color pages. Internationally distributed.

Canada

Computer Music Journal
School of Fine Art and Music, MacKinnon 214,
U. Guelph, Guelph, ON N1G 2W1
James Harley cmj-reviews@mitpress.mit.edu
mitpress.mit.edu/e-journals/Computer-Music-Journal
Covers digital audio signal processing and electro Acoustic music. When contacting, include "CMJ" in your Subject line.

musicworks
358-401 Richmond St. W. Toronto, ON M5V 3A8
PH: 416-977-3546 FX: 416-977-4181
sound@musicworks.ca
www.musicworks.ca
Exploration of new music and sound.

Europe

Belgium

l'entrepot
Mesesstraat 6, 2300 Turnhout, Belgium
Tom Wilms tom.wilks@skynet.be
users.skynet.be/entrepot
Resource center for unconventional tunes.

SIDE-LINE
90 rue Charles Degroux, 1040 Brussels, Belgium
PH: 0032-2-732-14-81 FX: 0032-2-732-14-81
info@side-line.com
www.side-line.com
Magazine on the Underground genre.

Uzine
PO Box 19 - B-2550 Kontich, Belgium
ultra@yucom.be
www.dma.be/p/ultra
Dealing with music, film, (multi)media and travel.

France

Guts of Darkness
Chris xian@gutsofdarkness.com
www.gutsofdarkness.com
Les archives du sombre et de l'expérimental.

Germany

Auf Abwegen
www.aufabwegen.de
The label, publisher and organizer for Experimental music.

de:bug
Brunnenstr. 196, 10119 Berlin, Germany
PH: 030-2838-4458 FX: 030-2838-4459
www.de-bug.de
News and reviews.

dense
Danziger Str. 16, 10435 Berlin, Germany
PH: +49-30-44-34-02-90 FX: +49-30-44-34-02-91
dense@dense.de
www.dense.de
Founded in order to promote sound visionaries. Please contact us before you send in any material.

Dominion Club
Karl-Schmidt-Str. 26-29, 39104 Magdeburg, Germany
PH: 0391-4018892 FX: 0391-4082899
dominionclub@aol.com
www.dominionclub.de
Events, reviews, news, interview and more.

e-lectric
info@e-lectric.de
www.e-lectric.de
Ein Online-Magazin, das sich mit der Musikrichtung Synthie-Pop beschäftigt.

MEMi
www.memi.com
The Magazine for Electronic Music on the Internet. We produce a yearly CD called "hiddentreasures" where home recording newcomers are presented.

NMZ
www.nmz.de
News, reviews, rezensionen, kulturpolitik, musicwirtschaft, musikforen...

re.fleXion
Zum Hasenkamp 8, 31552, Rodenberg, Germany
ingo@re-flexion.de
www.re-flexion.de
Neuigkeiten, kritiken, interviews, kozerte, termine, bands etc.

shift!
Choriner Strasse 50, D-10435 Berlin, Germany
PH: 49-030-693-7814 FX: 49-030-693-7844
info@shift.de
www.shift.de
Invites artists to create without compromise.

spex
Rolandstrasse 69, 50677 Koln, Germany
PH: 0221-579-7800 FX: 0221-579-7879
www.spex.de
News and reviews.

SynGate.net
Eibenweg 10, 53894 Mechernich, Germany
PH: 49-2443-903609
Lothar Lubitz mail@syngate.net
www.syngate.net
The gate to Synthesizer based music.

synthetics
Enzianweg 7, 41836 Huckelhoven, Germany
PH: 02433-95-99-808 FX: 0721-151201169
micha@synthiepop.de
www.synthiepop.de
BODY and SOUL come together.

Westzeit
Holger Seeling, Bahnhofstr. 6, 41334 Nettetal, Germany
PH: 02157-3858 FX: 02157-1760
info@westzeit.de
www.westzeit.de
Pop auf draht-musik, literature, kunst und film.

Italy

Neural
a.ludovico@neural.it
www.neural.it
New media art and Electronic music.

The Netherlands

Alfa Centauri Electronic Music Magazine
www.alfacentauri.nl
The only true Dutch and leading magazine on Synthesizer based music for fans of Electronic Music. We are investigating the borders of Electronic Music: we don't want to stick to traditional music styles only.

E-dition Magazine
Postbus 2171, 8203 AD Lelystad, The Netherlands
info@e-ditionmag.com
www.e-ditionmag.com
We will try to review ALL incoming products and we're accepting all types of music that you think belong in an Electronic Music magazine with a broad view It's possible that one of reviewers will contact you for an interview or an extended publication..

United Kingdom

Compulsion
PO Box 36, Enfield, EN1 1WS UK
tonycompulsion@hotmail.com
www.callnetuk.com/home/compulsion
Articles, interviews, news and music.

Computer Music
30 Monmouth St., Bath, BA1 2BW UK
PH: 01225-442244 FX: 01225-732353
Ronan.macdonald@futurenet.co.uk
www.computermusic.co.uk
Reviews of the latest gear/news as it happens.

DOT:ALT
xvscott@dot-alt.co.uk
dot-alt.co.uk
Covers progressive, creative music.

Future Music
30 Monmouth St., Bath, BA1 2BW UK
PH: 01225-442244 FX: 01225-732353
andy.jones@futurenet.co.uk
futuremusic.co.uk
Making music at the cutting edge of technology.

The Milk Factory
info@themilkfactory.co.uk
www.themilkfactory.co.uk
Reviews on Electronica, Dance and quality Pop.

Robots and Electric Brains
133 Green End Rd. Cambridge, CB4 1RW UK
Jimmy Possession rebzine@hotmail.com
come.to/robots
Eclectic zine for music with that extra something special.

Songsalive!

www.songsalive.org

Songsalive! is a non profit organization dedicated to the nurturing, support and promotion of songwriters and composers worldwide.

Songsalive! is run by songwriters for songwriters. It acts as an epicentre, a heart of the international songwriting community and music markets, bridging the gaps, tapping songwriters into the pulse of the business and at the same time giving them and their music the support they deserve.

Songsalive! gives life to songs, provide opportunities for collaboration, create awareness about original music, promote and educate through an amazing network of programs designed especially for songwriters and original music.

Support Songsalive! and help energize the business of songwriting and music. Join the Songsalive! network and become a link in the chain.

www.songsalive.org

The Wire
2nd Fl. E. 88-94 Wentworth St., London, E1 7SA UK
PH: 44-0207-422-5010 FX: 44-0207-422-5011
projects@thewire.co.uk
www.thewire.co.uk
Electronica, Breakbeat, Avant Rock, Free Jazz, Classical, Global and beyond.

Folk

Folk, Celtic, Singer/Songwriter, Roots, Acoustic, Traditional, Maritime

North America

United States

Acoustic Guitar Magazine
String Letter Publishing, 255 West End Ave.
San Rafael, CA 94901 Attn: Derk Richardson
PH: 415-485-6946 FX: 415-485-0831
editors.ag@stringletter.com
www.acousticguitar.com
Free lessons, giveaways, CD awards, gear reviews. We only review label recordings with widespread distribution or artist-owned recordings that have a significant, established Internet distribution channel.

Celtic Beat
4 Greenlay St., Nashua, NH 03063
PH: 603-880-3706
celt56@aol.com
www.mv.com/ipusers/celticbeat
Concert and CD reviews galore!

Celtic Cafe
Bernadette Price bernadette@celticcafe.com
www.celticcafe.com
Promotes Celtic culture. Mostly Irish dance.

Celtic Grove
PO Box 70227, Knoxville, TN 37938
crange@celticgrove.com
www.celticgrove.com
World's first and finest Celtic radio webcast and e-zine.

Dirty Linen
PO Box 66600, Baltimore, MD 21239-6600
PH: 410-583-7973 FX: 410-337-6735
info@dirtylinen.com
www.DirtyLinen.com
We welcome submission of audio Roots music.

eFolkMusic
artists@efolkMusic.org
www.efolkmusic.org
Traditional and Contemporary Folk music from around the world.

Folk & Acoustic Music Exchange
82 Leadmine Rd. Nelson, NH 03457
David N. Pyles dnpyles@acousticmusic.com
www.acousticmusic.com/fame/famehome.htm
Submit recordings and artist bio for review.

folklinks.com
David W. Johnson djohnson@ehc.edu
www.folklinks.com
Web presence for Folk and Acoustic music performers.

Folkwax
www.folkwax.com
Weekly Folk music e-zine with reviews.

Green Man Review
82 Rackleff St., Portland, ME 04103
Kim Bates kim@greenmanreview.com
www.greenmanreview.com
Focus on Folk music in all its aspects. You must send 2 copies of each CD that you want reviewed. No exceptions.

Kevin's Celtic & Folk Music CD Reviews
Kevin McCarthy celticfolkmusic@icogitate.com
www.icogitate.com/~celticfolkmusic
Reviewing Celtic, UK Folk and Folk music CDs.

Music Matters Review
PO Box 425, Smithtown, NY 11787
thefolks@mmreview.com
www.mmreview.com
Reviews of "under discovered" artists!

Puremusic
4505 Harding Rd. #157, Nashville, TN 37205
Frank Goodman frankgoodman@puremusic.com
www.puremusic.com
Bringing great music to the masses.

Rambles
1609 Ridgeview Ave. Lancaster, PA 17603
Tom Knapp editor@rambles.net
www.rambles.net
Folk & Traditional music.

Sign up for The Indie Contact Newsletter
www.indiebible.com

Roots Network
PO Box 397, Black Creek, NC 27813
PH: 252-243-8700
tellme@ibluegrass.com
www.rootsnetwork.com
Advances the cause of Acoustic-related music.

Sing Out!
PO Box 5460, Bethlehem, PA 18015
PH: 610-865-5366 FX: 610-865-5129
info@singout.org
www.singout.org
Feature articles and interviews, tons of recording and book reviews, the most comprehensive and up-to-date Folk festival and camp listing anywhere, plus regular columns on the Folk process, songwriting, storytelling and Children's music.

thedigitalfolklife.org
John McLaughlin john-mclaughlin@comcast.net
www.thedigitalfolklife.org
Folk interviews, CD and show reviews.

Canada

Celtic Heritage
PO Box 8805, Stn. A, Halifax, NS B3K 5M4
Attn: Cliff
PH: 902-835-6244 FX: 902-835-0080
editorial@celticheritage.ns.ca
celticheritage.ns.ca
Includes reviews of the latest in Celtic music, including independent labels.

Independent Reviewer - Paul Emile Comeau
PO Box 142, Saulnierville, NS B0W 2Z0
PH: 902-769-3288
pcm.comeau@ns.sympatico.ca
Does reviews for Dirty Linen, Penguin Eggs, Global Rhythm, No Depression, Goldmine and more! Reviews Roots Music in a wide sense of the word.

Penguin Eggs
10942 80th Ave. Edmonton, AB T6G 0R1
PH: 780-433-8287 FX: 780-437-4603
penguineggs@ hotmail.com
www.penguineggs.ab.ca
Canada's Folk, Roots and World music magazine.

Europe

France

Trad Magazine
BP 27, 62350 Saint Venant, France
PH: 03-21-02-52-52 FX: 03-21-27-16-70
tradmag@wanadoo.fr
www.tradmagazine.com
Französisches Magazin für Folk und Traditionelle Musik.

Germany

Folker!
Postfach 1269, 53582 Bad Honnef, Germany
PH: 02224-76510 FX: 02224-71464
info@folker.de
www.folker.de
Das deutsche Musikmagazin. Folk, Blues, Cajun...

FolkWorld
editors@folkworld.de
www.folkworld.de
Contributions from you are welcome!

The Netherlands

Bridge Guitar Reviews
Korenmolenweg 7, 7241 VA Lochem,
The Netherlands
acousticreviews@xs4all.nl
www.xs4all.nl/~guitars
Reviews albums of a high level of Acoustic guitar music.

Newfolksounds
info@newfolksounds.nl
www.newfolksounds.nl
Een Nederlands tijdschrift dat één keer in de twee maanden verschijnt.

The Real Roots Café
Lincolnstraat 2, 6566 CT Millingen aan de Rijn,
The Netherlands
Jan Janssen rrc@realrootscafe.com
www.realrootscafe.com
Promotes fabulous American Roots music musicians.

United Kingdom

BBC Folk and Acoustic Page
www.bbc.co.uk/radio2/folk
Info, news, reviews, radio, events and more.

Celtic Ways
'Murhy', Keash, Ballymote, Co. Sligo, Ireland
PH: 353-71-918-9377
John Willmott john@celticways.com
celticways.com
MP3s of Celtic, Folk, World Fusion and World Tradition music. Free services.

Folk and Roots
info@folkandroots.co.uk
www.folkandroots.co.uk
Gigs, reviews, interview featured artists and more.

Folk Roots
PO Box 337, London, N4 1TW UK
PH: 44-020-8340-9651 FX: 44-020-8348-5626
froots@frootsmag.com
www.frootsmag.com
Roots, Folk and World music magazine.

Folking.com
PH: +44 (0) 7956-430-221
Darren Beech folkmaster@folking.com
www.folking.com
Album/gig reviews, CD of the month, MP3s.

Tradition Magazine
9 Burwash, Witnesham,
Ipswich Suffolk, IP6 9EL UK
paul@salmonp56.fsnet.co.uk
www.traditionmagazine.com
Magazine for world custom and tradition.

Trad Music / Music Maker Magazine
c/o Magnet Publishing Ltd. 28 Grafton Terrace,
London, NW5 4JJ UK
PH: 020-7424-0027
Brian Healey tradmusic@btinternet.com
www.tradmusic.net
The official journal of the Music Maker Association. Dedicated to the promotion of independent record labels, songwriters & performers. Folk to Country, Rock, Jazz and World Music.

worldmusic.org.uk
Barry Miller reviews@worldmusic.org.uk
www.worldmusic.org.uk
Reviews are for World/Folk/Roots music (widely defined) albums, DVDs etc.

Australia

Trad&Now
PO Box 1125, Wollongong, NSW 2500 Australia
PH: 02-4225-3792 FX: 02-4229-9368
David De Santi david@tradandnow.com
www.tradandnow.com
Promotes Traditional and Contemporary Folk music.

GLBT

365Gay.com
editor@365Gay.com
www.365gay.com/entertainment/MusicChannel/Musicchannel.htm
CD reviews and artist profiles are covered in the Music Section.

Chicago Free Press
c/o Gregg Shapiro, 3845 N. Broadway 2nd Fl.
Chicago, IL 60613
GREGG1959@aol.com
www.chicagofreepress.com
I write about music, film and literature, in a variety of capacities. I also write for several other publications including afterelton.com, HX (NYC), Bay Area Reporter (SF), The Bottom Line (Palm Springs), In Newsweekly (Boston), Outsmart Magazine (Houston) and many others!

Curve Magazine
4523 Iberville St., New Orleans, LA 70119
Margaret Coble "DJ Mags" djmags@djmags.com
www.djmags.com
Currently my main gig is with Curve Magazine (though i occasionally still freelance for The Advocate and Lesbianation.com), so female, lesbian/bi, and trans indie artists of any genre can submit their press kits/cds to me the above address.

Freelance Reviewer Jason Victor Serinus
PO Box 3073, Oakland, CA 94609-0073
Jason Victor Serinus jserinus@planeteria.net
www.jasonserinus.com
OutMusic Awards judge. Writes and reviews for gay, alternative, New Age, and audiophile publications nationwide. Jason's main genres are Singer-Songwriter, Classical, World, New Age, Light Jazz, and Blues. Cannot respond to queries or audition via the web. Be sure your submission is in final form and includes artwork and contact information. If your disc/DVD is reviewed, I will let you know.

gayhiphop.com
mistermaker mister@gayhiphop.com
www.gayhiphop.com
Promoting and featuring both gay and regular artists from the urban scenes around the world equally.

Girlfriends Magazine
3415 Cesar Chavez #101, San Francisco, CA 94110
PH: 415-648-9464
editorial@girlfriendsmag.com
www.girlfriendsmag.com
A national monthly magazine for lesbians. We review all kinds of music by women.

Pride Christian Music
PO Box 1083, Farmington, MI 48332
PH: 386-290-3795
email@pridechristianmusic.org
www.pridechristianmusic.org
A FREE networking resource for singers, musicians, & music industry professionals to communicate.

Queerpunks.com
Adam@punkk.com
www.queerpunks.com
Add your news, CD and show reviews etc. Covers Punk and all other Alternative genres.

Woman's Monthly
1718 M St. NW #198, Washington, DC 20036
PH: 202-965-5399
womo@womo.com
www.womo.com
DC's magazine for lesbians.

Goth

Goth, Industrial, EBM, Ethereal, Synthpop, DeathRock and Darkwave.

North America

United States

13thTrack.com
2351 S. Shore Cn. PO Box 141,
Alameda, CA 94501-5723
Mark Harvey reviews@13thTrack.com
www.13thtrack.com
We review any and all Halloween related items.

Absolute Zero Media
3655 W. Anthem Way, #A-109 Pmb 212,
Anthem, AZ 85086
magazine@absolutezeromedia.us
www.absolutezeromedia.us
Experimental, Dark Industrial/Ambient, Noise and Doom label, mail order, label and zine.

Beautiful Cruelty Magazine
PO Box 605, Round Lake, IL 60073
submissions@beautifulcruelty.com
beautifulcruelty.com
Open forum for everything Gothic, Nu-Metal, Industrial, Grave and beyond.

BiteMe!
6038 Hayes Ave. #1A, Los Angeles, CA 90042
PH: 626-359-5338
Nikki J1Fix@aol.com
www.bitemezine.net
Interviews, commentary. Also reviews demos.

The City Morgue
PO Box 4128, Alexandria, VA 22303
damion@thecitymorgue.com
www.thecitymorgue.com
Got something you want to send us?

Dark Culture Magazine
Cinka submissions@darkculture.net
www.darkculture.net
An open forum for writers to get their words read.

Dark Realms Magazine
4377 W. 60th St., Cleveland, OH 44144
Music Editor goth@monolithgraphics.com
www.monolithgraphics.com/darkrealms.html
Visit for guidelines to submitting your music.

Dead Angel
PO Box 1468, Buda, TX 78610-1468
monorecs@monotremata.com
www.monotremata.com/dead
E-zine with Underground music reviews.

Deluge US Edition
4802 Lawndale Dr. Greensboro, NC 27455-1924
Chris Alfano deluge71@msn.com
delugezine.com
Contact us first to let us know about your music.

EsoTerra
5500 Prytania, #216, New Orleans, LA 70115
Chad Hensley hecate999@msn.com
www.esoterra.org
Interviews with musicians, writers and artists existing on society's fringes.

Gothic Beauty
4110 SE Hawthorne Blvd. #501,
Portland, OR 97214
FX: 503-249-8844
Constantine info@gothicbeauty.com
www.gothicbeauty.com
Send us your press kit.

gothicsociety.net
713 Willow Bend Dr. Chesapeake, VA 23323
PH: 304-216-3632
gothicsociety@gothicsociety.net
www.gothicsociety.net
Looking for reviews for music and print.

Grave Concerns
PO Box 38174, Albany, NY 12203
Julie Johnson gothgirl@berk.com
www.graveconcernsezine.com
Gothic and Industrial music resource for CD reviews, interviews etc.

Haunted Attraction *Underground DJ*
PO Box 220286, Charlotte, NC 28222
PH: 704-366-0875 FX: 704-366-0876
info@hauntedattraction.com
www.hauntedattraction.com
Get an expert opinion on the best in Haunted music.

Industrial Nation
PO Box 2717, Oakland, CA 94602
PH: 208-575-7234 FX: 208-575-7234
info@Industrialnation.com
www.Industrialnation.com
Covers all music Electronic.

Morbid Outlook
PO Box 838, 128 E. Broadway,
New York, NY 10002-9998
mistress@morbidoutlook.com
www.morbidoutlook.com
Feel free to send your CDs and press kits to us

Newgrave
contact@newgrave.com
www.newgrave.com
Preservation of Dark and Gothic culture.

Outburn
PO Box 3187, Thousand Oaks, CA 91359-0187
outburn@outburn.com
www.outburn.com
In-depth interviews with popular musicians and established Underground favorites.

Propaganda
PO Box 296, Dept W. New Hyde Park,
New York 11040
FX: 516-248-8143
propazine@aol.com
www.propagandamagazine.net
Music reviews, band interviews and more.

RealmGothica
PO Box 841358, Houston, TX 77284-1358
Naika Malveaux naika@realmgothica.com
www.realmgothica.com
Seeks talent submissions for online feature section.

Regen Magazine
c/o Nick Garland, 4032 19th St.
San Francisco, CA 94114
PH: 510-676-5129 FX: 859-259-1256
submissions@regenmag.com
www.regenmag.com
We feature IDM, Industrial, Goth, Synthpop etc.

Sentimentalist
PO Box 174, Murray Hill Stn. New York, NY 10156
PH: 212-679-1287 FX: 212-679-1287
sentimentalist@asthetik.com
www.asthetik.com/sentimentalist
Alternative music, art, film and fashion magazine.

StarVox
6 Camden, Irvie, CA 92620
Blu Ashton blu@starvox.net
www.starvox.net
Promoting Deathrock, Goth, Psychobilly/Gothabilly, Ethereal, Industrial, Post Punk and dark Alternative Country.

Swag Magazine
8033 Sunset Blvd. #4500, W. Hollywood, CA 90046
PH: 323-466-3069
styleguide@swagmag.com
www.swagmag.com
All about everything the successful Rock stars need.

Vampirefreaks.com
jet@vampirefreaks.com
www.vampirefreaks.com
News about everything Gothic.

VIAL Magazine
PO Box 22514, San Francisco, CA 94122
omen@disinfo.net
www.vialmagazine.com
A dream must accompany your CD.

Voidstar Productions
240 Jackson St. #610, Lowell, MA 01852
David Dodson deftlyd@nauzeeaun.com
www.voidstarproductions.com
Our reviews give constructive criticism directly to the artists.

World Horror Network
390 E. Woodlake Dr. #95, Salt Lake City, UT 84107
Shane Diablo shane_diablo@diemonsterdie.net
worldhorrornetwork.com
If you are in a band and would like WHN to review your CD. Please make sure it is a finished product. It will be reviewed on all levels.. recording quality, packaging, and talent. so PLEASE dont send a cd-r with black marker all over it.

Canada

Rue Morgue
700 Queen St. E. Toronto, ON M4M 1G9
info@rue-morgue.com
www.rue-morgue.com
Reviews (no demos) Horror related music.

Sick Among the Pure
PO Box 72043, Ottawa, ON K2K 2P4
PH: 360-513-9121
Daemon submit@sickamongthepure.com
www.sickamongthepure.com
Is your band of the Alternative / Industrial / Metal / Electronic genre (or sub-sub-sub-genre?) Do they just plain fucking rock? SATP is always interested in bringing established, up-and-coming, and underground artists to the forefront of everyone's attention.

Wrapped in Wire
64 Lardner St., Cambridge, ON N3C 4L2
mediawhore@wrappedinwire.com
www.wrappedinwire.com
CD reviews, humor, music news and more.

Europe

Belgium

Darker than the Bat
Peter Jan Van Damme pj.vandamme@scarlet.be
www.proservcenter.be/darkerthanthebat
CD reviews, interviews and airplay for Indies.

De Kagan Kalender
Geerdegemstraat 23, 2800 Mechelen, Belgium
PH: +32 (0)15-424363
info@kagankalender.com
www.kagankalender.com
Each promo is assured to get a review and will be played on our radio show.

Croatia

Elektronski Zvuk
info@elektronskizvuk.com
www.elektronskizvuk.com
We review Electronic music from bands around the world.

Czech Republic

teenage.cz
ebm@teenage.cz
teenage.cz
School sucks. Music Rocks!

Finland

Kaos Kontrol
Yliopistonkatu 8 D 81, FIN-20100 Turku, Finland
info@kaos-kontrol.org
www.kaos-kontrol.org
Focuses on 'Industrial' sounds.

France

Cynfeirdd
2 sente des Godeurs, 78250 Hardricourt, France
info@cynfeirdd.com
cynfeirdd.com
Data storage about this dark culture we share.

Darkface
postmaster@dark-face.com
dark-face.com
Se donne le but de faire connaître le mouvement Electro & Goth, faire circuler le maximum d'informations.

D-Side
3 bis, rue Pasteur, 94270 Le Kremlin Bicetre, France
PH: 33-01-47-77-80-28 FX: 33-01-46-77-53-82
Monsieur Bruce ab@d-side.org
www.d-side.org
Gothic, Rock Metal, Electro, Industrial, Electronica, Darkwave.

Germany

Astan Magazine
PF 1247, 48629 Metelen, Germany
astanmagazin@t-online.de
www.astan-magazin.de
Gothic / Electro zine. News, reviews, interviews...

Back Again
Behringstr. 93B, 22763 Hamburg, Germany
Alexander Pohle sam@backagain.de
www.backagain.de
CD-Kritiken und Interviews aus dem Independentbereich.

The Black Gift
Ahornweg 25, 50226 Frechen, Germany
PH: 02234-497793 FX: 0721-151 447655
office@the-black-gift.de
www.the-black-gift.de
Gothicmagazin. News, reviews, interviews.

Black Rain
Altendorfer Strasse 96, 09113 Chemnitz, Germany
FX: 0049-0-371-3899450
www.blackrain.de
Mail your demos in for review.

Blacklight Magazin
c/o Niels Menke,
Postfach 10 26 04, 34026 Kassel, Germany
Redaktion@blacklight-magazin.de
www.blacklight-magazin.de
Darkzine, Gothic magazin.

The Dark Site
Postfach 1130, 61451 Konigstein im Taunus, Germany
contact@wavegothic.de
www.wavegothic.de
Schickt einfach euer Material an unsere Anschrift und gebt uns ein paar Wochen Zeit (wir müssen die CDs ja auch intern verteilen).

Dark Spy Magazine
Demo, Postfach 11 03 01, 46123 Oberhausen, Germany
info@dark-spy.com
www.dark-spy.com
Send your CD to the above address, or e-mail us with the word "DEMO" in the subject heading. Stay Dark And Enjoy The Fetish!

Darkbeat.Net
Bernadottestr. 84, 60439 Frankfurt, Germany
info@darkbeat.net
www.darkbeat.net
Reviews, events, radio etc.

electric diary
Thomas Tröger thomas@electric-diary.com
www.electric-diary.com
Dark-Alternative Musikmagazin. News, interviews, reviews, tips etc.

Electric Tremor
Karl-Liebknecht-Str. 88, 04275 Leipzig, Germany
contact@electric-tremor.org
www.electric-tremor.de
Home of degenerated music, events and art.

Electricafé
info@electricafe.de
www.electricafe.de
Fan-E-Zine für Elektronische Musik. Der Schwerpunkt liegt bei Electro, EBM und Industrial.

e-lectric.de
Scharrenbroicher Str. 55c, 51503 Rosrath, Germany
Andreas Wolf wolf@e-lectric.de
www.e-lectric.de
Synthie-Pop und der etwas "härteren" Variante Future-Pop beschäftigt.

||Electronic Body Music||dot com
info@electronic-body-music.com
www.electronic-body-music.com
Features a newcomers section.

electrowahn.de
Nachtigallenstr. 26, 41466 Neuss, Germany
demo@electrowahn.de
www.elektrowahn.de
Electro/EBM/Industrial. Includes a "Demo" zone.

elektrauma
Gustav-Heinemann-Ring 64, 81739 Munchen, Germany
Andreas Romer andi@elektrauma.com
www.elektrauma.de

Gothic Magazin
Selmastrasse 3, 30451 Hannover, Germany
PH: 0511-261-58-31 FX: 0511-47-333-46
info@gothic-magazin.de
www.gothic-magazin.de
Gothic magazin und community.

Gothic Magazine
Konviktstrasse 4, D-72488 Sigmaringen, Germany
Martin Sprissler Martin@dark-media.de
www.gothic-magazine.de
News, reviews, newsletter, links and more!

Gothic Paradise
Birkbuschstraße 76/77, 12167 Berlin, Germany
PH: +49-179-7514371 FX: +49-1212-529-705-763
Freya Diepenbrock info@GothicParadise.de
www.gothicparadise.de
Onlinemagazin für die Szene - Gothic, EBM, Alternative, Industrial, Metal, Konzertberichte Tourdaten

Gothic World
gothicworld@ritchies.de
www.the-gothicworld.de
Unabhängiges Internet-Magazin für die Gothicszene.

Klangwald
Munsterstrasse 1b-44575 Castrop-Rauxel, Germany
info@klangwald.de
www.klangwald.de
Rezensionen, interviews, news & more.

Medienkonverter
Kriegersiedlung 69, D-81369 München, Germany
Bertram Uhner redaktion@medienkonverter.de
www.medienkonverter.de
Das eZine für die subkulturellen Töne. Darkwave, Wave, EBM, Gothic, Gothicrock...

MeltingClose
Volker Riehl, Waldallee 45, 65817 Eppstein, Germany
PH: 0177-7134884
darkon@reanimation-club.de
www.meltingclose.de
Eletronic Music Magazin.

Noise Nation
Postfach 2107, D-96012 Bamberg, Germany
redaktion@noisenation.de
www.noisenation.de
Interviews, rezis, konzerte, bands, troudaten...

La Nuit Obscure
Grünhundsbrunnen 2, 96049 Bamberg, Germany
PH: +49-951-519-00-05
Ulrich Herwig uli@subkultur.com
www.lanuitobscure.de
Dark Wave, Gothic, EBM...

pandaimonix.de
Krokusweg 37, 76199 Karlsruhe, Germany
PH: 0721-98929933
Stefan Thiel public@pandaimonix.de
www.pandaimonix.de
Provides information (mostly) about Gothic, Metal and "dark" music, i.e. news, reviews, stories, photos and more.

Sinful Gothic
webmaster@sinfulgothic.com
www.sinfulgothic.com
If you'd like exposure, contact me.

Sonic Seducer
Schmachtendorfer Str. 5, 46147 Oberhausen, Germany
PH: 0208-699370 FX: 0208-6993715
info@sonic-seducer.de
www.sonic-seducer.de
Musicmagazin: Gothic, EBM, Alternative, Dark.

subKultur.com
Postfach: 580664 - 10415 Berlin, Germany
PH: 030-446-780-86 FX: +49 (0) 721-151-281-383
www.subkultur.com
Cd-kritiken, interviews, termine, MP3, galerien.

Zillo Musikmagazin
Sereetzer Weg 20, 23626 Ratekau, Germany
PH: 04504-606680 FX: 04504-60668-10
info@zillo.de
www.zillo.de
Dark wave, Alternative, Industrial music.

Italy

Angelic North-East Alternative Bands Club
info@angelic.it
www.angelic.it
Guide to the Dark Italian scene.

Chain D.L.K.
www.chaindlk.com
News, reviews, interviews and radio show. You don't have to email us to ask permission to send material! We have many different reviewers, each covering a particular style of music, so please check our site to see where to send your material.

Kronic.it
info@kronic.it
www.kronic.it
Encouraging music addiction since 2002.

Ver Sacrum
via Rosa Luxemburg 10/P, 56010 Orzignano (PI) - Italy
Marzia Bonato redazione@versacrum.com
www.versacrum.com
Rivista Gotica di letteratura, cinema, musica e arte.

The Netherlands

Funeral Procession
Postbus 5034, 3502 JA Utrecht, The Netherlands
Hans D. hansd@funprox.com
www.funprox.com
Covers all Gothic.

Norway

Musique Machine
info@musiquemachine.com
www.musiquemachine.com
Reviews, interviews, editorial columns and MP3s.

Russia

Deluge *Russian Edition*
PO Box 47, Russia, Novosibirsk, 630132
Andrew Kugaevskiy anri@skeptik.net
delugezine.com
Contact us first to let us know about your music.

Industrial Onego
Industrial@onego.ru
Industrial.onego.ru
Music Reviews Archive.

Russian Gothic Page
PO Box 129, Moscow 119331, Russia
coroner@gothic.ru
www.gothic.ru
An underground project promoting Gothic subculture in Russia.

Spain

Sonidobscuro
Apartado de Correos 11009, 18007 Granada, Spain
reviews@sonidobscuro.com
www.sonidobscuro.com
Webzine de musica oscura.

Sweden

Moving Hands
Heleneborgsgatan 6C, SE-117 32 Stockholm, Sweden
Robert Eklind robert.eklind@movinghands.net
www.movinghands.net
We review Synth, Industrial, Electronica, EBM, Postpunk etc.

Release
V Stillestorpsg 23, S-417 Gothenburg, Sweden
PH: 46-31-775-00-83
info@releasemagazine.net
www.releasemagazine.net
Features, reviews, news, classified ads etc.

Switzerland

HeAvYmeTaL.ch
c/o Roderick Zeig, Im Trichtisal 12, CH-8053
Zürich, Switzerland
rzeig@gmx.ch
www.heavymetal.ch
The Metal / Gothic portal of Switzerland.

heimdallr
Le Camion Blanc, Case Postale 270, CH-1618
Chatel St. Denis, Switzerland
Stéphane stephane@heimdallr.ch
www.heimdallr.ch
Bands, Labels... send us any news, promotional records, CDs, vinyl, tapes!

Sanctuary
spiderb@sanctuary.ch
www.sanctuary.ch
Promotes the musical alternative scene.

United Kingdom

DARKLIFE
The Small House, 138b Brownlow Rd.
London, GB-N11 2BP UK
G. Sciacca darklifezine@gmx.de
www.darklifezine.de
All CDs & tapes will be reviewed (Gothic/ Electro/ Industrial/ Experimental/ Avant-garde/ Ritual only).

DJ Martian's
altmartinuk@excite.com
djmartian.blogspot.com
Delivering cultural sound knowledge for the intelligent generation.

Fluxeuropa
BM Box 4392, London, England WC1N 3XX
rik@fluxeuropa.com
www.fluxeuropa.com
Dark-edged Alternative and Avant-garde music.

Hard Wired
6 Saxon Ct. Kingsway Gardens, Andover,
Hants, England SP 10 4BU
www.hard-wired.org.uk
Send items for review (demos/albums etc.).

Judas Kiss Magazine
judaskiss@freezone.co.uk
www.judaskissmagazine.co.uk
Capturing the very essence of the post-Industrial scene through the written medium.

MK Magazine
www.mk-magazine.com
News, reviews and interviews. Evil and funny.

The Slaghuis
sam@slaghuis.net
www.slaghuis.net
Gothic, Darkwave, Industrial Reviews & Radio Free Abattoir.

Ukraine

Ukrainian Gothic
stranger@gothic.com.ua
www.gothic.com.ua
Supports the Ukrainian Gothic/Industrial/Independent scene.

Hip Hop

North America

United States

allhiphop.com
PH: 877-499-5111
www.allhiphop.com
Articles, audio, reviews, chat, boards etc.

Altrap.com
mail@altrap.com
www.altrap.com
News, reviews, interviews and MP3s.

B-Boys.com
www.b-boys.com
Contribute some of your work or pieces to be featured on our site.

BIG BAER Alternative Music Magazine
Jack C. Baer promote@bigbaer.com
www.bigbaer.com
Feature interviews and articles by today's movers & shakers in the music world.

Bombhiphop.com
4104 24th St. #105, San Francisco, CA 94114
Attn: A&R Dept.
PH: 415-821-7965
usa@bombhiphop.com
www.bombhiphop.com
Artists, send in your demos for review.

Cellar Noise
cellarreviews902@aol.com
www.cellarnoise.com
News, reviews, interviews and more.

contrabandit
1320 Mohawk St. #1, Los Angeles, CA 90026
hollabandit@hotmail.com
www.contrabandit.com
Reviews, articles, commentary and more.

DaveyD's Hip Hop Corner
hiphopdaveyd@aol.com
www.daveyd.com
All the info on the Hip Hop scene.

eJams
PH: 803-237-3943
sales@ejams.com
www.ejams.com
Let us feature your new CD.

Elemental Magazine
71A Oak St., Brooklyn, NY 11222
PH: 718-218-0077 FX: 718-383-6378
mail@elementalmag.com
www.elementalmag.com
True, we never update the site. But we don't care. That's because we run a magazine.

The Elements
PO Box 233, Hollywood, CA 90028-0233
inquiries@hiphop-elements.com
www.hiphop-elements.com
Your #1 source for Hip Hop related issues.

Feedback Magazine
PO Box 81524, Austin, TX 78708
PH: 512-751-0107
www.feedbackmagazine.com
Covers the modern urban culture relating to music.

GlobalHipHop.com
globalhiphop@hotmail.com
www.globalhiphop.com
Reviews, interviews, mix shows & more.

GuerillaOne.com
webinfo@guerillaone.com
www.guerillaone.com
Music, graffiti, galleries and more.

Hip Hop Congress
www.hiphopcongress.org
Uplifting society through Hip Hop art and culture.

HipHopDX.com
Albert McCluster III editor@hiphopdx.com
www.hiphopdx.com
Hip Hop news, album reviews, links, release dates etc.

HipHopGame
PO Box 337, Manasquan, NJ 08736
Mr730@tmail.com
www.hiphopgame.com
Daily information from around the world.

HipHopSite.com
4700 S. Maryland Pkwy. #2, Las Vegas, NV 89119
PH: 702-933-2123 FX: 702-947-2290
mistapizzo@hiphopsite.com
www.hiphopsite.com
Reviews and interesting items related to Hip Hop.

Hood Grown
PO Box 733, Pocono Summit, PA 18346-0733
www.hoodgrown.com
Covering Urban music in a street oriented, yet intelligent manner. It's very important that you check out our submission policy on our website before contacting us.

Illtip
322 Harbour Way, #18, Richmond, CA 94801
PH: 510-215-6110 FX: 510-215-5112
contact@theilltip.com
www.theilltip.com
The last real street magazine.

Insomniac
PO Box 592722, Orlando, FL 32859
PH: 212-629-1797
insom@mindspring.com
www.insomniacmagazine.com
Nationally distributed Hip Hop industry trade magazine that is now converting to DVD format. Features interviews, articles and reviews pertaining to the world of Indie music and now film.

Last Word Online
900-306 Summit Walk Dr. Charlotte, NC 28270
PH: 704-364-9222
Mehka mehka_1@hotmail.com
www.lastwordonline.com
An online Hip Hop news magazine. We cover Hip Hop topics and music, as well as politics, business, sports and world news and events.

Manhunt
info@manhunt.com
www.manhunt.com
News, reviews and artist spotlight.

Murder Dog
164 Robles Dr. #257, Vallejo, CA 94591
PH: 707-553-8191
www.murderdog.com
America's #1 Rap magazine. Send us 2 copies of your CD for review.

MUSIC2G.com
PO Box 110-924, Brooklyn, NY 11211
charlie@music2g.com
www.music2g.com
Get featured in our "New Artist" section.

OHHLA
www.ohhla.com
Original Hip Hop lyrics archive.

Okay Player
dan@okayplayer.com
www.okayplayer.com
Artists, reviews, insights and much more.

OpenZine
PO Box 562243, Miami, FL 33256
humbyvaldes@openzine.com
www.openzine.com
Submit articles, graffiti art pictures & many other outlets.

Ozone Magazine
1516 E. Colonial Dr. #205, Orlando, FL 32803
PH: 407-447-6063 FX: 407-447-6064
Julia Beverly feedback@ozonemag.com
ozonemag.com
The southern voice of Hip Hop music!

Pass the Mic
4130 Heyward St., Cincinnati, OH 45205
PH: 718-213-4176
www.passthemic.com
Community for independent Hip Hop artists.

Phat Cat News
phatcatnews@urscene.com
www.urscene.com/Interviews.htm
We are in need of artist information for articles, interviews and CD reviews.

Phatmag
Theeditor@phatmag.com
www.phatmag.com
Real news, interviews and reviews.

Rap Scene
rapscene@hotmail.com
www.rapscene.com
Check out our "New Artist Showcase".

RapAttackLives
PH: 818-917-2217
nastynes1@aol.com
www.rapattacklives.com
The true voice of Hip Hop!

RapIndustry.Com
info@rapindustry.com
rapindustry.com
Showcase your talent!

Rapmusic.com
www.rapmusic.com
Your total source for Rap/Hip Hop.

Rapnetwork.com
www.rapnetwork.com
Source for the hottest Rap music on the planet.

rapreviews.com
PO Box 540938, Omaha, NE 68154
dj.flash@rapreviews.com
www.rapreviews.com
An independent site dedicated to up-and-coming artists.

Raptism.com
webmaster@raptism.com
www.raptism.com
Reviews, interviews, news etc.

Shine Magazine
PO Box 4314, Deerfield Beach, FL 33442
PH: 561-758-7127
editors@planetshine.com
www.planetshine.com
Music, fashion, entertainment and more.

Siccness-Dot-Net
PO Box 106, 5619 Lankershim Blvd. N.
Hollywood, CA 91601
bplease@siccness.net
www.siccness.net
CD Vendors, reviews, interviews etc.

Soundslam
nick@soundslam.com
www.soundslam.com
The latest music news, reviews, artist info, contests and more!

The Source *Unsigned Hype*
www.thesource.com
Profiles a talented unsigned artist each month.

Sphere of Hip Hop
Plastic webmaster@sphereofhiphop.com
www.sphereofhiphop.com
Reviews positive Hip Hop.

Stink Zone
Eric info@stinkzone.com
www.stinkzone.com
Reviews all kinds of Hip Hop, Funk and Reggae.

Stylus Wars
info@styluswars.com
www.styluswars.com
To have your mix tape reviewed send us a copy.

Suckarepellent.com
Katy Walker kcwalker@gmail.com
www.suckarepellent.com
Artist features, Real Audio, fashion and more.

Support Online Hip Hop
PO Box 374, Jersey City, NJ 07303-0374
www.sohh.com
Connect with the online Hip Hop community.

Tha Formula.com
PO Box 385, Gardena, CA 90248
info@thaformula.com
www.thaformula.com
Streaming radio station, news and much more.

THEULTIMATECDLINK.com
ultimatecdlink@yahoo.com
theultimatecdlink.com
Send your CD and promotional materials to us.

Trickology
opus@trickology.com
www.trickology.com
Archive of 12' singles and exclusive joints we got our hands on.

Undergroundhip-hop.net
1201 University Ave. #106, PO Box 179,
Riverside, CA 92507
josh@undergroundhip-hop.net
www.undergroundhip-hop.net
Spreads the word about Hip Hop talent.

UnderworldHipHop.com
Iwil murderu2@hotmail.com
www.underworldhiphop.net
The Rap ice age is over!

Unsigned the Magazine
PO Box 165116, Irving, TX 75016
Kitty Estes kitty@unsignedthemagazine.com
www.unsignedthemagazine.com
Gives unsigned artists and labels maximum exposure.

UrbanJoint.com
www.urbanjoint.com
Devoted to the varied essence of urban talents.

Vice Magazine
97 N. 10th St. #202, Brooklyn, NY 11211
PH: 718-599-3101 FX: 718-599-1769
vice@viceland.com
www.viceland.com
Online community and magazine. We have offices around the world. Check our site for a contact near you.

The Vinyl Exchange
PO Box 117, 1450 Sutter St.,
San Francisco, CA 94109
djbooth@vinylexchange.com
www.vinylexchange.com
Please do NOT send CDs for review. We only review vinyl.

XXL
1115 Broadway, New York, NY 10010
PH: 212-807-7100 FX: 212-620-7787
xxl@harris-pub.com
www.xxlmag.com
Features eye candy, street team, articles and more.

Canada

The CyberKrib.com
theichibanson@thecyberkrib.com
www.thecyberkrib.com
Just e-mail me and we'll get you some coverage.

HipHopHotSpot.com
PO Box 35534, ROP Strath Barton,
Hamilton, ON L8H 7S6
hiphophotspot.com
Free resources to give artists more promotion.

JACKHOUSE
PO Box 10617, 998 Bloor St. W.
Toronto, ON M6H 1L8
PH: 647-271-7736 FX: 647-4339-1411
info@urbnet.com
www.urbnet.com/Jackhouse
Web development, digital music delivery and more.

Peace Magazine
PO Box 124, Stn. B, Toronto, ON M5T 2T3
PH: 416-406-2088
info@peacemagazine.com
www.peacemagazine.com
Music. Fashion. Athletics. Lifestyle.

Pound Magazine
675 King St. W. #306, Toronto, ON M5V 1M9
PH: 416-656-7911 FX: 416-656-9388
chris@poundmag.com
www.poundmag.com
Send in all your stuff for review.

ThickOnline.com
3007 W. 7th Ave. Vancouver, BC V6K 1Z7
PH: 778-892-8670 FX: 778-892-8670
info@thickonline.com
www.thickonline.com
Shedding light on unknown talent.

underground sound
PO Box 9622, Saskatoon, SK S7K 7G1
Noyz319@ugsmag.com
www.ugsmag.com
We post/review submitted Hip Hop MP3s.

Europe

Czech Republic

BBaRák CZ
Pribyslavska 10, 135 00 Praha 3, Czech Republic
PH: 420-296-330-993 FX: 420-296-330-993
info@bbarak.cz
www.bbarak.cz
Reviews local and international artists.

France

Just Like HipHop
Lot n°12 5 Boulevard de Creteil,
94100 Saint-Mauer Des Fosses, France
PH: 01-48-89-15-16 FX: 01-48-89-15-17
service-client@justlikevibes.com
www.justlikehiphop.com
News, reviews, interviews, downloads etc.

LeHiphop.com
www.lehiphop.com
We propose reviewz, interviewz, articlez, MP3 etc.

Germany

Backspin
Postfach 71 02 03, 22162 Hamburg, Germany
PH: 040-22-92-98-0 FX: 040-22-92-98-50
info@backspin.de
www.backspin.de
Marktplatz, forum, termine etc.

Heftig!
Am Holländer 15, 03238 Finsterwalde, Germany
PH: 49-3531-7190500 FX: 49-3531-7190600
Joern-A. Werner presse@heftig.com
www.heftig.com
Reviews, news, release dates, interviews etc.

hamburghiphop.de
Isladstr. 14a 22145, Hamburg, Germany
PH: 0162-3391575
info@hamburghiphop.de
www.hamburghiphop.de
News, reviews, interviews and MP3s.

MK Zwo
Jonasstrabe 47, 12053 Berlin, Germany
PH: 49-030-318-00-266 FX: 49-030-639-78-705
info@mkzwo.com
www.mkzwo.com
Magazin für Hip Hop, Dancehall und Raggae.

Rap.de
Blucherstr. 22, D-10961 Berlin, Germany
PH: 49-30-440-100-90 FX: 49-30-440-100-88
Basti Zeiger basti@rap.de
www.rap.de
Music, radio, video, shop, reviews, interviews.

Truehead.de
webmaster@truehead.de
www.truehead.de
Online community and magazine.

WebBeatz
Auf dem Kamp 13, 42799 Leichlingen, Germany
FX: +49-01212-5-59763024
Daniel Doege info@webbeatz.de
webbeatz.de
Hip Hop promotion platform.

The Netherlands

Globaldarkness
Postbus 11173, 2301 ED Leiden, Holland
info@globaldarkness.com
www.globaldarkness.com
Jungle, Electro-Funk, Hip Hop & Reggae.

theBoombap
Postbus 10804, 1001 EV Amsterdam, Netherlands
www.theboombap.nl
Nederlandsch meest gelezen Hip Hop magazine.

Spain

Hip Hop Yaik
hiphopyaik@gmail.com
www.hiphopyaik.com
Web dedicada al mundo del Hip Hop en Español..

Muevelo Hip Hop
C/ Sales y Ferre n°1, 1°, 41004 Sevilla, Spain
discos@muevelohiphop.com
www.muevelohiphop.com
Webzine de Hip Hop latino.

Sweden

Boom Bap
Hojdvagen 19, 291 41 Kristianstad, Sweden
J. Persson info@boom-bap.com
www.boom-bap.com
Send your demos to us.

hiphopper.org
info@hiphopper.org
www.hiphopper.org
All your Hip Hop news.

Street Zone
Flottbrovagen 23, 112 64 Stockholm, Sweden
Melin info@streetzone.com
www.streetzone.com
News, reviews, label and more.

Switzerland

Aight-Genossen
Postfach 3032, 8033 Zurich, Switzerland
PH: 41-043-535-31-30
info@aight-genossen.ch
www.aight-genossen.ch
Swiss Hip Hop online.

Cosmic Hip Hop
27 ch. De Champ-Manon, 1233 Bernex, Suisse
staff@cosmichiphop.com
www.cosmichiphop.com
Web mag exclusively dedicated to Hip Hop.

Urban Smarts
Sturzbuchelstrasse 14, CH-9303 Wittenbach, Switzerland
PH: 71-298-58-26
get@urbansmarts.com
www.urbansmarts.com
Sheds light on independent Hip Hop artists from all coasts and continents.

United Kingdom

Big Smoke Magazine
PO Box 1002, Croydon, CRO 2UF UK
PH: 44-0-7966472051
Dirty Harry dirtyharry@bigsmokelive.com
www.bigsmokelive.com
Interviews, reviews, events, competitions and more!

Knowledge
1 Trafalgar Mews, Eastway, London, E9 5JG UK
PH: 0-208-533-9300 FX: 0-2008-533-9320
editor@knowledgemag.co.uk
www.knowledgemag.co.uk
The magazine for Drum 'n Bass, Jungle, Hip Hop, Breakbeat and urban culture.

RAGO Magazine
PO Box 1668, Wolverhampton, England WV2 3WG
info@ragomagazine.com
www.ragomagazine.com
Interviews, features, news and mixed tape, album, single & video reviews.

spinemagazine
4 Ganton St., London, England W1F 7QN
PH: +44 (0)20 7494 4401
FX: +44 (0)020 7494 4402
Zaid zaid@spinemagazine.com
www.spinemagazine.com
In-depth music reviews.

Australia

Stealth
PO Box 666, Sydney, NSW 2001 Australia
info@stealthmag.com
www.stealthmag.com
Australia's premier Hip Hop magazine.

StreetHop.com
PO Box 2102, Salisbury Downs, Adelaide,
SA 5108 Australia
info@streethop.com
www.streethop.com
Promoting the Hip Hop culture: news, interviews, artist directory, music reviews...

Africa

Africasgateway
PO Box 1087, Woodstock, 7915, South Africa
info@africasgateway.com
www.africasgateway.com
Africa's largest platform for independent artists and record labels. Interact with fans and submit press releases to an audience from over 100 countries.

Direct traffic to your website -
www.indielinkexchange.com/ile

Jam Band

An Honest Tune
PO Box 1362, Oxford, MS 38655
PH: 662-281-0753
Tom Speed tspeed@anhonesttune.com
www.AnHonestTune.com
Mostly Jam bands, Americana, Alt-Country & Roots music.

ebong.org
info@ebong.org
ebong.org
We are an international collective of "special folk" who wish to provide a venue for creativity.

Glide Magazine
c/o Eric Ward, PO Box 640414, Flushing, NY 11364
reviews@glidemagazine.com
www.glidemagazine.com
Covering today's most innovative artists.

High Times
419 Park Ave. S.16th Fl. New York, NY 10016
PH: 212-387-0500 x 249
hteditor@hightimes.com
www.hightimes.com
Presenting the true independent voice of today.

Hittin' the Note
info@hittinthenote.com
www.hittinthenote.com
Americana sounds of Blues, Rock & Jazz.

Jamaholic.com
submissions@jamaholic.com
www.jamaholic.com
A place where those who are afflicted with music addiction can feel at home and not be ashamed of their condition. If you would like to send your latest CD for review consideration, send me an email and I'll send you my mailing address.

JamBands.com
dean@jambands.com
www.jambands.com
An on-line web zine devoted to Improvisational music.

Jammed Online
dan@jammedonline.com
www.jammedonline.com
A place for people to come and read independent stories, reviews and interviews about their favorite artists and music.

KyndMusic
906 Prince St. #301, Alexandria, VA 22314
bandsubmittal@kyndmusic.com
www.kyndmusic.com
We cover the national and regional Jam scene as well as other music of interest to music fans like ourselves, including Folk, World, Indie Rock, Jazz and Blues.

Relix Magazine
180 Varick St. #410, New York, NY 10014
PH: 646-230-0100 FX: 646-230-0200
Steve Bernstein steve@relix.com
www.relix.com
Covering other, non-mainstream, types of music.

The Watercooler
5929 Ridgecrest Cir. Peoria, IL 61615
PH: 309-691-1323
Sam Tayyari webmaster@thewatercooler.org
www.thewatercooler.org
We cover all areas of Jam/Jazz music.

Jazz

North America

United States

All About Jazz
761 Sproul Rd. #211, Springfield, PA 19064
PH: 610-690-0326
mricci@visionx.com
www.allaboutjazz.com
Jazz & Blues magazine/resource.

allJaZZGuiTar
webmaster@alljazzguitar.com
www.alljazzguitar.com
Resource site for the Jazz guitar enthusiast!

American Rag
20137 Skyline Ranch Dr. Apple Valley, CA 92308
PH: 760-247-5145 FX: 760-247-5145
don@americanrag.com
www.americanrag.com
Commentary, news, articles of interest and reviews.

Any Swing Goes
doug@anyswinggoes.com
www.anyswinggoes.com
Publication that allows Indie CDs for review.

AsianImprov.com
1375 Sutter St. #110, San Francisco, CA 94109
PH: 415-353-5732 FX: 415-353-5733
promotions@asianimprov.com
www.asianimprov.com
Resource for new directions by Asian Americans.

Atomic Mag
4230 Fairway Dr. #6210, Carrolton, TX 75010
PH: 972-939-5417
info@atomicmag.com
www.atomicmag.com
The essential guide to retro culture.

Contemporary Jazz
11131 Colorado, Kansas City, MO 64137
Jeff Charney cjazz@contemporaryjazz.com
www.contemporaryjazz.com
News, reviews, interviews and release listings.

DownBeat.com
102 N. Haven Rd. Elmhurst, IL 60126
editor@downbeat.com
www.downbeat.com
Send in your material for review.

Independent Reviewer - Frank Matheis
frank@matheisproductions.com
www.frankspicks.com
Writes a weekly column as music critic for Taconic Press.

Jazz & Blues Report
19885 Detroit Rd. #320, Rocky River, OH 44116
PH: 216-651-0626 FX: 440-331-0886
Bill Wahl billwahl@jazz-blues.com
www.jazz-blues.com
Features show listings and reviews.

Jazz Improv
PO Box 26770, Elkins Park, PA 19027
PH: 215-887-8808
jazz@jazzimprov.com
www.jazzimprov.com
100 detailed Jazz CD reviews in each issue.

Jazz Nation
PO Box 218362, Houston, TX 77218
PH: 832-439-3560
Baldwin "Smitty" Smith smittyjazz@sbcglobal.net
www.thejazznation.com
Covers the ever-changing music called Jazz.

Jazz Now
PO Box 19266, Oakland, CA 94619-0266
jazznow@sbcglobal.net
www.jazznow.com
Covering the hottest up-and-coming stars.

Jazz Online
contact@jazzonline.com
www.jazzonline.com
Fresh reviews of fresh Jazz music.

Jazz-Sax.Com
ericdano@jazz-sax.com
www.jazz-sax.com
Post your own reviews.

Jazz Times
8737 Colesville Rd. 9th Fl.
Silver Spring, MD 20910-3921
PH: 301-588-4114 FX: 301-588-5531
info@jazztimes.com
www.jazztimes.com
World's leading Jazz publication.

Jazz USA
2613 NE MLK Blvd. #B, Portland, OR 97212
jazzmaster@jazzusa.com
jazzusa.com
Submit music that you would like reviewed.

Jazziz
2650 N. Military Trail, Fountain Sq. II Bldg. #140,
Boca Raton, FL 33431
PH: 561-893-6868 FX: 561-893-6867
www.jazziz.com
The voice of a new Jazz culture.

JazzReview.com
10033 W. Ruby Ave. Milwaukee, WI 53225
Morrice Blackwell morrice@jazzreview.com
www.jazzreview.com
Promotes all styles of Jazz music.

The Mississippi Rag
9448 Lyndale Ave. S. #120,
Bloomington, MN 55420
PH: 952-885-9918 FX: 952-885-9943
editor@mississippirag.com
www.mississippirag.com
New bands are highlighted in each issue.

Mr. Lucky
PO Box 3227, Napa, CA 94558
PH: 415-420-9163 FX: 661-420-6943
editor@mrlucky.com
www.mrlucky.com
Our only criteria are harmony, melody and rhythm.

One Final Note
1311 St. Albans St. N. St. Paul, MN 55117
PH: 651-489-3412
Scott Hreha scott@onefinalnote.com
onefinalnote.com
Jazz & Improvised music webzine.

Saxophone Journal
www.dornpub.com/saxophonejournal.html
Publishes reviews that are positive in nature. Visit our site to find which reviewer covers your style of music.

Turbula.net
PO Box 3497, Escondido, CA 92033
Jim Trageser jt@trageser.com
www.turbula.net
An odd little online publication to which truly talented people seem strangely compelled to send interesting works for others to enjoy.

Canada

eJazzNews
news@ejazznews.com
www.ejazznews.com
News, profiles, interviews, reviews and more.

Smooth Jazz Now
main@smoothjazznow.com
SmoothJazzNow.com
News, reviews and interviews. Also covers New Age music.

Europe

Austria

jazzeit.at
Große Sperlgasse 2, A-1020 Wien, Austria
jazzzeit@jazzzeit.at
www.jazzzeit.at
Information and CD reviews.

Belgium

Dragon Jazz
BP 25 - BXL 44, 13 Avenue de la Brise, B-1020 Bruxelles, Belgium
Pierre Dulieu pierre.dulieu@skynet.be
users.skynet.be/sky19290
Accent mis sur les productions Européennes et Belges en particulier. Jazz, Blues, Avant-Garde, Fusion, World Jazz, Jazz Européen...

Denmark

JAZZ SPECIAL
Havnegade 41, DK-1058 K, Denmark
PH: 45-33-33-87-60
jazzspecial@sundance.dk
www.jazzspecial.dk
The world's most distributed Jazz magazine!

France

Citizen Jazz
127, Ave. Marcel ouvrier,
91550 Paray Vieille Poste, France
PH: 33-01-69-38-06-26
redaction@citizenjazz.com
www.citizenjazz.com
CD review, articles, interviews, audio and radio.

Culturekiosque
editors@culturekiosque.com
www.culturekiosque.com
Worldwide A & E guide. We do Jazz and Classical music reviews.

Jazz Break
info@jazzbreak.com
www.jazzbreak.com
Covers the worldwide Jazz scene.

Jazz Hot
BP 405, 75969 Paris cedex 20, France
PH: 33-01-43-66-74-88 FX: 33-01-43-66-72-60
jazzhot@wanadoo.fr
www.jazzhot.net
La revue internationale du Jazz depuis 1935.

Jazz Magazine
18-24 quai de la Marne,
75164 Paris, Cedex 19, France
info@jazzmagazine.com
www.jazzmagazine.com
Interviews, articles, exhibitions, concert dates, news reviews etc.

Sudden-Thoughts.com
17 rue Augereau, 75007 Paris, France
Charles Walker charles@sudden-thoughts.com
www.sudden-thoughts.com
To ensure both radio play and review, send at least (2) copies of your CD.

Germany

Jazz Pages
Friedrich Ebert Str 75, 69239 Neckarsteinach, Germany
PH: 06229-28-20-7 FX: 06229-28-20-8
Frank Schindelbeck jazz@jazzpages.com
www.jazzpages.com
All about Jazz in Germany.

Jazz Thing
Verlag Azel Stinshoff, Sulzburgstr. 74,
50937 Koln, Germany
PH: 0221-941-488 FX: 0221-413-166
redaktion@jazzthing.de
www.jazzthing.de
Die Zeitschrift für weltoffene Musikliebhaber von heute.

Jazzdimensions
Postfach 36 03 10, 10973 Berlin, Germany
PH: 49-30-612-850-68 FX: 49-30-695-08-273
info@jazzdimensions.de
www.jazzdimensions.de
News, reviews, interviews and articles.

jazzlive
PH: 02-587-68-63
jazzlive@aon.at
www.onstage.at/jazzlive
Magazin für zeitgenössische musik.

Italy

All About Jazz
302A W. 12th St. #204, New York, NY 10014
PH: 610-690-0326 FX: 240-359-2349
mricci@visionx.com
www.allaboutjazz.com/italy
All the info on the Italian Jazz scene.

CiaoJazz
www.ciaojazz.com
Artist bios, MP3s and much, much more.

Jazzer
Francesco Soliani info@jazzer.it
www.jazzer.it
Jazzer doesn't mean only Jazz, it means also Classical, Rock, Alternative etc... because music hasn't frontiers.

Poland

ERA JAZZU
erajazzu@jazz.pl
www.jazz.pl
Send us samples of CDs, DVD, publications, press-kits, promo-sets etc.

Russia

Jazz News
home.nestor.minsk.by/jazz
A monthly magazine on Jazz and Blues.

Spain

Cuaderno de Jazz
cuadernos@cuadernosdejazz.com
www.cuadernosdejazz.com
Articles about Jazz musicians.

Switzerland

Smooth Jazz Vibes
Blattenstr. 8, Postfach 55, 9450 Altstätten, Switzerland
PH: 41-71-755-07-90
Peter Böhi pboehi@boehi.ch
www.smoothvibes.com
Please visit the site for submission details.

United Kingdom

Jazz UK
132 Southwark St., London, SE1 0SW UK
PH: 44-020-7928-9089 FX: 44-020-7401-6870
www.jazzservices.org.uk
Jazz publication in the UK.

Jazzwise
2B Gleneagle Mews, Ambleside Ave.
London, SW16 6AE UK
PH: 44-020-8664-7222 FX: 4-020-8677-7128
admin@jazzwise.com
www.jazzwise.com
From cutting-edge to Jazz club crossover and World Jazz.

King's Jazz Review
ds.dial.pipex.com/jazzitoria
A voice for all forms of Jazz in the UK.

Asia

CyberFusion
webmaster@jazzfusion.com
jazzfusion.com
CD reviews, interviews, live reports.

Warta Jazz.com
info@wartajazz.net
www.wartajazz.com
The ultimate source for Indonesian Jazz lovers.

Latin

La Banda Elástica
PO Box 2608, West Covina, CA 91793-2608
rock@labandaelastica.com
www.labandaelastica.com
Latin Alternative music magazine.

BoomOnline.com
PO Box 398752, Miami Beach, FL 33239
PH: 305-718-3612 FX: 305-468-1983
promotions@boomonline.com
www.boomonline.com
The community site for Latin Rock and Pop.

Brownpride Online
PO Box 3852, Fullerton, CA 92834
FX: 714-792-3806
info@digitalaztlan.com
www.brownpride.com
Everything about the Latino scene.

HispanicOnline.com
rperez@hisp.com
www.hispaniconline.com
Does reviews and has an artist-of-the-month feature.

LA FACTORÍA DEL RITMO
Apd. 647. CP 39080, Santander - Cantabria, Spain
info@lafactoriadelritmo.com
www.lafactoriadelritmo.com
El primer magazine musical en Español via Internet.

Flamenco-world.com
Huertas 62, local, 28014 Madrid, Spain
PH: + (34) 913600865 FX: + (34) 91 3690244
magazine@flamenco-world.com
www.flamenco-world.com
Your one stop shop for anything and everything Flamenco!

LaMusica.com
Luis Moreno lmoreno@sbsnewyork.com
www.lamusica.com
News, events, artists and some independent reviews.

MUSICA SALSA
Schomburgstr. 54 a, D- 22767 Hamburg, Germany
stefan.renz@salsayazucar.com
www.musicasalsa.de
Events and Latin-American culture in Germany, Colombia and more...

Picadillo
bishikawa@picadillo.com
www.picadillo.com
Resource for info on Latin music and bands, CD reviews, articles, music sources, listening sites, and links... for the serious Latin music aficionado.

PicanteXpress
2335 Jane St. #1701, Downsview, ON M3M 1A7
PH: 416-245-4907 FX: 416-245-1469
info@picantexpress.com
www.picantexpress.com
Toronto's Latin entertainment magazine.

'LA'Ritmo.com
info@laritmo.com
www.laritmo.com
Interviews and reviews of established and up-and-coming artists.

SalsaPower.com
Jacira Castro & Julián Mejía jacira@salsapower.com
www.salsapower.com
We only review artists who do Salsa, Timba, and other related Afro-Cuban rhythms.

Salsaroots.com
rita@salsacrazy.com
www.salsaroots.com
CD reviews of everything new, old and sizzling.

Timba.com
6800 Bird Rd. #267, Miami, FL 33155
mail@timba.com
www.timba.com
News, some independent reviews and concert information.

Vista USA
2107 D West Commonwealth Ave. # 420, Alhambra, CA 91803
PH/FX: 626-282-9047
editor@vistausa.com
vistausa.com
Extensive coverage of Tropical music and more.

Metal
All styles of Metal as well as Hard Rock, Modern Rock and Stoner Rock

North America
United States

666metal.com
metal@popstar.com
www.666metal.com
If you are in a band, and are interested in reviews/interviews, please, contact the author whose tastes you think match your style most.

Abrasive Rock
PO Box 828, Olympia, WA 98507
PH: 360-789-0703
www.abrasiverock.com
Covers any and all forms of abrasive Rock.

Absolut Metal
editor@absolutmetal.com
www.absolutmetal.com
Reviews, local tour dates/shows and more.

Adrenalin Metal Fanzine
PO Box 296, Waunakee, WI 53597
Mike Burmeister adrenalin@adrenalinfanzine.com
www.adrenalinfanzine.com
Promotes bands of the various Metal styles.

AllThingsMetal.net
108 St. Michelle, Apt G, Hawk Point, MO 63349
Jennifer Shipley jennifer@allthingsmetal.net
www.allthingsmetal.net
We are bringing them together...the signed & the unsigned.

Anvil
731 Heatherstone Dr.
High Ridge, MO 63049
PH: 636-677-5925
anvilmag@charter.net
www.anvilmagazine.com
The unholy bible of Extreme music.

Archaic Metallurgy
lane@archaicmetallurgy.com
www.archaicmetallurgy.com
We review every release in earnest. Contact us for our physical address.

Aversion Online
PO Box 5084, Richmond, VA 23220
aversiononline@holyterror.com
www.aversiononline.com
Exposure for all forms of Extreme/Underground music.

BallBusterHardMUSIC.com
PO Box 58368, Louisville, KY 40268-0368
PH: 502-447-2568 FX: 502-447-2568
ballbusterhard@webtv.net
www.ballbusterhardmusic.com
Without prejudice, 100% lead for your head!

The Beer Pit
godofmetal@thebeerpit.com
www.thebeerpit.com
If you would like to be considered for inclusion on the site please fill out our online form and let us know what your poison is.

Blabbermouth.net
PO Box 8234, White Plains, NY 10602
bmouth@bellatlantic.net
www.roadrun.com/blabbermouth.net
All the latest Heavy Metal / Hard Rock news and reviews. Updated daily

Black Metal Reviews
info@evilmusic.com
www.evilmusic.com/reviews
We promote the Metal artists that ignore trends and superficial music.

Bleeding for Metal
c/o Jimmy Hymiller, 8733 McKendree Rd.
Wesley Chapel, FL 33544
contact@bleeding.de
www.bleeding.de
Please address demos, promo-materials etc. to the above address.

Chronicles of Chaos
NorthAmerica@ChroniclesOfChaos.com
Europe@ChroniclesOfChaos.com
RestOfTheWorld@ChroniclesOfChaos.com
www.chroniclesofchaos.com
Extreme music webzine. Updated daily! Contact the reviewer in your region for our mailing address.

Crave Magazine
1013 NE 68th St., Vancouver, WA 98665
PH: 360-991-9332 FX: 501-694 8061
Robin Steeley robinsteeley@hotmail.com
www.cravemagazine.com
Your guide to extreme culture.

Crusher Magazine
1924 2nd Ave. #3B, New York, NY 10029
PH: 646-215-8522
Christine Natanael editatrix@crushermagazine.com
www.crushermagazine.com
Covers the ever-changing loud music scene.

DBN Magazine
PO Box 3547, Lantana, FL 33465-3547
Tim Maher dbn@gsta.net
www.dbnmagazine.com
We cover a wide range of musical genres.

Death Metal and Black Metal
PO Box 1004, Alief, TX 77411-1004
S.R. Prozak prozak@anus.com
www.anus.com/metal
Reviews of Metal, Grindcore, Punk, Thrash as evolving history.

deathgrind.com
jash@deathgrind.com
www.deathgrind.com
You must record your demo/CD/LP/EP whatever with a raw production.

DigitalMetal.com
PO Box 295, Drexel Hill, PA 19026
FX: 610-734-3716
info@digitalmetal.com
www.digitalmetal.com
News, reviews and interviews.

Doomed Nation
Cyphlon Studio, 4149 W. 80th Pl.
Chicago, IL 60652
Tom Denney cyphlon@yahoo.com
www.bakulasaves.com
A project developed to document and illustrate a specific genre of music that no one in video media really cares about.

The Edge
5555 Rangeland, San Antonio, TX 78247
PH: 210-564-0088 FX: 210-655-6586
Toni Torres edgemag@satx.rr.com
www.theedgemagazine.com
Supports national and unsigned bands.

ElectricBasement.com
PO Box 472, 1442 E. Lincoln Ave.
Orange, CA 92865
PH: 877-301-7351
contact@electricbasement.com
www.electricbasement.com
See guidelines before submitting.

Feast of Hate and Fear
PO Box 560069, Miami, FL 33156
A. Souto 156@feastofhateandfear.com
feastofhateandfear.com
Dark archives, travelogs, strange articles, music reviews...

FuBARM
7832 W. Manchester Ave. #3,
Playa del Rey, CA 90293
anubis@fubarm.com
www.fubarm.com
Full blown-ass ripping Metal.

FUELMYPAIN.COM
W2433 Twin Pine Ln. Porterfield, WI 54159
Ben Steimle admin@fuelmypain.com
www.fuelmypain.com
Heavy Metal, Hard Rock community.

Future Impact
Robert Beneux rbeneux@futureimpactmag.com
www.futureimpactmag.com
Bringing you the sounds of unknown artists.

The Gauntlet
174 W. Foothill Blvd. #235, Monrovia, CA 91016
moshpit@thegauntlet.com
www.thegauntlet.com
Huge archive of Metal Indie musicians, reviews...

Glam-Metal.com
Thomas S. Orwat contact@glam-metal.com
glam-metal.com
Dedicated to bringing you the most updated information on the best Hard Rock bands on the face of the planet.

The Grimoire of Exalted Deeds
PO Box 1987, Clifton, NJ 07011
PH: 973-478-3743
masterzebub@aol.com
www.thegrimoire.com
A Death Metal magazine for assholes, by assholes.

Hammerhead
hamhedzine@aol.com
www.hammerheadzine.com
Resource of Metal music and more.

The Hard Rock Society
2621 14th St. S. #4, Fargo, ND 58103
mmd@hardrocksociety.com
www.hardrocksociety.com
A Hard Rock/Heavy Metal site with reviews.

Hardrock Haven
John Kindred webmaster@hardrockhaven.net
www.hardrockhaven.net
Contact us about submitting your material for review.

Harvest Moon Music
PO Box 385, Howell, MI 48844
Dave Knoch tattooz@harvestmoonmusic.com
www.harvestmoonmusic.com
Rock and Heavy Metal reviews and information.

Headbanger's Delight
2497 Plymouth Rock, Holland, MI 49424
info@headbangersdelight.com
www.headbangersdelight.com
Get your material reviewed here.

HitThePit.Com
derek@hitthepit.com
www.hitthepit.com
Pick any writer to review your material.

HMAS.org *Heavy Metal Appreciation Society*
374 1st St. N. Huntingdon, PA 15642
John Brighenti webmaster@hmas.org
www.hmas.org
We review ONLY Heavy Metal, and its various sub genres.

Hyperblast
Cleric Curst grammaton1st@aol.com
www.hyperblastmetal.com
Heavy Metal news, CD reviews, show reviews etc.

In Depth
Anthony ConcertRag@aol.com
www.indepthzine.com
Show and album reviews and live pictures.

Inside Metal
Sam Humphreys info@insidemetal.net
www.insidemetal.net
Reviews and promotes independent bands and labels.

Into Obscurity
bane@into-obscurity.com
www.into-obscurity.com
Reviews, interviews, tour dates, events and more!

Jen's Metal Page
JensMetalPage@comcast.net
www.jensmetalpage.com
News, reviews, interviews, MP3s etc.

Justin's Heavy Metal Site
Justin "Battle Angel" Harvey
thelearning@comcast.net
justinsmetalwebsite.com
Reviews all kinds of Metal music.

lambgoat.com
PO Box 15106, Reading, PA 19612
info@lambgoat.com
www.lambgoat.com
News, reviews, interviews, audio samples and more.

Lamentations of the Flame Princess Weekly
lotfp@lotfp.com
www.lotfp.com
The interviews in LotFP are as informative and in-depth as any ever done on Planet Earth..

Maximum Metal
6305 Greenway Dr. Roanoke, VA 24019
Frank Hill news@maximummetal.com
www.maximummetal.com
We will review every promo and demo we receive!

Loudside
1549 Burnside Ave. Ventura, CA 93004 Attn: Jono
Jono jon@loudside.com
www.loudside.com
Send in your stuff for review.

Maelstrom
3234 Clay St., San Francisco, CA 94115
Roberto Martinelli roma@maelstrom.nu
www.maelstrom.nu
Live/album reviews, interviews and more.

Metal Core
PO Box 622, Marlton, NJ 08053
metalczine@aol.com
www.metalcorefanzine.com
Review section for signed and unsigned bands.

Metal Coven
PO Box 580326, Houston, TX 77258
Angel Bollier webmistress@metalcoven.com
www.metalcoven.com
Extremely informative online Metal webzine promoting Heavy Metal and the Underground Metal scene.

Metal Crypt
michelr@metalcrypt.com
www.metalcrypt.com
Submit your Metal CDs/demos for review.

Metal Fanatix
70 Patrick Cir. Fulton, NY 13069
legion59@aol.com
www.metalfanatix.com
News, reviews, interviews of Metal music.

Metal Hordes
emile@metalhordes.com
www.metalhordes.com
Extreme Metal community. Profiles, reviews, interviews.

Metal Judgement
PO Box 979, Santa Monica, CA 90406-0979
info@metaljudgment.com
www.metaljudgment.com
In-depth reviews on the world of Heavy Metal.

Metal Life Magazine
Attn: Terry Bunch 10942 Poblado Rd. #2921,
San Diego, CA 92127
www.metallife.com
Contact databases, concert info, reviews, interviews, bands, sounds, pics, Metal lifestyle information and much more.

Metal Maniacs
PO Box 263, Denton, MD 21629
Attn: Label consideration
metalmaniacsnews@aol.com
www.metalmaniacs.com
News, reviews etc.

Metal Meltdown
drmetal@metalmeltdown.com
www.metalmeltdown.com
Metal interviews, radio, reviews, news and pictures.

Metal Reigns Unsigned Artist page
www.metalreigns.com
You can learn about up and coming metal bands, or just hear some cool new metal music. There will be a new unsigned artist each week.

Metal Reviews
contact@metalreviews.com
www.metalreviews.com
Loads of reviews. Updated weekly!

Metal Sludge
PO Box 3024, Gary, IN 46403-3024
Donna Anderson metalsludge@metalsludge.tv
www.metalsludge.tv
The minimum number of CDs we need is TWO. Don't send just one!

Metal Update
Laura German editor@metalupdate.com
www.metalupdate.com
Up to date and complete Metal news.

METALREVIEW.COM
PO Box 25097, Woodbury, MN 55125
www.metalreview.com
Album reviews, concert reviews, band interviews.

metalunderground.com
9008 Harris St., Frederick, MD 21704
metalunderground.com
Send promo CDs, demos, stickers, t-shirts etc.

Midwest Metal Magazine
PO Box 612, Downers Grove, IL 60516
Tom midwestmetal@comcast.net
www.midwestmetalmagazine.com
Send CDs, cassettes, vinyl and contact/photos.

MidwestMetal.info
Review Dept. PO Box 39023, St. Louis, MO 63139
Maggot maggot@midwestmetal.info
www.midwestmetal.info
To get a review of your CD, please mail your Demo/CD to us. Please include your Bands name, website address & E-mail address.

Mourning the Ancient
PO Box 45637, Omaha, NE 68145
sunlessdawn@mourningtheancient.com
www.mourningtheancient.com
Black and Death Metal interviews, samples and more.

Music Incider
musicincider@earthlink.net
www.musicincider.com
"The truth is out there".

Music Mayhem
musicmayhem@knology.net
www.musicmayhem.com
Interviews, reviews, concert shots etc.

Neo-Zine
PO Box 144, Asheville, PA 16613
neo-zine@earthlink.net
www.Neo-Zine.com
We are involved in all kinds of Noise, Death Metal, Black Metal, Experimental, Punk, Ambient, ... everything extreme or underground.

Noize Pollution
PH: 310-914-3081
info@noizepollution.com
noizepollution.com
Send us your CDs, website address and contact info.

On Track Magazine
1752 E. Ave. J #243, Lancaster, CA 93535
David Priest priest@ontrackmagazine.com
www.ontrackmagazine.com
Coverage of your favorite Hard music bands.

Open Up And Say
www.openupandsay.com
Rock/Metal reviews, interviews, news and links.

Pit Magazine
PO Box 9545, Colorado Springs, CO 80932
PH: 719-633-5752 FX: 719-633-8081
Wendy Perelstein wendy@pitmagazine.com
www.pitmagazine.com
The Extreme music magazine.

PiTRiFF Online
PO Box 1101, Twinsburg, OH 44087
richwithhatred@pitriff.com
www.pitriff.com
News, reviews, radio etc.

Pivotal Rage
c/o Leevan Macomeau, 665 S. Banana River Dr.
Merritt Island, FL 32952
bidou333 bidou333@pivotalrage.com
www.pivotalrage.com
If you can send extra copies of your CDs, or send any kind of merch or goodies, please feel free to do so since we like to use them for giveaways on our website.

The Plague
PO Box 5965, Bellevue, WA 98006
Dan Hinds plaguelord@triple-point.net
the-plague.net
Covers all types of Metal and other Dark music.

The Pure Rock Shop
403 Pin Oak Dr. McDonald, PA 15057
music@tprs.com
www.tprs.com
Contact to get reviewed/featured.

Raginpit Magazine
PH: 209-203-0002
John Southworth edge@raginpit
raginpit.com
The world's loudest magazine. Heavy Metal and Hardcore CD reviews, interviews, show reviews, MP3s and more...

Revolver
1115 Broadway, New York, NY 10010
PH: 212-807-7100
letters@revolvermag.com
www.revolvermag.com
The world's loudest Rock magazine!

RIFTrock
Jason Lutjen jason@riftrock.com
www.riftrock.com
Rock promotion and daily news.

Rock and a Hard Place Zine
812 Countryside Pk. Fargo, ND 58103
Torch rockhardtorch@hotmail.com
www.rockhardplace.com
CD reviews, independent Rock, Metal and AOR.

ROCKBOTTOM Zine
Marcy marcy@rockbottomzine.com
www.rockbottomzine.com
Each issue features lots of reviews. Visit our website for details on how to become "band of the month".

Rocknation
info@rocknation.tv
www.rocknation.tv
Reviews and interviews. Demos accepted.

Rough Edge
PO Box 5160, Ventura, CA 93005
PH: 805-293-8507 FX: 805-293-8507
info@roughedge.com
www.roughedge.com
CD and live reviews, news, photos and more.

Score! Music Magazine
Bands@ScoreMusicMagazine.com
www.scoremusicmagazine.com
Covers today's Indie artists. To get your CD reviewed, fill out the submissions form on our website.

Screachen Publications
PO Box 16352, Phoenix, AZ 85011-6352
Editor@Screachen.com
www.screachen.com
Hard Rock news, interviews, reviews and more.

Seeds of Evil
3720 E Tuttle Ave. Terre Haute, IN 47805-1940
Ron Moody zan@seedsofevil.com
www.seedsofevil.com
We do reviews, band interviews and concert reviews.

Silent Uproar
5614 Split Oak Dr. Raleigh, NC 27609
p-layer@silentuproar.com
www.silentuproar.com
We cover a wide range of Alternative, Metal, Hardcore music.

siN's Metal News
aidan@SMNnews.com
www.smnnews.com
News, reviews, interviews.

Sleazegrinder
PO Box 51446, Boston, MA 02205
sleazegrinder@gmail.com
www.sleazegrinder.com
Preservation of full-tilt, high octane, blistering Rock.

Sociopathic Despair Magazine
PO Box 10025, Bowling Green, KY 42102-4825
sociod@hotmail.com
come.to/despair
Bands, record labels and zines can send items for review.

Soul Killer
neil@soulburn3d.com
www.soulkillerwebzine.com
The very best in Death, Grind, Classic and New Metal.

stonerrock.com
PO Box 78, Carmen, ID 83462
El Danno dan@stonerrock.com
www.stonerrock.com
News, reviews, interviews, galleries and more.

Strigl's Music News
PO Box 4112, New York, NY 10163
Mark mark.strigl@unistudios.com
striglsmusicnews.com
We do a couple reviews each month. Some of the people who run this site are on-air commentators for VH1. Please send GUITAR ROCK ONLY - Metal, Punk, Glam, Emo, Grunge, etc.

Tad Loud Productions
PMB 226, 5815 82nd St. #145, Lubbock, TX 79424
PH: 505-762-7346
Sean Pruitt tadloudrocks@door.net
www.tadloudrocks.com
Helping to promote Indie artists by posting links, articles, CD reviews, interviews, news and more.

That's So Metal.com
PO Box 273, Union NJ, 07083
Rich rich@thatssometal.com
www.thatssometal.com
Send your promos and product.

Theundergroundscene.net
28 Brookside Ave. Boylston, MA 01505
Michael Byrne mike@theundergroundscene.net
www.theundergroundscene.net
Send your album our way and we'll see what we can do.

Transcending the Mundane
5 Hudson Ave. Bohemia, NY 11716
Ladd Everitt Ladd@BasementBar.com
tmetal.com
Quality reviews of newly-released Heavy Metal albums.

Ultimate Metal Reviews
info@metal-reviews.com
www.metal-reviews.com
Small fee required with your CD/promo kit.

UltimateMetal.com
mail@ultimatemetal.com
www.ultimatemetal.com
Supporting the Metal underground. Forums, discussion, interviews, reviews.

Unchain the Underground
PO Box 15, Stony Point, NY 10980
al@unchain.com
www.unchain.com
Reviews and interviews of all forms of Extreme music.

Uranium Music
Mike Smathers smathers@uraniummusic.com
www.uraniummusic.com
Our goal is to remain on the cutting edge of Metal's most extreme flavors and cover bands that don't receive the attention they deserve. Reviews/interviews/tour sponsors for Metal and Rock bands.

Vibrations of Doom
PO Box 1258, Suwanee, GA 30024-0963
Steven Cannon vibrationsofdoom@hotmail.com
vibrationsofdoom.com
Resource for Metal artists and fans.

VOXonline.com
PO Box 712412, Los Angeles, CA 90071
vox@voxonline.com
www.voxonline.com
We will listen to all submissions and publish reviews for those that we favor.

Worm Gear
PO Box 426, Mayfield, MI 49666
korgull@chartermi.net
www.crionicmind.org/wormgear
Interviews, news, reviews, merchandise and more.

Canada

Blistering.com
C.P. St Dorothee, PO Box 69023,
Laval, QC H7X 3M2
PH/FX: 450-689-7106
Rob Cotter rob@blistering.com
www.blistering.com
Submit your CDs and demos. Bands can sell their CDs at our store. We also feature downloads.

Brave Words and Bloody Knuckles
368 Yonge St., Toronto, ON M5B 1S5
PH: 416-229-2966 FX: 416-586-0819
bwbk@bravewords.com
www.bravewords.com
Metal news, features, columns, reviews...

martinpopoff.com
PO Box 65028, 358 Danforth Ave.
Toronto, ON M4K 2Z2
Martin Popoff martinp@inforamp.net
www.martinpopoff.com
Reviews editor and writer for HardReviews (on HardRadio.com).

The Metal Observer
770 Sherbrooke W. #1750, Montréal, QC H3A 1G1
Mark McKenna mark@metal-observer.com
www.metal-observer.com
Contact us about sending your promo/demo/CD in for review.

Metallian.com
34 Okanagan Dr. #1129,
Richmond Hill, ON L4C 9R8
metallian@canada.com
www.metallian.com
Promotes all sub-genres of Heavy Metal.

Midnight Metal
PO Box 1325, Chetwynd, BC V0C 1J0
PH: 250-788-9452
mike@midnightmetal.com
www.midnightmetal.com
I will review, sample or preview your album on air.

theprp.com
wookubus@theprp.com
www.theprp.com
We work relentlessly all year round providing news, reviews and uncovering the very latest acts.

Sleaze Roxx
PO Box 142, Minto, MB R0K 1M0
Skid skid@sleazeroxx.com
www.sleazeroxx.com
Your Hard Rock and Heavy Metal resource.

Stoner Rock Chick
201 Sherbourne St. #2209, Toronto, ON M5A 3X2
Deanna St.Croix deanna@stonerrockchick.com
www.stonerrockchick.com
Bands and Labels, send your CDs for review.

Teufel's Tomb
PO Box 54519, Highgate Village, 7155 Kingsway,
Burnaby, BC V5E 4J6
Eric Crookes info@teufelstomb.com
www.teufelstomb.com
Brutal isn't just a way of life... it's also stupid!

UNRESTRAINED!
5625 Glen Erin Dr. #57, Mississauga, ON L5M 6V2
PH: 416-483-7917
Adam Wasylyk adam@unrestrainedmag.com
www.unrestrainedmag.com
Every demo is taken into review/interview consideration.

South America

Eye of Shiva
Rua D, N° 106, Cj. Milton Gomes, Feira de
Santana-BA - Brazil CEP: 44031-580
corpsegrinder@eyeofshiva.com.br
www.eyeofshiva.com.br
Extreme Metal zine.

himnosrituales
PO Box 1451, Popayan, Colombia
himnosrituales@yahoo.com
www.himnosrituales.com
Please send in only Metal!!!

Kuravilu
PO Box 548, Valdivia, Chile
carlos@kuravilu.cl
www.kuravilu.cl
Reviews, videos, interviews etc.

Metal Fashion Videos
Lord Tato ibalassanian@arnet.com.ar
www.metalfashionvideos.com.ar
Para enviar material a ser revisado o promociones, contactarse a lord tato para recibir posteriores instrucciones.

Music Extreme
Billinghurst 2380 2-A, (C1425DTV) Buenos Aires,
Argentina
info@musicextreme.com
www.musicextreme.com
Lots of new reviews every month!

Roadie Crew
metal@roadiecrew.com
www.roadiecrew.com
A revista de Heavy Metal do Brasil.

Valhalla
Rua Luzerne Proenca Arruda, 128 Sorocaba, SP
CEP: 18081-021, Brazil
PH: 55-15-232-5192 FX: 55-15-211-1621
Eliton Tomasi eliton@valhalla.com.br
www.valhalla.com.br
A revista Underground mais Metal do Brasil.

Europe

Austria

Arising Realm
Sechshauserstr. 59/6, A-1150 Vienna, Austria
PH: 0043-1-9665357
Redaktion@arisingrealm.at
www.arisingrealm.at
Reviews, interviews etc.

DarkScene
c/o Thomas Kernbichler, Gumppstr. 77/21,
6020 Innsbruck, Austria
redaktion@darkscene.at
www.darkscene.at
The magazine about Metal and Gothic, where you can find many pictures, interviews, reviews and more about your favorite bands!

deathmetal.at
Markus [h3ll] h3ll@deathmetal.at
www.deathmetal.at
Brutal Death Metal zine.

Resurrection
info@resurrection.at
www.resurrection.at
News, reviews, interviews, tour dates and more.

Belgium

Beyond Webzine
22 rue Reniers, 1090 Jette, Belgium
Nicolas Arnaud info@beyondwebzine.com
www.beyondwebzine.com
We review all Rock and Metal material. Signed or unsigned bands.

BMU
Temsestraat 27, 9150 Rupelmonde, Belgium
heavy.metal@telenet.be
bmu.lasseel.be
Promoting the underground in Belgium.

The Dark Towers of Lugburz
rc@lugburz.be
www.dma.be/p/lugburz
A support site for Belgian Black & Death Metal bands.

Still Online
Overpoortstraat 29, B 9000 Gent, Belgium
Ronny Van Huffel grindkiller@stillonline.be
www.stillonline.be
News and reviews.

Strickle
Osystraat 31 Bus 6, 2060 Antwerpen, Belguim
www.strickle.com
Review site for the Stoner-Rock genre.

Denmark

Antenna
Lars Lolk lolk@antenna.nu
www.antenna.nu
Contact me to get my address. Please notice that we don't review Mp's or cd-r's without any sleeves. If we're interested in doing interviews, we'll contact you. Don't ask us to contact you when we've reviewed your product.

Intromental Webzine
Nørrebrogade 200B, 4tv, DK-2200 Copenhagen N, Denmark
PH/FX: +45-38344833
Claus Jensen webzine@intromental.com
www.intromental.com/webzine
Paying tribute to all the hard working Metal bands and record labels out there. All labels and bands are welcome to send us their Metal and Hard Rock related titles for review and interview.

mighty music
Skelmosen 1, 2670 Greve, Denmark
PH: 45-332-956-959 FX: 45-33-141-406
Michael H. Andersen Michael@targetdistribution.dk
www.mightymusic.dk
Send material for review.

RevelationZ Magazine
Gebauersgade 2, 4. sal, -3, 8000 Aarhus C, Denmark
Steen Jepsen steen@revelationz.net
www.revelationz.net
Your Heavy Metal and Hard Rock resource.

Finland

Imperiumi
www.imperiumi.net
Dedicated fully to Heavy music, covering anything from Hard Rock to Extreme Metal. Visit our website to see which reviewer covers your particular style of Metal.

meteli.net
tapahtumat@meteli.net
www.meteli.net
Metal in Finland.

RockUnited.Com A&R Dept.
"Wally" Wallström urban@rockunited.com
rockunited.com
With this column we intend to give young, fresh, unsigned bands the opportunity to let their voices be heard. We review demos or independent releases of unsigned bands looking for promotion.

France

Les Acteurs de l'Ombre
52 Avenue du 8 mai 1945,
13240 Septemes les Vallons, France
Cyril Planard webmaster@lesacteursdelombre.com
www.lesacteursdelombre.com
Pour que le Metal survive et se propage!!!

Burn Out
2, rue de la colinette, 51110 Bourgogne, France
PH: 33-0-326-892-668
Phil Kieffer burn.out@wanadoo.fr
www.burnoutzine.net
Chroniques, interviews, concerts, distro...

Decibels
Isabelle Carriot decibels@metal-extreme.com
www.metal-extreme.com
Le Metal Extreme.

Decibels Storm
Boite Postale 7165, Lyon cedex 07, France
decibelsstorm@free.fr
decibelsstorm.free.fr
Le site de Metal par les fans, pour les fans.

Heavy Metal Universe
c/o Ludovic Castelbou, 343, chemin de la Treille,
83500 la Seyne-sur-mer, France
www.heavymetaluniverse.com
International Webzine - from AOR to Grind Death. Once you receive a message from us telling you that we did get your promo material, then you just need to be patient. The review will come

Leprozy.com
webmonster@leprozy.com
www.leprozy.com
Send us news, tour dates about your band or activity. If you want your stuff reviewed send it along by mail. Contact us for our mailing address. Get in touch!!

Lords of Winter
lord-of-winter@wanadoo.fr
lordsofwinter.free.fr
News, reviews, articles etc.

Metallian
B.P 41. 38242, Meylan Cédex, France
PH: +33-0-4-76-90-01-38 FX: +33-0-4-76-41-17-80
headoffice@metallian.net
www.metallian.net
Published every 3 months. You can send Demos, Self-Released CD with complete biography and photo to the above address.

Metalorgie.com
c/o Eric Cambray, 11 rue Sully, Apt. 5,
44 000 Nantes, France
bacteries@metalorgie.com
www.metalorgie.com/metal
Essayez d'envoyer des démos avec un son correcte, on en reçoit beaucoup la sélection commence souvent selon la qualité du son.

METALUZINE
5, rue Drouin - Rés. Saint Georges - 54000 Nancy, France
metaluzine@free.fr
metaluzine.free.fr
Groupes, Labels & Distribs n'hésitez pas à prendre contact.

ObsküR[e]
Emmanuel H. emmanuel.obskure@gmail.com
www.obskure.com
Metal Gothique, Electro, Indus, Death, Black, Progressif, Ambient, Heavy.

Santagore
c/o Pierre NOËL, 10 rue pierre Bouvier, 69270
Fontaines sur Saône, France
pierrot@santagore.com
www.santagore.com
Chroniques, interviews, photos ...

Spirit of Metal
Kivan kivan@spirit-of-metal.com
www.spirit-of-metal.com
Reviews, biographies, reports etc.

La Terre Des Immortels
latem@metal-immortel.com
www.metal-immortel.com
Metal, Rock Prog etc. Si vous êtes un label ou un groupe et que vous voulez voir des chroniques de vos productions sur le site, écrivez un mail à cette adresse.

Snakepit
La Calloterie, 72210 Voivres Les Le Mans, France
Laurent Ramadier snakepit2@free.fr
truemetal.org/snakepit
Around 200 reviews per issue.

Underground Society
13 rue John Kennedy, Lotissement Du Lac, 40990 Saint Paul Les Dax, France
Duarte Philippe duarteph@wanadoo.fr
undersociety.free.fr
Si vous êtes un label / distributeur / PR et que vous voulez nous envoyer votre matériel promos, merci de nous contacter et de nous envoyer vos packages à notre adresse ci contre uniquement.

Versus Magazine
1, boulevard de Strasbourg, 75010 Paris, France
PH: 01-53-34-66-45 FX: 01-53-34-66-46
info@versusmagazine.net
www.versusmagazine.net
Magazine mensuel spécialisé dans tous les Rock.

Germany

21st Century Metal Net
webmaster@21stcenturymetal.net
www.21stcenturymetal.net
Heavy Metal, Hard Rock, Thrash, Black, Death ...

Allschools Network
PO Box 230229, 44639 Herne, Germany
Simone Jäger simone@allschools.net
www.allschools.net
Online Hardcore fanzine. Send demos to the above address.

Amboss
Postfach 1119, 32001 Herford, Germany
info@amboss-mag.de
www.amboss-mag.de
Heavy Metal and Gothic music magazine.

Ancient Spirit
Burdastr. 4, 77656 Offenburg, Germany
dominikvoigt@web.de
www.ancientspirit.de
News, interviews, tour dates, live/CD reviews.

Bleeding for Metal
c/o Madhouse Of Cain, PO Box 39 23, 30039 Hannover, Germany
contact@bleeding.de
www.bleeding.de
Please address demos, promo-materials etc. to the above address.

Bloodchamber
info@bloodchamber.de
www.bloodchamber.de
CD and DVD reviews, interviews and MP3s.

BloodDawn.de
gevatter.tod@blooddawn.de
www.blooddawn.de
News, reviews and featured bands.

Break Out
Verlag Michael Möller, Postfach 1336, D - 69141 Neckargemünd, Germany
PH: +49-0-6229 / 7666 FX: +49-0-6229 / 2714
info@breakoutmagazin.de
www.breakoutmagazin.de
Hardrock, AOR, Melodic Rock, Progressive Rock, Heavy Metal ...

Bright Eyes
Herzog Friedrich Str. 69, 24103 Kiel, Germany
PH: +49 (0) 431 94693 FX: +49 (0) 431 6793221
info@brighteyes.de
www.bright-eyes.de
Updates, interviews, reviews, tour dates, festival-news und vieles mehr ...

Bullet Music Explorer
c/o Michael Jakob, Richard-Böhm-Str.5, Rauenstein, Thüringen, 96528, Germany
PH: 036766 80691 FX: 036766 80693
www.bullet-music-explorer.de
News, reviews, concerts etc.

Carnage
Leif Timm, Herderstr. 76, D - 28203 Bremen, Germany
blasphegor@compuserve.de
carnagedeathmetal.de
Death Metal fanzine.

Daredevil
Kantstr 31, 68723 Oftersheim, Germany
Ralf Burkart daredevil-mag@web.de
www.daredevil.de
If you want your stuff reviewed just send it to us.

Dark Tales
Michael Wohde dark-tales@gmx.de
www.dark-tales.de
Rock, Hard, Death, Black, Speed, Thrash ...

Deathgrind
mail@deathgrind.de
www.deathgrind.de
News, reviews and much more.

Die Geister, die ich rief
Findorffstr. 51, 28215 Bremen, Germany
PH: 0421-377750 FX: 0421-3777511
geister.bremen@gmx.de
www.geister-bremen.de
Covering the German Metal scene.

echoes-online.de
Klauprechtstr. 21, 76137 Karlsruhe, Germany
redaktion@echoes-online.de
www.echoes-online.de
Tons of reviews.

Eternity
Straßmannstr. 49, 10249 Berlin, Germany
redaktion@eternitymagazin.de
eternitymagazin.de
News, interviews, specials, diskussionen, festivalberichte, dates...

Evil Rocks Hard
Groß-Gerauer-Str. 6, 65468 Trebur, Germany
Nils Manegold nils@evilrockshard.de
www.evilrockshard.de
Wir sind ein Musik-Magazin für Hard-Rock, Independent, Metal, Punk & Ska!

Evilized
c/o Markus Wirth, Geusaer Straße 88 - WH12, 06217 Merseburg, Germany
markus.wirth@evilized.de
www.evilized.de
Death Metal, Swedishmetal, Melodic Death Metal.

FFM-Rock.de
www.ffm-rock.de
Interviews, CD reviews, live reviews etc.

Guts Fuck Magazine
loebnitz@t-online.de
members.tripod.com/BSBB
Underground, Hardcore Gore/Grind.

Heavy-Magazine.de
bandzone@heavy-magazine.de
www.heavy-magazine.de
Habt Ihr Info Material, eine Promo CD, einen Song oder ein neues Album? Dann nehmt Kontakt per E-Mail.

Heavy-Metal.de
Amtsgerichtstr. 10, 47119 Duisburg, Germany
PH: 49-0203-666-804 FX: 49-0203-66-93-253
mail@heavy-metal.de
www.heavy-metal.de
News, reviews, interviews, festival/tour dates...

Home of Rock
Kolumbusstr. 17, 81543 München, Germany
Fred Schmidtlein webmaster@home-of-rock.de
www.home-of-rock.de
Rock, Heavy Metal news, reviews etc.

Lärmbelästigung
Marienstrasse 67, 21073 Hamburg, Germany
Karim Daire laermbelaestigung@gmx.de
www.laermbelaestigung.net
News, reviews, interviews. Death-Metal, Grind.

Metal District
Schlaifhausen 135, 91369 Wiesenthau, Germany
P. Weinstein redaktion@metal-district.de
www.metal-district.de
We review all styles of Metal.

Metal-Dungeon.de
www.metal-dungeon.de
Metallheadz meet Metalheadz.

Metal Inside
torben@metal-inside.de
www.metal-inside.de
News, reviews, interviews, tour dates & more.

METALMESSAGE.de
Brückenring 39a, 86916 Kaufering, Germany
PH: +49 (0)8191-6970
Markus Eck info@metalmessage.de
www.metalmessage.de
Reviews and Interviews in German & English.

Metal1.info
c/o Andi Althoff, Eidinghausener Str. 168, 32549 Bad Oeynhausen, Germany
webmaster@metal1.info
www.metal1.info
Falls ihr - Bands, Labels, Veranstalter etc. - daran Interesse habt, hier auf Metal1.info vertreten zu sein - egal ob Bandinfo, Interview, CD-Reviews etc. - oder mit uns zusammenzuarbeiten, dann mailt uns!

Metal2Metal
Jahnstr. 7, 46145 Oberhausen, Germany
Dennis Hemken ambiguity@metal2metal.de
www.metal2metal.de
The ultimate (online) Metal-fanzine / magazin.

Metal.de
Postfach 11 30, 6141 Konigstein im Taunus, Germany
contact@metal.de
metal-online.de
The dark site.

Metalglory
Im Moore 16 A, 30167 Hannover, Germany
metal@metalglory.de
www.metalglory.de
Heavy, Thrash, Black, Doom Metal reviews, interviews...

Metalius Multizine
Deisterweg 12, 31515 Wunstorf, Germany
PH: 050-31-51-68-41 FX: 050-31-51-68-42
Michael Schild michael.schild@metalius.de
www.metalius.de
Reviews of band CDs and videos.

Metalnews
www.metalnews.de
Metal, Heavy Metal, Blackmetal, Deathmetal, Darkmetal, Gothicmetal etc.

Mind-Fire.de
Martin Sch. Weischer, An der Spinnerei 5, 48249 Dülmen, Germany
PH: 0162/7037796
sarumann@web.de
www.mind-fire.de
Heavy Metal reviews, interviews, mp3, news...

Morrigan's Pit
c/o Silkie Gerold, PO Box 1720, 33247 Guetersloh, Germany
morrigan@morrigans-pit.org
www.morrigans-pit.org
We aim to promote metal ranging from Melodic/Symphonic/Progmetal to Power/Thrash to Death/Metalcore/(Melodic)Blackmetal. You might want to check with us first in case of doubt!

MyRevelations.de
www.myrevelations.de
Don't spit on those who chose to pose!

NecroSlaughter
www.necroslaughter.tk
We DO reviews and other support for independent bands/musicians. But we do this only for metal bands playing Death Metal, Thrash Metal, Grind Core or comparable style.

New-Core.de
Saargemünderstrasse 121, 66119 Saarbrücken, Germany
FX: 01212-5-594-05-315
my-stuff@new-core.de
www.new-core.de
Online magazine for Harder Music.

Nocturnal Hall
c/o Dajana Winkel, Rüschhausweg 14-16, 48161 Münster, Germany
PH.: +49 (0) 251 / 867493
office@nocturnalhall.com
www.nocturnalhall.de
We use a scale from 1 to 10 (1 = biggest crap ever to 10 = fucking brilliant).

Powermetal.de
Taunus Straße 44, 72622 Nürtingen, Germany
PH: 49-7022-951091 FX: 49-1212-512760667
weihrauch@powermetal.de
www.powermetal.de
CD and show reviews and interviews

Rock Hard Online
Postfach 11 02 12, 44058 Dortmund, Germany
PH: 0231-56-20-14-0 FX: 0231-56-20-14-13
Hansi Daberger hansi@rockhard.de
www.rockhard.de
Ist sowohl in der Printausgabe als auch online das groesste Rock- und Metal-Magazin Europas.

Rock It!
Seilandstr. 40, 59379 Selm, Germany
PH: 02592-918-599 FX: 02592-918-598
Birgitt Schwanke bschwanke@rock-it-magazine.de
www.rock-it-magazine.de
*Das AOR * Hard Rock * Metal Magazin.*

Rockbytes
Ubierstrasse 11, 53173 Bonn, Germany
Mia Walter miaw@rockbytes.de
www.rockbytes.de
Covers local and international Metal.

Schweres-Metall.de
Sandy Cutter sandy@schweres-metall.de
www.schweres-metall.de
Das Onlinemagazin für Rock und Metal.

Silentium Noctis
Viktor-Renner-Str. 55, D-72074 Tubingen, Germany
Manuel Niess info@silentium-noctis.de
www.silentium-noctis.de
MP3s, interviews, news, reviews and more.

Sonny's Rock & Metal Heaven
webmaster@sonny1968.de
www.sonny1968.de
If you want send me a promotional copy of your CD (for review/ interview) plus information material, please contact me.

Sounds Of Eternal War
soew_webzine@web.de
www.soew-webzine.de.vu
Dedicated to all fucking, true Black, Death, Thrash Metal and Grindcore- maniacs out there! Contact us for submission details.

Tiefgang
Gutenbergstr. 1, 33615 Bielefeld, Germany
Marius Neugebauer info@tiefgang-online.de
www.tiefgang-online.de
News, interviews, MP3s, tour dates, reviews etc.

Tinnitus
Spannskanmp 26, 22527 Hamburg, Germany
Haiko Nahm haiko@tinnitus-mag.de
www.tinnitus-mag.de
Für Adressen für Demos und Promos bitte die entsprechenden Mitarbeiter kontaktieren.

Underground Empire Metal Magazine
Rothenbacher Hauptstr. 71, 90449 Nurnberg, Germany
FX: 0911-6421-923
www.underground-empire.de
Prasentiert Deutschlands fuhrendes Metal e-mag.

Underground Empire the Online Empire
Postfach 1602, D - 72006 Tübingen, Germany
Stefan Glas redaktion@underground-empire.com
www.underground-empire.com
News, interviews, reviews etc.

vampyria
c/o G.J. Schroeder,
Bergstrasse 2, 27367 Sottrum, Germany
www.vampyria.de
The Northern Metal site. Send CDs, demos, promos etc. to the above address.

Vampster
Reichenberger Strasse 9, 71711 Steinheim, Germany
PH: 49-7144-894099 FX: 49-7144-894088
kontakt@vampster.com
www.vampster.com
Bands! labels! veranstalter! schickt daten, promos, demos etc.

Voices from the Darkside
www.voicesfromthedarkside.de
The magazine for brutal Death, Thrash and Black Metal!

Vönger
webmaster@voenger.de
www.voenger.de
Deutsche Black Metal seite mit reviews, konzertberichten, interviews, merchandise...

Whiskey Soda
Postfach 42 01 02, 12061 Berlin, Germany
PH: 030-75-76-59-52
Sascha & Jens info@whiskey-soda.de
www.whiskey-soda.de
Alternative Rock/Metal music community.

Greece

Metal Eagle
Kerasouintos St. 33-35, Nea Smirni, 17124, Athens, Greece
battlerager@metaleagle.com
www.metaleagle.com
News, reviews, interviews and more.

Metal Temple
Alamanas 17, Metamorphosi Chalandriou, 15234, Athens, Greece
PH: 306938416392
webmaster@metal-temple.com
www.metal-temple.com
Spread the word, the Metal religion has its own temple! If you live OUTSIDE of Europe, check our website for details on where to send your music.

The Temple of Metal
Alamanas 17, T.K. 152 34, Metamorphosi Xaladriou, Athens, Greece
Michael Dalakos thetempleofmetal@yahoo.com
www.thetempleofmetal.gr
News, reviews, galleries, links etc.

Tombstone.gr
Agelos Kanarelis, Epidamnou 21, 112-54, Athens, Greece
info@tombstone.gr
www.tombstone.gr
By Metalheads.....for Metalheads.

Italy

Babylon Magazine
news@babylonmagazine.net
www.babylonmagazine.net
Metal underground.

Heavy Metal Portal
Alessandro Ballini ztm@hmp.it
www.hmp.it
News, reviews, interviews, tour dates and more.

Kult Rock
Via a.Cristiano 4, 80028 Grumo Nevano (NA), Italy
Enrico D'Aniello info@kultrock.com
www.kultrock.com
Supports all music with particular regard to Rock and Metal.

Shapeless Zine
PO Box 113, 20030 Senago (MI), Italy
Carlo Paleari hellvis@shapeless.it
www.shapeless.it
We review all Metal bands, except nu-Metal bands.

Silent Scream
Via Benedettina Inferiore, 1, 98050 - Terme Vigliatore (ME), Italy
Fulvio Adile industry@silentscreamzine.com
www.silentscreamzine.com
Metal and Alternative music site.

The Netherlands

Aardschok
PO Box 7, 5690 AA Son, The Netherlands
mike@aardschok.com
www.aardschok.com
You can send all CDs, demos and bios.

Brutalism
Markiezaatpad 5, 5628 BR Eindhoven, The Netherlands
PH: +31-6-231-33-859 FX: +31 (0) 847-16-59-67
Twan Sibon twan@brutalism.com
www.brutalism.com
Interviews, reviews etc. You can also have your band/label promoted on our site for free!

Lords of Metal
Postbus 756, 1780 AT Den Helder, The Netherlands
Horst Vonberg lordsofmetal@quicknet.nl
www.lordsofmetal.nl/english
CD reviews, gig reviews and new interviews.

Roadburn
Walter Hoeijmakers walter@roadburn.com
www.roadburn.com
Contribute all your CDs, LPs, demos, gifts etc. to us.

Rock-E-Zine
Klaproos 16, 4102HN, Culemborg, The Netherlands
info@rockezine.com
www.rockezine.net
It's all about Rock 'n' Roll but we like it hard. We provide you with up to date interviews, concert reviews and CD reviews of all genres and much, much more!

Vampire Magazine
c/o Ricardo Mouwen, Kapittelhof 34, 4841 GX Prinsenbeek, The Netherlands
vampire-magazine.com
Covering the world of Underground Metal. Please send your promos, demos and other material to us for a fair review. Don't forget to include some background information!

Norway

Beat the Blizzard
AJ. Blisten, Ostover, N-2730 Lunner, Norway
blizzard@tiscali.no
home.world-online.no/blizzard
Labels and bands are welcome to ship CDs for review.

Enslaved by Metal
Erling Høviks veg 21, 7058 Jakobsli, Norway
Ole Markus With contact@enslavedbymetal.com
www.enslavedbymetal.com
If you want us to review a demo/promo, contact us.

Metal Express Radio Show
Ovrefoss 14, N-0555 Oslo, Norway Attn: Nordahl
mail@metalexpress.no
www.metalexpress.no
Streaming radio, news, reviews, interviews...

Scream Magazine
scream@scream.no
www.screammagazine.com
Norway's biggest Metal magazine!

The Streets
Renvikveien 47, 8160 Glomfjord, Norway
PH: 480-93-990
Even Knudsen even@streetswebzine.com
www.streetswebzine.com
Dedicated to Heavy Metal music.

Poland

diabolous.com
Lord Darnok darnok@diabolous.com
diabolous.com
Before sending any promo materials please contact us.

Masterful
OUPT ul. Lubelska, PO Box 19, 24-100 Pulawy, Poland
Aleksander Krzeczkowski olo@masterful.art.pl
www.masterful.art.pl
Dedicated to the most brutal genres of Metal music.

Multum In Parvo
Ul. Zagorna 17, 05-230 Kobylka, Poland
PH: 0-691-34-89-20
mechatronika@interia.pl
www.mip.av.pl/mip
MP3, zdjecia, ogloszenia, konkursy...

rockmetal.pl
rockmetal@rockmetal.pl
www.rockmetal.pl
Rock i Metal po polsku.

Russia

Black Minds
Engels str. 10-2, Goryachiy Kluych, 353293, Russia
Eugene Sivokon cannibalius@pisem.net
blackminds.tk
We support Extreme Metal bands from Europe.

Musica Must Die
30-81, Leskova str. Moscow, 127560, Russia
musica@mustdie.ru
musica.mustdie.ru
Everything about Metal music.

totalmetal.net
info@totalmetal.net
www.totalmetal.net
Russian's #1 Heavy Metal site.

Slovenia

firegoat.com
reviews@firegoat.com
www.firegoat.com/eng
Covering Metal from Slovenia and around the world!

Spain

Alfa:Omega
C/Pintor Balaca,5 1º A, 30205 - Cartagena (Murcia), Spain
PH: 679397683
Jose E. Ricondo correo@alfaomega.info
www.alfaomega.info
Webzine musical indpependente para metnes inquietas.

Basa Rock
info@rafabasa.com
www.rafabasa.com
Portal en Castellano dedicado al Heavy Metal.

Canedo Rock
Apartado de Correos: 1027, 32001 - Ourense, Spain
canedorock@canedorock.com
www.canedorock.com
Webzine dedicado al Rock en todas sus variantes Metal, Heavy, Punk, etc... Con Noticias, discos, conciertos, Mp3, entrevistas, fotos, etc...

Cuerdas de Acero
contacto@cuerdasdeacero.com
www.cuerdasdeacero.com
Tu portal de Rock Nacional.

Heavy Weight
Rodrigo rodrigomayayo@ono.com
www.truemetal.org/heavyweight
Reviews, interviews, demos, news and more.

Inside Out Webzine
correo@insideoutwebzine.com
www.insideoutwebzine.com
Musica, Metal, Rap-Metal, Nu-Metal, noticias, conciertos, discos, listas...

The Metal Circus
Sergi Ramos sergi@themetalcircus.com
www.themetalcircus.com
Tu webzine de Metal.

Portaldelrock.com
portaldelrock@terra.es
www.portaldelrock.com
Un portal de musica Rock y Metal, con lo ultimo en noticias, grupos, conciertos, todo sobre los ultimos discos que aparecen en el mercado y mucho mas.

Rock Angels
PO Box 156, 50080 ZARAGOZA, Spain
PH: 657803368
carlosdestroyer@rockangels.com
www.rockangels.com
Metal, AOR etc.

Rock Circus
Iván Ortega, APDO. 146, 28820 COSLADA
(MADRID), Spain
rockcircus@arrakis.es
www.rockcircus.net
Tu revista de Rock en Internet.

ROCK ESTATAL
rockestatalrockestatal.com
rockestatal.com
Rock nacional estatal Heavy Metal y Punk.

TodoRock.net
info@todorock.net
www.todorock.tk
Un portal dedicado al mundillo loco este del Rock, en esta web encontrarás noticias, información de grupos, reseñas discográficas, cronicas de conciertos etc.

Vampiria Magazine
PO Box 1848, 20080 Donostia, Gipuzkoa, Spain
info@castleofvampiria.com
www.castleofvampiria.com
We review CDs, demos and promos.

XTREEM MUSIC
PO Box 1195, 28080, Madrid, Spain
info@xtreemmusic.com
www.xtreemmusic.com
Portal devoted to Extreme music.

Sweden

Close Up
PO Box 4411, SE-102 69, Stockholm, Sweden
PH: 46-8-462-02-14 FXA: 46-8-462-02-15
mail@closeupmagazine.net
www.closeupmagazine.net
A forum for all types of Extreme and Heavy music!

Extreme Terror
Sadesbingen 26, lgh 71, vån 3, 461 61 Trollhattan, Sweden
Micke Backelin info@extreme-production.com
www.extreme-terror.com
News, profiles, reviews etc.

Metal Heart
Skivyxvägen 19, 723 53 Västerås, Sweden
David Noaksson noak@metalheart.se
www.metalheart.se
Mainly focused on Metal and Hard Rock.

metal-only
36 70220 Orebro, Sweden
webmaster@metal-only.com
www.metal-only.com
Review, interviews, write your own review or read the latest Metal news.

Swedish Metal
Olstorpsvägen 4, 616 30 ÅBY, Sweden
Fredrik Kreem fredrik@swedishmetal.net
www.swedishmetal.net
News, reviews, interviews, downloads etc.

Tartarean Desire
Rydsvagen 218A, S-584 32 Linkoping, Sweden
Vincent Eldefors tartareandesire@yahoo.com
embark.to/tartareandesire
Metal and Dark music with reviews, interviews etc.

Switzerland

Schwermetall
steiner@schwarzmetall.ch
www.schwarzmetall.ch
Dark, Black, Trash Metal etc.

Swiss Metal Factory
PO Box 809, 5401 Baden, Switzerland
PH: 41-0-79-638-1021
metal@metalfactory.ch
www.metalfactory.ch
Reviews, interviews, concerts etc.

United Kingdom

Black Velvet
336 Birchfield Rd.
Webheath, Redditch, Worcs, B97 4NG, UK
editor@blackvelvetmagazine.com
www.blackvelvetmagazine.com
Features Glam, Punk, Rock, Metal and more.

doom-metal.com
122 Colwith Rd. London, W6 9EZ UK
reviews@doom-metal.com
www.doom-metal.com
Please see submission guidelines before sending.

I Will Be Heard
reviews@iwillbeheard.co.uk
www.iwillbeheard.co.uk
Heavy Metal e-zine. Features, news, reviews and interviews.

Justin-Case.co.uk
PO Box 1055, Market Harborough,
Leicestershire, LE16 7ZL UK
PH: 0116-858464678
justin@justin-case.co.uk
www.justin-case.co.uk
Rock album reviews.

Kerrang! Magazine
Mappin House, 4 Winsley St.,
London, W1W 8HF UK
PH: 020-7436-1515
kerrang@emap.com
www.kerrang.com
The world's biggest selling weekly Rock magazine.

Live 4 Metal
PO Box 819, Harrow, Middlesex, HA3 8TS UK
Steve Green live4metal666@aol.com
www.live4metal.com
The best of the Metal world.

Lykos
Sam Wright editor@lykoszine.co.uk
www.lykoszine.co.uk
Interviews, reviews, free email etc.

Metal Hammer
99 Baker St., London, W1U 6FP UK
Attn: Reviews editor
www.metalhammer.co.uk
Send a copy of your latest demo.

Metal Mayhem
Chris Rogers chris@metal-mayhem.co.uk
www.metal-mayhem.co.uk
Death, Thrash, Doom, Black and Power Metal Reviews, interviews, news etc. Please contact us for the address to send stuff to.

Metal Pigeon
www.metalpigeon.com
Dedicated to straight up Metal, as well as elements of Extreme Metal, Hardcore and Hard Rock.

Metalliville
9 Street Farm Close, Harthill, Sheffield,
South Yorkshire, S26 7UH UK
PH: 44-79-6923-8178
Robert Milligan metalliville@hotmail.com
www.metalliville.com
The UK's finest Rock & Metal webzine!!!

New Breed
amy@newbreedonline.co.uk
newbreedonline.co.uk
Promoting signed and unsigned bands. Features CD reviews, live reviews and interviews.

Planet-Loud
PO Box 2581, Reading, Berks, England RG1 7GT
info@planet-loud.com
www.planet-loud.com
The loudest music site on the net!

Powerplay
PO Box 159, York, YO24 3WT UK
PH/FX: 01904-783939
webmaster@powerplaymagazine.co.uk
www.powerplaymagazine.co.uk
Hard, Heavy, Power, Prog, Progressive, Speed, AOR, FM, Death, Extreme and Black.

Raw Nerve Promotions
22 Eastdean Grange, Leeds,
West Yorkshire, LS14 1HA UK
Paul Priest paulrawnerve@ntlworld.com
www.rawnervepromotions.co.uk
News, interviews, reviews, articles, profiles, shows, gigs etc.

Rock Midgets.com
www.rockmidgets.com
The phrase "Rock Midgets" refers to the idea of up-and-coming bands with not quite a following large enough to be referred to as Rock Gods. We focus on Rock, Metal and Punk.

ROCK SOUND
#22, Jack's Pl., 6 Corbet Pl., Spitalfields,
London, E1 6NN UK
Darren darren.taylor@rock-sound.net
www.rock-sound.net
Monthly music magazine in the UK.

ROCKREVIEW.co.uk
8 Orpington Ct. Halberton, EX16 7DD UK
Liam Martin liam@rockreview.co.uk
www.rockreview.co.uk
News and reviews from the world of Rock and Metal.

Terrorizer
#36, 10-50 Willow St., London, EC2A 4BH UK
PH: 44-20-7729-7666 FX: 44-20-7739-0544
editorial@terrorizer.com
www.terrorizer.co.uk
Magazine for Extreme music of ANY kind.

Yugoslavia

ROCK express
PO Box 666, 11000 Belgrade, Yugoslavia
PH: 38111-657-416 FX: 38111-656-356
rockexpr@eunet.yu
www.rockexpress.org
The only Yugoslav Rock magazine!

Australia

The Buzz
PO Box 55, Dromana, VIC 3936 Australia
PH: 61-3-59812979 FX: 61-3-59861449
psutton@r150.aone.net.au
www.ozonline.com.au/buzz
CD reviews, interviews and coverage of local artists.

Crustymusic.com
PO Box 1483, Warrnambool, VIC 3280 Australia
www.crustymusic.net
Metal, Rock, Alternative and Hardcore. Crusty just fucking loves his music, more than anything! Send in an album or EP and it may get reviewed.

FasterLouder.com.au
PO Box 1964, Strawberry Hills,
NSW 2012 Australia
PH: 02-8353-7070 FX: 02-8353-7099
www.fasterlouder.com.au
Gig info, interviews, reviews etc.

Loud! Online
23 Yester Rd. Wentworth Falls, NSW 2782 Australia
B. Fischer-Giffin goreripper@maxi.net.au
www.geocities.com/SunsetStrip/Stage/4599
Promotion of Australian Heavy Metal music.

MelodicRock.com
GPO Box 1770, Hobart, TAZ 7001 Australia
PH: +61-3-6229-3113
Andrew J. McNeice ajm@melodicrock.com
www.melodicrock.com
Reviews Melodic and Hard Rock.

Asia

Armageddawn.com
c/o Afidz Che Rosli, PO Box 1029 / 30820, Ipoh, Perak, Malaysia
vorn666@armageddawn.com
www.armageddawn.com
Send your cd complete with the tracklist and remember to specify which track you want to be featured on our site. We only support quality Extreme, Death, Black, Thrash, Grind, and Heavy Metal music.

HeavyMetal.co.il
www.heavymetal.co.il
Supporting the Israeli Metal scene.

New Age

Amazing Sounds
Apartado de Correas 727, PO Box 08220, Tarrasa, Barcelona, Spain
amazingsounds@amazings.com
www.amazings.com
News, articles, interviews, album reviews...

Awareness Magazine
7441 Garden Grove Blvd. #C,
Garden Grove, CA 92841
PH: 714-894-5133 FX: 714-890-1664
info@awarenessmag.com
www.awarenessmag.com
Holistic magazine with music and video reviews.

Body and Soul Magazine
42 Pleasant St., Watertown, MA 02472
PH: 617-926-0200 FX: 617-926-5021
editor@bodyandsoulmag.com
www.bodyandsoulmag.com
Reviews of current books and music.

Changes
comments@changes.org
www.changes.org
New CD review page on our site.

EarthLight Magazine
111 Fairmount Ave. Oakland, CA 94611
PH: 510-451-4926
klauren@earthlight.org
www.earthlight.org
We do very occasional CD reviews.

Innerchange
1602 S. Wade Ave. Garner, NC 27529
PH: 919-661-2282 FX: 919-779-9136
Karen Newton editor@innerchangemag.com
innerchangemag.com
Magazine website with music reviews.

Kindred Spirit
Foxhole Dartington Totnes Devon, TQ9 6EB UK
PH: 01803-866686 FX: 01803-866591
mail@kindredspirit.co.uk
www.kindredspirit.co.uk
The UK's leading guide for body, mind and spirit.

Magical Blend
PO Box 600, Chico, CA 95927-0600
PH: 530-893-9037 FX: 530-893-9076
info@magicalblend.com
www.magicalblend.com
An entertaining and thoroughly unique look at the modern spiritual lifestyle.

Mysteries Magazine
PO Box 490, Walpole, NH 03608-0490
PH: 603-352-1645 FX: 603-352-0232
Kim Guarnaccia editor@mysteriesmagazine.com
www.MysteriesMagazine.com
We review CDs of World Music, New Age music, healing/meditation/yoga music etc.

New Age Retailer
1300 N. State St. #105, Bellingham, WA 98225
PH: 360-676-0789 FX: 360-676-0932
www.newageretailer.com
Two independent music review columns.

New Age Reporter
650 Poydras #2523, New Orleans, LA 70130
RJ Lannan nar@newagereporter.com
www.newagereporter.com
We will review New Age, World, Celtic, Folk and Neo-Classical works.

New Frontier Magazine
PO Box 17397, Asheville, NC 28816
PH: 828-254-6620
info@newfrontier.com
www.newfrontier.com
Reviews of New Age music and videos.

New Renaissance
Weisenauer Weg 4, 55129 Mainz, Germany
PH: 49-6131-834262 FX: 49-6131-834628
www.ru.org
Reviews of books, recordings and events.

Solo Piano Publications
Kathy Parsons kathypiano@comcast.net
www.solopianopublications.com
Helping to promote New Age and Classical piano music in hopes of reaching new ears and audiences. Contact Kathy directly about CD review submissions and interviews.

Spirit of Change
PO Box 405, Uxbridge, MA 01569
PH: 508-278-9640 FX: 508-278-9641
info@spiritofchange.org
www.spiritofchange.org
Welcomes independent music reviews and all music releases.

Wind and Wire
4040 46th Ave. S., Minneapolis, MN 55406
PH: 612-724-9391
www.windandwire.com
Ambient and New Age music – please send Instrumental music only!

Writings by Serge Kozlovsky
PO Box 410, 220050 Minsk, Belarus
S.Kozlovsky@gtp.by
mkmk.com/kozlovsky
Articles, interviews and reviews.

Yoga Journal
2054 University Ave. Berkeley, CA 94704
PH: 510-841-9200 FX: 510-644-3101
webmaster@yogajournal.com
www.yogajournal.com
The voice of Yoga online.

Yoga Magazine
26 York St., London, W1U 6PZ UK
PH: 44-020-7729-5454 FX: 44-020-7739-0025
Laura McCreddie laura@yogamagazine.co.uk
www.yogamagazine.co.uk
Willing to listen to anything you send.

Progressive Rock

Progressive Rock, AOR, Jazzrock, Melodic Rock, Progressive Metal, Spacerock, Krautrock, Psychedelic and Improvisational Rock

North America

United States

EER-MUSIC.com
John W. Patterson eermusic@nc.rr.com
eer-music.com
We seek to offer free promo to all the artists ignored by major corporate labels. Reviews to Jazz Rock Fusion, non-rhythmic, Atmospherix, Ambient Space musicks and select Progressive Rock.

Exposé
6167 Jarvis Ave. #150, Newark, CA 94560-1210
ptlk@expose.org
www.expose.org
Focuses on Progressive and Experimental Rock.

ghostland.com
chad@ghostland.com
ghostland.com
Your source for Progressive Rock on the web. Contact us for mailing address.

Ground and Sky
1820 Ontario Pl. Washington, DC 20009
webmaster@progreviews.com
www.progreviews.com
Extensive, in depth reviews. Please do not e-mail us asking if it's OK to send us your CD. Just send it in and we'll make the judgment based on the music.

Heavy Harmonies
webmaster@heavyharmonies.com
heavyharmonies.com
Submit your CDs, no Demos.

Music Street Journal
musicstreetjournal@hotmail.com
www.musicstreetjournal.com
News, reviews, interviews ...

Prog Archives
www.progarchives.com
Post your reviews on our site.

Prog4you.com
PO Box 687, Coatesville, PA 19320
info@prog4you.com
www.prog4you.com
We are always looking for new material, that we can listen to and review.

ProGGnosis
webmaster@proggnosis.com
www.proggnosis.com
Our goal is to further the success of Progressive and Fusion music genres.

Progression Magazine
PO Box 7164, Lowell, MA 01852
PH: 978-970-2728 FX: 978-970-2728
progzine@aol.com
www.progressionmagazine.com
News, reviews, interviews and features.

Progressive Ears
1594 6th St., Trenton, NJ 08638
Floyd Bledsoe floyd@progressiveears.com
progressiveears.com
Progressive Rock discussion, polls and reviews.

ProgressiveWorld.net
PO Box 1476, Glendora, CA 91740-1476
Stephanie sollows@progressiveworld.net
www.progressiveworld.net
We review Prog Rock, Prog Metal, Ambient/Electronic and similar genres.

ProgNaut.com
PO Box 266, Santa Monica, CA 90406-0266
reviews@prognaut.com
www.prognaut.com
Vessel for Southern California Progressive music.

progrock.com
www.progrock.com
Visit our site for instructions on how to submit your music for review and airplay.

ProgScape.Com
www.progscape.com
Get your CD or DVD reviewed.

Sea of Tranquility
53 Old Country Rd. Monroe, NY 10950
www.seaoftranquility.org
Journal of Fusion and Progressive Rock.

Ytsejam.com
www.ytsejam.com
We try to review all CDs we receive.

South America
Argentina

Nucleus
Horacio Cestino nro 709, Ensenada, Codigo Postal 1925, Buenos Aires, Argentina
nucleus@netverk.com.ar
www.nucleusprog.cjb.net
Sitio especializado en Rock Sinfonico, Progresivo Symphonic, Progressive.

Planeta-Rock
info@planeta-rock.com.ar
www.planeta-rock.com.ar
New, reviews, radio etc.

Brazil

Progressive Rock & Progressive Metal
Rua Tailandia 426, Bras de Pina, Cep 21011350, Rio de Janeiro, Brasil
Carlos Vaz carlosvaz@br.inter.net
www.progressiverockbr.com
Reviews, interviews and much more.

Rock Progressivo Brasil
www.rockprogressivo.com.br
Site sobre Rock Progressivo no Brasil/Mundo com resenhas e entrevistas.

Europe
Belgium

Prog Nose
Beekstraat 1, 2640 Mortsel, Belgium
Claeskens Jany info@prog-nose.org
www.prog-nose.be
Promoting Progressive Rock in general.

Prog-résiste
c/o Gilles Arend, avenue de l'Equinoxe, 8, B-1300, Wavre, Belgium
PH: 32-0-10-41-35-71 FX: +32-0-10-41-05-49
webmaster@progresiste.com
www.progresiste.com
We publish (in French only) a quarterly, 132 pages magazine with reviews, news, rumors, events...

Rock Report
Collegestraat 129, B-8310 Assebroek, Belguim
PH: 32-050-35-87-72 FX: 32-050-35-87-72
info@rockreport.be
www.rockreport.be
A new medium, totally dedicated to AOR.

France

Acid Dragon
20 rue Ferrandiere, 69002 Lyon, France
PH: 33-04-78373733 FX: 33-04-72373909
T. Sprtouche acidrag@club-internet.fr
perso.club-internet.fr/acidrago/ad2.htm
We have an international readership. We also host a radio show.

AmarokProg
webmaster@amarokprog.net
www.amarokprog.net
All about Progressive Rock, Metal, Alternative Rock and Electro with band pages, concert guides, news, reviews and much more!

Big Bang
17 ave. de la Monta, 38120 St. Egreve, France
PH: 33-04-76580290 FX: 33-04-76580290
redaction@bigbangmag.com
www.bigbangmag.com
Une revue Français consacrée aux musiques Progressives.

KOID'9
51, avenue Wilson, 45500 Gien, France
koid9@club-internet.fr
koid9.fanzine.free.fr
Un fanzine trimestriel très complet, réalisé par des passionnés, traitant avec humour de l'actualité du Rock Progressif, Metal Progressif et Rock Alternatif.

Progressia.net
promotion@progressia.net
www.progressia.net
Rock Progressif, Metal Progressif, Jazz Expérimental, Fusion, Post-Rock.

somethingprog.com
webmaster@somethingprog.com
www.somethingprog.com
Rock Progressif, Métal Progressif, Death Metal, Doom ...

Traverses
c/o Stéphane Fougère, 16, avenue d'Alfortville, 94600 Choisy le Roi, France
traversesmag.org
Musiques presque nouvelles et autrement Prprogressia.neogressives.

Germany

AOR Heaven
Landshuter Strasse 11, 84051 Altheim, Germany
PH: 49-8703-8517 FX: 49-8703-8568
georg.siegl@aorheaven.com
www.aorheaven.com
If you have a demo feel free to contact us.

Babyblaue Prog-Reviews
Grünwalder Straße 117, D-81547 München, Germany
PH: 089-64260946
Udo Gerhards promos@babyblaue-seiten.de
www.babyblaue-seiten.de
Die Prog-Enzyklopädie der Mailingliste.

Bright Eyes
Herzog Friedrich Str. 69, 24103, Kiel, Germany
PH: 49-0431-94693 FX: 49-0431-6793221
info@brighteyes.de
www.brighteyes.de
Interviews und Reviews aus der Metal und HardRock Szene.

Jesters News
Wolfgang Volk, Eichenweg 25, 64711 Erbach/Odw, Germany
www.jesters-news.de
Progressive, Rock und Metal fanzine.

Progressive Newsletter
Postfach 1806, D-71208 Leonberg, Germany
Kristian Selm Kristian@Progressive-Newsletter.de
www.progressive-newsletter.de
Reviews, interviews, gig dates etc.

Italy

Arlequins
Via Paparoni 6, 53100 Siena, Italy
Alberto Nucci info@arlequins.net
www.arlequins.it
Covers the Progressive Rock underground scene.

MovimentiPROG
staff@movimentiprog.net
www.movimentiprog.net
Riflessioni scritte sulla musica che evolv.

The Netherlands

Axiom of Choice
PO Box 80-089, 3508TB Utrecht, The Netherlands
jur@cs.uu.nl
www.cs.uu.nl/people/jur/progrock.html
Progressive Rock music and related genres.

Background Magazine
PO Box 3155, 1620 GD Hoorn, The Netherlands
info@backgroundmagazine.nl
www.backgroundmagazine.nl
High quality information on Progressive Rock and closely related music on an international level.

The Dutch Progressive Rock Page
c/o B. Mulvey, 29 Lutton Cres.
Billingham, TX22 5DZ UK
dprp@vuurwerk.nl
www.dprp.vuurwerk.nl
Internet magazine on Progressive Rock.

The iO Pages
Stichting iO, Postbus 67, 2678 ZH De Lier,
The Netherlands
FX: +31-174-51-12-13
io@net4u.nl
www.net4u.nl/io
Magazine devoted to Progressive Rock and all its related genres such as Electronic Music, Jazzrock, Progmetal, Progressive Pop, Spacerock and Psychedelic Rock.

Progwereld
t.a.v. Maarten Goossensen, Vogeldreef 22, 2727 AM
Zoetermeer, Holland
info@progwereld.org
www.progwereld.org
News, reviews, interviews, columns etc.

Psychedelic Music Database
webmaster@psychedelic-music.net
www.psychedelic-music.net
Submit reviews, information on your band etc. Contact us before you send your music. Try to give us a chance to listen to your MP3 files first.

Strutter Magazine
Zandrak 82, 2924 BC Krimpen Aan Den Ijssel,
The Netherlands
Gabor gabor.fabian@wxs.nl
www.strutter.8m.com
Promotes deserving AOR/Melodic Rock bands.

Norway

Tarkus
Mollefaret 48B, N-0750 Oslo, Norway
Sven Eriksen sven@tarkus.org
www.tarkus.org
We cover a wide spectre of Progressive music.

Portugal

Prog PT
Travessa de Monserrate N 32, 3 Dto. 4450-199
Matosinhos, Portugal
António Santos info@prog-pt.com
www.prog-pt.com
Promoting Progressive music in all of its sub-genres.

Spain

Prog Visions
Alfonso Algora algora@progvisions.net
www.progvisions.net
Center of information about Progressive Rock. English & Spanish Reviews!

United Kingdom

Acid Attack
19 Belper Row, Dudley W. Midlands, DY2 9LP UK
martyn@acidattackmusic.co.uk
www.acidattackmusic.co.uk
Reviews and news on mostly independent music.

Hairless Heart Herald
Jem Jedrzejewski info@hairlessheartherald.co.uk
www.hairlessheartherald.co.uk
Specialises in the Progressive Rock and Jazz-Fusion genres.

Mood Swings
nigel@mswings.com
www.mswings.com
News, links, interviews, reviews etc.

New Horizons
feedback@elrose.demon.co.uk
www.elrose.demon.co.uk
Progressive, Classic and Melodic Rock on the web.

Silhobbit.com
17 Maddox Rd. Hemel Hempstead,
Herts, HP2 4QF England
silhobbit@silhobbit.com
www.silhobbit.com
Reviews, gig guide, features...

Uzbekistan

ProgressoR
Vitaly Menshikov, PO Box 4065, Tashkent, 700100,
Uzbekistan
www.progressor.net
Send your CDs to us for review.

Punk

Punk, Hardcore, Emo, oi, Garage, Ska and Anti-Folk

North America

United States

A Thousand Apologies
Brian Roberts webmaster@athousandapologies.com
www.athousandapologies.com
Interviews, reviews, badass music news and info!

Absolute Punk
jason.tate@absolutepunk.net
www.absolutepunk.net
Submit your demo, album or ep to us.

The Agro
1884 Florida Rd. Pell City, AL 35125
agroradio@theagro.com
www.theagro.com
An Underground Hardcore and Metal website.

Alarm Press
2506 N. Clark, Chicago, IL 60614
music@alarmpress.com
www.alarmpress.com
Bi-monthly magazine. Covers Northeast concerts.

All Ages Zine.com
allageszine@sbcglobal.net
www.AllAgesZine.com
Dedicated to music of all kinds. From bands just starting out in their garage to bands on world tours. We do reviews, interviews, post tour dates, band information, you think it up, we will do it.

ALLALOM Music
RR3 Box 385, Ted Hunt Rd. Los Fresnos, TX 78566
PH: 541-350-1607
Samuel-Aaron Thomas samuel@allalom.com
www.allalom.com
Interviews, reviews, MP3s, booking, management and promotion services for alternative music.

Americore Magazine
546 Vanguard Way #L, Brea, CA 92821
larry@americoremagazine.com
www.americoremagazine.com
Reviews, interviews, gear, shows, listings, the works.

American Music Press
PO Box 1070, Martinez, CA 94553
Scoot@ampmagazine.com
ampmagazine.com
Interviews, reviews, columns, articles etc.

Annoyance
PO Box 21, Bound Brook, NJ 08805-0021
zine@annoyances.com
www.annoyances.com/zine.html
Punkin' up da web with fun and silliness.

ANTIFOLK ONLINE
PO Box 250, 15105-D John J. Delaney Dr.
Charlotte, NC 28277
Brad Willis Brad@AntifolkOnline.com
www.antifolkonline.com
Share music, ideas, stories and opinions.

anti-popmusic.com
Danny danny@anti-popmusic.com
www.anti-popmusic.com
Promotes all types of Rock bands.

Arm the Pit
Joel Blackout Joel_Blackout@armthepit.com
www.armthepit.com
An independent music collective. We are here to help you, the artist, by using the most powerful and useful promoting tool we know of... word of mouth.

Askew Reviews
PO Box 684, Hanover, MA 02339
denis@askewreviews.com
www.askewreviews.com
We cover, review and promote music.

Asylum Magazine
PO Box 32208, Euclid, OH 44132
info@asylummagazine.com
www.asylummagazine.com
Covering all the genres that matter: Punk Industrial, Hardcore, Ska, Indie, Techno ...

Audiocratic
joeydied@hotmail.com
www.audiocratic.com
Don't hesitate, send us your demos today!! The sooner we receive your (predominantly) fantastic demos, the sooner we can put a review on our site, which in the long run is just more publicity for yourself.

Breaking Custom
info@breakingcustom.com
www.BreakingCustom.com
Specializing in all genres; from Indie to Death Metal.

bushmado
39D Lower Boone Dr. Turtle Creek, PA 15145
dj@bushmado.com
www.bushmado.com
Helping Underground Heavy bands get exposure.

Bystander Fanzine
PO Box 10392, Albany, NY 12201
info@bystanderfanzine.com
www.bystanderfanzine.com
Covering the Hardcore scene.

centerfuse.net
reviews@centerfuse.net
www.centerfuse.net
Dedicated to the independent music scene.

Chain-Whipped Magazine
2976 Washington Blvd.
Cleveland Heights, OH 44118
PH: 216-397-1191
Warren Davis chain-whipped@chain-whipped.com
www.chain-whipped.com
Artist interviews, CD reviews, DVD reviews, and miscellaneous bollocks. Born in the back alleys of Tokyo and spreading like a virus worldwide.

Chaos and Fruit Punch
PO Box 13380, Mill Creek, WA 98082
Adam Chaos adam@operationphoenixrecords.com
www.operationphoenixrecords.com/zine.html
Reviews music while publishing personal stories.

Chord Magazine
Gus Peña gus@chordmagazine.com
PO Box 56821, Sherman Oaks, CA 91413
www.chordmagazine.com
National magazine published 6 times a year. Features Emo, Punk, Metal, Hardcore...

The Continental Magazine
PO Box 4336, Bellingham, WA 98227-4336
Sean Berry records@dblcrown.com
www.dblcrown.com
Surf/Instrumental and Garage Rock n' Roll.

Corn 'Zine
206 Elm St., Elkview, WV 25071
www.cornzine.com
Covering Hardcore, Punk, Ska, Indie, Emo etc.

Culture Bunker
PO Box 480353, Los Angeles, CA 90048
culturebunker@culturebunker.com
www.culturebunker.com
Indiscriminate, wholesale, erotic, power-mad killing...

Da' Core
4407 Bowes Ave. W. Mifflin, PA 15122
PH: 412-462-0203
dacorerecords@yahoo.com
www.da-core.com
A Hardcore label and magazine.

Deadtide.com
4503 North Troy St. Unit 1, Chicago, IL 60625
Jason Muxlow jason@deadtide.com
www.deadtide.com
If you'd like to your album, concert, musical instrument, or other items reviewed send them to the above address.

Decoy Music Magazine
PO Box 6078, Atascadero, CA 93423
Aaron Troy aaron@decoymusic.com
www.decoymusic.com
Covering everything from Punk to Metal to Indie to Hip Hop. Industry revealing interviews and more.

Delusions of Adequacy
PO Box 23558, Rochester, NY 14692
www.adequacy.net
Music reviews, interviews, concert reviews and more.

emotionalpunk.com
PO Box 363, Littleton, CO 80160
Andrew Martin andrew@emotionalpunk.com
www.emotionalpunk.com
If you are an artist or promoter and want a "guaranteed" review, be sure to e-mail me first.

EpiMag.com
121-61 6th Ave. College Point, NY 11356
jeremy@epimag.com
www.epimag.com
Opinions, reviews, interviews... whatever.

ePunk-Zine.com
alexx@epunk-zine.com
epunk-zine.com
Where we review it first!

graynoise.net
29731 Stagecoach Blvd. Evergreen, CO 80439
PH: 303-669-9939 FX: 303-669-6636
www.graynoise.net
Connect to the Punk music community.

Hand Carved Magazine
10495 Flanders Pl. San Diego, CA 92126
mail@hcmagazine.com
hcmagazine.com
We are always accepting albums to be reviewed.

hardcoremusic.com
greg@hardcoremusic.com
www.hardcoremusic.com
Tons of reviews.

hardcorewebsite.net
nycore@hardcorewebsite.net
www.hardcorewebsite.net
I only support bands that support our scene.

How's Your Edge?
72 Rockland Rd. Auburn, MA 01501
Brian Murphy murphy@howsyouredge.com
www.howsyouredge.com
News, reviews, shows etc.

ihateyour.com
560 Pine Ct. Sequim, WA 98382
press@ihateyour.com
www.ihateyour.com
Send us your press kit, along with your latest release.

Independent Clauses
8820 S. 75th E. Ave. Tulsa, OK 74133
IndependentClauses@hotmail.com
www.independentclauses.com
Dedicated to the reviewing of unknown music, be it independent or 'signed'. We want to hear your band.

Intellectos
intellectos@care2.com
www.intellectos.com
From Electro to Pop to Hardcore and more.

Juice
13900 Tahiti Way #201, Marina Del Ray, CA 90292
PH: 310-578-7575 FX: 310-578-7575
Terri Craft JuiceMagazineLA@aol.com
www.juicemagazine.com
Sounds, surf and skate.

Laminated
1134 22nd St. #6, San Pedro, CA 90731
email@laminated.org
www.laminated.org
CD/show reviews, interviews and photographs.

The Lance Monthly
PO Box 613, Sandia Park, NM 87047
rvstewartproductions@yahoo.com
www.lancerecords.com
'60s Surf and Garage band music.

Last Life Media
greg@lastlifemedia.com
www.lastlifemedia.com
Reviews, tabs, features, downloads.

Lollipop
PO Box 441493, Boston, MA 02144
PH: 617-623-5319
Scott Hefflon scott@lollipop.com
www.lollipop.com
We cover all that fiercely Alternative music.

Music Overload
111 Oak Lawn Ct. #207, Schaumburg, IL 60195
Amber amber@music-overload.com
www.music-overload.com
Interviews, reviews, featured bands etc.

Music Spork
aeiou@musicspork.com
www.musicspork.com
Guide to new Indie Rock, Garage, Electronica etc.

Neu Futur
308 S. Maple St., Lancaster, OH 43130
James McQuiston editor@neufutur.com
www.neufutur.com
I review anything that comes across my desk.

neus subjex.net
PO Box 18051, Fairfield, OH 45018
mail@neussubjex.net
www.neussubjex.net
Send in vinyl, CDs, cassettes and zines. No MP3s.

Overated Magazine
OveratedMag@aol.com
www.overatedmag.com
Punk Rawk, Metal, Ska, Grunge, Alternative and just plain old Rock & Roll.

On the Rag
PO Box 251, Norco, CA 92860-0251
PH: 909-478-5208 FX: 909-478-5208
webmistress@ontherag.net
www.ontherag.net
Info on the California Punk Rock scene.

pastepunk
1600 S. Eads St. #319S, Arlington, VA 22202
jordan@pastepunk.com
www.pastepunk.com
Tons of reviews, interviews and columns.

Psychobilly Homepage
roy@wreckingpit.com
www.wreckingpit.com
Concerts, news, reviews interviews and more.

Punk Magazine
PO Box 675, 200 E. 10th St., New York, NY 10003
Editor@punkmagazine.com
www.punkmagazine.com
Send all promo material, CDs and other hard copy to us.

Punk N Metal
Ashley Shirreff punknmetalwebsite@hotmail.com
www.punknmetal.com
The latest reviews, audio, news and more.

Punk-it.net
sev@punk-it.net
www.punk-it.net
Interviews, show and CD reviews, columns...

Punkmusic.com
www.punkmusic.com
News, interviews, reviews, links and more.

punknews.org
338 Streets Run Rd. Pittsburgh, PA 15236-2007
Attn: Brian Shultz
www.punknews.org
Submit your material for review.

punkplanet.com
4229 N. Honore, Chicago, IL 60613
PH: 773-248-7172 FX: 773-248-7189
punkplanet@punkplanet.com
www.punkplanet.com
We will make every attempt to include you in our reviews section.

punkrockreviews.com
4133 W. Melrose St., Chicago, IL 60641-4641
Bart Niedzialkowski info@punkrockreviews.com
www.punkrockreviews.com
Accepts all your material. No MP3s.

punkROCKS.net
148 San Federico Ave. Santa Barbara, CA 93111
Kevin Wade kevin@punkrocks.net
www.punkrocks.net
Show reviews, interviews, up-to-date news and more.

READ Magazine
PO Box 3437, Astoria, NY 11103
editor@readmag.com
www.readmag.com
Want to send us something? We review everything!

Rebel Rawk
Julia Gariepy slowdownnsmile@hotmail.com
rebelrawk.mess-up.org
We are an online music magazine, devoted to all different genres of Alternative music.

Rock n Roll Purgatory
PO Box 771153, Lakewood, OH 44107
rocknrollpurgatory@yahoo.com
www.rocknrollpurgatory.com
We review Rockabilly, Surf, Punk, oi, Swing, Psychobilly and then some...

Shredding Paper
PO Box 2271, San Rafael, CA 94912
shreddingpaper@netscape.net
www.shreddingradio.com/sp.html
Reviews Underground Pop of all kinds.

Ska, Punk and Other Junk
407 Regency Ct., Middletown, NY 10940
Bryan Kremkau
webmaster@skapunkandotherjunk.com
www.skapunkandotherjunk.com
CD, DVD, concert reviews, interviews, etc.

Skratch Magazine
17300 17th St. J-123, Tustin, CA 92780
Scott scott@SkratchMagazine.com
www.SkratchMagazine.com
Covers Garage Rock, Punk, Hardcore and Emo.

Skyscraper
PO Box 1595, New York, NY 10276
skyscraperzine@hotmail.com
www.skyscrapermagazine.com
Music, print, live reviews and more.

Someday Never
somedaypress@yahoo.com
www.somedaynever.com
Honest and thorough coverage of music.

Soundnova.com
PH: 410-627-1733
Corey Evans corey@soundnova.com
www.Soundnova.com
Covering mainstream and underground acts.

soundriot
mail@sound-riot.com
www.sound-riot.com
News, reviews, interviews and more!

Strictly Locals!
Pocrow's Nest, 550. S. Broadway #38,
Blythe, CA 92225
Sonny Malvolio Malvoliocybercafe@hotmail.com
www.strictlylocals.2ya.com
Down with the underground. Submit your demo!

Super Bitch Magazine
PO Box 973 Royal Oak, MI 48068
John Davies superbitchmagazine@yahoo.com
www.punkrockchicks.com
Dedicated to Girls, Booze, Music,....and more Girls. Music reviews that don't follow the norm.

Switch Magazine
PO Box 3623, Myrtle Beach, SC 29578
switch@switchmagazine.com
switchmagazine.com
We do mostly Punk and Hip Hop reviews.

TheScout.Net
420 San Pedro St. #422, Los Angeles, CA 90013
thekillingmoon@aol.com
www.thescout.net
News and show reviews.

The Toilet
ralph@thetoiletonline.com
www.thetoiletonline.com
Submit anything you have to offer.

Torpedo Magazine
PO Box 35070, Syracuse, NY 13235
Gregg Yeti torpedomag@hotmail.com
torpedomag@hotmail.com
www.torpedomag.com
Indie Rock, Punk, Experimental Rock, Pop focus with fiction, interviews and reviews.

Tragic Endings
2 Stephanie Ln. Lakeville, MA 02347
Stephanie DeMoura stephanie@tragicendings.net
www.tragicendings.net
We're not about money or being into the 'scene' or any of that nonsense. We love to help out the bands. That will never change.

truepunk.com
301 E. 34th St. #103, Austin, TX 78705
staff@truepunk.com
www.truepunk.com
News, reviews, interviews and a message board.

Undevoured
PO Box 15367, Boston, MA 02215
jessica@undevoured.com
www.undevoured.com
Hardcore, Industrial, Emo, Metal...

Canada

Ambush The Night
28 Industrial St. #116, Toronto, ON M4G 1Y9
info@ambushthenight.com
www.ambushthenight.com
Send your CD in for review!

Caustic Truths
PO Box 92548, 152 Carlton St.,
Toronto, ON M5A 2K0
PH: 416-703-6429
www.caustictruths.com
Punk, Hardcore, Garage and other noisy music.

Flex Your Head
11067 146 A St., Surrey, BC V3R 3V3
info@flexyourhead.net
flexyourhead.vancouverhardcore.com
Reviews, audio samples, interviews, links and more.

The Heard
PO Box 3034, Hanmer, ON P3P 1J6
Trevor support@theheard.org
www.theheard.org
Reviews, comics, articles and all that good stuff.

punkhardcore.com
PO Box 25442, London, ON N6C 3P5
Ryan Izzard ryan@punkhardcore.com
www.punkhardcore.com
Up to date news, interviews, CD reviews and more.

punkinternational.com
Tim Krysko tim@punkinternational.com
www.punkinternational.com
We review CDs only.

Scandalized Human Zine
www.shzine.com
Get in touch and we'll send you our mailing address. If possible, please include a link to where a sample of your band or project can be heard or read about.

Scene It All
20355 Erie Peat Rd. Port Colborne, ON L3K 5V4
PH: 905-835-0355
Louie Baribeau info@sceneitall.net
sceneitall.net
Built to better serve the music scene with CD reviews, mp3 teasers, live footage, concert pictures, interviews, lyrics and message boards.

Europe

Belgium

Mashnote.Magazine
Asstraat 4/2, 2400 Mol, Belgium
Jim Faes info@mashnote.net
www.mashnote.net
Interviews, reviews, news and more. Contact us before sending in your music.

Nameless
Rue de Warnoumont, 53, 4140 Sprimont, Belgium
www.webzinenameless.net
News, reviews, interviews and more.

Punk Updates
St-Hubertusplein 52/1, 3290 Schaffen, Belgium
Hein Terweduwe hein@punkupdates.com
www.punkupdates.com
Send in stuff for review or put up links.

Finland

Hardcoresounds
Riskusillankatu 5, 65300 VAASA, Finland
Tero Känsäkangas tero_a_k@hotmail.com
hardcoresounds.net
If you want to send us an album for review or other material, you can do it by mailing it to the above address.

France

Headinstars.com
Erick equipe-666@headinstars.com
www.headinstars.com
Hardcore, Emo, Punk, Metal, Rock, Pop.

Kill...What?
9 Ave. de la Gare, 34440, Nissan, France
Kelly Saux kelly@killwhat.com
www.killwhat.com
Send in your promo material.

Metalorgie.com
www.metalorgie.com/punk
There are different contacts covering the various sub-genres of Punk. Visit our site to see who you should be getting in touch with.

Punk (is) For Dummies
anne@punk4dummies.com
punk4dummies.com
News, reviews, interviews, mp3s...

Sans Tambour ni Trompette
9, rue Bartholdi, 56700 Hennebont, France
info@stnt.org
www.stnt.org
Interactive ezine & radio show from France with news (a lot!), reviews, links, interviews...

SDZ
Impasse Janine, 95220, Herblay, France
L. Levy sdzfanzine@hotmail.com
sdz.free.fr
Rock'n'Roll magzine with reviews, news, etc.

Walked in Line Fanzine
BP 04-60t840 Breuil le Sec, France
PH: 03-44-50-23-63
thewilteam@wilrecords.com
www.wilrecords.com
French Underground label with tons of reviews.

Worst
BP 5195, 57075 Metz cedex 03, France
PH: 00-33-03-87-69-13-02
worsty@wanadoo.fr
www.toutankeupon.com/worst
Concert dates, news, reviews, interviews and more.

Germany

4P Fanzine
Benrather Schlossalee 64, 40597 Dusseldorf, Germany
PH: 0049-0211-5839646
Nico Spielmann nico@beerandmusic.de
www.4p-fanzine.de
Beer and music.

Allschools Network
PO Box 911116, 30431 Hannover, Germany
Torben Utecht torben@allschools.de
www.allschools.de
Network Hardcore eZine.

Back to the Boots
Postfach 360127, Berlin, Germany
info@bttb.de
www.bttb.de
Home of dirty Crust-n-Punk.

Broken Violence
Hofstattstr. 36, 70825 Munchingen, Germany
PH: 07150-2380
Thomas Jansch tomofdeath@brokenviolence.de
www.brokenviolence.de
E-Zine für Hardcore, Punk, Indie und Metal.

CORE Ground
RehmstraBe 119, #501, 49080 Osnabruck, Germany
Holger Straede holger@coreground.de
www.coreground.de
Hardcore fanzine. Send in your material.

Daredevil Magazine
Kantstr. 31, 68723 Oftersheim, Germany
Ralf Burkart daredevil-mag@web.de
www.daredevil.de
Send in your material to get reviewed.

Enough
PO Box 12 07 50, 68058 Mannheim, Germany
info@enoughfanzine.com
www.enoughfanzine.com
DIY punk/HC/Ska/Indie e-zine for the scene!

In-Your-Face
Postfach 65 71, D- 30065, Hannover, Germany
Ralf Sonnenberg redaktion@in-your-face.de
www.in-your-face.de
Punk, Hardcore, Emo, Metal, Nu Metal...

Moloko Plus
Feldstr. 10, 46286 Dorsten, Germany
info@moloko-plus.de
www.moloko-plus.de
News, dates, gigs, zines and more.

Online Zine
Aulgasse 131, 53721 Seigburg, Germany
PH: 016-25-60-2999
Boguslaw Cala bogus@onlinezine.de
www.onlinezine.net
The voice of subculture. Reviews, news and more.

Ox Fanzine
PO Box 102225, 42766 Haan, Germany
PH: 49-700-7865-7625 FX: 49-2104-810830
redaction@ox-fanzine.de
www.ox-fanzine.de
Germany's biggest Punk Rock & Hardcore zine.

Plastic Bomb
Postfach 100205, 47002 Duisburg, Germany
PH: 0203-730613 FX: 0203-734288
info@plastic-bomb.de
www.plastic-bomb.de
News, reviews, interviews and much more.

purerock.de
Diesterwegstr. 9c, 10405 Berlin, Germany
PH: 030-420-22-917 FX: 030-420-22-917
Steffen Lehmann tour@purerock.de
www.purerock.de
Your Alternative Rock community.

Skinhead World
Postfach 6177, 33071 Paderborn, Germany
PH: 0049-05254-936648 FX: 0049-05254-936649
eds@skinhead-world.com
www.skinhead-world.com
Ska, skinheads & scooterists. Info, gig list, reviews & more.

Trust Fanzine
Postfach 11 07 62, 28087 Bremen, Germany
PH: 0421-49-15-88-0 FX: 0421-49-15-88-1
dolf@trust-zine.de
www.trust-zine.de
German online resource for Hardcore, Punk Rock, emo.

Waste of Mind
Oranienstr. 6, 10997 Berlin, Germany
wom@wasteofmind.de
www.wasteofmind.de
News, reviews, tour dates, MP3s and much more.

XSEBX.com
www.xsebx.com
Contact us via our online form before sending in your music.

Italy

Be Nice to Mommy
theguru@benicetomommy.com
www.benicetomommy.com
Fanzine italiana dedicata al Punk-Rock.

Freak Out
Vittorio Emanule 43, 80059, Torre del Greco, Italy
FX: 0039-081-8822687
freakout@libero.it
www.freakout-online.com
Independent music magazine. Postrock noise, emo, Metal...

In Your Eyes
Via N.Cantalupo 15h/5b, 17019 Varazze (SV) Italy
Simone Benerecetti simone@iyezine.com
www.iyezine.com
About what we think and what we feel.

komakino
Paolo yrkomakino@libero.it
www.inkoma.com
Write me a brief introduction about your band. If you can direct me to a couple of MP3's, I'll check them out and get in touch.

The Netherlands

Asice.net
W. Kluinveenweg 28, 7641 AR Wierden, The Netherlands
info@asice.net
www.asice.net
Get your stuff reviewed, promoted or whatever!

Inside Knowledge
Mgr. Nolensstaat 14, 6043 BV Roermond, The Netherlands
info@insideknowledge.net
www.insideknowledge.net
We review everything we get (including Ska, Metal, Indie Rock).

Pitfather.com
Hoofdstraat 55a 7811ED Emmen, Holland
PH: 0591-643838 FX: 0591-642359
info@pitfather.com
www.pitfather.com
Hardcore, Punk and Metal community.

Norway

punkbands.com
Haldensvingen 31, 1387 Asker, Norway
reviews@punkbands.com
www.punkbands.com
Promotes Punk/Ska/oi- bands from all over the world.

Spain

I wanna
PO Box 156.103, 28080, Madrid, Spain
www.ipunkrock.com
On-line Punk-Rock'n'roll zine in Spanish.

iPunkRock
Rafael Peláez, PO Box 156.103, 28080 - Madrid, Spain
www.ipunkrock.com
Punk, PunkRock, Garage, PowerPop, Rock and Roll

Iron Skies
info@ironskies.com
www.ironskies.com
Get your music reviewed in the best Spanish online magazine.

RockCore
www.rockcore.com
Hardcore, Rock, Metal y Punk.

Sweden

Doomsday Magazine
Gamlestadsvägen 19F, 41502 Göteborg, Sweden
Andreas Hedberg doomsday@home.se
www.doomsdaymag.com
News, interviews, reviews and more.

Happy as Raw Sewage (HARS)
Vallavagen 8.213, SE-582 Linkoping, Sweden
Hjertstrand contact@happyasrawsewage.com
www.happyasrawsewage.com
Covers Ska, Swing, Punk, emo and Hardcore.

United Kingdom

Brain Love
brain.love@btinternet.com
www.brainlove.co.uk
Interviews, news, reviews and much, much more.

Bubblegum Slut
27 Stores Ln. Tiptree, Essex, CO5 0LH UK
bubblegumslutzine@gmail.com
www.bubblegumslutfanzine.1hwy.com
The online home of the UK's only fake-fur covered glammy / sleazy / punky / gothy fanzine! We promise to review every single CD we receive. This is NOT the place for emo, Skate Punk, Grunge and things ending in 'core' okay.

collective
18 Waterloo Close, Horsham St. Faith, Norwich, Norfolk, NR10 3JA UK
you-guys@collective-zine.co.uk
www.collective-zine.co.uk
Music reviews zine covering the Indie scene.

Hardcore Times
Papion, Erskine Ave. Grestones, Co. Wicklow, Ireland
info@hardcore-times.com
www.hardcore-times.com
News, reviews, interviews, listings and more.

Organ Zine
c/o The Old Gramophone Works, 326 Kensal Rd. London, W10 5BZ UK
Sean organ@organart.demon.co.uk
www.organart.com
We're mostly interested in Punk/Metal/Alternative/ Prog and music of a left field guitar nature.

Real Overdose
64 Chatsworth Dr. Rushmere Park, Ipswich, Suffolk, England IP4 5XD
tard@realod.com
www.realod.com
Always review a ton o' wax, a heap o' zines and a stack o' shows.

R*E*P*E*A*T Online
PO Box 438, Cambridge, CB4 1FX UK
rosey@repeatfanzine.co.uk
www.repeatfanzine.co.uk
Focuses on the Underground music scene.

Sonic Dirt
lee@sonicdirt.co.uk
www.sonicdirt.co.uk
Punk news, reviews, interviews etc.

State Of Emergency.net
Footloose Farm, Crediton Devon, EX17 4RX UK
info@stateofemergency.net
www.stateofemergency.net
Send promos and any other promotional materials.

Tokolosheonline.com
thealienalf@hotmail.com
tokolosheonline.com
This website was created to support the local British music scene and introduce people to new bands both from Britain and from around the world.

trakMARX.com
c/o Nee Ltd, 1st St. NAC Coventry, CV8 2LZ UK
PH: 07786-261821
wastebin@trakMARX.com
www.trakmarx.com
We bring you the juice on young upstarts.

vanity project
43 Hartley Cr. Woodhouse, Leeds, LS6 2LL UK
skif@vanityproject.co.uk
www.vanityproject.co.uk
Informative interviews, reviews and articles.

Vendetta Zine
vendettazineuk@hotmail.com
www.vendettazine.co.uk
Send us your music, demos, t-shirts and sex toys.

Africa

zapunx.com
Matt matt@zapunx.com
www.zapunx.com
Alternative music community website. Share your views on CDs, EPs, LPs, VHS Tapes, DVDs, anything!

Sign up for The Indie Contact Newsletter
www.indiebible.com

Reggae

Reggae, Ska, Rocksteady and Dancehall.

The Beat Magazine
PO Box 65856, Los Angeles, CA 90065
PH: 818-500-9299 FX: 818-500-9454
editor@getthebeat.com
www.getthebeat.com
A bimonthly publication of Reggae, African, Caribbean and World music, providing information, news, reviews, interviews, discographies and cultural features.

The Dainty Crew
PO Box 7825, Birmingham, England B42 1RA
PH: 44-07958-411-009 FX: 44-0-870-137-6489
info@daintycrew.com
www.daintycrew.com
Interviews, reviews, headlines, Black history and more.

DerDude Goes SKA.de
Emser Straße 18, 56076 Koblenz, Germany
Achim Fricke nuhr@gmx.de
www.derdude-goes-ska.de
SKA ist nicht einfach eine Musik!

Dizzybeat *Australia*
Glen Smyth dizzybeat@topstatus.com
dizzybeat.com
Ska, Reggae, Punk, Life. We encourage people to contribute photos, reviews, news and articles.

JahWorks.org
PO Box 9207, Berkeley, CA 94709
info@jahworks.org
jahworks.org
A web-based project which portrays Caribbean and African-based music and culture with enthusiasm and integrity.

Jammin Reggae
4584 G. W. Pt. Loma Blvd. San Diego, CA 92107
PH: 619-226-6108 FX: 619-226-6108
eznoh@niceup.com
niceup.com
The gateway to Reggae Music on the internet!

Planet Ska
89 Hillside St. #2, Boston, MA 02120
Niff niff007@hotmail.com
www.planetska.com
Send your stuff for review.

Reggae in Germany
Hamburger Str. 16, D-45481 Mülheim / Ruhr, Germany
Peter Beckhaus node@reggaenode.de
www.reggaenode.de
Covers the Reggae scene in Germany.

Reggae in Rio
www.reggaeinrio.com.br
Reggae in Rio de Janeiro-Brazil.

Reggae News
18 Dalberg Rd. Brixton, London, SW2 1AN UK
info@reggaenews.co.uk
www.reggaenews.co.uk
We review a very wide selection of Reggae music. From UK Reggae, to Dancehall, to the latest re-issues of classic music. We get the music on promo so reviews are often on the site before the title has been released.

Reggae Report
21300 NE 24 Ct. Miami, FL 33180
PH: 305-933-9918 FX: 305-933-9918
mpq@reggaereport.com
www.reggaereport.com
All the info on the Reggae scene.

The Reggae Source
303 E. 119th St., Chicago, IL 60628
PH: 773-785-7536 FX: 773-785-7536
service@reggaesource.com
www.reggaesource.com
Solid information on this crucial music form.

Reggae Train.com
info@reggaetrain.com
reggaetrain.com
Comprehensive Reggae music portal on the web.

Reggae Vibes
Pieter Brueghelstraat 5, 6181 DJ Elsloo, The Netherlands
PH: 31-46-4373228 FX: 31-46-4376427
info@reggae-vibes.com
www.reggae-vibes.com
Spread the "Reggae Vibes"...anyway & anywhere!

Reggaefrance.com
6, rue maurice delafosse, 92100 Boulogne, France
redaction@reggaefrance.com
www.reggaefrance.com
Retrouvez la référence Reggae Dancehall, nombreuses interviews d'artistes Jamaïquains & Français.

Roots Garden Promotions
info@rootsgarden.com
3 Kings Mews, Hove, BN3 2PA UK
www.rootsgarden.com
Dedicated to promoting the best of the UK Roots and culture scene. Specialise in playing and promoting strictly conscious Reggae and Dub music new and old.

RudeGal.com
rudegal@rudegal.com
www.rudegal.com
Dancehall Reggae music - the internet resource.

Ska Summit
www.nhsph.tk
The #1 site for info on Ska scenes around the world. View and post shows, bands, venues, profiles and so much more!

The Ska Tipz
skatipz@neoska.com
neoska.com
A site for Japanese Ska bands and other Ska music.

Ska Wars
c/o Karl Peterz, Forskarbacken 9/0604, 104 05 Stockholm, Sweden
johan@skawars.nu
www.skawars.nu
Guide to Ska, Reggae and Rocksteady.

SkaFreaks.com
www.skafreaksonline.com
There is an artist list, discography, lyrics, mp3s, videos, radio and more.

skanews.net
10 rue Andrieu, 95340 Persan, France
skanews@wanadoo.fr
skanews.net
Ska, Reggae, Rocksteady, Nutty sound dub....

Surforeggae
contato@surforeggae.com.br
www.surforeggae.com.br
All the info on the Reggae scene.

WhereItzAt Magazine
PH: 718-591-9424
PO Box 120584, Jamaica, NY 11412
info@whereitzatlive.com
www.whereitzatlive.com
Created to satisfy the entertainment needs of an increasingly sophisticated Caribbean-American marketplace that is influenced by Reggae, Soca, Calypso, Hip Hop and R&B, while providing a platform for artistic and entrepreneurial expression.

Soul / R&B

United States

Gedup.com
www.gedup.com
We are into artists with actual talent, people with something to say and music with originality. We like artists who have more noble goals than just becoming celebrities.

RHYTHMflow.net
PO Box 130, Bronx, NY 10467
editor@rhythmflow.net
www.rhythmflow.net
Entertainment and lifestyle e-zine covering R&B, Urban, Jazz and Soul music. If you are an artist or publicity coordinator and would like to have your project considered for an upcoming issue, please e-mail us your information.

Soul Tracks
chris@soultracks.com
www.soultracks.com
Reviews, biographies and group updates.

WFNK.com
20 E. Central Pkwy. #66, Cincinnati, OH 45202
wfnk@wfnk.com
www.wfnk.com
Welcome to Earth's Funk super site!

Finland

Soul Express
Box 105, 02101 ESPOO, Finland
soulexpress@kolumbus.fi
PH: 358-9-759-40401
www.kolumbus.fi/soulexpr
Music Magazine specialising in real Soul and Funk.

Germany

Groove Attack Magazine
Schanzenstrasse 36 / Gbd 31, 51063 Cologne, Germany
PH: +49 (0) 221-990750 FX: +49 (0) 221-99075990
info@grooveattack.com
www.grooveattack.com
News, new releases and profiles. We also deal with distribution and promotion.

Jazz not Jazz
Chateauneufstrasse 5, 20535 Hamburg, Germany
PH: +49-40-41260844
Dirk Binsau feedback@jazz-not-jazz.com
blog.jazz-not-jazz.com
Specialising in Neo-Soul and quality Indie Soul releases. If you like to see your music reviewed on this site, please contact me via e-mail prior to sending anything.

Sonic Soul
Eichendorffstrasse 6c, D-30916 Isernhagen, Germany
Joerg Michael Schmitt jms@soulsite.de
www.soulsite.de/sonic
The home of Soul in Germany.

Italy

La Pelle Nera
lapellenera@fastwebnet.it
www.lapellenera.com
Predominantly 'Northern'-orientated with sound samplers and CD reviews.

United Kingdom

Blues & Rhythm
82 Quenby Way, Bromham,
Bedfordshire, MK43 8QP UK
PH: +44 (0)123-482-6158
Tony Burke tonyburke@bluesandrhythm.co.uk
www.bluesandrhythm.co.uk
Europe's leading Blues, R&B and Gospel mag.

Blues & Soul Magazine
153 Praed St., London, W2 1RL UK
Bob Kilbourn bob@bluesandsoul.com
www.bluesandsoul.com
Covers all the latest UK and US Urban music info, including news, charts, reviews, events and clubs, as well as in-depth interviews

funkjunkiez.biz
www.funkjunkiez.biz
Soul, R&B, Urban Music etc. Reviews of the latest albums, singles and even live gigs.

futureboogie
PO Box 2051, Bristol, BS6 9ZY UK
demos@futureboogie.com
www.futureboogie.com
Soul & Funk news, reviews and interviews. We're looking for new music to release. please send your demos to us (no attachments please).

In The Basement Magazine
193 Queens Park Rd.
Brighton, East Sussex, BN2 9ZA UK
PH: 00-44-1273-601217 FX: 00-44-1273-601217
David Cole itb@basement-group.co.uk
www.basement-group.co.uk
60's, 70's-style Soul music specialist magazine. Happy to receive CDs for review.

Life and Soul Promotions
PH: +44 (0) 1934-642121
Mike Ashley mike@lifeandsoulpromotions.co.uk
www.lifeandsoulpromotions.net
We have many pages of reviews of Soul Music and related genres – independent and major, Urban, Reggae and more.

Soul Sorts
soulboydodge@clara.co.uk
www.soulsorts.co.uk
News, reviews and events.

Straight No Chaser
17D Ellingfort Rd. London, E8 3PA UK
Paul Bradshaw info@straightnochaser.co.uk
straightnochaser.co.uk
We review mostly "music from the African diaspora" - Jazz, Hip Hop, Ragga, Jungle/d&b, Latin, Brazilian + African musics. Review editors: LPs - Amar Patel / singles: Dom Servini.

ViBIN
info@vibinmusic.co.uk
www.vibin.co.uk
Submitting your work for the unsigned artist section:
Our Unsigned Artist section is designed to showcase unsigned or up & coming artists on the R&B scene. If you wish to be considered in the unsigned artist section then send me a sample of your work (CD or mp3) along with a bio & a couple of pictures.

Women in Music

Most of the publications in the section review exclusively Women's Music. However, there are a few that will accept the music of male musicians as well.

United States

3BlackChicks Review
PO Box 871883, New Orleans, LA 70187-1883
Cassandra Henry cass@3blackchicks.com
www.3blackchicks.com
Interested in submissions from Black artists.

Bamboo Girl
PO Box 507, New York, NY 10159-0507
BambooGirl@aol.com
www.bamboogirl.com
Reviews Indie/Progressive/Hip Hop female music.

The Beltane Papers
PO Box 29694, Bellingham, WA 98229-1694
PH: 360-647-1264
beltane@az.com
www.thebeltanepapers.net
We review the music of independent female artists.

Bitch
1611 Telegraph Ave. #515, Oakland, CA 94612
PH: 510-625-9390
Lisa Jervis lisa@bitchmagazine.com
www.bitchmagazine.com
Covers all female music/musicians.

CandyforBadChildren.Com
PO Box 51446, Boston, MA 02205
editor@candyforbadchildren.com
www.candyforbadchildren.com
Send us press kits, promos and screeners for review.

Cha Cha Charming
284 Lafayette St. #5D, New York, NY 10012
editor@chachacharming.com
www.chachacharming.com
Covering female Pop stars from Tokyo to Paris.

Church of Girl
1405 SE Belmont #65, Portland, OR 97214-2669
PH: 503-819-9201
girl@churchofgirl.com
www.churchofgirl.com
A showcase of emerging female artists and all female/female fronted bands. We do reviews, interviews, have an internet radio station, and offer publicity/promotion/media relations services to bands and artists.

Collected Sounds
3010 Hennepin Ave. S. #630,
Minneapolis, MN 55408
Amy Lotsberg amy@collectedsounds.com
www.collectedsounds.com
A site dedicated to women in music.

Cool Grrrls
PO Box 186, Balboa Island, CA 92662
PH: 714-960-2650 FX: 714-532-6829
editors@coolgrrrls.com
www.coolgrrrls.com
Show & CD reviews, interviews and more.

Daily Diva
2794 Seabreeze Dr. Fairfield, CA 94533
PH: 916-821-0773
webmaster@dailydiva.com
www.dailydiva.com
Fashion, music, culture and fine women of color. We review Independent music.

Ectophile's Guide
PO Box 30187, Seattle, WA 98113-0187
www.ectoguide.org
Submit your material for reviews.

Female Musician
PO Box 623, Northport, NY 11768
fm@femalemusician.com
www.femalemusician.com
Interviews & CD reviews with independent artists.

FemMuse
PO Box 727, Los Angeles, CA 90078
PH: 323-687-7420
shredmistress@femmuse.com
www.femmuse.com
Female musicians and artists network.

FEMMUSIC.com
1550 Larimer St. #511, Denver, CO 80202
PH: 720-341-8567
alexteitzmedia@yahoo.com
www.femmusic.com
Magazine devoted to emerging women in music.

Gilded Serpent
PO Box1928, San Anselmo, CA 94979
PH: 415-455-8455
editor@gildedserpent.com
www.gildedserpent.com
Digital community for Middle Eastern performers and other adventurers.

Girlposse
www.girlposse.com
We review Independent artists from time to time.

GirlPunk.Net
PO Box 177, Roebling, NJ 08554
FX: 609-298-6566
jessica@girlpunk.net
www.girlpunk.net
News, reviews, articles, featured bands etc.

Girly Thing
christina@girlything.com
www.girlything.com
Entertainment news with a touch of all things girly.

Glittergrrrls.com
PO Box 186, Balboa Island, CA 92662
PH: 714-960-2650 FX: 714-532-6829
Laura Encarnado glittergrrrls@hotmail.com
www.glittergrrrls.com
The online teen mag for grrrls that Rock!

GoGirlsMusic.com
PO Box 16940, Sugar Land, TX 77496-6940
Madalyn Sklar info@gogirlsmusic.com
www.gogirlsmusic.com
Promoting women in music. You must be a GoGirls Elite member to get your CD reviewed. Info at www.gogirlselite.com.

Grrl.com
430 Broadway, Redwood City, CA 94063
Bonnie Burton bonnie@grrl.com
www.grrl.com
Send your material in for review.

GuitarGirls.com
Lynn Cary Saylor Lynn@guitargirls.com
www.guitargirls.com
Music reviews of women artists on a one on-one basis.

GURLmusic
c/o iVillage, 500 7th Ave. 14th Fl.
New York, NY 10018
staff@gURL.com
www.gurl.com
Online community and content site for teenage girls.

GyrlsRock.com
1238 Comm Ave. #36, Boston, MA 02134
Sara Hamilton webmaster@gyrlsrock.com
www.gyrlsrock.com
100% devoted to the female musician.

Heartless Bitches International
supremebitch@heartless-bitches.com
www.heartless-bitches.com
Music for the heartless bitch in all of us.

Jade Magazine
PO Box 915, Village Stn. New York, NY 10014
FX: 781-634-6457
ellen@jademagazine.com
audrey@jademagazine.com
www.jademagazine.com
The voice of English-speaking Asian women around the world.

Lilith's Child
44 Rooney St. #2, Clifton, NJ 07011
PH: 973-945-3562
Erin P. Capuano ErinP@lilithschild.com
www.lilithschild.com
We focus on indie female musicians. We offer artist highlights, interviews, CD & concert reviews, with reoccurring columns. Send us your press kit and we'll get you exposure!

MS. Magazine
433 S. Beverly Dr. Beverly Hills, CA 90212
webmstress@msmagazine.com
www.msmagazine.com
We do publish music reviews, but not in every issue.

musical discoveries
rwelliot@hotmail.com
www.musicaldiscoveries.com
Reviews of Contemporary, Progressive and Crossover recordings.

MusiqQueen.com
PO Box 30337, Memphis, TN 38130
PH: 901-332-3504
Charla Littlejohn queen@musiqqueen.com
www.musiqqueen.com
Meet other women, gather resources and more.

Purple Pyjamas
Martine editor@purplepjs.com
www.purplepjs.com
Reviews CDs, musical shows and concerts.

Rockrgrl
3220 1st Ave. S., #203, Seattle, WA 98134
PH: 206-624-7131 FX: 206-624-7037
info@rockrgrl.com
www.rockrgrl.com
For women involved in music.

She Caribbean
PO Box 1146, Castries, St. Lucia, WI
PH: 758-450-7827 FX: 758-450-8694
waynem@candw.lc
www.shecaribbean.com
We are only interested in Caribbean labels or artists, especially women.

Venus Magazine
2000 W. Caroll #402, Chicago, IL 60612
PH: 312-738-3701 FX: 312-738-3702
feedback@venuszine.com
www.venuszine.com
Women in music, art, film and more.

Women of Country
staff@womenofcountry.com
www.womenofcountry.com
Features undiscovered female Country musical gems.

Womanrock.com
PO Box 1460, New York, NY 10009
PH: 800-610-4867
Brenda Kahn bkahn@womanrock.com
www.womanrock.com
Promotion of women's music on the web.

xsisterhoodx.com
1430 Ella T. Grasso Blvd. New Haven, CT 06511
kelly@xsisterhoodx.com
www.xsisterhoodx.com
Promotes girls in Hardcore and Straightedge.

Canada

absolutedivas
3-1750 The Queensway #327,
Toronto, ON M9C 5H5
www.absolutedivas.com
We gladly accept album releases for review as well as submissions for an artist feature.

Germany

Melodiva Net Club
Roßdorfer Str. 24, D-60385 Frankfurt/M, Germany
PH: 69-4960-848 FX: 69-4960-800
musik@melodiva.de
www.frauenmusikbuero.de
News, reviews, interviews etc.

The Netherlands

Metal Maidens
PO Box 230, 4140 AE Leerdam, The Netherlands
metalmaid@globalxs.nl
www.metalmaidens.nl
CDs, seven inches, demo tapes and concert reviews and dates.

Reviews of Women Composers
Patricia Werner Leanse patricia@dds.nl
www.patricia.dds.nl/cds.htm
Does reviews of Classical Music CDs by women.

Sweden

Darling
red@drrling.se
darling.spray.se

United Kingdom

AMP: IT'S THE TITS!
PO Box 30639, London, E1 6GA UK
amp@ampnet.co.uk
www.ampnet.co.uk
For chicks and dicks and... just about anybody, really.

Celestial Voices Reviews
16 Atlantic House, Waterson St. Shoreditch,
London, England E2 8HH
www.loobie.com
Promoting ethereal female vocals on the internet.

Australia

Femail Magazine
8 East Concourse, Beaumaris, VIC 3193 Australia
Michelle Warmuz michelle@femail.com.au
femail.com.au
Empowering every woman! Please try to assist us by including a subject heading in your enquiry; ie. product reviews, competitions, gig guide, entertainment, news etc.

Girl Power Magazine
8 East Concourse, Beaumaris, VIC 3193 Australia
Michelle Warmuz michelle@femail.com.au
girl.com.au
Magazine empowering girls worldwide. Please try to assist us by including a subject heading in your enquiry; ie. product reviews, competitions, gig guide, entertainment, news etc.

World Music

Allafrica.com
920 M Street SE, Washington, DC 20003
PH: 202-546-0777 FX: 202-546-0676
allafrica.com/music
Distributor of African news/music worldwide.

Global Rhythm
PH: 212-868-4354
edit@globalrhythm.net
www.globalrhythm.net
World music, culture & lifestyle.

globalvillageidiot.net
cnicks@seanet.com
www.globalvillageidiot.net
Find the latest news in World music.

Jewish Entertainment Resources
PO Box 12692, Alexandria, LA 71315
PH: 318-442-3346 FX: 318-442-3356
info@jewishentertainment.net
www.jewishentertainment.net
Jewish music resources. Get your music reviewed.

Klezmer Shack
ari@ivritype.com
www.klezmershack.com
Good klezmer and the music inspired by it.

Mondomix
9, Cité Paradis, 75010 Paris, France.
PH: + 33 (0)1-56-03-90-89
FX: + 33 (0)1-56-03-90-84
info@mondomix.com
www.mondomix.com
The electronic media of reference for World Music.

Musical Traditions
1 Castel St., Stroud, Glos, GL5 2HP UK
PH: 01453-759475
rod@mustrad.org.uk
www.mustrad.org.uk
Traditional music throughout the world.

New World Buzz
116 Farmcrest Dr. Oakdale, PA 15071-9332
info@NewWorldBuzz.com
www.newworldbuzz.com
Promotes artists of music genres from all over the world.

The Piper & Drummer
editor@piperanddrummer.com
www.piperanddrummer.com
Devoted solely to piping and drumming.

Whispering Wind Magazine
PO Box 1390, Folsom, LA 70437-1390
PH: 985-796-5433 FX: 985-796-9236
www.whisperingwind.com
We offer Native American musicians a place to get their Indie music reviewed.

World Music Central
552 Parkview Dr. Burlington, NC 27215-5036
PH: 336-437-0762
info@worldmusiccentral.org
www.worldmusiccentral.org
We accept news stories/articles/reviews, and other contributions. There is an online form that you need to fill. If you have photos to go along with the story, please e-mail us the JPEG.

World Music Magazine
Via Alfiera 19, 10121 Torino, Italy
PH: +39-011-5591849 FX: +39-011-2307034
worldmusic@edt.it
www.worldmusiconline.it
Since 1991, the only World Music magazine in Italy.

If you know of a resource that should be listed, please contact indiebible@rogers.com

COLL AUDIO

Canada's premier choice for complete backline requirements!!!

We rent guitar/bass amplifiers, keyboards, synthesizers, Hammond Organs, Leslies, drums & percussion and more...

Proudly supplying venues throughout Ontario and surrounding areas, festivals, recording studios, touring bands, and the movie industry since 1986.

3595 St. Clair Ave. East, #19
Toronto, Ontario, Canada M1K 1L8
Tel: 416-264-1188 Fax: 416-264-1190
mail@collaudio.com

www.collaudio.com

SECTION TWO: REGIONAL PUBLICATIONS AND RESOURCES

"Getting that first article written about you can be quite a challenge. Two great places to start are your local town papers and any local fanzine" - **Ariel Hyatt, Ariel Publicity**

The resources listed in this section can help you to gain exposure in your local area, whether it be a CD review, allowing you to post information about your band, post info on a new release, upcoming shows etc. Most of the organizations listed (Folk, Jazz, Blues etc.) publish a newsletter that will review your CD. Note that many of these resources will promote music from outside of their region, but give preference to local talent.

North America

United States

boulevards.com / Associated Cities
www.boulevards.com
A network of the world's premier "city.com" websites. In the music and nightlife section you can find out about bars in most major cities. You can also have a link to your band posted (you must link back).

Citysearch
www.citysearch.com
Entertainment guide. Has a separate website for ALL major US cities. Extensive coverage of the local music scene. Post your shows and events in your local city and any city that you will be playing in.

Craigslist
PO Box 225159, San Francisco, CA 94122-5159
www.craigslist.org
Restoring the human voice to the Internet, in a humane, non-commercial environment. Originating in San Francisco, now available for communities all over the world. Get the word out about your music, gigs etc.

donewaiting.com
616 S. Lazelle St., Columbus, OH 43206
Robert Duffy duffy@donewaiting.com
www.donewaiting.com
Discussing local music scenes around the world.

Evite
www.evite.com
Free online invitations and local event listings. Want to tell people about an event in your area? Post it on Evite.

Golistenlive.net
www.golistenlive.net
News and information about local bands in most major cities.

Home Town News
www.hometownnews.com
Providing direct links to more than 2,600 Daily and Weekly U.S. Newspapers!

Journalism Resources on the Web
www.library.arizona.edu/library/teams/sst/jour/web/resources.html#newspapers
Links to newspapers, magazines, broadcasters, television/radio and news services.

The Local Mix
PO Box 8407,Cranston, RI 02920
info@thelocalmix.com
www.thelocalmix.com
Promoting local bands and artists and providing them with global exposure.

Local Band Network
1341 W. Fullerton #232, Chicago, IL 60614
PH: 773-868-1441 FX: 707-922-2306
fitz@localband.net
www.localband.net
Information about local bands and music venues... no matter where "local" is to you.

Local Music Edge
PO Box 5202, Vernon Hills, IL 60061
PH: 847-577-2249
Dave Rohrer admin@edge-inc.net
edge-inc.net/local
Find local bands and music near you and help support these bands.

Local Music Now
localmusicnow@gmail.com
www.localmusicnow.net
Fostering community through music...one city at a time. Get your band listed. Submit your gigs.

MusicJamCentral.com
kevin@musicjamcentral.com
MusicJamCentral.com
A state-by-state listing of bands. Submit yours!

MYLOCALBANDS.com
958 Palm Ave. #115, W. Hollywood, CA 90069
PH: 310-657-8078 FX: 310-507-0291
concerts@mylocalbands.com
www.mylocalbands.com
Add information about your band as well as your MP3s. Sign up to play at local venues.

NewsDirectory College Newspapers
www.newsdirectory.com/college_news.php
Links to hundreds of college newspapers.

Newspaper & News Media Guide
www.abyznewslinks.com
Links to over 12,000 newspapers worldwide.

openmikes.org
comments@openmikes.org
www.openmikes.org
A listing of music open-mike nights in the US and Canada. Anything open (by invitation, sign-up, etc.) to the general public, where live music may be performed, may be included here.

roundmusic.com
vin@roundmusic.com
www.roundmusic.com
General info covering the music scene in various US cities.

State of Music
128 Louisville Ave. Neptune, NJ 07753
PH: 908-433-8963
JoeD@StateofMusic.com
stateofmusic.com
A network of local music sites that include new releases, downloads, upcoming gigs etc. Our mission is to assist the fans and the artists in providing quick and easy detailed information of the local music scene throughout the country.

United States Newspapers and News Media Database
www.abyznewslinks.com/unite.htm
Links to hundreds of US newspapers.

US Newspaper List
www.usnpl.com
Links to newspapers throughout the country.

YourLocalHipHop
yourlocalhiphop.com
A network of nationwide Hip Hop sites. Submit the details on MC Battles, B Boy Competitions and Hip Hop artist showcases near you.

ZBands.com
Barbara White barb@zbands.com
ZBands.com
Finally, musicians and venues can quickly & easily post their information and the general public can quickly & easily retrieve it. ZBands is now open in almost every large city in the U.S.

Alabama

al.com
www.al.com/music
Online presence for the Birmingham News, Huntsville Times and Mobile Register. Local music section.

Alabama Bluegrass Music Association
PO Box 220, Leeds, AL 35094
webmaster@alabamabluegrass.org
www.alabamabluegrass.org
Promoting Bluegrass music in the state of Alabama.

Alabama Blues Project
alablues@aol.com
www.alabamablues.org
Dedicated to the preservation of Blues music as a traditional American art form.

AlabamaLine.com
Wayne Mills WayneMillsBand@hotmail.com
www.alabamaline.com
Promoting singers, songwriters, artists and musicians from Alabama.

Bama Hip Hop
2216 Christine Ave. Anniston, AL 36207
PH: 256-282-0799 FX: 925-475-7458
bamahiphop@hotmail.com
bamahiphop.homestead.com
Lists your bio, company profile, concert/festival schedule, release dates and booking contacts.

Bands of Bama
launch.groups.yahoo.com/group/bandsofbama
groups.msn.com/alabamamusiciansmessageboard
List your gigs, find available players/singers and find gigs in Alabama.

Birmingham Buzz
PO Box 660686, Vestavia Hills, AL 35266
PH: 205-602-6872
Tim Taylor timt@bhambuzz.com
screamsophie.net/ezine
Dedicated to covering the local Rock music scene in Birmingham.

Black & White
1312 20th St. S. Birmingham, AL 35205
PH: 205-933-0460
www.bwcitypaper.com
Birmingham's city paper. Events, concerts and live music sections.

Cajun-Zydeco Connection of Huntsville
webmaster@czdance.com
www.czdance.com
Dedicated to Cajun and Creole music, dancing and culture in the North Alabama area.

Crimson White
PO Box 2389, Tuscaloosa, AL 35403-2389
PH: 205-348-7845 FX: 205-348-8036
www.cw.ua.edu
University of Alabama newspaper.

fleabomb.com
www.fleabomb.com
Promotes local bands in Birmingham. We cover Punk, Grindcore, Indie Rock/Pop, emo, Hip Hop, and not much else.

Indie Community
9495 Brook Forest Cir. Helena, AL 35080
PH: 205-492-3284
info@indiecommunity.com
www.indiecommunity.com
Alabama's network for independent Christian bands and artists.

Magic City Blues Society
PO Box 55895, Birmingham, AL 35255
PH: 205-822-7387
www.magiccityblues.org
Encourages the performances of the Blues and develops an appreciation within the community.

MobileSucks
webmaster@mobilesucks.net
www.mobilesucks.net
Covering the Punk scene in Mobile.

The Toe
PH: 240-643-9434
Robin Moore ramoore@TheToe.cc
www.thetoe.cc
North Alabama's premiere music and nightlife site. Email us to set up your profile.

Alaska

AK Ink
PO Box 244235, Anchorage, AK 99524
jennink@hotmail.com
www.geocities.com/akinkzine
Anchorage based Punk zine covering local and international bands.

AK This Month
PO Box 202941, Anchorage, AK 99520
akthismonth@hotmail.com
www.alaskathismonth.com
Free guide to entertainment in the 49th State!

Alaskan Folk Music And More!
gary@alaskafolkmusic.org
www.mosquitonet.com/~gcn
Comprehensive local and statewide Folk and traditional music happenings.

The Anchorage Press
PO Box 241841, Anchorage, AK 99524-1841
PH: 907-561-7737
calendar@anchoragepress.com
www.anchoragepress.com
An A&E weekly newspaper.

YourAnchorageRadio.com
youranchorageradio.com
An online music community. Post shows, reviews, events etc.

Arizona

602 Streets.com
PO Box 506, Peoria, AZ 85345
info@602streets.com
www.602streets.com
Arizona Rap and Hip Hop network.

Acoustic Music Arizona
PO Box 1554, Queen Creek, AZ 85242
PH: 480-888-1692
info@acousticmusicaz.com
www.acousticmusicaz.com
Promoting Acoustic music and Arizona based Acoustic musicians.

Arizona Bluegrass Association
PO Box 8139, Glendale, AZ 85312-8139
PH: 602-993-6801 FX: 602-863-4861
www.azbluegrass.org
Up-to-date information about news, events, festivals and Bluegrass bands.

Arizona Hip Hop Network
PO Box 86545, Phoenix, AZ 85080-6545
Ryan "Creepz" Piercey creepz@cox.net
www.ArizonaHipHop.com
Album reviews, artist interviews, monthly features and more!

Arizona Irish Music Society
9867 Roundup Ct. Sun City, AZ 85373
PH: 602-770-8077 FX: 602-977-0050
aims@azirishmusic.com
www.azirishmusic.com
News, events, listings etc.

Arizona Music Club
9920 S. Rural Rd. #108, Tempe, AZ 85284
PH: 480-206-3435 FX: 480-753-7021
music@blackdogpromotions.com
www.arizonamusicclub.com
Help us spread the word about the great music of Arizona!

Arizona Music Scene
414 S. Mill, #110, Tempe, AZ 85281
PH: 480-966-5558 FX: 503-214-8181
directory@arizonamusicscene.com
www.ArizonaMusicScene.Com
Arizona band index, local music news, CD reviews, free promotional tools etc.

Arizona Old-Time Fiddlers Association
7470 Derryberry Dr. Flagstaff, AZ 86004
www.arizonaoldtimefiddlers.org
Created to preserve and promote the art of Old-Time fiddling.

Arizona Open Mics
chris@azopenmic.com
azopenmic.com
Includes pictures and artist profiles.

ASU Web Devil
PH: 480-727-6941
webdevil@asu.edu
www.statepress.com
Arizona State University online publication.

AZ Local Music
2030 W. Deer Valley Rd. #B, Phoenix, AZ 85027
PH: 623-580-7386
matt@azlocalmusic.com
www.azlocalmusic.com
Covering the Arizona music scene.

AZPunk.com
Chris Lawson chris@azpunk.com
www.AZPunk.com
Arizona's #1 source for Punk Rock!

CollectiveUnderground.com
www.collectiveunderground.com
Dedicated to Arizona's heaviest music.

Desert Bluegrass Association
7878 E. Cloud Rd. Tucson, AZ 85750-2819
PH: 520-591-2614
desertbluegrass@yahoo.com
www.desertbluegrass.org
Developing and promoting Bluegrass music in the Greater Tucson area.

In Your Ear
PO Box 85304, Tucson, AZ 85754
PH: 520-624-9979
info@in-your-ear.net
www.in-your-ear.net
We have a focus on Arizona music because we are based in Tucson; however, we cover national and other independent artists too.

LiNK Music
Site 51, 2308 E. Boston St., Chandler, AZ 85225
PH: 480-814-9768
Rachel@linkmusicaz.com
www.linkmusicaz.com
Musician directory, classifieds and calendar of events.

Phoenix Band Guide
Melissa Ostrow mp3@phx.com
phoenixbandguide.com
Post your band info, Take advantage of our services including unlimited downloads of MP3s.

Phoenix Blues Society
PO Box 36874, Phoenix, AZ 85067-6874
PH: 602-252-0599
info@phoenixblues.org
www.phoenixblues.org
Promotes and perpetuates local and national Blues music.

Phoenix Early Music Society
PO Box 16839, Phoenix, AZ 85011-6839
PH: 602-234-5724
info@pems.org
www.pems.org
Keeps you up to date on local events from the Medieval, Renaissance and Baroque eras.

A Documentary Film by Dave Cool

WHAT IS INDIE?

A Look into the World of Independent Musicians

FEATURING: EMBER SWIFT TIM RIDEOUT PAUL CARGNELLO ANDREA REVEL ATHENA REICH BLOODSHOT BILL BIONIC KARYN ELLIS THE RIPCORDZ KALI ANNABELLE CHVOSTEK MYSTIC & MIRANDA PENNY LANG MATTHEW LARGE...AND THE SAGA CONTINUES NEEMA MALCOLM BAULD JEAN-FRANÇOIS FORTIER NAILA KELETA MAE

PLUS INDUSTRY EXPERTS:
DEREK SIVERS - CD BABY   SUZANNE GLASS - INDIE-MUSIC.COM
DAVID WIMBLE - INDIE BIBLE   DAYLLE DEANNA SCHWARTZ - AUTHOR
PANOS PANAY - SONIC BIDS   PETER SPELLMAN - MUSIC BUSINESS SOLUTIONS

Available on DVD in 2006...
Special features packed with tons of resources for indie artists!

STANDALONERECORDS.COM

Phoenix New Times
PO Box 2510, Phoenix, AZ 85002
PH: 602-271-0040 FX: 602-253-4884
www.phoenixnewtimes.com
Free weekly alternative paper. Thursday has local reviews.

Prescott Jazz Society
PO Box 26096, Prescott Valley, AZ 86312
PH: 928-925-1422
milt@pjazz.org
www.pjazz.org
Presenting, promoting and celebrating Jazz performance and education in northern Arizona.

Rock in Phoenix
PO Box 61432, Phoenix, AZ 85082
rockinphoenix@hotmail.com
www.rockinphoenix.org
A Spanish Rock/Punk/Metal website dedicated to the Spanish Rock scene in Phoenix.

RockThis.net
PO Box 20783, Bullhead City, AZ 86439
PH: 928-201-0300
nikki@rockthis.net
www.rockthis.net
Serving Bullhead City, Kingman, and Lake Havasu City. Local musicians forums, chatroom, articles, photos and more!

Southwest Acoustic Music Association
925 W. Baseline, #105-G6, Tempe, AZ 85283
SAMcomment@aol.com
www.acousticscene.com
Articles, events, CD reviews, venues, open mic listings, poetry and more.

Tucson Guitar Society
info@tucsongs.org
www.tucsongs.org
Organizes classic guitar concerts in the Tucson area for local, national and international talent.

Tucson Friends of Traditional Music
PO Box 40654, Tucson, AZ 85717-0654
PH: 520-293-3783
www.tftm.org
Sponsors and promotes concerts, dances, workshops and informal music sessions.

Tucson Jazz Society
PO Box 1069, Tucson, AZ 85702-1069
PH: 520-903-1265 FX: 520-903-1266
office@tucsonjazz.org
www.tucsonjazz.org
Promotes Jazz across southern Arizona with concerts, festivals and media activities.

Tucson Weekly
PO Box 27087, Tucson, AZ 85726-7087
PH: 520-792-3630 FX: 520-792-2096
Stephen Seigel musiced@tucsonweekly.com
www.tucsonweekly.com
Free weekly paper. Indie record reviews. Publish the annual "Tucson Musician's Register".

Zia Record Exchange
1940 W. Indian School Rd. Phoenix, AZ 85015
PH: 602-241-0313
www.ziarecords.com
Can set you up with a consignment arrangement.

Arkansas

Delta Boogie
1710 Henry St., Jonesboro, AR 72401
www.deltaboogie.com
Information about music, art and entertainment in Northeast Arkansas and the Mississippi Delta.

Dinky Music
www.freewebs.com/dinkymusic
Supporting and promoting bands from Northeast Arkansas & beyond.

Fayetteville Free Weekly
PO Box 843, Fayetteville, AR 72702
PH: 479-521-4550
www.freeweekly.com
Entertainment weekly. Covers local music.

Followmearound
josh@followmearound.net
followmearound.net
Got a band that wants to be linked up or an upcoming show?

GodbeyGirl
Kelsey Murphy KelciRenae@yahoo.com
www.godbeygirl.bravehost.com
Covering the Russellville scene.

Little Rock Hardcore
Adam Peterson adam@littlerockhardcore.com
www.littlerockhardcore.com
Interviews, concert and album reviews, downloads etc.

Little Rock Scene
www.littlerockscene.com
Improving our local music scene. News, reviews, gallery etc.

MalvernMusic.com
www.malvernmusic.com
All the Shizzle that's Fizzle to Priznizzle.... Features include news, show dates, pictures, flyers, forums, instant messaging and more...

Midsouth Metal Society
midsouthmetal.com
Online community where you can post shows, news, releases etc.

Nightflying
PO Box 250276, Little Rock, AR 72225
PH: 501-354-8577 FX: 501-354-1994
info@nightflying.com
www.nightflying.com
Free monthly alternative magazine. Live music guide, CD reviews, features and previews.

Ozark Blues Society
www.ozarkblues.com
Promoting public knowledge of local, national, and international Blues music.

Spa City Blues Society
PO Box 4270, Hot Springs, AR 71902
ken-lynne@spacityblues.com
www.spacityblues.com
Preserving and promoting Blues music and musicians.

Under the Ground
gforce@undertheground.com
www.undertheground.com
Covering the Little Rock Hip Hop scene.

California

The (916) Magazine
5001 Freeport Blvd. Sacramento, CA 95822
PH: 916-452-2482
the916@comcast.net
www.the916.com
Hip Hop magazine providing information about the best in local talent in Northern California.

All Access Magazine
15981 Yarnell St. #122,
Rancho Cascades, CA 91342
PH: 818-833-8852
allaccessmgzn@aol.com
www.allaccessmagazine.com
A free bi-weekly music and entertainment publication. Keeping the local music alive!

Amoeba Music *Home Grown*
www.amoebamusic.com
Our Home Grown artists are nominated by Amoeba staff, and must be local to Berkeley, Hollywood or San Francisco.

American Guitar Society
18111 Nordhoff St., Northridge, CA 91330
PH: 818-677-2339
www.csun.edu/~igra/ags
Provides an opportunity for you to perform before an appreciative audience.

Barflies.net
PO Box 1367, Orange, CA 92856-1367
www.barflies.net
Weekly concert calendar, weekly cd/show reviews and a bi-monthly features magazine.

Bluegrass West
PO Box 614, Los Olivos, CA 93441
PH: 805-688-9894 FX: 805-688-0366
peterf@silcom.com
www.bluegrasswest.com
Presenting Bluegrass music and selected performers in shows throughout the Southern California area.

Butte Folk Music Society
PO Box 3406, Chico, CA 95927
bobharrison@mindspring.com
www.bfms.freeservers.com
Supports traditional and Folk music through concert venues and other music-related activities.

CaBands.com
PO Box 661254, Sacramento, CA 95866
PH: 916-247-9024
www.cabands.com
Robert Michael Lockwood II robert@cabands.com
We do concert and CD reviews and list over 7,000 local CA bands. Now offering bands a 10 page website where they can upload MP3s, pictures, news, info on upcoming shows etc. (only $5 month!).

California Aggie
25 Lower Freeborn, 1 Shields Ave.
Davis, CA 95616
PH: 530-752-0208
www.californiaaggie.com
UC Davis Student paper is distributed free on the UC Davis campus and in the Davis community.

California Bluegrass Association
PO Box 9, Wilseyville, CA 95257-0009
PH: 209-293-1559
rcornish@sjcoe.net
www.cbaontheweb.org
Dedicated to the furtherance of Bluegrass, Old-Time and Gospel music.

California Hardcore
nick@calihardcore.com
www.calihardcore.com
The latest information on the bands, zines, record labels, distros and more from the Bay area.

California Lawyers for the Arts
1641 18th St., Santa Monica, CA 90404
PH: 310-998-5590 FX: 310-998-5594
cla@calawyersforthearts.org
www.calawyersforthearts.org
Provides lawyer referrals, dispute resolution services, publications and a resource library.

California State Old-Time Fiddler's Association
Mimi Wolf mimi@mimi.com
www.fiddle.com/calfiddle
Dedicated to the preservation of Old-Time fiddle music.

California Traditional Music Society
4401 Trancas Pl. Tarzana, CA 91356-5399
PH: 818-817-7756 FX: 818-817-7734
info@ctmsfolkmusic.org
www.ctmsfolkmusic.org
Dedicated to the preservation and dissemination of traditional Folk music, dance and related Folk arts

California Newspapers
www.usnpl.com/canews.html
www.usnpl.com/canews2.html
Links to newspapers throughout the state.

Carmel Classic Guitar Society
PO Box 6543, Carmel, CA 93921
PH: 831-484-5848 FX: 831-484-5746
CarmelClassicGuitar@starrsites.com
www.starrsites.com/CarmelClassicGuitar
Promotes the Classical guitar through education, recitals and gatherings.

The Catalyst
PO Box 279214, Sacramento, CA 95827
submissions@thecatalystonline.com
thecatalystonline.com
Monthly art culture and political newspaper geared to provide independent artists, organizations, and businesses a forum with fresh perspectives. Please, send us your recorded materials (audio and video) and literature.

CentralCali.com
www.centralcali.com
Covers the Hip Hop scene in California, featuring message boards and news on local events.

Chico News and Reviews
353 E. 2nd St., Chico, CA 95928
PH: 530-894-2300 FX: 530-894-0143
www.newsreview.com/chico
Provides extensive coverage of grassroots issues and the local music scene.

chico underground show info
chicolist@synthesis.net
www.chicolist.com
Promotes the local Indie/punk/Hardcore scene in the Chico area. Emphasize unity in the scene.

DIG Music
1831 V St., Sacramento, CA 95818
PH: 916-442-5344 FX: 916-442-5382
Holly Holt holly@digmusic.com
www.digmusic.com
Independent record label and Artist Management company. AAA, Roots/Americana, Singer/Songwriter. The artists we manage put a record out with us as a part of their management deal. We also sell CDs by approved artists on our site. Right now, we mainly have relationships with local/regional acts.

Digress Magazine
Annie Knight (Mable) mable@digressonline.com
www.digressonline.com
An Indie publication that promotes artists from Riverside and beyond.

East Bay Express
1335 Stanford Ave. Emeryville, CA 94608
PH: 510-879-3700 FX: 510-601-0217
editor@EastBayExpress.com
www.eastbayexpress.com
Extensive coverage of local music including weekly reviews and gig listings.

Egomania Records
PO Box 370069, Reseda, CA 91337-0069
PH: 818-708-8454
Jon Dunmore dunmore@egomaniarecords.com
egomaniarecords.com
An agency providing video & CD production, press kits for bands and musicians, photography, providing live entertainment for weddings, festivals, corporate, any social function. Online Listings for musicians & bands, web design.

The Fresno Bee
1626 E St., Fresno, CA 93786-0001
PH: 559-441-6356 FX: 559-441-6457
features@fresnobee.com
www.fresnobee.com
Central California's leading daily newspaper. Local entertainment section.

Fresno Folklore Society
PO Box 4617, Fresno, CA 93744
PH: 559-224-1738
patwolk@yahoo.com
home.pacbell.net/ckjohns/
Preserves Folk arts, especially traditional music, in California's San Joaquin Valley.

Good Times
PO Box 1885, Santa Cruz, CA 95061
PH: 831-458-1100 FX: 831-458-1295
events@gdtimes.com
www.gdtimes.com
Santa Cruz news and entertainment weekly. Extensive coverage of the local music scene.

GrooveTV
marco@groovetv.net
www.groovetv.net
Featuring the best from the Santa Cruz Groove and Jam music scene.

HDBands.com
PH: 760-963-6516
contact@hdbands.com
www.HDBands.com
Covering the High Desert Punk scene. Specializing in photography, reviews, interviews and more!

Humboldt Folklife Society
PO Box 1061, Arcata, CA 95518
PH: 707-822-5394
folk@humboldtfolklife.org
www.humboldtfolklife.org
Working to bring together Folk dancers, musicians and music lovers.

HumboldtMusic.com
mike@humboldtmusic.com
www.humboldtmusic.com
Provides an extensive and searchable directory of local musicians and music resources.

HumGuide
517 3rd St. #8 Eureka, CA 95501
PH: 707-444-9566 FX: 707-476-8049
info@humguide.com
www.humguide.com
Event calendars, bands, art and more in Humboldt County.

In 2 The Red
rachel@in2thered.com
in2thered.com
Serving the Northstate including Redding, Chico and more! Find a favorite band, the perfect venue or the show you can't miss??

Inland Empire Music
PH: 909-318-0686
William Gould CEO@InlandEmpireMusic.com
www.InlandEmpireMusic.com
Bands from the Inland Empire area can post two promo pictures, a bio and four MP3s for free.

inTUNE: SoCal Bluegrass News
inTUNEnews1@aol.com
members.aol.com/intunenews
Profiles regional Bluegrass folks. The DISCoverings column lets you know which CDs to buy.

Jazz Connection
jazzconnection@hotmail.com
jazzconnectionmag.com
Celebrating the fine art of Jazz music in Northern California.

Jazz Society of Santa Cruz County
editor@santacruzjazz.org
santacruzjazz.org
Promotes Jazz with a bulletin board, musician's directory service and news and views of Jazz.

The List
PO Box 2451, Richmond, CA 94802
skoepke@stevelist.com
jon.luini.com/thelist
stevelist.com
Southern California funk-punk-thrash-ska upcoming shows of interest.

The Living Tradition
PH: 949-559-1419
livingtradition@hotmail.com
www.thelivingtradition.org
Sponsors regular contra dances, Folk music concerts and Folk music jams in Bellflower and Anaheim.

Mach Turtle
FX: 310-823-2227
jamie@machturtleprods.com
www.machturtleprods.com
Listing of Live Surf music events in Southern California.

MetroSantaCruz
115 Cooper St., Santa Cruz, CA 95060
PH: 831-457-9000 FX: 831-457-5828
msc@metcruz.com
www.metcruz.com
Free weekly alternative paper. Indie music reviews.

Modesto Area Musician Association
4300 Finch Rd. Modesto, CA 95357
FX: 209-572-0221
mama@modestoview.com
www.modestoview.com/mama
News, reviews, MP3s etc.

Moshking.com
PO Box 1605, Glendora, CA 91740
moshking@moshking.com
www.moshking.com
Info on all Metal and Hard Rock concerts, events and bands in the SoCal area.

New Times
505 Higuera St., San Luis Obispo, CA 93401
PH: 805-546-8208 FX: 805-546-8641
calendar@newtimesslo.com
www.newtimes-slo.com
San Luis Obispo County's news & entertainment weekly.

norcalmusic.com
zac@norcalmusic.com
www.norcalmusic.com
Community board for Norcal musicians.

North Bay Bohemian
216 E. St., Santa Rosa, CA 95404
FX: 707-527-1288
editor@bohemian.com
www.metroactive.com/sonoma
Arts and entertainment weekly. Covers the local music scene.

Northern California Metal Underground
caioneach@yahoo.com
www.ncmu.com
100% uncompromised Underground Metal.

OC Punk
www.ocpunk.com
A resource for Orange County Punk bands and their fans.

OC Weekly
1666 N. Main St. #500,
Santa Ana, CA 92701-7417
PH: 714-550-5950 FX: 714-550-5903
letters@ocweekly.com
www.ocweekly.com
Orange County A&E weekly. Lots of local music coverage.

OnStageNow.net
3140 Red Hill Ave. #150, Costa Mesa, CA 92626
support@onstagenow.net
www.onstagenow.net
Get info and schedules for bands and clubs in S. California or find musicians for your band.

Open Mikes in California
www.openmikes.org/calendar/CA

Orange County Bands
admin@ocbands.com
www.ocbands.com
Band listings, post gigs, find band members or clubs that need bands.

The Orion
College of Communication, Cal State U., Chico, CA 95926-0600
PH: 530-898-5625 FX: 530-898-4799
www.orion-online.net
California State U. Chico's student publication.

Pacific Sun
PO Box 5553, Mill Valley, CA 94942
PH: 415-383-4500 FX: 415-383-4159
steve.mcnamara@pacificsun.com
www.pacificsun.com
North Bay's weekly paper.

Palo Alto Weekly
PO Box 1610, Palo Alto, CA 94302
PH: 650-326-8210 FX: 650-326-3928
editor@paweekly.com
www.paloaltoonline.com
Semi-weekly newspaper. Post your events online

Pasadena Weekly
50 S. DeLacey Ave. #200, Pasadena, CA 91105
PH: 626-584-1500 FX: 626-795-0149
Julie Riggott julier@pasadenaweekly.com
www.pasadenaweekly.com
Pasadena's A&E weekly. Lists gigs by local bands, reviews CDs, writes features etc.

Powerslave.com
1308 Borregas Ave. #130, Sunnyvale, CA 94089
PH: 408-745-1690 FX: 408-745-9928
info@powerslave.com
www.powerslave.com
NoCal underground Metal scene with show and album reviews.

Reviewer Magazine
PO Box 87069, San Diego, CA 92138
PH: 619-992-9211
reviewermag@yahoo.com
www.reviewermagazine.com
Southern California music, entertainment and lifestyle magazine.

Rose Street Music
1839 Rose St., Berkeley, CA 94703
PH: 510-594-4000
rosestreetmusic@yahoo.com
www.rosestreetmusic.com
A Berkeley house concert venue featuring women musicians and songwriters.

Sacramento Guitar Society
Greg Williams gregorwilliams@comcast.net
www.sacguitar.org
Provides education and performance opportunities to all cultures, ages, abilities and economic means.

Santa Barbara Blues Society
PO Box 30798, Santa Barbara, CA 93130
PH: 805-897-0060 FX: 805-899-4100
www.sbblues.org
Dedicated to keeping the African-American Blues tradition alive in the Santa Barbara area.

Santa Barbara Choral Society
PO Box 3324, Santa Barbara, CA 93130-3324
PH: 805-965-6577
info@sbchoral.org
www.sbchoral.org
Provides qualified singers with an opportunity to study and perform great works of music.

Santa Barbara Independent
122 W. Figueroa St., Santa Barbara, CA 93101
PH: 805-965-5205 FX: 805-965-5518
arts@independent.com
www.independent.com
The county's news and entertainment paper.

Santa Clara Valley Fiddlers Association
PO Box 2666, Cupertino, CA 95015-2666
www.scvfa.org
Dedicated to the preservation of traditional American music such as Old-Time, Bluegrass and Gospel.

Santa Clarita Valley Blues Society
scvblues@earthlink.net
www.home.earthlink.net/%7Escvblues
Preserving and promoting Blues music.

Santa Cruz Sentinel
207 Church St., Santa Cruz, CA 95060
PH: 831-423-4242
www.santacruzsentinel.com
Entertainment section includes a calendar of music events.

Seven South
webmaster@sevensouth.com
sevensouth.com
Covering the Santa Barbara music scene.

Seven South Record Shop
382 N. La Cumbre Rd. Santa Barbara, CA 93110
PH: 805-898-0710
recordshop@sevensouth.com
sevensouth.com/recordshop
Sell recordings at our shop if you're from the Santa Barbara / Ventura area.

Skinnie
10184 6th St. #A Rancho Cucamonga, CA 91730
PH: 909-476-0270 FX: 909-476-5931
jimmy@skinniezine.com
www.skinniezine.com
A monthly entertainment and lifestyles magazine based out of Rancho Cucamonga.

skipsintune.com
2740 Auburn Blvd. Sacramento, CA 95821
FX: 916-484-1916
info@skipsintune.com
www.skipsintune.com
Welcomes and encourages your submissions of band photos, bios, gigs and CD releases.

Socal-Breaks Community
Robtronik robtronik@socal-breaks.com
www.socal-breaks.com
News, promotion, events etc.

SoCalMonthly.com
mail@socalmonthly.com
www.socalmonthly.com
Show listings, CD reviews and more. Mainly Punk but sometimes special features on other types of music.

Sonoma County Blues Society
PO Box 7844, Santa Rosa, CA 95407
mikeah@pacbell.net
www.sonomacountybluessociety.org
Interviews and CD reviews in our monthly newsletter.

Sonoma County Folk Society
PO Box 9659, Santa Rosa, CA 95405-9659
Kathi Carney knccarney@yahoo.com
socofoso.org
Promotes the knowledge and performance of traditional and contemporary Folk music.

Sonoma Tunes
webmaster@sonomatunes.com
www.sonomatunes.com
Dedicated to live Blues in Northern California in general and Sonoma County in particular.

Southern California Blues Society
PO Box 1007, Los Alamitos, CA 90720
PH: 714-229-0643 FX: 714-229-9950
SleepingBootie@hotmail.com
www.socalblues.org
Presentation of Blues music through teaching, publications, festivals and concerts.

Southern California Early Music Society
PO Box 544, Pacific Palisades, CA 90272-0504
PH: 310-358-5967
Bim Erlenkotter info@earlymusicla.org
www.earlymusicla.org
Supports the study, performance and enjoyment of Medieval, Renaissance, Baroque and Classical music. Baroque periods, defined as music written before 1750. Our support in terms of musicians are those who interpret the music and play the instruments of these specific historical periods.

Southland Blues
6475 E. Pacific Coast Hwy. #397,
Long Beach, CA 90803
PH: 562-498-6942 FX: 562-498-6946
info@southlandblues.com
www.southlandblues.com
The hub of the Blues in Southern California.

SouthWest Bluegrass Association
5206 Calle de Ricardo, Torrance, CA 90505
swba@s-w-b-a.com
www.s-w-b-a.com
Bi-monthly newsletter with information about festivals and house jams. Members get free web page.

Supergiant Productions
2109 W. St. #4, Sacramento, CA 95818
PH: 916-501-4799
Gina Azzarello gina@supergiantproductions.com
www.supergiantproductions.com
We promote and book bands in the Sacramento area.

The Switchboard
ladynoir@socalgoth.com
www.socalgoth.com
Southern California Goth directory. Contact us to be included on the site.

Top Secret Records
mike@humboldtmusic.com
www.humboldtmusic.com/tsr
Owned by musicians solely to produce music under the total control of the musicians themselves.

Valley Scene Magazine
6520 Platt Ave. #336, West Hills, CA 91307
PH: 818-888-2114 FX: 818-888-7142
contact@valleyscenemagazine.com
www.valleyscenemagazine.com
Provides the most current information on entertainment, restaurants, retail, services and more.

Ventura Reporter
PH: 805-658-2244
editor@vcreporter.com
www.vcreporter.com
Ventura County's news and entertainment weekly. Covers local music with articles and show listings.

VenturaMusicScene.com
PH: 805-794-4714
mail@venturamusicscene.com
www.venturamusicscene.com
The complete guide to upcoming music events for Ventura County.

webookbands.com
7095 Hollywood Blvd. #794,
Hollywood, CA 90028
PH: 323-651-1582 FX: 323-651-2643
info@webookbands.com
www.webookbands.com
Books talent and promotes for over 30 venues, both club and theatre, in California and Seattle.

West Coast Performer
475 Haight St. #4, San Francisco, CA 94117
PH: 415-255-8567
Kjersti Egerdahl wcpeditorial@performermag.com
www.performermag.com
Want your CD reviewed? Do you have news on your band? Send your CDs and press releases.

Westcoast Worldwide
Mike xhatex@earthlink.net
www.westcoastworldwide.com
Covers the Punk/Hardcore scene. Has a message board, zine, CD reviews, gig listings, bookings etc.

Your Best Bet Magazine
POBox 1062, Lake Isabella, CA 93240
YourBestBet4oc@hotmail.com
yourbestbet4oc.tripod.com
Serving the Southern California area. Looking for bands to interview. Looking to help spread the word on any and all up and coming local bands.

Your Music Magazine
PH: 831-465-1305
mikelyon@yourmusicmagazine.com
www.yourmusicmagazine.com
Metal magazine distributed throughout Southern California.

The Bay Area

Bay Area Blues Society
Ronnie hipwayblues@yahoo.com
www.bayareabluessociety.net
Dedicated to the preservation, promotion and representation of Blues, Jazz and gospel.

Bay Area Bunch Newsletter
bab_news@yahoo.com
www.geocities.com/SunsetStrip/Venue/9842
Highlights live Acoustic music performed by women singer-songwriters in the Bay Area.

Bay Area Improvisers Network
johnlee@bayimproviser.com
www.bayimproviser.com
Find musician's information, upcoming concert info, reviews, links to other sites and more.

Bay Area Ska Page
PO Box 4233, Hayward, CA 94540-4233
info@bayareaska.com
www.bayareaska.com
Reviews are broken up between albums or demos by a band, compilations and shows.

Bay Area Underground Music
groups.myspace.com/BayAreaMusic
Designed to expose local Rap artists, producers, groups & vocalists to dedicated fans.

Bay Guardian
135 Mississippi, San Francisco, CA 94107-2536
PH: 415-255-3100 FX: 415-255-8762
www.sfbg.com
Free weekly alternative paper. Local Indie music, concert reviews and artist interviews.

BayInsider.com
PO Box 22222, Oakland, CA 94623
PH: 510-834-1212
bayinsider@ktvu.com
www.bayinsider.com
Entertainment zine sponsored by KTVU TV.

BayProg
don@till.com
www.bayprog.org
San Francisco area Progressive Rock community.

Bluegrass by the Bay
134 Serrano Dr. San Francisco, CA 94132
deirdre@deirdre-cassandra.com
www.scbs.org/bbb.htm
Contains reviews and articles about shows, venues, albums, artists and upcoming Bluegrass event.

Cruzin' the Bluz
Dave "Doc" Piltz dmpiltz53@aol.com
www.cruzinbluz.com
Blues news and reviews from Santa Cruz and the Bay Area.

Dub Beautiful Collective
Maer Ben-Yisrael maer@dub-beautiful.org
www.dub-beautiful.org
Presents live Electronic music events. We record all of our shows and stream the best recordings.

East Bay Recorder Society
darrellstaley@yahoo.com
www.sfems.org/ebrs
Hosts monthly meetings for amateur recorder players to play Renaissance and Baroque music.

Five Spot
sayhi2@fivespot.com
www.fivespot.com
Find out who artists are and where they're playing, hear their music, order their CDs.

Flavorpill SF
985 Howard St. San Francisco, CA 94103
sf_events@flavorpill.net
sf.flavorpill.net
A publishing company that seeks out the best in arts, music and culture and delivers its findings.

Happa.com
www.happa.com
Your 24/7 online source for Hip Hop shows in the greater Bay Area.

Hip Hop Slam
DnZ tfsdjz@hotmail.com
www.hiphopslam.com
A mixed media company with a record label, radio show, videotape series and website.

illstatic
Selino Valdes selino@illstatic.com
www.illstatic.com
Focused on bringing the current listings in Hip Hop, Dirty House, Electro, DnB, Indie, DIY and more. Post your events!

JazzWest.com
Wayne Saroyan wayne@jazzwest.com
www.jazzwest.com
The Bay area's online Jazz network. Reviews, articles, new releases etc.

KFOG's Local Scene
55 Hawthorne St. #1000,
San Francisco, CA 94105
PH: 415-817-5364 FX: 415-995-6867
kfog@kfog.com
www.kfog.com/local_scene/local_scene.html
Turning the spotlight on up and coming Bay Area musicians.

KUSF Entertainment Calendar
2130 Fulton St., San Francisco, CA 94117
kusf@usfca.edu
kusf.org/calendar.shtml
Please send only calendar listings to this address.

Laughing Squid
PO Box 77633, San Francisco, CA 94107
www.laughingsquid.org
An online resource for underground art and culture of San Francisco and beyond.

Metro San Jose
550 S. 1st St., San Jose, CA 95113
PH: 408-298-8000 FX: 408-298-0602
letters@metronews.com
www.metroactive.com/metro
Silicon Valley's leading weekly newspaper.

Metroactive
www.metroactive.com
A Northern California meta-site specializing in A&E information.

North Bay Music
info@northbaymusic.com
www.northbaymusic.com
An online guide to live music in the San Francisco area.

oakland.com Local Bands Page
www.oakland.com/nightlife/localbands.shtml
Does your band have a web site? E-mail us to get your band linked here.

On The Tip of My Tongue
ceemoon@yahoo.com
www.tipofmytongue.net
We produce a cable video show in San Francisco that focuses on local Bay Area talent.

Outsound
www.outsound.org
Tries to raise public awareness of music by presenting public performance, promotion and education.

Redwood Bluegrass Associates
PO Box 390515, Mountain View, CA 94039-0515
PH: 650-691-9982
bruce@rba.org
www.rba.org
Serving the Bay area to promote Bluegrass and related Acoustic music through concerts and workshops.

San Francisco Bay Area Early Music Concert Listings
1071 Blair, Sunnyvale, CA 94087
FX: 408-245-6901
Jonathan Salzedo listings@albanyconsort.com
www.albanyconsort.com/concerts
A resource for working musicians and concert-goers.

San Francisco Bay Salsa & Latin Jazz
info@salsasf.com
www.salsasf.com
Your info site for Northern California and beyond.

San Francisco Classical Guitar Society
560 19th St., San Francisco, CA 94107
PH: 415-731-7336
mail@sfcgs.org
www.sfcgs.org
Promoting the awareness, understanding and appreciation of the Classical guitar.

San Francisco Classical Voice
225 Bush St. #500, San Francisco, CA 94104
Editor@SFCV.org
www.sfcv.org
The Bay Area's website journal of Classical music criticism. Features reviews of musical performances.

San Francisco Early Music Society
PO Box 10151, Berkeley, CA 94709
PH: 510-528-1725
sfems@sfems.org
www.sfems.org
Creates a supportive environment for the performance of Medieval, Renaissance and Baroque music.

San Francisco Traditional Jazz Foundation
41 Sutter St., San Francisco, CA 94104
info@sftradjazz.org
www.sftradjazz.org
Helps foster live, high quality traditional Jazz, regionally and worldwide.

sanfranciscohiphop.com
John Harrison click411@aol.com
www.sanfranciscohiphop.com
Bay Area's biggest Hip Hop/R&B site. Interviews and contacts.

San Jose Jazz Society
60 S. Market St. #210, San Jose, CA 95113
PH: 408-288-7557 FX: 408-288-7598
jazzmaster@sanjosejazz.org
www.sanjosejazz.org
Presents free concerts, festivals, hands-on workshops, clinics and master classes.

San Jose Mercury News
750 Ridder Park Dr. San Jose, CA 95190
PH: 408-920-5000 FX: 408-288-8060
letters@mercurynews.com
www.bayarea.com/mld/mercurynews
Entertainment section covers the local music scene.

SF JAZZ
3 Embarcadero Ctr. Lobby Level,
San Francisco, CA 94111
PH: 415-398-5655 FX: 415-398-5569
mailbox@sfjazz.org
www.sfjazz.org
Devoted to Jazz at the highest level, with concert performers ranging from acknowledged masters to the newest and most promising talents on the international, national, and San Francisco Bay Area scenes.

SF Music Online
webmaster@sfmusiconline.com
www.sfmusiconline.com
Your online source for local music information here in the SF Bay Area.

SF Weekly
185 Berry #3800, San Francisco, CA 94107
PH: 415-536-8100 FX: 415-541-9096
feedback@sfweekly.com
www.sfweekly.com
San Francisco's smartest publication. Local music section.

SFBAYou
sfbayou@sfbayou.com
www.sfbayou.com
Will keep you informed on Bay Area events, new CDs and books and Cajun-Zydeco news.

SFBlues.net
Rich Piellisch peach@sfblues.net
www.sfblues.net
Your source of information on San Francisco's Blues scene.

sfcelticmusic.com
jim@sfcelticmusic.com
www.sfcelticmusic.com
Traditional Celtic music of Ireland, Scotland, Cape Breton and Brittany in the Bay Area.

sfgoth.com
www.sfgoth.com
Provided for free to the SF net.goth community for hosting Gothic or Industrial club pages.

SFMPB.com
eric@sfmpb.com
www.sfmpb.com
Exists to promote Brazilian music in the San Francisco Bay Area.

sfstation.com
3528 17th St., San Francisco, CA 94110
PH: 415-552-5588 FX: 415-552-5587
www.sfstation.com
San Francisco's independent information resource.

Sister SF
PO Box 6, 1001 Page St.,
San Francisco, CA 94117
sistersf@sistersf.com
www.sistersf.com
Providing a supportive, friendly platform for any female DJ, MC or live performer.

sodachrome
Sarah Guerin bbq4sale@hotmail.com
www.sodachrome.com/indie.shtml
Online community covering all things Indie in the San Francisco area.

South Bay Folks
contact-sbf@SouthBayFolks.org
www.SouthBayFolks.org
Dedicated to promoting Folk music in the greater San Jose area.

South Bay Guitar Society
72 N. 5th St., #18, San Jose, CA 95112
PH: 408-292-0704
sbgs@sbgs.org
www.sbgs.org
Promotes Classical and related guitar music by providing performance opportunities to professional and amateur musicians.

Thrasher Magazine
1303 Underwood Ave. San Francisco, CA 94124
PH: 415-822-3083 FX: 415-822-8359
greg@thrashermagazine.com
www.thrashermagazine.com
Covers SF Punk and Hardcore music scene.

Transbay Creative Music Calendar
1510 8th St., Oakland, CA 94607
PH: 510-893-2840
mail@transbaycalendar.org
transbaycalendar.org
Concert listings for non-commercial, adventurous new music in the Bay Area.

True Skool
Ren dj_ren@true-skool.org
true-skool.org
Dedicated to preserving Hip Hop and Funk. We are your number one resource for the Bay Area's up and coming musicians and events.

urban delicious
Alex Pleasant alex@urbandelicious.com
www.urbandelicious.com
San Francisco event calendar.

Voice is Venom
Denise Mauro venomous@voiceisvenom.com
www.voiceisvenom.com
Bay area resource for women who Rock. We do reviews of local unsigned bands only. The only reviews we do of non-local bands are if they are coming through the SF Bay Area and playing with our local bands.

Walfredo.com
adam@walfredo.com
www.walfredo.com
Covering the Bay Area jam band scene.

West Coast Songwriters
1724 Laurel St. #120, San Carlos, CA 94070
PH: 650-654-3966 FX: 650-654-2156
info@westcoastsongwriters.org
www.westcoastsongwriters.org
Promotes, educates and provides tools and opportunities to songwriters from Alaska to California.

Zero Magazine
12 S. 1st St. #300, San Jose, CA 95113
PH: 408-971-8511
Larry Trujillo larry@zero.cc
www.zeromag.com
San Jose free monthly magazine. Alternative record reviews, articles and interviews plus local spotlight. Please contact me by e-mail before you send your music in.

Los Angeles

The Americana Music Circle
Lauren Adams lauren@laurenadams.com
www.americanacircle.com
A place for songwriters to enjoy themselves, stretch out and meet new comrades each month. The format of our show is to have a local artist open the show. Next, a four artist song circle takes the stage and then, a touring artist or artist of note to close our show.

AOL City Guide Los Angeles *Music*
home.digitalcity.com/losangeles
Contains feature articles plus highlights, a running music poll and interactive message board.

Entertainment Today
2325 W. Victory Blvd. Burbank, CA 91506
PH: 818-566-4030 FX: 818-566-4295
www.ent-today.com
Weekly A&E magazine. Does cover local music.

Flavorpill LA
la_events@flavorpill.net
la.flavorpill.net
A publishing company that seeks out the best in arts, music and culture and delivers its findings.

folkWorks
PO Box 55051, Sherman Oaks, CA 91413
PH: 818-785-3839
mail@folkworks.org
www.folkworks.org
A newspaper dedicated to promoting Folk music, dance and other folk arts.

groophug
Daniel Ryder redelvis@pacbell.net
groophug.originalfools.com
Get the latest information about music related events in the Los Angeles/Orange County.

The Hive Music and Media Complex
2894 Rowena Ave. Los Angeles, CA 90039
PH: 323-664-2899
LJ Scott info@buzzplay.com
www.hivehollywood.com
A recording and rehearsal facility.

hollywoodband.com
2510-G Las Posas Rd. #200,
Camarillo, CA 93010-3496
PH: 805-322-4265
web2@venturaphoto.com
www.hollywoodband.com
Underground band directory. Rock, Pop, Punk, Metal etc. reviews, news, shows...

JesusJams.com
PH: 301-289-5635
jjid@jesusjams.com
www.jesusjams.com
L.A. area Christian music concerts and events.

Jointz Magazine
1800 S. Robertson #0420,
Los Angeles, CA 90035
PH: 213-351-1006 FX: 323-417-4977
listings@jointzmag.com
www.jointzmag.com
Provides expansive coverage of club listings and events, as well as trends in music.

KC Productions
49 Thornton Ave. #2, Venice, CA 90291
PH: 310-399-3942 FX: 310-399-0815
info@kcntp.com
www.kcntp.com
Live music & film/ video production services, included stage & lighting design.

LA Weekly
PO Box 4315, Los Angeles, CA 90078
PH: 323-465-9909
letters@laweekly.com
www.laweekly.com
LA arts and entertainment. Local music coverage includes spotlight artists, reviews and gig listings.

LAmusic.com
dean@lamusic.com
www.lama.com
Promotes artists with little or no access to airwaves due to economic rather than creative reasons.

LAReggaeClubs.com
10008 National Blvd. #144,
Los Angeles, CA 90034
White Lightning admin@lareggaeclubs.com
www.lareggaeclubs.com
Your one stop for reggae entertainment in Los Angeles.

LOL Records
PO Box 5148, Beverly Hills, CA 90209
PH: 310-790-5689 FX: 208-460-2903
Gerry Davies info@lolrecords.com
www.lolrecords.com
A record label gearing up to sign more music, and help Indie artists get their careers off the ground.

Los Angeles Goes Underground
5850 West 3rd St. PMB 274,
Los Angeles, CA 90036
lagu.somaweb.org
Showcasing Los Angeles based Underground, Alternative & Indie Rock bands.

Los Angeles Jazz Society
5959 W. Century Blvd. #736,
Los Angeles, CA 90045
PH: 310-216-9100 FX: 310-216-7515
info@lajazz.org
www.lajazzsociety.org
Keeps its members informed through its quarterly newsletter, "Quarter Notes."

The Los Angeles Music Guide
editor_losangeles@citysearch.com
losangeles.citysearch.com
Extensive coverage of the local music scene. Post your shows and events.

Los Angeles Music Productions (L*A*M*P)
PH: 800-783-5267
Leslie Waller leslie@lamusicproductions.com
www.lamusicproductions.com
Offers tangible success tools for songwriters, composers, performers, producers, engineers, and Indie record labels through seminars, events, and artist development programs.

Los Angeles Gothic-Industrial Network
marytemp@lagoth.net
www.lagoth.net
If you are in a Goth/Industrial/Deathrock band, and are local to LA/OC, then submit a band form.

Los Angeles Songwriters' Network
PH: 626-818-0047
songnet@songnet.org
www.songnet.org
Career-minded artists supporting each other through network events, seminars and collaboration.

The Los Angeles Swing Times
www.nocturne.com/swing
Covering all things Swing in L.A.

Los Angeles Times
202 W. 1st St., Los Angeles, CA 90012
PH: 213-237-5000
www.latimes.com
Covers local and national music scene.

LosAngeles.com
www.losangeles.com/music
Our insider's look at the L.A. music scene.

LosAngelesPunk.com
jason@losangelespunk.com
www.losangelespunk.com
Show reviews, news, gigs etc.

Music Plus TV
517 North Alvarado St., Los Angeles, CA 90026
PH: 213-572-0240
Marc Cubas marc@musicplustv.com
www.musicplustv.com
We air undiscovered and indie artists of all genres 24/7 on our cable and Web TV stations.

Planet Shark Productions
Sally sohosharky@aol.com
www.planetsharkproductions.com
Produces, markets, and promotes film, record, and DVD release parties & other industry events.

Pork TarTare
Rebecca Hill rebecca@porktartare.com
www.porktartare.com
A Los Angeles online magazine that wants to get CDs / tapes and even records to review.

Rock City News
7030 De Longpre Ave. Hollywood, CA 90028
PH: 323-461-6600 FX: 323-461-6622
webmaster@rockcitynews.com
www.rockcitynews.com
Covering local bands, clubs and other social gatherings.

Techno4.us
PO Box 280633, Northridge, CA 91328-0633
FX: 775-269-1388
staff@techno4.us
www.techno4.us
Dedicated to promote the underground party culture of Los Angeles. Get your event flyers posted online.

thelamusicscene.com
7210 Jordan Ave. #C50, Canoga Park, CA 91304
Seth Schwartz seth@thelamusicscene.com
www.thelamusicscene.com
LA music scene site featuring artists / bands, clubs, reviews, show dates, a discussion forum and more!

TheSceneLA.com
editor@thescenela.com
www.thescenela.com
Articles, reviews, release information...

Venice Magazine
PO Box 1, Venice, CA 90294-0001
venicemag@venicemag.com
www.venicemag.com
Los Angeles A&E magazine.

Webookbands.com
7095 Hollywood Blvd. #794,
Hollywood, CA 90028
PH: 323-651-1582 FX: 323-651-2643
info@webookbands.com
www.webookbands.com
A booking service giving local unsigned talent easy access to clubs throughout Los Angeles.

WHERE Magazine
3679 Motor Ave. #300, Los Angeles, CA 90034
PH: 310-280-2880 FX: 310-280-2890
art@wherela.com
www.wherela.com
List your upcoming events.

YourLocalScene.com Los Angeles
PO Box 41669, Long Beach, CA 90853
Eric eric@yourlocalscene.com
la.yourlocalscene.com
Los Angeles' home on the internet for local music information, bands, venues and more!

San Diego

Accretions
PO Box 81973, San Diego, CA 92138
PH: 619-299-5371
sounds@accretions.com
www.accretions.com
An artist-based label with an ear towards Experimental, Improvisational and Global sounds.

Blues Lovers United of San Diego
PO Box 34077, San Diego, CA 92163
PH: 619-256-1124
info@blusd.org
www.blusd.org
Presenting and supporting local and national Blues artists and culture.

Oly's San Diego Open Mic Schedule
PH: 720-985-7423
Scott "Oly" Olson olyjams@yahoo.com
webspawner.com/users/sdopenmic
A comprehensive list of various open mic events in the San Diego area.

San Diego Acoustic Music Scene
Kelley Martin kelley@acousticpie.com
www.acousticpie.com/SanDiego.html
San Diego is fast catching up with Austin and Boston as a hotbed of Acoustic Singer/Songwriters and a springboard for national talent.

San Diego CityBEAT
3550 Camino Del Rio N. #207,
San Diego, CA 92108
PH: 619-281-7526 FX: 619-281-5273
www.sdcitybeat.com
Has "locals only" section.

San Diego Early Music Society
3510 Dove Court, San Diego, CA 92103-3904
PH: 619-291-8246 FX: 619-688-1684
sdems@sdems.org
www.sdems.org
Showcasing the musical treasures of Europe's Medieval, Renaissance and Baroque periods.

San Diego Local Metal
raymond@sdmetal.com
www.sdmetal.com
Presenting the best of San Diego's local Metal bands.

San Diego Magazine
1450 Front St., San Diego, CA 92101
PH: 619-230-9292 FX: 619-230-0490
www.sandiego-online.com
We welcome information on upcoming events in the San Diego area.

San Diego Musicians Network
PH: 858-344-2294
info@sdmusicnet.com
www.sdmusicnet.com
Featured artists section plus show dates, new bands, and new projects by your favorite artists.

San Diego NSAI
EAxford@aol.com
www.pianopress.com/nsai.htm
We do writing exercises as well as group song critiques. Every month we feature our "Night of Original Songs" Showcase at Claire de Lune.

San Diego Reader *Music Scene*
PO Box 85803, San Diego, CA 92186
PH: 619-235-3000 FX: 619-231-0489
e-music@sdreader.com
www.sdreader.com/ed/calendar/music.html
San Diego's most complete and accurate listings for concerts, clubs and bands.

San Diego Songwriter's Guild
3368 Governor Dr. #F-326,
San Diego, CA 92122
sdsongwriters@hotmail.com
www.sdsongwriters.org
Assisting in the advancement of songwriting skills through educational programs, and to expose original songs to the recording, television and motion picture industries via pitch sessions with entertainment professionals.

San Diego Swings
PO Box 460084, Escondido, CA 92046-0084
FX: 760-740-1732
www.sandiegoswings.com
Your source for Swing and Big Band music in America's finest city.

San Diego Troubadour
sdtroubadour@yahoo.com
gothere.com/sandiego/Troubadour
A free publication aimed at bridging the gap in covering music not often represented in other publications. Specializing in American Roots music, which encompasses Alt Country, Folk, Gospel and Bluegrass.

San Diego Union-Tribune
PO Box 120191, San Diego, CA 92112-0191
PH: 619-718-5200 FX: 619-260-5081
Maya Kroth maya.kroth@uniontrib.com
www.uniontrib.com
Submit a music event or take a look at what's going on in San Diego in our music community database.

SanDiegoPunk.com
joel@sandiegopunk.com
www.sandiegopunk.com
Coverage includes show listings, pictures, interviews, places to hang out and buy records and more.

SDAM.com *(San Diego Area Music)*
PO Box 151648, San Diego, CA 92175-1648
PH: 619-286-6873
webmaster@sdam.com
www.sdam.com
Will stream your audio, post your bios and gigs on our calendar and sell your CD.

sdmetal.org
webmaster@sdmetal.org
www.sdmetal.org
San Diego's online realm for Metal.

Trummerflora Collective
c/o Accretions, PO Box 81973,
San Diego, CA 92138
PH: 619-299-5371
rubble@trummerflora.com
www.trummerflora.com
An independent group of music makers dedicated to Experimental and Improvisational music.

Colorado

Black Rose Acoustic Society
PO Box 165, Colorado Springs, CO 80901-0165
PH: 719-633-3660
feedback@blackroseacoustic.org
www.blackroseacoustic.org
Dedicated to the education, performance and preservation of all types of traditional music.

Boulder Weekly
690 South Lashley Ln. Boulder, CO 80303
PH: 303-494-5511 FX: 303-494-2585
www.boulderweekly.com
Free weekly alternative paper. CD and concert reviews, club listings.

Classical Guitar Society of Northern Colorado
PH: 970-267-8705
Frank Gordon classguitarsoc@aol.com
www.coloradoguitar.com
Brings both Classical and Acoustic guitar players and friends together each month in a pleasant cafe.

Colorado Art Rock Society
Philip Satterley progrocktv@hotmail.com
www.coloradoprog.com
A society for like minded and intelligent odd-metered music connoisseurs.

Colorado Arts Net
Box 300-245, Denver, CO 80203
letters@coarts.net
www.coloradoarts.net
The ultimate, the most informative and most exciting tool any local fan of the arts.

Colorado Bluegrass Music Society
PO Box 68, Louisville, CO 80027
PH: 303-281-9473
cbms@coloradobluegrass.org
www.coloradobluegrass.org
Promotes and encourages the development, performance and preservation of bluegrass.

Colorado Blues Society
620 Oak St., Windsor, CO 80550
WebMaster@COBlues.com
www.coblues.com
Creating a wider appreciation of the American indigenous art form, the Blues.

Colorado Friends of Cajun/Zydeco Music and Dance
3331 S. Dayton St., Denver, CO 80231
PH: 303-745-9577
webmaster@rockymountainweb.com
cfcz.org
Your guide for the best in Cajun and Zydeco music in the front range area of Colorado.

Colorado Music Association *(COMA)*
8 E. 1st Ave. #107, Denver, CO 80203
PH: 720-570-2280
info@coloradomusic.org
www.coloradomusic.org
Presents music festivals showcasing and celebrating local talent.

Colorado Springs Independent Newsweekly
235 S. Nevada, Colorado Springs, CO 80903
PH: 719-577-4545 FX: 719-577-4107
Kathryn Eastburn kathryn@csindy.com
www.csindy.com
Colorado Springs weekly A&E paper.

ColoradoRock.com
webmaster@coloradorock.com
www.coloradorock.com
Resource site and TV show.

Commotion Music Promotion
PH: 303-921-5271
www.commotionpromotion.com
We offer you a full range of Internet and traditional publicity services. We're not some faceless corporate giant that doesn't care. We get to know you. We come to your shows and we offer extra advice to help you toward your goals.

THE DIRT
unholiestgoddess@yahoo.com
denver.erebusmusic.com
Colorado's live Metal music network.

Fort Collins Colorado Music Index
cbk@seldomfed.com
www.seldomfed.com/fcmusic.htm
We list musician's pages, artists, music projects, venues, stores and more. Learn about the music biz.

Hapi Skratch Entertainment
1151 Eagle Dr. #324, Loveland, CO 80537-8020
PH: 970-613-8879 FX: 775-256-2501
info@hapiskratch.com
www.hapiskratch.com
Offers a complete line of service essential to the growth and development of any band.

Independent Records and Video
3030 E. Platte Ave. Colorado Springs, CO 80909
PH: 719-473-0882
independent@beindependent.com
www.beindependent.com
Since 1978, fulfilling Southern Colorado's music needs.

JamSpace.net
PH: 303-915-8578
www.jamspace.net
Covering Colorado Jam music scene.

Kaffeine Buzz
PO Box 181261, Denver, CO 80218
PH: 303-394-4959
info@kaffeinebuzz.com
www.kaffeinebuzz.com
An online music and entertainment source for Colorado and beyond.

KGNU's Bluegrass Calendar
Cuz'N Nickles bluegrass@kgnu.org
www.kgnu.org/bluegrass
List your upcoming Bluegrass event.

MileHighMusicStore.com
1151 Eagle Dr. #324, Loveland, CO 80537-8020
PH: 970-613-8879
info@milehighmusicstore.com
MileHighMusicStore.com
We want to sell all CDs that have a Colorado and Rocky Mountain connection.

Production and Distribution
1151 Eagle Drive #324,
Loveland, CO 80537-8020
PH: 970-613-8879
info@productionanddistribution.com
productionanddistribution.com
We work closely with Hapi Skratch Records and major one-stops for our fulfillment to large online retailers and direct retail brick and mortar accounts around the country.

Reggae Movement
1233 Flower Cir. #C, Lakewood, CO 80218
Larry Leiber larry@reggaemovement.com
www.reggaemovement.com
An organization dedicated to the spread and cultivation of Reggae music.

Rock on Colorado!
1550 Larminer St. #608, Denver, CO 80202
David Webmaster@RockOnColorado.com
www.rockoncolorado.com
A Celebration of Colorado's music scene!

Rocky Mountain Bullhorn
238 Walnut St., Fort Collins, CO 80524
PH: 970-416-7957 FX: 970-221-5539
www.rockymountainbullhorn.com
Fort Collins weekly A&E paper. Alternative to the traditional mainstream press.

Scene Magazine
PO Box 489, Fort Collins, CO 80522
PH: 970-490-1009 FX: 970-490-1266
editor@scenemagazine.info
www.scenemagazine.info
Ft. Collins arts and music information covering local and national acts. Profiles bands and reviews CDs.

Denver

3A Records
PO Box 29593, Denver, CO 80229
hiphop3a@hiphop3a.com
www.hiphop3a.com
We have 3 related businesses under one roof. We feel these businesses are the key to your albums finished product. (Studio, Production & Publishing).

blood.sweat.tears music syndicate
Rob Tatum bloodsweattears@comcast.net
www.bloodsweattears.net
Punk zine. News, reviews, band of the month and more.

Creative Music Works
PO Box 480552, Denver, CO 80248
PH: 303-759-1797 FX: 303-759-1220
info@creativemusicworks.org
creativemusicworks.org
Provides educational and performance opportunities for Jazz and other contemporary music.

Denver Musicians Association
1165 Delaware St., Denver, CO 80204-3607
PH: 303-573-1717
PVriesenga@aol.com
www.dmamusic.org
Provides the finest professional Classical, symphonic, Jazz, Rock, Country and commercial musicians.

Denver Post
PO Box 1560, Denver, CO 80202
PH: 303-825-1010
ourreaders@denverpost.com
www.denverpost.com
Album reviews, previews upcoming shows. Friday calendar listings.

DenverBoulderMusic.com
info@denverbouldermusic.com
www.denverbouldermusic.com
The finest site on the web to find the best music in Denver, Boulder and all over Colorado.

DenverMix.com
PO Box 11081, Englewood, CO 80151
PH: 303-722-6322
submit@denvermix.com
denver.mixliving.com
Denver's hippest online entertainment guide. Submit your bands information and website address for free.

EyeOnDenver.com
endlessproductions@eyeondenver.com
www.eyeondenver.com
Send us info on you or your band. Post show dates and view music videos.

KTCL's Locals Only Calendar
4695 S. Monaco St., Denver, CO 80237
PH: 303-713-8000
www.area93.com
Post your upcoming shows.

Swallow Hill Music Association
71 East Yale, Denver, CO 80210
PH: 303-777-1003
info@swallowhill.com
www.swallowhill.com
Denver's home for Folk and Acoustic music. Publishes the Swallow Hill Quarterly.

Underground Network
www.undergroundnet.net
Submit events, club nights, links, event reviews, CD or DJ reviews and much more.

Westword
PO Box 5970, Denver, CO 80217
PH: 303-296-7744 FX: 303-296-5416
www.westword.com
Denver free weekly alternative paper. Reviews CDs and normally does a full bio on one local band each week.

Connecticut

Club CT Live Bands
24 Wilfred Rd. Manchester, CT 06040
PH: 860-680-4756
info@clubct.com
www.clubct.com/bands.htm
Submit your band if playing in Connecticut. Also contains a band of the month feature.

Connecticut Area Blues Bands and Musicians
www.megablues.com/conn.htm
Features local band links, photos, area venues and more!

Connecticut Bluegrass Music Association
PO Box 2042, Salem, CT 06420
PH: 860-859-2696
ctbma@yahoo.com
www.ctbluegrass.org
Preserves Bluegrass music in Connecticut and the surrounding area.

Connecticut Blues Society
PO Box 651, Higganum, CT 06441
www.ctblues.org
Promoting a sense of community through our newsletters and special events.

Connecticut Classical Guitar Society
PO Box 1528, Hartford, CT 06144-1528
PH: 860-249-7041
info@ccgs.org
www.ccgs.org
Serving Classical guitarists by providing a forum for listening, learning, performing and teaching.

Connecticut Post
410 State St., Bridgeport, CT 06604
PH: 203-333-0161
www.connpost.com
Bridgeport daily paper. Covers local music.

Connecticut Songwriters Association
PO Box 511, Mystic, CT 06355
Bill Pere bill@billpere.com
www.ctsongs.com
Weekly newsletter full of helpful information, news, classified ads and upcoming events.

Connecticut Songwriting Academy
PO Box 511, Mystic, CT 06355
PH: 860-984-6508
info@ctsongwriting.com
www.ctsongwriting.com
We teach the art of success! You set your goals, we'll help you to reach them.

CT Punx
www.ctpunx.com
News, reviews, profiles and MP3s.

CT Ska Productions
33 Central Ave. Naintic, CT 06357
info@ctska.com
www.ctska.com
Working to supply CT with quality information on the state's Ska scene as well as to provide Ska bands with the opportunity to spread their music.

CTBEATS.COM
webmaster@ctbeats.com
www.ctbeats.com
Intended to be a tool for those in the Connecticut and Massachusetts music industry. Forums, gig listings etc.

CTFolk.com
www.ctfolk.com
Current info on the Connecticut Folk music scene.

CTLocal.com
c/o IndepenDisc, PO Box 183,
North Haven, CT 06473
info@ctlocal.com
www.ctlocal.com
Are you a Connecticut Artist? Want to include your CD on CTLocal.com? Then head over to our Artist Submission page to find out how.

CTMusic.com
Keith Wilkinson email@ctmusic.com
www.ctmusic.com
Connecticut's definitive music web resource.

CTMusicians.org
PH: 860-298-8689
Tomaca Govan info@ctmusicians.org
ctmusicians.org
Featuring musicians and bands from the greater Connecticut area.

entertainment.ctcentral.com
Weekend, New Haven Register, 40 Sargent Dr.
New Haven, CT 06511
FX: 203-865-7894
entertainment.ctcentral.com
CTCentral's hub for entertainment news. Phone or fax your shows. Do not send by e-mail!

Fairfield County Weekly
3 Quincy St., Norwalk, CT 06850
PH: 203-838-1825 FX: 203-838-1872
www.fairfieldweekly.com
Free weekly paper. CD and concert reviews, previews shows, interviews bands.

Hartford Advocate
100 Constitution Plaza, Hartford, CT 06103
PH: 860-548-9300 FX: 860-548-9335
www.hartfordadvocate.com
CD reviews. Local Bands and Happenings. Updated every Thursday.

Hartford Courant
285 Broad St., Hartford, CT 06115
www.ctnow.com
Accepts CD for review if playing in Connecticut. Previews shows and interviews bands.

Hartford Jazz Society
116 Cottage Grove Rd. Rm. 202,
Bloomfield, CT 06002-3200
PH: 860-242-6688 FX: 860-243-8871
hartjazzsocinc@aol.com
www.hartfordjazzsociety.com
Improves Jazz as America's gift to the music world and fosters an appreciation and love for Jazz.

Live Bands in Connecticut
24 Wilfred Rd. Manchester, CT 06040
clubct2@clubct.com
www.clubct.com/bands.htm
Is your Band performing in Connecticut? Submit your info!

New Haven Advocate
900 Chapel St. #1100, New Haven, CT 06510
PH: 203-789-0010 FX: 203-787-1418
jmamis@newhavenadvocate.com
www.newhavenadvocate.com
New Haven's weekly newspaper. Local bands and happenings, updated every Thursday.

openmikeonline.com
www.openmikeonline.com
Features pictures and news from CT open mics. Site includes a "featured artist".

Soundwaves
PO Box 710, Old Mystic, CT 06355
PH: 860-572-5738 FX: 860-572-5738
editor@swaves.com
www.swaves.com
Southern New England's entertainment guide. In-depth band & club info.

Delaware

302 Music
de_302music@yahoo.com
302music.brenewilson.com
Promoting original bands & artists in Newark, Delaware & surrounding areas.

Brandywine Friends of Old-Time Music
PO Box 3672, Greenville, DE 19807
PH: 302-475-3454 FX: 302-798-2088
bfotm@dca.net
www.brandywinefriends.org
Preserving and presenting traditional American music.

Delaware Friends of Folk
PO Box 1006, Dover, DE 19903-1006
PH: 302-465-0805
jan@flutecake.com
www.delfolk.org
Furthering the cause of Folk music and Folk musicians in our area.

DelawareOnline
PO Box 15505, Wilmington, DE 19850
PH: 302-324-2500
www.delawareonline.com/entertainment
Concerts, clubs and local nightlife around Delaware and Philadelphia.

Delaware Today
3301 Lancaster Ave. #5-C,
Wilmington, DE 19805
PH: 302-656-1809 FX: 302-656-5843
www.delawaretoday.com
List your upcoming events.

Diamond State Blues Society
PO Box 4098, Wilmington, DE 19807-0098
PH: 302-376-6298
mrbluz2@aol.com
www.diamondstateblues.com
Supporting local Blues artists as well as to bring national acts to the Diamond State.

freedelaware.com
PH: 302-421-9377 FX: 302-421-8365
info@freedelaware.com
freedelaware.com
Includes a message board, MP3 service area and search engine.

Key of DE
101 Leslie Dr. Dover, DE 19901
PH: 302-697-9034
info@keyofde.com
www.keyofde.com
Delaware's premiere source for entertainment information.

Newark Arts Alliance
100 Elkton Rd. Newark, DE 19711
PH: 302-266-7266
info@newarkartsalliance.org
www.newarkartsalliance.org
Community A&E calendar accepts events.

Project Unity
PO Box 129, Hockessin, DE 19707
xprojectunityx@hotmail.com
www.projectunity.cjb.net
We have a spot for local up and coming bands to play and gain exposure.

Florida

Alligator MP3
PO Box 14257, Gainesville, FL 32604-2257
PH: 352-376-4458 FX: 352-376-4467
www.alligator.org
Read about bands in Gainesville, listen to their music and find out where they're playing.

AM Marketing/AM Publications
PO Box 20044, St. Petersburg, FL 33742
PH: 727-577-5500
Al Martino AMPUBS@aol.com
www.ampubs.com
Entertainment magazine in Central Florida. Covers many Indie CDs.

Apalachee Blues Society
PO Box 7617, Tallahassee, FL 32314-7617
PH: 850-668-5863 FX: 850-201-2945
info@apalacheebluessociety.org
www.apalacheebluessociety.org
We are willing to support any and all Blues activities in our area whenever possible.

aquaunderground.com
aquaunderground2001@yahoo.com
www.aquaunderground.com
Experience some of Florida's finest artists, bands and DJ's. Get exposure and recognition. Post your MP3s!

Axis Magazine
116 S. Orange Ave. Orlando, FL 32801
PH: 407-839-0039
rwheeler@axismag.com
www.axismag.com
Orlando's A&E magazine.

Boca Raton News
5801 N. Congress Ave. Boca Raton, FL 33487
PH: 561-893-6400
www.bocanews.com
Posts a calendar of events.

Broward Folk Club
3256 NW 113th Ave. Sunrise, FL 33323
PH: 954-742-9236
Pete Larson plarson@lci-aerospace.com
www.browardfolkclub.com
Promotes Folk and Acoustic music.

Central Florida Future
3361 Rouse Rd. #200, Orlando, FL 32817
PH: 407-447-4555 FX: 407-447-4556
indie@ucfnews.com
www.ucffuture.com
University of Central Florida student paper.

City Link
PO Box 14426, Fort Lauderdale, FL 33302
PH: 954-356-4943
jcline@citylinkmagazine.com
www.citylinkmagazine.com
Your link to news, A&E in Broward & Palm Beach County.

Clear Da Corner Entertainment
Robin cdce225@yahoo.com
cdce.topcities.com
We are currently reaching out across the entire Orlando area to embrace our talented youth, remove them from the street corners, and help them to take that next step into the spotlight where they belong.

Coffee Stain
PO Box 50802, Sarasota, FL 34232
PH: 941-323-2545
joe@coffeestain.com
www.coffeestain.com
Band news, reviews, interviews, listings etc.

Country Grapevine
PO Box 380219, Murdock, FL 33938
PH: 941-625-8486 FX: 941-625-1172
Roxanne Moore roxanne@countrygrapevine.com
www.countrygrapevine.com
A grassroots newspaper concerning Country music, dance and fun.

First Street Live Records
412 N. 1st St., Jacksonville Beach, FL 32250
PH: 904-435-1640
Spade McQuade spade@firststreetlive.com
firststreetlive.com
A label looking for fresh talent North Florida.

Fla.vor Alliance
7809 N. Orleans Ave. Tampa, FL 33604
PH: 813-935-8887 FX: 813-935-0535
info@flavoralliance.com
www.flavoralliance.com
Supports local Christian Hip Hop music and artists.

Florida East Coast Classical Guitar Society
1710 Canterbury Dr.
Indialantic, FL 32903-4017
PH: 321-725-5181
dale31@earthlink.net
home.earthlink.net/~dale31
Sponsors concerts featuring promising young artists as well as acclaimed musicians.

Florida Freaks
nigma@floridafreaks.com
www.floridafreaks.com
Gothic/Industrial site. Submit your band info and we'll put it online for you.

Florida Harpers and Friends
PO Box 2256, Marco Island, FL 34146
florida@harper.org
www.florida.harper.org
An organizing force for Florida harpers and other instrumentalists.

Florida Spins
PH: 704-841-4904
info@spinsmusic.com
spins.us/florida
Promotes Florida Dance music, Electronic music, DJs, artists and community.

Florida State Fiddlers Association
PO Box 713, Micanopy, FL 32667
www.nettally.com/fiddler
Hold a yearly convention and fiddle contest.

Florida Stuff *Local Bands*
www.floridastuff.com/events
Weekly music & art listings and resource pages for local bands and musicians.

FloridaBackstage.com
PO Box 354361, Palm Coast, FL 32135-4361
PH: 386-446-8785
info@FloridaBackstage.com
www.floridabackstage.com
Resource for musicians, bands and artists to communicate, collaborate, discuss and showcase.

FloridaLocalMusic.Com
11348 Torchwood Ct. W. Palm Beach, FL 33414
PH: 561-346-0293
herman@floridalocalmusic.com
www.floridalocalmusic.com
Find information on the Florida local music scene.

Folio Weekly
9456 Philips Hwy. #11, Jacksonville, FL 32256
PH: 904-260-9770 FX: 904-260-9773
www.folioweekly.com
Jacksonville free weekly alternative paper with complete concert calendar.

Folk Music in Orlando
halsey@cffolk.com
cffolk.com
All about Folk music & related stuff in & around Orlando.

Fort Pierce Jazz Society
1165 Hwy. 1 #12, Fort Pierce, FL 34950
PH: 772-631-4548
CVivino@adelphia.net
www.jazzsociety.org
A cultural, educational and entertainment resource for Jazz.

Friends of Florida Folk
4411 Bee Ridge Rd. Sarasota, FL 34233
PH: 941-378-3553
news@foff.org
www.foff.org
Publicizes, sponsors and produces newsletters, film, records, festivals and other events.

Gainesville Band Family Tree
gbft@gainesvillebandfamilytree.com
www.gainesvillebandfamilytree.com
A list of every band that has ever been in Gainesville.

Gainesville Friends of Jazz and Blues
PO Box 12769, Gainesville, FL 32604-0769
PH: 352-379-0300
friendsofjazznetwork@gnvfriendsofjazz.org
www.gnvfriendsofjazz.org
Promotes and supports Jazz and Blues music in Gainesville and surrounding area.

Girlz Like Us
PH: 407-929-4348
girlzlikeusfl@aol.com
www.girlzlikeus.com
Produces and promotes events for lesbians throughout central Florida. Post your event.

Gulf Coast Bluegrass Music Association
5026 Willard Norris Rd. Milton, FL 32570
gcbma@cox.net
members.cox.net/gcbma
Bringing Bluegrass music to northwest Florida and southern Alabama.

Gulf Jazz Society
PO Box 1535, Panama City, FL 32402
PH: 850-235-1659
www.gulfjazzsociety.com
Sponsors Jazz clinics, awards music scholarships and stages Jazz festivals and concerts.

Heat Beat
3100 Boca Raton Blvd. #201,
Boca Raton, FL 33431
PH: 877-525-0052 FX: 561-826-0338
info@heatbeat.com
www.heatbeat.com
A South Florida guide to red-hot Jazz, Blues and Big Band music!

Hiphopelements
PH: 954-977-7886 FX: 775-249-0062
webmaster@hiphopelements.com
www.hiphopelements.com
Supports the Florida Hip Hop scene.

JaxBands
PO Box 14315, Jacksonville, FL 32238-1315
webmaster@JaxBands.com
www.jaxbands.com
Dedicated to supporting Jacksonville local bands!

Jazz Club of Sarasota
330 S. Pineapple Ave. #111, Sarasota, FL 34236
PH: 941-366-1552 FX: 941-366-1553
admin@jazzclubsarasota.com
www.jazzclubsarasota.com
Provides Jazz and community programs for Florida's West Coast.

JungleTV
info@jungletv.com
www.jungletv.com
TV program featuring the best in South Florida music.

localrocksite.com
localrock@cfl.rr.com
localrocksite.com
Local live music schedules, venues and band bios covering Brevard County.

METAL MASTERS
2780 E. Fowler Ave. #224, Tampa, FL 33612
info@metalmasters.net
www.metalmasters.net
A one hour video/interview show, showcases top names and up and coming new artists.

Movement Magazine
1650-302 Margaret St. PMB 132,
Jacksonville, FL 32204
movementmagazine@aol.com
www.movementmagazine.com
Underground music magazine. Interviews with local and world renowned musicians.

MusicPensacola.com
tiger@gulfbreeze.net
www.musicpensacola.com
Pensacola's weekly live entertainment guide. Local artists, concerts, festivals and services.

New Times Broward Palm Beach
PO Box 14128, Ft. Lauderdale, FL 33302-4128
PH: 954-233-1600 FX: 954-233-1521
www.newtimesbpb.com
Weekly paper with local music coverage. Reviews and previews bands playing the area.

North Florida Bluegrass Association
PO Box 2830, Orange Park, FL 32067-2830
PH: 904-284-8901
info@nfbluegrass.org
www.nfbluegrass.org
Promotes and preserves Bluegrass music.

Orlando Weekly
111 W. Jefferson St. #200, Orlando, FL 32801
PH: 407-377-0400 FX: 407-377-0420
feedback@orlandoweekly.com
www.orlandoweekly.com
Free weekly alternative paper. Covers local music scene, reviews new CD releases.

OrlandoCityBeat.com
feedback@orlandocitybeat.com
www.orlandocitybeat.com/citybeat/music
The definitive guide to the Orlando music scene.

OrlandoSwing.com
swing-info@orlandoswing.com
www.orlandoswing.com
Delivers the latest swing news and events.

Rag Magazine
8930 State Rd. 84 #322,
Ft. Lauderdale, FL 33324
PH: 954-234-2888 FX: 954-727-1797
info@ragmagazine.com
www.ragmagazine.com
South Florida's music magazine.

Realitysnap.com
5401 65th Ter. N Suite A,
Pinellas Park, FL 33781
PH: 727-520-7540
Ken Thomas Ken@realitysnap.com
www.realitysnap.com
A comprehensive Tampa Bay music resource.

Rivot Rag
www.myspace.com/rivotrag
Tampa Bay's ONLY Underground Metal magazine.

South Florida Blues Society
PO Box 772548, Coral Springs, FL 33077-2548
bluesbobby2@aol.com
www.soflablues.org
Promoting, teaching, and advancing the Blues through networking with fans and musicians.

Southeast Jambands
info@southeastjambands.com
www.southeastjambands.com
There was a clear need for a community of bands in the Southeast to work together and fight for each other. This is our attempt to unite the scene, and work as a team.

Space Coast Jazz Society
louflorida@msn.com
www.spacecoastjazzsociety.com
Promotes, preserves, and educates Jazz-music lovers and Jazz-music makers.

Suncoast Blues Society
PO Box 4232, Tampa, FL 33677
bands@suncoastblues.org
www.suncoastblues.org
Dedicated to upholding the traditions of the Blues.

Tampa Bay Entertainment Guide
PO Box 17674, Clearwater, FL 33762
webmster@oltb.com
tampabayentertainment.com
Promoting Tampa Bay's Entertainment industry.

TampaBayMusician.com
admin@tampabaymusician.com
www.tampabaymusician.com
Resources for Tampa Bay area musicians.

tampahiphop.com
kramtronix@tampahiphop.com
www.tampahiphop.com
Covering the local scene.

Veltrox Local
PO Box 816127, Hollywood, FL 33081
PH: 954-249-8233
info@veltrox.com
www.veltroxlocal.com
Post ads, events, gig dates. Links to music industry professionals.

Weekly Planet
1383 5th St., Sarasota, FL 34236
PH: 941-365-6776 FX: 941-365-6854
scott.harrell@weeklyplanet.com
www.weeklyplanet.com
Tampa free weekly alternative paper. Covers local scene and reviews Indie CD releases.

Miami

CityLink Online
PO Box 14426, Fort Lauderdale, FL 33302
PH: 954-356-4943
jcline@citylinkmagazine.com
www.citylinkonline.com
South Florida's alternative news magazine.

CLOSER Magazine
520 Clematis St. W. Palm Beach, FL 33401
submissions@closermagazine.com
www.closermagazine.com
Networks for you. Meet artists from Palm Beach to Miami.

GoPBI.com
2751 S. Dixie Hwy. West Palm Beach, FL 33405
PH: 561-820-3700 FX: 561-820-3722
gopbi@pbpost.com
www.gopbi.com/events/music
Music guide for the Palm Beaches and South Florida.

Miami New Times Online
PO Box 011591, Miami, FL 33101-1591
PH: 305-576-8000 FX: 305-571-7677
feedback@miaminewtimes.com
www.miaminewtimes.com
Online paper with local music section.

Slammie Productions
PO Box 5891, Lake Worth, FL 33461
PH: 954-532-4333
feedback@slammie.com
www.Slammie.com
An independent concert promoter presenting club shows in South Florida.

South Florida's Entertainment News & Views
hsalus@entnews.com
www.entnews.com
Miami's premiere A&E weekly.

South Florida Jams
13855 Langley Pl. Davie, FL 33325
PH: 954-424-8728 FX: 954-424-8902
ethanschwartz@southfloridajams.com
www.southfloridajams.com
Bringing the best live music to South Florida.

South Florida Sun-Sentinel
1800 N. Commerce Pkwy. Weston, FL 33326
PH: 954-385-7900
www.sun-sentinel.com
Entertainment section contains a local events calendar.

South Florida Zydeco Society
Amy Rodriguez soflozydeco@aol.com
www.soflozydeco.com
Educating and encouraging Zydeco music in South Florida.

TheHoneyComb.com
623 Selkirk St. W. Palm Beach, FL 33405
steven@thehoneycomb.com
thehoneycomb.com
This site is an "underground" resource module for the So-Fla area.

Georgia

Athens Folk Music and Dance Society
PO Box 346, Athens, GA 30603
PH: 706-208-0985
www.uga.edu/folkdance
Promotes Folk music by providing an opportunity to perform in the area.

Augusta Goth
www.angelfire.com/sc2/nocturn
Info on the Goth scene in Augusta, Georgia.

Chunklet Magazine
PO Box 2814, Athens, GA 30612-0814
PH: 404-627-8883 FX: 801-469-6869
www.chunklet.com
Chafing America's ass since 1992.

Connect Savannah
1800 E. Victory Dr. #7, Savannah, GA 31404
PH: 912-231-0250 FX: 912-231-9932
letters@connectsavannah.com
www.connectsavannah.com
Weekly news, A&E publication. Extensive coverage of local music.

Georgia Music Industry Association
3063 Clairmont Rd. NE, Atlanta, GA 30329
PH: 404-633-7772
www.gmia.org
Educates the songwriter and performer on all aspects of the music industry.

Georgia Spins
PH: 704-841-4904
info@spinsmusic.com
spins.us/georgia
Dedicated to Georgia Dance music, electronic music, DJ's and artists.

JPM Records
1126 Floyd Road, Columbus, GA 31907
PH: 706-562-1702
Melonie teea@sowega.net
jpmrecords.topcities.com
An independent record label and recording facility specializing in the sounds of the dirty South.

Lokal Loudness
1017 Broad St.,
Augusta, GA 30901
PH: 706-823-0779
John "Stoney" Cannon
info@lokalloudness.com
www.lokalloudness.cjb.net
Covering the Augusta music scene.

Metropolitan Spirit
PO Box 3809, Augusta, GA 30914-3809
PH: 706-738-1142 FX: 706-733-6663
spirit@metrospirit.com
www.metrospirit.com
Augusta's most popular newsweekly.

Nuçi's Space
396 Oconne St., Athens, GA 30601
PH: 706-227-1515 FX: 706-227-1524
space@nuci.org
www.nuci.org
A resource center for musicians located in Athens.

redandblack.com
540 Baxter St., Athens, GA 30605
PH: 706-433-3000 FX: 706-433-3033
webmaster@randb.com
www.redandblack.com
University of Georgia student publication.

Rock Athens
PH: 706-208-2328
www.onlineathens.com/rockathens
Get your music heard if you are an Athens musician/band.

SLABMusic.com
3340 Haverhill Rowe, Lawrenceville, GA 30044
Chris Horton info@slabmusic.com
www.slabmusic.com
No Games. No Politics. Just Music.

Southeast Performer
449½ Moreland Ave. #206 Atlanta, GA 30307
Mike Misiak sepeditorial@performermag.com
www.performermag.com
Want your CD reviewed? Do you have news on your band? Send your CDs and press releases.

South Eastern Bluegrass Association
PO Box 20286, Atlanta, GA 30325
PH: 770-961-5974
chairman@sebabluegrass.org
www.sebabluegrass.org
Promotes Bluegrass activities through a newsletter.

Technique
353 Ferst Dr. Atlanta, GA 30332-0290
entertainment@technique.gatech.edu
cyberbuzz.gatech.edu/nique
Georgia Tech's student newspaper.

Whatz Happenin' TV
1529 Spring Rd. #E, Smyrna, GA 30080
PH: 770-437-0002 FX: 770-319-6694
Rodney Lundy sales@whtv1.com
www.whtv1.com
TV program on Broadcast Television that has videos and interviews.

Atlanta

Art Rock in Atlanta
www.gnosisarts.org/aria
News, references and resources for the Atlanta Art Rock community.

Atlanta Blues Society
PO Box 352, 931 Monroe Dr. #102,
Atlanta, GA 30308
PH: 404-237-9595
absmail@mindspring.com
www.atlantablues.org
Keeping the Blues alive.

SoundsAtlanta
Studio & Location Recording - Mastering
(404) 329-9438
Email: SoundsAtlanta@aol.com
www.SoundsAtlanta.com

"Power Up Your Music©!!"

Atlanta Journal
PH: 404-522-4141
www.accessatlanta.com
Arts and entertainment online resource.

Atlanta Magazine
260 Peachtree St. #300, Atlanta, GA 30303
PH: 404-527-5500 FX: 404-527-5575
www.atlantamagazine.com
List your upcoming events online.

Atlanta Music Guide
878 Peachtree St. NE #504, Atlanta, GA 30309
PH: 404-892-1533 FX: 404-254-2749
info@atlantamusicguide.com
www.atlantamusicguide.com
Atlanta bands, news, concerts, reviews, venues and radio stations.

AtlantaJamz.com
4514 Chamblee Dunwoody Rd. #279,
Atlanta, GA 30338
PH: 678-476-3726
atlantajamz.com
We provide more than just an "online store" for your music. We also offer full-service promotion and marketing so you can concentrate more on your craft of making great music.

AtlantaJazz Discussion Group
groups.yahoo.com/group/AtlantaJazz
Supports and encourages the proliferation of Jazz music.

AtlantaLocalMusic.com
326 Nelson St. Loft 509, Atlanta, GA 30313
PH: 404.428.8045
info@atlantalocalmusic.com
www.atlantalocalmusic.com
Search engine/website that keeps you in tune with the Atlanta local music scene.

atlantashows.com
shows@atlantashows.com
www.atlantashows.com
Information on how to get recognition for your band.

atlantashows.org
darian@atlantashows.org
www.atlantashows.org
Listing of Metro Atlanta and surrounding area shows.

Creative Loafing Atlanta
750 Willoughby Way, Atlanta, GA 30312
PH: 404-688-5623 FX: 404-614-3599
Heather Kuldell
heather.kuldell@creativeloafing.com
www.atlanta.creativeloafing.com
Free weekly alternative paper. Covers local music scene and reviews CDs.

DryerBuzz
PH: 770-912-2217 FX: 877-576-1895
support@dryerbuzz.com
www.dryerbuzz.com
Atlanta's Urban entertainment magazine.

Jamgrrl.com
gen@jamgrrl.com
www.jamgrrl.com
Supporting Atlanta's Jam scene.

Metro Atlanta Country Music Club
www.macmc.net
Promotes Country, Bluegrass and Southern Gospel music in the Atlanta area.

RockSocial.com
seanrox@rocksocial.com
www.rocksocial.com
Atlanta's Rock Social Club. Plan and co-promote prime acts and venues.

Sounds Atlanta
PO Box 49266, Atlanta, GA 30359
PH: 404-329-9438 FX: 404-325-8401
Bill Tullis SoundsAtlanta@aol.com
soundsatlanta.com
Studio & Remote Recording - Mastering.

Stage 96
c/o 96 Rock, 1819 Peachtree Rd. Ste. 700,
Atlanta, GA 30309
nick@96rock.com
www.96rock.com/stage96
Sponsored by 96 Rock, dedicated to bringing you the finest in local music.

Hawaii

808shows.com
PO Box 11871, Honolulu, HI 96828
Jason Miller hwnexp@aol.com
www.808shows.com
Bands can list their upcoming shows on this site.

Aloha Joe
alohajoe@alohajoe.com
www.alohajoe.com
Will review any music created on the Island.

BuyHawaiianMusic.com
1145 Kilauea, Hilo, HI 96720
PH: 888-652-2212 FX: 808-935-7761
info@buyhawaiianmusic.com
www.buyhawaiianmusic.com
All your favorite Hawaiian CDs and new releases.

Hawaiian Express Records
Jason Miller hwnexp@aol.com
www.HwnExp.com
Rock, Punk, Ska & more, from the islands of Hawaii.

Hawaiian Music Concerts & Workshops
www.mele.com/ConcertCalendar.cgi
Post your music concerts, workshops, concerts, calendars etc.

Hawaiian Steel Guitar Association
45-600 Kamehameha Hwy. Kaneohe, HI 96744
PH: 808-235-4742
hsga@lava.net
www.hsga.org
Promotes traditional Hawaiian music.

HawaiiEventsOnline.com
4380 Lawehana St., Bay C, Honolulu, HI 96818
FX: 808-421-1448
admin@hawaiieventsonline.com
www.hawaiieventsonline.com
Includes listings of live shows going on throughout Hawaii.

Honolulu Advertiser *TGIF*
PO Box 3110, Honolulu, HI 96802
PH: 808-525–8056 FX: 808-525–8037
tgif@honoluluadvertiser.com
www.honoluluadvertiser.com/tgif
Weekly arts section. Covers local music and events.

Honolulu Weekly
1200 College Walk #214, Honolulu, HI 96817
PH: 808-528-1475 FX: 808-528-3144
calendar@honoluluweekly.com
www.honoluluweekly.com
Honolulu's A&E weekly.

Maui Time Weekly
658 Front St. #126A-7278, Lahaina, HI 96761
PH: 808-661-3786 FX: 808-661-0446
www.mauitime.com
Maui weekly A&E paper.

mele.com
PO Box 223399, Princeville, HI 96722
auntie@mele.com
www.mele.com
The Internet's largest in-stock catalog of Hawaiian music CD titles.

NahenaheNet
Keola Donaghy keola@nahenahe.net
www.nahenahe.net
Breaking news on new releases, gigs and concerts.

Idaho

The Arbiter
1910 University Dr. Boise, ID 83725
PH: 208-345-8204 FX: 208-426-3198
www.arbiteronline.com
Boise State University's student newspaper.

Argonaut
UI Argonaut, 301 Student Union,
Moscow, ID 83844
PH: 208-885-8924 FX: 208-885-2222
www.argonaut.uidaho.edu
University of Idaho's student paper.

Boise Area WOMEN Musicians!
PO Box 768, Boise, ID 83701
yffn@yffn.org
www.yffn.org/admin/women
Send in your calendar or booking info, phone and other contact info.

Boise Blues Society
PO Box 2756, Boise, ID 83701
neb@fiberpipe.net
www.boiseblues.org
Promoting the Blues as an American art form.

Idaho Bluegrass Association
PO Box 477, Star, ID 83669
DobroBob@att.net
www.smithfowler.org/bluegrass/IdahoBGindex.htm
Promoting Bluegrass music in Idaho.

Zidaho
5407 Fairview Ave. Boise, ID 83706
PH: 208-321-5720
kedmunds@ktvb.com
www.ktvb.com/zidaho
Everything in Idaho from A to Z. Add your event listing.

Illinois

Blues Blowtorch Society
PO Box 1092, Bloomington, IL 62702-1092
PH: 309-662-2780
www.bluesblowtorch.com/society
Promotes local artists as well as regional and national talents.

Buzz
57 E. Green St., Champaign, IL 61820
buzz@dailyillini.com
illinimedia.com/buzz
Weekly entertainment magazine. Music reviews, calendar of events and feature stories.

Central Illinois Jazz Society
5427 N. James Rd. Peoria, IL 61615
PH: 309-692-5330
jazz@flink.com
www.midil.com/cijs.html
Provides opportunities for Jazz artists to play.

findusat309.com
carlathornquist@hotmail.com
findusat309.com
Exposes local residents to the great Quad City music scene.

Fox Valley Blues Society
PO Box 797, Oswego, IL 60543
www.foxvalleyblues.org
Promotes the Blues through festivals, CD reviews etc.

Illinois Times
PO Box 5256, Springfield, IL 62705
PH: 217-753-2226 FX: 217-753-2281
editor@illinoistimes.com
www.illinoistimes.com
Springfield's A&E weekly.

Northern Illinois Bluegrass Association
PO Box 653, Sheridan, IL 60551
webmaster@nibaweb.org
www.nibaweb.org
Promotes Bluegrass music by sponsoring events.

Peoria Shows
peoriashows@hotmail.com
www.angelfire.com/il2/PeoriaShows
Everything you need to know about the Peoria music scene.

River City Blues Society
PO Box 463, Peoria, IL 61651
www.rivercityblues.com
Submit news items, CD reviews and articles for the newsletter.

Southern Illinois Music E-Zine
Tad VanDyke ld_manager45@hotmail.com
www.sime-zine.com
Submit your gig and information online.

Chicago

American Gothic Productions
PMB 258, 2506 N. Clark St., Chicago, IL 60614
PH: 773-278-4684
scaryladysarah@aol.com
www.americangothicprod.com
Send your recordings for review.

AOL City Guide Chicago *Music*
home.digitalcity.com/chicago
Weekly feature articles plus weekend entertainment highlights.

Association for the Advancement of Creative Musicians
410 S. Michigan Ave. #943, Chicago, IL 60680
PH: 312-922-1900 FX: 312-922-1900
greatblackmusic@aacmchicago.org
aacmchicago.org
A collective of musicians and composers dedicated to nurturing, performing, and recording serious, original music.

Barbershop Hip Hop
c/o Kevin Slimko, 3452 W. Irving Park Rd. Chicago, IL 60618
slimthebarber@barbershophiphop.com
barbershophiphop.com
TV program showcasing the finest talent in Chicago's underground Hip Hop scene. Send your video to the above address (check our website for formats). Artists hoping to be on the show while in Chicago, e-mail mental@barbershophiphop.com

Bluegrass Chatterbox Discussion Group
launch.groups.yahoo.com/group/bgrass-chatbox-illinois
Join for info on bands, musicians, festivals, jam sessions, concerts, and more.

Cafe Ballistico
DArren Coltman rdecline@yahoo.com
cafeballistico.com
A unique co-operative of musicians, artists and fans of music living in and around the Chicago area.

Centerstage Chicago
3540 N. Southport Ave. #280, Chicago, IL 60657
PH: 847-784-0095 FX: 773-442-0190
centerstage.net
Find and post gigs, announce auditions, buy & sell gear!

chi-improv Discussion Group
launch.groups.yahoo.com/group/chi-improv
Discussion about the Chicago creative and Improvised music scene.

Chicago Cajun Connection
PH: 708-361-2321
cajunconnx@earthlink.net
home.earthlink.net/~cterra440
Lists local events featuring traditional Cajun and Zydeco music.

Chicago Classical Guitar Society
PO Box 4485, Skokie, IL 60076
PH: 847-475-7877
chicagocgs@bizland.com
www.chicagoclassicalguitarsociety.org
Sponsors recitals, master classes, evaluated recitals and lectures.

Chicago Flame
222 S. Morgan #3E, Chicago, IL 60607
PH: 312-421-0480 FX: 312-421-0491
chicagoflame@chicagoflame.com
www.chicagoflame.com
Independent student newspaper of the U. Illinois.

Chicago Fusion
www.chicagofusion.com
Promotes your venue or special event.

Chicago Harmony and Truth
PO Box 578456, Chicago, IL 60657
www.chatmusic.com
Creates a more hospitable music business environment.

Chicago Jazz Magazine
PO Box 737, Park Ridge, IL 60068
PH: 847-322-3534
reviews@ChicagoJazz.com
www.chicagojazzmagazine.com
News, reviews, shows etc.

Chicago Magazine
500 N. Dearborn, #1200, Chicago, IL 60610-4901
letters@chicagomag.com
www.chicagomag.com
Covers local music scene. News, reviews.

Chicago Music Guide
chicago.citysearch.com
Extensive coverage of local music. Post your shows and events.

Chicago Open Mics
2248 W. Farwell, #2, Chicago, IL 60645
PH: 773-820-2970
info@risingstarmusic.com
www.risingstarmusic.com/ommonday.html
List of places to play in the Chicago area. Reviews are posted of each venue.

Chicago Punk & Ska
tony@coppoletta.net
www.cpsw.net
Live shows listings, images, bands, message board and articles.

Chicago Reader
11 E. Illinois St., Chicago, IL 60611
PH: 312-828-0350
musiclistings@chicagoreader.com
www.chicagoreader.com
Free weekly paper. Chicago's essential music guide.

Chicago-Scene.com
1151 N. State St. #297, Chicago, IL 60610
PH: 312-587-3474 FX: 312-587-7397
www.chicago-scene.com
Chicago's leading online entertainment guide.

Chicago Songwriter's Collective
559 Foxford Rd. Bartlett, IL 60103
Jill Dawson info@chicagosongwriters.com
chicagosongwriters.com
Our purpose is to work for the community of artists by networking, showcases and educational seminars.

Chicago Stoner Rock
1573 N. Milwaukee Ave. PMB 488, Chicago, IL 60622
PH: 773-276-4474
www.chicagostonerrock.com
Reviews heavy, stoner, drug Metal, and Space Rock CDs and live shows.

ChicagoAfterhours.com
PH: 312-286-3832 FX: 413-691-4783
info@chicagoafterhours.com
www.chicagoafterhours.com
Provides information on Chicago's brightest night clubs, DJ's and artists.

ChicagoGigs.com
PO Box 2419, Palatine, IL 60078-2419
contact@chicagogigs.com
www.Chicagogigs.com
Covers both local and national touring acts.

ChicagoGroove.com
2318 S. Oakley, #3, Chicago, IL 60608
ramiros@chicagogroove.com
www.chicagogroove.com
Pics and audio sets from local DJs.

ChicagoJazz.com
Contact@ChicagoJazz.com
www.chicagojazz.com
Online version of Chicago Jazz Magazine.

ChicagoRockabilly.com
amy@rockabilly.net
www.rockabilly.net/chicago
Find out what's rockin' in Chicago. Post your gig.

ChiCds.com
980 N. Michigan Ave. One Magnificent Mile,
#1400, Chicago, IL 60611
PH: 312-214-3521 FX: 775-264-7137
chiradio@hotmail.com
www.chicds.com
Rap and Soul online CD store.

Columbia Chronicle
623 S. Wabash Ave. #205, Chicago, IL 60605
PH: 312-344-7253
www.ccchronicle.com
Student publication of Columbia College. Has an A&E section.

Daisy Glaze Entertainment
1658 N. Milwaukee Ave. #267, Chicago, IL 60647
info@daisyglaze.com
www.daisyglaze.com
Artist management and consulting for bands in the Chicago area.

Early MusiChicago
1133 S. Grove Ave. Oak Park, IL 60304-1908
Robert Osterlund,
webmaster@earlymusichicago.org
www.earlymusichicago.org
We are trying to help lower the barriers to participation in and enjoyment of this captivating but strangely under-appreciated art form that we call Early Music.

Entertainment Law Chicago
PO Box 558023, Chicago, IL 60655
PH: 773-882-4912 FX: 708-206-1663
info@entertainmentlawchicago.com
www.entertainmentlawchicago.com
Entertainment, music, and intellectual property legal issues.

Gothic Chicago
davidb@gothicchicago.com
www.gothicchicago.com
We want to be your resource to events in the Chicago Gothic Community.

Illinois Entertainer
124 W. Polk St., Chicago, IL 60605
PH: 312-922-9333 FX: 312-922-9369
www.illinoisentertainer.com
Chicago A&E weekly. Loads of local music coverage!

Intergrüv Networks
3247 S. Maple, Berwyn, IL 60402
info@intergruv.net
www.intergruv.net
Builds events to expand Chicago's entertainment scene.

Jazz Institute of Chicago
410 S. Michigan Ave. Chicago, IL 60605
PH: 312-427-1676 FX: 312-427-1684
www.JazzInstituteOfChicago.org
Preserving and perpetuating Jazz.

JstreetZine.com
PO Box 126, Waukegan, IL 60079
PH: 847-589-1396
jesse@jstreetzine.com
www.jstreetzine.com
Focuses on unsigned, talented, hardworking artists.

Live Music Chicago
webmaster@livemusicchicago.com
www.livemusicchicago.com
The premier source for Chicago live music entertainment and DJs for all occasions.

Local 101's CD Reviews
230 Merchandise Mart, Chicago, IL 60654
PH: 312-527-8348 FX: 312-527-8348
www.q101.com/local101
We review CDs of Chicago artists.

Mathbat Records
www.mathbat.com
We have been recording and releasing our warped brand of Dark and Funky music out of Chicago since 1997.

Newcity Chicago
770 N. Halsted, #306, Chicago, IL 60622
David Chamberlain chamberlain@newcity.com
www.newcitychicago.com
Chicago's free A&E publication.

Revolutionslive.com
2521 N. Artesian Ave. #2, Chicago, IL 60647
Sean seanorr@revolutionslive.com
www.revolutionslive.com
An online provider of tour dates, show reviews, promotions, live music, venue info, and more for the Chicago area.

Rising Star Music
2248 W. Farwell #2, Chicago, IL 60645
PH: 773-820-2970
risingstarmusic@ameritech.net
www.risingstarmusic.com
Presents recording artists to an international audience.

Silver Wrapper Productions
5352 N. Lockwood Ave. Chicago, IL 60630
bands@silverwrapper.com
www.silverwrapper.com
Concerts, Jazz, Funk, Electronic, Creole and Soul music.

Start A Revolution
1635 W. Julian, Chicago, IL 60622
Michael Bambacht editor@startarevolution.com
www.startarevolution.com
Focuses on the Chicago Jam Band and Prog Rock scene.

Suburban NiteLife
PO Box 428, W. Chicago, IL 60186
PH: 800-339-2000 FX: 630-653-2123
Bart Loiacono bart@nitelife.org
www.nitelife.org
Chicago entertainment magazine.

Triple Dot MAS
2549 Waukegan Rd. # 178,
Bannockburn, IL 60015-1510
PH: 773-406-3434
Michael Berg berg@3dmas.com
www.3dmas.com
A movement towards unity and harmony amongst creative people through our multimedia events.

UR Chicago Magazine
655 W. Irving Park Rd. #209, Chicago, IL 60613
PH: 773-529-5100 FX: 773-529-5101
www.urchicago.com
New releases, local shows and more.

VIP Records
Dallas dallas@viprecordsinc.com
viprecordsinc.com
Our mission is to propel the Chicago music scene into the forefront of the industry.

Windy City Media Group
1940 W. Irving Park Rd. Chicago, IL 60657
editor@windycitymediagroup.com
www.wctimes.com
The voice of Chicago's gay, lesbian, bisexual and transgendered community. Has a music section. Post your upcoming shows.

Windyhop
www.windyhop.org
Covering the Chicago swing scene.

Women With Guitars
contact@womenwithguitars.com
www.womenwithguitars.com
Are you a woman? Are you a singer-songwriter? Do you play guitar? Do you feel ready to share your talents with Chicagoland audiences? You're invited to submit your promotional materials to be considered a Women With Guitars showcase slot.

Indiana

6 String Design
sixstring@6string.net
www.6string.net
Northwest Indiana's #1 musician's resource.

BandNut
www.bandnut.com
Local Band connection for the Evansville Tri-State area local bands.

CarpeMidwest
grunt@carpemidwest.com
www.carpemidwest.com
Regional Darkwave, EBM, World, Ambient & Experimental events.

Central Indiana Folk Music & Mountain Dulcimer Society
1322 Cool Creek Dr. Carmel, IN 46033-2315
PH: 317-844-4101
muzikhaus@iquest.net
www.indianafolkmusic.org
Promoting and preserving American Folk music and Acoustic instruments.

Crush Entertainment
booking@crushentertainment.com
www.crushentertainment.com
Provides promotional needs for your product, service, or event. We are your promotional hand in the Indianapolis Metropolitan area!

Empress Alyda Productions
PO Box 421302, Indianapolis, IN 46242
Alyda Stoica empress@alyda.com
www.alyda.com
Books Goth, Industrial, Alternative Pop and Rock and Worldbeat bands in Indianapolis.

EvansvilleScene.com
Adam Ferguson webmaster@evansvillescene.com
www.evansvillescene.com
Promoting local talent in the area.

Flatfun Bloomington Music Calendar
bloomingmusic.net
Bands can submit sites, MP3s, photos and other info.

FortWayneMusic.com
bands@fortwaynemusic.com
www.fortwaynemusic.com
Exposing as many people as possible to the excellent Fort Wayne music scene.

Indiana SKAlendar
thomska@yahoo.com
php.indiana.edu/~tgatkins/ska.html
Upcoming Ska shows in the Indiana area.

Indianapolis Musicians
325 N. Delaware St., Indianapolis, IN 46204
PH: 317-636-3595 FX: 317-636-3596
indymusicians@sbcglobal.net
www.indymusicians.com
Promoting the music profession in Indiana.

IndianapolisMusic.net
5260 Hinesley Ave. Indianapolis, IN 46208
matt@indianapolismusic.net
indianapolismusic.net
Sparking interest in local music. Features Indy MP3 project.

IndianaRap.com
604 W. Taylor St. #201, Kokomo, IN 46901
Alex Clark reviews@indianarap.com
www.IndianaRap.com
If you would like your music reviewed, send 2 CDs to the above address.

indygoth Discussion Group
groups.yahoo.com/group/indygoth
Discussion for Goths living in/around Indianapolis.

Midwest BEAT Magazine
2613 41st St., Highland, IN 46322
PH: 219-972-9131
tom@midwestbeat.com
www.midwestbeat.com
A&E weekly publication throughout the Midwest.

MidWestBands.com
PO Box 558, Owensville, IN 47665
PH: 877-731-1081 FX: 509-351-9927
mwbcontact@midwestbands.com
www.midwestbands.com
Provides a wealth of resources to aid bands and individuals.

Naptown Reggae
the_lioness@naptownreggae.com
www.naptownreggae.com
Covering the Indianapolis Reggae scene.

Northern Indiana Bluegrass Association
5034 Wapiti Ct. Fort Wayne, IN 46804-4946
PH: 260-432-4485
Jim Winger nibga@mixi.net
www.bluegrassusa.net
Info on Bluegrass and all Acoustic music in a 200 mile radius of Fort Wayne.

NUVO Newsweekly
3951 N. Meridian St., Indianapolis, IN 46208
PH: 317-254-2400 FX: 317-254-2405
www.nuvo.net
Indianapolis free weekly alternative paper. Covers local music scene!

NWiLive.com
PO Box #551, Schererville, IN 46375
admin@nwilive.com
www.nwilive.com
Northwest Indiana's premium source for local music info.

The Observer
PO Box Q, Notre Dame, IN 46556
PH: 574-631-7471 FX: 574-631-6927
www.ndsmcobserver.com
The student-run newspaper serving Notre Dame and Saint Marys.

One Kind Radio
PO Box 127, Hobart, IN 46342
jbowles@onekindradio.com
www.onekindradio.com
Promoting local and independent music from NW Indiana, Chicago and beyond.

punkrocknight.com
PH: 317-920-0853
greg@punkrocknight.com
www.punkrocknight.com
Resource with reviews, forums, audio, video etc. covering the Indianapolis Punk scene.

TheMuncieScene.com
PH: 765-215-5440
Phantom phantom@TheMuncieScene.com
themunciescene.com
Assisting local artists in the creation and distribution of their music.

Whatzup Magazine
2305 E. Esterline Rd. Columbia City, IN 46725
PH: 260-691-3048
whatzup@whatzup.com
www.whatzup.com
Indianapolis based entertainment magazine. Show listings and reviews of local bands.

Iowa

515 Crew/ Iowa Hardcore
4710 Steinbeck #103, Ames, IA 50014
Greg Rice greg@ttecore.com
www.515crew.org
Covering the Iowa Hardcore scene. News, shows, band listings etc.

Cedar Rapids Gazette
PO Box 511, Cedar Rapids, IA 52406
319-398-8333
www.gazetteonline.com
Up to date news, sports and entertainment coverage of Eastern Iowa.

Central Iowa Blues Society
PO Box 13016, Des Moines, IA 50310
PH: 515-830-4213
www.cibs.org
Keeping the Blues alive through appreciation and education.

Des Moines Register
PO Box 957, Des Moines, IA 50304-0957
PH: 515-284-8000
www.desmoinesregister.com
Daily A&E paper. Covers new music and Indie bands.

Iowa HomeGrown Music
PO Box 23265, Nashville, TN 37202
PH: 615-244-0570 FX: 615-242-2472
bronson@iowahomegrown.com
www.iowahomegrown.com
Represents songwriters and artists with a variety of musical styles.

Linn County Blues Society
PO Box 2672, Cedar Rapids, IA 52406-2672
PH: 319-399-5105
www.lcbs.org
Preserving Blues music in Eastern Iowa.

Lizard Creek Blues Society
2161 179th St., Fort Dodge, IA 50501
PH: 515-573-5964
bobwood@frontiernet.net
www.lizardcreekblues.org
Promoting the local Blues scene.

Mississippi Valley Blues Society
102 S. Harrison St. #300,
Davenport, IA 52801-1811
PH: 563-322-5837 FX: 563-322-5832
mvbs@revealed.net
www.mvbs.org
Educating the general public about the Blues through performances.

Mushroom Cloud Records
3006 46th St., Des Moines, IA 50310-3530
PH: 515-278-4485
Rob mushroomcloudrecords@yahoo.com
www.mushroomcloudrecords.com
Providing an outlet for artists to have their music heard and seen.

River Cities' Reader
532 W. 3rd St., Davenport, IA 52801
PH: 563-324-0049 FX: 563-323-3101
info@rcreader.com
www.rcreader.com
Davenport news & entertainment weekly.

Kansas

F5
216 S. Market, Wichita, KS 67202
PH: 316-219-3440 FX: 316-219-0250
editorial@f5wichita.com
www.f5wichita.com
Wichita's alternative news magazine.

Kansas Christian Artists
Deb Rempel kca@kansaschristianartists.com
kansaschristianartists.com
We are a hub for Christian musicians and songwriters to network with others in the Wichita area.

Kansas Prairie Pickers Association
11408 Hwy. 75, Hoyt, KS 66440
John Payne fidlnjohn@yahoo.com
www.accesskansas.org/kppa
Preserving Bluegrass and Old-Time Acoustic music.

Lawrence.com
Phil pcauthon@ljworld.com
www.lawrence.com
Good coverage of local music scene.

LawrenceHipHop.com
PO Box 336, Lawrence, KS 66044
lawrencehiphop@hotmail.com
www.lawrencehiphop.com
Uniting Hip Hop artists in the KC area.

Lawrencerock.com
www.lawrencerock.com
Promotes local music and other cultural events.

Manhattan Mercury
PO Box 787, Manhattan, KS 66505
PH: 785-776-8808 FX: 785-776-8807
net@themercury.com
www.themercury.com
Contact us if you would like your band showcased.

Pipeline Productions
c/o The Bottleneck, 737 New Hampshire,
Lawrence, KS 66044
Julie music@pipelineproductions.com
www.pipelineproductions.com
Presents concerts in Lawrence & Kansas City. Visit our site for submission details.

RockKansas.com
616 SE Jefferson, Topeka, KS 66607
PH: 800-777-7171
JJ Duncan jj.duncan@cjonline.com
www.RockKansas.com
Band directory, calendar, rk radio, news, interviews and reviews

Kentucky

Amplifier
PO Box 27, Dunbar, KY 42219
PH/FX: 270-526-2987
Don Thomason don@amplifier.ky.net
amplifier.ky.net
Bowling Green monthly music & entertainment magazine.

Bluegrass Anonymous
PO Box 21281, Louisville, KY 40221-0281
PH: 502-368-1831
www.bluegrass-anonymous.org
Promoting Bluegrass music in the Louisville area.

Kentuckiana Blues Society
PO Box 755, Louisville, KY 40201-0755
membership@kbsblues.org
kbsblues.org
Accepts and lists cds from local acts.

Leobeat.com
640 S. 4th St. #100, Louisville, KY 40402
leobeat@leoweekly.com
www.leobeat.com
Your complete guide to the city's musical goings-on.

Louisville Music Index
www.louisvillemusicindex.org
Listings for bands playing in the area.

Louisville Music Industry Alliance
Lesa Seibert lesa@lmiacentral.com
www.lmiacentral.com
Supporting and furthering of the Louisville original music scene.

Louisville Music News
3705 Fairway Ln. Louisville, KY 40207
PH: 502-893-9933 FX:502-721-7482
editor@louisvillemusic.com
www.louisvillemusic.com
Free monthly music paper. Covers regional music scene.

Louisville Scene
www.louisvillescene.com
Extensive music review section.

Louisiana

BRCentral
brcentral.com
Baton Rouge info site. Has a weekly entertainment guide.

Caffeine Music
1515 Poydras St. #1900, New Orleans, LA 70112
PH: 504-488-7435
caffeinemusic@yahoo.com
www.satchmo.com/caffeinemusic
An independent contemporary music publisher.

Cajun French Music Association
PO Box 92575, Lafayette, LA 70509-2575
president@cajunfrenchmusic.org
www.cajunfrenchmusic.org
Preserves and promotes traditional French Cajun music.

Cajunfun.com
412 Travis St., Lafayette, LA 70503
PH: 337-769-1466
info@cajunfun.com
www.cajunfun.com
Acadiana's premier entertainment resource.

Cox.net NewOrleans.com Music
9544 Fenway Ave. Baton Rouge, LA 70809
PH: 225-923-0860
neworleans.cox.net
Got a show? Let us know!

Gambit Weekly
response@gambitweekly.com
www.bestofneworleans.com
New Orleans' alternative weekly magazine.

girl gang productions
4523 Iberville St., New Orleans, LA 70119
Margaret Coble info@girlgangproductions.com
www.girlgangproductions.com
Promoting live music shows, drag king shows, dance parties, spoken word and other performances and events by, for and about women and GLBT performers.

Gumbo Pages
18111 Nordhoff St., Northridge, CA 91330-8312
www.gumbopages.com
Dedicated to the music and culture of New Orleans.

HisMusic.com
PH: 985/781-083
David Grant info@HisMusic.com
www.hismusic.com
Provides Christian concert listings for New Orleans.

Lafayette Local Entertainment
www.lafayettelocalentertainment.com
Created to cover and feature Lafayette area acts who are producing original material, and are presenting it live.

LiveNewOrleans.com
jason@liveneworleans.com
www.LiveNewOrleans.com
Dedicated to covering the New Orleans music scene with reviews and photographs.

Louisiana Blues Preservation Society
PO Box 80823, Lafayette, LA 70598-0823
BluesPreserve@yahoo.com
www.geocities.com/Bluespreserve
Preserving and supporting Blues music throughout.

Louisiana Folk Roots
118 W. Vermilion, Lafayette, LA 70501
PH: 337-234-8360 FX: 337-234-8361
info@lafolkroots.org
www.lafolkroots.org
Nurturing the unique Folk art scene in Louisiana.

Louisiana Jukebox
2120 Canal St., New Orleans, LA 70112
PH: 504-304-7345
goodemedia@kfbol.com
www.louisianajukebox.com
Live music television show. Post your CD release.

Louisiana Music Commission
3330 N. Causeway Blvd. #438, Meairie, LA 70002
PH: 504-838-5600 FX: 504-838-5280
www.louisianamusic.org
Promoting and developing the Louisiana music industry.

Louisiana Music Factory
210 Decatur St., New Orleans, LA 70130
PH: 504-586-1094
info@louisianamusicfactory.com
www.louisianamusicfactory.com
Resources for artists in Louisiana.

Louisiana Songwriters Association
PO Box 80425, Baton Rouge, LA 70898-0425
PH: 504-443-5390
info@lasongwriters.org
www.lasongwriters.org
Holds workshops to increase understanding of the music industry.

MojoNO.com
PH: 504-914-6860
staff@mojono.com
www.mojono.com
Free band listings and personal gig calendar.

Mothership Entertainment
219 S. Clark St., New Orleans, LA 70119
PH: 504-488-3865 FX: 504-488-1574
funk@mothershipentertainment.com
www.MotherShipEntertainment.com
Aids artists by building a strategy designed for success.

New Orleans Bands.com
Thaddeus Frick thaddeus@nolabands.com
www.neworleansbands.com
Providing a network to help New Orleans talent become successful.

New Orleans Bands.net
c/o 504 Productions, 4453 East Falk St.,
New Orleans, LA 70121
www.neworleansbands.net
Bringing a new dimension to the local music scene in the Big Easy.

New Orleans Blues Project
1112 9th St., New Orleans, LA 70115
PH: 504-895-0739 FX: 504-895-6070
contact@bluesproject.com
www.bluesproject.com
Promotes communication, dialogue and understanding of the Blues.

New Orleans Live
jdonley@nola.com
www.nolalive.com/music
News and reviews of local music.

NewOrleansOnline.com
www.neworleansonline.com/neworleans/music
Extensive coverage of local music.

NOLA Life
nolalife@yahoo.com
www.nolalife.com
Where New Orleans talent networks online!

Offbeat
4211 Frenchmen St. #200,
New Orleans, LA 70116-2506
PH: 504-944-4300 FX: 504-944-4306
offbeat@offbeat.com
www.offbeat.com
Louisiana's music and entertainment magazine.

Pershing Well's South Louisiana Music Site
150 Shady Arbors Cr. #17-D, Houma, LA 70360
PH: 985-209-2229
pershing@pershingwells.com
www.pershingwells.com
Provide free listings for Louisiana artists.

Satchmo.com
3726 Loyola Dr. #245, Kenner, LA 70065
PH: 504-469-5958 FX: 212-504-7918
editor@satchmo.com
www.satchmo.com
New Orleans & Louisiana music news, CD reviews, listings etc.

Sauteed Entertainment
Jody Taylor sauteed77@hotmail.com
sauteed.implode.com
Lists a show calendar for regional and national acts.

Shrevepunx
www.shrevepunx.com
Post pictures and info on your upcoming shows.

South Louisiana Bluegrass Association
PO Box 51672 Lafayette, LA 70505
PH: 337-280-9763
info@southlouisianabluegrass.org
www.southlouisianabluegrass.org
Promoting and preserving Bluegrass music.

Times of Acadiana
215 Garfield St., Lafayette, LA 70501
PH: 337-237-3560 FX: 337-233-7484
Arsenio Orteza arsenioort@aol.com
www.timesofacadiana.com
Lafayette's A&E weekly.

Where y'at Magazine
5500 Prytania St. #248, New Orleans, LA 70115
PH: 504-891-0144 FX: 504-891-0145
info@whereyatnola.com
www.whereyatnola.com
New Orleans' monthly entertainment magazine.

Maine

Bluegrass Music Association of Maine
PO Box 1010, Brunswick, ME 04011
bluegrass@bmam.org
www.bmam.org
Supports local Bluegrass musicians.

Down East
PO Box 679, Camden, ME 04843
PH: 207-594-9544 FX: 207-594-7215
editorial@downeast.com
www.downeast.com
Monthly magazine. Post your upcoming events.

Entertainment in Maine Today.com
390 Congress St., Portland, ME 04104
PH: 207-822-4060 FX: 207-879-1042
entertainment.mainetoday.com
Maine music resource including reviews and previews.

FACE
PO Box 336, Bar Harbor, ME 04609-0336
PH: 207-288-4500 FX: 207-288-0220
www.facemag.com
The entertainment magazine/calendar for Maine.

Maine Songwriters Association
Judd@tlmgi.com
www.mesongwriters.com
Supporting songwriters and their art.

MaineList.com
www.mainelist.com
Submit your Maine-based web site.

MaineMusic.Org
997 State St., Bangor, ME 04401
PH: 207-775-9056
www.mainemusic.org
Supporting artists of all genres throughout Maine.

Portland Maine Music
anton@portlandmainemusic.com
www.portlandmainemusic.com
Supports original music created in Maine.

Portland Phoenix
482 Congress St., Portland, ME 04101
PH: 207-773-8900 FX: 207-773-8905
submit@phx.com
www.portlandphoenix.com
Local band coverage including MP3s from locally based musicians.

Maryland

Baltimore Blues Society
PO Box 2915, Baltimore, MD 21229
PH: 410-744-2291
bob@mojoworkin.com
www.mojoworkin.com
Reviews CD releases by national, regional and local artists.

The Baltimore Buzz
staff@buzz-magazine.com
www.buzz-magazine.com
Accepts submissions for the genres of Rock and Metal music. Contact us for our mailing address.

Baltimore City Paper
812 Park Ave. Baltimore, MD 21201
PH: 410-523-2300 FX: 410-523-2222
Bret McCabe bmccabe@citypaper.com
www.citypaper.com
Baltimore's weekly news and entertainment paper. Covers local music.

Baltimore Classical Guitar Society
4607 Maple Dr. Baltimore, MD 21227
PH: 410-247-5320
president@bcgs.org
www.bcgs.org
Organizes concerts for local and national classic guitarists.

BaltimoreBands.com
www.baltimorebands.com
Classifieds, gigs, plus the ultimate list of Baltimore and Maryland's finest music makers.

Cajun/Zydeco in the Mid-Atlantic Region
Pat Yaffe patyaffe@yahoo.com
www.wherewegotozydeco.com
Cajun and Zydeco music and dance guide for the Baltimore-Washington area.

Frederick Blues Society
28 S. Court St., Frederick, MD 21701
PH: 301-698-5300
fredblues@frederickblues.org
www.frederickblues.org
Supporting the Blues in the Frederick area.

Maryland Music.com
www.marylandmusic.com
Listings of venues, bands, media etc.

Maryland Night Life.com
PH: 410-239-2817
www.marylandnightlife.com
Free online entertainment guide with local music section.

Maryland Spins
spins.us/maryland
Highlights Dance & Electronic music, DJ's and artists.

MarylandParty.com
409 Lee Dr. Baltimore, MD 21228
PH: 443-697-0210
www.mdparty.com
Guide to live music in Maryland and surrounding states.

Music Monthly
2807 Goodwood Rd. Baltimore, MD 21214
PH: 410-426-9000 FX: 410-426-4100
kcmusicmonthly@comcast.net
www.musicmonthly.com
Baltimore monthly music magazine. Register your band.

Potomac River Jazz Club
10005 Evergreen Ave. Columbia, MD 21046
PH: 410-997-0704
prjcweb@prjc.org
www.prjc.org
Encouraging and promoting traditional Jazz.

Rockbottom Promotions
Marcy marcy@rockbottomzine.com
www.rockbottomzine.com/RBProduct.html
I book Alternative bands into a club in Hagerstown, MD.

Street Legal Entertainment
PH: 410-467-7797
Mark "LB" Carey billboard@streetlegalent.com
www.streetlegalent.com
Indpendent Urban record label. We lead "The Middle East Revolution", the rise of Mid-Atlantic Hip Hop artists into national prominence.

Tri-State Bluegrass Association
PO Box 215, Brunswick, MD 21716
comments@tri-statebluegrass.com
www.tri-statebluegrass.com
Promotes interest in Bluegrass and Old-Time music.

Walther Productions
PO Box 116, Jefferson, MD 21755
FX: 301-834-3373
info@walther-productions.com
www.walther-productions.com
Hosts tons of awesome Jam band shows in the Baltimore & DC areas. While we always welcome promotional packages, this is a highly competitive market which makes it virtually impossible to feature every band who vies for a club show play.

Massachusetts

angeldustrial.com
bobby@angeldustrial.com
www.angeldustrial.com
News about the local New England Electro/Industrial/Noise scene.

Cambridge Society for Early Music
PO Box 380-336, Cambridge, MA 02238-0336
PH: 617-489-2060
info@csem.org
www.cscm.org
Enlightening, educating and promoting the rich musical culture of five centuries.

capecodmusic.com
www.capecodmusic.com
Extensive listing of events in the area. Post yours.

Concert and Venue Listings for New England
concertlistings@yahoo.com
www.geocities.com/concertlistings
Listings of concerts and hundreds of venues in MA, CT, NH, ME, RI and VT.

Country Dance and Song Society
132 Main St., PO Box 338,
Haydenville, MA 01039-0338
PH: 413-268-7426 FX: 413-268-7471
office@cdss.org
www.cdss.org
Celebrating English and Anglo-American Folk dance and music.

Folk Arts Center of New England
42 W. Foster St., Melrose, MA 02176
PH: 781-662-7475
fac@facone.org
www.facone.org
Promoting traditional Dance, music and related Folk arts..

Imagine News
185 Mt. Auburn St. #3, Cambridge, MA 02138
PH: 617-576-0773 FX: 617-864-4923
publisher@imaginenews.com
www.imaginenews.com
Your Source for media arts news in the Northeast.

in newsweekly
450 Harrison Ave. #414, Boston, MA 02118
PH: 617-426-8246 FX: 617-426-8264
arts@innewsweekly.com
www.innewsweekly.com
Companion publications to New England's gay and lesbian news & entertainment weekly.

Link2Rock
22 Bridge St., Wilbraham, MA 01095
PH: 413-543-2022
Kingkevinis@hotmail.com
www.link2rock.com
Focuses on the Western Mass Indie Rock scene.

Massachusetts Spins
spins.us/massachusetts
Dedicated to the Massachusetts Dance music community.

MassConcerts
MassMediaGirl@aol.com
www.massconcerts.com
Find information about music and entertainment events in the northeast United States.

Media Factory TV / Media Factory Radio Show
718 Enfield St. Space B, Enfield, CT 06082
PH: 860-741-8801
Peter Wesley Bastone earformusik02@aol.com
www.netshows.us
TV and Radio shows. Send us material that will promote you in a positive way. Musicans send us your videos and music CDs.

Music For Robin
535 Concord Ave. Lexington, MA 02421-8011
PH: 781-862-7837 FX: 425-650-9584
bhockett@music-for-robin.org
www.music-for-robin.org
Concerts, Folk & Celtic resources covering Mass.

NBROCK
www.nbrock.net
Lists bands, shows etc. in the New Bedford area.

NBVIP.org
4 Kimberly Way, Acushnet, MA 02743
Eric Marcelino booking@nbvip.org
www.nbvip.org
Brings you the hot shows and the hot dance parties in New Bedford area. We spotlight all the upcoming local events and hot spots. You can mail your music / press kit to be considered for an NBVIP show by sending it to the above address.

New England Country Music Club
dm1972a@cs.com
www.necmc.homestead.com
Promoting Country music and local talent!

New England Entertainment Digest
PO Box 88, Burlington, MA 01803
JulieAnn Charest jacneed@aol.com
www.jacneed.com
Covering all of New England and New York.

New England Jazz Alliance
200 Washington Ave. Winthrop, MA 02152
PH: 617-567-6364
info@nejazz.org
www.nejazz.org
Celebrating and perpetuating the tradition of Jazz in New England.

NeHipHop.com
www.nehiphop.com
Covering the New England Hip Hop scene.

NewEARS
newears@newears.org
www.newears.org
A community dedicated to sharing and promoting Progressive Rock in the New England area.

newenglandrock.com
www.newenglandrock.com
New England area live entertainment resource.

Northeast Performer / Midwest
285 Washington St., Somerville, MA 02143
nepeditorial@performermag.com
www.performermag.com
Want your CD reviewed? Send your CDs and press releases.

PACE Arts Magazine
41 Union St., Easthampton, MA 01027
PH: 413-527-3700
Sonia Fried Oppenheim pace@pioneerarts.org
pioneerarts.org
Supporting the arts in Massachusetts.

Skope Magazine
47 Mellen St., Framingham, MA 01702
www.skopemagazine.com
Taking local music global!

TRP/NME Wreckidz
9 Hutchins Ct. Gloucester, MA 01930
PH: 978-394-0751
Mr. Dilligence mrdilligence@aol.com
www.NMEwreckidz.com
Indie Record Label/grassroots distributor for Massachusetts (and beyond) rappers/R+B singers.

uglyfuzz
Ben Weller b@uglyfuzz.com
www.uglyfuzz.com
Underground music portal for Cape Cod and the rest of Massachusetts.

Valley Advocate
116 Pleasant St., Easthampton, MA 01027
PH: 413-529-2840 FX: 413-529-2844
kthurlow@valleyadvocate.com
www.valleyadvocate.com
Springfield free weekly alternative paper. Local bands and happenings section.

Worcester County Jazz Scene
PH: 508-238-7432
FHaigh3879@aol.com
www.donricklin.com/worcjazz
Everything you want to know about Jazz in Worcester County.

Worcester Magazine
PH: 508-755-8004 x258 FX: 508-775-8860
Chet Williamson chetw@worcestermag.com
www.worcestermag.com
Worchester's A&E weekly.

Wormtown
bgoslow@yahoo.com
www.wormtown.org
Info on the Worcester, MA scene. Free listings.

Boston

Boston Beats
PR Dept. 195 Tower St., Dedham, MA 02026
PH: 781-381-2856 FX: 206-237-2473
contact@boston-beats.com
boston-beats.com
Interviews, artist and venue listings, weekly events, streaming local music and more!

Boston Bluegrass Union
PO Box 650061, W. Newton, MA 02465-0061
PH: 617-782-2251
info@bbu.org
www.bbu.org
Promoting and supporting the wealth of regional bands.

Boston Blues Society
PO Box 51438, Boston, MA 02205
mcg101@hotmail.com
www.bostonblues.com
Preserving and promoting the Blues.

Boston Classical Guitar Society
alec.donna@verizon.net
www.bostonguitar.org
Bimonthly newsletter. Submit your info to get posted.

The Boston Hip-Hop Alliance
askdarcie@hotmail.com
bostonhha.tripod.com
A collective of people with a common goal to make the experience of Hip Hop artists, producers, promoters, etc. better in the city of Boston, and to increase our visibility and voice.

Boston Irish Reporter
150 Mt. Vernon St., Boston, MA 02125
PH: 617-436-1222 FX: 617-825-5516
pstevens@bostonirish.com
www.bostonirish.com
New England's monthly Irish American newspaper.

Boston Jazz Fest
Chris Allen centralarteryproject@yahoo.com
bostonjazzfest.com
Promoting Jazz in the Boston area.

Boston Phoenix
126 Brookline Ave. Boston, MA 02215
PH: 617-536-5390 FX: 617-536-1463
feedback@phx.com
www.bostonphoenix.com
Entertainment magazine covering the New England region.

Boston Society of Mechanics
submit@bsm.us
www.bsm.us
Contains every resource artists need.

BostonHipHopBoard.com
www.bostonhiphopboard.com
Post info about upcoming shows, lyrics etc.

BostonNoise.org
1200 Massachusetts Ave. #28W,
Cambridge, MA 02138
Karl Giesing submit@bostonnoise.org
bostonnoise.org
Submit your Noise act and MP3s to our site. It's best to contact us first.

BostonRap.com
www.bostonrap.com
Covering the Boston Rap scene. New releases, downloads, videos etc.

Folk Song Society of Greater Boston
PO Box 492, Somerville, MA 02143
PH: 617-623-1806
fssgb@fssgb.org
www.fssgb.org
Providing opportunities for everyone to make, enjoy and support this music.

GyrlsRock Boston
1238 Comm Ave. #36, Boston, MA 02134
Sara Hamilton webmaster@gyrlsrock.com
www.gyrlsrock.com
100% devoted to female musicians in Boston.

Improper Bostonian
142 Berkeley St., Boston, MA 02116
PH: 617-859-1400
music@improper.com
www.improper.com
Boston's A&E magazine.

The Noise
74 Jamaica St., Boston, MA 02130
PH: 617-524-4735
www.thenoise-boston.com
Free zine covering the local music scene.

Purerockfury.com
Deek deek@purerockfury.com
www.purerockfury.com
Covering the Hard Rock/Metal scene. Includes a local band spotlight.

SalsaBoston.com
salsaboston.com
Boston's premiere Latin music and dance website.

WBUR Online Arts
890 Commonwealth Ave. 3rd Fl. Boston, MA 02215
PH: 617-353-0909
Bill Marx bmarx@wbur.bu.edu
www.publicbroadcasting.net/wbur/arts.artsmain
Covers the local Boston Music scene.

Michigan

Ann Arbor Classical Guitar Society
www.society.arborguitar.org
Bringing performances of Classical guitar music to Michigan.

Ann Arbor Council for Traditional Music and Dance
info@aactmad.org
thedance.net/~aactmad
Dedicated to the promotion and preservation of Acoustic Folk, Traditional, and Ethnic music only.

The Ark
316 S. Main St., Ann Arbor, MI 48104
PH: 734-761-1818
www.theark.org
Presenting and encouraging Folk, Roots and Ethnic music.

Between the Lines
20793 Farmington #25, Farmington, MI 48336
PH: 888-615-7003
editor@pridesource.com
www.pridesource.com
Farmington's Gay & Lesbian news & entertainment weekly.

Capital Area Blues Society
PO Box 1004, Okemos, MI 48805-1004
PH: 517-349-0006
www.cabsblues.org
Reviews of new album releases every month.

Current Magazine
212 E. Huron St., Ann Arbor, MI 48104
FX: 734-668-0555
music@sgipub.com
ecurrent.com
Free monthly A&E magazine. Covers local music scene, news and reviews.

Flint Folk Music Society
PO Box 1000, Flint, MI 48501
jim@flintfolkmusic.org
www.flintfolkmusic.org
Promoting Folk music through performances and workshops.

Folk Alliance Region Midwest
PO Box 300322, Waterford, MI 48330
info@farmfolk.org
www.farmfolk.org
Promotes the growth of Folk music and dance.

From the Garage
Sarah imthesparker@yahoo.com
www.fromthegarage.com
This site lists Punk, Ska, emo, & Hardcore bands and shows from all over Michigan.

Grand River Folk Arts Society
2520 Russit Dr. NE. Grand Rapids, MI 49525
Pete grfasbooker@grfolkarts.org
www.grfolkarts.org
Contact to perform in West Michigan.

GRD's Local Music Page
50 Monroe NW Ste. 500, Grand Rapids, MI 49503
grdbrian@yahoo.com
www.wgrd.com/localmusic
If you are in a local band, submit your news.

Great Lakes Acoustic Music Association
PO Box 50781, Kalamazoo, MI 49005
www.geocities.com/glacoustic
Promoting Bluegrass and Acoustic music.

Hearts On Fire Records
PO Box 852, Marshall, MI 49068
PH: 800-381-1063
Bob Shell info@heartsonfirerecords.com
www.heartsonfirerecords.com
Kalamazoo, Michigan Rock!

JAM RAG
Box 20076, Ferndale, MI 48220
PH: 248-336-9243
jamrag@glis.net
jamrag.com
Promotes local artists and the local music economy.

Kalamazoo Valley Blues Association
PO Box 2413, Kalamazoo, MI 49003-2413
PH: 269-381-6514 FX: 269-381-3818
kvba@kvba.org
www.kvba.org
Preserving Blues music around Kalamazoo.

K'zoo Folklife Organization
PO Box 51421, Kalamazoo, MI 49005-1421
peggy91193@yahoo.com
www.geocities.com/Vienna/Studio/5893
Promotes multi-cultural, traditional and contemporary Folk music.

LocalMichiganMusic.com
www.localmichiganmusic.com
Submit your band info as well as an image file, an mp3 or video file.

Magazine of Country Music
PO Box 1412, Warren, MI 48090
PH: 586-755-0471
staff@magazineofcountrymusic.com
www.magazineofcountrymusic.com
Monthly publication. Features national and local Country music.

Michiana Listings
info@michianalistings.com
www.michianalistings.com
Find details on events, concerts and entertainment.

Michigan Artists
contactus@michiganartists.com
www.michiganartists.com
Supporting Michigan artists with postings of history, bios, pictures and more!

Michigan Bands dot Com
mitch@michiganbands.com
www.michiganbands.com
Submit news and press releases and add links to your band page.

MichiganMetal
webmaster@michiganmetal.com
www.michiganmetal.com
Michigan's Heavy Metal resource. Downloads, gigs and more!

Michigan Television Network
PO Box 765, Royal Oak, MI 48068-0765
PH: 248-376-4162
MichiganTV@hotmail.com
mitvnet.tripod.com/home.html
Increasing public awareness of Michigan's homegrown talent.

Michigan Times
303 E. Kearsley St., Flint, MI 48502-1950
PH: 810-762-3475
www.themichigantimes.com
The student voice of the University of Michigan.

Michigan Womyn's Music Festival
PO Box 22, Walhalla, MI 49458
PH: 231-757-4766
www.michfest.com
Festival week offers 40 performances, workshops and a film festival.

MLive
www.mlive.com
Michigan's home on the net. CD and concert reviews, music news.

Northern Express
PO Box 209, Traverse City, MI 49685-0209
PH: 231-947-8787 FX: 231-947-2425
info@northernexpress.com
www.northernexpress.com
Covering Northern Michigan. Does features on local musicians.

Northern Michigan Bands
www.northernmichiganmusicscene.com
Any new CD releases, Big events, you would like me to promote?

Southeast Michigan Jazz Association
2385 W. Huron River Dr.
Ann Arbor, MI 48103-2241
PH: 734-662-8514
www.semja.org
Monthly newsletter and free online listings.

State News
345 Student Services Bldg. East Lansing, MI 48824
PH: 517-455-3447 FX: 517-353-6355
www.statenews.com
Michigan State University's student paper.

Tawas Bay Blues Society
PO Box 213, East Tawas, MI 48730-0213
BluesByTheBayTawas@hotmail.com
www.bluesbythebaytawas.com
Promoting and preserving Blues music and culture.

TRAVERSE
148 E. Front St., Traverse City, MI 49684
PH: 231-941-8174 FX: 231-941-8391
www.traversemagazine.com
Northern Michigan's magazine. Does features on local artists.

West Michigan Blues Society
PO Box 6985, Grand Rapids, MI 49516-6985
PH: 616-241-9247
webmaster@wmbs.org
www.wmbs.org
Promotes Blues appreciation by sponsoring concerts, festivals and community events.

West Michigan Jazz Society
304 Paris SE, Grand Rapids, MI 49503
PH: 616-458-0125 FX: 616-235-7330
james.l.akins@att.net
www.wmichjazz.org
Promotes numerous events and local artists.

West Michigan Music
listen@westmichiganmusic.com
www.westmichiganmusic.com
The area's one-stop place for the best information on the unique and exciting West Michigan music scene.

WGRD Local Music Page
PO Box 96, Grand Rapids, MI 49501
PH: 616-451-4800 FX: 616-451-4807
grdbrian@yahoo.com
www.wgrd.com/localmusic
Helping Western Michigan bands promote themselves and to keep fans up to date on local happenings.

Wheatland Music Organization
Box 22, Remus, MI 49340
PH: 989-967-8879 FX: 989-967-8562
wmo@wheatlandmusic.org
www.wheatlandmusic.org
Resource center for the preservation and presentation of traditional music and arts.

Detroit

DetMusic.com
www.detmusic.com
A local artist boards community. Promote your CD or upcoming shows.

Detroit Beat Club
PO Box 27, Roseville, MI 48066
PH: 586-873-7482
Jay Mills booking@detroitbeatclub.com
www.detroitbeatclub.com
Online Hip Hop community.

Detroit Blues Society
PO Box 488, Goodrich, MI 48438
detroitblues@flash.net
home.flash.net/~dbsblues
Promotes the Blues to the general public.

Detroit Metro Times
733 Saint Antoine, Detroit, MI 48226
PH: 313-961-4060 FX: 313-961-6598
feedback@metrotimes.com
www.metrotimes.com
Free weekly alternative. CD reviews, concert reviews and previews.

DetroitCountryMusic.com
11449 Fleming St., Hamtramck, MI 48212
larry@detroitcountrymusic.com
www.detroitcountrymusic.com
Promotes and showcases local talent.

Jazz n Jams
22516 Telegraph Rd. Southfield, MI 48034
PH: 248-353-5299 FX: 248-353-5291
Lynn Koretz lynn@jazznjams.com
www.jazznjams.com
Specializing in all genres of Jazz. There is a section where Detroit Jazz artists can sell their music from.

TheHeadlessHorsemen.com
onslaught@theheadlesshorsemen.com
www.theheadlesshorsemen.com
Features an Underground artist page!

Motor City Rocks
PH: 313-982-0607 FX: 313-982-0607
Ryan Sult ryan@motorcityrocks.com
www.motorcityrocks.com
Our mission is to promote Detroit musicians and Detroit music venues.

Nestor in Detroit
hectop@peoplepc.com
www.nestorindetroit.com
News, releases and show reviews of the local Punk scene.

Online Bands
joe@onlinebands.com
www.onlinebands.com
Visit our site where you will find exciting fresh music from Detroit area bands.

Renaissance Soul Detroit
PMB #323, 23205 Gratiot Ave.
Eastpointe, MI 48021
Kelly "K-Fresh" Frazier djkfresh@rensoul.com
rensoul.com
The Detroit Urban alternative. Dedicated to Detroit Hip Hop.

Minnesota

Christian World Today Television
Joseph Mckenzie ntwbroadcasting@msn.com
www.christianworldtodaytelevision.net
Gives Christian artists exposure in the Minneapolis and Midwest area.

Indie Journal Minnesota Made CD Store
indiejournal@hotmail.com
www.indiejournal.com/indiejournal/cds

KXXR's Loud & Local Page
2000 SE. Elm St., Minneapolis, MN 55414
PH: 612-617-4000
Patrick loudandlocal@93xrocks.com
www.93x.com/loudnlocal.asp
Submit news on your local band.

Midwest Movement
2520 Silver Ln NE #205, Minneapolis, MN 55421
PH: 651-308-1469
info@midwestmovement.com
www.midwestmovement.com
Covering the Midwest Punk scene. Reviews, interviews, spotlight bands etc.

Minnesota Bluegrass and OT Music Association
PO Box 16408, Minneapolis, MN 55416
PH: 612-285-9133
waltzmn@skypoint.com
www.minnesotabluegrass.org
Host's Bluegrass and Old-Time music events and celebrations.

Minnesota Music Directory
401 N. 3rd St. #550, Minneapolis, MN 55401
PH: 612-375-1015
mmd@citypages.com
www.citypages.com/mmd
Magazine resource for local musicians.

MusicScene
1998 Bluestem Ln. Shoreview, MN 55126-5013
PH: 612-747-0894 FX: 612-605-1299
Conal "Reverend Gonzo" Garrity
gonzo@musicscene.org
www.musicscene.org
Submit your band, gig, news etc. Send your Demos and CDs for review.

Ripsaw News
12 E. Superior St. #208, Duluth, MN 55802
PH: 218-279-5253 FX: 218-279-2732
cdean@ripsawnews.com
www.ripsawnews.com
Duluth news and entertainment weekly.

Springboard for the Arts
308 Prince St. #270, St. Paul, MN 55101
ph: 651-292-3206
Chris Osgood chris@springboardforthearts.org
www.springboardforthearts.org
Provides affordable management information for Indie artists.

STATIC magazine
729 S. 2nd St., Manakato, MN 56001
PH: 507-344-2141 FX: 507-344-1404
info@freestaticonline.com
www.freestaticonline.com
Arts & Entertainment zine for Southern Minnesota.

Minneapolis/St. Paul

Blues on Stage
PO Box 582983, Minneapolis, MN 55458
mnblues@aol.com
www.mnblues.com
Reviews and posts your Blues demos.

D.U. Nation Underground Hip Hop
PH: 612-770-8357
hype@dunation.com
www.dunation.com
Provides info about upcoming concerts and local events.

freenoise.org
wrongjohn@freenoise.org
www.freenoise.org
Provides info on Underground sound.

Pulse of the Twin Cities
3200 Chicago Ave. S. Minneapolis, MN 55407
PH: 612-824-0000 FX: 612-822-0342
musiceditor@pulsetc.com
pulsetc.com
Weekly alternative paper. CD reviews and concert previews.

Rake Magazine
800 Washington Ave. N. #504,
Minneapolis, MN 55401
PH: 612-436-2880 FX: 612-436-2890
therake@rakemag.com
www.rakemag.com
Provides entertaining reading for the Twin Cities.

Skyway
1115 Hennepin Ave. S. Minneapolis, MN 55403
PH: 612-825-9205 FX: 612-825-0929
skywaynews@skywaynews.net
www.skywaynews.net
Covers the Twin Cities music scene.

Twin Cities Jazz Society
PO Box 4487, St. Paul, MN 55104
PH: 651-633-0329
tcjs@tcjs.org
www.tcjs.org
Sponsors local Jazz concerts, workshops and education programs.

Twin Cities Music Network
23 SE. 4th St. #213, Minneapolis, MN 55414
PH: 612-605-7960
email@tcmusic.net
www.tcmusic.net
List performances, band info and sell your CDs online.

Mississippi

Dead Man Dancing Promotions
201A S. 14th Ave. Hattiesburg, MS 39401
PH: 601-466-5861
TC Byrd deadmandancing@gmail.com
www.deadmandancing.com
Source for the Hattiesburg music scene.

DeepGrass
Barry Collins bacfire@netdoor.com
deepgrass.vgninc.com
Discussion forum for Mississippi Bluegrass music.

Magnolia State Bluegrass Association
250 Maxine Cir. Pearl, MS 39208-4908
www.geocities.com/magnoliabluegrass
Promotes Bluegrass music in the Deep South.

Mississippi Link
PO Box 11307, Jackson, MS 39283-1307
PH: 601-896-0084 FX: 601-896-0091
mslink@misnet.com
www.mississippilink.com
Jackson weekly paper.

Mississippi Old Time Music Society
Alvin Hudson hollycrk@netdoor.com
www.fiddlemania.com/motmsweb
Sponsors several events and jams throughout the state.

Planet Weekly
PH: 601-714-4719
feedback@planetweekly.com
www.planetweekly.com
Weekly newspaper. A&E section covers the local music scene.

The Reflector
PH: 662-325-7906
Dustin Barnes life@reflector.msstate.edu
www.reflector-online.com
Mississippi State University's student paper.

Missouri

Blues Society of the Ozarks
PO Box 8133, Springfield, MO 65801
PH: 417-869-9188
bsoeditor@yahoo.com
www.ozarksblues.org
Encourages performance of the Blues at clubs, at festivals and on radio.

CapeScene.com
scott@capescene.com
www.capescene.com
Covering upcoming events in the Cape Girardeau music scene.

Central Plains Jam Band Society
4741 Central, #256, Kansas City, MO 64112
john.bollin@cpjs.org
www.cpjs.org
Promotes the arts, music and spirit of Jam Band music.

Columbia360.com
PMB249 503 E. Nifong Blvd. Columbia, MO 65201
submit@columbia360.com
www.columbia360.com
List your band, event, news etc.

COMOmusic
justinglow@gmail.com
www.comomusic.com
Columbia's definitive guide to local music. Post your profile, CD and show reviews etc.

Gufbal.com
james@gufbal.com
www.gufbal.com
Springfield's source for live music.

Heavy Frequency
13415 15th St., Grandview, MO 64030
PH: 816-995-0460
Heather Bashaw heather@heavyfrequency.com
www.heavyfrequency.com
Features promising Heavy Metal and Hardcore acts emerging from the depths of the Midwest underground.

Maneater
214 Brady Commons, Columbia, MO 65211
PH: 573-882-5500
maneater@themaneater.com
www.themaneater.com
Student newspaper of the University of Missouri - Columbia.

Missouri Area Bluegrass Committee
www.bluegrassamerica.com
Promoting Bluegrass music across the US.

MO Blues Association
PO Box 105758, Jefferson City, MO 65110
Chris Puyear promo-reviews@moblues.org
www.moblues.org
Artist photos, merchandise, CD reviews, and more!

MOHeads.com
brooks@moheads.com
www.moheads.com
Post your news, listings, events etc.

MOrawk.com
aaron@morawk.com
www.morawk.com
Supporting Independent music in Missouri.

Tri-State Bluegrass Association
c/o Erma Spray, RR 1, Box 71, Kahoka, MO 63445
PH: 573-853-4344
Ed Spray edspray@marktwain.net
k0bkl.org/tristate.htm
Publishes both a yearly festival guide and quarterly newsletter.

Unsigned Hype: Midwest Promoter
PH: 206-984-4973
info@unsignedhype.org
unsignedhype.stlhiphop.com
Hip Hop artist promotion and services.

Voxmagazine
320 Lee Hills Hall, Columbia, MO 65211
PH: 573-882-6432 FX: 573-884-1870
vox@missouri.edu
www.voxmagazine.com
Columbians weekly guide to area new, arts and entertainment.

Kansas City

Banzai Magazine
PO Box 7522, Overland Park, KS 66207
PH: 913-642-2262
Jim Kilroy banzaimagazine@hotmail.com
www.banzaimagazine.net
Kansas City's Rock & Roll Headquarters.

eKC online
Brandon Whitehead kinginyellow@juno.com
www.kcactive.com
Metro Kansas City news and entertainment.

Heart of America Bluegrass and Old-Time Music
www.pars.net/~habot
Performances, jam sessions, newsletter, gigs etc.

hiphopkc.com
mark@transparentsolutions.com
www.hiphopkc.com
The virtual Hip Hop community of Kansas City.

Kansas City Blues Society
PO Box 32396, Kansas City, MO 64171
PH: 816-474-4774
info@kcbluessociety.com
www.kcbluessociety.com
Keeping the Blues alive.

Kansas City Concert Page
concerts@hearditontheradio.com
www.hearditontheradio.com/concerts.aspx
Submit your Kansas City concert.

Kansas City Guitar Society
133813 S. Shannan St., Olathe, KS 66062
PH: 913-526-6042
kcguitarsociety@aol.com
www.kansascityguitarsociety.org
Encourages artistry of the Classical guitar.

Kansas City Infozine
PO Box 22661, Kansas City, MO 64113
PH: 913-432-2661
info@infozine.com
www.infozine.com
Post your show information on the music page.

Kansas City Jazz Ambassadors
PO Box 36181, Kansas City, MO 64171
info@jazzkc.org
www.jazzkc.org
Publishes Jam Magazine. Submit Cds for review.

Kansas City Magazine
118 SW. Blvd. Kansas City, MO 64108
PH: 816-421-4111 FX: 816-221-8350
www.kcmag.com
Submit your demo for review.

Kansas City Music
PH: 816-520-8430
valentine@boxofchalk.com
www.kansascitymusic.com
Find musicians, their gigs, as well as posting your own.

KC Christian Music
17300 Gray Dr. Pleasant Hill, MO 64080
Connie Whitlock info@kcchristianmusic.com
www.kcchristianmusic.com
KCCM is about artists coming together to help each other grow in our ministries.

KC Gothic and Industrial List
groups.yahoo.com/group/kcgoth-indus
Discussion forum for all dark music.

KCLocalBands
info@kclocalbands.com
kclocalbands.com
News, interviews, forums, radio etc.

Pitch Weekly
1701 Main, Kansas City, MO 64108
PH: 816-561-6061 FX: 816-756-0502
feedback@pitch.com
music.pitch.com
Kansas City free weekly alternative. Reviews new CDs, focuses on local music scene.

Songwriters Circle of Kansas City
5921 Charlotte, Kansas City, MO 64110
PH: 816-363-1917
David Hakan davidhakan@kc.rr.com
www.songwriterscircle.org
Supporting local Indie songwriters.

St. Louis

The Commonspace
615 N. Grand Blvd. St. Louis, MO 63103-1008
info@thecommonspace.org
www.thecommonspace.org
A progressive, monthly, online magazine for grassroots culture.

gtp-inc.com
shaunbrooks@gtp-inc.com
www.gtp-inc.com
Dedicated to the St. Louis music scene.

THE metro i
PH: 314-965-4788
www.themetroi.com
St. Louis arts & entertainment. Local band coverage and reviews.

playback
PO Box 9170, St. Louis, MO 63117
PH: 314-952-6404 FX: 877-204-2067
Laura Hamlett editor@playbackstl.com
www.playbackstl.com
St. Louis pop culture. Send your info and news.

Pulse
pulse@localmp3.com
www.stl-pulse.com
St. Louis' music source. Downloads, featured artists, events and more!

Riverfront Times
6358 Delmar Blvd. #200,
St. Louis, MO 63130-4719
PH: 314-754-5966 FX: 314-754-5955
www.rftstl.com
St. Louis free weekly A&E paper. Covers local music scene.

Spin City Record
748 N. Hwy. 67 #279, Florissant, MO 63031
spincityrecordz@spincityrecordz.com
www.spincityrecordz.com
Record label formed to market Hip Hop artists from St. Louis.

St. Louis Concert Web
Plugthis@stl-music.com
www.stl-music.com
Reviews local shows and CD releases.

St. Louis Donna Page
o2bkjn@swbell.net
home.swbell.net/o2bkjn
Featuring this weeks Cajun and Zydeco music and dance events.

St. Louis Front Page Entertainment Guide
PO Box 1354, St. Louis, MO 63188
PH: 314-771-0200 FX: 314-771-0300
editor@slfp.com
www.slfp.com
A St. Louis Internet-only publication. Post your event.

St. Louis Gothic
skeletal13@hotmail.com
www.stlouisgothic.com
Your source for St. Louis Darkwave events and information!

St. Louis Magazine
1034 S. Brentwood Blvd. #1220,
St. Louis, MO 63117
PH: 314-727-0900
egrant@stlmag.com
www.stlmag.com
What's happening in the arts, music, politics, the media and more.

St. Louis Punk Page
PO Box 63207, St. Louis, MO 63163
jerome@stlpunk.com
www.stlpunk.com
Post your band info and events.

STLBlues
stlouisblues@swbell.net
www.stlblues.net
E-mail to get your band listed here!

STLScene
PO Box 300575, St. Louis, MO 63130
info@stlscene.com
www.stlscene.net
Connecting St. Louis music.

STLtoday.com
www.stltoday.com/entertainment
Extensive local music coverage. News, reviews, spotlights etc. Submit your band's info.

Montana

Exponent
exponent.montana.edu
Montana State University's student newspaper.

Hansen Music
1819 Grand Ave. Billings, MT 59102
PH: 406-245-4544 FX: 406-256-3649
pat@hansenmusic.net
www.hansenmusic.net
Contact to get your band listed.

Lively Times
1152 Eagle Pass Trail, Charlo, MT 59824
PH: 406-644-2910
writeus@livelytimes.com
www.livelytimes.com
Montana's complete A&E calendar.

Missoula Folklore Society
PO Box 9296, Missoula, MT 59807
mtfolk@montanafolk.org
www.montanafolk.org
Preserving contemporary and traditional music.

Missoula Independent
115 S. 4th St. W. Missoula, MT 59801
PH: 406-543-6609 FX: 406-543-4367
www.missoulanews.com
Free weekly alternative paper. CD and concert reviews, interviews and previews.

Montana Kaimin
Journalism 206, U of Montana,
Missoula, MT 59801
PH: 406-243-6541 FX: 406-243-4303
editor@kaimin.org
www.kaimin.org
The University of Montana's student paper.

Nebraska

Blues Society of Omaha
blues@bluesgroup.com
www.bluesgroup.com
Promoting Blues music in the greater Omaha-Lincoln area. News, reviews, newsletter, upcoming shows...

free Lincoln
services@freelincoln.com
www.freelincoln.com
Community website. Post your upcoming shows/events.

The Gateway
6001 Dodge St., Omaha, NE 68182
PH: 402-554-2470
www.unogateway.com
University of Nebraska, Omaha's student paper.

Great Plains Bluegrass & Old-Time Music Association
3714 Forest Lawn Ave. Omaha, NE 68112-2025
jenni_w-g@tconl.com
gpbotma.homestead.com
Promoting Bluegrass and Old-Time music in and around Omaha.

KIBZ Radio's Local Bands Page
4630 Antelope Creek Rd. Lincoln, NE 68506
PH: 402-484-8000 FX: 402-483-9138
luna@kibz.com
www.kibz.com/localbandscalendar.html
Local radio station. Online band listings.

Lazy-i
743 J.E. George Blvd. Omaha, NE 68132
timmymac29@aol.com
www.timmcmahan.com/lazyeye.htm
Interviews and band profiles, reviews and hype.

Lincoln Live Music
lincolnlivemusic@hotmail.com
www.lincolnlivemusic.com
News, links, interviews, downloads, album and show reviews.

OMAHAMUSIC.com
4535 Leavenworth St., Omaha, NE 68106
PH: 402-553-5818 FX: 402-553-5819
oma@omahamusic.com
www.omahamusic.com
Official website of the Omaha Musician's Association. Band and event listings.

The Reader
5015 Underwood Ave. Omaha, NE 68132
PH: 402-341-7323 FX: 402-341-6967
www.thereader.com
Alternative news zine. Submit your info/events.

SLAM Omaha
PO Box 391264, Omaha, NE 68139-1264
mick@slamomaha.com
www.slamomaha.com
Local music, featured bands, new releases etc.

Someday Never
jimmy@somedaynever.com
www.somedaynever.com
Omaha music web site with band list, show calendar and reviews.

Starcityscene.com
Tery info@astropopweb.com
www.starcityscene.com
Your guide to the Lincoln music scene.

Nevada

Las Vegas

Guitar Society of Las Vegas
4950 W. Craig Rd. #3, Las Vegas, NV 89130
lvcge@yahoo.com
www.gslv.org
Promoting the art of Acoustic guitar.

Jazzlasvegas.com
jazzlasvegas@mediaband.net
www.jazzlasvegas.com
Emphasis on Jazz in the Las Vegas area.

Las Vegas City Life
1385 Pama Ln. #111, Las Vegas, NV 89119
PH: 702-871-6780
keene@lvpress.com
www.lvcitylife.com
Extensive music section with profiles and reviews of musicians.

Las Vegas Jam Band Society
www.lvjbs.org
Exists to help create a more supportive music community in southern Nevada for the musicians of the Jam Band genre. The goal is to educate ourselves and the community through grass roots promotions and concert events.

Las Vegas Jazz Society
PO Box 60396, Las Vegas, NV 89160
PH: 702-313-6778
pjgaffey@earthlink.net
www.vegasjazz.org
Publishes and reviews concerts, club dates and special events.

Las Vegas Weekly
PO Box 230040, Las Vegas, NV 89123-0011
PH: 702-990-2411 FX: 702-990-2400
www.lasvegasweekly.com
Extensive coverage of both local and touring bands.

Neon
PO Box 70, Las Vegas, NV 89125
PH: 702-383-0211
www.reviewjournal.com/neon
Entertainment section of the Las Vegas Review-Journal.

onethirtyeight.org
ge138@onethirtyeight.org
onethirtyeight.org
Devoted to the REAL Las Vegas Punk Rock scene.

Vegas News *Music Buzz*
Jim Wilson wilpro@cox.net
vegasnews.squarespace.com/music-buzz
Send in any of your press releases.

Reno

Reno Blues Society
PO Box 10742, Reno, NV 89510
PH: 775-331-5494
soulman@renoblues.org
www.renoblues.org
One stop source for the Blues in Reno.

Reno News & Review
708 N. Center St., Reno, NV 89501
PH: 775-324-4440 FX: 775-324-4572
www.newsreview.com
Reno's news and entertainment weekly.

New Hampshire

Blues Audience Newsletter
62 Cricket Hill Rd. Harrisville, NH 03450
Diana dshonk@bluesaudience.com
www.bluesaudience.com
Supports New England's fine Blues musicians and clubs.

Foster's Online *Showcase Magazine*
333 Central Ave. Dover, NH 03820
showcase@fosters.com
www.fosters.com
Dover weekly A&E magazine.

Monadnock Folklore Society
54 Brook St., Keene, NH 03431
PH: 603-352-8616
info@monadnockfolk.org
www.monadnockfolk.org
Offering support to local musicians' projects.

Northeast In-Tune
PO Box 355, Epping, NH 03042-0355
PH: 603-767-4440
Bob Donovan Editor@northeastintune.com
www.northeastintune.com
Indie Music, Arts/Body Art publication focusing on music of the Northeast (NJ, NY, New England).

Peterborough Folk Music Society
PO Box 41, Peterborough, NH 03458
PH: 603-827-2905
deb@pfms.mv.com
www.acousticmusic.com/pfms/index.htm
Supporting musicians in the Monadnock Region.

Spotlight Magazine
spotlight@seacoastonline.com
www.seacoastonline.com/calendar/nightlife.htm
Portsmouth's A&E magazine.

Union Leader
PO Box 9555, Manchester, NH 03108-9555
PH: 603-668-4321 FX: 603-668-0382
writeus@theunionleader.com
www.theunionleader.com
Interviews, previews and reviews bands. Accepts CDs for review.

New Jersey

Acoustic Musicians Guild
PO Box 4247, Brick, NJ 08723
denise_and_son@yahoo.com
www.amg.org
Promoting and preserving Acoustic music.

All-Access-Minus
87 Gless Ave. 2nd. Floor Belleville, NJ 07109
PH: 732-266-9828
M. Pimentel minus@minusp.com
www.minusp.com
Site for upcoming Hip Hop artists in the Tri-State area.

Aquarian Weekly
52 Sindle Ave. PO Box 1140, Little Falls, NJ 07424
PH: 973-812-6766 FX: 973-812-5420
chrisf@theaquarian.com
www.theaquarian.com
Covers the area of New York, New Jersey and Connecticut.

AsburyMusic.com
Gary Wien gary@asburymusic.com.
www.asburymusic.com
The portal for Jersey Shore music fans and artists.

Basically-HipHop.Com
PO Box 7093-WOB, West Orange, NJ 07052
Max-Jerome maxjerome@basically-hiphop.com
www.basically-hiphop.com
Represents Underground music, artists and MC's.

Blow Up Radio
PO Box 664, Old Bridge, NJ 08857
lazlo@blowupradio.com
BlowUpRadio.com
Posts news, reviews, downloads and concert listings.

Bluegrass and OT Music Association of NJ
president@newjerseybluegrass.org
www.newjerseybluegrass.org
Promoting Bluegrass and Old-Time music.

Central NJ Song Circle
711 Raritan Ave. #27, Highland Park, NJ 08904
info@jerseysongs.com
www.jerseysongs.com
A friendly, in-the-round get-together for testing out new songs.

Chorus and Verse
editor@chorusandverse.com
www.chorusandverse.com
Provides exposure and insight into the New Jersey scene.

Composers Guild of New Jersey
wanderso@mail.slc.edu
www.cgnj.org
Focuses on local contemporary music.

Cookmanave.com
PH: 732-773-3631
Jason Thomson info@cookmanave.com
www.cookmanave.com
Dedicated to music and art in Asbury Park.

Create A Vibe
booking@createavibe.com
www.createavibe.com
Northern New Jersey's Jam music promoters. Send detailed information and links to website, MP3s, Videos, etc. If we're interested, we will send you the mailing address to send your promo kits.

Crooked Beat
feedback@crooked-beat.com
www.crooked-beat.com
Band pages and gig listings for NY and NJ bands.

Folk Project
PO Box 41, Mendham, NJ 07945
PH: 908-771-0187
secretary@folkproject.org
www.folkproject.org
Sponsors Folk music and dance activities in the NJ area.

Hammonton Gazette
PO Box 1228, Hammonton, NJ 08037
PH: 609-704-1939 FX: 609-704-1938
Jim Calder jcalder@mail.hammontongazette.com
www.hammontongazette.com
A&E section includes show and Indie music reviews.

Hudson Current
current@hudsonreporter.com
www.hudsoncurrent.com
Hoboken weekly news and entertainment paper Covers Hudson County bands..

Jersey Beat
418 Gregory Ave. Weehawken, NJ 07086
jim@jerseybeat.com
www.jerseybeat.com
Will accept all CDs, but local releases get the highest priority.

Jersey Jam
www.@jerseyjam.com
www.jerseyjams.com
If you're a New Jersey artist, or in a band, you may add your web site to the list! Our staff will continually visit your web site, listen to your music, see what you're up to and decide if you should be the SpotLight Artist of the month!

Jersey Shore Jazz and Blues Foundation
PO Box 8713, Red Bank, NJ 07701
PH: 732-933-9473
info@jsjbf.org
www.jsjbf.com
Formed to preserve, promote and perpetuate Jazz, Blues, and other indigenous music forms in New Jersey.

JERSEYMUSIC.COM
jerseymusic.com
Connect to the local music scene.

JerseyShoreRocks
1137 Hope Rd. Asbury Park, NJ 07712-3162
PH: 732-542-2688
info@JerseyShoreRocks.com
www.jerseyshorerocks.com
Lists bands, bars, clubs and venues.

New Jersey Jazz Society
187 Watchung Ave. Chatham, NJ 07928
PH: 800-303-6557 FX: 215-483-7045
Joe Lang pres@njjs.org
www.njjs.org
Monthly magazine with feature articles, reviews and event calendar.

Newark Star-Ledger
1 Star-Ledger Plaza, Newark, NJ 07102-1200
PH: 973-392-4141
eletters@starledger.com
www.starledger.com
Considers submissions of bands playing in the area.

Night & Day
PO Box 202, Spring Lake, NJ 07762
PH: 732-974-0047 FX: 732-974-0163
info@ndmag.com
www.ndmag.com
Covers movies, concerts, local bands and more.

NJ State of Music
128 Louisville Ave. Neptune, NJ 07753
PH: 908-433-8963
JoeD@StateofMusic.com
nj.stateofmusic.com
Will stream your demo, post shows, news and sell merchandise.

NJMUSIC.net
info@njmusic.net
www.njmusic.net
Post your band's info to get connected in the NJ music scene.

Planet Verge
15 Albert Terrace, Bloomfield, NJ 07003
PH: 973-338-0560
planet_vergemagazine@yahoo.com
www.planetverge.com
Interviews up-and-coming Punk/Rock bands.

PressofAtlanticCity.com
1000 W. Washington Ave. Pleasantville, NJ 08232
PH: 609-272-7000
dbergen@pressofac.com
www.pressofatlanticcity.com
Covers local music scene.

Princeton Folk Music Society
PO Box 427, Princeton, NJ 08542-0427
PH: 609-799-0944
info@princetonfolk.org
www.princetonol.com/groups/pfms
Encourages the growth of Folk music.

Showcase
PO Box 306, Trenton, NJ 08625
PH: 800-843-2787
info@jerseyarts.com
www.jerseyarts.com
Increasing the awareness of and participation in the arts in New Jersey.

South Jersey Underground.com
36 Elmer St., Bridgeton, NJ 08302
Bob Headley sjunderground@aol.com
www.southjerseyunderground.com
Covering the local Punk and Metal scene.

SouthJerseyClubs.com
300 N. Broadway, Gloucester City, NJ 08030
PH: 856-456-8080
info@southjerseyclubs.com
www.southjerseyclubs.com
Info on clubs, events and local bands.

Steppin' Out Magazine
381 Broadway, Westwood, NJ 07675
stepoutmag@aol.com
www.steppinoutmagazine.com
North Jersey/NYC music weekly.

TheNJScene.com
mike@thenjscene.com
thenjscene.com
Info site for fans and bands alike.

Tri-State Punk
Stumpy stumpy@tristatepunk.com
www.tristatepunk.com
Informing the tri-state area about all musical events.

Upstage Magazine
PO Box 140, Spring Lake, NJ 07762
Gary Wien info@upstagemagazine.com
www.upstagemagazine.com
Supporting the original arts scene of Central New Jersey.

New Mexico

Albuquerque Live Music
patrique@albuquerquemusicscene.com
www.abqlivemusic.com
The hottest place on the web to find where your favorite band is playing.

Albuquerque Music Scene
500 Tyler NE, Albuquerque, NM 87113
PH: 505-341-3916
patrique@albuquerquemusicscene.com
www.albuquerquemusicscene.com
Band listings, band websites, band promotion and lots of music!

Alibi
2118 Central Ave. SE #151
Albuquerque, NM 87106-4004
PH: 505-346-0660 FX: 505-256-9651
rockstar@alibi.com
alibi.com
Albuquerque's weekly A&E paper. Extensive local music coverage.

Hyper Active Music Magazine
11024 Montgomery PMB 253,
Albuquerque, NM 87111
PH: 505-293-0594
Allison Shaw allie@hyperactivemusicmag.com
hyperactivemusicmag.com
Created to cater to the hungry-ears of Southwesterners; to provide them with an appealing & colorful menu replete with the full variety of musical cuisine that the local & national bands are cooking up. We also support national bands that are from, or are touring through the Southwest.

New Mexico Folk Music & Dance Society
PO Box 40421, Albuquerque, NM 87196-0421
board@folkmads.org
www.folkmads.org
Promoting and teaching traditional music and dance.

New Mexico Music Portal
info@nmmusic.com
www.nmmusic.com
Band listings, events, classifieds etc.

NewMexicoEvents.com
5104 Gaviota NW, Albuquerque, NM 87120
FX: 505-922-8775
Mark Hendricks mark@nmevents.com
www.newmexicoevents.com
Submit events and band info to get listed.

Santa Fe Buzz
369 Montezuma Ave. Box 454, Santa Fe, NM 87501
Nancy Nielsen nn@santafebuzz.com
www.santafebuzz.com
Santa Fe's online magazine for good news, good people and good works.

Santa Fe Reporter
132 E. Marcy St., Santa Fe, NM 87504
PH: 505-988-5541 FX: 505-988-5348
culture@sfreporter.com
www.sfreporter.com
Weekly news and culture paper. Covers local music scene.

Southwest Traditional and Bluegrass Music Association
PO Box 90145, Albuquerque, NM 87199
www.southwestpickers.org
Promoting Acoustic music through jams and workshops.

Taos News
PO Box U, Taos, NM 87571
PH: 505-758-2241 FX: 505-751-3026
tempo@taosnews.com
www.taosnews.com
Weekly paper. Spotlights local and regional music, interviews, previews and reviews.

New York

A Place for Jazz
1221 Wendell Ave. Schenectady, NY 12308
jerrygordon@juno.com
timesunion.com/communities/jazz
Supports Jazz through concerts and workshops.

AlmostPunk NY
almostpunkny@hotmail.com
www.geocities.com/almostpunkny
Promoting local Punk Rock bands in the area.

Artvoice
810-812 Main St., Buffalo, NY 14202
PH: 716-881-6604 FX: 716-881-6682
editorial@artvoice.com
www.artvoice.com
Buffalo free weekly A&E paper Reviews album releases and profiles new bands.

Bands of New York State
ableals@juno.com
www.yrbook.com/music
Supporting upstate NY groups and artists.

The Blues Society of Western New York
PO Box 129, Kenmore Branch, Buffalo, NY 14217
Rich Schneider BluesBeatM@aol.com
www.wnyblues.org
Promoting Blues events, record releases and club scenes.

Buffalo Music Online
www.wnymusic.com
Submit your band news, info and events.

Buffalobarfly.com
162 Elmwood Ave. Buffalo, NY 14201
PH: 716 886-4785 FX: 716 886-5481
info@buffalobarfly.com
www.buffalobarfly.com
Promoting nightlife and entertainment in the Buffalo area.

BuffaloBluegrass.com
PH: 716-627-9010
Mark Panfil markpanfil@hotmail.com
www.buffalobluegrass.com
Dedicated to promoting Bluegrass music in the Buffalo area.

BUMlocal
1699 W. Glenville Rd. Amsterdam, NY 12010
PH: 518-399-6604
editor@bumrock.com
www.bumrock.com
All the info on the Albany, NY area modern Rock music scene.

Capital Region Unofficial Musicians and Bands Site
andy@crumbs.net
www.crumbs.net
Online music resource for the Albany area.

Central New York Bluegrass Association
PO Box 491, Baldwinsville, NY 13027
rhayden357@aol.com
www.cnyba.com
News, calendar, classifieds, jams, festivals etc.

Central New York Friends of Folk
www.folkus.org/fof
Supporting Folk and Acoustic music.

Central New York Music
PO Box 1526, Auburn, NY 13021
PH: 315-255-4650
Steve Johnson cnymwebmaster03@cnymusic.com
www.cnymusic.com
Promoting and supporting live music in and around Central New York State.

Empyre Lounge
11 Atkins St. #3, Brighton, MA 02135
PH: 781-801-8674
ian@empyrelounge.com
www.empyrelounge.com
Focuses on the upstate NY Indie music scene.

Folkus Project
PO Box 99, Syracuse, NY 13214
PH: 315-457-2290
joe@folkus.org
www.folkus.org
Presents Folk and Acoustic music. Includes artist spotlight.

Freetime Magazine
850 University Ave. Rochester, NY 14607
PH: 585-473-2266
www.freetime.com
Rochester A&E mag. Covers local and national music.

Golden Link
PO Box 92398, Rochester, NY 14692
PH: 585-234-5044
goldenlink@goldenlink.org
www.goldenlink.org
Rochester publication containing everything about Folk music.

Hudson Valley Bluegrass Association
hvba@optonline.com
www.hvbluegrass.org
Contains Bluegrass news, show schedules, CD reviews, newsletter etc.

Hudson Valley Folk Guild
PO Box F, Poughkeepsie, NY 12602
HVFOLKS@aol.com
www.hvfg.org
Produces events and nurtures new Folk artists.

HudsonNights.com
www.hudsonnights.com
Local shows and venues in the Hudson Valley. Also does band promotion.

In-Music
johnpatgallagher@aol.com
www.in-nyc.com/in-music
Submit your music info and MP3s to be featured here.

INSIDEOUT Magazine
PO Box 908, New Paltz, NY 12561
Attn: Music Editor
PH: 845-255-6500 FX: 845-255-5533
Linda Boyd Kavars info@insideouthv.com
www.insideouthv.com
The Hudson Valley magazine for the LGBT community.

Ithaca Times
PO Box 27, Ithaca, NY 14851
PH: 607-277-7000 FX: 607-277-1012
Jessica del Mundo jdelmundo@ithacatimes.com
www.ithacatimes.com
Free weekly alternative paper. Local concert reviews, accepts CDs for review.

IthacaMusic.com
tpcannan@yahoo.com
www.ithacamusic.com
Created to spotlight the wonderful musical resources that Ithaca has to offer.

Metroland
419 Madison Ave. Albany, NY 12210
PH: 518-463-2500 FX: 518-463-3712
advertise@metroland.net
www.metroland.net
Albany's alternative newsweekly.

Mohawk Valley Bluegrass Association
6447 W. Carter Rd. Rome, NY 13440
PH: 315-339-2771
lmarti1@twcny.rr.com
www.mvbga.com
Building a base of members in an area that is rich in musicians.

Music 315
PO Box 4796, Rome, NY 13442
FX: 866-851-3851
Zoe zoe@music315.com
www.music315.com
Area code 314 bands contact us to get your site listed.

Musicians On Call
216 W. 18th St. #201B, New York, NY 10011
PH: 212-741-2709 FX: 212-741-3465
info@musiciansoncall.org
www.musiciansoncall.org
Providing musical healing to the community.

MyRochester.com
www.myrochester.com
Rochester's ultimate online music guide.

Nadeau Music
PO Box 6511, Watertown, NY 13601
PH: 315-785-8484
nadeaumusic@aol.com
www.nadeaumusic.net
Promoting local, independent and international Blues and Rock artists.

New York Newspapers
www.usnpl.com/nynews.html
Links to newspapers throughout the state.

New York Open Mikes
www.openmikes.org/calendar/NY

New York/Tri-State Area Bluegrass/Old Time Music Scene
benfreed@optonline.net
www.banjoben.com
Send details of your gig to get posted.

Northeast Blues Society
2 Sheffield Circle, Loudonville, NY 12211
www.timesunion.com/communities/nebs
Exposing regional Blues talent to the largest possible audience.

Prog 90
3150 Weidrick Rd. Walworth, NY 14568
Michael Martin progonthe90@yahoo.com
www.prog90.com
Gives Progressive Rock bands in New York support with gigs, contact, recording and promotional outlets.

The Pulse
PH: 315-797-1208
www.thepulse.com
City Guide for Utica. Post your gigs.

PRIMO PR 716
PO Box 1622, Buffalo, NY 14231
Mark Weber primopr716@juno.com
www.primopr.com
Specializes in getting the word out to Buffalo and beyond about upcoming concerts and events put on by Christian artists.

The Refrigerator
dearrefrigerator@therefrigerator.net
www.therefrigerator.net
Rochester A&E online zine.

Rochester Groove
7758 Newco Dr. Hamlin, NY 14464
webmaster@rochestergroove.com
www.rochestergroove.com
An effort to promote local bands in this genre who are making the effort & playing around the region. In a local / regional Groove or Jam Band? Send a CD & we'll be glad to put it into the mix.

Rochester Music Coalition
PO Box 26378, Rochester, NY 14626
rochestermusiccoalition@hotmail.com
rochestermusiccoalition.org
Supports and promotes artists of all genres.

Syracuse New Times
1415 W. Genesee St., Syracuse, NY 13204-2156
PH: 315-422-7011 FX: 315-422-1721
snt@syracusenewtimes.com
newtimes.rway.com
Provides extensive A&E information for the Syracuse area.

Syracuse Ska scene
danny@wxxe.org
syracuseska.com
Shows, classifieds, MP3s and more!

Tribal Jams Magazine
tribaljm@bestweb.net
www.tribaljams.com
Information on festivals and local venues for the "tie-die" jam band music scene for all you hippies, nomads, and tribesmen out there. We cover the northeastern region of the U.S.

TriStateBands.com
PH: 917-232-4624
Kevin Rath kevin@tristatebands.com
www.TriStateBands.com
For NY, NJ and CT bands. List your band, bio and other info.

Underground Music Television
7492 Hillside Rd. #1, Baldwinsville, NY 10327
PH: 315-652-9383
Rich Stahle rich@umtv.info
umtv.info
A TV show that features local, unsigned and underground artist's music videos.

Upstate NY Reggae
Ras Adam Simeon rasadam@yahoo.com
go.to/NYreggae
Postings for concerts, radio shows, shops, venues, contacts etc.

Western New York / S. Ontario Raves
www.wnysor.net
Promoting all upcoming events.

Wild Cauldron
submit@wildcauldron.com
www.wildcauldron.com
Music news, reviews, interviews and show information for the NY and NJ area local band scene.

Long Island

AOL CityGuide Long Island *Music*
home.digitalcity.com/longisland
Regional music column and forum.

AURAL FIX
PO Box 6054, N. Babylon, NY 11703
auralfix@optonline.net
www.auralfix.com
Covering the local Indie scene.

Club Long Island
info@clublongisland.com
www.clublongisland.com
Has a Local Band feature.

Island Songwriter Showcase
mcspeed@optonline.net
www.islandsongwriters.org
Support original music through workshops and showcases.

Long Island Blues Society
PO Box 557, E. Setauket, NY 11733
lbbluznews@aol.com
www.liblues.org
Band listings, newsletter, events etc.

Long Island Classical Guitar Society
182 Parkside Ave. Miller Place, NY 11764
PH: 631-821-5270
licgs@licgs.us
www.licgs.us
Hosts a quarterly mixer to showcase local talent.

Long Island Entertainment News
1 Carr Ct. Nesconset, NY 11767
PH: 631-979-2608 FX: 631-979-2048
Richard L'Hommedieu publisher@lienews.com
www.lienews.com
Free A&E newspaper. Accepts and reviews demos.

Long Island Press
1103 Stewart Ave. Garden City, NY 11530
PH: 516-629-4327 FX: 516-992-1801
mnelson@longislandpress.com
www.longislandpress.com
Bi-weekly A&E paper. Reviews concerts, profiles and interviews bands.

Long Island Punx
lipunx@gmail.com
77.lipunx.com:6080
Covering the Long Island scene. News, reviews, gig calendar.

LongIsland.com *Nightlife*
feedback@longisland.com
nightlife.longisland.com
Long Island band pages, calendar, interviews, bulletin boards and more.

LongIslandClubs.com
info@liclubs.com
www.liclubs.com
A complete listing of Long Island and NYC Night Clubs, Bars and Bands

longislandmusicscene
groups.yahoo.com/group/longislandmusicscene
Discussing the LI original music scene.

longislandmusicscene.com
PO Box 417, E. Rockaway, NY 11518-0417
PH: 516-887-0923 FX: 516-887-0923
webguy@longislandmusicscene.com
www.longislandmusicscene.com
Provides free exposure and resources for musicians.

NetTowns of Long Island
PH: 631-586-7925
davekot@yahoo.com
www.nettowns.com/music.htm
Free gig postings. E-mail your info.

Sick Promotions
www.sickpromotions.com
Promotion company. Hosts a yearly Indie concert.

TheFreezer.com
PO Box 211, Saint James, NY 11780
PH: 631-948-8781
mike@thefreezer.com
www.thefreezer.com
News, band and gig listings for Long Island bands.

New York City

Absolute Indie TV
PO Box 97, New York, NY 10156
PH: 631-827-3000 FX: 419-831-3032
Andrew Herzman andy@qopelrecords.com
www.absoluteindie.com
A TV show that plays Independent music videos from all over the world.

Acoustic Live!
51 MacDougal St. PO Box #254,
New York, NY 10012
ricco@earthlink.net
www.acousticlive.com
Monthly newsletter showcasing all Acoustic performances in NY.

Antifolk.net
PO Box 20469, Tompkins Sq. Stn.
New York, NY 10009
info@antifolk.net
www.antifolk.net
The home for the NYC Antifolk scene.

AOL CityGuide New York *Music*
home.digitalcity.com/newyork
Regional music column and forum.

Associated Musicians of Greater New York
322 W. 48th St., New York, NY 10036
PH: 212-245-4802
Joseph Eisman jeisman@local802afm.org
www.local802afm.org
Musicians union fighting for your well-being.

Attention Deficit Television *(ADD-TV)*
contact@add-tv.com
www.add-tv.com
We welcome submissions of all types of media including experimental film and video, animation, multimedia works and websites.

Big Apple Jazz
Gordon Polatnick gordon@bigapplejazz.com
www.bigapplejazz.com
Reinvigorating the Jazz scene in NYC, by introducing fans to the more authentic and hidden Jazz events that occur.

Black Rock Coalition
PO Box 1054, Cooper Stn. New York, NY 10276
PH: 212-713-5097
www.blackrockcoalition.org
Represents a united front musically and politically progressive Black artists and supporters.

Crashin' In
204 Powers St. #1, Brooklyn, NY 11211
Lio dj@crashinin.com
www.crashinin.com
For album reviews, band interviews, online listening parties, and all other inquiries, send us an email.

CelticTV.com
7 Sterling Pl. Edgewater, NJ 07020
PH: 201-491-4055 FX: 419-781-0744
William A. Phillips celticv@yahoo.com
www.celtictv.com
All things Celtic Rock and Irish music in NYC.

Chicks With Guitars
PH: 917-969-6409
Jeanette Palmer info@chickswithguitars.com
chickswithguitars.com
Provides cooperative promotional publishing and performing opportunities for emerging and established musicians.

ComposersCollaborative
210 Riverside Dr. New York, NY 10025-6883.
ccooke@composerscollab.org
www.composerscollab.org
Promotes new music as an integral part of our lives and culture. We help creative and performing artists connect with audiences by encouraging big ideas, fueling vital collaborations, and producing innovative multidisciplinary performances.

The Deli
info@thedelimagazine.com
www.thedelimagazine.com
Provides news and in-depth interviews with local bands, analyses of where the scene is headed, CD and equipment reviews and features.

Elizabeth Records
PO Box 22049, Brooklyn, NY 11202
PH: 212-330-7082
info@elizabethrecords.com
www.elizabethrecords.com
Promotes Indie Folk artists.

eXtreme NY
info@extremeny.com
www.extremeny.com
Contains a calendar with reviews of Extreme music events.

Fearless Music TV Show
mail@fearlessmusic.tv
www.fearlessmusic.tv
Weekly show featuring Indie bands.

Flavorpill NYC
594 Broadway #1212, New York, NY 10012
PH: 212-253-9309 FX: 212-313-9833
nyc_events@flavorpill.net
flavorpill.net
A publishing company with a weekly e-mail events list.

Free Williamsburg
311 Graham Ave. Brooklyn, NY 11211
www.freewilliamsburg.com
Providing you with cutting edge music.

Gay City News
487 Greenwich St. #6A, New York, NY 10013
PH: 646-452-2500 FX: 646-452-2501
Email: Editor@gaycitynews.com
gaycitynews.com
Covers local GLBT music events and does the occasional CD review.

GO TIME Music
105 Buckingham #4A, Brooklyn, NY 11228
info@gotimemusic.com
www.gotimemusic.com
Creating a tangible community of support among musicians, bands, promoters, venues, managers agents and fans.

GothamJazz
webmaster@gothamjazz.com
www.gothamjazz.com
Shedding light on lesser known, Indie performers.

Greenwich Village Gazette
PO Box 1023 Island Hts., NJ 08732
www.nycny.com
Weekly news & entertainment paper.

Greenwich Village Gazette *Jazz Listings*
www.nycny.com/entertainment/jazz/index.html
Complete listing of NYC Jazz events.

HelloBrooklyn.com
PH: 917-754-3537
events@hellobrooklyn.com
www.hellobrooklyn.com
Send your calendar listings by e-mail.

HUGE!
hugemassif@gmail.com
www.hugemassif.com
Focuses on the NYC rave scene.

Indie Sounds NY
indiesoundsny.com
Each month we cover the musicians, the people and the places that combine to make up one of the most creative and vibrant artistic communities on the planet.

JACKMUSIC
332 Bleeker St. G7, New York, NY 10014
PH: 212-279-3941
info@jack-music.com
www.jack-music.com
We represent the music of NYC's best small label and unsigned talent.

Jazz Clubs in Brooklyn and Queens
www.ny.com/clubs/jazz/brooklyn&queens.html

Jazz Clubs in Manhatten
www.ny.com/clubs/jazz

Jazz Composers Collective
info@jazzcollective.com
www.jazzcollective.com
Advancing the development and presentation of music.

JazzNewYork – Art Attack
musicmargaret@earthlink.net
www.jazznewyork.org
For & about liberation musicians in NYC.

The L Magazine
20 Jay St. #207, Brooklyn, NY 11201
PH: 718-596-3462
info@thelmagazine.com
thelmagazine.com
A distillation of the best music and special events the city has to offer. A little window into what's happening in our lunatic city.

Mass Appeal
689 Myrtle Ave. #2A, Brooklyn, NY 11205
PH: 718-858-0979 FX: 347-365-2159
Gavin Stevens gavin@massappealmag.com
www.massappealmag.com
Focuses on urban culture, music, art and fashion.

Neatness.com
webmaster@neatness.com
www.neatness.com
Music resource for the NYC area. Photos, calendar and more!

Neitherland
www.neitherland.com
Guide to the Gothic, Industrial, vampyre and fetish scene.

New York Blues and Jazz Society
134 Overlook St., Mt. Vernon, NY 10552
info@nybluessociety.org
www.nybluesandjazz.org
Blues news, reviews, listings etc.

New York Blade
333 7th Ave. 14th Fl. New York, NY 10001
PH: 212-268-2701 FX: 212-268-2069
www.nyblade.com
A weekly newspaper covering the New York Gay communities.

New York City Area Bluegrass Music Scene
benfreed@optonline.net
banjoben.com
A calendar of Bluegrass events. Submit your info.

New York City Classical Guitar Society
www.nyccgs.com
Providing a dynamic community for Classical guitarists in New York City.

New York Cool
newyorkcoolstuff@aol.com
www.newyorkcool.com
Entertainment site that gives great coverage of local musicians and events.

New York Metro
444 Madison Ave. 4th Fl. New York, NY 10022
www.newyorkmetro.com/arts/theweek/music
A&E magazine. Covers local music.

New York Metropolitan Country Music Assc.
PO Box 260201, Bellrose, NY 11426-0201
PH: 718-763-4328
www.nymcma.org
Promoting Country music and dance in the metropolitan area. We produce a series of free concerts in public parks during the summer. These concerts feature at least one local band.

New York Music Guide
newyork.citysearch.com
Extensive coverage of the local music scene. Post your shows and events.

New York Musician
PH: 917-576-3745
listing@newyorkmusician.com
www.newyorkmusician.com
Free guide to NYC music industry.

New York Pinewoods Folk Music Club
450 7th Ave. #972, New York, NY 10123
PH: 212-563-4099
nypinewood@aol.com
www.folkmusicny.org
Concerts and events plus a monthly newsletter.

New York Press
333 7th Ave. 14th Fl. New York, NY 10001
PH: 212-244-2282 FX: 212-244-9864
listings@nypress.com
www.nypress.com
Free weekly A&E paper. Reviews CDs and concerts by Indie artists. We also help out local artists by listing them in our weekly calendar.

NewYorkCity.com
235 Pinelawn Rd. Melville, NY 11747-4250
PH: 516-843-2000
ndstaff@newsday.com
www.nyc.com
Guide to New York music and clubs.

Notorious Marketing & Promotion
31-15 30th St. #3R, Astoria, NY 11106
PH: 718-545-9816
Notorious L.I.Z. notorious@notoriousradio.com
www.notoriousradio.com
Promotes Alternative/Rock Indie bands and artists.

NY JAZZ REPORT
WillWolf@NYJazzReport.com
www.nyjazzreport.com
News and links about jazz in NYC. Musicians, clubs, concerts, poetry, music, interviews etc.

NY Rock
PO Box 563, Gracie Stn. New York, NY 10028
PH: 212-426-4657
www.nyrock.com
Reviews full length CDs.

NY Waste
PO Box 20005, W. Village Stn.
New York, NY 10014
FX: 212-243-7252
info@newyorkwaste.com
www.newyorkwaste.com
New York's Punk Rock newspaper. News, reviews and attitude.

NYC Gothic Events
nygothic@razorwire.com
anon.razorwire.com/events
Add your news or upcoming events.

NYC Music Places
61 W. 23rd St. 4th Fl. New York, NY 10010-4205
PH: 212-886-2503 FX: 212-737-1496
info@nycmusicplaces.org
www.nycmusicplaces.org
Find rehearsal and performance spaces in NYC.

NYC Reggae
rasadam12@hotmail.com
web.syr.edu/~affellem/nycshows.html
Covering concerts, shows and dances in the NYC area.

NYMusicLife.com
mlo4ny@aol.com
nymusiclife.com
Linking NYC bands and fans together.

PAPERMAG
365 Broadway, New York, NY 10013
PH: 212-226-4405 FX: 212-226-0062
edit@papermag.com
www.papermag.com
Guide to urban culture, events, people, news and entertainment.

Popular Music Venues in NYC
www.ny.com/clubs/pop
Virtually every band that steps foot in the United States plays some dates in or around New York City and the City's Rock clubs have a history of discovering and showcasing new acts.

Real Magic TV
PO Box 264, Bedford Hills, NY 10507-0264
PH: 917-495-0741
www.realmagictv.com
Send your band's material in for a chance to get booked.

Roulette Television
228 W. Broadway, New York, NY 10013
PH: 212-219-8242 FX: 212-219-8773
info@roulette.org
www.roulette.org
Presents New Jazz, World Music, Experimental Rock, Improvisation, Traditional and Hybrid ensembles from New York City and around the world.

Songwriter's Beat
PO Box 20086, W. Village Stn.
New York, NY 10014
val@valghent.com
songwritersbeat.com
Create an environment where musicians can share their experiences.

SoundArt
PO Box 70, Stottville, NY 12172
PH: 518-828-0131
soundarts@soundart.org
www.soundart.org
New York City's source for information on concerts of contemporary music.

Suburban Clash
PO Box 5651, Hauppauge, NY 11788
Gaelen Harlacher gaelen@suburbanclashzine.net
www.suburbanclashzine.net
Information on the Long Island/NYC Hardcore scene. News, reviews etc.

Time Out New York
475 10th Ave. 12th Fl. New York, NY 10018
PH: 646-432-3000 FX: 646-432-3010
music@timeoutny.com
www.timeoutny.com
The obsessive guide to impulsive entertainment.

UMO Music
10 West 15 St. #313, New York, NY 10011
PH: 212-727-1352
Ernest Budnick umo@umo.com
www.umo.com
Provides online artist promotional accounts, live music events and compilation CDs.

Video City TV
PO Box 1607, New York, NY 10013
Attn: A&R Department
212-613-0072
videocitytv@aol.com
www.videocity.tv
Cable show that spotlights Indie music.

The Village Broadsheet
302 E. 3rd St. #5A, New York, NY 10009
eric@ericfeig.com
www.villagebroadsheet.com
CD and show reviews.

Village Voice
36 Cooper Sq. New York, NY 10003
PH: 212-475-3333
www.villagevoice.com
Alternative weekly newspaper. Extensive A&E section.

Vocal Area Network
890 West End Ave. #11B,
New York, NY 10025-3521
steve.friedman@van.org
www.van.org
Dedicated to the advancement of vocal ensemble music in the New York City area. Our information-sharing services are offered for the benefit of the vocal ensemble community.

Volunteer Lawyers for the Arts
1 E. 53rd St. 6th Fl. New York, NY 10022-4201
PH: 212-319-2787 FX: 212-752-6575
askvla@vlany.org
www.vlany.org
Pro bono legal services for artists.

Webtunes
39-37 50th St., Woodside, NY 11377
FX: 718-426-6346
John Elder tunemaster@webtunes.com
www.webtunes.com
New York City's premier music guide.

ZydecoRoad.com
zydecoroad@yahoo.com
www.zydecoroad.com
Covering Zydeco and Cajun music in New York City and on Long Island.

North Carolina

A. WarnerEntertainment
3615-B St Johns Ct. Wilmington, NC 28403
Annette Warner awarnerentertainment@ec.rr.com
www.awarnerentertainment.com
Catering to a variety of up and coming local and regional Singer/Songwriter's, bands and entertainers.

Asheville Citizen Times
PO Box 2090, Asheville, NC 28802
PH: 828-232-5855
tkiss@citizen-times.com
www.citizen-times.com
Reviews CDs and interviews bands if playing in the area.

Banjo in the Hollow
8700 Foggy Bottom Dr. Raleigh, NC 27613
PH: 919-676-9118
banjointhehollow@earthlink.net
www.rtpnet.org/~bith
Preserving and promoting Bluegrass and Old-Time music.

Blues Society of the Lower Cape Fear
PO Box 1487, Wilmington, NC 28402-1487
PH: 910-350-8822
cfblues01@capefearblues.org
www.capefearblues.com
Welcomes listeners, musicians and Blues enthusiasts.

Cape Fear Live
PO Box 4741, Wilmington, NC 28406
PH: 910-392-9887
webmaster@cflive.com
www.cflive.com
Wilmington's A&E magazine.

Carolina Spins
spins.us/Carolina
Showcasing North and South Carolina electronic Dance music.

Central Carolina Songwriters Association
1144 Amber Acres Ln. Knightdale, NC 27545
PH: 919-266-5791
ccsa_raleigh@yahoo.com
www.ccsa-raleigh.com
Promotes songwriting and music in NC.

Charlotte Blues Society
PO Box 32752, Charlotte, NC 28232-2752
PH: 704-331-8871
www.charlottebluessociety.org
Presents Blues concerts, forums, workshops, and educational programs.

Charlotte Chapter NSAI
PH: 704-846-3873
www.secondwindmusic.com/NSAICLT
Supporting songwriters through workshops, festivals and concerts.

Charlotte Folk Society
PO Box 36864, Charlotte, NC 28236-6864
PH: 704-372-3655 FX: 704-563-5382
shsnow@mindspring.com
www.folksociety.org
Promoting contemporary Folk music, dance and crafts.

Charlotte Live Music.com
PO Box 34726, Charlotte, NC 28234-4726
www.charlottelivemusic.com
Guide for live music, bands, venues and the local music scene.

The Chronicle
PO Box 90858, Durham, NC 27708
PH: 919-684-2663
www.chronicle.duke.edu
Duke University's student paper.

Creative Loafing Charlotte
6112 Pineville Rd. Charlotte, NC 28217
PH: 704-522-8334 FX: 704-522-8088
backtalk@creativeloafing.com
charlotte.creativeloafing.com
Free weekly alternative paper. Covers local and national music.

Dalloway Records
PO Box 4751, Greensboro, NC 27404 Attn: A & R
Christina Lewis clewis@dallowayrecords.com
www.dallowayrecords.com
An independent record label based in North Carolina.

East Carolinian
2nd Fl. Old Cafeteria Complex,
Greenville, NC 27858
PH: 252-328-6366 FX: 252-328-6558
listmaster@theeastcarolinian.com
www.theeastcarolinian.com
East Carolina University's student paper.

Eastern North Carolina Bluegrass Association
PH: 252-523-5735
adam1@icomnet.com
www.encbluegrass.freeservers.com
Promoting Bluegrass across the region.

Edge Magazine
PO Box 478, Swansboro, NC 28584
edgeguy@edgemagazineonline.com
www.edgemagazineonline.com
The only magazine in Eastern NC that doesn't suck!

Encore
PO Box 12430, Wilmington, NC 28405
PH: 910-791-0688 FX: 910-791-9177
email@encorepub.com
www.encorepub.com
Covers local music with interviews, previews and reviews.

Fiddle & Bow Society
PO Box 10447, Winston-Salem, NC 27108
PH: 336-727-1038
fb@fiddleandbow.org
www.fiddleandbow.org
Preserving Folk music, dance and related arts.

gate city noise
401 Tate St., Greensboro, NC 27403
PH: 336-272-7883 FX: 336-272-5994
gatecitynoise@mindspring.com
www.gatecitynoise.com
Covering the Greensboro music scene.

goTriad.com
sales@thedepot.com
www.gotriad.com
Covering A&E in Greensboro.

Guitartown
webmaster@guitartown.org
www.guitartown.org
Features news of the thriving North Carolina Roots music scene.

Infinite Limits Publishing
821 Shadyside Ln, Todd, NC 28684
PH: 336-877-3533
Greg Taylor infinitelimits@quickspeed.net
www.infinitelimits.net
I provide music publishing, graphic design for CD covers and promo packages and website design. I also accept CDs to sell online and list bands in the Performing Acts section.

Independent Weekly
PO Box 2690, Durham, NC 27715
PH: 919-286-1972 FX: 919-286-4274
Kirk Ross kross@indyweek.com
indyweek.com
Interviews bands, previews and reviews CDs and concerts.

ListeningRoomTour.com
3615-B St Johns Ct. Wilmington, NC 28403
Annette Warner awarnerentertainment@ec.rr.com
ListeningRoomTour.com
Dedicated to building and maintaining the largest database of 'Listening Room' atmospheres for Live Music, Poetry and Stand-Up Comedy acts.

Lumber River Regional Bluegrass Association
PO Box 565, Lumberton, NC 28359
PH: 910-739-2935 FX: 910-739-9800
rgs-lubt@carolina.net
www.lrrba.com
Keeping alive the Bluegrass traditions of our country.

Mountain Xpress
PO Box 144, Asheville, NC 28802
PH: 828-251-1333 FX: 828-251-1311
webmaster@mountainx.com
mountainx.com/ae/music.php
Has music section covering the Asheville area music scene.

musicomet
PO Box 31725, Charlotte, NC 28231
PH: 704-527-7570
Samir Shukla cometriderx@yahoo.com
www.musicomet.com
I am the current Listing Editor and Music Writer for the weekly alternative newspaper - Creative Loafing (Charlotte).

NC Goth DOT COM
steve@ncgoth.com
www.ncgoth.com
All the info on the North Carolina Goth scene.

NCMusic.com
PO Box 17383, Winston-Salem, NC 27116-7383
noel@ncmusic.com
www.ncmusic.com
Opinions and reviews about music in North Carolina.

NCSC Buzz
www.ncscbuzz.com
The largest Carolinas music portal on the web.

NCScene.com
63 John Lewis Rd. Walstonburg, NC 27888
webmaster@ncscene.com
www.ncscene.com
All bands and artists may submit music and/or press material.

North Carolina Songwriters Co-op
joey@joeytownsend.com
www.ncsongwriters.org
Promoting songwriters in the state of North Carolina.

Piedmont Blues Preservation Society
PO Box 9737, Greensboro, NC 27429
info@piedmontblues.org
www.piedmontblues.org
Preserving the fine art of American Blues.

Raleigh Underground
dj-joey@raleighunderground.com
www.raleighunderground.com
Lists info on Raleigh's Underground music scene.

Raleighmusic.com
joanna@raleighmusic.com
www.raleighmusic.com
Marketing local artists to a regional audience.

SongwritersSoapbox.com
c/o A. Warner Ent. 3615-B St Johns Ct. Wilmington, NC 28403
PH: 910-793-1507
Annette Warner awarnerentertainment@ec.rr.com
www.SongwritersSoapbox.com
Creating the perfect ambiance for listening and enjoying a songwriter in their rawest form.

Stwrongtone
PH: 252-714-2296
Tony Murnahan tony@stwrongtone.com
www.stwrongtone.com
Dedicated to offering resources to North Carolina area bands and musicians.

Technician
323 Witherspoon Student Ctr. NCSU, Raleigh, NC 27695
PH: 919-515-2411 FX: 919-515-5133
diversions@technicianonline.com
technicianonline.com
NCSU student newspaper.

Up & Coming Magazine
PH: 910-484-6200
www.upandcomingmag.com
Weekly A&E paper. Artist interviews, CD and concert reviews.

Wilkes Acoustic/Folk Society
PO Box 2038, N. Wilkesboro, NC 28659-2038
PH: 336-838-2425
kwatts@wilkes.net
www.wilkesfolks.com
Educating the public in music appreciation.

WilmingtonNCMusic.com
3615-B St Johns Ct. Wilmington, NC 28403
Annette Warner awarnerentertainment@ec.rr.com
wilmingtonncmusic.com
We provide venue and musician pages, free musician and venue listings, CD reviews, press releases and articles.

ZSpotlight
PH: 919-215-5000
webmaster@ZSpotlight.com
www.zspotlight.com
Information on who's playing where in the Triangle.

North Dakota

Barking Dog Records
coates@barkingdogrecords.com
www.barkingdogrecords.com
Promoting outstanding artists from the Upper Midwest.

BUSTHQ.com
busthq.fargousa.com
Supporting independent music in the Northern Plains!

DickinsonBands.com
PH: 701-483-0491
Kyle Thiel gonaweigh@dickinsonbands.com
DickinsonBands.com
Created to promote local and area talent in Dickinson, ND.

FargoUnderground.com
fargounderground.com
A whole new site for Fargo-Moorhead nightlife & entertainment.

ndin.tv
ndintv@hotmail.com
www.vastlane.org/ndintv
An internet video show featuring all regional bands (primarily ND). Live videos, band promotions, websites, mp3 links, interviews, comedy, and most importantly, the promotion of local talent.

North Dakota Indie Nation
www.ndindienation.com
A discussion forum dedicated to the ND indie music scene.

North Dakota State University Spectrum
www.ndsuspectrum.com
Campus publication. Covers local music.

Saboingaden.com
www.saboingaden.com
Fargo Electonica community & center of the Electronica earth. Dedicated to news and events in the ND and MN region.

Vastlane.org
contact@vastlane.org
www.vastlane.org
Grand Forks' community driven resource. Music, poetry, calendar etc... it all comes from members or passers by who feel an idea, opinion, story, event, or discussion is important.

Ohio

Athens Musician's Network
amn@frognet.net
www.athensmusician.net
Covers the local music scene around Athens.

Blues, Jazz & Folk Music Society
PO Box 2122, Marietta, OH 45750
PH: 740-373-6640
bjfm@bjfm.org
www.bjfm.org
Promoting Blues, Jazz & Folk music in the Mid-Ohio Valley.

Central Ohio Bluegrass Association
5858 S. Alley, Columbus, OH 43230
www.centralohiobluegrass.com
Preserving Bluegrass in the central Ohio area.

CowTownMusic.com
PO Box 144, Orient, OH 43146
sixis@columbus.rr.com
www.cowtownmusic.com
Source for live entertainment in central Ohio.

Highlands of Ohio
637 Edgewood Rd. Mansfield, OH 44907
PH: 419-522-5058
highlands@neo.rr.com
www.highlandsofohio.com
Keeps the local community informed of Celtic concerts and other events.

Midwest Invasion
PO Box 422, Youngstown, OH 44501-0422
www.midwestinvasion.com
Offers Hip Hop CD reviews, MP3s, streaming radio, a store and more.

Ohio Bands Online
PH: 330-206-0564
ohiobandsonline@yahoo.com
www.ohiobandsonline.com
A listing of Ohio bands by city and genre.

Ohio Hystairical Musick Society
Jimi Imij jimi_imij1us@yahoo.com
ohms.nu
We list the shows and venues where bands can get gigs. Send in your band and gig info.

Ohio Online Magazine
www.ohioonline.com
Supporting the local music scene.

OhioRap.com
cr4zyt@ohiorap.com
www.ohiorap.com
A free website designed for artists and fans. Our goal is to help put Ohio on the map.

Utter Trash
PO Box 200496, Cleveland, OH 44120
trashmag@uttertrash.net
www.uttertrash.net
Covering the best underground entertainment in Northeast Ohio and beyond.

Cincinnati

Cincinnati CityBeat
811 Race St. 5th Fl. Cincinnati, OH 45202
PH: 513-665-4700 FX: 513-665-4368
letters@citybeat.com
www.citybeat.com
Covers news, A & E, reviews CDs and posts gigs.

Cincinnati Music Online
PO Box 54096, Cincinnati, OH 45254
cincymusic.com
Free promotion of Cincinnati artists and music.

Cincinnati Shows
PO Box 42815, Cincinnati, OH 45242-0815
cincyshows@niceguyrecords.com
www.cincinnatishows.com
Show listings, downloads, links, pictures etc. of Cincinnati bands.

Cincinnatibands.com
cincinnatibands.com
Covering everything about local bands.

Greater Cincinnati Blues Society
PO Box 6098, Cincinnati, OH 45206
PH: 513-684-4227
info@cincyblues.org
www.cincyblues.org
Advancing the culture and tradition of Blues music.

Greater Cincinnati Guitar Society
gtr2971@fuse.net
www.cincinnatiguitarsociety.org
Get in touch with the local Acoustic scene.

Cleveland

ClePunk
mark.vocca@clepunk.com
www.clepunk.com
All the info on the local Punk scene.

Cleveland-Ain't It Fun
157 Fair St., Berea, OH 44017
comp@cleveland-aintitfun.com
www.cleveland-aintitfun.com
The majority of the acts featured on this site fall underneath the genres of Punk, Hardcore, Metal, emo etc.

Cleveland Composers Guild
jaquick@en.com
my.en.com/~jaquick/ccg.html
Promoting the music of composers living in Northeast Ohio.

Cleveland Free Times
800 W. St. Clair Ave. 2nd Fl.
Cleveland, OH 44113-1266
PH: 216-479-2033
Jeff Niesel jniesel@freetimes.com
www.freetimes.com
Covers local music scene. CD and concert previews and reviews.

Cleveland Metal
joe@cleveland-metal.com
www.cleveland-metal.com
News, reviews, downloads etc.

Cleveland Metal Connection
submissions@clevmetalconn.org
www.clevmetalconn.org
Connect to the Metal scene. Features a band of the month.

Cleveland Punk Scene.com
PO Box 21263, Cleveland, OH 44121
www.clevelandpunkscene.com
Send in your reviews, interviews, gigs etc.

Cleveland Scene
PO Box 15029, Cleveland, OH 44115-0029
PH: 216-241-7550 FX: 216-802-7212
jason.bracelin@clevescene.com
www.clevescene.com
Alternative news weekly.

Cleveland.com
entertainment@cleveland.com
www.cleveland.com/music
Create a free web site for your band.

ClevelandWeirdness
PO Box 771398, Lakewood, OH 44107
audio@clevelandweirdness.com
www.clevelandweirdness.com
We highlight different local talent every month.

Domain Cleveland
PO Box 609127, Cleveland, OH 44109
Dougless R. Esper dougless@domaincleveland.com
www.domaincleveland.com
A booking and promotions company for all genres.

The North Coast STARS
c/o MAPATV, PO Box 111285,
Cleveland, OH 44111
visitor@ncstars.tv
www.ncstars.tv
Video magazine that showcases original material submitted by artists.

Proartist
PO Box 609105, Cleveland, OH 44109
PH: 216-269-6607
proartist@ncstars.tv
www.ncstars.tv/proartist.htm
We are concentrating our efforts to promote artists through the North Coast Stars video program.

Starvation Army Zine
11124 Clifton Blvd. #9, Cleveland, OH 44102
starvationarmyzine@yahoo.com
groups.myspace.com/starvationarmyzine
All things in the DIY world!!! Mostly CLEVELAND shite.

Columbus

Columbus Alive
1079 N. High St., Columbus, OH 43201
PH: 614-221-2449 FX: 614-221-2456
Stephen Slaybaugh stephen@columbusalive.com
www.columbusalive.com
Covers local Indie music with concert previews and reviews.

Columbus Blues Alliance
1350 W. 5th Ave. #10-D, Columbus, OH 43212
PH: 614-486-4575
info@columbusblues.com
www.colsbluesalliance.org
Encourages ties between traditional and electric Blues.

ColumbusArts.com
100 E. Broad St. #2250 Columbus, OH 43215
PH: 614-224-2606 FX: 614-224-7461
tkauffman@gcac.org
www.columbusarts.com
Resource for Central Ohio culture and arts.

columbusMUSIC.com
1800 West 5th Ave. Columbus, OH 43212
columbusmusic.com
Dedicated to providing local music fans with Central Ohio's best online local music resource.

columbusound.com
paul@artclix.com
www.columbusound.com
Central Ohio's #1 music directory!

Cringe
PO Box 10276, Columbus, OH 43201
PH: 614-421-7589
webmaster@cringe.com
www.cringe.com
Accepts nearly all submissions from the Columbus area.

The Lantern
242 W. 18th Ave. Columbus, OH 43210
PH: 614-292-2031 FX: 614-292-3722
Lantern@osu.edu
www.thelantern.com
Ohio State University's student paper.

musicohio
5579 Valencia Park Blvd. Hilliard, OH 43026
PH: 614-771-4243
Jason Perlman jason@musicohio.com
www.musicohio.com
Un-known artists get recognition. Covers mostly the Columbus area.

The Other Paper
5255 Sinclair Rd. Columbus, OH 43229
PH: 614-847-3800 FX: 614-848-3838
www.theotherpaper.com
Covers Indie music with band interviews, CD and concert previews and reviews.

Dayton

Dayton Band Resource Page
1408 Poplar Dr. Fairborn, OH 45324
PH: 937-878-4937
Tony Hurley info@DaytonBands.com
www.daytonbands.com
Helping Indie local musicians become successful.

H.M.D. Music Resource Guide
251 W. Central Ave. #292,
Springboro, OH 45066-1103
PH: 937-746-4426
Sonny Thomas contact@thehmd.com
www.thehmd.com
Gem City resource where "unsigned" means you're a star here!

NiteOnTheTown.com
3430 S. Dixie Dr. #200, Dayton, OH 45439
PH: 937-297-3052 FX: 937-293-4523
webmaster@niteonthetown.com
www.niteonthetown.com
Guide to local nightlife. Includes local music listings.

WXEG's Local Band Page
101 Pine St., Dayton, OH 45402
PH: 937-224-1137 FX: 937-224-9965
Shoom shoom@wxeg.com
www.wxeg.com/pages/local_bands.html
Always keeping you up to date on the music that you love.

Toledo

Renegade Concerts
2542 Heatherhills Rd. #E, Toledo, OH 43614
chris@renegadeconcerts.com
PH: 419-283-2818
www.renegadeconcerts.com
We have produced over 100 concerts since 1999. Local, regional and unsigned touring acts, please visit our website to find out what we require in a press kit, and how to get it to us.

Toledo Jazz Society
425 N. St. Clair, Toledo, OH 43604
PH: 419-241-5299 FX: 419-241-4777
toledojazz@toledojazzsociety.org
www.toledojazzsociety.org
Increasing the appreciation of Jazz.

Toledopunks.com
www.toledopunks.com
All the contacts, bands and info needed on the Toledo Punk scene.

T-townmusic.com
scott-stamp@t-townmusic.com
www.t-townmusic.com
Your source for NorthwestOhio and Southeast Michigan's local music scene.

Oklahoma

91FM Local Music Page
www.kokf.com/localbands.html
We'll post your band's info. You must be a Oklahoma Christian band.

The Bartlesville Music Scene
Bridget Martin bridgetkt@cableone.net
www.thebartlesvillemusicscene.com
Promotes local bands in and around Bartlesville. Interviews, photos, blog, calendar, etc. for all in the community to use.

BestofTulsa.com *Music*
4821 S. Sheridan #228, Tulsa, OK 74145
PH: 918-632-0000
info@bestoftulsa.com
bestoftulsa.com/html/music.shtml
Listings, spotlights, events etc.

Celtic Oklahoma
celticoklahoma@yahoo.com
www.celticoklahoma.com
Information about sessions, concerts, festivals, or anything else that might be of interest to players and lovers of Celtic music.

The Collegian
600 S. College, Tulsa, OK 74104
PH: 918-631-3818 FX: 918-631-2885
collegian@utulsa.edu
www.utulsa.edu/collegian
University of Tulsa's student paper.

Green Country Bluegrass Association
PO Box 2002, Owasso, OK 74055-2002
Don Casady gcbg_editor@cox.net
www.gcba.homestead.com
Promoting Bluegrass in Northeast Oklahoma.

Homegrown Music Jam
www.homegrownmj.com
Our mission is to help promote bands, songwriters and artists of all types.

MidwestVenues.com
Pat O'Reilly Midwestvenues@aol.com
www.midwestvenues.com
Providing the music community with info on thousands of venues in the greater Midwest region where bands/artist perform or are scheduled to perform.

The Norman Transcript
PO Drawer 1058, Norman, OK 73070
PH: 405-321-1800 FX: 405-366-3516
pop@normantranscript.com
www.normantranscript.com
Pop section covers the local music scene.

NormanMusicScene.com
511 Highland Parkway, Norman, OK 73069
pchelp@normanmusicscene.com
www.normanmusicscene.com
Linking local musical artists, events & venues.

NormanNow.com
sales@normannow.com
www.normannow.com
Post your band info and upcoming shows.

OKC Live
PH: 405-410-7360
info@okclive.com
www.okclive.com
Oklahoma City's online entertainment source.

Oklahoma Blues Society
PO Box 76176, Oklahoma City, OK 73147-2176
PH: 405-523-0110
www.okblues.org
CD reviews, news, gig listings etc.

Oklahoma Bluegrass Events
Charles Donaghe cdonaghe@cableone.net
myweb.cableone.net/cdonaghe/bgrassfest.htm
Add information about your upcoming shows.

Oklahoma City Traditional Music Association
PO Box 60087, Oklahoma City, OK 73146
www.octma.org
Learning, teaching and playing Acoustic Folk music.

Oklahoma Country Music Association
ocma@oklahomacma.com
www.oklahomacma.com
Created to promote and advance Country & Western music and its artists in the State of Oklahoma.

Oklahoma Music Guide
author@oklahomamusicguide.com
www.oklahomamusicguide.com
Up to date news about the local music scene.

Oklahoma Music Magazine
7134 S. Yale, Ste. 720, Tulsa, OK 74136
PH: 866-656-6241 FX: 918-491-9946
www.oklahomamusic.biz
The only magazine devoted entirely to the heritage, sounds, people and events that shape the music and entertainment scene in our state.

OklahomaHardcore.com
admin@oklahomahardcore.com
www.oklahomahardcore.com
Shows, news, message boards...

OklahomaPunkscene.com
Barb spano25@hotmail.com
www.oklahomapunkscene.com
Articles, interviews, photos, reviews and more!

OklahomaRock.com
Ryan LaCroix ryan@oklahomarock.com
www.oklahomarock.com
A website helping others to realize what great talents are out there in Oklahoma. News, reviews etc.

Omnizine
PO Box 35854, Tulsa, OK 74153
Joe Cinocca zingali@omnizine.com
www.omnizine.com
Independent music zine featuring album reviews, concert reviews and more.

The Oracle
7777 S. Lewis Ave. Tulsa, OK 74171
PH: 918-495-6346 FX: 918-495-6345
oraclechief@oru.edu
www.oru.edu/oracle
Student paper. Does spotlights on local musicians.

Payne County Line Promotions
3333 E. 68th St., Stillwater, OK 74074
PH: 405-612-5477
Stan Moffat stan@paynecountyline.com
www.paynecountyline.com
Working hard to support Oklahoma live music!

Red Dirt Scene
jtq4x4@aol.com
www.reddirtscene.com
Oklahoma is the birthplace of "Red Dirt" music, launching some of today's' most respected working musicians out into the arms of the music nation. We offer up to date news of these bands.

Southwest Songwriters Association
PH: 580-354-1402
music@sirinet.net
www.swsongwriters.com
Place for musicians looking for bands, or bands looking for musicians.

StillOK Records
re: Demo Submission, 1822 N. Perkins Rd. #1124, Stillwater, OK 74075
PH: 405-533-1885
info@stillokrecords.com
www.stillokrecords.com
Discovering & developing unsigned artists in the Midwest and Texas regions.

Stillwater Scene
916 North Duck, Stillwater, OK 74075
PH: 405-762-9733
jared@stillwaterscene.com
www.stillwaterscene.com
Magazine with local music news, reviews, intererviews etc.

Tulsa Music Pulse
www.tulsamusicpulse.com
Tulsa Bands heard here. Cuz every band was local at some point. Protect endangered music.

Tulsa Rock 'n' Roll
8530 E. 131st St. S., Bixby, OK 74008
Emmett Lollis Jr. emmett@tulsarocknroll.com
www.tulsarocknroll.com
Home of the Tulsa Rock music scene. If you would like to be considered for a CD review or interview please mail us your press kit .

TulsaBands.com
tulsabands.com
Oklahoma's #1 website for Tulsa Bands and Music!!!

tulsajazz.com
PH: 918-232-0157
Tim DeMoss tim@tulsajazz.com
www.tulsajazz.com
Providing an online portal to the activities of the Tulsa Jazz community.

TulsaMusicScene.com
www.tulsamusicscene.com
Showing the world the sea of musical talent that Tulsa has to offer.

Urban Tulsa Weekly
710 S. Kenosha, Tulsa, OK 74120
PH: 918-592-5550 FX: 918-592-5970
urbantulsa@urbantulsa.com
www.urbantulsa.com
Free weekly A&E paper. Covers local music scene.

Yawn Records
PO Box 35854, Tulsa, OK 74153
yawnrecords2@hotmail.com
www.yawnrecords.com
Tulsa-based record label focusing on local artists.

Oregon

Cascade Blues Association
PO Box 14493, Portland, OR 97293-0493
PH: 503-223-1850
cbastaff@cascadeblues.org
www.cascadeblues.org
Promoting Blues and Roots music in the Great Northwest.

Creative Music Guild
PO Box 40564, Portland, OR 97240-0564
PH: 503-772-0772
cmg@creativemusicguild.org
www.creativemusicguild.org
Promotes new music that advances the art of composition.

Early Music Guild of Oregon
PO Box 593, Oregon City, OR 97045
www.cmgo.org
Bulletin board of news and events related to Early music.

Eugene Weekly
1251 Lincoln, Eugene, OR 97401
Melissa Bearns melissa@eugeneweekly.com
www.eugeneweekly.com
Eugene's A&E publication.

IndieAvenue.com
8152 SW Hall Blvd. #103, Beaverton, OR 97008
PH: 503-961-2998 FX: 717-828-8257
boyd@indieavenue.com
www.indieavenue.com
Database of Northwest musicians, bands and venues.

Jazz Society of Oregon
PO Box 986, Portland, OR 97207
PH: 503-234-1332 FX: 503-452-4009
info@jsojazzscene.org
www.jsojazzscene.org
Promotes Jazz musicians, Jazz education and Jazz appreciation.

Kingbanana
kngbanana@aol.com
www.kingbanana.net
Covering the Portland Punk/Hardcore/Metal scene.

NAIL Distribution
14134 NE Airport Way, Portland, OR 97230
PH: 888-6245-462 FX: 503-257-9061
info@naildistribution.com
www.naildistribution.com
Placing independent music in Northwest stores.

Nexus Underground
jeremy@nexusunderground.com
www.nexusunderground.com
Indie distribution center offering free distribution, MP3s and more.

NightPiper Productions
c/o Sabala's Mt. Tabor, 4811 SE Hawthorne Blvd.
Portland, OR 97215
PH: 503-819-5979
info@nightpiper.com
nightpiper.com
Booking company featuring local acts, clubs and upcoming events.

Northeast Oregon Folklore Society
PO Box 433, LaGrande, OR 97850
info@neofs.us
www.neofs.us
Promotes traditional forms of music and dance.

Oregon Bluegrass Association
PO Box 1115, Portland, OR 97207
PH: 503-507-1947
Darlene G. Rominger romcom@comcast.net
www.oregonbluegrass.org
Promotes, encourages, fosters and cultivates bluegrass. The Bluegrass Express is our bi-monthly newsletter.

Oregon Live
kcosgrov@oregonlive.com
www.oregonlive.com/music
All the info on the Oregon music scene.

PDX Bands.com
PO Box 17509, Portland, OR 97217
info@pdxbands.com
pdxbands.com
What Portland sounds like.

Portland Folklore Society
PO Box 1448, Portland, OR 97207-1448
PH: 503-697-8159
mail@portlandfolklore.org
www.portlandfolklore.org
Promoting Folk music and arts in the greater Portland area.

Portland Mercury
605 NE 21st Ave. #200, Portland, OR 97232
PH: 503-294-0840 FX: 503-294-0844
events@portlandmercury
www.portlandmercury.com
Portland's A&E weekly. Submit your info.

Portland Songwriters Association
PO Box 42389, Portland, OR 97242
PH: 503-914-1000
info@portlandsongwriters.org
www.portlandsongwriters.org
Developing the talents of our members.

portlandmusicians.com
1802 SE Clatsop St., Portland, OR 97202
PH: 503-230-4854
tim@portlandmusicians.com
www.portlandmusicians.com
Your online connection to the Portland music scene.

Two Louies Magazine
2745 NE 34th, Portland, OR 97212
PH: 503-284-5931
twolouie@aol.com
www.twolouiesmagazine.com
Portland monthly music paper. CD and concert reviews.

Willamette Week
825 SW 10th Ave. Portland, OR 97205
PH: 503-243-2122 FX: 503-243-1115
mbaumgarten@wweek.com
www.wweek.com
A weekly calendar of live music in venues throughout the city.

Pennsylvania

AK Music Scene
bill@akmusicscene.com
www.akmusicscene.com
Based in the Alle-Kiski Valley, we provide free resources to help promote unsigned bands, including: show calendar, an affiliation with Indie Band Radio and much more!

Arts & Music PA
mary02@epix.net
www.artsandmusicpa.com
Guide to the arts, music and local cultures of Pennsylvania.

AudioXposure
616 West Schuylkill Rd. Ste. 359,
Pottstown, PA 19465
Jennifer Mattern info@audioxposure.com
audioxposure.com
Promoting unsigned and independent musicians in Southeastern and Southcentral PA. We also highlight select non-local artists each month.

Berks Tonight
info@berkstonight.com
www.berkstonight.com
The source for what's happening in Reading PA and Berks County.

Billtown Blues Association
PO Box 935, Williamsport, PA 17737
PH: 570-323-1624
bbaweb88@suscom.net
www.billtownblues.org
Providing opportunities for area residents to experience Blues music. Our newsletter is the Blues Note.

Black Thorn Entertainment
dimensions@pa.net
blackthornentertainment.com
Assisting local talent in the entertainment business.

Bucks County Blues Society
PO Box 482, Levittown, PA 19058-0482
tjc3@voicenet.com
www.bucksbluessociety.com
Keeping the Blues alive in Bucks county!

Bucks County Folk Song Society
info@bucksfolk.org
www.bucksfolk.org
Furthering the interest and appreciation of Folk music.

Central PA Friends of Jazz
PO Box 10738, Harrisburg, PA 17105
PH: 717-540-1010 FX: 717-540-7735
cpfj@pajazz.org
www.pajazz.org
Presenting and promoting local and national Jazz artists.

Central Pennsylvania Blues Calendar
blueslinks@delta-blues.com
www.delta-blues.com/PABLUES.HTM
Listing Blues events in & around central PA.

ErieShows.com
Mike Torti miketorti@erieshows.com
www.erieshows.com
Covering the Erie Punk scene.

Fly Magazine
22 E. McGovern Ave. Lancaster, PA 17602
PH: 717-293-9772 FX: 717-295-7561
info@flymagazine.net
www.flymagazine.net
Central PA's most complete guide to entertainment.

Gallery of Sound
nardone@galleryofsound.com
www.galleryofsound.com
Monthly publication reviewing CDs along with interviews with new musicians.

Harrisburg Online
4401 N. 6th St. #222, Harrisburg, PA 17110
PH: 717-231-7019
info@hbgonline.com
www.hbgonline.com
Central PA's entertainment guide.

Homegrown Bands
PO Box 3530, York, PA 17402
webmaster@homegrownbands.net
www.homegrownbands.net
Central PA's home for promoting local bands.

The LAB (Local Area Bands)
2417 Cambridge Rd. York, PA 17402
admin@thelab-pa.com
www.thelab-pa.com
Encouraging the local area bands.

Lehigh Valley Blues Network
517 N. 6th St., Allentown, PA 18102
PH: 610-437-3217
jcm46@earthlink.net
www.lvbn.org
Promoting the Blues in the Lehigh Valley area.

Lehigh Valley Folk Music Society
402 S. 18th St., Allentown, PA 18104
PH: 610-433-8899
kristbenj@aol.com
lvfolkmusicsociety.org
Promoting the appreciation of the Old-Time American Folk music.

Northeast PA Blues Society
PO Box 124, Clarks Summit, PA 18411
greeneyedlady@happyhippie.com
www.nepablues.org
Creating an appreciation for live Blues and Roots music.

Out On the Town
100 Temple Blvd. Palmyra, NJ 08065
PH: 856-786-1600 FX: 856-786-1450
ootme2@aol.com
www.ootweb.com
Entertainment trade paper covering PA and NJ.

PABands.com
info@pabands.com
www.pabands.com
Sign your band up today. Free unlimited listing.

PaMidstate
tom@pamidstate.com
www.pamidstate.com
You're A&E guide to the Midstate region of PA.

Patriot News
2214 Market St., Camp Hill, PA 17011-4600
PH: 717-255-8161 FX: 717-255-8456
citydesk@pnco.com
www.patriot-news.com
Interviews bands, previews and reviews CDs and concerts.

PaXposure
1278 West Liberty Rd. Reynoldsville, PA 15851
PH: 814-894-5570
mail@paxposure.com
www.paxposure.com
Your most extensive source for PA's best indie artists.

Pennsylvania Musician
admin@pennsylvania-musician.com
www.pennsylvania-musician.com
Designed for PA and Maryland musicians to chat, find members, find gigs and help each other with playing tips and tricks.

Pennsylvania Musician Magazine
PO Box 362, Millerstown, PA 17062
PH: 717-444-2423
rnoll@pamusician.net
www.pamusician.net
Guide and marketing tool for the entertainment industry in PA.

Pennsylvania Ska Page
paska@kozlek.com
paska.kozlek.com
This page covers every aspect of the PA Ska scene.

Pennsylvania's Southern Gospel Website
www.southerngospelpa.com
All the info on the PA Gospel scene.

Pocono Bluegrass and Folk Society
PH: 570-421-0997
felixpap@ptd.net
www.poconobluegrass.org
Dedicated to the promotion and preservation of authentic Acoustic music.

Pulse Weekly
930 N. 4th St. #205, Allentown, PA 18102
PH: 610-437-7867 FX: 610-437-7869
Michael Faillace michaelf@pulseweekly.com
www.pulseweekly.com
Covering the A&E scene in the Lehigh Valley and beyond.

Rock in PA
andy@rockinpa.com
www.rockinpa.com
Information about local bands, concerts, clubs etc.

ROCKPAGE
www.rockpage.net
We're doing our best to serve the local and regional music community here in PA. Set up your own band page, list gigs etc.

Seven Mountains Bluegrass Association
827 New Valley Rd. Marysville, PA 17053-9716
www2.epix.net/~7mtns
Preserving and promoting Bluegrass music.

The Snapper
Student Memorial Center,
Millersville, PA 17551-0302
PH: 717-872-3516 FX: 717-872-3515
snapper@marauder.millersville.edu
www.thesnapper.com
Millersville University's student paper.

Sonicdrift.com
sonic_drift79@yahoo.com
www.sonicdrift.com
Southwestern PA's source for local music and more.

StateCollegeMusic.com
1907 Fairwood Ln. State College, PA 16803
PH: 814-360-3946
info@statecollegemusic.com
www.statecollegemusic.com
One-stop resource for local musicians.

Susquehanna Folk Music Society
378 Old York Rd. New Cumberland, PA 17070
PH: 717-763-5744
info@sfmsfolk.org
www.sfmsfolk.org
Preserving and encouraging the traditional arts in Central PA.

Susquehanna Life
637 Market St. PO Box 421, Lewisburg, PA 17837
PH: 570-522-0149 FX: 570-524-7796
www.susquehannalife.com
Central Pennsylvania's lifestyle magazine. Only info pertaining to this region is of interest to us.

Swarthmore Phoenix
Swarthmore College, 500 College Ave.
Swarthmore, PA 19081-1390
phoenix@swarthmore.edu
www.sccs.swarthmore.edu/org/phoenix
Student paper. A&E section.

The Underground
c/o After Midnight Media, PO Box 535,
Altoona, PA 16603
chris@theundergroundtv.com
www.theundergroundtv.com
A TV show filmed and produced in Central PA, featuring the region's best unsigned bands and musicians.

WebJHN.com
6393 Penn Ave. #319, Pittsburgh, PA 15206-4010
PH: 412-216-6790 FX: 412-362-3841
johng@webjhn.com
webjhn.com
Taking Hip Hop entertainment in Pittsburgh to the next level.

The Weekender
15 N. Main St., Wilkes-Barre, PA 18711
PH: 570-829-7101
www.timesleader.com
Free weekly A&E paper. Interviews bands and previews concerts.

Philadelphia

The 13th Child
info@the13thchild.com
the13thchild.com
Philadelphia Gothic & Industrial promotions & productions.

Groove Lingo
trishy@groovelingo.com
www.groovelingo.com
Covering the Philadelphia music scene. News, reviews and interviews.

HOSH Productions
Attn: Booking, 1304 E. 9th St. Apt #1,
Eddystone, PA 19022
PH: 610-800-9154
Chuck Clapper hoshproductions@hotmail.com
hoshproductions.cjb.net
Independent firm outside of Philadelphia that helps with basic web design, promoting and booking.

Jazzmatazz
4 E. Mt. Pleasant Ave. Philadelphia, PA 19119
Alan Lankin lankina@att.net
www.Jazzmatazz.info
I concentrate on Jazz and Jazz-related releases. List of upcoming shows.

Local Music Network
LMN Reviews, 112A Bala Ave.
Bala Cynwyd, PA 19004
Brain brain@localmusicnetwork.com
localmusicnetwork.com
The resource for discovering local music in the Philadelphia area. To get a review, send 2 copies of your CD to the above address.

maneo.com
www.maneo.com
Philadelphia's online nightlife guide. Spotlights local bands. Local events guide.

Origivation Magazine
PO Box 1412, Havertown, PA 19083
Anthony info@origivation.com
www.origivation.com
All-original music publication and hosts Philadelphia's most popular message board.

Philadelphia Ambient Consortium
Aharon Varady aharon@simpletone.com
www.simpletone.com
Unifying the city's Ambient, Chill Drum 'n Base, intelligent community.

Philadelphia City Paper
123 Chestnut St. 3rd Fl. Philadelphia, PA 19106
PH: 215-735-8444
pat@citypaper.net
citypaper.net
Free weekly alternative paper. Covers all music styles.

Philadelphia Classical Guitar Society
2038 Sansom St., Philadelphia, PA 19103
PH: 215-567-2972
membership@phillyguitar.com
www.phillyguitar.org
Encouraging Classical guitar activities in the area.

Philadelphia Musician Resource Kitchen
submissions@PhiladelphiaMRK.com
www.philadelphiamrk.com
Has areas designated to the uploading of just about anything you could possess.

Philadelphia Songwriters Project
PO Box 69, Ardmore, PA 19003
PH: 610-896-7664
dena@phillysongwriters.com
www.phillysongwriters.com
Local artists can showcase their music and advance their career.

Philadelphia Weekly
1500 Sansom St. 3rd Fl. Philadelphia, PA 19102
PH: 215-563-7400
Doree Shafrir dshafrir@philadelphiaweekly.com
www.philadelphiaweekly.com
Free weekly alternative paper. Does CD reviews.

Philly at Night
PO Box 52664, Philadelphia, PA 19115
PH: 215-673-0661 FX: 267-200-0084
info@phillyatnight.com
www.phillynightlife.com
Free listings for businesses and artists.

Philly Blues
phillyblues@comcast.net
www.phillyblues.com
A comprehensive list of Blues bands, events, and websites.

Philly Local Concert Listings
online@xpn.org
www.xpn.org/concerts.php
Submit your concert & event information. Be sure to include the date, artist, time, venue and hyperlink information.

Philly Goth
1429 Locust St., Norristown, PA 19401
jules@fusion-web.org
www.fusion-web.org/phillygoth
All the info on the local Goth scene.

Philly Prog Rock Connection
PO Box 687, Coatesville, PA 19320
info@pprcmusic.com
www.pprcmusic.com
Dedicated to bringing Progressive and intense music to the forefront.

PhillyHipHop.com
8500 Henry Ave. #124,
Philadelphia, PA 19128-2111
PH: 215-552-8812
info@phillyhiphop.com
www.phillyhiphop.com
Covers the local Hip Hop scene. Reviews CDs.

phillyjunglemassive.com
www.phillyjunglemassive.com
Covering the Philadelphia Jungle music scene.

phillymusic.com
www.phillymusic.com
All the latest on the Philly music scene.

phillytown.com
PO Box 63325, Philadelphia, PA 19114
webmaster@phillytown.com
www.phillytown.com
Add events and get your music reviewed.

Pipedreams Newsletter
3604 Calumet St., Philadelphia, PA 19129
Jim Calder jccalder2000@yahoo.com
New print newsletter doing music reviews of all types of music. Distributed in Philadelphia. Send CDs for review.

Showcase Underground Productions
www.showcaseunderground.com
Bringing the area's best artists together. We produce dynamic events which include live music, DJ's, dance and video recording.

tbtmo.com
PO Box 63619, Philadelphia, PA 19147
info@tbtmo.com
www.tbtmo.com
Covering the Philadelphia Electronic music scene.

Urban Web Link
PO Box 38922, Philadelphia, PA 19104
PH: 888-628-2618
admin@urbanweblink.com
www.urbanweblink.com
Your source for Urban Christian events in the Philadelphia area.

Wonkavision Magazine
PO Box 63642, Philadelphia, PA 19147
PH: 215-413-2136 FX: 775-261-5247
jeff@wonkavisionmagazine.com
www.wonkavisionmagazine.com
Entertainment magazine covering Rock and Punk in the Philly area.

WXPN Musicians On Call
Attn: Volunteer Musicians,
216 West 18th St. #201B, New York, NY 10011
www.xpn.org/moc.php
Brings live music to the bedsides of patients in healthcare facilities throughout the region.

Pittsburgh

Flidop
info@flidop.com
www.flidop.com
Our mission is to revive the Pittsburgh music scene by providing a resource for local bands to post gigs, upload MP3s, and communicate through our message board.

Lady Fox Productions
info@ladyfoxproductions.com
www.ladyfoxproductions.com
If you are in a band and interested in being our featured band of the month, email us for details.

pghgoth.com
www.pghgoth.com
Covering the local Goth scene.

PghLocalMusic.com
PO Box 17970, Pittsburgh, PA 15235
info@pghlocalmusic.com
www.pghlocalmusic.com
All the info on the local music scene.

pittpunk.com
www.pittpunk.com
CD and show reviews, event calendar and MP3s.

Pittsburgh Beat.com
www.pittsburghbeat.com
Discussion board for all things music in Pittsburgh

Pittsburgh Blues Women
www.pghblueswomen.com
Showcasing the local female Blues talent.

Pittsburgh City Paper
650 Smithfield St. #2200, Pittsburgh, PA 15222
PH: 412-316-3342 FX: 412-316-3388
driscoll@steelcitymedia.com
www.pghcitypaper.com
Free weekly A&E paper.

Pittsburgh Folk Music Society
#10 Bedford Sq. Pittsburgh, PA 15203
PH: 412-432-0333 FX: 412-432-0335
calliope@calliopehouse.org
www.calliopehouse.org
Promotes traditional and contemporary Folk music.

Pittsburgh Jazz Society
PO Box 1333, Pittsburgh, PA 15230
PH: 412-343-9555 FX: 412-343-5959
info@pittsburghjazz.org
www.pittsburghjazz.org
Preserving and perpetuating local Jazz music.

Pittsburgh Live Music
mediawebsource@yahoo.com
www.mediawebsource.com/pittsburghlive
Band websites, event and concert listings, venue directory etc.

PittsburghHipHop.com
6393 Penn Ave. #3319, Pittsburgh, PA 15206-4010
www.pittsburghhiphop.com
Your local Pittsburgh Hip Hop authority.

PittsburghRock.com
manny@PittsburghRock.com
www.pittsburghrock.com
Advancing the local presence in the national independent music scene.

Renaissance and Baroque Society of Pittsburgh
303 S. Craig St., Pittsburgh, PA 15213
PH: 412-682-7262 FX: 412-682-5253
director@rbsp.org
www.rbsp.org
Presents performances of the music of the middle ages.

RiverCityRock
zer0code zer0code@rivercityrock.com
www.rivercityrock.com
Our goal is to bring local music into the foreground of the Pittsburgh music scene.

Treelady Studios
630 Brown Ave. Turtle Creek, PA 15145
PH: 412-816-0300 FX: 412-291-3032
Garrett Haines garrett@treelady.com
www.treelady.com
A state-of-the art recording studio located in Pittsburgh, PA. Although the main studio focus is mastering, a brand new tracking room was added in 2004 (ProTools HD3 and 2" analog). Co-owner Garrett Haines is the Recording Tips Editor for Tape Op Magazine, and a columnist for EQ Magazine and Rockrgrl.

Ultimate Pittsburgh-Area Band Link Page
yairi@lhtc.net
www.randombrothers.com/bandlink.htm
Supporting Pittsburgh music. Link up your band page!

Rhode Island

Lotsofnoise
chris@lotsofnoise.com
www.lotsofnoise.com
Devoted to Providence-area Indie shows, leaning towards Noise and Punk Rock.

Providence Arts & Culture
25 Dorrance St., Providence, RI 02903-3215
PH: 401-421-7740
www.providenceri.com/as220/music.html
Covering the Providence local music scene.

Providence Phoenix
150 Chestnut St., Providence, RI 02903
PH: 401-273-6397 FX: 401-351-1399
www.providencephoenix.com
Free weekly alternative paper. CD and concert reviews.

Rhode Island Songwriters Association
PO Box 367, Harmony, RI 02829
PH: 401-949-0757
hearinri@ids.net
www.risongwriters.com
An organization dedicated the art of songwriting.

Sauga Records
418 Wickham Rd. North Kingstown, RI 02852
Dave Dave@SaugaRecords.com
www.SaugaRecords.com
A record label for hometown bands in North Kingstown, Rhode Island.

South Carolina

Charleston City Paper
1049 B Morrison Dr. Charleston, SC 29403
PH: 843-577-5304 FX: 843-853-6899
www.charlestoncitypaper.com
Free weekly A&E paper. CD and concert previews and reviews.

Charleston Swing!
info@charlestonswing.com
www.charlestonswing.com
Promoting Swing music and dancing in Charleston.

CharlestonRocks
PH: 843-532-2545
shawnte@charlestonrocks.com
CharlestonRocks.com
Promoting the local music of Charleston.

Chuck Nice Inc.com
2827 Truman St., Columbia, SC 29204
PH: 803-254-2464 FX: 803-933-0497
chuckinc@bellsouth.net
www.chuckniceinc.com
South Carolina's #1 entertainment website.

Creative Loafing Greenville
letters.atl@creativeloafing.com
www.cln.com
Free weekly A&E paper. Interviews artists, previews and reviews concerts and CDs.

Free Times
6904 N. Main St., Columbia, SC 29203
PH: 803-765-0707 FX: 803-765-0727
music@free-times.com
www.free-times.com
Free A&E paper. CD and concert previews and reviews.

Greenville Chapter NSAI
PH: 864-467-0987
www.nsaigreenville.com
Learn about songwriting and find out how the music business works.

GRITZ
24 Vardry St. #101-G, Greenville, SC 29601
PH/FX: 864-467-1699
Michael Buffalo Smith editor@gritz.net
www.gritz.net
A national print magazine with a sister e-zine. We review CDs, DVDs, books- all Southern flavored, from Southern Rock to Americana, Southern Soul, Bluegrass, Classic Rock and Blues.

Rivertown Bluegrass Society
PO Box 1921, Conway, SC 29526-1921
PH: 843-365-3570
Steve Tradaway sptread@excite.com
www.rivertownbluegrasssociety.com
Supports local Bluegrass musicians/events.

SChiphop.com
reviews@schiphop.com
www.schiphop.com
An online community of the hottest Underground talent in SC.

South Carolina Bluegrass and Traditional Music Assoc.
710 Meeting St. W. Columbia, SC 29169
scbtma@expresswebs.com
expresswebs.com/scbtma
Host's Bluegrass concerts and workshops to promote the art.

Southeastern Bluegrass Association of South Carolina
PO Box 4743, Florence, SC 29502
ccalder@sc.rr.com
www.sebga.org
Preserving the love of Bluegrass music.

The State
PO Box 1333, Columbia, SC 29202
PH: 800-888-5353
stateeditor@thestate.com
www.thestate.com
Covers local music scene with interviews, previews and reviews.

South Dakota

Black Hills Music
PH: 605-348-3770 FX: 270-712-8507
barb@blackhillsbusiness.com
blackhillsmusic.com
Covering all aspects of the Black Hills music scene.

C-Sharp Productions
421 N. Edgerton, Mitchell, SD 57301
PH: 605-996-0232
live@sharpmusic.com
www.sharpmusic.com
Production company and label that signs and develops acts.

Panache Magazine
editor@panachepages.com
www.panachepages.com
Free A&E magazine. Accepts press kits.

Rapid City Journal
507 Main St., Rapid City, SD 57701
PH: 605-394-8300
debbie.renner@rapidcityjournal.com
www.rapidcityjournal.com
Covers local music scene with CD and concert reviews.

Sioux Falls Jazz and Blues Society
123 S. Main Ave. Ste. 204, PO Box 88904,
Sioux Falls, SD 57109
PH: 605-335-6101 FX: 605-367-1764
info@sfjb.org
www.sfjb.org
Promoting Jazz and Blues through events and education.

South Dakota Friends of Traditional Music
PO Box 901, Sioux Falls, SD 57101-901
info@fotm.org
www.fotm.org
Promoting traditional music for generations of South Dakotans.

Wipe Your Eyes and Face the Day
811 S. Minnesota, Sioux Falls, SD 57104
PH: 605-728-4635
jayson_jweihs@hotmail.com
wye.slyink.com/board
Report of the local Punk scene.

Tennessee

BlueSpeak
25 Linden Ave. Memphis, TN 38103
info@bluespeak.com
www.bluespeak.com
Features and reviews of Memphis music and related information.

CIA Music
info@ciamusic.com
www.ciamusic.com
Supporting Chattanooga independent artists.

DecadentArtWorks.com
PO Box 1203, Smyrna, TN 37167
David Goodman
davidgoodman@decadentartworks.com
decadentartworks.com
Label dedicated to pushing the edge of music.

Down-South.com
DownSouth@Comcast.net
www.down-south.com
Reviews local and major Hip Hop albums.

Enigma Online
PO Box 825, Chattanooga, TN 37401
PH: 423-267-6072 FX: 423-265-0120
www.enigmaonline.com
We support the local Indie music scene.

jungleroom.com
elvis@jungleroom.com
www.jungleroom.com
Memphis local music notes. Post news about your upcoming release.

KnoxGothic.com
www.knoxgothic.com
Knoxville and East Tennessee's Gothic source.

Knoxville Metro Pulse
505 Market St. Level 300, Knoxville, TN 37902
PH: 865-522-5399 FX: 865-522-2955
editor@metropulse.com
www.metropulse.com
A&E section allows local bands to list info and post MP3s.

KnoxShows
info@knoxshows.com
www.knoxshows.com
Post band info, upcoming events, links etc.

Memphis Acoustic Music Association
PO Box 41528, Memphis, TN 38174-1528
PH: 901-276-1010
jkitts1662@aol.com
www.mamamusic.org
Sponsors Acoustic music, both American Folk and Celtic.

Memphis Area Bluegrass Association
PO Box 171152, Memphis, TN 38187-1152
webmaster@memphis-bluegrass.org
www.memphis-bluegrass.org
Info on the Bluegrass scene. Reviews CDs.

Memphis Commercial Appeal
495 Union Ave. Memphis, TN 38103
PH: 901-529-2345
www.commercialappeal.com
Covers the tri-state music scenes. Profiles touring bands, reviews CDs.

Memphis Flyer
460 Tennessee St., Memphis, TN 38103
PH: 901-521-9000 FX: 901-521-0129
letters@memphisflyer.com
www.memphisflyer.com
Free weekly paper. Covers local scene and bands playing the area.

The Memphis Mojo
www.memphismojo.com
Focusing on local music, where it's played and by whom.

Memphis Music Commission
47 Union Ave. Memphis, TN 38103
PH: 901-543-5334 FX: 901-543-5351
www.memphismusic.org
We want to develop a comprehensive on-line directory to help you find the resources you need, and help people who want your services to find you. Be heard. GET LOUD!

Memphis Songwriters Association
4746 Spottswood #191, Memphis, TN 38117-4815
admin@memphissongwriters.com
www.memphissongwriters.org
All the resources local songwriters need.

MemphisRap.com
PO Box 30337, Memphis, TN 38130
PH: 901-332-3504
feedback@memphisrap.com
www.MemphisRap.com
Artists can submit news, links, demos, audio files and more!

Rebourne Entertainment
1102 Llano Cove, Memphis, TN 38134-7908
PH: 901-388-2988
Bill & Holly Simmers simmers@rebourne.net
www.rebourne.net
A network of bands, vocalists, musicians, and songwriters who are committed to using their talents to make a positive impact on the world around them.

Sensored
2817 West End Ave. #126296, Nashville, TN 37203
PH: 615-498-6069
Ken Scruggs ken@sensored.com
www.sensored.com
Introducing lesser known artist to a larger audience.

Smoky Mountain Blues Society
PO Box 10866, Knoxville, TN 37939-0866
cptanalog@fastermac.net
www.smokymountainblues.com
Serving Maryville, Knoxville and all of East Tennessee.

Tennessee Jazz & Blues Society
PO 121293 Nashville, TN 37212-1293
PH: 615-255-5580
www.jazzblues.org
Submit news, articles, CDs for review and more.

Tennessee Songwriters Association
PO Box 2664, Hendersonville, TN 37077-2664
PH: 615-969-5967
AskTSAI@aol.com
www.clubnashville.com/tsai.htm
Educating, assisting and representing all songwriters.

Tennessee Spins
spins.us/tennessee
Dance music, electronic music, DJ's, artists and community.

Websites Unlimited
curtis@curtisj.com
curtisj.com
Memphis music events and news.

Nashville

American Music Showcase
9 Music Sq. S. #210, Nashville, TN 37203
ams@nashvilleconnection.com
www.americanmusicshowcase.com
Promote your music on Comcast 75 TV.

Eyemix Magazine
PO Box 121462, Nashville, TN 37212
PH: 615-320-7379
Covering the Nashville music scene.

Music City Blues
PO Box 22852, Nashville, TN 37211
PH: 615-876-4520
Tom Bottigliero tomkat@musiccityblues.org
www.musiccityblues.org
Hosts performances and programs to sustain this music.

Music Row
1231 17th Ave. S. Nashville, TN 37212
PH: 615-321-3617 FX: 615-329-0852
news@musicrow.com
www.musicrow.com
Nashville's music industry publication.

Nashville Ear
4636 Lebanon Pike #144, Hermitage, TN 37076
steve@NashvilleEar.com
NashvilleEar.com
A venue for songwriters and singers to get their music out on the Internet to gain exposure. We want to help you get your music, CD and website noticed.

Nashville Gothic
djneph@nashvillegothic.com
www.nashvillegothic.com
Serving the needs of the Gothic community in the area.

Nashville Scene
2120 8th Ave. S. Nashville, TN 37204-2204
PH: 615-244-7989
editor@nashvillescene.com
www.nashscene.com
Free weekly alternative paper. Covers local music scene.

Nashville Songwriter's Association International (NSAI)
1701 W. End Ave. 3rd Fl. Nashville, TN 37203
PH: 615-256-0034 FX: 615-256-0034
nsai@nashvillesongwriters.com
www.nashvillesongwriters.com
Protecting the rights and serving songwriters in all genres.

NashvilleConnection.com
9 Music Sq. S. # 210 Nashville, TN 37203
PH: 615-826-4141
info@nashvilleconnection.com
www.NashvilleConnection.com
Your source for info about the business of music in Nashville.

NashvilleRock.net
PH: 615-319-1773
Chris Work info@nashvillerock.net
nashvillerock.net
The latest local Rock news, reviews and concert information.

Nashvillerockscene.com
4649 Woodview Circle, Old Hickory, TN 37138
Penny Samson bands@nashvillerockscene.com
nashvillerockscene.com
Online community covering the local scene.

The Rage
1100 Broadway, Nashville, TN 37203
PH: 615-664-2270 FX: 615-664-2280
www.nashvillerage.com
Nashville free A&E weekly.

Tunesmith
info@tunesmith.net
www.tunesmith.net
Presents some of Nashville's best undiscovered songwriting!

Vanderbilt Hustler
2301 Vanderbilt Pl. VU Stn B, Box 1504, Nashville, TN 37235
PH: 615-343-0967
vibe@vanderbilthustler.com
www.vanderbilthustler.com
Vanderbilt U. student paper.

Writer/Artist Showcase
PO Box 1346, Hendersonville, TN 37077
PH: 615-826-9550
mail@writerartist.com
www.writerartist.com
A tool for success for aspiring songwriters and artists.

Texas

CD TEX
8806 Lockway, San Antonio, TX 78217
contact@bgmnetwork.com
www.cd-tex.com
CD store for Texas and Americana Music.

Central Texas Bluegrass Association
PO Box 9816, Austin, TX 78766-9816
PH: 512-261-9440
ctba@centraltexasbluegrass.org
www.centraltexasbluegrass.org
Post events and get your CD reviewed.

corpusmusic.com
corpusmusic.com
Band information, show dates and song downloads of local artists.

Country Line Magazine
16150 IH 35, Buda, TX 78610
PH: 512-295-8400
TJ Greaney tj@countrylinemagazine.com
www.countrylinemagazine.com
A Country Music magazine distributed throughout Texas. Special ad rates for Indies.

Denton Rock City
www.dentonrockcity.com
An information source for Denton musicians, bands, venues and music writers.

East Texas Gig Guide
webmaster@easttexasgigguide.com
www.easttexasgigguide.com
A resource for finding live entertainment and fun things to do throughout the Arklatex region.

El Paso Scene
PO Box 13615, El Paso, TX 79913
PH: 915-542-1422 FX: 915-542-4292
epscene@epscene.com
www.epscene.com
Free monthly A&E paper. Concert previews and CD reviews.

ElDoradoUnderground.com
www.eldoradounderground.com
Resource for the local music scene. Post your news, MP3s etc.

The Foghorn
Entertainment_fg@delmar.edu
www.delmar.edu/foghorn
Del Mar College student paper.

Gruene With Envy
1215 W. Slaughter Ln. #2513, Austin, TX 78748
Katie Ross katie@gruenewithenvy.com
www.gruenewithenvy.com
Texas/Americana music reviews plus a radio show.

Harmonica Organization of Texas
PH: 214-327-5008
Jerl Welch dfwhoot@flash.net
www.hoottexas.com
Promoting the art of playing the harmonica.

HillCountryScene.com
PH: 702-340-6748
Roy Al Rendahl trimordial@thefaro.com
www.thefaro.com/hillcountryscene.html
Covering the Central Texas Hill Country scene - music and arts.

iGotMusic.com
www.igotmusic.com
San Antonio musician directory. Free listing, events calendar, message board etc.

The Juice
210 S. Grimes #108, San Antonio, TX 78203
PH: 210-226-1939 FX: 866-378-1258
avista@thejuiceonline.com
www.thejuiceonline.com
San Antonio's A&E magazine.

Left Ear Entertainment
2611 N. Beltline Rd. #111, Sunnyvale, TX 75182
PH: 469-233-9563
Chaz info@fullforceproductions.com
www.hearleftear.com
We are looking towards the future to help artists make the right decisions to reach their goals of success.

Lone Star Music
1243 Gruene Rd. New Braunfels, TX 78130
PH: 830-627-1992 FX: 830-624-0976
www.lonestarmusic.com
Reviews, tour dates, contests, prizes and much more.

Lubbockonline.com
PH: 806-762-8844
webmaster@lubbockonline.com
www.lubbockonline.com
Local paper. A&E section.

MyTexasMusic.com
PO Box 148, Linden, TX 75563
PH: 903-756-8944 FX: 888-693-9379
Lucky Boyd MyTexasMusic@aol.com
www.mytexasmusic.com
We are doing more for musicians in Texas than other online vendors could ever pretend to do.

MusicTexas.Com
Doug LaRue larue@glaze.net
www.musictexas.com
A local independent music community.

musicTX.com
musictx@musictx.com
musictx.com
Show postings for Texas Underground/Alternative bands.

SA Music Scene
PH: 210-367-2572
Jess Garcia jess@samusicscene.net
www.samusicscene.net
Promotes Texas bands and all acts touring through there.

SAMPLE Press
PO Box 471159, Fort Worth, TX 76147
Jason Manriquez jason@samplepress.com
samplepress.com
Features independent Rock bands, primarily (but not entirely) from Texas.

San Antonio Blues Society
PO Box 33952, San Antonio, TX 78265
PH: 210-641-8192
www.sanantonioblues.com
Preserving various styles of Blues music.

San Antonio Rocks
SanAntonioZine@aol.com
www.sanantoniorocks.fr.st
Covering the local Christian Rock scene.

San Antonio Weekly Music News
PO Box 201090, San Antonio, TX 78220
PH: 210-227-4821 FX: 210-225-5009
editor@sambe.org
sambe.org
An online newsletter with all that's going on in the SA music scene.

The Shorthorn
Box 19038, Arlington, TX 76019
PH: 817-272-3188 FX: 817-272-5009
www.theshorthorn.com
U. Texas at Arlington campus paper.

Shroom Productions
9340 W. Sahara Ste. 103, Las Vegas, NV 89117
PH: 702-480-7036
Richard S. Patz shroom@trinicom.com
www.shroomangel.com
Promoting and selling Texas Prog, Stoner and Hard Rock.

Spring Creek Bluegrass Club *(SCBC)*
9410 Dundalk St., Spring, TX 77379
PH: 281-376-2959
bluegrass22@ev1.net
www.springcreekbluegrass.com
An organization dedicated to preserving the wonderful tradition of Bluegrass music.

State of Texas Gospel Announcers Guild
texgag@worldnet.att.net
www.texasgag.com
Increasing the penetration of Gospel music in cities in America.

Texarkana Blues Society
PO Box 1592, Texarkana, TX 75504
PH: 903-223-5464
www.texarkanablues.com
Dedicated to preserving blues history, supporting blues education, and promoting the ongoing development of Blues music.

Texarkanarocks.com
webmaster@texarkanarocks.com
www.texarkanarocks.com
An attempt to create community and provide useful information about music-related issues and events in and around Texarkana.

Texas Monthly
PO Box 1569, Austin, TX 78767-1569
PH: 512-320-6900 FX: 512-476-9007
www.texasmonthly.com
Magazine covering music, the arts and cultural events.

Texas Music Chart
2500 Tanglewilde #106, Houston, TX 77063
PH: 713-952-9221 FX: 713-952-1207
katie@shanemedia.com
www.texasmusicchart.com
The industry standard weekly compilation of radio airplay for Texas artists and their fans.

Texas Music Magazine
PO Box 50273, Austin, TX 78763
PH: 512-472-6630 FX: 208-485-0347
info@txmusic.com
www.txmusic.com
Promoting original Indie Texas music.

Texas Music Movement
PO Box 161038, Fort Worth, TX 76161
Cary Wrinkle cary@texasmusicmovement.com
www.texasmusicmovement.com
Connecting Texas artists and their fans.

Texas Music Round-Up
PO Box 49884 Austin, TX 78765-9884
PH: 512-480-0765 FX: 512-499-0207
info@texasmusicroundup.com
www.texasmusicroundup.com
Your independent Texas music superstore!

Texas Talent Register
PO Box 13246, Austin, TX 78711
PH: 512-463-6666 FX: 512-463-4114
music@governor.state.tx.us
www.governor.state.tx.us/music
Listing of Texas born or based recording artists.

texasmetalundeground.com
www.texasmetalunderground.com
Band profiles, interviews, articles etc.

TexasMusicGuide.com
PO Box 2032, Allen, TX 75013-0036
PH: 214-547-1699
www.texasmusicguide.com
Texas music festivals, events, venues, CD releases and artist links.

TexasReggae.org
texasreggaelist@earthlink.net
www.texasreggae.org
Covering all things Reggae in Texas.

West Texas Country
webmaster@westtexascountry.com
www.westtexascountry.com
Enjoy the spice of the West Texas area through WTC's unique artists and their music.

Women in Jazz
PO Box 200576, Austin, TX 78720
PH: 512-258-6947 FX: 512-258-7072
Hartbeat@swbell.net
www.womeninjazz.org
Provides opportunities for amateur women to perform.

Austin

All Access Live TV Show
2414 Elmglen Dr. Austin, TX 78704
PH: 512-445-7117
Gigi Greco info@allaccesslive.com
www.allaccesslive.com
We feature a very hot up and coming Indie act each season but they would have to have a big buzz.

Austin 360 *Ultimate Austin Band List*
305 S. Congress Ave. Austin, TX 78701
PH: 512-912-2591 FX: 512-912-2926
music@cim.austin360.com
www.austin360.com
List your band, events etc.

Austin Celtic Association
PO Box 684163, Austin, TX 78768-4163
PH: 512-218-6973
www.austincelts.org
Promoting Celtic culture through music, dance and the arts in Central Texas.

Austin Classical Guitar Society
PO Box 49704, Austin, TX 78765
PH: 512-420-0542
www.austinclassicalguitar.org
Link between amateur and professional guitarists and the community.

Austin Friends of Traditional Music
PO Box 49608, Austin, TX 78765-9608
PH: 830-825-3108
erhunt@austin.rr.com
www.main.org/aftm/aftmhome.htm
Preserving all genres of traditional music.

Austin Metal Music
i_amm_ironman@yahoo.com
www.austinmetalmusic.homestead.com
Bringing you info about the Underground Heavy Metal scene in Austin.

Austin Metro Entertainment
PO Box 1583, Pflugerville, TX 78691-1583
PH: 512-251-1882 FX: 512-251-1909
info@austinmetro.com
www.austinmetro.com
An entertainment guide for Austin and Central Texas.

Austin Music Foundation
PO Box 4309, Austin, TX 78765
PH: 512-323-0787
info@austinmusicfoundation.org
www.austinmusicfoundation.org
Professional development and economic advancement of local musicians.

AustinExperience.com
PO Box 140404, Austin, TX 78714-0404
content@austinexperience.com
www.austinexperience.com
Send your CDs, press packets or anything else you'd like to share.

austinlive.com
10204 Vaquero Trail, Austin, TX 78759
lisa@austinlive.com
www.austinlive.com
News, reviews and band info.

Blues Society of Austin
PO Box 150052, Austin, TX 78715-0052
PH: 512-809-3357
info@bluessocietyofaustin.org
www.bluessocietyofaustin.org
Information and updates on all of your favorite local Blues artists.

INsite Magazine
1704½ S. Congress #J, Austin, TX 78704
PH: 512-462-9260 FX: 512-326-4923
mail@insiteaustin.com
www.insiteaustin.com
Features with local up-in-coming acts.

Jupiter index
PO Box 2024, Austin, TX 78768-2024
Gabrielle Burns jupiterindex@netropolis.net
www.jupiterindex.com
Helping musicians by connecting them with a wider audience.

MusicAustin
www.musicaustin.com
A catalog of the Austin music scene.

Texas Observer
307 W. 7th St., Austin, TX 78701
PH: 512-477-0746
observer@texasobserver.org
texasobserver.org
Austin news & entertainment weekly.

Dallas/Fort Worth

Booksomebody.com
PO Box 33257, Fort Worth, TX 76162
David Bratton dbratton@booksomebody.com
www.booksomebody.com
A booking service for musicians, singers/vocalists, bands, DJ's and anyone else who provides their talents as a contract service.

Buzz-Oven
aden@buzz-oven.com
www.buzz-oven.com
A grass-roots movement set up by music fans to deliver talented new music to the ears, eyes and minds of a new generation of music fans.

Dallas Classic Guitar Society
PO Box 190823, Dallas, TX 75219
PH: 214-528-3733
www.dallasguitar.org
Holds concerts and outreach efforts.

Dallas Hardcore
www.dallashardcore.com
Promoting the Hardcore scene.

Dallas Music Guide
660 Preston Forest Ctr. #218, Dallas, TX 75230
PH: 214-739-5300 FX: 214-696-6249
Paul Salfen psalfen@dallasmusicguide.com
www.dallasmusicguide.com
Online music magazine in the Dallas/Ft. Worth area.

Dallas, Tyler, Shreveport Underground
www.dtsunderground.com
This site is for all the guys and gals in the music scene that are still grateful when someone like me comes up after a show and tells them they kicked ass.

Dallas Songwriter's Association
3630 Harry Hines Blvd. Box 20, Dallas, TX 75219
PH: 214-750-0916
info@dallassongwriters.org
www.dallassongwriters.org
Enhancing the overall personal growth and professionalism of our members.

dallas.com
www.dallas.com
The Dallas area music scene: clubs, concerts, bars, nightlife and a local band directory.

dallasmusic
4912 Wedgeview Dr. Hurst, TX 76053
Darin Wakely dallasmusic@hotmail.com
www.dallasmusic.com
Live reviews, CD reviews, interviews and more!

dallastexasmusic.com
PO Box 2718, Glen Rose, TX 76043
PH: 254-898-9418 FX: 254-898-9418
Tommy Randall tommy@triasite.com
www.dallastexasmusic.com
Promoting bands/artists in the Dallas/Fort Worth and surrounding areas in Texas.

DFW Hip Hop Society
James Castro castro77us@msn.com
dfwhiphopsociety.com
Covering Hip Hop events in Dallas/ Ft. Worth.

Fort Worth Songwriters Association
PO Box 162443, Fort Worth, TX 76161
PH: 817-654-5400 FX: 817-626-7458
www.fwsa.com
Improving musical work through fellowship, workshops and education.

Fort Worth Weekly
1204-B W. 7th St. #201, Fort Worth, TX 76102
PH: 817-321-9700 FX: 817-335-9575
feedback@fwweekly.com
www.fwweekly.com
Fort Worth's A&E weekly.

ftworthmusic.com
1912 RiverBend Rd. Arlington, TX 76104
Grady Smith ftworthmusic@hotmail.com
ftworthmusic.com
Live reviews, CD reviews, interviews and more!

GuideLive.com
508 Young St., Dallas, TX 75202
PH: 214-977-8861 FX: 214-977-8177
editor@guidelive.com
www.guidelive.com
Covers the local music scene. Post your shows and events.

Harder Beat
PO Box 781702, Dallas, TX 75378
PH: 972-484-8030
linda@harderbeat.com
www.harderbeat.com
Local band features, show and CD reviews and more.

Southwest Blues
PO Box 710475, Dallas, TX 75371
PH: 214-887-1188 FX: 972-642-6999
southwestblues@aol.com
www.southwestblues.com
We feature and spotlight Blues artists that deserve the recognition.

Spune Productions
1009 Andrew Dr. Burleson, TX 76028
PH: 817-426-0264
info@spune.com
www.spune.com
Promotes quality artists. Reviews demos, posts events and more.

Wave Capsule Promotion/Booking/Event Planning
3000 S. Hulen, #124, PMB 148,
Ft. Worth, TX 76109
PH: 214-274-5544
Jeff Pollard wavecapsule@yahoo.com
www.wavecapsule.com
We book Industrial/Darkwave/Goth/Electronic bands in various venues in Dallas. If you are going to come through Dallas on your tour, let us set it up for you.

Houston

Bay Area Bluegrass Association
4327 Townes Forest Rd.
Friendswood, TX 77546-4254
PH: 713-235-7336
www.bayareabluegrass.org
Promotes Bluegrass music in the Houston area and beyond.

Best In Texas Magazine
2500 Tanglewilde, Ste. 106, Houston, TX 77063
PH: 713-952-9221
Ed Shane smsofc@shanemedia.com
www.bestintexasonline.com
News, reviews and profiles, plus reports on new releases, live shows, events etc.

Guitar Houston
4149 Bellaire Blvd. #229, Houston, TX 77025
PH: 281-497-5187
mail@guitarhouston.org
www.guitarhouston.org
Supports developing artists through free concerts.

Houston Band Coalition
hbcpromotions@sbcglobal.net
www.hbclive.com
Houston bands working together to bring Houston music to the masses. Includes a forum for musicians, fans and industry pros.

Houston Beat
heyhb@houstonbeat.com
www.houstonbeat.com
List your bands, shows and special events.

Houston Blues Society
PO Box 7809, Houston, TX 77270
PH: 713-942-9427
president@houstonbluessociety.org
www.houstonbluessociety.org
Blues education, special events and a monthly jam session.

Houston Folklore & Folk Music Society
PO Box 720314, Houston, TX 77272-0314
longoap@ev1.net
www.houstonfolkmusic.org
Promoting folklore and Folk music.

Houston/Fort Bend Songwriters Association
www.hfbsa.org
Supports and encourages the art and craft of songwriting.

Houston Press
1621 Milam, #100, Houston, TX 77002
PH: 713-280-2400 FX: 713-280-2444
feedback@houstonpress.com
www.houstonpress.com
Major news and entertainment weekly.

Houston Women's Festival
PO Box 70102, Houston, TX 77270
www.hwfestival.org
Festival for/by women featuring the performing arts.

houstonbands.net
10250 Lands End #304, Houston, TX 77099
webmaster@houstonbands.net
www.houstonbands.net
The network for Houston bands on the internet. Send your CDs. I can't guarantee a review, but if I like it, I'll write about it.

Jazz Houston
www.jazzhouston.com
Gig listings, profiles, recordings, news and more.

North Star News
2700 W. Thorne Dr. Houston, TX 77073-3499
PH: 281-765-7808 FX: 281-618-5585
nsnews@nhmccd.edu
www.northstarnewsonline.com
The college/community newspaper of North Harris College.

Silver Dragon Records Artist of the Month
3452 Palmer Hwy. PMB#308, Texas City, TX 77590
PH: 409-939-0897 FX: 409-948-4409
punkbrady@silver-dragon-records.com
www.silver-dragon-records.com/Houston_bands.htm
A free resource for local band promotion in the Houston dedicated to our local artist of the month. Artists must play locally!

Space City Rock
PO Box 541010, Houston, TX 77254
gaijin@spacecityrock.com
www.spacecityrock.com
Covering the Houston music scene.

Utah

diemonsterdie
info@diemonsterdie.net
www.diemonsterdie.net
Helping Indie bands find gigs in Salt Lake City.

Draztikbeatz.net
www.draztikbeatz.net
The Hip Hop/Rap resource for the Salt Lake City area!

Intermountain Acoustic Music Association
PO Box 520521, Salt Lake City, UT 84152
PH: 801-339-7664
iama@sisna.com
www.iamaweb.org
Preserving Acoustic music, including Bluegrass, Folk etc.

LDS Music World
www.ldsmusicworld.com
News, reviews, features, music downloads, internet radio and more.

LDSMusicians.com
www.ldsmusicians.com
Discussion forum for LDS musicians and fans.

Music Utah
info@MusicUtah.com
www.musicutah.com
Event calendar, venue directory, band directory, classifieds and more.

The Rock Salt
staff@therocksalt.com
www.therocksalt.com
Bringing you the Rock from the Great Salt Lake.

Salt Lake City Weekly
248 S. Main St., Salt Lake City, UT 84101
PH: 801-575-7003
comments@slweekly.com
www.slweekly.com
Free weekly alternative paper. Band interviews, CD and concert previews and reviews.

Salt Lake Under Ground *(SLUG)*
351 W. Pierpont Ave. 4B, SLC, UT 84101
PH: 801-487-9221 FX: 801-487-1359
info@slugmag.com
www.slugmag.com
Covers local music scene with concert and Indie CD reviews.

The Seldom Scene
contact@theseldomscene.com
www.theseldomscene.com
Community of local artists promoting local artists.

SLC Billy Central
slcbillygirl@yahoo.com
www.rockabilly.net/slc
Rockabilly, Swing and Country in Salt Lake City.

UtahBands.com
info@fungusent.com
www.utahbands.com
Music posting service for band members to promote their concerts.

Vermont

artvt
artvt@together.net
www.artvt.com
A listing of Vermont musical artists.

Deerfield Valley News
PO Box 310, West Dover, VT 05356
PH: 802-464-3388 FX: 802-464-7255
events@vermontmedia.com
www.dvalnews.com
Southern Vermont's source for entertainment.

Early Music Vermont
163 Waterworks Rd. Lincoln, VT 05443
PH: 802-453-3016
info@earlymusicvermont.org
www.earlymusicvermont.org
Connecting artists and fans of Early music.

Seven Days
PH: 802-864-5684 FX: 802-865-1015
Pamela Polston pamela@sevendaysvt.com
www.sevendaysvt.com
Weekly A&E paper. Accepts CDs for review.

Vermont Bluegrass
andy@vtbluegrass.org
www.vtbluegrass.org
Everything Bluegrass in Vermont. Send your info!

Vermont Collegian
PO Box 698, Burlington, VT 05402-0698
PH: 802-658-0774 FX: 802-658-0244
www.vtliving.com/newspapers/vtcollegian
Burlington biweekly student paper. A&E section.

Vermont MIDI Project
sandi@vtmidi.org
www.vtmidi.org
Online music mentoring project for student K-12.

Vermont Music Shop
PO Box 428, Burlington, VT 05402
PH: 800-3033-1590 FX: 802-865-6200
musicshop@bigheavyworld.net
www.vermontmusicshop.com
Selling local musicians CDs. Consign your CDs with us.

Virginia

Acoustic Charlottesville
SalPal5000@Juno.com
www.geocities.com/acousticcharlottesville
Promotes local, original music in the area.

Americana Rhythm
PO Box 450, Dayton, VA 22821
PH: 540-746-0360
Greg E. Tutwiler greg@americanarhythm.com
www.americanarhythm.com
Regional publication that review's CDs of regional artists and those touring through the area. Americana, Roots, Bluegrass, Folk from throughout the Central VA.

Bluegrass Connection
9908 Brightlea Dr. Vienna, VA 22181
PH: 703-927-1875
pmilano@emailservice.com
www.gotech.com
Band, performer and festival home pages for the Virginia area.

The Breeze
G1, Anthony-Seeger Hall, MSC 6805, Harrisonburg, VA 22807
PH: 540-568-6127 FX: 540-568-7889
www.thebreeze.org
James Madison U. student paper.

C-Ville Weekly
106 E. Main St., Charlottesville, VA 22902
PH: 434-817-2749 FX: 434-817-2758
music@c-ville.com
www.c-ville.com
Charlottesville free weekly paper. Covers local music scene.

Cavalier Daily
PO Box 400703, Charlottesville, VA 22904-4703
PH: 434-924-1086 FX: 434-924-7290
cavdaily@cavalierdaily.com
www.cavalierdaily.com
University of Virginia's student newspaper.

Charlottesville Monthly
301 E. Market St., Charlottesville, VA 22902
PH: 804-295-9004 FX: 434-293-5618
artsmonthly.com
Monthly A&E magazine. Covers local music scene.

Collegiate Times
121 Squires Student Center, Blacksburg, VA 24061
PH: 540-231-9865
www.collegiatetimes.com
Virginia Polytechnic Institute's student paper.

Dan River Region Blues and Folk Society
livemusic@danriverregion.com
www.danriverregion.com/bluessociety
Supports local artists. Gig calendar, artist info, etc.

Fredericksburg Songwriters' Showcase
122 Laurel Ave. Fredericksburg, VA 22408
PH: 540-898-0611
showcase@bobgramann.com
www.webliminal.com/songwrite
A forum for local songwriters with monthly showcases.

GetRockedOut.com
www.getrockedout.com
Helping the music scene in Blacksburg and surrounding areas. Shows, band listings etc.

HamptonRoads.com
PH: 757-446-2989
www.hamptonroads.com
News, information, calendars, reviews and more.

The Hook
100 2nd St., Charlottesville, VA 22902
PH: 434-295-8700 FX: 434-295-8097
Mark tunes@readthehook.com
www.readthehook.com
A&E weekly. Covers local music scene.

James River Blues Society
P.O Box 4064, Lynchburg, VA 24502-0064
PH: 434-237-8080
jamrivblusoc@aol.com
www.jamesriverblues.org
Promoting and preserving Blues music in the area.

MEONA
meona@bellatlantic.net
www.meona.net
Supporting the local music scene in the SE Virginia area.

Natchel Blues Network
PO Box 1773, Norfolk, VA 23501-1773
PH: 757-456-1675
bluzq@hotmail.com
www.natchelblues.org
Blues newsletter, reviews, gig listings and a "spotlight artist" feature.

NorVaGoth.Net
figurehead@norvagoth.net
www.norvagoth.net
The Norfolk/Tidewater area Goth Industrial guide.

Phat Cats Entertainment
6483 Fenestra Ct. #100, Burke, VA 22015
PH: 202-415-9268
Enrique Lopez bookings@phatcats.com
www.phatcats.com
Management/entertainment company that brings the best talent to the DC, MD and VA area.

Playmaker Entertainment
c/o A&R Dept. PO Box 963,
Richmond, VA 23218-0963
PH: 804-439-0475
dinkydogg@comcast.net
www.playmakerentertainment.com
Record label specializing in Hip Hop, R&B. Utilizing our relationship with the Atlanta and Virginia music scenes, we provide guidence and opportunity to driven individuals and bands.

Reload
3729 Colonial Pkwy. Virginia Beach, VA 23452
webmaster@710.com
www.710.com/reload
Promoting the local talent of Hampton Roads and Richmond, Virginia.

Richmond.com
1427 W. Main St., Richmond, VA 23220
PH: 804-355-4500 FX: 804-355-3110
calendar@richmond.com
www.richmond.com
Online guide to Richmond events. Submit your gig.

Richmond Jazz Society
PO Box 25753, Richmond, VA 23260-5723
PH: 804-643-1972 FX: 804-643-1974
admin@vajazz.org
www.vajazz.org
Promotes Jazz through performances, lectures and workshops.

Richmond Music Journal
PO Box 8372, Richmond, VA 23226
PH: 804-569-6283 FX: 804-569-6284
Mariane Matera rmjournal@mindspring.com
www.mindspring.com/~rmjournal
Monthly magazine. Covering local music in Richmond. Please do NOT send us CDs if you are not from Richmond!

River City Blues Society
107 S. Pine St., Richmond, VA 23220
PH: 309-267-4425
Bob Kieser bob@rivercityblues.com
www.rivercityblues.com
Educating and enlightening the metropolitan area on the Blues.

Roanoke Fiddle & Banjo Club
PO Box 12043, Roanoke, VA 24022-2043
roanokefidbanclub.tripod.com
Fostering and preserving Old-Time and Bluegrass music.

Roanoke Times
PO Box 2491, Roanoke, VA 24010-2491
PH: 800-346-1234
shawna.morrison@roanoke.com
www.roanoke.com
Covers Southern Virginia music scene.

SevenZeroThree
info@sevenzerothree.com
www.sevenzerothree.com
Raising awareness about the local music scene.

Style Weekly
1707 Summit Ave. #201, Richmond, VA 23230
PH: 804-358-0825 FX: 804-358-1079
info@styleweekly.com
www.styleweekly.com
Richmond's magazine of news, culture and opinion.

Tidewater Classical Guitar Society
PO Box 1171, Norfolk, VA 23501
tcgs@mac.com
www.tcgs.cx
Concert schedule features local performers.

Tidewater Friends of Folk Music
PO Box 9606, Norfolk, VA 23505
PH: 757-626-3655
tffm@tffm.org
www.tffm.org
Promotes traditional and contemporary Folk music in Southeast Virginia.

Tidewater Rocks!
edrocker@tidewaterrocks.com
www.tidewaterrocks.com
Get the lowdown on Hampton local bands.

The Undersound
AlexWinfield@theundersound.com
theundersound.com
The voice of the underground, Virginia Beach local music scene. Punk, Hardcore...all types of music. Listen to the bands and read about the venues.

VABEST
www.vabest.com
Extensive A&E section with events calendar.

VaRockBands.com
812 Moorefield Park Dr. #300,
Richmond, VA 23236
Jason Smith jason@varockbands.com
www.varockbands.com
Linking fans with Virginia's best bands.

Virginia Organization of Composers and Lyricists
PO Box 34606, Richmond, VA 23225
PH: 804-342-0550
www.vocalsongwriter.org
Promoting the art and craft of songwriting and musical composition.

Virginia Spins
spins.us/virginia
Guide to Virginia Dance music, DJ's, artists and community.

Wadi Magazine
PO Box 70129, Richmond, VA 23255
www.wadimagazine.com
Virginia's freaky bi-weekly. Send us your CDs!

WCFStudios
3540 Holland Rd. Ste. 113 PMB 103,
Virginia Beach, VA 23452
PH: 757-651-5063 FX: 757-468-6988
indiebible@wcfstudios.us
local-scene.wcfstudios.com
Supports the Hampton Roads and beyond music scene: recording studio, promotions, event listings, web design, promo packs and more!

Washington

AnacortesOnline.com
1717 Commercial Ave. Anacortes, WA 98221
www.anacortesonline.com
Covers local music.

Bellingham Independent Music Association
PO Box 234, Ferndale, WA 98248
PH: 360-714-1630
info@bima.com
www.bima.com
Independent musicians and music supporters promoting local arts.

Blues to Do
PO Box 22950, Seattle, WA 98122-0950
PH: 206-328-0662
info@bluestodo.com
www.bluestodo.com
Source of information about live Blues in the Northwest!

ForceWeb.com
chris@forceweb.com
www.forceweb.com
Puget Sound Live Music.

Inland Empire Blues Society
PO Box 9126, Spokane, WA 99209-9126
PH: 509-534-1081
ieblues@ieblues.org
www.ieblues.org
Promoting the Blues in the Northwest.

Inland Northwest Bluegrass Association
PO Box 942, Spokane, WA 99210
www.spokanebluegrass.org
Host's Bluegrass concerts, jams, festivals and other events.

Northwest Artist Management
PH: 503-774-2511
www.nwmusicpro.com
Represents the best artists in the Northwest.

Northwest Dance music Association
10522 Lake City Way NE #C204,
Seattle, WA 98125-7767
PH: 206-440-9780
john.england@nwdma.org
www.nwdma.org
The premier record pool covering the Pacific Northwest.

Northwest Folklife
305 Harrison St., Seattle, WA 98109-4623
Attn: General
PH: 206-684-7300 FX: 206-684-7190
folklife@nwfolklife.org
www.nwfolklife.org
The most visible advocate of the traditional arts in the Northwest region.

Northwest Music Network
PO Box 46401, Seattle, WA 98146
info@northwestmusic.net
www.northwestmusic.net
Online guide to all things musical in the Northwest!

Northwest Tekno
www.nwtekno.org
Electronic music community.

NWBlues.com
PO Box 551, Stanwood, WA 98292
PH: 360-629-8027
carol@nwblues.com
www.nwblues.com
Promoting Blues and Blues artists in the Northwest.

Old Time Music in Portland
nkm@bubbaguitar.com
www.bubbaguitar.com
Lists Old-Time music gigs and music gatherings in the Portland area.

Olymusic.com
webbies@olymusic.com
www.olymusic.com
Site for Olympia musicians.

Pacific Northwest Inlander
1020 W. Riverside Ave. Spokane, WA 99201
PH: 509-325-0638
www.theinlander.com
Spokane weekly that reviews and covers local music.

Songwriters of the Northwest Guild
scotth@qualdata.com
www.songnw.com
Helps songwriters define and pursue their artistic goals.

Spokanebands.com
PH: 509-701-0333
Dan spokanebands@hotmail.com
www.spokanebands.com
Events, bands, news, forums, venues and much more.

Tacoma New Music
3701 Tacoma Ave. S. Tacoma, WA 98418
kim@new-music.org
www.new-music.org
Creates opportunities for new chamber music in the area.

Three Rivers Folklife Society
PO Box 1098, Richland, WA 99352
PH: 509-528-2215
Micki mail@3rfs.org
www.owt.com/3r-folkmusic
Promoting Folk music in the Tri-Cities area.

Three6oh Productions
12218 NW 11th Ave. Vancouver, WA 98685
PH: 360-606-3359 FX: 360-574-6776
three6oh@three6oh.com
www.three6oh.com
We are a street team that promotes primarily Urban Music releases (Putting up your posters in retail/lifestyle, clubs, concerts & streets). We do feedback and push singles to radio in Seattle WA, Portland, OR and Boise, ID. The best Street Team in the Pacific Northwest!

Walla Walla Blues Society
PO Box 906, Walla Walla, WA 99362
wwbs@bmi.net
www.wwbs.org
Keeping the public in touch with our American musical heritage.

Washington Bluegrass Association
PO Box 490, Toledo, WA 98591
www.washingtonbluegrassassociation.org
Promotes understanding and enjoyment of Bluegrass and other closely related music.

Washington Blues Society
PO Box 70604, Seattle, WA 98107
www.wablues.org
News, CD reviews, classifieds etc.

Seattle

Early Music Guild of Seattle
2366 Eastlake Ave. E. #335,
Seattle, WA 98102-3399
PH: 206-325-7066 FX: 206-860-9151
emg@earlymusicguild.org
www.earlymusicguild.org
Supports early music artists through concerts and programs.

Earshot Jazz
3429 Fremont Pl. #309, Seattle, WA 98103
FX: 206-547-6286
jazz@earshot.org
www.earshot.org
Supports Jazz and increases awareness in the community.

Gospel Music Workshop of America Pacific
PH: 253-941-4014
pacificnwc@aol.com
www.pacificnwchapter.com
Promoting Gospel and all its beliefs in the community.

KNDD The End's Seattle Music Page
1100 Olive Way #1650, Seattle, WA 98101
PH: 206-622-3251
www.1077theend.com/seattlemusic.asp
Here's where you'll find out about the best bands in Seattle - pictures, bios, music and links to the bands' official websites.

Seaspot.com
info@seaspot.com
www.seaspot.com
Covering the entertainment scene in the Seattle area.

Seattle Booking & Entertainment
PO Box 1250, N. Bend, WA 98045-9998
PH: 425-831-5697 FX: 425-831-5721
Tonya Terbrueggen tonya@seattlebooking.com
www.seattlebooking.com
A booking, promotions and management company.

Seattle Classic Guitar Society
PO Box 31256, Seattle, WA 98103-1256
PH: 206-365-0845
scgs@seattleguitar.org
www.seattleguitar.org
Events calendar, local news, articles of interest and more.

Seattle Composer's Alliance
PO Box 19604, Seattle, WA 98109
questions@seattlecomposers.org
www.seattlecomposers.org
Uniting Seattle composers to share ideas.

Seattle Drummer
aarongrey@seattledrummer.com
www.seattledrummer.com
Helping musicians achieve their personal and professional goals.

Seattle Folklore Society
PO Box 30141, Seattle, WA 98103
PH: 206-528-8546
members@seafolklore.org
seafolklore.org
Promoting Folk and traditional arts in the Seattle area.

Seattle Gay News
1605 12th Ave. Ste. 31, Seattle, WA 98122
PH: 206-324-4297 FX: 206-322-7188
sgn2@sgn.org
www.sgn.org
Post your shows and events.

Seattle Metal Online
PO Box 46661, Seattle, WA 98146-6661
smo-webmistress@comcast.net
www.seattlemetal.com
A complete resource for Metal fans and bands alike.

Seattle Weekly
1008 Western Ave. #300, Seattle, WA 98104
PH: 206-623-0500 FX: 206-467-4338
info@seattleweekly.com
www.seattleweekly.com
Covers local music scene with artist interviews, CD and concert previews and reviews.

SeattleSounds.com
3444 24th Ave. W., Seattle, WA 98199
PH: 253-951-8153
tavislemay@seattlesounds.com
www.seattlesounds.com
Post all your band info free. Downloads, bios, and more.

The Stranger
1535 11th Ave. 3rd Fl. Seattle, WA 98122
PH: 206-323-7101 FX: 206-323-7203
postmaster@thestranger.com
www.thestranger.com
Seattle free weekly alternative paper. Covers local music with concert previews and CD reviews.

Tablet
1122 E. Pike St. PMB 1435,
Seattle, WA 98122-3934
PH: 206-374-8678
Dan Halligan dan@tabletmag.com
www.tabletmag.com
A forum for the exchange of information in the Seattle area.

The Tentacle
PO Box 45655, Seattle, WA 98145-0655
tentacle@tentacle.org
www.tentacle.org
Local artists can post their info, gigs, releases, etc.

Washington DC

AOL CityGuide Washington *Music*
home.digitalcity.com/washington
Regional music column and forum.

DC Bluegrass Union
PO Box 903, Warrenton, VA 20188
PH: 800-380-3228
www.dcbu.org
Promoting and supporting Bluegrass music in the area.

DC Blues Society
PO Box 77315, Washington, DC 20013-7315
PH: 202-962-0112
webmaster@dcblues.org
www.dcblues.org
Dedicated to preserving and promoting the Blues.

DC Freaks
dcfreaks.com
Washington DC Goth resource.

DC Hip Hop Network
launch.groups.yahoo.com/group/dchiphopnetwork
Share music, drop rhymes, post show info and more.

DC Music Net
info@dcmusicnet.com
www.dcmusicnet.com
Washington's scene for local talent.

DC Rap Television
3815 Jay St. NE #1, Washington, DC 20019
PH: 202-396-7209
Skinny Corleone skinny@dcraptv.com
www.dcraptv.com
Showcasing new upcoming, and established underground Hip Hop/Rap artists and groups. If you have a music video or live performance video recorded in VHS, Mini DV, High-8, CDR or DVD, send us a copy. We also do CD reviews.

DCGoGo.COM
5814 Clay St. NE. Washington, DC 20019
PH: 202-257-7992 FX: 202-398-8299
www.dcgogo.com
Source for Go Go music in our nations capital.

DCjazz.com
PH: 202-882-6573
www.dcjazz.com
MP3s, videos, CD store and more!

dcMusicNews
www.dcmusicnews.com
Resource sites for independent musicians in the area.

DCShows.net
strangebeer@dcshows.net
www.dcshows.net
Local Punk, Metal and Hardcore shows for the mid-Atlantic.

dcska.com
Michelle dcskagirl@dcska.com
www.dcska.com
Reviews, show dates, interviews, multimedia and more.

District of Columbia Spins
spins.us/dc
Connect with DC Dance music, electronic music, DJ's, artists and community.

Exotic Fever Records
PO Box 297, College Park, MD 20741-0297
www.exoticfever.com
Supports local and regional independent music/writing/art.

Folklore Society of Greater Washington
6009 84th Ave. New Carrollton, MD 20784
PH: 202-546-2228
webmaster@fsgw.org
www.fsgw.org
Promoting the traditional Folk music and folklore of the American people.

House of Musical Traditions
7040 Carroll Ave. Takoma Park, MD 20912
PH: 301-270-9090 FX: 301-270-3010
hmtrad@hmtrad.com
www.hmtrad.com
We have one of the most extensive collections of recordings done by musicians local to the DC area.

Left Off the Dial
917 N. Wayne St. #305, Arlington, VA 22201
editor@leftoffthedial.com
www.leftoffthedial.com
Provides exposure for ignored Indie music. Accepts and reviews CDs.

On Tap
4238 Wilson Blvd. #3078, Arlington, VA 22203
PH: 703-465-0500 FX: 703-465-0400
Jeff Jones jeff@ontaponline.com
www.ontaponline.com
Arts & entertainment magazine for the DC area.

Pheer.com
pablo@pheer.com
www.pheer.com
Shows listing for Punk/Hardcore bands. Post your MP3s.

Rhythmplaza.com
PH: 202-234-8635
contact@rhythmplaza.com
www.rhythmplaza.com
Source for Hip Hop artists, club listings, videos, go-go music and more.

The SalsaNews
note@thesalsanews.com
www.thesalsanews.com
Information on salsa classes, clubs, concerts and special events.

Society of Art Rockers
info@dc-soar.org
www.dc-soar.org
Promoting the musical form called Art Rock or Progressive Rock in the Metropolitan Washington, DC area.

Songwriters' Association of Washington
4200 Wisconsin Ave. NW, PMB 106-137,
Washington, DC 20016
PH: 301-654-8434
Membership@saw.org
saw.org
Resource for professional songwriters to further their careers.

Washington Area Lawyers for the Arts
901 New York Ave. NW, Suite P1,
Washington, DC 20001-4413
PH: 202-289-4440 FX: 202-289-4985
legalservices@thewala.org
www.thewala.org
Provides legal service to the arts community.

Washington Area Music Association
6263 Occoquan Forest Dr.
Manassas, VA 20112-3011
PH: 202-338-1134 FX: 703-393-1028
dcmusic@wamadc.com
wamadc.com
Promotes local music regardless of genre.

Washington City Paper
2390 Champlain St. NW, Washington, DC 20009
PH: 202-332-2100 FX: 202-332-8500
mail@washcp.com
www.washingtoncitypaper.com
Covers the local music scene and previews upcoming A&E events.

Washington Post
1150 15th St. NW, Washington, DC 20071
PH: 202-334-7582
Michael ombudsman@washpost.com
www.washingtonpost.com
Considers Indie albums for review. Covers local music scene.

washingtonpost.com MP3
mp3@wpni.com
mp3.washingtonpost.com
Self-publishing by and for the Metro region's music community.

West Virginia

304live.com
303 Del Ray Dr. St. Albans, WV 25177
www.304live.com
Accepts CDs from local Hip Hop artists.

The Daily Athenaeum
1374 VanVoorhis Rd. Lot D14,
Morgantown, WV 26505
www.da.wvu.edu
West Virginia University's daily paper. We're always looking for new things to write about. My next article could be your CD review!

Graffiti
519 Juliana St., Parkersburg, WV 26101
PH: 304-485-1911
Matt Burdette mburdette@graffitiwv.com
www.grafwv.com
Covers local music scene with interviews, concert and CD reviews.

Honeking Productions
PO Box 113, London, WV 25126
Bryan King bryanking@honekingproductions.com
www.honekingproductions.com
Booking/production company dedicated to exposing local bands to the national eye.

The Picket
PO Box 3210, Shepherdstown, WV 25443
PH: 304-876-5687 FX: 304-876-5100
pickweb@shepherd.edu
www.shepherd.edu/pickweb
Shepherd College's student paper.

West Virginia Music Center
max@wvmc.com
www.wvmc.com
Information on professional live-performance acts working in WV.

Wisconsin

bluescds.com
PO Box 11145, Milwaukee, WI 53211
FX: 414-962-4995
Steve info@bluescds.com
www.bluescds.com
Offers Blues CDs from all over the world.

Cty Murph's Music Page
cty@ctymurph.com
www.ctymurph.com
Listing of Wisconsin bands and show dates.

FolkLib Index
PO Box 1447, Oshkosh, WI 54903-1447
henkle@pobox.com
www.folklib.net/index/wi
Information of Wisconsin Folk, Bluegrass, Celtic, Acoustic and Blues artists. Everything related to Wisconsin music and musicians in all genres of music. Working on 2006 book, "Wisconsin Discography, 1948-2005" to include all Wisconsin recording artists.

Fond du Lac Features
PO Box 2265, Fond du Lac, WI 54936-2265
PH: 920-924-2368
info@fdlfeatures.com
www.fdlfeatures.com
Fond du Lac's online community. Add your event in the entertainment section.

Fondy Acoustic Music Alliance
PO Box 1875, Fond du Lac, WI 54936-1875
PH: 920-923-0662
fondyacoustic@yahoo.com
www.fondyacoustic.org
Providing listening and playing opportunities for fans of Acoustic music.

Great Northern Blues Society
PO Box 2276, Wausau, WI 54402-2276
www.gnbs.org
Encourages member's artistic growth and helps them thrive by providing opportunities to perform.

Greater Milwaukee Today
webmaster@conleynet.com
www.gmtoday.com
Entertainment section covers local music and events.

Isthmus
101 King St., Madison, WI 53703
PH: 608-251-5627
Dean Robbins robbins@isthmus.com
www.thedailypage.com
Madison's news & entertainment weekly.

Kenosha Music
Rhianon kenoshamusic@yahoo.com
www.kenoshamusic.cjb.net
Covering the Punk/Hardcore scene in Kenosha.

mad.city.hard.core
www.MadHC.com
A Madison/Milwaukee area music site focusing on Punk, Metal, Hardcore and Rock.

Madison Blues Society
PO Box 3202, Madison, WI 53704-0202
PH: 608-221-7332
info@madisonbluessociety.com
www.madisonbluessociety.com
Keeping the Blues alive in the Madison area.

Madison Folk Music Society
PO Box 665, Madison, WI 53701
madfolk@charter.net
www.madfolk.org
Dedicated to fostering Folk Music in the Madison area.

Madison Jazz Society
PO Box 8866, Madison, WI 53708-8866
PH: 608-850-5400 FX: 608-850-5401
mjs@madisonjazz.com
www.madisonjazz.com
Preserving and promoting Jazz music.

Madison Music Online
www.madison-online.com/music
All the info on the local music scene.

MadisonSongwriters.com
PO Box 8142, Madison, WI 53708
info@madisonsongwriters.com
www.madisonsongwriters.com
Provides education and networking opportunities within the music business.

MadisonMusicians.Net
admin@madisonmusicians.net
www.madisonmusicians.net
Connect with the local music scene.

Maximum Ink
PH: 608-245-0781 FX: 608-245-0782
Rokker Rokker@maximumink.com
www.maximumink.com
Music magazine featuring interviews/stories, CD reviews, events and more.

Milwaukee-Hardcore.com
xbaxterx@hotmail.com
www.milwaukee-hardcore.com
Covering the Milwaukee Punk/Hardcore scene.

OnMilwaukee.com
1504 E. North Ave. Milwaukee, WI 53202
PH: 414-272-0557
www.onmilwaukee.com
Milwaukee music guide. Add your band to our local music database.

OnWisconsin.com Live: Music and Night Life
www.onwisconsin.com/music
Your LIVE guide for Wisconsin music.

Rick's Cafe
PO Box 137, Mt. Horeb, WI 53572
PH: 608-437-6867
Rick Tvedt rick@rickscafe.org
www.rickscafe.org
A local music newspaper near Madison. CD and live show reviews.

The Scene
300 N. Appleton St. #2, Appleton, WI 54911
PH: 920-733-5743 FX: 920-733-5783
info@valleyscene.com
www.valleyscene.com
Appleton A&E weekly.

Shepherd Express
413 N. 2nd St., Ste. 150, Milwaukee, WI 53203
PH: 414-276-2222 FX: 414-276-3312
editor@shepherd-express.com
www.shepherd-express.com
Milwaukee free daily alternative paper. Covers local music scene.

Southern Wisconsin Bluegrass Music Association
3109 Hermina St., Madison, WI 53714
www.swbmai.org
News about Bluegrass events, profiles of area bands and reviews.

WISCONLINE
8832 N. Port Washington Rd. Box 150,
Milwaukee, WI 53217
PH: 800-575-9781 FX: 88-204-3278
reception@wisconline.com
www.wisconline.com
Everything Wisconsin. Submit your music event.

Wisconsin Alliance for Composers
653 Charles Ln. Madison, WI 53711
www.wiscomposers.org
Supports the performance of new music by Wisconsin composers.

Wisconsin Area Music Industry
PO Box 510826, Milwaukee, WI 53202-0816
PH: 414-431-8719
wamimusic@yahoo.com
www.wamimusic.com
Our purpose is to educate and recognize the achievements and accomplishments of individuals in the Wisconsin music industry.

Wisconsin Musical Groups
regent@execpc.com
www.execpc.com/~regent
Wisconsin's music resource! Submit your band/gig info.

Wyoming

Jackson Hole Online
610 W. Broadway, WY 83001
PH: 377-733-5681
info@jacksonholenet.com
www.jacksonholenet.com
Entertainment section covers local music.

Wyoming Companion
PO Box 1111, Laramie, WY 82073-1111
editor@wyomingcompanion.com
www.wyomingcompanion.com
Wyoming's visitor guide. Covers local music events.

Canada

20hz.ca
www.20hz.ca
Discussion board covering the local scene across Canada.

A Better World
601 Magnetic Dr. # 8, Toronto, ON M3J-3J2
mastermail@abetterworld.ca
www.abetterworld.ca
Created to inform and encourage artists, songwriters, performers to convey 'Better World' themes and messages in their words through their art form.

ANR Lounge
www.mincanada.com
Promote CDs through e-mail to stations across Canada.

Association of Canadian Women Composers
20 St. Joseph St., Toronto, ON M4Y 1J9
webmaster@acwc.ca
www.acwc.ca
Active in the promotion of music written by Canadian women composers, and endeavours to help these composers achieve a higher profile in the community.

AtlanticSeabreeze.com
283 Valermo Dr. Toronto, ON M8W 2L2
PH: 416-255-3127 FX: 416-255-8192
info@AtlanticSeabreeze.com
www.atlanticseabreeze.com
Supports Celtic, East Coast and Country music in Canada.

Bedlam Society
Lesley Benchina lesley@bedlamsociety.com
www.bedlamsociety.com
Emo, Rock, Punk...from BC to PEI, we've got you covered! Find local show listings, read reviews, or just turn your mind to mush on the message board!

Borealis Recording Company
225 Sterling Rd. #19, Toronto, ON M6R 2B2
PH: 416-530-4288 FX: 416-530-0461
info@borealisrecords.com
www.borealisrecords.com
Supports Folk and Roots music in Canada.

Canada.com
www.canada.com
Post your event news! (check for the contact e-mail for your city).

Canadian Amateur Musicians
85 Cammac Rd. Harrington, QC J8G 2T2
PH: 819-687-3938
national@cammac.ca
www.cammac.ca
Creating opportunities for musicians of all levels.

Canadian Celtic Music
Kimberley kimberley@islandviewcreations.com
members.shaw.ca/kimberleyw/canadaceltic music
Musician's websites, tour date, news and more.

Canadian Copyright Act
webadmin@justice.gc.ca
laws.justice.gc.ca/en/C-42
Important information on the Canadian copyright act.

Canadian Country Music Association
626 King St. W. #203, Toronto, ON M5V 1M7
PH: 416-947-1331 FX: 416-947-5924
country@ccma.org
www.ccma.org
Developing Canadian Country music.

Canadian Electroacoustic Community
7142 Sherbrooke St. W. Montreal, QC H4B 1R6
cec@vax2.concordia.ca
cec.concordia.ca
Network for the flow and exchange of information and ideas.

Canadian Gospel Music Association
50 Gervais Dr. #507, Toronto, ON M3C 1Z3
info@cgmaonline.com
www.cgmaonline.com
Promoting the growth and ministry of the Christian music arts in Canada.

Canadian Guitar Players Association
RR#2, Lion's Head, ON N0H 1W0
PH: 519-592-5756 FX: 519-592-5756
www.guitarassociation.org
Sharing information and helping one another in developing individual talents.

Canadian Intellectual Property Office
50 Victoria St. Room C-229,
Gatineau, QC K1A 0C9
PH: 819-953-7620
cipo.contact@ic.gc.ca
strategis.gc.ca/sc_mrksv/cipo
Responsible for intellectual property (copyright and trademarks) in Canada.

Canadian Music Center
20 St. Joseph St., Toronto, ON M4Y 1J9
PH: 4160961-6601 FX: 416-961-7198
info@musiccentre.ca
www.musiccentre.ca
Collecting, distributing and promoting music by Canada's composers.

Canadian Musical Reproduction Rights Agency (CMRRA)
56 Wellesley St. W. #320, Toronto, ON M5S 2S3
PH: 416-926-1966 FX: 416-926-7521
inquiries@cmrra.ca
www.cmrra.ca
Represents the vast majority of music copyright owners (usually called music publishers) doing business in Canada. Issues licenses and collects royalties for the use of music on CDs and other products.

Canadian Music Direct
PO Box 21056, Bower Pl. Red Deer, AB T4R 2M1
PH: 403-343-0109
Chad Gillies chad@canadianmusicdirect.com
www.canadianmusicdirect.com
Highlights independent Canadian musicians.

Canadian Musician
23 Hannover Dr. #7, St., Catharines, ON L2W 1A3
PH: 905-641-3471 FX: 905-641-1648
mail@nor.com
www.canadianmusician.com
Showcases unsigned Canadian acts.

Canadian Newspaper and News Media Database
www.abyznewslinks.com/canad.htm
Links to hundreds of Canadian newspapers.

Canadian Society for Traditional Music
PO Box 4232, Stn. C, Calgary, AB T2T 5N1
sparling@post.queensu.ca
www.yorku.ca/cstm
Articles, notices and reviews on all aspects of Canadian Folk music.

CanadianBands.com
canconrox@excite.com
www.canadianbands.com
Submit band info, gigs, reviews, etc.

canEHdian.com
PO Box 119, Heatherton, NS B3M 4H4
info@canehdian.com
www.canehdian.com
Everything music for Canada. Professional review site.

CBC Records
PO Box 500 Stn. A, Toronto, ON M5W 1E6
PH: 416-555-1212 FX: 416-205-2139
cbcrecords@toronto.cbc.ca
www.cbcrecords.cbc.ca
Making the music of Canadian performers available to music lovers around the world.

Chart Magazine
41 Britain St. #200, Toronto, ON M5A 1R7
PH: 416-363-3101 FX: 416-363-3109
chart@chartattack.com
www.chartattack.com
Canadian college radio and retail charts, reviews and lots more.

COBA Collective Of Black Artists
610 Queen St. W. 2nd Fl. Toronto, ON M6J 1E3
PH: 416-658-3111 FX: 416-658-9980
info@cobainc.com
www.cobainc.com
Dedicated to the creation and production of dance and music while preserving cultural traditions of the African Diaspora.

Composers.ca
200 N. Service Rd. 1-211, Oakville, ON L6M 2Y1
office@composers.ca
www.composers.ca
Features information and support for active composers of all genres.

Country Music News
PO Box 7323 Vanier Terminal, Ottawa, ON K1L 8E4
PH: 613-745-6006 FX: 613-745-0576
Larry Delaney larry@countrymusicnews.ca
www.countrymusicnews.ca
The voice of Country music in Canada.

Devilous
1670 Heron Rd. Ottawa, ON K1V 0C0
PH: 1866 8477436
Billy info@soulcanada.com
www.soulcanada.com
Street Hip Hop. Showcasing the many talents of Canada to the World!

Earshot Concerts
23 Herman Ave. Toronto, ON M6R 1Y1
PH: 416-538-2006
Scott Good ad@earshotconcerts.ca
www.earshotconcerts.ca
Produces concerts of new Canadian Art music. Since our founding, we have produced numerous concerts featuring new works by the rising generation of Canadian composers.

EventInfo.ca
contact@eventinfo.ca
www.eventinfo.ca
We'll list any type of event in Canada for free. We also list artist profiles, venue locations, event promoter profiles etc.

!*@# Exclaim!
7-B Pleasant Blvd. #966, Toronto, ON M4T 1K2
PH: 416-535-9735
Ian Danzig ian@exclaim.ca
www.exclaim.ca
Coverage of new music across all genres of Canadian cutting-edge artists.

Federation of Canadian Music Festivals
3954 Parkdale Rd. Saskatoon, SK S7H 5A7
PH: 306-343-1835 FX: 306-373-1390
www.fcmf.org
An umbrella organization for 230 local and provincial festivals.

Festival Distribution
1351 Grant St., Vancouver, BC V5L 2X7
PH: 604-253-2662 FX: 604-253-2634
fdi@festival.bc.ca
www.festival.bc.ca
Distributor of Canadian Indie music of all genres.

Folk Alliance Canada
info@folkalliancecanada.org
www.folkalliancecanada.org
Helps you create, perform and market your Folk music here and internationally.

Great White Noise.ca
bandsubs@greatwhitenoise.ca
www.greatwhitenoise.ca
Canadian independent music exposed.

Groove Music Canada
1930 Yonge St. #1010, Toronto, ON M4S 1Z4
services@groovemusiccanada.com
www.groovemusiccanada.com
Pop / R&B record label with National & international distribution.

GuitarsCanada
www.guitarscanada.com
Helps out any up and coming Canadian Bands. Submit your info.

HERIZONS
PO Box 128, Winnipeg, MB R3C 2G1
PH: 888-408-0028
Penni Mitchell editor@herizons.ca
www.herizons.ca
Feminist magazine. We focus on Canadian female musicians, Indie for the most part.

hiphopcanada.com
532 Montreal Rd. #493, Ottawa, ON K1K 4R4
PH: 613-749-7777 FX: 613-747-9317
submissions@hiphopcanada.com
www.hiphopcanada.com
Send artist press kits, new updates etc.

Indie Pool
118 Berkeley St., Toronto, ON M5A 2W9
PH: 416-424-4666 FX: 416-424-4265
mail@indiepool.com
www.indiepool.com
Provides an affordable distribution alternative.

IndieMusic.ca
www.indiemusic.ca
Directory of indie bands and musicians in Canada. Add your band's website!

jambands.ca
kevo@jambands.ca
www.jambands.ca
Bringing together great bands and appreciative fans.

JamHub.ca
www.jamhub.ca
Canada's online Jam Bands community.

Jazz Canadiana
bebop@sympatico.ca
www.jazzcanadiana.on.ca
For people everywhere who enjoy Jazz and the artists who make it happen.

JazzPromo.com
650 Dupont St. #503, Toronto, ON M6G 4B1
jazz@jazzpromo.com
www.jazzpromo.com/canadajazz.php
Showcasing Canadian artists. Artist of the month feature.

kickinthehead.com
46 Lepage Ct. Toronto, ON M3J 1Z9
PH: 416-638-9895 FX: 416-638-8167
info@kickinthehead.com
www.kickinthehead.com
Web database that lets artists add and update their own information for free.

Linear Reflections
344 Farview Rd. Victoria, BC V9C1V8
PH: 250-474-0693
Naomi de Bruyn nai@shaw.ca
www.linearreflections.com
An arts review e-zine, which deals with all genres of music.

LiveTourArtists
1451 White Oaks Blvd. Oakville, ON L6H 4R9
PH: 905-844-0097 FX: 905-844-9839
info@livetourartists.com
www.livetourartists.com
International booking agency representing talented artists.

MapleMusic
30 St. Clair Ave. W. #103, Toronto, ON M4V 3A1
PH: 416-961-4332
justcurious@maplemusic.com
www.maplemusic.com
Submit your info, gigs, sell your CD from our site and more.

Music By Mail Canada
ck580@freenet.carleton.ca
www.musicbymailcanada.com
Canadian source for music.

New Music Canada
PO Box 4600, Vancouver, BC V6B 4A2
PH: 877-955-6565 FX: 604-662-6594
mymusic@newmusiccanada.com
www.newmusiccanada.com
Send us your MP3s and we put it up on the site.

Newbands.ca
newbands@newbands.ca
www.newbands.ca
Post comments, upload your mp3's and more.

Northern Journey Online
gene@wilburn.ca
www.northernjourney.com
Promoting lesser-known Canadian Folk artists.

Opera.ca
215 Spadina Ave. #210, Toronto, ON M5T 2C7
PH: 416-591-7222 FX: 416-536-3463
www.opera.ca
Keeps members abreast of issues relating to artistic quality and creativity, education and audience development.

Orchestras Canada
56 The Esplanade #203, Toronto, ON M5E 1A7
PH: 416-366-8834 FX: 416-366-1780
info@oc.ca
www.oc.ca
The national service organization for all Canadian orchestras.

Salsa Canada
PH: 604-771-7750
info@salsacanada.com
www.salsacanada.com
Canada's premier Salsa dance site with sections on events, bands and clubs.

SMASHING LUMBER.COM
313-40 Baif Blvd. Richmond Hill, ON L4C 5M9
info@smashinglumber.com
www.smashinglumber.com
Created to provide exposure opportunities for Canadian artists and help them navigate the tricky waters of the music business.

Society of Composers, Authors and Music Publishers of Canada (SOCAN)
41 Valleybrook Dr. Toronto, ON M3B 2S6
PH: 416-445-8700 FX: 416-445-7108
socan@socan.ca
www.socan.ca
We represent individuals who make their living creating music.

Songwriters Association of Canada
26 Soho St. #340, Toronto, ON M5T 1Z7
PH: 416-961-1588 FX: 416-961-2040
sac@songwriters.ca
www.songwriters.ca
Exclusively for Canadian composers, lyricists and songwriters.

Stamm'ler International
303 Robinson St., Oakville, ON L6J 1G7
PH: 905-842-2822 FX: 905-842-2823
ragna@sympatico.ca
www.stammlerinternational.com
Covers all marketing/promotion aspects for the arts.

Supernova.com
www.supernova.com
Our goal is to empower bands with valuable tools to promote, advance and excel independent music.

UmbrellaMusic
30 St. Clair Ave. W. #103, Toronto, ON M4V 3A1
PH: 416-961-4332 FX: 416-343-9986
info@umbrellamusic.com
www.umbrellamusic.com
Check our site every week for Umbrella's weekly pick.

Urban Music Association of Canada
675 King St. W. #210, Toronto, ON M5V 1M9
PH: 416-916-2874
aisha@umac.ca
www.umac.ca
Domestic and international promotion and development of Canadian Urban music.

URBNET.COM
PO Box 10617, Toronto, ON M6H 1L8
PH: 647-271-7736 FX: 647-439-1411
info@urbnetrecords.com
www.urbnet.com
Reviews, CDs and downloads of Techno, House, etc.

Words & Music
socan@socan.ca
www.socan.ca
Society of Composers, Authors and Music Publishers of Canada's (SOCAN) publication. Music news and bios are done on a few members each month. New releases are also listed.

Zone Francophone
450, rue Rideau, bureau 405, Ottawa, ON K1N 5Z4
PH: 613-241-8770 FX: 613-241-6064
fccf@zof.ca
www.francoculture.ca
A site dedicated to francophone culture and arts.

Zoilus.com
Carl Wilson c/o The Globe and Mail,
444 Front St. W., Toronto, ON M5V 2S9
cwilson@globeandmail.ca
www.zoilus.com
I am an editor and critic at the Toronto Globe & Mail. My music column Overtones appears there every Saturday. Send me your CDs for review.

Alberta

ALBERTA Metal
1919B 4th St. SW #195, Calgary, AB T2S 1W4
Christine Garton info@albertametal.net
www.albertametal.net
Canadian Metal bands may submit a profile and MP3.

Alberta Music Network
621 Columbia Rd. Lethbridge, AB T1K 5K3
PH: 403-381-1885 FX: 403-329-1248
www.albertamusic.net
Provides convergence for all Alberta music.

Alberta Rock
Jake jake@albertarock.com
www.albertarock.com
A website/publication that reviews independent music. Helping artists to gain more exposure!

ALTAsound Independent Bands Site
PH: 905-890-1122
Eddy Costa epcosta@sympatico.ca
www.altasound.com
A site for Alberta bands and artists, with mp3's, charts, spotlights, band stores, biographoes, contacts...

Bignote Entertainment
87 Tuscany Springs Way NW, Calgary, AB T3L 2N4
PH: 403-668-0880 FX: 403-286-5773
Jim Samuelson jim@bignote.net
bignote.net
Our mission is simple: to bring audiences and artists together in the creation of great musical experiences!

The Bricklayer
PO Box 5005, Red Deer, AB T4N 5H5
PH: 403-343-1877 FX: 403-343-8510
thebricklayer@canoemail.com
www.sardc.ab.ca/public_brick.htm
Red Deer College's student publication.

Calgary Music
kenny@bassguitar.com
www.calgarymusic.com
Free listing for artists/agents/promoters.

CalgaryPlus.ca
PH: 403-228-1800 FX: 403-240-5669
www.calgaryplus.ca
Post your music events.

Dark Calgary
webmaster@darkcalgary.com
www.darkcalgary.com
A means for local Goth artists and organizers to promote their creations.

Dose Calgary
1450 Don Mills Rd. Toronto, ON M3B 2X7
info@dose.ca
www.dose.ca/calgary
A free daily online magazine. One of the key areas of our website is promotion of indie bands. Upload profiles, tracks and images as we feature an indie artist weekly.

Dose Edmonton
1450 Don Mills Rd. Toronto, ON M3B 2X7
info@dose.ca
www.dose.ca/edmonton
A free daily online magazine. One of the key areas of our website is promotion of indie bands. Upload profiles, tracks and images as we feature an indie artist weekly.

Edmonton Composers' Concert Society
PO Box 52204, Edmonton, AB T6G 2T5
PH: 780-432-1618
piotrgm@shaw.ca
www.eccsociety.com
Our vision is to ensure that the musical works of composers from Edmonton, as well as Alberta, Canada, and the rest of the world, are made fully accessible to and for the Canadian public.

EdmontonPlus.ca
PH: 403-228-1800 FX: 403-240-5669
www.edmontonplus.ca
Online A&E magazine covering the local music scene.

FFWD
1902-B 11th St. SE Calgary, AB T2G 3G2
PH: 403-244-2235 FX: 403-244-1431
Jason Lewis jlewis@ffwd.greatwest.ca
www.ffwdweekly.com
Calgary's news and entertainment weekly.

Foothills Bluegrass Music Society
PO Box 22094, Banker's Hall, Calgary, AB T2P 4J5
fbms@melmusic.com
www.melmusic.com/fbms
Promoting Bluegrass music in Calgary.

The Gateway
Suite 3-04, Students' Union Bldg. UA,
Edmonton, AB T6G 2J7
PH: 780-492-7052 FX: 780-492-6665
entertainment@gateway.ualberta.ca
www.gateway.ualberta.ca
University of Alberta's student paper.

The Gauntlet
Rm 319, MacEwan Students' Ctr.
2500 University Dr. NW, Calgary, AB T2N 1N4
PH: 403-220-4376
entertainment@gauntlet.ucalgary.ca
gauntlet.ucalgary.ca
U. of Calgary's student paper. Large music section.

indecline
band@markbirtlesproject.com
www.indecline.net
Covering the Edmonton Punk scene.

Megatunes *Calgary*
932 17th Ave. SW, Calgary, AB T2T 0A2
PH: 403-229-3022
customer.service@megatunes.com
www.megatunes.com
An independent music store in Calgary.

Megatunes *Edmonton*
10355 Whyte Ave. Edmonton, AB T6E 1Z9
PH: 780-434-6342
edmt.customer.service@megatunes.com
Independent music store in Edmonton.

Red Deer Express
5301 43rd St. #121, Red Deer, AB T4N 1C8
PH: 403-346-3356 FX: 403-347-6620
express@reddeer.greatwest.ca
www.reddeerexpress.com
Cover local music.

SEE Magazine
10275 Jasper Ave. #200, Edmonton, AB T5J 1X8
PH: 780-430-9003 FX: 780-432-1102
info@see.greatwest.ca
www.seemagazine.com
Edmonton's weekly source for news, arts and entertainment.

British Columbia

Abbotsford Times
30887 Peardonville Rd. Abbotsford, BC V2T 6K2
PH: 604-854-5244 FX: 604-854-1140
editorial@abbotsfordtimes.com
www.abbotsfordtimes.com
Covers local music in the "Showtime!" section.

B.C. Country Music Association
20290 Industrial Ave. Langley, BC V3A 4K7
PH: 604-533-5088 FX: 604-533-5054
bccountrymusic@telus.net
www.bccountry.com
Promotes the BC Country music community.

BC Touring Council
PO Box 547, Nelson, BC V1L 5R3
PH: 250-352-0021 FX: 250-352-0027
fyi@bctouring.org
www.bctouring.org
Expands touring opportunities for artists.

Brand X Media
106-715 Vancouver St., Victoria, BC V8V 3V2
Jesse Ladret jesse@brandxmedia.ca
www.brandxmedia.ca
An online alternative arts and music magazine that reviews music predominantly from Western Canada, covering all genres of music.

CFOX New Music Page
#2000-700 W. Georgia, Vancouver, BC V7Y 1K9
PH: 604-684-7221 FX: 604-331-2755
webmaster@cfox.com
www.cfox.com/shows/indie_night.cfm
Are you a local band looking for some exposure? (Music exposure, that is... keep your clothes on!). Want to be on our New Music page? Got some songs we can put up? Contact us!

Chilliwack Times
45941 Trethewey Ave. Chilliwack, BC V2P 1K4
PH: 604-792-9117 FX: 604-792-9300
editorial@chilliwacktimes.com
www.chilliwacktimes.com
Community newspaper. Showtime A&E section.

Cowichan Folk Guild
PO Box 802, Duncan, BC V9L 3Y1
PH: 250-748-3975
info@folkfest.bc.ca
www.folkfest.bc.ca
Preserves and promotes local Folk artists.

C~VUE Local Music Profiles
www.civu.net/local.html
Submit a photo your info to be featured online.

Festival Distribution Inc.
1351 Grant St., Vancouver, BC V5L 2X7
PH: 604-253-2662 FX: 604-253-2634
fdi@festival.bc.ca
www.festival.bc.ca
Markets independently produced recordings.

Gothic BC
atratus@gothic.bc.ca
www.gothic.bc.ca
British Columbia's Gothic source.

Hornby Island Blues Society
Savoie 1-6, Hornby Island, BC V0R 1Z0
PH: 250-335-2581 FX: 250-335-1954
doucette@mars.ark.com
www.hornby-blues.bc.ca
Connects listeners and players of Blues music.

liquidbeat.com
liquidbeat@email.com
www.liquidbeat.com
Underground Dance community site catering to the BC interior.

Monday Magazine
PH: 250-382-6188 x132
John Threlfall johnt@mondaymag.com
web.bcnewsgroup.com/portals/monday
Victoria's weekly entertainment magazine.

The Nerve Magazine
508-825 Granville St., Vancouver, BC V6Z 1K9
PH: 604-734-1611 FX: 604-684-1698
info@thenervemagazine.com
www.thenerveonline.com
The North West's Rock & Roll magazine.

The Pacific Music Industry Association
425 Carrall St. #501, Vancouver, BC V6B 6E3
PH: 604-873-1914 FX: 604-873-9686
Amanda Schweers amanda@musicbc.org
www.musicbc.org
Supports and promotes the spirit, development, and growth of the BC music community.

Rave Victoria
ariz0na ariz0na@ravevictoria.com
www.ravevictoria.com
Provides DJ sets for download by the community. This is a great way to get your sound out to the promoters and the people who attend shows.

Rek Magazine
1450 Chestnut St. #817, Vancouver, BC V6J 3K3
bands@rekmagazine.ca
www.rekmagazine.ca
Committed to Western Canadian Punk / Hardcore / Metal talent and business.

SaltSpringMusic.Com
328 Lower Ganges Rd.
Salt Spring Island, BC V8K 2V3
PH: 250-475-5896 FX: 250-537-2613
info@saltspringmusic.com
www.saltspringmusic.com
We have begun to expand to take in other Western Canadian artists.

Victoria Fiddle Society
467 Fraser St., Victoria, BC V9A 6H2
info@bckitchenparty.com
www.bckitchenparty.com
A fiddle community for all persons interested in fiddle music in the Victoria region.

Victoria Jazz Society
250-727 Johnson St., Victoria, BC V8W 1M9
PH: 250-388-4423 FX: 250-388-4407
vicjazz@pacificcoast.net
www.vicjazz.bc.ca
Presenting high quality Jazz to the community.

Westcoast Indie
#507, 2005 Pendrell St., Vancouver, BC V6G 1T8
PH: 604-505-9492
Waynerd webmaster@westcoastindie.com
www.westcoastindie.com
Online music community for West Coast musicians to connect, post shows and news. Also does reviews.

West Kootenay Bluegrass Site
pickingrinin@shaw.ca
www.westkootenaybluegrass.com
All the info on the local Bluegrass scene.

Vancouver

At Both Ends Magazine
#207 - 555 E. 6th Ave. Vancouver, BC V5T 1K9
Stephen Fallis stephen@atbothendsmagazine.com
atbothendsmagazine.com
Covers Hardcore/Punk related topics from all over the world with special attention to the Vancouver and Pacific Northwest areas.

Coastal Jazz & Blues Society
316 W. 6th Ave. Vancouver, BC V5Y 1K9
PH: 604-872-5200 FX: 604-872-5250
cjbs@jazzvancouver.com
www.jazzvancouver.com
Covering the Jazz scene both locally and nationally.

Cosmic Debris
PO Box 90, Duncan, BC V9L 3X1
Guy Langlois cosmic@cvnet.net
www.cvnet.net/cosmic
Entertainment magazine covering the local music scene.

Devil Doll Promotions
141-757 Hasting St. W. #169,
Vancouver, BC V6C 1A1
PH: 604-340-1466
Johanna Dolenuck info@devildollpromotions.com
www.devildollpromotions.com
Artist management, development, PR and event coordinating. A fresh company with ample attitude helping you to get more recognition.

DISCORDER
c/o CITR, #233-6138 SUB Blvd.
Vancouver, BC V6T 1Z1
PH: 604-822-3017 x3
discorder.citr.ca
An Indie review magazine published by CITR FM.

Dose Vancouver
1450 Don Mills Rd. Toronto, ON M3B 2X7
info@dose.ca
www.dose.ca/vancouver
A free daily online magazine. One of the key areas of our website is promotion of indie bands. Upload profiles, tracks and images as we feature an indie artist weekly.

Live Music In Vancouver
kristine@livemusicinvancouver.com
www.livemusicinvancouver.com
The main focus of the website is photos of local bands.

Local Authority
info@thelocalauthority.net
www.thelocalauthority.net
We don't charge for our promotional services, we don't expect anything in return except for you to help spread the word around town and a return link on your website if you have one.

Rogue Folk Club
1465 Lamey's Mill Rd. #31,
Vancouver, BC V6H 3W1
PH: 604-736-3022 FX: 604-736-3012
roguefolk@hotmail.com
www.roguefolk.bc.ca
Vancouver area folk dancing, jam sessions, etc.

Georgia Straight
1770 Burrard St. 2nd Fl. Vancouver, BC V6J 3G7
PH: 604-730-7000 FX: 604-730-7010
info@straight.com
www.straight.com
Mag covering the active urban West Coast lifestyle.

Greater Vancouver Alliance for Arts and Culture
938 Howe St. #100, Vancouver, BC V6Z 1N9
PH: 604-681-3535 FX: 604-681-7848
info@allianceforarts.com
www.allianceforarts.com
Represents and serves the local arts community.

LiveMusicVancouver.com
PH: 604-871-0477
Sati Muthanna sati@LiveMusicVancouver.com
livemusicvancouver.com
Covering local music with news, gigs, resources etc.

The Nerve Magazine
508-825 Granville St., Vancouver, BC V6Z 1K9
PH: 604-734-1611
Bradley editor@thenervemagazine.com
www.thenervemagazine.com
Independent, underground culture magazine.

North Shore News
1139 Lonsdale Ave. N. Vancouver, BC V7M 2H4
PH: 604-985-2131 FX: 604-985-2104
editor@nsnews.com
www.nsnews.com
The voice of Vancouver. Covers local music.

North Shore Outlook
#104-980 West 1st St.,
North Vancouver, BC V7P 3N4
PH: 604-903-1000
newsroom@northshoreoutlook.com
www.northshoreoutlook.com
Vancouver paper. Lifestyles section covers local events.

oscillations.ca
comments@oscillations.ca
oscillations.ca
The source for New Music events and performances in Vancouver and the surrounding region.

Pacific Bluegrass and Heritage Society
1343 E. 14th Ave. Vancouver, BC V5N 2C7
PH: 604-439-2583
pacificbluegrass@yahoo.ca
www.pacificbluegrass.bc.ca
Host's jams, workshops, concerts and other special events.

The Peak
2901 Maggie Benston Bldg. 8888 U. Dr.
Burnaby, BC V5A 1S6
PH: 604-291-4630 FX: 604-291-3786
arts@mail.peak.sfu.ca
www.peak.sfu.ca
SFU's independent student newspaper.

Spawner Records
PO Box 93046, Langley, BC V3A 8H2
staff@spawnerrecords.com
www.spawnerrecords.com
Label run by bands for bands from Vancouver.

Terminal City
#300-211 Columbia St., Vancouver, BC V6A 2R5
PH: 604-689-7559 FX: 604-689-7097
music@terminalcity.ca
www.terminalcity.ca
Covering Vancouver arts & entertainment. Covers local music.

The Ubyssey
6138 Student Union Blvd. Vancouver, BC V6T 1Z1
FX: 604-822-1658
culture@ubyssey.bc.ca
www.ubyssey.bc.ca
UBC Student newspaper.

VanCityBands.com
www.vancitybands.com
Showcasing unsigned Vancouver Indie music!

Vancouver Courier
1574 W. 6th Ave. Vancouver, BC V6J 1R2
PH: 604-738-1411
Mick Maloney mmaloney@vancourier.com
www.vancourier.com
Vancouver news and entertainment. Covers local music.

vancouverJazz.com
www.vancouverjazz.com
Reviews, news, interviews etc.

Vancouver World Music Collective
PH/FX: 604-253-6292
Diana Stewart-Imbert
contact@vancouverworldmusic.org
www.vancouverworldmusic.org
Promoting our music and city internationally.

VancouverDiy
PO Box 21530, 1424 Commercial Dr.
Vancouver, BC V5L 5G2
vancouverdiy@hotmail.com
www.vancouverdiy.org
Helping to build the Vancouver DIY community.

Westender
1490 W. Broadway #200, Vancouver, BC V6H 4E8
PH: 604-742-8686
editor@westender.com
www.westender.com
Vancouver's urban voice. Covers local music.

Western Front Society
303 E. 8th Ave. Vancouver, BC V5T 1S1
PH: 604-876-9343 FX: 604-876-4099
music@front.bc.ca
www.front.bc.ca
Produces and promotes contemporary media.

Manitoba

Blues Music in Winnipeg
webmaster@winnipegblues.com
www.winnipegblues.com
Blues reviews, news, previews and more.

Conifera
PO Box 185, RPO Corydon,
Winnipeg, MB R3M 3S7
info@conifera.ca
www.conifera.ca
Network that will help you develop your skills.

dig!
65 Dafoe R. U. Manitoba, Winnipeg, MB R3T 2N2
jazzmag@umanitoba.ca
www.umanitoba.ca/schools/music/jazz/dig
Designed to mirror the growth and gauge the health of Winnipeg's Jazz scene.

Manitoba Audio Recording Industry Association
1-376 Donald St., Winnipeg, MB R3B 2J2
PH: 204-942-8650 FX: 204-942-6083
info@manitobamusic.com
www.manitobamusic.com
Helps anyone involved with music in Manitoba.

Manitoba Blues Society
PO Box 52, Winnipeg, MB R2L 1M0
PH: 204-667-3491
flkraft@shaw.ca
www.mbblues.mb.ca
Promotes, fosters and supports the Blues in Manitoba.

Manitoba OldTyme & Bluegrass Society
101-3281 Pembina Hwy. Winnipeg, MB R3V 1T7
PH: 204-864-2921
whittakerr@shaw.ca
www.manitobabluegrass.ca
All the info on the local Bluegrass scene.

Musicians Network
90 Greensboro Sq. Winnipeg, MB R3T 4L1
Mike Garbutt riffvandal@mts.net
www.bytes4u.ca
Join a band, form a band, tour, record or jam and more.

newWinnipeg
137 Langside St., Winnipeg, MB R3C 1Z5
PH: 204-783-0935
info@newwinnipeg.com
www.newwinnipeg.com
Winnipeg's A&E magazine.

Uptown Magazine
#202-63 Albert St., Winnipeg, MB R3B 1G4
PH: 204-949-4370 FX: 204-949 4376
email: source@uptownmag.com
www.uptownmag.com
Winnipeg's online source for arts, entertainment & news.

Winnipeg Classical Guitar Society
Box 3037, Winnipeg, MB R3C 4E5
PH: 204-775-0809
www.winnipegclassicalguitarsociety.org
Promoting the Classical guitar in Winnipeg.

Winnipeg Early Music Society
PH: 204-474-2360
Monica Hultin mhultin@mts.net
www.mts.net/~mhultin/wems.htm
Gives members opportunities to perform.

Winnipeg Metal
winnipegmetal.cjb.net
Online Metal community. Post shows, reviews, news etc.

New Brunswick

Argosy
152 Main St., Sackville, NB E4L 1B3
PH: 506-364-2236
argosy@mta.ca
argosy.mta.ca
Mount Allison U. independent student journal

The Brunswickan
21 Pacey Dr. #35, Fredericton, NB E3B 5A3
PH: 506-453-4983 FX: 506-453-5073
bruns@unb.ca
www.unb.ca/web/bruns
U. NB campus paper.

canadaeast.com
www.canadaeast.com
Local music covered in the entertainment section.

Deleted Scene
setsfire@hotmail.com
deletedscene.brinkster.net
A Fredericton Punk show journal. Add your info.

giraffecycle.com
webmaster@giraffecycle.com
www.giraffecycle.com
Dedicated to the Saint John Hardcore music scene.

Maritime Metal
www.discorporatemusic.com/MessageBoard
A forum is meant exclusively for Maritime Metal Bands to make announcements, talk about their music, promote their merchandise and post information about upcoming shows.

monctonlocals.com
admin@monctonlocals.com
www.monctonlocals.com
Covering the local music scene. Post your info!

Music New Brunswick
PO Box 1638, Moncton, NB E1C 9X4
PH: 506-383-4662 FX: 506-383-4329
mnb@nb.aibn.com
www.musicnb.org
Promoting and developing the New Brunswick music industry.

Saint John Now!
krista@sjnow.com
www.sjnow.com
List your upcoming event.

Newfoundland

AtlanticCanadianMusic.com
PO Box 847, Mount Pearl, NL A1N 3C8
PH: 709-744-5037 FX: 709-737-0912
info@atlanticcanadianmusic.com
www.atlanticcanadianmusic.com
We offer over 300 titles of music and audio books from Atlantic Canada.

Bluegrass and Oldtime Country Music Society of NFLD & Labrador
www.bluegrass-nl.ca
Fosters the awareness, development and growth of Bluegrass & Oldtime Country music in the province.

Music Industry Association of NFLD & Labrador
155 Water St. #102, St. John's, NL A1C 1B3
PH: 709-754-2574 FX: 709-754-5758
dparker@nfld.com
www.mia.nf.ca
Provides opportunities for local bands to grow. Our newsletter, "The Measure" features local artists.

nflocals.com
Steven Musgrave: xstevemx@hotmail.com
www.nflocals.com
The very best in underground culture.

Nova Scotia

Cape Breton Music Online
info@cbmusic.com
cbmusic.com
Cape Breton music on the Internet.

Cape Bretoner Magazine
PO Box 220, Sydney, NS B1P 6H1
PH: 902-567-6400 FX: 902-539-2040
editorial@capebretoner.com
www.capebretoner.com
The latest Cape Breton releases, performances etc.

Castlebay Music
904 Castlebay Rd. Cape Breton, NS B1T 1J6
PH: 902-379-2343
www.castlebaymusic.com
Cape Breton and East Coast music.

cblocals.com
Eli Richards bands@cblocals.com
www.cblocals.com
Covering the Cape Breton underground culture.

Celtic Music Interpretive Centre
PO Box 157, Judique, Inverness Cove, NS B0E 1P0
PH: 902-787-2708
celtic.music@ns.sympatico.ca
www.celticmusicsite.com
Promoting the traditional music of Cape Breton Island through education and performance.

Charlie's Music
14614 Cabot Trail, PO Box 516,
Cheticamp, NS B0E 1H0
PH: 902-224-3782 FX: 902-224-1441
charlie@ns.sympatico.ca
www.capebretonisland.com/Music/Charlies
Recorded music from Atlantic Canada.

The Coast
5435 Portland Pl. Halifax, NS B3K 6R7
PH: 902-422-6278 FX: 902-425-0013
Tara Thorne tarat@thecoast.ca
www.thecoast.ca
Submit info about your event, performance or gig to us.

East Coast Catalogue Company Ltd.
45 Madeira Cr. Dartmouth, NS B2W 6G7
PH: 800-461-3361 FX: 902-492-8770
www.eastcoastcatalogue.com
Mail order retailer of Atlantic Canadian products.

East Coast Music Online
Wendy Gilmour wendy@eastcoastmusiconline.com
www.eastcoastmusiconline.com
News, reviews and links to music industry related websites.

halifaxlocals.com
Sean MacGillivray admin@halifaxlocals.com
www.halifaxlocals.com
Connect to the Halifax underground culture.

JazzEast
PO Box 33043, Halifax, NS B3L 4T6
PH: 902-492-2225
www.jazzeast.com
Presents live Jazz concerts and workshops.

The Madrigal
5640 Spring Garden Rd. #207,
Halifax, NS B3J 3M7
PH: 902-423-6453
madrigal@mirror.org
www.themadrigal.com
Online Indie record shop.

Maritime Metal
www.maritimemetal.net
Atlantic Canada's Metal community.

Music Industry Association of Nova Scotia
PO Box 36119, Halifax, NS B3J 3S9
PH: 902-423-6271 FX: 902-423-8841
info@mians.ca
www.mians.ca
Promotes the local music industry in Nova Scotia.

Nova Scotia Punk Resource
www.punk.hfxns.org
Post your shows, news etc.

Rock In Halifax
Adrian bruhma@hotmail.com
www.rockinhalifax.net
News, updates, show listings etc.

Ontario

Barrie Folk Society
51 Henry St., Barrie, ON L4N 1C6
princess@barriefolk.com
www.barriefolk.com
Supports artistic talent, style and creative vision.

The Barrie Music Scene
www.barriemusic.com
News, forums, gigs etc.

BayToday.ca
348 Worthington St. E. #16,
North Bay, ON P1B 1H3
PH: 705-497-9619 FX: 705-497-9671
info@baytoday.ca
www.baytoday.ca
North Bay A&E publication. Post your news and events.

Brantford Folk Club
22 Spartan Dr. Brantford, ON N3R 6C7
PH: 519-759-7676
folk@rogers.com
www.brantford.folk.on.ca
Keeping the tradition alive!

Brock Press
www.brockpress.com
Brock U. campus paper.

Canada South Blues Society
PO Box 28037, Windsor, ON N8X 5E4
ThePrez@BluesSociety.ca
www.bluessociety.ca
Helping to keep the Blues alive in SW Ontario.

Christian Underground Rock In Ontario
www.curio.org
Uniting the Christian music scene in Ontario.

Cornwall Underground
The_Nads@hotmail.com
www.geocities.com/cornwallunderground
The best website for all the latest news in the Cornwall music scene.

Cuckoo's Nest Folk Club
folk@iandavies.com
www.cuckoosnest.folk.on.ca
Promoting traditional Folk music in London.

Dogbus Music
16 Rosemary Dr. Lindsay, ON K9V 4P8
Ryan Oliver ryanoliver@dogbusonline.com
www.dogbusonline.com
We're always looking for new Punk bands to support and help grow their message.

ECHO Weekly
19 King St. E. 2nd Fl. Kitchener, ON N2G 2K4
PH: 519-220-1594 FX: 519-743-7491
www.echoweekly.com
Weekly alternative magazine covering the greater Kitchener/Waterloo/Cambridge/Guelph area.

The Ford Plant
1 King St., Brantford, ON N3R 3V9
PH: 519-754-4859
www.thefordplant.ca
Founded to help re-vitalize Brantford's struggling art and music community.

Hammer-rock Discussion Group
groups.yahoo.com/group/hammer-rock
Discussing Hamilton's music scene.

Imprint
Student Life Center, Rm 1116, U. Waterloo,
Waterloo, ON N2L 3G1
PH: 519-888-4048 FX: 519-884-7800
board@mail.imprint.uwaterloo.ca
imprint.uwaterloo.ca
U. Waterloo's student paper.

The Journal
272 Earl St., Kingston, ON K7L 2H8
PH: 613-533-2800 FX: 613-533-6728
journal_news@ams.queensu.ca
www.queensjournal.ca
Queens University's student paper.

Kingston Jazz Society
203-117 Park St., Kingston, ON K7L 5P6
kingstonjazz.com
Preserving Jazz music in the Limestone City.

KingstonMp3.com
807-L Blackburn Mews, Kingston, ON K7P 2N6
Ryan ryan.donaven@kingstonmp3.com
www.kingstonmp3.com
Created to expand and promote the strong independent music scene that is constantly overlooked in Kingston.

KW Music
dadmobile@hotmail.com
www.kwmusic.ca
Covering the Kitchener/Waterloo Punk scene.

London INDIE
www.londonindie.com
We are attempting to re-establish the London scene.

London Hardcore
www.londonhardcore.com
Local discussion board. Talk about upcoming shows, reviews, news etc.

The London Musicians' Association
240 Commissioners Rd. W. Unit G,
London, ON N6J 1Y1
PH/FX: 519-685-2540
crescendo@londonmusicians.com
www.londonmusicians.com
Benefits include our Booking Referral Service.

London Ontario Music Scene
www.cleverjoe.com/local
Lists venues, events, resources etc.

London Ontario Rox
1225 Wonderland Rd. N., PO Box 8051,
London, ON N6G 1Z1
Josie info@londonontariorox.com
www.londonontariorox.com
Advertise your band, post your events...what's happening in and around London.

LondonPunkRock.Kicks-Ass.org
Laurie ljwedge@shaw.ca
londonpunkrock.kicks-ass.org
If you would like to submit photos, add a link, promote a band, a CD or an upcoming gig, get in touch with us.

The Northern Bluegrass Committee
PO Box 148, River Valley, ON P0H 2C0
PH: 705-758-9049
Tony Deboer bgypsy@northernbluegrass.com
www.northernbluegrass.com
Promoting the local Bluegrass scene.

Northern Blues
225 Sterling Rd. #19, Toronto, ON M6R 2B2
PH: 416-536-4892 FX: 416-536-1494
info@northernblues.com
www.northernblues.com
Bringing you the best in world class Blues.

Ontario Council of Folk Festivals
410 Bank St., #225, Ottawa, ON K2P 1Y8
PH: 866-292-6233 FX: 613-560-2001
info@ocff.ca
www.ocff.ca
Exists to foster and promote traditional, contemporary and multicultural Folk Music and related arts. Website includes a list of upcoming Folk festivals.

Ontario Metal Pages
Tina tina@ontariometal.net
www.ontariometal.net
The ultimate authority on Metal in Ontario!

The Ontarion
U. Center Room 264, U. Guelph,
Guelph, ON N1G 2W1
PH: 519-824-4120 FX: 519-824-7838
ontarion@uoguelph.ca
www.uoguelph.ca/~ontarion
U. Guelph's campus publication.

ontariopunk.com
PH: 416-499-3079
Shane Macaulay shane@ontariopunk.com
www.ontariopunk.com
News, reviews, interviews, contests etc.

Open Mics in Ontario
www.openmikes.org/calendar/ON

Orillia Folk Society
17 Maria St., Elmvale, ON L0L 1P0
cyberfolkie@hotmail.com
www.geocities.com/liveatjives/ofs1.html
Focus on local contemporary and traditional Folk music.

Our Scene
the_scene01@hotmail.com
www.ourscene.tk
Covering the Windsor Punk/Hardcore scene.

overhear
490 Castlefield Ave. Toronto, ON M5N 1L6
PH: 416-480-0788
webmaster@overhear.com
www.overhear.com
Listings for Ontario Indie artist and bands.

PartyInKingston.com
www.partyinkingston.com
Submit gig info, album reviews etc.

Pulse Niagra
243 Church St. #208, St. Catharines, ON L2R 3E8
PH: 905-682-5999 FX: 905-682-1414
info@pulseniagara.com
www.pulseniagara.com
The Niagra region's weekly alternative paper.

Rock Crew Productions
324 Princess St. #324, Kingston, ON K7L 5S9
PH: 613-539-8438
chris@rockcrew.ca
www.rockcrew.ca
A concert promotion company based in Kingston. Rock Crew is at the forefront of the Kingston live music industry, presenting local, Canadian, and international talent in Kingston's premier live venues.

royalcitymusic.ca
info@royalcitymusic.ca
www.royalcitymusic.ca
An online community for artists and fans from a variety of genres in the Guelph area.

SarniaPunk.tk
Christine White christine@sarniapunk.tk
www.sarniapunk.tk
Covering the Sarnia Punk scene. Gigs, pictures etc.

Sault Music Scene.com
saultmusic@hotmail.com
www.thesaultmusicscene.com
Covers the local Hardcore scene.

Scene Magazine
PO Box 2302, London, ON N6A 4E3
PH: 519-642-4780 FX: 519-642-0737
music@scenemagazine.com
www.scenemagazine.com
London arts & entertainment magazine.

The Silhouette
McMaster U. Student Ctr. Rm B110,
1280 Main St. W., Hamilton, ON L8S 4S4
FX: 905-529-3208
thesil@msu.mcmaster.ca
www.msu.mcmaster.ca/sil
McMaster University student newspaper.

Steel City Music
feedback@steelcitymusic.ca
www.steelcitymusic.ca
Website dedicated to the promotion of the Hamilton, Ontario music scene.

tbshows.com
www.tbshows.com
Covering the Thunder Bay Punk scene.

Thunder Bay Blues Society
236 Elron Cres. Thunder Bay, ON P7C 5T5
PH: 807-475-4597
info@thunderbaybluessociety.ca
www.thunderbaybluessociety.ca
Supports local, national and international Blues artists.

Traditions Folk Club
80 Broadway, Orangeville, ON L9W 1J9
PH: 519-942-6258 FX: 519-940-9367
info@acoustictraditions.com
www.acoustictraditions.com/folkclub.html
Showcases local performers.

The Underground
1265 Military Trail, Rm. 207, Students Ctr.
Scarborough, ON M1C 1A4
PH: 416-287-7054 FX: 416-287-7055
info@the-underground.ca
the-underground.ca
U of T Scarborough student publication.

Upfront Magazine
325 Chatham St. W., Windsor, ON N9A 5M8
PH: 519-254-5268 FX: 519-254-6110
info@upfrontwindsor.com
www.upfrontwindsor.com
Windsor's independent news, music and art culture magazine.

VIEW Magazine
20 Jackson St. #300, Hamilton, ON L8P 1L2
PH: 905-527-3343 FX: 905-527-3721
info@viewmag.com
www.viewmag.com
Greater Hamilton's weekly alternative.

Wow! Sudbury
contact@wowsudbury.com
www.wowsudbury.com
Sudbury's entertainment website. Covers local music.

XEN Magazine
www.xenmagazine.com
Kitchener-Waterloo's A&E magazine. Post your gigs, events etc.

Ottawa

The Bear's Soundcheck
soundcheck@thebear.fm
www.thebear.fm
Classified ads for musicians in Ottawa.

Blues4U
67 North St., Gatineau, QC J9H 2W8
steam@allblues4u.com
www.allblues4u.com
Covering the Ottawa Blues scene.

Dark Ottawa
www.darkottawa.com
An alternative guide to Canada's capital.

Dose Ottawa
1450 Don Mills Rd. Toronto, ON M3B 2X7
info@dose.ca
www.dose.ca/ottawa/music
A free daily online magazine. One of the key areas of our website is promotion of indie bands. Upload profiles, tracks and images as we feature an indie artist weekly.

Flat and Black Records
2515 Bank St. PO Box 40029,
Ottawa, ON K1V 0W8
flatblack@spincom.on.ca
www.spincom.on.ca/flatblack
Looking to work with new bands for live shows, recording and distribution.

The Fulcrum
07-85 University Private, Ottawa, ON K1N 6N5
PH: 613-562-5260 FX: 613-562-5259
arts@thefulcrum.com
www.thefulcrum.com
U. Ottawa's student paper.

Musician's Conversation Circle Ottawa
mccottawa.proboards17.com
Discussion board for Ottawa musicians. Post your shows, new releases etc.

Ottawa Blues, Jazz and Swing Guide
bu932@ncf.ca
ottawabluesjazz.ca
Ottawa's one-stop Blues and Jazz event site.

Ottawa Blues Society
PO Box 708, Stn. B, Ottawa, ON K1P 5P8
www.ottawabluessociety.com
Cconcert reviews and information on the scene.

Ottawa Chamber Music Society
Box 20583, Ottawa, ON K1N 1A3
PH: 613-234-8008 FX: 613-234-7692
webmaster@chamberfest.com
www.chamberfest.com
Dedicated to presenting Chamber music of the highest possible artistic standard.

Ottawa Metal
Eric Mulligan d_a_t_a_g_r_a_m@hotmail.com
www.ottawametal.com
Covering Metal music in the Ottawa/Gatineau region.

Ottawa Music Connection
omc@spincom.on.ca
www.spincom.on.ca/omc.htm
Up-to-date listings of what's happening in Canada's National Capital.

The Ottawa Musician
www.theottawamusician.com
With continuing support, The OM site has a NEW feature promoting talented artist Mp3s from the greater Ottawa area.

Ottawa Underground
ottawaunderground@yahoo.com
www.geocities.com/ottawaunderground
Covering the Ottawa Punk scene.

Ottawa Valley Bluegrass Music Association
PO Box 328, Woodlawn, ON K0A 3M0
webmaster@valleygrass.ca
www.valleygrass.ca
Promotes and publicizes Bluegrass music and activities.

Ottawa Valley Music Association
PO Box 2, Renfrew, ON K7V 4A2
www.ovmas.ca
Promoting music in and about the Ottawa Valley.

Ottawa XPress
396 Cooper St. #204, Ottawa, ON K2P 2H7
PH: 6133-237-8226 FX: 613-237-8220
info@ottawaxpress.ca
www.ottawaxpress.ca
Weekly paper. Coverage of local music.

OttawaJazz.com
kgrace@entrenet.com
www.ottawajazz.com
Lists upcoming gigs and special events.

OttawaMusicians.com
www.ottawamusicians.com
Artist bios, pictures, gigs and contact information.

OttawaMusicScene.Com
editor@ottawamusicscene.com
OttawaMusicScene.Com
Promotes the Ottawa area music scene.

OttawaPlus.ca
www.ottawaplus.ca
Online A&E guide. Submit your info.

OttawaRocks.ca
webmaster@ottawarocks.ca
www.ottawarocks.ca
Dedicated to all artists and musicians in our nation's capital.

OttawaStart
23 Elm St., Ottawa, ON K1R 6M9
PH: 613-2234-0017
ottawastart.com
Add your events for free to our calendar.

punkottawa.com
PO Box 57043, Ottawa, ON K1R 6P0
PH: 613-234-7869
info@punkottawa.com
www.punkottawa.com
Covers the local Punk scene.

VOIR.ca Ottawa
396 Cooper #204, Ottawa, ON K2P 2H7
PH: 613-237-8226 FX: 613-237-8220
www.voir.ca
A&E magazine. In French.

Women's Voices Festival
artistic_submissions@womensvoices.on.ca
womensvoices.on.ca
Hosts a variety of music festivals.

Toronto

2 The Beat
161 Spadina Ave. Toronto, ON M5V 2L6
PH: 416-598-8120 FX: 416-598-9031
brian@2thebeat.com
2thebeat.com
Offers Electronic/Techno physical and online sales.

The Ambient Ping
2141 Kipling Ave. PO Box 30119,
Etobicoke, ON M9W 6T1
info@theambientping.com
www.theambientping.com
Weekly musical performance event.

ARRAYMUSIC
60 Atlantic Ave. #218, Toronto, ON M6K 1X9
PH: 416-532-3019 FX: 416-532-9797
info@arraymusic.com
www.arraymusic.com
Site for composers of all levels.

Citygigs *Toronto*
#2 116 Pembroke St., Toronto, ON M5A 2N8
PH: 416-926-3711 FX: 416-926-3711
toronto@citygigs.com
www.citygigs.com
Reviews, interviews, concert previews and more!

Classic Jazz Society of Toronto
25 The Esplanade, #2305, Toronto, ON M5E 1W5
PH: 416-777-9235
www.classicjazztoronto.com
Promotes the original form of Jazz.

Dose Toronto
1450 Don Mills Rd. Toronto, ON M3B 2X7
info@dose.ca
www.dose.ca/toronto
A free daily online magazine. One of the key areas of our website is promotion of indie bands. Upload profiles, tracks and images as we feature an indie artist weekly.

eye
70 Peter St., Toronto, ON M5V 2G5
PH: 416-596-4393
Stuart Berman sberman@eye.net
www.eye.net
Toronto's A&E weekly. Local music covered.

The Eyeopener
380 Victoria St. Rm A54, Toronto, ON M5B 1W7
PH: 416-595-1490 FX: 416-595-1374
entertainment@theeyeopener.com
www.theeyeopener.com
Ryerson's independent student newspaper.

Flying Cloud Folk Club
292 Brunswick Ave. Toronto, ON M5S 2M7
PH: 416-410-3655
flying_cloud_folk@sympatico.ca
www3.sympatico.ca/flying_cloud_folk
Information about the Toronto Folk music scene.

Guitar Society of Toronto
9 Gibson Ave. Toronto, ON M5R 1T4
PH: 416-922-8002 FX: 416-968-0525
eli.kassner@utoronto.ca
www.guitar-toronto.on.ca
Promoting the Classical guitar and artists.

Indie-Music-Toronto
79564-1995 Weston Rd. Toronto, ON M9N 3W9
LiANA Di Marco guitarbabe@hotmail.com
www.indie-music-toronto.ca
All about music, songwriting and the business of entertainment.

Jazz in Toronto
3 St. Patrick St., Toronto, ON M5T 1T9
PH: 416-599-5486
jazz@jazzintoronto.com
www.jazzintoronto.com
The official guide to Jazz in Toronto.

kid with camera
david@kidwithcamera.com
www.kidwithcamera.com
Print and online zine. Chronicle of photography and journal entries covering the Toronto Punk scene.

Maple Blues
910 Queen St. W. #B04, Toronto, ON M6J 1G6
PH: 416-538-3885
info@torontobluessociety.com
www.torontobluessociety.com/maple.htm
Toronto Blues Society's magazine promoting local artists.

Music Gallery
197 John St., Toronto, ON M5T 1X6
PH: 416-204-1080 FX: 416-204-9986
staff@musicgallery.org
www.musicgallery.org
Center for new and unusual music.

New Adventures in Sound Art
401 Richmond St. W. #358, Toronto, ON M5V 3A8
PH: 416-910-7231
naisa@soundtravels.ca
www.soundtravels.ca
Produces performances and installations spanning the entire spectrum of Electroacoustic and Experimental Sound Art.

Nocturnal
info@nocturnalmagazine.net
www.nocturnalmagazine.net
Guide to the music and artists of Toronto.

NOW
189 Church St., Toronto, ON M5B 1Y7
PH: 416-364-1301
entertainment@nowtoronto.com
www.nowtoronto.com
Extensive coverage of local music.

Small World Music
29 Gwynne Ave. Toronto, ON M6K 2C2
PH: 416-536-5439 FX: 416-536-2742
Alan Davis alan@smallworldmusic.com
www.smallworldmusic.com
Created to promote World Music activity in Toronto by presenting artists of the highest calibre, emphasizing Canadian performers and audience development through community outreach.

Spill
3055 Harold Sheard Dr. Mississauga, ON L4T 1V4
PH: 905-677-8337 FX: 905-677-9705
info@spillmagazine.com
www.spillmagazine.com
Concert listings, show and CD reviews and more.

TORO
119 Spadina Ave. #502, Toronto, ON M5V 2L1
PH: 416-785-9446 FX: 416-785-9434
info@toromagazine.ca
www.toromagazine.ca
Toronto A&E publication.

Toronto Blues Society
910 Queen St. W. #B04, Toronto, ON M6J 1G6
PH: 416-538-3885 FX: 416-538-6559
info@torontobluessociety.com
www.torontobluessociety.com
Promoting and preserving the Blues.

Toronto Downtown Jazz
82 Bleecker St., Toronto, ON M4X 1L8
PH: 416-928-2033 FX: 416-928-0533
tdjs@tojazz.com
www.torontojazz.com
Our missions is to promote the art of Jazz and engage a diverse public through an internationally-renowned organization devoted to year round activities and initiatives.

Toronto Early Music Players Organization
90 Wayland Ave. Toronto, ON M4E 3C9
PH: 416-699-0517
dresher@chass.utoronto.ca
www.chass.utoronto.ca/~dresher/TEMPO
Nurtures and encourages all early music.

Toronto-goth.com
reviews@toronto-goth.com
www.toronto-goth.com
Resource for Toronto's Gothic/Industrial scene.

Toronto Hip Hop Online
RR #3, Parkhill, ON N0M 2K0
FX: 519-238-1224
matt@megacityhiphop.com
www.megacityhiphop.com
Gets exposure for your work. Reviews CDs.

ToRonTo HisPaNo.com
PH: 416-694-1834
info@torontohispano.com
www.torontohispano.com
Covering music in the Toronto Hispanic community.

Toronto Musicians' Association
15 Gervais Dr. #500, Toronto, ON M3C 1Y8
PH: 416-421-1020 FX: 416-421-7011
www.torontomusicians.org
Our experience and support can help you achieve your goals.

toronto.com
info@toronto.com
www.toronto.com
Covers the local music scene.

TOsalsa.com
info@tosalsa.com
www.tosalsa.com
Interviews and articles in the Latin music section.

The Varsity
21 Sussex Ave. Toronto, ON M5S1J6
PH: 416-946-7600 x205
review@thevarsity.ca
www.thevarsity.ca
U. Toronto's student newspaper.

Wavelength
868 Dovercourt Rd. Toronto, ON M6H 2X5
howdy@wavelengthtoronto.com
www.wavelengthtoronto.com
Underground music from Toronto and beyond.

Word Magazine
6-295 Queen St. E., #370, Brampton, ON L6W 4S6
PH: 905-799-1630 FX: 905-799-2788
word@wordmag.com
www.wordmag.com
Toronto's Urban Culture magazine.

Prince Edward Island

Alchemy Music
www.alchemymusic.net
PEI's leading music news and discussion website.

The Buzz
PO Box 1945, Charlottetown, PE C1A 7N5
PH: 902-628-1958 FX: 902-628-1953
buzzon@isn.net
www.buzzon.com
What's going on in the lively cultural scene of PEI.

East Coast Music Association
145 Richmond St., Charlottetown, PE C1A 1J1
PH: 902-892-9040 FX: 902-892-9041
ecma@ecma.ca
www.ecma.ca
Promote/celebrates music locally and globally.

peilocals.com
admin@peilocals.com
www.peilocals.com
The very best in the PEI underground scene.

Quebec

33-MTL.com
info@33-mtl.com
www.33mtl.com
Covering the Montreal Urban music scene.

Bandeapart.fm
1400 boul. Rene-Levesque E. 8ᵉ etage
Montreal, QC H2L 2M2
PH: 514-597-5909 FX: 514-597-7373
bap@radio-canada.ca
www.bandeapart.fm
Magazine internet sur les musiques Alternatives francophones.

Club Culture
plazzart@club-culture.com
club-culture.com
A site which posts French Canadian MP3s.

FOLQUÉBEC
Dana Whittle info@folquebec.com
www.folquebec.com
Increases recognition of Québéc's Folk Music and dance culture.

Hour
355 W. St. Catharine 7th Fl. Montreal, QC H3B 1A5
PH: 514-848-0777 FX: 514-848-9004
info@hour.ca
www.hour.ca
Weekly news. Extensive coverage of local music.

Jazz Montreal
webmaster@jazzmontreal.com
www.jazzmontreal.com
Add your into, listings, releases etc.

MetalQuebec.com
www.metalquebec.com
Critiques, MP3, Vidéos etc.

Montreal Mirror
465 McGill St. 3rd Fl. Montreal, QC H2Y 4B4
PH: 514-393-1010 FX: 514-393-3173
letters@mtl-mirror.com
www.montrealmirror.com
Weekly A&E paper. Covers local music.

Montreal Shows
www.montrealshows.com
Send in info about your upcoming gigs.

Montrealgroove
3750 Cremazie E. #305, Montreal, QC H2B 1A6
PH: 514-727-2737 FX: 514-727-2737
info@montrealgroove.com
www.montrealgroove.com
CD Vendor for local Montreal artists.

MontrealMusicScene.com
info@montrealmusicscene.com
www.montrealmusicscene.com
Providing a networking vehicle for musicians and artists to help them gain public exposure while informing locals about the Montreal music scene and to unify them through a stronger growing community.

MontrealPlus.ca
english.montrealplus.ca
Online A&E magazine covering the local music scene.

orcasound
5202 Mountain Sights, Montreal, QC H3W 2Y2
PH: 514-483-6722
orcasound@videotron.ca
www.orcasound.com
Reports the hottest musical attractions and recordings.

Quebec Hardcore
898 Short #2 Sherbrooke, QC J1H 2G2
www.qchc.com
Promoting local bands, labels and organizations.

Quebec Punk Scene
660 Ave. Chouinard #4, Quebec City, QC G1S 3E4
info@quebecpunkscene.net
www.quebecpunkscene.net
La source #1 de la scène Punk Québécoise.

QuebecPlus.ca
www.quebecplus.ca
Online A&E magazine covering the local music scene.

Rien à Déclarer
Nelson nelson001@sympatico.ca
www.radzine.com
Covering the Montreal Punk scene.

Rimouski Metal
106 St. Germain E. #16, Rimouski, QC G5L 1A6
www.rimouskimetal.net
News, reviews, gig dates etc.

Sang Frais
PO Box 32111, Montreal, QC H2L 4Y5
info@sangfrais.com
www.sangfrais.com
Le 'zine métal Québécoise 100% francophone.

SOPREF
info@sopref.org
www.sopref.org
Société pour la promotion de la relève musicale de l'espace francophone.

SubQuebec.com
186 Boul. Indutriel #201,
Saint-Eustache, QC J7R 5C2
PH: 450-974-9339
webmestres@subquebec.com
www.subquebec.com
Covering the hard music scene in Quebec.

Sur Scene
webmaster@surscene.qc.ca
www.surscene.qc.ca
Quebec music and arts scene.

TechnoQuebec.com
info@musiquebec.com
www.technoquebec.com
La porte d'entrée la plus électronique du web.

Thirty Below
1108 rue Dollar, Val-Belair, QC G3K 1W6
FX: 418-847-9815
thirtybelow@trentesouszero.com
www.trentesouszero.com
Quebec traditional and Folk music site.

Trois-Rivieres Metal
584 rue Principale, St-Bonifae, QC G0X 2L0
PH: 819-535-3777
info@troisrivieresmetal.com
www.troisrivieresmetal.com
Ce site est une référence Metal pour la région de Trois-Rivières.

Voir
internet@voir.ca
www.voir.ca
A&E magazine with editions for Montreal and Quebec City.

Saskatchewan

The Carillon
Room 227 Riddell Center, U. Regina, SK S4S 0A2
PH: 306-586-8867 FX: 306-586-7422
carillon@ursu.uregina.ca
www.carillon.uregina.ca
U. Regina's student publication.

Regina Jazz Society
PO Box 24054, 2202 Broad St., Regina, SK S4P 4J8
contact@reginajazz.ca
www.reginajazz.ca
Our newsletter covers local Jazz events.

Saskatchewan Country Music Association
PO Box 271, Saskatoon, SK S7K 3L3
PH: 306-978-7262
scma@scma.sk.ca
www.scma.sk.ca
Promoting Saskatchewan Country music.

Saskatchewan Recording Industry Association
2001 Cornwall St. #114, Regina, SK S4P 3X9
PH: 306-347-0676 FX: 306-347-7735
info@saskrecording.ca
www.saskrecording.ca
The sound recording industries of Saskatchewan.

The Saskatoon Blues Society
PO Box 21035, Saskatoon, SK S7H 5N9
info@saskatoonbluessociety.ca
www.saskatoonbluessociety.ca
Celebrates Blues music throughout Saskatchewan.

Saskatoon Jazz Society
245 3rd Ave. S. Saskatoon, SK S7K 1M3
PH: 306-683-2277
www.jazzbassment.com
Jazz Rag newsletter covers local music events.

Saskmetal.com
www.saskmetal.com
Online Metal community. Post shows, reviews, news etc.

The Sheaf
93 Campus Dr. Room 108 Memorial Bldg.
Saskatoon, SK S7N 5B2
PH: 306-966-8688 FX: 306-966-8699
Sheaf.editors@usask.ca
www.thesheaf.com
U. Saskatchewan students' newspaper.

Threeohsix.org
1002 14th St. E. #3, Saskatoon, SK S7H 0E2
PH: 306-934-3444
setaside@threeohsix.org
threeohsix.org
A cross-genre Underground music webzine.

Yukon

Jazz Society of Yukon
Box 31307, 211 Main St., Whitehorse, YT Y1A 5P7
PH: 867-633-3300 FX: 867-633-3310
info@jazzyukon.ca
www.jazzyukon.ca
Our mandate is to develop, promote and present jazz in Yukon.

MusicYukon
108 Elliott St. Ste. 416, Whitehorse, YT Y1A 6C4
PH: 867-456-8742 FX: 867-668-3450
Mark Smith mark@musicyukon.com
www.musicyukon.com
Formed to help promote Yukon recording artists and help them get themselves export ready.

Europe

American Voices
Klarastrasse, 35a D-79106, Freiburg, Germany
PH: 49-179-461-3035 FX: 49-179-461-3035
Liz.Smailes@americanvoices.org
www.americanvoices.org
Dedicated to the promotion of quality American music.

euromusic
webmaster@euromusic.com
www.euromusic.com
Register and create your page on Euromusic.

European Bluegrass Music Association
Steinenweg 8, CH-4133 Pratteln, Switzerland
FX: 41-61-821-83-64
bluegrasseurope@datacomm.ch
www.europe-bma.org
Promotes European Bluegrass musicians and bands.

Europe Jazz Network
49 Blvd. Marcel Sembat, 93200 Saint-Denis France
info@europejazz.net
www.europejazz.net
Promotes collaboration among the professionals in the field of Jazz.

Riotgrrl Europe
6 Melrose Ave. Mitcham, Surrey, CR4 2EG UK
ms_scarlet@btinternet.com
riotgrrrleurope.net
Underground-feminist bands, zines, distros, groups, projects etc.

Rocksie
Kultur Kooperative Ruhr, Guntherstr. 65, 44143 Dortmund, Germany
PH: 0231-557521-18 FX: 0231-557521-29
rocksie@rocksie.de
www.rocksie.de
European music network for Women.

France

3AM Magazine
12 rue de Tournon, 75006, Paris, France
andrew@3ammagazine.com
www.3ammagazine.com
The hottest in online literature, entertainment and music.

France Bluegrass Musique Association
www.france-bluegrass.org
Un site pour les amateurs et les professionels du Bluegrass en France.

Societe Des Auteurs Compositeurs Et Editeurs De Musique (SACEM)
225 ave. Charles de Gaulle 92528 Neuilly-sur-Seine Cedex, France
PH: 01-47-15-47-15
communication@sacem.fr
www.sacem.fr
An advocate for French performers.

Germany

CrossOver - Network For Youth Culture
Roland Ludwig, Untere Schoenauer Strasse 16, D-04654 Frohburg, Germany
PH: 49-0-34348-53293 FX: 49-0-34348-53293
crossover@ag-musik.de
www.crossover-agm.de
ALL styles of music are being reviewed by a review team of about 12 people.

GEMA
Bayreuther St. 37, 10787, Berlin, Germany
PH: 030-21245-00 FX: 030-21245-950
gema@gema.de
www.gema.de
German performing rights society.

MP3.de
www.mp3.de
Germany's largest MP3 site.

Italy

hotmc.com
Casella 290, Via Valparaiso, 11, 20144 Milano, Italy
s.lippolis@hotmc.com
news.hotmc.com
News, articles and reviews, mainly on Italian hiphop scene.

Italian Jazz Musicians
PH: 39-080-3929215
www.ijm.it
News, reviews, MP3s and online CD sales.

MP3.it
www.mp3.it
Italy's largest MP3 site.

Music Italiana
Tarrikone@hotmail.com
musicaitaliana.com
All the info on the Italian music scene.

Societa Italiana Degli Autori Ed Editori
Musica@siae.it
www.siae.it
Performing Rights Association of Italy.

The Netherlands

Dutch Gothic
troy@dutchgothic.org
www.dutchgothic.org
Info on the Dutch Goth scene.

Hip Hop in je Smoel
yid@hiphopinjesmoel.nl
www.hiphopinjesmoel.nl
Reviews for everything Dutch in Hip Hop.

Holland Rocks
Prins Hendrikkade 142, 1011 At Amsterdam, Holland
PH: 030-4284288 FX: 020-4284287
info@npi.nl
www.hollandrocks.com
Music-related news from the Netherlands.

MP3.nl
www.mp3.nl
Large database with information about tracks, albums and artists.

MusicFrom.NL
Heemraadssingel 188, 3021 DM Rotterdam, The Netherlands
PH: 010-4761318 FX: 020-5241677
info@musicfrom.nl
www.musicfrom.nl
Netherlands musician's resource. Interviews, news, columns etc.

Urban Legends
www.urbanlegends.nl
For everything in Dutch Hip Hop. Local artists etc.

Poland

MP3.pl
www.mp3.pl
Poland's largest MP3 site.

Russia

MP3.ru
www.mp3.ru
Russia's largest MP3 site.

Spain

SpanishPop.net
www.spanishpop.net
Información y opinión sobre música independiente.

Sweden

Sweden Songs
PO Box 15210, SE-10465 Stockholm, Sweden
PH: +4686485762
Keith Almgren info@swedensongs.se
www.swedensongs.se
Music publishing service.

United Kingdom

AFunk
Angharad Williams funky@afunk.co.uk
www.afunk.co.uk
Interviews and reviews with UK Urban artists.

AllThingsMusic.co.uk
webmaster@allthingsmusic.co.uk
www.allthingsmusic.co.uk
A resource directory dedicated to UK musicians and entertainers, and of course we act as a go between for entertainment bookers and artists.

antifolk.co.uk
info@antifolk.co.uk.
www.antifolk.co.uk
Dedicated to the Antifolk scene in the UK.

Association of British Orchestras
20 Rupert St., London, England W1D 6DF
PH: 020-7287-0333 FX: 020-7287-0444
Rebecca Guest info@abo.org.uk
www.abo.org.uk
Exists to support, develop and advance the interests and activities of the orchestras in the UK.

Association of Independent Music
Lamb House, Church St., London, England W4 2PD
PH: 020-89945599 FX: 020-89945222
www.musicindie.org
Designed to increase the market share & business potential of the UK Independent Music Industry.

BandBase Online
enquiries@bandbase.co.uk
bandbase.co.uk
Promote your band, up-to-the-minute "Gig Guide" and more!

Big-Gig Guide to Live Music
3 Eastbourne Gate, Taunton,
Somerset, TA1 1SZ UK
PH: 01823-353-608
www.big-gig.co.uk
A music events guide, UK festival guide and live music forum section.

BIGMOUTH
PH: 01159-934-169
info@bigmouth.co.uk
www.bigmouth.co.uk
Ticket sales for most UK gigs, links to artists sites and more.

British Academy of Composers & Songwriters
25-27 Berners St., London, England W1T 3LR
PH: 020-7636-2929
info@britishacademy.com
www.britishacademy.com
Representing the interests of over 3,000 UK music writers.

British Horn Society
6206 Kings Hill, West Malling, ME19 4TA UK
mike@british-horn.org
www.british-horn.org
Dedicated to the art, craft and fun of horn playing.

British Music Information Centre *(BMIC)*
75 Westminster Bridge Rd. Lambeth N.
London, England
PH: 00-44-0-20-7499-8567
FX: 00-44-0-20-7499-4795
info@bmic.co.uk
www.bmic.co.uk
Information on composers, live events programs and more.

British Music Rights
26 Berners St., London, England W1T 3LR
PH: 44-0-20-7306-4446 FX: 44-0-20-7306-4449
britishmusic@bmr.org
www.bmr.org
Promotes the interests of composers, songwriters and music publishers.

British Musician's Union
60/62 Clapham Rd. London, England SW9 0JJ
PH: 020-7582-5566 FX: 020-7582-9805
info@musiciansunion.org.uk
www.musiciansunion.org.uk
Loads of resources and benefits for members.

BritishHipHop.co.uk
PH: 07780-707-468 FX: 07884-52-11-62
peter@low-life.fsnet.co.uk
www.britishhiphop.co.uk
Showcases unknown Hip Hop acts from the UK.

Cajun UK
PH: 01530-263-421
cajun.uk@ntlworld.com
www.cajunuk.freeserve.co.uk
Raises awareness of the UK Cajun and Zydeco music and dance scene.

Country Music In Britain
iain@cmib.co.uk
www.cmib.co.uk
All the info on the Country music scene in the UK.

The Crate Estate
Ollie ollie@thecrateestate.co.uk.
www.thecrateestate.co.uk
Promotes the Hip Hop scene in the United Kingdom.

falmusic.co.uk
PH: +44 (0)20-8816-8374
info@falmusic.co.uk
www.falmusic.co.uk
Forum for musicians and venues near Falmouth.

Federation of Guitar Societies
Shellwood, Forest Rd. E. Horsley, Surrey Kent, 24 5BA UK
martin.shaw1@connectfree.co.uk
www.federationofguitarsocieties.org.uk
Promoting the Classical guitar and related instruments.

folkWISE
PO Box 649, Dunstable, Beds, LU5 4XD UK
PH: +44 (0) 1582-475655 FX: +44 (0) 1582-475739
Brian Heywood brianh@folkwise.org
folkwise.org
Our aim is to support and encourage professional Folk performers from Wales Ireland, Scotland and England in all aspects of their work and career.

GigSwap UK
6 Watts Close, Southampton, SO16 9WA UK
PH: 023-8070-1025 FX: 023-8070-1025
info@gigswapuk.com
www.gigswapuk.com
Providing unsigned bands with the opportunity to perform in other cities across the country.

Jazz in Britain
john.r@ision.co.uk
www.jazz-in-britain.com
All the info on the British Jazz scene.

Jazz Services
www.jazzservices.org.uk
Promotes and develops Jazz in the UK.

Jim's Jazz Mag
info@jimsjazzmag.co.uk
www.jimsjazzmag.co.uk
Many different bands of all styles from the UK.

lovealbatross
albatross@lovealbatross.com
www.lovealbatross.com
Free promotion for unsigned bands in the UK.

Mechanical Copyright Protection Society
Elgar House, 41 Streatham High Rd.,
London, SW16 1ER UK
classicalquery@mcps-prs-alliance.co.uk
www.mcps.co.uk
Licenses the recording and use of music.

Music Jobs UK
info@interbase.co.uk
uk.music-jobs.com
The UK's Music Industry central point for employment seekers & employers.

Musical Index
Davo info@musicalindex.co.uk
www.musicalindex.co.uk
Search facility for every aspect of the music industry.

Musician-Online.com
29-33 Berners St., London, W1T 3AB UK
www.musician-online.com
Advertise yourself, your band and concerts for free.

musicians-web.co.uk
webmaster@musicians-web.co.uk
www.musicians-web.co.uk
Connect with musicians across the land.

MusicOf.com
20 St. Catherines, Newark Rd. Lincoln,
England LN5 8LY
PH: 44-0-7833347439
Vincent Wegner office@musicof.com
www.musicof.com
Promoting independent music, primarily by bands from the UK.

OurBand.net
Studio 2, Keystone House, Exeter Rd.
Bournemouth, BH2 5AR UK
PH: 01202-298882 FX: 01202-298883
promotions@ourband.net
www.ourband.net
Promotion service for local bands.

Performing Arts Media Rights Association *(PAMRA)*
PO Box 4398, London, England W1A 7RU
PH: 0207-534-1234 FX: 020-7543-1383
office@pamra.org.uk
www.pamra.org.uk
The UK's collecting society for performers.

Real UK Music
www.realukmusic.co.uk
Resource for events, venues, festivals, clubs performers, concerts studios, etc.

SERIOUSLY GROOVY
3rd Fl. 28 D'Arblay St., Soho,
London, England W1F 8EW
PH: 44-020-7439-1947 FX: 44-020-7734-7540
info@seriouslygroovy.com
www.seriouslygroovy.com
Newest Alternative, Indie, and Rock records coming out of the UK.

Society for the Promotion of New Music *(spnm)*
4th Fl. St. Margaret's House, 18-20 Southwark St.,
London, England SE1 1TJ
PH: 020-7407-1640 FX: 020-7403-7652
spnm@spnm.org.uk
www.spnm.org.uk
Promotes music composed by musicians born in the UK.

Sound Devastation
56 Milne St. Oldham, Manchester,
Lancashire, OL9 0HU UK
Chris sounddevastation@yahoo.co.uk
www.sounddevastation.tk
Focuses upon the UK's rapidly growing (in size AND quality) underground Metal scene.

swampmusic
PO Box 94, Derby, DE22 1XA UK
chrishall@swampmusic.co.uk
www.swampmusic.demon.co.uk
Guide to all things Cajun & Zydeco in the UK.

The Talent Scout
PO Box 10349, London, England NW1 9WJ
PH: 0207-864-1300
info@thetalentscout.co.uk
www.thetalentscout.co.uk
Gives unsigned bands the chance to get recognized.

talentSTAR
#11C, Ever Ready Industrial Park, Tanfield Lea, Stanley, County Durham, England DH9 9QF
PH: 01207-236-555
info@talentstar.net
www.talentstar.net
The UK's biggest service of its kind, giving opportunities through performing and promotion to up and coming music performers.

Traffic Online
6 Stucley Pl. London, NW1 8NS UK
teams@trafficonline.net
www.trafficonline.net
We build, maintain and coordinate street teams in the UK for bands and record labels as well as for a whole host of other projects.

tourdates.co.uk
dean@ita1.co.uk
www.tourdates.co.uk
Listings of all major local upcoming events.

UK-Flava *(Strictly UK)*
5 Florence Nightingale House, London, N1 2PL UK
hello@uk-flava.com
www.uk-flava.com
Working with local artists. Accepts demos.

UK Gospel
reviews@ukgospel.com
www.ukgospel.com
Reviews some of the best Urban projects in the country.

UK Mix
www.ukmix.net
Your guide to the UK music scene starts here.

UK Newspaper and News Media Database
www.abyznewslinks.com/uking.htm
Links to hundreds of UK newspapers.

UKbands.net
support@ukbands.net
www.ukbands.net
THE one-stop music promotion portal for UK artists.

ukevents.net
PH: 07733-295387
Michelle@ukevents.net
www.ukevents.net
Guide to music events in the UK.

ukhh.com *(UK Hip Hop)*
info@ukhh.com
www.ukhh.com
A chance to gain exposure for all UK Hip Hop acts.

UKmusicsearch
38 Whitchurch Rd. Tavistock,
Devon, PL19 9BD UK
Mike Bond mike@ukmusicsearch.co.uk
www.ukmusicsearch.co.uk
News, reviews and more. Send us your music!

The Ultimate Showcase
PH: 07830-119190
Mike Deal mike@halcyonsounds.co.uk
www.halcyonsounds.co.uk
An excitingopportunityy for unsigned Christian artists in the UK to get their music heard by record industry representatives and the public alike.

Unsigned UK
www.unsigneduk.com
Resource for the UK's new and established bands.

Vitamin UK
20 Orange St., London, WC2H 7NN UK
PH: 44-020-7766-4000 FX: 44-020-7766-4001
info@vitaminic.co.uk
www.vitaminic.co.uk
MP3s of British artists.

England

AcoustiCity.co.uk
21 Constantine Rd. Colchester,
Essex, England CO3 3DU
info@acousticity.co.uk
www.acousticity.co.uk
Reviews, links & listings for local Acoustic based music.

Barratt Folk
richard@barrattfolk.co.uk
www.barrattfolk.co.uk
Focusing on Folk Music around the Central South Coast of England.

BEDFORD METAL
bedfordmetal@hotmail.com
www.Bedfordmetal.co.uk
Created to promote the local Rock, Punk, Goth and Metal scene in the Bedford & surrounding area. News, Interviews, CD Reviews etc.

Bedford Unplugged
music@bedfordunplugged.co.uk
www.bedfordunplugged.co.uk
If you want your Bedford area 100% live music listed FREE, please send us an e-mail.

Birmingham Jazz
19 Selwyn Rd. Edgbaston,
Birmingham, England B16 OSH
PH: 0121-454-2371
www.birminghamjazz.co.uk
Providing the best in Jazz and contemporary music.

Birmingham Music Network
PO Box 9121, Birmingham, England B13 8AU
info@birminghammusicnetwork.co.uk
www.birminghammusicnetwork.co.uk
Promotes all related music businesses operating within the region.

Bromley Guitar Society
denstock@spanguitar.freeserve.co.uk
www.bromleyguitarsociety.org.uk
Created to encourage local interest in the Classical guitar.

Classical London
sub@classical-london.com
welcome.to/classicallondon
CD, DVD and concert reviews, information about competitions and more.

Concrete Chaos
info@concretechaos.co.uk
www.concretechaos.co.uk
News, reviews, interviews etc. covering the Buckingham scene.

Connect Magazine
Withall's Gardens, Lympstone,
Devon, England EX8 5JH
PH: 01395-270157
www.connect-magazine.co.uk
Free magazine. Covers local music scene.

Devon Folk Music
devonfolk@devonfolk.co.uk
www.devonfolk.co.uk
Serving the whole of Devon in all aspects of Folk.

Dorset Blues Society
webmaster@bluesnights.co.uk
www.bluesnights.co.uk
For Blues lovers everywhere.

Dorset Guitar Society
www.dorsetguitarsociety.org.uk
Promoting music via solo and ensemble performances, master classes, workshops and concerts.

eat the beat
11 St. Nicholas St., Bristol, BS1 1UE UK
PH: 01179251691
info@eatthebeat.co.uk
www.eatthebeat.co.uk
Bristol's online Dance music specialists.

Eerie Powers
andrewk@eeriepowers.co.uk
www.eeriepowers.co.uk
Guide to the Doncaster music scene.

English Folk Dance & Song Society
Cecil Sharp House, 2 Regent's Park Rd.
London, England NW1 7AY
PH: 0207-485-2206
www.efdss.org
Provides support and assistance to anyone interested in the Folk arts.

Essex Folk Association *efn Magazine*
37 Sidwell Ave. Benfleet, Essex, England SS7 1LF
PH: 44-01268-793905
essex_folk_news@hotmail.com
www.pvcw.freeserve.co.uk
Folk articles, record reviews, songs and tunes.

Fat Northerner Records
Langley Lane Farm, Middleton,
Manchester, M24 5LJ UK
PH: 0161-610-7516
staff@fatnortherner.com
www.fatnortherner.com
Developing and releasing music by good musicians from the North of England.

Folk Around Bristol
woolley101@hotmail.com
folkaroundbristol.co.uk
Gives local and new Folk bands a chance.

Folk London
4A Kenilworth Rd. Petts Wood,
Kent, England BR5 1DY
PH: 44-01-689-825-263
folklondon@hotmail.com
www.grove-cottage.demon.co.uk/folklon
Folk clubs and events in London and the South-east of England.

Folk North West
7, Sunleigh Rd. Hindley, Wigan,
Lancashire, WN2 2RE UK
webmaster@folknorthwest.co.uk
www.folknorthwest.co.uk
News, reviews of live events, CDs & more.

Folk Talk
57, Lloyds Ave. Scunthorpe N. Lincolnshire,
England DN17 1BY
PH: 01724-844241
Jim@folktalk.co.uk
www.folktalk.co.uk
The magazine for Folk music in Lincolnshire & East Yorkshire.

Folkus
55 The Strand, Fleetwood, Lancs,
England FY7 8NP
PH: 01253-872317 FX: 01253-878382
www.folkus.co.uk
Deals with local and international talent.

Fresh Sounds
PO Box 2760, Caterham, CR3 6WW UK
PH: 0870-609-3683 FX: 0870-486-0348
Michael East contact@fresh-sounds.co.uk
www.fresh-sounds.co.uk
Showcases unsigned bands in Britain.

Gigwise
4th Fl. Gostins Bldg. 32-34 Hanover St.,
Liverpool, England L1 4LN
andy@gigwise.com
www.gigwise.com
Covering the Liverpool music scene. Gigs, reviews, news etc.

GlassWerk Media
38-B Ventnor Rd. Wavetree,
Liverpool, England L15 4JF
PH: 44-0151-280-9679
editor@glasswerk.co.uk
www.glasswerk.co.uk
The Northwest's premier website for unsigned musical artists.

GogetWise.co.uk
5 Pretoria Villas, De Grey St., Hull, E. Yorkshire,
HU5 2RT UK
Darren Bunting darren@gogetwise.co.uk
www.gogetwise.co.uk
I am the music editor and am happy to receive CDs to review as well as relevant music news/gig dates for the Hull and East Yorkshire region of the UK.

Greenwood Classical Guitar Society
Martin Shaw martin@greenwoodgs.org.uk
www.greenwoodgs.org.uk
Encouraging and developing Classical guitar playing.

Herts & Essex Live Band Photos
phil@livebandphotos.co.uk
www.livebandphotos.co.uk
Live bands, pubs & music venues in the Herts & Essex Area. Includes Herts & Essex area band news.

The Insight
1st Fl. E. Globe House, 3 Morley St.,
Brighton, England BN2 9RA
PH: 44-01273-245956 FX: 44-01273-245960
listings@theinsight.co.uk
www.theinsight.co.uk
Listings magazine for the city of Brighton and Hove.

irLondon
PH: 07717-798-483
matty@irLondon.co.uk
www.irlondon.co.uk
Online club/gig guide as well as reviews & news.

josaka
PO Box 5027, Reading, Berkshire, RG6 7ZN UK
PH: +44-118-826-1440
Kevin Harrington kevin@josaka.info
www.josaka.com
Supporting live music in Berkshire. Gig and CD reviews, venue information, news and a lot more.

Know The Ledge
getintouch@knowtheledge.net
www.knowtheledge.net
Keeping you in the know about left field music and urban culture, with a focus on London and New York City.

Kent and East Sussex Gig Guide
The Cedars, Elvington Ln. Hawkinge, Folkestone,
Kent, CT18 7AD UK
PH: 01303-893472 FX: 01303-893833
chris@kentgigs.com
kentgigs.com
Listings are updated every week!

leeds music scene
PH: 07005-964-458
info@leedsmusicscene.net
www.leedsmusicscene.net
The primary music resource for new and existing bands based in Leeds and West Yorkshire. Includes an extensive CD review, live, news and interview archive, gig guide and previews.

Lemonrock
editor@lemonrock.com
www.lemonrock.com
The live music guide for London and the South East. It contains gig listings, a powerful search facility, MP3 clips and gig reviews.

Live Circuit
c/o Roger, 14 John Barker Pl. Hitchin,
Hertfordshire, SG5 2PE UK
roger@livecircuit.net.
www.livecircuit.net
Dedicated to providing facilities to nurture Hertfordshire's up and coming original music talent.

London Musicians Collective
Rm 3.6, 3rd. Fl. Lafone House, 11 - 13
Leathermarket St., London, SE1 3HN UK
PH/FX: 020-7403-1922
lmc@lmcltd.demon.co.uk
www.l-m-c.org.uk
Promotes Improvised and Experimental music via concerts and an annual festival.

londonimprov.com
admin@londonimprov.com
www.londonimprov.com
Home for the London Improv scene.

LondonNet *London Music Guide*
ahoy-talkback@londonnet.co.uk
www.londonnet.co.uk
News and reviews of local music.

Low Life Records
19 Devonshire St., London, England W1G 7AH
PH: 44-020-7637-8555 FX: 44-020-7637-0111
info@lowliferecords.co.uk
www.lowliferecords.co.uk
The place to check for quality British Rap.

manchestermusic.co.uk
PO Box 1977, Manchester, M26 2YB UK
enquiries@music-dash.co.uk
www.manchestermusic.co.uk
Information regarding local music and bands.

Midnight Mango
21 Kings Dr. Westonzoyland, England TA7 OHJ
PH: 07779723061
gigs@midnightmango.co.uk
www.midnightmango.co.uk
Covers all things to do with local bands.

musicmk.org.uk
ndmweb@hotmail.com
musicmk.org.uk
This site aims to provide you with a single resource to refer to music in Buckinghamshire, Bedfordshire and Hertfordshire.

North Herts Ska Punk Hardcore
nhsph@hotmail.com
www.nhsph.tk
Whether you're Hardcore, Punk, Ska, Metalcore, Pop-Punk or anything else there will be a home for you here. We'll do as much as we can to help you!

North West Bluegrass News
1 Woodlands Rd. Saltney, Chester, CH4 8LB UK
PH: 01244-683563
www.nwbn.freeserve.co.uk
British Bluegrass Magazine. Photos, reviews, tablature etc.

Northampton Bands
www.northamptonbands.co.uk
Bands can use our site as an up-to-date information source for their fans.

nwdnb.co.uk
asok@nwdnb.co.uk
www.nwdnb.co.uk
Central hub of information for Drum 'n Bass in Liverpool and Manchester.

Peterborough Folk Diary
fenfolk@glowinternet.com
www.fenfolk.glowinternet.net
Your guide to music and Folk events in Peterborough.

Plymouth Music
administration@plymouthmusic.co.uk
plymouthmusic.co.uk
Everything you need to know about your local music scene.

Punk & Oi in the UK
PO Box 158, Leeds, England LS27 7XP
rebecca@punkoiuk.co.uk
www.punkoiuk.co.uk
Information on the current Punk & oi scene.

Rhythm and Booze
32 Barnes Way, Worcester, England WR5 3AP
PH: 01905-731615
chrisbennion@netbreeze.co.uk
www.rhythmandbooze.net
Covering the Birmingham music scene.

Rocklands
therocklands@yahoo.com
welcome.to/rocklands
Festivals, events, counter culture, venues and more.

Sandman Magazine
PO Box 3187, Sheffield, England S7 1WA
PH: 0114-278-6727
info@sandmanmagazine.co.uk
www.sandmanmagazine.co.uk
Sheffield's independent music magazine.

Skippy's Cage
skippyscage@yahoo.com
www.skippyscage.com
Showcasing the best bands around London.

South Riding Folk Network
PH: 44-0114-233-6539
info@folk-network.com
www.folk-network.com
Maintaining the strength and vibrancy of the Folk arts.

South Yorkshire Folk
editor@syfolk.co.uk
www.syfolk.co.uk
News, festivals and CD reviews.

Southampton Classical Guitar Society
David Tripp enquiries@scgs-guitar.org.uk
www.scgs-guitar.org.uk
Focal point for those playing the Classical guitar in South Hampshire.

Southern Country
53 Windsor Rd. Alresfor, Hants, SO24 9HU UK
PH: 0044-0-1962-734401
SueMac@southerncountry.fsnet.co.uk
angelfire.com/sd/scountry
Reviews, news, features and articles on related subjects.

Southwest Gig Guide
PO Box 116, Exmouth, Devon, EX8 5ZA UK
FX: 0870-161-9638
info@southwestgigguide.co.uk
www.southwestgigguide.co.uk
Artist listings, gigs and more.

Stirrings
251 Cemetery Rd. Sheffield, S11 8FS UK
PH: 0114-2551782
stirrings@taproot.demon.co.uk
www.stirrings.co.uk
Folk, Roots and Acoustic music in South York and beyond.

Sussex Folk Guide
3 Chester Terrace, Brighton, BN1 6GB UK
PH: 01273-559750
folk@brighton.co.uk
whatson.brighton.co.uk/folk
Free publication listing Folk events in Brighton and Hove.

This is Essex
webeditor@thisisessex.co.uk
www.thisisessex.co.uk
Band biographies, pictures and sound files from around Essex.

This is Wiltshire
digitalmedia@newswilts.co.uk
www.thisiswiltshire.co.uk
Covers local bands and events.

totallywired
PO Box 70, Brighton, England BN1 1YJ
PH: 01273-244144
listings@totallywired.co.uk
www.totallywired.co.uk
Covering the Brighton music scene.

The Viper Label
PO Box 48, Liverpool, England L17 7JE
info@the-viper-label.co.uk
www.the-viper-label.co.uk
Label that releases Underground music.

The Virtually Acoustic Club
50 Liden Close, London, E17 8HQ UK
PH: 07885-600-165
David Sherwood david@thevac.co.uk
www.viac.co.uk
The Longest-Established Open Mic Club in London with open mic listings for many clubs in London and the UK.

Wiltshire Folk Association
PH: 01980-625019
user@wiltsfolka.fsnet.co.uk
www.wiltsfolka.fsnet.co.uk
All the info on the local Folk music scene.

Ireland

Anglo-Celt
Middle Abbey St., Dublin 1, Ireland
PH: 353-0-1-705-5333 FX: 353-0-1-872-0304
www.unison.ie/anglo_celt
Online newspaper for Cavan, Fermanagh and Monaghan, Ireland.

Association of Irish Composers *(AIC)*
Copyright House, Pembroke Row, Dublin 2, Ireland
PH: 353-1-4961484
info@composers.ie
www.composers.ie
The representative body of composers in Ireland.

Bluegrass In Ireland
kgill@cit.ie
www.bluegrassireland.150m.com
Information on Bluegrass activities in Ireland.

CLUSA
webmaster@cluas.com
www.cluas.com
Lending an ear to life & adventure in Ireland.

Contemporary Music Centre
19 Fishamble St., Temple Bar, Dublin 8, Ireland
PH: 353-1-673-1922 FX: 353-1-648-9100
info@cmc.ie
www.cmc.ie
Promotes contemporary Irish concert music.

CPU Media
www.cpu.ie
An unsigned band site dedicated to Irish Bands within the Republic of Ireland and abroad. Downloads, reviews, news etc.

Dublin Jazz Society
info@dublinjazz.com
dublinjazz.com
Promoting live mainstream Jazz in Dublin.

fastfude
www.fastfude.com
Northern Ireland's music scene.

Folktalk
57, Lloyds Ave. Scunthorpe, N. Lincolnshire, Ireland DN17BY
PH: 01724-844241
Jim Hancock jim@folktalk.co.uk
www.folktalk.co.uk
Folk news, CD reviews, gig listings and more.

Irish Music Magazine
11 Clare St., Dublin 2, Ireland
PH: 353-0-1-662-2266 FX: 01-662-4881
mag.irish-music.net
CD reviews, live reviews, articles and more!

Irish Music Rights Organization *(IMRO)*
Pembroke Row, Lower Baggot St., Dublin 2, Ireland
PH: 353-1-661-4844 FX: 353-1-661-3789
info@imro.ie
www.imro.ie
Collects and distributes royalties arising from the public performance of copyright works.

IrishBandsList.com
96 Swanbrook, Southern Cross, Bray,
Co. Wicklow, Ireland
kevin@irishbandslist.com
www.irishbandslist.com
A tool for unsigned bands to promote their music, gigs, merchandise and art to the world.

IrishUnsigned.com
Ron Healy ron@IrishUnsigned.com
www.IrishUnsigned.com
Promotes any unsigned Irish artists, anywhere.

Journal of Music in Ireland
Edenvale, Esplanade, Bray, Co. Wicklow, Ireland
PH: 353-0-1-2867292 FX: 353-0-1-2867292
editor@thejmi.com
www.thejmi.com
Articles, essays and reviews by composers and musicians working in the fields of traditional, Classical and Jazz music.

Music Network
The Coach House, Dublin Castle, Dublin 2, UK
PH: 353-1-6719429 FX: 353-1-6719430
info@musicnetwork.ie
www.musicnetwork.ie
Established to develop Classical, traditional and Jazz music nationwide.

Music Scene Ireland
mail@musicsceneireland.com
www.musicsceneireland.com
Community site for unsigned and new music in Ireland.

Northern Ireland Music Industry Commission
#2, Northern Whig House, Bridge St.,
Belfast, Ireland BT1 1LU
PH: 44-28-9092 3488
Tony Talbot tonyt@nimusic.com
www.nimusic.com
Supports artists in any genre. International promotion.

Thumped
thumped.com
Irish Underground Music. Interviews, reviews, listings, mp3, real audio, real video.

Wales

Sound Nation
Ty Cefn, Rectory Rd. Canton,
Cardiff, CF5 1QL Wales UK
james@soundnation.net
www.soundnation.net
Wales only national music magazine.

Australia

Artists helping Artists
join@ahadirect.com.au
www.ahadirect.com.au
Generates more work and a friendlier working environment for all involved.

Arts Law Centre of Australia
The Gunnery, 43-51 Cowper Wharf Rd.
Woolloomooloo, NSW 2011 Australia
PH: 02-9356-2566 FX: 02-9358-6475
artslaw@artslaw.com.au
www.artslaw.com.au
Advice and information for all artists.

Association of Independent Record Labels
Lvl 1, 148 Brunswick St. PO Box 878,
Fortitude Valley, QLD 4006 Australia
PH: 61-0-7-3257-1838 FX: 61-0-7-3257-0087
info@air.org.au
www.air.org.au
Largest Australian music online database. New releases and back catalogue info. If you're an Oz indie label, join us.

AUSMUSIC
PO Box 307, Port Melbourne, VIC 3207 Australia
PH: 03-9696-2422 FX: 03-9696-2879
info@ausmusic.org.au
www.ausmusic.org.au
Promotional opportunities for the Australian music industry.

Ausradiosearch Distribution
PO Box 532, Newcastle, NSW 2300 Australia
PH: 61-02-49270290
www.isonliveradio.com
Can get your film clips on to Aussie TV.

Australasian Mechanical Copyright Owners Society *(AMCOS)*
6-12 Atchison St., St Leonards, NSW 2065 Australia
PH: 02-9935-7900 FX: 02-9935-7999
www.apra.com.au
Represents music publishers in Australia and New Zealand.

Australian Christian Artists Network
PO Box 650, Belmot, VIC 3216 Australia
PH: 03-5243-0855
nationaloffice@acan.org.au
www.acan.org.au
Bringing you Australia's finest Christian artists.

Australian Copyright Council
PO Box 1986, Strawberry Hills,
NSW 2012 Australia
PH: 61-2-9318-1788 FX: 61-2-9698-3536
www.copyright.org.au
Technical info on the music business.

Australian Hip Hop Online
hiphop.net.au
Covers the Australian Hip Hop culture.

Australian Music Association
MBE 148/45 Glenferrie Rd. Malvern,
VIC 3144 Australia
PH: 03-9527-6658 FX: 03-9507-2316
info@australianmusic.asn.au
www.australianmusic.asn.au
Furthering the interests of the music industry.

Australian Music Info
geoff@australianmusic.info
www.australianmusic.info
Music news, discussion, promotion and more!

Australian Music Online
PO Box 2227, Sydney, NSW 2001 Australia
PH: 61-2-8353-6900 FX: 61-2-8353-6999
www.amo.org.au
Promotes all new Australian music.

Australian Music Web Site
webmistress@amws.com.au
www.amws.com.au
Resource for tracking down anything to do with Australian music.

Australian Songwriters Association
PO Box 217, Erindale LPO, ACT 2903 Australia
PH: 02-6231-1452
dennyb@asai.org.au
www.asai.org.au
Supports and promotes developing Australian songwriters.

The Blurb Magazine
feedback@theblurb.com.au
www.theblurb.com.au
New releases, albums and music events.

Bombshell Zine
PO Box 8032, Werrington County,
NSW 2747 Australia
info@bombshellzine.com
www.bombshellzine.com
News, reviews, MP3s etc.

Buywell.com
PO Box 1010, Willagee Central, WA 6156 Australia
sales@buywell.com
www.buywell.com
We specialize in Classical music CDs produced in Australia.

ChaosMusic
45 Collins St., E. Melbourne, VIC 3000 Australia
PH: 61-3-9654-1144 FX: 61-3-9654-2333
info@chaos.com
www.chaosmusic.com
Promotes local music to a global audience.

Country Music Association of Australia
PO Box 298, Tamworth, NSW 2340 Australia
PH: 02-6766-1577 FX: 02-6766-7314
info@countrymusic.asn.au
www.countrymusic.asn.au
Promotes all aspects of the Australian Country music industry.

Country Music Store
PO Box 3000, Brisbane, QLD 4000 Australia
PH: 07-3221-3000 FX: 07-3221-3983
cmstore@countrymusic.com.au
www.countrymusic.com.au
Online resource for all your Australian Country Music.

Crusty Music.net
PO Box 1483, Warrnambool, VIC 3280 Australia
crusty@crustymusic.net
www.crustymusic.net
Showcases Metal/Rock Aussie bands.

Folk Alliance Australia
PO Box 536, Canberra, ACT 2600 Australia
PH: 08-8352-8034
thefolk@folkaustralia.com
www.folkalliance.org.au
Preserving the Folk arts. Reviews CDs.

Folk Australia
reviews@folkaustralia.com
www.folkaustralia.com
Promoting Folk music in Australia.

grooveloader.com
PH: 61-2-9555-8060
info@grooveloader.com
www.grooveloader.com
Highlights music CDs, links and information from Australian musicians.

HowlSpace
PO Box 305, Elwood, VIC 3184 Australia
PH: 61-3-9531-0885
howlspace@howlspace.com.au
www.howlspace.com.au
An open encyclopedia of Australian and New Zealand music which encourages contributions from everyone.

In Music & Media
PH: 02-9557-7766
Phil Tripp tripp@themusic.com.au
www.themusic.com.au
Australian music news and resource site.

Indie-CDs
85 Oakfords Rd. Wattle Grove, TAS 7109 Australia
PH: 03-6295-0735 FX: 03-6295-0835
www.indie-cds.com
Music by independent Australian artists.

Loud! Online
23 Yester Rd. Wentworth Falls, NSW 2782 Australia
goreripper@maxi.net.au
www.geocities.com/SunsetStrip/Stage/4599
Promotion and exposure for Australian Heavy Metal music in all its forms.

Middle Eight Music
PO Box 1443, St., Kilds South, VIC 3182 Australia
PH: 61-3-9510-5109 FX: 61-3-9521-5219
mem@bigpond.net.au
www.middle8.com
Online CD shop specializing in Australian artists.

Move Records
1 Linton St., Ivanhoe, VIC 3079 Australia
PH: 03-9497-3105 FX: 03-9497-4426
move@move.com.au
www.move.com.au
Independent Classical label supporting Australian composers and performers.

MP3.com.au
Level 2, Bldg. 10, 658 Church St., Richmond,
VIC 3121 Australia
PH: 03-8415-9111 FX: 03-8415-9100
info@MP3.com.au
www.mp3.com.au
Listen to both unsigned and commercial artist's music.

New Music Network
PO Box A661, Sydney South, NSW 1235 Australia
PH: 61-02-9362-5711 FX: 61-02-9362-5834
nmn@chilli.net.au
www.newmusicnetwork.com.au
Hosts performances of new Australian music.

Oz Music Central
PO Box 559, Toronto, NSW 2283 Australia
PH: 0417-275-042
ozmusic-central@bigpond.com
www.ozmusic-central.com.au
Australian music resource. Reviews, featured artists and more!

Oz Music Project
PO Box 329, Epping, NSW 1710 Australia
jaz@ozmusicproject.net
www.ozmusicproject.net
Resource for any Australian musician/band.

OzRock.com
PO Box 7227, Baulkham Hills, NSW 2153 Australia
www.ozrock.com
Independent, unsigned and undiscovered artists, bands and music.

revolve.com.au
dstrahan@revolve.com.au
www.revolve.com.au
Recordings of modern Australian Classical music.

Rockus
PO Box 2221, Warwick, WA 6024 Australia
PH: 0403-223-012
Steph Edwardes mail@rockus.com.au
www.rockus.com.au
Specializing in the Indie, Pop and Rock genres. Australian artists only!

SCALA News
PO Box 228, Kensington Park, SA 5068 Australia
PH: 618-8431-4063 FX: 618-8332-1013
scala@scala.org.au
www.scala.org.au
Provides info and support for songwriters in Australia.

SUBSTRATA
PO Box 6001, Collingwood North,
VIC 3066 Australia
PH: 61-3-9417-6888
info@substrata.com.au
www.substrata.com.au
Previews, interviews, news, reviews, charts and more!

Tamworth Songwriters' Association Inc.
PO Box 618, Tamworth, NSW 2340 Australia
PH: 02-6765-8558 FX: 02-6762-3361
tsa@tpgi.com.au
www.tsaonline.com.au
Represents Australian Country music songwriters.

Time Off
PO Box 515, Brisbane, QLD 4001 Australia
PH: 07-3252-9666 FX: 07-3252-9761
timeoff@timeoff.com.au
www.timeoff.com.au
Covers all genres of music. Dedicated Dance music section.

New South Wales

3D World Magazine
Level 2, 25 Cooper St., Surry Hills,
NSW 2010 Australia
PH: 612-9211-1222 FX: 612-9281-4193
editor@threedworld.com.au
www.threedworld.com.au
Free circulating street press music magazine.

Bathurst After Dark
bathurstafterdark.com
Promote local music. Mp3s, gig guide and more!

CanberraRootsMusic.com
www.canberrarootsmusic.com
Dedicated to promoting Roots music venues, gigs and musicians in the Canberra region.

JAM - Folk Federation of NSW
38 Alleyne Ave.
North Narrabeen,
NSW 2101 Australia
Wayne Richmond
inquiries@folkfednsw.org.au
jam.org.au
Presents & supports Folk music, song and dance.

I-94 Bar
PO Box 105, Mortdale,
NSW 2223 Australia
barman@i94bar.com
www.i94bar.com
Covers the rock action in the area.

Newcastle Music
PO Box 985, Newcastle,
NSW 2300 Australia
contact@newcastlemusic.net
www.newcastlemusic.net
Covers the Newcastle music scene. Bands, albums, downloads, gigs etc.

Sydney Friction
info@sydneyfriction.com
www.sydneyfriction.com
Sydney drum 'n' bass resource.

Sydney Gothic
PO Box 284, Newtown,
NSW 2042 Australia
PH: 61-2-9519-0618
Zoog zoog_angelspit@yahoo.co.uk
www.sydneygothic.com
The online hub of Sydney's Gothic / Industrial / Neo-Cyberpunk community - submissions for reviews and interviews welcome.

Sydney Music Guide
sydney.citysearch.com.au
Extensive coverage of the local music scene. Post your shows and events.

Sydney Music Web
27 1st Ave. Coolum Beach, QLD 4573 Australia
PH: 07-5446-1919 FX: 07-5446-1919
iangav@tpg.com.au
www.sydneymusicweb.com
Everything you need to know about the Sydney music scene.

Queensland

Blues Association of South East Queensland
PO Box 329, Annerley, QLD 4103 Australia
PH: 07-3397-3265
helenf@uqconnect.net
baseq.tripod.com
Promoting local Blues musicians locally and globally.

brispop.com
PO Box 103, Spring Hill, QLD 4004 Australia
PH: 61-0409-204-424
admin@brispop.com
www.brispop.com
Portal for local bands, gigs, and more.

Hellbane
amber@hellbane.net
www.hellbane.net
Covering the Brisbane Goth scene.

South Australia

MusicSA
Music House, Level 1, Corner North Tce & Morphett St., Adelaide, SA 5000 Australia
PH: 08-8218-8404 FX: 08-8218-8122
Elizabeth Reid info@musicsa.com.au
www.musicsa.com.au
Offering South Australian artists free listings (including space for MP3s & video clips), reviews and other free promotional opportunities.

Rip it Up
93 King William St., Kent Town, SA 5067 Australia
PH: 08-8132-7000 FX: 08-8363-4190
maryanneagostino@ripitup.com.au
www.ripitup.com.au
Adelaide's leading street press magazine.

South Australian Blues Society
53 Cooinda Ave. Redwood Park, SA 5097 Australia
PH: 0408-085-821
bluessa@senet.com.au
www.sablues.org
Promoting the Blues in South Australia.

Victoria

Beat Magazine
3 Newton St., Richmond, Melbourne,
VIC 3121 Australia
PH: 613-9428-3600 FX: 613-9428-3611
music@beat.com.au
www.beat.com.au
Free weekly paper. Focus on local music.

Early Music Society of Victoria
182 Berringa Rd. Park Orchards,
VIC 3114 Australia
emsv4viols@yahoo.com.au
home.vicnet.net.au/~emsv
Promotes the performance of early music.

GrooveOn.com.au
PO Box 7572, Melbourne, VIC 8004 Australia
info@grooveon.com.au
www.grooveon.com.au
RnB / HipHop / Latin news, events, clubs and more.

MELBAND
1/43-45 Melverton Dr. Hallam, VIC 3803 Australia
PH: 03-9702-3244
Geoff Mison info@melband.com.au
www.melband.com.au
Listing of all things music in Melbourne.

The Melbourne Ska Page
Mike Williams mike@better-access.com
www.melbourneska.dhs.org
All about the Melbourne Ska scene.

Pith Records
www.pithrecords.com
Independent label that promotes local bands.

Raven Sphere Creations
PO Box 1 Richmond, VIC 3121 Australia
PH: 0411-854-553
Sona Sefflova sona@ravensphere.com
www.ravensphere.com
Information on local artists, venues and more.

Victorian Folk Music Club
PO Box 2025, Melbourne, VIC 3001 Australia
PH: 613-9478-9656
vfmc@bigpond.net.au
users.bigpond.net.au/vfmc
Folk music organization in Australia.

Western Australia

Perth Blues Club
PO Box 2023, Dog Swamp, WA 6060 Australia
info@perthbluesclub.org.au
www.perthbluesclub.org.au
Supporting local & international Blues & Roots music.

Perthbands.com
www.perthbands.com
Gives Perth bands national and international exposure.

Scoop Magazine
#3-266 Hay St., Subiaco, WA 6008 Australia
PH: 08-9388-8188 FX: 08-9388-8199
editorial@scoop.com.au
www.scoop.com.au
Western Australian lifestyle magazine.

Western Front
Clay clay@wf.com.au
www.wf.com.au
Info on Western Australia's Metal music scene.

Westska *Western Ska Online*
submit@westska.ii.net
westska.ii.net
All about Western Australian Ska.

XPress Magazine
73 Railway Parade, City W. Business Cn. W. Perth,
WA 6872 Australia
PH: 6618-9213-2888 FX: 618-9213-2882
localmusic@xpressmag.com.au
www.xpressmag.com.au
Interviews, reviews and news on the local music scene.

South Africa

zaZone.com
PO Box 142, Bothasig 7441,
Cape Town, South Africa
PH: 082-898-0648 FX: 086-610-4157
zazone.com
An entertainment industry website which promotes and supports South African music of all genres.

Bill Wence Promotions

RADIO PROMOTION FOR THE INDEPENDENT ARTIST

GET YOUR MUSIC HEARD! NOW WORKING WITH OVER 400 ADVENTUROUS RADIO STATIONS THAT AREN'T AFRAID TO TAKE A CHANCE

**Radio Interviews
Tours & Support
Weekly Tracking**

RADIO AIRPLAY/ON THE CHARTS! JERRY JEFF WALKER • JAMES TALLEY • AMAZING RHYTHM ACES • RONNY ELLIOTT • RED MEAT • TOM T. HALL • JONELL MOSSER • RUTHIE & THE WRANGLERS • BOBBY BARE • WOODSONGS & MORE...

PROMOTING THE MUSIC OF SOME OF THE MOST TALENTED PEOPLE IN THE WORLD

RECENT ALBUMS GONZO STEW - Jerry Jeff Walker • THIRTEEN - Red Meat • TOUCHSTONES - James Talley • THE OUTLAWS - Waylon Jennings, Jessi Colter, Willie Nelson, Tompall Glaser • HEP - Ronny Elliott • ENOUGH ROPE - Jonell Mosser • CHOC FULL OF COUNTRY - Amazing Rhythm Aces • HOMEGROWN - Tom T. Hall • LONESOMERS - Mare Winningham • OLD DOGS - Waylon Jennings, Bobby Bare, Mel Tillis, Jerry Reed • STILL THE ONE, LIVE - Orleans • ALAMEDA COUNTY LINE - Red Meat • DRAG QUEENS IN LIMOUSINES - Mary Gauthier and more...

**Bill Wence Promotions
PO Box 39 • Nolensville, TN 37135
615-776-2060** Fax 776-2181
email: billwencepro@earthlink.net

All major credit cards accepted

www.billwencepromotions.com

AMA (Americana Music Association - founding member) • IBMA • CMA • NARAS • ASCAP • AFM #257

SECTION THREE: RADIO STATIONS AND SHOWS THAT ARE WILLING TO PLAY INDEPENDENT MUSIC

"Following a DJ's set list is mandatory. I find it annoying when someone contacts me asking if I have received their CD, when I have already played them once or twice. It shows me that they would rather bother me than do the work to find out themselves." - Angela Page, Host of Folk Plus on WJFF Radio

Promotional Services

United States

Backstage Entertainment
2560 Senator Ave. Harbor City, CA 90710
PH: 310-325-2800 FX: 310-427-7333
www.backstageentertainment.net
A marketing information company which focuses its management abilities throughout all aspects of the music industry.

Bryan Farrish Radio Promotion
14230 Ventura Blvd. 2nd Fl.
Sherman Oaks, CA 91423
PH: 818-905-8038 x14
airplay@radio-media.com
www.radio-media.com
Offering promotion packages which obtain airplay for bands and labels.

Creativity In Music
PO Box 3481, Bridgeport, CT 06605
Gi Dussault npsfunk@optonline.net
www.creativityinmusic.com
Radio Promotion on all genres and locations, concert promotion, submission of press releases to local, national and international media plus business advice/consultation.

DemoDaze
2134 Curtis St. Bldg. 1, Denver, CO 80205
tracy@demodaze.com
www.demodaze.com
New music – serious play.

DG Systems
750 W. John Carpenter Fwy. #700,
Irving, TX 75039
PH: 800-335-4347
www.dgsystems.com
Private digital network with over 7500 radio stations across the US and Canada.

Indiego Promotions
3650 Osage St., Denver, CO 80211
Attn: Artist Development
info@indiego.com
www.indiego.com
Radio is the backbone of successful music promotion.

Jerome Promotions & Marketing
2535 Winthrope Way, Lawrenceville, GA 30044
PH: 770-982-7055 FX: 770-982-1882
Bill Jerome hitcd@bellsouth.net
www.jeromepromotions.com
We call the music directors and program directors of over 250 stations several times a week in order to help our artists get airplay and the recognition that they deserve with the goal of helping them make a deal with a major label.

Jerry Lembo Entertainment Group
742 Bergen Blvd. 2nd Fl. Ridgefield, NJ 07657
PH: 201-840-9980 FX: 201-840-9921
Jerry Lembo jerry@lemboentertainment.com
www.lemboentertainment.com
A music consulting firm specializing in Radio Promotion, Artist Management, Music Publishing, Publicity and more.

KDM Promotion
721 E. Temperence St., Kent, WA 98030
PH: 253-852-0218 FX: 253-852-0241
Kathleen Monahan kdmpromo@mindspring.com
www.mc-kdm.com
We introduce new music and artists to radio stations focusing on Jazz, Blues, Adult Eclectic, World, Celtic, Ambient, Native American, Spoken Word, Acoustic and Folk programming.

Loggins Promotion
2530 Atlantic Ave. #C, Long Beach, CA 90806
PH: 888-325-2901
promo@logginspromotion.com
www.logginspromotion.com
Most advanced system for tracking radio airplay.

Mediaguide
1000 Chesterbrook Blvd. #150, Berwyn, PA 19312
Paul E. Wright AMSales@mediaguide.com
www.artistmonitor.com
A technology-based music monitoring company that provides radio airplay information products on nearly 2,500 college, non-commercial and commercial broadcast stations to music industry professionals, artists, and radio stations.

MiaMindMusic
259 W. 30th St. #12FR, New York, NY 10001-2809
PH: 212-564-4611 FX: 212-564-4448
MiMiMus@aol.com
www.miamindmusic.com
Radio tracking and working with CMJ and R&R surveyed radio stations.

Michelle Sounds
176-25 Union Tpk. #398,
Fresh Meadows, NY 11365
michelles@michellesounds.com
www.michellesounds.com
We promote to 500 college radio stations across the United States.

New Music Weekly Magazine
26239 Senator Ave. Harbor City, CA 90710
PH 310-325-9997 FX: 866-243-4357
editor@newmusicweekly.com
www.newmusicweekly.com
Covers the Radio and Music industry with its 24+ page weekly magazine, website, NMW mail and fax services. Has become the standard for tracking radio airplay nationwide.

BRYAN FARRISH
RADIO PROMOTION

Billboard #22 AC
Billboard Top5 Most Added AC
R&R #24 AC
R&R Top5 Most Added AC
R&R Rock Specialty #11
FMQB #15 AC
FMQB #1 Most Added AC
CMJ #1 Most Added Hip Hop, RPM, Loud Rock
CMJ #3 Most Added Top200
Living Blues #3
Roots Music #5
New Age Reporter #15
Folk DJ List charting

310-998-8305
airplay@radio-media.com
www.radio-media.com

Nice Promotion
6418 28th Ave S.
Seattle, WA 98108
PH: 206-284-8528
Dave Radford ownerdave@nicepromo.com
www.nicepromo.com
Providing college radio promotion to labels and indie musicians alike. Genres: Alternative, Rock, Pop, Electronic and more!

Planetary Group
PO Box 52116,
Boston, MA 02205
PH: 617-451-0444
FX: 617-451-0888
adam@planetarygroup.com
www.planetarygroup.com
Full promotional services as well as targeted radio mailing services.

Protocol Entertainment
4610 Peachtree Industrial Blvd.
Atlanta, GA 30071
PH: 770-993-6565
FX: 770-518-3471
info@protocolentertainment.com
www.protocolentertainment.com
Providing labels and artists with radio promotion.

Radio & Retail Promotions
PH: 323-876-7027
Jon Flanagan promotions@radioandretail.com
www.radioandretail.com
Build a fan base through radio airplay and retail promotion.

Radio Station Library
info@radiostationlibrary.com
www.radiostationlibrary.com
Allows labels and independent artists to place their music in the library in the category of their particular genre of music. Categories are then accessed by pre-qualified, radio stations for inclusion in play lists.

RadioWave
areich68@comcast.net
www.radiowavemonitor.com/artists.html
Offers a comprehensive suite of services that will help you to concentrate your efforts on getting your music heard by potentially thousands of Internet radio listeners.

RAM (Realtime Airplay Metrics)
151 W. 25th St. 12th Fl. New York, NY 10001
PH: 917-606-1908 FX: 917-606-1914
ram@cmj.com
www.cmj.com/ram
A revolutionary airplay tracking service.

RCI Music Promotion
2000 Mallory Ln. #130-151, Franklin, TN 37067
Attn: Evaluations Dept.
PH: 615-599-5722
rcimusic@bellsouth.net
www.rcimusicpromotion.com
Radio airplay music promotion for independent music promotion.

Sheheshe Music Services
303 W. 2nd St., Eldon, MO 65026-1589
PH: 573-480-6647
Angel Davis-Blake angeldb@charter.net
www.sheheshe.com
We offer major quality with indie prices, check them out yourself! It's a one time fee! NOT WEEKLY! We promote all genres of music. We do mastering as well!

Space 380
2008 Swindon Ave. Columbia, MO 65203-8985
PH: 573-446-7221 FX: 309-210-9037
Mat Matlack indiebible@space380.com
www.space380.com
We develop name recognition for independent artists & labels of ALL genres.

The Syndicate
1801 Willow Ave. Weehawken, NJ 07086-6614
PH: 201-864-0900
Matt college@thesyn.com
musicsyndicate.com
We work mainly with artists and labels that are completely ready, with all the puzzle-pieces in place, ready for a serious radio campaign to compliment their marketing plan.

Tinderbox Music
Krista Vilinskis krista@tinderboxmusic.com
www.tinderboxmusic.com
Music promotion and distribution company.

Triplearadio.com
228 Commercial St., Nevada City, CA 95959-2507
PH: 530-477-2224 FX: 530-477-5599
Dave Chaney dave@triplearadio.com
www.triplearadio.com
Helps anyone who will be working their music to Triple A radio.

TRS Music Promotion
36625 N. 7th St. Bldg. 4, Phoenix, AZ 85086
PH: 800-616-3270 FX: 602-465-0395
TRS@radiopromo.com
www.radiopromo.com
Makes sure your music is getting attention.

Canada

dB Promotions & Publicity
1365 Yonge St. #204, Toronto, ON M4T 2P7
PH: 416 928 3550 FX: 416 928 3401
Dulce Barbosa info@dbpromotions.ca
www.dbpromotions.ca
National radio promotion and artist publicity.

www.indielinkexchange.com/ile

formatted and playlisted alternative, rock, pop, electronica.
real time artist/title info, voting, charting, chat and more

www.eoRadio.com | eoRadio)))

ListenEasy.com
PH: 905-790-3493
Sean Paddison paddisonclan@sympatico.ca
listeneasy.com
Offers a vast array of Internet radio and podcast promotional programs for independent artists, including radio feature spots, revenue generating podcast solutions and audio ad and CD giveaway programs.

RadioDirectX
650 Dupont St. #503, Toronto, ON M6G 4B1
PH: 888-746-7234
radio@radiodirect.com
www.radiodirectx.com
We've focused on developing a service that offers artists the opportunity to gain an international listening audience.

United Kingdom

Anglo Plugging
www.angloplugging.co.uk
Radio, television and internet promotion for bands and artists.

Stations that Play a Variety of Genres

*Most stations listed in the Variety section have weekly shows that cater to every style of music – Pop, Rock, Folk, Jazz, Various Metals, Punk, Goth, Industrial, Electronic, Hip Hop, Country, Blues etc. As one Music Director pointed out, when contacting these stations, it is **crucial** to add: **ATTENTION - MUSIC DIRECTOR** in the Subject: heading of your e-mail, as well as on the **package** you mail to the station.*

North America

United States

Alabama

WBLZ *U. Alabama*
151 Hill U. Center, 1400 U. Blvd.
Birmingham, AL 35294
PH: 205-975-9259 FX: 205-975-9261

WEGL
116 Foy Union Blvd. Auburn U. AL 36849-5231
PH: 334-844-4114 FX: 334-844-4118
wegl@auburn.edu
wegl.auburn.edu

WLJS *Jacksonville State U.*
700 Pelham Road N. Jacksonville, AL 36265
PH: 256-782-5572 FX: 256-782-5645
www.jsu.edu/92j

WUAL
PO Box 870370, Tuscaloosa, AL 35487-0370
PH: 205-348-6644 FX: 205-348-6648
www.wual.ua.edu

Alaska

KBBI
3913 Kachemak Way, Homer, AK 99603
PH: 907-235-7721
kim@kbbi.org
www.kbbi.org

KBRW
PO Box 109, Barrow, AK 99723
PH: 907-852-6811
info@kbrw.org
www.kbrw.org

KCAW
2B Lincoln St. #B, Sitka, AK 99835
PH: 907-747-5877 FX: 907-747-5977
ravenradio@ak.net
www.ravenradio.org

KCHU
PO Box 467, Valdez, AK 99686
PH: 800-478-5080
kchu@alaska.net
www.alaska.net/~kchu

KHNS
PO Box 1109, Haines, AK 99827
PH: 907-76-2020 FX: 907-766-2022
khns@khns.org
www.khns.org

KMXT
620 Egan Way, Kodiak, AK 99615-6487
PH: 907-486-5698 FX: 907-486-2733
kmxt@ptialaska.net
www.kmxt.org

KRUA *U. Alaska Anchorage*
3211 Providence Dr. Anchorage, AK 99508
PH: 907-786-6805
aykrua1@uaa.alaska.edu
www.uaa.alaska.edu/krua

KSUA *U. Alaska Fairbanks*
PO Box 750113, Fairbanks, AK 99775
PH: 907-474-7054 FX: 907-474-6314
ksuamusic@uaf.edu
ksua.uaf.edu

KTOO
360 Egan Dr. Juneau, AK 99801-1748
PH: 907-586-1670 FX: 907-586-3612
www.ktoo.org

Arizona

KAMP *U. Arizona*
PO Box 3605, Tucson, AZ 85722
Attn: Music Director
PH: 520-626-4460 FX: 520 626-5986
kamp.arizona.edu

KASC *Arizona State U.*
Stauffer Hall A231, Tempe, AZ 85287-1305
PH: 480-965-4163
md@theblaze1260.com
www.theblaze1260.com

KXCI
220 S. 4th Ave. Tucson, AZ 85701
PH: 520-623-1000
kxcimd@kxci.org
www.kxci.org

Radio Limbo
limbo103@yahoo.com
www.radiolimbo.org

Arkansas

KABF
2101 S. Main St., Little Rock, AR 72206
PH: 501-372-6119 FX: 501-376-3952
kabf@acorn.org
www.kabfradio.org

KHDX *Hendrix College*
1600 Washington Ave. Conway, AR 72032
PH: 800-277-9017
khdxStaff@ mercury.hendrix.edu

KSWH Henderson State U.
HSU Box 7872 Arkadelphia, AR 71999
PH: 870-230-5185
kswh@hsu.edu
stuwww.hsu.edu/kswh

KUAF U. Arkansas
PO Box 180554, Fort Smith, AR 72918
PH: 479-648-3993 FX: 479-648-9252
kuafinfo@uark.edu
www.kuaf.com

KXUA U. Arkansas
A665 Arkansas Union, Fayetteville, AR 72701
PH: 479-575-5883
charts@uark.edu
www.kxua.com

Live at Acoustic Sounds Cafe KUAR
2801 S. U. Little Rock, AR 72204
PH: 501-569-8485 FX: 501-569-8488
Joe.Henry@AcousticSoundsCafe.org
www.acousticsoundscafe.org/radioshow.htm
Artist interviews and live recordings of performances at the Acoustic Sounds Cafe. It's not a drop-in, just-show-up, open-mic kind of situation. We book 6-12 months in advance.

California

Demolisten KXLU
LMU Dr. Los Angeles, CA 90045
PH: 310-338-2866 FX: 310-338-5959.
kxlu889fm@hotmail.com
www.kxlu.com
Submit your homemade music on cassettes and CDRs. We expose the unexposable.

DMX
11400 W. Olympic Blvd. #1100,
Los Angeles, CA 90064-1507
PH: 310-444-1744 FX: 310-444-1717
www.dmxmusic.com
We are the global leader in delivering unparalleled personal music experiences via digital cable, satellite and the Internet to over 10 million homes, 180,000 businesses and 30 airlines.

Indie 103
5700 Wilshire Blvd. #250, Los Angeles, CA 90036
PH: 877-452-1031
feedback@indie1031.fm
indie1031.fm

iRADIO Los Angeles
561 S. Calvados Ave. Covina, CA 91723
PH: 626-780-6323 FX: 626-974-4776
Mark Coon iradiola@yahoo.com
www.iradiola.com
We are an independent radio station playing only independent artists and bands.

KALX U. California Berkeley
26 Barrows Hall #5650, Berkeley, CA 94720-5650
PH: 510-642-1111
kalxmail@media.berkeley.edu
kalx.berkeley.edu

KAPU Azusa Pacific U.
PO Box 9521, #5168 Azusa, CA 91702
music@kapuradio.com
kapu.apu.edu

KAZU
PO Box 210, 167 Central Ave.
Pacific Grove, CA 93950
PH: 831-375-7275 FX: 831-375-0235.
mail@kazu.org
www.kazu.org

KBeach
1212 Bellflower Blvd. USU #110,
Long Beach, CA 90815
PH: 562-985-1624
md@kbeach.org
www.kbeach.org

KCBL
4623 T St. #A, Sacramento, CA 95819-4743
PH: 916-456-8600 x144 FX: 916-451-9601
www.sacramento.org/stations/kcbl

KCIA California Inst. of the Arts
24700 McBean Pkwy. Valencia, CA 91355
PH: 661-255-1050 x2011
info@music.calarts.edu
shoko.calarts.edu

KCPR California Poly State U.
Graphic Arts Bldg 26 #201,
San Luis Obispo, CA 93407
PH: 805-756-2965
kcprmd@kcpr.org
www.kcpr.org

KCR San Diego College
5200 Campanile Dr. San Diego, CA 92182
PH: 619-594-7014 FX: 619-594-6092
md@KCRlive.com
kcr.sdsu.edu

KCRW
1900 Pico Blvd. Santa Monica, CA 90405
PH: 310-450-5183 FX: 310-450-7172
mail@kcrw.org
www.kcrw.org

KCSB U. California
PO Box 13401, Santa Barbara, CA 93107-3401
PH: 805-893-3757
external.music@kcsb.org
www.kcsb.org

KCSC California State U.
Cal State U. Chico, Chico, CA 95929
PH: 530-898-6229
kirt@kcsradio.com
kcsradio.com

KCSN California State U.
18111 Nordhoff St., Northridge, CA 91330-8312
PH: 818-677-3090
www.kcsn.org

KCSS California State U. Stanislaus
801 W. Monte Vista Ave. Turlock, CA 95380
PH: 667-3378 FX: 667-3901
www.kcss.net

KCXX
242 Airport Dr. #106, San Bernardino, CA 92408
PH: 909-384-1039 FX: 909-888-7302
www.x1039.com

KDNZ U. San Francisco
2130 Fulton St., UC402, San Francisco, CA 94117
PH: 415-422-6880

KDVS U. California
14 Lower Freeborn, Davis, CA 95616
PH: 530-752-0728
musicdept@kdvs.org
www.kdvs.org

KFJC
12345 El Monte Rd. Los Altos Hills, CA 94022
PH: 650-949-7260 FX: 650-948-1085
music@kfjc.org
www.kfjc.org

KFSR California State
Mail Stop SA #119, 5201 N. Maple,
Fresno, CA 93740
PH: 559-278-2598 FX: 559-278-6985
kfsr_musicdirector@hotmail.com
www.csufresno.edu/kfsr

KGFN Grossmont College
8800 Grossmont College Dr. El Cajon, CA 92020
PH: 619-644-7288.
kgfnfm@yahoo.com
www.grossmont.net/kgfn

KHUM Humboldt State U.
PO Box 25 Ferndale, CA 95536
PH: 707-786-5104 FX: 707-786-5100
info@khum.com
www.khum.com

KITS Soundcheck
865 Battery St. 2nd Fl. San Francisco, CA 94111
PH: 415-402-6700
www.live105.com

KKSM Palomar College
1140 W. Mission Rd. San Marcos, CA 92069
PH: 760-744-1150 x3149
www.palomar.edu/kksm

KKUP
PO Box 820, Cupertino, CA 95015
PH: 408-260-2999
admin@kkup.org
www.kkup.com

KMUD
PO Box 135, 1144 Redway Dr.
Redway, CA 95560-0135
PH: 707-923-2513 FX: 707-923-2501
Kate Klein md@kmud.org
kmud.org

KNAB Chapman U.
1 University Dr. Orange, CA 92866
PH: 714-744-7020
musicdirector@chapmanradio.com
www.ChapmanRadio.com

KOZT
110 South Franklin St., Fort Bragg, CA 95437
PH: 707-964-7277 FX: 707-964-9536
thecoast@kozt.com
www.kozt.com

KPCC Pasadena City College
1570 E. Colorado Blvd. Pasadena, CA 91106-2003
PH: 626-585-7000
mail@kpcc.org
www.kpcc.org

KPFA
1929 MLK Jr. Way Berkeley, CA 94704
PH: 510-848-6767 FX: 510-848-3812
postmaster@kpfa.org
www.kpfa.org

KRBS
PO Box 9, Oroville, CA 95965
www.radiobirdstreet.org

KRCB
5850 Labath Ave. Rohnert Park, CA 94928
PH: 707-585-8522 FX: 707-585-1363
www.krcb.org/radio

KRFH Humboldt State U.
c/o Dept. of Journalism, HSU, Arcata, CA 95521
PH: 707-826-3257
www.humboldt.edu/~krfh

KRSH
3565 Standish Ave. Santa Rosa, CA 95407
PH: 707-588-0707
www.krsh.com

KSAK Mt. San Antonio College
1100 N. Grand Ave. Walnut, CA 91789
PH: 909-594-5611 x5725
ksak@mtsac.edu
www.ksak.com

KSCR U. Southern California
STU 404, Los Angeles, CA 90089-0895
PH: 213-740-1483
music@kscr.org
www.kscrradio.com

KSCU Santa Clara U.
500 El Camino Real #3207, Santa Clara, CA 95053
PH: 408-554-4413
music@kscu.org
www.kscu.org

KSDT U. California San Diego
kbmitchell@ucsd.edu
scw.ucsd.edu

KSFS San Francisco State U.
1600 Holloway Ave. San Francisco, CA 94132
PH: 415-338-2428
ksfs@sfsu.edu
userwww.sfsu.edu/~ksfs

KSJS San Jose State U.
Hugh Gillis Hall #132, San Jose, CA 95192-0094
PH: 408-924-4548 FX: 408-924-4558
programdirector@ksjs.org
www.ksjs.org

KSMC St. Mary's College
PO Box 3223, Moraga, CA 94575-3223
PH: 925-631-4252 x1
ksmc@stmarys-ca.edu

KSPC Pomona College
Thatcher Music Bldg. 340 N. College Ave.
Claremont, CA 91711
PH: 909-621-8157 FX: 909-607-1259
www.kspc.org

KSRH San Rafael H.S.
185 Mission Ave., San Rafael, CA 94901
PH: 415-457-5314

KSSB California State U.
5500 University Pkwy. San Bernadino, CA 92407
PH: 909-880-5772

KSSU California State U.
c/o ASI, 6000 J St., Sacramento, CA 95819
PH: 916-278-3343

KSUN Sonoma State U.
1801 E. Cotati Ave. Rohnert Park, CA 94928
PH: 707-664-2622
Tom Shields ksunmusic@yahoo.com
www.sonoma.edu/ksun

KUCI U. California
PO Box 4362, Irvine, CA 92616
PH: 949-824-6868
md@kuci.org
www.kuci.org

KUCR U. California
Riverside, CA 92521
PH: 909-787-3737 FX: 909-787-3240
kucrmusic@hotmail.com
www.kucr.org

KUSF U. San Francisco
2130 Fulton St., San Francisco, CA 94117
PH: 415-386-5873
kusf@usfca.edu
www.kusf.org

KUSP
PO Box 423, Santa Cruz, CA 95061
PH: 831-476-2800
gjs@kusp.org
kusp.org

KVMR
401 Spring St., Nevada City CA 95959
PH: 530-265-9073 FX: 530-265-9077
music@kvmr.org
www.kvmr.org

KWRF Santa Monica College
1900 Pico Blvd. Santa Monica, CA 90405
PH: 310-434-4583

KXLU Loyola - Marymount U.
1 LMU Dr. Malone 402, Los Angeles, CA 90045
PH: 310-338-2866 FX: 310-338-5959
kxlu889fm@hotmail.com
www.kxlu.com

KYDS El Camino H.S.
4623 T St., Sacramento, CA 95819-4743
PH: 916-456-8600 x144
www.sacramento.org/voice

KZSC U. California
Student Music E. Santa Cruz, CA 95064
PH: 831-459-2811 FX: 831-459-4734
kzsc.org

KZSU Stanford U.
PO Box 20510, Stanford, CA 94309
PH: 650-725-4868 FX: 650-725-5865
music@kzsu.stanford.edu
kzsu.stanford.edu

KZYX
PO Box 1, Philo, CA 95466
PH: 707-895-2451 FX: 707-895-2554
musicdir@kzyx.org
www.kzyx.org

Morning Becomes Eclectic KCRW
1900 Pico Blvd. Santa Monica, CA 90405
PH: 310-450-5183 FX: 310-450-7172
mbe@kcrw.org
www.kcrw.org

Penguin Radio Dominican U. California
50 Acacia Ave. San Rafael, CA 94901
PH: 482-3587
radio@dominican.edu
radio.dominican.edu

Radio Goethe
2130 Fulton St., San Francisco, CA 94117
PH: 415-386-5873
Arndt Peltner info@radiogoethe.de
www.radiogoethe.org
The German voice. News, reviews, interviews.

Rock-it Radio
4756-4 Telephone Rd. #225, Ventura, CA 93003
PH: 805-477-2502
Bennie Dingo Rockitradio@aol.com
www.palmsradio.com/main.html

Titan Internet Radio California State U.
PO Box 6868, Fullerton, CA 92834-6868
PH:714-278-5505 FX:714-278-5514
titanradio@fullerton.edu
titaninternetradio.com

UCLA Radio
118 Kerckhoff Hall, 308 Westwood Plaza,
Los Angeles, CA 90024
PH: 310-825-6955
info@uclaradio.com
www.uclaradio.com

WPMD Cerritos College
11110 Alondra Blvd., Norwalk, CA 90650
PH: 562-860-2451 FX: 562-467-5005
wpmd@cerritos.edu
www.cerritos.edu/wpmd

Colorado

etown
207 Canyon, Ste. 302, Boulder, CO 80302
PH: 303-443-8696 FX: 303-443-4489
Nick & Helen Forster info@etown.org
www.etown.org
We're heard from coast to coast on both NPR and commercial stations. We present a variety of musical styles and talent, from household names to regional artists and emerging performers. Live performances and interviews.

iSAMI
1420 Austin Bluffs Pkwy. PO Box 7150,
Colorado Springs, CO 80933-7150
radio.uccs.edu

KAFM
PO Box 4167, Grand Junction, CO 81502
PH: 970-241-8801 x5 FX: 970-241-0995
md@kafmradio.org
www.kafmradio.org

KCSU Colorado State U.
Student Ctr. Box 13, Lory Student Ctr.
Fort Collins, CO 80523
PH: 970-491-7611 FX: 970-491-7612
kcsufm.com

KDNK
PO Box 1388, Carbondale, CO 81623
PH: 970-963-0139 FX: 970-963-0810
www.kdnk.org

KDUR *Ft. Lewis College*
1000 Rim Dr. Durango, CO 81301
PH: 970-247-7628
kdur_pd@fortlewis.edu
www.kdur.org

KEPC *Pikes Peak College*
Box 49, 5675 S. Academy Blvd.
Colorado Springs, CO 80906
PH: 719-540-7455
kepc@ppcc.edu
www.ppcc.cccoes.edu/NewsEvents/KEPC

KGNU
4700 Walnut St., Boulder, CO 80301
PH: 303-449-4885
Elaine C. Erb music@kgnu.org
www.kgnu.org

KMSA *Mesa State College*
1100 N. Ave. Grand Junction, CO 81501-3122
PH: 970-248-1718
www.mesastate.edu/kmsa

KOTO
PO Box 1069, 207 N. Pine St., Telluride, CO 81435
PH: 970-728-4334 x2
kotofm@yahoo.com
koto.org

KRCC *Colorado College*
912 N. Weber St., Colorado Springs, CO 80903
PH: 719-473-4801
jeff@krcc.org
www.krcc.org

KRCX *Regis U.*
3333 Regis Blvd. Denver, CO 80221
PH: 303-964-5392
insite.regis.edu/insite.asp?sctn=krcx

KSRX *U. Northern Colorado*
928 20th St., Greeley, CO 80639
PH: 970-336-1004 FX: 305-489-8256
www.unco.edu/ksrx

KVCU *U. Colorado*
Campus Box 207, Boulder, CO 80309
PH: 303-492-5031 FX: 303-492-1369
kvcumd@stripe.colorado.edu
www.colorado.edu/StudentGroups/KVCU

KVNF
PO Box 1350, Paonia, CO 81428
PH: 970-527-4866 FX: 970-527-4865
kvnf@kvnf.org
www.kvnf.org

KWSB *Western State College*
Taylor Hall, Rm 111, Gunnison, CO 81230
PH: 970-943-3033

Connecticut

Offbeat *WPKN*
244 U. Ave. Bridgeport, CT 06604
PH: 203-331-9756
Rich Kaminsky wpkn@wpkn.org
www.wpkn.org
Exposes and critiques the latest musical releases, reviewing sounds and styles that fly just beneath the radar of commercial radio stations.

Upper Room with Joe Kelley
PO Box 3481, Bridgeport, CT 06605
Gi Dussault or Joe Kelley npsfunk@optonline.net
www.upperroomwithjoekelley.com
On the air since 1982, recognized worldwide for interviews, in-house concerts series and support of indie artists in all kind of music. Email us before sending a CD.

WCNI *Connecticut College*
PO Box 4972, 270 Mohegan Ave.
New London, CT 06320
PH: 860-439-2853 FX: 860-439-2805
www.wcniradio.org

WECS *Eastern Connecticut State U.*
PH: 860-465-5354
WECS@hotmail.com
www.easternct.edu/depts/wecs

WESU *Wesleyan U.*
222 Church St., Middletown, CT 06459
PH: 860-685-7703 FX: 860-685-3744
www.wesleyan.edu/wesu

WFCS *Central Connecticut State U.*
1615 Stanley St., New Britain, CT 06050
PH: 860-832-1883 FX: 860-832-3757
WFCS1077@yahoo.com
clubs.ccsu.edu/wfcs

WHRT *Sacred Heart U.*
5151 Park Ave. Fairfield, CT 06852
PH: 203-371-7962

WHUS *U. Connecticut*
1501 Storrs Road Storrs, CT 06269-3008
PH: 860-486-4007
nfo@whus.org
whus.org

WKZE
67 Main St., Sharon, CT 06069
PH: 860-364-5800 FX: 860-364-0129
info@wkze.com
www.wkze.com

WNHU *U. New Haven*
300 Orange Ave. West Haven, CT 06516
PH: 203-934-8888 FX: 203-931-6055
wnhu@newhaven.edu
www.newhaven.edu/wnhu

WPKN
244 U. Ave. Bridgeport, CT 06604
PH: 203-331-9756
Phil Bowler philcbowler@aol.com
www.wpkn.org

WRTC *Trinity College*
300 Summit St., Hartford, CT 06106
PH: 860-297-2439
www.wrtcfm.com

WSAM *U. Hartford*
200 Bloomfield Ave. W. Hartford, CT 06117
music@wsam.hartford.edu
wsam.hartford.edu

WSIN *Southern Connecticut State U.*
501 Crescent St., New Haven, CT 06456
PH: 203-392-6930
wsin1590@gmail.com
radio.southernct.edu

WVOF *Fairfield U.*
1073 N. Benson Rd. Box R,
Fairfield, CT 06430-5195
PH: 203-254-4144 FX: 203-254-4224
musicdirector@wvof.org
www.wvof.org

WWUH *Hartford U.*
Attn: Music Director, 200 Bloomfield Ave.
West Hartford, CT 06117
PH: 860-768-4701 FX: 860-768-5701
wwuh@mail.hartford.edu
www.wwuh.org

WXCI *Western Connecticut State U.*
181 White St., Danbury, CT 06811
PH: 203-837-8387
wxcigm@yahoo.com
www.myspace.com/wxci

WYBC *Yale U.*
142 Temple St. #203, New Haven, CT 06510
PH: 203-776-4118
md@wybc.com
www.wybc.com

Delaware

WVUD *U. Delaware*
Perkins Student Ctr. Newark, DE 19716
PH: 302-831-2701 FX: 831-1399
wvudmusic@udel.edu
www.wvud.org

Florida

Sonic Detour *WMNF*
1210 E. MLK Blvd. Tampa, FL 33603-4449
PH: 813-238-8001 FX: 813-238-1802
Flee wmnf@wmnf.org
www.wmnf.org
A Rock-based mix of eclectic music: new releases, old favorites, contemporary singer-songwriters and unpredictable surprises..

WBRY *Barry U.*
11300 NE 2nd Ave. Miami Shores, FL 33161-6695
PH: 305-899-3463
www.barry.edu/communication/facilities/wbry.htm

WBUL *U. South Florida*
4202 E. Fowler Ave. CTR 2487, Tampa, FL 33620
PH: 813-974-4906
www.ctr.usf.edu/wbul

WECX *Eckerd College*
4200 54th Ave. S. Box D, St. Petersburg, FL 33711
PH: 727-864-8419

WERU *Embry-Riddle Aeronautical U.*
600 S. Clyde Morris Blvd.
Daytona Beach, FL 32114-3900
PH: 386-226-7056 FX: 386-226-6083
www.eaglesfm.com

WFCF *Flagler College*
PO Box 1027, St. Augustine, FL 32085-1027
PH: 904-829-6940
www.flagler.edu/news_events/wfcf.html

WKNT *U. Central Florida*
PO Box 163230, Orlando, FL 32816
PH: 407-823-4584 FX: 407-823-5899
music@knightcast.org
www.knightcast.org

WKPX *Piper H.S.*
8000 NW 44th St., Sunrise, FL 33351
PH: 954-572-1321
www.wkpx.freeservers.com

WMNF *Tampa College*
1210 E. MLK Blvd. Tampa, FL 33603-4449
Attn: Music Director <your genre>
PH: 813-238-8001 FX: 813-238-1802
wmnf@wmnf.org
www.wmnf.org

WNSU *Nova Southeastern U.*
3301 College Ave. Ft. Lauderdale, FL 33314
PH: 954-262-8457 FX: 954-262-3928
wnsu@nova.edu
radiox.nova.edu

WOSP *U. North Florida*
4567 St. John's Bluff Rd. S. Jacksonville, FL 32224
PH: 904-620-2908 FX: 904-620-1560
canopenersunion@hotmail.com
ospreyradio.tk

WOWL *Florida Atlantic U.*
777 Glades Rd. U. Ctr. #207D,
Boca Raton, FL 33431
PH: 561-297-3759 FX: 561-297-3771
owlradio@wowl.fau.edu
wowl.fau.edu

WPBZ *Smith College*
www.buzz103.com

WPRK *Rollins College*
1000 Holt Ave. 2745, Winter Park, FL 32789
PH: 407-646-2241 FX: 407-646-1560
wprkfm@rollins.edu
www.rollins.edu/wprk

WRGP *Florida International U.*
11200 SW 8th St., U. Park, GC 319,
Miami, FL 33199
PH: 305-348-3071 FX: 305-348-6665
wrgpmusic@hotmail.com
wrgp.fiu.edu

WVFS *Florida State U.*
420 Diffenbaugh Bldg. Tallahassee, FL 32306-1550
music@wvfs.fsu.edu
www.wvfs.fsu.edu

WVUM *U. Miami*
PO Box 248191, Coral Gables, FL 33124
PH: 305-284-3131 FX: 305-284-3132
info@wvum.org
wvum.org

Georgia

Indie Access
PH: 706-340-6303
info@indieaccessonline.com
www.indieaccessonline.com
We feature the best Indie bands from all over the country.

Just Off the Radar *WUGA*
U. Georgia, 1197 S. Lumpkin St., Athens, GA 30602
PH: 706-542-9842 FX: 706-542-6718
Joe Silva wuga@uga.edu
justofftheradar.com
The best of Folk to Techno, and everything in between.

WGHR *Southern Tech Inst. College*
1100 S. Marietta Pkwy. Marietta, GA 30060
PH: 770-528-7354 FX: 770-528-7409
wghr@spsu.edu
wghr.spsu.edu

WMRE *Emory U.*
PO Drawer AG, Atlanta, GA 30322
PH: 404-727-9672 FX: 404-712-8000
www.students.emory.edu/wmre

WRAS *Georgia State U.*
33 Gilmer St. SE #8, Atlanta, GA 30303-3088
PH: 404-651-2240
wrasgm@yahoo.com
www.wras.org

WREK *Georgia Tech*
165 8th St. NW, Atlanta, GA 30332-0630
PH: 404-894-2468 FX: 404-894-6872
music.director@wrek.org
www.wrek.org

WRFG
1083 Austin Ave. NE, Atlanta, GA 30307-1940
PH: 404-523-3471
info@wrfg.org
www.wrfg.org

WUOG *U. Georgia*
Box 2065 Tate Student Ctr. Athens, GA 30602
PH: 706-542-7100 FX: 706-542-0070
md@wuog.org
wuog.org

WVVS *Valdosta State U.*
Valdosta, GA 31698
PH: 333-7314
www.valdosta.edu/wvvs

Hawaii

KKCR
PO Box 825, Hanalei, HI 96714
PH: 808-826-7774
kkcr@kkcr.org
www.kkcr.org

KTUH *U. Hawaii*
2445 Campus Rd. Hemenway Hall #203,
Honolulu, HI 96822
PH: 808-956-5288 FX: 808-956-5271
music@ktuh.org
ktuh.hawaii.edu

Idaho

KISU *Idaho State U.*
Campus Box 8014, Pocatello, ID 83209
PH: 208-282-3691
kisufm91@isu.edu
www.kisu.org

KUOI *U. Idaho*
3rd Fl. Student Union Bld. Campus Box 444272,
Moscow, ID 83844-4272
PH: 208-885-6433 FX: 208-885-2222
kuoi@uidaho.edu
kuoi.asui.uidaho.edu

Illinois

Decatur Community Radio
2024 E. Damon Ave. Decatur, IL 62526
PH: 217-233-3018 FX: 217-233-3019
dcr1650@yahoo.com
www.decaturcommunityradio.com

UIC Radio *U. Illinois Chicago*
750 S. Halsted #318, 118 M/C, Chicago, IL 60607
PH: 312-413-5085
uicradio.pages.uic.edu

WAUG *Augustana College*
639 38th St., Rock Island, IL 61201
PH: 309-794-7513
waug@augustana.edu
waug.augustana.edu

WCRX *Columbia College*
600 S. Michigan Ave. Chicago, IL 60605
PH: 312-344-8160
www.colum.edu/crx/snoble

WDBX
224 N. Washington St., Carbondale, IL 62901
PH: 618-457-3691 FX: 618-529-5900
Brian Powell wdbx@globaleyes.net
www.wdbx.org

WDGC *Downers Grove H.S.*
4436 Main St., Downers Grove, IL 60515
PH: 630-795-8491 FX: 630-795-8400
wdgcfm@hotmail.com
www.csd99.k12.il.us/wdgc

WEFT
113 N. Market St., Champaign, IL 61820
PH: 217-359-9338
weft@weftfm.org
www.weft.org

WEIU *Eastern Illinois U.*
PH: 217-581-5956
weiu@weiufm.org
www.weiufm.org

WESN *Illinois Wesleyan U.*
PO Box 2900, Bloomington, IL 61701
PH: 309-556-2638 FX: 309-556-2949
www.iwu.edu/~wesn

WHPK *U. Chicago*
5706 S. U. Ave. Chicago, IL 60637
PH: 773-702-8289 FX: 773-834-1488
whpk.uchicago.edu

WIDB *Southern Illinois U.*
Mailcode 4428, Carbondale, IL 62901
PH: 618-536-2361
pd@widb.net
www.widb.net

WIIT *Illinois Inst. of Technology*
3300 S. Federal St., Chicago, IL 60616
PH: 312-567-3087 FX: 312-567-7042
wiit@iit.edu
radio.iit.edu

WLUW *Loyola U.*
6525 N. Sheridan Rd. Chicago, IL 60626
PH: 773-508-8080 FX: 773-508-8082
musicdept@wluw.org
www.wluw.org

WMCR *Monmouth College*
700 E. Broadway Monmouth, IL 61462
PH: 309-457-3060 FX: 309-457-2141
department.monm.edu/wmcr

WNUR *Northwestern U.*
1920 Campus Dr. Evanston, IL 60208-2280
PH: 847-491-7102 FX: 847-467-2058
rock-md@wnur.org
www.wnur.org

WONC North Central College
30 N. Brainard St., Naperville, IL 60540-4690
PH: 630-637-5969 FX: 630-637-5900
feedback@wonc.org
www.wonc.org

WPCD Parkland College
2400 W.Bradley Ave. Champaign, IL 61821
PH: 217-373-3790
wpcd@eudoramail.com
www.parkland.edu/wpcd

WQNA Springfield
2201 Toronto Rd. Springfield, IL 62712
PH: 217-529-5431 x164 FX: 217-529-7861
www.wqna.org

WQUB Quincy U.
1800 College Ave., Quincy, IL 62301-2699
PH: 217-222-8020
www.quincy.edu/wqub

WRDP Depaul U.
802 W. Belden Ave. #110, Chicago, IL 60614
PH: 773-325-7342
wrdpmanagement@depaul.edu
radio.depaul.edu

WRRG Triton College
2000 5th Ave., River Grove, IL 60171
PH: 708-583-3110
info@wrrg.org
www.wrrg.org

WVJC Wabash Valley College
2200 College Dr. Mount Carmel, IL 62863
PH: 618-262-8989
www.iecc.cc.il.us/wvjc

WVKC Knox College
PO Box K-254 2 E. S. St., Galesburg, IL 61401
PH: 309-341-7441
wvkc@knox.edu
deptorg.knox.edu/wvkc

WXAV St. Xavier U.
3700 W. 103rd St., Chicago, IL 60655
PH: 773-298-3376 FX: 773-298-3381
wxavmusic@yahoo.com
web.sxu.edu/wxav

WZND Illinois State U.
007 Fell Hall, Normal, IL 61790-4481
PH: 309-438-5490 FX: 309-438-2652
znd@hotmail.com
www.wznd.com

WZRD Northeastern Illinois U.
5500 N. St. Louis Ave. Chicago, IL, 60625-4699
PH: 773-442-4578
wzrd@neiu.edu
www.WZRDChicago.com

Indiana

City of Music
7399 N. Shadeland Ave. #284,
Indianapolis, IN 46250
information@cityofmusic.com
www.cityofmusic.com

WBAA Purdue U.
712 3rd St., W. Lafayette, IN 47907-2005
PH: 765-494-5920
www.purdue.edu/wbaa

WCRD Ball State U.
BC 132, Muncie, IN 47306
PH: 765-285-1467
wcrd@bsu.edu
wcrd.net

WECI Earlham College
Earlham College, Richmond, IN 47374
PH: 765-983-1246 FX: 765-983-1641
www.earlham.edu/~weci

WFHB
PO Box 1973, Bloomington, IN 47402
PH: 812-323-1200 FX: 812-323-0320
wfhb@wfhb.org
www.wfhb.org

WGRE DePauw U.
609 Locust St., Greencastle, IN 46135
PH: 765-658-4641
wgre@depauw.edu
www.depauw.edu/univ/wgre

WISU Indiana State U.
217 Dreiser, Terre Haute, IN 47809
PH: 812-237-FM90 FX: 812-237-8970
wisu.indstate.edu

WIUS Indiana U.
326 Sallee Hall, Macomb, IL 61455
PH: 309-298-3217
www.wiu.edu/thedog

WMHD Rose-Hulman Inst. Tech
5500 Wabash Ave. Terre Haute, IN 47803
PH: 812-877-8350
musicdir@wmhd.rose-hulman.edu
wmhd.rose-hulman.edu

WMRH Purdue U.
Owen Hall, West Lafayette, IN 47906
WMRH@expert.cc.purdue.edu
expert.cc.purdue.edu/~wmrh

WPUM St. Joseph's College
US Hwy. 231, PO Box 870, Rensselaer, IN 47978
PH: 219-866-6000 Ext 6905
wpum@saintjoe.edu
www.saintjoe.edu/~wpum

WUEV U. Evansville
1800 Lincoln Ave. Evansville, IN 47722
PH: 812-479-2022 FX:812-479-2320
wuevfm@evansville.edu
www2.evansville.edu/wuevweb

WVFI U. Notre Dame
200 LaFortune Hall, Notre Dame, IN 46556
PH: 574-631-6400
wvfi@nd.edu
www.nd.edu/~wvfi

WVUR Valparaiso U.
32 Schnabel Hall, 1809 Chapel Dr.
Valparaiso, IN 46383
PH: 219-464-5383
www.valpo.edu/student/wvur

Iowa

KALA St. Ambrose U.
518 W. Locust St., Davenport, IA 52803
PH: 563-333-6450
kala@sau.edu
sau.edu/kala

KBVU Buena Vista U.
610 W. 4th St., Storm Lake, IA 50588
PH: 712-749-1234 FX: 712-749-2037
KBVU@bvu.edu
edge.bvu.edu

KDIC Grinnell College
PO Box.V.4, Grinnell, IA 50112
PH: 641-269-3335
kdic.grinnell.edu

KICB Iowa Central College
330 Ave. M, Fort Dodge, IA 50501
PH: 515-576-0099 ext. 2353
www.iccc.cc.ia.us/kicb

KLIF Briar Cliff College
3303 Rebecca St. PO Box 2100,
Sioux City, IA 51104-2100
PH: 712-279-1624

KMSC Morningside College
1501 Morningside Ave. Sioux City, IA 51106
PH: 712-274-5665
fusion@morningside.edu
webs.morningside.edu/masscomm/KMSC

KRNL Cornell College
810 Commons Cir. Mount Vernon, IA 52314
PH: 319-895-4431
www.cornellcollege.edu/krnl

KRUI U. Iowa
129 Grand Ave. Ct. Iowa City, IA 52246-2504
PH: 319-335-9525
krui@uiowa.edu
www.uiowa.edu/~krui

KSTM Simpson College
701 NC St., Indianola, IA 50125
Phone: 515-961-1536

KULT U. Northern Iowa
L045 Maucker Union, Cedar Falls, IA 50614
PH: 319-372-6935
kult@uni.edu
www.uni.edu/kult

KURE Iowa State U.
1199 Friley Hall, Ames, IA 50012
PH: 515-294-4332 FX: 515-294-4332
music@kure885.org
www.kure885.org

KWAR
100 Wartburg Blvd. Waverly, IA 50677
PH: 319-352-8209
theone@kwar.org
www.kwar.org

KWLC Luther College
700 College Dr. Decorah, IA 52101-1045
PH: 563-387-1571 FX: 563-387-2158
kwlcam@luther.edu
kwlc.luther.edu

Onion River Radio
300 Bel Aire #6, Burlington, IA 52601
PH: 319-752-4075
feedback@onionriverradio.com
www.onionriverradio.com

Kansas

KFHS *Fort Hays State U.*
600 Park St., Hays, KS 67601
PH: 785-628-4198
kfhs@fhsu.edu
www.fhsu.edu/int/kfhsradio

KJHK *U. Kansas*
2051A Dole Ctr. 1000 Sunnyside Ave.
Lawrence, KS 66045
PH: 785-864-4747
kjhkmusic@ku.edu
kjhk.org

KSDB *Kansas State U.*
105 Kedzie Hall, Manhattan, KS 66506-1501
PH: 785-532-2769
radio@ksu.edu
wildcatradio.ksu.edu

Kentucky

The Indie Connection *WKMS*
2018 University Stn. Murray, KY 42071
PH: 270-762-4359
John Gibson john.gibson@gmail.com
www.indieconnection.blogspot.com
www.myspace.com/indieconnection
A weekly program focusing on independent and local bands. I am no longer accepting unsolicited material; I have gotten a lot of great music, but I also have gotten a lot of material that does not fit my format, and I can't play it. So, I would prefer artists to email me first, with a link to their music.

Lexrock.com
PH: 650-345-7400 FX: 650-345-7497
Steve lexrock@insightbb.com
www.lexrock.com
Playing Indie music from across the globe.

WFPK
HSA Broadband Bldg. 619 S. 4th St.,
Louisville, KY 40202
PH: 502-814-6500
www.wfpk.org

WMMT
91 Madison St., Whitesburg, KY 41858
PH: 606-633-1208
wmmtfm@appalshop.org
www.appalshop.org/wmmt

WRFL *U. Kentucky*
777 U. Stn. Lexington, KY 40506-0025
PH: 859-257-4636 FX: 859-323-1039
music@wrfl.uky.edu
wrfl.uky.edu

Louisiana

KLPI *Louisiana Tech*
PO Box 8638, Tech Stn. Ruston, LA 71272
PH: 318-257-4851 FX: 318-257-5073
www.latech.edu/tech/orgs/klpi

KNSU *Nicholls State U.*
PO Box 2664, Thibodaux, LA 70310
PH: 985-448-4447 FX: 985-449-7106
www.nicholls.edu/knsu

KSCL *Centenary College*
2911 Centenary Blvd. Shreveport, LA 71104
kscl@centenary.edu
www.centenary.edu/life/kscl

KSLU *Southern Louisiana U.*
D. Vickers Rm 112, SLU 10783,
Hammond, LA 70402
PH: 985-549-2330 FX: 985-549-3960
ksluradio@hotmail.com
www.selu.edu/kslu

KXUL *U. Louisiana*
130 Stubbs Hall, ULM Monroe, LA 71209-8821
PH: 318-342-5986
kxul.com

WTUL
Tulane U. Center, New Orleans, LA 70118
PH: 504-865-5887 FX: 504-463-1023
md1@wtul.fm
www.wtul.fm

Maine

WBOR *Bowdoin College*
Smith Union, Brunswick, ME 04011
PH: 207-725-3210
wbor@bowdoin.edu
studorgs.bowdoin.edu/wbor

WERU
PO Box 170, 1186 Acadia Hwy E.
Orland, ME 04431
PH: 207-469-6600 FX: 207-469-8961
info@weru.org
www.weru.org

WHSN *Husson College*
1 College Cir. Bangor, ME 04401
PH: 888-877-1876 FX: 207-947-3987

WMEB *U. Maine*
5748 Memorial Union, Orono, ME 04469-5748
PH: 207-588-2333 FX: 207-581-4343
www.umaine.edu/wmeb

WMHB *Colby College*
4000 Mayflower Hill, Waterville, ME 04901
PH: 207-872-3686
wmhb@colby.edu
www.colby.edu/wmhb

WMPG *U. Southern Maine*
96 Falmouth St., Portland, ME 04104-9300
PH: 207-780-4943
programdirector@wmpg.org
www.wmpg.org

WRBC *Bates College*
31 Frye St., Lewiston, ME 04240
PH: 207-777-7532 FX: 207-795-8793
www.bates.edu/people/orgs/wrbc

WUMF *U. Maine*
111 S. St., Farmington, ME 04938
PH: 207-778-7352 FX: 207-778-7113
wumf@umf.maine.edu
wumf.umf.maine.edu

WUPI *U. Maine Presque Isle*
PO Box 525, 181 Main St., Presque Isle, ME 04769
PH: 207-768-9742
stationmanager@wupiradio.com
www.umpi.maine.edu/~wupi

Maryland

WFWM *Frostburg State U.*
Frostburg, MD 21532
PH: 301-687-7096
wfwm@frostburg.edu
www.wfwm.org

WMBC *U. Maryland*
U. Ctr. 101, 1000 Hilltop Cir. Baltimore, MD 21250
PH: 410-455-3192 FX: 410-455-3067
headmd@wmbc.umbc.edu
www.wmbc.umbc.edu

WMTB *St. Mary's College*
16300 Old Emmitsburg Rd.
Emmitsburg, MD 21727
PH: 301-447-5239
campuslife@msmary.edu
www.msmary.edu/wmtb

WMUC *U. Maryland*
3130 S Campus Dining Hall,
College Park, MD 20742-8431
PH: 301-314-7868
md@wmuc.umd.edu
www.wmuc.umd.edu

WXSU *Salisbury U.*
PO Box 3151 Salisbury, MD 21801
orgs.salisbury.edu/wxsu

XTSR *Towson U.*
8000 York Rd., Media Ctr. Rm 005,
Towson, MD 21252
PH: 410-704-5308
xtsr@hotmail.com
wwwnew.towson.edu/xtsr
Towson's commercial free Rock station.

Massachusetts

All Independent Radio *New England Inst. of Art*
10 Brookline Pl. W., Brookline, MA 02445
PH: 617-277-8616
www.neia.aiiradio.com

BCR
radio@babson.edu
radio.babson.edu

Exploit Boston! Radio
343 Medford St. #2A Somerville, MA 02145
PH: 781-420-9660
contact@exploitboston.com
www.exploitboston.com
Features Boston pop and Rock bands past and present. Regional and national acts coming to town (publicists, etc.) should contact us, too. The show is not just for local bands.

The Patchwork Majority *WXOJ*
60 Masonic St., Northampton, MA 01060
Arjuna Greist arjunagazette@yahoo.com
www.valleyfreeradio.com
Send in music and spoken word in any genre, as long as it embraces and addresses issues such as feminism, environmentalism etc. I'd like a ONE PAGE bio which highlights the ways you or your band work towards progressive goals through your art and other activisms.

Three Ring Circus *WMBR*
3 Ames St., Cambridge, MA 02142
PH: 617-253-4000
Joan Hathaway circus@wmbr.org
wmbr.mit.edu
Roots Rock, Indie, Blues, Garage, Surf/instro, and all the billies (Rocka, Hill and Psycho).

WAMH *Amherst College*
AC #1907 Campus Ctr. Amherst, MA 01002-5000
PH: 413-542-2224
wamh@Amherst.edu
wamh.amherst.edu

WAVM *Maynard HS*
1 Tiger Dr. Maynard, MA 01754
PH: 978-897-5179
studio@wavm.org
www.wavm.org

WBIM *Bridgewater State College*
Campus Ctr. 109, Bridgewater, MA 02325
PH: 508-531-1366 FX: 508-531-1786
wbimmd@hotmail.com
www.bridgew.edu/wbim

WBRS *Brandeis U.*
415 S. St. Waltham, MA 02453-2728
Attn: (genre)
PH: 781-736-4785
music@wbrs.org
www.wbrs.org

WBTY *Bentley College*
175 Forest St., Waltham, MA 02452
PH: 781-891-2808
musicmail@wbty.com
www.wbty.com

WCCS *Wheaton College*
Box W0977, Norton, MA 02766
PH: 508-286-3819
wccsmd@wheatoncollege.edu
wccs.wheatonma.edu

WCFM *Williams College*
Baxter Hall, Williamstown, MA 01267
PH: 413-597-3265 FX: 413-597-2259
wcfmbd@wso.williams.edu
wcfm.williams.edu

WCHC *College of the Holy Cross*
1 College St., Worcester, MA 01610
PH: 508-793-2474
wchc@holycross.edu
college.holycross.edu/wchc

WCUW
910 Main St., Worcester, MA 01610
PH: 508-753-1012
wcuw@wcuw.com
www.wcuw.com

WDOA
128 Mechanic St., Spencer, MA 01562
FX: 253-323-1606
wdoainfo@wdoa.com
www.wdoa.com

WERS *Emerson College*
120 Boylston St., Boston, MA 02116
PH: 617-824-8891
info@wers.org
www.wers.org

WGAJ *Deerfield Academy*
wgajradio@yahoo.com
www.geocities.com/wgajradio

WMBR *Mass Inst. Technology*
3 Ames St., Cambridge, MA 02142
PH: 617-253-4000
music@wmbr.org
wmbr.mit.edu

WMFO *Tufts U.*
PO Box 65, Medford, MA 02155
PH: 617-625-0800
md@wmfo.org
www.wmfo.org

WMHC *Mt. Holyoke College*
Blanchard Student Ctr. South Hadley, MA 01705
PH: 413-538-2019 FX: 413-538-2431
www.mtholyoke.edu/org/wmhc

WMLN *Curry College*
1071 Blue Hill Ave. Milton, MA 02186
PH: 617-333-0311
www.curry.edu/WMLNWeb

WMUA *U. Massachusetts*
105 Campus Ctr. Amherst, MA 01003
PH: 413-545-2876 FX: 413-545-0682
wmua@wmua.org
wmua.org

WOMR
14 Ctr. St. PO Box 975, Provincetown, MA 02657
PH: 800-921-9667
programming@womr.org
www.womr.org

WOZQ
Campus Ctr. Northampton, MA 01063
PH: 413-585-4956
wozq@email.smith.edu
sophia.smith.edu/org/wozq

WRBB *Northeastern U.*
360 Huntington Ave. Boston, MA 02115
PH: 617-373-4338 FX: 617-373-5095
wrbbradio.org

WRNX
98 Lower Westfield Rd. Holyoke, MA 01040
PH: 413-536-1105 FX: 413-536-1153
www.wrnx.com

WRSI
100 Main St., Northampton, MA 01060
PH: 413-585-9555 FX: 413-585-8501
Johnny Memphis johnny@wrsi.com
www.wrsi.com

WSFR *Suffolk U.*
41 Temple St., Boston, MA 02114
PH: 617-305-6337
radio@suffolk.edu
www.suffolk.edu/radio

WSHL *Stonehill College*
320 Washington St., North Easton, MA 02357
PH: 508-565-2612 FX: 508-565-5722
wshl@stonehill.edu
wshl.stonehill.edu

WSKB *Westfield State College*
577 Western Ave. Westfield, MA 01086
PH: 413-572-5579 FX: 413-572-5625
WSKB89_5FM@yahoo.com
wskb.tripod.com

WSMU *U. Mass/Dartmouth*
285 Old Westport Rd. N. Dartmouth, MA 02747
PH: 508-999-8149 FX: 508-999-8173
wsmu@umassd.edu
www.wsmu.org

WTBU *Boston U .*
640 Commonwealth Ave. Boston, MA 02215
PH: 617-353-6401 FX: 617-353-6403
www.wturadio.com

WUML *U. Massachusetts*
1 U. Ave. Lowell, MA 01854
PH: 978-934-4975
md@wuml.org
wuml.org

WWPI *Worcester Polytechnic Inst.*
100 Institute Rd. Worcester, MA 01609
PH: 508-831-5956
radio@wpi.edu
radio.wpi.edu

WXOJ
60 Masonic St., Northampton, MA 01060
info@valleyfreeradio.org
www.valleyfreeradio.org

WZBC *Boston College*
McElroy Commons, 107 Chestnut Hill, MA 02467
PH: 617-552-3511 FX: 617-552-1738
music@wzbc.org
www.wzbc.org

WZLY *Wellesley College*
Schneider Ctr. 106 Central St., Wellesley, MA 02481
PH: 781-283-2791
md@wzly.net
wzly.net

Michigan

Free Radio Jackson
Aaron Childs aaronchilds@ameritech.net
www.live365.com/stations/aaronchilds
A mixture of Rock, Blues, Alternative, Jazz and Electronica from both major label, small label, and unsigned artists.

Lake FX Radio *Muskegon College*
221 S. Quarterine Rd. Muskegon, MI 49437
PH: 231-777-0330
info@lakefxradio.com
lakefxradio.com

WBLD *West Bloomfield HS*
4925 Orchard Lake Rd. W. Bloomfield, MI 48323
PH: 248-865-6754
wbld_fm@hotmail.com
wbld893.tripod.com

WCBN *U. Michigan*
530 Student Activities Bldg.
Ann Arbor, MI 48109-1316
PH: 734-763-3501
music@wcbn.org
www.wcbn.org

WCKS *Grand Valley State U.*
104 Commons Bldg. Allendale, MI 49401
PH: 616-331-2875
www.wcks.org

WHFR *Henry Ford College*
5101 Evergreen Rd. Dearborn, MI 48128
PH: 313-845-9776 FX: 313-317-4034
whfr@hfcc.net
whfr.hfcc.net

WIDR *Western Michigan U.*
1511 Faunce Student Service Bldg.
Kalamazoo, MI 49008-6301
PH: 269-387-6305
widr-music@groupwise.wmich.edu
www.widr.org

WLBN *Albion College*
611 E. Porter St., Albion, MI 49224
PH: 517-629-1000
wlbn@albion.edu
www.albion.edu/wlbn

WLSO *Lake Superior State U.*
650 W. Easterday Ave, Sault Ste. Marie, MI 49783
PH: 888-800-LSSU FX: 906-635-2111
wlso@gw.lssu.edu
www.lssu.edu/wlso

WMHW *Central Michigan U.*
183 Moore Hall Mt. Pleasant, MI 48859
PH: 989-774-7287
wmhw@mail.cmich.edu
www.bca.cmich.edu/WMHW

WMTU *Michigan Technological U.*
G03 Wadsworth Hall, 1703 Townsend Dr.
Houghton MI 49931-1193
PH: 906-487-2333 FX: 906-483-3016
wmtu@mtu.edu
wmtu.mtu.edu

WNMC *Northwestern Michigan College*
1701 E. Front St., Traverse City, MI 49686
PH: 231-995-1135
information@nmc.edu
www.wnmc.org

WPHS *Warren Cousino HS*
30333 Hoover Rd. Warren, MI 48093
PH: 586-698-4501 FX: 586-571-3755
wphs@wphs.com
www.wphs.com

WQAC *Alma College*
614 W. Superior Alma, MI 48801
PH: 989-466-7095
wqaccharts@blazemail.com
students.alma.edu/organizations/wqac

WUMD *U. Michigan Dearborn*
4901 Evergreen Rd. Dearborn, MI 48128
PH: 313-593-5439 FX: 313-593-3503
WUMD_GM@hotmail.com
www.umd.umich.edu/wumd

WUPX *Marquette U.*
1204 U. Ctr. Marquette, MI 49855
PH: 906-227-1844 FX: 906-227-2344

WXOU *Oakland U.*
69 Oakland Ctr. Rochester, MI 48309
PH: 248-370-2845 FX: 248-370-2846
wxoumusic@yahoo.com
www.oakland.edu/org/wxou

WYCE
711 Bridge St. NW, Grand Rapids, MI 49504
PH: 616-459-4788 FX: 616-742-0599
comments@wyce.org
www.wyce.org

Minnesota

KAXE
1841 E. Hwy. 169, Grand Rapids, MN 55744
PH: 218-326-1234 FX: 218-326-1235
kaxe@kaxe.org
www.kaxe.org

KBSB *Bemidji State U.*
1500 Birchmont Dr. NE, Bemidji, MN 56601-2699
PH: 218-755-4120 FX: 218-755-4048
fm90@bemidjistate.edu
www.fm90.org

KFAI
1808 Riverside Ave. Minneapolis, MN 55454
PH: 612-341-3144 FX: 612-341-4281
richmond@kfai.org
www.kfai.org

KGSM *Gustavus Adolphus College*
800 W. College Ave. St. Peter, MN 56082
PH: 507-933-8000 x8783.
www.gac.edu/oncampus/orgs/kgsm

KMSC *Minnesota State U. Moorhead*
Owens Hall Box 356, Moorhead, MN 56563
PH: 218-477-2116
kmsc1500am@yahoo.com
www.dragonradio.org

KMSU *Minnesota State U.*
PH: 800-722-0544
www.mnsu.edu/kmsufm

KQAL
PO Box 5838, Winona, MN 55987
PH: 507-453-2222 FX: 507-457-5226
music@kqal.org
www.kqal.org

KSMR *St. Mary's U.*
2500 Park Ave. Minneapolis, MN 55404-4403
PH: 866-437-2788
ksmr@smumn.edu
www2.smumn.edu/studorg/~ksmr

KSTO *St. Olaf College*
1500 St. Olaf Ave. Northfield, MN 55057
PH: 507-646-3603
ksto@stolaf.edu
www.stolaf.edu/orgs/ksto

KUMM *U. Minnesota*
600 E. 4th St., Morris, MN 56267
PH: 320-589-6076
kumm@kumm.org
www.kumm.org
Hard Alternative music.

KUOM *U. Minnesota*
610 Rarig Ctr. 330 21st Ave. S.
Minneapolis, MN 55455
PH: 612-625-3500 FX: 612-625-2112
music@radiok.org
www.radiok.org

KVSC *Saint Cloud State U.*
720 4th Ave. S. 27 Stewart Hall,
St. Cloud, MN 56301-4498
PH: 320-308-3126 FX: 320-308-5337
music@kvsc.org
www.kvsc.org

Radio Rumpus Room *KFAI*
1808 Riverside Ave. Minneapolis, MN 55454
PH: 612-341-3144 FX: 612-341-4281
rumpus2@bitstream.net
www.radiorumpusroom.com
Surf, Hot Rod, Rockabilly, '60s Garage, Hillbilly, Psychedelia, Back-to-the-Roots Country…

WELY
133 E. Chapman St., Ely, MN 55731
PH: 218-365-4444
info@wely.com
www.wely.com

WMCN *Manchester College*
1600 Grand Ave. Saint Paul, MN 55105
PH: 651-696-6082
wmcn@macalester.edu
www.macalester.edu/~wmcn

WTIP
PO Box 1005, Grand Marais, MN 55604
PH: 218-387-1070 FX: 218-387-1120
wtip@boreal.org
wtip.org

Mississippi

WMSV *Mississippi State U.*
PO Box 6210 Student Media Ctr. MS 39762-6210
PH: 662-325-8034 FX: 662-325-8037
wmsv@msstate.edu
www.wmsv.msstate.edu

WMUW *Mississippi U. for Women*
1100 College St., Columbus, MS 39701
PH: 662-329-4750
wmuw@muw.edu
www.muw.edu/wmuw

WUMS *U. Mississippi*
PO Box 1848, UM, 38677-1848
PH: 662-915-7566
www.olemiss.edu/orgs/wums

WUSM *U. Southern Mississippi*
PO Box 10045, Hattiesburg, MS 39406-0045
PH: 601-266-4287 FX: 601-266-4288
www.usm.edu/wusm

Missouri

3WK Undergroundradio
PO Box 160161, St. Louis, MO 63116.
wandagm@3wk.com
www.3wk.com

KCFV *Florissant Valley College*
3400 Pershall Rd. St Louis, MO 63135-1499
PH: 414-595-4463 FX: 314-595-4217
www.stlcc.cc.mo.us/fv/kcfv

KCLC
209 S. Kingshighway, St Charles, MO 63301
PH: 636-949-4880
fm891@lindenwood.edu
www.891thewood.com

KCOU *U. Missouri*
101f Pershing Hall, Columbia, MO 65201
PH: 573-882-7820
kcou@mu.org
kcou.missouri.edu

KDHX
3504 Magnolia, St. Louis, MO 63118
PH: 314-664-3955 FX: 314-664-1020
musicdepartment@kdhx.org
www.kdhx.org

KGLX *Webster U.*
470 E. Lockwood, St. Louis, MO 63119
PH: 314-968-7162
www.kglx.org

KKFI
PO Box 32250, Kansas City, MO 64171
PH: 816-931-3122 x106
www.kkfi.org

KMNR *U. Missouri*
113E U. Ctr. W. 1870 Miner Cir.
Rolla, MO 65409-1440
PH: 573-341-4273 FX: 573-341-6021
www.umr.edu/~kmnr

KNSX
PO Box 93, St. Peters, MO 63376
PH: 314-921-9330
x93@knsx.com
www.knsx.com
Rock format. If it's good, we'll play it!

KOPN
915 E. Broadway Columbia, MO 65201
PH: 573-874-1139 FX: 573-499-1662
mail@kopn.org
www.kopn.org/artist_sub.htm

KSLU *St. Louis U.*
20 N. Grand Blvd, St. Louis, MO 63108
PH: 314-977-1574 FX: 314-977-1579
kslu@slu.edu
kslu.slu.edu

KWUR *Washington U.*
Campus Box 1205, 1 Brookings Dr.
St. Louis, MO 63105
PH: 314-935-5952
kwur.wustl.edu

Sonic Spectrum *KCUR*
4825 Troost Ave. #202, Kansas City, MO 64110
PH: 816-235-1551 FX: 816-235-2864
Robert Moore moorerb@umkc.edu
www.kcur.org
Blues to Drum n' Bass, Indie Rock to Honky Tonk.

Montana

KBGA *U. Montana*
U. Ctr. Missoula, MT 59812
PH: 406-243-5715
music@kbga.org
www.kbga.org

KGLT
MSU Box 17424, Bozeman, MT 59717-4240
PH: 406-994-6483 FX: 406-994-1987
wwwkglt@montana.edu
www.kglt.net

KMSM *Montana Tech*
1300 W. Park St. #117, Butte, MT 59701
PH: 406-496-4601 FX: 406-496-4702
kmsm@mtech.edu
www.mtech.edu/kmsm

Nebraska

KBUL *U. Nebraska Omaha*
6001 Dodge St., Omaha, NE 68182
PH: 402-554-2800
maverickradio@netscape.net
www.mavradio.org

KDNE *Doane College*
1014 Boswell Ave. Crete, NE 68333
PH: 402-826-8677
kdne@Doane.edu
webcast.doane.edu

KFKX *Hastings College*
PO Box 269, Hastings, NE 68901
PH: 402-461-7367 FX: 402-461-7442
kfkx@hastings.edu

KRNU *U. Nebraska*
PO Box 880466, Lincoln, NE 68588-0466
PH: 402-472-8277
krnu@unl.edu
krnu.unl.edu

KZUM
941 "O" St., Lincoln, NE 68508
PH: 402-474-5086 FX: 402-474-5091
programming@kzum.org
www.kzum.org

New Hampshire

The Crop *WFRD*
PO Box 957, Hanover, NH 03755
PH: 603-646-3313 FX: 603-643-7655
music@wfrd.com
www.wfrd.com
Emo Kid and Pilot Irish play the best in Indie Rock.

RadioSNHU *S. New Hampshire U.*
2500 N. River Rd. Manchester, NH 03106-1045
PH: 603-629-4695
radiosnhu@snhu.edu
radio.snhu.edu

WDCR *Dartmouth College*
theradio@dartmouth.edu
www.dartmouth.edu/~wdcr

WFPR *Franklin Pierce College*
20 College Rd. Rindge, NH 03461-0060
twingo4291@aol.com
members.tripod.com/~Sheep_Pimp

WFRD *Dartmouth College*
PO Box 957, Hanover, NH 03755
PH: 603-643-7625 FX: 603-643-7655
www.wfrd.com
Mostly Rock format.

WKNH *Keene State College*
PH: 603-358-2420
music@wknh.org
www.wknh.org

WPCR *Plymouth State College*
music@wpcr.plymouth.edu
mindwarp.plymouth.edu

WSCA
PH: 603-430-9722 FX: 603-430-9822
PO Box 6532, Portsmouth, NH 03802
Jay Boucher jay@portsmouthcommunityradio.org
www.wscafm.org

WSCS *Colby-Sawyer College*
100 Main St., New London, NH 03257
PH: 603-526-3493
wscs@colby-sawyer.edu
www.colby-sawyer.edu/wscs

WUNH *U. New Hampshire*
music@wunh.org
wunh.org

YourOnLive.com *Manchester*
Jim theshow@youronlive.com
www.youronlive.com
Come sit in for an interview and we'll play your music.

New Jersey

The Pipeline Radio Show
P O Box 1242, Voorhees, NJ 08043
Bullwinkle thepipeline@comcast.net
All styles of artists are urged to send their music to us for airplay consideration.

RLC *Rutgers U. Livingston*
#117 Student Ctr. Joyce Kilmer Ave.
Piscataway, NJ 08854
PH: 732-445-4100
thecoremusic@hotmail.com
www.thecore.rutgers.edu

WBZC *Burlington County College*
County Rt. 530, Pemberton, NJ 08068-1599
PH: 609-894-9311 x7223 FX: 609-894-9440
mail@wbzc.org
staff.bcc.edu/radio

WCCR *Rutgers U. Camden*
Camden, NJ 08102
www.clam.rutgers.edu/~wccr

WFDU *Fairleigh Dickinson U.*
Metropolitan Campus, 1000 River Rd.
Teaneck, NJ 07666
PH: 201-692-2806 FX: 201-692-2807
wfdu.fm

WFMU
c/o Brian Turner, PO Box 5101, Hoboken, NJ 07030
PH: 201-521-1416
www.wfmu.org

WGLS *Rowan U.*
201 Mullica Hill Rd. Glassboro, NJ 08028
PH: 856-863-WGLS FX: 856.256.4704
wgls@rowan.edu
wgls.rowan.edu

WJTB *New Jersey Inst. of Tech.*
323 MLK Blvd. Newark, NJ 07102
PH: 973-596-5816
www.wjtb.org

WMCX *Monmouth U.*
400 Cedar Ave. W. Long Branch, NJ 07764
PH: 732-571-3482 FX: 732-263-5145
wmcxradio@monmouth.edu
hawkmail.monmouth.edu/~wmcx

WMSC *Montclair State U.*
1 Normal Ave. Upper Montclair, NJ 07043
PH: 973-655-4387 FX: 973-655-7433
music@wmscradio.com
www.montclair.edu/orgs/WMSC

WNTI *Centenary College*
400 Jefferson St., Hackettstown, NJ 07840
PH: 908-979-4355
Amanda Socko wntimd@aol.com
www.wnti.org

WPRB *Princeton U.*
30 Bloomberg Hall, Princeton, NJ 08544
PH: 609-258-3655 FX: 609-258-1806
music@wprb.com
www.wprb.com

WRNU *Rutgers U.*
350 MLK Blvd. Rm 315 Newark, NJ 07102
PH: 973-353-5746 FX: 973-353-5187
wrnu@yahoo.com
pegasus.rutgers.edu/~wrnu

WRSU *Rutgers U.*
126 College Ave. New Brunswick, NJ 08901
PH: 732-932-7800 FX: 732-932-1768
wrsu@wrsu.rutgers.edu
www.wrsu.org

WSOU *Seton Hall U.*
400 S. Orange Ave. South Orange, NJ 07079
PH: 973-761-9768
wsou@shu.edu
www.wsou.net

WTSR *College of New Jersey*
Kendall Hall, PO Box 7718, Ewing, NJ 08628
PH: 609-771-2420 FX: 609-637-5113
tsrmusic@tcnj.edu
www.wtsr.org

New Mexico

KTEK *New Mexico Tech.*
PH: 505-835-6013
ktek@nmt.edu
infohost.nmt.edu/~ktek

KUNM *U. New Mexico*
MSC06 3520, Onate Hall 1,
Albuquerque, NM 87131-0001
PH: 505-277-4806
music@kunm.org
www.kunm.org/home

New York

106 VIC *Ithaca College*
118 Roy H. Park Hall, Ithaca, NY 14850
PH: 607-274-1059
vic@ithaca.edu
www.ithaca.edu/radio/vic

Emotional Rescue *WJFF*
4765 State Rt. 52, PO Box 546,
Jeffersonville, NY 12748
PH: 845-482-4141 FX: 845-482-9533
Kae Kotarski rescue@wjffradio.org
www.wjffradio.org
A weekly, 90 minute music show covering most genres.

The Indie Show *WBER*
2596 Baird Rd. Penfield, NY 14526
PH: 585-419-8190
wber@monroe.edu
wber.monroe.edu
2 hours of music exclusively from Independent labels.

Radio Liberation Front *WXXE*
826 Euclid Ave. Syracuse, NY 13210
PH: 315-455-5624 FX: 315-701-0303
Dale R. Gowin wxxeradio@yahoo.com
www.wxxe.org
Featuring a mix of explicitly political music from many genres, including Rock, Punk, Reggae, Folk, Country, and unclassifiable Experimental music.

RocklandWorldRadio.com
c/o Independent Music, 30A Chestnut St.,
Suffern, NY 10901
info@modernmetro.com
www.RocklandWorldRadio.com
Download our release form and send it with your CD.

The Tuesday Night Rock & Roll Dance Party *WUSB*
Student Union Bld. SUNY,
Stony Brook, NY 11794-3263
PH: 631-632-6500 FX: 631-632-7182
musicwusb·fm
wusb.fm
Contact us to lay down a set of music.

WAIH *SUNY Potsdam*
9050 Barrington Dr.
Potsdam, NY 13676
PH: 315-267-7692
waih@potsdam.edu
www2.potsdam.edu/WAIH

WALF *Alfred U.*
1 Saxon Dr. Alfred, NY 14802
PH: 607-871-2200
FX: 607-871-2287
WALF@alfred.edu
jobs.alfred.edu/~walf

WAMC
PO Box 66600,
Albany, NY 12206
PH: 518-465-5233
FX: 518-432-6974
mail@wamc.org
www.wamc.org

WBAI
120 Wall St.10th Fl.
New York, NY 10005
PH: 212-209-2800
FX: 212-747-1698
info@wbai.org
www.wbai.org

WBAR *Barnard College*
3009 Broadway,
New York, NY 10027-6598
PH: 212-854-6538
wbar@columbia.edu
www.wbar.org

WBER *Monroe College*
2596 Baird Rd. Penfield, NY 14526
PH: 585-419-8190
wber@monroe.edu
wber.monroe.edu

WBMB *Baruch College*
55 Lexington Ave. Box 3-280,
New York, NY 10010
PH: 646-312-4722
www.geocities.com/wbmbradio

WBNY *Buffalo State U.*
1300 Elmwood Ave. Buffalo, NY 14222
PH: 716-878-3080 FX: 716-878-6600
wbny@buffalostate.edu
www.wbny.org

WBSU *SUNY Brockport*
Seymour Union, Brockport, NY 14420
PH: 716-395-2580
www.891thepoint.com

WCDB *U. Albany*
Campus Ctr. 316 1400 Washington Ave.
Albany, NY 12222
PH: 518-442-5262 FX: 518-442-4366
wcdb@albany.edu
www.albany.edu/~wcdb

WCOT *SUNY Utica*
wcot@sunyit.edu
clubs.sunyit.edu/wcot

WCWP *Long Island U.*
C.W. Post Campus 720, Northern Blvd.
Brookville, NY 11548-1300
PH: 516-299-2626 FX: 516-299-2767
wcwp@cwpost.liu.edu
www.liu.edu/cwis/cwp/radio/wcwp

WDST
PO Box 367, Woodstock, NY 12498
PH: 845-679-7266 FX: 845-679-5395
www.wdst.com

WDYN
2844-46 Dewey Ave. Rochester, NY 14616
PH: 585-621-6270 FX: 585-621-6278
wdyn@wdyn.net
dynamicradio.net
Plays ONLY Local and Indie music every day.

WFNP *SUNY*
SUB 413, New Paltz, NY 12561-2443
PH: 845-257-3094 FX: 845-257-3099
wfnp@newpaltz.edu
www.newpaltz.edu/wfnp

WFUV *Fordham U.*
Bronx, NY 10458
PH: 718-817-4550
thefolks@wfuv.org
www.wfuv.org

WGFR *Adirondack College*
640 Bay Rd. Queensbury, NY 12804
PH: 518-743-2300 x2376
wgfr@wgfr.org
www.wgfr.org

WHCL *Hamilton College*
198 College Hill Rd. Clinton, NY 13323
PH: 315-859-4200
www.whcl.org

WHPC *Nassau College*
1 Education Dr. Garden City, NY 11530-6793
PH: 516-572-7438 FX: 516-572-7831
whpc@ncc.edu
www.sunynassau.edu/dptpages/whpc/whpc.htm

WHRW *Binghampton U.*
PO Box 2000, Binghamton, NY 13902-6000
PH: 607-777-2139 FX: 607-777-6501
pd@whrwfm.org
www.whrwfm.org

WICB *Ithaca College*
118 Park Hall, Ithaca, NY 14850
PH: 607-274-1040 x1 FX: 607-274-1061
Will VanDyke wicbmusic@yahoo.com
www.ithaca.edu/radio/wicb

WITR *Rochester Institute of Tech.*
PO Box 20563, Rochester, NY 14602-0563
PH: 585-475-5643 FX: 585-475-4988
musicdirector@modernmusicandmore.com
www.modernmusicandmore.com

WJFF
4765 State Rt. 52, PO Box 546,
Jeffersonville, NY 12748
PH: 845-482-4141 FX: 845-482-9533
wjff@wjffradio.org
www.wjffradio.org

WLMU *Le Moyne College*
1419 Salt Springs Rd. Syracuse, NY 13214
PH: 315-445-4586
www.lemoyne.edu/wlmu

WNYO *SUNY Oswego*
9B Hewitt Union, Oswego, NY 13126
PH: 315-312-2101 FX: 315-312-2907
wnyo@oswego.edu
www.oswego.edu/~wnyo

WNYU *New York U.*
194 Mercer St. 5th Fl. New York, NY 10012
PH: 212-998-1660 FX: 212-998-1652
music@wnyu.org
www.wnyu.org

WONY
Hunt Union Bldg. Oneonta, NY 13820
PH: 607-436-2712
WONY@oneonta.edu
www.oneonta.edu/WONY

WPOB *JFK H.S.*
PH: 516-937-6375
www.wpob.com

WQKE *Plattsburgh State U.*
110 Angell College Ctr. Plattsburgh, NY 12901
PH: 518-564-2726
chia1230@mail.plattsburgh.edu
clubs.plattsburgh.edu/wqke

WRCU *Colgate U.*
13 Oak Dr. Hamilton, NY 13346
PH: 315-228-7104 FX: 315-228-7028
wrcu@mail.colgate.edu
wrcu.colgate.edu

WRHO *Hartwick College*
1 Hartwick Dr. Oneonta, NY 13820O
PH: 607-431-4555 FX: 607-431-4064
Alex Cameron wrho@hartwick.edu
users.hartwick.edu/wrho

WRHU *Hofstra U.*
Room 127, Hempstead, NY 11549-1000
PH: 516-463-3674
WRHUmusic@wrhu.org
www.wrhu.org

WRKL *(Polskie Radio New York)*
1551 Rte. 202, Pomona, NY 10970
PH: 845-354-2000 FX 845-354-4796
WRKL@polskieradio.com
www.polskieradio.com
Polish radio. Plays Independent music.

WRPI *Rensselaer Polytechnic Inst.*
1 WRPI Plaza, Troy, NY 12180
PH: 518-276-2648 FX: 518-276-2360
wrpi-md@rpi.edu
www.wrpi.org

WRUB *SUNY U. Buffalo*
174/175 MFAC. Buffalo, NY 14261
PH: 716-645-3405
WRUBmusic@hotmail.com
www.subboard.com/wrub

WRUR *U. Rochester*
PO Box 277356, Rochester, NY 14627
PH: 585-275-6400 FX: 585-256-3989
music@wrur.org
wrur.rochester.edu

WSBU *St. John's U.*
PO Box O, St. Bonaventure, NY 14778
PH: 716-375-2307

WSGU *SUNY at Geneseo*
1 College Cir. Geneseo, NY 14454
PH: 585-245-5211
wgsu@geneseo.edu
onesun.cc.geneseo.edu/~wgsu

WSIA *College of Staten Island*
2800 Victory Blvd. Rm 1C-106,
Staten Island, NY 10314
PH: 718-982-3057 FX: 718-982-3052
music@wsia.csi.cuny.edu
wsia.fm

WSPN *Skidmore College*
815 N. Broadway, Saratoga Springs, NY 12866
PH: 518-580-5787
wspn@skidmore.edu
www.skidmore.edu/~wspn

WSUC *State U. New York*
7060 State Rt. 104, Oswego, NY 13126
PH: 315-312-3690 FX: 315-312-3174
wrvo@wrvo.fm
www.wrvo.com

WTSC *Clarkson U.*
PO Box 8743, Potsdam, NY 13699
PH: 315-268-7658
radio@clarkson.edu
radio.clarkson.edu

WUSB *SUNY Stoneybrook*
Union Building, Stony Brook, NY 11794-3263
PH: 631-632-6501 FX: 631-632-7182
musicwusb·fm
wusb.fm

WVBR
957 Mitchell St. #B, Ithaca, NY 14850
PH: 607-273-4000 FX: 607-273-4069
www.wvbr.com

WVKR *Vassar College*
Box 726, 124 Raymond Ave.
Poughkeepsie, NY 12604
PH: 845-437-5476 FX: 845-437-7656
music@wvkr.org
www.wvkr.org

WXBA *Brentwood H.S.*
Brentwood, NY 11717
PH: 631-434-2581
www.88x.net

WXXE
826 Euclid Ave. Syracuse, NY 13210
PH: 315-455-5624 FX: 315-701-0303
info@wxxe.org
www.wxxe.org

North Carolina

The New Music & Indie Label Show
801 E. Morehead St. #200, Charlotte, NC 28202
PH: 704-376-1065
Divakar 90minutes@1065.com
www.1065.com/newmusic.html
Features new music & bands from all over the country.

Wake Radio *Wake Forest U.*
PO Box 7760, Winston-Salem, NC 27109
PH: 336-758-4894 FX: 336-758-4562
radio.wfu.edu

WASU *Appalachian State U.*
Wey Hall #332, Boone, NC 28608
PH: 828-262-3170 FX: 828-262-2543
music@wasurocks.com
www.wasurocks.com

WDCC *Central Carolina College*
1105 Kelly Dr. Sanford, NC 27330
PH: 919-718-7257
bfreeman@cccc.edu
www.wdccfm.com

WKNC *North Carolina State U.*
Mail Ctr. Box 8607, Raleigh, NC 27695-8607
PH: 919-515-2401 FX: 919-213-2353
wknc.org

WNCW *Isothermal College*
PO Box 804, Spindale, NC 28160
PH: 828-287-8000 x334
info@wncw.org
www.wncw.org

WQFS *Guilford College*
17714 Founders Hall, 5800 W. Friendly Ave.
Greensboro, NC 27410
PH: 336-316-2352
wqfs@guilford.edu
www.guilford.edu/wqfs

WSGE *Gaston College*
201 Hwy. 321 S. Dallas, NC 28034
PH: 704-922-6552 FX: 704-922-2347
www.wsge.org

WSOE *Elon College*
Campus Box 6000, Elon, NC 27244
PH: 336-278-7211 FX: 336-278-7298
wsoe@elon.edu
www.elon.edu/wsoe

WUAG *U. North Carolina Greensboro*
PO Box 26170, Greensboro, NC 27402
PH: 336-334-4308
wuagmd@hotmail.com
www.uncg.edu/wua

WVOD
637 Harbor Rd. Wanchese, NC 27981
PH: 252-475-1888
thesound@cbobx.com
www.wvod.com

WXDU *Duke U.*
PO Box 90689, Duke Stn. Durham, NC 27708
PH: 919-684-2957
music_director@wxdu.org
www.wxdu.duke.edu

WZMB *East Carolina U.*
Mendenhall Student Ctr.
PH: 252-328-4751
ket0518@mail.ecu.edu
wzmb.ecu.edu

Ohio

ACRN *Ohio U.*
9 S. College St. #315, Athens, OH 45701
PH: 740-593-2276
acrn@ohiou.edu
www.acrn.com

BearCast Radio *U. Cincinnati*
2217 Mary Emery Hall, PO Box 210003,
Cincinnati, OH 45221
PH: 513-556-4525
bearcastmusicdirector@gmail.com
www.bearcast.uc.edu

KBUX *Ohio State U.*
1739 N. High St. #15-S, Columbus, OH 43210
PH: 614-688-3780 FX: 614-688-5788
pd@underground.fm
www.underground.fm

Radio U *Westerville*
PO Box 1887, Westerville, OH 43086
PH: 614-890-9977 FX: 614-839-1329
www.radiou.com

Radio Free Canton
radiofreecanton@neo.rr.com
www.radiofreecanton.net

WAIF
1434 E. McMillan Ave. Cincinnati, OH 45206
PH: 513-961-8900
WAIF@WAIF883.org
www.waif883.org

WBGU *Bowling Green State U.*
120 West Hall, Bowling Green, OH 43403
PH: 419-372-8657 FX: 419-372-9449
www.wbgufm.com

WBWC *Baldwin-Wallace College*
275 Eastland Rd. Berea, OH 44017
PH: 440-826-2145 FX: 440-826-3426
www.wbwc.com

WCSB *Cleveland State U.*
Rhodes Tower 956, 2121 Euclid Ave.
Cleveland, OH 44115-2214
PH: 216-687-3721 FX: 216-687-2161
musdirwcsb@yahoo.com
wcsb.org

WCWS *College of Wooster*
Wishart Hall, Wooster, OH 44691
PH: 330-263-2240 FX: 330-263-2690
wcws@wooster.edu
www.wooster.edu/wcws

WJCU *John Carroll U.*
20700 N. Park Blvd. U. Heights, OH 44118
PH: 216-397-4937 FX: 216-397-4438
directors@wjcu.org
www.wjcu.org

WKSR *Kent State U.*
C306 Music & Speech, Kent, OH 44242
wksr.kent.edu

WMCO *Muskingum College*
163 Stormont St., New Concord, OH 43762
PH: 740-826-8907
wmco@muskingum.edu
muskingum.edu/~wmco

WMSR *Miami U.*
221 Williams Hall, Oxford, OH 45056
PH: 513-529-1269
wmsr@muohio.edu
www.orgs.muohio.edu/wmsr

WOBC *Oberlin College*
Wilder Hall 319, 135 W. Lorain St.,
Oberlin, OH 44074
PH: 440-775-8107 FX: 440-775-6678
music.wobc@oberlin.edu
www.wobc.org

WONB *Ohio Northern U.*
Freed Center, Ada, OH 45810
PH: 419-772-1194 FX: 419-772-2794
wonb@onu.edu
www.onu.edu/wonb

WOXY
5120 College Corner Pike, Oxford, OH 45056
PH: 513-523-4114
Matt Shiv shiv@woxy.com
www.woxy.com

WRMU *Mount Union College*
1972 Clark Ave. Alliance, OH 44601
PH: 800-992-6682, ext. 3777 FX: 330-823-4913
wrmu@muc.edu
www.muc.edu/wrmu

WRUW *Case Western Reserve U.*
11220 Bellflower Rd. Cleveland, OH 44106
PH: 216-368-2207 FX: 216-368-5414
Wade Tolleson md@wruw.org
www.wruw.org

WSLN *Ohio Wesleyan U.*
HWCC Box 1366, Delaware, OH 43015
PH: 740-368-2239
wsln.owu.edu

WUDR *U. Dayton*
300 College Park K.U. #215, Dayton, OH 45409
PH: 937-229-3058
flyer-radio.udayton.edu

WWCD *Independent Playground, Indie Playground Deux*
503 S. Front St. #101, Columbus, OH 43215
PH: 614-221-9923 FX: 614-227-0021
Tom Butler tbutler@cd101.com
www.cd101.com
Award winning Independent music shows.

WWSU *Wright State U.*
W022 Student Union, Dayton, OH 45435
PH: 937-775-5554 FX: 937-775-5553
www.wright.edu/studentorgs/wwsu

WXUT *U. Toledo*
2801 W. Bancroft, SU2515, Toledo, OH 43606
PH: 419-530-4172 FX: 419-530-2210
883wxut@gmail.com
www.wxut.com

WZIP *U. Akron*
Akron, OH 44325-1004
PH: 330-972-7105
wzip@uakron.edu
www.wzip.fm

Oklahoma

KRSC *Rogers State U.*
1701 W. Will Rogers Blvd. Claremore, OK 74017
PH: 918-343-7913
www.rsu.edu/krsc/fm

WIRE *U. Oklahoma*
860 Van Vleet Oval, Norman, OK 73019
PH: 405-325-0121 FX: 405-325-7565
wiremusic@ou.edu
wire48.ou.edu

Oregon

Guitar Shop Radio *KPSU*
PO Box 751-SD, Portland, OR 97207
PH: 503-725-5669
guitarshop@guitarshopradio.com
www.guitarshopradio.com
Presents Rock, Classical, Jazz and Blues guitarists.

KBVR *Oregon State U.*
210 Memorial Union E. Corvallis, OR 97331
PH: 541-737-6323 FX: 541-737-4545
oregonstate.edu/dept/kbvr

KEOL *Eastern Oregon State College*
1 University Blvd. La Grande, OR 97850
PH: 541-962-3698
keol@eou.edu
www3.eou.edu/~keol

KLC *Lewis and Clark College*
0615 SW Palatine Hill Rd. Portland, OR 97219
PH: 503-768-7104 FX: 503-768-7130
klc@lclark.edu
www.lclark.edu/~klc

KPSU *Portland State U.*
PO Box 751-SD, Portland, OR 97207
PH: 503-725-4071 FX: 503-725-4079
kpsumd@pdx.edu
www.kpsu.org

KRVM *Eugene*
2455 Willakenzie Rd. Eugene, OR 97401
PH: 800-285-2895
www.krvm.org

KSLC *Linfield College*
#A498 900 SE Baker St., McMinnville, OR 97128
PH: 503-883-2550 FX: 503-883-2665
kslc@linfield.edu
www.linfield.edu/kslc

KTEC
PO Box 2009, Klamath Falls, OR 97601
PH: 541-885-1840 FX: 541-885-1857
ktec@oit.edu
www.oit.edu/d/ktec

KWVA *U. Oregon*
PO Box 3157, Eugene, OR 97403
PH: 541-346-4091 FX: 541-346-0648
gladstone.uoregon.edu/~kwva

Pennsylvania

The Harrisburg Broadcast Network
223 Walnut St., Harrisburg, PA 17101
PH: 717-255-6545
info@hbnradio.org
www.hbnradio.org

Musician Showcase with Sherri Mullen
PO Box 177, Middletown, PA 17057
Sherri musicshowcase@sherrimullen.com
www.sherrimullen.com/musicshowcase
Attention ALL-INDIE artists!!!! Check it out! Get YOUR music heard!

WARC *Allegheny College*
520 N. Main St. Box C, Meadville, PA 16335
PH: 814-332-3376
warc@allegheny.edu
warc.allegheny.edu

WBUQ *Bloomsburg U.*
1250 McCormick Ctr. 400 E. 2nd St.,
Bloomsburg, PA 17815
PH: 570-389-4686 FX: 570-389-2718
orgs.bloomu.edu/wbuq

WCLH *Wilkes U.*
84 W. S. St., Wilkes Barre, PA 18766
PH: 570-408-2908 FX: 570-408-5908

WDCV *Dickinson College*
PO Box 1773, Carlisle, PA 17013
PH: 717-245-1444
wdcv@dickinson.edu
omega.dickinson.edu/~wdcv

WDIY
301 Broadway, Bethlehem, PA 18015
PH: 610-694-8100 FX: 610-954-9474
info@wdiyfm.org
www.wdiyfm.org

WDNR *Widener U.*
1 U. Pl. Chester, PA 19013
PH: 610-499-4000
wdnr895@mail.widener.edu
www.wdnr.com

WEHR *Penn State*
120 S. Burrowes St. Box 30, U. Park, PA 16801
PH: 814-865-0897
www.clubs.psu.edu/wehr

WERG *Gannon U.*
U. Square, Erie, PA 16541
PH: 814-871-5841
werg@gannon.edu
www.wergfm.com

WESS *East Stroudsburg U.*
200 Prospect St., E. Stroudsburg, PA 18301-2999
PH: 570-422-3512
www.esu.edu/wess

WFSE *Edinboro U. of Pennsylvania*
Edinboro, PA 16444
PH: 814-732-2888 FX: 814-732-2427
wfse@flashmail.com
piper.edinboro.edu/cwis/wfse

WHRC *Haverford College*
370 Lancaster Ave. Haverford, PA 19041
PH: 610-896-2920
www.whrcradio.com

WIUP *U. Pennsylvania*
121 Stouffer Hall, Indiana, PA 15705
PH: 724-357-5652
www.coe.iup.edu/wiupfm

WIXQ *Millersville U.*
Student Memorial Ctr. Millersville, PA 17551-0302
PH: 717-872-3333
music.director@wixq.com
www.wixq.com

WJRH *Lafayette College*
Farinon Center, PO Box 9473, Easton, PA 18042
PH: 610-330-5316 FX: 610-330-5318
wjrh@lafayette.edu
www.lafayette.edu/~wjrh

WKDU *Drexel U.*
3210 Chestnut St., Philadelphia, PA 19104
PH: 215-895-2580
musicdir@wkdu.org
www.wkdu.org

WKPS *Penn State U.*
125 HUB-Robeson Ctr. U. Park, PA 16802-6600
PH: 814-865-7983 FX: 814-865-2751
www.lion-radio.org

WKVR *Juniata College*
1005 Juniata College, Huntingdon, PA 16652
PH: 814-641-3341 FX: 814-643-4477
wkvr@juniata.edu
clubs.juniata.edu/wkvr

WLVC *Lebanon Valley College*
Box 244 College Ctr. Annville, PA 17003
PH: 717-867-6171
wlvc@lvc.edu

WLVR *Lehigh U.*
27 Memorial Dr. W. Bethlehem, PA 18015
PH: 610-758-3000
www.wlvr.org

WMSS *Middletown HS*
214 N. Race St., Middletown, PA 17057-2242
PH: 717-948-9136
www.wmssfm.com

WMUH *Muhlenberg College*
2400 Chew St., Allentown, PA 18104
PH: 484-664-3239 FX: 484-664-3539
wmuh@muhlenberg.edu
www.muhlenberg.edu/cultural/wmuh

WNTE *Mansfield U.*
PH: 570-662-4653
mustuweb.mnsfld.edu/wnte

WPTC *Pennsylvania College of Tech.*
1 College Ave. Williamsport, PA 17701
PH: 570-326-3761 x7214
wptc@pct.edu
www.pct.edu/wptc

WPTS *U. Pittsburgh*
411 William Pitt Union, Pittsburgh, PA 15260
PH: 412-648-7990 FX: 412-648-7988
wptsmusicdirector@hotmail.com
www.wpts.pitt.edu

WPUR *Philadelphia U.*
School House Lane, Philadelphia, PA 19144-5494
PH: 215-951-2728
wpur@philau.edu
orgs.philau.edu/wpur

WQHS *U. Pennsylvania*
3905 Spruce St., Philadelphia, PA 19104
PH: 215-898-3500
WQHS_programming@sharpsharpsharp.com
www.wqhs.org

WQSU *Susquehanna U.*
514 University Ave. Selinsgrove, PA 17870
PH: 570-372-4030
wqsufm@susqu.edu
www.susqu.edu/wqsu-fm/default.html

WRCT *Carnegie Mellon U.*
1 WRCT Plaza, 5000 Forbes Ave.
Pittsburgh, PA 15213
PH: 412-621-0728
info@wrct.org
www.wrct.org

WRLC *Lycoming College*
700 College Pl. Williamsport, PA 17701
PH: 570-321-4054
wrlc@lycoming.edu
www.lycoming.edu/orgs/wrlc

WRKC *Kings College*
133 N. Franklin St., Wilkes Barre, PA 18711
PH: 570-208-5931
wrkc@kings.edu
www.kings.edu/wrkc

WRSK *Slippery Rock U.*
C-211 U. Union, Slippery Rock, PA 16057
PH: 724-738-2931 FX: 724-738-2754
radiowrsk@hotmail.com
www.wrsk.org

WSRN *Swarthmore College*
500 College Ave. Swarthmore, PA 19081
PH: 610-328-8335
wsrn.swarthmore.edu

WSYC *Shippensburg U.*
3rd Fl. CUB, 1871 Old Main Dr.
Shippensburg, PA 17257
PH: 717-532-6006 FX: 717-477-4024
wsyc@wsyc.org
www.wsyc.org

WTGP *Thiel College*
75 College Ave. Greenville, PA 16125
PH: 724-589-2224
www.thiel.edu/studentlife/student%5Forg/wtgp

WUSR *U. Scranton*
800 Linden St., Scranton, PA 18510
PH: 570-941-7648 FX: 570-941-4628
academic.uofs.edu/organization/wusr

WVBU *Bucknell U.*
Box C-3956, Lewisburg, PA 17837
PH: 570-577-1174
www.orgs.bucknell.edu/wvbu

WVCS *California U.*
428 Hickory St., California, PA 15419
PH: 724-938-4330 FX: 724-938-5959

WVMW *Marywood U.*
PH: 570-348-6202
wvmwurbanmusicdirector@hotmail.com
www.marywood.edu/departments/commarts/wvmw.html

WVYC *York College*
Country Club Rd. York, PA 17405-7199
PH: 717-815-1311 FX: 717-849-1602
music@wvyc.org
www.ycp.edu/wvyc

WXLV *Lehigh Carbon College*
4525 Education Park Dr. Schnecksville, PA 18078
PH: 610-799-4141 FX: 610-799-1571
wxlv@hotmail.com
www.wxlvfm.com

WXPN *U. Pennsylvania*
3025 Walnut St., Philadelphia, PA 19104
PH: 215-898-6677 FX: 215-898-0707
wxpndesk@pobox.upenn.edu
xpn.org

WXVU *Villanova U.*
210 Dougherty Hall, 800 Lancaster Ave.
Villanova, PA 19085-1699
PH: 610-519-7200
wxvu.villanova.edu

WYBF *Cabrini College*
610 King of Prussia Rd. Radnor, PA 19087
PH: 610-902-8457
www.wybf.com

WYEP
2313 E. Carson St., Pittsburgh, PA 15203
PH: 412-381-9131
info@wyep.org
www.wyep.org

WZBT *Gettysburg College*
www.gettysburg.edu/college_life/osa/orgs/
media/WZBT

Rhode Island

WBRU *Brown U.*
88 Benevolent St., Providence, RI 02906-2046
PH: 401-272-9550 FX: 401-272-9278
wbru.com

WBSR *Brown U.*
PO Box 1930, Providence, RI 02912
PH: 401-863-9600
music.director@bsrlive.com
www.bsrlive.com

WDOM *Providence U.*
549 River Ave. Providence, RI 02918-0001
PH: 401-865-2460 FX: 401-865-2822

WRIU *U. Rhode Island*
326 Memorial Union, Kingston, RI 02881
PH: 401-874-4949 FX: 401-874-4349
fmpd@wriu.org
www.wriu.org/index2.html

WXHQ
PO Box 3541, Newport, RI 02840
PH: 401-847-1955
info@radionewport.org
www.radionewport.org

WXIN *Rhode Island College*
600 Mt. Pleasant Ave. Providence, RI 02908
PH: 401-456-8288 FX: 401-456-1988
music@ricradio.org
www.ricradio.org

South Carolina

WPLS *Furman U.*
3300 Poinsett Hwy. Greenville, SC 29613
PH: 864-294-3045
www-student.furman.edu/WPLS

WSSB *South Carolina State U.*
PO Box 7619, Orangeburg, SC 29117
PH: 803-536-8196
www.scsu.edu/Services/Radio

WUSC *U. South Carolina Columbia*
343 Russell House U. Union, 1400 Greene St.,
Columbia, SC 29208
PH: 803-777-7000
wuscmd@gwm.sc.edu
wusc.sc.edu

South Dakota

KAOR *U. South Dakota*
414 E. Clark St., Vermillion, SD 57069
PH: 605-677-5215
kaor@usd.edu
www.usd.edu/kaor

KAUR *Augustana College*
2001 S. Summit Ave. Sioux Falls, SD 57197
PH: 605-274-4386.
kaurfm89@hotmail.com
inst.augie.edu/~kaur

KBHU *Black Hills State U.*
1200 University St. #9000, Spearfish, SD 57799
PH: 605-642-6265
kbhufm@hotmail.com
www.bhsu.edu/studentlife/organizations/kbhu

KCFS *U. Sioux Falls*
1101 W. 22nd St., Sioux Falls, SD 57105
PH: 605-331-6691 FX: 605-331-6615
kcfs@usiouxfalls.edu
www.thecoo.edu/campus/radio

KTEQ *South Dakota School of
Mines and Tech.*
Old Gym, 501 E. St. Joseph St.,
Rapid City, SD 57701
PH: 605-394-2231
nmidzak@hotmail.com
www.hpcnet.org/kteq

Tennessee

The Songwriter Sessions *WPLN*
630 Mainstream Dr. Nashville, TN 37228-1204
PH: 615-760-2903 FX: 615-760-2904
songwritersessions@comcast.net
www.wpln.org/songwriters
Features 3 Indie guests each week.

WAWL *Chattanooga State Tech College*
4501 Amnicola Hwy. Chattanooga, TN 37406-1097
Don Hixson don.hixson@chattanoogastate.edu
www.chattanoogastate.edu/media_services/mewawl.
html

WEVL
PO Box 40952, Memphis, TN 38174
PH: 901-528-0560
wevl@wevl.org
wevl.org

WMTS *Middle Tennessee State U.*
Box 58, 1301 E. Main St., Murfreesboro, TN 37132
PH: 615-898-2636 FX: 615-898-5682
wmts@frank.mtsu.edu
www.mtsu.edu/~wmts

Writer's Block *WDVX*
PO Box 18157, Knoxville, TN 37928
PH: 865-494-2020
Karen E Reynolds writersblockinfo@aol.com
www.writersblockonline.com
*Created to bring attention to original artists that
deserve being listened to. Whether you like Blues,
Folk, Rock or Americana the show offers something
for every listener. With interviews, a new live
performance series and in studio performances.*

WRLT
401 Church St. Fl. 30, Nashville, TN 37219-2206
PH: 615-242-5600 FX: 615-523-2199
www.wrlt.com

WRVU *Vanderbilt U.*
PO Box 9100, Stn. B, Nashville, TN 37235
wrvu@vanderbilt.edu
wrvu.org

WTPL *Tusculum College*
PO Box 5036, 60 Shiloh Rd. Greeneville, TN 37743
PH: 1-800-729-0256 FX: 423-638-7166
wtpl@tusculum.edu
wtpl.tusculum.edu

WUTK *U. Tennessee*
P103 Andy Holt Tower, Knoxville, TN 37996-0333
PH: 865-974-2229 FX: 865-974-2814
www.wutkradio.com

WUTM *U. Tennessee*
220 Gooch Hall, U. St. Martin, TN 38238
PH: 731-587-7000
wutm@utm.edu
www.utm.edu/~wutm

WUTS *Sewanee U.*
735 U. Ave. Sewanee, TN 37383
PH: 931-598-1206
wuts@sewanee.edu
angels.sewanee.edu/wuts

WVCP *Volunteer State College*
1480 Nashville Pike, A-201,
Gallatin, TN 37066-3188
PH: 615-230-3618 FX: 615-230-4803
holly.nimmo@volstate.edu
www2.volstate.edu/wvcp

Texas

The All-You-Can-Eat Texas Music Cafe
TMC/Media Communications 3801 Campus Dr.
Waco, TX 76705
Paula Unger info@texasmusiccafe.com
www.texasmusiccafe.com
Variety music television and radio program.

The Indy Show *KACV*
PO Box 447, Amarillo, TX 79178 Attn: Shanna
kacvfm90@actx.edu
www.kacvfm.org
*It's two hours of music the big labels don't want you
to hear.*

KACV *Amarillo College*
PO Box 447, Amarillo, TX 79178
PH: 806-371-5222
kacvfm90@actx.edu
www.kacvfm.org

KANM *Texas A&M U.*
Student Services Bldg. 1236 TAMU, College Station, TX 77843-1236
PH: 979-862-2516 FX: 979-847-8854
md@kanm.tamu.edu
kanm.tamu.edu

KAZI
8906 Wall St. #203, Austin, TX 78754
PH: 512-836-9544 FX: 512-836-9563
kazimusic@sbcglobal.net
www.kazifm.com

KEOS *College Station*
PO Box 78, College Station, TX 77841
PH: 979-779-5367
John Roths jroths@mail.tca.net
www.keos.org

KFAN
PO Box 311, Fredericksburg, TX 78624
PH: 830-997-2197 FX: 830-997-2198
txradio@ktc.com
www.texasrebelradio.com

KGSR
8309 N. IH 35, Austin, TX 78753
PH: 512-832-4000 FX: 512-908-4902
www.kgsr.com

KNON
PO Box 710909, Dallas, TX 75371
PH: 214-828-9500 x234
md@knon.org
www.knon.org

KOOP
PO Box 2116, Austin, TX 78768-2116
PH: 512-472-1369 FX: 512-472-6149
koopradio@yahoo.com
www.koop.org

KPFT
419 Lovett Blvd. Houston, TX 77006
PH: 713-526-4000 FX: 713-526-5750
music@kpft.org
www.kpft.org

KSAU *Stephen F. Austin State U.*
1936 North St., Nacogdoches, TX 75961
PH: 936-468-4000

KSHU *Sam Houston State U.*
PO Box 2207, Huntsville, TX 77341
PH: 936-294-1111
www.kshu.org/Kshu-Radio

KTCU *Texas Christian U.*
Box 298020, Fort Worth, TX 76129
PH: 817-257-7631
ktcu@tcu.edu
www.ktcu.tcu.edu

KTRU *Rice U.*
PO Box 1892, Houston, TX 77251
PH: 713-348-5878
ktru@ktru.org
www.ktru.org

KTSW *Southwest Texas State U.*
601 U. Dr. Old Main Rm 106,
San Marcos, TX 78666
PH: 512-245-3485
ktswmusic@txstate.edu
www.ktsw.swt.edu

KTXT *Texas Tech*
PO Box 43081, Lubbock, TX 79409
PH: 806-742-3916 FX: 806-742-3906
ktxtfm@yahoo.com
www.ktxt.net

KUT/KUTX *U. Texas*
1 University Stn. A0704, Austin, TX 78712
PH: 512-471-1631 FX: 512-471-3700
music@kut.org
www.kut.org

KVRX *U. Texas/Austin*
PO Box D, Austin, TX 78713-7209
PH: 512-471-5106
kvrx@kvrx.org
www.kvrx.org

KWTS *West Texas A & M U.*
2501 4th Ave. Canyon, TX 79016-0001
PH: 806-651-2000
kwts@mail.wtamu.edu
www.wtamu.edu/kwts

Utah

KRCL
1971 W. N. Temple, Salt Lake City, UT 84116
PH: 801-359-9191 FX: 801-533-9136
musicdirector@krcl.org
www.krcl.org

KSUU *Southern Utah U.*
351 W Ctr. Cedar City, UT 84720
PH: 435-865-8224 FX: 435-865-8352
ksuu@suu.edu
www.suu.edu/ksuu

KWCR *Weber State U.*
Ogden, UT 84408
PH: 801-626-6450
organizations.weber.edu/kwcr

KZMU
PO Box 1076, 1734 Rocky Rd. Moab, UT 84532
PH: 435-259-8824 FX: 435-259-8763
music-director@kzmu.org
www.kzmu.org

Vermont

Download *WEQX*
PO Box 102.7 Manchester, VT 05254
PH: 802-362-4800 FX: 802-362-5555
www.weqx.com
3 Hours of the new music every Sunday night!

Early Warning *WBTZ*
PO Box 999, Burlington, VT 05402
PH: 877-893-2899
mailbag@999thebuzz.com
www.999thebuzz.com
New music from Buzz bands, new artists and unheard of bands.

WGDR *Goddard College*
PO Box 336, Plainfield, VT 05667
PH: 802-454-7667
wgdr@goddard.edu
www.wgdr.org

WJSC *Johnson State College*
337 College Hill, Johnson, VT 05656
PH: 802-635-1355 FX: 802-635-1202
WJSC907@hotmail.com
www.wjsc.findhere.org

WRMC *Middlebury College*
Middlebury, VT 05753
PH: 802-443-6324 FX: 802-443-5108
wrmc@wrmc.middlebury.edu
wrmc.middlebury.edu

WRUV *U. Vermont*
Billings Student Ctr. UVM Burlington, VT 05405
PH: 802-656-0796
wruv@zoo.uvm.edu
www.uvm.edu/~wruv

WVTC *Vermont Tech College*
Randolph Ctr., VT 05061-0500
PH: 800-442-8821
www.wvtc.net

WWPV *Saint Michael's College*
Box 274, Winooski Park, Colchester, VT 05439
PH: 802-654-2334 FX: 802-654-2336
wwpv@smcvt.edu
personalweb.smcvt.edu/wwpv

Virginia

WCWM *College of William and Mary*
Campus Ctr. PO Box 8793, Williamsburg, VA 23186
PH: 757-221-3287 FX: 757-221-2118
wcwmmd@wm.edu
www.wcwm.org

WDCE
Box 85, U. Richmond, VA 23173
PH: 804-289-8698 FX: 804-289-8996
wdce@richmond.edu
www.student.richmond.edu/~wdce

WEBR
2929 Eskridge Rd. #S, Fairfax, VA 22031
PH: 703-573.1090 FX: 703-573.1210
webr@fcac.org
www.fcac.org/webr/webr.htm

WEHC *Emory & Henry College*
PO Box 947, Emory, VA 24327-0947
PH: 276-944-4121
WEHC@ehc.edu
www.ehcweb.ehc.edu/masscomm/WEHC/WEHC_index.htm

WFFC *Ferrum College*
Ferrum, VA 24088
PH: 540-365-4483
wffc@ferrum.edu
www.ferrumradio.com

WGMU *George Mason U.*
4400 University Dr. MS4B7,
Fairfax, VA 22031-4444
PH: 703-993-2940 FX: 703-993-2941
music@wgmuradio.com
www.wgmuradio.com

WMWC *Mary Washington College*
Box WMWC, 1301 College Ave.
Fredericksburg, VA 22401
PH: 540-654-1152
station@wmwc.org
www.wmwc.org

WNRN
2250 Old Ivy Rd. #2, Charlottesville, VA 22903
PH: 434-971-4096 FX: 434-971-6562
wnrs@sbc.edu
wnrs.sbc.edu

WODU *Old Dominion U.*
2102 Webb Ctr. Norfolk, VA 23529
PH: 757-683-3441
music@woduradio.com
www.woduradio.com

WTJU *U. Virginia*
PO Box 400811, Charlottesville, VA 22904-4811
PH: 434-924-0885 FX: 434-924-8996
wtju@virginia.edu
wtju.net

WUVT *Virginia Tech*
350 Squires Student Ctr.
Blacksburg, VA 24061-0546
PH: 540-231-9880 FX: 208-692-5239
wuvtamfm@vt.edu
www.wuvt.vt.edu

WVAW *Virginia Wesleyan College*
1584 Wesleyan Dr. Virginia Beach, VA 23502
PH: 757-455-3200
dlbroomell@vwc.edu
facultystaff.vwc.edu/~comm/radio.htm

WVCW *Virginia Commonwealth U.*
920 W. Franklin St., Richmond, VA 23284
PH: 804-828-1057
wvcw@hotmail.com
www.wvcw.cc

WVRU *Radford U.*
PO Box 6973, Radford, VA 24142
PH: 540-831-6059. FX: 540-831-5893
wvru@radford.edu
www.runet.edu/~wvru

WXJM *James Madison U.*
MSC 6801 Seeger Hall, Harrisonburg, VA 22807
PH: 540-568-7939 FX: 540-568-7907
wxjm@jmu.edu
www.jmu.edu/wxjm

Washington

KAEP *Seattle*
PH: 509-444-6714
www.1057thepeak.COM

KAOS *Evergreen State College*
CAB 301 2700 Evergreen Pkwy.
Olympia, WA 98505
PH: 360-867-6896
kaos_music@evergreen.edu
www.kaosradio.org

KCCR *Pacific Lutheran U.*
Pacific Lutheran U. Tacoma, WA 98447
PH: 253-535-8860
kccr@plu.edu
www.plu.edu/~kccr

KCWU *Central Washington U.*
400 E. U. Way, Ellensburg, WA 98926-7594
PH: 509-963-2283
md@cwu.edu
www.881theburg.com

KEXP *U. Washington*
113 Dexter Ave. N. Seattle, WA 98109
PH: 206-520-5833 FX: 206-520-5899
info@kexp.org
www.kexp.org

KGRG *Green River College*
12401 SE 320th St., Auburn, WA 98092-3699
PH: 253-833-9111 ext.2192 FX: 253-288-3439
music@kgrg.com
www.kgrg.com

KNDD
1100 Olive Way #1650, Seattle, WA 98101
PH: 206-622-3251
www.1077theend.com
Rock format.

KOHO
7475 KOHO Place, Leavenworth, WA 98826
PH: 509-548-1011 FX: 509-548-3222
www.kohoradio.com

KSER
2623 Wetmore Ave. Everett, WA 98201
PH: 425-303-9070 FX: 425-303-9075
Ann McCoy annkser@aol.com
www.kser.org

KSUB *Seattle U.*
900 Broadway, Seattle, WA 98122-4340
PH: 206-296-6036
ksubmd@seattleu.edu
www.seattleu.edu/ksub

KSVR *Skagit Valley College*
2405 E. College Way, Mount Vernon, WA 98273
PH: 360-416-7711
mail@ksvr.org
www.ksvr.org

KUPS *U. Puget Sound*
1500 N. Warner, Tacoma, WA 98416
PH: 253-879-2974
kupsmusic@ups.edu
kups.ups.edu

KWCW *Whitman College*
200 E. Boyer Ave. Walla Walla, WA 99362.
PH: 509-527-5285
music@kwcw.net
www.kwcw.net

KWRS *Whitworth College*
300 W. Hawthorne Rd. Spokane, WA 99251
PH: 509-777-4575
kwrsmd@whitworth.edu
www.whitworth.edu/KWRS

KZUU *Washington State U.*
CUB Rm 311, Pullman, WA 99164
PH: 509-335-2208
md@kzuu.org
www.kzuu.org

Washington DC

WGTB *Georgetown U.*
432 Leavey Ctr. Washington, DC 20057
PH: 202-687-3702 FX: 202-687-8940
wgtb.music@gmail.com
georgetownradio.com

WRGW *George Washington U.*
800 21st St. NW #G02, Washington, DC 20052
PH: 202-994-7554 FX: 202-994-4551
wrgw@gwu.edu
www.gwradio.com

WVAU *American U.*
Mary Graydon Ctr. 256, 4400 Massachusetts Ave. NW, Washington, DC 20016
PH: 202-885-1212
www.wvau.org

West Virginia

WMUL *Marshall U.*
1 John Marshall Dr. Huntington, WV 25755-2635
PH: 304-696-2295 FX: 304-696-3232
wmul@marshall.edu
www.marshall.edu/wmul

WVWC *West Virginia Wesleyan*
Box 167, 59 College Ave.
Buckhannon, WV 26201-2999
PH: 304-473-8292
c92studio@wvwc.edu
www.wvwc.edu/c92

WWVU *West Virginia U.*
PO Box 6446, Morgantown, WV 26506-6446
PH: 304-293-3329 FX: 304293-7363
u92@mail.wvu.edu
www.wvu.edu/~u92

Wisconsin

KUWS *U. Wisconsin*
Belknap and Catlin, PO Box 2000,
Superior, WI 54880
PH: 715-394-8530 FX: 715-394-8404
kuwsmd@yahoo.com
kuws.fm

Power 100 *U. Wisconsin*
Menomonie, WI 54751
PH: 715-232-2332
power100@robword.com
www.power100.uwstout.edu

WBCR *Beloit College*
Box 39, 700 College St., Beloit, WI 53511
PH: 608-363-2402 FX: 608-363-2718
wbcr@www.beloit.edu
www.beloit.edu/~wbcr

WCCX *Carroll College*
100 N. E. Ave. Waukesha, WI 53186
PH: 262-524-7355
wccx@cc.edu
wccx.cc.edu

WLFM *Appleton*
Music Ctr. 420 E. College Ave. Appleton, WI 54911
PH: 920-832-6567 FX: 920-832-6904
wlfm@lawrence.edu
www.lawrence.edu/sorg/wlfm

WMMM
7601 Ganser Way, Madison, WI 53719
PH: 608-826-0077 FX: 608-826-1245
1055triplem@entercom.com
www.1055triplem.com

WMSE *Milwaukee School of Engineering*
1025 N. Broadway, Milwaukee, WI 53202
PH: 414-277-6942 FX: 414-277-7149
www.wmse.org

WMUR *Marquette U.*
1131 W. Wisconsin Ave. #421
Milwaukee, WI 53233
PH: 414-288-7541 FX: 414.288.0643
marquetteradio.mu.edu

WORT
118 S. Bedford St., Madison, WI 53703-2692
PH: 608-256-2001 FX: 608-256-3704
Sybil Augustine sybil@terracom.net
www.wort-fm.org
Our Friday afternoon show features interviews with Independent artists.

WRFW *U. Wisconsin*
306 N. Hall, 410 S. 3rd St., River Falls, WI 54022
PH: 715-425-3689 FX: 715-425-3532
music@pureradio887.com
www.uwrf.edu/wrfw

WRPN *Ripon College*
300 Seward St., Ripon, WI 54971
PH: 920-748-8147 FX: 920-748-7243
wrpnfm@yahoo.com
wrpnfm.homestead.com

WSRI *U. Wisconsin Eau Claire*
132 Davies Ctr. UWEC Eau Claire, WI 54702
PH: 715-836-5819

WSUM *U. Wisconsin Madison*
PO Box 260020, Madison, WI 53726-0020
PH: 265-WSUM
music@wsum.wisc.edu
wsum.wisc.edu

WSUP *U. Wisconsin Platteville*
42 Pioneer Tower, 1 U. Plaza, Platteville, WI 53818
PH: 608-342-1165 FX: 608-342-1290

WSUW *U. Wisconsin Whitewater*
1201 Anderson Library, Whitewater, WI 53190
PH: 262-472-1323 FX: 262-472-5029
wsuw@uww.edu
www.wsuw.org

WWSP *U. Wisconsin Steven's Point*
105 CAC Reserve St., Stevens Point, WI 54481
PH: 715- 346-4722
tbehn001@uwsp.edu
www.uwsp.edu/stuorg/wwsp

Canada

Canadian Satellite Radio (CSR)
Canada Trust Tower, BCE Place, #2300,
PO Box 222, 161 Bay St., Toronto, ON M5J 2S1
info@cdnsatrad.com
www.cdnsatrad.com
Formed to provide subscription-based satellite radio service to Canadians.

Creative Radio
431 Barton St. E., #3, Hamilton, ON L8L 2Y5
cradio@creativeradiocentral.com
www.creativeradiocentral.com
Get the exposure you deserve.

Galaxie - The Continuous Music Network
PO Box 3220, Stn. C, Ottawa, ON K1Y 1E4
PH: 877-425-2943 FX: 613-562-8889
information@galaxie.ca
www.galaxie.ca
We recognize Canadian talent by supporting the development and promotion of our home-grown musicians. Our "Rising Stars" program encourages Canada's up-and-coming stars.

radioKAOS
1067 Bruce Ave. Windsor, ON N9A 4Y1
PH: 519-984-2377
radio@radiokaos.com
radiokaos.com
Featuring many live shows and welcomes requests 24/7.

RadioMOI
#1-1555 Dublin Ave. Winnipeg, MB R3E 3M8
PH: 204-786-3994 FX: 204-783-5805
www.radiomoi.com
We accept submissions from Independent artists.

Soul Shine Indie Radio
20 Gilroy Dr. Scarborough, ON M1P 1Z9
PH: 416-751-3884
info@soulshine.ca
www.soulshine.ca
The best in Canadian Indie. If you'd like to be heard, contact us.

UMFM
48 Abell St. Studio 223, Toronto, ON M6J 3H2
radio@umfm.net
www.umfm.net
If you are a band, musician, DJ, producer or other musical artist, we would love to hear your music.

Alberta

Cellular Pirate Radio *Banff*
sin-d@radio90.fm
radio90.fm

CJSR *U. Alberta*
0-09 Students' Union Bldg. Edmonton, AB T6G 2J7
PH: 780-492-2577 x232 FX: 780-492-3121
Jay Hannley wormsnot@cjsr.com
www.cjsr.com

CJSW *U. Calgary*
#127 MacEwan Hall, Calgary, AB T2N 1N4
PH: 403-220-3902 FX: 403-289-8212
cjswfm@ucalgary.ca
www.cjsw.com

CKUA
10526 Jasper Ave. Edmonton, AB T5J 1Z7
PH: 780-428-7595 FX: 780-428-7624
music.director@ckua.org
www.ckua.org

CKUL *U. Lethbridge*
SU164, Student's Union Bldg. 4401 U. Dr. W.
Lethbridge, AB T1K 3M4
PH: 403-329-2335 FX: 403-394-3919
home.uleth.ca/~ckul

British Columbia

CFBX *U. College of the Cariboo*
900 McGill Rd. House 8 Kamloops, BC V2C 5N3
PH: 250-377-3988 FX: 250-372-5055
radio@cariboo.bc.ca
www.thex.ca

CFML *BC Inst. Tech*
Building SE-10, 3700 Willingdon Ave.
Burnaby, BC V5G 3H2
PH: 604-432-8510
allofus@radiocfml.com
www.radiocfml.com

CFRO
110-360 Columbia St., Vancouver, BC V6A 4J1
PH: 604-684-8494 x250
music-department@coopradio.org
www.coopradio.org

CFUR *UNBC*
3333 University Way, Prince George, BC V2N 4Z9
cfurradio@hotmail.com
www.cfur.ca

CFUV *U. Victoria*
PO Box 3035, Victoria, BC V8W 3P3
PH: 250-721-8702
musiccfuv@yahoo.ca
cfuv.uvic.ca

CHET
PO Box 214, Chetwynd, BC V0C 1J0
PH: 250-788-9452 FX: 250-788-9402
info@peacefm.ca
www.chetradio.com

CHLS
Box 2124, Lillooet, BC V0K 1V0
PH: 250-256-2457 FX: 250-256-7405
www.lss.sd74.bc.ca/chls

CHLY *Malaspina U. College*
#2-34 Victoria Rd. Nanaimo, BC V9R 5B8
PH: 250-716 3410
music@chly.ca
www.chly.ca

CITR
#233-6138 SUB Blvd. Vancouver, BC V6T 1Z1
PH: 604-822-8733 FX: 604-822-9364
citrmusic@club.ams.ubc.ca
www.citr.ca

CJLY
Box 767, Nelson, BC V1L 5R4
PH: 250-352-9600 FX: 250-352-9653
music@kootenaycoopradio.com
www.kics.bc.ca/kcr

CJSF *Simon Fraser U.*
TC 216, Burnaby, BC V5A 1S6
PH: 604-291-3727 FX: 604-291-3695
cjsfmusc@sfu.ca
www.cjsf.bc.ca

CKMO *Camosun College*
3100 Foul Bay Rd. Victoria, BC V8P 5J2
PH: 250-370-3658 FX: 250-370-3679
Doug Ozeroff doug@village900.ca
www.village900.ca

CVUE
PO Box 2288, Sechelt, BC V0N3A0
PH: 604-885-0800
cvue@dccnet.com
www.civu.net

Manitoba

CKUW *U. Winnipeg*
Rm 4CM11, 515 Portage Ave.
Winnipeg, MB R3B 2E9
PH: 204-786-9782 FX: 204-783-7080
ckuw@uwinnipeg.ca
www.ckuw.ca

Native Communications Inc.
1507 Inkster Blvd. Winnipeg, MB R2X 1R2
PH: 204-772-8255 FX: 204-779-5628
info@ncifm.com
www.ncifm.com
An Aboriginal service organization offering radio programming throughout Manitoba.

UMFM
Room 308 U. Ctr. Winnipeg, MB R3T 2N2
PH: 204-474-7027 PH: 204-269-1299
www.umfm.com

New Brunswick

CFMH *U. New Brunswick*
CFMH, PO Box 5050, Saint John, NB E2L 4L5
PH: 506-648-5667 FX: 506-648-5541
cfmh@unbsj.ca
www.unbsj.ca/cfmh

CHMA Mount Allison U.
Mount Allison U. Sackville, NB E4L 1E4
PH: 506-364-2269
chma_music@mta.ca
www.mta.ca/chma

CHSR U. New Brunswick
PO Box 4400, Fredericton, NB E3B 5A3
PH: 506-453-4985 FX: 506-453-4999
chsrmd@unb.ca
www.unb.ca/web/chsr

CJPN
715 rue Priestman, Fredericton, NB E3B 5W7
PH: 506-454-2576 FX: 506-453-3958
cjpn@nbnet.nb.ca
www.centre-sainte-anne.nb.ca/cjpn

CJSE
96 rue Providence, Shédiac, NB E4P 2M9
PH: 506-532-0080 FX: 506-532-0120
cjse@cjse.ca
www.cjse.ca

Newfoundland

CHMR Memorial U. Newfoundland
Box A-119 St. John's, NL A1C 5S7
PH: 709-737-4777 FX: 709-737-7688
chmr@mun.ca
www.mun.ca/chmr

The Songwriters CHMR
Box A-119 St. John's, NL A1C 5S7
PH: 709-744-3429
Terry Parsons t.parsons@roadrunner.nf.net
www.geocities.com/chmrshows
If you are a Singer/Songwriter and would like to be a guest, contact me.

Nova Scotia

CAPR
UCCB, PO Box 5300, Sydney, NS B1P 6L2
PH: 902-563-1475
info@capr.uccb.ns.ca
capr.uccb.ns.ca

CKDU
Dalhousie Stud. Union Bldg. 6136 U. Ave.
Halifax, NS B3H 4J2
PH: 902-494-6479
Jessica Whyte jessica@ckdu.ca
www.ckdu.ca

Ontario

C101.5 Mohawk College
135 Fennell Ave. W. PO Box 2034,
Hamilton, ON L8N 3T2
PH: 905-575-2175 FX: 905-575-2385
program.director@mohawkcollege.ca
www.mohawkcollege.ca/msa/cioi

CFFF Trent U.
715 George St., N. Peterborough, ON K9H 3T2
PH: 705-748-4761
info@trentradio.ca
www.trentu.ca/trentradio

CFMU McMaster U.
Student Ctr. Rm B119, Hamilton, ON L8S 4S4
PH: 905-525-9140 x22053
cfmumusic@msu.mcmaster.ca
cfmu.mcmaster.ca

CFRC Queens U.
Carruthers Hall Kingston, ON K7L 3N6
PH: 613-533-2121 FX: 613-533-6049
cfrc@ams.queensu.ca
www.cfrc.ca

CFRE
3359 Mississauga Rd. Mississauga, ON L5L 1C6
PH: 905-569-4712 FX: 905-569-4713
music@feelthevibe.org
www.cfreradio.com

CFRU U. Guelph
U.C. Level 2 Guelph, ON N1G 2W1
PH: 519-824-4120 x56919 FX: 519-763-9603
music@cfru.ca
www.cfru.ca

CHRW U. Western Ontario
Rm. 250, U. Community Ctr.
London, ON N6A 3K7
PH: 519-661-3601 FX: 519-661-3372
chrwmp@uwo.ca
www.chrwradio.com

CHRY York U.
4700 Keele St. Rm 413, Student Ctr.
Toronto, ON M3J 1P3
PH: 416-736-5145
chry@yorku.ca
www.yorku.ca/chry

CHUO U. Ottawa
372 Rideau St. #201, Ottawa, ON K1N 1G7
PH: 613-562-5965 FX: 613-562-5969
music@chuo.fm
www.chuo.fm

CIUT U. Toronto
91 St. George St., Toronto, ON M5S 2E8
PH: 416-978-0909 x214 FX: 416-946-7004
Ron Burd r_burd@ciut.fm
www.ciut.fm

CJAM U. Windsor
401 Sunset Ave. Windsor, ON N9B 3P4
PH: 519-253-3000 ext.2527 FX: 519-971-3605
progcjam@uwindsor.ca
www.uwindsor.ca/cjam

CJLX Loyalist College
PO Box 4200, Belleville, ON K8N 5B9
PH: 613-966-0923 FX: 613-966-1993
cjlx@loyalistc.on.ca
cjlx.loyalistc.on.ca

CKCU Carleton U.
Rm 517 U. Center, 1125 Colonel By Dr.
Ottawa, ON K1S 5B6
PH: 613-520-2898
music@ckcufm.com
www.ckcufm.com

CKDJ Algonquin College
PH: 613-727-4723 x7740
www.algonquincollege.com/ckdj

CKLN Ryerson
380 Victoria St., Toronto, ON M5B 1W7
PH: 416-595-1477
music@ckln.fm
www.ckln.fm

CKLU Laurentian U.
935 Ramsey Lake Rd. Sudbury, ON P3E 2C6
PH: 705-673-6538 FX: 705-675-4878
music@cklu.ca
www.cklu.ca

CKMS U. Waterloo
200 University Ave. W. Waterloo, ON N2L 3G1
PH: 519-886-2567 FX: 519-884-3530
ckmsfm@web.ca
watserv1.uwaterloo.ca:80/~ckmsinfo

CKRG Glendon College
2275 Bayview Ave. Toronto, ON M4N 3M6
PH: 416-487-6739
ckrg.glendon.yorku.ca

CKON Akwesasne Mohawk Nation Radio
PO Box 1496, Cornwall, ON K6H 5V5
PH: 613-575-2100 FX: 613-575-2566
ckon@ckonfm.com
www.cnwl.igs.net/~ckon

CKVI Kingston Collegiate
235 Frontenac St., Kingston, ON K7L 3S7
PH: 613-544-7864 FX: 613-544-8795
www.thecave.ca

CKWR (YOUR FM)
375 U. Ave. E. Waterloo, ON N2K 3M7
PH: 519-886-9870
general@yourfm.ca
www.yourfm.ca

Indie Hour CFNY
1 Dundas St. W. #1600 Toronto, ON M5G 1Z3
PH: 416-408-3343 FX: 416-847-3300
Dave Bookman INDIEHOUR@edge.ca
www.edge102.com/station/sp_indie_hour.cfm
*We do not accept CDs anymore. Send us **one** MP3 for the show.*

Krankit Radio Paris
www.krankit.com

Off the Beaten Track CKCU
Rm 517 U. Center, 1125 Colonel By Dr.
Ottawa, ON K1S 5B6
PH: 613-520-2898
info@ckcufm.com
Far reaching Underground Rock based, general music show with an emphasis on "organic" sounds.

Radio Laurier
3rd Fl. Fred Nichols Campus Ctr. WLU, 75
University Ave. W., Waterloo, ON N2L 3C5
PH: 519-884-0710 x2192
info@radiolaurier.com
www.radiolaurier.com

Spirit Live Radio Ryerson Polytechnic U.
350 Victoria St., Toronto, ON M5B 2K3
PH: 416-979-8151 FX: 416-979-5246
spiritliveradio@yahoo.com
www.spiritlive.net

Quebec

CFAK U. Sherbrooke
2500, boul. de l'Université,
Sherbrooke, QC J1K 2R1
PH: 819-821-8000 poste 2693 FX: 819-821-7930
musique@cfak.qc.ca
www.cfak.qc.ca

CFLX
67, rue Wellington nord, Sherbrooke, QC J1H 5A9
PH: 819-566-2787 FX: 819-566-7331
cflx@cflx.qc.ca
www.cflx.qc.ca

CFOU
3351, boul. des Forges,
Trois-Rivières, QC G9A 5H7
PH: 819-376-5184 FX: 819-376-5239
www.cfoufm.com

CHAA
91, rue St. Jean, Longueuil, QC J4H 2W8
PH: 450-646-6800 FX: 450-646-7378
info@fm1033.ca
www.fm1033.ca

CHGA
163 Laurier, Maniwaki, QC J9E 2K6
PH: 1-819-449-3959 FX: 819-449-7331
www.chga.qc.ca

CHYZ *U. Laval*
Local 0236, Pavillon Pollack, QC G1K 7P4
PH: 418-656-2131 FX: 418-656-2365
chyz-fm@public.ulaval.ca
www.chyz.qc.ca

CIBL
1691, boul Pie IX, Montréal, QC H1V 2C3
PH: 514-526-2581 FX: 514-526-3583
www.cibl.cam.org

CISM *U. de Montréal*
2332 Edouard Montpetit, C-1509 C.P. 6128,
Montréal, QC H3C 3J7
PH: 514-343-CISM FX: 514-343-2418
musique@cam.org
www.cismfm.qc.ca

CJLO
7141 Sherbrooke St. Ouest, #CC-430,
Montreal, QC H4B 1R6
PH: 514-848-8663 FX: 514-848-7450
program@cjlo.com
www.cjlo.com

CJMQ *Bishops U.*
Box 2135, Lennoxville, QC J1M 1Z7
PH: 819-822-9600 ext. 2689
cjmq@ubishops.ca
www.cjmq.uni.cc

CKRL *Québec City*
405, 3ᵉ Ave. Québec City, QC G1L 2W2
PH: 418-640-2575 FX: 418-640-1588
studio@ckrl.qc.ca
www.ckrl.qc.ca

CKUT *McGill U.*
3647 U. St., Montreal, QC H3A 2B3
PH: 514-398-6787 FX: 514-398-8261
music@ckut.ca
www.ckut.ca

Muzik Paradise
C.P. 151, Bromont, QC J2L 1A9
info@muzikparadise.org
www.muzikparadise.org
La radio internet du top chrétien Francophone!

Saskatchewan

CFCR
PO Box 7544, Saskatoon, SK S7K 4L4
PH: 306-664-6678 FX: 306-933-0038
cfcr@cfcr.ca
www.cfcr.ca

Six Strings & A Million Possibilities
c/o Bob Evans, PO Box 334 Stn. Main,
Regina, SK S4P 3A1
SixStrings@BobEvansGuitar.com
www.bobevansguitar.com/six_strings.html
I'm open to almost anything where the guitar is the featured instrument.

Mexico

Eufonia Radio
Postal 2146 Sucursal de Correos "J" 64841
Monterrey, N.L. México
PH: 5281-8387-0665
programa@eufonia.net
www.eufonia.net
2hrs weekly of Indie Rock and other non commercial genres.

XHUG *Radio U. de Guadalajara*
#976, PISO 12A.P. 4-29 C.P. 44100 Guadalajara,
Jalisco, México
PH: 0133-3825-6000 FX: 0133-3826-1848
server.radio.udg.mx

South America

New Releases by Murilo de Oliveira
Exclusiva FM
Rua Gonçalves Dias, 89/804 - Centro, 20050-030,
Rio de Janeiro - RJ, Brazil
Murilo de Oliveira exclusiva.fm@br.inter.net
www.exclusiva979.com.br
We welcome all genres of music. Contact me for submission details.

Europe

Austria

FM4 *Linz U.*
PH: 0800-226-996 FX: 01-50101-18900
fm4.orf.at

Freier Rundfunk Oberösterreich
GmbH Kirchengasse 4 A-4040 Linz, Austria
PH: 43-732-71-72-77 FX: 43-732-71-72-77 -155
fro@fro.at
www.fro.at

Orange 94.0 *Free Radio in Wien*
1090 Wien, Schubertgasse 10, Austria
PH: 43-1-3190999 FX: 43-1-3190999-14
www.orange.or.at

Radio 1476
ORF, 1476 Argentinierstr. 30a A-1040 Wien, Austria
1476@orf.at
1476.orf.at

UniRadio Salzburg *U. Salzburg*
Rudolfskai 42, 5020 Salzburg, Austria
www.unitv.sbg.ac.at/uniradio/mambo

Belgium

Belgischer Rundfunk
11 4700 Eupen, Belgium
PH: 087-591111 FX: 087-591199
musik@brf.be
www.brf.be

FM Brussel
Eugène Flageyplein 18, Bus 18 - 1050 Elsene,
Belgium
PH: 02-800-0-808 FX: 02-800-0-809
info@fmbrussel.be
www.fmbrussel.be

Radio 1
Auguste Reyerslaan 52 1043, Brussels, Belgium
PH: 02-741-38-93-kantooruren FX: 02-736-57-86
info@radio1.be
www.radio1.be

Radio 101
PO Box 2, B-4851 Gemmenich, Belgium
radio101.de

Radio 21
Blvd. Reyers, 52 à 1044 Bruxelles, Belgium
PH: 02-737-27-69
mima@rtbf.be
www2.rtbf.be/radio21

Radio Campus Bruxelles
cp 166/21 22 av. paul héger 1000 Bruxelles,
Belgium
PH: 32-2-640-87-17 FX: 32-2-650-34-63
rcampus@ulb.ac.be
radiocampus.ulb.ac.be

Radio Canteclaer
Gentsesteenweg 204 B-9800 Deinze, Belgium
PH: 32-9-380-80-90 FX: 32-9-386-86-33
info@canteclaer.be
www.canteclaer.be

Radio Panik
Caserne Prince Baudouin Place Dailly, 4 1030
Bruxelles, Belgium
cp@radiopanik.org
www.radiopanik.org

Radio Scorpio
Meiersstraat 5, 3000 Leuven, Belgium
PH: 32-016-222-300
demo@radioscorpio.com
www.radioscorpio.com

RUN
OREFUNDP ASBL, Rue du Séminaire, 22/15 5000
Namur, Belgium
run@fundp.ac.be
www.run.be

Urgent FM *U. Ghent*
Sint-Pietersnieuwstraat 43, 9000 Gent, Belgium
muziek@urgent.fm
urgent.fm

Czech Republic

THC Radio
submit@thcradio.net
www.thcradio.net

Denmark

Station 10
Stationsvej 10 9400 Nørresundby, Denmark
PH: 98-19-47-00
station10@station10.dk
www.station10.dk

Universitetsradioen Nalle Kirkväg
Krystalgade 14, 1172 København K, Denmark
PH: 35-32-39-39 FX: 35-32-39-38
info@universitetsradioen.dk
www.uradio.ku.dk

Radio Østsjælland
Vinkældertorvet 2A Postboks 34 4640 Fakse, Denmark
PH: 56-71-30-03 FX: 56-71-39-51
fakse@lokalradio.dk
www.lokalradio.dk

Finland

Radio Extrem
Helsingfors Radio X3M pb 13 00024 YLE, Finland
PH: 358-9-14801
www.yle.fi/extrem

Radio Robin Hood
Itäinen Rantakatu 64 20810 TURKU, Finland
PH: 02-2773-666 FX: 02-2500-905
info@radiorobinhood.fi
www.radiorobinhood.fi/rrh

France

Alternantes FM
19, rue de Nancy, BP 31 605, 44 316 Nantes cedex 3, France
PH: 02-40-93-26-62 FX: 02-40-93-04-98
alternantes@presse-radio.com
www.alternantesfm.net

Le Biplan
19 rue colbert 59000 LILLE, France
PH: 33-03-20-420-227
lebiplan.programmation@wanadoo.fr
www.lebiplan.org

Canal B Rennes
BP 7147, 35171 BRUZ Cédcx, France
PH: 33-0-2-99-52-77-66 FX: 33-0-2-99-05-39-07
canalb@rennet.org
www.rennet.org/canalb

Chameleons
Radio Beton, 90, avenue Maginot, 37100 TOURS, France
PH: 02-47-51-03-83
www.radiobeton.com
Emission Indie pop-Rock.

Coloriage
Ferme de la Vendue 21500 Fain les Moutiers, France
03 80 96 40 76 FX:03 80 96 34 99
coloriage@free.fr
coloriage.free.fr

Couleur 3 Lausanne
Av. du Temple 40, case postale 78, CH-1010 Lausanne, France
PH: +41-21-318-15-42
la.radio@couleur3.ch
www.couleur3.ch

C'rock radio
BP 231, 38201 Vienne cedex, France
PH: 04-74-53-28-91 FX: 04-74-31-59-07
prog@crockradio.com
www.crockradio.com

Dig It! Radio Show *Canal Sud*
32, rue Pharaon, 31000 Toulouse, France
FX: 05-61-14-06-28
DJ Dildas Cosperec digitfanzine@chez.com
www.chez.com/digitfanzine
Globally popular Rock 'n' Roll radio show.

L'Eko des Garrigues
BP5555 34070 Montpellier Cedex 3, France
PH: 04-67-70-80-86 FX: 04-67-70-93-65
info@ekodesgarrigues.com
www.ekodesgarrigues.com

FMR
9 bd. Minimes, 31200 Toulouse, France
PH: 05-61-58-35-12 FX: 05-61-58-37-04
raskal@radio-fmr.net
www.radio-fmr.net

JetFM
11 rue de Dijon 44800 St., Herblain, France
PH: 0240586363
contact@jetfm.asso.fr
www.jetfm.asso.fr

Ocean Radio
2, place du Foirail 81220 St Paul Cap de Joux, France
eole@ocean-music.com
www.ocean-music.com

Planet Claire
denis@planet-claire.org
planet-claire.org

Planet of Sound
planet_of_sound@lemoneyes-radio.com
www.lemoneyes-radio.com/music

Pop Corn
Radio Beton, 90, avenue Maginot, 37100 TOURS, France
PH: 02-47-51-03-83
franck7@hotmail.com
www.popcornweb.com

Radio 666
BP 666, 14203 Hérouville Saint Clair Cedex, France
PH: 02-3194-6666
radio666@radio666.com
www.radio666.com

Radio Alpine Meilleure
Rue du Sénateur Bonniard 05 200 Embrun, France
PH: 04-92-43-37-38 FX: 04-92-43-54-43
ram05@wanadoo.fr
perso.wanadoo.fr/jb.oury/RAM.htm

Radio Beton
90, avenue Maginot, 37100 TOURS, France
PH: 02-47-51-03-83
info@radiobeton.com
www.radiobeton.com

Radio Campus
16 rue degeorges 63000 CLERMONT-FD, France
PH: 04-73-140-158
clermont@radiocampus.org
clermont.radio-campus.org

Radio Campus Grenoble
av. Centrale Domaine universitaire 38402 Saint Martin d'Hères cedex, France
PH: 04-56-52-85-20
grenoble@radio-campus.org
www.grenoble.radio-campus.org

Radio Campus Lille
campus@campuslille.com
www.campuslille.com

Radio Campus Orléans
4, rue de Tours 45072 ORLEANS La Source, France
PH: 02-38-64-00-42
www.orleans.radio-campus.org

Radio Campus
50, rue des Tournelles, 75 003 Paris, France
PH: 01-49-96-65-45
musique@radiocampusparis.org
www.radiocampusparis.org

Radio Canal Sud
40, rue alfred duméril 31400 Toulouse, France
PH: 05-61-25-95-43
canalsud@canalsud.net
www.canalsud.net

Radio Canut
24, rue Sergent Blandan 1er arrdt - BP 1101 - 69201 LYON Cedex, France
PH: 04-78-39-18-15 FX: 04-78-29-26-00
radio@radiocanut.org
regardeavue.com/radiocanut

Radio Dio
BP 51, 42002 St-Etienne Cédex, France
PH: 0477250594 FX: 0477417916
radiodio.org

Radio En Construction
BP124, 67069 Strasbourg Cedex, France
PH: 33-0-3-88-600-915
contact@radioenconstruction.com
www.recfm.com

Radio Grenouille
La Friche la Belle de Mai 23, Rue Guibal 13003 Marseille, France
PH: 04-95-04-95-15 FX: 04-95-04-95-00
radio.grenouille@lafriche.org
www.lafriche.org/grenouille

Radio Grésivaudan
94, rue du Brocey, 38920 CROLLES, France
PH: 04-76-08-91-91
webmaster@radio-gresivaudan.org
www.radio-gresivaudan.org

Radio Pluriel
BP 106 69801 Saint-Priest Cedex, France
PH: 04-78-21-83-49 FX: 04-78-21-46-58
prog@plurielfm.org
www.plurielfm.org

Radio Primitive
13, rue. Flodoard BP 2169 51081 REIMS Cedex, France
PH: 33-03-26-02-33-74 FX: 33-03-26-02-68-30
radio.primitive@wanadoo.fr
perso.wanadoo.fr/primitive

Radio Pulsar
15, rue. des Feuillants 86035 Poitiers Cedex, France
PH: 05-49-88-33-04 FX: 05-49-88-07-99
info@radio-pulsar.org
www.radio-pulsar.org

RadioCeros
126 rue Oberkampf, 75011 Paris, France
PH: 33-0-1-45-79-12-70 FX: 33-0-1-45-79-12-77
rhino@radioceros.com
www.radioceros.com

RCT
BP 2001-69603 Villeurbanne Cedex, France
PH: 33-04-78-89-59-48 FX: 33-04-72-44-34-42
liberte@radio-rct.com
www.radio-rct.com

RCV
41 Bis Bd Vauban, 59046 Lille Cedex, France
PH: 33-03-20-54-12-11 FX: 33-03-20-30-40-51
rcv.lille@wanadoo.fr
www.rcv-lille.com

Sauvagine
3 rue Ferbos 33800 Bordeaux, France
PH: 05-56-92-98-99 FX: 05-56-91-95-96
contact@radio-sauvagine.com
www.radio-sauvagine.com

Germany

ALPHAbeat Radio
c/o DJ Ottic Westerwaldstr.35 D-53489 Sinzig, Germany
PH: 49-2642-43385 FX: 49-30-484983193
info@ottic.de
www.ottic.de

Bayerischer Rundfunk
Rundfunkplatz 1 80300 München, Germany
PH: (089) 59-00-01
info@br-online.de
www.br-online.de

Campus-Welle Köln
Kölncampus-Das Kölner Hochschulradio Albertus-Magnus-Platz 50923 Köln, Germany
PH: 0221-470-4831 FX: 0221-470-6712
musik@koelncampus.com
www.koelncampus.com

coloRadio
Jordanstraße 5 01099 Dresden, Germany
PH: 0351-317-9227 FX: 0351-317-9226
coloradio@freie-radios.de
www.freie-radios.de/coloradio

Eins live
WDR, 50600 Köln, Germany
PH: 0180-5678-111
einslive@wdr.de
www.einslive.de

elDOradio!
Martin-Schmeißer-Weg 13 44227 Dortmund, Germany
PH: 0231-79-49-815 FX: 0231-79-49-816
musik@elDOradio.de
www.eldoradio.de

Freies Radio für
Rieckestr. 24 70190 Stuttgart, Germany
PH: 0711-64-00-444 FX: 0711-64-00-443
info@freies-radio.de
www.freies-radio.de

FRITZ Radio
Postfach 90 9000 14439 Potsdam, Germany
PH: 0331-70-97-110 FX: 0331-731-39-83
fritz@fritz.de
www.fritz.de

HSF Studentenradio
e.V. Postfach 100 565 D-98684 Ilmenau, Germany
PH: 49-3677-694-222 FX: 49-3677-694-216
info@radio-hsf.de
www.hsf.tu-ilmenau.de

ju: N ai
UNI, radio über Otto-von-Guericke-Universität PF 4120 39016 Magdeburg, Germany
uni-radio@uni-magdeburg.de
www.uni-magdeburg.de/uniradio

Kontrast Radio
www.kontrastradio.net
Berlin's finest Alternative radio. Does reviews too.

Lord Litter's Radio Show
LordLitter@LordLitter.de
www.LordLitter.de
www.CyberStormRadio.com - the weekly show
www.radiomarabu.de - the German on demand show
Indie bands-submit your music for worldwide airplay.

M945
Schwere-Reiter-Str. 35 Gebäude 40a 80797 München, Germany
PH: 089-360-388-0 FX: 089-360-388-59
m945@afk.de
m945.afk.de/m

NiceSurf Radio
GmbH Vahrenwalder Strasse 205 30165 Hannover, Germany
PH: 05-11- 37-29-44 FX: 05-11-37-29-45
www.NiceSurf.de

Oldenburg Eins
Bahnhofstr.11 26 122 Oldenburg, Germany
PH: 0441 21-888-44 FX: 0441 21-888-40
info@oeins.de
www.oeins.de

POPSCENE with J*A*L*A*L
Elisabethstr.120, 28217 Bremen, Germany
info@popscenewithjalal.com
www.popscenewithjalal.com
One of the leading Indie radio shows in Europe.

QUERFUNK
Steinstraße 23 76133 Karlsruhe, Germany
PH: 0721 38-50-30 FX: 0721 38-50-20
info@querfunk.de
www.querfunk.de

Radio 0815
PH: 0170/5246953 FX: 09122/887400
Tomo Masic tomo@radio-0815.de
www.radio-0815.de

Radio 19/4
Vennheideweg 49 D-48165 Münster, Germany
PH: 0049-251-13-66-855
andy@radio19-4.de
www.radio19-4.de

Radio Blau
V.i.S.d.P Paul-Gruner-StraBe 62 04107 Leipzig, Germany
PH: 0341-301-00-97 FX: 0341-301-00-07
musik@radioblau.de
www.radioblau.de

Radio C.T.
Ruhr-Universität 44780 Bochum, Germany
PH: 0234-971-90-80 FX: 0234-971-90-82
info@radioct.de
www.radioct.de

Radio Dreyeckland
Betriebs GmbH Adlerstr. .12, D - 79098 Freiburg, Germany
PH: 0761-31028 FX: 0761-31868
verwaltung@rdl.de
www.rdl.de

Radio Flora
Zur Bettfedernfabrik 1 30451 Hannover, Germany
PH: 0511-219-79-0 FX: 0511-219-79-19
postbox@radioflora.apc.de
radioflora.apc.de

Radio Mittweida
Leisniger Straße 9, 09648 Mittweida, Germany
programm@radio-mittweida.de
www.radio-mittweida.de
Our format is rooted in Hot AC with a touch (big touch!) of Alternative and Rock music.

Radio Neckarburg
August-Schuhmacher-Straße 10, 78664 Eschbronn-Mariazell, Germany
PH: 07403-8000 FX: 07403-8002
info@radio-neckarburg.de
www.radio-neckarburg.de

Radio Rheinwelle
Postfach 4920 65039 Wiesbaden, Germany
PH: 0611-609-9333
info@radio-rheinwelle.de
www.radio-rheinwelle.de

Radio SIRUP
AVMZ Adolf-Reichwein-Str.2 57068 Siegen, Germany
PH: 0271-2-383-666 FX: 0271-740-25-26
info@radio-sirup.de
sirup.avmz.uni-siegen.de

Radio T
Karl-Liebknecht-Str. 19 09111 Chemnitz, Germany
PH: 0371-350-235 FX: 0371-350-234
info@radiot.de
www.radiot.de

RadioActiv
Rhein-Neckar e.V.U. Mannheim Schloß, Postfach 144 68131 Mannheim, Germany
PH: 0621-1-81-18-11 FX: 0621-1-81-18-12
musikred@radioaktiv.org
www.radioaktiv.org

recordcaster
Mahnkopfweg 12-14 13595 Berlin, Germany
PH: 49-30-362-85-422 FX: 49-30-362-85-421
mail@recordcaster.de
www.recordcaster.de

uniRadio
Malteser Str. 74-100/ Haus M 12249 Berlin, Germany
PH: 030-841-727-101 FX: 030-841-727-109
redaktion@uniradio.de
www.uniradio.de

Uniwelle Tübingen
Gmelinstr. 6/1 72076 Tübingen, Germany
PH: 07071-297-7688 FX: 07071-29-5881
uniradio@uni-tuebingen.de
www.uni-tuebingen.de/uniradio

YOU FM
60222 Frankfurt a.M. Germany
PH: 069-55-30-40 FX: 069-55-88-06
www.youfm.de

Greece

ERA Aigaiou
www.aegean.gr/era_aegean

Hot Station
info@hotstation.gr
www.hotstation.gr

Rhodes Radio Rhodes U.
PH: 0241-99090
radio@Rhodes.aegean.gr
www.rhodes.aegean.gr/radio.htm

Hungary

Tilos Rádió
Tilos Rádió, 1462 Budapest, Pf: 601, Hungary
radio@tilos.hu
tilos.hu

Italy

Kristall Radio
Via Ludovico Il Moro 165 - 20142 Milano, Italy
PH: 0039-02-8912 FX: 0039-02-0212
info@kristallradio.it
www.kristallradio.it

Radio Beckwith
PH: 0121-954194
redazione@rbe.it
web.tiscalinet.it/rbeonline

Radio Onda Rossa
Via dei Volsci 56 00185 Rome, Italy
PH: 06-491-750 FX: 06-446-3616
www.ondarossa.info

Luxembourg

Eldoradio Dortmund
B.P. 1344 L-1013, Luxembourg
PH: 352-409-509-1 FX: 352-409-509-509
eldoradio@eldoradio.lu
www.eldoradio.lu

Radio ARA
3, rue principale, L-9183 Schlindermanderscheid, Luxembourg
Greg Sylvester radioara@mindless.com
www.ara.lu

The Netherlands

3FM
Postbus 26444 1202 JJ Hilversum, The Netherlands
3fm.omroep.nl

B92
Bulevar AVNOJ-a 64 11000 Beograd, The Netherlands
PH: 381-11-301-2000 FX: 381-11-301-2001
www.b92.net

PopScene Radio
PH: 31-0-6-5264-1135
Nicole Blommers nicole@popscene.nl
www.popscene.nl
Dutch Indie radio show.

Radio Netherlands
Box 222, 1200 JG Hilversum, The Netherlands
PH: 31-35-672-4211 FX: 31-35-672-4239
www.rnw.nl

Radio Patapoe
patapoe@freeteam.nl
freeteam.nl/patapoe

A Shake Of Music
Vreelust 26, 2804 LJ Gouda, The Netherlands
Sjaak Sekeris sjajol@planet.nl
www.realrootscafe.com/shakeofmusic.html
A lot of different styles like Pop, R&B, Country-Rock, Symphonic Rock, Soul, Gospel, Americana, Singer-Songwriter, Roots, Cajun and Swamp.

Stadsomroep
Dullertstraat 27 - 6828 HJ Arnhem, The Netherlands
PH: 026-442-2282 FX: 026-443-1547
radio@stadsomroeparnhem.nl
www.stadsomroeparnhem.nl

WFM
Omroepstichting Milbergen Postbus 111 6573 ZK Beek Ubbergen, The Netherlands
PH: 0481-434-343 FX: 0481-434-444
wfmradio@hetnet.nl
www.wfmradio.nl

Zeilsteen Radio
Bosma Multimedia Skoallestrjitte 11 9125ED Oostrum, The Netherlands
PH: 0519-292-980
info@bosma-multimedia.nl
www.zeilsteen.com

Norway

Independentradio.no
info@independentradio.no
www.independentradio.no
Listen to the best from the Norwegian independent scene.

Radio Nova
Slemdalsveien 7 Postboks 1162 Blindern 0317 Oslo, Norway
PH: 22-85-70-00 FX: 22-84-44-194
nova@radionova.no
www.radionova.no

Radio Tango
Norge AS Nedre Vaskegang 6 0186 Oslo, Norway
PH: 22-99-94-00 FX: 22-99-94-10
musikk@radiotango.no
www.radiotango.no

Studentradioen i Bergen
Parkveien 1, 5007 Bergen, Norway
PH: 47-55-54-51-29 FX: 47-55-32-84-05
studentradioen.uib.no

Studentradio'n i Trondheim
Elgesetergt. 1 7030 Trondheim, Norway
PH: 47-73-51-88-88 FX: 47-73-89-96-69
www.studentradion.no/rogue/index.php

Poland

Radio Akademickie
INDEX ul. Podgórna 50 DS 1 65-246 Zielona Góra, Poland
PH: 0-68-328-22-25 FX: 0-68-324-55-93
radio@index.zgora.pl
www.index.zgora.pl

Radio Sfera
U. Mikolaja Kopernika Rozglosnia U. Gagarina 17, 87-100 Torun', Poland
PH: 48-56-611-49-00 FX: 48-56-611-45-84
redakcja@sfera.umk.pl
www.sfera.umk.pl

Portugal

Rádio Universitária do Minho
apartado 3061, 4711-906 braga, Portugal
PH: 351-253-200-630
rum@rum.pt
www.rum.pt

Tráfico Alternativo Viriato FM
Rua Prof. Aristides Amorim Girão Lote 70, 2°dir, Moinho de vento, 3500-041 Viseu, Portugal
Nuno Polónio trafico@viriatofm.com
www.viriatofm.com
Special attention on international independent releases, new bands and live acts.

Viriato FM
Rua Prof. Aristides Amorim Girão Lote 70, 2°dir, Moinho de vento, 3500-041 Viseu, Portugal
www.viriatofm.com

Romania

Radio DELTA RFI
OP 32 - CP 108, Bucuresti, Romania
PH: 021-223-19-20 FX: 021-229-19-24
deltarfi@deltarfi.ro
www.deltarfi.ro

Russia

Special Radio
PO Box 424, Moscow, 119017, Russia
admin@specialradio.ru
www.specialradio.ru

Serbia

Alternatives Show Radio 021
Rodoljuba Colakovica, 6, 21000 Novi Sad, Serbia & Monte Negro
Predrag Strazmester sipa1@InfoSky.net
www.radio021.co.yu
I have been promoting Independent music for over 10 years.

Slovakia

Radio Mars
Gosposvetska cesta 83, 2000 Maribor, Slovakia
PH: 386-2-228-19-20 FX: 0386-2-25-25-489
urednistvo@radiomars.si
www.radiomars.si

Slovenia

Radio Student Ljubljana
PO Cesta 27. aprila 31 1000 Ljubljana, Slovenia
PH: 386-1-24-28-800 FX: 386-1-24-28-808
www.radiostudent.si

Spain

Ràdio Despí
Avda. Barcelona, 64, 08970 Sant Joan Despí, Barcelona, Spain
radiodespi@infonegocio.com
www.radiodespi.com

Radio PICA
PO Box 9242, 08080 Barcelona, Spain
pica@gracianet.org
www.radiopica.net

Sweden

Mick 102
Box 7652 907 13 Umeå, Sweden
PH: 090-786-90-40 FX: 090-13-09-28
studion@mick102.nu
www.mick102.nu

Radio AF
Sandgatan 2 223 50 Lund, Sweden
PH: 046-14-60-00 FX: 046-14-60-01
radioaf@radioaf.com
radio.af.lu.se

Rocket Radio
THS 10044 Stockholm, Sweden
PH: 468-790-9869
eric@rocket.fm
www.rocket.fm

Switzerland

Frequence Banane
Centre Est, EPFL 1015 Lausanne, Switzerland
PH: 41-0-21-693-40-25 ou 59 93
FX: 41-0-21-693-40-24
programmation@frequencebanane.ch
fbwww.epfl.ch

Radio Lora
Postfach 1036, CH-8026 Zürich, Switzerland
PH: 01-241-59-59 FX: 01-241-35-80
lora@lora.ch
www.lora.ch

radio RaBe
Randweg 21 Postfach 297 3000 Bern 11, Switzerland
PH: 031-330-99-90 FX: 031-330-99-92
rabe@rabe.ch
www.rabe.ch

United Kingdom

2010fm.com
PO Box 212, Baldock, SG7 6ZR UK
info@2010fm.com
www.2010fm.com
Live webcasts of unsigned bands and DJ's.

Alternative Devon
tom@alternativedevon.co.uk
www.alternativedevon.co.uk

BBC Radio 1 *Indie*
www.bbc.co.uk/radio1/alt
Home page of the BBC Radio 1's various Indie Music shows. Info, shows, contacts etc.

BBC Radio 2 *Rock and Pop*
www.bbc.co.uk/radio2/r2music/rockandpop
Home page of the BBC Radio 2's various Rock and Pop shows. Info, shows, contacts etc.

BCB Radio
11 Rawson Rd. Bradford,
West Yorkshire, BD1 3SH UK
PH: 01274-771677 FX: 01274-771680
www.bcb.yorks.com

The Beatscene
Four Winds Pavilion 1a Pacific Quay
Glasgow, G51 1EB UK
Jim Gellatly jim@beat106.com
www.beatscene.co.uk
The home of new music in Scotland.

Celtica Radio Wales
PO Box 48, Bridgend, CF32 9ZY UK
info@celticaradio.com
www.celticaradio.com
A platform for artists who have been denied elsewhere.

Clare FM
Abbeyfield Ctr. Francis St. Ennis,
Co. Clare, Ireland UK
PH: 353-0-65-68-28-888 FX: 353-0-65-68-29-392
info@clarefm.ie
www.clarefm.ie

Downtown Radio
Kiltonga Ind. Est. Newtownards
County Down, BT23 4ES UK
PH: 028-9181-5555 FX: 028-9181-5252
www.downtown.co.uk

Drive 105
2 St Josephs Ave. Derry, N. Ireland BT48 6TH
enquiries@drivefm.com
www.drive105fm.com
Send us your demo (CD/mini-disc/MP3).

Ellesmere Radio
PH: 07813-724082
Andy admin@ellesmereradio.co.uk
www.ellesmereradio.co.uk
Playing the best of the unknown.

Eternal Fusion *SpydaRadio*
42-43 Lower Marsh Waterloo
London, SE1 7RG UK
PH: 023-92-263-933
Gary Fosster eternalfusion@eternalfusion.org
www.eternalfusion.org
www.spydaradio.co.uk
Free from radio show for Indie/Alternative, Electronica, Psychedelia, Folk and Progressive.

Forest of Dean Radio
1 Berisford Ct. Cinderford,
Gloucestershire, GL14 2BS UK
PH: 01594-820722
contactus@fodradio.org
www.fodradio.org

Fresh Air FM
5/2 Bristo Sq. Edinburgh, EH8 9AL UK
PH: 44-0-131-650-2656 FX: 44-0-131-668-4177
music@freshairfm.co.uk
www.freshairfm.co.uk

Gravity FM *Grantham*
webfeedback@prioryfm.co.uk
www.prioryfm.co.uk

HFM Radio
PO Box 1055, Market Harborough,
Leicestershire, LE16 7ZL UK
info@harboroughfm.co.uk
www.harboroughfm.co.uk

Imperial College Radio
Beit Quad Prince Consort Rd. S. Kensington,
London, SW7 2BB UK
PH: 020-7594-8100 FX: 020-7594-8101
info@icradio.com
icradio.su.ic.ac.uk

Jimmy Possession's Radio Show
c/o r+eb 133 Green End Rd.
Cambridge, CB4 1RW UK
rebzine@hotmail.com
come.to/robots
Band demos, unreleased tracks and (as yet) undiscovered bands from all over the world.

jockrock radio
PO Box 13516, Linlithgow, EH49 6WB UK
FX: 070-92-011-439
jockrock@vacant.org.uk
www.vacant.org.uk/jockrock/jockrock.html

Jolly Roger Radio International
PO Box 39, Waterford, Ireland
jr_radio@hotmail.com
listen.to/jrri
Indie, C&W, Folk, New world & Ambient music.

Kick FM
The Studios 42 Bone Ln.
Newbury Berkshire, RG14 5SD UK
PH: 01635-841600 FX: 01635-841010
mail@kickfm.com
www.kickfm.co.uk

Kooba Radio
Studio 12 37 Tanner St., London, SE1 3LF UK
contact@koobaradio.co.uk
www.KoobaRadio.co.uk
Internet radio exclusively for the unsigned.

Last.fm
86C Greenfield Rd. London, E1 1EJ UK
PH: +44-20-7247-0292
labels@last.fm
www.last.fm/labels
Mega star or an unsigned band, on Last.fm every song gets the same starting point. The listeners, decide what's great music and what's rubbish.

LiveIreland
www.liveireland.com
Five stations that play Irish influenced music.

Luton FM *U. Luton*
Rm A315, U. Luton, Park Sq., Park St., Luton,
Bedfordshire, LU1 3JQ UK
PH: 015-82-703-020
lutonfm@hotmail.com
www.lutonfm.net

Magazine *SkyWave Radio*
155 Coventry Rd. Ilford, Essex, England IG1 4RD
PH: +44 (0) 20-8554-2219
Richard Allen bclstudios@aol.com
www.skywaveradio.com
Programme for new up and coming and unsigned artists to air their views and their music. Please feel free to contact us and/or send your material on CD enclosed with a biography.

Matchbox Radio 24
33 Bath St., Abingdon, Oxfordshire, OX14 3RH UK
info@matchboxrecordings.co.uk
www.matchboxrecordings.co.uk
We broadcast continuous new Independent music 24 hours a day.

Moon Radio
info@moonradio.co.uk
www.moonradio.co.uk
Buckle up and enjoy the sounds.

Music Maker Web Radio
c/o Magnet Publishing Ltd. 28 Grafton Terrace,
London, NW5 4JJ UK
PH: 020-7424-0027
Brian Healey tradmusic@btinternet.com
www.musicmaker-web.co.uk
Music covering different styles from Folk to Country, Rock, Jazz and World music. If you have produced a CD you would like to hear broadcast on this station, just send a copy to the Editor.

The Musical Mystery Tour *BBC Radio Wales*
Adam Walton, Library and Arts Ctr. Rhosddu Rd.
Wrexham, LL11 1NF UK
adam.walton@bbc.co.uk
www.themysterytour.co.uk

OneMusic *BBC Radio 1*
London, W1A 7WW UK
onemusic@bbc.co.uk
www.bbc.co.uk/radio1/onemusic
Resources for unsigned bands – articles, downloads, radio shows etc.

Phantom FM
PO Box 6721 Dun Laoghaire Co. Dublin, Ireland
PH: 353-1-478-0363 FX: 353-1-476-2138
music@phantomfm.com
www.phantomfm.com

Phoenix FM
Hutton Poplars Lodge, Rayleigh Rd. Hutton,
Brentwood, CM13 1BA UK
PH: 01277-234555 FX: 0870-706-1174
www.phoenixfm.com

PuLSE Radio
LSE Houghton St., London, England WC2A 2AE
PH: 44-0-20-7405-7686
www.pulsefm.co.uk
Playing Independent music over the net.

Pulse Unsigned
Enterprise House, Woodgreen Industrial Estate,
Salhouse, Norwich, NR13 6NY UK
PH: +44 (0) 870-1423456 FX: FX: +44 (0) 1603-735160
info@pulseunsigned.com
www.pulseunsigned.com
We exist to promote YOUR music through our website and on our Digital Satellite and Internet Radio stations. Send us your music for inclusion on our playlist. You must include fill out our Submission Pack to be considered for airplay. Visit our site for details.

Radio Gets Wild
17 London Rd. Kings Lynn Norfolk, PE30 5PY UK
Tim Daymond tim@radiogetswild.com
www.radiogetswild.com
Indie artists interviewed live on air; have your music featured. We also have a download section where visitors can vote, review, comment etc. on the music they hear.

Radio Telefís Éireann
Donnybrook, Dublin 4, Ireland
radio1@rte.ie
www.rte.ie/radio
The Irish national public service broadcasting organization.

Radio Warwick
U. Warwick Student's Union
Coventry, CV4 7AL UK
PH: 024-765-73077
studio@radio.warwick.ac.uk
www.raw.warwick.ac.uk

RadioReverb
170 North Street, Brighton,
East Sussex, BN1 1EA UK
PH: +44 (0) 1273-323-040
office@radioreverb.com
radioreverb.com

RamAir
Communal Bldg. U. Bradford, BD7 1DP UK
PH: 012-74-233-269
info@ramair.co.uk
www.ramairfm.co.uk

rare FM
UCL Union 25 Gordon St.,
London, WC1H 0AY UK
PH: 44-020-7679-2509
hom.rarefm@ucl.ac.uk
www.rarefm.co.uk

Reptor Productions Radio
16 Llys Glyndwr, Towyn,
Abergele, Conwy, LL22 9PA UK
PH: 44-0-1745-343-777
Dug submissions@reptorproductions.co.uk
www.reptorproductions.co.uk
We offer radio play online to unsigned artists and although we are based in the UK, we air the works of many USA artists – some of which are now gaining success in the music industry.

Scotland Rocks
SR56Kbps Indies, 28B Atholl St.,
Perth, PH1 5NP UK
Alasdair Macleod webmaster@scotlandrocks.co.uk
www.scotlandrocks.co.uk
Guitar oriented Blues and Rock, Metal and more.

Skywave Radio
#2, Quayside Offices, Basin Rd. S., Portslade,
Brighton, E. Sussex, BN41 1UH UK
PH: +44 (0) 1273-422553
studio@skywaveradio.com
www.skywaveradio.com

Solid Steel
c/o SBN 109A Regents Park Rd. Primrose Hill
London, NW1 8UR UK
PH: 020-7691-4777 FX: 020-7691-4666
solidsteel@ninjatune.net
www.ninjatune.net/solidsteel

Spirit FM
9-10 Dukes Ct. Bognor Rd. Chichester,
West Sussex, PO19 8FX UK
PH: 01243-539000 FX: 01243-786464
info@spiritfm.net
www.spiritfm.net

SpydaRadio
42-43 Lower Marsh Waterloo
London, SE1 7RG UK
PH: 023-92-263-933
info@spydaradio.co.uk
www.spydaradio.co.uk

SURE
U. Sheffield Union Students Western Bank,
Sheffield, S10 2TG UK
PH: 0114-222-8750 x28750 FX: 0114-275-2506
radio@sureradio.com
www.shef.ac.uk/sure

Tapp Out Radio
tor@tappoutradio.co.uk
www.tappoutradio.co.uk
We're always on the look out for music to add to our growing playlist. We cover many genres now from Hip Hop and RnB right through to different types of Rock and Alternative music.

thesunmachine.net Radio
234/5 Marionville Rd. Edinburgh,
Midlothian, EH7 6BE UK
Aynsley Watson tsmradio@thesunmachine.net
www.thesunmachine.net/radio
Discover a whole new world of music.

Today FM
124 Upper Abbey St., Dublin 1, Ireland
PH: 01-8049000
www.todayfm.com

totallyradio
PO Box 107, Brighton, East Sussex, BN1 1QG UK
www.totallyradio.com
Packed with new music across the board.

University Radio York
c/o Vanbrugh College, U. York, Heslington,
York, YO10 5DD UK
PH: 01904-433840 FX: 01904-433840
ury@york.ac.uk
ury.york.ac.uk

"The Unknown" Radio Show
Langley Ln. Farm, Middleton,
Manchester, M24 5LJ UK
PH: 0161-610-7516
Ruth Daniel ruth@fatnortherner.com
www.fatnortherner.com
Mail your demos, complete with biographies and press releases.

URN *U. Nottingham*
Students Union U. Park Nottingham, NG7 2RD UK
PH: 0115-935-1122
music@urn1350.net
urn1350.net

Virgin Radio
No.1 Golden Sq. London, W1F 9DJ UK
Attn: Head of Music
PH: 08707-30-1215 FX: 08707-30-1197
www.virginradio.co.uk
We have a tight playlist policy, and only a small handful of tracks get added each week, usually from established artists or those signed to major record labels. However, we're always keen to hear new bands and new music.

Wired Radio *Goldsmiths College*
wired@gold.ac.uk
www.wired.gold.ac.uk

Wrexham FM
www.wrexham.fm

XFM
30 Leicester Sqr London, WC2H 7LA UK
PH: 020-7766-6000
xfm.co.uk

Yugoslavia

Radio Free Belgrade
B92 Bulevar AVNOJ-a 64 11000 Beograd,
Yugoslavia
PH: 381-11-301-2000 FX: 381-11-301-2001
www.b92.net

Australia

2AAA
Cnr. Coleman & Young St., Wagga Wagga, NSW 2650 Australia
PH: 61-02-6925-3000 FX: 61-02-6925-2300
fm107@2aaafmradio.org.au
www.2aaafmradio.org.au

2ARM
PO Box 707, Armidale, NSW 2350 Australia
PH: 6772-1486
2arm@northnet.com.au
users.northnet.com.au/~2arm

2BBB
PO Box 304, Bellingen, NSW 2454 Australia
PH: 02-6655-0718 FX: 02-6655-1888
2bbb@midcoast.com.au
www.2bbb.midcoast.com.au

2CCR
PO Box 977, Baulkham Hills, NSW 1755 Australia
PH: 9686-3888 FX: 9639-5618
mail@2ccr-fm.com
www.2ccr-fm.com

2CHY
30 Orlando St., Coffs Harbour, NSW 2450 Australia
PH: 02-6651-1104
info@chyfm.com
www.chyfm.midcoast.com.au

2EAR
PO Box 86, Moruya, NSW 2537 Australia
PH: 02-4474-3443 FX: 02-4474-3500
info@earfm.com
www.earfm.com

2MCE
Panorama Ave. Bathurst, NSW 2795 Australia
PH: 02-6338-4790 FX: 02-6338-4402
2mce@csu.edu.au
www.csu.edu.au/2MCE

2NCR
PO Box 5123, E. Lismore, NSW 2480 Australia
PH: 02-66203-929 FX: 02-66-203884
fm2ncr@scu.edu.au
www.2ncr.org.au

2NSB
PO Box 468, Chatswood, NSW 2057 Australia
PH: 02-9419-6969 FX: 02-9413-1684
manager@2nsb.org.au
www.2nsb.org.au

2NUR
U. Newcastle, NSW 2308 Australia
PH: 61-2-4921-5555 FX: 61-2-4921-7158
contact@2nurfm.com
2nurfm.com

2RRR
PO Box 644, Gladesville, NSW 1675 Australia
PH: 61-29816-2988 FX: 61-2-9817-1048
www.2rrr.org.au

2SER
U. Tech. Sydney, Fl. 26, Bldg. 1, 1 Broadway, Ultimo, NSW 2007 Australia
PH: 61-2-9514-9514 FX: 61-2-9514-9599
info@2ser.com
www.2ser.com

2TEN
PO Box 93, Tenterfield, NSW 2372 Australia
PH: 02-6736-3444 FX: 02-6736-2197
twotenfm@halenet.com.au
www.halenet.com.au/~twotenfm

2UNE
UNE, Armidale, NSW 2351 Australia
PH: 02-677-323-99 FX: 02-677-27-633
radio@tunefm.une.edu.au
2une.une.edu.au

2UUU
PO Box 884, Nowra, NSW 2541 Australia
PH: 02-4422-1700 FX: 02-4421-8222
manager@tripleu.org.au
www.shoalhaven.net.au/jukebox

2VOX
PO Box 1663, Wollongong, NSW 2500 Australia
PH: 02-4227-3436 FX: 02-4226-5922
www.vox.1earth.net

2VTR
PO Box 248, Windsor, NSW 2756 Australia
PH: 02-45-879-899 FX: 02-45-878-865
webmaster@hawkradio.org.au
www.hawkradio.org.au

2XX
PO Box 812, Canberra, ACT 2601 Australia
PH: 02-6247-4400 FX: 02-6248-5560
comrad@2xxfm.org.au
www.2xxfm.org.au

3CR
PO Box 1277, Collingwood, Melbourne, VIC 3065 Australia
PH: 03-9419-8377 FX: 03-9417-4472
programming@3cr.org.au
www.3cr.org.au

3GCR
PO Box 579 Morwell, VIC 3840 Australia
PH: 61-3-5134-8444 FX: 61-3-5133-0555
3gcr@gippsland.net.au
www.3gcrfm.org.au

3MBR
PO Box 139, Murrayville, VIC 3512 Australia
PH: 03-5095-2045 FX: 03-5095-2346
3mbr@riverland.net.au
www.riverland.net.au/~3mbr

3MGB
PO Box 555, Mallacoota, VIC 3892 Australia
PH: 03-5158-0929 FX: 03-5158-0079
cootafm@vicnet.net.au
home.vicnet.net.au/~cootafm

3MR
c/o Monash U. VIC 3800 Australia
PH: 03-990-55-151 FX: 61-3-9905-4007
yoyo.cc.monash.edu.au/groups/3MU

3ONE *Shepparton*
onefm@mcmedia.com.au
www.welcome.to/onefm

3PBS
PO Box 2917 Fitzroy MDC, VIC 3065 Australia
PH: 61-3-8415-1067 FX: 61-3-8415-1831
music@pbsfm.org.au
www.pbsfm.org.au

3RIM
PO Box 979, Melton, VIC 3337 Australia
PH: 03-9747-8500 FX: 03-9747-0405
www.979fm.net

3RPP
PO Box 602, Somerville, VIC 3912 Australia
PH: 03-5978-8200 FX: 03-5978-8551
rpp@peninsula.hotkey.net.au
www.3rpp.asn.au

3RRR
25 Victoria St, PO Box 304, Fitzroy, VIC 3065 Australia
PH: 61-3-9419-2066 FX: 61-3-9417-1841
3rrr@rrr.org.au
www.rrr.org.au

3SER
PO Box 977 Cranbourne DC, VIC 3977 Australia
PH: 03-5996-6977 FX: 03-5996-6900
dlentin@3ser.org.au
www.3ser.org.au

3WAY
PO Box 752 Warrnambool, VIC 3280 Australia
PH: 03-5561-2666 FX: 03-5561-2585
3wayfm@standard.net.au
www.standard.net.au/~3wayfm

3WPR
PO Box 605, Wangaratta, VIC 3676 Australia
PH: 572-215-69 FX: 03-5722-3443
wprfm@netc.net.au
home.netc.net.au/~wprfm

4CCR
PO Box 300m Manunda, QLD 4870 Australia
PH: 61-7-4053-6891 FX: 61-7-4053-2085
info@cairnsfm891.org
www.4ccr-fm.org.au

4CLB
PO Box 2101 Logan City DC, QLD 4114 Australia
PH: 07-3808-8101 FX: 07-3808-7787
admin@101fm.asn.au
www.101fm.asn.au

4CRM *Mackay*
PO Box 1075, Mackay, QLD 4740 Australia
PH: 49531411 FX: 49535649
4crm@4crm.com.au
www.4crm.com.au

4RED
PO Box 139, Redcliffe, QLD 4020 Australia
PH: 07-3284-5000 FX: 07-3283-4527

4ZZZ
PO Box 509, Fortitude Valley, QLD 4006 Australia
PH: 07-3252-1555 FX: 07-3252-1950
info@4zzzfm.org.au
www.4zzzfm.org.au

5PBA
PO Box 433 Salisbury, SA 5108 Australia
PH: 61-8-8250-3735 FX: 61-8-8281-7495
pbafm@pbafm.org.au
www.pbafm.org.au

5 UV
228 N. Ter. Adelaide, SA 5000 Australia
PH: 08-8303-5000 FX: 08-8303-4374
radio@adelaide.edu.au
radio.adelaide.edu.au

96.5 Family FM
PO Box 965, Milton BC, QLD 4064 Australia
PH: 07-3217-5999 FX: 07-3217-5888
admin@96five.com
www.96five.org.au

The Basement
Level 1 / No. 2 Bulletin Pl. Sydney,
NSW 2000 Australia
PH: 02-9251-2797 FX: 02-9252-3007
base29@bigpond.net.au
www.thebasement.com.au

Bay FM
PO Box 1003, Cleveland, QLD 4163 Australia
PH: 07-3821-0022 FX: 07-3286-9166
bayfm@bayfm.org.au
www.bayfm.org.au

Bondi FM
PO Box 7588 Bondi Beach, NSW 2026 Australia
PH: 61-0-2-9365-55-88
team@bondifm.com.au
www.bondifm.com.au

City Park Radio
PO Box 1501, Launceston, TAS 7250 Australia
PH: 03-6334-7429
cityparkradio@cityparkradio.com
www.cityparkradio.com

Contact! *2RDJ FM*
contact2001@bigpond.com
www.users.bigpond.com/celt1969
International Indie/Alternative/New Wave Pop, broadcast across Australia. Demos too.

FM 98.5
PO Box 6824, Shepparton, VIC 3632 Australia
PH: +61-3-58317282 FX: +61-3-58312722
music@fm985.com.au
www.onefm.com.au

ISON Live Radio
PO Box 532, Newcastle, NSW 2300 Australia
PH: 6102-49270290 FX: 6102-49270290
Sean Ison info@isonliveradio.com
www.isonliveradio.com

JOY Melbourne
PO Box 907, S. Melbourne, VIC 3205 Australia
PH: 61-03-9699-2949 FX: 61-03-9699-2646
info@joy.org.au
www.joy.org.au

KAOSFM
Ison Live Radio, PO Box 532, Newcastle,
NSW 2300 Australia
PH: 6102-49270290 FX: 6102-49270290
Sean Ison info@isonliveradio.com
www.isonliveradio.com/kaosfm.php

The Planet *ABC Radio*
GPO Box 9994, Perth, WA 6848 Australia
PH: 02-8333-2821 FX: 02-8333-1366
Doug Spencer spencer.doug@abc.net.au
www.abc.net.au/rn/music/planet/default.htm
Plays good, heartfelt, inspiring music from around the world.

QBN FM
PO Box 230, Braidwood, NSW 2622 Australia
PH: 02-48-422-241 FX: 02-48-421-149
admin@qbnfm.com.au
www.qbnfm.com.au
Air time is given to Independent artists of all genres.

RTR FM
PO Box 949, Nedlands, WA 6909 Australia
PH: 61-8-9380-3380 FX: 61-8-9380 1092
rtrfm@rtrfm.com.au
www.rtrfm.com.au

Southern FM
PO Box 2132, Moorabbin, VIC 3189 Australia
PH: 03-9553-5444 FX: 03-9553-5244
info@southernfm.org.au
www.southernfm.org.au

Sub Fm
Union Bldg. La Trobe U. VIC 3086 Australia
PH: 613-03-9479-3835
Simon Knight s.knight@latrobe.edu.au
www.subfm.org

Three D Radio
PO Box 937, Stepney, SA 5069 Australia
PH: 61-8-83633937
mail@threedradio.com
www.threedradio.com

Triple H *Sydney*
PH: 9476-0105 FX: 9482-1662
programming@hhhfm.org.au
www.hhhfm.org.au

Triple J
PO Box 9994, Canberra, NSW Australia
PH: 1-800-0555-36
www.abc.net.au/triplej

Triple U
PO Box 884, Nowra, NSW 2541 Australia
PH: 02 4422-1193 FX: 02 4421-8222
manager@tripleu.org.au
www.tripleu.org.au

WYN
PO Box 155, Werribee, VIC 3030 Australia
PH: 9216 8089
wynfm@wynfm.org.au
www.wynfm.org.au

New Zealand

95b FM
PO Box 4560 Shortland St.,
Auckland 1001 New Zealand
PH: 64-9-309-4831 FX: 64-9-366-7224
95bfm@95bfm.com
www.95bfm.co.nz

Radio Active
PO Box 11-971 Wellington, New Zealand
PH: 64-4-801-9089
studiolive@radioactive.co.nz
www.radioactive.co.nz

Radio Kidnappers
PO Box 680, Hastings, New Zealand
PH: 06-876-6914 FX: 06-876-6914
enquiries@radiokidnappers.org.nz
www.radiokidnappers.org.nz

Asia

Psychic Vibe Bot Radio
108-902 Suenaga, Takatsu-ku, Kawasaki-shi,
Kanagawa-ken, JAPAN 213-0013
PH: 011-81-044-866-1422
Drew Golden botanist@psychicvibe.com
www.psychicvibe.com
An internet radio station specializing in interesting music from all genres.

Yellow Beat *Shonan Beach FM*
Gremlin and Baby Magic
ciao_babies@yellowbeat.net
www.yellowbeat.net
We can be a key step to introducing your into the Japanese market.

Internet Radio, Syndicated Shows and Podcasts

24-7 Indie Radio
BCNI c/o 2 Go Group, 123 Birch Ave.
Kitchener, ON N2H 4W6
PH: 519-742-6907 FX: 519-742-0992
admin@247radiogroup.com
www.247indie.com
Want to be heard on 24-7 New Artist? Contact us.

247 On-Air
BCNI c/o 2 Go Group, 123 Birch Ave.
Kitchener, ON N2H 4W6
PH: 519-742-6907 FX: 519-742-0992
admin@247radioonair.com
www.247radioonair.com
Indie Artists must sign an artist agreement in order to get airplay.

2kool4radio
music@2kool4radio.com
www.2kool4radio.com
Alternative, Indie, Punk, Hip Hop, and more.

3wk
PO Box 160161, St. Louis, MO 63116
wandagm@3wk.com
www.3wk.com
Promoting Underground/Indie artists.

440MUSIC.COM
3200 N. Lake Shore Dr. #1103, Chicago, IL 60657
PH: 773-477-8738
www.440MUSIC.COM
We play only original music from independent bands.

8BallRadio
newmusic@8ballradio.com
www.8ballradio.com
Combining mainstream Rock with independent artists.

AccuRadio
119 W. Hubbard #4E Chicago, IL 60610
PH: 312-527-3879
artist-contact@accuradio.com
www.accuradio.com
Plays all genres.

AdrenalineRadio.com
PH: 562-945-6469
www.adrenalineradio.com
Contact to get your music featured.

Adult Alternative Music Weekly
aamw@spotdawg.com
www.spotdawg.com/aamw
Plays the top 20 songs in Adult Alternative (AAA) music.

Airbubble
info@airbubble.com
www.airbubble.com
Free form radio covering various genres of music.

Aiiradio.net
postmaster@aiiradio.net
www.aiiradio.net
Featuring worldwide independent recording artists.

Alexa Digital Internet Radio
www.alexadigitalmusic.com
webmaster@alexadigitalmusic.com
alexadigitalmusic.com
The best mix of Indie music on the web.

All Songs Considered *NPR*
635 Mass. Ave. NW, Washington, DC 20001
Bob Boilen allsongs@npr.org
www.npr.org/programs/asc
Full versions of the music snippets played on NPR's afternoon news program. Check our site for submission details.

Allan Handelman Show
PH: 704-596-4718
ahshow@vnet.net
ifitrocks.com
Rock & Roll and the Rock Culture. The talk show that rocks!

alternative nu
board@alternative.nu
www.alternative.nu
Send in your music video for play on our rerun stream.

American Radio Network *ARN*
5287 Sunset Blvd. Hollywood, CA 90027
PH: 323-464-4580 FX: 323-962-1936
arninc@earthlink.net
www.kclafm.com

AMPCAST Radio
28 Ledgeland Dr. Mystic, CT 06355
www.ampcast.com/radio
Fully interactive, completely live and totally ad-hoc radio program.

Angry Coffee Radio Show
hello@angrycoffee.com
www.angrycoffee.com
We will compliment online marketing efforts to Indie and major record labels alike.

ArtistFirst Internet Radio
1062 Parkside Dr. Alliance, OH 44601
PH: 330-823-2264
info@artistfirst.com
www.artistfirst.com
If you have a CD, you can have a 1hr prime-time radio show here.

ArtistLaunch.com
14852 Dasher Allen Park, MI 48101
PH: 313-492-5657
www.artistlaunch.com
Live showcases, internet and real-world radio outlets, reviews and artist pages.

The Artistlaunch Hour
Paul dos Santos cavalierhome@aol.com
RadioFreeTunes.com
Showcases the music of Artistlaunch.com subscribers.....outstanding independent artists from all over the planet. The show is aired on FM and AM stations in the US, UK, Canada and Sweden.

AudioRealm.Com
504 N. Hockley Main, Ropesville, TX 79405
PH: 806-562-3838
www.audiorealm.com
Operates the AudioRealm Broadcast Network with currently over 200 active affiliates and growing. Over 800 active stations.

Artists Without a Label Radio
PO Box 879, Ojai, CA 93024
PH: 805-640-7399 FX: 805-646-6077
info@awal.com
www.awal.com
Discover great new music and artists.

Audio Independence
PO Box 73193, Metairie, LA 70033-3193
Wesley Clark wesley@wesleyclark.com
www.audioindependents.com
Features a new independent artist each week for a one hour show.

AURICAST
PO Box 459, 16420 SE McGillivary #103,
Vancouver, WA 98683-3461
www.auricast.com
Would you like your sound in rotation at thousands of retail locations?

BAGeL Radio
209 11th Ave. San Francisco, CA 94118-2101
Ted feedback@bagelradio.com
www.bagelradio.com
Playlists include Indie & Alternative Rock, and Noisy Pop. Mostly guitar music...no testosterock.

BandsRadio.com
www.bandsradio.com
Funk, Boogie, Groove, New Grass, Americana and Southern Rock.

BlackLight Radio
Gene Savage postmaster@blacklightradio.com
www.blacklightradio.com
We WILL play independent artists, and if requested we can review CDs. We welcome submissions in all genres.

Blazin' Mics FM
PO Box 25668, Baltimore, MD 21224
Hector Rivera blazinmicsfm@yahoo.com
www.blazinmicsfm.com
#1 unsigned hype internet station. 24/7 365 days of non stop music!

The Box Music Network
Tyler Woodward tylerwoodward@planetradio.us
www.theboxmusicnetwork.com
I would be more the willing to run any indie bands or artist on The Box. We are majority a Rock station but also air Top40 style music. We'll take a listen to anything and see if it's a good fit for our station.

Bumpskey.com
jerry@bumpskey.com
www.Bumpskey.com
Live show featuring all independent music.

Cactus Radio
1220 E. Silverwood Dr. Phoenix, AZ 85048-8655
www.cactusradio.com
Visit website for submission details.

CDTV.NET
67 Wall St. 22nd Fl. New York, NY 10005
PH: 212-696-7890
support@cdtv.net
www.cdtv.net
Accepts demo CDs/music videos from all genres.

Celebrate Radio
PO Box 72174, Oakland, CA 94612
PH: 510-464-4677
Don Fass celebrateradio@yahoo.com
www.celebrateradio.com
We want your music. All languages, all genres (except Classical, Hip Hop, Metal, or Jazz).

Cyber Storm Radio
alcocchi@cyberstormradio.com
www.cyberstormradio.com
The newest releases from known and unknown recording artists.

Dark Side of the Radio
2288 Sharon Depoy Rd. Greenville, KY 42345
hollywood@kih.net
www.dsotr.8m.com
Indie Section: www.dsotr.8m.com/indy.htm
No MP3s. See submission guidelines.

D'Art Radio
PO Box 303, W. Long Branch, NJ 07764
Arlene Smith dart1@mail.com
www.dartradio.com
An Indie music internet radio station for Rock, Techno, Pop, R&B, Rap and Hip Hop. An artist may submit one MP3 for free.

Dynamic Indie Radio
2844-46 Dewey Ave. Rochester, NY 14616
PH: 585-621-6270 FX: 585-621-6278
wdyn@wdyn.net
www.dynamicindieradio.com
Send your CD. Include the form found at our website.

Echoes of Sound
moofious_c@hotmail.com
www.live365.com/stations/moofious_c
Ranging from House, Jazz, Downtempo and Indie Rock. Streaming this radio station fuels the insomnia at night.

eoRadio
PO Box 441234, Aurora, CO 80014-1234
PH: 303-808-8140
Ryan Smith webmaster@eoradio.com
www.eoradio.com
The best free music from unsigned artists from around the globe.

erika.net
PO Box 7858, Ann Arbor, MI 48107
programming@erika.net
erika.net
Sounds and styles you won't hear on other radio stations.

Evolving Artist
18 Mill St., Southbridge, MA 01550-2757
Attn: Derek Tremblay
PH: 508-764-9500 FX: 508-764-9501
Craig Frand craig.frand@evolvingartist.com
evolvingartist.com
Submit your CDs/ MP3s for consideration for ENGAGE Internet Radio. You can also submit your DVDs/ MPEGs for consideration for Evolving Artist Internet Television.

Excellent Radio Online
www.excellentonline.com
The home for North American fans of UK music.

ExtraPlay.com Radio
Nicholas Cope marketing@extraplay.com
www.extraplay.com
Unsigned band and unsigned artist songs from both the UK and the US. We'd like to hear your music. If you'd like to make your sound available and broadcast on our radio, register today.

The FatCat Radio Network
FatCat_Radio@ieatcatsforfun.com
www.freewebs.com/fatcatradio
Submit via our online submission form. Your music must come from a funender.com site. (No exceptions. It's the OMD that powers our station). Must be lo-fi (48kbps max.). Use the 'lo-fi creator' in the ADMIN section at Funender.

FlagAss Radio!
PO Box 297, Frankenmuth, MI 48734
PH: 989-652-9520
Rev. Dan radio@flagass.com
www.FlagAssRadio.com
Features local, independent and underground acts.

FNR Unsigned Radio
www.fnr-radio.com
Playing the best in unsigned 24/7!

FreeWorldRadio.com
152 Meads Cross Rd. Stormville, NY 12582
PH: 800-259-7130
Paul dos Santos cavalierhome@aol.com
FreeWorldRadio.com
Music news, artist bios, album reviews, exclusive interviews and performances.

FreshBlend Radio
PO Box 85, Bell Buckle, TN 37020
requests@freshblendradio.com
www.freshblendradio.com
The latest music from a variety of styles.

Garage Radio
John Foxworthy roadrash@garageradio.com
www.garageradio.com
Promoting independent artists via Internet radio stream. Please visit our site for submission details.

Get Indie Radio
4080 Paradise #242, Las Vegas, NV 89109
PH: 702-880-5717 FX: 702-248-8564
www.getindie.com/indexlowhigh.cfm
22 different radio stations in one location.

Gimme Noise
246 Bradhurst Ave. #44, New York, NY 10039
www.gimmenoise.com
Get your music featured here.

GotRadio
8100 Mulrany Way, Antelope, CA 95843
programmer@gotradio.com
www.gotradio.com
Send your CD to our address and mention the STATION you are contacting ie: "New Age".

Growth House Radio
Package Receiving, 2215-R Market St. #199,
San Francisco, CA 94114
PH: 415-863-3045
info@growthhouse.org
www.growthhouse.org
Entertainment with a mission: to improve the quality of compassionate care for people who are dying. We offer several different channels with music and easy-listening education features on end-of-life care. In order to be considered for promotion your album must be available for purchase either at CDBaby.com or at Amazon.com. Visit our site for submission details.

Hidden Planet Radio
PO Box 131, Selah, WA 98942
Jason Moore Jason@hiddenplanetradio.com
www.hiddenplanetradio.com
Streaming the best unsigned indie bands & artists in the world, 24/7.

IMC Radio
PO Box 2366, Madison, MS 39130-2366
PH: 601-605-9691
Duane Lamb braintrust@imcradio.com
www.imcradio.com
Open format internet radio station. The home of "The Better Music Mix"!

INcast
Mick mickwainman@sbcglobal.net
www.live365.com/stations/310349
Adult Rock for those who refuse to grow up!

The Independent Anthem
PO Box 1166, Rancho Cucamonga, CA 91729-1166
David Betz theanthem@nodavidmedia.com
theanthem.nodavidmedia.com
Podcast featuring independent artists from all over the world and offers an eclectic mix of really good music. I broadcast two shows. I also do reviews and have a "feature artist" section on my site.

Indie Airplay
1857 N. Wilton Pl. #205, Los Angeles, CA 90028
PH: 323-960-0145 FX: 626-579-1705
Jakob Nielsen jakob@suite108.com
www.suite108.com
Delivers weekly news via Podcast from SoCal about indie bands and their gig info.

Indie Artist Radio
943 Old Mars Hill Hwy. #5, Weaverville, NC 28787
submissions@indieartistradio.com
indieartistradio.com
We are now a licensed radio station with ASCAP, BMI, Soundexchange and SESAC. We email weekly play reports to ALL artists with their song plays and what time their songs were played for the previous week.

Indie Band Radio
105 Rosewood Texarkana, TX 75501
PH: 903-223-7205
Chris Hawthorne chris@indiebandradio.com
indiebandradio.com
Devotes itself to playing and promoting unsigned music 24/7. All unsigned. All the time!

indie cent exposure radio
8949 Sunset Blvd. #201,
West Hollywood, CA 90069
PH: 310-943-7164 FX: 310-919-3091
Justin Goldberg justin@indie911.com
www.indie911.com
Changing the way people discover and get paid for making music. As people listen to streamed music from Indie911's media player, qualifying artist accounts are paid for online airplay via their PayPal account.

The Indie Limelight Radio Show
James St. James info@iarnetworks.com
indieartistradio.com
Each Week the show brings over 1.3 million listeners music and interviews from the best independent music from around the world.

Indie Radio Live
16837 64th Pl. N. Loxahatchee, FL 33470
PH: 561-790-3791 FX: 561-790-3791
Merrick merrick@indieradiolive.com
www.indieradiolive.com
Playing the music of international Indie artists.

Indie Shop
PO Box 92077, Long Beach, CA 90809-2077
PH: 562-860-2451 x2626
indieshop@hotmail.com
www.indieshop.org
Features the best in Brit Pop & Rock.

INDIE Warehouse Radio
PO Box 511, Louisville, KY 40201
information@indiewarehouse.com
www.indiewarehouse.com
Bringing additional awareness to your CD.

IndieFan Radio
John Jorgensen info@indiefan.com
www.indiefan.com
Broadcasting Rock, Punk, Metal, Hip Hop and Electronica nightly.

IndieFeed
Chris MacDonald info@indiefeed.com
www.indiefeed.com
Podcast that plays most genres. Please visit our site for submission details.

indieradio.org
whatscooking@indieradio.org
www.indieradio.org
Groundbreaking music by independent artists/labels. I may consider reviewing the release and post it to the reviews and commentary section. Contact me for the mailing address.

InRadio
PO Box 6882, Minneapolis, MN 55406
PH: 612-332-9606 FX: 612-338-6043
info@inradio.net
www.inradio.net
Encourages music and ideas not found on mainstream FM radio.

Inside the Music Business *Indie Artist Radio*
PH: 828-658-0984
Chad LaGrone info@Iarnetworks.com
info@iarnetworks.com
iarnetworks.com
Any artist looking to submit music to the station and/or programs should visit www.indieartistradio.com to view their submission requirements. We feature an unsigned artist showcase each show.

Direct traffic to your website - www.indielinkexchange.com/ile

Instatone Radio
Aaron Cohen aaron@instatone.com
www.instatone.com
Community Indie Radio guarantees internet air time for unsigned bands and offers unique feedback mechanism to create great rotation. All genres welcome!

The Jaci Rae Show *ArtistFirst Radio*
PO Box 1118, Felton, CA 95018
PH: 727-443-7115
Jaci Rae info@jacirae.com
jacirae.com/jacishow.html
Weekly talk show covering various aspects of the music business. Often interviews Indie artists.

Jack and Jill Radio
PO Box 450967, Sunrise, FL 33345
PH: 954-741-7233
Grant Porter djradiojack@jackandjillradio.com
www.jackandjillradio.com
Acoustic, Folk, Blues, Bluegrass, Country and Light Pop.

Kulak's Woodshed
5230? Laurel Canyon Blvd. N.
Hollywood, CA 91607
PH: 818-766-9913
Paul Kulak paulkulak@earthlink.net
www.kulakswoodshed.com
Live internet video web casts and Acoustic music showcases.

Kweevak Music Magazine
38 Oliver Pl. Ringwood, NJ 07456
PH: 973-556-5400
Rich Lynch info@kweevak.com
www.kweevak.com
A weekly, 1-hour syndicated program now on five station and growing.

IgoRADIO
info@lgoradio.com
www.lgoradio.com
Our goal is to give all musicians an online location where they can show what they have worked so hard to create.

LIQUID-A RADIO
PO Box 356, Fort Monmouth, NJ 07703
PH: 732-495-6375
liquidaradio1@yahoo.com
www.liquidasite.citymax.com
Profiles unsigned/underground artists from around the world.

Liquid Radio Live
New Music Dept. 1490 Lafayette St. #203,
Denver, CO 80218
lrl@liquidcompass.net
www.liquidradiolive.com
A free service allowing online listeners to access new, independent artists!

Little Radio
558 Westminster Ave. Venice, CA 90291
dave@littleradio.com
littleradio.com
A variety of shows that welcome submissions.

Live365.com
1291 E. Hillsdale Blvd. #200,
Foster City, CA 94404
PH: 650-345-7400 FX: 650-345-7497
www.live365.com
Over 3 million visitors per month and 5,000 radio stations.

Live365 Record Pool
1291 E. Hillsdale Blvd. #200,
Foster City, CA 94404
PH: 650-345-7400 FX: 650-345-7497
travis@live365.com
www.live365.com/labelservices/index.live
Submit your track or album to the Live365 Record Pool and reach thousands of DJs.

Live Discs Radio
PO Box 89, Ambler, PA 19002
PH: 215-641-9989
submit@livediscsradio.com
www.livediscsradio.com
Submit tracks for inclusion in our playlists.

LUVeR
PO Box 11445 Berkeley, CA 94712
Frank Moore fmoore@eroplay.com
www.luver.com
Shows created/webcasted by individuals around the world.

M3 Radio
259 W. 30th St. 12th Fl. New York, NY 10001
PH: 917-351-1021
Tony-O m3radio@aol.com
www.m3radio.com
Gets independent musicians some airplay.

M4 Radio
463 Boxwood Ct. Kissimmee, FL 34743
PH: 407-344-1902
Banzai banzai@m4radio.com
www.m4radio.com
All Indie Music. The Invasion Continues.

Magazine *Skywave Radio*
Richard Allen magazine@skywaveradio.com
www.skywaveradio.com
Features interviews with artists, engineers, producers and unsigned bands on a global level.

The Michael Anthony Show
PO Box 1284, Hillsville, VA 24343
Michael Anthony fmyshow@gmail.com
www.michaelanthonyshow.com
We play, review and promote any and every genre of music by unsigned and Indie artists (except religious oriented music).

Miz B's Porch
c/o Paula Bright, 8530 White Ave.
St. Louis, MO 63144
Crazy Miz B paula@crazedcowboys.com
mizbsporch.com
All genres are welcome, but I should warn you that my personal tastes lean away from really Hard Rock, Metal and related styles. But I'm open to trying anything. Ya just never know, ya know?

Monks Media Radio Network
44 N. 9th St. #202, Noblesville, IN 46060
PH: 317-776-4127 FX: 317-776-4128
Jeffrey S. Monks jeff@monksmedia.com
www.monksmedia.com
We will be launching a new weekly show to showcase Indie Artists. Prizes are... 1st Place: Artist/Band will open at a venue in Central Indiana in July, 2005 in front of 15,000 people! 1st-3rd: 5 Hour recording session to cut your new demos!

MUSIC CHOICE
Attn: Unsigned Material, 525 7th Ave. 12th Fl.
New York, NY 10018
PH: 215-784-5842
www.musicchoice.com
44 genre specific non-stop digital quality music channels.

Music Forte
154 E. Bailey Rd. #G, Naperville, IL 60565
PH: 888-659-2867
Greg Percifield greg@musicforte.com
www.musicforte.com
An unprecedented online program that is fast becoming the world's foremost community for music, education and business!

Music Places
200A Linville St., Morganton, NC 28655
Wayne Fetherbay mail@musicplaces.com
www.musicplaces.com
Our free music promotion will stream your music worldwide.

Music Sojourn
PO Box 509, Gibsonia, PA 15044-0509
www.musicsojourn.com
You must fill out our online artist submission form before sending your CD.

Musicians.net
1000 Singleton Blvd. Dallas, TX 75212
peri@musicians.net
www.musicians.net
Provides independent artists and musicians all of the tools to get their music heard.

Musiconradio.com
PH: 251-550-7947
Damon Collins info@musiconradio.com
www.musiconradio.com
Our broadcast is dedicated to original talent. We'll also sell your CD from our site. Visit our site for submission details.

NBT Radio
info@nbtradio.net
nbtradio.net
Mostly independent artists as well up-and-comers. Stylistically almost anything goes at NBT Radio. Although Singer-Songwriters dominate, you'll find Reggae, Hard Rock, Jam Bands and Jazz here.

NEKKID Radio
pd@nekkidradio.com
www.nekkidradio.com
DJs from around the world and the widest mix of music anywhere on the NET!

NeverEndingWonder Radio
16 S.W. 3rd #18, Portland, OR 97204
PH: 503-219-6741
Lee Widener new@neverendingwonder.com
www.neverendingwonder.com/radio.htm
Plays a wide variety of music & comedy including Rock, Pop, Alt, Folk, Jazz, Electronic, New Age, World, Goth, and other styles with an emphasis on the Experimental & unusual. NOT interested in Rap, Hip Hop or "Dance."

New Artist Radio
490 S. Main Pleasent Grove, UT 84062
PH: 801-380-0215 FX: 801-785-2157
Theda Messic tmc@newartistradio.net
www.newartistradio.net
A FREE service offered to bands & new artists that would like to get their music heard worldwide on a Top 40 show & 8 other radio shows. Sign Up Today!!

newFremontradio
Jeff Yost myost1@woh.rr.com
www.live365.com/stations/freetreejeff?play
Send me a good quality CD for my listening pleasure; or send me an email letting me know where I can download an mp3.

Null Set Rock Radio
min@whitemusic.tv
www.nullset.tv

On The Horizon *New Artist Radio*
490 S. Main Pleasent Grove, UT 84062
PH: 801-380-0215 FX: 801-785-2157
John Anderson aharvest@newartistradio.net
www.newartistradio.net
A weekly show that plays independent music and interviews independent artists.

OnlyPiano.com
PO Box 144, Bothell, WA 98011
info@onlypiano.com
www.onlypiano.com
Dedicated to promoting piano music and the people who play it. Visit our site for submission details.

Outsight Communications
5224 Shoreline Blvd. Waterford, MI 48329-1670
PH: 248-842-5850
Tom Schulte outsight@usa.net
www.new-sounds.net
Brings to light non-mainstream music.

PittRadio
PH: 202-483-6864
Marc Sylvestre pittradio@bottomlesspitt.com
pittradio.bottomlesspitt.com
Streaming the cutting edge artistry of the independents. Upload your music today!

Pod Heads Radio
The E-man eman@podheadsradio.com
podheadsradio.com
We feature music...all kinds...whatever floats our boat. We'll play it in our podcasts.

Popbang.com
PO Box 6522, St. Paul, MN 55106
Jay Anderson jay@popbang.com
www.popbang.com
Newer power Pop and other Rock!

PopStorm Radio
requests@popstormradio.com
www.popstormradio.com
Plays both signed and unsigned artists.

Pulse Now
171 Pier Ave. # 498, Santa Monica, CA 90405-5363
PH: 310-216-9047
office@pulsenowmail.com
pulsenow.com
All indie music! Send us your music for consideration, and you may be included on our play list. Just print & complete our online Submission Pack, and send it in along with your CD.

Radio Crystal Blue
3655 Shore Pkwy. #1F, Brooklyn, NY 11235
PH: 718-646-0158
Dan Herman cblue456@optonlinedotnet
www.radiocrystalblue.com
Featuring the best of the independents & the unsigned. Send your latest CD to the above address.

Radio Free Tunes
PH: 412-818-1131
Paul Carosi radiofreetunes@yahoo.com
www.radiofreetunes.com
I promote Indie musicians from around the world from a wide range of genres.

Radio Free Virgin
5670 Wilshire Blvd. #2500, Los Angeles, CA 90036
PH: 323-933-3399 FX: 323-939-7211
feedback@radiofreevirgin.com
www.radiofreevirgin.com
Creating a format for unsigned artists.

Radio Free World
PO Box 444, Idyllwild, CA 92549
webmaster@radiofreeworld.com
www.radiofreeworld.com
Almost 12 hrs of Indie music per day.

Radio Indie Pop
175 E. 2nd St. #1B New York, NY 10009
Rob Sacher LunaSeaRecords@nyc.rr.com
www.radio-indie-pop.com
Music by independent label artists with no commercial radio airplay.

Radio Indie Rock
schroeder@radioindierock.com
www.radioindierock.com
Daily radio broadcasts of indie music. Listener supported, commercial free.

RADIO IV
radioiv.com
Offering free airtime for all dedicated bands/musicians. We will air your demo tunes and get them heard!

Radio Muse
Jodi Krangle jodi@musesmuse.com
www.musesmuse.com/radiomuse.html
Features independent songwriters. The idea behind the show is to bring together the very best indie music from songwriters at all levels and stages of their musical journey. Please visit our site for submission details!

Radio Paradise
PO Box 3008, Paradise, CA 95967
bill@radioparadise.com
www.radioparadise.com
We welcome CDs from artists & record labels.

Radio X
PO Box 42448, Middletown, OH 45042
promos@usradiox.com
www.usradiox.com
We Are Indie Music Friendly!

RadioAid.com
1006 Banister Ln. #1101, Austin, TX 78704
Rob Vining support@radioaid.com
www.RadioAid.com
We do not accept hard copy CDs from artists. However, artists upload their own music on our site and select which songs they want to appear in our streaming radio player.

RadioAOL
375 Alabama St. #350, San Francisco, CA 94110
music.channel.aol.com
We have a few indie radio stations, and lots of specialty channels.

RadioINDY.com
PO Box 230581, Encinitas, CA 92023
support@radioIndy.com
www.radioindy.com
Home for Independent music on the web.

radioio
PO Box 1449, Graham, NC 27253
www.radioio.com
Alternative Rock, cutting-edge Pop, contemporary Folk, Blues and Jazz.

RadioMike
PO Box 2631, Austin, TX 78768-2631
Mike Perazzetti
galahad@theferedbrainofradiomike.com
www.theferedbrainofradiomike.com
Our mission ...is to make the world safe for good music around the world to thrive and multiply on the Radio and be the best damn Music Supervisor, at the Movies with Great Independent Music. It's very simple really.

RadioMojo
radiomojo.com
We play Modern and Alternative Rock with some Rap/Electronica mixed in for good measure.

RadioNonsense.com
459 Holly Ave. St. Paul, MN 55102
PH: 651-647-0275
Scott Sosna nonsense@buddhadata.com
www.radiononsense.com
I love to put new music on for others to enjoy.

RadioU
PO Box 1887, Westerville, OH 43086
PH: 614-890-9977
radiou.com
We play the stuff corporate radio doesn't.

RadioXY
Chaos aceking@pobox.com
radioxy.com
Underground Alternative music.

RelaxRadio
Ron Trigwell relaxradio@perthinternet.com
www.relaxradio.net.au
Australian Internet Radio Station supporting Independent Artists worldwide. We play most genres of music except Heavy Alternative.

Riot Radio
2956 Willow Bend, Orlando, FL 32808
PH: 407-445-3096 FX: 407-445-3096
Justin riotradio@hotmail.com
www.riotradio.4t.com
Radio station offering free studio time, airplay, venues, bios, distribution of CD etc.

Rock Solid Pressure
4254 Whistlewood Cir. Lakeland, FL 33811
rocksolidpressure@yahoo.com
rocksolidpressure.com
The only independent music game show on the net! Now exclusively on M4radio.com. We are now focusing exclusively on 'Rock' music, which falls into many genres.. Hard Rock, Pop Rock, Soft Rock, Punk Rock, Industrial Rock etc. Check our site for submission info.

Rule Radio
1114 Magnolia St. 2nd Fl. Greensboro, NC 27401
PH: 336-324-6784 FX: 336-274-5431
theruler@ruleradio.com
ruleradio.net
Taking control of your music means doing something to make it available. Adding your music to Rule Radio is an affordable and powerful way to do just that.

SayHy Radio
9442 Leo Dr. Brighton, MI 48116
PH: 517-861-9380
Ron Howard info@sayhyradio.com
www.sayhyradio.com
An internet radio station that plays only indie and unsigned music 24/7 365!

Scrub Radio
info@scrubradio.com
www.scrubradio.com
A station dedicated to unsigned artists.

SiaNet Radio
PO Box 18686, Minneapolis, MN 55418
sianetradio@understream.net
www.sianetradio.com
Dedicated to unsigned and small label original bands.

Sirius Satellite Radio
1221 Ave. of the Americas, New York, NY 10020
PH: 212-584-5100
www.siriusradio.com
The best music you've ever heard and never heard.

Sloth Radio
www.slothradio.com
Playing the best in modern and classic Synthpop and New Wave.

SomaFM
1594 Treat Ave. San Francisco, CA 94110
Attn: (channel name)
dj@somafm.com
www.somafm.com
Internet broadcasts that reach around the world.

SP Radio One
PO Box 5766, Irvine, CA 92616
Tazy SPradio1@aol.com
www.skaparade.com
New Music! Live Bands! 24+ Genres!

SpiderBiteRadio.com/SpiderBite Records
435 Elm S. Manchester, NH 03101
PH: 603-645-1449 FX: 603-657-7202
Tracy Vail Tracy@Spiderbiteradio.com
www.spiderbiteradio.com
A FREE Internet based radio station streaming independent/unsigned bands 24/7. Includes live acoustic performances and interviews.

Sunnymead Internet Radio
PO Box 277, Waterloo, QC J0E 2N0
PH: 450-539-2098 FX: 450-539-5176
info@sunnymead.org
www.sunnymead.org
A virtual village of independent artists.

Texas Online Radio
music@texasonlineradio.com
www.texasonlineradio.com
We're not your usual online radio station, and we're not limited to Texas Artists! We support the growth and promotion of new artists everywhere!

Thunderground Radio
Rich Gardner rich@thundergroundradio.com
www.thundergroundradio.com
Streaming Internet Radio featuring the BEST Independent Bands we can find!

TraceLength.com
8623 SW Holly St. #707, Wilsonville, OR 97070
tlradio@tracelength.com
tlradio.tracelength.com
Songs sent must be of MP3 format and at least 128kbit/sec.

TruSonic
7835 Fay Ave. Ste. LL-A, La Jolla, CA 92037
PH: 858-623-7006
www.truSONIC.com
Music and messaging service used by various businesses. We're always on the lookout for fresh upcoming acts with artistic vision and control of their own content. Visit our site for instructions on how to upload your music.

URSCENE Radio
Attn: Playlist, 7468 Village Green Dr.
Landover, MD 20785
PH: 877-379-7062
radio@urscene.com
www.urscene.com
Totally dedicated to the advancement of unsigned artists. 700,000 listeners worldwide. All genres all the time!!!

Way Out There Radio
info@wayoutthere.net
www.wayoutthere.net
You can be sure to hear our DJs play local bands and unsigned artists from their area and everywhere.

WCH Radio
GW Carver House, 3035 Bell Ave.
St. Louis, MO 63106
FX: 270-682-9474
John ODay wchradio1@lycos.com
wchradio.com
We try to play as much Indie music as possible.

WebRadioPugetSound.com
6310 203rd St. Ct. E. Spanaway, WA 98387
www.webradiopugetsound.com
See website for submission guidelines/forms.

What Sound
Adrian datzaboy@msn.com
www.live365.com/stations/daturaboy
An eclectic mix of Rock, Trip Hop, Techno, & assorted musical stylings for the open minded.

Whole Wheat Radio
PO Box 872, H St., Talkeetna, AK 99676
radio2@wholewheatradio.org
www.talkeetna-alaska.com/radio.php
We play independent music exclusively.

World Café *WXPN*
3025 Walnut St., Philadelphia, PA 19104
David Dye wxpndesk@pobox.upenn.edu
worldcafe.org
Send TWO compact discs (no cassettes or tapes).

WSVN Radio
PO Box 132, Thornton, IL 60476-0132
wsvnradio@yahoo.com
www.wsvnradio.net
Send your CD and additional info. E-mail to get MP3 address.

XM SATELLiTE RADiO
1500 Eckington Place NE,
Washington, DC 20002-2194 Attn: Billy Zero
FX: 202-380-4065
Billy Zero yzero@xmradio.com
radiounsigned.com
unsigned.xmradio.com
Submit your CD with genre labeled. No MP3s.

XMU *XM Radio*
xmu.xmradio.com
We play what's next...now! It's Indie Pop, Indie Rock, Electronic, Down Tempo and Underground Hip Hop. It's XMU...it's about the music!

Blues Radio

Internet Radio and Syndicated Shows

United States

Bandit Blues Radio
3586 Ridgefield Dr. Murfreesboro, TN 37129
mgr@banditbluesradio.com
www.banditbluesradio.com
We are willing to help new and up coming artists gain exposure. We also do reviews.

Beale Street Caravan
66 Monroe Ave. #101, Memphis, TN 38103
PH: 901-527-4666 FX: 901-529-4030
info@bealestreetcaravan.com
www.bealestreetcaravan.com
Aired weekly on over 280 public, community and college radio stations nationwide.

Blue Icewater Radio
www.blueicewater.com
Plays an eclectic blend of swampy, Jazzy, Rock, Acoustic and spiritual Blues.

Blues Before Sunrise
PO Box 272, Forest Park, IL 60130
Steve Cushing
steve.cushing@bluesbeforesunrise.com
www.bluesbeforesunrise.com
Each Saturday night this Chicago-based, nationally syndicated public radio program explores, preserves, and popularizes the various eras and genre of Blues Heritage.

Blues Train
steviegeo@charter.net
www.live365.com/stations/steviegeo
Guitar driven Blues you can jam to! Get reacquainted with some old friends and meet lots of new ones!

Cybro Radio
info@cybroradio.us
www.cybroradio.com
Blues, R&B, Jazz, Big Band, Swing, Cajun and Gospel music.

ElectricBlues Radio
PO 1370, Riverview, FL 33568-1370
GoodBlues@ElectricBluesRadio.com
web.tampabay.rr.com/ebradio
Sizzlin' electric Blues guitar.

Every Day I Have The Blues
www.thebluesnet.com
We promote Independent Blues groups, artists, and songwriters heavily.

Incensemans Groove
incenseman@sbcglobal.net
www.live365.com/stations/309897
Blues you won't hear anywhere else, Grooves, some Jazz and music from new artists in The San Francisco area!

MasterpieceNetBlues
HomerDylan@comcast.net
www.live365.com/stations/70253
Blues, Folk and Rock from all eras. From old masters to current artists. Plus a few surprises!

Smokestack Lightnin' WUCF
200 Shell Point W. Maitland, FL 32751
blues@smokestacklightnin.com
www.smokestacklightnin.com
Syndicated show playing Blues, Rhythm & Blues, Soul, Funk, Blues/Rock and Zydeco.

California

Ann the Raven's Blues Show KCSN
18111 Nordhoff St., Northridge, CA 91330-8312
Ann the Raven anntheraven@aol.com
www.kcsn.org/programs/anntheraven.html
Delivering the best Blues sounds in Southern California for over 20 years.

Rollin' and Tumblin' KUSP
PO Box 423, Santa Cruz, CA 95061
PH: 408-476-2800 FX: 408-476-2802
www.kusp.org
Send any promotional items for airplay, giveaway or review.

Two Steps from the Blues KUSP
Blues Programming, 203 8th Ave.
Santa Cruz, CA 95062
PH: 408-476-2800 FX: 408-476-2802
www.kusp.org
Send any promotional items for airplay, giveaway or review.

Connecticut

Sunday Night Blues WCCC
1039 Asylum Ave. Hartford, CT 06105
Beef Stew beefstew@wccc.com
www.megablues.com/program.htm
Six hours of ass kickin' Blues!

Illinois

Basement of Blues WMKB
Chicago Slim chicagoslim@basementofblues.com
www.basementofblues.com
Blues from classic artists to current local talents.

Indiana

The Blues Revue WVPE
2424 California Rd. Elkhart, IN 46514
PH: 888-399-9873
Ole Harv oleharv@worldnet.att.net
www.wvpe.org/blues_revue.html
Celebrating over 20 years of the Blues!

Minnesota

Rollin & Tumblin KFAI
1808 Riverside Ave. Minneapolis, MN 55454
PH: 612-341-3144
Jacquie Maddix diamondblue@qwest.net
www.kfai.org/programs/roll_tum.htm
A synthesis of Blues and Big Band.

Nebraska

Confessin' The Blues KZUM
941 "O" St., Lincoln, NE 68508
PH: 402-474-5086 FX: 402-474-5091
Bill Wagner confessintheblues@yahoo.com
www.confessintheblues.org
I'm always looking for new or established talent to have on the show.

Mystic Mile KZUM
941 "O" St., Lincoln, NE 68508
PH: 402-474-5086 FX: 402-474-5091
Mike Flowers mflowers@lps.org
www.kzum.org/mystic
Nothing but the very best of Blues with the classics and new releases.

New York

Across the Tracks WFDU
Metropolitan Campus, 1000 River Rd. T-WFDU,
Teaneck, NJ 07666
PH: 201-692-2806 FX: 201-692-2807
Dave Grogan grogans@aol.com
wfdu.fm
Blends both classic Blues and Soul with new artists who perform in the traditional style.

Bad Dog Blues Radio Show WITR
PO Box 20563, Rochester, NY 14602-0563
PH: 585-475-5643 FX: 585-475-4988
www.baddogblues.com
We span the history of the Blues bringing you everything from Barrelhouse Piano to searing Electric Blues.

Sunday Night Blues WAER
795 Ostrom Ave. Syracuse, NY 13244-4601
PH: 315-443-4021 FX: 315-443-2148
Tom Townsley waer@syr.edu
waer.org
For over 12 years supplying Blues fans a healthy dosage of both national and local Blues talent.

Texas

On the Roadside KMBH
PO Box 2147, Harlingen, TX 78551
PH: 956-421-4111 FX: 956-421-4150
Chris Maley kmbhkhid@aol.com
www.kmbh.org/radio/roadside.htm
The best in classic & latest Blues.

Virginia

Blues Valley WMRA
PO Box 1292, Harrisonburg, VA 22803
PH: 540-568-6221 FX: 540-568-3814
Gregory Versen versengr@cisat.jmu.edu
www.jmu.edu/wmra/blues.html
I accept Indie releases, give them a listen, and if it fits, I play it.

Canada

Natch'l Blues CKUA
10526 Jasper Ave. Edmonton, AB T5J 1Z7
PH: 780-428-7595 FX: 780-428-7624
holger.petersen@ckua.org
www.ckua.org
Canada's longest running Blues program. Over 33 years old!

Saturday Night Blues CBC
PO Box 555, Edmonton, AB T5J 2P4
PH: 780-468-7472
Holger Petersen snb@edmonton.cbc.ca
www.cbc.ca/snb
Concerts, interviews, artist features, new releases.

France

Midnight Special Blues Radio
Paul Bondarovski, 14, rue Olier, 75015 Paris, France
PH: +33-1-45323893 FX: 2062030639
Paul Bondarovski bonda@ms-blues.com
www.ms-blues.com
We provide support for independent artists, and take part in this important and joyful movement - Keeping The Blues Alive!

The Netherlands

Blue Ears
E. Samsonstraat 5, 1103 MR Amsterdam Z-O,
The Netherlands
info@BlueEars.com
www.blueEars.com
Independent radio station for adventurous Blues (y) music.

Blueprint
Tjariet 34, 9642 KD Veendam, The Netherlands
Thomas Kaldijk thomasharm@planet.nl
www.realrootscafe.com/blueprint.html
Honest and genuine music styles like Southern Soul, Blues, Country and Rock & Roll. Roots music from past and present with heart and soul.

Triple R Blues
triplerblues@home.nl
www.live365.com/stations/radioton21
I play Blues music of all kinds. I'm not a critic, I just love the music, no......I eat it, I'm a Blues animal!

United Kingdom

The Blue Front Blues Room Forest of Dean Radio
1 Berisford Ct. Cinderford,
Gloucestershire, GL14 2BS UK
PH: 01594-820722
contactus@fodradio.org
www.fodradio.org
A monthly mix of Traditional and Modern, Acoustic and Electric Blues.

Children's Radio

Alphabet Soup WBRS
Brandeis U. 415 South St.,
Waltham, MA 02453-2728
PH: 781-736-4785
music@wbrs.org
www.wbrs.org
The best children's music on the airwaves.

CBC 4 Kids Music
PO Box 500 Stn. A, Toronto, ON M5W 1E6
PH: 866-306-4636
kids@cbc.ca
www.cbc.ca/kids
Features interviews and music from Canadian music stars.

Children's Corner *KUFM*
MPR, 32 Campus Dr. U. Montana,
Missoula, MT 59812-8064
PH: 406-243-4931 FX: 406-243-3299
www.kufm.org
Delightful stories and music for children.

Children's Hour *KRZA*
528 9th St., Alamosa, CO 81101
PH: 719-589-8844
programming@krza.org
www.krza.org

Children's Hour *KUNM*
MSC06 3520, Onate Hall, 1 U. New Mexico,
Albuquerque, NM 87131-0001
PH: 505-277-4806
kunmkids@unm.edu
www.kunm.org
Music and stories for children of all ages.

Children's Stories & Music *KMUD*
PO Box 135, 1144 Redway Dr.
Redway, CA 95560-0135
PH: 707-923-2513 FX: 707-923-2501
Kate Klein md@kmud.org
www.kmud.org
An inspirational blend of stories and music for children of all ages.

Christian Pirate Radio Kids Show
701 N. Brand Blvd. #550, Glendale, CA 91203
PH: 888-321-2469 FX: 818-956-7030
ahoy@mycpr.com
www.mycpr.com
Programs for kids and kids at heart.

HIS KIDS RADIO
PO Box 151515, Grand Rapids, MI 49515-1515
mail@HisKidsRadio.net
hiskidsradio.gospelcom.net
A Christian station for the young heart.

Kids Corner *WXPN*
3025 Walnut St., Philadelphia, PA 19104
PH: 215-898-6677 FX: 215-898-0707
Kathy O'Connell & Robert Drake
Robert@kidscorner.org
kidscorner.org
Entertaining and educational programming for children.

Kids on Fire for Jesus
mail@praiseonfire.com
www.praiseonfire.com/KIDS
Saturday morning kids programming block.

Kids Play *WLUW*
6525 N. Sheridan Rd. Chicago, IL 60626
PH: 773-508-8080 FX: 773-508-8082
Sheila Donlan kidsplay@wluw.org
wluw.org
Features new and old releases of kids' music.

KidMixRadio
Box 5173, Norwell, MA 02061
Kimberly Robasky editor@boopadoo.net
www.KidMixRadio.com
Please send your CDs with contact information and expressed written permission to play your titles. You can also send your MP3s via e-mail.

Over the Moon *KGLP*
c/o Jonathan Dooley, 200 College Dr.
Gallup, NM 87301
PH: 505-863-7626 FX: 505-863-7633
www.kglp.org/moon
Music for Children of all ages incorporates a wide variety of themes that include the best in Children's music and literature.

Pea Green Boat *KUFM*
MPR, 32 Campus Dr. Missoula, MT 59812-8064
PH: 406-243-4931 FX: 1-406-243-3299
www.kufm.org
Stories, songs, poetry and special guests for kids.

Radio Lollipop
6 St Andrew St., London, EC4A 3LX UK
PH: 44-0-208-661-0666
info@radiolollipop.org
www.radiolollipop.org
Providing smiles and laughter to children during their stay in the hospital.

Tell Us a Tale *WTJU*
PO Box 400811, U. Virginia,
Charlottesville, VA 22904-4811
PH: 434-978-3603 FX: 434-978-4935
Peter@tellusatale.com
www.tellusatale.com
Send us your CDs for radio airplay consideration or review.

We Kids Radio
PO Box 444, Paradise, CA 95969
Mr.Nick@WeKids.org
www.wekids.org
Pointing little people and their families to God.

We Like Kids! *KTOO*
360 Egan Dr. Juneau, AK 99801-1748
PH: 907-586-1670 FX: 907-586-3612
Jeff Brown jbrown@alaska.net
www.ktoo.org
Weekly Children's music show.

Christian Radio
Promoters

HMG-Nashville Radio Promotions
PO Box 100584, Nashville, TN 37224
PH: 615-248-8105 FX: 615-248-8505
info@powersourcemusic.com
ccma.cc/hmg
Country, Christian Country, Southern Gospel, Bluegrass & Bluegrass Gospel etc.

Stations
United States

A-Blazin Grace Radio
2060 3rd Ave. #12-A, New York, NY 10029
PH: 978-984-3106
www.kay3music.com
Keeping the Gospel airwaves hot!

Air 1
5700 W. Oaks Blvd. Rocklin, CA 95765
PH: 888-937-2471 FX: 888-329-2471
www.AIR1.com
If you have something with exceptional sound quality, contact us.

Arraz Radio
240 Fleetwood Dr, Hot Springs, AR 71913
PH: 501-844-7748
Andrew Bonds bonds@arraz.net
arraz.net
Playin' GODCORE music for a HARDCORE world. 24/7 Christian: Rock, Metal, & Rap.

Bread-n-Jam *WRXV*
Erik Lane erik@breadnjam.net
www.breadnjam.net
Rock & Roll 2 feed your soul!

Black Gospel Radio
4142 Ogletown-Stanton Rd. #138,
Newark, DE 19713
PH: 215-227-5026
Alicia Hall dj@blackgospelradio.net
www.blackgospelradio.net
Playing the best in Black Gospel Music on the internet.

Christian Blues Radio
john@christianblues.net
www.christianblues.net
The web's most complete resource for Christian Blues music and Christian Blues artists.

Christian Music Corner
diane13dj@yahoo.com
live365.com/stations/dianedj13
Whatever touches my heart, I will play and pray it blesses anyone listening.

Christian Pirate Radio
701 N. Brand Blvd. #550, Glendale, CA 91203
PH: 888-321-2469 FX: 818-956-7030
Ahoy@mycpr.com
www.mycpr.com
Playing independent artists, modern Rock and contemporary Christian music.

Christian Pirate Xtreme
701 N. Brand Blvd #550, Glendale, CA 91203
PH: 888-321-2469 FX: 818-956-7030
ahoy@mycpr.com
www.cprxtreme.com
Expanding Modern Christian Music into the realms of Ska, Punk, Rock, Loud, Swing etc.

Christian Rock Radio
online@christianrockradio.com
www.christianrockradio.com
We also do album and concert reviews.

ChristianRock.net
333 Park Central E. #610, Springfield, MO 65806
PH: 417-865-1283 x41 FX: 417-865-9062
mail@christianrock.net
www.christianrock.net
Listen to what they play on the station and only send it if it matches the style.

Classic Christian Rock Radio
hdcr365@earthlink.net
www.hdcr365.com
Features Rock music from artists who proclaim themselves to be Christians and who have demonstrated Christian attributes in their lives.

CMRadio.Net
PO Box 687, Allentown, PA 18105-0687
FX: 610-746-4053
musicmakers@cmradio.net
www.cmradio.net
Worldwide source of Christ inspired music.

Cornerstone *KXUL*
130 Stubbs Hall, ULM Monroe, LA 71209-8821
PH: 318-342-5662
kxul.com
A non-sectarian presentation of contemporary Christian music.

DeltaWav
c/o WEJF Radio, 2824 Palm Bay Rd.
Palm Bay, FL 32905
Rick & Kevin info@deltawav.com
deltawav.com
Dedicated to playing Indie artists. We are bringing Indie Christian music to the air waves.

Effect Radio
PO Box 271, Twin Falls, ID 83301
PH: 208-734-2049 FX: 208-736-1958
effectradio@hotmail.com
www.effectradio.com
We play music as led by the Spirit of the living God of the Bible.

eJNM.net
6550 Maurice-Duplessis,
Montréal-Nord, QC H1G 6K9
PH: 514-324-2190
Gene Kelley englishprogram@ejnm.net
eJNM.net
A source of blessing for our brothers & sisters ...the independant Christian artist. We have programming in English, French, Italian & Spanish.

En Sound Radio
PO Box 319, Bronx, NY 010453
PH: 718-741-3271 FX: 801-340-1126
Delroy ensound@ensoundentertainment.com
www.ensoundentertainment.com
Listing of Gospel music anywhere on the web.

The Fish 95.9
PO Box 29023, Glendale, CA 91209
PH: 818-956-5552
fishfeedback@thefish959.com
www.TheFish959.com

God Gets The Glory Radio
Cedric Bullock cedricmbullock@netscape.ne
www.live365.com/profiles/jordan23ww?
Expect to hear the best in Gospel.

The Gospel Connection *WRBB*
360 Huntington Ave. #174, Curry Student Ctr.
Boston, MA 02115
PH: 617-373-4339 FX: 617-373-5095
WRBBGOSPEL1@yahoo.com
wrbbradio.org
The longest running Gospel show in Boston!

The Gospel Experience *KPFA*
1929 MLK Jr. Way Berkeley, CA 94704
PH: 510-848-6767 FX: 510-848-3812
Emmit Powell emmitap@aol.com
www.kpfa.org
One of the longest running gospel music shows in the Bay Area.

Gospel Harmony Mix *KSGM*
1023 N. Pine St., DeRidder, LA 70634
PH: 337-463-2040
Tony Partigianoni inkognito@earthlink.net
www.ksgm.com
A nice blend of Southern Gospel Music and Country Gospel Music.

The Gospel Hiway
PO Box 34321, Houston, TX 77234-4321
Attn: Music Director
dj@thegospelhiway.org
www.thegospelhiway.org
Submissions must be on CD, professionally produced along with a bio on the group or artist so we can know more about you.

Gospel House Music Radio
PO Box 583151, Minneapolis, MN 55458
Thomas@gospelhousemusic.com
www.gospelhousemusic.com
Your original source for Gospel House music.

Gospel Jazzations *WFDU*
1000 River Rd. Teaneck, NJ 07666
PH: 201-833-0694
Tony Smith gospeljazzations@yahoo.com
www.gospeljazzations.com
Focuses on the instrumental side of Gospel Jazz.

Gospel Revelations *WFDU*
1000 River Rd. Teaneck, NJ 07666
PH: 201-692-2806 FX: 201-692-2807
Stacy Wendell gospelrevelations@yahoo.com
www.wfdu.fm
Bringing you the very best variety of Traditional Gospel Music.

The Gospel Sound
1023 N. Pine St., DeRidder, LA 70634
PH: 337-463-2040
Tony Partigianoni inkognito@earthlink.net
thegospelsound.com
Southern Gospel Music featuring quartet-style singing and close harmony.

The Gospel Truth *WNCW*
PO Box 804, Spindale, NC 28160
PH: 828-287-8000 x328 FX: 828-287-8012
www.wncw.org
Bluegrass Gospel. Send 2 CDs to the attention of the Music Director. Make sure to include a one-sheet (bio).

Gospel Twang Radio
1023 N. Pine St., DeRidder, LA 70634
PH: 337-463-2040
Tony Partigianoni inkognito@earthlink.net
gospeltwang.com
A nice blend of Christian Country and Bluegrass Gospel Music.

Gospel's Glory Road *KOHO*
7475 KOHO Place, Leavenworth, WA 98826
PH: 509-548-1011 FX: 509-548-3222
John T. Humphreys johnt@kohoradio.com
www.kohoradio.com
An exciting blend of music and artists.

HCJB World Radio
PO Box 39800, Colorado Springs, CO 80949-9800
PH: 719-590-9800 FX: 719-590-9801
info@hcjb.org
www.hcjb.org
Broadcasts the Gospel in nearly 120 languages.

HCR *Huntington College*
2303 College Ave. Huntington, IN 46750
Attn: Music Director
www.hcradio.net

Holy Hip Hop Radio
PO Box 1023, Pine Lake, GA 30072
www.holyhiphop.com/radio
Over 200 domestic & international markets. Please send 2 CDs!

The Indie Rock Show
PO Box 120358, Clermont, FL 34712-0358
www.theindierockshow.com
Home of the hottest Indies on the Planet!

Indy Live
PO Box 2552, Lakeside, AZ 85929
Bill Freeland kwkmbillman@yahoo.com
indylive.gq.nu
We only air positive mindset, non-degrading, or Christian-Spiritual based materials.

Intense Radio
PO Box 1477, Mt. Juliet, TN 37121-1477
www.IntenseRadio.com
Christian Rock. Programs, great music, interviews and more.

JamX Radio
jamxradio@gmail.com
www.jamxradio.net
Your recordings don't even need to be in studio quality! Garage/home recordings sound real cool to us! Unlike most radio stations which demand submitted songs to be professionally recorded, here at JamX Radio, we embrace the "raw" feel of home recordings.

KCMS
19303 Fremont Ave. N. Seattle, WA 98133
PH: 206-546-7350 FX: 206-546-7372
tom@spirit1053.com
www.spirit1053.com

KCWJ
4200 Blue Ridge Blvd. #LF18,
Kansas City, MO 64133
PH: 816-313-0049 FX: 816-313-1036
Paul@1030thelight.com
www.1030thelight.com

Kingdom Keys Network
PO Box 8088, Amarillo, TX 79114-8088
PH: 806-359-8855 FX: 806-354-2039
kjrt@kingdomkeys.org
www.kingdomkeys.org
Teaching, preaching, music, news, talk and commentaries.

KJTX
PO Box 150151, Longview, TX 75615
PH: 903-759-1243
kjtx@jeffersontx.com
www.kjtxgospel.com
High energy Gospel. Will play independent artists.

KLRC *John Brown U.*
2000 W. University, Siloam Springs, AR 72761
PH: 479-524-7101 FX: 479-524-7451
klrc@klrc.com
www.klrc.com

KOBC *Ozark Christian College*
1111 N. Main Joplin, MO 64801
PH: 417-781-6401 FX: 417-782-1841
kobc@kobc.org
www.kobc.org

KTIS *Northwestern College*
3003 Snelling Ave N. Saint Paul, MN 55113-1598
PH: 651-631-5000
studio@ktis.org
www.ktis.org

KTCU *Texas Christian U.*
TCU Box 298020, Fort Worth, TX 76129
PH: 817-257-7631
ktcu@tcu.edu
www.ktcu.tcu.edu/ktcu

KWAM
2650 Thousand Oaks Blvd. #4100,
Memphis, TN 38118
PH: 901-259-1300 FX: 901-259-6445
www.am990.com

Mariner Radio
6485 Omaha Blvd. #4,
Colorado Springs, CO 80915-2633
PH: 719-574-2310
Jeffrey J. Roediger radio@marinerministries.org
www.marinerministries.org
Christian Internet Radio. A non-profit ministry reaching the world for Christ.

Nightowl Radio *WIOJ*
10055 Beach Blvd. Jacksonville, FL 32246
PH: 904-641-1010 FX: 9046411022
wioj@wioj.net
www.wioj.net
Christian Rock, Punk, Electronic and Techno show.

Power FM
11061 Shady Trail, Dallas, TX 75229
PH: 214-353-8970
Eddie Alcaraz eddie@kvrk.com
897powerfm.com
A full time Christian Rock station in North Texas

Rebourne Radio
1102 Llano Cove, Memphis, TN 38134
PH: 901-388-2988
Bill Simmers radio@rebourne.net
www.rebourneradio.com
Indie positive CD submissions are welcome!

Reign Radio
PO Box 10252, Daytona Beach, FL 32120-0252
md@reignradio.com
www.reignradio.com
Christian Rock. Helping Christian artists get heard!

RevFM
925 Houserville Rd. State College, PA 16801
PH: 814-867-1922
info@revfm.net
www.revfm.net
We seek to play modern Christian music, but do so with a specific goal of encouraging believers to grow spiritually and to share the message of Jesus with unbelievers.

Rhythm N' Praise Radio
370 W. Pleasantview Ave. #289,
Hackensack, NJ 07601
RNPRADIO@optonline.net
www.rhythmandpraise.com
Contemporary Gospel music 24 hours a day. 75% of the music we play is independent. We will also review your music.

Savagerock
PH: 866-868-9824
Shane Timson shane@savagerock.com
savagerock.com
Our goal is to provide the world with great Hard Rock focused on Jesus Christ.

Serious Comedy Radio
1023 N. Pine St., DeRidder, LA 70634
PH: 337-463-2040
Tony Partigianoni inkognito@earthlink.net
seriouscomedyradio.com
Family-friendly comedy featuring many Christian artists.

sglive365.com
903 Rogers St., Clinton, TN 37716
dj@sglive365.com
www.sglive365.com
Southern Gospel radio. Feel free to send us your music!

SGM Radio
rob@sgmradio.com
www.sgmradio.com
Today's best Southern Gospel and Christian Country Music. We'll also review your album.

Shine / Extreme Worship *KHPE*
PO Box 278, Albany, OR 97321
PH: 541-926-2431
Paul Hernandez paul@hope1079.com
www.khpeonline.com

Silent Planet Radio *WCLH*
641 N. Washington St., Wilkes-Barre, PA 18705
PH: 570-417-3818 FX: 570-822-5848
Mark Blair mark@silentplanetradio.com
www.silentplanetradio.com
Progressive Christian music.

Smooth Pizzazz
David@songsofdavid.com
songsofdavid.com
Jazz With Pizzazz! Featuring Christian artists.... lively, energetic, and intoxicating Jazz that touches the soul!

Solid Gospel
402 BNA Dr. #400 Nashville, TN 37217
PH: 615-367-2210 FX: 615-367-0758
info@solidgospel.com
www.solidgospel.com

Sound of Light
PO Box 2212, Spartanburg, SC 29304
PH: 888-765-4487
mail@soundoflight.com
www.soundoflight.com
We do play Indie music, so send it along.

Southern Fried Gospel *WDCB*
College of DuPage, 425 Fawell Blvd.
Glen Ellyn, IL 60137
PH: 630-942-4200 FX: 630-942-2788
Harry Rohde RohdeH@wdcb.org
wdcb.org
Reflecting a branch of the rich Southern culture.

sglive365.com RADIO
903 Rogers St., Clinton, TN 37716
dj@sglive365.com
www.sglive365.com
The nation's Southern Gospel station.

The Spirit Radio
PO Box 245, Pendleton, IN 46064
PH: 317-501-2242 FX: 317-428-4675
info@thespiritradio.com
www.thespiritradio.net
Christian artists ranging from Easy Listening to Heavy Metal. Most artist pages have songs for you to sample, in addition to bios, tour dates, news and more.

Spiritco1.com Radio
6178 Oxon Hill Rd. #101, Oxon Hill, MD 20745
PH: 301-567-5349
Henry W. Harris Spiritco1@aol.com
www.spiritco1.com
The Internet allows us to reach the world and spread the Gospel Ministry of Music and Messages to the Internet Radio Community. Spiritco1.com has established a relationship with our customers that will last a lifetime.

Star93fm.com
PO Box 4048, Clinton, MS 39058
PH: 925-3548 FX: 925-3337
www.star93fm.com

StreetRadio.com
c/o WOTS Ministries, PO Box 1636,
Indian Trail, NC 28079
programdir@streetradio.com
streetradio.com
Featuring some of the most positive programs on the web.

Sunday Night Gospel Show
c/o 24 Hour Gospel Network / KNES Radio,
PO Box 1184, Crockett, TX 75835
PH: 936-546-8291 FX: 270-837-1977
Reverend Reginald Marshall, Sr.
info@24hourgospelnetwork.org
www.24hourgospelnetwork.org
Accepting Black Gospel and Gospel Jazz music for airplay consideration.

Three Angels Broadcasting Network
PO Box 220, W. Frankfort, IL 62896
PH: 618-627-4651 FX: 618-627-2726
www.3abn.org

Train to Glory *KUNM*
MSC06 3520, Onate Hall 1 U. New Mexico,
Albuquerque, NM 87131-0001
PH: 505-277-4806
music@kunm.org
www.kunm.org
Black Gospel music featuring traditional, contemporary and local church choirs.

trancedomain.com
trancelott@aol.com
www.trancedomain.com
Bringing you the best talent in the Electronic music industry. We are always looking for mix sets and original material to feature on our website.

Uncle Samoo's Zoo *WITR*
sammep@aol.com
www.thelivingrock.com
Featuring independent & import artists from all around the globe!

Uneon Entertainment
PH: 310-384-0386
Bryant Johnson info@uneonentertainment.com
www.uneonentertainment.com
Spiritual Hip Hop.

WAY-FM
1012 McEwen Dr. Franklin, TN 37067
PH: 615-261-9293 FX: 615-261-3967
waym@wayfm.com
waym.wayfm.com
We use radio to encourage youth and young adults in their Christian walk.

WBL2Radio
PO Box 92055, Nashville, TN 37209
PH: 615-230-0870
wbl2radio@yahoo.com
wbl2radio.com
Your source for Christian Country, Classic Country and Gospel Music.

WBCS *Bethel College*
3900 Bethel Dr. St. Paul, MN 55112-6999
PH: 651-638-6283
wbcs@bethel.edu
www.bethel.edu/Majors/Communication/wbcs

WCDR *Cedarville College*
PO Box 601, Cedarville, OH 45314
PH: 1-800-333-0601 FX: 1-937-766-7927
cdrradio@cdrradio.com
www.cdrradio.com

WCNO
2960 SW Mapp Rd. Palm City, FL 34990
PH: 772-221-1100 FX: 772-221-8716
wcno@wcno.com
www.wcno.com
Adult Contemporary Christian Music and programming.

WCSE
126 Sharp Hill Rd. Uncasville, CT 06382
PH: 860-848-7400
Steve Harper stepharper@snet.net
A Christian station that plays the music of independent artists.

WETN *Wheaton College*
501 College Ave. Wheaton, IL 60187
PH: 630-752-5074
wetn@wheaton.edu
www.wheaton.edu/wetn

WFCA *French Camp Academy*
Route 1, Box 12, French Camp, MS 39745
PH: 662-547-6414 FX: 662-547-9451
events@wfcafm108.com
www.wfcafm108.com
All Southern Gospel radio.

WGEV *Geneva College*
c/o Dept. of Communication, 3200 College Ave. Beaver Falls, PA 15010
PH: 724-846-5100
web@geneva.edu
www.wgev.net

WGRN *Greenville College*
315 E. College Ave. Greenville, IL 62246
PH: 618 664 6789
WGRNMusicDirector@greenville.edu
wgrn.greenville.edu

WGTS *Columbia U. College*
7600 Flower Ave. Takoma Park, MD 20912
PH: 301-270-1800 FX: 301-270-9191
wgts@wgts.org
www.wgts.org

What's the Buzz *WCNI*
247 Haley Rd. Ledyard, CT 06339
PH: 860-572-2705
John Fogg Jr. buzzradiowcni@aol.com
www.wcniradio.org
A weekly 3 hour show. Christian Rock, Pop & Hip Hop. I am happy to play the music of independent artists.

Whitedove Radio
Crystal Clear, HCR 82 Box 62-A, Salem, MO 65560
www.whitedoveradio.com
If your music is selected to be played on our station, there is a $25 fee.

WMHK *Columbia International U.*
PO Box 3122, Columbia, SC 29230
PH: 803-754-5400 FX: 803-714-0849
www.wmhk.com

WOCG *Oakwood College*
7000 Adventist Blvd. Huntsville, AL 35896
PH: 256-726-7420 FX: 256-726-7417
wocg@wocg.org
www.wocg.org

WRCM *Columbia International U.*
PO Box 17069, Charlotte, NC 28227
PH: 704-821-9293 FX: 704-821-9285
info@newlife919.com
www.newlife919.com

WRVL *Liberty U.*
1971 U. Blvd Lynchburg, VA 24502
PH: 434-582-3688 FX: 434-582-2994
wrvl@liberty.edu
www.liberty.edu/wrvl

WSAE *Spring Arbor College*
106 E. Main St., Spring Arbor, MI 49283
PH: 517-750-9723 FX: 517-750-6619
wsae@arbor.edu
www.arbor.edu/wsae

WTBC
PO Box 18891, Huntsville, AL 35804
Mike T. miket@wtbcradio.com
www.wtbcradio.com
Gospel and Holy Hip Hop.

Canada

CHRI
1010 Thomas Spratt Pl. #3, Ottawa, ON K1G 5L5
PH: 613-247-1440 FX: 613-247-7128
chri@chri.ca
chri.ca

GospelCity.com Radio
1410 Stanley St. #1020, Montreal, QC H3A 1P8
PH: 800-858-3207
promotions@corp.gospelcity.com
www.gospelcity.com/radio
We play Traditional, Contemporary, Urban/Inspirational, Rap/Hip Hop, & Quartet Gospel.

Malta

Maltanetworkresources Praise and Worship Internet Radio
PH: 356-99882177
Clyde Meli streamingprobs@catholichealing.com
www.maltanetworkresources.com
A 24 hour Catholic Christian internet radio from Malta playing a range of praise and worship songs as well as contemporary Christian artists.

United Kingdom

Branch FM
PH: 01924-465600
studio@branchfm.co.uk
www.branchfm.co.uk
Christian music 24/365 available across the globe.

Cross Rhythms Radio
PO Box 1110, Stoke on Trent, ST1 1XR UK
PH: 44-8700-118-008 FX: 44-8700-117-002
radio@crossrhythms.co.uk
www.crossrhythms.co.uk/radio
Predominantly contemporary Christian music.

Australia

Rhema FM
PO Box 886, Belmont, VIC 3216 Australia
PH: 61-3-5241-6550 FX: 61-3-5241-6552
rhema@rhemafm.org.au
www.rhemafm.org.au
A station that can change lives for good and the promotion of family values.

Classical Radio

North America

United States

Classical Excursions *KTCU*
TCU Box 298020, Fort Worth, TX 76129
PH: 817-257-7631
Rosemary Solomons R.Solomons@tcu.edu
www.ktcu.tcu.edu/ktcu/html/classical_excursions.html
www.ktcu.tcu.edu
Two uninterrupted hours of music from the Baroque to the present.

Classical 89.3 *WCAL*
1520 St. Olaf Ave. Northfield, MN 55057
PH: 612-798-9225 FX: 612-798-8614
Accepts quality Indie submissions.

Classical Music with Jeff Esworthy *MPR*
45 E. 7th St., Saint Paul, MN 55101
PH: 651-290-1212
Jeff Esworthy mail@mpr.org
music.mpr.org/programs/mttnight
Featuring performances by the outstanding artists of our region alongside recordings by the world's finest music makers.

ClassicalGuitar.cc
Michae Cervane info@classicalguitar.cc
ClassicalGuitar.cc
Music for the Classical guitar, including solos, chamber pieces, and concertos.

ClassicalMusicAmerica.com
PH: 248-324-2600 FX: 248-324-0439
Pat McElroy
patmcelroy@classicalmusicamerica.com
www.classicalmusicamerica.com
Local events, music and recording artists are prominent in the mix.

Colorado Public Radio
2249 S Josephine St., Denver, CO 80210
PH: 800-722-4449 FX: 303-733-3319
cpr.org
Presents the full range of Classical music.

The Composer's Voice *MPR*
45 E. 7th St. Saint Paul, MN 55101
PH: 651-290-1212
John Zech mail@mpr.org
music.minnesota.publicradio.org/programs/
composersvoice
The program that asks current composers: Who are you? - What does your music sound like? Why does it sound the way it does?

Contemplation Connection *KKUP*
PO Box 820, Cupertino, CA 95015
PH: 408-260-2999
Roger Werner wernerr@pacbell.net
www.yosquare.com/rogerwerner/html_files
www.kkup.com
Visionary and Classical music for contemplation. Quotes for self-awareness.

From the Top
295 Huntington Ave. Boston, MA 02115
PH: 617-437-0707 FX: 617-262-4267
info@fromthetop.org
www.fromthetop.org
Showcases the nation's most exceptional pre-college age Classical musicians.

GoldMedia Showcase
compaxx@012.net.il
www.live365.com/stations/compaxx
Classical all day - the finest of 16th-19th century masterpieces.

Harmonia *WFIU*
1229 E. 7th St., Bloomington, IN 47405
PH: 812-855-1357
Angela Mariani harmonia@indiana.edu
www.indiana.edu/~harmonia
Brings the music of these earlier periods to life.

Here of a Sunday Morning *WBAI*
120 Wall St., New York, NY 10005
PH: 212-209-2900
Chris Whent mail@hoasm.org
www.hoasm.org
The very best in Early music.

In the Spotlight *WBNI*
3204 Clairmont Ct. PO Box 8459,
Fort Wayne, IN 46898-8459
PH: 260-452-1189 FX: 260-452-1188
Janice Furtner jfurtner@nipr.fm
www.nipr.fm/wbni/spotlight
We often broadcast performances by local musicians and ensembles.

The Kalvos & Damian New Music Bazaar *WGDR*
176 Cox Brook Rd. Northfield, VT 05663
Dennis Báthory-Kitsz dennis@maltedmedia.com
www.kalvos.org
Bringing composers to the wider world through their music, interviews, artwork, ideas etc.

KANU
1120 W. 11th St., U. Kansas, Lawrence, KS 66044
PH: 785-864-4530 FX: 785-864-5278
Rachel Hunter rhunter@ku.edu
kanu.ku.edu
We do play music by independent Classical musicians.

KBIA
409 Jesse Hall, Columbia, MO 65211
PH: 573-882-3431 FX: 573-882-2636
kbia@kbia.org
www.kbia.org
We love to play music from new and independent Classical artists.

KBPS
515 NE 15th Ave. Portland, OR 97232
PH: 503-916-5828 FX: 503-916-2642
music.info@allclassical.org
www.allclassical.org
Happy to receive any CDs by Indie performers of standard Classical.

KBYU *Brigham Young U.*
2000 Ironton Blvd. Provo, UT 84606
PH: 800-298-5298
www.kbyu.org
New material is reviewed and aired if deemed appropriate.

KCME
1921 N. Weber St., Colorado Springs, CO 80907
PH: 719-578-5263 FX: 719-578-1033
jazz@kcme.org
www.kcme.org
We play independent labels Classical and Jazz music.

KCSC *U. Central Oklahoma*
100 N. University Dr. Edmond, OK 73034
PH: 405-974-3333 FX: 405-974-3844
kanderson@kcscfm.com
www.kcscfm.com

KDFC
455 Market St. #2300,
San Francisco, CA 94105-2446
PH: 415-975-5332 FX: 415-777-4611
rmalone@kdfc.com
www.kdfc.com
We don't discriminate against struggling musicians!

KEDM
ULM 225 Stubbs Hall Monroe, LA 71209-6805
PH: 318-342-5565 FX: 318-342-5570
kedm@ulm.edu
www.kedm.org
We do play Classical music by independent musicians/composers/producers.

KFUO
85 Founders Ln. St. Louis, MO 63105
PH: 314-725-0099 FX: 314-725-3801
Jim Connett jconnett@classic99.com
www.classic99.com

KING
10 Harrison St. #100, Seattle, WA 98109
PH: 206-691-2981 FX: 206-691-2982
Tom Olsen tomo@king.org
www.king.org
We do air independent musician's recordings.

KNAU *Northern Arizona U.*
Bldg 83 Box 5764, Flagstaff, AZ 86011
PH: 928-523-5628
knauradio.org

KNPR *Nevada Public Radio*
1289 S. Torrey Pines Dr. Las Vegas, NV 89146
PH: 702-258-9895 FX: 702-258-5646
Florence Rogers flo@knpr.org
www.knpr.org
I try to play as many independents as I can.

KRPS
PO Box 899, Pittsburg, KS 66762
PH: 620-235-4288
www.krps.org
Any music received is first reviewed by our Program Director.

KSUI
710 S. Clinton St., Iowa City, IA 52242-1030
PH: 319-335-5730 FX: 319-335-6116
Joan Kjaer Kirkman joan-kirkman@uiowa.edu
ksui.uiowa.edu
We welcome the music of Independent Classical musicians.

KUAT
PO Box 210067, Tucson, AZ 85721-0067
PH: 520-621-5828
www.kuat.org
A "serious" Classical station. NO recordings from New-Age noodlers.

KUFM *Morning Classics*
U. Montana, Missoula, MT 59812-8064
PH: 406-243-4931 FX: 406-243-3299
www.kufm.org
We play a wide variety of Classical music.

KUHF
4343 Elgin, Fl. 3 Houston, TX 77204-0887
PH: 713-743-0887 FX: 713-743-0868
www.kuhf.org
As long as your performances and recordings are of professional quality, we'll play 'em.

KUSC
PO Box 77913, Los Angeles, CA 90007-0913
PH: 213-225-7400
kusc@kusc.org
www.kusc.org
Making Classical music a more important part of more people's lives.

KWAX *U. Oregon*
Agate Hall, Eugene, OR 97403
PH: 541-345-0800
kwax@qwest.net
www.uoregon.edu/~kwax
Classical music 24-hour a day.

KWIT *West Iowa Tech College*
4647 Stone Ave. PO Box 5199,
Sioux City, IA 51106
PH: 712-274-6406 FX: 712-274-6411
www.kwit.org

KXMS *Missouri Southern State U.*
3950 E. Newman Rd. Joplin, MO 64801-1595
PH: 417-625-9356 FX: 417-625-9742
kxms@mssu.edu
www.kxms.org
Happy to highlight independent Classical CDs. Please send only Classical Music!

Millennium of Music
2775 S. Quincy St., Arlington, VA 22206
radman@weta.com
www.classicstoday.com/mom
Features the evolution of Sacred Music, East and West. Our one-hour national weekly program is heard on over 190 public radio stations across the country.

Modern Masterpieces *WBHM*
650 11th St. S. Birmingham, AL 35294
PH: 205-934-2606 FX: 205-934-5075
info@wbhm.org
www.wbhm.org
Features music by acknowledged Classical masters as well as emerging composers of merit.

A Musical Meander *KRCU*
1 U. Plaza, Cape Girardeau, MO 63701
PH: 573-651-5070 FX: 888-651-5070
Alan Journet ajournet@semo.edu
www4.semo.edu/krcu/meander.html
The basic theme is Classical music in the broadest sense.

The New Edge *WMBR*
3 Ames St., Cambridge, MA 02142
PH: 617-253-4000
Ken Field newedge@wmbr.org
newedge.home.att.net
wmbr.mit.edu
Creative and innovative, mostly instrumental new music, composed and improvised at the intersection of classical, jazz and world styles.

New Releases-Adventures in Good Music *WITF*
1982 Locust Ln. PO Box 2954, Harrisburg, PA 17105-2954
PH: 717-236-6000
Karl Haas fm@witf.org
www.witf.org
Heard on over 180 stations. Glad to receive CDs for consideration on the program.

New Sounds *WNYC*
1 Centre St. 24th Fl. New York, NY 10007
PH: 212-669-3333 FX: 212-669-3312
John Schaefer newsounds@wnyc.org
www.wnyc.org/shows/newsounds
New works from the Classic and Operatic to Folk and Jazz.

Pipedreams *MPR*
45 E. 7th St., St. Paul, MN 55101
PH: 651-290-1212
Michael Barone mail@mpr.org
pipedreams.mpr.org
The finest organ music from around the world.

Saint Paul Sunday *MPR*
45 E. 7th St., Saint Paul, MN 55101
PH: 651-290-1212
sunday@mpr.org
www.stpaulsunday.org
Host opens the studio to the world's best Classical artists.

Sound and Spirit *PRI*
125 Western Ave. Boston, MA 02134
PH: 617-300-4415
Alice Abraham alice_j_abraham@wgbh.org
www.wgbh.org/wgbh/pages/pri/spirit
Blends Classical, Traditional and World music.

Sunday Baroque *WSHU*
5151 Park Ave. Fairfield, CT 06825
PH: 203-365-6604
Bill McGlaughlin SundayB@wshu.org
www.sundaybaroque.org
An exploration of Baroque and Early music.

Sunday Classical Show *WIUS*
815 E. 8th St., Bloomington, IN 47408-3842
PH: 812-320-1955
Thom Pease thompease@yahoo.com
www.wius.org

Taste of Classics *WBCX*
Brenau U., 500 Washington St. SE, Gainesville, GA 30501
PH: 770-538-4708
Vanessa Hyatt vhyatt@brenau.edu
www.brenau.edu/about/wbcx/Taste-of-Classics.htm
Promotes "local" artists or anyone of quality and would like some air time.

Thursday Evening Classics *WWUH*
Attn: Music Director,
200 Bloomfield Ave. West Hartford, CT 06117
PH: 860-768-4701 FX: 860-768-5701
Steve Petke sdpetke@snet.net
www.wwuh.org
Offers a broad range of music from the Middle Ages to the present, highlighting Renaissance Choral music and lesser-known works by familiar and obscure composers.

WBJC
2901 Liberty Heights Ave.
Baltimore, MD 21215-7893.
PH: 410-462-8444
wbjcinformation@wbjc.com
www.wbjc.com
The Baltimore region's only Classical music station.

WCLV
26501 Renaissance Pkwy. Cleveland, OH 44128
PH: 216-464-0900
wclv@wclv.com
www.wclv.com
Spotlights new Classical CDs.

WCNY *Syracuse*
506 Old Liverpool Rd. Liverpool, NY 13088-6259
www.wcny.org/classicfm
Features performances by numerous local musical institutions.

WCPE
PO Box 897, Wake Forest, NC 27588
PH: 919-556-5178
wcpe@wcpe.org
www.wcpe.org
Makes great Classical music available to the public.

WDAV
PO Box 7178, 423 N. Main St.,
Davidson, NC 28035-7178
PH: 704-894-8900 FX: 704-894-2997
wdav@davidson.edu
www.wdav.org
We have numerous independently produced recordings as part of its regular music rotation.

WDIY
301 Broadway 3rd Fl. Bethlehem, PA 18015
PH: 610-694-8100 FX: 610-954-9474
info@wdiyfm.org
www.wdiyfm.org
We will certainly consider the efforts of independent musicians!

WDPR
126 N. Main St., Dayton, OH 45402
PH: 937-496-3850 FX: 937-496-3852
dpr@dpr.org
dpr.org
The voice for our region's performing and fine arts organizations.

WETA
2775 S. Quincy St., Arlington, VA 22206
PH: 703-998-2600 FX: 703-998-3401
www.weta.org
Feel free to submit your music.

WFCR *U. Massachusetts*
Hampshire House, 131 County Cir.
Amherst, MA 01003-9257
PH: 413-545-0100 FX: 413-545-2546
radio@wfcr.org
www.wfcr.org

WFMR
5407 W. McKinley Ave.
Milwaukee, WI 53208-2540
PH: 414-978-9000 FX: 414-978-9001
Steve Murphy smurphy@wfmr.com
www.wfmr.com

WFMT
5400 N. St. Louis Ave. Chicago, IL 60625-4698
PH: 773-279-2020
www.networkchicago.com/wfmt
We do play some self-produced CDs.

WGMS
3400 Idaho Ave. NW, Washington, DC 20016
PH: 202-895-5000
www.wgms.com

WHRO
5200 Hampton Blvd. Norfolk, VA 23508
PH: 757-889-9400 FX: 757-489-0007
info@whro.org
www.whro.org
Will consider any independent Classical recordings for possible airplay.

WILL
Campbell Hall 300 N. Goodwin Ave.
Urbana, IL 61801-2316
PH: 217-333-0850 FX: 217-244-9586
willamfm@uiuc.edu
www.will.uiuc.edu
Send us your Classical, Jazz and Traditional/Ethnic music.

WITF
1982 Locust Ln. PO Box 2954,
Harrisburg, PA 17105-2954
PH: 717-236-6000
fm@witf.org
www.witf.org
Offering Classical music and news.

WKAR *Michigan State U.*
283 Communication Arts Bldg. E.
Lansing, MI 48824-1212
PH: 517-432-9527 FX: 517-353-7124
mail@wkar.org
wkar.org/radio

WKSU *Kent State U.*
PO Box 5190, Kent, OH 44242-0001
PH: 330-672-3114 FX: 330-672-4107
letters@wksu.org
www.wksu.org

WMNR
PO Box 920, Monroe, CT 06468
PH: 203-268-9667
info@wmnr.org
www.wmnr.org
Non-commercial Classical and Fine Arts music.

WMRA *James Madison U.*
PO Box 1292, Harrisonburg, VA 22803
PH: 540-568-6221 FX: 540-568-3814
wmra@jmu.edu
www.jmu.edu/wmra
Interested in hearing contemporary composer's music.

WMUH *Muhlenberg College*
2400 Chew St., Allentown, PA 18104-5586
PH: 484-664-3239 FX: 484-664-3539
wmuh@muhlenberg.edu
www.muhlenberg.edu/cultural/wmuh
We play Independent Classical 4 hrs/week.

WNPR
240 New Britain Ave. Hartford, CT 06106
PH: 860-278-5310 FX: 860-244-9624
info@wnpr.org
www.wnpr.org
We welcome the music of Independent Classical musicians.

WQED
4802 5th Ave. Pittsburgh, PA 15213
PH: 412-622-1300 FX: 412-622-1488
music@wqed.org
www.wqed.org
You are more than welcome to send CDs for consideration.

WQXR
122 5th Ave. New York, NY 10011
PH: 212-633-7600 FX: 212-633-7730
listener.mail@wqxr.com
www.wqxr.com
Welcomes submissions from independent artists.

WRTI
1509 Cecil B. Moore Ave, 3rd Fl.
Philadelphia, PA 19121-3410
PH: 215-204-3393 FX: 215-204-7027
Jack Moore jack@wrti.org
www.wrti.org
Plays some Classical/Jazz independent music.

WSCL
PO Box 2596, Salisbury, MD 21802.
PH: 410-543-6895
wscl@salisbury.edu
www.wscl.org
Will accept quality Indie submissions.

WWFM
PO Box B, Trenton, NJ 08690
PH: 1-800-622-9936 FX: 1-609-586-4533
smith@mccc.edu
www.wwfm.org
Playing the finest Classical music available.

WXPR
303 W. Prospect St., Rhinelander, WI 54501
PH: 715-362-6000 FX: 715-362-6007
wxpr@wxpr.org
www.wxpr.org

WXXI
280 State St. PO Box 30021,
Rochester, NY 14603-3021
PH: 585-258-0200
wxxi@wxxi.org
www.wxxi.org
We do play the music of Independent artists.

Yellowstone Public Radio
1500 U. Dr. Billings, MT 59101
PH: 406-657-2941 FX: 406-657-2977
mail@yellowstonepublicradio.org
www.yellowstonepublicradio.org

Canada

Music Around Us *CBC*
PO Box 500, Stn. A, Toronto, ON M5W 1E6
Keith Horner musicaroundus@cbc.ca
www.cbc.ca/musicaroundus
Presenting concerts recorded across Ontario.

Northern Lights *CBC*
PO Box 160, Winnipeg, MB R3C 2H1
Andrea Ratuski northernlights@cbc.ca
radio.cbc.ca/programs/northernlights
I sometimes play Indie Classical artists.

Our Music *CBC*
PH: 403-521-6241
Catherine McClelland ourmusic@cbc.ca
www.cbc.ca/ourmusic
Presenting the best of Alberta's many talented Classical musicians.

Shades of Classics *CKUW*
Rm. 4CM11 U. Winnipeg, 515 Portage Ave.
Winnipeg, MA R3B 2E9
PH: 204-786-9782 FX: 204-783-7080
John Iverson shades@mts.net
www.jliverson.com/ckuw
Promoting the music of local musicians/ensembles.

Sound Advice *CBC*
PO Box 500 Stn. A, Toronto, ON M5W 1E6
PH: 416-205-3700 FX: 416-205-6040
Rick Phillips soundadvice@toronto.cbc.ca
www.radio.cbc.ca/programs/advice
A weekly guide to the world of Classical music and recordings.

Symphony Hall *CBC*
PH: 403-521-6109 FX: 403-521-6232
Katherine Duncan symphony@calgary.cbc.ca
www.cbc.ca/symphonyhall
A showcase for Canadian orchestras and their musicians.

Two New Hours *CBC*
CBC Radio, Box 500, Stn. A,
Toronto, ON M5W 1E6
PH: 416-205-8577 FX: 416-205-6040
Larry Lake twonewhours@toronto.cbc.ca
www.cbc.ca/2newhours
The world of new concert music by Canadian and international composers.

Westcoast Performance *CBC*
PO Box 4600 Vancouver, BC V6B 4A2
PH: 604-662-6000
Michael Juk westcoast@vancouver.cbc.ca
www.cbc.ca/wcp
Presenting the finest music by British Columbia Classical artists.

Europe

Czech Republic

Cesky rozhlas 3 - Vltava
Vinohradská 12 120 99 Prague, Czech Republic
PH: 420-221-552-647 FX: 420-221-552-676
bvitek@cro.cz
www.rozhlas.cz/vltava
Live broadcasts Opera, Classical music and Jazz from all over the world.

Denmark

P2musik
Rosenorns Allé 22 DK 1999 Frederiksberg C,
Denmark
PH: 45-3520-3040 FX: 45-3520-2644
hpl@dr.dk
www.dr.dk/p2musik

Germany

NDR kultur
Rothenbaumchaussee 132 134 20149 Hamburg,
Germany
PH: 49-040-41-56-0 FX: 49-040-44-76-02
www.ndrkultur.de
The Classical station of Northern Germany.

Hungary

Bartók Radio
Hungarian Radio P.L.C. Bródy Sándur utca 5-7.
1800 Budapest, Hungary
PH: 36-1-328-8108 FX: 36-1-328-7004
nki@radio.hu
www.radio.hu
Magyar's Classical station.

Italy

Filodiffusione
isoradio@rai.it
www.radio.rai.it/isoradio
Il palinsesto del V canale "Auditorium".

The Netherlands

AVRO Klassiek
klassiek@avro.nl
klassiek.avro.nl

Classic FM
Postbus 1088 1400 BB Bussum, The Netherlands
PH: 035-699-79-99 FX: 035-699-79-98
classicfm@classicfm.nl
www.classicfm.nl

The Concertzender
www.concertzender.nl
Presenting remarkable programmes with lots of genuine Jazz and Classical music.

Norway

NRK - NRK Alltid Klassisk
PH: 815-65-900
info@nrk.no
www.nrk.no/kanal/nrk_alltid_klassisk
The Classical station of the Norwegian Public Radio.

Portugal

antena2
Antena2 Av. Duarte Pacheco, 26 1070 - 110 Lisboa,
Portugal
PH: 213-820-000 FX: 213-873-986
www.rdp.pt
Broadcasting Classical music from all epochs and styles.

Switzerland

Espace 2
espace2@rsr.ch
www.rsr.ch
The Classical channel of Radio Suisse Romande.

United Kingdom

BBC Radio 3 *Classical*
www.bbc.co.uk/radio3/classical
Home page of the BBC Radio 3's various Classical shows. Info, shows, contacts etc.

BBC Radio 2 *Easy Listening and Classical*
www.bbc.co.uk/radio2/r2music/easy
Home page of the BBC Radio 2's various Easy Listening and Classical shows. Info, shows, contacts etc.

BBC Radio 3
London, W1N 4DJ UK
PH: 087-00-100-100
www.bbc.co.uk/radio3/classical
The mother of all Classical radio stations!

Hear and Now *BBC*
Radio 1, London, W1N 4DJ UK
PH: 087-00-100-100
www.bbc.co.uk/radio3/hearandnow
Features live concerts, studio sessions from the best new music groups.

Lyric FM
Cornmarket Sq. Limerick, Ireland
PH: 353-0-61-207300 FX: 353-0-61-207390
lyric@rte.ie
www.lyricfm.ie
Irish Classical music station.

Australia

5UV Radio
228 N. Ter. Adelaide, SA 5000 Australia
PH: 61-8-8303-5000 FX: 61-8-8303-4374
radio@adelaide.edu.au
radio.adelaide.edu.au
We particularly love independents!

ABC Classical Music
PO Box 9994, Melbourne, VIC 3001 Australia
PH: 03-9626-1600 FX: 03-9626-1633
www.abc.net.au/classic
Programs that feature new Australian Classical music.

Sundayz *JOY FM*
PO Box 907, South Melbourne, VIC 3205 Australia
PH: 61 (03) 9699-2949 FX: 61 (03) 9699-2646
Beau Vigushin sundayze@joy.org.au
www.joy.org.au
A great mix of Australian and International Chillout music, combined with the "Classical meets Contemporary" music style that is taking the world by storm.

Country Radio

Includes Country, Bluegrass, Old-Tyme, Rockabilly, Alt-Country, Americana and Fiddle music

Radio Promoters

Airplay Specialists Radio Promotion
1100 18th Ave. S., Nashville, TN 37212
PH: 877-999-9975 FX: 615-321-2244
Kezia Murphy Airplay4U@aol.com
www.AirplaySpecialists.com
Calls 650 radio stations per month including 400+ secondary Country stations, Music Row, Texas, Americana.

Bill Wence Promotions
PO Box 39, Nolensville, TN 37135
PH: 615-776-2060 FX: 615-776-2181
Bill Wence info@billwencepromotions.com
www.billwencepromotions.com
Hundreds of singles and albums have been charted for our clients.

Billy James Productions
PO Box 5496, Deptford, NJ 08096
PH: 856-468-7889
gobillygo@netzero.com
www.wnjc1360.com/Shows/Billy_James/billy_james.html
We offer promotion for artists and bands.

CounterPoint Music Group
PO Box 24650, Nashville, TN 37202
PH: 615-341-0060 FX: 615-341-0072
info@americana-music.com
americana-music.com
Promoting progressive, non-mainstream & Roots Country artists.

E. H. King Music
PO Box 40, Santa Fe, TX 77517
PH: 409-925-4539
Ed & Barbara Ekingehk@cs.com
www.wingnut.net/ehk.htm
We'll mail out your CDs for you!! We get airplay!!

Syndicated and Internet Broadcasts

NorthAmerica

United States

Internet and Syndicated

Angel Radio Bluegrass
Stormin Norman norm@angelradio.net
angelradio.net
Bluegrass old and new.

Bluegrassbox
admin@bluegrassbox.com
www.bluegrassbox.com
We encourage visitors to purchase the releases of the bands represented here.

The Cosmic Cowboy
gerrich@crosswinds.net
www.live365.com/stations/c_bar_dick
A down-home brew of Americana. Off the beaten' path, down the road a bit and sometimes way out there!

Country Shufflemania
Shufflemania@aol.com
www.live365.com/stations/hillbillyoldiesman
Where the Country Shuffle, aka Texas Two-Step, is king. Toe-Tappin' Traditional Country - Old & new, famous & not-so-famous - but ALL good!

Gearjammin' Gold Radio
truckinradio@yahoo.com
www.live365.com/stations/97637
50+ years of truckin' favorites, blending Alt.Country, Bluegrass, Country Rock, Western Swing, & Classic Country!

Gruene With Envy Radio
1215 W. Slaughter Ln. #2513, Austin, TX 78748
Dave Lytle dlytle@gruenewithenvy.com
www.gruenewithenvy.com
Playing music from all of your favorite Texas and Americana artists.

Independent Music Network
8424 Santa Monica Blvd. S. #776,
West Hollywood, CA 90069
PH: 323-654-2182
Gary Hendrix gary@independentmusicnetwork.com
independentmusicnetwork.com
We have mainstream and Country versions of our weekly syndicated radio show featuring the best independent artists in the universe!

Olde Surber Station
578 Old Rail Rd. Eagle Rock, VA 24085
Jack Lewis JackLewis@surberstation.com
www.surberstation.com/radio
Bringing you great Bluegrass, Gospel and Old Time Mountain music from independent bands.

Radio Louisiana
kcq6230@hotmail.com
www.gatorsbackyard.com
A nice blend of Country, 60's and a touch of G-Rated comedy.

RAM Radio
Pam McCluskey pam@ramradio.net
www.ramradio.net
Playing music from the legends of Country as well as today's vibrant independent artists.

Roots Rock Radio
PO Box 1307, Sykesville, MD 21784
Richard Richard@RRRadio.com
RRRadio.com
Showcases the best indie Roots Rock, Americana, Alt Country, Indie Pop/Rock, indie Garage Rock, indie Rockabilly, and rockin Rhythm and Blues from around the globe. Now accepting CDs from indie Roots Rock artists.

SmokiN Turtle
sabrina@smokinturtle.net
www.smokinturtle.net
I like Singer/Songwriters and have a tendency to fall in love with some songs, enjoying hearing newer, progressive interpretations of traditional favorites as well as new works. Country, Americana and Bluegrass.

Traditional Country Music Radio
Dusty Owens dusowens@hotmail.com
www.tcmradio.com
Presents the most qualified work from artists.

Twangtown USA
Dick Shuey dick@dickshuey.com
www.twangtownusa.com
Broadcasting a variety of Country Music shows.

Alaska

The Arctic Cactus Hour *KNBA*
c/o Jim Stratton, 818 E. 9th Ave,
Anchorage, AK 99501
stratto@alaska.net
www.alaska.net/~stratto
Covering all that Rocks and honky tonks.

Arizona

Bluegrass Gospel Drive *KWXT*
PH: 479-968-1337
Shirley & Dennis mugwump@cei.net
www.eversongbluegrass.com
Bluegrass groups are invited to submit gospel CDs or CDs with gospel cuts on them for review and possible airplay.

KFMM/KCUZ
PO Box 1330, Safford, AZ 85548-1330
PH: 928-428-0916 FX: 928-428-7797
mike@kfmmradio.com
www.kfmmradio.com
Best mix of old and new Country.

M-PAK Radio
PO Box 3262, Gilbert, AZ 85299-3262
Mike Mikels mikemikels@cox.net
www.mpakproductions.com
Internet radio station that plays independent Country/Texas country/and Americana artists. We also review or recommend certain CDs.

California

Bluegrass, Etc. *KCSN*
18111 Nordhoff St., Northridge, CA 91330-8312
Frank Hoppe fhoppe@kcsn.org
kcsn.org/programs/bluegrassetcetera.html
Features traditional Bluegrass, Old-Time and early Country Music to move your heart and your feet.

The Bluegrass Show *KMUD*
PO Box 135, 1144 Redway Dr.
Redway, CA 95560-0135
PH: 707-923-2513 FX: 707-923-2501
Kate Klein md@kmud.org
www.kmud.org
Enjoy two hours of Bluegrass music.

Bluegrass Signal *KALW*
500 Mansell St., San Francisco, CA 94134
PH: 415-841-4121 FX: 415-841-4125
Peter Thompson bgsignal@comcast.net
www.kalw.org
Bluegrass - "Folk Music in overdrive." That unique synthesis of Blues and Old-Time Country music, with elements of Celtic, Jazz, and a variety of Folk music.

Boot Liquor Radio
32 Park Groton Pl. San Jose, CA 95136-2519
roy@bootliquor.com
bootliquor.com
American Roots music for saddle-weary drunkards.

Cupertino Barndance *KKUP*
PO Box 2250, Cupertino, CA 95015
Attn: Music Director
Stompin' Steve Hathaway steve@westernswing.com
www.westernswing.com/barndance.html
Features Classic Country, Honky Tonk, Western Swing, Bluegrass and Rockabilly. The middle hour features a current release of either a new artist or reissue. Occasionally features a live in studio performances by local and touring Country and Rockabilly bands.

Down Home *KCSN*
18111 Nordhoff St., Northridge, CA 91330-8312
PH: 818-677-3090
chuck@downhome.org
www.downhome.org
Folk, Roots, Traditional base and beyond.

Down On the 'Pataphysical Farm *KUSP*
PO Box 423, Santa Cruz, CA 95061
PH: 831-476-2800
Leigh Hill bluegrass@kusp.org
www.kusp.org/playlists/pharm
If it's good, Acoustic and Country I'll play it.

Freight Train Boogie Radio
PO Box 4262, Santa Rosa, CA 95402
Bill Frater frater@freighttrainboogie.com
www.freighttrainboogie.com
An emphasis on Alt. Country or Americana music.

Howdylicous!
PO Box 4362, Irvine, CA 92616
PH: 949-824-6868
Wanda wanda@kuci.org
www.howdylicious.com
The best in new and old twangy music.

Lunch on the Back Porch *KZYX*
Mary Aigner - PD, PO Box 1, Philo, CA 95466
PH: 707-895-2324 FX: 707-895-2451
Diane Hering gm@kzyx.org
kzyx.org/show_profiles/lunch_on_porch.htm
Traditional and contemporary Bluegrass.

Semi-Twang
59 36th Way, Sacramento, CA 95819
Paul A. Hefti semitwang@yahoo.com
www.angelfire.com/indie/semitwang
Classic Country.

Tangled Roots *KCSN*
18111 Nordhoff St., Northridge, CA 91330-8312
PH: 818-677-3090
Pat Baker pat@kcsn.org
www.kcsn.org
Features Alternative Country, Folk, Folk/Rock, Gospel, Blues and music from the singer-songwriter tradition resulting in an eclectic mix of Roots based music.

Tied To The Tracks *KCSN*
18111 Nordhoff St., Northridge, CA 91330-8312
PH: 818-677-3090
Martin Perlich (Program Directory)
mperlich@kcsn.org
kcsn.org/programs/tiedtothetracks.html
Features harmonious string-backed vocals, great fiddles and mandolins, honky-tonk piano, Acoustic Blues, harmonicas and squeezeboxes and lots more. Host: Larry Wines.

Wildwood Flower *KPFK*
3729 Cahuenga Blvd. W.
North Hollywood, CA 91604
PH: 818-985-2711 FX: 818-763-7526
Ben Elder weissenben@earthlink.net
www.kpfk.org
Your music MUST be Bluegrass, Old-Time or Traditional Country to be considered for airplay.

Colorado

The Conman Radio Show
9697 E. Mineral Ave. Englewood, CO 80112
Chris Conn conmanfm@aol.com
www.countrydj.com/conman
Bar Bands & Basement Tapes is one our special features.

Honky Tonk Heroes *KGNU*
4700 Walnut St., Boulder, CO 80301
PH: 303-449-4885
music@kgnu.org
www.kgnu.org
Old and new Country & Western music!

KCUV
1201 18th St. #250, Denver, CO 80202
PH: 303-296-7025
www.kcuvradio.com
Americana music.

KSUT
PO Box 737, 123 Capote Dr. Ignacio, CO 81137
PH: 970-563-0255 FX: 970-563-0399
www.ksut.org
An eclectic Triple A and Americana music mix.

Old Grass GNU Grass
4700 Walnut St., Boulder, CO 80301
PH: 303-449-4885
www.kgnu.org
The oldest! The Gnuest! You bet your grass!

Connecticut

Go Kat Go! *WNHU*
PO Box 5392, Milford, CT 06460
PH: 203-934-9296
Michelle gokatgo13@hotmail.com
www.gokatgoradio.com
Spinning the latest and greatest Rockabilly and Psychobilly.

Swingin' West *WVOF*
Fairfield U. 1073 N. Benson Rd.
Fairfield, CT 06824
PH: 203-254-4000
mike@swinginwest.com
www.swinginwest.com
Western Swing and Western Music (not Country).

U-H Radio Bluegrass *WWUH*
Attn: Music Director, 200 Bloomfield Ave.
West Hartford, CT 06117
PH: 860-768-4701 FX: 860-768-5701
Kevin Lynch KLbgrass@aol.com
www.wwuh.org
Traditional to contemporary Bluegrass music with the latest news, as well as occasional live performances by national, regional and local artists.

Delaware

Rural Free Delivery *WVUD*
Perkins Student Ctr. U. Delaware,
Newark, DE 19716
PH: 302-831-2701 FX: 831-1399
www.wvud.org
Devoted to Bluegrass, Old-Time and Classic Country music.

Florida

CountryBear.com
PO Box 758, Lake Placid, FL 33862
PH: 863-531-0102 FX: 863-531-0103
sbc48@hotmail.com
www.countrybear.com
All material must be licensed thru one of the licensing companies.

This is Bluegrass *WMNF*
1210 E. MLK Blvd. Tampa, FL 33603-4449
PH: 813-238-8001 FX: 813-238-1802
Tom Henderson wmnf@wmnf.org
www.wmnf.org
Old and new Bluegrass.

Illinois

Live-N-Kickin Bluegrass
6525 N. Sheridan Rd. Chicago, IL 60626
PH: 773-508-8080 FX: 773-508-8082
Billy J. Ivers BillyJ@wluw.org
www.wluw.org
Recorded and live Bluegrass music in the studio with featured artist.

Southbound Train *WNUR*
1920 Campus Dr. Evanston, IL 60208-2280
PH: 847-491-7102 FX: 847-467-2058
www.wnur.org

WWHP
407 N. Main St., Farmer City, IL 61842
PH: 309-928-9876 FX: 309-928-3708
wwhp@farmwagon.com
www.wwhp.com
Blues, Bluegrass, Rock, Gospel and American Roots music.

Kansas

Trail Mix *KPR*
1120 West 11th St. U. Kansas, Lawrence, KS 66044
PH: 785-864-4530 FX: 785-864-5278
Bob McWilliams radiobob@ku.edu
kpr.ku.edu/trailmix.shtml
Celtic, Folk, Old-Time and Bluegrass.

Kentucky

Americana Crossroads *WMKY*
c/o Jonese Franklin, MSPR, UPO Box 903,
Morehead U., Morehead, KY 40351
PH: 606-783-2001 FX: 606-783-2335
Nelson Gullett wmky@moreheadstate.edu
www.moreheadstate.edu/units/wmky/ac.htm
www.morehead-st.edu/units/wmky
Blending Folk, Traditional, Bluegrass, Alternative Country and Acoustic Blues in a music format known as Americana.

Blue Yodel # 9 *WRFL*
PO Box 777, University Stn.
Lexington, KY 40506-0025
PH: 859-257-4636 FX: 859-323-1039
Joe Takacs shadygrove@prodigy.net
wrfl.uky.edu
Country an Americana.

The Cecilian Bank Bluegrass Hour *WLVK*
519 N. Miles St. PO Box 2087,
Elizabethtown, KY 42702-2087
PH: 270-766-1055
theboman@theboman.com
www.theboman.com/cecilian.html
Bluegrass ain't just a kind of music, it's a way of life. Once Bluegrass music gets into your body, life as you know it will change forever.

H. Perkins Bluegrass *WBRT*
106 South 3rd. St., Bardstown, KY 40004
Howard Perkins h.perkins@juno.com
I have two hours of programming a week playing Bluegrass Music. I play a lot of Independent Musician's music. I have live bands drop by as well.

Roots n' Boots *WFPK*
619 S. 4th St., Louisville, KY 40202
PH: 502-814-6500
Michael Young myoung@wfpk.org
www.wfpk.org/programs/rootsandboots.html
There's room for outlaws, preachers, rockers and prophets.

Sunday Bluegrass *WFPK*
HSA Broadband Bldg. 619 S. 4th St.,
Louisville, KY 40202
PH: 502-814-6500
Berk Bryant bbryant@wfpk.org
www.wfpk.org/programs/bluegrass.html
If it fits the format of the show, I'll play it.

WHAY
PO Box 69, Whitley City, KY 42653
PH: 606-376-2218 FX: 606-376-5146
whayradio@highland.net
www.hay98.com

Louisiana

American Routes
U. New Orleans, 1118 Royal St.,
New Orleans, LA 70116
mail@amroutes.org
amroutes.cc.emory.edu
Presenting a broad range of American music — Blues and Jazz, Gospel and Soul, Old-Time Country and Rockabilly, Cajun and Zydeco...

AmericanaRama *KEDM*
ULM 225 Stubbs Hall Monroe, LA 71209-6805
PH: 318-342-5556 FX: 318-342-5570
Mike Luster luster@aol.com
kedm.org/americanarama
Blues, Celtic, Western Swing, Honky Tonk etc.

Maine

The Blue Country *WMPG*
96 Falmouth St., Portland, ME 04104-9300
PH: 207-780-4943
Blizzard Bob blizbob@maine.rr.com
www.wmpg.org
Where the Bluegrass grows high, under a clear country sky.

Maryland

Rockabilly Radio
PO Box 5046, Baltimore, MD 21220
www.rockabillyradio.net
The voice of independent Rockabilly artists.

Massachusetts

American Primitive *WMBR*
3 Ames St., Cambridge, MA 02142
PH: 617-253-4000
Jay Beek primitive@wmbr.org
wmbr.mit.edu
Some Gospel for you sinners. Not the same old Blues crap.

American Roots Radio
146 Copperfield Rd. Lower Level,
Worcester, MA 01602
PH: 508-792-2876 FX: 508-795-7659
Troy Tyree womp@womp.com
www.womp.com/radio.html
ROOTS steeped DEEP in the tradition of Folk, Rock, Cajun, Blues, Bluegrass and Country.

Bluegrass Junction *WICN*
6 Chatham St., Worcester, MA 01609
PH: 508-752-0700 FX: 508-752-7518
T.Banyai@worldnet.att.net
www.bluegrassjunction.org
Back to days when the radio was the center of family entertainment.

Bradford Street Bluegrass *WOMR*
PO Box 975, Provincetown, MA 02657
PH: 800-921-9667
Bob Seay bob@womr.org
www.womr.org

Hillbilly at Harvard *WHRB*
389 Harvard St., Cambridge, MA 02138
PH: 617-495-4818
mail@whrb.org
www.whrb.net
The best Country/Western show in New England.

Lost Highway *WMBR*
3 Ames St., Cambridge, MA 02142
PH: 617-253-4000
Doug Gesler highway@wmbr.org
wmbr.mit.edu
Americana, Alt-Country, Blues, Bluegrass, Cajun, Zydeco and Hawaiian.

Southern Rail *WBRS*
Brandeis U. 415 S. St., Waltham, MA 02453-2728
PH: 781-736-4785
music@wbrs.org
www.wbrs.org
A blend of Bluegrass, Folk, Country, Western and Acoustic music.

Michigan

Progressive Torch and Twang *WDBM*
G-4 Holden Hall, MSU East Lansing, MI 48824
PH: 517-353-4414
nealdoug@egr.msu.edu
www.msu.edu/~depolo
Home of hip-shakin', soul-swayin' music!

Minnesota

Good 'n' Country *KFAI*
1808 Riverside Ave. Minneapolis, MN 55454
PH: 612-341-0980
Ken Hippler vintagecountry@hotmail.com
www.kfai.org/programs/goodnc.htm
One of KFAI's oldest programs.

Missouri

Bluegrass Breakdown *KDHX*
3504 Magnolia St. Louis, MO 63118
PH: 314-664-3955 FX: 314-664-1020
Walter & Willa Volz bluegrassbreakdown@kdhx.org
www.kdhx.org
Part of each show will be dedicated to Homegrown Grass.

Country Function Bluegrass Junction *KDHX*
3504 Magnolia, St. Louis, MO 63118
PH: 314-664-3955 FX: 314-664-1020
Gene & Larry cfandbj@kdhx.org
www.kdhx.org
Featuring local artists and unknown artists.

Down Yonder *KDHX*
3504 Magnolia St. Louis, MO 63118
PH: 314-664-3955 FX: 314-664-1020
Keith Dudding, downyonder@kdhx.org
www.kdhx.org
Bluegrass and Old-Time music.

Fishin' with Dynamite *KDHX*
3504 Magnolia St. Louis, MO 63118
PH: 314-664-3955 FX: 314-664-1020
Fred Friction fishinwithdynamite@kdhx.org
www.kdhx.org
Features the finest Alt-Country, cow-Punk, and Roots Rock.

Montana

Americana Backroads *KGLT*
MSU Box 174240, Bozeman, MT 59717-4240
PH: 406-994-3001 FX: 406-994-1987
wwwkglt@montana.edu
www.kglt.net

The Bluegrass Show *KCLC*
209 S. Kingshighway, St. Charles, MO 63301
PH: 636-949-4880
mwall@lindenwood.edu
www.891thewood.com

Bluegrass Traditions *KGLT*
MSU Box 174240, Bozeman, MT 59717-4240
PH: 406-994-3001 FX: 406-994-1987
wwwkglt@montana.edu
www.kglt.net

New Jersey

Bluegrass Jam *WBJB*
765 Newman Springs Rd. Lincroft, NJ 07738
PH: 732-224-2252
www.wbjb.org/bluegrass
Old-time, contemporary and Gospel Bluegrass.

Burlington County Bluegrass *WBZC*
County Rte. 530 Pemberton, NJ 08068-1599
PH: 609-894-8900 FX: 609-894-9440
Nancy Longenecker clongen@aol.com
www.wbzc.org
Bluegrass with a mixture of Celtic fiddle tunes and Folk music mixed with African rhythms. Welcomes projects by independent artists!

Honky Tonk Roadhouse *WDVR*
PO Box 191, Sergeantsville, NJ 08557
PH: 609-397-1620 FX: 609-397-5991
www.wdvrfm.org

On the Sunny Side *WFDU*
Metro. Campus, 1000 River Rd. T-WFDU,
Teaneck, NJ 07666
PH: 201-692-2806 FX: 201-692-2807
Dave Gross onthesunnyside891@yahoo.com
wfdu.fm
I play Bluegrass and other Acoustic music.

The Radio Thrift Shop *WFMU*
PO Box 5101, Hoboken, NJ 07030
PH: 201-521-1416
Laura Cantrell laura@wfmu.org
www.radiothriftshop.com/radiothriftshop/index.htm
Has a Country-and-western format.

Trash, Twang and Thunder *WFMU*
c/o Brian Turner, PO Box 5101, Hoboken, NJ 07030
PH: 201-521-1416
www.wfmu.org/playlists/MO
Twang Rock for now cowboys. Lots of live music too.

WDVR
PO Box 191 Sergeantsville, NJ 08557
PH: 609-397-1620 FX: 609-397-5991
host@wdvrfm.org
www.wdvrfm.org
Quite a few of the DJ's play Indie artists.

New Mexico

Green Chile Revival & Medicine Show *KGLP*
200 College Rd. Gallup, NM 87301
PH: 505-863-7626 FX: 505-863-7633
Tom Funk chile@kglp.org
www.kglp.org/chile
An eclectic mix of Country, Alt-Country, Blues, Zydeco, Tex - Mex, Folk, Singer-Songwriter, Big Band Jazz. In short - Roots music.

High Lonesome Bluegrass *KGLP*
200 College Rd. Gallup, NM 87301
PH: 505-863-7626 FX: 505-863-7633
David Lang kglp_bluegrass@hotmail.com
www.kglp.org

The Santa Fe Opry *KSFR*
PO Box 31366, Santa Fe, NM 87504-1366
PH: 505-428-1527 FX: 505-428-1237
www.ksfr.org
steveterrell.blogspot.com
Stephen W. Terrell robotclaww@msn.com
Hardcore, Alternative, Outlaw, Insurgent, No Depression.

New York

All Together Now *WBNY*
Buffalo State, 1300 Elmwood Ave.
Buffalo, NY 14222
PH: 716-878-3080 FX: 716-878-6600
Al Riess riessaf@buffalostate.edu
www.wbny.org
All styles of Country, Folk and Bluegrass.

Bluegrass Ramble *WCNY*
PO Box 2400, Syracuse, NY 13220-2400
Bill Knowlton udmacon@aol.com
www.wcny.org/classicfm
www.fmhs.cnyric.org/notes/knowlton-bio.html

The Bristol Brothers Show *WDYN*
2844 Dewey Ave. Rochester, NY 14616
Brother Don drk@dynrec.com
dynrec.com/bristolbrothers
Old time Bluegrass music. I play independent artists only.

Salt Creek Show *WVBR*
957 Mitchell St., Ithaca, NY 14850
PH: 607-273-4000 FX: 607-273-4069
Peter Fraissinet pf13@cornell.edu
wvbr.com/salt.html
Old-Time, Bluegrass, Old and Alt-Country with a sprinkling Cajun, Blues and Gospel.

String Fever *NCPR*
St. Lawrence U. Canton, NY 13617-1475
PH: 315-229-5356 FX: 315-229-5373
radio@ncpr.org
www.northcountrypublicradio.org/programs/local/string.html
Instrumental finger picking guitar for GREAT musicians.

North Carolina

Goin' Across The Mountain *WNCW*
PO Box 804, Spindale, NC 28160
PH: 828-287-8000 x328 FX: 828-287-8012
www.wncw.org
Traditional and contemporary Bluegrass music. Send 2 CDs to the attention of the Music Director. Make sure to include a one-sheet (bio).

The Good-Tyme Bluegrass Show *WFSS*
1200 Murchison Rd. Fayetteville, NC 28301
PH: 910-672-1919 FX: 910-672-1964
Bob and Sara Barden monkous@nc.rr.com
www.wfss.org

Topsoil *WXDU*
PO Box 90689, Durham, NC 27708
PH: 919-684-2957
Steve Gardner steve@topsoil.net
www.topsoil.net
A non-commercial free-form Roots radio show.

Ohio

D28+5 *WOUB*
9 S. College St., Athens, OH 45701
PH: 740-593-1771 FX: 740-593-0240
radio@woub.org
woub.org/bluegrass
Bluegrass Roots radio for SE Ohio.

Roots 'n' Offshoots *WCBE*
540 Jack Gibbs Blvd. Columbus, OH 43215
PH: 614-365-5555 FX: 614-365-5060
mbrennan@wcbe.org
www.wcbe.org
Folk, Bluegrass, Rockabilly and more.

Oregon

Early Morning Gumbo *KBOO*
20 SE 8th Ave. Portland, OR 97214
PH: 503-231-8032 FX: 503-231-7145
Diane Karl dkarl@ipns.com
www.kboo.fm
Features Acoustic Blues, Texas Folk, Cajun, Old-Time, Bluegrass etc.

Music From the True Vine *KBOO*
20 SE 8th Ave. Portland, OR 97214
PH: 503-231-8032 FX: 503-231-7145
rockmd@kboo.org
www.kboo.fm
Bluegrass show featuring live performances and interviews.

Pennsylvania

The Bluegrass Jam Session *WYEP*
2313 E. Carson St., Pittsburgh, PA 15203
PH: 412-381-9131 FX: 412-381-9126
Bruce Mountjoy mtjoypgh@aol.com
www.wyep.org
Explores Bluegrass music from its 1940's creation by Kentuckian Bill Monroe into the new century.

The Bluegrass Show *WQSU*
Susquehanna U. 514 U. Ave. Selinsgrove, PA 17870
PH: 570-372-4030
www.susqu.edu/wqsu-fm
Three hours of the best of Bluegrass.

Mountain Folk
PO Box 2266, Sinking Spring, PA 19608
mtnfolk@aol.com
www.mountainfolk.com
Indie artists are encouraged to send material.

Pure as Stone Country Music Jamboree *WQSU*
Susquehanna U. 514 U. Ave. Selinsgrove, PA 17870
PH: 570-372-4030
www.susqu.edu/wqsu-fm
Traditional Country and Western music.

Roots and Rhythm Mix *WYEP*
2313 E. Carson St., Pittsburgh, PA 15203
PH: 412-381-9131 FX: 412-381-9126
Kate Borger kateb913@hotmail.com
www.wyep.org
As well as playing Roots and Alt-Country, I'm also in to any regional rhythms - Tex-Mex, New Orleans, Cajun and Zydeco, Latin, etc.

Traditional Ties *WYEP*
2313 E. Carson St., Pittsburgh, PA 15203
PH: 412-381-9131 FX: 412-381-9126
John Trout johntrout91@hotmail.com
www.wyep.org
New Bluegrass releases and old favorites.

South Carolina

The Bluegrass Sound *ETV*
1101 George Rogers Blvd.
Columbia, SC 29201-4761
PH: 803-737-3420
www.etvradio.org/bgs
A mix of both traditional and contemporary Bluegrass music, some occasional Old Time mountain music. Covers independent labels and artists.

Tennessee

Bluegrass Breakdown *WPLN*
630 Mainstream Dr. Nashville, TN 37228-1204
PH: 615-760-2903 FX: 615-760-2904
Dave Higgs bluegrass@wpln.org
www.wpln.org/bluegrass
Our goal is to edify, educate, and entertain. We leave no instrument unpicked, no song unsung, and no interview undone.

The Bluegrass Special *WDVX*
PO Box 18157 Knoxville, TN 37928
PH: 865-494-2020
Tony Lawson mail@wdvx.com
www.wdvx.com/programs/bluegrassspecial.html
The best in Bluegrass music, old and new.

Clinch River Breakdown *WDVX*
PO Box 27568, Knoxville, TN 37927
PH: 865-494-2020
Charlie charlie_lutz@comcast.net
www.wdvx.com/Programs/Clinch.html
Bluegrass, Old-Time and Classic Country.

The Country Music Planet
1 Black Hawk Circle # D6,
Downingtown, PA 19335
PH: 610-518-1122
www.countrymusicplanet.com
Streams various online Country music and Gospel shows.

The Fiddler's Grove Bluegrass Show *WANT*
PO Box 399 Lebanon, TN 37088
PH: 615-449-3699 FX: 615-443-4235
info@wantfm.com
www.wantfm.com

Out on a Limb *WETS*
PO Box 70630, Johnson City, TN 37614-1709
PH: 423-439-6440 FX: 423-439-6449
Mike Strickland gmstrickland@prodigy.net
www.wets.org
Progressive sounds of current Americana music.

WDVX
PO Box 27568, Knoxville, TN 37927
PH: 865-494-2020
mail@wdvx.com
www.wdvx.com
We play all types of Country, Celtic and Folk.

WSM
2804 Opryland Dr. Nashville, TN 37214
PH: 615-889-6595 FX: 615-458-2445
mail@wsmonline.com
www.wsmonline.com

Texas

Humble Time
PO Box 310490, New Braunfels, TX 78130
PH: 830-625-9400
humble@humbletime.com
www.humbletime.com

The LoneStar JukeBox *KPFT*
620 West 21st St., Houston, TX 77008
PH: 713-222-0709 FX: 713-222-0666
Rick Heysquierdo rick@lonestarjukebox.com
www.lonestarjukebox.com
Promotes Americana and Alt-Country genres.

Third Coast Music Network *KSYM*
7519 Dell Oak San Antonio, TX 78218-2634
PH: 210-733-2787
David Ludwig dludwig@ev1.net
www.accd.edu/tcmn

WCUB
4493 US Hwy 67, Stephenville, TX 76401
PH: 254-965-4132
Carroll Parham opry@countryopry.com
www.cubradio.com
Has a weekly Country, Bluegrass & Gospel show that plays Independent artists.

Utah

The Amarillo Highway *KZMU*
PO Box 1076, 1734 Rocky Rd. Moab, UT 84532
PH: 435-259-8824 FX: 435-259-8763
Professor Purple music-director@kzmu.org
www.kzmu.org
Hillbilly, Alt.Country, Alterna-twang, No Depression, left-wing Country, hard core Honky Tonk.

Monday Breakfast Jam *KRCL*
1971 W. North Temple, Salt Lake City, UT 84116
PH: 801-363-1818 FX: 801-533-9136
The Iceman iceman@krcl.org
www.krcl.org/~iceman
Eclectic mix of Insurgent Country, contemporary Singer Songwriter, Folk and Rock.

Virginia

Allegheny Mountain Radio
users.htcnet.org/wvls/AMR.html
Country, Bluegrass, Gospel, Rock, Classical and Jazz.

WGRX
4414 Lafayette Blvd. Ste #100,
Fredericksburg, VA 22408
PH: 540-891-9696 FX: 540-891-1656
Stephanie Taylor staylor@thunder1045.com
www.thunder1045.com
A mainstream Country station that mixes in Americana and Southern Rock. We air a two hour Americana/Bluegrass/Texas Country show on Sunday nights that incorporates independent artists.

WHEE
PO Box 3551, Martinsville, VA 24115
PH: 276-632-9811 FX: 276-632-9813
bill@wheeradio.com
wheeradio.com

TwangCast Radio
PO Box 293, Orange, VA 22960
PH: 540-661-1245
R.W. Shamy Jr. twangradio@twangcast.com
www.twangcast.com
We play independent artists of several genres.

Washington

KSER *The Bluegrass Express*
2623 Wetmore Ave. Everett, WA 98201
PH: 425-303-9070
Sandy sandraq@compuserve.com
www.kser.org
Live performances from our studio.

Front Porch Bluegrass *KPBX*
2319 N. Monroe St., Spokane, WA 99205
PH: 509-328-5729 FX: 509-328-5764
Kevin Brown bluegrass@kpbx.org
www.kpbx.org/programs/frontporch
Classic Bluegrass and its progressive offshoots.

KBCS Americana Music
3000 Landerholm Cir. SE
Bellevue, WA 98007-6484 Attn: Music Director
PH: 425-564-6194 x1
Christine Linde clinde@bcc.ctc.edu
kbcs.fm
Send your CD to see if it fits within our Americana format.

Washington DC

Bluegrass Overnight *WAMU*
American U. 4400 Massachusetts Ave. NW,
Washington, DC 20016-8082
PH: 202-885-1200
Lee Michael Demsey demsey@wamu.org
www.wamu.org
Six lively hours of Bluegrass every week.

bluegrasscountry.org
4000 Brandywine St. NW, Washington, DC 20016
bluegrasscountry.org
Traditional and contemporary Bluegrass.

The Ray Davis Show *WAMU*
American U. 4400 Massachusetts Ave. NW,
Washington, DC 20016-8082
PH: 202-885-1200
feedback@wamu.org
www.wamu.org/programs/rd
Traditional and Gospel Bluegrass.

Stained Glass Bluegrass *WAMU*
American U. 4400 Mass. Ave. NW,
Washington, DC 20016-8082
PH: 202-885-1200
Red Shipley rs@ns.gemlink.com
www.wamu.org/programs/sgbg
Receives and considers material from anyone.

WAMU *American U.*
American U. 4400 Mass. Ave. NW,
Washington, DC 20016-8082
PH: 202-885-1200
feedback@wamu.org
www.wamu.org

West Virginia

Sidetracks
c/o EIO Productions, 151 S. Mineral St.,
Keyser, WV 26726
PH: 304-788-0129
Ed McDonald emcdonald@mountain.net
www.wvpubcast.org/radio/sidetracks
A weekly syndicated program of Bluegrass, Folk, Country, Blues, and related styles of contemporary Acoustic music.

Wisconsin

Bluegrass on Saturday *WXPR*
303 W. Prospect Ave. Rhinelander, WI 54501
PH: 715-362-6000 FX: 715-362-6007
Brother Bill Kaul wxpr@wxpr.org
www.wxpr.org/program/bluegrass.cfm
Four big hours of Bluegrass every Saturday afternoon.

Canada

The Back Forty *CKCU*
Ron Moores, 56-121 Buell St.,
Ottawa, ON K1Z 7E7
PH: 819-827-0068
ron.moores@back40.ca
www.back40.ca
Traditional Country, Western and Bluegrass music.

Dagwood Country Radio
Cluade Camacho rambler@dagwoodradio.com
dagwoodradio.com
Today's Contemporary Country. Blue jeans, guitars, NASCAR. Two-steppin' fools and yahoos. Hell Yeah!! Today's Country Rocks!!

Pacific Pickin' *CITR*
#8-700 St. Georges Ave. N.
Vancouver, BC V7L 4T1
Arthur and Andrea Berman aberman@telus.net
www.citr.ca
Bluegrass, Old-Time music and its derivatives.

Radio Boogie *CKLN*
380 Victoria St., Toronto, ON M5B 1W7
Steve Pritchard s.pritchard1@sympatico.ca
www.ckln.fm
Bluegrass, Old-tyme, Acoustic and Traditional Country.

Six Strings & A Million Possibilities *CJTR*
PO Box 334 Stn. Main, Regina, SK S4P 3A1
PH: 306-525-7274 FX: 306-525-9741
Bob Evans SixStrings@BobEvansGuitar.com
www.cjtr.ca
Primarily, but not exclusively, instrumental.

Smokin' Bluegrass *CFMU*
16 Penlake Ct. Hamilton, ON L9C 5Y7
Jim Marino jlmarino@mountaincable.net
cfmu.mcmaster.ca
The best in Bluegrass. New music is welcome!

Spirit of the West
Hugh McLennan, Lot 1, Hyas Lake Rd.
Pinantan, BC V0E 3E1
PH: 250-573-5731 FX: 250-573-5731
www.cowboylife.com
Features talented Independent artists. The show is heard around the world.

Wide Cut Country *CKUA*
10526 Jasper Ave. Edmonton, AB T5J 1Z7
PH: 780-428-7595 FX: 780-428-7624
Allison Brock allison.brock@ckua.org
www.ckua.com
Traditional Hillbilly to Pop Country of today.

Europe

Austria

Archangel's Country Club
Wienerbruckstr. 87, A-2344 Maria-Enzersdorf, Austria
Kurt K. Gabriel archangel-country@kabsi.at
Weekly Country music show.

Go West Go Country *Radio Ostttirol*
Att. Hans Mair,
Amlacher Str. 2, A-9900 Lienz, Austria
hans.mair@hella.co.at
www.radio.osttirol.net
Send your promotional CDs to the above address.

Denmark

BJ the DJ
Radio Sindals, Her bor vi. Norgesgade 1 9870
Sindal, Denmark
PH: 989-342-00
bj-the-dj@mail.dk
www.dj.1go.dk
Playing independent artists from all over the world.

Bornholms Stemme
Gammeltoft 36 – 25, 3790 Hasle, Bornholm, Denmark
Lulu and Arne Andersen arne_lulu@country-vaerkstedet.dk
www.country-vaerkstedet.dk
On the local radio we air Country music 2 hours a week, plus entertain every second Saturday with mixed music for 3 hours.

Radio Oestsjaelland
Vinkældertorvet 2A Postboks 34 4640 Fakse, Denmark
PH: 56-71-30-03 FX: 56-71-39-51
Hans-Henrik Thamdrup country@lokalradio.dk
www.lokalradio.dk/voresprg/countrymusic
A lot of the indie music is at least as good as the music of famous artists.

Estonia

Bluegrass Radio 108
bluegrassradio@hot.ee
www.hot.ee/bluegrassradio
Devoted to the American Bluegrass and Grassroots music.

France

Along the Navajo Trail *Radio Canut*
24, rue Sergent Blandan 1er arrdt - BP 1101 - 69201
LYON Cedex, France
PH: 04-78-39-18-15 FX: 04-78-29-26-00
Bernard Boyat radio@radiocanut.org
regardeavue.com/radiocanut
Toutes les musiques "Roots" Américaines. Country, Blues, Hillbilly, Western Swing etc.

Country Cookin *Radio ALFA*
PH: 33-1-45109860
Viggo Jensen radio@radioalfa.net
www.radioalfa.net
Plays a wide variety of Country music.

Country Road Radio *Arc en Ciel*
RCT, BP 2001-69603 Villeurbanne Cedex, France
PH: 0033-04-78-89-59-48 FX: 0033-04-72-44-34-42
liberte@radio-rct.com
www.radio-rct.com

Germany

Country Special Radio *Countrymusic24*
Verantwortlicher i. S. d. P., Birgit Walter,
Hildburghauser Str. 35 in 12279 Berlin, Germany
CSR-BERLIN@t-online.de
www.countrymusic24.com
A weekly show that plays independent Country music.

Hillbilly Jukebox *Radio Rhein Welle*
Hauptstrasse 62, 65396 Walluf, Germany
FX: 012-126-744-372-84
Rolf Hierath cashville@gmx.de
www.cashville.de

Italy

Kristall Radio
Via Ludovico Il Moro 165 - 20142 Milano, Italy
PH: 0039-0-2-8912-0212
info@kristallradio.it
www.kristallradio.it
We give massive support to all independent artists.

Luxembourg

Country Club Music Show
2, rue de la Boucherie, L-1247, Luxembourg
radioara@mindless.com
www.ara.lu

The Netherlands

Alt Country Cooking
Gasthuislaan 31, 9671 JC Winschoten,
The Netherlands
Theo Oldenburg t.oldenburg@hetnet.nl
www.realrootscafe.com/altcountrycooking.html
Features Americana, Folk, Alt Country, Blues, Roots-Rock and Singer-Songwriter music.

B.R.T.O.
Burgemeester van Hasseltstraat 7,
4611 BG Bergen op Zoom, The Netherlands
redactie@brto.nl
www.brto.nl
Bluegrass, Gospel, Cajun, Zydeco, Tex Mex, Rockabilly and Modern Country.

Country Express Radio Rucphen
Zwaard 27 4871 DL ETTEN-LEUR,
The Netherlands
verwijmerenries@zonnet.nl
www.home.zonnet.nl/verwijmerenries
Please send me material (CDs & Bio) for my show.

Countryland Radio Barneveld
p/a Valkhof 63, 3772 EC Barneveld,
The Netherlands
PH: 0342-422-411
Dick Brink & Timen van Ark
countryland@radiobarneveld.nl
www.radiobarneveld.nl
Bluegrass, Old time Country, New Country, aandacht aan de Nederlandse artiesten en in mei geen artiest van de maand, maar Bluegrass maand!!

The Long Distance
Schout 48, 1625 BP Hoorn, The Netherlands
Nico Druyf nicodr@hetnet.nl
www.realrootscafe.com/longdistance.html
All kinds of Roots styles like Alt. Country, Cajun, Blues, Tex-Mex, Rockabilly, Singer-Songwriter, Zydeco etc.

PeelGrass
Akelei 10 5803 CA Venray, The Netherlands
Rein Wortelboer peelgras@xs4all.nl
www.xs4all.nl/~peelgras
Send a promotional CD for review and possible airplay.

Norway

Radio Risor
Klingra, Gjernes, N-4990 Sondeled, Norway
PH: 47-3715-4528 FX: 47-3715-2022
Dagfinn M. Pedersen dagfinn@bluegrass.no
www.bluegrass.no
All types of Bluegrass, including Gospel, Roots and music on the edges.

Spain

Solo Country *Elda FM*
Apartado Correos 224, Sax, Alicante, Spain
David Sutton-Rowe countryrowe@hotmail.com
I ONLY play Country Music and Country Gospel Music. No more, no less.

United Kingdom

Bob Harris Country *BBC 2*
PH: 08700-100-200
www.bbc.co.uk/radio2/shows/bobharriscountry
The best in Country, from cowboy classics to the newest sounds coming out of Nashville.

Brand New Opry *BBC Radio Scotland*
Queen Margaret Dr. Glasgow, G12 8DG UK
www.bbc.co.uk/scotland/radioscotland/programmes/other/brandnewopry.shtml
Features the best in new and old Country, Alt-Country and Americana music.

The Comfort Zone *SpydaRadio*
42-43 Lower Marsh Waterloo
London, SE1 7RG UK
PH: 023-92-263-933
Gail Comfort gail.comfort@spydaradio.co.uk
www.spydaradio.co.uk
Three hours of the sweetest of country music with the sweetest of country girls Gail Comfort.

Country Corner Radio Show *Claire FM*
Abbeyfield Ctr. Francis St. Ennis Co Clare, Ireland
PH: 353-0-65-682-8888 FX: 353-0-65-682-9392
Mike Gardiner mgardiner@clarefm.ie
www.clarefm.ie/progs/countrycorner.htm
Features Irish, American and European Country music, new and old.

Metro Country
ray@metrocountry.co.uk
www.metrocountry.co.uk
E-mail to submit your material.

The Stuart Cameron Show
Whinstay, Kilham,
Coldstream, Scotland, TD12 4QS
Stuart country@hotdisc.net
www.hotdisc.ukgateway.net/caroline.html
The very best of the latest independent Country music tracks from Europe and overseas.

Australia

Bay Breeze Country *Bay FM*
92 Serpentine Ck Rd. Redland Bay,
QLD 4165 Australia
Bob Atkins bob_atkins@iprimus.com.au
www.bayfm.org.au
Weekly show featuring independent artists.

Cool Country Radio
PO Box 2, The Entrance, NSW 2261 Australia
PH: 0415-616-431
941@coolcountry.com.au
www.coolcountry.com.au

Country For You *2NUR*
Unit 1-5 Sandgate Rd. Wallsend, Newcastle,
NSW 2287 Australia
Warren Fuller wassa@2nurfm.com
2nurfm.com
Weekly Country music show.

Country Roads *FM 98.5*
43 Harcourt St., Nathalia, VIC 3638 Australia
Pejay pejays1@mcmedia.com.au
www.onefm.com.au
Weekly show that plays some independent artists.

Make Mine Country *WYN*
PO Box 1011, St. Albans, VIC 3021 Australia
PH: +61-3-9364-0817
trudy-burke@bigpond.com
www.wynfm.org.au
You will hear some Australian, some overseas major label artists and a whole lot of independent Country music artists from around the world.

MCR Radio
PO Box 1420, Campbelltown, NSW 2560 Australia
PH: 02-4625-2768 FX: 02-4627-0670
2mcr.org.au/country
Our station features a variety of Country music shows.

Music from Foggy Hollow *Hawk Radio*
11 Fitzgerald St., Windsor, NSW 2756 Australia
PH: 02-45-775-662
foggyhollow@bluegrass.org.au
www.hawkradio.org.au/bluegrass
Our show is a new releases Bluegrass show.

Saturday Night Country *ABC*
PO Box 694 Townsville, QLD 4810 Australia
PH: +61-7-4722-3050 FX: 07-4722-3099
snc@your.abc.net.au
www.abc.net.au/snc
Your gateway to the best in Australian Country music.

Slinga's Independent Country *WYN*
PO Box 4221 MDC, Hoppers Crossing,
VIC 3029 Australia
PH: 61-1-03-9742-1868 FX: 61-1-03-9742-1868
Tony Slinga slinga1@slinga.com
slinga.com
Indie Country music from all over the world!

Dance Radio

North America

United States

1groovE.com
1groove@icebergradio.com
1groove.icebergradio.com
Drum n' Bass, Electronica, House etc.

Area 54 Radio
mike@area54.com
www.area54.com
Eclectically cool music every week on your radio.

astralwerks Radio
A+R Dept. 104 W. 29th St. 4th Fl.
New York, NY 10001
feedback@astralwerks.net
www.astralwerks.com
Limit your demo to your 3 best tracks. Please, no phone calls!

BassDrive
Submissions, 402 Newberry Dr.
Elk Grove Village, IL 60007
phix@bassdrive.com
www.bassdrive.com
The best of Drum 'n Bass & Jungle music.

Beats in Space *WNYU*
194 Mercer Str. 5th Fl. New York, NY 10012
PH: 212-998-1660 FX: 212-998-1652
Tim Sweeney tim@beatsinspace.net
www.beatsinspace.net
The sounds you'll hear are not limited to one style.

Club Radio Network
127 Wright Ave. Deer Park, NY 11729
Attn: Michael Manicone
www.clubradio.net
The very best that the Dance music scene has to offer.

ClubNetRadio.com
Attn: Submissions, 395 Bill France Blvd. #26N,
Daytona Beach, FL 32114-1383
contact@clubnetradio dot com
www.clubnetradio.com
We are always accepting submissions by artists, DJs and record labels who would like us to review their material for possible airing on our station.

Beta Lounge Radio Show
1072 Illinois St., San Francisco, CA 94107
support@betalounge.com
www.betalounge.com
Send a sample of your material.

Darkside Radio Internet Program (DRiP)
PO Box 1905, Boulder, CO 80306
stevyn@ironfeather.com
www.ironfeather.com
We welcome Dance & Electronica CDs, demos etc..

Digital Club Network
121 E. 24th St. 12th Fl New York, NY 10010
PH: 212-253-0600 FX: 212-253-8506
www.dcn.com
Recording and webcasting performances every night.

Digitally Imported Radio
demos@di.fm
www.digitallyimported.com
E-mail to get submission instructions.

djmixed.com
BPM Magazine, 8525 Santa Monica Blvd. W. Hollywood, CA 90069
PH: 310-360-7170 x107 FX: 310-360-7171
feedback@djmixed.com
www.djmixed.com
DJ culture and the Electronic music lifestyle.

dnbradio.com
info@dnbradio.com
www.dnbradio.com
24/7 Drum and Bass, Jungle, and Liquid Funk. If you are an artist and would like to submit your work to be featured on our stream, please contact us.

dublab Radio
707 Ridgewood Pl #201, Los Angeles, CA 90038
www.dublab.com
Positive, freeform music.

Global Electronic KDHX
3504 Magnolia, St. Louis, MO 63118
PH: 314-664-3955 FX: 314-664-1020
Paul Jove global@kdhx.org
www.kdhx.org
A dose of weekly electronic vibrations that will be sure to tantalize every nerve on your body.

Gruvsonic Dance Radio
720 Two Mile, Wisconsin Rapids, WI 54494
info@gruvsonic.com
www.gruvsonic.com
Willing to spin any Dance material via live mix shows.

The Hitchhiker's Dance Guide WEVL
518 S. Main Memphis, TN 38103
PH: 901-528-1990
Stephen Schocke stephen@wevl.org
www.thinkhead.com/guide
For 14 years we've provided the Mid-South air waves with the latest in electronic dance music, from progressive to breaks, house to trip hop, and just about everything in between.

Limbik Frequencies
320 E. Buffalo St. #605, Milwaukee, WI 53202
djsam@limbikfreq.com
www.limbikfreq.com
Our mix of Ambient, Downtempo, Ethereal, Industrial, and intelligent Techno, is an active exploration into deep and uncharted modes of existence.

m1live.com
musicone@m1live.com
m1live.com
Today's Dance music. We do reviews too.

Metropolis KCRW
1900 Pico Blvd. Santa Monica, CA 90405
PH: 310-450-5183 FX: 310-450-7172
Jason.bentley@kcrw.org
www.kcrw.org/show/mt
The hypnotic pulse of modern city life.

milk.audio
gani@milkaudio.com
www.milkaudio.com
If you like what you've seen and would like to support us by sending CDs or vinyl then contact me directly by emailing.

mypowermix.com
randys@c895fm.com
www.mypowermix.com
Seattle's No. 1 non-commercial Dance-Mixshow.

N*Soul Radio
1455 Burbank Blvd. N. Hollywood, CA 91601-2303
PH: 818-980-9088 FX: 818-980-9577
beats@nsoul.com
www.nsoul.com/radio
Trance, Electronic, House, Dance, Rave, Trip-Hop, Techno...

Phuture Frequency Radio
www.pfradio.com
Online music community & Drum and Bass radio station.

Proton Radio
Jay Epoch jason@protonradio.com
www.protonradio.com
The internet's gold standard for underground Dance music. Visit our site for submission details.

RadioValve
PO Box 7266, Boulder, CO 80306-7266
info@radiovalve.com
www.radiovalve.com
DJ sets, interviews and more!

The "So Very" Show KTUH
Honolulu, Hemenway Hall #203, 2445 Campus Rd. Honolulu, HI 96822.
PH: 808-956-4848
Ms. Angel thesoveryshow@gmail.com
ktuh.org/sovery
Groove to the sounds of Deep House.

Sovereign Glory! KDHX
3504 Magnolia St. Louis, MO 63118
PH: 314-664-3955 FX: 314-664-1020
Li'l Edit sovereignglory@kdhx.org
www.kdhx.org/programs/sovereignglory.htm
Li'l Edit spins beat music live without a net.

Streetbeat WNUR
1920 Campus Dr. Evanston, IL 60208-2280
PH: 847-491-7102 FX: 847-467-2058
streetbeat-md@wnur.org
streetbeat.wnur.org
Dance music that doesn't get exposure elsewhere.

Technodrome KUCI
PO Box 4362, Irvine, CA 92616-4362
www.technodromeweb.com
Trance, Techno, Electronica, House, Progressive etc.

Technomusic.com Radio
www.technomusic.com
Broadcasting live DJ Mixes, 24/7. Also does music reviews.

The Underground Sounds Show KTUH
Honolulu, Hemenway Hall #203, 2445 Campus Rd. Honolulu, HI 96822.
PH: 808-956-4848
G-Spot info@double-o-spot.com
www.double-o-spot.com
3 hours of the hottest and latest Dance tracks with a mix of past recordings, combining House, Trance, D & B, Trip hop etc.

Universal Vibes
info@universalvibes.com
www.universalvibes.com
Hosts a variety of shows. Has interviews and guest DJs.

Untamed Tongues Poetry Lounge Radio Show
7575 W Washington Ave, Ste. 127-171
Las Vegas, NV 89128
PH: 702-644-4688 FX: 702-474-4688
www.untamedtongues.com
The right blend of music and Spoken Word. We feature Neo-Soul, Jazz, Hip-hop, and Funk fusions.

VoyagerRadio
547 Gayley Ave. #1, Los Angeles, CA 90024
Harold J. Johnson
program_director@voyagerradio.com
www.voyagerradio.com
The only Internet radio station in the known universe webcasting Downtempo from outer space. Send your demos to the above address.

We Sold Our Souls For Techno
PH: 708-954-7996
Laurynas suomis@yahoo.com
www.technofor.us
100% Techno radio.

WMPH Mt. Pleasant H.S.
5201 Washington St. Ext. Wilmington, DE 19809
PH: 302-762-7199 FX: 302-762-7042
music@wmph.org
www.wmph.org
We accept Indie releases.

XTC Radio
2508 Constance St., Atlanta, GA 30344
DJ GradyZero GradyZero@XTCRadio.com
www.xtcradio.com
Trance, Hard and Acid Trance etc.

Canada

The Groove CKCU
Rm. 517 U. Ctr. 1125 Colonel By Dr.
Ottawa, ON K1S 5B6
PH: 613-520-2898
Elorius Cain music@ckcufm.com
www.ckcufm.com
Canada's longest running Disco show playing every variation.

Higher Ground CIUT
Jason Palma jasonpalma@rogers.com
www.highergroundradio.com
Along with the music I love so much, we also feature information on upcoming events, charts and mixes from some of the world's top DJs and much much more.

The Shakedown
DJ Joseph Martin shakedown@hotmail.com
www.liquidbeat.com
A well-balanced audio experience in Underground Dance music. Always looking for new talent!

Techno Prisoners
DJ Tykx tykxboy@hotmail.com
www.techno-prisoners.com
Techno, Hard House, and Electronica.

Tongue and Groove CKUA
10526 Jasper Ave. Edmonton, AB T5J 1Z7
PH: 780-428-7595 FX: 780-428-7624
Kevin Wilson kevin.wilson@ckua.org
www.ckua.com
Oasis of everything that grooves.

Tuned In Radio The New Rhythm Of The Nation
68 Walmer Rd. Richmond Hill, ON L4C 3X1
PH: 905-883-5773 FX: 905-883-4337
tunedin@tunedinradio.com
www.tunedinradio.com
Always looking for 'radio friendly' recording artists to interview.

Europe

Belgium

Beyondjazz Radio Show
Lange Boomgaardstraat 114a, b9000 Gent, Belgium
Jurriaan Persyn jurriaan.persyn@skynet.be
www.beyondjazz.net
We play, review and discuss on the show whatever we like and love. Broken Beats, Future Jazz, Space Funk...

Denmark

beats.dk
PH: 45-702-334-56
www.beats.dk
A funky LIVE and on demand musical website.

France

Galaxie Radio
BP 21-59392 Wattrelos Cedex, France
PH: 03-20-83-57-57 FX: 03-20-75-09-87
info@galaxiefm.com
www.galaxiefm.com

MaXXima
contact@maxxima.org
www.maxxima.org
Electronic, NuJazz, Lounge, Downtemp, DeepHouse, House, TekHouse...

Radio FG Paris
team@radiofg.com
www.radiofg.com
Broadcasting a variety of Dance music shows.

Radio Nova
33, rue du Faubourg Saint Antoine, 75011 Paris, France
PH: 01-53-33-33-15
radionova@radionova.com
www.novaplanet.com
Broadcasting on various stations throughout France.

Germany

Back to the Basics
NDR, Rothenbaumchaussee 132 20149 Hamburg, Germany
PH: 040-41-56-2788 FX: 040-41-56-3018
web@vinylizer.net
www.vinylizer.net
Presents new releases and exclusively recorded sessions by DJs from all over the world.

Klub Radio
kontakt@klubradio.de
www.klubradio.de
Brings you the worlds best DJs live from the best clubs in Germany.

Hungary

Rádió Eger
3300 Eger Trinitárius út 1, Hungary
PH: 36-410-450
radioeger@agria.hu
www.agria.hu/radio/r_eger

Italy

Fashion FM
Via ca' ricchi, 7/9-40068 San Lazzaro Di Savena-Bologna, Italy
PH: 051-627-0400 FX: 051-627-1679
fashion@fashionfm.it
www.fashionfm.it
Features a variety of shows.

The Netherlands

Radio X-Clusief
Reepstraat 33, 2583 XG 'S-Gravenhage, The Netherlands
PH: +316-12136870
info@exclusieffm.nl
The #1 Trance-Station of the Hague.

Cybernetic Broadcasting System
robotdjx@cybernetic-broadcasting.net
www.cybernetic-broadcasting.net
Electro, Electronica, House.

Switzerland

Basic.ch
Boulevard St-Georges 21 PO Box 166, CH1211 Geneva 8, Switzerland
PH: 41 22 800 22 32 FX: 41 22 800 22 33
basic@basic.ch
live.basic.ch
Covering quality Electronic music and more.

lounge-radio.com
Haegelerstrasse 75, CH-5400 Baden, Switzerland
PH: 0041-79-681-73-92
Thomas Zumbrunnen dj@lounge-radio.com
www.lounge-radio.com
Fresh beats of NuJazz - dipped with a smile of Brazil and served with a breath of Ambient. We play lot of stuff from independent artists.

Radio Couleur 3
Av. du Temple 40, Case Postale 78, CH-1010 Lausanne, Switerland
PH: +41-21-318-15-42
www.couleur3.ch

SwissGroove
Spyristrasse 48, CH 8044 Zürich, Switzerland
Patrik Jungo mail@swissgroove.ch
swissgroove.ch
Our sound is a mix of Acid, Nu, Smooth-Jazz, Trip-Hop, Funk, Soul, RnB, Lounge & Latin.

United Kingdom

B2B Radio
PO Box 41, Tipton, DY4 7YT UK
PH: +44 (0) 7946-768-278
JB & Spice studio@back2basicsrecords.co.uk
back2basicsrecords.co.uk
The best in up front Drum & Bass.

BBC Radio 1 Dance Music
www.bbc.co.uk/radio1/dance
Home page of the BBC Radio 1's various Dance Music shows. Info, shows, contacts etc.

BBC Radio 1xtra Drum & Bass
www.bbc.co.uk/1xtra/drumbass
Home page of the BBC 1xtra's various Drum & Bass shows. Info, shows, contacts etc.

BBC Radio 1xtra Garage
www.bbc.co.uk/1xtra/garage
Home page of the BBC 1xtra's various Garage shows. Info, shows, contacts etc.

Breaks FM
www.breaksfm.com
Playing host to the worlds leading breaks djs/labels & artists.

The Electric Hour Forest of Dean Radio
1 Berisford Ct. Cinderford, Gloucestershire, GL14 2BS UK
PH: 01594-820722
Joe Williams contactus@fodradio.org
www.fodradio.org/TheElectricHour.htm
Playing the latest unreleased and upfront tracks from my record box.

freakin
info@freakin.org
www.freakin.org
Underground House music.

ministryofsound radio
103 Gaunt St., London, SE1 6DP UK
PH: 44-0-20-7740-8600 FX: 44-0-20-7403-5348
studio@ministryofsound.com
www.ministryofsound.com
The biggest digital dance floor on the planet.

Power FM
PO Box 3517, Dublin 1, Ireland UK
PH: 353-87-6668114
info@powerfm.org
www.powerfm.org
Streaming live Dance music from Dublin.

Radio Magnetic
Argyle House, 16 Argyle Ct. 1103 Argyle St., Glasgow, Scotland, G3 8ND
PH: 44-141-226-8808 FX: 44-141-226-8818
dougal@radiomagnetic.com
www.radiomagnetic.com
Covers the UK and Scottish Dance music scenes.

UK Rumble
info@ukrumble.com
www.ukrumble.com
Webcasting a varied style of Dance music.

UrbanBreakzFM.com
3 Bolshaw Close, Leighton, Crewe,
Cheshire, CW1 3WX UK
PH: 07969-164390
www.urbanbreakzfm.com
Playing a whole spectrum of music from Funky House to Speed Garage.

Vibe FM
Reflection House Olding Rd. Bury St. Edmunds
Suffolk, UK IP33 3TA
PH: 012-84-715-300
www.vibefm.co.uk
England's #1 Dance music radio station.

Australia

Australian Underground Dance Station
Ison Live Radio, PO Box 532, Newcastle,
NSW 2300 Australia
PH: 6102-49270290 FX: 6102-49270290
Sean Ison info@isonliveradio.com
www.isonliveradio.com
Underground Dance music from all around the world!

Fresh FM
Unit Level 2, 230 Angas St., Adelaide,
SA 5000 Australia
PH: 08-8232-7927 FX: 08-8224-0922
music@freshfm.com.au
www.freshfm.com.au
The rhythm of Adelaide's youth.

Mix Up
PO Box 9994, Sydney, NSW 2001 Australia
www.abc.net.au/triplej/mixup/default.htm
Grab your clubbin' outfit, your water bottle and jump into your fav dancing shoes.

Spraci
PH: 61-0-402-605-188 FX: 1-603-691-5915
support@spraci.com
spraci.cia.com.au
An extensive list of weekly Dance music radio shows heard around the Sydney area.

Wild FM
admin@wild-online.info
www.wild-online.info
Like a nightclub in your lounge room without the glow sticks.

Experimental Radio

North America

United States

420 Train Wreck
rocksanne@calsoni.com
www.live365.com/stations/rocksanne
Psychedelic, Stoner Rock, Space & Heavy groove.

Alchemical Radio
1364 W. 7th Ave. #B, Columbus, OH 43212
Jerry Kranitz stonepremonitions@fsmail.net
www.aural-innovations.com/radio/alchemy.html
Transmitting truly innovative music and lyrics.

Aural Innovations SpaceRock Radio
1364 W. 7th Ave. #B, Columbus, OH 43212
jkranitz@aural-innovations.com
www.aural-innovations.com/radio/radio.html
Space Rock, Psychedelia and eclectic forms of Progressive Rock.

Bohemian Radio
BohemianRadio@comcast.net
www.bohemianradio.com
An eclectic selection of Electronic music, mixed in with Sci-Fi tunes.

Cyberage Radio KUNM
MSC06 3520, Onate Hall 1 U. New Mexico
Albuquerque, NM 87131-0001
PH: 505-277-4806
Tommy T tommyt@dsbp.cx
www.cyberage.cx
Electronic music and Underground sounds.

Dr. Demento On the Net
PO Box 884, Culver City, CA 90232
DrDemento@drDemento.com
www.drdemento.com
www.krellan.com/demento
Nationally renowned for his weekly two-hour radio festival of mad music and crazy comedy heard on well over 100 stations coast to coast. It's a free-wheeling unpredictable mix of music and comedy.

Esoterica WQNA
PO 1233, Springfield, IL 62705
PH: 217-528-8466
Ted Keylon eted@blowingthewhistle.org
www.thespectra.net/esoterica
Experimental, Electronica, unsigned and unusual.

Galactic Travels WDIY
PO Box 632, Nazareth, PA 18064-0632
Bill Fox billyfox@soundscapes.us
wdiy.org/programs/gt
An Electronic, Ambient and Space music show. Inquire by e-mail before submitting music.

The Greatest Show From Earth WWUH
Attn: Music Director,
200 Bloomfield Ave. West Hartford, CT 06117
PH: 860-768-4701 FX: 860-768-5701
Mark DeLorenzo teltanman@cox.net
www.teltan.org
Focuses on Psychedelic, Electronic and Progressive music.

KSPC Pomona College
Thatcher Music Bldg. 340 N. College Ave.
Claremont, CA 91711 Attn: Josh Weide
PH: 909-621-8157 FX: 909-607-1259
www.kspc.org
Electronic, Ambient, Noise, Industrial, Experimental and strange music.

The Latest Score WOMR
14 Centre St. PO Box 975,
Provincetown, MA 02657
PH: 800-921-9667
www.womr.org
Basically I play everything that comes in.

Music For Nimrods KXLU
1 LMU Dr. Los Angeles, CA 90045
PH: 310-338-2866 FX: 310-338-5959
Reverend Dan ReverendDan@Hotmail.com
www.musicfornimrods.net
Looking for degenerate music of all styles.

The Musical Transportation Spree KFAI
316 Hennepin Ave. #300, Minneapolis, MN 55414
Chris Waterbury mts@mtsradio.com
www.mtsradio.com
We prefer home recordings.

My First Cassette WMBR
3 Ames St., Cambridge, MA 02142
PH: 617-253-4000
mfc@wmbr.org
wmbr.mit.edu
Cut up and cross-stitched. Electronic music and storytelling in fragments. Evil music science.

New Dreamers KLCC
Lane College 4000 E. 30th Ave.
Eugene, OR 97405-0640
PH: 541-726-2212 FX: 541-744-3962
Chris Owen & Kent Willocks klcc@efn.org
www.klcc.org
Electronic and Synthesized sounds from this world and beyond. The full spectrum of Electronic music, from Classical to Progressive Rock, Avant Garde to Spacemusic.

No Pigeon Holes Radio Show KKUP
PO Box 9162, Santa Rosa, CA 95405
PH: 408-260-2999
Don Campau campaudj@jps.net
lonelywhistle.tripod.com/playlists
I accept all styles of music for airplay.

Other Music KZUM
941 "O" St., Lincoln, NE 68508
PH: 402-474-5086 FX: 402-474-5091
Thad, Erik, Malcom & Jeff om_kzum@yahoo.com
othermusic.freeservers.com
We mostly delve into Experimental types of Jazz, Electronica, Rock, Spoken Word, and Free-Form Improvisation..

Press the Button WRUW
11220 Bellflower Rd. Cleveland, OH 44106
PH: 216-368-2208 FX: 216-368-5414
info@pressthebutton.com
pressthebutton.com
An Experimental radio show of found sound collage.

Psych-Out WREK
350 Ferst Dr. NW #224, Atlanta, GA 30332-0630
PH: 404-894-2468 FX: 404-894-6872
oncomouse@gmail.com
andrew.technobastards.net/psychout
www.wrek.org
Specializing in the best Psychedelic music from around the globe.

Psych Rock 101 KMBH
RT8 Box 613, Brownsville, TX 78520
Texas Joe Valles Jr. vallescream@aol.com
www.vallesbrothersband.com
Showcasing old and new bands in the Psych Rock format only! No other types of music are accepted! CDs new shrinkwrapped, retail ready only! No CDr's or homemade tapes etc. Free to email me before sending submissions.

Pushing The Envelope WHUS
1501 Storrs Rd. Storrs, CT 06269-3008
PH: 860-486-4007
info@whus.org
www.whus.org
The finest in Avant Ephemera.

Screamin' Streamin' Audio
richius@voicenet.com
www.richius.com
Psychedelic, Drone and Space Rock music. If you have music you'd like to submit to SSA for possible airplay, send me an e-mail and I will get back to you with contact information.

Some Assembly Required
3010 Hennepin Ave. S. #145,
Minneapolis, MN 55408
PH: 612-990-0460
Jon Nelson assembly@detritus.net
www.some-assembly-required.net
Focuses exclusively on "tape manipulations, digital deconstructions and turntable creations."

Something Else WLUW
6525 N. Sheridan Rd. Chicago, IL 60626
PH: 773-508-8080 FX: 773-508-8082
somethingelse@wluw.org
www.stopgostop.com/somethingelse
A weekly radio program of Sound Art & New/Experimental music.

Spank Radio
13410 Preston Rd. #1378, Dallas, TX 75240
Angela info1@spankradio.com
spankradio.com
Featuring an avant blend of Indie, Emo, Spacerock, Electro-clash, Dream-Pop, Fusion and anything else that defies explanation. Check our website for submission details.

(((Thump))) Radio KUSF
2130 Fulton St., San Francisco, CA 94117
PH: 415-386-5873
info@thumpradio.com
www.thump-radio.com
Exposing local talent and artists worldwide.

Transfigured Night WKCR
2920 Broadway Mailcode 2612,
New York, NY 10027
PH: 212-854-9920
newmusic@wkcr.org
www.columbia.edu/cu/wkcr
An overnight exploration of new releases of Experimental music, with an emphasis on Electronic works

Ultra Radio KVMR
401 Spring St., Nevada City, CA 95959
PH: 530-265-9073 FX: 530-265-9077
Kevin Kormylo ultraradio@kvmr.org
www.ultraradio.org
Bringing new music, sound sculptures and rarely heard recordings together into a seamless flow of electrifying radio experience.

The Weekly World Noise WORT
118 S. Bedford St., Madison, WI 53703-2692
PH: 608-256-2001 FX: 608-256-3704
www.wort-fm.org/schedule/noise.htm
Experimental, Avant-Garde and "difficult listening" music.

Weirdsville!
PO Box 936, Northampton, MA 01061
weirdo@weirdsville.com
www.weirdsville.com
We are constantly on the hunt for strange, bizarre, and righteous music to blow your minds.

Well-Rounded Radio
59 Forest Hills St., Jamaica Plain, MA 02130-2935
PH: 617-233-6613
Charlie McEnerney charlie@wellroundedradio.net
www.wellroundedradio.net
An interview program that finds what inspires and influences artists work.

Canada

Adventures In Plasticland CKWR
19 Norfolk Ave. Cambridge, ON N1R 3T5
Spaceman Stan spacedman40@hotmail.com
www.romislokus.com/eng/stan.html
Progressive, Acid, Stoner, Psychedelic, Garage, Indie and Rock music of the 60's up to now.

Brave New Waves Radio Show CBC
PO Box 6000, Montreal, QC H3C 3A8
PH: 514-597-5923
Patti Schmidt bnw@cbc.ca
www.bravenewwaves.ca
Anything from Indie Rock to Dance, Experimental Electronic and more.

Cranial Explosions: Sounds That Blow Minds! CJTR
PO Box 334 Stn. Main, Regina, SK S4P 3A1
PH: 306-525-7274 FX: 306-525-9741
programs@cjtr.ca
www.cjtr.ca
Submit your impacting music to us and if it moves us, we will play it on our show!!

Do Not Touch This Amp CFBX
House 8, U. College of the Cariboo, 900 McGill Rd.
Kamloops, BC V2C 5N3
PH: 250-377-3988 FX: 250-372-5055
Steve Marlow dntta@yahoo.ca
www.geocities.com/dntta
www.thex.ca
An Experimental/Electronic/Industrial program that runs every Friday night.

Feedback Monitor CIUT
158 Close Ave. 2nd Fl. Toronto, ON M6K 2V5
Greg Clow greg@feedbackmonitor.com
www.feedbackmonitor.com
Electronic and Experimental music.

Le Navire Night
navire@radio-canada.ca
radio-canada.ca/radio/navire
Electro-Acoustique, expérimantation.

plutonian nights CITR
#233-6138 SUB Blvd. Vancouver, BC V6T 1Z1
PH: 604-822-2487
info@plutonia.org
plutonia.org
Musical content is predominantly Electronic based.

Two New Hours CBC
PO Box 500, Stn. A Toronto, ON M5W 1E6
PH: 416-205-8577 FX: 416-205-6040
Larry Lake twonewhours@toronto.cbc.ca
www.radio.cbc.ca/programs/2newhours
We're always interested in discovering new composers.

Europe

Germany

Lametta Radio
FX: 49-251-37030
lametta@gmx.net
www.muenster.org/lametta
Alternative, Electronic and Progressive Pop music

Radio Future 2
radiofuture2@hotmail.com
www.radiofuture2.purespace.de
Electro, Industrial, Crossover, Dark Wave...

Radio "Morituri te salutant"
Semperstr. 115 44801 Bochum, Germany
PH: 0049-234-333-8427
Holger Ackermann madrego@radio-morituri.de
www.radio-morituri.de
Interviews, CD comments, chat etc.

Radio Neandertal
Elberfelder Straße 81, 40822 Mettmann, Germany
PH: 02104-91-90 20 FX: 02104-91-90-89
verkauf@radioneandertal.de
www.radioneandertal.de
Mostly instrumental.

Latvia

Ozone
RIXC, 11. Novembra Krastmala 35-201 LV 1050,
Riga, Latvia
PH: 722-8478 FX: 722-8477
rixc@rixc.lv
ozone.re-lab.net

United Kingdom

BBC Radio 3 New Music
www.bbc.co.uk/radio3/newmusic
Home page of the BBC Radio 3's various New Music shows. Info, shows, contacts etc.

Resonance FM
9 Denmark St., London, WC2H 8LS UK
PH: 020-7836-3664
Ed Baxter info@resonancefm.com
www.resonancefm.com
London's first Radio Art station, brought to you by London Musicians' Collective.

Xfm Dublin
Xfm, PO Box 200, Dublin 1, Ireland UK
www.xfmdublin.com

Australia

Musicality Tune FM
c/o U.N.E, Armidale, NSW 2351 Australia
PH: 02-677-323-99 FX: 02-677-276-33
airtime@tunefm.une.edu.au
tunefm.une.edu.au
Experimental compositions, great improvisations and more.

Sound Quality ABC
PO Box 9994, Canberra, NSW Australia
PH: 02-8333-2051 FX: 02-8333-1381
Tim Ritchie soundquality@your.abc.net.au
www.abc.net.au/rn/music/soundqlt
The interesting, the evolutionary, the inaccessible and the wonderful.

Folk Radio

North America

United States

Internet Radio and Syndicated Shows

Acoustic Café
PO Box 7730, Ann Arbor, MI 48107-7730
Rob Reinhart rob@acafe.com
www.acafe.com
Rare Acoustic cuts, classic tracks and more.

Acoustic Pie Radio
Kelley Martin kelley@acousticpie.com
www.acousticpie.com/Radio.htm
Devoted to Acoustic Singer/Songwriters.

Celtic Grove Radio
PO Box 70227, Knoxville, TN 37938
chris.range@celticgrove.com
www.celticgrove.com
The best Celtic radio programming on the Internet.

Celtic Melt
Mike mike@distantsuns.com
www.distantsuns.com/celticmelt.html
Playing the best of Celtic and Celtic inspired tunes.

The Folk Sampler
PO Box 517, Siloam Springs, AR 72761
Mike Flynn mike@folksampler.com
www.folksampler.com
Folk, Traditional, Bluegrass and Blues.

FolkScene
PO Box 707, Woodland Hills, CA 91365
PH: 818-883-7557
folkscene@folkscene.com
www.folkscene.com
Live music, interviews and remote recordings.

GidaFOLK
multithd@hotmail.com
gida.tzo.net/RadioDB
Playing whatever sounds good.

Grassy Hill Radio
c/o Indie Submissions Editor, PO Box 160,
Lyme, CT 06371
radio@grassyhill.org
radio.grassyhill.org
Streaming lesser known/self released songs.

Highlander Radio
www.CelticRadio.net
Scottish, Irish and Celtic music.

Hober Radio
PO Box 5748, Takoma Park, MD 20913
PH: 301-270-1734
gregor@hober.com
hober.com
An attempt to bring human warmth to the computer environment. Hober brings unvarnished sounds into a glossy space.

Internet Folk Festival
PO Box 331173, Elmwood, CT 06133-1173
feedback@internetfolkfestival.com
www.internetfolkfestival.com
Send your CDs and information to us.

Ironandwine
iron_to_wine@yahoo.com
www.live365.com/stations/ironandwine
www.myspace.com/14237691
I play music that echo's within your soul and rebounds off the diaphragm of your existence. I play music that has a very strong emphasis on lyrics, enchanting rhythms and unbelievable sound.

Online Folk Festival
580 E. Town St. #101, Columbus, OH 43215
PH: 614-224-2906
Greg Grant greg@onlinefolkfestival.com
www.onlinefolkfestival.com
Freeform Folk and Folk related music.

radiowayne
PO Box 17742, Shreveport, LA 71138
Wayne Greene radiowayne@att.net
www.radiowayne.com
An eclectic mix of Folk, Singer/Songwriter, Acoustic, Swing and more.

Renradio
4243 Enchantedgate, Spring, TX 77373
Michael Harris rengeek@renradio.com
renradio.com
The music and spirit of Renaissance and Celtic Festivals.

Roots Music
rwtate@avenuecable.com
www.live365.com/stations/rwtate1
You can expect to hear an eclectic mix of Bluegrass, Celtic, Louisiana, and Blues music.

Singer Magazine's Indie Artists Showcase
PO Box 1288, Harrisburg, VA 22803
Greg Tutwiler greg@singermagazine.com
www.live365.com/stations/singermagazine
The voice of the independent musician and songwriter. It's the new American music revolution!

Whole Wheat Radio
PO Box 872 H St., Talkeetna, AK 99676
radio2@wholewheatradio.org
www.wholewheatradio.org
We focus on independent music.

Woodsongs Old-Time Radio Hour
PO Box 200, Lexington, KY 40588
Attn: Submissions
FX: 859-225-4020
radio@woodsongs.com
www.woodsongs.com
Introducing new, grassroots independent artists.

Your Folk Connection *KRCU*
1 U. Plaza, Cape Girardeau, MO 63701
PH: 573-651-5070 FX: 888-651-5070
comments@yourfolkconnection.org
www.yourfolkconnection.org
Folk artists, performers, and songwriters.

Alaska

Acoustic Accents
PO Box 89, Tok, AK 99780 Attn: Bud Johnson
www.acousticaccents.net
In-depth interviews and songs from some of the best performers around.

It's All Folk *KEUL*
Glacier City Radio, PO Box 29,
Girdwood, AK 99587
PH: 907 754-2489
Karen Rakos keulkaren@hotmail.com
www.glaciercity.us
I play Folk, Roots, Bluegrass and Old-Time music.

Arkansas

From Albion and Beyond *KUAR*
2801 S. University, Little Rock, AR 72204
PH: 501-569-8485 FX: 501-569-8488
home.swbell.net/lholton/fromalbionandbeyond.html
Traditional, revival and contemporary Folk music.

California

Across the Great Divide *KPFA*
1929 MLK Jr. Way, Berkeley, CA 94704
PH: 510-848-6767 FX: 510-848-3812
www.kpfa.org
Folk and Acoustic music show.

Cool As Folk *KDVS*
14 Lower Freeborn, Davis, CA 95616
PH: 530-752-0728
Cornelius coolasfolk@hotmail.com
www.kdvs.org
Folk, Bluegrass, Americana, Indie Singer-Songwriter and other Acoustic based music. I also welcome weekly in-studio guests.

Don't Get Trouble on Your Mind *KMUD*
PO Box 135, 1144 Redway Dr.
Redway, CA 95560-0135
PH: 707-923-2513 FX: 707-923-2501
ED md@kmud.org
www.kmud.org
Each show ED plays 25 or so Folk and Blues songs.

Folk Music & Beyond *KALW*
500 Mansell St., San Francisco, CA 94134
PH: 415-841-4121 FX: 415-841-4125
kalwfolk@rahul.net
www.kalwfolk.org
Folk, traditional and original music.

Folk Roots *KSBR*
34031 Calle de Bonanza, #1,
San Juan Capistrano, CA 92675
Marshall Andrews ToMarshall@aol.com
www.ksbr.net
Independent artists are a staple of the wide range of Bluegrass, Old-Time, Celtic, Gospel and Folk music featured each time we're on the air.

KPIG
1110 Main St. #16, Watsonville, CA 95076
PH: 831-722-9000
sty@kpig.com
www.kpig.com
Great music and serious fun - Folk, Rock, Acoustic, Roots, Blues.

Heaven's Bar 'n Grill *KZSC*
126 Lennox St., Santa Cruz, CA 95060
PH: 831-459-2811 FX: 831-459-4734
Clytia Fuller clytia@cruzio.com
members.cruzio.com/~clytia
Showcases live guests playing in the area.

Music Along The Feather *KRBS*
PO Box 9, Oroville, CA 95965
www.radiobirdstreet.org
Contemporary folk. Bluegrass, Country and new Folk.

Music Without Boundaries
PO Box 60427, San Diego, CA 92166
PH: 619-226-1174 FX: 619-226-1181
Kenny Weissberg otissing@aol.com
members.aol.com/mwb98
Healthy doses of R&B, Folk, Blues, Gospel and more.

Nevada City Limits *KVMR*
401 Spring St., Nevada City, CA 95959
PH: 530-265-9073 FX: 530-265-9077
Dennis Brunnenmeyer dennisb@kvmr.org
www.kvmr.org
Americana to traditional and contemporary American Folk music with an occasional journey into Celtic, Old Time Bluegrass and early Country music styles. Please send 2 CDs.

A Patchwork Quilt *KALW*
500 Mansell St., San Francisco, CA 94134
PH: 415-841-4121 FX: 415-841-4125
Kevin Vance kevin_vance@yahoo.com
www.kalw.org
A program of Celtic and other traditional music.

Wild River Radio *KMUD*
PO Box 135, 1144 Redway Dr.
Redway, CA 95560-0135
PH: 707-923-2513 FX: 707-923-2501
Kate Klein md@kmud.org
www.kmud.org
Sometimes you can hear independent Folk artists. Looking for songs for social justice.

Colorado

The Folk Show *KRFC*
619 S. College Ave. #4, Fort Collins, CO 80524
PH: 970-221-5075
Leonard Epstein lsepstein2@aol.com
krfcfm.org
Send your music in.

Connecticut

AcousticConnections *WSHU*
5151 Park Ave. Fairfield, CT 06825
PH: 203-365-6604
Walt Graham graham@wshu.org
www.wshu.org/acoustic/acindex.asp
Acoustic music, Folk, Celtic and Bluegrass.

Folkrama *WWUH*
Attn: Music Director,
200 Bloomfield Ave. West Hartford, CT 06117
PH: 860-768-4701 FX: 860-768-5701
Ed McKeon EMckeon@aol.com
www.wwuh.org
The "Father" of the Folk Next Door concert series. Our most unusually progressive and eclectic Folk show.

Harmony Junction *WKZE*
Oblong Books & Music, PO Box 482,
Rhinebeck, NY 12572
Dick Hermans dickhermans@taconic.net
www.wkze.com
Review and promotional copies are welcomed. Please send to the above address.

Profiles in Folk *WSHU*
5151 Park Ave. Fairfield, CT 06825-1000
PH: 203-330-6203 FX: 203-365-0425
Steve Winters winters@wshu.org
www.wshu.org/profiles/prindex.asp
Traditional and Celtic Folk with Bluegrass.

Sunday Night Folk Festival *WHUS*
Box U-3008, U. Connecticut,
Storrs, CT 06269-3008
Susan Forbes Hansen flkczarina@aol.com
whus.org

Florida

Acoustic Highways *WPRK*
4041 Lake Forest, Mount Dora, FL 32757
PH: 407-646-2241 FX: 407-646-1560
Rich Pietrzak rapietrzak@hotmail.com
www.rollins.edu/wprk
A free-wheeling show devoted to bringing Folk music, performing songwriters, and other guitar-based acoustic music to the airwaves.

Eclectic Hours *1480 East Radio*
7824 Martha's Ln. Falls Church, VA 22043
PH: 703-698-0066
Paul A. Porzio eclectichours@cox.net
Playing a wide variety of Folk Music.

Folk & Acoustic Music *WLRN*
172 NE 15th St., Miami, FL 33132
PH: 305-995-2207 FX: 305-995-2299
Michael Stock mstock@wlrn.org
www.wlrn.org/radio/folkacoustic
Playing songs ignored by other stations.

Folk, Bluegrass and More *WFIT*
150 West U. Blvd. Melbourne, FL 32901-6975
PH: 321-674-8140 FX: 321-674-8139
Bill Stuart ukidnme@aol.com
www.wfit.org
Weekly Acoustic music show.

Messages *WFCF*
PO Box 1027, St. Augustine, FL 32085-1027
PH: 904-829-6940
Stu Weaver sw1191@aol.com
wfcf.freeservers.com
A two hour weekly radio broadcast of Acoustic Singer/Songwriters.

Noneyet Music *WFCF*
PO Box 2055, St. Augustine, FL 32085-2055
PH: 904-826-0743
Stu Weaver sw1191@aol.com
wfcf.freeservers.com
A two hour weekly radio broadcast of Acoustic Singer/Songwriters.

Georgia

Fox's Minstrel Show
182 Elizabeth St. NE, Atlanta, GA 30307
Harlon Joye sheartfiel@aol.com
www.wrfg.org
A mixture of Folk, Blues, Country, some Rock and even some early Jazz.

Green Island Radio Show *WSVH*
12 Ocean Science Cir. Savannah, GA 31411
PH: 912-598-3300 FX: 912-598-3306
Harry O'Donoghue wsvhirish@earthlink.net
www.wsvh.org/giarchive.htm
The very best Irish and Celtic music.

Idaho

Laz Spectrum *KBSU*
c/o Linda Laz, 1910 University Dr. MS 1915,
Boise, ID 83725
PH: 208-426-3663 FX: 208-344-6631
radio.boisestate.edu
A unique blend of Folk, Jazz, Blues, Bluegrass, International, Celtic and Singer/Songwriters. It's what Saturday morning is supposed to sound like.

Illinois

Celtic Connections *WSIU*
Southern Illinois U. Carbondale, IL 62901-6602
PH: 618-453-1884
Bryan Kelso Crow bcrow@siu.edu
www.celticconnectionsradio.org
The finest selections from new releases.

Continental Drift *WNUR*
1920 Campus Dr. Evanston, IL 60208-2280
PH: 847-491-7102 FX: 847-467-2058
drift-producer@wnur.org
www.wnur.org/drift
Roots and Folk music of cultures around the world.

Folk Fiasco *WDBX*
224 N. Washington St., Carbondale, IL 62901
PH: 618-529-5900 FX: 618-529-5900
Randy Auxier drauxier@yahoo.com
www.wdbx.org
Weekly Singer/Songwriter show.

Folkstage *WFMT*
PO Box 58, Mahomet, IL 61853
PH: 773-279-2020
Rich Warren folkdj@mchsi.com
www.midnightspecial.org/folkstage.html
About 23 concerts per year are broadcast live from our studio in front of an audience.

Midnight Special *WFMT*
PO Box 58, Mahomet, IL 61853
PH: 773-509-1111
Rich Warren folkdj@mchsi.com
www.midnightspecial.org
Folk music with a sense of humor.

Somebody Else's Troubles *WLUW*
1137 Noyes St., Evanston, IL 60201
PH: 847-475-1615,
John Wright jhwright@northwestern.edu
www.wluw.org
Open to all kinds of Acoustic music.

Indiana

The Back Porch *WVPE*
2424 California Rd. Elkhart, IN 46514
PH: 888-399-9873
Norm Mast nmast@wvpe.org
www.wvpe.org/backporch.html
The best of Folk and Bluegrass.

The Kitchen Party *WIUS*
815 E. 8th St., Bloomington, IN 47408-3842
PH: 812-320-1955
Thom Pease thompease@yahoo.com
www.wius.org
Celtic, Bluegrass, Old-Time, Folk and more.

Roots For Breakfast WFHB
PO Box 1973, Bloomington, IN 47402
Mark Richardson polskacat@hotmail.com
www.wfhb.org
The usual assortment of Old-Time, Blues, Alt-Country, Bluegrass and Folk songs/tunes are played.

Iowa

KUNI's Folk Music
U. Northern Iowa, Cedar Falls, IA 50614-0359
PH: 319-273-6400 FX 319-273-2682
www.kuniradio.org/kufolk.html
Traditional and contemporary Acoustic music.

Louisiana

Hootenanny Power WRKF
3050 Valley Creek Dr. Baton Rouge, LA 70808
Taylor Caffery tlcaffery@yahoo.com
www.hootenannypower.com
Folk and Acoustic music.

Music in the Glen WWOZ
PO Box 51840, New Orleans, LA 70151-1840
www.wwoz.org
Irish music show.

Maine

Jigs, Hoedowns and Songs O'Tragedy WMHB
Colby College, 4000 Mayflower Hill,
Waterville, ME 04901
PH: 207-872-3686
wmhb@colby.edu
www.colby.edu/wmhb

Us Folk WMPG
96 Falmouth St., Portland, ME 04104-9300
PH: 207-780-4976
Chris ctdarlin@maine.rr.com
www.wmpg.org
Promotes independent Folk artists from around the world.

Maryland

Detour WTMD
Towson U. 8000 York Rd. Towson, MD 21252
www.charm.net/~dirtylin/detour.html
An eclectic blend of Folk and World music.

Just Folks WSCL
PO Box 2596, Salisbury, MD 21802
PH: 410-543-6895 FX: 410-548-3000
John Kalb jdkalb@salisbury.edu
www.wscl.org
Contemporary Folk music (mostly Acoustic).

Roots and Wings WMUC
3130 S. Campus Dining Hall,
College Park, MD 20742-8431
PH: 301-314-7868
John McLaughlin john-mclaughlin@comcast.net
www.wmuc.umd.edu
Folk and Bluegrass.

Massachusetts

A Celtic Sojourn WGBH
125 Western Ave, Boston, MA 02134
PH: 617-300-4415
Alice Abraham alice_j_abraham@wgbh.org
www.wgbh.org
Traditional and contemporary music from the Celtic countries.

Against The Grain WICN
6 Chatham St., Worcester, MA 01609
PH: 508-752-0700 FX: 508-752-7518
David Ritchie david@wicn.org
www.wicn.org
Folk, Blues, traditional and Alt-Country, Roots, World music and more.

Alternate Currents
88 Zeno Crocker Rd. Centerville, MA 02632
Kerry Patk errypat@comcast.net
www.live365.com/stations/kerrypat
Adult album radio station featuring Americana, Folk and Singer/Songwriter.

Celtic Twilight WUMB
U. Mass, 100 Morrissey Blvd.
Boston, MA 02125-3393
PH: 617-287-6900 FX: 617-287-6916
wumb@umb.edu
www.wumb.org
Contemporary and traditional music from the British Isles.

Contemporary Cafe WICN
6 Chatham St., Worcester, MA 01609
PH: 508-752-0700 FX: 508-752-7518
Nick nick@wicn.org
www.angelfire.com/nd/satnight
Folk, Americana, Acoustic Blues and more.

The Fiddle & the Harp WOMR
14 Center St. PO Box 975,
Provincetown, MA 02657
PH: 800-921-9667
Dinah Mellin dinah164@capecod.net
www.womr.org
Irish, Scottish and Canadian Maritime music.

Folk and Good Music Show WMFO
PO Box 65 Medford, MA 02155
PH: 617-625-0800
Morgan Huke morganhuke@yahoo.com
www.wmfo.org
An experience of Acoustic and Electric tunes live from our studios. Features up and coming artists.

Folk is a Four Letter Word Creative Radio
POB 441444, Somerville, MA 02144
Sarah Woolf sarahw@sarahwoolf.com
www.sarahwoolf.com/4folk.htm
Please don't send photos or elaborate press kits. I don't care what you look like or where you have performed.

Folk on WGBH
125 Western Ave. Boston, MA 02134
PH: 617-300-4415
Alice Abraham alice_j_abraham@wgbh.org
www.wgbh.org
New and traditional Folk music by local and national musicians.

The Old Songs' Home WOMR
c/o Watch City Arts, PO Box 2171,
Orleans, MA 02653
Bob Weiser theoldsongshome@hotmail.com
www.womr.org
I will gladly review CDs for airplay. Folk and Acoustic music, traditional and contemporary.

Sounds of Erin Radio
Box 12, Belmont, MA 02428
PH: 617-926-IRISH
Soundoferinradio@comcast.net
soundoferinradio.com
Features interviews, music, book reviews, sports and other items of interest for the world-wide Celtic Community.

Valley Folk WFCR
Hampshire House, U. Mass, 131 County Cir.
Amherst, MA 01003-9257
PH: 413-545-0100 FX: 413-545-2546
folk@wfcr.org
www.wfcr.org/vfolk.html
Selections from local, national and international musicians.

The Watch City Coffeehouse WBRS
c/o Watch City Arts, PO Box 2171,
Orleans, MA 02653
Bob Weiser theoldsongshome@hotmail.com
www.wbrs.org
I will gladly review CDs for airplay. Folk and Acoustic music, traditional and contemporary.

WUMB U. Mass Boston
100 Morrissey Blvd. Boston, MA 02125-3393
PH: 617-287-6900 FX: 617-287-6916
wumb@umb.edu
www.wumb.org
The only full-time listener funded Folk station in the US.

Michigan

Folk Aire WNMC
1701 E. Front St., Traverse City, MI 49686
PH: 231-995-2562
www.wnmc.org
We don't care how famous our artists are (yet) - we just want to play good music!

Folks Like Us WEMU
PO Box 980350, Ypsilanti, MI 48198
PH: 734-487-8936
Matt Watroba matt@watrobanetwork.com
www.folkslikeus.org
Traditional and contemporary Folk music.

The Folk Tradition WKAR
283 Comm Arts Bldg. Michigan State U.
E. Lansing, MI 48824-1212
PH: 517 432-9527 FX: 517-353-7124
Bob Blackman blackman@wkar.org
wkar.org/folktradition
Traditional Folk songs, Celtic tunes and more.

Old Front Porch WXOU
2360 Oaknoll, Auburn Hills, MI 48326
Maggie Ferguson marmikdj@yahoo.com
www.oakland.edu/org/wxou
Pioneering progressive Folk, holding fast to Traditional Roots. We promote and support Michigan and regional artists.

The Spectra Show WIAA
PH: 800-441-9422
Bob Allen AllenRE@interlochen.org
www.spectrashow.org
Mix of contemporary songwriters, Folk, Blues and World.

Minnesota

Folk Migrations *KUMD*
Duluth Ent. Convention Ctr. 350 Harbor Dr.
Duluth, MN 55802
Bryan French bfrench@decc.org
www.kumd.org
If you would like your CDs considered for airplay, please send them to me at the above address.

Thirsty Boots *WTIP*
PO Box 1005, Grand Marais, MN 55604
PH: 218-387-1070 FX: 218-387-1120
wtip@boreal.org
wtip.org
Folk, Bluegrass, Americana and Celtic music!

Urban Folk *KFAI*
1808 Riverside Ave. Minneapolis, MN 55454
PH: 612-341-3144
www.kfai.org/programs/urb_folk.htm
Folk, Bluegrass, Blues and international Roots music.

Missouri

The Acoustic Edge *KRFC*
1731 B. S. 11th St., St. Louis, MO 63104-3459
PH: 314-588-9255
Naomi and Terry nstm1@yahoo.com
www.geocities.com/nstm1/acousticedge.html
Cool tunes each Sunday.

Blue Highways/No Limit *KOPN*
110 E. Hubbell Dr. Columbia, MO 65201
PH: 573-424-5331
Clint Harding thevoice@coin.org
www.kopn.org
The voice of Heartland Security. Please e-mail me before you send in your material, just to give me a heads up.

Family Reunion *KDHX*
3504 Magnolia, St. Louis, MO 63118
PH: 314-664-3955 FX: 314-664-1020
Judy Stein musicdepartment@kdhx.org
www.kdhx.org
Often featuring artists who will be performing locally.

Sunday Morning Coffeehouse *KOPN*
1907 Juniper Dr. Columbia, MO 65201-3862
Steve Jerrett sjerrett@coin.org
www.kopn.org
Traditional Folk, Bluegrass, Country, Celtic and Singer-Songwriter expressions of the ever-evolving Folk process.

Montana

The Folk Show *KUFM*
MPR, 32 Campus Dr. U. Montana,
Missoula, MT 59812-8064
PH: 406-243-4931 FX: 406-243-3299
www.kufm.org
A potpourri of Folk music from around the world.

Nebraska

Celtic Heartland *KZUM*
Grace McKinley, 941 "O" St. #1025,
Lincoln, NE 68508
PH: 402-474-5086 FX: 402-474-5091
Grace McKinley grace@celticheartland.org
www.celticheartland.org
If you're a performer of Celtic music and would like to be a guest on the show, either by phone or in person, please e-mail me.

New Hampshire

The Folk Show *NHPR*
207 N. Main Street, Concord, NH 03301-5003
PH: 603-228-8910 FX: 603-224-6052
Kate McNal folkshow@nhpr.org
www.nhpr.org
Traditional and contemporary Acoustic and Folk Music. In-studio guests as well.

Writers in the Round *WITR*
c/o Portsmouth Radio, PO Box 6532,
Portsmouth, NH 03802
PH: 603-430-9722 FX: 430-9822
Deidre Randall WITR@deidrerandall.com
www.deidrerandall.com/witr.html
A weekly showcase of live music with two songwriters and one poet.

New Jersey

The Legacy Program *WTSR*
2000 Pennington Rd. Ewing, NJ 08628-0718
PH: 609-771-2420 FX: 609-637-5113
Peter Kernast wtsrlegacy1@cs.com
www.wtsr.org
Folk and New World Music. Features live guests.

The Mists of Avalon *WDVR*
PO Box 191, Sergeantsville, NJ, 08557
PH: 609-397-1620 FX: 609-397-5991
walt@themistsofavalon.com
www.themistsofavalon.com
Features Celtic, Medieval, Renaissance and Folk music.

Music You Can't Hear On the Radio *WPRB*
79 Rittenhouse Rd. Stockton, NJ 08559
PH: 609-258-3655 FX: 609-397-9016
John Weingart VerySeldom@aol.com
www.veryseldom.com
Folk music, String band music, Bluegrass, Blues and humor.

The Roots Rock Review *WBZC*
County Rt. 530, Pemberton, NJ 08068-1599
PH: 609-894-9311 x7223 FX: 609-894-9440
Greg Gaughan no9mngmt@enter.net
staff.bcc.edu/radio
This show mixes Rock n' Roll, Folk, Blues, Bluegrass, even Country.

Traditions *WFDU*
1000 River Rd. Teaneck, NJ 07666
Ron Olesko rolesko@optonline.net
wfdu.fm
Sharing the unique and expansive world of Folk music. Continuing its long "tradition" of introducing new artists to its audience.

New York

A Thousand Welcomes *WFUV*
Fordham U. Bronx, NY 10458
PH: 718-817-4550 FX: 718-365-9815
Kathleen Biggins kathleenbiggins@wfuv.org
www.wfuv.org/wfuv/kathleen.html
Celtic traditional music.

After Midnight *WXXE*
PO Box 35091, Syracuse, NY 13235
Dale R. Gowin wxxeradio@yahoo.com
luminist.org/radio
An eight-hour Roots and Acoustic music program.

Bound for Glory *WVBR*
957 B Mitchell St., Ithaca, NY 14850
PH: 607-273-4000
www.wvbr.com/bfg.html
Provides free, live Folk concerts.

Common Threads *WAER*
795 Ostrom Ave. Syracuse, NY 13244-4601
PH: 315-443-4021 FX: 315-443-2148
Larry Hoyt friendoffolk@netscape.net
waer.org/threads.html
Traditional Folk and Acoustically-based music.

Dancing on the Air *WAMC*
PO Box 66600, Albany, NY 12206
PH: 800-323-9262 FX: 518-432-6974
dancingontheair.com
Live musical performances. Folk, Celtic, Swing, Cajun, Zydeco, Old-Time Country, Bluegrass, Rockabilly, Blues, Jazz, Pop, and more.

Folk Plus *WJFF*
45 Dwyer Ave. Liberty, NY 12754
Angela Page folkplus@wjffradio.org
www.wjffradio.org/FolkPlus
I explore the music and artists that I call FOLK.

Folk, Rock & Roots *WVKR*
Box 726, Vassar College, 124 Raymond Ave.
Poughkeepsie, NY 12604
PH: 845-437-5476 FX: 845-437-7656
Andrew Tokash aptokash@aol.com
members.aol.com/aptokash/vkr-frr.html
Playing Folk, Alt.Country, Rock, Blues, guitar instrumentals and Roots Rock.

The Folk Show *WSLU*
St. Lawrence U. Canton, NY 13617
Mike Alzo folkshow@ncpr.org
www.northcountrypublicradio.org/programs/local/folk.html
Traditional and contemporary Folk music.

Hootenanny Cafe *WTBQ*
62 N. Main St., Florida, NY 10921
PH: 845-651-1110 FX: 845-651-1025
Jon Stein musicnow@frontiernet.net
www.wtbq.com
Acoustic music show.

Hudson River Sampler *WAMC*
PO Box 66600, Albany, NY 12206
PH: 800-323-9262 FX: 518-432-6974
Wanda Fischer wanda@wamc.org
www.wamc.org/hurisam.html
Folk, Bluegrass and Blues.

It's Folk Music, It's For Folks *WBNY*
Buffalo State College, 1300 Elmwood Ave.
Buffalo, NY 14222
PH: 716- 673-3260
Ken "Dr. K" Nagelberg kenfolkdj@yahoo.com
www.wbny.org
Features Folk and Acoustic Singer/Songwriters on independent and self-published labels.

Light Show *WBAI*
120 Wall St. 10th Fl. New York, NY 10005
PH: 212-209-2800 FX: 212-747-1698
Frederick Geobold lightshow@wbai.org
www.lightshownycwbaifm.org
Folk songs, tale of struggle, people's poetry, drama, liturgy, theology, professional wrestling — narrative forms that proclaim the values of a civilization striving to be born.

Nonesuch *WVBR*
957 Mitchell St. #B, Ithaca, NY 14850
PH: 607-273-4000 FX: 607-273-4069
nonesuch@wvbr.com
www.wvbr.com
Music in the Folk tradition.

Sunday Street *WUSB*
Student Union Bld. SUNY,
Stony Brook, NY 11794-3263
PH: 631-632-6500 FX: 631-632-7182
Charlie Backfish sundaystreetwusb@aol.com
wusb.fm
An Acoustic-oriented program on the air since 1978.

A Variety of Folk *WRUR*
PO Box 277356, Rochester, NY 14627
PH: 585-275-6400 FX: 585-256-3989
Tom Bohan tombohan@rochester.rr.com
home.rochester.rr.com/bohan
Folk, Bluegrass, Old Time, Singer Songwriter etc.

North Carolina

Back Porch Music *WUNC*
120 Friday Ctr. Dr. Chapel Hill NC 27517
PH: 919-966.5454 FX: 919-966-5955
Freddy Jenkins fjenkins@wunc.org
www.wunc.org/backporchmusic
A wide range of Acoustic-based Folk music.

Celtic Winds *WNCW*
286 ICC Loop Road, Spindale, NC 28160
PH: 828-286-3636
info@wncw.org
www.wncw.org
Celtic music from around the world and around the corner. Send 2 CDs to the attention of the Music Director. Make sure to include a one-sheet (bio).

Ohio

Below the Salt *WOUB*
9 S. College St., Athens, OH 45701
PH: 740-593-1771 FX: 740-593-0240
Keith Newman belowthesalt@woub.org
woub.org/belowthesalt
An eclectic mix of Folk music.

FolkAlley.com
PO Box 5190, 1613 E. Summit St., Kent, OH 44242
David Fuente letters@folkalley.com
www.folkalley.com
The online gateway to the world of Folk music!

Folk Music *WKSU*
PO Box 5190, Kent, OH 44242–0001
PH: 330-672–3114 FX: 330-672–4107
letters@wksu.org
www.wksu.org/folk
We air 13 hours of Folk music weekly!

Toss the Feathers *WCBE*
540 Jack Gibbs Blvd. Columbus, OH 43215
PH: 614-365-5555 FX: 614-365-5060
Doug Dickson music@wcbe.org
www.wcbe.org
Featuring the best of Celtic and British Folk - Rock.

Visiting The Folks *WJCU*
7666 N. Gannett, Sagamore Hills, OH 44067
PH: 216-397-4937 FX: 216-397-4438
Fred Dolan dolan@en.com
www.wjcu.org
Folk, Acoustic, Celtic, Classic Country, & Bluegrass vocals.

Oklahoma

Different Roads *KCSC*
U. Central Oklahoma, 100 N. University Dr.
Edmond, OK 73034
PH: 405-974-3333 FX: 405-974-3844
Kent Anderson kanderson@kcscfm.com
www.kcscfm.com/programming/program_roads.asp
Devoted to Folk-oriented Acoustic music.

Folk Salad *KWGS*
U. Tulsa, 600 S. College Ave. Tulsa, OK 74104
PH: 918-836-4354
Richard & Scott folksalad@kwgs.org
kwgs.org/folksalad.html
Contemporary and traditional offerings in Folk.

Oregon

The Raggle Taggle Gypsy *KPSU*
1100 W. 9th St, The Dalles, OR 97058
Judith Gennett gennett@gorge.net
www.columbiagypsy.net/kpsu.htm
I play European and euro-influenced music on the radio.

The Saturday Cafe *KLCC*
PO Box 50698, Eugene, OR 97405
Frank Gosar fgosar@efn.org
www.klcc.org
Mostly Acoustic, Folk and Singer/Songwriter music.

Pennsylvania

Acoustic Eclectic
114 Braithwaite Ln. Quakertown, PA 18951
www.acousticeclectic.org
Contemporary Singer/Songwriters and Acoustic instrumental music.

In The Tradition *WDIY*
3681 Huckleberry Rd. Allentown, PA 18104
PH: 610-395-5908
Tom Druckenmiller producer/host littlecat@enter.net
www.WDIY.org
Features traditional based North American and Celtic music.

Roots *WVUD*
PO Box 701, Unionville, PA 19375
Todd Tyson folkbloke@kennett.net
www.wvud.org
All kinds of Folk, for all kinds of folks.

The Saturday Light Brigade *WRCT*
PO Box 100092, Pittsburgh, PA 15233
PH: 412-761-5144 FX: 412-761-3625
slb@slbradio.com
www.slbradio.com
Acoustic music and family fun.

Transitions Radio Magazine *KBAC*
17 Alondra Rd. Santa Fe, NM 87508
Alan Hunter & Elizabeth Rose
hosts@transradio.com
www.transradio.com
Music crosses over typical industry classifications to provide a wide range of vocals and instrumentals, Acoustic and Electronic styles, from the familiar to the unique.

Rhode Island

Traditions *WRIU*
326 Memorial Union, Kingston, RI 02881
PH: 401-874-4949 FX: 401-874-4349
folk@wriu.org
www.wriu.org
The place to hear new Folk & Roots releases.

Texas

Folk Fury *KTEP*
500 W. U. Ave. #200, El Paso, TX 79968-0001
PH: 915-747-5152 FX: 915-747-5641
Dan Alloway ktep@utep.edu
www.ktep.org
Unique blends of Bluegrass, Blues, Western Swing, Progressive Country and of course, Folk music.

Folkways *KUT*
1 University Stn. A0704, Austin, TX 78712
PH: 512-471-1631 FX: 512-471-3700
Ed Miller edmiller@io.com
www.kut.org
Six hours of assorted Folk music.

Some Call it Folk *KEDT*
4455 S. Padre Island Dr. #38, Corpus Christi, TX 78411-4481
PH: 361-855-2213 FX: 361-855-3877
Pat Smith stewartjacoby@kedt.org
www.kedt.org
Featuring today's Singer/Songwriters and yesterday's Folk legends.

Utah

Fresh Folk *UPR*
Utah State U. Logan, UT 84322-8505
Blair Larsen blair@mfire.com
upr.org/programs/FreshFolk.htm
Folk, Blues, Bluegrass and Celtic new releases.

Saturday Sagebrush Serenade *KRCL*
1971 W. N. Temple, Salt Lake City, UT 84116
PH: 801-359-9191 FX: 801-533-9136
Dave S. davesa@krcl.org
www.krcl.org
Folk and Acoustic Rock to ease you from your morning cup of coffee through your Sunday afternoon..

Sunday Sagebrush Serenade *KRCL*
1971 W. North Temple, Salt Lake City, UT 84116
PH: 801-363-1818 FX: 801-533-9136
Phil phill@krcl.org or Lori lorir@krcl.org
www.krcl.org
Folk and Acoustic Rock every Sunday.

Thursday Breakfast Jam *KRLC*
1752 S. 600 E. Salt Lake City, UT 84105
PH: 801-363-1818 FX: 801-533-9136
Susanne Millsaps susannem@krcl.org
www.krcl.org/~susannem
Folk, Jazz, world, eclectic mix.

The Wayward Wind *KZMU*
PO Box 1076, 1734 Rocky Rd. Moab, UT 84532
PH: 435-259-8824 FX: 435-259-8763
Becky Thomas and Dave Condie music-director@kzmu.org
www.kzmu.org
Adventure into Folk, Country, Jazz....

Vermont

All the Traditions *Vermont Public Radio*
20 Troy Ave. Colchester, VT 05446
PH: 802-655-9451 FX: 802-655-2799
Robert Resnik rresnik@vpr.net
www.vpr.net/music/traditions.shtml
Folk, Country, Old Time etc.

The Folk Show *WWPV*
St. Michael's College, Box 274, Winooski Park,
Colchester, VT 05439
PH: 802-654-2334 FX: 802-654-2336
John Sheehey wwpv@smcvt.edu
personalweb.smcvt.edu/wwpv
Contemporary Folk, Celtic, Blues and more.

Virginia

Acoustic Café *WMRA*
PO Box 1292, Harrisonburg, VA 22803
PH: 540-568-6221 FX: 540-568-3814
slottca@jmu.edu
www.jmu.edu/wmra/folk.html
Cover up and coming artists.

Atlantic Weekly II *WTJU*
PO Box 400811, U. Virginia,
Charlottesville, VA 22901-4811
Terry Carpenter etc56@aol.com
wtju.net
Celtic-flavored music based in Britain and Ireland with excursions to Scandinavia and the Continent.

The Electric Croude *WCVE*
c/o George Maida, 23 Sesame St.,
Richmond, VA 23235
www.wcve.org
I like to support Indie music.

Eclectic Hours *WEBR*
2929 Eskridge Rd., #S, Fairfax, VA 22031
PH: 703-573-1090 x1018
www.fcac.org/webr/webr.htm
Singer/Songwriter & Folk music.

Out O' the Blue Radio Revue *WCVE*
PO Box 1117, Mechanicsville, VA 23111-6117
PH: 804-559-8855 FX: 804-559-0516
Page@PageWilson.com
www.pagewilson.com/ootbrr.html
Folk, Blues, Bluegrass, Country, Cajun/Zydeco, Rock & Roll, Irish and more.

Sunset Road *WTJU*
PO Box 400811, U. Virginia,
Charlottesville, VA 22901-4811
Terry Carpenter etc56@aol.com
wtju.net
Folk show featuring local, regional, national, and international artists. Also, what's happening at local and regional venues, new releases, interviews, featured artists, and more.

Washington

Inland Folk *KWSU*
PO Box 2184-CS, Pullman, WA 99165
PH: 509-332-5047
Dan Maher dmaher@wsu.edu
www.kpbx.org/programs/inlandfolk.htm
Music of local and national Folk artists.

Lunch With Folks *KBCS*
3000 Landerholm Cir. SE,
Bellevue, WA 98007-6484
PH: 425-564-2427
John Sincock john.sincock@verizon.net
kbcs.fm
Every weekday a different host features 3 hours of flavorful Folk music.

Our Saturday Tradition *KBCS*
3000 Landerholm Cir. SE,
Bellevue, WA 98007-6484
PH: 425-564-2427
Hal Durden asubdude@att.net
kbcs.fm
Traditional Folk music including Bluegrass, Old-Time, British and American contemporary.

Sunday Brunch *KMTT*
1100 Olive Way #1650, Seattle, WA 98101
PH: 206-233-1037 FX: 206-233-8978
Drew Dundon adundon@entercom.com
www.kmtt.com
Selections from the lighter side of the music library.

Washington DC

Traditions *WETA*
2775 S. Quincy St., Arlington, VA 22206
PH: 703-998-2600 FX: 703-998-3401
Mary Cliff traditions@weta.com
www.marycliff.net
A mix of traditional, revival, Singer/Songwriter, Ethnic and World music.

Wisconsin

Acoustic Revival *WWSP*
105 CAC UWSP Reserve St.,
Stevens Point, WI 54481
PH: 715-346-3755 FX: 715-346-4012
Granddad granddad90fm@hotmail.com
www.uwsp.edu/stuorg/wwsp/AR_Main.htm
The best selections of Acoustic mMusic in Central Wisconsin.

Diaspora *WORT*
PO Box 3247, Madison, WI 53704
PH: 608-256-2695 FX: 608-256-3704
Terry O'Laughlin diaspora@terryo.org
diaspora.terryo.org
Folk and World music.

Folkways *WOJB*
Rte. 2, Box 2788 Hayward, WI 54843
Mark Pedersen pedersen@chibardun.net
www.wojb.org
From American Roots music to contemporary Singer/Songwriters.

Northwoods Cafe *WXPR*
303 W. Prospect Ave. Rhinelander, WI 54501
PH: 715-362-6000 FX: 715-362-6007
Marcia Barkus wxpr@wxpr.org
www.wxpr.org/program/northcafe.cfm
Folk, Roots, World, Blues, Cajun, Zydeco...

Simply Folk *Wisconsin Public Radio*
821 University Ave. Madison, WI 53706
PH: 800-747-7444
Judy Rose rosej@wpr.org
www.wpr.org/simplyfolk
Bringin you concerts recorded here in Wisconsin.

Wyoming

Morning Music With Don Woods *WPR*
U. Wyoming, Dept: 3984 1000 E. U.
Laramie, WY 82071
PH: 307-766-4240 FX: 307-766-6184
Don Woods dwoods@uwyo.edu
uwadmnweb.uwyo.edu/WPR
Daily 3 hour show.

US Virgin Islands

The Doug Lewis Show *WVGN*
PO Box 6786, St. Thomas, VI 00804-6786
PH: 340-777-6035
Doug Dick cddick@viaccess.net
www.wvgn.org
Blues, Folk, Classic Rock & Roll and Country.

Canada

Acoustic Roots *CHUO*
117 Carruthers Ave. Ottawa, ON K1Y 1N4
PH: 613-729-1106
L.J. Bouchard ljbouchard@rogers.com
www.chuo.fm
We play acoustic guitar-focused singer-songwriters, traditional music from Celtic to Americana, acoustic Blues, Old-timey music, World music - on occasion, Newgrass, Bluegrass, (some) Country.

Acoustic Routes *CKLN*
168 Combe Ave. Toronto, ON M3H 4K3
Joel Wortzman jwortzman@sympatico.ca
www.ckln.fm
Contemporary Acoustic Singer/Songwriter.

The Celtic Show *CKUA*
10526 Jasper Ave. Edmonton, AB T5J 1Z7
PH: 780-428-7595 FX: 780-428-7624
Andy Donnelly andy.donnelly@ckua.org
www.ckua.com/celticshow
Traditional ballads to hard-driving Rock tunes.

Folk Roots/Folk Branches *CKUT*
235 Metcalfe Ave. #402, Westmount, QC H3Z 2H8
Mike Regenstreif mike@ckutfolk.com
www.ckutfolk.com
Broadly-defined Folk-oriented program.

Folk Routes *CKUA*
10526 Jasper Ave. Edmonton, AB T5J 1Z7
PH: 780-428-7595 FX: 780-428-7624
Tom Coxworth tom.coxworth@ckua.org
www.ckua.org
Tracing Folk music from around the world.

For the Folk *CHRW*
Allison muckfluckchuckbuk@hotmail.com
www.geocities.com/folkie4
Folk, Roots, Traditional, Celtic, Singer-Songwriter.

Freewheeling Folk Show *CFMU*
16 Penlake Ct. Hamilton, ON L9C 5Y7
Jim Marino jlmarino@mountaincable.net
cfmu.mcmaster.ca
Folk and Celtic music with a touch of Bluegrass and an emphasis on local talent.

Jigs and Reels *CKWR*
c/o Dean Clarke, 6-130 Columbia St. W.,
Waterloo, ON N2L 3K9
general@yourfm.ca
www.yourfm.ca
East Coast style music show.

Just Us Folk CKPC
571 West St., Brantford, ON N3T 5P8
PH: 519-759-1000 FX: 519-753-1470
Jan Vanderhorst production@ckpc
www.ckpc.on.ca
Sunday night Folk show.

Prairie Ceilidh CKJS
96 Erlandson Dr. Winnipeg, MB R3K 0G8
Lyle Skinner pceilidh@shaw.ca
members.shaw.ca/pceilidh
Traditional and contemporary Celtic music.

Regina's Mighty Shores
PO Box 334, Stn. Main, Regina, SK S4P 3A1
mightyshores@hotmail.com
regie2.phys.uregina.ca
Featuring Folk, Roots, Celtic, Bluegrass etc.

Roots and Wings CBC
Philly Markowitz, PO Box 500, Stn. A,
Toronto, ON M5W 1E6
PH: 416-205-3700 FX: 416-205-6040
rootsandwings@cbc.ca
radio.cbc.ca/programs/roots
Send in any and all music.

Roots & Writers UMFM
153 Emerson Ave. Winnipeg, MB R2G 1E8
Len Osland lennytunes@shaw.ca
www.umfm.com
A weekly cocktail of Roots/ Blues/ Country & rockin' Folk tunes served up by songwriters and independents you may well never have heard of before.

Steel Belted Radio
126 Meadow Lake Dr. Winnipeg, MB R2C 4K3
PH: 204-224-1663
Terry Wilson steelbeltedradio@shaw.ca
www.steelbeltedradio.com
Specializing in Roots, Country and all the down and dirty stuff those wimps at other radio stations won't play!

Sunday Coffee House CJLX
PO Box 4200, Belleville, ON K8N 5B9
Greg Schatzmann sundaycoffeehouse@yahoo.ca
www.cjlx.fm
Folk/Acoustic/Celtic/Roots music & beyond.

Tell the Band to Go Home
7 Brownell Bay, Winnipeg, MB R3R 1L8
PH: 204-474-7027
Jeff Robson BandGoHome@shaw.ca
members.shaw.ca/bandgohome
Weekly Singer/Songwriter radio show. I also review CDs and write music articles for local publications.

Waxies Dargle UMFM
Room 308 U. Ctr. Winnipeg, MB R3T 2N2
PH: 204-474-7027 FX: 204-269-1299
Lyle Skinner waxies@shaw.ca
www.umfm.com
Traditional and Contemporary Celtic-edged Folk/Pop/Rock music from near and afar.

Window of Opportunity CKCU
61 Highmont Ct. Kanata, ON K2T 1B2
Laurie-Ann Copple lcopple@ncf.ca
www.ncf.ca/~eh202/window.html
We support up-and-coming Folk, Blues and Jazz artists. Or maybe you represent a genre that is somewhere in between - this is still good - Bluegrass, Celtic, World; these are also featured.

Europe

Belgium

Psyche van het Folk
PO Box 28, 2570 Duffel, Belgium
PH: 0472-769207
Gerald.Van.Waes@pandora.be
psychevanhetfolk.homestead.com
World progressive music, Acoustic crossovers, Acid Folk...

Germany

Folkladen
Radio Neckarburg, Lucian-Reich-Str. 30, 78050 VS-Villingen, Germany
Heinrich Wesolly hwesolly@gmx.de
www.radio-neckarburg.de
Features Singer/Songwriter, Bluegrass, Folk and Alt-Country.

Keine Heimat
Sedanstrasse 12, 79098 Freiburg, Germany
PH: 49-761-35329 FX: 49-761-35329
Christian Rath info@keine-heimat.de
www.keine-heimat.de
The Euro-Folk-show on Radio Dreyeckland.

Radio ISW
Mozartstraße 3a, 84508 Burgkirchen/Alz, Germany
PH: 08679-9827-0 FX: 08679-9827-30
Hansjoerg Malonek hajomalo@iiv.de
www.inn-salzach-welle.de
Folk & Country Music.

Radio ZuSa
Scharnhorststr. 1, 21335 Lueneburg, Germany
Juergen Kramer j.kramer@zusa.de
www.zusa.de
I do a show on all kinds of Folk, Acoustic and Traditional music from around the world. I'm looking for more or less Acoustic material without loads of drums and gimmicks.

Italy

"Highway 61" and "Un Mondo Di Musica" (A World Of Music)
PO Box 12, 15040 San Michele, Alessandria, Italy
PH: 39-131-225791 FX: 39-131-225791
Massimo Ferro highway61@interfree.it
www.highway61.it
The two radio shows of Italian DJ Massimo Ferro on Radio Voce Spazio 93.800, Italy. Highway 61 plays American Roots based music (Folk, Country, Bluegrass, Blues but also Roots Rock, Americana, Alternative Country, etc.) Un Mondo Di Musica deals with every form of Folk, Roots & World Music from around the globe.

The Netherlands

Crossroads Radio BRTO
Smitsstraat 13, 4623 XP Bergen op Zoom,
The Netherlands
Jos van den Boom crossroads@brto.nl
www.crossroadsradio.nl
Roots and Singer/Songwriter music. Once a month musicians from all over the world are invited to record an acoustic session in front of an audience of about 50 people.

Landslide
Tarwestraat 99, 1446 CC Purmerend,
The Netherlands
Tel: 00-31-0-299-463138
Michael van Bruggen landslide@planet.nl
www.realrootscafe.com/landslide.html
A wide variety of American Roots music, like Country, Folk, Blues, Singer Songwriters, Cajun, Zydeco etc. We're always looking for new talent!

Under the Tree
Hoogewaard 39, 2396AC Koudekerk aan den Rijn,
The Netherlands
PH.: 00-31-0-713-414-647
Hans Hoogeveen hanshoogeveen@planet.nl
www.realrootscafe.com/underthetree.html
www.ttfc.nl
Traditional and modern days Folk music, as well as Singer-Songwriters, a little Blues, Americana and Country, some World music and sip of Pop and Rock every now and then.

United Kingdom

Acoustic Freeway Clare FM
Abbeyfield Ctr. Francis St. Ennis,
Co. Clare, Ireland UK
PH: 353-0-65-68-28-888 FX: 353-0-65-68-29-392
Michelle Harding acoustic@clarefm.ie
www.clarefm.ie
Michelle has gift for spotting talent and she isn't afraid to showcase new artists, who aren't getting airplay elsewhere.

BBC Radio 2 Folk and Acoustic
www.bbc.co.uk/radio2/r2music/folk
Home page of the BBC Radio 2's various Folk and Acoustic shows. Info, shows, contacts etc.

BBC Radio 2 Folk and Country
www.bbc.co.uk/radio2/r2music/folkandcountry
Home page of the BBC Radio 2's various Folk and Country shows. Info, shows, contacts etc.

FOLK MUSIC with Chris Arscott Forest of Dean Radio
1 Berisford Ct. Cinderford,
Gloucestershire, GL14 2BS UK
PH: 01594-820722
contactus@fodradio.org
www.fodradio.org/folk_music_with_chris_arscott.htm
Featuring CD tracks of and interviews with artists visiting the local Folk clubs and sessions.

The Late Session RTÉ
PH: 01-2082040 FX: 01-2083092
Áine Hensey brownep@rte.ie
www.rte.ie/radio1/thelatesession
Irish traditional and Folk music.

Roots Around the World Spirit FM
9-10 Dukes Ct. Bognor Rd. Chichester,
West Sussex, PO19 8FX UK
PH: 01243-539000 FX: 01243-786464
Mark Ringwood mark.ringwood@spiritfm.net
rootsaroundtheworld.info
www.spiritfm.net
A weekly showcase of the best in Folk, Blues, World and Country music, including the latest gig news, exclusive airplays and interviews.

Australia

A Dog's Breakfast
Glenn Morrow glen@saturdaybreakfast.com
saturdaybreakfast.com
Playing a mixture of Blues, Folk, Roots, Country, and World music.

Celtic World
PO Box 9014, Deakin, ACT 2600 Australia
postmaster@celtic-world.net
www.celtic-world.net
Today's top performers, from the traditional to the very modern.

Come All Ye *2MCE*
Panorama Ave. Bathurst, NSW 2795 Australia
PH: 02-6338-4790 FX: 02-6338-4402
Bruce Cameron cameron@ix.net.au
www.csu.edu.au/2MCE
The longest running Folk program on Australian radio. Preview CDs are welcomed.

Folk till Midnight / Good Morning Folk *5EB*
PO Box 250, Nairne, SA 5252 Australia
Henk de Weerd hdeweerd@hotkey.net.au
www.5ebi.com.au
Please send in your promotional CDs.

Northside Folk *Triple H*
26 Awatea Rd. St Ives, NSW 2075 Australia
Jude & Mart Fowler fowlermj@bigpond.net.au
www.hhhfm.org.au
Promotional material welcome. Please send to the above address.

Sidestream
PO Box 139, Redcliffe, QLD 4020 Australia
www.red997.com
Folk & Roots, Singer/Songwriter, Acoustic, World, Celtic, Bluegrass & Blues.

New Zealand

Folk on Sunday
1214 Louie St., Hastings, New Zealand 4201
PH: 64-6-8785395
Mitch and Robyn Park mfpark@xtra.co.nz
www.radiokidnappers.org.nz
Ballads, Shanties, Blues, Gospel, Bluegrass etc.

Town & Country
21 Redvers Drive, Belmont,
Lower Hutt 6009, New Zealand
Eddie O'Strange blue.smoke@actrix.gen.nz
Folk and Roots music.

GLBT Radio

After Hours *KPFT*
400 Westmoreland #2, Houston, TX 77006
PH: 713-526-4000 FX: 713-526-5750
Jimmy Carper afterhours@kpft.org
www.kpft.org
Queer weekly variety show, generally 6-8 GLBT songs per show.

Amazon Country *WXPN*
3025 Walnut St., Philadelphia, PA 19104
PH: 215-898-6677. FX: 215-898-0707
Debra D'Alessandro amazon@xpn.org
www.xpn.org/amazon.php
One of the longest-running gay and lesbian/feminist radio shows in America.

Audiofile
info@audiofile.org
PO Box 66648, Houston, TX 77006
www.audiofile.org
The monthly radio review of new music of interest to the gay, lesbian, bisexual and transgender communities. Audiofile airs on over 125 stations around the world as a regular feature of This Way Out, the international lesbian and gay radio magazine.

Bear Radio Network
261 W. Squire Dr. #1, Rochester, NY 14623-1735
Joe Maulucci Poetbear@BearRadio.net
www.BearRadio.Net
We're looking for submissions from artists in the GLBT community and those musicians who are gay friendly. Independent artists with quality demos are welcomed!

Beat FM
PH: 02-9516-1771
info@beatfm.com.au
www.beatfm.com.au
The very best gay programming and even better Dance music!

Dykes on Mics *3CR*
PO Box 1277, Collingwood, Melbourne, VIC 3065 Australia
PH: 03-9419-8377 FX: 03-9417-4472
programming@3cr.org.au
www.3cr.org.au

Dykes On Mykes *4ZZZ*
PO Box 509, Fortitude Valley, QLD 4006 Australia
dykesonmykes@hotmail.com
www.queerradio.org/dykesonmykes.html
100% women-presented and women-focused.

Dykes on Mykes *CKUT*
3647 U. St., Montreal, QC H3A 2B3
PH: 514-398-6787 FX: 514-398-8261
music@ckut.ca
www.ckut.ca
Dyke radio for everyone. Even Barbie listens.

Face the Music *WCUW*
910 Main St., Worcester, MA 01610
PH: 508-753-1012
wcuw@wcuw.com
www.wcuw.com
Syndicated lesbian/feminist music program.

Fresh Fruit *KFAI*
1808 Riverside Ave. Minneapolis, MN 55454
PH: 612-341-3144 x842
Leigh Combs peaceluv@bitstream.net
www.kfai.org/programs/frshfrut.htm
Interviews with activists, authors and musicians from all over the country. It offers recorded music, live music, news and more.

Gay Spirit *WWUH*
Attn: Music Director,
200 Bloomfield Ave. West Hartford, CT 06117
PH: 860-768-4701 FX: 860-768-5701
wwuh@hartford.edu
www.wwuh.org
Greater Hartford's only gay news program featuring contemporary issues, music, and special guests.

GaydarRadio.com
PH: +44-700-4429-327
studio@gaydarradio.com
www.gaydarradio.com
Featuring great music and interviews.

Generation Q *WRSU*
21 Southside Ave, Somerville, NJ 08876
Pedro Serrano gd4nuttin@operamail.com
wrsu.rutgers.edu
Out music, interviews & conversation. On the air for over 25 years!

Highest Common Denominator *WRSU*
21 Southside Ave, Somerville, NJ 08876
Bill Stella realman@att.net
wrsu.rutgers.edu
Champions great under appreciated musicians. Gay/Queer/Out music + political & passionate songs.

Homo Radio *WRPI*
51 Park Avenue, Albany, NY 12202-1722
PH: 518-276-2648 FX: 518-276-2360
Sean McLaughlin HomoRadio@yahoo.com
www.wrpi.org
Mix of talk and music by GLBT artists of all genres.

Homophobic *PlanetOut Radio*
PO Box 500, San Francisco, CA 94104-0500
PH: 415-834-6500 FX: 415-834-6502
www.planetout.com/pno/radio
A music show bringing you interesting, hip and relevant artists from the past, present and future.

IMRU Radio *KPFK*
11333 Moorpark St. PMB 456,
Studio City, CA 91602
imru@kpfk.org
www.imru.org
Focusing on issues affecting the GLBT community in Southern California. We welcome CD submissions from all "out" LGBT artists. If you would like us to review your CD for play on our show please send it to the above address.

K-BEAR Radio
Okumba@mailpanda.com
k-bear101.tripod.com
Rock, Dance and a few surprises.

Lesbian Power Authority *KFAI*
1808 Riverside Ave. Minneapolis, MN 55454
PH: 612-341-3144
kfai.org/programs/l_p_a.htm
Lesbian music, interviews, announcements...

Lesbian Radio
PO Box 13-0021, Christchurch, New Zealand
info@lesbianradio.org.nz
www.lesbianradio.org.nz
A weekly half-hour magazine that is primarily focused on lesbians and queer women. Usually 3 songs per show but every few weeks a whole show is dedicated to new and old music.

Out, Loud, & Queer *WJFF*
4765 State Rt. 52, PO Box 546,
Jeffersonville, NY 12748
PH: 845-482-4141 FX: 845-482-9533
Kathy Rieser kathy@wjffradio.org
www.wjffradio.org
Working to make known the music of out musicians and share the humor, culture, and diversity of the gay community—showcasing local talent and issues whenever possible.

PCM Radio
PO Box 1083, Farmington, MI 48332
PH: 386-290-3795
ilisten@pcmradio.com
www.pcmradio.com
The voice of Pride Christian music!

PrideNation
pridenation.com/radio.htm
24 hour Dance music with Trance, House, Techno and more.

Queer Ear for Far and Near *KZYX*
2000 Grand View Dr. Redwood Valley, CA 95470
Lark Letchworth LarkLet@Lycos.com
www.kzyx.org
I'm very interested in indie art, but only the queer kind for our radio show.

Queer Corps *CKUT*
3647 U. St., Montreal, QC H3A 2B3
PH: 514-398-6787 FX: 514-398-8261
music@ckut.ca
www.ckut.ca

Queer Radio *4ZZZ*
82 Main Ave. Wavell Heights, QLD 4012 Australia
Ph: +61-7-3350-1562
John Frame jvframe@bigpond.net.au
www.queerradio.org
Support, talk, music and news for GLBT.

Queer Voices *KPFT*
c/o Queer Music Heritage Radio,
4643 Wild Indigo #402, Houston, TX 77027
JD Doyle qmheritage@aol.com
www.kpft.org
It's a public affairs show but that doesn't stop me from slipping in a number of new songs each week.

Queer Waves *KOOP*
2819 Foster Lane, F122, Austin, TX 78757
PH: 512-472-1369 FX: 512-472-6149
Taylor Cage cagetaylor@aol.com
www.koop.org
A weekly showcase for GLBT and just plain Queer musicians.

Q'zine *WXPN*
3025 Walnut St., Philadelphia, PA 19104
PH: 215-898-6677. FX: 215-898-0707
Robert Drake qzine@xpn.org
www.xpn.org/qzine.php
Celebrates queer arts and culture with a mix of interviews, commentary and music from out artists worldwide.

Rainbow World Radio
info@stonewallsociety.com
www.stonewallsociety.com/rainbowworldradio.htm
Promoting GLBT artists, GLBT music and the GLBT community with music choices and interviews!

SIRIUS OutQ
1221 Ave of the Americas, New York, NY 10020
PH: 212-584-5334 FX: 212-584-5200
Charlie Dyer cdyer@siriusradio.com
www.sirius.com/outq
America's only 24/7 radio station for the gay, lesbian, bisexual and transgender community. Provocative, entertaining-even titillating! Plus news, interviews and music from GLBT recording artists.

Think Pink *WLUW*
6525 N. Sheridan Rd. Chicago, IL 60626
PH: 773-508-8080 FX: 773-508-8082
Erik and Ali thinkpink@wluw.org
www.wluw.org
Chicago's only all music radio show for the queer community, Think Pink focuses on music made by the GLBT community but will also include music with queer themes and music targeting the queer audience.

This Way Out
PO Box 38327, Los Angeles, CA 90038-0327
PH: 818 986 4106
TWOradio@aol.com
www.thiswayout.org
Internationally syndicated gay and lesbian radio news magazine. Plays music between segments; particularly interested in "out" songs that are relevant to current events and can be used for intro/outro related news and features.

Windy City Radio *WCKG*
PH: 773-871-7610
Danica Milich DanicaMilich@aol.com
www.windycityradio.com
A fun program that allows for a new and creative outlet to cover the GLBT community.

WKJCE
c/o GLBT RADIO, 1216 Constitution Blvd. 1st Fl.
New Kensington, PA 15068
Joanne Lynn garfield25_tg@yahoo.com
scorpius.spaceports.com/~wkjce
A GLBT community radio station. May the voices in the wilderness be heard through low power radio.

Goth Radio

North America

United States

A Feast Of Friends *KTUH*
Hemenway Hall #203, 2445 Campus Rd.
Honolulu, HI 96822
PH: 808-956-4848
Nocturna feast@hawaii.rr.com
afeastoffriends.net
Features Gothic, Industrial, Ethereal, Dark Wave, Death Rock and Dark Narrative Rock music. The music is dark and we do our best to keep it there.

ampedOut
Stoicite stoic@ampedout.net
ampedout.net
A source for music other than the pre-fab radio bullshit.

Arzachel's Dreaming
PH: 206-321-4109
franklin@oz.net
www.live365.com/stations/290062
Industrial, Ambient, Goth show.

Bats in the Belfry *WMBR*
3 Ames St., Cambridge, MA 02142
PH: 617-253-4000
Mistress Laura bats@wmbr.org
wmbr.mit.edu
Moody, dark, and atmospheric – beginning with ancient music and chant, to the newest Gothic Rock, Darkwave, Goth-Industrial, and Dark-Ambient.

The Black Cauldron *KUCI*
PO Box 4362 Irvine, CA 92616
PH: 949-824-6868
Matthew Brown morven@byz.org
www.kuci.org/~mbrown/cauldron.html
Goth, Industrial, Pagen, Ethereal, Electronica and Darkwave.

Black Wings
evilhasnoboundaries@hotmail.com
www.live365.com/stations/302964
Goth/Industrial station.

The Circle of Souls Pagan Radio
radio@circleofsouls.net
www.circleofsouls.net
If you are a musical artist, a record label promoter, or other authorized representative of a musical artist or group, please contact us regarding promotion via our online radio broadcasts and website.

Closed Caskets for the Living Impaired *KUCI*
PO Box 4362 Irvine, CA 92616
PH: 949-824-5824
Dach dach@kuci.org
www.closedcaskets.com
The most popular Goth radio show of all time.

Dark Horizons *WMNF*
6006 N. Branch Ave. Tampa, FL 33604
PH: 813-239-9663
www.darkhorizonsradio.com
Ethereal, Gothic, Industrial and Synthpop bands.

Dark Nation Radio
cypher@bound.org
www.live365.com/stations/297970
Features a mix of Gothic, Industrial, Deathrock and Ambient.

Detroit Industrial Underground
brian@detroitIndustrial.org
www.detroitIndustrial.org
Questions, comments, and playlist suggestions are always welcome. Free CDs from bands and labels are even more welcome.

Digital Gunfire
shirow@digitalgunfire.com
www.digitalgunfire.com
Industrial, EBM and Electronic all day, every day. We play the music of Independent artists.

Factory 911 *WEGL*
116 Foy Union Bldg. Auburn U., AL 36849-5231
PH: 334-844-4113 FX: 334-844-4118
Robert Dykes wegl@auburn.edu
wegl.auburn.edu
An Industrial and Electronic show.

Generation Death *KSPC*
Thatcher Music Bldg. 340 N. College Ave.
Claremont, CA 91711
PH: 909-621-8157 FX: 909-607-1259
www.kspc.org
Gothic, Industrial, Ethereal, Darkwave and Shoegazer. Host: Wednesday

Gothic Paradise Radio
jacob001@comcast.net
www.Gothicparadise.com
Gothic, Industrial, Darkwave, EBM, Ethereal and Synthpop.

GotBlack.com Radio
5501 N. 7th Ave. PMB 721, Phoenix, AZ 85013
joe@gotblack.com
www.gotblack.com/radio
Plays Gothic, Industrial, and Electronic music. We are currently accepting CDs and press kits.

In Perpetual Motion Radio
314 Kensington Ave. Ferndale, MI 48220-2359
G. R. Perye III ipm@ipmradio.com
www.ipmradio.com
Indie artists of the Gothic, Industrial and Electronic genres.

The Industrial Factory *WZBC*
Boston College 107, Chestnut Hill, MA 02467
PH: 617-552-3511 FX: 617-552-1738
Brian Industrialfactory@hotmail.com
www.geocities.com/sunsetstrip/disco/5053
Underground Cyber-Electro Industrial music.

DJ I.Z.
1515 W. Veterans Pkwy. Marshfield, WI 54449
www.djizmusic.com
Industrial/Darkwave bands. I'm always accepting promos and demos to use in my DJing. Send your promo material (CD, CD-R and vinyl are acceptable) and a little info about you, your band, or record label.

Liquid Gothic Radio
PO Box 3421, Westport, MA 02790
Michael Brown michael@liquidgothic.net
www.liquidGothic.net
Web Radio to Die For!

The Machineries of Joy
nebenabsicht@hotmail.com
www.live365.com/stations/289591
Gothic/Industrial/EBM. From the spankin' new to the tried-and-true...MOJ streams a little bit of everything.

The Mr. Winky Show
mrwinkyshow@hotmail.com
www.live365.com/stations/295506
Playing the random tunes you have come to love, and hate. Goth, Industrial and Electronica.

Nevermind Radio
nemesis2207@attbi.com
www.live365.com/stations/nemesis2207
A mix of Gothic, Synthpop, Industrial, EBM...along with the occasional strange songs you can't really classify!

Pagan Radio Network
PH: 651-457-0912
Paul Ieson arizonatramp@hotmail.com
paganradio.thewitchesbrew.net
Pagan Rock with attitude. PLEASE, send only PAGAN music!

Radio Free Abattoir
PO Box 190792, Miami Beach, FL 33119-0792
PH: 305-434-8651 FX: 305-531-5609
Sam Bradford radiofreeabattoir@slaghuis.net
www.radiofreeabattoir.com
Gothic, Darkwave and Industrial.

Radio Free Satan
Matt G. Paradise matt@purgingtalon.com
www.radiofreesatan.com
Corrupting the minds of the youth since 2000.

Radio Satan 666
www.radiosatan666.com
Various shows including Goth, Metal etc.

Seismic Radio
Teri teri@comcast.net
www.seismicradio.com
Have your band featured/interviewed.

The Shape of Things to Come *WFDU*
Bob Westphal theonebob@aol.com
www.theonebob.com
The longest running and best dark music show to air in NYC.

Sounds and Visions of Tomorrow Today
PO Box 54771, Philadelphia, PA 19148
Losafa@aol.com
www.drugmusic.com
Drug and Drone Music.

sursumcorda Radio
5115 Excelsior Blvd. #235, Minneapolis, MN 55416
FX: 612-677-3272
www.sursumcorda.com
New directions in Electronic organic groove.

Thaljana's Chartreuse Translucent
PO Box 0172, Brightwaters, NY 11718-0172
DJ Thaljana thaljana@chartrans.com
www.chartrans.com
Neo-synthpop, Electro, Darkwave and Gothic music.

This is Corrosion
4317 Harlem Rd. Amherst, NY 14226
legion@thisiscorrosion.com
www.thisiscorrosion.com
Please send only CDs.

The Vapour Treatment *WUSB*
Student Union Bld. SUNY,
Stony Brook, NY 11794-3263
PH: 631-632-6500 FX: 631-632-7182
DJ Datura vapourtreatment@yahoo.com
www.geocities.com/radiovt
Modern Electronic music, Industrial, New Wave, Synth Pop, Electro and more.

Waiting for the Blackouts
death@perkigoth.com
www.live365.com/stations/c_death
I play a wide range of music that lean mostly towards Goth and Industrial.

Canada

The Alcove
PO Box 24052, Hazeldean RPO,
Kanata, ON K2M 2C3
Nikki info@thealcove.ca
www.thealcove.ca
Ottawa's only Gothic/Industrial radio show.

Distorted Circuitry
RaZoRGrrL info@razorgrrl.com
www.razorgrrl.com
The best in crunchy and harder-edged Industrial and EBM.

EBM *CIUT*
91 St. George St., Toronto, ON M5S 2E8
PH: 416-978-0909 x214 FX: 416-946-7004
Sophia & Burt ebm@ciut.fm
www.ciut.fm
Electronic Music for the body and mind. Industrial/Noise, EBM, Synth-pop, Darkwave and Gothic.

The Electric Front
djlee@theelectricfront.com
www.theelectricfront.com
Industrial, Electronic, Synth, Goth and Dark-Rock songs.

Electrosynthesis
promo@electrosynthesis.ca
www.electrosynthesis.ca
Goth, Industrial, Experimental, Ambient, Techno...

Les Mouches Noires *CISM*
1094 Martial, Laval, QC H7P 1E5
Francois Richer lesmouchesnoires@videotron.ca
www.lesmouchesnoires.com
Send your press kit and CD or demo to us.

Maleus Maleficarum *CJSR*
Room 0-09 Students' Union Bldg. U.
Alberta, Edmonton, AB T6G 2J7
PH: 780-492-2577 x232 FX: 780-492-3121
DJ Nik Rofeelya tsangbang@cjsr.com
www.cjsr.com
Showcases, but not limited to, Industrial, Metal, Goth, EBM & Punk.

RantRadio
Box 18121, 1215-C 56 St., Delta, BC V4M 2M4
www.rantradio.com
Industrial and Punk station. Please contact me if you'd like your band to be played on RantRadio. Also upload your songs to the ftp site or provide a place for me to download your songs (or if you really want, mail me your CD). If you're good and your band fits the format then you're in!

The Real Synthetic Audio Show
2515 Bathurst St. #B01, Toronto, ON M6B 2Z1
Todd Clayton todd@synthetic.org
www.synthetic.org
The most listened to Industrial net-radio show.

Europe

Belgium

Darker than the Bat
ZRO, Pierets-De Colvenaerplein 7a,
9060 Zelzate, Belgium
PH: 32-0-9-345-54-55 FX: 32-0-9-342-99-38
www.proservcenter.be/darkerthanthebat/radio.html
Special Gothic/Wave/Industrial/Electro/EBM/... show.

Kagan *Radio Scorpio*
info@kagankalender.com
www.kagankalender.com
Wave, Gothic, Electro, Industrial. Each promo is assured a review and airplay.

France

Coquille Felee Radio
jeckel@coquille-felee.net
coquille-felee.net
Goth, Industrial and Electronica music.

Meiose
Meiose RCT, BP 2001 69603 Villeurbanne Cedex, France
PH: 04-78-94-37-37
kb69@free.fr
meiose.free.fr
Industriel, Gothique, Expérimental, Electro dark, Dark Folk, Médiéval.

Schizophonia
24 rue Pasteur, 51000 Châlons en Champagne, France
Philippe Chrétien schizophonia@duskofhope.com
schizophonia.duskofhope.com
Industrial, Neofolk, Rhythmic Electronics & Noise.

Germany

Black Channel Radio Show
c/o Tobias Kuechen Baldung-Grienstr. 5 D-79312
Emmendingen, Germany
PH: 49-160-8532545 FX: 49-7641-9373-13
info@blackchannel.org
www.blackchannel.org
Wave, Gothic, Industrial, Dark Techno, Electro, Ritual etc.

Dead or Alive
Radio R1live, Engelbert Eichhorn D-96047
Bamberg, Germany
PH: 49-0-175-703-706-1 FX: 012-12-5-110-23-008
www.r1live.de
Darkwave & Gothic radio.

(((EBM Radio)))
Kleine Düwelstrasse 13a, 30171 Hannover, Germany
Michael Stoll radiomaster@ebm-radio.de
www.ebm-radio.de
Strange music 4 strange people.

Radio Morituri
vlad.tepecz@radio-morituri.de
radio-morituri.de
Featuring Goth and Industrial music.

Italy

Chain the Door Radio Show
c/o Ferruccio Milanesi, Via G. Jannelli 45/D, 80131
Napoli, Italy
www.chaindlk.com
Promote your music through our show.

Radio Blackout
via Antinori 3 10129 Torino (Turin) Italy
PH: 39-011-580-68-88
blackout@ecn.org
www.ecn.org/blackout
L'unica Radio libera In piemonte. Sostieni la frequenza libera!

The Netherlands

Tormentor Radio Show
Funprox, PO Box 5034 3502 JA Utrecht, The Netherlands
PH: +33(0)1-43-71-89-40
tormentor@free.fr
www.exabrupto.net/tormentor
Dark, Electro, Industrial.

Spain

La Hora Muerta *(The Dead Hour)*
PO Box 5138, 31010 Baranain, Spain
Rafa Cros lahoramuerta@hotmail.com
www.sonidobscuro.com/lahoramuerta
Goth, Industrial, ebm etc.

United Kingdom

Hidden Sanctuary Radio
www.darkcelldigitalmusic.net
Gothic, Ethereal, Alternative and Electronic.

Spiderpower Sounds
4, Ballyoran Pk. Portadown, County Armagh, N. Ireland BT62 1JN
spiderpower.net
Send me demos, talk to me. Let me promote YOU!!!

TotalRock
1 Denmark Pl. London, WC2H 8NL UK
info@totalrock.com
www.totalrock.com
Tune in to hear the latest Goth new releases.

Australia

Darkwings Radio Show *RTR*
PO Box 949, Nedlands, WA 6909 Australia
PH: 08-6488-3380
rtrfm@rtrfm.com.au
www.rtrfm.com.au
For all your Industrial and Gothic wants.

Dawntreader *RTR*
PO Box 949, Nedlands, WA 6909 Australia
PH: 08-6488-3380
rtrfm@rtrfm.com.au
www.rtrfm.com.au
Post-Punk, pre-pop tack, Industrial and more.

Sacrament *2RRR*
PO Box 644 Gladesville, NSW 1675 Australia
FX: 61-2-9817-1048
info@sacramentradio.org
www.sacramentradio.org
Gothic music & information program.

Slave to the Grave *Three D Radio*
asickpervertedcorpsegrinder@hotmail.com
www.slavetothegrave.com
Deathrock, Gothabilly, Psychobilly, Batcave, Post Punk & Horror Punk.

Hip Hop Radio

Radio Promoters

Mo' Better Music
77 Bleecker St. #C115, New York, NY 10012
PH: 212-388-0597 FX: 212-388-0592
mobettermusic@earthlink.net
www.mobettermusic.com
A National marketing and promotion company.

Insomniac Media & Promotions
PO Box 592722, Orlando, FL 32859
PH: 212-629-1797
insom@mindspring.com
www.insomniaconline.com/services
Get your Hip Hop release on radio stations nationally.

Looking4airplay
PO Box 630372, Houston, TX 77263
support@looking4airplay.com
www.looking4airplay.com
We will digitally deliver your next hit single DIRECTLY to people who ACTUALLY decide what gets played over the airwaves.

Raw Talent
rawtalent@hiphopdx.com
PH: 888-753-6291 x0
www.rawtalentdx.com
We can get you the exposure you crave through radio airplay, record distribution, showcases and even recording deals.

Shocksoundpromotions.com
3840 E. Robinson Rd. #200, Amherst, NY 14228
PH: 716-578-0097
shocksoundpromo@yahoo.com
www.shocksoundpromotions.com
National radio promotions, event consulting etc.

Stations and Shows

North America

United States

2hot4radio
1616 McCaskill Ave. #207-A,
Tallahassee, FL 32310
PH: 850-350-0347
Jovan Myrick or Torentha Clark
ncmgmusic@yahoo.com
2Hot4Radio.net
Radio Promotion and broadcast specializing playing the music of independent artists. Genres: Hip Hop, R&B and Pop.

The Bassment Online Radio
1112 Montana Ave. #122, Santa Monica, CA 90403
djspider@thebassment.com
www.thebassment.com
Send us your music!

Beatsauce *KUSF*
2130 Fulton St., San Francisco, CA 94117
J-Boogie info@jboogie.com
www.beatsauce.com
San Francisco's premier Underground Hip Hop mixshow. We create a positive vibe for local and out of town artists to showcase their talent and promote their skills for the entire Bay Area, and beyond.

The Big Drew Show *WHRW*
Binghamton U. PO Box 2000,
Binghamton, NY 13902-6000
PH: 607-777-2139 FX: 607-777-6501
pd@whrwfm.org
www.whrwfm.org
Underground and unsigned Hip Hop as well as live Interviews.

bsideMX.net
lynwah@bsideMX.net
www.bsidemx.net
Hip Hop 24 hours a day. Music, information and news.

Club Dub *WXCI*
181 White St., Danbury, CT 06811
PH: 203-837-8387
WXCIDanbury@yahoo.com
www.myspace.com/wxci
The station's oldest show. The best in Hip Hop.

Chiradio.com
980 N. Michigan Ave. 1 Magnificent Mile #1400,
Chicago, IL 60611
PH: 312-214-3521 FX: 775-264-7137
chiradio@hotmail.com
www.chiradio.com
Features a Rap and Soul station.

Dedicated *WNUR*
Campus Dr. Evanston, IL 60208-2280
PH: 847-491-7102 FX: 847-467-2058
dj3rdrail@dj3rdrail.com
dj3rdrail.com/main.htm
www.wnur.org
To those who continue to represent Hip Hop.

The Difference
c/o Illvibe Media, 5555 Wissahickon Ave. #L8,
Philadelphia, PA 19144
Statik statik@illvibe.net
illvibe.net
You can expect to hear anything from Funk to Traditional Jazz, from Hip Hop to Bossanova and Soulful House.

Earthbound Radio
PH: 619-392-7359
info@twelvez.com
www.twelvez.com
From Hip Hop to Jazz and Acoustic to Electronic, music of all genres and forms have shown to be a universal language, with no limits and no boundaries.

The Fresh Connection KPSU
1825 S.W. Broadway #443 Portland, OR 97201
PH: 503-725-4071 FX: 503-725-4079
freshconnection@hotmail.com
freshconnection.cjb.net
www.kpsu.org
Portland's hottest Hip Hop show!

GMS Music Group
16100 Van Aken Blvd. #207, Cleveland, OH 44120
PH: 216-798-4199
James Thomas marketing@gmsradio.com
www.gmsradio.com
We are an underground Hip Hop radio station. We feature unsigned artists and post Hip Hop events.

Hip Hop Central WFCS
1615 Stanley St., New Britain, CT 06050
PH: 860-832-1077 FX: 860-832-3757
trees@undergroundhiphop.com
www.hiphopcentral.cjb.net
Email with 'Radio Airplay' as the subject.

Hip Hop FundaMentalz Radio
Attn: PrizMatiK, 4940 Merrick Rd. # 311,
Massapequa Park, NY 11762 - 3803
info@hiphopfundamentalz.com
www.hiphopfundamentalz.com
Streaming Hip Hop 24/7. Send all promo material to the above address.

Hip Hop Lounge Radio
DJ Watts djwatts@hiphoplounge.net
www.hiphoplounge.net
Do you think you got the skills to hold your own on the mic? Do you want to get your music heard and promote your name? If you answered yes, then you have come to the right place.

Jaywhy.com
PO Box 693, Brooklyn, NY 11229-0693
www.jaywhy.com
Hip Hop that'll knock your fuckin' teeth out!

KBXX Houston
24 Greenway Plaza, #900 Houston, TX 77046
latinagirl1979@yahoo.com
www.kbxx.com
#1 for Hip Hop and R&B.

KMEL
340 Townsend St. 4th Fl. San Francisco, CA 94107
Big Von Johnson vonjohnson@clearchannel.com
www.106kmel.com
Both Independent and mainstream music.

KTOP
3337 Hunter Blvd. S. Seattle, WA 98144
DJ Topspin topspin@topsyte.com
www.topsyte.com
Seattle's only Hip Hop Station in FM Stereo!!!*

Last Crate
www.unifiedbeats.com
Supports Underground music. Get recognition!

The Last Hip-Hop
c/o Jerome Ford, PO Box 7093-WOB,
West Orange, NJ 07052
www.basically-hiphop.com/lastshow
Submit your music.

Mic Check
djreadycee@mail.com
www.miccheckradio.com
Contact us to get your material played on the show.

Movement Radio
www.movementradio.com
We have 3 streams featuring the best in Underground Hip Hop, Reggae and Jungle/Drum and Bass.

Outside The Box Radio
530 Main St. #653, New Rochelle, NY 10801
PH: 914-879-8837
ty@otbradio.com
www.otbradio.com
The tri-states' #1 station for Underground and unsigned Hip Hop.

Planet X Radio
c/o Nothing But Nett Web Productions,
1011 NE 109th St., Portland, OR 97218
hiphopmuzik@nothingbutnett.com
www.planetxradio.com
Underground Hip Hop sounds. Download the release form from our website and send it in with your CD.

The Pro Flow Fa-Sho Show
PO Box 8287, Akron, OH 44320
MaD MaXxx M3@maxheat.com
www.m4radio.com/main/shows/pro_fo_fla.htm
Ranging from theatrical audio productions of from every genre of music to intellectually stimulating, precise, unscripted word schemes and industry critiques from the host. The show has a strong hip hop origin.

SimplyRadio.com
3080 Hidden River Ct. Oviedo, FL 32766
Ken Darby kendarby@simplyradio.com
www.simplyradio.com
Unreleased and pre released material from artists you know, and artists you never knew existed.

SOL of HIPHOP Radio TIR
PO Box 6868, Fullerton, CA 92834-6868
PH: 714-278-5505 FX: 714-278-5514
DJ Buddhabong buddhabong@solofhiphop.com
www.solofhiphop.com
Streamin' live every Friday 4-7 PM pst.

Subsoniq XM Radio
subsoniq@xmradio.com
xmu.xmradio.com
Underground, Progressive Hip Hop...it's beats and rhymes...it's a way of life!

Sunday Night Jams KTXT
Texas Tech U. PO Box 43081, Lubbock, TX 79409
PH: 806-742-3916 FX: 806-742-3906
ktxtfm@yahoo.com
www.ktxt.net
The #1 rated Urban Show in Lubbock!!

The SureShot
c/o Illvibe Media, 5555 Wissahickon Ave. #L8,
Philadelphia, PA 19144
Statik statik@illvibe.net
illvibe.net
A taste of new Underground Hip Hop, mixed with some classics, some Funk, exclusives and whatever else we think is dope!

Tables of Content KCSN
18111 Nordhoff St., Northridge, CA 91330-8312
Anthony Valadez antonio.valadez@kcsn.org
www.kcsn.org/programs/tablesofcontent.html
Transcends mainstream so-called Hip Hop stations by exposing listeners to non-corporate motivated musical acts.

theabstractbeatworkshop
Honolulu, Hemenway Hall #203, 2445 Campus Rd.
Honolulu, HI 96822.
PH: 808-956-4848
joan9 abstract@ktuh.org
ktuh.org/beat
Hip Hop | beats | bunnies.

themerchgirl.com Radio
PO Box 51222, Phoenix, AZ 85076
PH: 480-471-6195
Mattx admin@themerchgirl.com
www.themerchgirl.com
Underground Hip Hop and indie artists featuring some of the dopest shit you have never heard.

Third Floor Radio
c/o Titan Comm, PO Box 6868,
Fullerton, CA 92834-6868
Roslynn thirdfloorla@yahoo.com
ThirdFloorRadio.com
A journey through Hip Hop's past, present and future....

True Unda-ground WCSB
Rhodes Tower 956, 2121 Euclid Ave.
Cleveland, OH 44115-2214
PH: 216-687-3721 FX: 216-687-2161
www.wcsb.org
Alien Hip-hop - most of these groups you can only hear HERE!

The Underground Railroad WBAI
120 Wall Street, 10th Fl. New York, NY 10005
PH: 212-209-2800 x2931
Jay Smooth jsmooth@hiphopmusic.com
www.hiphopmusic.com
The first DJ on radio to explore mixing classic Jazz cuts with the latest underground Hip Hop.

WFNK
wfnk@wfnk.com
wfnk.com/radio
Covering every aspect of Alternative Black music.

WJPZ Syracuse U.
PH: 315-443-4689 FX: 315-443-4379
www.z89.com
"LIVE" weekend mixshows with everything u want and everything u need!!

WKXN
PO Box 369, Greenville, AL 36037
PH: 334-286-9301 FX: 334-382-7770
wkxn@wkxn.com
www.wkxn.com
Hip Hop, Gospel and R&B.

Canada

Hip Hop 101 *UMFM*
Room 308 U. Ctr. Winnipeg, MB R3T 2N2
PH: 204-474-7027 FX: 204-269-1299
Kinetik kinetikaljoints@hotmail.com
www.umfm.com
The best in independent and underground Hip Hop. Constantly introducing the city to brand new artists and flavas!

The Lounge *CKUW*
Rm 4CM11, 515 Portage Ave.
Winnipeg, MB R3B 2E9
PH: 204-786-9782 FX: 204-783-7080
thelounge@mailcity.com
www.ckuw.ca
Online radio show playing Hip Hop, R&B and Dancehall Reggae.

The Wax Jungle *CKMS*
200 University Ave. W. Waterloo, ON N2L 3G1
PH: 519-886-2567 FX: 519-884-3530
ckmsfm@web.ca
watserv1.uwaterloo.ca/~ckmsinfo
The show focuses on Hip Hop and R&B beats.

Europe

France

Skyrock
Skyrock.com, 37 bis rue Grenéta 75002 Paris, France
www.skyrock.com
Rap, Hip Hop, R&B...

Norway

The National Rapshow
P.B. 4663, Sofienberg, 0506 Oslo, Norway
tp@teeproductions.com
www.teeproductions.com
Send us your music/demo for review/ airplay.

Sweden

P3 Hip-Hop
Sveriges Radio, 211 01 Malmö, Sweden
Timbuktu & Dj Amato musik.p3@sr.se
www.sr.se/p3/hiphop
Y'all need to peep this, because it's slammin! Nuff said!

Switzerland

BoomBox.net
c/o beatmap.com, Ackerstrasse 11, CH-8005 Zurich, Switzerland
www.boombox.net
Send us your private mix tapes and live-shows on Cassette, MiniDisc or DAT!

United Kingdom

BBC Radio 1xtra *Hip Hop*
www.bbc.co.uk/1xtra/hiphop
Home page of the BBC 1xtra's various Hip Hop shows. Info, shows, contacts etc.

BBC Radio 1 *Urban Music*
www.bbc.co.uk/radio1/urban
Home page of the BBC Radio 1's various Urban Music shows. Info, shows, contacts etc.

Grand Theft Audio
PH: 07919-437120
info@grandtheftaudio.co.uk
grandtheftaudio.co.uk
An urban internet radio station that plays Hip Hop, Drum and Bass, Garage etc. Providing an opportunity for producers and DJs to have their talents displayed.

Australia

Open Source *2SER*
U. Tech. Sydney, Level 26, Building 1,
1 Broadway, Ultimo, NSW 2007 Australia
PH: 61-2-9514-9514 FX: 61-2-9514-9599
opensource@2ser.com
www.opensourceradio.net
Electronic and Hip Hop.

New Zealand

True School Hip Hop Show *95bFM*
PO Box 4560, Shortland St.,
Auckland 1001 New Zealand
PH: 64-9-309-4831 FX: 64-9-366-7224
music@95bfm.com
www.95bfm.co.nz
The phattest coverage of local and international Hip Hop.

Africa

Bay FM
Shop M3, The Bridge at Greenacres, Greenacres, South Africa
PH: 041-363-6788 FX: 041-363-7085
info@bayfm.co.za
www.bayfm.co.za
Have regular Hip Hop shows.

Jam Band Radio

Finding The Groove *KUMD*
U. Minnesota, 130 Humanities, 1201 Ordean Ct.
Duluth, MN 55812
PH: 218-726-7181 FX: 218-726-6571
kumd@kumd.org
www.kumd.org
A collection of Jam Bands from all over the U.S. & the world.

Home Grown Radio
PO Box 340, Mebane, NC 27302
PH: 919-563 4923
leeway@homegrownmusic.net
www.homegrownmusic.net/radio.html
Discover new bands and kind music.

Honest Tunes Radio Show *KXUA*
383 Fletcher Ave. Fayetteville, AR 72701
Daniel Gold goodgold@gmail.com
www.dgold.info/radio
Covering a wonderful array of Songwriters, Jam Bands and Roots music, including Blues, Jazz, Bluegrass, Folk, Improv, and live Electronic. Please send CD's and press kits.

Jam Band Extravaganza *KIWR*
2700 College Rd. Council Bluffs, IA 51503
PH: 712-325-3254 FX: 712-325-3391
Junior jambandextravaganza@yahoo.com
www.897theriver.com
Specializing in automated hydro phonic growing systems and the cutting edge of Rock.

Jambana *WPGU*
#107, 24 E Green St., Champaign, IL 61801
PH: 217-244-3000 FX: 217-244-3001
music@wpgu.com
www.wpgu.com
Jam Band music.

Jamnation *WXPN*
3025 Walnut St., Philadelphia, PA 19104
PH: 215-898-6677. FX: 215-898-0707
online@xpn.org
www.xpn.org/jamnation.php
Dedicated to the broad variety of musical output often grouped under the "Jam Band" umbrella.

The Side Trip *WQNR*
5810 Goener Ave. St. Louis, MO 63116
PH: 314-832-5529
James Mullin jamesm@thesidetrip.com
www.thesidetrip.com
Groove and Jam Music.

Stumble In The Dark *KDHX*
3504 Magnolia St. Louis, MO 63118
PH: 314-664-3955 FX: 314-664-1020
James Mullin volunteerdj@stumbleinthedark.com
www.stumbleinthedark.com
An eclectic mix of Rock, Jazz, Funk and Bluegrass. Features some of the best live music from today's best Jam bands.

Jazz Radio

North America

Promotional Services

United States

Lisa Reedy Promotions
275 Bonnie Briar Pl. Reno, NV 89509
PH: 775-826-0755
Lisa Reedy reedylm@aol.com
www.jazzpromotion.com
A full-service radio promotions company that specializes in Jazz and related music.

Internet Radio and Syndicated Shows

aTTeNTioN sPaN raDiO
www.attentionspanradio.net
The hippest, coolest mix of Jazz, Funk and Rock instrumentals available..

Big Band Jump
PH: 800-377-0022
Don Kennedy don@bigbandjump.com
www.bigbandjump.com
Featuring both original and later Swing music.

Cat Galaxy
catprotector@catgalaxymedia.com
www.catgalaxymedia.com
It is my hope that all of you cats and your humans will enjoy this station. Smooth Jazz, Classic Rock, Alternative, Funk, R&B and Swing.

Chill With Chris Botti
Chris info@chillwithchrisbotti.com
www.chillwithchrisbotti.com
Syndicated show playing NY Chill music. Chris also posts recommended CDs on his website.

Cobalt Stream 59
cobaltstream@rock.com
www.live365.com/stations/zen823
Kicking off an abstract mix of dangerously sexy music featuring Down Tempo, Jazz, Trip Hop, Nu Jazz and Funk.

Hammond Organ Plus
James Ferguson jamesferguson@email.com
www.live365.com/stations/leslieoverdrive
Like the sound of the Hammond B3 Organ? Then you'll love Hammond Organ Plus! Jazz, Funk and Blues.

Jazz After Hours
729 N. 66th St., Seattle, WA 98103
Jim Wilke jim@jazzafterhours.org
www.jazzafterhours.org
New and well-established Jazz artists regularly drop in for a chat.

Jazz, Then and Now *Healthy Life Radio*
PH: 949-231-8476
Bill Tannebring biltan@usa.net
www.healthylife.net
www.billtannebring.com
Showcases mainstream Jazz of all genres from around the world. I also invite established and up and coming players to talk about their careers and their music.

Jazz with Bob Parlocha
1216 Post St., Alameda, CA 94501
bob@jazzwithbobparlocha.com
www.jazzwithbobparlocha.com
Information about Jazz recordings, publications, musicians and live gigs.

JazzSet
Dee Dee Bridgewater jazzset@npr.org
www.npr.org/programs/jazzset
Jazz radio series presenting today's artists.

Jazztrax
611 S. Palm Canyon Dr. #7-458,
Palm Springs, CA 92264-7402
PH: 760-323-1171 FX: 760-323-5770
jazztrax@jazztrax.com
www.jazztrax.com
The very best songs, from the very best smooth Jazz albums.

LuxuriaMusic.com
PO Box 26290, San Francisco, CA 94126-6290
support@luxuriamusic.com
www.luxuriamusic.com
Outré lounge and Latin Jazz, breezy swinging instrumentals and vocals, Psychedelia, quirky oddities, Retro Pop and Surf music.

maroom c@fe
marooy2002@hotmail.com
www.live365.com/stations/marooy2002
Time flows gently with cool but a little warm atmospheric tracks. Smoothly crossing over genres like Jazz, Nu Jazz, Hip Hop, R&B, Brazilian and more!

New Orleans Radio
inquiry@lagniappe.la
www.neworleansradio.com
Produces and delivers regional custom music.

NPR Jazz
635 Massachusetts Ave. NW,
Washington, DC 20001
nprjazz@npr.org
www.nprjazz.org
Submit your CD for review consideration.

Quietmusic.com
www.quietmusic.com
Smooth Jazz.

OverXposure.FM
overxposure.fm
Looking for Downtempo, Chillout, Modern lounge, Electro Jazz, Nu Jazz. Please visit our site to see if your music fits our formats. No Smooth Jazz.

SkyJazz Internet Radio
info@skyjazz.com
www.skyjazz.com
Hear great Jazz from new and undiscovered artists.

Smoothjazz.com
PO Box 982, Pacific Grove, CA 93950
feedback@smoothjazz.com
www.smoothjazz.com
For on-air consideration, record representatives may e-mail our music department.

SmoothNetRadio.com
adultmix@hotmail.com
smoothnetradio.com
A mix of Smooth Jazz blended with soulful Slow Jams.

Sounds Of Boston Swing
m0nuz@qsl.net
www.live365.com/stations/307335
Big Band, Swing and Jazz music from the 30's to present day.

SoulfulSmoothJazz.com Radio
PO Box 660-100, Flushing, NY 11366
Blackwell contact@SoulfulSmoothJazz.com
www.SoulfulSmoothJazz.com
The world's hot spot for Soulful Smooth Jazz & R&B where you can request your music and hear it instantly. Commercial free all day, every day!

The Tamm E. Hunt Show *artistfirst.com*
1620 Bolton St., Baltimore, MD 21217-4316
PH: 410-462-8266 FX: 410-669-2009
Gina Hirschberg thetammehuntshow@aol.com
www.freewebs.com/thetammehuntshow
An Internet radio talk show with a focus on independent and major artists in the Jazz genre.

WNJL.com
1040 Riverview Dr. Florence, NJ 08518
PH: 609-922-1620 FX: 609-499-1971
wnjl@wnjl.com
www.wnjl.com
The home of Smooth Jazz On the Internet.

Alabama

Alabama Public Radio Evening Jazz
PO Box 870370, Tuscaloosa, AL 35487-0370
PH: 205-348-6644 FX: 205-348-6648
Alisa Beckwith abeckwith@apr.org
www.apr.org

WJAB *Alabama A&M*
PO Box 1687, Normal, AL 35762
Ellen C. Washington ewashington@aamu.edu
www.aamu.edu/wjab

Arizona

KJZA
226 N. Cortez St., Prescott, AZ 86301
PH: 928-541-1008

KJZZ
2323 W. 14th St., Tempe, AZ 85281
PH: 480-834-5627 FX: 480-774-8475
kjzz.mail@riomail.maricopa.edu
www.kjzz.org

KYOT
PH: 480-966-6236
www.kyot.com
Lots of known & unknown Jazz artists.

Arkansas

KASU *Arkansas State U.*
PO Box 2160, State U. AR 72467
PH: 870-972- 2200
www.kasu.org

California

The Annals of Jazz *KCSM*
1700 West. Hillsdale Blvd. San Mateo, CA 94402
PH: 650-524-6945
www.kcsm.org
Annals in Europe, Asia, Latin America or Back of Town anywhere.

Capital Public Radio
7055 Folsom Blvd. Sacramento, CA 95826
PH: 916-278-8900 FX: 916-278-8989
jazz@capradio.org
www.capradio.org

FreeFall *KUSF*
2130 Fulton St., San Francisco, CA 94117
PH: 415-386-5873
David Bassin freefall@pacbell.net
www.geocities.com/davidbassin/freefall.html
A mix of Future Jazz, Soul, Abstract Beats & World Rhythms.

Horizons *KIFM*
1615 Murray Canyon Rd. #710,
San Diego, CA 92108-4321
PH: 619-297-3698 FX: 619-543-1353
Kelly Cole kelly@kifm.net
www.kifm.com
An hour-long listen to the artists and music breaking ground in Smooth Jazz. Join me for a serious sampling of what's on the Horizon.

In the Groove *KUSP*
203 8th Ave. Santa Cruz, CA 95062
PH: 408-476-2800 FX: 408-476-2802
Mike Lambert kusp@kusp.org
www.kusp.org/playlists/synch
Send any promotional items for airplay, giveaway or review.

In Your Ear *KPFA*
1929 MLK Jr. Way, Berkeley, CA 94704
PH: 510-848-6767 FX: 510-848-3812
info@kpfa.org
www.kpfa.org
A cool fusion of Jazz and Latin music, giving voice to musicians deserving wider recognition, and showing that Jazz and Afro-Caribbean music are separate, but "branches of the same tree".

KCBX
4100 Vachell Ln. San Luis Obispo, CA 93401
PH: 805-549-8855
kcbx@kcbx.org
www.kcbx.org

KCLU *California Lutheran College*
60 W. Olsen Rd. #4400, Thousand Oaks, CA 91360
PH: 805-493-3900
www.kclu.org

KCSM
1700 W. Hillsdale Blvd. San Mateo, CA 94402
PH: 650-524-6945
jesse_varela@kcsm.net
www.kcsm.org/jazz91.html
E-mail Jesse to set up submissions etc.

KKJZ *California State U.*
1288 N. Bellflower Blvd. Long Beach, CA 90815
PH: 562-985-5566 FX: 562-597-8453
info@kkjz.org
www.kkjz.org

KKSF
340 Townsend St., San Francisco, CA 94107
Attn: Music Director
PH: 415-975-5555 FX: 415-975-5573
www.kksf.com
Send your CD to the Music Director at the above address. You will notified if we add it to rotation.

KPFK
3729 Cahuenga Blvd. W.
North Hollywood, CA 91604
PH: 818-985-2711 FX: 818-763-7526
pd@kpfk.org
www.kpfk.org

KRVR
961 N. Emerald Ave. #A, Modesto, CA 95351
PH: 209-544-1055
theriver@krvr.com
www.krvr.com

KSBR *Saddleback College*
28000 Marguerite Pkwy. Mission Viejo, CA 92692
PH: 949-582-4228 FX: 949-347-9693
twedel@saddleback.cc.ca.us
www.ksbr.net

KSDS
1313 Park Blvd. San Diego, CA 92101
PH: 619-234-1062 FX: 619-230-2212
Joe Kocherhans jkocherh@sdccd.net
www.ksds-fm.org

KTWV
8944 Lindblade St., Culver City, CA 90232
PH: 310-840-7182 FX: 310-815-8391
www.947wave.com

Madly Cocktail *KCSN*
Kat Griffin madlycocktail@aol.com
18111 Nordhoff St., Northridge, CA 91330-8312
PH: 818-677-3090
www.kcsn.org/programs/madlycocktail.html
An excellent mix of Cocktail Jazz, Latin Soul and Big Band mayhem all done up with a healthy dose of class.

Radio Sausalito
PO Box 397, Sausalito, CA 94966
PH: 415-332-5299
info@radiosausalito.org
www.radiosausalito.org
Several locally produced, Jazz oriented programs every week.

Tony Palkovic's Jazz Show *KSPC*
Thatcher Music Bldg. 340 N. College Ave.
Claremont, CA 91711-6340
TPJazzShow@cs.com
www.fortunecity.com/tinpan/lute/484
www.kspc.org/
A mix of Jazz-Fusion, Straight Ahead and Latin.

Colorado

KAJX
110 E. Hallam #134, Aspen, CO 81611
PH: 970-925-6445 FX: 970-544-8002
music@kajx.org
www.kajx.org

KCME
1921 N. Weber St., Colorado Springs, CO 80907
PH: 719-578-5263 FX: 719-578-1033
genmanager@kcme.org
www.kcme.org

KRFC
1705 Heatheridge D303, Fort Collins, CO 80525
PH: 970-221-5075
krfcfm.org

KRZA
528 9th St., Alamosa, CO 81101
PH: 719-589-8844
programming@krza.org
www.krza.org

KUNC *U. Northern Colorado*
822 7th St. #530, Greeley, CO 80631-3945
PH: 970-378-2579 FX: 970-378-2580
mailbag@kunc.org
www.kunc.org

KUVO
PO Box 2040, Denver, CO 80201-2040
PH: 303-480-9272
info@kuvo.org
www.kuvo.org

Connecticut

Out Here & Beyond *WWUH*
Attn: Music Director,
200 Bloomfield Ave. West Hartford, CT 06117
PH: 860-768-4701 FX: 860-768-5701
Chuck Obuchowski cobuchow@aol.com
www.wwuh.org
I attempt to capture the diversity of the modern Jazz realm, focusing on local artists, musicians from outside the U.S. and cutting-edge improvisers. I frequently feature interviews with the music-makers.

Florida

WDNA
PO Box 558636, Miami, FL 33255
PH: 305-662-8889 FX: 305-662-1975
feedback@wdna.org
www.wdna.org
Send in your serious Jazz.

WFIT *Florida Tech*
150 W. University Blvd. Melbourne, FL 32901
PH: 321-674-8140 FX: 321-674-8139
wfit@fit.edu
www.wfit.org

WKGC *Gulf Coast College*
PH: 850-873-3500
www.wkgc.org

WLOQ
170 W. Fairbanks Ave. #200, Winter Park, FL 32789
PH: 407-647-5557 FX: 407-647-4495
Brian Morgan bmorgan@wloq.com
www.wloq.com
CD Reviews- 'Smooth Jazz' shows all day.

WLRN
172 NE 15th St., Miami, FL 33132
PH: 305-995-2207 FX: 305-995-2299
info@wlrn.org
www.wlrn.org

WSJT
9721 Executive Ctr. Dr. N. #200,
St. Petersburg, FL 33702-2439
PH: 727-563-8830 FX: 727-568-9758
Kathy Curtis kcurtis@wsjt.com
wsjt.com
CD Reviews, concerts, interviews. Note that it's more difficult to get music on the air if you don't have any representation.

WUCF *U. Central Florida*
PO Box 162199, Orlando, FL 32816-2199
PH: 407-823-0899
wucf.ucf.edu

WUFT *U. Florida*
2206 Weimer Hall, Gainesville, FL 32611-8405
PH: 352-392-5200 x1119 FX: 352-392-5741
William Beckett bbeckett@wuft.org
radio@wuft.org
www.wuft.org/fm

WUWF
11000 University Pkwy. Pensacola, FL 32514
PH: 850-474-2787
wuwf@wuwf.org
wuwf.org

Georgia

The Jazz Spot *Georgia Public Radio*
260 14th St. NW, Atlanta, GA 30318
PH: 404-685-2400 FX: 404-685-2684
Masani jazz@gpb.org
www.gpb.org/public/radio
Mainstream and progressive contemporary impressions of Jazz music.

WBCX *Brenau U.*
PH: 770-538-4708
Scott Fugate sfugate@lib.brenau.edu
www.brenau.edu/about/wbcx
Promotes and supports local Jazz musicians.

WCLK *Clark Atlanta U.*
111 James P. Brawley Dr. SW, Atlanta, GA 30314
PH: 404-880-8273
www.wclk.com

WWGC *State U. West Georgia*
1600 Maple St., Carrollton, GA 30118
PH: 770-836-6500
wwgc@westga.edu
www.westga.edu/~wwgc

Hawaii

Jazz with Don Gordon *KIPO*
738 Kaheka St., Honolulu, HI 98614
PH: 808-955-8821 FX: 808-942-5477
Don Gordon dgordon@hawaiipublicradio.org
dongordon.net
www.hawaiipublicradio.org
Jazz is a very thick tree with deep roots and many branches and I try to cover the gamut.

The Real Deal *KIPO*
738 Kaheka St. #101, Honolulu, HI 96814
PH: 808-955-8821 FX: 808-942-5477
Seth Markow realdeal@lava.net
www.hawaiipublicradio.org
I do play independent music, namely Jazz (likely to expand soon to include more diverse Roots music).

Idaho

BSU Radio Network *Boise State U.*
1910 University Dr. Boise, ID 83725-1915
PH: 208-947-5660 FX: 208-344-6631
radio.boisestate.edu
Radio Vision and Idaho's Jazz Station.

Illinois

New Vintage *WDCB*
College of DuPage, 425 Fawell Blvd.
Glen Ellyn, IL 60137
PH: 630-942-4200 FX: 630-942-2788
Bill O'Connell OConnellB@wdcb.org
wdcb.org
Featuring the contemporary sounds of the vintage art form known as Big Band, The show celebrates the many successes of today's band leaders dedicated to furthering and promoting America's greatest contribution to world music history.

WBEZ
CPR, Navy Pier, 848 E. Grand Ave.
Chicago, IL 60611-3462
PH: 312-948-4855
www.wbez.org

WDCB
College of DuPage, 425 Fawell Blvd.
Glen Ellyn, IL 60137
PH: 630-942-4200 FX: 630-942-2788
www.cod.edu/wdcb
We're known for our eclectic music programming.

WGLT
8910 Illinois State U. Normal, IL 61790-8910
PH: 309-438-2255 FX: 309-438-7870
wglt@ilstu.edu
www.wglt.org

WILL *U. Illinois*
Campbell Hall, 300 N. Goodwin Ave.
Urbana, IL 61801-2316
PH: 217-333-0850 FX: 217-244-9586
www.will.uiuc.edu
Send us your Classical, Jazz and traditional/Ethnic music.

Indiana

Jazz By The Border *WVPE*
2424 California Rd. Elkhart, IN 46514
PH: 888-399-9873
Lee Burdorf lburdorf@wvpe.org
www.wvpe.org/border.html
We love to receive music from independent artists!

WBAA AM *Purdue U.*
712 3rd St. W. Lafayette, IN 47907-2005
PH: 765-494-3961
www.purdue.edu/wbaa

WFIU *Indiana U.*
1229 E. 7th St., Bloomington, IN 47405
PH: 812-855-1357
wfiu@indiana.edu
www.indiana.edu/~wfiu

WSND *U. Notre Dame*
315 LaFortune Student Ctr. Notre Dame, IN 46556
PH: 574-631-4069
wsnd@nd.edu
www.nd.edu/~wsnd

Iowa

KCCK *Kirkwood College*
6301 Kirkwood Blvd. SW, Cedar Rapids, IA 52406
PH: 319-398-5446 FX: 319-398-5492
Bob Stewart bobs@kcck.org
www.kcck.org

KHKE *U. Northern Iowa*
U. Cedar Falls, IA 50614-0359
PH: 319-273-6400 FX 319-273-2682
kuni@uni.edu
www.khke.org

Saturday Night Jazz *KWIT*
4647 Stone Ave. PO Box 5199,
Sioux City, IA 51106
PH: 712-274-6406 FX: 712-274-6411
www.kwit.org
Plays almost entirely new material.

WOI *Iowa State U.*
2022 Comm. Bldg. Iowa State U.
Ames, IA 50011-3241
PH: 515-294-2025 FX: 515-294-1544
info@woi.org
www.woi.org

Kansas

Jazz in the Night *U. Kansas*
1120 W. 11th St. U. Kansas, Lawrence, KS 66044
PH: 785-864-4530 FX: 785-864-5278
Bob McWilliams radiobob@ku.edu
kpr.ku.edu/Jazz

KMUW *Wichita State U.*
3317 E. 17th St. N. Wichita, KS 67208-1912
PH: 316-978-6789
info@kmuw.org
www.kmuw.org

Kentucky

WKMS *Murray State U.*
2018 U. Stn. Murray, KY 42071
PH: 270-762-4359 FX: 270-762-4667
mark.welch@murraystate.edu
www.wkms.org

WMKY *Morehead State U.*
132 Breckinridge Hall, Morehead, KY 40351
PH: 606-783-2001 FX: 606-783-2335
wmky@moreheadstate.edu
www.morehead-st.edu/wmky

WNKU *Northern Kentucky U.*
PO Box 337, Highland Heights, KY 41076
PH: 859-572-6500 FX: 859-572-6604
wnku@nku.edu
www.wnku.org

Louisiana

KEDM *Northeast Louisiana U.*
ULM 225 Stubbs Hall, Monroe, LA 71209-6805
PH: 318-342-5556 FX: 318-342-5570
kedmjazz.ulm.edu
www.kedm.org

KRVS *U. Southern Louisiana*
PO Box 42171, Lafayette, LA 70504
PH: 337-482-5787 FX: 337-482-6101
admin@krvs.org
www.krvs.org

WBRH *Baton Rouge Magnet H.S.*
2825 Government St., Baton Rouge, LA 70806
PH: 225-388-9030
www.baton-rouge.com/wbrh

WWOZ
PO Box 51840, New Orleans, LA 70151-1840
wwoz@wwoz.org
www.wwoz.org

Maryland

WHFC *Harford College*
401 Thomas Run Rd. Bel Air, MD 21015
PH: 410-836-4151

WTMD *Towson U.*
8000 York Rd. Towson, MD 21252
PH: 410-704-8938
wwwnew.towson.edu/wtmd

WYPR *Johns Hopkins U.*
2216 N. Charles St., Baltimore, MD 21218
PH: 410-235-1660 FX: 410-235-1161
www.wypr.org

Massachusetts

Jazz Safari *WFCR*
Hampshire House, U. Mass. 131 County Cir.
Amherst, MA 01003-9257
PH: 413-545-0100 FX: 413-545-2546
Kari Njiiri kari@wfcr.org
www.wfcr.org
African, Afro-Latin, Afro-Caribbean and other international Jazz styles.

WBUR *Online Arts*
890 Commonwealth Ave. 3rd Fl. Boston, MA 02215
PH: 617-353-0909
www.publicbroadcasting.net/wbur/arts.artsmain
Covers the local Boston Music scene.

WGBH *Boston*
125 Western Ave. Boston, MA 02134
PH: 617-300-4415
Alice Abraham alice_j_abraham@wgbh.org
www.wgbh.org

WHRB *Harvard U.*
389 Harvard St., Cambridge, MA 02138
PH: 617-495-4818
mail@whrb.org
www.whrb.net

WICN *Worcester*
6 Chatham St., Worcester, MA 01609
PH: 508-752-0700 FX: 508-752-7518
www.wicn.org
Many hours of Jazz, CD release parties and more!

Michigan

Nightside Jazz and Blues *CMU Public Radio*
1999 E Campus Dr. Mt. Pleasant, MI 48859
PH: 989-774-3105 FX: 989-774-4427
Jamie Lynn Gilbert gilbe1jl@cmich.edu
www.wcmu.org/radio/cmuradioproductions/nightside.html
Artists/Labels submit your music for airplay.

WDET *Wayne State U.*
4600 Cass Ave. Detroit, MI 48201
PH: 313-577-4146 FX: 313-577-1300
wdetfm@wdetfm.org
www.wdetfm.org

WEMU *Eastern Michigan U.*
PO Box 980350, Ypsilanti, MI 48198
PH: 734-487-2229
Linda Yohn linda.yohn@emich.edu
www.wemu.org

WGVU
301 W. Fulton Ave. Grand Rapids, MI 49504-6492
PH: 616-331-6666
www.wgvu.org/radio

WLNZ *Lansing College*
400 N. Capitol, #001, Lansing, MI 48933
PH: 517-483-1710 FX: 517-483-1894
www.lcc.edu/wlnz

Minnesota

Great Blend of Watercolors *KFAI*
1808 Riverside Ave. Minneapolis, MN 55454
PH: 612-341-3144
Dee Henry Williams deelin1@juno.com
www.kfai.org/programs/watercol.htm
Jazz, Blues, Rhythm & Blues, great interviews and mo' fun.

KBEM
1555 James Ave. N. Minneapolis, MN 55411
PH: 612-668-1735 FX: 612-668-1766
www.jazz88fm.com

Mississippi

WJSU *Jackson State U.*
PO Box 18450, Jackson, MS 39217
PH: 601-979-2140 FX: 601-979-2878
Bobbie Trussell Bobbie.Walker@jsums.edu
www.wjsu.org

WUSM *U. Southern Mississippi*
PO Box 10045, Hattiesburg, MS 39406-0045
PH: 601-266-4287 FX: 601-266-4288
Michael.Davis@usm.edu
www-dept.usm.edu/~wusm

Missouri

KSMU
901 South National, Springfield, MO 65804-0089
PH: 417-836-5878 FX: 417-836-5889
ksmu@smsu.edu
www.ksmu.smsu.edu

WSIE
0141 Dunham Hall, S. Illinois U. Box 1773,
Edwardsville, IL 62026
PH: 618-650-2228
www.siue.edu/WSIE

Nebraska

KIOS
3230 Burt St., Omaha, NE 68131
PH: 402-557-2777 FX: 402-557-2559
www.kios.org

Nevada

KUNV *U. Nevada Las Vegas*
1515 E. Tropicana Ave. #240, Las Vegas, NV 89119
PH: 702-798-9115
kunv.unlv.edu

New Jersey

The Groove Boutique
41 Watchung Plaza #387, Montclair, NJ 07042
Rafe Gomez music@thegrooveboutique.com
www.thegrooveboutique.com
An exhilarating listening experience that melds vibrant Jazz musicianship with dynamic, irresistible rhythms.

WBGO
54 Park Pl. Newark, NJ 07102
PH: 973-624-8880 FX: 973-824-8888
www.wbgo.org

WBJB *Brookdale College*
765 Newman Springs Rd. Lincroft, NJ 07738
PH: 732-224-2492
www.wbjb.org

New Mexico

KGLP
200 College Rd. Gallup, NM 87301
PH: 505-863-7626 FX: 505-863-7633
www.kglp.org

KRWG *New Mexico State U.*
PO Box 3000, Las Cruces, NM 88003-3000
PH: 505-646-4525 FX: 505-646-1974
krwgfm@nmsu.edu
www.krwgfm.org

KSFR *Santa Fe College*
PO Box 31366, Santa Fe, NM 87504-1366
PH: 505-428-1527 FX: 505-428-1237
info@ksfr.org
www.ksfr.org

New York

Jazz on the Air *WUSB*
Student Union Bld. SUNY,
Stony Brook, NY 11794-3263 Attn: Jazz Director
PH: 631-632-6500 FX: 631-632-7182
musicwusb·fm
wusb.fm
Showcases the best of the newest releases.

WAER
795 Ostrom Ave. Syracuse, NY 13244-4610
PH: 315-443-4021 FX: 315-443-2148
escohen@syr.edu
www.waer.org

WBFO *U. Buffalo*
205 Allen Hall, 3435 Main St.,
Buffalo, NY 14214-3003
PH: 716-829-6000
mail@wbfo.org
www.wbfo.buffalo.edu

WDWN *Cayuga County College*
197 Franklin St., Auburn, NY 13021
PH: 315-255-1743 ext 2284 FX: 315-255-2690
wdwn@hotmail.com
www.wdwn.fm

WEOS *Hobart and William Smith Colleges*
300 Pulteney St., Geneva, NY 14456
PH: 315-781-3812 FX: 315-781-3916
weos@hws.edu
www.weos.org

WFNP *SUNY New Paltz*
SUB 413, New Paltz, NY 12561-2443
PH: 845-257-3041 FX: 845-257-3099
wfnpmusic@newpaltz.edu
www.newpaltz.edu/wfnp

WGMC
750 Maiden Ln. Rochester, NY 14615
PH: 585-966-2660 FX: 585-621-8692
JazzInfo@jazz901.org
www.jazz901.org

WKCR *Columbia U.*
2920 Broadway, Mailcode 2612,
New York, NY 10027
PH: 212-854-9920
Paul Burkey jazz@wkcr.org
www.columbia.edu/cu/wkcr

WLIU *Long Island U.*
239 Montauk Hwy. Southampton, NY 11968
PH: 631-287-8289 FX: 631-287-8392
nancy.montgomery@liu.edu
www.wliu.org

WQCD
395 Hudson St. 7th Fl. New York, NY 10014
PH: 212-352-1019 FX: 212-929-8559
cd1019@cd1019.com
www.cd1019.com
Playing NY Chill. CD reviews, live events and concert series.

WSKG/WSQX
PO Box 3000, Binghamton, NY 13902-3000
PH: 607-729-0100 FX: 607-729-7328
Bill_Snyder@wskg.pbs.org
www.wskg.com/radiowskg.htm

North Carolina

WFSS
1200 Murchison Rd. Fayetteville, NC 28301
PH: 910-672-1919 FX: 910-672-1964

WSHA *Shaw College*
118 E. South St., Raleigh, NC 27601
PH: 919-546-8430 FX: 919-546-8315
wsha@shawu.edu
www.wshafm.org

WZRU
232 Roanoke Ave. Roanoke Rapids, NC 27870
PH: 252-308-0885 FX: 252-537-3333
www.wzru.org

Ohio

Mama Jazz *WMUB*
Williams Hall, Miami U. Oxford, OH 45056
PH: 513-529-5885 FX: 513-529-6048
mamajazz@yahoo.com
www.wmub.org/mamajazz
The best in Jazz from the classics to today.

WAPS
65 Steiner Ave. Akron, OH 44301
PH: 330-761-3099 FX: 330-761-3240
billgruber@913thesummit.com
www.wapsfm.com

WJZA
4401 Carriage Hill Ln. Columbus, OH 43220
PH: 614-451-2191 FX: 614-451-1831
www.columbusjazz.com
Live Jazz Concerts listing, lots of Jazz programming.

WMUB *Miami U.*
Williams Hall, Miami U. Oxford, OH 45056
PH: 513-529-5885 FX: 513-529-6048
wmub@wmub.org
www.wmub.org

WNWV
538 W. Broad St. PO Box 4006, Elyria, OH 44036
PH: 440-236-9283 FX: 440-236-3299
www.wnwv.com
Great Jazz and local concert listings for the area.

WYSO *Antioch U.*
795 Livermore St., Yellow Springs, OH 45387
PH: 937-767-6420
wyso@Antioch.edu
www.wyso.org

WYSU *Youngstown State U.*
1 University Plaza, Youngstown, OH 44555
PH: 330-941-3363
info@wysu.org
www.wysu.org

Oregon

KLCC
4000 E. 30th Ave. Eugene, OR 97405-0640
PH: 541-463-6000 FX: 541-463-6046
klcc@lanecc.edu
www.klcc.org

KMHD *Mt. Hood College*
26000 SE Stark St., Gresham, OR 97030
PH: 503-661-8900 FX: 503-491-6999
www.kmhd.org

KMUN
PO Box 269, Astoria, OR 97103
PH: 503-325-0010
kmun@kmun.org
www.kmun.org

Pennsylvania

WDUQ *Duquesne U.*
Pittsburgh, PA 15282
PH: 412-396-6030 FX: 412-396-5061
info@wduq.org
www.wduq.org

WPSU *Pennsylvania State U.*
102 Wagner Bldg. University Park, PA 16802
PH: 814-865-9778 FX: 814-865-3145
wpsu@psu.edu
wpsu.psu.edu

WVIA
100 WVIA Way, Pittston, PA 18640-6197
PH: 570-655-2808 FX: 570-655-1180
www.wvia.org/fm

South Dakota

KUSD
SDPB, 555 Dakota St. PO Box 5000,
Vermillion, SD 57069
PH: 800-456-0766
www.sdpb.org/radio

Tennessee

WETS *East Tennessee State U.*
PO Box 70630, Johnson City, TN 37614-1709
PH: 423-439-6440 Fax 423-439-6449
www.wets.org

WFSK *Fisk U.*
Nashville, TN 37208-3051
PH: 615-329-8754
Chris Nochowicz nock@tds.net
www.fisk.edu/wfsk

WMOT
MTSU, PO Box 3, Murfreesboro, TN 37132
PH: 615-898-2800 FX: 615-898-2774

WUMR *U. Memphis*
PH: 901-678-2766
WUMRJazz@memphis.edu
www.people.memphis.edu/~wumrjazz

WUOT *U. Tennessee*
209 Comm. Building, U. Tennessee,
Knoxville, TN 37996.
PH: 865-974-5375 FX: 865-974-3941
wuot@utk.edu
sunsite.utk.edu/wuot

WUTC *U. Tennessee*
615 McCallie Ave. Dept. 1151,
Chattanooga, TN 37403
PH: 423-265-9882 FX: 423-425-2379
mark-colbert@utc.edu
www.wutc.org

Texas

Jazz etc. *KUT*
1 University Stn. A0704, Austin, TX 78712
PH: 512-471-1631 FX: 512-471-3700
Jay Trachtenberg theloni760@aol.com
www.kut.org
Winding across the entire expanse of the Jazz spectrum from the 1920s to the present, with a particular emphasis on the Blues and modern and progressive styles.

KACU *Abilene Christian U.*
PO Box 27820, Abilene, TX 79699
PH: 325-674-2441
info@kacu.org
www.kacu.org

KNTU *U. North Texas*
PO Box 310881, Denton, TX 76203
PH: 940-565-3688 FX: 940-565-2518
kntu@unt.edu
www.kntu.unt.edu

KPVU *Prairie View A&M U.*
PO Box 519, Prairie View, TX 77446-0519
PH: 936-857-3311
kpvu_fm@pvamu.edu
www.pvamu.edu/kpvu

KTXK *Texarkana College*
2500 N. Robison Rd. Texarkana, TX 75599
PH: 903-838-4541 x3269 FX: 903-832-5030
smitchel@texarkanacollege.edu
www.tc.cc.tx.us/ktxk

KVLU *Lamar U.*
PO Box 10064, Beaumont, TX 77710
PH: 409-880-8164
Joe Elwell elwelljc@hal.lamar.edu
dept.lamar.edu/kvlu

KWBU *Baylor U.*
PO Box 97296, Waco, TX 76798-7296
PH: 254-710-3472 FX: 254-710-3874
www.baylor.edu/kwbu/index.php

Morning Jazz *KTEP*
500 W. University Ave. Cotton Memorial # 203,
El Paso, TX 79968
PH: 915-747-5152 FX: 915-747-5641
www.ktep.org
Mainstream Jazz, Big Band, traditional and up and coming Jazz artists.

Utah

KRCL
1971 W. North Temple, Salt Lake City, UT 84116
PH: 801-363-1818 FX: 801-533-9136
musicdirector@krcl.org
www.krcl.org

KUER *U. Utah*
101 S. Wasatch Dr. Salt Lake City, UT 84112
PH: 801-581-4997
Steve Williams swilliams@media.utah.edu
www.kuer.org

Vermont

WNCS
169 River St. Montpelier, VT 05602
PH: 802-223-2396 FX: 802-223-1520
feedback@pointfm.com
www.pointfm.com

Virginia

Soundwaves *WDCE*
PO Box 85, U. Richmond, VA 2317
PH: 8804-289-8698 FX: 804 289 8996
Herb King wdce@richmond.edu
www.student.richmond.edu/~wdce
Purist prepare for an expansive look at the Jazz idiom. Pronounced World music elements, spanning the globe in diversity, percolate throughout the highly eclectic, yet seamlessly flowing mix.

Washington

KBCS Jazz Music
3000 Landerholm Cir. SE Bellevue,
WA 98007-6484 Attn: Music Director
PH: 425-564-6194 x2
Gordon Todd gtodd@bcc.ctc.edu
kbcs.fm
Send your CD to see if it fits within our Jazz format.

KEWU *Eastern Washington U.*
104 R-TV Bldg. Cheney, WA 99004-2431
PH: 509-359-4282
jazz@mail.ewu.edu
www.kewu.ewu.edu

KPLU
1010 S. 122nd St., Tacoma, WA 98447-0885
PH: 253-535-7758 FX: 253-535-8332
info@kplu.org
www.kplu.org

Washington DC

Jazz Saturday Night *WAMU*
4400 Mass Ave. NW, Washington, DC 20016-8082
PH: 202-885-1200
Rob Bamberger hotjazz@wamu.org
www.wamu.org
On the air for over 22 years.

WPFW
2390 Champlain St. NW 2nd Fl.
Washington, DC 20009
PH: 202-588-0999 x0
www.wpfw.org

Wisconsin

WOJB *Lac Courte Oreilles Ojibwa College*
Route 2, Box 2788 Hayward, WI 54843
musicdirector@wojb.org
www.wojb.org

Wisconsin Public Radio *WPR*
821 University Ave. Madison, WI 53706
PH: 800-747-7444
www.wpr.org/regions

Canada

After Hours *CBC*
PO Box 160, Winnipeg, MB R3C 2H1
Andy Sheppard afterhours@winnipeg.cbc.ca
www.cbc.ca/afterhours
Entertaining, informing and challenging Jazz lovers.

Café Jazz Radio Show
669 Fairmont Rd. Winnipeg, MB R3R 1B2
PH: 204-777-5200 FX: 204-777-5323
info@jazzlynx.net
www.jazzlynx.net
Exposes and support new artists from around the world.

Dig Radio *UMFM*
Room 308 U. Ctr. Winnipeg, MB R3T 2N2
PH: 204-474-7027 FX: 204-269-1299
Kinetik kinetikaljoints@hotmail.com
dig_radio@hotmail.com
www.umanitoba.ca/schools/music/jazz/dig
If you've got label released, demo or live recordings, we would love to play them on air. Email for more info on submissions. Likewise if you have a Jazz event coming up, let us know and we'll spread the word.

In a Mellow Tone *CKCU*
Rm 517, U. Center, 1125 Colonel By Dr.
Ottawa, ON K1S 5B6
PH: 613-520-2898
Ron Sweetman ronsweetman@canada.com
www.ckcufm.com/inamellowtone.html
Jazz from every era and in every style.

Jazz Beat *CBC*
PO Box 6000, Montreal, PQ H3C 3A8
PH: 416-205-3700
Katie Malloch jazzbeat20@montreal.cbc.ca
radio.cbc.ca/programs/JazzBeat
Concert recordings and studio sessions, current and classic CD releases.

jazz for a sunday night *CHRW*
Rm 250, U. Community Ctr. U. Western Ontario,
London, ON N6A 3K7
PH: 519-661-3601 FX: 519-661-3372
Barrie Woodey jazz4a@yahoo.ca
www.chrwradio.com
Covers the whole spectrum of Jazz.

JAZZ.FM91
150 Mutual St., Toronto, ON M5B 2M1
PH: 416-595-0404 FX: 416-595-9413
info@jazz.fm
www.jazz.fm
Latest Jazz and Blues styles, artists and their music.

The Jazz Show *CiTR*
#233-6138 SUB Blvd. Vancouver, BC V6T 1Z1
PH: 604-822-8733 FX: 604-822-9364
citrmusic@club.ams.ubc.ca
www.citr.ca
Vancouver's prime time Jazz program.

Silence...on Jazz! *CBC*
PH: 604-662-6167 FX: 604-662-6161
Andre Rheaume silenceonjazz@vancouver.radio-canada.ca
radio-canada.ca/regions/colombie-britannique/Radio/silenceonjazz.shtml
Concerts from across the country, new CD releases and anecdotes.

Some Experiences in Jazz *CHRY*
4700 Keele St. Rm 413, Student Ctr.
Toronto, ON M3J 1P3
PH: 416-736-5293 FX: 416-650-8052
chry@yorku.ca
www.yorku.ca/chry
Mix of Jazz with heavy Canadian content.

Time for Jazz *CKUA*
10526 Jasper Ave. Edmonton, AB T5J 1Z7
PH: 780-428-7595 FX: 780-428-7624
Roger Levesque roger.levesque@ckua.com
www.ckua.com
Blending all eras of popular Jazz into three hours.

Europe

Belgium

In De Club *RADIO 1*
Auguste Reyerslaan 52, 1043 Brussels, Belgium
PH: 02-741-38-93 FX: 02-736-57-86
info@radio1.be
www.radio1.be

Germany

department deluxe
1425158 / Packstation 105, D-80636 Munich,
Germany
PH: +49 (0) 170-14-77-039
Jan Siegmund info@department-deluxe.org
www.department-deluxe.org
I would describe our style as NuJazz and Freestyle with a touch of Jazz. If someone wants to send me music I always request some mp3 samples to see if it fits our format.

jazz-network.com
PO Box 100 751, 73707 Esslingen, Germany
PH: 49-711-3966294 FX: 49-711-3966295
info@jazz-network.com
www.jazznradio.com
Traditional to modern, mainstream to Blues and World music.

JazzRadio.net
PO Box 390116, 14091 Berlin, Germany
PH: 030-80692050 FX: 030-80692051
info@jazzradio.net
www.jazzradio.net
Covering the world of Jazz - from Jazz news and reviews to the Jazz lifestyle.

The Netherlands

Jazz & Blues Tour
PO Box 471, 2400 Al Alphen a/d Rijn,
The Netherlands
Joost van Steen jazzbluestour@alphenstadfm.nl
www.jazzbluestour.nl
Send any promotion material for airplay.

NPS Radio
www.omroep.nl/nps/output
Jazz, World and beyond.

Norway

Jazz Scene
david@jazzscene.no
jazzscene.no
We welcome good Jazz music from any place on the planet.

Spain

All that Jazz Radio
Apartado de Correos 445, San Pedro de Alcantara,
29670, Malaga, Spain
PH: 34-95-278-56-16 FX: 34-95-278-39-04
Brian Parker bp@jazz-radio.fm
www.jazz-radio.fm
On-line 24 HOURS A DAY with the Best Jazz on the Net.

United Kingdom

BBC Radio 2 *Jazz and Big Band*
www.bbc.co.uk/radio2/r2music/jazz
Home page of the BBC Radio 2's various Jazz and Big Band shows. Info, shows, contacts etc.

BBC Radio 3 *Jazz*
www.bbc.co.uk/radio3/jazz
Home page of the BBC Radio 3's various Jazz shows. Info, shows, contacts etc.

Ejazz.fm
info@ejazz.fm
www.ejazz.fm
For real Jazz Heads!

JazzNet 247 Radio Channels
22, Watermill Rd. Feering, Essex,
CO5 9SR England
info@euroclubdejazz.com
EuroClubdeJazz.com
Promoting all genres of Jazz music and musicians. Also send us your major tour dates or press releases for inclusion in our news section.

In The Mood *SpydaRadio*
42-43 Lower Marsh Waterloo
London, SE1 7RG UK
PH: 023-92-263-933
Barry Everitt barry.everitt@spydaradio.co.uk
www.spydaradio.co.uk
Two hours of the best Jazz and Blues from across the styles.

Jazz FM
26-27 Castlereagh St., London, W1H 5DL UK
music@jazzfm.com
www.jazzfm.com
Latin Jazz, world Jazz, fusion, vocalists and more.

Australia

3MBS
146 Cotham Rd. Kew, VIC 3101 Australia
PH: 03-9816-9355 FX: 03-9817 3777
info@3mbs.org.au
www.3mbs.org.au
Jazz and Classical music.

Bitches' Brew *PBS*
PO Box 2917, Fitzroy MDC, VIC 3065 Australia
PH: 61-3-8415-1067 FX: 61-3-8415-1831
Len Davis lend@optushome.com.au
www.bitches-brew.com
A fusion of Jazz-Rock and other styles.

Quantumlounge
info@quantumlounge.net
www.quantumlounge.net
Featuring a range of quality 'Fusion Music'.

Latin Radio

Alma del Barrio *KXLU*
LMU Dr. Los Angeles, CA 90045
PH: 310-338-2866 FX: 310-338-5959
www.kxlu.com
Authentic and traditional Latin music.

Alma Latina *KDHX*
3504 Magnolia, St. Louis, MO 63118
PH: 314-664-3955 FX: 314-664-1020
Lydia and Carlos almalatina@kdhx.org
www.kdhx.org/programs/almalatina.htm
Caribbean beats, classic boleros and Latin-style Rock'n Roll.

Arriba *WDVR*
PO Box 191 Sergeantsville, NJ 08557
PH: 609-397-1620 FX: 609-397-5991
Carla Van Dyk host@wdvrfm.org
www.wdvrfm.org
Featuring Latin rhythms.

Batanga.com
2007 Yanceyville St., Greensboro, NC 27405
Attn: Programming
www.batanga.com
Plays several Hispanic genres.

The Best of Brazil *KZUM*
941 "O" St., Lincoln, NE 68508
PH: 402-474-5086 FX: 402-474-5091
Randy Morse somdobrasil@alltel.net
www.kzum.org/brazil
Featuring Brazilian musicians and composers.

Brazil Moods
pauloj.amaral@clix.pt
www.live365.com/stations/broadcastor
The finest in classic Bossa Nova, Jazz-Samba & contemporary MPB.

Cafe Brasil *WDNA*
PO Box, 558636, Miami, FL 33255
PH: 305-662-8889 FX: 305-662-1975
www.wdna.org
Brazilian Jazz/Bossa Nova music in all styles, interviews, and special in-studio musical guests.

Chicano Radio Network
7336 Santa Monica Blvd. #800,
Hollywood, CA 90046
PH: 480-636-8853 FX: 612-465-4500
info@crnlive.com
www.crnlive.com
Submit your recordings to be included for possible rotation.

Con Sabor *KPFA*
1929 MLK Jr. Way, Berkeley, CA 94704
PH: 510-848-6767 FX: 510-848-3812
Luis Medina comboson@aol.com
www.kpfa.org
Afro-Caribbean Dance music. A mix of Salsa, Afro-Cuban and Latin Jazz.

Con Salsa *WBUR*
890 Commonwealth Ave. 3rd Fl. Boston, MA 02215
PH: 617-353-0909
Jose Masso jmasso@consalsa.org
www.consalsa.org
Afro-Cuban music, Salsa, Latin-Jazz, Merengue, Nueva Trova and World Music.

Corriente *KGNU*
4700 Walnut St., Boulder, CO 80301
PH: 303-449-4885
music@kgnu.org
www.kgnu.org
Music, news, poetry and features.

Dimension Latina *WLUW*
6525 N. Sheridan Rd. Chicago, IL 60626
PH: 773-508-8080 FX: 773-508-8082
musicdept@wluw.org
wluw.org
Four hours of Latin music with occasional news.

Encanto Latino *WBEZ*
CPR, Navy Pier, 848 E. Grand Ave.
Chicago, IL 60611-3462
PH: 312-948-4855
Catalina Maria Johnson
Music@ChicagoPublicRadio.org
www.wbez.org
Spanning the globe for many different forms and styles. Reaching back to classic recordings and looking ahead for some of the best of today's emerging sounds, styles, and performers.

Horizontes *KUT*
1 University Stn. A0704, Austin, TX 78712
PH: 512-471-1631 FX: 512-471-3700
Michael Crockett mcrockett@caravanmusic.com
www.kut.org
Travel the musical airways of Latin America.

Jazz on the Latin Side *KKJZ*
1288 N. Bellflower Blvd. Long Beach, CA 90815
PH: 562-985-5566 FX: 562-597-8453
Jose Rizo info@kkjz.org
www.kkjz.org

Jazz Tropicale *WDCB*
College of DuPage, 425 Fawell Blvd.
Glen Ellyn, IL 60137
PH: 630-942-4200 FX: 630-942-2788
Marshall Vente VenteM@wdcb.org
www.cod.edu/wdcb
From traditional to contemporary, and Brazilian to Caribbean. It's a Jazz show with palm trees.

The Latin Breeze
PH: 949-388-0662
roxyxlnt@gmail.com
www.live365.com/stations/roxyxlnt
The best in California Classic Latin.

Latina Del Swing *WGMC*
750 Maiden Ln. Rochester, NY 14615
PH: 585-966-2660 FX: 585-621-8692
www.wgmc.org
Latin Pop music show.

Latino America Sonando *KMUD*
PO Box 135, 1144 Redway Dr.
Redway, CA 95560-0135
PH: 707-923-2513 FX: 707-923-2501
Kate Klein md@kmud.org
www.kmud.org
The latest in Salsa, Songo, Latin Jazz, Afro-Cuban Folkloric, music from all over Latin America, plus interviews and other specials.

Mejor Rock/Pop Espanol
aztecasrequest@comcast.NET
www.live365.com/stations/aztecas
Los clasicos y lo mas nuevo del Rock/Pop en tu idioma.

Noche de Ronda *KCSN*
18111 Nordhoff St., Northridge, CA 91330-8312
Betto Arcos betto@kcsn.org
kcsn.org/programs/nochederonda.html
Covering the vast territory of Latin music in a weekly 3-hour show.

Onda Nueva *WUSB*
Student Union Bld. SUNY,
Stony Brook, NY 11794-3263
PH: 631-632-6500 FX: 631-632-7182
Felix Palacios musicwusb-fm
wusb.fm
Everything from Sun to Salsa, Plena, Afro-Antillean, Latin-American music, interviews, history, live in-studio jams, and critique.

PlanetaTV.com
www.planetatv.com
Offers Latin music stations including Tropical, Salsa, Rock en Espanol and mainstream stations such as Pop, Rock and Hip Hop.

Radio Bilingue
PH: 559-455-5777 FX: 559-455-5778
www.radiobilingue.org
The only national distributor of Spanish-language programming in public radio.

Raices *KUNM*
MSC06 3520, Onate Hall, 1 U. NM,
Albuquerque, NM 87131-0001
PH: 505-277-4806
Henry Gonzales music@kunm.org
www.kunm.org
All genres of Hispanic music.

Raizes Radio Show KBCS
3000 Landerholm Circle SE,
Bellevue, WA 98007-6484
PH: 425-564-2427
kbcs.fm
Explores the music and culture of Brazil and its neighbors.

Ritmos Latinos KRBS
PO Box #9, Oroville, CA 95965
www.radiobirdstreet.org
Music from North, Central and South America, Europe and the Caribbean.

Rock Sin Anestesia WLUW
6525 N. Sheridan Rd. Chicago, IL 60626
PH: 773-508-8080 FX: 773-508-8082
spanishrock@wluw.org
wluw.org
The premiere Latin Alternative radio show in the US. Featuring: Indie-Rock, Electronica, Surf, Fusion, Ska, and more with commentary, interviews, and hard to find tracks that will kick your ass!!

SaborSalsa.com
PH: 323 666-2692
Adrian Treto adriantreto@saborsalsa.com
www.SaborSalsa.com
Playing the best of Tropical music.

Salsa Sabrosa KUNM
MSC06 3520, Onate Hall, 1 U. New Mexico,
Albuquerque, NM 87131-0001
PH: 505-277-4806
Wellington Guzman music@kunm.org
www.kunm.org
Friday nights are hot hot hot!

Son Pacifica KPFT
419 Lovett Blvd. Houston, TX 77006
luisalfonso59@hotmail.com
www.hometown.aol.com/alfnsrvr
The best of independent Latino music!

The Sounds of Brazil
5250 Grand Avenue, 14/111, Gurnee, IL 60031
PH: 847-855-8546 FX: 240-358-3096
www.connectbrazil.com
The best and the latest sounds from Brazil.

¡Tertulia! WFCR
Hampshire House, U. Mass, 131 County Cir.
Amherst, MA 01003-9257
PH: 413-545-0100 FX: 413-545-2546
Luis Meléndez tertulia@wfcr.org
www.wfcr.org/tertulia
Latin Jazz, Boleros, Salsa, Merengue, Nueva Trova, Tango and Folk music.

Tiene Sabor WWOZ
PO Box 51840, New Orleans, LA 70151-1840
Yolanda Estrada wwoz@wwoz.org
www.wwoz.org
I want to be the first to play a new record!

La Voz Hispana WWGC
State U. W. Georgia, 1600 Maple St.,
Carrollton, GA 30118
PH: 770-836-6500
wwgc@westga.edu
www.westga.edu/~wwgc
Spanish news, music and information are featured.

WKCR Columbia U.
2920 Broadway, Mailcode 2612,
New York, NY 10027
PH: 212-854-9920
latin@wkcr.org
www.columbia.edu/cu/wkcr
A leader in Latin music broadcasting.

WRTE Mexican Fine Arts Center
1401 W. 18th St., Chicago, IL 60608
PH: 312-455-9455 FX: 312-455-9755
www.wrte.org
Bilingual youth-operated, urban, community radio.

Metal Radio

Radio Promoters

Skateboard Marketing
1150 Agnes Ct. Valley Stream, NY 11580
Attn: Munsey Ricci
PH: 516-328-1103 FX: 516-328-1293
Munsey excuseking@aol.com
www.skateboard-marketing.com
Street marketing & commercial specialty shows, active Rock & college Metal radio promotion.

Stations and Shows

North America

United States

4Q Radio
andy@4qradio.com
www.4qradio.com
Station with a Metal and Punk Rock show.

Alaska's Tundra Trash Radio
www.tundratrashradio.com
We play Heavy Metal, Hardcore Rock and similar genres.

American Radio Network / Megarock Radio
1000 Bates St., St. Louis, MO 63111
Robert Winkelmann megarock@sbcglobal.net
www.myamericanradio.net
Producers of Garageband ROCK, a syndicated independent Rock, Alternative and Hard Rock music show on 20 radio stations.

Audio Aggression
Metal Mark metalmark55@hotmail.com
www.geocities.com/SunsetStrip/Frontrow/2430/MMP.html
Our intention here is to focus on the true independent Heavy Metal underground and not those MTV or FUSE video bands. No Glam bands please!

Axecaliber WITR
Generations Underground, PO Box 16303,
Rochester, NY 14616
geno@heavyrock.com
www.heavyrock.com/radioshow.html
Promotes the undiscovered Heavyrock artist.

Bad Attitude Radio
c/o K.T. Productions, PO Box 604,
Kewaskum, WI 53040
cormws@charter.net
www.kissthis.com
If you would like to submit your band's music for inclusion in our play list - send us a press kit, a copy of your CD, a short bio, links to your website, contact information and a written letter stating that you give us permission to air your music.

Brutality Radio
The Mistress 36804 Farmbrook Dr. B13,
Clinton Twp. MI 48035
www.xwarp.net
Playing only the most brutal Death Metal from around the world!!!

Dementia Radio
www.dementiaradio.com
We encourage Indies to submit their music to us.

CD Smash Radio
109 Poe Ave. Poteau, OK 74953
Kerry D. Plummer cdsmash@clnk.com
www.cdsmash.com
A show featuring Glam Rock, Hard Rock, Power Pop & some Metal. "All Indie, All The Time!"

Doom Metal Radio
info@doom-metal.com
www.doom-metal.com/radio.html
All Doom and closely related music 24 hours a day, 7 days a week.

Electric Eye Radio
requests@electriceyeradio.com
www.electriceyeradio.com
Classic, Hard and Modern Rock, Heavy Metal, Goth and Punk.

Embrace of the Darkness & Metal WMUA
105 Campus Ctr. U. Mass, Amherst, MA 01003
PH: 413-545-2876 FX: 413-545-0682
DJ Solveig embraceofthedarkness@yahoo.com
www.embraceofthedarkness.com
European Metal (Death, Black etc.) Sunday nights.

Ground Zero WRBC
Box 339, Bates College, Lewiston, ME 04240
Justin vmpyre2k@aol.com
www.geocities.com/gzwrbc/gzwrbc.html
All request fun & mayhem.

Guitar Central
snootee@aol.com
www.live365.com/stations/trixi17
All instrumental GUITAR oriented jams. Get in touch with your inner 6 string!

HeavyMetalRadio.com
Marc Schoech webmaster@heavymetalradio.com
www.heavymetalradio.com
The loudest site on the Internet!!!

High Octane 525.com
contact525@525.com
www.525.com
Hard Rock and Heavy Metal. We support unsigned artists and we would like to play your material.

HoTMetaLradio
www.hotmetalradio.com
We play the music that YOU want to hear.

www.indielinkexchange.com/ile

Humble's House of Rock
House_of_Rock@bellsouth.net
www.live365.com/stations/dorknozle
Here you will hear AOR/Melodic/Glam/80's/Hair Rock. Be ready to hear some old stuff that you haven't heard in a while & some new bands

The Independent Recording Group Radio
109 Poe Ave. Poteau, OK 74953
Steve Harris irgradio@classicnet.net
www.irgradio.com
We are looking for music in the Rock genre.

Into the Pit KUPD
Marcus Meng, 1900 W. Carmen, Tempe, AZ 85283
www.98KUPD.com
The shit your mama don't want you to hear.

K666 Radio /StonerRock.com
PO Box 78, Carmen, ID 83462
El Danno dan@stonerrock.com
www.stonerrock.com
If you're disgusted with the pathetic state of popular music, you've come to the right place.

L.A. Metal.com
Tizzod2 biglantonian@yahoo.com
www.live365.com/stations/tizzod2
Loud and Aggressive Metal! Brutal, Melodic, Hardcore etc.

The Last Exit for the Lost WVBR
957 Mitchell St. #B, Ithaca, NY 14850
PH: 607-273-4000 FX: 607-273-4069
lastexit@thelastexit.org
www.thelastexit.org
Supports Indie Metal, Goth, Punk, Industrial, etc.

Livehardrock.com
Livehardrock@livehardrock.com
www.livehardrock.com
Carries Hard Rock shows with DJs from around the world.

Maddog Rock Radio
www.heavymetalradio.net
Broadcasting from Kailua, Hawaii, but hey, even in paradise, we need to crank up the amps to 11 once in awhile! Check out the site for submission details.

Megatrends in Brutality WRBC
Box 339, Bates College, Lewiston, ME 04240
Psycho megabrutal@excite.com
home.gwi.net/~jiminmaine
If it is heavy and Metal ... I play it.

Metal Faction Radio
www.vampire-magazine.com/listen_mf.asp
Metal, Thrash, Hardcore, Industrial and Punk. We like to give the 'little guys' a chance to receive air play and encourage bands to contact us.

Metal Reigns Live LV ROCKS
www.metalreigns.com
Tune in to hear the latest Metal releases.

Metal Rock WDCB
College of DuPage, 425 Fawell Blvd.
Glen Ellyn, IL 60137
PH: 630-942-4200 FX: 630-942-2788
Steve James JamesS@wdcb.org
www.cod.edu/wdcb
Keeping hard rock alive in the greater Chicago area. Specializing in cuts rarely heard on commercial radio and music from local talent.

Metalradio.com
1321 Campbell Ave. La Salle, IL 61301
FX: 806-261-8138
webmaster@metalradio.com
www.metalradio.com
The only station for a Metal Nation! Send us your demos or press releases and we'll get 'em up on the site.

PulverRadio.com
115 Broadhollow Rd. Ste. 225, Melville, NY 11747
PH: 631-961-8998 FX: 631-293-3996
Mikey McClenathan mikey@pulver.com
www.pulverradio.com
We're ready to blast your eardrums with cutting edge tunes from the world of in-your-face, up-all-night, guitar smashing Rock!

Rampage Radio
KUSF, 2130 Fulton St., San Francisco, CA 94117
Dirty Sanchez rampageradio@hotmail.com
www.rampageradio.com
The Bay Area's Heaviest Radio Show since 1981. Please send any promo CDs to the address above. If your band wants to be interviewed on the show, e-mail me.

Rapture Radio
1932 E. Lindsey #212, Norman, OK 73071
Wes raptureradio@msn.com
www.raptureradio.net
We support indie artists 100%!!!!!

RIFF Radio
2621 14th St. S. #4, Fargo, ND 58103
Dan mmd@hardrocksociety.com
www.hardrocksociety.com
New, reviews and new releases are posted.

The RoadRash Bash
RoadRash roadrash@newartistradio.net
www.newartistradio.net/The%20Roadrash%20Bash.htm
Spotlighting all forms of Rock and Metal from around the world. Hear the bands the way they were meant to be heard ... complete with commentary, news and interviews.

Rock Hard Place Radio Show
812 Countryside Park, Fargo, ND 58103
Torch rockhardtorch@hotmail.com
www.rockhardplace.com
Looking for new Rock, Metal, Industrial, Punk, Goth and other loud music!

The Root Of All Evil KFAI
1808 Riverside Ave. Minneapolis, MN 55454
PH: 612-341-3144
Earl Root root@rootofallevil.com
www.rootofallevil.com
Molten Metal meltdowns, demented and deranged; totally tasteless; rotten mean and nasty.

SINDradio
SEtrendkill@comcast.net
www.live365.com/stations/the_six
Metal, Industrial and Alternative. Hardcore to not-so Hardcore.

Snakenet Metal Radio
snake@snakenet.com
www.snakenetmetalradio.com
Contact to send CDs/promotional material.

Sound of the Fury WLUW
6525 N. Sheridan Rd. Chicago, IL 60626
PH: 847-424 1931
Kimberly Tester kim@uraniummusic.com
www.soundofthefury.com
The best in Death, Black, Power, Thrash, Hardcore, and Progressive Metal as well as bands fusing their own unique style across metal genres.

Spin 180
6400 N. Beltline Rd. #210, Irving, TX 75063
Matt Mungle info@spin180.net
www.spin180.net
If you would like to have your tunes added to our play list please submit a CD, bio and lyric sheet to the above address (CDs only please!). Rock and Alternative only.

Sudden Death Overtime WITR
PO Box 20563, Rochester, NY 14602-0563
PH: 585-475-5643 FX: 585-475-4988
ron@suddendeathovertime.com
suddendeathovertime.com
Every sub-genre is represented: Death, Thrash, Power, Traditional, Doom and more! Just send you music to us!

The Tink's Metal Show WVUD
PO Box 9284, Wilmington, DE 19809
PH: 302-798-0144
The Tink thetinksinc@lycos.com
www.thetinksinc.com/radio.htm
The TINK is metal incarnate. Radio. Video. Online. And, In Person. He is the Godfather. He is the man, the myth, the legend and the entity that makes it possible for the rest of us to be metal.

Vomit Radio
PO Box 93006, Albuquerque, NM 87199-3006
vomitbag@vomitradio.com
vomitradio.com
Heavy and uncensored 24 hours a day!

WGCC
1College Rd. Batavia, NY 14020
PH: 585-343-0055 x6420
Jared Ingersoll Ingus18@yahoo.com
wgcc-fm.com
A mixture of Rock, Metal and Punk programming.

Canada

Blistering Radio 1
C.P. St Dorothee, PO Box 69023,
Laval, QC H7X 3M2
PH/FX: 450-689-7106
Rob Cotter rob@blistering.com
www.blistering.com
A spiritual, political, and musical journey via a totally random and massive selection of songs from all Heavy genres and some that you may not consider so.

Bourreau Metallique CIBL
1691, boul Pie IX, Montréal, QC H1V 2C3
PH: 514-526-2581 FX: 514-526-3583
bourreaumetallique@hotmail.com
www.sangfrais.com/bourreau

The Darkest Hours
info@thedarkesthours.com
www.thedarkesthours.com
Send us your Demos, promos & press kit!

Feel The Rage CJIQ
Dan Kieswetter rage@gto.net
www.cjiq.fm/feeltherage.asp
Weekly Heavy Metal radio show featuring all sub-genres of Metal!

Hard Beyond Driven
PO Box # 47665, 939 Lawrence Ave. E.
Don Mills, ON M3C 3S7
metalmike@hardbeyonddriven.com
www.hardbeyonddriven.com
Heavy Metal bands send your promos/CDs to us.

Metal Canvas CHUO
372 Rideau St. #201, Ottawa, ON K1N 1G7
metalcanvas@yahoo.com
www.chuo.fm
Presents Metal as splashes of blood, bile, excrement intertwined like a tapestry with sunshowers, butterflies, tulips surrounded by a soft mist creating a beautiful tropical lagoon of death. If you send it, Metal Canvas will broadcast it!

Métal Pesant CFLX
67 rue Wellington nord, Sherbrooke, QC J1H 5A9
PH: 819-566-2787 FX: 819-566-7331
metalpesant@hotmail.com
www.cflx.qc.ca
Where the word Metal finds all its meaning.

MetalNetRadio.com
1 Selkirk Rd. W. Lethbridge, AB T1K 4N4
programdirector@metalnetradio.com
www.metalnetradio.com
We maintain our independence and play only what we think is good and what our listeners think is good.

Metalurgy's "Live Evil" CFCR
PO Box 21068, Grosvenor Park,
Saskatoon, SK S7H 5N9
Larry Lava metalurgy@shaw.ca
members.shaw.ca/metalurgy/main.htm
The most Extreme & brutal radio show to be heard on the Canadian airwaves.

Midnight Metal CHET
Mike Sabulsky, PO Box 1325,
Chetwynd, BC V0C 1J0
PH: 250-788-1663
mike@midnightmetal.com
www.midnightmetal.com
Get your album reviewed, sampled and played.

Mind Compression CJSR
Room 0-09 Students' Union Bldg. U. Alberta,
Edmonton, AB T6G 2J7
PH: 780-492-2577 x232 FX: 780-492-3121
www.cjsr.com
Canada's longest running Heavy Metal show! Metal John plays Old School Metal, Hardcore, Classic Metal, and anything else he wants.

Space in Your Face CKMS
200 University Ave. W. Waterloo, ON N2L 3G1
PH: 519-886-2567 FX: 519-884-3530
siyf@gto.net
www.angelfire.com/on/siyf
Features Metal news, interviews, giveaways and more!

L'Ulcère de vos nuits CISM
2332 Edouard Montpetit, C-1509 C.P. 6128,
Montréal, QC H3C 3J7
PH: 514-343-CISM FX: 514-343-2418
uglydj@videotron.ca
pages.infinit.net/danko
Intense, powerful, dark Metal.

Europe

Finland

Chrominance Metal
chrominance@rock.com
www.live365.com/stations/anhaapal
Different Metal genres featuring many underground bands.

Meteliä Maan Alta Rado Show
c/o Lähiradio, 5 Linja 3 A 1, 00530 Helsinki,
Finland
radio@diypunk.net
diypunk.net/radio

France

Kerosene Radio
6 bis, rue d'Echange, 35000 Rennes, France
kfuel@kfuel.org
www.kfuel.org
Rock, Noise, Hard/emo core, Experimental, Punk, Pop....

Rock'One
Poste Restante Paris beaubourg, 90 rue St. Denis,
75001 Paris, France
stephanek@rock-1.com
www.rock-1.com
La Webradio Rock.

Germany

InfraRot
Amtsgericht HRA 10032 Memmingen, Germany
PH: 49-0-8333/93113 FX: 49-0-8333/93114
Jörg Wolfgram gott@infrarot.de
www.infrarot.de
Fresh music for rotten people.

Radio Melodic
Postfach 3144, 70777 Filderstadt, Germany
PH: +49-7158-956611 FX: +49-7158-956611
radio@radiomelodic.de
www.radiomelodic.de
Each show is full of new CDs, news, interviews, concert reports and more.

Rock of Ages Bermuda-Funk
c/o Georg Lögler, Krappmühlstrasse 32, 68165
Mannheim, Germany
georg.loegler@web.de
www.bermudafunk.org
All styles of Rock/Metal. No Death Metal. My emphasis is on UNKNOWN bands.

Rock Station Kiel
Lämmerstücken 7, 24111 Kiel, Germany
Heiko Mangels rockstation@kielfm.de
www.rockstationkiel.de
We play all styles from AOR to Metal in 2 Shows. Please send promotional stuff to the above address.

Rockin` Radio
Banderbacher Str. 24, 90513 Zirndorf, Germany
PH/FX: 0911-60-95-95
info@rockin-radio.de
www.rockin-radio.de
Das Beste fur Franken in Sachen Rock.

Stahlwerk-Hannover Radio Show
FLORA, Zur Bettfedernfabrik 1, D-30451
Hannover, Germany
PH: 49-511-219790 FX: 49-511-2197919
stahlwerk-hannover@gmx.de
www.stahlwerk-hannover.de
Different bands without a recent record deal are featured.

Norway

Metal Express Radio Show
att: Nordahl, Ovrefoss 14, N-0555 Oslo, Norway
mail@metalexpress.no
www.metalexpress.no
straight Heavy Metal and closely related genres.

Portugal

S.O.S Heavy Metal Radio Show
PO Box 408, 4703 Braga Codex, Portugal
Filipe Marta mail@sosradio.online.pt
www.sosradio.online.pt
Online and screaming fucking loud!

United Kingdom

One Louder Radio
richard@onelaudermedia.com
www.OneLouderRadio.co.uk
If you do not have any MP3s, you can e-mail us for our mailing address.

Sex to 9 with María TotalRock
1 Denmark Pl. London, WC2H 8NL UK
maria@sexto9.com
www.totalrock.com
Rock and Metal like you've never heard it before... with a touch of exotic Latin passion.

Zed's Psycholopedia of Rock TotalRock
1 Denmark Pl. London, WC2H 8NL UK
Zaid 'Zed' Couri zed@psycholopedia.co.uk
www.psycholopedia.co.uk
A kick-arse Rock/Heavy Metal show.

Australia

Critical Mass Radio Show RTR FM
PO Box 949, Nedlands, WA 6909 Australia
PH: 08-6488-3380
cmass@optusnet.com.au
www.wf.com.au/criticalmass
Stay Heavy Metal and bang your heads.

Full Metal Racket Triple J
GPO Box 9994, Melbourne, VIC 3000 Australia
PH: 1-800-0555-36
Andrew Haug fullmetalracket@triplej.abc.net.au
www.triplej.abc.net.au/racket
Covering a wide range of the latest and greatest heavy sounds with news updates, interviews, local and international tour announcements and tonnes more. Send in your demo CDs and tapes.

Metal Head Radio Show Triple U
PO Box 1488, Nowra, NSW 2541 Australia
metalhead@dodo.net.au
www.tripleu.org.au/metalhead.html
Four Hours of Metal with the Chief Metallurgist.

New Age Radio

United States

Ageless Music for a New World KEDT
4455 S. Padre Island Dr. #38,
Corpus Christi, TX 78411-4481
PH: 361-855-2213 FX: 361-855-3877
W.C. Welz stewartjacoby@kedt.org
www.kedt.org
A unique mix of New Age and World Beat music that will please the ears and soothe the mind.

Alpha Rhythms WYSO
Antioch U. 795 Livermore St.,
Yellow Springs, OH 45387
PH: 937-767-6420
Lori ltaylor@uc-council.org Jerry
allank@earthlink.net
www.wyso.org/alpharhythms.htm
4 hours of Ambient and New Age music.

Ambience WWUH
Attn: Music Director,
200 Bloomfield Ave. West Hartford, CT 06117
PH: 860-768-4701 FX: 860-768-5701
Susan teltanman@cox.net
www.teltan.org
Ambient and Atmospheric Electronic music to drift into Sunday morning with.

AM/FM WMUH
PO Box 632, Nazareth, PA 18064-0632
Bill Fox billyfox@soundscapes.us
soundscapes.us/amfm
Electronic, Ambient, Space, Acoustic, Electric, Pop, New Age, Progressive Rock and whatever strikes my fancy. Inquire by e-mail before submitting music.

Astreaux World
www.astreauxworld.com
Ambient/ New Age / Space Music. We're always looking for new artists and music to introduce to our listeners. If you have songs/materials/events that we should know about, contact us. Visit our website to find out submission details.

Audioscapes KCPR
Graphic Arts Bldg 26, Rm 201, Cal Poly State U.
San Luis Obispo, CA 93407
PH: 805-756-2965
audioscapes@yahoo.com
www.geocities.com/audioscapes
www.kcpr.org
A Classical, Electronic and Progressive music merge.

Audiosyncracry KTEP
c/o Jamey Osborne, 500 W. University Ave.
Cotton Memorial #203, El Paso, TX 79968
PH: 915-747-5152 FX: 915-747-5641
www.ktep.org
Covers a wide range of music, from Acoustic to Electronica. A good deal of Jazz and Classical is played with an occasional dash of World music.

Audiosyncrasies WVXU
1648 Herald Ave. Cincinnati, OH 45207
PH: 513-458-3143
Lee Hay lhay@xstarnet.com
www.xstarnet.com
A nightly eclectic musical excursion ranging from New Age to World music and nearly everything in between.

BRAINWAVES KXCI
220 S. 4th Ave. Tucson, AZ 85701
PH: 520-623-1000
Doug Wellington brainwaves@kxci.org
www.brainwavesradio.com
New Age, Ambient, Experimental, electro-Acoustic Classical, World music.

Changes Radio
comments@changes.org
www.changes.org
We review Folk, Rock, Trance, Ethnic, Classical and New Age.

CheezMuzik WTUL
Tulane U. Center, New Orleans, LA 70118
PH: 504-865-5887 FX: 504-862-3072
Chris Albright cheez@wtul.fm
www.wtul.fm
We feel the music is healthy and beautiful.

Common Threads KRBS
PO Box #9, Oroville, CA 95965
www.radiobirdstreet.org
Spiritual music, poetry and speeches.

Cosmic Island
kevin@thecosmicisland.com
TheCosmicIsland.com
Peaceful and relaxing, quiet and soothing... the best mix of New Age and Ambient music.

The Crystal Ballroom NetRadioLink.com
info@netradiolink.com
www.netradiolink.com/id1.html
Quiet Brilliance! Piano, Keyboard and Progressive Electronic music.

Different Standards KMBH
PO Box 2147, Harlingen, TX 78551
PH: 956-421-4111 FX: 956-421-4150
Kim Menard kmbhkhid@aol.com
www.kmbh.org/radio
Features many genres of Instrumental and Ambient music from the classic sounds right up to the newest releases with a few musical surprises thrown in.

Earth Tones KVLU
PO Box 10064, Beaumont, TX 77710
PH: 409-880-8164
dept.lamar.edu/kvlu
Elizabeth French Elizabeth.French@lamarpa.edu
Two hours of quiet time music. I gladly accept independent music for the show.

Echoes
PO Box 256, Chester Springs, PA 19425
FX: 610-827-9614
echoes@echoes.org
www.echoes.org
Send submissions for airplay (CDs only).

ethnosphere KRCL
450 S. 300 West, Salt Lake City, UT 84101
Sohrab Mafi sohrabm@krcl.org
www.krcl.org
www.krcl.org/%7Esohrabm
A meditative journey into the world of consciousness through music. All submissions are greatly appreciated and seriously considered for inclusion.

Galactic Voyager KCSN
18111 Nordhoff St., Northridge, CA 91330-8312
PH: 818-677-3090
Meishel Menachekanian meishel@kcsn.org
www.kcsn.org
A blend of Electronic and New Age music.

Gift of Peace WJFF
4765 State Rt. 52, PO Box 546,
Jeffersonville, NY 12748
PH: 845-482-4141 FX: 845-482-9533
Lisa Brody & Jim McKeegan
jimandlisa@catskill.net
www.wjffradio.org
The New Age music has to have a certain feel to it. I guess you could call it spiritual, but not sappy. The World music is usually very mellow. Jim likes long, spacey, Ambient pieces, so we play a lot of these too.

The Great Awakening WXCI
181 White St., Danbury, CT 06811
PH: 203-837-8387
WXCIDanbury@yahoo.com
www.myspace.com/wxci
New Age readings, meditations and the latest in soothing sounds.

Hearts of Space Radio
PO Box 5916, Sausalito, CA 94966
PH: 415-331-3200 FX: 415-331-3280
radio@hos.com
www.hos.com/radio.html
Submit your music, send CD & promo info.

Inner Visions WNMC
1701 E. Front St., Traverse City, MI 49686
PH: 231-995-2562
www.wnmc.org
A mix of sounds and textures that could not be more appropriate for a Sunday morning.

Instrumental Saturdays WMSE
1025 N. Broadway, Milwaukee, WI 53202
PH: 414-277-6942 FX: 414-277-7149
Mary Bartlein meab@execpc.com
www.wmse.org
New Age, Ambient and World Music.

Internet Oasis
Tammy tjw_2001@yahoo.com
www.internetoasisradio.com
A mix of New Age, Instrumental and Ambient music. For airplay consideration, send me an email via the form on my website. Tell me about your music, instruments, target genre and anything else you want.

Iridium Radio KZYX/KZYZ
c/o Iridium Hosts, PO Box 1, Philo, CA 95466
Kitty & Creek Iridiumradio@starband.net.
www.iridiumradio.com
We welcome CD's of your music for review and airplay! Everything received will be acknowledged. Currently we are interested in exploring your offerings in New Age, World and Cool Jazz.

KUAT U. Arizona
PO Box 210067, Tucson, AZ 85721-0067
PH: 520-621-5828
www.kuat.org
Classical or New Age artists may submit.

The Lighthouse KCHO
Cal State U. Chico 95929-0500
PH: 530-898-5896 FX: 530-898-4348
www.kcho.org
Mellow and uplifting music.

Lucid Sounds *WZBC*
Boston College, McElroy Commons 107,
Chestnut Hill, MA 02467
PH: 617-552-3511 FX: 617-552-1738
music@wzbc.org
www.wzbc.org
Expanding awareness.

Midnight Light *KKUP*
PO Box 820, Cupertino, CA 95015
PH: 408-260-2999
Joseph Leight admin@kkup.org
www.kkup.com
Providing the Listeners, soundscapes, spoken words, occasionally taped interviews with the thoughts to foster peaceful states of mind

The Moonlight Space Hour *KCHO*
Cal State U. Chico 95929-0500
PH: 530-898-5896 FX: 530-898-4348
www.kcho.org
Electronic Music.

Morning Breeze *KSBR*
28000 Marguerite Pkwy. Mission Viejo, CA 92692
PH: 949-582-4221
Donna Jo Thornton themorningbreeze@gmail.com
www.ksbr.net
A mixture of New Age, World, Acoustic Instrumental and Spacey Electronic music.

The Morning Fog *WVUD*
Perkins Student Ctr. U. Delaware,
Newark, DE 19716
PH: 302-831-2701 FX: 302-831-1399
Gary Dunham morningfogman@yahoo.com
www.wvud.org
Early morning Ambience for sleeping or waking.

Music From Beyond the Lakes *WDBX*
224 N. Washington St., Carbondale, IL 62901
PH: 618-457-3691
wdbx@globaleyes.net
www.wdbx.org
New Age music show.

Music from the Cosmic Wheel *WSCS*
Postmaster, E. Andover, NH 03231
PH: 603-735-5586
Brad Hartwell brad@cosmicwheel.net
www.cosmicwheel.net
New Age, Ambient/Electronic/Space, World Fusion, Native, Celtic etc. Taped interviews and live performances are an occasional feature.

Music of the 21st Century with Chris Hickey *WXXI*
280 State St. PO Box 30021,
Rochester, NY 14603-3021
PH: 585-258-0200
wxxi.org
New Age, Celtic, Jazz and World music that is energetic, rhythmic and melodic. It is a journey through a pleasing, surprising and sometimes startling musical landscape.

Musical Starstreams
info@starstreams.com
www.starstreams.com
Mid to downtempo, exotic Electronica. If you think your stuff fits, send your release on regular CD only (no mp3s) to our mailing address and then watch our playlists to see if it worked for us.

Mystic Music *KKUP*
PO Box 820, Cupertino, CA 95015
Eric Mystic admin@kkup.com
www.kkup.com/ericm.html
Something special and out of the ordinary. Lifts and awakens you above normal consciousness.

Mystic Soundscapes
PO Box 50128, Albuquerque, NM 87181-0128.
www.mysticsoundscapes.com
We make it our mission to promote your music to our large listener base. If your music fits the New Age, World Music, Celtic, Ambient or Instrumental genre, we'd love to hear from you.

Neptune Currents *KKUP*
PO Box 2250, Cupertino, CA 95015
Attn: Music Director
Steve Davis & Carol Joyce
neptuneradio@earthlink.net
www.kkup.com
Tranquil, expressive, meditative. Emphasis on electronic & electro-acoustic music, plus music of the Far East and other World music.

New Age Collage *SDPR*
555 Dakota St. PO Box 5000, Vermillion, SD 57069
PH: 800-456-0766
programming@sdpb.org
www.sdpb.org
2 hours of modern instrumental music.

New Age Music Mix *WEBR*
2929 Eskridge Rd. #S, Fairfax, VA 22031
PH: 703-573-1090 x1018
webr@fcac.org
www.fcac.org/webr/webr.htm

New Age Sampler *WWSP*
105 CAC Reserve St., Stevens Point, WI 54481
PH: 715- 346-4722
BEAR nasbear@bearheartltd.com
www.bearheartltd.com/nas
Ambient, Celtic, Instrumental, New Age, Orchestral, Smooth Jazz, Space & World Music.

The New Edge *WMBR*
3 Ames St., Cambridge, MA 02142
PH: 617-253-8810
Ken Field newedge@wmbr.org
wmbr.mit.edu
Mostly instrumental creative new music, composed and improvised at the intersection of Classical, Jazz, and World styles.

New Frontiers *WXDU*
PO Box 90689, Duke Stn. Durham, NC 27708
Attn: Marty
PH: 919-684-2957
music_director@wxdu.org
www.wxdu.duke.edu
Two hours of Space Music - almost-Ambient, almost-Trance, & almost-Folk.

New Music Gallery *WMNR*
PO Box 920, Monroe, CT 06468
PH: 203-268-9667
info@wmnr.org
www.wmnr.org

Night Breeze *KCCK*
6301 Kirkwood Blvd. SW, Cedar Rapids, IA 52406
PH: 319-398-5446 FX: 319-398-5492
Mark Jayne nightbreeze@kcck.org
www.kcck.org
The most relaxing evening in radio. An exotic blend of mellow Jazz with new Instrumental and Ambient sounds.

Night Tides *KCUR*
4825 Troost Ave. #202, Kansas City, MO 64110
PH: 816-235-1551 FX: 816-235-2864
Renee Blanche blanchea@umkc.edu
www.kcur.org
An eclectic blend of contemplative Instrumental & Electronic music that combines upbeat grooves and dubs with soothing melodies that whisper (softly) to the soul.

Nightcrossings *Radio Kansas*
815 N. Walnut #300, Hutchinson, KS 67501-6217
PH: 620-662-6646
Sara Sayers comments@radiokansas.org
www.radiokansas.org/nc.cfm
New Age music with light Jazz and Classical.

Nightstreams *KASU*
PO Box 2160, State University, AR 72467
PH: 870-972- 2200
Marty Scarbrough kasu@astate.edu
www.kasu.org
Relaxing, contemporary instrumental music.

Nitelite *KEDM*
ULM 225 Stubbs Hall, Monroe, LA 71209-6805
PH: 318-342-5556 FX: 318-342-5570
Don Dixon kedm@ulm.edu
kedm.ulm.edu/nitelitegallery/default.htm
Acoustic music styles, instrumental hybrids and deep-space explorations.

Nocturnes *KEDM*
ULM 225 Stubbs Hall, Monroe, LA 71209-6805
PH: 318-342-5556 FX: 318-342-5570
kedm.ulm.edu/
Mixes Acoustic and Classical music forms.

Oasis *Montana Public Radio*
U. Montana, Missoula, MT 59812-8064
Attn: Joan Richarde
PH: 406-243-4931 FX: 406-243-3299
www.mtpr.net
Electronic and Acoustic New Age music.

Open Space District *KRCB*
5850 Labath Ave. Rohnert Park, CA 94928
PH: 707-585-8522 FX: 707-585-1363
John Katchmer listener@krcb.org
www.krcb.org/radio
A weekly slide through the dreamy, dopey, sexy world of contemporary Electronica.

PACIFICnoir *KEDM*
ULM 225 Stubbs Hall, Monroe, LA 71209-6805
PH: 318-342-5556 FX: 318-342-5570
Don Dixon kedm@ulm.edu
kedm.ulm.edu/nitelitegallery/default.htm
Typically this program features new and vintage Space/Ambient releases, but on occasion, will feature thematic oriented programs.

Planetary Prismatic Psonics *WKNH*
PH: 603-358-2420
music@wknh.org
www.wknh.org

The Smiling Ear
PO Box 1241, Hilo, HI 96721
smilingear@yahoo.com
www.smilingear.com
A soothing mix of deeply relaxing, healing, meditative music and sounds from all ages and into the future. Ambient, New Age, Meditative, Classical, Hawaiian, World, Electronic, Space, Trance and much more.

Solitudes WXPR
303 W. Prospect Ave. Rhinelander, WI 54501
PH: 715-362-6000 FX: 715-362-6007
wxpr@wxpr.org
www.wxpr.org/program/solitudes.html
An hour of New Age or "Space" music.

Soundscape WSKG
PO Box 3000, Binghamton, NY 13902
PH: 607-729-0100 x315
Crystal Sarakas Crystal_Sarakas@wskg.pbs.org
www.wskg.com/Soundscape
New Age & World Music.

Star's End WXPN
PO Box 22, Upper Darby, PA 19082-0022
Chuck van Zyl info@starsend.org
www.starsend.org
A non-stop drifting blend, drawing from many genres including: Electronic, Ambient, Spacemusic, Chillout, Avant-Garde, Low-Intensity Noise, New Age, International, Spoken Word and Classical.

Sunday CD Spotlight WSHU
5151 Park Ave. Fairfield, CT 06825
PH: 203-365-6604
Julie Freddino spotlight@wshu.org
www.wshu.org/spotlight/spotlight.asp
New Age and Space Music.

Sunday Session WKZE
67 Main St., Sharon, CT 06069
PH: 860-364-5800 FX: 860-364-0129
Steve Utterback info@wkze.com
www.wkze.com
An interesting mix of Contemporary Jazz, Native, World Beat and New Age music.

Sunday Sunrise KRVR
961 N. Emerald Ave. #A, Modesto, CA 95351
PH: 209-544-1055
theriver@krvr.com
www.krvr.com
Acoustic, New Age and World music.

Sunrise WUTC
615 McCallie Ave. Dept. 1151,
Chattanooga, TN 37403
PH: 423-265-9882 FX: 423-425-2379
Rabbit rabbit@celticradio.org
www.wutc.org
Soothing Acoustic, New Age and World music. Quiet and reflective moments provide an opportunity to begin your weekend with a peaceful atmosphere of relaxing music.

Tangents KALW
500 Mansell St., San Francisco, CA 94134
PH: 415-841-4121 FX: 415-841-4125
Dore dore@tangents.com
www.tangents.com
A program that explores the bridges connecting various styles of music, such as World and Roots music, and Creative Jazz hybrids.

Tonal Vision WICN
6 Chatham St., Worcester, MA 01609
PH: 508-752-0700 FX: 508-752-7518
karen@wicn.org
www.wicn.org
New Age, Acoustic, Ambient and World music.

Visionary Activist KPFA
1929 MLK Jr. Way, Berkeley, CA 94704
PH: 510-848-6767 FX: 510-848-3812
www.visionaryactivism.com/radioshow.htm
Insights on nature of magic and reality.

Canada

Night Music CKUA
10526 Jasper Ave. Edmonton, AB T5J 1Z7
PH: 780-428-7595 FX: 780-428-7624
tony.dillon-davis@ckua.org
www.ckua.org
Jazz, Folk, Pop, New Age, Aboriginal, East Indian, Arabic and Asian.

Germany

Sounds of Syn
Steffen Thieme Redaktion@Sounds-of-Syn.de
www.sounds-of-syn.de
It's a program for syntheszier music.

The Netherlands

Time Trek
Jelke Bethlehem timetrek@omroeprijnwoude.nl
timetrek.nl
Het programma neemt u mee op een ontspannende reis door de wereld van de New Age muziek.

Sound Sounding
Ronald boortman@presenteert.nl
boortman.presenteert.nl
Smooth moods, which one can bring spiritual emotions.

Spain

Musical Trip Radio Iliberis
Miguel Angel Espigares Flores, Plaza Los Caquis Nº1, Maracena, GranadaI CP 18200, Spain
PH: +34-958-420310
otrasmusicas.net
Promoting and popularizing your creative work. We want to be the first in discovering it. New Age, Symphonic Rock, Jazz Fusion, Soundtracks, Lounge and Contemporary Electronic Music.

Australia

Hybrid PBS
PO Box 812, Parkville, VIC 3052 Australia
Andrew Hollo ahollo@connexus.net.au
www.listen.to/hybrid
Experimental, Jazz, chamber and fourth world music.

Japan

Earth Feeling Love FM
2-18-1-501 Kusagae, Chuo-ku, Fukuoka, 810-0045, Japan
PH/FX: 81-92-716-8848
Jeffrey Martin earthfeeling@yahoo.com
www.lovefm.co.jp
Features relaxing kinds of sounds and music that is described in Japan as "healing music," known more popularly in Europe and America as New Age. Ambient, Electronic, New Age, Contemporary Instrumental, Jazz, World and Classical.

Progressive Rock Radio

North America

United States

Afterglow WMUH
PO Box 632, Nazareth, PA 18064-0632
Bill Fox billyfox@soundscapes.us
soundscapes.us/afterglow
Mixed bag of Acoustic, Electric, Pop, New Age and Progressive Rock. Inquire by e-mail before submitting music.

Aural Moon
Davin Flateau avian@auralmoon.com
www.auralmoon.com
A large portion of our playlist is from Independent artists.

CP Radio/The Canvas Prog Hour
Canvas Productions c/o Matt Sweitzer,
411 Lorraine Blvd. Pickerington, OH 43147
canvas@insight.rr.com
www.canvasproductions.net
Genre - Jazz Fusion, Prog & Art Rock.

Dreams Wide Awake WOSP
11800 UNF Drive, HB #2565,
Jacksonville, FL 32224
Jason Ellerbee jeller@unf.edu
www.unf.edu/~jeller/dreams.html
Features Progressive Rock and related music.

Epic Rock Radio
Kailef submissions@epicrockradio.com
www.epicrockradio.com
We regularly feature independent artists, as long as the style (Symphonic / Melodic / Power Metal) matches with what we play.

Gagliarchives WBZC
645 S. Forklanding Rd. #18,
Maple Shade, NJ 08052
PH: 609-332-2019 FX: 609-894-9440
Tom Gagliardi gagliarchives@yahoo.com
gagliarchives.com
A Progressive and Art Rock program.

Groove Traffic Control WHCL
198 College Hill Rd. Clinton, NY 13323
Sean stice@hamilton.edu
www.whcl.org
New and up-coming jam oriented music.

Koolkat's Odd Sky
Koolkat koolkatsoddsky@verizon.net
groups.msn.com/KoolkatsOddSky
Prog Rock Internet station.

Newgrass, Prog & More!
HCR 66, Box 1999, Mathews, VA 23109
Steve Sikes-Nova/virginiaprograsser MFSB@SAFe-mail.net
www.live365.com/stations/virginiaprograsser
www.progressiveradiocat.com
The best in Newgrass, Progressive Rock, Indie & Alternative. Musicians are welcome to submit CDs.

Night Vision WITR
PO Box 20563, Rochester, NY 14602-0563
PH: 585-475-5643 FX: 585-475-4988
jluminous@hotmail.com
www.modernmusicandmore.com
The best in Progressive Rock from all across the globe! If you have a band looking for a new audience, get in touch with us about airplay.

Open-Ears
dj@open-ears.com
www.open-ears.com
Comments, suggestions and submissions are always welcomed here!

The Pit WYBF
c/o Joe Stevenson, 610 King of Prussia Rd.
Radnor, PA 19087
PH: 610-902-8457
www.wybf.com
The authority on Progressive Rock, Jazz, Jam and New Age music.

Planet Prog
PO Box 04512, Milwaukee, WI 53204
Mark Krueger markakrueger@hotmail.com
planetprog.com
Playing Progressive Rock from around the globe. You are invited to send your promotional discs and information for airplay consideration to the above address.

Plastic Tales from the Marshmallow Dimension WNYU
c/o Music Director, 194 Mercer St. 5th Fl.
New York, NY 10012
The Paisley Piper plastictales@wnyu.org
www.wnyu.org/plastictales
Blow your mind with a weekly 'dose' of Psychedelic, Garage, Mod...

Progged Radio
6435 W. Wenden Way, Tucson, AZ 85743
Chan Weinmeister chan@proggedradio.com
www.proggedradio.com
Focuses on the harder edge of Progressive music.

progradio.com
pdirector@progradio.com
www.progradio.com
Progressive music for your mind!

Progressive Positivity Radio
Attn: Mark Stephens, 3301 Claymore Dr.
Plano, TX 75075
musicoptimist@yahoo.com
www.progpositivity.com
launch.groups.yahoo.com/group/progpositivity
We are very proud to feature the best (and most positive) Independent Progressive Rock bands on our station and on our e-mail discussion list. We play a wide variety of Progressive Rock!

The Progressive Rock Radio Network
progradio@progradio.net
www.progradio.net
Discover the joys of Progressive music.

Progressive Soundscapes Radio
artist-contact@progressivesoundscapes.com
progressivesoundscapes.com
Supports independent or signed to small labels bands.

The Prog-Rock Diner WEBR
2929 Eskridge Rd. #S, Fairfax, VA 22031
PH: 703-573-1090 x1018
www.fcac.org/webr/webr.htm
Prog from all over the world.

progrock.com
www.progrock.com
Can only accept Ogg Vorbis files with the quality set to 5 for playback.

Starstream
Anthony starstream@paracom.net
starstream.musiconnect.com
Broadcasting many of the Progressive sub-genres.

The Trip WRFL
U. Kentucky, PO Box 777,
Lexington, KY 40506-0025
Clay Gaunce thetrip@pop.uky.edu
www.uky.edu/~wrfl/trip/trip.html
Send us your music.

WEER Radio
John W. Patterson eermusic@nc.rr.com
www.JazzRock-Radio.com
Jazz Rock Fusion show. Each show is guaranteed as good or better than the show aired last week!

Ytesjam Radio
webmaster@ytseradio.com
www.ytseradio.com
Progressive Rock, Progressive Metal.

Canada

The Dividing Line
9 - 32442 Dahlstrom Ave. #694,
PO Box 8000, Stn. Main, Abbotsford, BC V2S 6H1
promotions@thedividingline.com
www.thedividingline.com
Promotes artists by playing their music and broadcasting interviews.

La Villa Strangiato CHUO
Gary Lauzon and Gilles Potvin lavilla@yantz.com
www.yantz.com/lavilla
Are you in a Prog band wanting airplay on the radio to get the recognition you deserve? Drop me an email and I will be glad to give you my address and play your material on my show!

South America

The Musical Box Argentina
eventos@themusicalbox.com.ar
www.themusicalbox.com.ar
Progressive Rock radio show.

Europe

France

Instinct Progressif
c/o RCF Accords, 226 rue de Bordeaux, 16021
Angoulême Cedex, France
Arnaud metalnono@free.fr
instinct.prog.free.fr
Pour les groupes qui souhaiterais être diffusés durant l'émission, vous pouvez nous envoyer vos démos à l'adresse de la radio, accompagnées d'une petite biographie du groupe.

Morow.com
info@morow.net
morow.com
THE Prog Radio!

Opposition de phase
41bis bvd Vauban, 59046 LILLE cedex, France
PH: 33-03-20-54-12-11 FX: 33-03-20-30-40-51
Sebastien Petit petit.sebastien@online.fr
membres.lycos.fr/sleeprev/menu.html
Progressive Rock, new and creative music radio show with reviews and discographies.

Germany

Progdependent Rockin` Radio
Banderbacher Str. 24, 90513 Zirndorf, Germany
PH/FX: 0911-60-95-95
progdependent@rockin-radio.de
www.rockin-radio.de

The Netherlands

Mark From Holland Radio Show
Simon van Haerlemstraat 34, 1962 VC Heemskerk,
The Netherlands
PH: ++31-251-246497
Mark C. Deren mcd@wanadoo.nl
www.markfromholland.com
It is recommended to "follow-up" submissions of music with a request via e-mail for a Sunday night "on air" interview. The conversations usually last 5-7 minutes.

Paperlate
Andre Steijns, Boompjesdijk 102, 4671 PT
Dinteloord, The Netherlands
PH: 31-0-167566111 FX: 31-0-167566111
paperlte@westbrabant.net
home.concepts.nl/~paperlte
Concentrates on Classic, Progressive and Psychedelic Rock.

Psychedelicatessen Radio Patapoe
f.renier@kennisnet.nl
freeteam.nl/patapoe
Psychedelic and Progressive music show.

Symfomania
symfomania@xs4all.nl
home.wanadoo.nl/symfomania
Progressive, Symphonic & Melodic Rock show. If you have new material that you would like us to play, get in touch!

Punk Radio

North America

United States

The Anti-Emo Empire! WNHU
PO Box 5392, Milford, CT 06460
PH: 203-934-9296
Jeff Terranova theantiemoempire@earthlink.net
www.theantiemoempire.com
Spinning the best rare old school and new school Hardcore/Punk.

BaconBitz Radio
Eddie Barella eddie@baconbitzradio.com
www.baconbitz.com
The Heinz 57 of Rock radio with an Alternative focus.

The Bitter Sky Tonight *WBWC*
275 Eastland Rd. Berea OH, 44017
PH: 440-826-2145 FX: 440-826-3426
www.wbwc.com
3 hours of Rock influenced emo, Indie, and emo-Hardcore.

The Cherry Blossom Clinic *WFMU*
Attn: Terre T, PO Box 5101,
Hoboken, NJ 07030
www.wfmu.org/playlists/TT
Please DON'T send any attached files of any type (no flyers, MP3s, etc). Also, DON'T contact me and ask if I played your CD or demo. Check my playlist to find out.

Coffee n' Smokes *WMFO*
PO Box 65, Medford, MA 02153
PH: 617-625-0800
coffeensmokes@verizon.net
coffeensmokes.freeservers.com
Garage/Punk, Surf, Psychedelic, Rockabilly, Pop obscurities...

DIY Radio *WAPS*
65 Steiner Ave. Akron, OH 44301
PH: 330-761-3099 FX: 330-761-3240
diy@diyradio.net
www.diyradio.net
A Punk Rock radio show.

Etiquette of Violence *KDHX*
3504 Magnolia, St. Louis, MO 63118
PH: 314-664-3955 FX: 314-664-1020
Cricket O'Neill etiquetteofviolence@kdhx.org
www.kdhx.org
A tasteful array of Pop/Rock/Punk/Country.

Hussieskunk
PO Box 1599, Reynoldsburg, OH 43068
Matt mattg@hussieskunk.com
www.hussieskunk.com
Every CD we receive is reviewed and promoted on our site, as well as featured on our show.

idobi.com Radio
1825 New Hampshire Ave. #407,
Washington, DC 20009
pr@idobi.com
www.idobi.com/radio
Broadcasts Alternative Rock and Punk music. We are committed to bringing you the best of the known (and not-so-well-known) artist from around the world.

In Your Ear *KRCB*
5850 Labath Ave. Rohnert Park, CA 94928
PH: 707-585-8522 FX: 707-585-1363
Rosa Corn rosacorn@sonic.net
www.krcb.org
We feature new independent music of the "Alternative" flavor.

Mohawk Radio
10862 Coronel Rd. #B, Santa Ana, CA 92705
Rich Z. richz@mohawkradio.com
www.mohawkradio.com
Punk Rock streaming radio and MP3s. Hundreds of bands and Punk MP3s for download. Check our site for submission guidelines.

Music to Spazz By *WFMU*
c/o Brian Turner, PO Box 5101, Hoboken, NJ 07030
PH: 201-521-1416
www.wfmu.org/~spazz
Hillbilly chimpanzee Punk Rock rhythm n' Blues surf garage radio show!

The Next Big Thing *KALX*
26 Barrows Hall #5650, Berkeley, CA 94720-5650
PH: 510-642-1111
Marshall Stax robins@ix.netcom.com
kalx.berkeley.edu
Showcase for demo and pre-released music. CD-Rs and cassette formats OK... NO vinyl, no mass-produced CDs. Featuring material available only on CD-Rs and cassettes. I want Punk, Hardcore, emocore...anything with an edge, passion or purpose.

The No Show *KDHX*
3504 Magnolia, St. Louis, MO 63118
PH: 314-664-3955 FX: 314-664-1020
Brett Underwood noshow@kdhx.org
www.kdhx.org
Punk, post-Punk, noisy and no-wave and more..

the pAved earth
www.thepavedearth.com
Exposes new and refreshing music to people.

Punk 45
info@pwrgrrl.com
www.radiopower.org
Punk Rock and New Wave Vinyl. Raw, timeless, anthems of dissent.

Punk University *WSOU*
400 S. Orange Ave. South Orange, NJ 07079
PH: 973-761-9768
wsou@shu.edu
www.wsou.net
Underground Punk and Ska.

Punk Up the Volume *KIWR*
2700 College Rd. Council Bluffs, IA 51503
PH: 712-325-3337
KC Jones riverpunk897@yahoo.com
www.897theriver.com
Punk music every Sunday night!

Rock Hell Radio
James Saltzman rockhellradio@yahoo.com
www.Rockhellradio.com
We accept music submissions from any Punk band.

Shredding Radio
PO Box 2271, San Rafael, CA 94912
shreddingpaper@netscape.net
www.shreddingradio.com
Underground Pop, Britpop, J-pop, New Wave, Riot Grrrl and Shoegazer!

Super Fun Happy Hour *KDHX*
3504 Magnolia, St. Louis, MO 63118
PH: 314-664-3955 FX: 314-664-1020
Tim, Matt and Heather
superfunhappyhour@kdhx.org
www.kdhx.org
Punk Rock from the 70's to the latest independent and major label releases of today.

The Super Rock Fun Show
Dave thesuperrockfunshow@excite.com
www.geocities.com/superrockfunshow
The best in Punk/Indie/Underground Rock.

Total Punk Radio
PO Box 64862, Phoenix, AZ 85082-4862
chris@totalpunkradio.com
www.totalpunkradio.com
Send us your CD/demo/press info and we'll get you on the radio!!

Under the Big Top *WMUA*
105 Campus Ctr. U. Mass, Amherst, MA 01003
PH: 413-545-2876 FX: 413-545-0682
www.wmua.org/index2.shtml
Punk to Ska, Emo to Hardcore and more.

The Wayback Machine *KDHX*
3504 Magnolia, St. Louis, MO 63118
PH: 314-664-3955 FX: 314-664-1020
www.garagepunk.com
Bands and labels, submit material for airplay.

WDOA.com
128 Mechanic St., Spencer, MA 01562
FX: 253-323-1606
Mike Malone wdoainfo@wdoa.com
wdoa.com
We actively encourage independent bands and artists to send us their music.

Canada

Danko Radio
240 Clayton St. E., Listowel, ON N4W 2G1
Paul Cardiff citizenk@danko-radio.com
danko-radio.com
Home of the best underground Punk, Metal, Rock and whatever else we feel like playing.

Flex Your Head Radio Show *CITR*
#233-6138 SUB Blvd. Vancouver, BC V6T 1Z1
PH: 604-822-8733 FX: 604-822-9364
info@flexyourhead.net
www.flexyourhead.net
Long running Hardcore/Punk radio program.

PunkRadioCast
6-295 Queen St. E. #388, Brampton, ON L6W 4S6
PH: 905-495-6003
info@punkradiocast.com
www.punkradiocast.com
Features a variety of Punk related shows.

Europe

France

Ecrasons La Vermine *Radio Campus Lille*
Kalimero, BP 21, 59007 Lille cedex, France
chpunk@chpunk.org
chpunk.org/elv
Punk, Hardcore, oi!, Crust, Ska...

United Kingdom

Generica
Genericaradio@hotmail.com
www.live365.com/stations/omegamoses
Features music from numerous genres, haphazardly and amateurishly thrown together for your enjoyment. Alternative, Punk and Indie.

Hardcore Street Sounds *TotalRock*
Anne Maria1 Denmark Pl. London, WC2H 8NL UK
annmahss@aol.com
www.hardcorestreetsounds.com
Punk and Hardcore with Oi!, Ska and Metal.

Radio Nowhere
Christopher radionowhere@talk21.com
www.live365.com/stations/297531
Alternative, Emo and Indie music show.

Reggae Radio

United States

400 Years: Radio Free Mondo *KZUM*
941 "O" St., Lincoln, NE 68508
PH: 402-474-5086 FX: 402-474-5091
Josh Jakoubek cv2109@columbia.edu
www.kzum.org
Roots Reggae show.

Beast Reggae *KTUH*
Honolulu, Hemenway Hall #203, 2445 Campus Rd.
Honolulu, HI 96822.
PH: 808-956-4848
Big Bar bigbar@ktuh.org
ktuh.org/beastreggae
Roots Reggae show. Our "Progression Session" segment features all new releases.

Creation Steppin'
John Reichle jreichle@scottsboro.org
www.creation-steppin.com
Classic and modern Roots Reggae; many of whom are independent artists.

Dub Mixture *KDHX*
3504 Magnolia, St. Louis, MO 63118
PH: 314-664-3955 FX: 314-664-1020
www.kdhx.org
The hottest Reggae in the classic Dub style with DJ Ranx.

Everything Off Beat *WLUW*
6525 N. Sheridan Rd. Chicago, IL 60626
PH: 773-508-8080 FX: 773-508-8082
musicdept@wluw.org
wluw.org
The world's premier Ska oriented radio show.

Ithaska *WVBR*
957 Mitchell St. #B, Ithaca, NY 14850
PH: 607-273-4000 FX: 607-273-4069
ithaska@ithaska.com
ithaska.com
Despite our name, we play all sorts of music.

Jammin Reggae Radio
eznoh@niceup.com
niceup.com
The Gateway to Reggae Music on the Internet!

Kingston Beat *WXXE*
826 Euclid Ave. Syracuse, NY 13210
PH: 315-455-5624 FX: 315-701-0303
wxxe.org
Explorations in Ska, Rock Steady and Reggae, with an emphasis on new interpretations of the more traditional Jamaican forms.

The Night Shift *KDHX*
3504 Magnolia, St. Louis, MO 63118
PH: 314-664-3955 FX: 314-664-1020
Kevin Straw roots@kdhx.org
www.kdhx.org
Reggae, Dub, and Groove.

Play I Some Music *WXXE*
826 Euclid Ave. Syracuse, NY 13210
PH: 315-455-5624 FX: 315-701-0303
Papa Andy playisomemusic@email.com
wxxe.org
The best in Reggae, African and Caribbean music, covering all eras and styles.

Positive Vibes *WXCI*
181 White St., Danbury, CT 06811
PH: 203-837-8387
WXCIDanbury@yahoo.com
www.myspace.com/wxci
Over 10 years on the air. Where it's warm and sunny and the vibes are positive.

Positive Vibrations *KDHX*
3504 Magnolia, St. Louis, MO 63118
PH: 314-664-3955 FX: 314-664-1020
Professor Skank pskank@kdhx.org
Michael Kuelker positivevibes_michael@kdhx.org
www.kdhx.org
For the latest - and the greatest - in Reggae music.

Reggae Rhythms *WAPS*
412 Bettie St. #A, Akron, OH 44306-1212
PH: 330-761-3099 FX: 330-761-3240
B. E. Mann theenergyman@cs.com
www.bemann.com/reggaerhythms.html
www.913thesummit.com
Reggae music from the US and abroad.

The Reggae Ride *WDNA*
PO Box 558636, Miami, FL 33255
PH: 305-662-8889 FX: 305-662-1975
Flagga Dupes flagga@wdna.org
www.wdna.org
Authentic Reggae music from Ska (60's) to present.

The Reggae Train *KRBS*
PO Box #9, Oroville, CA 95965
www.radiobirdstreet.org
Classic Roots Reggae music.

reggaemania.com
rnelson@reggaemania.com
www.reggaemania.com
Discover the pulse of the dancehall.

Rocket Ship Ska Trip *KFAI*
1808 Riverside Ave. Minneapolis, MN 55454
PH: 612-341-3144
Capt. 2much FREETIME capt2much@yahoo.com
www.kfai.org/programs/rocketst.htm

Roots, Rock, Reggae *KUSP*
PO Box 423, Santa Cruz, CA 95061
PH: 831-476-2800
www.kusp.org/playlists/rrr
The best from the Reggae world.

Saturday's a Party *WUSB*
Student Union Bld. SUNY,
Stony Brook, NY 11794-3263 Attn: Music Director
PH: 631-632-6500 FX: 631-632-7182
musicwusb·fm
wusb.fm
The longest-running Reggae-politics mix (RPM) in the USA. Den de Dubwise playyyyyyy, it play, it play!!! Hosted by Lister Hewan-Lowe.

Ska*Anarchy
skashow@yahoo.com
www.geocities.com/skashow
This is your Ska station!

Ska's The Limit *KDHX*
3504 Magnolia, St. Louis, MO 63118
PH: 314-664-3955 FX: 314-664-1020
Paul Stark stlska@mindspring.com
home.mindspring.com/~stlska/ska.htm
A weekly all-Ska radio show.

Tropical Reggae *KGLP*
200 College Dr. Gallup, NM 87301
PH: 505-863-7626 FX: 505-863-7633
Steve Buggie buggie@unm.edu
www.kglp.org/tropicalreggae
You'll hear the finest in Reggae music from the Caribbean, Africa or elsewhere.

Tunnel One *WNYU*
194 Mercer Str. 5th Fl. New York, NY 10012
PH: 212-998-1660 FX: 212-998-1652
Dee Jay Mush One tunnelone@wnyu.org
www.wnyu.org
Old school, Rocksteady and third wave Ska.

Vibes of the Time *KRUA*
PO Box 20-2831, Anchorage, AK 99520
PH: 907-223-4531
Ras Jahreal dready@gci.net
reggaealaska.com/jahreal
The longest running show on KRUA (12 years strong!). After the Most High, in Reggae we trust. Featuring Roots Reggae, Dancehall Dub and Lovers Rock.

West Indian Rhythms *WWUH*
Attn: Music Director,
200 Bloomfield Ave. West Hartford, CT 06117
PH: 860-768-4701 FX: 860-768-5701
Philip Mitchell pearl286@aol.com
www.wwuh.org
A blend of music and information straight from the Caribbean. A rich mixture of Calypso and Reggae.

Canada

Caribbean Linkup *CJSW*
caribbeanlinkup@shaw.ca
members.shaw.ca/caribbeanlinkup
Dedicated to the Caribbean - news, views and music. E-mail for address to submit.

Reggae in the Fields *CKCU*
U. Center Rm 517, 1125 Colonel By Dr.
Ottawa, ON K1S 5B6
PH: 613-520-2898
Junior Smith reggaeinthefields@canada.com
www.ckcufm.com
The longest-running Reggae program in Canada.

Scratch
scratch@azevedo.ca
www.azevedo.ca/scratch
Early-1960's Ska, through Rocksteady, Reggae and on to modern-day Dub.

Ska Party *CIUT*
c/o Music Dept, 91 St. George St.,
Toronto, ON M5S 2E8
DJ Skip skaparty@ciut.fm
www.skapages.com/skip
Features interviews, news, reviews and some schmooze. How can we spread the word if we don't know about it? Send your goods and info!

Jamaica

IrieFM.net
Coconut Grove, Ocho Rios, St. Ann, Jamaica
PH: 876-974-5051 FX: 876-974-5943
info@iriefm.net
www.iriefm.net
24-hour all-Reggae station.

Belgium

Reggae Connection
68 rue de Roux. 6140 Fontaine l'Evêque, Belgium
Salvatore Baldacchino reggaeconnection@be.tf
www.reggaeconnection.be.tf
If you have new promo releases press info, send them to the above address.

France

Dance Hall Style *Radio Mega*
DJ Prince Thierry princethierry@wanadoo.fr
www.dancehallstyle.net
All styles of Reggae with a little bit emphasis on Roots, Oldies and Dub.

Dub Action *Radio Canut*
24, rue Sergent Blandan 1er arrdt - BP 1101 - 69201
LYON Cedex, France
PH: 04-78-39-18-15 FX: 04-78-29-26-00
Bassta bassta69@hotmail.com
regardeavue.com/radiocanut
Ici toute les composantes de la musique jamaïcaine sont d'actualité: du Mento, du Ska, du Rock Steady, du Reggae etc.

Germany

Freedom Sounds
Radio Flora, Zur Bettfedernfabrik 1, 30451
Hannover, Germany
Peter Roth info@freedomsounds.de
www.freedomsounds.de
Reggae show based in Germany on Radio Flora.

United Kingdom

BBC Radio 1xtra *Dancehall*
www.bbc.co.uk/1xtra/dancehall
Home page of the BBC 1xtra's various Dancehall shows. Info, shows, contacts etc.

Israel

Reggae Power
Dr. Reggae drreggae@irielion.com
www.irielion.com/israel/reggae_power.htm
The best Reggae vibes from the best radio station!

Soul / R&B Radio

Radio Promotion

Monet Radio Promotions
PH: 832-545-0998
Arsdale Harris monetproductions@comcast.net
www.monetproductionsinc.com/monetradiopromo.html
Over 100 radio program directors and DJs in our contact database.

Stations

United States

African New Dawn *WRSU*
126 College Ave. New Brunswick, NJ 08901
PH: 732-932-8800 FX: 732-932-1768
wrsu@wrsu.rutgers.edu
wrsu.rutgers.edu
Promotes new, unknown and un(der)exposed music artists and music companies.

blackmusicamerica.com
support@bossnetworks.com
www.blackmusicamerica.com
Music, information, culture and entertainment for the Black community.

BlakeRadio.com
PO Box 403, Massapequa Park, NY 11762
PH: 866-269-7197
CustomerService@BlakeRadio.com
www.blakeradio.com
R&B, Jazz, Soul and Reggae slow jams.

Blame it on the Media
starseed105@yahoo.com
www.live365.com/stations/starseed
Eclectic Hip Hop, Electronica, Funk and Rock. A place where anything goes...don't get trapped in one reality...

Broke N' Beat Radio
221 Poplar St. Rear Apt. Philadelphia, PA 19123
brokenbeatradio@gmail.com
www.brokenbeatradio.com
Pushing the latest Broken Beat, Nu Jazz and Soul sounds.

Chocolate City *KCRW*
1900 Pico Blvd. Santa Monica, CA 90405
PH: 310-450-5183 FX: 310-450-7172
Garth Trinidad garth.trinidad@kcrw.org
www.kcrw.org
A progressive mix of Soul, Hip Hop and World Rhythms.

Etherbeat Radio
14781 Memorial Dr. #1791, Houston, TX 77079
www.etherbeat.com
Free and Funky internet radio. Funk, Soul, Jazz, Latin, World, Afro, Reggae..

Fusebox *WRSU*
126 College Ave. New Brunswick, NJ 08901
PH: 732-932-8800 FX: 732-932-1768
DJ Fusion shortmary@ureach.com
wrsu.rutgers.edu
Supports new, unknown and un(der)exposed music artists.

Invincible Radio
#107, 203 Mare Studios, London, E8 3QE UK
PH: +44-0208-525-4131
info@invincibleradio.com
www.invincibleradio.com
The world's market-leading radio station for new music, bringing you the future today.

Key56
PH: 619-835-9614
key56radio@yahoo.com
www.Key56internetradio.com
Classic Soul, R&B, Jazz, Funk and today's R&B.

KJLH
161 N. La Brea Ave. Inglewood, CA 90301
PH: 310-330-2200 FX: 310-330-5555
www.kjlhradio.com
To get your music played, call us to set up an appointment.

KPOO
PO Box 423030, San Francisco, CA 94142
PH: 415-346-5373 FX: 415-346-5173
www.kpoo.com
The first Black station in the country to be on-line. Specializes in Jazz, Reggae, Salsa, Blues, Gospel and Hip Hop.

KPVU *Waller County*
PO Box 519 Prairie View, TX 77446-0519
PH: 936-857-5788
www.pvamu.edu/kpvu

Liquid Sound Lounge *WBAI*
120 Wall Street, 10th Fl. New York, NY 10005
PH: 212-209-2800 x2931
radio@liquidsoundlounge.com
www.liquidsoundlounge.com
Devoted to exposing Soul infused grooves of all persuasions.

LiquidSoulRadio.com
875 Lawrenceville-Suwanee Rd. #310-120,
Lawrenceville, GA 30043
PH: 866-323-8074
www.liquidsoulradio.com
A vast array of musical genres of Neo-Soul, R&B, Jazz and Hip Hop.

The Listening Lounge with Alysia Cosby *WEIB*
Alysia submissions@thelisteninglounge.com
thelisteninglounge.com
A hip and groovy mix of Chillout, Jazz, Soul, Brazilian, Latin and World rhythms.

Love Radio
238 Auburn Ave. Atlanta, GA 30303
PH: 404-523-2656
tdavis@dr-love.com
www.dr-love.com
Channels include Blues, R&B, Rap, Hiphop, World and Reggae.

The Love Zone *WHCR*
1026 6th Ave #301 S., New York, NY 10018
PH: 917-545-2169
Maurice Watts MauriceWatts@MauriceWatts.com
www.mauricewatts.com
For over 22 years playing some of the best R&B love songs of the past and present.

projectVIBE
submissions@projectvibe.net
projectvibe.net
Representing the best of Soul-influenced music online. From Neo-Soul rhythms to Deep House, from Jazz to Classic R&B. Visit our site for submission details.

Radio Host DJ Come of Age
PH: 850-276-2188
DJ Come of Age djcomeofage@yahoo.com
www.djcoa.com
I have mix shows on several Internet stations. If you play Soul, R&B, Funk, Jazz, or anything mellow then contact me to have your track or full-length CD featured for a show.

RadioBlack.com
webmaster@mail.radioblack.org
www.radioblack.com
A guide to radio stations around the world.

RHYTHMflow Radio
PO Box 130, Bronx, NY 10467
rhythmflowradio@rhythmflow.net
www.rhythmflow.net/Radio.html
We're always looking for R&B, Jazz, Gospel, and other neglected music genres (sorry, no Rap or Hip Hop) to add to our playlist.

Slow Jam
1528 6th St. #501, Santa Monica, CA 90401
Kevin James slowjam@verizon.net
www.slowjam.com
The best R&B slow jams, both old & new. I do mix in some independent music.

smoothbeats.com
www.smoothbeats.com
Streaming non-stop beats 24 hours a day.

Solar Radio
PH: +44-8707-451-879
info@solarradio.com
www.solarradio.com
The best in Soul, Jazz, Funk and other related music.

The Soul Lounge / Groovenation
2870 Peachtree Rd. #404, Atlanta, GA 30305
PH: 877-636-7685
www.groovenation.net
Your online resource to the Soul community.

Soul Patrol Radio
Bob Davis earthjuice@prodigy.net
www.soul-patrol.com
A celebration of great Black Music from the Ancient to the future. It's all about Soul, Jazz, Blues, Rock, Funk and the culture they evolved from.

Soul Spectrum *WMBR*
3 Ames St., Cambridge, MA 02142
PH: 617-253-4000
Josh McDermott soul@wmbr.org
wmbr.mit.edu
Soul sounds from past and present. From Classic Soul, Rare Grooves, Disco and Boogie up to current Nu-Soul and Deep House.

SoulSis Radio
stephanie@soulsis.net
www.soulsis.net/radio.html
Programming ranges from R&B to Hip Hop to Jazz...I will eventually incorporate some Gospel!

Southern Exposure *KRUA*
3211 Providence Dr. Anchorage, AK 99508
PH: 907-786-6805
Marcus lrd47@hotmail.com
www.uaa.alaska.edu/krua
Rap and R&B by a lot of artists outside of the Top 20.

Urban Landscapes
1029 Southwood Dr. #D,
San Luis Obispo, CA 93401
Velanche Stewart mail@urbanlandscapes.org
www.urbanlandscapes.org
I play a choice selection of music, including Funk & Soul (old school & new sounds), Latin/Brazilian, Soulful House. Feel free to send materials (vinyl preferred, but CDs & minidiscs are acceptable) for airplay/club play/review consideration.

UrbanSoulNation
music@smoothfm.com
admin@urbansoulnation.com
urbansoulnation.com
#1 Destination for Urban lifestyle and streaming R&B music. We also feature and review the music of independent artists.

WHCR *City College of New York*
138th and Convent Ave. Nac Building, Rm 1515,
New York, NY 10031
PH: 212-650-7481
whcr903fm@yahoo.com
www.whcr.org

WMOC
info@mocradio.com
www.mocradio.com
R&B to Hip Hop to Old School to House Music.

WNAA *North Carolina A & T State U.*
200 Price Hall, Greensboro, NC 27411
PH: 336-334-7936 FX 336-334-7960
Mamie J. wnaafm@ncat.edu
wnaalive.ncat.edu

France

Right On FM
7 Rue du Stade, 57050 Longeville - Les - Metz, France
PH/FX: +33 (0) 3-87-63-86-54
contact@righton-fm.com
www.righton-fm.com
A melting pot of Jazz, Soul, Funk, DnB, NuJazz etc.

Touchofsoul
Céline touchofsoul@free.fr
touchofsoul.free.fr

The Netherlands

Royal Groove
royalgroove@royalgroove.org
www.royalgroove.org
We have grown to encompass all types of black music, historical and contemporary, starting with Funk and Soul, and going from Jazz to Bossa Nova, from Hip Hop to Latin, Afro-Beat and everything in between.

SaveOurSoul
crew@saveoursoul.nl
saveoursoul.nl
Playing the best in today's R&B and Classic Soul. We also review and interview some of the artists we play.

United Kingdom

The Basic Soul Radio Show
www.basic-soul.co.uk
Syndicated show broadcasting through various stations online.

BBC Radio 1xtra *RnB*
www.bbc.co.uk/1xtra/rnb
Home page of the BBC 1xtra's various RnB shows. Info, shows, contacts etc.

BBC Radio 2 *Blues, Soul and Reggae*
www.bbc.co.uk/radio2/r2music/blues
Home page of the BBC Radio 2's various Soul and Reggae shows. Info, shows, contacts etc.

boombastic radio
27 Franklin St., Brighton, BN2 3AL UK
www.boombastic.org
Free and funky Internet radio. Funk, Soul, Jazz, Hip Hop, Latin...

Choice FM
291 - 299 Borough High St., London, SE1 1JG UK
PH: 0207 378 3969 FX: 0207 378 3911
www.choicefm.net
The future of Urban music radio & culture.

Women in Music Radio

North America

United States

Amazon Radio Show *WPKN*
PO Box 217, New Haven, CT 06513
Pamela S. Smith psmith@amazonradio.com
www.amazonradio.com
Welcomes music from women everywhere, all styles.

Assorted Women *WDIY*
301 Broadway, Bethlehem, PA 18015
PH: 610-694-8100 FX: 610-954-9474
info@wdiyfm.org
www.wdiyfm.org
From Folk-Rockers to Jazz greats, from soul divas to torch singers: It's not just chicks with guitars...

The Bonus Cup Radio Show *WOWL*
777 Glades Road U. Ctr. Rm 207D,
Boca Raton, FL 33431
PH: 561-297-3759 FX: 561-297-3771
thundergrrl@rocketmail.com
listen.to/thebonuscup
If you are in a Punk or Indie oriented band with at least one female member, drop me an email and let me know about you!!!

Bread & Roses *KBOO*
20 SE 8th Ave. Portland, OR 97214
PH: 503-231-8032 FX: 503-231-7145
www.kboo.fm
Public Affairs radio produced and engineered by women.

Chick Rock Radio
4065 S. Braeswood Blvd. #148, Houston, TX 77025
Attn: Jenny Morgan
www.chickrockradio.com
Covers ALL genres. Please submit your CD or MP3 files w/track listing, email address, and a few photos to be added to our featured artist section.

Chicks Rock Radio
info@gogirlsmusic.com
www.live365.com/stations/gogirlsrock
Featuring unknown, and undiscovered female fronted bands across the country. If you know a great female band in your local town or are in one, send me an email and I'll get 'em on the station!

Church of Girl Radio
1405 SE Belmont #65, Portland, OR 97214-2669
PH: 503-819-9201
Mary Ann Naylor radiogirl@churchofgirl.com
www.churchofgirl.com
An Internet radio station featuring 14 different rotations of lady-made music.

Circle of Women *KBOO*
20 SE 8th Ave. Portland, OR 97214
PH: 503-231-8032 FX: 503-231-7145
Annelise Hummel annelieseh99@yahoo.com
www.kboo.fm
Covering women's issues and all genres of music.

Country Girls Only Radio
CountryGirlsOnly@yahoo.com
www.live365.com/stations/140113
The newest songs of your favorite female artists.

Diva Radio *KUSF*
2130 Fulton St., San Francisco, CA 94117
PH: 415-386-5873
kusf@usfca.edu
www.kusf.org
A focus on women's independently produced music.

The Eclectic Woman *WTJU*
PO Box 400811, Charlottesville, VA 22904-4811
PH: 434-924-0885 FX: 434-924-8996
wtju.radio.virginia.edu/eclectic
Showcases female singer-songwriters.

Enchantress Radio *Radio Free Tunes*
Paul Carosi radiofreetunes@yahoo.com
www.artistlaunch.com/enchantressradio
An online streaming music station that features female artists

the ESTROGEN zone
Red redone@redontheweb.net
www.redontheweb.net
Music beyond bimbos. No trashy fluffy music. Just real women making real music that's real good.

Estrogenius
arhythmius@hotmail.com
www.arhythmius.com
Features ONLY female artists. Alternative, Indies, Trance, Rock and even Pop.

EVE OUTLOUD *WICB*
118 Park Hall, Ithaca, NY 14850
PH: 607-274-1040 x1 FX: 607-274-1061
wicbmusic@yahoo.com
www.ithaca.edu/radio/wicb
We're ALWAYS looking to promote new artists!

Every Woman *WAIF*
PO Box 6126, Cincinnati, OH 45206
PH: 513-961-8900
waif@waif883.org
www.waif883.org
Women's music and issues. Send material.

The Female Form *KBGA*
University Center, Missoula, MT 59812
PH: 406-243-5715
kbga@selway.umt.edu
kbga.org
All female artists and bands: from Country to Punk.

Female Musician Radio
157 Fort Salonga Rd. Northport, NY 11768
tj@femalemusician.com
www.femalemusician.com
Promotes and empowers women pursuing a music career.

The Feminine Groove
Barb Hill brnshuga61@yahoo.com
www.cyberstationusa.com
The best music, from today's women artists.

Feminist Magazine *KPFK*
3729 Cahenga Blvd. W.
North Hollywood, CA 91604
feministmagazine@yahoo.com
www.feministmagazinc.org
Public affairs show that eagerly spotlights the work of women in all walks of life.

La Femme Fatale *WBRS*
Brandeis U. 415 South St.,
Waltham, MA 02453-2728
PH: 781-736-4785
music@wbrs.org
www.wbrs.org
Dedicated to dangerous women and their music.

Femme FM *KUT*
1 University Stn. A0704, Austin, TX 78712
PH: 512-471-1631 FX: 512-471-3700
Teresa Ferguson sanferg@austin.rr.com
www.kut.org
Music performed by women artists of all genres.

General Eclectic *WCVF*
115 McEwen Hall, SUNY Fredonia,
Fredonia, NY 14063
Tom Bingham mason2042@gmail.com
As the title indicates, this is an ALL-GENRE show. I am VERY much open to women artists on indie labels. All material for airplay should be sent to the above address.

Girlpowder Radio
PO Box 1841, Lafayette, CA 94549
PH: 866-475-7937 FX: 925-871-0365
info@girlpowder.com
www.girlpowder.com
Girlpowder has chosen to incorporate music.

The Girl's Room *KWVA*
PO Box 3157, Eugene, OR 97403
PH: 541-346-4091 FX: 541-346-0648
kwva@gladstone.uoregon.edu
gladstone.uoregon.edu/~kwva
Dedicated solely to female artists.

Grrrlville *WIDR*
1511 Faunce Student Service Bldg.
Kalamazoo, MI 49008-6301
PH: 269-387-6305
widr-music@groupwise.wmich.edu
www.widr.org
Delivering a diverse mix of female-fronted bands and singer-songwriters.

Her Infinite Variety *WORT*
118 S. Bedford S. Madison, WI 53703-2692
PH: 608-256-2001 FX: 608-256-3704
www.wort-fm.org
Showcases women in all genres/styles of music.

In Other Words *KUFM*
MPR, 32 Campus Dr. U. Montana,
Missoula, MT 59812-8064
PH: 406-243-4931 FX: 406-243-3299
www.kufm.org
Women's program of music, international news...

Instrumental Women *KSDS*
1313 Park Blvd. San Diego, CA 92101
PH: 619-234-1062 FX: 619-230-2212
jkocherh@sdccd.net
www.ksds-fm.org
Highlights women in Jazz.

Into the Light *KMFA*
3001 N. Lamar #100, Austin, TX 78705
PH: 512-476-5632 FX: 512-474-7463
Kathryn Mishell kmishell@austin.rr.com
www.kmfa.org
Devoted to the music of Classical women composers.

Kickin' Judy *KRCL*
1971 W. North Temple, Salt Lake City, UT 84116
Tracy and Angie kickinjudy@krcl.org
www.krcl.org/~tracyb
Alternative and Indie Rock!

Ladies First *WKNC*
NCSU Mail Ctr. Box 8607,
Raleigh, NC 27695-8607
PH: 919-515-2401 FX: 919-213-2353
wknc.org

The Ladies of Daemon
www.daemonrecords.com/beta/radio
Webcast playing the artists of Daemon Records.

Luscious Voices
Paul Cattro cattrone@hotmail.com
www.live365.com/stations/103350
Promotes the female vocalists/artists/sounds.

Moving On
PO Box 10652, Portland, OR 97296
L.C. Hansen lchansen@spiritone.com
www.KBOO.org
Political, feminist, pro guitar.

Murphy's Magic Mess *KZUM*
941 "O" St., Lincoln, NE 68508
PH: 402-474-5086 FX: 402-474-5091
Nadine Murphy programming@kzum.org
www.kzum.org
Alternative spirituality, New Age and Women's music.

Musique du Mouchette
mouchette@bust.com
www.live365.com/stations/254596
Grrrl Vocals Only!! (Punk, Riot Grrrl, Indie).

Nette Radio
7738 Forest Ln. #284, Dallas, TX 75230
Annette Conlon info@netteradio.com
www.netteradio.com/submit.html
Dedicated to promoting unsigned women musicians. From piano to Punk - it's great music by fab women artists, as well as discussion of current events and upcoming showcases around the country. PLEASE visit our website for submission details.

Nowhere To Go Radio
814 N 15th St., San Jose, CA 95112
Ursula Romanowski ursula@ntgradio.com
www.ntgradio.com
We play strictly women artists, both indie and mainstream. Please visit our website for submission details.

Odd Man Out *WUOG*
Box 2065 Tate Student Ctr. Athens, GA 30602
PH: 706-542-7100 FX: 706-542-0070
Haley Zapal programming@wuog.org
wuog.org
From Hardcore to Riot Grrrl, Punk to ambient and soothing melodies.

Other Voices *WORT*
118 S. Bedford S. Madison, WI 53703-2692
PH: 608-256-2001 FX: 608-256-3704
wort@terracom.net
www.wort-fm.org
Women composers, performers and conductors.

Pleasure Kittens *WXCI*
181 White St., Danbury, CT 06811
PH: 203-837-8387
WXCIDanbury@yahoo.com
www.myspace.com/wxci
Chick Rock!

The Red Spot *KCPR*
Graphic Arts Bldg 26, Rm 201, Cal Poly State U.
San Luis Obispo, CA 93407
PH: 805-756-2965
Bobbie Sox kcprMD@kcpr.org
www.kcpr.org
Featuring women in music of all genres.

Rocket Girl Radio
Trisha admin@rocketgirls.net
www.rocketgirls.net
We want girls that are eclectic, yet entertaining.

Sirens' Muse *WEVL*
PO Box 40952, Memphis, TN 38174
PH: 901-528-0560
brian@wevl.org
wevl.org
A variety of genres of contemporary music by women.

Sister Sound *KAOS*
CAB 301, 2700 Evergreen Pkwy.
Olympia, WA 98505
PH: 360-867-6896
kaos@evergreen.edu
www.kaosradio.org
Music and information for, by and about women.

Sisters *KLCC*
4000 E. 30th Ave. Eugene, OR 97405-0640
PH: 541-463-6000 FX: 541-463-6046
Nanci LaVelle lavellen@lanecc.edu
www.klcc.org
Features the best of female performances in virtually every genre of music.

Sisters *KVSC*
720 4th Ave. S., 27 Stewart Hall,
St. Cloud, MN 56301-4498
PH: 320-308-3126 FX: 320-308-5337
music@kvsc.org
www.kvsc.org
Women's music Sundays from 2-5pm.

Something About the Women *WMFO*
PO Box 65 Medford, MA 02155
PH: 617-625-0800
Susan Edelman suedelman@hotmail.com
www.wmfo.org
The voices of woman artists in all genres.

The Sound Job *WNCI*
PO Box 4972, 270 Mohegan Ave.
New London, CT 06320
PH: 860-439-2853 FX: 860-439-2805
wcni@conncoll.edu
www.wcniradio.org
All styles, all eras. Music by women only - so leave your dick at home.

Stroke the Goddess *WMHB*
Colby College, 4000 Mayflower Hill,
Waterville, ME 04901
PH: 207-872-3686
Annie aandandy@somtel.com
www.colby.edu/wmhb
A show devoted to music by female artists..

Suffragette City *KDHX*
3504 Magnolia, St. Louis, MO 63118
PH: 314-664-3955 FX: 314-664-1020
René Saller suffragette@kdhx.org
www.suffragettecity.org
The mood and pace? Challenging but not jarring; beautiful but not sappy; fun but not mindless.

Suffragette Station *KTUH*
2445 Campus Rd. Hemenway Hall #203,
Honolulu, HI 96822
PH: 808-956-5288 FX: 808-956-5271
Lori Saeki ssonktuh@ktuh.org
listen.to/ssonktuh
Showcasing the diversity of women's voices in contemporary Folk music.

T.G.I. Femmes *KZUM*
941 "O" St., Lincoln, NE 68508
PH: 402-474-5086 FX: 402-474-5091
Tad Frazier programming@kzum.org
www.kzum.org
An eclectic selection of women's music: Folk, Rock and fun.

Under the Skirt *WDBX*
224 N. Washington St., Carbondale, IL 62901
PH: 618-457-3691
wdbx@globaleyes.net
www.wdbx.org
Playing women vocalists (Jazz, Rock, Indie etc.)

Venus Rising *KRBS*
PO Box #9, Oroville, CA 95965
www.radiobirdstreet.org
Music by women. Local and underplayed.

Voices of Women *WRIU*
326 Memorial Union, Kingston, RI 02881
PH: 401-874-4949 FX: 401-874-4349
jpthabigga@aol.com
www.wriu.org

WCCS *Wheaton College*
Box W0977, Norton, MA 02766
PH: 508-286-3819
wccsmd@wheatoncollege.edu
wccs.wheatonma.edu
Various shows which focus on woman's music.

Wild Women Radio *WNHU*
300 Orange Ave. West Haven, CT 06516
PH: 203-934-8888 FX: 203-931-6055
wnhu@newhaven.edu
www.newhaven.edu/wnhu

The Wimmin's Music Program *KKUP*
PO Box 820 Cupertino, CA 95015
PH: 408-260-2999
Laura Testa rinaldi@cruzio.com
www.kkup.com
www.sans-serif.com/music.html
Music by, about and for women.

The Wimmin's Show *KZUM*
941 "O" St., Lincoln, NE 68508
PH: 402-474-5086 FX: 402-474-5091
thewimminsshow@hotmail.com
www.kzum.org
WANTED: Recorded music by, for, and about women.

Woman Song *KKFI*
PO Box 32250, Kansas City, MO 64171
PH: 816-931-3122 x106
www.kkfi.org
Music by Women for Women.

Woman Voices *KUNV*
1515 E Tropicana Ave. #240, Las Vegas, NV 89119
PH: 702-798-9115
kunv.unlv.edu
Want to hear some singing women?

Woman to Woman *KKFI*
PO Box 32250, Kansas City, MO 64171
PH: 816-931-3122 x106
www.kkfi.org
A public affairs show that plays the music of women artists.

Womanifesto *WUSC*
343 Russell House U. Union, 1400 Greene St.,
Columbia, SC 29208
PH: 803-777-7000
wuscsm@gwm.sc.edu
wusc.sc.edu
Two hours to honor women in music.

Womanotes *KBCS*
3000 Landerholm Cir. SE,
Bellevue, WA 98007-6484
PH: 425-564-2427
Mary Brabec & Tracey Wickersham
kbcsdj@ ctc.edu
kbcs.fm
Enjoy Jazz music by women.

Womanwaves *WFPK*
HSA Broadband Bldg. 619 S. 4th St.,
Louisville, KY 40202
PH: 502-814-6500
www.wfpk.org
Female artists (or fronted bands) send your stuff.

Women Hold Up Half the Sky *KALX*
26 Barrows Hall #5650, Berkeley, CA 94720-5650
PH: 510-642-1111
kalxmail@media.berkeley.edu
kalx.berkeley.edu
Talk radio and music by and about women.

Women in the 3rd Decade *KRCL*
1971 W. North Temple, Salt Lake City, UT 84116
PH: 801-363-1818 FX: 801-533-9136
Babs DeLay babs@urbanutah.com
www.krcl.org
News, information and mainly music by women.

Women in the Arts *KALX*
26 Barrows Hall #5650, Berkeley, CA 94720-5650
PH: 510-642-1111
kalxmail@media.berkeley.edu
kalx.berkeley.edu
Interviews, reviews, roundtables, music, artist spotlight segments.

Women In Music *NPR*
P.O. Box 15465, Boston, MA 02215
Laney Goodman WomenOnAir@aol.com
www.womenonair.com
Looking for exciting new female talent to add to our playlists!

Women In Music *WERS*
120 Boylston St., Boston, MA 02116
PH: 617-824-8891
womeninmusic@wers.org
www.wers.org

Women in Music *KRVM*
Sheldon HS, 2455 Willakenzie Rd.
Eugene, OR 97401
PH: 687-3381
Leigh wimusic@hotmail.com
www.myspace.com/womeninmusic
www.krvm.org
From Blues to New Wave to the most current to the obscure.

Women In Music *WTIP*
PO Box 1005, Grand Marais, MN 55604
PH: 218-387-1070 FX: 218-387-1120
wtip@boreal.org
wtip.org
A new perspective to women and their music, featured artists and interviews.

Women in Rock *WEFT*
113 N. Market St., Champaign, IL 61820
PH: 217-359-9338
weft@weftfm.org
www.weft.org

Women of the 90's *Live365*
PH: 440-228-6479
Mark Collins mecollins@ameritech.net
www.live365.com/stations/yngemcee
Features the music of women from the 90's to today.

Women of Jazz *KEWU*
E. Washington U. 104 R-TV Bldg.
Cheney, WA 99004-2431
PH: 509-359-4282
www.kewu.ewu.edu
Three hours of music from dazzling divas.

Women on Wednesday / One of Her Voices *KMUD*
PO Box 135, 1144 Redway Dr.
Redway, CA 95560-0135
PH: 707-923-2513 FX: 707-923-2501
Kate Klein md@kmud.org
www.kmud.org
Women's voices, women's issues and women's music.

Women on Women Music Hour *WLUW*
6525 N. Sheridan Rd. Chicago, IL 60626
PH: 773-508-8080 FX: 773-508-8082
wowmusichour@wluw.org
wluw.org
Focusing on female musicians from all genres.

Women Rock!
Chrystal chcjcamo@hotmail.com
www.live365.com/stations/49832?
Features women in many different genres.

Women Who Rock
152 Meads Cross Rd. Stormville, NY 12582
PH: 800-259-7130
Paul dos Santos cavalierhome@aol.com
www.freeworldradio.com

Women's Blues and Boogie *KZUM*
941 "O" St., Lincoln, NE 68508
PH: 402-474-5086 FX: 402-474-5091
Carol Griswold. cbluelf@aol.com
www.kzum.org
Legendary and contemporary female vocals.

Women's Collective *KVMR*
401 Spring St., Nevada City, CA 95959
PH: 530-265-9073 FX: 530-265-9077
womenscollective@kvmr.org
www.kvmr.org
A group of broadcasters dedicated to bringing women's voices and women's experiences to the airwaves.

Women's Independent Music Show
1940-2 Harrison St., Hollywood, FL 33020
Diane Ward info@wims.ws
www.wims.ws
Turning listeners on to great independent music.

Women's Music *KMUN*
PO Box 269, Astoria, OR 97103
PH: 503-325-0010
www.kmun.org

Women's Music Hour *WXPN*
3025 Walnut St., Philadelphia, PA 19104
PH: 215-898-6677. FX: 215-898-0707
wxpndesk@pobox.upenn.edu
xpn.org
Sixty minutes devoted to women's music.

Women's Music Radio *WMSE*
1025 N. Broadway, Milwaukee, WI 53202
PH: 414-799-1917
Jenny, Maria & Rose
musicwomen91_7@hotmail.com
www.geocities.com/musicwomen91_7
www.wmse.org
Every week we do our best to bring you the best in music from a wide variety of women artists!

Women's Music Show *KUMD*
130 Humanities, 1201 Ordean Ct.
Duluth, MN 55812
PH: 218-726-7181 FX: 218-726-6571
kumd@d.umn.edu
www.kumd.org
Music by women in all genres, with local interviews and information..

Women's Radio
2121 Peralta St. #138, Oakland, CA 94607
PH: 510-891-0004 FX: 510-891-0003
goladies@womensradio.com
www.womensradio.com
The music of every woman artist your heart desires.

Women's Rock *KBVR*
210 Memorial Union E. Corvallis, OR 97331
PH: 541-737-6323
oregonstate.edu/dept/kbvr

The Women's Show *WMNF*
1210 E. MLK Blvd. Tampa, FL 33603-4449
PH: 813-238-8001 FX: 813-238-1802
www.wmnf.org
An eclectic feminist/womanist radio magazine.

Women's Voices *KZYX*
PO Box 1, Philo, CA 95466
PH: 707-895-2451 FX: 707-895-2554
musicdir@kzyx.org
www.kzyx.org

Women's Windows *WERU*
PO Box 170, 1186 Acadia Highway E.
Orland, ME 04431
PH: 207-469-6600 FX: 207-469-8961
info@weru.org
www.weru.org

Womenfolk *KFAI*
1808 Riverside Ave. Minneapolis, MN 55454
PH: 612-341-3144
Ellen Stanley womenfolk@earthlink.net
www.kfai.org/programs/womenflk.htm
Bringing you the best in Women's Folk & Acoustic music.

Womansoul *KBOO*
20 SE 8th Ave. Portland, OR 97214
PH: 503-231-8032 FX: 503-231-7145
Annelise Hummel annelieseh99@yahoo.com
www.kboo.fm
Women's music with rotating hosts.

Womyn Making Waves *WEFT*
113 N. Market St., Champaign, IL 61820
PH: 217-359-9338
weft@weftfm.org
www.weft.org
Features live interviews and performances with local women as well as women from around the world. All genres of music are played.

World Woman *KOPN*
Attn: Music Director, 915 E. Broadway,
Columbia, MO 65201
Leigh Lockhart and Rhitu Chatterjee
mail@kopn.org
www.kopn.org
Playing local artists and women's music from around the globe.

Canada

Audible Woman *CIUT*
91 St. George St., Toronto, ON M5S 2E8
PH: 416-978-0909 x214 FX: 416-946-7004
Sarah speeb@sympatico.ca
www.sarahpeebles.net/audwoman.htm
www.ciut.fm
Explore Avant-garde music & performance. Visit our site for submission details.

Babae(h) Mama *CIUT*
91 St. George St., Toronto, ON M5S 2E8
PH: 416-978-0909 x214 FX: 416-946-7004
Danielle and Donna babaehmama@yahoo.ca
www.ciut.fm
Local and global feminist perspectives.

Big Broad Cast *CFUV*
PO Box 3035, Victoria, BC V8W 3P3
PH: 250-721-8702
musiccfuv@yahoo.ca
cfuv.uvic.ca

Broadly Speaking *CHRW*
Rm 250, U. Community Ctr. U. Western Ontario,
London, ON N6A 3K7
PH: 519-661-3601 FX: 519-661-3372
broadlyspeaking@chrwradio.com
www.chrwradio.com
Occasional shows on women musicians and have then play a song or two.

Hersay *CKUT*
3647 U. St., Montreal, QC H3A 2B3
PH: 514-398-6787 FX: 514-398-8261
music@ckut.ca
www.ckut.ca

Lois' Jazz Lane and Jazz Coach *CHRW*
Rm 250, U. Community Ctr. U. Western Ontario,
London, ON N6A 3K7
PH: 519-661-3601 FX: 519-661-3372
chrwmp@uwo.ca
www.chrwradio.com
A female perspective on Jazz. Lots of vocalists and lots of swing.

A Madwoman's Underclothes *CFRU*
U.C. Level 2, Guelph, ON N1G 2W1
PH: 519-824-4120 x56919 FX: 519-763-9603
music@cfru.ca
www.cfru.ca
Words and music made mostly by women.

The Neo Brideshead *CHLY*
#2-34 Victoria Rd. Nanaimo, BC V9R 5B8
PH: 250-716 3410
music@chly.ca
www.chly.ca
Female emPOWERed music.

Radio Active Femminism *CKLN*
380 Victoria St., Toronto, ON M5B 1W7
PH: 416-595-5068
music@ckln.fm
www.ckln.fm
A news program for and about issues that concern women and feminism.

Spinsters On Air *CKDU*
Dalhousie Stud. Union Bldg. 6136 U. Ave.
Halifax, NS B3H 4J2
PH: 902-494-6479
music@ckdu.ca
www.ckdu.ca
Pro-woman, Pro change Radio.

Women on Air *CFUV*
PO Box 3035, Victoria, BC V8W 3P3
PH: 250-721-8702
musiccfuv@yahoo.ca
cfuv.uvic.ca
Music, news and interviews on diverse women's voices.

Womenspin *CKMS*
200 University Ave. W. Waterloo, ON N2L 3G1
PH: 519-886-2567 FX: 519-884-3530
Elaine womenspin@hotmail.com
www.amaruit-asha.ca/womenspin
watserv1.uwaterloo.ca/~ckmsinfo
Women's music, news and views for everyone.

Womyn's words *CHRY*
4700 Keele St. Rm 413, Student Ctr.
Toronto, ON M3J 1P3
PH: 416-736-5145
chry@yorku.ca
www.yorku.ca/chry
International documentaries on women and feminism.

The XX Show *CIOI*
135 Fennell Ave. W. PO Box 2034,
Hamilton, ON L8N 3T2
PH: 905-575-2175 FX: 905-575-2385
radiomgr@mohawkcollege.ca
www.mohawkcollege.ca/msa/cioi
Music written and performed by women.

Europe
France

Babes in Boyland *Clapas FM*
Le Polynice Bat B, appt 48, 34000 Montpellier, France
babes@babesinboyland.info
www.babesinboyland.info
Entirely dedicated to women in music, especially "Rock" but it nevertheless remains open to any digression. Feel free to send us stuff.

panx radio
Panx, BP 5058, 31033 Toulouse Cedex, France
PH: 33-0-561612145 FX: 33-0-561114895
infos@panx.net
www.panx.net
HardCore, Punk, CyberThrash, Grindcore, TechnoBruit, Crades Mélodies.

The Netherlands

Radio Monalisa Amsterdam FM
Patricia Werner Leanse monalisa@dds.nl
www.radiomonalisa.nl
A weekly program of women's Classical Music.

United Kingdom

Girls and Guitars *Forest of Dean Radio*
1 Berisford Ct. Cinderford,
Gloucestershire, GL14 2BS UK
PH: 01594-820722
Sue Brindley contactus@fodradio.org
www.fodradio.org/darren.htm
Featuring female Singer/Songwriters.

Australia

Behind the Lines, Frock Off, Women with Attitude *2XX*
PO Box 812, Canberra, ACT 2601 Australia
PH: 02-6247-4400 FX: 02-6248-5560
www.2xxfm.org.au
As part of our commitment 2XX Women in Radio present these three weekly programs: Behind the Lines, Frock Off, Women with Attitude. 2XX's music programs endeavour to give a fair representation to performances by women.

Burning Down The House *RTR FM*
PO Box 949, Nedlands, WA 6909 Australia
PH: 08-6488-3380
rtrfm@rtrfm.com.au
www.rtrfm.com.au
Women's issues and interests plus women in music.

Drastic On Plastic *RTR FM*
PO Box 949, Nedlands, WA 6909 Australia
PH: 08-6488-3380
rtrfm@rtrfm.com.au
www.rtrfm.com.au
Featuring women in music of all genres.

Freewaves *3RPP*
PO Box 602, Somerville, VIC 3912 Australia
PH: 03-5978-8200 FX: 03-5978-8551
rpp@peninsula.hotkey.net.au
www.3rpp.asn.au
Promoting the achievements of women in all walks of life and particularly women artists.

Girly is Good *3CR*
PO Box 1277, Collingwood, Melbourne,
VIC 3065 Australia
PH: 03-9419-8377 FX: 03-9417-4472
Emily Hayes girlyisgood@today.com.au
www.3cr.org.au
Featuring women musicians, visual artists....basically any art form that is girly.

The Grrrly Show *2RRR Sydney*
PO Box 644 Gladesville, NSW 1675 Australia
PH: 61-29816-2988 FX: 61-2-9817-1048
Giselle & Alison thegrrrlyshow@coolgrrrls.com
www.2rrr.org.au
Riot Grrrl to Indie Pop, Electronica and Folk, interspersed with music news, interviews and artist info.

MegaHerz *4ZZZ*
4ZZZ, PO Box 509, Fortitude Valley,
QLD 4006 Australia
PH: 07-3252-1555 FX: 07-3252-1950
info@4zzzfm.org.au
www.4zzzfm.org.au
Women's issues and music.

Playing Like A Girl *3CR*
PO Box 1277, Collingwood, Melbourne,
VIC 3065 Australia
PH: 03-9419-8377 FX: 03-9417-4472
programming@3cr.org.au
www.3cr.org.au

Wayward Girl and Wicked Woman *3CR*
PO Box 1277, Collingwood, Melbourne,
VIC 3065 Australia
PH: 03-9419-8377 FX: 03-9417-4472
Lotti & Marijana
waywardgirlswickedwomen@yahoo.com.au
www.3cr.org.au
Features interviews, live performances, special genre shows and helpful info.

Women on Waves *JOY Radio*
PO Box 907, South Melbourne, VIC 3205 Australia
PH: 61-03-9699-2949 FX: 61-03-9699-2646
womenonwaves@joy.org.au
www.joy.org.au/womenwaves
The latest and best eclectic mix of basically Alternative "women's music". Regular features include the Comedy Shot, Jazz Segment, and Artist In Focus to provide a broad flavour and an in-depth look at performers.

World Radio
United States

Afropop Worldwide
688 Union St. Storefront, Brooklyn, NY 11215
www.afropop.org
Dedicated to African music and the music of the African Diaspora. Does CD reviews too.

alterNATIVE Voices *KUVO*
PO Box 2040, Denver, CO 80201-2040
producer@alternativevoices.org
www.alternativevoices.org
We entertain, educate and generally promote positive excellence and appropriate role models by and for, American Indian people.

Ambiance Congo *WRIR*
1311 Wentbridge Rd. Richmond, VA 23227
David Noyes davidn4010@yahoo.com
www.motherlandinfluence.com
Bringing you the best Dance music out of Central Africa.

The American Indian Radio
PO Box 83111, Lincoln, NE 68501
airos@unl.edu
airos.org
A national distribution system for Native programming to Tribal communities and to general audiences.

Channel Africa
www.channelafrica.org
Playlists include illustrious musicians on all the continents...along with exceptional, underexposed international artists.

Culture Cafe *WWUH*
Attn: Music Director,
200 Bloomfield Ave. West Hartford, CT 06117
PH: 860-768-4701 FX: 860-768-5701
Brian Grosjean abgrosjean@earthlink.net
www.wwuh.org
Folk music from the rest of the world - African, Latin, Flamenco, Native American, Asian music and much more.

Earthsongs
PO Box 187, Walnut Creek, CA 94597
Gregg McVicar earthsongs@radiocamp.com
www.earthsongs.net
Exploring the Native influences that help shape and define contemporary American music.

Folks of the World *KDHX*
3504 Magnolia, St. Louis, MO 63118
PH: 314-664-3955 FX: 314-664-1020
Harriet Shanas folksoftheworld@kdhx.org
www.kdhx.org
A wealth of old and new ethnic music from Asia, Europe, and the Mid East.

Giramondu *KUSP*
PO Box 423, Santa Cruz, CA 95061
PH: 831-476-2800
Gypsy Flores gypsy_flores@yahoo.com
www.kusp.org
An eclectic blend of music from everywhere.

The Indestructible Beat *WITR*
PO Box 20563, Rochester, NY 14602-0563
PH: 585-475-5643 FX: 585-475-4988
Terry Lindsey
musicdirector@modernmusicandmore.com
www.modernmusicandmore.com
Devoted to World music. A wide range of sound, from early 20th century field recordings to the latest cutting edge world fusions.

KBCS World Music
3000 Landerholm Cir. SE
Bellevue, WA 98007-6484 Attn: Music Director
PH: 425-564-6194 x3
Barbie-Danielle DeCarlo bdecarlo@bcc.ctc.edu
kbcs.fm
Send your CD to see if it fits within our World Music format.

KGOU *U. Oklahoma*
Kaufman Hall, Rm 339, Norman, OK 73019-2034
PH: 405-325-3388 FX: 405-325-7129
kholp@ou.edu
www.kgou.org

KIDE *Hoopa Radio*
PO Box 1220, Hoopa, CA 95546
PH: 530-625.4245
www.hoopa-nsn.gov/departments/kide.htm
Tribally owned and operated community radio.

International Pulse! *WVKR*
Box 726, Vassar College, 124 Raymond Ave.
Poughkeepsie, NY 12604
PH: 845-437-5476 FX: 845-437-7656
Michel Joseph msanonjoseph@hotmail.com
www.musicalmix.org
The rhythmic music of Afro-Caribbean, South/Central America and Eurasia.

Joyous Noise Radio
20644 Keeney Mill Rd. Freeland, MD 21053
PH: 410-329-8304
jmadill@joyousnoise.com
www.joyousnoise.com/radio
Didjeridu music.

Kindbeat *KGLP*
c/o Lester Kien, 200 College Dr. Gallup, NM 87301
PH: 505-863-7626 FX: 505-863-7633
www.kglp.org/moon
With a belief in honoring cultural diversity and a strong commitment to community awareness of social concerns, Lester brings his sense of rhythm to this unique blend of World Music.

Morning Breeze *KSBR*
28000 Marguerite Pkwy. Mission Viejo, CA 92692
PH: 949-582-4221 FX: 949-347-9693
Donna Jo Thornton themorningbreeze@gmail.com
www.ksbr.net
World / New Age music.

The Motherland Influence *WRIR*
1311 Wentbridge Rd. Richmond, VA 23227
David Noyes davidn4010@yahoo.com
www.motherlandinfluence.com
The best of African, Latin & Caribbean music.

Music From Everywhere But Here *WBGU*
120 West Hall, BGSU, Bowling Green, OH 43403
PH: 419-372-8657 FX: 419-372-9449
David Scars dsears@bgnet.bgsu.edu
www.wbgufm.com
Weekly World music show.

Music of the World *KEUL*
Glacier City Radio, PO Box 29,
Girdwood, AK 99587
PH: 907 754-2489
Karen Rakos keulkaren@hotmail.com
www.glaciercity.us
Get ready to dance to the beat of the latest World music.

New World Buzz Radio
116 Farmcrest Dr. Oakdale, PA 15071-9332
info@newworldbuzz.com
www.newworldbuzz.com
Provides a showcase to promote the composers, artists and performers of music genres from all over the world.

Planet of Sound *KTUH*
Honolulu, Hemenway Hall #203, 2445 Campus Rd.
Honolulu, HI 96822
PH: 808-956-4848
Ling planet_sound@ktuh.org
www.geocities.com/planet_sound/pos.html
I am willing to play stuff I've never heard of, thus each show is unique and has different styles/sounds.

Radio Afrodicia
PO Box 19866, Los Angeles, CA 90019
PH: 323-938-0720 FX: 206-279-3020
Nnamdi and Donna afrodicia@yahoo.com
www.afrodicia.com
Afrobeat, Afropop, World and Fuji music.

RadioOFIndia.com
www.radioofindia.com
Bollywood hits along with the best of regional music.

sakapfet.com
PO Box 66-9303, Miami, FL 33166
PH: 305-599-8060 FX: 305-599-1005
support@sakapfet.com
www.sakapfet.com
Your cyber-highway to Haiti.

Sound Travels *WERU*
PO Box 170, 1186 Acadia Hwy E.
Orland, ME 04431
PH: 207-469-6600 FX: 207-469-8961
Sue Aripotch info@weru.org
www.weru.org
World Music show.

Spin the Globe *KAOS*
CAB 301, Evergreen State College,
Olympia, WA 98505
PH: 360-867-6896
Scott Stevens spintheglobe@earball.net
www.earball.net/spintheglobe
World music news and reviews.

Vibe FM
KujA Moto, 29193 Northwestern Hwy. #605,
Southfield, MI 48034-1023
PH: 248-358-8702 FX: 248-358-8702
eth@KujAMoto.com
www.vibefm.com.gh
The music of Ghana.

WLIB
PH: 212-889-1190 FX: 212-447-5193
Richard rl@wlib.com
www.wlib.com

World Fusion Radio
1452 Oak Ave. #2S, Evanston, IL 60201
worldfusionradio.com
We play only certain genres of music that fit under the "World Fusion" or "World Beat" umbrella. Listen to our station first and see if what you play fits with one of our shows.

The World Music Show *WTUL*
Tulane U. Ctr. New Orleans, LA 70118
PH: 504-865-5887 FX: 504-862-3072
md1@wtul.fm
www.wtul.fm

World Party *KEWU*
E. Washington U. 104 R-TV Bldg.
Cheney, WA 99004-2431
PH: 509-359-4282
Tronyak@mail.ewu.edu
www.kewu.ewu.edu
Music from around the globe: Latin, Brazilian, African, European, Hawaiian, Reggae and others.

Worldbeat Transfusion KEDT
4455 S. Padre Island Dr. #38,
Corpus Christi, TX 78411-4481
PH: 361-855-2213 FX: 361-855-3877
W.C. Welz stewartjacoby@kedt.org
www.kedt.org
Tastes of Middle Eastern, Ethno-Ambient, Latino Salsa, Celtic, and Light Fusion musical selections that flow together and become more than the sum of their parts developing a captivating sonic spell.

Canada

CKMO
3100 Foul Bay Rd. Victoria, BC V8P 5J2
PH: 250-370-3658 FX: 250-370-3679
www.village900.ca
Our music programming is a format called Global Roots, a contemporary mix of Folk, Roots and World Beat music.

Espace Musique CBC
Pierre Fortier pierre_fortier@radio-canada.ca
www.radio-canada.ca/folkalliance
Canada's leading broadcaster of World Music. We're always on the look-out for new talent.

Global Village CBC
PO Box 500, Stn. A, Toronto, ON M5W 1E6
PH: 416-205-3700 FX: 416-205-6040
Jowi Taylor globalvillage@cbc.ca
www.radio.cbc.ca/programs/global
Reports on musical life from 305 places in 108 countries.

Germany

radiomultikulti
Masurenallee 8-14, 14057 Berlin, Germany
PH: +49 (0)30-3031-1680 FX: +49 (0)30-3031-1689
Tobias Maier tobias.maier@rbb-online.de
www.multikulti.de
Ethnic music station.

SFB4 MultiKulti
RBB Standort Berlin, radiomultikulti,
14046 Berlin, Germany
PH: 49-0-30-3031-1680 FX: 49-0-30-3031-1689
multikulti-online@rbb-online.de
www.multikulti.de

United Kingdom

BBC Radio 3 World Music
www.bbc.co.uk/radio3/worldmusic
Home page of the BBC Radio 3's various World Music shows. Info, shows, contacts etc.

Australia

4EB
PO Box 7300, East Brisbane, QLD 4169 Australia
PH: 07-3240-8600 FX: 07-3240-8633
admin@4eb.org.au
www.4eb.org.au

The Global Village
PBS, PO Box 2917, Fitzroy MDC,
VIC 3065 Australia
PH: 61-3-8415-1067 FX: 61-3-8415-1831
Roger Holdsworth r.holdsworth@unimelb.edu.au
www.geocities.com/rogermhold
Traditional and contemporary music from around the world, emphasising acoustic sounds and distinctive fusions.

Radio Shows that Spotlight Local Musicians

"Local" is a relative term. For some stations, "Local" is defined as any artist who lives within the city limits. Others consider "Local" to be anyone that lives within the listening area. There are many shows that consider "Local" to be musicians from anywhere within the state, province or territory, while others consider "Local" to be artists from the host country. If you're not sure whether you qualify for airplay with a particular show, get in touch with the station (or host) and in most cases they will happily respond and clarify what they consider to be "Local" talent.

North America
United States
Alabama

WBHM Tapestry
650 11th St. S. Birmingham, AL 35294
PH: 205-934-2606 FX: 205-934-5075
info@wbhm.org
www.wbhm.org/tapestry
Music magazine that has a segment featuring local musicians.

WEGL Home Grown
116 Foy Union Bld. Auburn U. AL 36849-5231
PH: 334-844-4114 FX: 334-844-4118
wegl@auburn.edu
wegl.auburn.edu

Alaska

KRUA Locals Only
PSB Rm. 254, 3211 Providence Dr.
Anchorage, AK 99508
PH: 907-786-6805
www.uaa.alaska.edu/krua
An eclectic mix of Anchorage-area and statewide music.

KSUP The Next Step
Attn: Rockin Ron Davis, 1107 W 8th St. #2,
Juneau, AK 99801
ksup@ptialaska.net
www.ptialaska.net/~ksup
Music from artists and groups from S.E. Alaska, the interior, and our Canadian neighbors to the north. No Rap, Hip Hop or Country.

Arizona

KASC Underground Terminal
Stauffer Hall A231, Tempe, AZ 85287-1305
PH: 480-965-4163
md@theblaze1260.com
www.theblaze1260.com
Showcases a lot of AZ Hip Hop and other tight shit. If you send us local music, it will be heard!

KEDJ Local Frequency
7434 E. Stetson Dr. #265, Scottsdale, AZ 85251
Gadger gadger@theedge1039.com
www.theedge1039.com
Three songs from Arizona's best local bands every week night at midnight!

KRXS Jukebox Cantina
Stu D. Baker stubaker@jukeboxcantina.com
www.jukeboxcantina.com
American Roots Rock music. I have a passion for the music of Arizona artists, some of whom have made significant national marks themselves but had difficulty getting local airplay.

KXCI Locals Only
220 South 4th Ave. Tucson, AZ 85701
PH: 520-623-1000
kxcimd@kxci.org
www.kxci.org

KZGL Local Z
2690 E. Huntington Dr. Flagstaff, AZ 86004
www.radioflagstaff.com/kzgl/ZHome.htm
Present the best Arizona has to offer!

Arkansas

KXUA NW Arkansas Local
A665 Arkansas Union, Fayetteville, AR 72701
PH: 479-575-5883
charts@uark.edu
www.kxua.com
Bringing you the best in local and regional music.

WXFX The Fox Consumer Guide to New Rock
1 Commerce St. #300, Montgomery, AL 36104
PH: 334-240-9274 FX: 334-240-9219
Rick Hendrick thefox@wxfx.com
www.wxfx.com/guide
Playing the best new Rock.

California

dnbradio.com 916Junglist
Billy Lane 916junglist@916junglist.com
www.916junglist.com
Sacramento based Drum n Bass show.

KALX KALX Live!
26 Barrows Hall #5650, Berkeley, CA 94720-5650
PH: 510-642-1111
kalxmail@media.berkeley.edu
kalx.berkeley.edu
Musicians of varied styles perform at the beginning of the show, then at around 10:30 PM, the will be a live broadcast from a local club.

KCXX Local Spotlight
242 Airport Dr. #106, San Bernardino, CA 92408
PH: 909-384-1039 FX: 909-888-7302
John Desantis john@x1039.com
www.x1039.com
Features bands in the San Bernadino area.

KIOZ Local Music
www.kioz.com
We have several shows that feature music from San Diego bands. Send us an e-mail and include information like: band name, website address, show dates, any audio and video.

KIOZ Another State of Mind
rock1053@clearchannel.com
www.kioz.com
Local Hard Rock and Metal specialty.

KOZT Local Licks
110 South Franklin St., Fort Bragg, CA 95437
PH: 707-964-7277 FX: 707-964-9536
thecoast@kozt.com
www.kozt.com
Mendocino County musicians playing a variety of music.

KPIG Local Show
1110 Main St. #16, Watsonville, CA 95076
PH: 831-722-9000
sty@kpig.com
www.kpig.com

KPRI
5015 Shoreham Pl. #102, San Diego, CA 92122
PH: 858-678-0102 FX: 858-320-7024
info@authenticrock.com
www.authenticrock.com
We are dedicated to playing fresh music from new artists. Mondays we increase the number of newer tracks we play.

KRFH Local Lixx
Humboldt State U. Arcata, CA 95521
PH: 707-826-3257
www.humboldt.edu/~krfh
Live music in the studio.

KRXQ Local Licks
5345 Madison Ave. Sacramento, CA 95841
PH: 916-334-7777 FX: 916-339-4293
www.krxq.net/local_licks
The best local bands in Sacramento along with the occasional interview and special in-studio guest.

KSDS Local Jazz Corner
1313 Park Blvd. San Diego, CA 92101
PH: 619-234-1062 FX: 619-230-2212
jkocherh@sdccd.net
www.ksds-fm.org

KZSU Wednesday Night Live
PO Box 20510, Stanford, CA 94309
PH: 650-725-4868 FX: 650-725-5865
music@kzsu.stanford.edu
kzsu.stanford.edu
In studio performances and interviews.

West Coast Live
2124 Kittredge Ave. #350, Berkeley, CA 94704
PH: 510-549-1475
Producers producers@wcl.org
www.wcl.org
Music, ideas and humor from a rich mix of musicians, writers and thinkers from the Bay Area and around the country.

XTRA Loudspeaker
9660 Granite Ridge Dr. San Diego, CA 92123
www.91x.com
Our local show featuring bands from and in San Diego.

Z90
9660 Granite Ridge Dr. San Diego, CA 92123
PH: 858-292-2000 FX: 858-715-3190
z90rico@yahoo.com
www.z90.com
Plays the music of local artists. Mostly Dance and Hip Hop.

Colorado

KCSU The Local Show
Student Ctr. Box 13, Lory Student Ctr.
Fort Collins, CO 80523
PH: 970-491-7611 FX: 970-491-7612
www.kcsufm.com

KGNU Kabaret
4700 Walnut St., Boulder, CO 80301
PH: 303-449-4885
music@kgnu.org
www.kgnu.org/kabaret
Live music/spoken word program.

KTCL Locals Only
4695 S. Monaco St., Denver, CO 80237
PH: 303-713-8000
www.area93.com
Check out new music from some of Colorado's best musicians.

KVCU Basementalism
c/o Local Music, Campus Box 207,
Boulder, CO 80309
PH: 303-492-3243
us@basementalism.com
www.basementalism.com
We are a strong supporter of the Colorado Hip Hop Scene. We have an open door policy with new music and we'd be happy to enter it into our library of local music.

KVCU Local Shakedown
Campus Box 207, U. Colorado, Boulder, CO 80309
PH: 303-492-5031 FX: 303-492-1369
localshakedown@yahoo.com
localshakedown.com

Connecticut

UltraRadio.com
242-B College St., New Haven, CT 06510
PH: 203-772-3922 FX: 203-772-3956
Randy Borovsky StationManager@ultraRadio.com
UltraRadio.com
We play lots of independent Rock artists, as long as they are from Connecticut.

WHUS Bluesline, One World Radio
1501 Storrs Road Storrs, CT 06269-3008
PH: 860-486-4007
info@whus.org
whus.org
Music programming covers everything from polka to techno.

WKZE Off the Beaten Track
67 Main St., Sharon, CT 06069
PH: 860-364-5800
Todd Mack info@wkze.com
www.wkze.com
The show spotlights music from unsigned and independent artists residing within the WKZE listening area.

WPKN Live Music Special
244 U. Ave. Bridgeport, CT 06604
PH: 203-331-9756
wpkn@wpkn.org
wpkn.org
All forms of audio performance completely LIVE in our WPKN mega studios.

WPLR Local Band Show
PO Box 6508, Whitneyville, CT 06517
Rick Allison allison@thehotspot.com
www.thelocalbandsshow.com
We do promise to listen to everything that comes from within the WPLR listening area.

Delaware

WOSC Local Lixx
351 Tilghman Rd. Salisbury, MD 21804
PH: 410-572-6781
roxi@96rocksyou.com
www.96rockdelmarva.com
An hour of non stop local Rock. Interviews, live performances, traxx etc.

WOSC Local on the 8s
351 Tilghman Rd. Salisbury, MD 21804
PH: 410-572-6781
briancleary@clearchannel.com
www.96rockdelmarva.com
Plays local Rock.

WSTW Hometown Heroes
PO Box 7492, Wilmington, DE 19803
Johnny B. johnnyb@wstw.com
www.wstw.com
Spotlighting the best music from the Delaware Valley! We'll even bring some of the artists into the studio to perform live on the air.

Florida

97X Local Motion
11300 4th St. N. #300, St. Petersburg, FL 33716
localmotion@97xonline.com
97xonline.com
The best and brightest of our local music scene. Check out who's been in the studio, who's playing where, submit a gig...

Orlando Underground Radio Network
orlandounderground@yahoo.com
www.thefuzionradio.com
Various shows featuring local artists.

Rock 104 Locals Only
PO Box 14444, Gainesville, FL 32604
PH: 352-392-0771 FX: 352-392-0519
Philip Nyguen pandamight@hotmail.com
www.rock104.com
Exploring the Gainesville music scene, featuring music by local and regional bands.

Sunday Blues The Local Set
WKPX, 8000 NW 44th St., Sunrise, FL 33351
DAR dar@blueatheart.com
www.blueatheart.com
Local Blues bands, send in your CDs!

WFYV
8000 Belfort Pkwy. Jacksonville, FL 32256
PH: 904-245-8500
rock@rock105i.com
www.wfyv105.com
We don't specifically have a show but if something good comes down the pipe, we will definitely give it consideration for airplay!

WJBX Local X
20125 S. Tamiami Trail, Estero, FL 33928
PH: 239-495-2100 FX: 239-992-8165
99x@99xwjbx.com
www.99xwjbx.com
A magical journey through Southwest Florida's local music scene.

WJRR Native Noise
2500 Maitland Center Pkwy. #401,
Maitland, FL 32751
PH: 407-916-7800
DJ dj@realrock1011.com
www.wjrr.com
Join DJ as he brings you the best from the local music scene.

WNMF Live Music Showcase
1210 E. MLK Blvd. Tampa, FL 33603-4449
PH: 813-238-8001 FX: 813-238-1802
www.wmnf.org

WPBZ *Local Band Of The Month*
www.buzz103.com
A local band from South Florida visits the Buzz studios to perform.

WPRK *Local Music*
1000 Holt Ave. 2745, Winter Park, FL 32789
Attn: Russell
PH: 407-646-2241 FX: 407-646-1560
wprkfm@rollins.edu
www.rollins.edu/wprk
The local scene, our scene, is extremely important to us here at 91.5 fm. This is your opportunity to get: airplay, exposure, and most importantly—your music heard!

WVFS *Hootenanny*
420 Diffenbaugh Bldg. Tallahassee, FL 32306-1550
music@wvfs.fsu.edu
www.wvfs.fsu.edu
Local music, interviews and live performances.

WVUM *Locals Only*
PO Box 248191, Coral Gables, FL 33124
PH: 305-284-3131 FX: 305-284-3132
info@wvum.org
wvum.org

Georgia

Joe Stevenson Music / Homegrown
2536 Henry St. Augusta, GA 30904
PH: 706-364-7614 FX: 706-790-6857
Meredith Jenkins meredith@joestevensonmusic.com
www.joestevensonmusic.com
Special event promotion & artist development company. We produce 95 Rock's Homegrown radio program, featuring the Southeast US's best up and coming artists. Check our site for submission details.

SLAB Radio *(Southern Local Area Bands)*
3340 Haverhill Rowe, Lawrenceville, GA 30044
Chris Horton info@slabmusic.com
www.slabmusic.com
Playing the music of bands from the Southeast United States.

WMRE *Local Outbreak*
PO Drawer AG Atlanta, GA 30322
PH: 404-727-9672 FX: 404-712-8000
www.students.emory.edu/wmre

WPUP *Local Noise*
1010 Tower Place, Bogart, GA 30622
PH: 706-549-6222 FX: 706-353-1967
Chris Brame brame@rock1037.com
www.rock1037.com
Three hours of the best in local music.

WRAS *Georgia Music Show*
33 Gilmer St. SE #8, Atlanta, GA 30303-3088
PH: 404-651-2240
www.wras.org
If you "used" to live in Georgia and now live elsewhere, you are no longer local.

WREK *Live at WREK*
165 Eighth St. NW, Atlanta, GA 30332-0630
PH: 404-894-2468 FX: 404-894-6872
music.director@wrek.org
www.wrek.org
Music you don't hear on the radio.

WUOG *Live in the Lobby*
Box 2065 Tate Student Ctr. Athens, GA 30602
PH: 706-542-7100 FX: 706-542-0070
lmd@wuog.org
www.uga.edu/wuog/localmusic
We book artists for station remotes and help out with events involving local musicians. Twice a week we welcome an Athens band into the studio for Live in the Lobby.

Hawaii

KIPO *Aloha Shorts*
c/o Cedric Yamanaka, 738 Kaheka St. #101, Honolulu, HI 96814
PH: 808-955-8821 FX: 808-942-5477
hprmusic@hawaiipublicradio.org
www.hawaiipublicradio.org
A program of local literature, local authors, local actors and local music.

KTUH *Monday Night Live*
2445 Campus Rd. Hemenway Hall #203, Honolulu, HI 96822
PH: 808-956-5288 FX: 808-956-5271
live@ktuh.org
ktuh.hawaii.edu/mnl.php
Featuring occasional interviews with the band du jour. At 10pm is Monday Night Live proper, featuring an hour of original music from one of Hawaii's best local bands.

Illinois

ChiRap.com
www.ChiRap.com
Listen to tha hottest Rap acts outta tha Chicago area!!!

Mac and Slater *Fearless Radio*
401 W. Ontario #150, Chicago, IL 60610
PH: 312-224-8270 FX: 312-423-6598
www.fearlessradio.com
A Chicago based show hosted by Mac and Slater that features local personalities.

WBEZ *Performance Space*
CPR, Navy Pier, 848 East Grand Ave.
Chicago, IL 60611-3462
PH: 312-948-4855
Music@ChicagoPublicRadio.org
www.wbez.org
Concerts and other live productions from Chicago-based artists.

WDCB *Folk Festival*
College of DuPage, 425 Fawell Blvd.
Glen Ellyn, IL 60137
PH: 630-942-4200 FX: 630-942-2788
Lili Kuzma KuzmaL@wdcb.org
www.cod.edu/wdcb
An entertaining blend of music in the Folk tradition, including Old Time to Classic Folk and live performance interviews with local and regional artists.

WDCB *Strictly Bluegrass*
College of DuPage, 425 Fawell Blvd.
Glen Ellyn, IL 60137
PH: 630-942-4200 FX: 630-942-2788
RobinsonL@wdcb.org
www.cod.edu/wdcb
Bluegrass expert and aficionado Larry Robinson presents the music he loves, along with information on local groups and Bluegrass concerts.

WEFT *Local and Live*
113 N. Market St., Champaign, IL 61820
PH: 217-359-9338
weft@weftfm.org
www.weft.org

WESN *The Local Music Show*
PO Box 2900, Bloomington, IL 61701
PH: 309-556-2638 FX: 309-556-2949
wesn@sun.iwu.edu
www.iwu.edu/~wesn

WLUW *Radio One Chicago*
6525 N. Sheridan Rd. Chicago, IL 60626
PH: 773-508-8080 FX: 773-508-8082
Mike Gibson mike@lovehasnologic.com
wluw.org
Interviews, music and guests explore Chicago's independent music scene.

WONC *Local Chaos*
30 N. Brainard, PO Box 3063, Naperville, IL 60566
PH: 637-5965 x3 FX: 630-637-5900
www.wonc.org
Local music every Sunday night.

WPGU *Inner Limits*
#107, 24 E Green St., Champaign, IL 61801
PH: 217-244-3000 FX: 217-244-3001
DrewPatterson1071@yahoo.com
www.wpgu.com
One hour of local music.

WRRG *chicagocore*
2000 Fifth Ave. River Grove, IL 60171
PH: 708-583-3110
info@wrrg.org
www.wrrg.org
We accept music / Spoken-Word submissions in the following formats: CD, vinyl, minidisc and cassette. It must be a professional quality recording.

WXRT *Local Anesthetic*
4949 W. Belmont Ave. Chicago, IL 60641
PH: 773-777-1700 FX: 773-777-5031
Richard Milne rankenter@aol.com
www.wxrt.com
WXRT will only accept recorded materials that are clearly labeled as such. Any packages with hand written "send to" or "received from" information will not be accepted into the station.

Indiana

IndianaRap.com
www.indianarap.com
Listen to tha hottest Rap acts outta tha Indiana area!!!

MWB Radio
PO Box 558, Owensville, IN 47665
PH: 877-731-1081 FX: 509-351-9927
Mark and Jenny Lush
mwbcontact@midwestbands.com
www.mwbmusic.com/MWBRadio
You need to complete a permission form. Go to:www.midwestbands.com/permissionform.htm

One Kind Radio *Local & Indie Show*
PO Box 127, Hobart, IN 46342
John Bowles jbowles@onekindradio.com
www.onekindradio.com
A mixture of local and Indie music from Chicagoland and beyond.

WFHB *The Local Show*
PO Box 1973 Bloomington, IN 47402
PH: 812-323-1200 FX: 812-323-0320
wfhb@wfhb.org
www.wfhb.org

Iowa

KAZR *Local Licks*
1416 Locust St., Des Moines, IA 50309
PH: 515-280-1350
Suzi suzi@lazer1033.com
www.lazer1033.com
If your band is releasing a CD, send me an email with all of the info.

KIWR *New Day Rising*
2700 College Rd. Council Bluffs, IA 51503
PH: 712-325-3254 FX: 712-325-3391
Dave & Beau ndrdave@cox.net
www.897theriver.com
The best in fresh, new Rock before you will hear it anywhere else. The possibilities are endless with the latest from artists from all different genres.

KIWR *Planet O!*
2700 College Rd. Council Bluffs, IA 51503
PH: 712-325-3254 FX: 712-325-3391
Kady Jaymes & James Patrick
www.897theriver.com
Omaha's longest running local music show! Accept NO substitute!!!!

KKEZ *Fort Dodge*
PO Box 578, 540 A. St., Fort Dodge, IA 50501
PH: 515-576-0000 FX: 515-955-4250
www.kkez.com
No specific show, but we'll play the music of local artists.

KUNI *Live from Studio One*
U. Northern Iowa, Cedar Falls, IA 50614-0359
PH: 319-273-6400 FX 319-273-2682
Karen Impola karen.impola@uni.edu
www.kuniradio.org/kustud.html
Unique weekly live broadcast featuring local and national artists.

Kansas

KJHK *Plow the Fields*
2051A Dole Ctr. 1000 Sunnyside Ave.
Lawrence, KS 66045
PH: 785-864-4747
kjhkmusic@ku.edu
kjhk.org

KLZR *Local Lazer Music*
3125 W. 6th St., Lawrence, KS 66046
Newman newman@lazer.com
www.lazer.com
Wanna be on the radio? Send those CDs and concert updates to us. If you have an MP3, you can email it to me.

KSDB *Kansas State U.*
105 Kedzie Hall, K-State,
Manhattan, KS 66506-1501
PH: 785-532-2769
radio@ksu.edu
wildcatradio.ksu.edu
Local show every Saturday.

Kentucky

WTFX *Louisville Rocks*
4000 #1 Radio Dr. Louisville, KY 40218
Scott Clark jamf@clearchannel.com
www.foxrocks.com/louisville_rocks.html
Get your CDs to us if you want 'em on the air. Keep in mind that if they suck, we won't play them.

Louisiana

KBON
109 South 2nd St., Eunice, LA 70535
PH: 337-546-0007 FX: 337-546-0097
101.1@KBON.com
www.kbon.com
About 70% of the music on KBON is the music of Louisiana recording artists.

New Orleans Radio
info@neworleansradio.com
www.neworleansradio.com
We've now built the site to allow for mp3 uploads of music or syndicated shows.

Radio Free New Orleans
www.neworleansonline.com/neworleans/music/rfno.html
You can tune into the world's happiest music right here, broadcasting from the pleasure center of your brain.

WTUL *Local Music Show*
Tulane U. Ctr. New Orleans, LA 70118
PH: 504-865-5887 FX: 504-862-3072
Tom Connor localmusic@wtul.fm
www.wtul.fm

Maine

WMPG *Local Motive*
96 Falmouth St., Portland, ME 04104-9300
PH: 207-780-4976
Jan Wilkinson localmotives@yahoo.com
www.wmpg.org
Every Friday night, we bring a the sounds of a local Portland band.

WMPG *The Locals*
96 Falmouth St., Portland, ME 04104-9300
PH: 207-780-4976
www.wmpg.org
Highlights local acts, singers, bands and producers who are some how, some way local.

Maryland

98 Rock *Noise in the Basement*
c/o Matt Davis, 3800 Hooper Ave.
Baltimore, MD 21211
PH: 410-481-1098 FX: 410-467-3291
mattdavis@hearst.com
www.98online.com/noise_in_the_basement.html
Baltimore's local music outlet. For airplay consideration send your material to the above address. Please include a contact number. CD only please!

WWDC *Local Lix*
1801 Rockville Pike #405, Rockville, MD 20852
Roche roche@dc101.com
dc101.com
Devoted to the many great local bands in the D.C. Metropolitan area.

Massachusetts

Folkadelica Radio
2 Northwood Terr. Haverhill, MA 01830
PH: 978-373-9199 FX: 978-373-9359
Shawna Torres Shawna@folkadelica.com
folkadelica.com
Plays local RI and Massachusetts Singer/Songwriters.

WAAF *Bay State Rock*
20 Guest St. 3rd Fl. Boston, MA 02135-2040
PH: 617-931-1112 FX: 617-931-1073
Carmelita baystaterocklistings@yahoo.com
www.baystaterock.com
Playing the music of bands from the Boston area. We feature 4 song acoustic sets from bands at 11:30 each Sunday night.

WAMH *Live Concert*
AC #1907 Campus Ctr. Amherst, MA 01002-5000
PH: 413-542-2224
wamh.amherst.edu

WBCN *Boston Emissions*
1265 Boylston St., Boston, MA 02215
PH: 617-536-8000
Shred shred@wbcn.com
www.wbcn.com
Features local artists plus a band of the month.

WBRS *Watch City Coffeehouse*
Brandeis U. 415 South St.,
Waltham, MA 02453-2728
PH: 781-736-4785
music@wbrs.org
www.wbrs.org

WFNX *New England Product*
25 Exchange St., Lynn, MA 01901
PH: 781-595-6200
fnxradio@fnxradio.com
fnxradio.com
Live in-studio performances and interviews. We focus on bringing you the best up-and-coming acts.

WICN Jazz *New England*
6 Chatham St., Worcester, MA 01609
PH: 508-752-0700 FX: 508-752-7518
Joe Zupan jzupan@wicn.org
www.wicn.org
Music from regional artists, conversations about their music.

WICN *The Contemporary Café*
6 Chatham St., Worcester, MA 01609
PH: 508-752-0700 FX: 508-752-7518
Nick DiBiasio nick@wicn.org
www.wicn.org
The finest acoustic performances of Folk, Blues and Americana music by the biggest names in New England and around the world.

WICN *Live From Café Fantastique*
6 Chatham St., Worcester, MA 01609
PH: 508-752-0700 FX: 508-752-7518
www.wicn.org
Some of the best local and nationally acclaimed musicians in Folk, Blues and Country music.

WMBR *Pipeline!*
3 Ames St., Cambridge, MA 02142
PH: 617-253-4000
pipeline@wmbr.org
wmbr.mit.edu
Proof that there are geographical solutions to emotional problems! Local bands and a live in-studio performance every single week.

WMVY *The Local Music Cafe*
PO Box 1148, Tisbury, MA 02568
PH: 508-693-5000 FX: 508-693-8211
www.mvyradio.com
Music from some of the best local musicians on Cape Cod and the Islands of Martha's Vineyard and Nantucket.

WPXC *Homegrown*
154 Barnstable Rd. Hyannis, MA 02601
PH: 508-778-2888 FX: 508-790-4967
Suzanne Tonaire rockbabe@pixy103.com
www.pixy103.com
Cape Cod's original local artists showcase. Includes band of the month.

WTBU *Sublimity*
640 Commonwealth Ave. Boston, MA 02215
PH: 617-353-6401 FX: 617-353-6403
www.wtburadio.com

WUML *Live from the Fallout Shelter*
1 University Ave. Lowell, MA 01854
falloutshelter@wuml.org
fallout.wuml.org
A variety of Indie, Punk, Alt-Country, Jazz, and any and all other Underground music.

WZBC *Mass. Avenue and Beyond*
Boston College, McElroy Commons 107,
Chestnut Hill, MA 02467
PH: 617-552-3511 FX: 617-552-1738
gm@wzbc.org
www.wzbc.org
Local Rock, focusing on new music. Includes interviews from local musicians, artists etc.

Michigan

The Sonic Chronicles *M4 Radio*
aaronchilds@ameritech.net
www.m4radio.com
Plays Rock, Blues, Jazz and Electronica genres, with an emphasis on the local music scene in South Central Michigan.

WCBN *The Local Music Show*
530 Student Activities Bldg.
Ann Arbor, MI 48109-1316
PH: 734-763-3501
music@wcbn.org
www.wcbn.org

WDBM *The Basement*
G-4 Holden Hall, East Lansing, MI 48825
PH: 517-353-4414 FX: 517-355-4237
www.impact89fm.org
The best in local music from Mid-Michigan and the rest of the Great Lakes State.

WDET *The Martin Bandyke Program*
4600 Cass Ave. Detroit, MI 48201
PH: 313-577-4146 FX: 313-577-1300
wdetfm@wdetfm.org
www.wdetfm.org

WIDR *It Came From Next Door*
1511 Faunce Student Service Bldg.
Kalamazoo, MI 49008-6301
PH: 269-387-6305
widr-music@groupwise.wmich.edu
www.widr.org
Hear Michigan music before everyone else.

WIDR *West Michigan Radio*
listen@westmichiganmusic.com
www.westmichiganmusic.com
Playing the music of West Michigan artists. For information on how your band can be considered for airplay or a studio appearance, please e-mail us.

WRIF *Motor City RIFFS*
Attn: Shaffee, 1 Radio Plaza, Detroit, MI 48220
PH: 248-547-0101 FX: 248-542-8800
Doug and Jay jay@wrif.com
www.wrif.com
WRIF puts the local scene in the spotlight every Sunday night.

Minnesota

KFAI *Local Sound Department (LSD)*
1808 Riverside Ave. Minneapolis, MN 55454
PH: 612-341-3144
lsdkfai@yahoo.com
www.kfai.org
Dedicated to playing music created by Minnesota artists.

KQRS *KQ Homegrown*
2000 SE Elm St., Minneapolis, MN 55414
PH: 612-617-4000 FX: 612-623-9292
www.radiohomegrown.com
Music, interviews and in studio performances by your favorite local groups.

KTCZ *Minnesota Music*
1600 Utica Ave. S. #400, St. Louis Park, MN 55416
PH: 952-417-3000
Jason Nagle Jason@Cities97.com
www.cities97.com
In addition to playing local artists' tunes throughout the week, we dedicate a full hour to them Sunday nights.

KVSC *Monday Night Live*
720 4th Ave. S. 27 Stewart Hall,
St. Cloud, MN 56301-4498
PH: 320-308-3126 FX: 320-308-5337
stephanie@kvsc.org
www.kvsc.org
Every Monday it's an hour of live music from our studio featuring the best in Minnesota music.

KXXR *Loud & Local*
2000 S.E. Elm St., Minneapolis, MN 55414
PH: 612-617-4000
Patrick loudandlocal@93xrocks.com
www.93x.com
Send in info on your band.

KUOM *Off the Record*
610 Rarig Ctr. 330 21st Ave. S.
Minneapolis, MN 55455
PH: 612-625-3500 FX: 612-625-2112
music@radiok.org
www.radiok.org
Local music and a live band in Studio K.

WHMH *Minnesota Homegrown*
1010 2nd St. N. Sauk Rapids, MN 56379
Tim Ryan tim@rockin101.com
www.rockin101.com
If you have a band and want some exposure send CDs and bios to us.

Mississippi

WMSV *Homegrown*
PO Box 6210 Student Media Ctr.
Mississippi State, MS 39762-6210
PH: 662-325-8034 FX: 662-325-8037
wmsv@msstate.edu
www.wmsv.msstate.edu

Missouri

300 KC Jazz Stars
George Simms Sol 300ep@300kcjazzstars.com
www.300kcjazzstars.com
Internet Jazz station featuring only Kansas City Jazz artists.

EchoMidwest
support@echomidwest.com
www.echomidwest.com
The only radio station (online or not) that features only Midwestern artists and their music.

KC Christian Music Radio
17300 Gray Dr. Pleasant Hill, MO 64080
Connie Whitlock info@kcchristianmusic.com
www.kcchristianmusic.com
Plays the music of Kansas City Christian artists.

KPNT *The Local Show*
800 Union Stn. Powerhouse Bldg,
St. Louis, MO 63103 Attn: Cornbread
PH: 314-231-1057 FX: 314-621-3000
www.kpnt.com
Get in on STL's bitchin' local scene and hear the Indie bands that might become tomorrow's Rock superstars.

KWUR *The Side Trip*
Washington U. Campus Box 1205,
One Brookings Dr. St. Louis, MO 63105
PH: 314-935-5952
kwur.wustl.edu

TheGrowl
901 S. National, Springfield, MO 65804
PH: 417-836-6286
thegrowl@smsu.edu
thegrowl.smsu.edu

WVRV *The River Home Grown*
11647 Olive Blvd. St. Louis, MO 63141
PH: 314-983-6000
feedback@wvrv.com
www.wvrv.com

Montana

KBGA *The Local Show*
University Center, Missoula, MT 59812
PH: 406-243-5715
programming@kbga.org
kbga.org

KUFM *Musician's Spotlight*
32 Campus Dr. U. Montana,
Missoula, MT 59812-8064
PH: 406-243-4931 FX: 406-243-3299
www.kufm.org
Montana and regional musicians performing in KUFM's studios or in area theaters or clubs.

Nebraska

KEZO *Z-92's Homegrown*
c/o Scott Murphy, 11128 John Galt Blvd. #192,
Omaha, NE 68137
PH: 402-592-5300 x5316
www.z92.com
Features the best music from local Rock bands every Sunday night.

KRNU *Heresy*
PO Box 880466, Lincoln, NE 68588-0466
PH: 402-472-8277
Robert krnu_heresy@yahoo.com
www.geocities.com/krnu_heresy
My radio show is strictly for Metal and Hardcore music. The unsigned bands I play are from the Lincoln/Omaha area Contact us for requests, demos, interviews on air!!

KZUM *Alive in Lincoln*
941 "O" St., Lincoln, NE 68508
PH: 402-474-5086 FX: 402-474-5091
Hardy strawberry67@earthlink.net
www.kzum.org
Variety of local artists of all genres.

KZUM *River City Folk*
941 "O" St., Lincoln, NE 68508
PH: 402-474-5086 FX: 402-474-5091
www.kzum.org
Interviews and regional Folk artists.

Nebraska Public Radio *Live From the Mill*
1800 N. 33rd St., Lincoln, NE 68583
PH: 402-472-2200 FX: 402-472-2403
William Stibor wstibor2@unl.edu
netnebraska.org/radio
Discussion and performances with featured guests representing a broad range of arts topics, including writing, dance, music and theatre.

Nevada

KOMP *The Home Grown Show*
8755 W. Flamingo, Las Vegas, NV 89147
PH: 702-876-1460 FX: 702-876-6685
Laurie Steele homegrown@komp.com
www.komp.com
Showcasing the best local bands in Las Vegas.

KRZQ *The Scene*
Mary Jane contact@krzqfm.com
www.krzqfm.com
Every Sunday I play an hour of the best local music. Local show announcements, and special guests in studio every week.

KTHX
300 E. 2nd, 14th Fl. Reno, NV 89501
PH: 775-333-0123 FX: 775-333-0110
info@globalstudio.com
www.kthxfm.com
We play local music every night at 10pm, and have Acoustic performances on several of our shows.

KXTE *It Hurts When I Pee*
6655 W. Sahara Ave. #c-202, Las Vegas, NV 89146
homie@xtremeradio.com
www.xtremeradio.fm/pee
The new music show with a really goofy name. Local and Indie bands.

LV Rocks *Sounds of Sin*
PH: 866-587-6257
www.lvrocks.com
Features interviews and live performances from some of Vegas' hottest musicians & bands.

New Hampshire

The Studio
Mojo Music Studio, PO Box 536,
Franconia, NH 03580
PH: 603-823-5691
info@mojomusicstudio.com
www.mojomusicstudio.com/studio.asp
Featuring Artists of most genres from the Northeastern US. Note, you must fill out our License and Release form before we can play your music.

WGIR *Homegrown*
195 McGregor St., Manchester, NH 03102
www.wgir.com/homegrown.html
Supporting your local music scene.

WSCA *Hear Us Out*
PH: 603-430-9722 FX: 603-430-9822
PO Box 6532, Portsmouth, NH 03802
radio@portsmouthcommunityradio.org
www.wscafm.org
Features New Hampshire artists.

New Jersey

AsburyMusic.com *Upstage Radio*
info@upstageradio.com
www.loudcity.net/stations/upstageradio
www.asburymusic.com
Shows for most genres of music and some involving artist interviews and in-studio performances.

WDHA *Homegrown Spotlight*
PH: 973-455-1055 FX: 973-538-3060
www.wdhafm.com
Weeknights at 7:30.

WDVR *Heartlands Hayride*
PO Box 191, Sergeantsville, NJ 08557
PH: 609-397-1620 FX: 609-397-5991
www.wdvrfm.org/hayride.htm
www.wdvrfm.org
Live Country music show. The show invites participation to new and upcoming local talent who would not ordinarily have access to performing on the radio.

WFMU
c/o Brian Turner, PO Box 5101, Hoboken, NJ 07030
PH: 201-521-1416
www.wfmu.org
Many local acts perform live in the studio.

WSOU *Street Patrol*
400 S. Orange Ave. South Orange, NJ 07079
PH: 973-761-9768
wsou@shu.edu
www.wsou.net
Highlighting the area's top local Hard Rock acts. We also feature regular interviews and live performances.

New Mexico

KTAO *Acoustic Café*
PO Box 1844, Taos, NM 87571
PH: 505-758-5826 FX: 505-758-8430
ktao@newmex.com
www.ktao.com

New York

Brooklyn Heights Radio
smetrick@aol.com
www.brooklynheightsradio.com
To those artists and musicians in Brooklyn, who struggle to have their efforts heard THIS IS FOR YOU.

Radio Free Ithica
webmaster@radiofreeithaca.net
www.radiofreeithaca.net
Comprised solely of Ithaca-based bands and musicians.

WAIH *Local Bands*
9050 Barrington Dr. SUNY, Potsdam, NY 13676
waih@potsdam.edu
www2.potsdam.edu/WAIH
Talk about or promote your music through on-air interviews and live performances?

WBAB *The Homegrown Show*
555 Sunrise Hwy. West Babylon, NY 11704
PH: 631-587-1023 FX: 631-422-1023
Fingers fingers@cox.com
wbab.com/homegrown
For over 20 years WBAB has supported the local Long Island music scene, playing Long Island's best bands.

WBNY *The Local Show*
WBNY, 1300 Elmwood Ave. Buffalo, NY 14222
PH: 716-878-3080 FX: 716-878-6600
wbny@buffalostate.edu
www.wbny.org

WCWP *Aural Fix Transmission*
PO Box 6054, N. Babylon, NY 11703
auralfix@optonline.com
www.auralfix.com
Features artists from the Long Island, New York region.

WGFR *The Local Show*
640 Bay Rd. Queensbury, NY 12804
PH: 518-743-2300 x2376
wgfr@wgfr.org
www.wgfr.org

WICB *Home Brew*
118 Park Hall, Ithaca, NY 14850
PH: 607-274-1040 x1 FX: 607-274-1061
wicbmusic@yahoo.com
www.ithaca.edu/radio/wicb
Join Taz for local music news and in studio performances.

WLIR *Tri-State Sound*
3075 Veterans Memorial Hwy. #201,
Ronkonkoma, NY 11779
www.wlir.fm
Harlan Friedman showcases the best up and coming musicians from Long Island, NYC, CT and NJ.

WUSB *Local Insomniac Music*
Student Union Bld. SUNY, Stony Brook, NY
11794-3263 Attn: Music Director
PH: 631-632-6500 FX: 631-632-7182
musicwusb·fm
wusb.fm
The best in original local music from the Tri-State area, in a variety of genres.

WUSB *The Music Never Stops*
Student Union Blvd. Stony Brook, NY 11794-3263
Attn: Music Director
PH: 631-632-6500 FX: 631-632-7182
Bill Frey musicnostop@webtv.net
community-2.webtv.net/musicnostop/
THEMUSICNEVERSTOPS
Radio show featuring Long Island musicians in a live performance & interview format.

WVKR *Scene Unseen*
Box 726, Vassar College, 124 Raymond Ave.
Poughkeepsie, NY 12604
PH: 845-437-5476 FX: 845-437-7656
music@wvkr.org
www.wvkr.org
Featuring bands and music artists from the listening area. Local music news, interviews and live musical performances.

North Carolina

WGWG *Carolina Drive*
PO Box 876, Boiling Springs, NC 28017
info@wgwg.org
www.gardner-webb.edu/wgwg/home.html
Spotlighting artists of all styles across the Carolinas. Rock, Country, Blues, Bluegrass, Gospel, Classical, Jazz, Anything goes!

WSQL *Southern Exposure*
PO Box 1240, Brevard, NC 28712
PH: 828-877-5252 FX: 828-877-5253
aandl@citcom.net
www.wsqlradio.com
Summer show live show from the Essence of Thyme featuring local musicians.

The END 106.5 *90 Minutes*
801 E. Morehead St. #200, Charlotte, NC 28202
PH: 704-376-1065
Divakar 90minutes@1065.com
www.1065.com
The best local & regional music around with 90 minutes hosted by Divakar.

WKNC *North Carolina State U.*
NCSU Mail Center Box 8607,
Raleigh, NC 27695-8607
PH: 919-515-2401 FX: 919-213-2353
wknc.org
We play one local/regional artist an hour & every Friday noon to 2 PM we have a local music show.

WXNR *Local 99*
207 Glenburnie Dr. New Bern, NC 28560
Crash crash@wxnr.com
www.wxnr.com

WZMB *Locals Only*
PH: 252-328-4751
www.wzmb.ecu.edu

North Dakota

104.7 *The Boneyard*
T-Bone tbone1047thedam@yahoo.com
www.thedamrockstation.com/boneyard.html
The Rock of the Upper Midwest.

Ohio

KBUX *Tones of Home*
1739 N. High St. #15-S. Columbus, OH 43210
PH: 614-688-3780 FX: 614-688-5788
pd@underground.fm
www.underground.fm
A selection of the best in Ohio music. We also have slots once or twice every hour where djs have to play local artists.

OhioRap Radio
cr4zyt@ohiorap.com
www.ohiorap.com
Listen to tha hottest Rap acts outta tha Ohio area!!!

WAIF *Kindred Sanction*
PO Box 6126, Cincinnati, OH 45206
PH: 513-961-8900
kindredsanction@hotmail.com
www.waif883.org
Local, regional music and interviews.

WAIF *Live City Licks*
1434 E. McMillan Ave. Cincinnati, OH 45206
PH: 513-961-8900
waif@waif883.org
www.waif883.org

WAIF *Spin Cincinnati*
1434 E. McMillan Ave. Cincinnati, OH 45206
PH: 513-961-8900
spincincinnati@spincincinnati.com
www.spincincinnati.com
The best in local music.

WAPS *DIY Radio*
65 Steiner Ave. Akron, OH 44301
PH: 330-761-3099 FX: 330-761-3240
Ron & Ed diy@diyradio.net
www.diyradio.net
Two hours of Punk Rock, past and present, with spotlights on the local music scene.

WCSB *Blue Monday*
Rhodes Tower 956, 2121 Euclid Ave.
Cleveland, OH 44115-2214
PH: 216-687-3721 FX: 216-687-2161
musdirwcsb@yahoo.com
www.wcsb.org
The finest local and national Blues artists are heard.

WDUB
351 Cornwall, Rocky River, OH 44116
PH: 740-587-3008
WDUB@denison.edu
www.wdub.org
If you're an artist or band from the Northern Ohio area, we want your music.

WJCU *The Local Mix*
20700 N. Park Blvd. University Heights, OH 44118
PH: 216-397-4437 FX: 216-397-4438
www.wjcu.org
Local Hip Hop, R&B, Blues, Rock, etc.

WMSR *Local Band Showcase*
221 Williams Hall, Oxford, OH 45056
PH: 513-529-1269
wmsr@muohio.edu
www.orgs.muohio.edu/wmsr

WOUB *Showdown Concerts*
9 South College St., Athens, OH 45701
PH: 740-593-1771 FX: 740-593-0240
radio@woub.org
woub.org/bluegrass
We present local and regional Bluegrass and Old-Time music bands in concert .

WXEG *Joe's Garage*
101 Pine St., Dayton, OH 45402
PH: 937-224-1137 FX: 937-224-9965
www.wxeg.com
The best of the local scene on Sunday nights.

WXUT *Local Show*
2801 W. Bancroft, SU2515, Toledo, OH 43606
PH: 419-530-4172 FX: 419-530-2210
883wxut@gmail.com
www.wxut.com
Featuring acts from Toledo and all over the Midwest in any vein of musical styling.

Oklahoma

KMYZ *HomeGroan*
5810 E. Skelly Dr. #801, Tulsa, OK 74135
PH: 918-665-3131 FX: 918-663-6622
www.edgetulsa.com
Featuring local and regional talent.

Tulsa Music Pulse Radio
jordanius@tulsamusicpulse.com
www.tulsamusicpulse.com
Contact me about getting your music played online.

Oregon

JamminFM.com *Tha Undaground Show*
0234 SW Bancroft, Portland, OR 97201
PH: 503-243-7595 FX: 503-417-7653
StarChile starchile@jamminfm.com
www.jamminfm.com
Portland'z #1 ALL Hip Hop Show!!!! This is the ONLY show the gives MAJOR LUV 2 North West Artist!!!

KBOO
20 SE 8th Ave. Portland, OR 97214
PH: 503-231-8032 FX: 503-231-7145
rockmd@kboo.org
www.kboo.fm
We have several shows that play the music of local artists.

KBPS *Played in Oregon*
515 NE 15th Ave. Portland, OR 97232-2897
PH: 503-916-5828 FX: 503-916-2642
Robert McBride robert@allclassical.org
www.allclassical.org
There needs to be some Oregon connection and it needs to be "Classical" music.

KBVR *Locals Live*
210 Memorial Union E. Corvallis, OR 97331
PH: 541-737-6323 FX: 541-737-4545
oregonstate.edu/dept/kbvr
A 2 hour show that gives local musicians the chance to perform live on KBVR.

KEOL
One University Blvd. La Grande, OR 97850
PH: 541-962-3698
www3.eou.edu/~keol
We have many locals only shows. Some for the local area; others for all of Oregon and still others for eastern WA and ID.

KINK *Local Spotlight*
1501 SW Jefferson, Portland, OR 97201
PH: 503-517-6000 FX: 503-517-6100
Kevin Welch kwelch@kink.fm
www.kinkfm102.com
Tuesday through Friday at 9:20 p.m we spotlight a couple of tracks from a local artist or group.

KLCC *Friends and Neighbors*
4000 East 30th Ave. Eugene, OR 97405-0640
PH: 541-463-6000 FX: 541-463-6046
Kobi Lucas klcc@lanccc.edu
www.klcc.org
Very Acoustic Folk music. A focus on new releases and local music, both recorded and live.

KLRR *Homegrown Music Showcase*
711 NE Butler Market Rd. Bend, OR 97701
PH: 541-389-1088 FX: 541-388-0456
clear@clear1017.fm
www.klrr.com
A full hour of music you won't hear anywhere else. If you are a musician or band from Oregon, we want to hear from you.

KMHD *Homegrown Jazz*
26000 SE Stark St., Gresham, OR 97030
PH: 503-661-8900 FX: 503-491-6999
Mary Burlingame burlingm@mhcc.edu
www.kmhd.org

KNRQ *Native Noise*
1200 Executive Pkwy. #440, Eugene, OR 97405
PH: 541-684-0979
www.nrq.com
Local music show.

NW-Radio.com
8992 SW Gravenstein Ln. Tigard, OR 97224
www.nw-radio.com
Dedicated to bands from the Northwest United States and Lower West Canada. If you're interested in being featured on our site, as well as getting your music played on our streaming audio, fill in the form on our web site.

Pennsylvania

Indie Band Radio *The Pennsylvania Rock Show*
bill@akmusicscene.com
www.parockshow.info
Featuring the best unsigned Rock Pennsylvania has to offer.

Old School House Radio
201 Ross Ave. #B, New Cumberland, PA 17070
PH: 717-920-0905
info@OSHRadio.com
www.oshradio.com
Reviews, interviews and you can also post your MP3s. Several shows covering the Harrisburg entertainment scene.

PaXposure Radio
320 Jackson St., Reynoldsville, PA 15851
xposureradio@paxposure.com
www.paxposure.com/paxradio.asp
Playing PA's best indie artists. Send us a copy of your CD so we can encode it to our broadcasting specifications. Note: we do not download music or accept it in e-mail attachments.

The Phil Stahl Show *WXLV*
PO Box 231, Pennsburg, PA 18073
Phil songman@ptd.net
philstahl.indiegroup.com
Features unsigned local music acts only.

Philadelphia: Musician Resource Kitchen Radio
bill@philadelphiamrk.com
www.live365.com/stations/philadelphiamrk
It's about getting local music more attention in Philadelphia. We play everything from Indie to Metal, to World to Fusion Jazz.

The Pulse *OSH Radio*
c/o HBGOnline, 4401 N. 6th St. #222, Harrisburg, PA 17110
Big Jim jimo@hbgonline.com
www.hbgonline.com/radio
Your #1 source for band news, show listings and of course great music from Harrisburg and area bands!!! Send your CDs and press kits to the above address.

RevFM Local Christian Music
925 Houserville Rd. State College, PA 16801
PH: 814-867-1922
info@revfm.net
www.revfm.net
We are glad to bolster local Christian music ministries, as well as inform the public about area concerts.

WBXQ *The Backyard Rocker*
www.wbxq.com
A 2 hour weekly local music program.

WERG *The Local Show*
Gannon U. University Sq. Erie, PA 16541
PH: 814-871-5841
werg@gannon.edu
wergfm.com

WPTS *Live Show*
411 William Pitt Union, Pittsburgh, PA 15260
PH: 412-648-7990 FX: 412-648-7988
wptsmusicdirector@hotmail.com
www.wpts.pitt.edu

WQXA *Under the Radar*
919 Buckingham Blvd. Elizabethtown, PA 17022
maria@1057thex.com
1057thex.com
Local and regional music.

WRVV *Open Mic Night*
600 Corporate Circle, Harrisburg, PA 17110
PH: 717-671-9973
Michael - Anthony Smith
requestsomething@yahoo.com
www.river973.com
Join us every Sunday nights for 2 hours of the best local and regional Rock & Roll.

WSKR
#2-5533 W. Thompson St., Philadelphia, PA 19131
fivedeucemanager@yahoo.com
www.geocities.com/wskr_5deuce/ArtistSubmissionInfo.html
Promoting Philly music. We require a "Fee" to play your music. Without this small support we can not survive, so please understand the donation requirement. This is NOT payola but a MEMBERSHIP!

WXPN *Philly Local*
3025 Walnut St., Philadelphia, PA 19104
PH: 215-898-6677. FX: 215-898-0707
Helen Leicht phillylocal@xpn.org
www.xpn.org/phillylocal.php
Each weekday at 1pm I put the spotlight on one song from an up and coming local artist. Please do not send your bios, demos etc. by e-mail!

The WYEP 10 O'clock Local News
2313 E. Carson St., Pittsburgh, PA 15203
Kyle Smith kyle@wyep.org
www.wyep.org
Highlighting new local CD releases and up and coming talent from the Pittsburgh and surrounding region. Check our site for formats we play. CD must be available locally in stores and not a demo recording.

WZZO *Backyard Bands*
1541 Alta Dr. #400, Whitehall, PA 18052-5632
PH: 610-720-9595 FX: 610-434-9511
Brother Joel wzzobyb@aol.com
www.wzzo.com
Eastern PA's #1 radio showcase for regional unsigned bands.

Rhode Island

WBRU *Home BRU'd*
88 Benevolent St., Providence, RI 02906-2046
PH: 401-272-9550 FX: 401-272-9278
HomeBRUd@wbru.com
wbru.com
We play stuff hot off the local music presses, chat about gigs around the area and dish out the latest in local music news.

WHIY *Soundcheck*
75 Oxford St., Providence, RI 02905
PH: 401-224-1994 FX: 401-467-1103
Big Jim bigjim@whjy.com
www.whjy.com
Our local music show.

WRIU *Vocalists & Localists*
326 Memorial Union, Kingston, RI 02881
PH: 401-874-4949 FX: 401-874-4349
www.wriu.org
A showcase for the many talented Jazz artists who call New England home.

WXHQ *Digging It Up In New England*
PO Box 3541, Newport, RI 02840
PH: 401-847-1955
info@radionewport.org
www.radionewport.org
Focusing on local New England artists and recordings and featuring independent labels, live recordings, and demos..

South Carolina

WUSC *Locals Only*
343 Russell House U. Union, 1400 Greene St., Columbia, SC 29208
PH: 803-777-7000
wuscmd@gwm.sc.edu
wusc.sc.edu

South Dakota

KAUR *Local Rock*
2001 S. Summit Ave. Sioux Falls, SD 57197
PH: 605-274-4386
kaurfm89@hotmail.com
inst.augie.edu/~kaur
Midnight for the coolest in Sioux Falls area Rock and way awesome regional bands too.

Tennessee

NashvilleRap.Com
PO Box 846, Hermitage, TN 37076
PH: 615-506-8069
Robert Grady info@nashvillerap.com
www.NashvilleRap.com
Armed with experience, personality and drive, we are ready to take the world by storm with a new radio show that will showcase Cashville artists dubbed NashvilleRap.Com. Our mission is to expose the hidden secret Nashville Rap talent and industry.

WDVX Live At Laurel
PO Box 18157, Knoxville, TN 37928
PH: 865-494-2020
Brent Cantrell cantrellb@netstarcomm.net
www.wdvx.com
Performances recorded Live directly from the historic Laurel Theater in Knoxville.

WEVL The Memphis Beat
PO Box 40952, Memphis, TN 38174
PH: 901-528-0560
wevl@wevl.org
www.myspace.com/memphisbeat
wevl.org

WRVU Local Music Rule
PO Box 9100, Stn. B, Nashville, TN 37235
wrvu@vanderbilt.edu
wrvu.org

Texas

Austin Music Network
4209 Airport Blvd. Austin, TX 78722
PH: 512-451-1777
www.austinmusicnetwork.org
Each day features original music videos and uninterrupted concert performances with a short list of national artists mixed in.

Humble Time Texas Radio Showcase
humble@humbletime.com
www.humbletime.com

KACV TexTunes
PO Box 447, Amarillo, TX 79178
PH: 806-371-5222
kacvfm90@actx.edu
www.kacvfm.org
Sunday mornings, it's all about Texas Music. Join Marcie Lane for three hours of tunes from artists who live and Rock in the Lone Star State.

KCUB
471 Harbin Dr. #102, Stephenville, TX 76401
PH: 254-968-7459 FX: 254-968-6258
Pamela Stone pamela@kcubonline.com
www.kcubonline.com
A unique blend of Traditional Country and Texas music geared to music fans of the Lone Star State.

KFAN Local Licks
PO Box 311, Fredericksburg, TX 78624
PH: 830-997-2197 FX: 830-997-2198
txradio@ktc.com
www.texasrebelradio.com
Features unsigned local and regional Texas Musicians.

KHRO Steppin' Out
5426 N. Mesa, El Paso, TX 79912
jojo@herorocks.com
www.herorocks.com
Keep in touch with the best in independent, and local music.

KHYI Texas Music Review
660 N. Central Expressway #120, Plano, TX 75074
PH: 972-633-0953 FX: 972-633-0957
www.khyi.com

KISS Texas Traxx
8930 Four Winds Dr. #500, San Antonio, TX 78239
PH: 210-646-0105 FX: 210-871-6116
Brian Kendall brian.kendall@cox.com
www.kissrocks.com
Local music from throughout the state of Texas. Monday nights starting at midnight.

KOOP Around the Town Sounds
PO Box 2116, Austin, TX 78768-2116
PH: 512-472-1369 FX: 512-472-6149
Charlie Martin charliemuz@aol.com
www.koop.org
Covering the many genres and ethnic shades of the contemporary local club scene.

KOOP Live Bait
PO Box 2116, Austin, TX 78768-2116
PH: 512-472-1369 FX: 512-472-6149
koopradio@yahoo.com
www.koop.org
Rock 'n Roll comes alive once a week. The show that features local and touring acts.

KPFT Spare Change
419 Lovett Blvd. Houston, TX 77006
PH: 713-526-4000 FX: 713-526-5750
music@kpft.org
www.kpft.org

KPLX The Front Porch
3500 Maple Ave. #1600, Dallas, TX 75219
PH: 214-526-2400 FX: 214-520-4343
Justin Frazell Justin@995thewolf.com
www.995thewolf.com/porch.html
Proud and Honored to play TEXAS MUSIC.

KSTV Texas Style Saturday Night
PO Box 289, Stephenville, TX 76401
PH: 254-968-2141
erin@kstvfm.com
www.kstvfm.com

KSTX Sunday Nite Session
8401 Datapoint Dr. #800,
San Antonio, TX 78229-5903
PH: 210-614-8977
www.tpr.org
Features interviews, live music and recordings of contemporary musicians from San Antonio and around Texas.

KTRU The Local Show
PO Box 1892, Houston, TX 77251
PH: 713-348-KTRU
ktru@ktru.org
www.ktru.org

KTXT Domestics
PO Box 43081, Lubbock, TX 79409
PH: 806-742-3914 FX: 806-742-3906
www.ktxt.net
Lubbock's only local music show. Giving you the best from all around the hub city.

KUT/KUTX Live Set
1 University Stn. A0704, Austin, TX 78712
PH: 512-471-1631 FX: 512-471-3700
www.kut.org
Some of the best darned music you'll hear anywhere on the planet!

KUT Austin Music Minute
1 University Stn. A0704, Austin, TX 78712
PH: 512-471-1631 FX: 512-471-3700
Teresa Ferguson austinmusic@austin.rr.com
www.kut.org
Just one more way for KUT to promote live music events in Austin.

KVLU Lamar U.
PO Box 10064, Beaumont, TX 77710
PH: 409-880-8164
KVLU@hal.lamar.edu
dept.lamar.edu/kvlu
Texas artists are featured on all of our local programs.

KVRX Local Live
PO Box D, Austin, TX 78713-7209
PH: 512-471-5106
local_live@kvrx.org
www.kvrx.org
Handmade according to an ancient Austin recipe, using only the choicest barley, hops and spring water.

Live and Local Show
1 2611 N. Beltline Rd. #111, Sunnyvale, TX 75182
Chaz Chaz@TexasRadio1.com
www.liveandlocalshow.com
Bands that would like to be featured please mail your CD and contact info.

Texas Radio 1
2611 N. Beltline Rd. # 111 Sunnyvale, TX 75182
PH: 972-203-8886
www.texasradio1.com
Each show features Texas Music, News, Interviews, and LIVE Performances from Texas Artists.

Vermont

WBTZ Buzz Homebrew
255 S. Champlain St., Burlington, VT 05401
Attn: Homebrew Crew
mailbag@999thebuzz.com
www.999thebuzz.com
A show for local acts to prove that good music comes in all forms and genres.

WEQX EQX-Posure!!
PO Box 1027, Manchester, VT 05255
PH: 802-362-4800
Andy fueled_by_coffee@yahoo.com
www.weqx.com
The BEST Local/Regional music!

Virginia

The Electric Croude WCVE
23 Sesame St., Richmond, VA 23235
PH: 804-560-8172
George Maida George_Maida@wcve.pbs.org
wcve.org
As far as music goes, the show is very eclectic and I play both acoustic and electric. The only genre I don't play is Rap.

WCFS
3540 Holland Rd. Ste. 113 PMB 103,
Virginia Beach, VA 23452
PH: 757-651-5063 FX: 757-468-6988
indiebible@wcfsradio.us
www.wcfsradio.us
A streaming internet broadcast providing all original, non- stop, commercial free, broadcasting of local bands to Hampton Roads (and beyond).

WFSO *Locals Only*
1617 Cedar Rd. Chesapeake, VA 23322
PH: 757-547-1036
wfoslocalsonly@yahoo.com
www.wfoslocalsonly.com
Dedicated to local bands throughout the great state of Virginia.

WNOR *Homegrown*
870 Greenbrier Circle #399, Chesapeake, VA 23320
PH: 757-366-9900 FX: 757-366-9870
Shelley shelley@fm99.com
www.fm99.com
Featuring local and regional bands, plus live interviews and performances.

WNRN *Local Motive*
2250 Old Ivy Rd. #2, Charlottesville, VA 22903
PH: 434-971-4096 FX: 434-971-6562
wnrs@sbc.edu
wnrs.sbc.edu
Spotlights local & regional music covering VA & DC.

Washington

KNDD *The Young and The Restless*
1100 Olive Way #1650, Seattle, WA 98101
Attn: John Richards
PH: 206-622-3251
www.1077theend.com/seattlemusic.asp
Two hours of Northwest bands.

KOHO *Icicle Jazz*
7475 KOHO Place, Leavenworth, WA 98826
PH: 509-548-1011 FX: 509-548-3222
www.kohoradio.com
The Seattle Jazz scene is explored with new release music from Seattle artists and labels every week.

KPLU *Jazz Northwest*
1010 S. 122nd St., Tacoma, WA 98447-0885
PH: 253-535-7758 FX: 253-535-8332
Jim Wilke kplu@plu.edu
kplu.org/jandb/wilke.html
Focuses on the regional Jazz scene from Portland to Vancouver.

West Virginia

WAMX *Loud and Local*
ATTN: Erik on the X, 134 4th Ave.
Huntington, WV 25701
PH: 304-525-7788 x143 FX: 304-525-3299
Erik erikonthex@yahoo.com
www.x1063.com
The Original Local & Regional Rock Show.

WKLC *Homegrown 105*
100 Kanawha Ter., St. Albans, WV 25177
homegrown105@wklc.com
www.wklc.com
Features West Virginia's best Rock bands.

WWVU *The Morgantown Sound*
PO Box 6446, Morgantown, WV 26506-6446
PH: 304-293-3329 FX: 304293-7363
Orville Weale oweale@yahoo.com
www.wvu.edu/~u92
The exclusive source of live local music in the area.

Wisconsin

WLZR *Local Licks*
5407 W. McKinley Ave. Milwaukee, WI 53208
PH: 414-978-9000 FX: 414-978-9003
Marcus Allen mallen@lazer103.com
www.lazer103.com
If your band has a cd, you can send it to me, along with a one page bio.

WMSE *Midnight Radio*
1025 N. Broadway, Milwaukee, WI 53202
PH: 414-277-6942 FX: 414-277-7149
Mike bereiter@msoe.edu
www.wmse.org

WORT *Hootenanny*
118 S. Bedford S. Madison, WI 53703-2692
PH: 608-256-2001 FX: 608-256-3704
Dave Zero davezero@tds.net
fridayhoot.com
Rock & Roll, live music, local bands, insurgent Country, dirty Blues, Punk, Indie.

WSUW *Local Edge*
1201 Anderson Library, UW-Whitewater,
Whitewater, WI 53190
PH: 262-472-1323 FX: 262-472-5029
wsuw@uww.edu
www.wsuw.org

WWSP *Club Wisconsin*
105 CAC Reserve St., Stevens Point, WI 54481
PH: 715- 346-4722
Jeff clubwi@hotmail.com
www.uwsp.edu/stuorg/wwsp
The best in Moo-town music. Local concert information and interviews of bands playing in the area.

Canada

120 Seconds *CBC*
Box 4600, Vancouver, BC V6B 4A2
PH: 877-955-6565 FX: 604-662-6594
info@120seconds.com
www.120seconds.com
A showcase for the latest in Canadian bite-sized entertainment. Videos, spoken word, music and film.

Bandwidth *CBC*
PO Box 3220, Stn. C, Ottawa, ON K1Y 1E4
PH: 613-562-8570
Amanda Putz bandwidth@cbc.ca
www.cbc.ca/bandwidth
Eclectic mix of Canadian music.

CIUT *Back To The Sugar Camp*
100 Bain Ave. 19 The Lindens,
Toronto, ON M4K 1E8
PH: 416-465-9464
steve@backtothesugarcamp.com
www.backtothesugarcamp.com
Weekly radio show featuring Canadiana music.

CKCU *Canadian Spaces*
Rm 517, U. Ctr. 1125 Colonel By Dr.
Ottawa, ON K1S 5B6
PH: 613-520-2898
Chopper McKinnon chopper@nutshellmusic.com
www.ckcufm.com
Canada's most respected Folk and Roots music and interview show.

CKDU *Canadian Bacon*
Dalhousie Stud. Union Bldg. 6136 University Ave.
Halifax, NS B3H 4J2
PH: 902-494-6479
Derek Huffman & Kathy Crosby music@ckdu.ca
www.ckdu.ca
Canadian Rock and pop.

Definitely Not the Opera *CBC*
Attn: Anna Lazowski,
Box 160, Winnipeg, MB R3C 2H1
PH: 204-788-3182
Sook-Yin Lee dnto@cbc.ca
www.cbc.ca/dnto
We like to play Canadian Indie bands on the show and we're always looking for new music.

Indie Night in Canada *CFOX*
#2000-700 W. Georgia, Vancouver, BC V7Y 1K9
PH: 604-684-7221 FX: 604-331-2755
Cory Price cprice@cfox.com
www.cfox.com/shows/indie_night.cfm
Independent bands from Vancouver and across the country plus interviews and special live performances.

just concerts *CBC Radio 3*
PO Box 4600, Vancouver, BC V6B 4A2
PH: 877-955-6565 FX: 604-662-6594
info@justconcerts.com
justconcerts.com
Interviews, audio and video coverage of the latest concerts, Indie and mainstream!

Madly Off in All Directions *CBC*
PO Box 500 Stn. A, Toronto, ON M5W 1E6
PH: 416-205-6103
radio.cbc.ca/programs/madlyoff
Music, improvisation and satirical stand-up from all across Canada.

Roots Music Canada *CBC*
info@rootsmusiccanada.com
www.rootsmusiccanada.com
Canadian Roots and Folk music, is based on the longstanding music of various communities across Canada.

The Roundup *CBC*
PO Box 4600, Vancouver, BC V6B 4A2
PH: 604-662-6082 FX: 604-662-6098
Tetsuro Shigematsu roundup@vancouver.cbc.ca
www.cbc.ca/roundup
The music we play is everything from the latest smart pop melody to the songs your grandpa used to sing after his second glass of sherry!

Schmoozebuzz
schmoozequeen@hotmail.com
www.schmoozequeen.tv
A weekly radio and online entertainment talk show focusing on established and rising Canadian Film, Music & New Media Stars featuring interviews, news, reviews and more!

Sounds Like Canada *CBC*
700 Hamilton St. PO Box 4600,
Vancouver, BC V6B 4A2
PH: 604-662-6608 FX: 604-662-6025
Shelagh Rogers soundslikecanada@cbc.ca
www.cbc.ca/soundslikecanada
Our goal is to drench the airwaves with voices and sound from all over the country and bring the listener what is new, surprising and thought provoking.

The Sunday Edition CBC
PO Box 500 Stn. A, Toronto, ON M5W 1E6
PH: 416-205-3700 FX: 416-205-6461
Michael Enright thesundayedition@cbc.ca
radio.cbc.ca/programs/thismorning/sunday.html
Here you will also find a particularly eclectic mix of music.

Vinyl Café CBC
PO Box 500 Stn A, Toronto, ON M5W 1E6
PH: 416-205-3700
Stuart McLean vinylcafe@toronto.cbc.ca
www.cbc.ca/vinylcafe
Features music, both live and recorded.

Waxing Deep CKUT
235 Metcalfe Ave. #402, Westmount, QC H3Z 2H8
waxingdeep@ckut.ca
www.waxingdeep.org
Specialises in Canadian and Quebecois Bossa, Jazz, Funk, Breaks, Soul, Disco, Latin, and everything in between.

Alberta

CFBR Red, White & New
#100-18520 Stony Plain Rd.
Edmonton, AB T5S 2E2
PH: 780-486-2800 FX: 780-489-6927
Park Warden park@bear.fm
www.TheBearRocks.com
The latest, greatest Canadian Rock from homegrown to our international superstars.

CKUA Alberta Sessions
10526 Jasper Ave. Edmonton, AB T5J 1Z7
PH: 780-428-7595 FX: 780-428-7624
radio@ckua.org
www.ckua.com
A platform for artists based in this province to perform before an audience of open minded, earnest listeners in a state of the art theatre.

Key of A CBC
PH: 780-468-7472 FX: 780-468-7468
Katherine Duncan keyofa@cbc.ca
www.cbc.ca/keyofa
We go behind the scenes with musicians and performers from across Alberta.

British Columbia

CiTR Local Kids Make Good
#233-6138 SUB Blvd. Vancouver, BC V6T 1Z1
PH: 604-822-8733 FX: 604-822-9364
citrmusic@club.ams.ubc.ca
www.citr.ca
Local music of all sorts. The program most likely to play your band!"

CJSF Sonic Heights
TC 216, Burnaby, BC V5A 1S6
PH: 604-291-3727 FX: 604-291-3695
cjsfmusc@sfu.ca
www.cjsf.bc.ca
From BC and across Canada; various musical genres along with a focus on New Music/Electroacoustic works. Interviews, discussions, and listings related to the local music and art scene.

CVUE The All Canadian Show
PO Box 2288, Sechelt, BC V0N3A0
PH: 604-885-0800
Mike McMillan cvue@dccnet.com
www.civu.net
Fabulous Canadian music from 'then' & 'now' with lots of music by local musicians & other artists from around BC.

North by Northwest CBC
Box 4600, Vancouver, BC V6B 4A2
PH: 604-662-6089
Sheryl MacKay nxnw@cbc.ca
www.cbc.ca/nxnw
Presenting creative people and what they create. Artists, writers, performers and "just plain folks" talking about what they do and what others do.

On the Island CBC
1025 Pandora Ave. Victoria, BC V8V 3P6
PH: 250-360-2227 FX: 250-360-2600
Susan Elrington victoria@cbc.ca
www.cbc.ca/ontheisland

Radio Bandcouver
#110, 360 Columbia St., Vancouver, BC V6A 4J1
Mark Bignell mark@bandcouver.com
www.bandcouver.com
Artists & Bands send your CDs and press kits in.

Westcoast Performance CBC
Box 4600, Vancouver, BC V6B 4A2
PH: 604-662-6076
Michael Juk westcoast@vancouver.cbc.ca
www.cbc.ca/wcp
Presenting the finest music British Columbia Classical and World music artists.

The Zone's Band of the Month
The Zone, Top Fl. 2750 Quadra St.,
Victoria, BC V8T 4E8
PH: 250-475-6611
Kate Graham kate@TheZone.fm
www.thezone.fm
Our featured band will receive feature play of their music and will be highlighted in a mini audio bio that will air between five and seven times each day.

Manitoba

CKUW Beer For Breakfast
1 Neptune Bay, Winnipeg, MB R3T 0Z6
Broose Tulloch b2ware@hotmail.com
beerforbreakfast.org
I focus entirely on the Winnipeg scene including Manitoba, Nunavut, Saskatchewan, North Dakota, Minnesota, or Northern Ontario. I only play local or visiting artists. We always have time for live interviews.

Weekend Morning Show CBC
PH: 204-788-3612 FX: 204-788-3674
Ron Robinson weekend@winnipeg.cbc.ca
www.cbc.ca/weekendmorning
Features eclectic music, comedy, entertainment events, interesting people and special features.

New Brunswick

Mainstreet New Brunswick CBC
PO Box 2358, Saint John, NB E2L 3V6
PH: 506-632-7743 FX: 506-632-7761
Gary Mittelholtz mainstreet@cbc.ca
www.cbc.ca/mainstreetnb
Provincial, national and international news, as well as some fun features and East Coast music.

Newfoundland

CHMR Upon this Rock
Box A-119 St. John's, NL A1C 5S7
PH: 709-737-4777 FX: 709-737-7688
chmr@mun.ca
www.mun.ca/chmr
Two hours of the best in Newfoundland and Labrador music. From Traditional to Alternative.

MUSICRAFT CBC
Francesca Swann musicraft@cbc.ca
www.cbc.ca/musicraft
Musical events from across the province and discussions with the people who bring the music to life.

On the Go CBC
PH: 709-576-5270
Ted Blades onthego@cbc.ca
www.cbc.ca/onthego
A lively package of news, weather, interviews, mini-documentaries and the best in local music.

The Performance Hour CBC
theperformancehour@cbc.ca
www.cbc.ca/performancehour
Newfoundland's finest Singers and Songwriters recorded live at the LSPU Hall in St. Johns.

Nova Scotia

All The Best CBC
PO Box 30000, Halifax, NS B3J 3E9
PH: 902-420-4426 FX: 902-420-4089
www.cbc.ca/allthebest
The show presents music ranging from Classical through classic Jazz to traditional. Host: Shauntay Grant

Atlantic Airwaves CBC
PO Box 30000, Halifax, NS B3J 3E9
PH: 902-420-4426 FX: 902-420-4089
www.cbc.ca/atlanticairwaves
Music and profiles of music makers from Canada's four Atlantic Provinces as well as national and international Artists appearing throughout the region. Host: Stan Carew

CIGO East Coast Rising
11 MacIntosh Ave. Port Hawkesbury, NS B9A 3K4
PH: 902-625-1220 FX: 902-625-2664
1015thehawk@1015thehawk.com
www.1015thehawk.com/ecr.asp
Tune in to get updates on the East Coast music scene!!

CIGO Highland Fling
11 MacIntosh Ave. Port Hawkesbury, NS B9A 3K4
PH: 902-625-1220 FX: 902-625-2664
1015thehawk@1015thehawk.com
www.1015thehawk.com/highland.asp
Committing to focus on Cape Breton fiddle, piano, Gaelic song and bagpipes. Interviews with artists and those associated with the Cape Breton style of music.

CKDU Halifax
Dalhousie Stud. Union Bldg. 6136 U. Ave.
Halifax, NS B3H 4J2
PH: 902-494-6479
Jessica Whyte music@ckdu.ca
www.ckdu.ca
We like to help promote new music by local musicians by providing publicity for CD release performance/parties etc.

CKDU *The One Inch Punch*
Dalhousie Stud. Union Bldg. 6136 U. Ave.
Halifax, NS B3H 4J2
PH: 902-494-6479
Jessica Whyte music@ckdu.ca
www.ckdu.ca
Punk focusing on the local scene.

CKDU *Saturday Morning Musical Box*
Dalhousie Stud. Union Bldg. 6136 U. Ave.
Halifax, NS B3H 4J2
PH: 902-494-6479
Jessica Whyte music@ckdu.ca
www.ckdu.ca
Classical music. Interviews with local performers.

Connections *CBC*
PO Box 30000, Halifax, NS B3J 3E9
PH: 902-420-4248 FX: 902-420-4089
Olga Milosevich connections@halifax.cbc.ca
www.cbc.ca/connections
An uplifting mixture of music - largely Maritime and ranging from Classical to Folk, Jazz, pop and world-beat.

MainStreet Halifax *CBC*
PO Box30000, Halifax, NS B3J 3E9
PH: 902-420-4378 FX: 902-420-4357
Carmen Klassen mainstreet@halifax.cbc.ca
www.cbc.ca/mainstreetns
The latest on the news of the day...and of course, some great music.

Musically Yours *CBC*
PO Box 30000, Halifax, NS B3J 3E9
Adrian Hoffman ahoffman@halifax.cbc.ca
novascotia.cbc.ca/radio/musicallyyours
The music ranges from Classical to Atlantic Folk, with plenty of traditional, Jazz and popular selections thrown in for good measure.

WEEKENDER
PO Box 30000, Halifax, NS B3J 3E9
PH: 902-420-4378 FX: 902-420-4357
Peter Togni weekender@halifax.cbc.ca
www.radio.cbc.ca/programs/weekender
Music that's engaging, fun, brought to you from all over the world and played by the best in the business.

Ontario

All in a Day *CBC*
PO Box 3220, Stn. C, Ottawa, ON K1Y 1E4
PH: 613-562-8442 FX: 613-562-8810
Brent Bambury allinaday@cbc.ca
www.cbc.ca/allinaday
In any given program, you're likely to hear Rock, Jazz, Pop, World Beat, Classical or Blues.

CFFF *Good 'n Country*
715 George St. N. Peterborough, ON K9H 3T2
PH: 705-748-4761
Barb Holtmann restorix@nexicom.net
www.trentu.ca/trentradio
Blending the old, the new and the unusual in Country music. News, views and interviews with local and area artists.

CFFF *Smooth Operator*
715 George St. N. Peterborough, ON K9H 3T2
PH: 705-748-4761
trentradio@trentu.ca
www.trentu.ca/trentradio
Listen to local music along with interviews with interesting people from the Peterborough area.

CHUO *L'Express Country*
372 rue Rideau St. #201, Ottawa, ON K1N 1G7
www.chuo.fm
groups.msn.com/RobertGuindonAnimateur
Musique Country francophone d'artistes connus dans la région.

CJLX *The Spin on Quinte*
PO Box 4200, Belleville, ON K8N 5B9
Steve Fisher cjlx@loyalistc.on.ca
www.cjlx.fm
Folk/Acoustic/Celtic/Roots music & beyond. Each week host we spin some of the best music Quinte has to offer....whatever the genre. Local bands and musicians are encouraged to submit their material for airplay.

Fresh Air *CBC*
PO Box 500, Stn. A, Toronto, ON M5W 1E6
PH: 416-205-3700
Jeff Goodes freshair@toronto.cbc.ca
www.cbc.ca/freshair
A variety of music and stories. It's like sitting around the kitchen table with old friends.

Ottawa Morning
PO Box 3220, Stn. C, Ottawa, ON K1Y 1E4
PH: 613-562-8442 FX: 613-562-8810
Anthony and Lucy ottawamorning@cbc.ca
www.cbc.ca/ottawamorning
Matthew Crosier is your ear on entertainment and the local music scene.

Prince Edward Island

Island Music Radio
115 Richmond St., Charlottetown, PE C1A 1A7
PH: 902-368-6176 FX: 902-368-4418
peiarts@peiartscouncil.com
www.gov.pe.ca/radio
If you are an Island musician and would like to have your music included, please contact the PEI Council of the Arts for details.

Quebec

A Propos *CBC*
Box 6000, Montreal, QC H3C 3A8
PH: 514-597-6000 FX: 514-597-4423
Jim Corcoran performance@montreal.cbc.ca
www.cbc.ca/apropos
The most popular tunes coming out of Quebec.

Saskatchewan

Morning Edition *CBC*
2440 Broad St., Regina, SK S4P 4A1
PH: 306-347-9540 FX: 306-347-9797
Sheila Coles amradio@regina.cbc.ca
www.cbc.ca/morningedition
Lifestyle features, music and a good sprinkling of humour are major components of our program.

Sign up for
The Indie Contact Newsletter!

Every month you will receive a new list of places to send your music for review, radio play etc.

www.indiebible.com

Europe

United Kingdom

BBC Radio 1
London, W1N 4DJ UK
PH: 08700-100-100
www.bbc.co.uk
National Variations. `Steve Lamacq - the Evening Session'. Session tracks and new music. For listeners in Scotland only: `The Session in Scotland'. With Gill Mills and Vic Galloway. For listeners in Wales only: `The Session in Wales'. With Bethan Elfyn and Huw Stephens. For listeners in Northern Ireland only: `The Session in N Ireland'. With Colin Murray and Donna Legge.

BBC Radio Scotland
Rm 206, Music Dept. Queen Margaret Dr.
Glasgow, Scotland, G12 8DG
enquiries.scot@bbc.co.uk
www.bbc.co.uk/scotland/music

Forest of Dean Radio *Juke Box Jury*
1 Berisford Ct. Cinderford,
Gloucestershire, GL14 2BS UK
PH: 01594-820722
Darren Crook contactus@fodradio.org
www.fodradio.org/darren.htm
Spinning the finest local music that the Forest of Dean and Gloucestershire as whole as to offer with a studio panel passing judgment and comment on what's being played. The show also features a comprehensive gig guide.

Homegrown Cuts *BBC*
c/o 1Xtra, PO Box 1X, London, W1A UK
Ras Kwame homegrown@bbc.co.uk
www.bbc.co.uk/1xtra/djs/raskwame.shtml
Dance, Hip Hop etc.

Radio Free MK
PO Box 3595, Newport, Pagnell,
Bucks, MK16 0BF UK
live@radiofreemk.co.uk
www.radiofreemk.co.uk
Our aim is to provide a station for music from Milton Keynes and its so-called 'catchment area' (cos trust us, we know how you feel, we have to live here).

Rock3.co.uk
4 Sturdee, Frimley, Surrey, GU16 8DL UK
info@rock3.co.uk
www.rock3.co.uk
We review and play new and unsigned Bands from the British Isles.

Vic's Demo Derby *BBC*
Radio 1 Scotland, Queen Margaret Dr.
Glasgow, Scotland G12 8DG
Vic Galloway vic@bbc.co.uk
www.bbc.co.uk/vicandgill
Every week, two unsigned bands square up to one another. If you're in a band, based in Scotland, and want to get your music heard, then send your demo to us.

Australia

2RRR *Sydney Sounds*
PO Box 644 Gladesville, NSW 1675 Australia
PH: 61-29816-2988 FX: 61-2-9817-1048
www.2rrr.org.au
Interviews and Recordings by Garage/Surf/Punk/Psychobilly & Power Pop Bands from around Sydney.

2SER *Electro-plastique*
U. Tech. Sydney, Level 26, Building 1, 1 Broadway, Ultimo, NSW 2007 Australia
PH: 61-2-9514-9514 FX: 61-2-9514-9599
info@2ser.com
www.2ser.com
www.clananalogue.org
A policy of playing 100% Australian Electronic music.

2VOX *Australian Independent Music Show*
PO Box 1663, Wollongong, NSW 2500 Australia
PH: 02-4227-3436 FX: 02-4226-5922
Ben Hession vox@1earth.net
www.vox.1earth.net

2XX *Know Your Product*
PO Box 812, Canberra, ACT 2601 Australia
PH: 02-6247-4400 FX: 02-6248-5560
www.2xxfm.org.au
Local and National music featuring new releases and interviews.

3CR *Local and Live*
PO Box 1277, Collingwood, Melbourne, VIC 3065 Australia
PH: 03-9419-8377 FX: 03-9417-4472
programming@3cr.org.au
www.3cr.org.au
Featuring music and interviews with local musicians, live-to-air performances and gig guides.

3D *Local and Live*
48 Nelson St, Stepney, SA 5069 Australia
PH: 08-8363-3937 FX: 08-8362-6937
www.threedradio.com
All the Best Local Music

3MR *OZ Rock, H.A.T.*
c/o Monash U. VIC 3800 Australia
PH: 03-990-55-151 FX: 61-3-9905-4007
inquiries@monash.edu.au
yoyo.cc.monash.edu.au/groups/3MU

3PBS *Big Mob*
PO Box 2917, Fitzroy MDC, VIC 3065 Australia
PH: 61-3-8415-1067 FX: 61-3-8415-1831
www.pbsfm.org.au
Contemporary & traditional Indigenous music.

3RRR *Local and or General*
PO Box 304, Fitzroy, VIC 3065 Australia
localgeneral@hotmail.com
localgeneral.tripod.com
Music from around the country, as well as local independent artists. Live-to-air performances and interviews.

5PBA *Max Radio*
PO Box 433 Salisbury, SA 5108 Australia
PH: 61-8-8250-3735 FX: 61-8-8281-7495
www.pbafm.org.au/max
Live bands, interviews, feature albums, giveaways, music news, gossip, laughter and more.

5UV *Adelaide Concert Hour*
228 North Terrace Adelaide, SA 5000 Australia
PH: 61-8-8303-5000 FX: 61-8-8303-4374
Alastair Mackintosh radio@adelaide.edu.au
radio.adelaide.edu.au
Local Classical performances recorded live.

5UV *Local Noise*
228 North Terrace Adelaide, SA 5000 Australia
PH: 61-8-8303-5000 FX: 61-8-8303-4374
Darren Leach darren.leach@mail.com
radio.adelaide.edu.au
Local bands live to air from Studio 1.

ABC Backyard *Local Radio Music*
Bill Riner riner.bill@abc.net.au
www.abc.net.au/backyard/rinermusic.htm

ABC Radio National *Live On Stage*
Paul Petran petran.paul@abc.net.au
www.abc.net.au/rn/music/liveos
Live recordings of the best musicians touring this country. Local and overseas talent.

Aussie Bar-B-Que *4ZZZ*
PO Box 509, Fortitude Valley, QLD 4006 Australia
PH: 07-3252-1555 FX: 07-3252-1950
Tracey tracey-@hotmail.com
www.4zzzfm.org.au
100% Australian artists and bands.

The Australian Real Underground Music Show
PO Box 532, Newcastle, NSW 2300 Australia
PH: 61-02-49270290
info@isonliveradio.com
www.isonliveradio.com
Features great new Australian music each week.

Bay FM *Australian Music*
PO Box 1003 Cleveland, QLD 4163 Australia
PH: 07-3821-0022 FX: 07-3286-9166
bayfm@bayfm.org.au
www.bayfm.org.au

City Park Radio *OZ Muster*
PO Box 1501, Launceston, TAS 7250 Australia
PH: 03-6334-7429 FX: 03-6334-3344
country@cityparkradio.com
www.cityparkradio.com
All Australian Country music.

Gippsland FM *Oz Factor*
PO Box 579 Morwell, VIC 3840 Australia
PH: 61-3-5134-8444 FX: 61-3-5133-0555
3gcr@gippsland.net.au
www.3gcrfm.org.au

Heartland FM
68 High St. Robina Town Ctr., QLD 4228 Australia
PH: 61-7-5578 7870 FX: 61-7-5578-7871
admin@heartlandfm.com
www.heartlandfm.com
Features live broadcasts of local Country artists.

JOY FM *The Local*
PO Box 907, South Melbourne, VIC 3205 Australia
PH: 61 (03) 9699-2949 FX: 61 (03) 9699-2646
thelocal@joy.org.au
www.joy.org.au
A celebration of all things local, with an emphasis on Australian music content, as well as all that's going down in our great city.

Music Deli
PH: 03-9626-1623 FX: 03-9626-1621
Paul Petran musicdeli@your.abc.net.au
www.abc.net.au/rn/music/deli
Folk, Traditional and Acoustic music and what is commonly known as World music. There's a strong emphasis on Australian performances.

PBS FM *No Frills*
PO Box 2917, Fitzroy MDC, VIC 3065 Australia
PH: 61-3-8415-1067 FX: 61-3-8415-1831
Claire Stuchbery claire@beat.com.au
www.pbsfm.org.au
Showcasing the hard working, often under represented sector of the Australian music industry.

RTR FM *Homegrown*
PO Box 949, Nedlands, WA 6909 Australia
PH: 08-6488-3380
rtrfm@rtrfm.com.au
www.rtrfm.com.au
Local music scene news, reviews and interviews

Triple H *HOME BREW*
C- 4/48 Florence St., Hornsby, NSW 2077 Australia
homebrewradio@yahoo.com.au
www.homebrewradio.com.au
100% Australian Music

Triple J *Home and Hosed*
GPO Box 9994 Canberra, NSW Australia
www.abc.net.au/triplej/homeandhosed
Australian music from all over. Music, interviews, chat, news live sounds and much more.

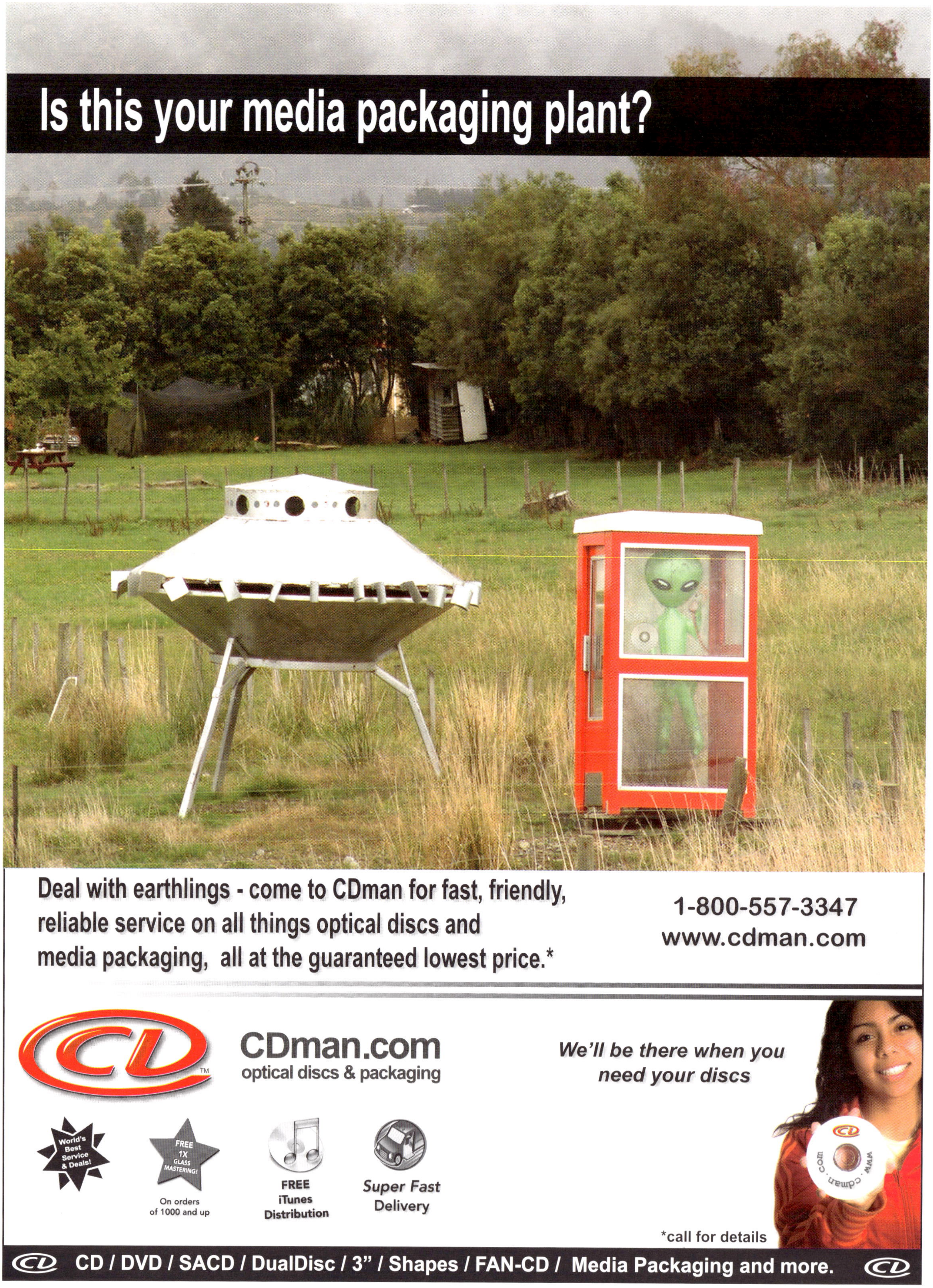

Is this your media packaging plant?

Deal with earthlings - come to CDman for fast, friendly, reliable service on all things optical discs and media packaging, all at the guaranteed lowest price.*

1-800-557-3347
www.cdman.com

CDman.com
optical discs & packaging

We'll be there when you need your discs

FREE iTunes Distribution

Super Fast Delivery

*call for details

 CD / DVD / SACD / DualDisc / 3" / Shapes / FAN-CD / Media Packaging and more.

SECTION FOUR: SERVICES THAT WILL HELP YOU TO SELL YOUR MUSIC

"You must believe in yourself. Realize that you don't need a label to be a success. Don't be egotistical, but be confident. Be optimistic – believe you are good enough and can get what you want. If you don't have faith in yourself – no one else will." - **Bernard Baur, Music Connection Magazine**

Promotional Services

United States

2 Generations SPA Music Management
300 E. 34th St. #28B, New York, NY 10016
PH: 212-842-8478
management@2generations.com
www.2generations.com
Consulting company representing unsigned bands/artists.

AFBPromotions
Wednesday Elektra wednesday@aidforbands.com
www.aidforbands.com
Currently we are an international street team service specializing in online and offline promotions and marketing for Underground artists.

The Almighty Institute of Music Retail
11724 Ventura Blvd. Suite B, Studio City, CA 91604
PH: 323-851-2430 FX: 815-642 0806
Clark Benson clark@almightyretail.com
www.almightyretail.com
Services record labels and youth culture companies looking to promote their product in record stores and other outlets that sell prerecorded music.

AlphaMusicGroup
1133 Broadway, #706, New York, NY 10010
PH: 212-696-7934
Sylvie Harris
sylvieharris@alphamusicgroup.com
www.alphamusicgroup.com
A selective independent A & R company that strives to be the most reliable source for unsigned artists/bands looking for help in getting a record deal.

Ariel Publicity Artist Relations and Cyber Promotions
325 W. 38th St. #505, New York, NY 10018
PH: 212-239-8384 FX: 212-239-8380
Ariel Hyatt ariel@arielpublicity.com
www.arielpublicity.com
Professional promotional services for Indie artists.

Arrow/ATM Distributing Company
1373 Grandview Ave. #212, Columbus, OH 43212
PH: 800-552-3472 FX: 877-249-6787
Matt E. Earley mee@arrdis.com
www.arrdis.com
National distribution of college music to retailers, bookstores & mass merchants. Specializing in East Coast and Midwest distribution.

Art Attack Promotions
2414 Elmglen Dr. Austin, TX 78744
PH: 512-445-7117 FX: 512-447-2493
Gigi Greco info@artattackpromotions.com
www.artattackpromotions.com
Full service entertainment marketing company specializing in grassroots marketing, online promotions, lifestyle campaigns, and street team development.

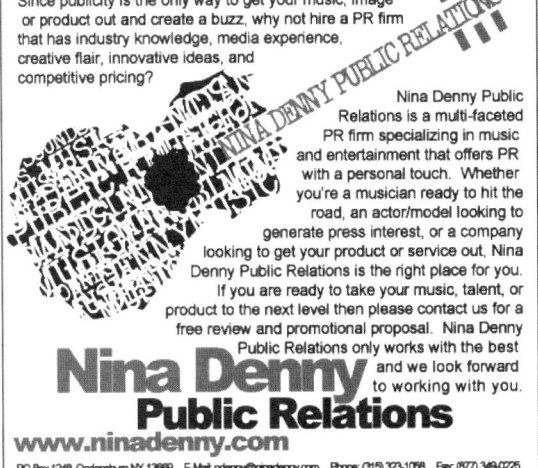

Bill Wence Promotions
RADIO PROMOTION FOR THE INDEPENDENT ARTIST

GET YOUR MUSIC HEARD! NOW WORKING WITH OVER 400 ADVENTUROUS RADIO STATIONS THAT AREN'T AFRAID TO TAKE A CHANCE

**Radio Interviews
Tours & Support
Weekly Tracking**

Bill Wence Promotions
PO Box 39 • Nolensville, TN 37135
615-776-2060 Fax 776-2181
email: billwencepro@earthlink.net

All major credit cards accepted

RADIO AIRPLAY/ON THE CHARTS! JERRY JEFF WALKER • JAMES TALLEY • AMAZING RHYTHM ACES • RONNY ELLIOTT • RED MEAT • TOM T. HALL • JONELL MOSSER • RUTHIE & THE WRANGLERS • BOBBY BARE • WOODSONGS & MORE...

PROMOTING THE MUSIC OF SOME OF THE MOST TALENTED PEOPLE IN THE WORLD

RECENT ALBUMS GONZO STEW - Jerry Jeff Walker • THIRTEEN - Red Meat • TOUCHSTONES - James Talley • THE OUTLAWS - Waylon Jennings, Jessi Colter, Willie Nelson, Tompall Glaser • HEP - Ronny Elliott • ENOUGH ROPE - Jonell Mosser • CHOC FULL OF COUNTRY - Amazing Rhythm Aces • HOMEGROWN - Tom T. Hall • LONESOMERS - Mare Winningham • OLD DOGS - Waylon Jennings, Bobby Bare, Mel Tillis, Jerry Reed • STILL THE ONE, LIVE - Orleans • ALAMEDA COUNTY LINE - Red Meat • DRAG QUEENS IN LIMOUSINES - Mary Gauthier and more...

www.billwencepromotions.com

AMA (Americana Music Association - founding member) • IBMA • CMA • NARAS • ASCAP • AFM #257

Artist Toolbox
289 S. Robertson Blvd. #200,
Beverly Hills, CA 90211
PH: 818-442-9294
info@warriorgirlmusic.com
www.artisttoolbox.net
A program designed to fill the gaps in independent music production, marketing, promotion and distribution.

Assembly Entertainment
8961 Sunset Blvd. West Hollywood, CA 90069
PH: 310-888-4040 FX: 310-288-8301
Seth Owen info@AssemblyEntertainment.com
www.AssemblyEntertainment.com
Artist management company seeking new artists.

Baker/Northrop Media Group
16255 Ventura Blvd. Ste 1016, Encino, CA 91436
PH: 818-986-5200 FX: 818-986-1174
Sheryl Northrop sheryl@bakernorthrop.com
bakernorthrop.com
We are committed to excellence in providing creative, thoughtful press campaigns for a diverse client roster ranging from high-profile artists and personalities to independent musicians in multiple genres.

bandpromote.com
PO Box 4102, Hollywood, CA 90078
PH: 323-276-1000 FX: 323-276-1001
Mike Galaxy mgalaxy@bandpromote.com
www.bandpromote.com
Distribute your music to thousands of record execs.

Blackcat Talent & Entertainment/ Blackcat Music Publishing
PO Box 26174, El Paso, TX 79926
David O. Samaniego info@blackcattalent.com
www.blackcattalent.com
A multi-service company within the music & film industry. BC Talent & Entertainment is a Management & Special Events Productions Co. BC Music Publishing: Publishing, Licensing and Representation, BC Multi Media features Media studio creations & productions and BC Music Group is an Indie Label.

Broken Record Productions
1210 Gamma, Pasadena, TX 77504
PH: 832-457-7790
Devon Mikeska
devon@brokenrecordproductions.com
www.brokenrecordproductions.com
A full service music/live event video production company as well as artist management/development.

BTM Communications
1325 Corcoran St. NW, Washington, DC 20009
PH: 202-483-1105
BuildTheMountain@aol.com
www.buildthemountain.com
We offer publicity services for the touring artist including press and radio advance work, press release writing and launch, and ensuring posters and photos are sent to venues in a timely fashion to further your career.

Canary Promotion + Design
PO Box 4377, Philadelphia, PA 19118-8377
PH: 215-242-6393
Megan Wendell info@canarypromo.com
www.canarypromo.com
Publicity and graphic design services for web and print.

CD Register
PO Box 182492, Shelby Twp., MI 48318
PH: 586-480-3000
info@cdregister.com
cdregister.com
Do you currently have a CD available? Get your music in the hands of DJs, magazine writers, film & TV Producers and A&R staff from around the world.

conqueroo
13351-D Riverside Dr. #655,
Sherman Oaks, CA 91423-2450
PH: 818-501-2001
Cary Baker cary@conqueroo.com
conqueroo.com
A music industry publicity firm started up in 2004 by an ex label executive.

Cooch Music
22 Williams Way S. PO Box 340,
Baiting Hollow, NY 11933
Joseph Cuccia info@coochmusic.com
www.coochmusic.com
Full service music publishers!

Deluxxe Media & Management
4509 Interlake Ave. N. #201, Seattle, WA 98103
PH: 206-634-0345 FX: 206-633-0054
Barbara Mitchell cocktailhr@aol.com
Publicity and management firm. Also handles national and tour press.

Drophit.com
7075 W. Gowan Rd. #2021, Las Vegas, NV 89129
PH: 702-951-0294 FX: 702-446-5352
Alicia Cohen z@drophit.net
www.drophit.com
Artist Booking - Publicity - Radio - Public Relations. Guaranteed the lowest prices in the industry!

Earl R. Dingman Productions
211 4th St., Troy, NY 12180
PH: 518-274-6299
R. John info@erdprod.com
www.erdprod.com
Media marketing, promotion, production and consultation.

Embrace Encouragement
2136 Ford Pkwy. #206, St. Paul, MN 55116
Wendy Vickers wendyvcoach@aol.com
www.embraceencouragement.com
I work with creative artists who want to get out in front of new, bigger and better audiences. I specialize in working with musicians, speakers and writers. I do this by being their "biggest fan" and giving support, encouragement and inspiration.

enexes.com
60 E. 9th St., Upland, CA 91786
PH: 909-840-7133 FX: 909-920-9029
Dileone Dileone@enexes.com
www.enexes.com
Your entertainment gateway. Online distribution and promotion.

Evolution Promotion
24 Bartlett St., Melrose, MA 02176
PH: 781-662-5278
info@evolutionpromotion.com
www.evolutionpromotion.com
As a full service company we offer all the key essentials necessary for a successful campaign.

Explosive PR
PO Box 31227, Los Angeles, CA 90031
PH: 323-223-2767
Kim Cooper explosivepr@gmail.com
www.explosivepr.com
We offer low cost press release writing and media mailings to a huge network of online, print and radio journalists.

Fanatic Promotion
135 W. 29th St. #1101, New York, NY 10001
PH: 212-616-5556
Josh Bloom josh@fanaticpromotion.com
www.fanaticpromotion.com
Our goal is to turn on the world to talented new artists.

Foley Entertainment
PO Box 358, Greendell, NJ 07839
PH: 908-684-9400
Eugene Foley EugeneFoleyMusic@aol.com
FoleyEntertainment.com
Providing a wide range of music industry disciplines, including artist development, marketing, promotion, advertising, songwriting, composing, arranging, intellectual property, publishing, touring, distribution, producing and merchandising.

Free Music Report
c/o 3000 Records, PO Box 182492,
Shelby Twp., MI 48318
PH/FX: 586-480-3000 Toll Free: 888-463-4336
www.freemusicreport.com
Do you currently have a CD available? Get your music in the hands of radio station DJs, magazine editors, film & TV producers and A&R staff from around the world.

FourFront Media & Music
1245 S. 128th St., Seattle, WA 98186
PH: 206-282-6116
Chris info@4frontmusic.com
www.knab.com
Consultation and education service for Indie musicians.

The Gate Media Group
1270 Springbrook Rd. Suite H,
Walnut Creek, CA 94597-3995
PH: 925-256-1770 FX: 925-256-1774
helpdesk@gatemedia.com
www.gatemedia.com
Develops successful Indie music promotional campaigns.

Green Galactic
1680 N. Vine St. #211, Los Angeles, CA 90028
PH: 323-466-5141 FX: 866-703-5344
lynn@greengalactic.com
www.greengalactic.com
A marketing and production media company specializing in youth culture.

Head First Entertainment
1146 N. Mesa Dr. #102-103, Mesa, AZ 85201
PH: 480-827-8686 FX: 480-733-7870
Dave Tedder dave@headfirstentertainment.com
www.headfirstentertainment.com
An independent management, marketing and publicity firm.

The Hennessy Group
4236 Franklin Ave. Hollywood, CA 90027
PH: 323-371-2895 FX: 323-953-8592
Tom tom@thehennessygroup.net
www.thehennessygroup.net
Talent management for bands and solo artists. Management and promotions tailored to your needs.

Holiday Matinee
920 E. St. #301, San Diego, CA 92101
www.holidaymatinee.com
Campaigns that produce increased exposure, profitability and brand awareness.

Impact Artist Promotions
PO Box 568, Gilbertsville, PA 19525
PH: 610-473-7377 PH: 610-369-7795
www.artistpromo.com
We provide strategies and tools for marketing your music.

Impact Entertainment
1640 W. Oak Knoll Cir. Fort Lauderdale, FL 33324
PH: 954-370-7000 FX: 954-370-7005
Rob Cohen impactent@aol.com
www.impactentertainmentgrp.com
Full service artist management for unsigned artists.

In House Booking
PH: 650-585-2239
info@inhousebooking.com
www.InHouseBooking.com
A new approach to booking and securing performances. We make the calls, you play the halls!

Incubation Music
PO Box 20425, New York, NY 10025
PH: 212-807-6397 FX: 646-390-7241
Jennifer Grimmer
jennifer.grimmer@incubationmusic.com
incubationmusic.com
A full service production and music publishing company representing songwriters throughout the country. We specialize in Rock, Pop, Urban and Roots genres. To submit your music to us, please send us an email.

Independent Records
PO Box 510, Blairstown, NJ 07825
PH: 908-362-5524
customerservice@indierec.com
www.indierec.com
Imagine your CD sitting in your local Record Store display window! Think it's impossible? WRONG!!!!

The Indie Edge
4341 Spring St. #47, La Mesa, CA 91941
PH: 619-301-3279
Lonny Brooks
lb@theindieedge.com
www.theindieedge.com
Artist management, guerrilla marketing and PR for the Indie artist.

indie911.com
8949 Sunset Blvd. #201, West Hollywood, CA 90069
PH: 310-943-7164
FX: 310-919-3091
Justin Goldberg
justin@indie911.com
www.indie911.com
Label and managment company. Helps indie musicians and labels sustain their livelihoods and increase their revenues by managing and monetizing their most valuable asset, their own music.

The Industry Resource
101 West 23rd St. #2152, New York, NY 10011
PH: 800-878-6113
FX: 800-878-6114
www.theindustryresource.com
Home to today's top industry professionals from management companies, booking agents, labels and publishing firms. These executives are actively seeking new and exciting talent.

IRL Music Group
31441 Santa Margarita Pkwy. #A 366, Rancho Santa Margarita, CA 92688
PH: 949-766-7979
Johnny Mendola
jmendola@earthlink.net
www.johnnyrock.com/join
Get Exposed to over 3,500 labels Worldwide! Free online service. Join Now!

→FREE←
15-min. marketing consultation with no strings attached, really!
Call PJ at 303-444-9575
(Tues.-Fri. 10 am - 4pm Mountain Time)
& learn how to take it to the next level.

87% of Musik International clients are repeat customers who refer us to their friends and fellow musicians.

GOT DISTRIBUTION?
We secured over 50 deals for clients in 2004; their CDs are in stores now...are yours? We also arrange international distribution.

NEED RADIO PLAY OR CD REVIEWS?
Our clients hit radio charts every week and get reviewed in major publications; are you getting enough airplay & visibility?

WANT IN-STORE SALES?
Sure, you're selling CDs online, but we get real stores to play your CD for their customers and display your materials to stimulate sales.

☑

WHO ARE WE?
MUSIK INTERNATIONAL
WWW.MUSIKINTERNATIONAL.COM
Call Toll-Free 888-476-8745
info@musikinternational.com

IndieBible Discount!!!
Mention this ad and get 15% off your promotion

OUR TEAM CAN ALSO HELP YOU WITH DIGITAL DOWNLOADS & FORMATTING
TOUR SUPPORT • CD/DVD PACKAGING
GRAPHIC DESIGN • AND MUCH MORE

wampus multimedia
What would you do if you knew you couldn't fail?
wampus.com
localmusicstore.com

cafebar 401, tvfordogs, arms of kismet, alice despard, casey abrams, johnny j blair, kowtow popof, amateur god, wampeters

Jerome Promotions & Marketing

Always looking for new talent

Radio Promotion is our specialty

Office: 770.982.7055
Fax: 770.982.1882

2535 Winthrope Way
Lawrenceville, GA 30044
email: hitcd@bellsouth.net

www.jeromepromotions.com

Just Rock PR
2976 Washington Blvd.
Cleveland Heights, OH 44118
PH: 216-397-1192
Ren Scarab publicity@justrockpr.com
justrockpr.com
We are media professionals that know how and why things get into print.

Kari Estrin Artist Career Consulting
PO Box 60232, Nashville, TN 37206
PH: 615-262-0883
kari@kariestrin.com
www.kariestrin.com
Consulting, artist services and special projects.

Kari-On Productions
PO Box 436, Evans, GA 30809
PH: 706-294-9996 FX: 706-210-9453
Kari Gaffney karionprod@knology.net
www.karigaffney.com/publicity.html
Solicits all major magazines, network television morning/weekend news programming, online publications & critics for reviews, interviews and appearances. Creates online image awareness.

Kathy Acquaviva Media
PH: 818-893-8458
Kathy Acquaviva KathyMedia@aol.com
A music publicist with over 15 years experience.

Kings of A&R
3 Scott Rd. Port Monmouth, NJ 07758
dean@kingsofar.com
www.kingsofar.com
Exposes unsigned acts to the music industry.

Liner Entertainment Group
Attn: Demo Submissions
PO Box 2853,
Baytown, TX 77522
PH: 888-239-6564
Diana Liner info@linerentertainmentgroup.com
www.linerentertainmentgroup.com
An artist management and booking agency. Our Goal is to provide encouragement and growth to artists seeking a face in mainstream entertainment. Please visit our site for submission guidelines.

Luck Media & Marketing
8900 Olympic Blvd.
Beverly Hills, CA 90211
PH: 310-860-9170
Steve Levesque
steve@luckmedia.com
luckmedia.com
Our staff has a well-deserved and well-earned reputation as one of the most creative, productive, and successful PR organizations.

MakingaStar.com
info@makingastar.com
makingastar.com
Your personal A&R vehicle. Music and film related companies contact us with their current needs.

Massive Music America
5130 Chase St.,
Denver, CO 80212
PH: 877-571-4521
questions@massivemusicamerica.com
www.massivemusicamerica.com
Independent promotions company that offers radio, media/print, internet and tour support..

Mazur Public Relations
PO Box 2425, Trenton, NJ 08607-2425
PH: 609-890-4550 FX: 609-890-4556
Michael Mazur michael@mazurpr.com
www.mazurpr.com
Full service PR company that represents all genres.

M-Squared Productions
POB 1331, Oklahoma City, OK 73101
PH: 405-601-1479
Mark Maxey m-squared@m-squared.org
m-squared.org
Graphic designs, photography, public relations...marketing. Over 20 years experience in the arts industry.

The Music Oven Network
701 Brazos, #500, Austin, TX 78701
PH: 512-334-6270
editor@musicoven.com
www.musicoven.com
Provides free promotional services to independent artists.

MUSIK INTERNATIONAL Distribution and Promotion
154 Betasso Rd. Boulder, CO 80302
Toll Free: 888-476-8745
PH: 303-444-9575 FX: 303-444-9122
info@musikinternational.com
www.musikinternational.com
Promotion, Marketing and Consulting to the worldwide entertainment community. ***We are offering you a FREE 15-minute consultation! I am best reached between 10 am and 4 pm (Mountain time) Tuesday-Friday. Genres of Music covered: Rock, World, Jazz, Latin, Hip Hop, R&B, Folk, Blues, Singer-Songwriter, Acoustic, Electronic, Ambient, New Age, Contemporary Classical/Crossover. NO Country, Gospel or Christian, please.

MWS Media
PO Box 402081, Hesperia, CA 92340-2081
PH: 760-964-8044
Matthew Wayne Selznick mws@mwsmedia.com
www.mwsmedia.com
Resources, community, and services for DIY, independent creative endeavors.

Namaste' Inernational
Robin McNeil robin@namastepromotions.com
namastepromotions.com
Your one-stop promotion, event coordination, management, and image consultation firm.

NeedPromo.com
28870 US Hwy. 19 N. 3rd Fl. Clearwater, FL 33761
PH: 800-708-0907
Maurice Evans info@NeedPromo.com
www.needpromo.com
Management, development and promotion services. Contact us before sending material.

New Game Media
332 N. La Brea Ave. Los Angeles, CA 90036
PH: 949-650-6229
Ken Tamplin Ken@NewGameMedia.Com
www.NewGameMedia.com
A strategic entertainment marketing investment company focussing on talent with pre-exiting fan bases and taking them to the next level. We look for exceptional Indie artists that we can help with corporate endorsements, TV, Film etc.

Nina Denny Public Relations
PO Box 1248, Ogdensburg, NY 13669
PH: 315-323-1058 FX: 877-349-0225
www.ninadenny.com
PR with a personal touch, affordable rates and music expertise.

Omni Entertainment/Caprice Records
5919 Greenville Ave. #361, Dallas, TX 75206
PH: 214-452-3726 FX: 214-452-3726
Don Brooks donb@omnicaprice.com
www.omnicaprice.com
A full service management, booking, marketing and promotions company.

On Target Media Group
6464 W. Sunset Blvd. Suite 829,
Hollywood, CA 90028
PH: 323-461-4230 FX: 323-461-4229
Jason Feinberg info@ontargetmediagroup.com
www.ontargetmediagroup.com
Internet marketing, publicity and promotion; music video and EPK editing as well as DVD authoring.

GET YOUR MUSIC IN INDEPENDENT FILMS

Make contact with independent filmmakers from around the globe
Place music in the next indie film, digital short, student project, or TV pilot
Have your profile and song samples sent to filmmakers weekly

Another service by promotion experts **VersusMedia**

info@versusmedia.com www.versusmedia.com

On That Note Entertainment
525 Mt. Pleasant Ave. West Orange, NJ 07052
PH: 973-486-0867 FX: 973-486-0875
Dan Balassone dan@onthatnote.net
www.onthatnote.net
A full service booking agency working with national and regional acts of all types and genres.

Posse Up Entertainment
7575 Tyler Blvd. Bldg C-31, Mentor, OH 44060
PH: 440-269-8311 FX: 440-269-8344
Jessica Hollenbach jessica@posseupent.com
www.PosseUpEntertainment.com
We are full service Management and publicity firm specializing in press kit design, radio promotion and more. We will get the "Buzz" going for up and coming talent and established artists.

Powderfinger Promotions
47 Mellen St., Framingham, MA 01702
PH: 800-356-1155 x.234
David Avery powderspam@aol.com
nimbit.com/promo
Offers customized publicity packages.

PR Buzz Campaign
www.musicdish.com/network/ex.php3
Through the MusicDish Network and its over 200 member sites, we are able to place your announcement and banner where your fans (and customers) are already surfing.

PR That Rocks
PO Box 1743, Novato, CA 94948
Christopher Buttner rockme@prthatrocks.com
prthatrocks.com
Public relations and marketing services for musicians.

The Press House
302 Bedford Ave #13, Brooklyn, NY 11211
PH: 718-302-1522
Dawn Kamerling dawn@thepresshouse.com
www.thepresshouse.com
Previews, reviews and live appearances for your band.

Prototype Entertainment
24-21 27th St., #2-B, Astoria, NY 11102
PH: 973.715.1101
Don Di Napoli don@prototypeentertainment.com
www.prototypeentertainment.com
Full service artist development company that handles all aspects from production to publicity.

Rainmaker Talent Group
8127 Mesa Dr.
PO Box 206-74,
Austin, TX 78759
PH: 512-485-3170
FX: 512-485-3171
info@rainmaker-talent.com
www.rainmaker-talent.com
Provides management, booking, promotional and financial support.

Red River Services
630 Quail Run,
Mitchell, IN 47446
PH: 812-849-6297
www.redriverservices.org
Are you tired of paying for promotion and nobody hears your music?

Sevier Productions
3110 West End Circle #4,
Nashville, TN 37203
PH: 615-500-4411
Chris Sevier
chris.sevier@vanderbilt.edu
www.sevierproductions.com
Artist development and A&R out sourcing. We help deserving artists make a record and build their team for success.

so much MOORE media
PO Box 120426, Nashville, TN 37212-0426
FX: 615-298-1446
Martha E. Moore martha@somuchmoore.com
www.somuchmoore.com
I am a full-time entertainment publicist working with Indie artists for 16 years.

Songwriters Showcases of America
608 McIntosh Rd. Ormond Beach, FL 32174
PH: 386-672-3789 FX: 775-249-3127
showstage@aol.com
www.ssa.cc
Creates showcases for songwriters and original bands.

Space 380
1705 Doris Dr. Columbia, MO 65202
PH: 573-449-7226 FX: 309-210-9037
www.space380.com
Creates name recognition for independent artists of all genres.

Publicity For Indie Musicians For Nine Years And Counting
www.ArielPublicity.com

Stretch the Skies
33 Sumner Park, Rochester, NY 14607
PH: 585-820-9353
Kenneth Fournier ken@stretchtheskies.com
www.stretchtheskies.com
Provides an all-encompassing system for artists to rise through the levels of a career in the music business, by implementing practical tools, industry education, artist development, and career paths that make sense.

Team Clermont Promotion
191 E. Broad St. #310, Athens, GA 30601
PH: 706-548-6008 FX: 706-548-0094
Nelson Wells nelsonwells@teamclermont.com
www.teamclermont.com
We get maximum exposure for the records we promote.

Need To Get Your Music In Stores?

Then you need the Almighty Institute of Music Retail

The only comprehensive source for detailed information on *every* U.S. music retail outlet

90% of all music is still sold at retail. If you want to show SoundScan sales and build a buzz, you gotta get your CD in stores

Almighty Offers:
- Retail Info Paks targeted to your region and style of music so you can get your music into all the right stores
- Retail marketing programs
- Email blasts to retail buyers

Find out which stores in your region:
- are SoundScan
- are near the venues you play
- carry consignment Cd's
- radio and more!

818.752.8000
www.almightyretail.com/diy

TekSunGirl Musician & Band Promotion
LaNita teksungrl909@aol.com
www.teksungirl.web.com
News, promotional tips, resources, local band listings and more!

Thompson Entertainment Group
1300 Division St. #105, Nashville, TN 37203
PH: 615-742-8004 FX: 615-742-8014
info@thompsonentertainmentgroup.com
www.thompsonentertainmentgroup.com
Artist development, media/marketing and management firm.

Tinderbox Music
600 Washington Ave. N. #102,
Minneapolis, MN 55401
PH: 612-375-1113 FX: 612-341-3330
Krista Vilinskis krista@tinderboxmusic.com
www.tinderboxmusic.com
Music promotion and distribution company.

True Music And Songs
7 Wild Flower Dr. Kings Park, NY 11754
PH: 631-896-9800
David Whittaker
davidwhittaker@truemusicandsongs.com
www.truemusicandsongs.com
Helps artists get their music to the right people in the music industry.

TwoShepsThatPass
476 Broome St. #5A, New York, NY 10013
PH: 646-613-1101 FX: 786-513-0692
Vera Sheps twoshepsthatpass@aol.com
www.twoshepsthatpass.com
Gives you a presence on and off the net.

UnderCover Records
526 W. Aurora Rd. #349,
Sagamore Hills, OH 44067
PH: 216-410-0366
FX: 330-468-9981
bill@undercoverrecords.com
www.undercoverrecords.com
A direct sales, distribution and marketing company dedicated to new and developing independent music.

Unite PR
113 NW 11th St.,
Gainesville, FL 32601
PH: 352-870-8036
Jessika
jessika@unitepr.com
www.unitepr.com
Independent publicity and promotional firm for Indies and unsigned acts.

United Global Artists Promotion
FX: 801-659-9406
Leigh Silberg
uga@email.com
www.u-g-a.com
We utilize various elements of promotion to implement the progress & growth of an individual artist's core fan base from a regional perspective to a global overview.

VersusMedia
556 S. Fair Oaks Ave. #245, Pasadena, CA 91105
PH: 877-633-8764
info@versusmedia.com
www.versusmedia.com
Provider of global publicity services.

Vigilant Promotions
PO Box 572, Princeton, MN 55371
Attn: Submissions
info@vigilantpromotions.com
www.vigilantpromotions.com
Using everything from street teams to radio promotion, press to the web.

Wiselephant
221 Columbia St., Brooklyn, NY 11231-1433
PH: 888-625-9258
info@wiselephant.com
www.wiselephant.com
Marketing tools geared specifically to promote you.

Xployted Hearts Promotions
11186 Spring Hill Dr. #174, Spring Hill, FL 34609
PH: 352-584-5676 FX: 352-688-4432
James Capone xploytedhearts@gmail.com
Xploytedhearts.orgfree.com
We offer full band promotions and also recording sessions and contacts with record labels.

Sign up for The Indie Contact Newsletter
www.indiebible.com

Vendors and Labels

Most of the online vendors listed in this section offer "non-exclusive" contracts. Non exclusive means you are allowed to sign up with as many of online vendors as you like without violating any agreement. The fees and/or commissions vary from site to site. I suggest you visit as many as you can to find out which sites you get a good feeling from. Be wary of large setup fees!

North America
United States

4CDMusic.com
Mike Tobin mike@4cdmusic.com
4CDMusic.com
If your CD is available through a distributor, such as the Orchard, then we should be able to get it in our catalog, just let us know the UPC and we'll get it listed.

AB-CD
shoptalk@ab-cd.com
www.ab-cd.com
We specialize in hard to find, rare and Indie music and media..

ALLindies
1321 W. 13th Ter. 3rd Level,
Kansas City, MO 64102-1055
PH: 816-283-8122 FX: 816-283-8126
info@harvest-mg.com
allindies.com
Providing independent artists and labels a creative and controlled environment for promoting, releasing and selling independent releases directly to retailers and on the internet.

AmazingCDs
15213 N. Bonnett, Mead, WA 99021
info@amazingcds.com
www.amazingcds.com
All CDs are accepted - all styles of music.

amazon.com Advantage Program
orders@amazon.com
www.amazon.com/advantage
Lets millions of customers find, discover and buy what you're selling.

American Eagle Recordings
13001 Dieterle Ln, St. Louis, MO 63127-1201
PH: 888-521-8146 FX: 314-984-0828
Dr. Charles "Max" E. Million
maxmillion1@earthlink.net
www.americaneaglerecordings.com
We believe that each artist should have a stake in the control of their destiny, in the direction that their careers are going.

Artist1Stop: Distributing Independent Artists
3650 Osage St., Denver, CO 80211
PH: 877-247-5046 FX: 303-433-8228
manager@artist1stop.com
www.artist1stop.com
We cater to independent artists/labels that need real physical brick and mortar store CD distribution, online distribution and "soon to come" digital distribution (itunes, Napster, etc.).

www.yourmusiconcd.com

100 BULK CDRS $59
Includes cdr, and duplication

100 BASIC CDRS $99
Includes cdr, on cd print, and jewelcase

100 FULL COLOR CDR PACKAGE $199
includes cdr, on cd print, color cover(4/1) & tray card(4/0)
assembly, jewel case, and shrinkwrap, from your artfiles

1000 FULL COLOR PACKAGE $999

100 BULK DVDRS - $224   100 BASIC DVDRS - $249
100 FULL PACKAGE DVDRS - $299   1000 FULL PACKAGE DVD - $1399

300 FULL COLOR PACKAGE $549

5000 4 x 6 flyers - $199

SNS DIGITAL INC

ATLANTA 678.442.0933
TOLL FREE 1.877.442.0933

Artopium.com
4400 Ave.B #121, Austin, TX 78751
Michael Betthauser mikeb@artopium.com
www.artopium.com
A place where artists, musicians, fashion designers, filmmakers and writers can come together to create and sell or show in a world wide art market.

awarestore.com
c/o Submissions, 3449 N. Southport Ave. #2,
Chicago, IL. 60657
PH: 800-292-7365
info@awarerecords.com
www.awarestore.com
Indie CD and merchandise shop.

AzOz
webmaster@azoz.com
www.azoz.com
Sell your CD here for $2/unit sold.

BandMecca.com
14255 Preston Rd. #421, Dallas, TX 75240
PH: 877-845-7864 FX: 240-384-2349
bands@bandmecca.com
www.bandmecca.com
We sell CDs and also have reviews of Indie music.

Bathtub Music
1990 N. Alma School Rd. #507 Chandler, AZ 85224
PH: 480-812-0622
David Tieman info@bathtubmusic.com
bathtubmusic.com
An online CD store dedicated to selling and promoting all genres of independent music with FREE SETUP for musicians.

BETA Records
Box 48,
Hollywood, CA 90028
PH 877-232-2382
support@betarecords.com
BetaRecords.com
Providing up-and-coming artists with an Internet platform to showcase their talent using a combination of personalized text, pictures, and music samples.

Billaweed.com
PO Box 1290,
Napavine, WA 98565
www.billaweed.com
We promote indie and unsigned bands. We work to get your music heard and your band exposed.

DIGITAL DYNAMICS AUDIO INC.

Everyone else is doing it, why can't we?

EMPLOYEE PRICING FOR EVERYONE
1000 CD Package*

$1050

Additional Offer:
Pay project in full up front (including estimated shipping) and if there is overage you get it free!

Package includes: 1000 CDs in jewel case with clear tray; 3 colors on disc, 4 page 4/1 book and 4/1 tray card; overwrap, bar code and free listing on **buythiscd.com**

Master and art must be supplied to DDAI spec.
Shipping not included.   +/-10% over/under run not included.

1-800-444-DDAI • www.4ddai.com

Our extensive list of services include: CD/SACD/DVD Replication • Audio Mastering • ISDN • Graphic Design • Custom Packaging

*To get special, mention the Indie Bible.
*offer expires January 31, 2006

Boosweet Records
PO Box 451594, Los Angeles, CA 90045
PH: 310-613-3535 FX: 909-877-9199
Vernon Neilly VNeillyI@aol.com
www.boosweet.com
Specializing in the recording and distribution of major acts as well as up and coming artists. We will promote and sell your products worldwide via the Internet. We can get any artist's material into the major digital download stores as well.

BrownJungle
PO Box 1143, Alameda, CA 94501-0117
customerservice@brownjungle.com
www.brownjungle.com
An online music store selling CDs for Indie artists.

Bu Hanan Records
113 Taylor, Chapel Hill, NC 27514-6632
Alex Lazara alexlazara@buhananrecords.com
www.buhananrecords.com
Independant record label based. Accepts submissions.

BuyIndieMusic.com
9920 S. Rural Rd. #108, Tempe, AZ 85284
PH: 480-206-3435 FX: 480-753-7021
music@blackdogpromotions. com
www.buyindiemusic.com
Sells Indie CDs and merchandise. Welcomes all styles of music.

buzz communications
PO Box 370105, Milwaukee, WI 53237-1205
PH: 414-431-8720
Andrea Hubbert andrea@buzzcommunicationsonline.com
www.buzzcommunicationsonline.com
A full-service public relations, marketing and business development firm.

buythiscd.com
buythiscd.com
There are great artists waiting to be heard. We want people to hear them!

Canadian American/Caprice International
PO Box 808, Lititz, PA 17543
PH: 717-627-4800
capricerecords@webtv.net
www.capricerecording.com/
Will distribute your album worldwide. 25% cut.

Can't Afford Em Records
demos@cantaffordem.com
www.cantaffordem.com
An Independent record label dedicated to underground Rock.

Captiva Records
1300 Guadalupe Ste. #206, Austin, TX 78701
PH: 512-322-9293 FX: 512-479.1805
Chris Perez captiva@captivagroup.com
www.captivarecords.com
Indie label with a focus on artist development.

CD Army
PO Box 225023, Dallas, TX 75222
PH: 214-943-7550 FX: 214-943-7550
Nic Climer Nic@cdarmy.com
www.cdarmy.com
Independent musicians web hosting and worldwide distribution of your music..

CD Baby
5925 NE 80th Ave. Portland, OR 97218-2891
PH: 503-595-3000 FX: 503-296-2370
cdbaby@cdbaby.com
www.cdbaby.com
We will expose your CD to 10,000 customers a day. We also have an amazing digital distribution service that is available to all CD Baby members.

CD Palace
174 W. Foothill Blvd. #235, Monrovia, CA 91016
manager@cdpalace.com
www.cdpalace.com
Will sell your CD for you. Accepts all genres.

The CD Party
236 Fairmont Ct. Nashville, TN 37203
PH: 615-293-8887 FX: 615-329-9831
Bill Lee McCleskey bill@thecdparty.com
www.TheCDparty.com
We sell and Promote indie music online and worldwide, representing all genres of music from Country, to Hip Hop, Blues, Jazz, Soul, Rock, Pop, Reggae, Spoken Word, Gospel, etc. Artists can sell and receive personal a page on our site for a one-time fee of $25.

CD Quest Music
FX: 801-751-4903
feedback@cdquest.com
www.cdquest.com
Reaches farther into the independent world than any other site.

CD Revolucion
8035 Culebra #104, San Antonio, TX 78251
info@cdrevolucion.com
www.cdrevolucion.com
Sells music for unsigned artists and Indie record labels.

CDFreedom.com
47 Mellen St., Framingham, MA 01702
FX: 508-820-7920
matt@nimbit.com
www.cdfreedom.com
CDfreedom takes a smaller cut than most on-line distributors!

CDfuse.com
PO Box 9615, Austin, TX 78766
info@cdfuse.com
cdfuse.com
An on-line record store for unsigned and Indie artists.

CDreview.com
30 Compton Way, Hamilton Square, NJ 08690
PH: 609-689-1711
info@CDreview.com
www.CDreview.com
Get 100% of your CD sale price. Type in the code "indiebible" to even waive the set up fee.

CDs-FROM-THE-ARTIST dot com
www.cdsfromtheartist.com
A community based Indie music site like no other.

Clefnote.com
PO Box 833728, Richardson, TX 75083
Dawn Hall-Jones dawn@nrntechnology.com
www.clefnote.com
A growing network of professional independent artists and musicians of every music genre. Sell your music downloads and CDs online.

ClubRoundtable.com
2320 Texoma Pkwy. #254, Sherman, TX 75090
FX: 513-297-4053
cds@clubroundtable.com
www.clubroundtable.com
We offer a comprehensive band profile at no cost. We offer consignment of your existing CDs.

Coach House Records
3503 S. Harbor Blvd. Santa Ana, CA 92704
PH: 714-545-2622 FX: 714-545-3490
Roger LeBlanc rogerl@thecoachouse.com
www.coachhouserecords.com
Introduces Indie releases into the retail market.

BOOSWEET RECORDS
INDEPENDENT LABEL OF THE FUTURE
ARE YOU READY TO TAKE YOUR MUSIC CAREER TO THE NEXT LEVEL!

WHAT WE OFFER:
- INTERNET DISTRIBUTION
- DIGITAL DISTRIBUTION
- RETAIL DISTRIBUTION
- ARTIST PROMOTION & MARKETING
- ARTIST DEVELOPMENT PACKAGES
- WEBSITE DESIGN
- MULTIMEDIA PACKAGING

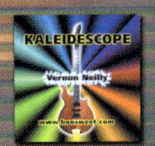   

FOR INFORMATION ON HOW TO SUBMIT YOUR MUSIC FOR WORLDWIDE EXPOSURE
CONTACT US AT (310) 613-3535 OR EMAIL US AT INFO@BOOSWEET.COM

Collekt Records
#555, 243 5th Ave. New York, NY 10016
PH: 917-406-5233
Kristian Sorge info@collekt.com
www.collekt.com
We are a beautifully shaped Indie Label. Please check us out!

Crafty Records
75 Earley St., Bronx, NY 10464
designsbydan@juno.com
www.craftyrecords.net
An independent, artist friendly record label.

Crooked Tooth Records
Casey Tolliver
ctolliver@crookedtoothindustries.com
www.crookedtoothindustries.com
We fulfill all the needs of unsigned bands.

Darla Records
2107 Camino Cantera, Vista, CA 92084
PH: 760-631-1731 FX: 760-454-1625
webmaster@darlashop.com
www.darla.com
Sells Indie CDs worldwide.

Delvian Records
1270 Springbrook Rd. Suite H,
Walnut Creek, CA 94597-3995
PH: 925-256-1770 FX: 925-256-1774
music@delvianrecords.com
www.delvianrecords.com
Specializing in Electronica, Darkwave, World and New Age.

DigitalCuts.com
2940 Heather Stone Way, Lawrenceville, GA 30043
www.digitalcuts.com
Offers artists the opportunity to develop and promote their music .

Digitone Records, LLC
PO Box 11284, Richmond, VA 23230
Gary Gaskin g@digitonerecords.com
www.digitonerecords.com
Indie record label. Accepts and reviews solicited and unsolicited material.

Disgraceland Records
PO Box 10882, Knoxville, TN 37939
paul@disgraceland.com
www.disgraceland.com
Online record label.

Dubxpress On-Demand Music Publishing
146 A McKnight Circle, Pittsburgh, PA 15237
PH: 412-519-8250
Peter Sysko pete@dubxpress.com
www.dubxpress.com
Free manufacturing and distribution integration for artists that cannot afford to manufacture their own products. For musicians that do offer their own products, they receive a merchant page and receive 95% of all sales.

Dynasonic
PMB #115, 4880 Lower Roswell Rd. Ste. 165,
Marietta, GA 30068-4385
PH: 770-984-8104 FX: 770-984-8105
info@dynasonic.com
www.dynasonic.com
Focused on traditional and mobile studio recording and online artist distribution services. We can enable you to efficiently record and distribute your music at a minimal cost using new technology.

earBuzz.com
77 Solano Sq. #159, Benicia, CA 94510
PH: 707-746-7537
Don Kimenker don@earbuzz.com
earbuzz.com
The only worldwide music site that returns 100% of the CD sale price to artists.

www.indielinkexchange.com/ile

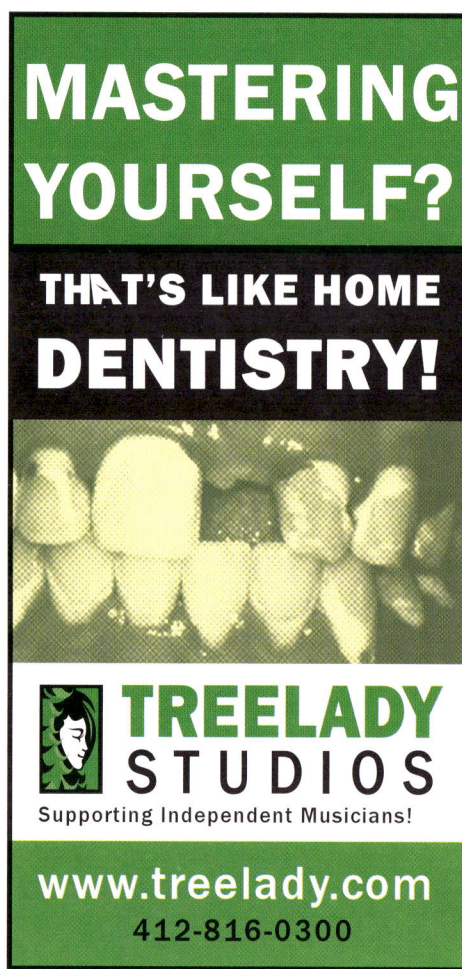

Epitone Records
103 Blaine Ave. East Meadow, NY 11793
PH: 516-489-7040 FX:
James Shields jshields@epitonerecords.com
www.epitonerecords.com
A full service independent record label.

Everfine Records
31 W. 26th St. 3rd Fl. New York, NY 10010
PH: 212-213-6101 FX: 212-213-6102
dave@everfinerecords.com
www.everfinerecords.com
Helps artists flourish and further develop their natural talents.

EvO:R
evor@evor.com
www.evor.com
Online store. Works with Indie musicians around the world.

eXtreme Sports Music
info@extremesportsmusic.com
www.eXtremeSportsMusic.com
Indie musicians into extreme sports can sell/distribute their CDs to loyal fans.

Factory Chime Records
Lance Leonnig factorychime@msn.com
www.factorychime.com
Independent online music distribution and sales.

FastLane Records
816 Platt Cir. Oklahoma City, OK 73170
PH: 405-703-1676
fastlanerecords@cox.net
www.fastlanerecords.com
An Indie label that specializes in Glam/Hard Rock/PowerPop.

Gadfly Records
PO Box 5231, Burlington, VT 05402
PH: 802-865-2406
gadfly1@aol.com
www.gadflyrecords.com
We specialize in offbeat and unique projects.

GEMM
PO Box 4062, Palm Springs, CA 92263
PH: 760-318-6251 FX: 760-318-6251
inquiry@gemm.com
www.gemm.com
Worlds largest music catalog. Submit your CD.

GoJangle.com
simon@gojangle.com
www.gojangle.com
This site is dedicated to musicians who want to advertise their music, fans of music who want a single source solution for all new music and record companies on the lookout for talent that have that extra buzz.

Greenwise Records
Scott Lykins scot.lykins@greenwiserecords.com
www.greenwiserecords.com
Artist reviews, artist promotions, quality reviews done by professionals with over 20 years experience.

Guitar Nine Records
8201 Hambledon Court, Raleigh, NC 27615
PH: 561-423-0741 FX: 561-423-0741
www.guitar9.com
Guitar worship. New releases and demos wanted!

Halogen Records
163 State St., Montpelier, VT 05602
PH: 206-338-3478
www.halogenrecords.com
Grassroots promotion, marketing, distribution and manufacturer.

Hearbox Recordings
info@hearbox.com
www.hearbox.com
Recommending great quality, Underground Rock.

Hill Billy Stew Records
PO Box 82625, San Diego, CA 92138-2625
Lee xhillxbillyx@hotmail.com
www.hillbillystew.com
Record label that puts out music by Indie/Punk/Folk/Country/ artists.

Hot Bands.com
PO Box 27722, Seattle, WA 98125-2722
webmaster@hotbands.com
www.hotbands.com
Accepts CDs for review. Covers all genres.

HotLocalMusic
PH: 504-606-6246
information@hotlocalmusic.com
hotlocalmusic.com
Empowers independent artists, venues, managers & labels with the tools and network interrelationships to reach music fans, build customer loyalty and increase profitability.

Ichiban Music
3809 Osage Dr. Rowlett, TX 75088
PH: 214-850-1102
Ty Keller tkeller@ichibanmusic.com
www.ichibanmusic.com
Supporting Indie artists and labels through Internet music sales and information.

iMusic
10900 Wilshire Blvd. #1400,
Los Angeles, CA 90024
imusic.artistdirect.com
Online music company that connects artists and fans.

Independent Musicians Marketplace
Rural Rd. 1, PO Box 497, Mansfield, PA 16933
PH: 877-263-3738
imm@secondfret.com
www.secondfret.com
Profiles, MP3's, CD sales, reviews and more.

IndepenDisc Music Club
PO Box 183, North Haven, CT 06473
feedback@independisc.com
www.independisc.com
We listen to every submittal for review, representation, & promotion, regardless of genre.

Indie Dude Music
1020 Stallings Rd. Matthews, NC 28104
PH: 704-821-3316
Gregg Spence gspence@sbstec.com
www.indiedude.com
We sell CDs and stuff for independent musicians!

The Indie Hot 100
Onno info@commuse.com
www.commuse.com
Accepts Indie CDs. Any genre, no setup fees, no commission.

Indie or Die Records
3160 N. Jog Rd. #11206,
West Palm Beach, FL 33411
PH: 561-762-0099
Frankie T. indieordierecords@pegrp.com
www.pegrp.com
Record label for DIY bands. No contracts and no BS. Demo's accepted 24/7.

indiecity.net
2100-F Townhill Rd. Baltimore, MD 21234
PH: 410-668-8575
artists@indiecity.net
indiecity.net
Sell and promote your music from our site.

Indie4Ever.com
Laban Johnson laban@indie4ever.com
www.indie4ever.com
Where you can sell your music without selling out!

IndiePro.com
PO Box 507, North Uxbridge, MA 01538-0507
artists@indiepro.com
www.indiepro.com
Submit your CD for review. Sell it online.

Indiespace
PO Box 5458, Santa Monica, CA 90409
PH: 310-399-4349 FX: 310-396-5489
editors@indiespace.com
www.indiespace.com
Indie artists can get their work out directly to their audience.

Insound
401 Broadway, 26th Fl. New York, NY 10013-3005
PH: 212-777-8056 FX: 212-777-8059
help@insound.com
www.insound.com
Brings the best underground culture to the surface.

InterMixx IndieGate
304 Main Ave. PO Box 287, Norwalk, CT 06851
PH: 203-483-1798
MixxMag@InterMixx.com
www.indiegate.com
The coolest place on the internet to buy Indie music!

IROCK Entertainment
PO Box 691247, Hollywood, CA 90069
PH: 310-246-0040 FX: 310-246-1044
Monte Malone mm@irock.com mm@irock.com
www.irock.com
An Indie label with major promotion & distribution.

ItsAboutMusic.com
275A Mill Ln.
Phoenixville, PA 19460
Dean Sciarra
dean@itsaboutmusic.com
www.itsaboutmusic.com
Connects artist with fans worldwide.

Juno Beach
723 NE University Ave.
Minneapolis, MN 55413
contact@junobeach.com
www.junobeach.com
News, reviews, sell your Indie CDs.

Kabukikore
fieldops@kabukikore.net
www.kabukikore.net
Record label specialising in tiny limited editions in hand made sleeves.

Kentland Records
1247 S. Elgin,
Forest Park, IL 60130
PH: 708-220-4387
Spiv simsimon@aol.com
www.kentlandrecords.com
Independent record label. Artist submissions welcome.

The Kitefishing Family
241 E. S. Temple #4,
Salt Lake City, UT 84111
PH: 801-637-2828
Camden camden@kitefishingfamily.com
www.kitefishingfamily.com
Dedicated to the promotion of all forms of Independent art.

Lakeshore-Records
9268 W. 3rd St.,
Beverly Hills, CA 90210
PH: 310-867-8000
FX: 310-300-3015
info@lakeshore-records.com
www.lakeshore-records.com
Dedicated to finding and developing unique new talent in addition to releasing soundtrack albums not only from our films, but also from other independent films of merit and interest.

LightningCD Corporation
4707 Aurora Ave. N. Seattle, WA 98103
distribution@lightningcd.com
www.lightningcd.com
Supports Indie artists with national distribution of their CDs.

Liquid Fusion
Liquid.fusion@verizon.net
www.liquidfusion.com
An independent record label.

Live Discs
PO Box 89, Ambler, PA 19002
PH: 215-641-9989
Lauren Samuels lauren@livediscs.com
www.livediscs.com
A variety of services for Indie bands.

Localeyez
fye.com
FYE, Strawberries, Coconuts, Spec's Music and Planet Music are giving local artists the opportunity to be seen & heard in our stores.

Locals Online
PH: 503-419-6402
sales@localsonline.com
www.localsonline.com
Global collection of local music.

KWEEVAK MUSIC MAGAZINE
on the web at WWW.KWEEVAK.COM!

- CD Reviews | Music News
- Weekly Radio Show & Artist Airplay
- Popular Online Music Community
- Industry Resources | Win Great Prizes!

LOL Records
PO Box 5148, Beverly Hills, CA 90209
PH: 310-790-5689 FX: 208-460-2903
info@lolrecords.com
lolrecords.com
Releases music overlooked by commercial recording companies.

LOUiPiMPS
1217 Silver St., New Albany, IN 47150
andrew@louipimps.com
www.louipimps.com
Internationally distributed Indie record label.

Lucky Unicorn Records
4339 Rialto St. #1, San Diego, CA 92107
PH: 619-246-3195
Mark Saalwaechter mark@comedymadness.com
www.luckyunicorn.com
Very small, independent record label interested in offbeat yet wildly talented bands. CDs sell for $5, with $1 going back to the band.

Magnanimous Records
Box 541, Shepherdstown, WV 25443
Curt info@magnanimous.org
www.magnanimousrecords.com
An independent label. We accept submissions for our radio broadcast as well as for potential album releases.

Maple Island Records
19030 Dreaming River Dr. Terrace, MN 56334
PH: 320-278-3019
island@mapleislandrecords.com
www.mapleislandrecords.com
Independent record producer & label.

MediaFeast
PMB #103, 2220 Otay Lakes Rd. #502,
Chula Vista, CA 91915
PH: 619-454-3996
support@mediafeast.com
www.mediafeast.com
Dedicated to helping independent artists bring new music to fans.

Merch Girl
PO Box 51222, Phoenix, AZ 85076
PH: 480-471-6195
Mattx admin@themerchgirl.com
store.themerchgirl.com
We sell ANYONES music, art or movies on consignment.

Milk Records
5500 Warwick Ct. #17, Lincoln, NE 68516
milk@milkrecords.com
milkrecords.com
Sell your Indie albums worldwide.

Minstrel Avenue Records
PO Box 1234, Cloudcroft, NM 88317-1234
PH: 505-682-1210
Paul Benshoof tmar@zianet.com
www.zianet.com/minstrel
Advertise and market your works independent of record distributors.

Moozikoo
PO Box 68247, Nashville, TN 37206-8247
Anthony Bates artist_services@Moozikoo.com
www.moozikoo.com
A bilingual (Russian and English) music Etailer. Our target market is the Russian-speaking community within the United States and consumers within the emerging markets of the former Soviet Union (especially Russia, Ukraine, Moldova, and Belarus), as well as specific English-speaking consumer groups.

Mordam Records
PH: 916-641-8900
info@mordamrecords.com
www.mordamrecords.com
We distribute labels. We don't work directly with artists.

Music Distributors.com
PH: 916-338-6881 FX: 916-338-6882
info@themusicdistributors.com
www.musicdistributors.com
We cater to independent artists and labels.

Music Loft
PH: 800-838-5638
www.music-loft.com
We will set up an individual page for your music which includes description and reviews, cover shot, audio clips, and a link to your website. No setup fee!

Musicheadz
45 Paper Mill Rd. PO Box 5008,
Springfield, PA 19064
PH: 610-543-2555 FX: 610-543-2799
pat@musicheadz.com
www.musicheadz.com
You send us your stock to sell, we worry about the rest!

MusicStack
contact@musicstack.com
www.musicstack.com
Individuals, collectors and record stores buy and sell each other's music.

MyGlobalSound.com
9898 SW 88th St. #102, Miami, FL 33176
Bensin info@myglobalsound.com
www.myglobalsound.com
Get your music heard globally.

NETUNES.com
359 San Miguel Dr. #200,
Newport Beach, CA 92660
PH: 949-498-3600 FX: 949-498-6900
Oracle@NETunes.com
www.netunes.com
You get a distribution agreement regardless of genre.

New Artist Direct
600 Washington Ave. N. #102,
Minneapolis, MN 55401
customerservice@newartistdirect.com
www.newartistdirect.com
Helping Indie artists make a living.

Nine 12 Records
275 Cathy Dr. Newbury Park, CA 91320
PH: 805-368-2251
Sara theman@nine12records.com
www.nine12records.com
Independent record label based in LA area. Individualized contracts based on artist goals.

Not Lame
PO Box 2266, Fort Collings, CO 80522
FX: 970-407-0256
Bruce popmusic@notlame.com
www.notlame.com
Label and online record store. Focus is Power Pop and Melodic Rock.

Number 3 Records
5870 Franklin Ave. #302, Los Angeles, CA 90028
PH: 323-605-8199
Toddrick Spalding toddrick@number3records.com
www.number3records.com
A diverse independent label formed from a true love of music. Also, the best records you never heard!

OEbase
www.oebase.com
We provide an artist development program, a way of creating community, and a means of building an audience by making full use of the Internet and other new media.

OneSource
PH: 215-661-1100 FX: 215-661-8959
onesource@pan.com
onesource.pan.com
Distribution system for the online sale of e-CDs.

Online Rock
2033 Ralston Ave. #50, Belmont, CA 94002
PH: 650-649-2304 FX: 650-649-2304
info@onlinerock.com
www.onlinerock.com
Bands can promote, distribute and sell their music online.

OnScene
21 Madera Ave. San Carlos, CA 94070
PH: 650-637-0763 FX: 650-637-0824
info@onscene.com
www.onscene.com
We'll proudly display your work, and help you find a market.

The Orange Spot
PO Box 15207, Fremont, CA 94539
PH: 510-353-1630 FX: 510-353-0573
oprstore@orangepeal.com
www.theorangespot.com
Sell all your merchandise here.

The Orchard
100 Park Ave. 17th Fl. New York, NY 10003
PH: 212-201-9280 FX: 212-201-9203
info@theorchard.com
www.theorchard.com
Supplier of independent music on the Internet.

OurGig.com
PH: 305-604-5256
info@ourgig.com
ourgig.com
Sell your music online all day, every day, worldwide.

OutBoundMusic.com
7037 Hwy. 6 N. PO Box 145, Houston, TX 77095
PH: 281-859-6715
info@outboundmusic.com
www.outboundmusic.com
Distribution and promotion services for Indie artists.

PeaceWork Music
PO Box 25102, Rochester, NY 14625
info@peacework.com
www.peaceworkmusic.net
International distribution at a low cost.

peermusic
3220 Blume Dr. #290, Richmond, CA 94806
PH: 510-222-9678 FX: 510-222-9676
sfcorp@peermusic.com
www.peermusic.com
Promotion and development with a personal touch.

Peppermint CDs
1170 15th Ave. SE #206, Minneapolis, MN 55414
PH: 800-633-7020 FX: 651-293-4421
mail@peppermintcds.com
www.peppermintcds.com
Wants full-time musicians with at least 2 CDs released.

Perris Records
PO Box 841533
Houston, TX 77284
PH: 281-550-0988
FX: 775-719-4768
Tom Mathers
perrisrecords@ev1.net
www.perrisrecords.com
80's Rock label, mail order & distribution company that sells worldwide. Perris is now Accepting CD's or CDR's for possible label consideration and distribution deals worldwide.

Planet CD
PO Box 19481,
Charlotte, NC 28219
PH: 704-560-2379
contact@planetcd.com
www.PlanetCD.com
We provide 2 custom designed pages for your listing - an "Info / Bio" page to tell about your music, the artist, or whatever message you want to get across - and a "CD page" which features a scan of your CD cover, a list of tracks and audio samples.

Point Five Limey
7536 E. Warren Dr.
#15-304,
Denver, CO 80231
PH: 303.306.7602
James Gardiner info@pointfivelimeyrecords.com
www.pointfivelimeyrecords.com
An online art, music, and culture website that strives to sell, promote, and display a variety art and music from around the world.

Pop Sweatshop
PO Box 460954,
Denver, CO 80246
PH: 303-525-5840
Chris Barber
chris@popsweatshop.com
www.popsweatshop.com
We work furiously, in sweatshop conditions, to make and distribute great Indie releases for bands.

Qopel Records
PO Box 97,
New York, NY 10156
PH: 631-827-3000
FX: 419-831-3032
Andrew Herzman
andy@qopelrecords.com
www.qopelrecords.com
We cover 3 areas: production, distribution and promotion. We don't book gigs, write music or do managing.

Jerome Promotions & Marketing
Always looking for new talent
Radio Promotion is our specialty
Office: 770.982.7055
Fax: 770.982.1882
2535 Winthrope Way
Lawrenceville, GA 30044
email: hitcd@bellsouth.net
www.jeromepromotions.com

CD's DVD's PROMO MATERIALS
complete manufacturing of retail ready packages
BEST PRICES
FAST TURNS
PERSONAL SERVICE
1000's of happy customers SINCE 1985
long or short runs • barcodes
posters • stickers • postcards
mastering • music videos
INTERNATIONAL AWARD WINNING DESIGN & PRODUCTION
Eastco Multi Media SOLUTIONS
www.eastcomultimedia.com
1-800-365-8273

PEACEWORK MUSIC NET
THE global distribution solution for independent artists and labels

Have an idea that you just can't seem to get down on paper? Let our talented staff turn your vision into cover art at a price that will amaze you. If you distribute through us, you'll receive a further discount and we'll even carry half your fees on account to be paid through your sales. Don't let the high cost of design work keep you from getting your music into the hands of music fans world wide!

Proud sponsoring partner of EvO:R
www.evor.com

Design

http://www.peaceworkmusic.net/

From cdr copies to full package manufacturing, you'll find us affordable and dependable with the fastest turnaround in the industry . . . never more than a week and usually 48 hours! As with all our services, if you distribute through us you'll recieve a discount and we'll carry half your fees on account to be paid through your sales. Don't let the high cost of manufacturing keep you from getting your music to music lovers world wide.

Duplication

We have offices in five countries, including Ukraine and China! This allows you to sell your music directly to fans all over the world in their native language and they even pay in their own currency! This gives you the opportunity to be heard by folks that would otherwise never have the opportunity.

Our basic package includes a buypage that you can use to market your album and the only cost to you is what it costs to send us one copy of your cd for our archives. Yes, the basic distribution service is totally free! An email to ibinquire@peaceworkmusic.net will get you all the details and you could be online and ready for business within a week.

We also have a Platinum Package which includes a shorter url to your buypage, up to 1,500 words of promotional text and up to five pictures.

Distribution

ibinquire@peaceworkmusic.net

PeaceWork Music Net officially launched on July 4, 2000 as a constant reminder to everyone that we're a new millennia company with the goal in mind to make the process of getting music from the artists' head to the ears of the public easy and affordable. The staff is 'composed' entirely of musicians and we truly understand on a personal level how much frustration and expense has been involved up till now. It is our mission, our way of doing business, that we make this process what it should have been all along. You make the music, you tell the fans where to buy your music and we give your music a home where you can send your fans. Email us today for the details, you'll be glad you did.

PEACEWORK MUSIC NET
The 21st Century Music Store

Post Office Box 25102   Rochester, New York   14625-0102   ibinquire@peaceworkmusic.net   http://www.peaceworkmusic.net/

Range Records
2730 E. County Line Rd. Ardmore, PA 19003
PH: 610-649-7100 FX: 610-649-7566
Joe Mattis Joem@rangeentertainment.com
www.rangeentertainment.com
Our expertise lies in artist development, recording, booking, management and promotion.

THE REC(o)RD LINK
PO Box 647, Orange, NJ 07051
mail@TheRecordLink.com
www.therecordlink.com
Will promote your recordings on the internet.

Reason Y
747 Barnett St. NE, #4, Atlanta, GA 30306
PH: 404-723-5098
Moe moe@reasonY.com
www.reasonY.com
Promotion and distribution for Indie bands of all genres.

Ritual Records Music
PH: 323-605-3429
Stacy Lande ritualrecords@hotmail.com
ritualrecordsmusic.com
An independent label providing full service artist development. We'll help you manage everything from booking gigs, to getting your CD designed, recorded and sold! We are always looking for talented new bands and musicians to promote! At Ritual Records we build Rock Stars!

ROA Records
6014 Chenango Ln. Orlando, FL 32807
Monica Rabino monica@roarecords.com
roarecords.com
Independent music label by artists for artists.

Rock-The-Web
Wayne Rogaczewski
info@mp3collegeradionetwork.com
www.mp3collegeradionetwork.com
Internet and grassroots promotion, buzz marketing concepts, and radio/media strategies.

Scarlet Shame Records
PO Box 20680, Park West Stn.
New York, NY 10025
PH: 646-221-6596 FX: 212-362-1864
mail@scarletshamerecords.com
www.scarletshamerecords.com
Independent label focusing on Americana, Rock and Electronica.

SCREACHEN
PO Box 16352, Phoenix, AZ 85011-6352
Al Harbison President@Screachen.com
www.screachen.com
Reviews, manages and produces local & national bands.

Shut Eye Records
1526 DeKalb Ave. #21, Atlanta, GA 30307
PH: 678-986-5110 FX: 404-584-5171
Pete Knapp knapp@shuteyerecords.com
www.shuteyerecords.com
Record label, publicity firm, CD manufacturing and more.

SignHere Online, Inc.
contact@signhereonline.net
www.signhereonline.net
Provides artists with an opportunity to promote original MP3 music and solicit recording contract offers.

Silk City Recording Company
PO Box 704,
West Paterson, NJ 07424
PH: 973-599-0236
FX: 973-599-0236
silkcitycd@aol.com
www.silkcitycd.com
An on-line retail site that sells Indie products.

something sacred
PO Box 15533, San Luis Obispo, CA 93401
PH: 805-235-4037
Jon Broyles bandinfo@somethingsacred.com
www.somethingsacred.com
Promotes Indie artists. Submit your material.

sonaBLAST!
141 W. 28th St. Stn. 300,
New York, NY 10001
PH: 212-541-4443
Matt Parker
gill@sonablast.com
www.sonablast.com
We are a label, management and publishing firm all wrapped into one.

SongRamp
444 Metroplex Dr. #B-104,
Nashville, TN 37211
PH: 615-333-7775
FX: 615-333-7728
admin@songramp.com
www.songramp.com
We offer independent artists an outlet to sell their CDs.

Sonic Garden
info@sonicgarden.com
www.sonicgarden.com
Free music, videos, tour info, song info and more!

SoundBarter
3100 NW 2nd Ave. #404,
Boca Raton, FL 33431
www.soundbarter.com
We bring together thousands of Musicians, Music Lovers and Industry Professionals from around the world to trade their skills & services, music items, original music CDs etc.

Stompinground.com
www.stompinground.com
Global independent promotion for local bands.

Strange Sandwich Music
www.strangesandwich.com
Independent musicians from various genres of music and three different countries.

100 Full Color Buttons Starting at $22!!!

100 1" Buttons-$22
100 2 1/4" Buttons-$27
100 3" Buttons-$38

****

We have some of the most affordable and highest quality buttons available for your needs

- Quick Turnaround
- Free Shipping
- Discounts for Bulk Orders
- Low or no service charges

****

In addition to bulk button orders, we also have individual buttons, t-shirts, and patches available.

Mention this ad when ordering and receive a 10% discount on your first order.

www.caebuttons.com

Strange Vibes
16000 Harrison St., Livonia, MI 48154-3499
Tracy Farley tracy@strangevibes.com
www.strangevibes.com
A free CD distribution site for Indie musicians.

SWRECORDS.NET
info@swrecords.net
www.swrecords.net
Support independent music and buy it online!

United For Opportunity Music
133 W. 25th St. 5th Fl. New York, NY 10001
PH: 212-414-0505 FX: 212-414-0525
www.ufomusic.com
An organization of experienced, independent-thinking music industry activists that have come together to create a new model for a record label/music distribution company.

Ventilator Records
ventilator@ventilatorrecords.com
www.ventilatorrecords.com
Independent musician/songwriter label.

Vochella Records
info@vochellarecords.com
www.vochellarecords.com
Indie label and artist promotions co-op.

Wampus Multimedia
5746 Union Mill Rd. #315,
Clifton, VA 20124
PH: 703-587-3972
FX: 703-968-0562
Mark Doyon
mail2@wampus.com
wampus.com
Record label, retail store, recording studio and marketing company.

Webcds.com
Paul Scaturro
info@webcds.com
www.webcds.com
Post photo, description, interviews, reviews, articles and links to songs.

Woodstock CD
PO Box 119,
Ruby, NY 12475
info@woodstockcd.com
www.woodstockcd.com
Distribute your Indie CD here.

The World Wide Songwriters Association
FX: 302-348-6409
contact@wwswa.com
www.wwswa.com
Here to assist and encourage songwriters, both amateur and professional, in all genres of music around the globe. Members can now sell their CDs from our site.

Xact Records
PO Box 1832,
Bangor, ME 04402-1832
info@xactrecords.com
xactrecords.com
Promotes unsigned bands and sells their merchandise.

Canada

Promotional Services

2nd Floor Music Management
5739-68 St. NE, Calgary, AB T3J 1W1
PH: 403-285-3047
Chris Perrault chris@2ndfloor.ca
www.2ndfloor.ca
Management company assisting artists with direction and development.

CatsAsk Music & Entertainment
PO Box 31029, Barrie, ON L4N 0B3
PH: 705-792-0394
Duss Rodgers info@catsask.com
www.catsask.com
Band consultation, bio assistance, song copyright assistance and monthly music reviews.

City Lights Entertainment
16 Wynford Ave. Ottawa, ON K2G 3Z4
PH: 613-265-9967
Michael Wood mike@citylightsent.com
www.citylightsentertainment.com
We do not promote artists directly. We offer consultation and guidance services among other things.

Danie Cortese Entertainment & Publicity
PH: 905-303-9910
Danie Cortese dcortese@platinum1.com
www.daniecortese.com
Publicity representing all talent. Management & Consulting. Radio releases. Film & Music division.

The Image Management
9332-63 Ave. Edmonton, AB T6E 0G4
Michelle Rogers
michelle@theimagemanagement.com
www.theimagemanagement.com
Works with artists to get them signed. We also help our artists to write hit songs and make the best music video possible (at the lowest price). We have many contacts in the industry to help make our clients successful or at least get noticed.

Kindling Music
Attn: Demos, 411 Queen St. W. 3rd Fl.
Toronto, ON M5V 2A5
PH: 416-506-9696 x1001
info@kindling.ca
www.kindlingmusic.com
Label for career artists: promotion, publicity, marketing, booking and tour support.

Last Tango Productions
29 Galley Ave. Toronto, ON M6R 1G9
PH: 416-538-1838 FX: 416-538-2633
lastango@pathcom.com
www.lasttangoproductions.com
National publicity & radio tracking. Tour support and promotions.

MassiveRecordProductions.com
10 Royal Orchard Blvd. #53081,
Thornhill, ON L3T 7R9
PH: 905-764-1246
Jerry Bader info@mrpwebmedia.com.
MassiveRecordProductions.com
A music production and marketing company. We produce and promote the music of talented independent musicians, bands, and Singer-Songwriters who want to take their fledgling careers to the next level.

MRPwebmedia
10 Royal Orchard Blvd. #53081,
Thornhill, ON L3T 7R9
PH: 905-764-1246
Jerry Bader info@mrpwebmedia.com
mrpwebmedia.com
Providing independent artists with the content, marketing material, and promotional tools needed to create a buzz in the competitive music industry.

S.L. Feldman & Associates
200-1505 W. 2nd Ave. Vancouver, BC V6H 3Y4
Attn: Watchdog
www.slfa.com
Canada's leading full-service entertainment agency. Please note we do our best to listen to all demos we receieve. We will only contact you if we are interested in obtaining more information.

SonicAwareness
155 E. Beaver Creek Rd. Unit 24 #121,
Richmond Hill, ON L4B 2N1
Zach zach@sonicawareness.com
www.sonicawareness.com
Actively promotes your music to listeners from all over the world!

SPEAK Music
20 Bloor St. E. Box 75102, Toronto, ON M4W 3T3
PH: 416-599-9079
Jennifer Claveau office@speak-music.com
www.speak-music.com
A management, publicity and promotions firm, dedicated to helping independent artists develop their public profile.

TEA South
101 Burlington St., Toronto, ON M8V 3W1
PH: 416-251-1501
Clay Phillips clay@teasouth.com
www.teasouth.com
We provide radio tracking / promotions, live showcases, Press Kits, press releases, biography writing, radio shows, and administrative services. Our goal is to help guide independent musicians into the right channels that fit their specific needs, budgets and goals. Always free consultations!

Vizou
Dana Whittle dana@vizou.com
www.vizou.com
Services include concept development, writing and content development, illustration, custom typography and digital photography.

White Eagle Music Promotions
122-250 The East Mall #1109,
Toronto, ON M9B 6L3
(US address) 342 Broadway #101,
New York, NY 10013
PH: 416-620-1231 FX: 416-620-5912
Maureen Smith maureen@whiteeaglerecords.ca
www.whiteeaglerecords.ca
Consulting can help you with getting all the marketing channels established and working together, while building your buzz and fan base, and/or just selling your CDs .

Vendors and Labels

Atomic Records
music@atomicrecords.com
www.atomicrecords.com
Assisting independent bands in the art of effective promotion.

BenT Music
32 Paul St., Toronto, ON M5A 3H3
bentmusic@bentmusic.ca
www.bentmusic.ca
Helps musicians get their music out to the public.

Betty Records
317 Adelaide St. W. #503, Toronto, ON M5V 1P9
PH: 416-598-8806 FX: 416-598-0884
eric@bettyrecords.com
www.bettyrecords.com
Exposes you to a large audience from around the globe.

Byte Music
PH: 250-544-8027
Jamie Cooper jamie@unibyte.com
www.bytemusic.ca
An online music store, digital download service, and marketplace for music fans, artists, and music retailers.

CANtunes.com
356 Ontario St. #311, Stratford, ON N5A 7X6
Stewart mail@brittlestar.ca
www.cantunes.com/indiebible.php
Sell your Independent CDs in Canada the easy way!

Crony Records
290 Bridge St. W. Waterloo, ON N2K 1L2
Brad Weber brad@cronyrecords.ca
www.cronyrecords.ca
Community based record label helping musicians promote each other through the label.

Cyclone Records
84 Martin Crossing Rise NE, Calgary, AB T3J 3P1
PH: 403-285-9586
Brad Trew info@cyclonerecords.ca
www.cyclonerecords.ca
Producer of high quality CD compilations at a local, regional, national and international level. We are always seeking new talent to promote to a wider audience.

SDR Music
170 Brockport Dr. #202, Etobicoke, ON M9W 5C8
sdrmusic@sprint.ca
www.sdrmusic.net
Dedicated to helping up-and-coming songwriters, musicians and artists get their music and talent heard by record business executives.

TuneVault.com
steve@tenvolt.com
www.tunevault.com
Reviews, news, calendar, artist pages and more. Sell your stuff!

Sign up for
The Indie Contact
Newsletter.
www.indiebible.com

Europe

Czech Republic

Indies Records
Stefánikova 8, Brno 602 00, Czech Republic
PH: +420-549-245-610 FX: +420-545-212-209
Premysl Stepanek indies@indiesrec.cz
www.indiesrec.cz
Supporting many young talented artists.

France

Ocean-Music
2, place du Foirail, 81220 St Paul Cap de Joux, France
eole@ocean-music.com
www.ocean-music.com
Listens to demos and promotes Indie artists.

Plastic Pancake Records
180 ch des Pitous, 82000, Montauban, France
Pierre Antoine plasticpancake@hotmail.com
www.plasticpancake.com
French Indie Pop label and website.

Sriracha Sauce
23 rue Emile, Zola 93400 St Ouen, France
possee@sriracha-sauce.com
www.sriracha-sauce.com
French based booking and management agency.

Germany

amazon.de
www.amazon.de
Online CD store for Germany.

Glitterhouse Records
Gruner Weg 25 D-37688 Beverungen, Germany
PH: 49-0-5273-36360 FX: 49-0-5273-363637
info@glitterhouse.com
www.glitterhouse.de
The ultimate Mail-order for Americana, Roots, Alternative and Folk CDs.

Music Marketing Service
Arte Leon Ltd., Albinsuweg 5, 06679 Hohenmoelsen, Germany
PH: 0049-34441-21184 FX: 0049-941-59-92-21-184
Michael Thurm info@music-marketing-service.com
www.music-marketing-service.com
We offer bands distribution throughout Germany and Europe with CD-On-Demand and digital distribution. We also do radio promotion!

RockCity Hamburg
Kleine Freiheit 1 D-22767 Hamburg, Germany
PH: 040-319-60-60 FX: 040-319-60-69
Claudia music@rockcity.de
www.rockcity.de
Resource for Indie musicians.

Scales Records
Kleygarten 14, 59302 Oelde, Germany
PH: 49-0-2522-838309 FX: 49-0-2522-838309
Joerg Pasler scales@gmx.net
www.scales.de
Label, producer, publisher & distributor of instrumental electric guitar music 'from Heavy Metal to Jazz and beyond' (since '97) & radio show 'Mad for Scales' of same musical direction (since '95).

UEBER Distribution
Strichweg 110, 27476 Cuxhaven, Germany
PH: +49-4721-666470 FX: +49-4721-666471
Oliver Lagemann Oliver@ueber.us
www.ueber.us
We are a distribution company looking for finished products. Rock, Pop or indie.

ZYX Music
Siemensstr. 9, 35797 Merenberg, Germany
PH: 49-0-6471-505-117 FX: 49-0-6471-505-107
info@zyx.de
www.zyx.de
Supports Indie music of all genres.

Gibraltar

Melodrift Productions
30 Halifax Court, Gibraltar, Europe
Wesley contact@melodrift.com
www.melodrift.com
Offering artists promotional advertising, and/or music distribution, licensing deals etc.

Hungary

Redstar Budapest
1144 Budapest, Tihany U 38-40, Hungary
Mikorka Kalman crvnazvezda@freemail.hu
redstarbudapest.tk
An independent label interested in all kinds of "do it yourself" activities.

Italy

Alma Music
Marco Broll info@almamusic.it
www.almamusic.it a
Promotes and sells Independent music from Italy and the rest of the world.

M.P. Records
Via Municipio, 5 - 35019 Tombolo - Padova, Italy
PH: 39-049-9470749 FX: 39-049-9470748
Vannuccio Zanella mprecords@mprecords.it
www.mprecords.it
A vendor/label that sells Independent music.

Music & Waves
Via D. Chelinie, 3 00197, Rome, Italy
PH: 39-068070486 FX: 39-0680662007
Robert Ruggeri info@omomworld.com
www.omomworld.com
Italian independent label.

RES - Registrazioni e Suoni
PO Box 292, 31100 Treviso Centrale, Italy
PH: +39-335-8409306 FX: +39-0422-235743
Joachim Thomas info@res-net.org
www.res-net.org
A record label always looking for new music.

New Zero Europe
Federica Furlotti via Tommaso Campanella 21, 00195 Rome, Italy
PH: 338 3100739
Federica federica@newzeroeurope.com
www.newzeroeurope.com
Booking and Promotion Agency.

Malta

Awaken Events
PO Box 07 Rabat, Malta,
PH: 356 9988 4824
Nick Grima manager@awakenevents.com
www.awakenevents.com
Awaken utilizes unique strategies and an honest, direct business approach to expose artists to the expertise that enables music industry success. We are also currently looking for retail ready music CDs and DVDs (all genres) to be placed with our on-line music store.

The Netherlands

Dying Giraffe Recordings
St. Anthoniusplaats 9, 6511, TR, NIJMEGEN, The Netherlands
Ingmar info@dyinggiraffe-recordings.com
redearexplosion-label.com
We are always looking forward to your work. We listen to all the stuff that comes in. You can send us some MP3 files by e-mail or mail a CD.

Norway

Abòn Records
P.B. 261, 2831 Raufoss, Norway
PH: +47-61-16-82-12
records@abon.info
www.abon.info
Dedicated to producing quality Alternative sound recordings.

ChewinPine Records/ HormonMelon Prod.
Serli gt.8A 0577, Oslo, Norway
chewinpine@chewinpine.no
www.chewinpine.no
Issues on Indie labels, booking, promotion and more.

Romania

Media Pro Music
Bd. Ferdinand 99, sector 2, Bucharest, Romania
PH: 4021-205-28-00 FX: 4021-205-28-01
office@mediapromusic.ro
www.mediapromusic.ro
Indie label promoting artists internationally.

Spain

ATIZA
info@atiza.com
www.atiza.com
Música, noticias, bares y conciertos en Barcelona.

DiscoWeb
PH: +34-93-208-15-70
disco@discoweb.com
www.discoweb.com
International music mega store.

popchild.com
c/o Masnou 23-24, Entlo. 2a,
08014 Barcelona, Spain
popchild@popchild.com
www.popchild.com
Promotes Indie/unknown artists.

pop-page.com
C/ Málaga 11, 18230 Atarfe (Granada), Spain
www.pop-page.com
Un e-zine dedicado a la música menos convencional (¿independiente, alternativa?).

Sweden

Fickle Fame
Alstromergatan 32:16, 1tr, 112 47 Stokholm, Sweden
Attn: Skogman
info@ficklefame.com
www.ficklefame.com
An independent record label and booking agency.

Top Five Records
M. Andersson, Dansbanev 37,
S-12631 Hagersten, Sweden
Mattias Andersson mattias@top-five-records.com
www.top-five-records.com
We are a mail order company that is starting to release records. Send us your demo. Indie, Alt. Rock, Electro, Garage, Pop etc.

Zorch Productions
Klostergatan 7-9, s70361, Orebro, Sweden
info@zorchproductions.com
www.zorchproductions.com
Label that release the best unsigned stuff from Scandinavia.

United Kingdom

Promotional Services

Crunchy Frog Management.
Geoff Osborne cfrogmanagement@aol.com
cfm.moonfruit.com
London management company with great contacts. We really don't have time to reply to any messages. Just send your link and who knows what could happen! We WILL visit every link and listen to the music, after all....It's our job

Evil Twin Promotions
29 Stoneway Rd, Cleveleys, Lancs, FY5 3AU UK
PH: 07863-352539
Alex eviltwins@tiscali.co.uk
www.eviltwinpromotions.com
Promotional agency catering to unsigned bands, solo artists, and freelance musicians for hire. We offer a full range of promotional services covering hundreds of companies, including live, recording, and film services.

Genius Entertainment
PO Box 111, Derwentside, England DH9 8YR
PH: 01207-236-555
info@genius-entertainment.com
www.genius-entertainment.com
Offers promotion to unsigned and signed bands.

Killer Bee UK Tours
Unit 14A Colenzo Dr., Andover,
Hants, SP10 1JN UK
PH: +44-1264-392495 FX: +44-1264-392368
Darren Smith info@killerbeetours.com
www.killerbeetours.com
We offer tours to the UK. You can use this either as a Rock 'n Roll vacation or as serious promotion.

Mosquito Records
PO Box 39375, London, SE13 5WP UK
PH: 442088520433 FX: 442088520433
London E. Taylor etaylor@mosquito-records.com
www.mosquito-records.com
London based Indie label promoting bands and solo artists.

panartist.com
1 Barnby St. Box 45502, Euston,
London, England NW1 2AX
indies@panartist.com
www.panartist.com
A physical and digital music service. We supply our physical catalogue to thousands of major retail and internet stores in the US, Canada and Europe and virtually all the major legitimate digital music services.

Pleb Records Promotions
records@plebrecords.co.uk
www.plebrecords.co.uk
Promotions and independent record company.

RPM Records - UK music Store
PO Box 679, Doncaster, DN3 3WW UK
PH: 44-0-1302-371791 FX: 44-0-1302-371791
questions@rpmrecords.uk.com
www.rpmrecords.uk.com
Online Indie CD/memorabilia shop. All genres.

Traffic Online
6 Stucley Pl. London, England NW1 8NS
teams@trafficonline.net
trafficonline.net
Promotions, street teams and more for UK bands.

Vendors and Labels

25 Records
PO Box 3006, Poole, England BH12 2HU
info@25records.com
www.25records.com
Discovers new and exciting bands and brings them to the world's attention.

amazon.co.uk
www.amazon.co.uk
Simple, direct and profitable way for sell your music.

Astral Records
PH: +61-3-9849-1484 FX: +61-3-9878-6277
Mike Puskas puskas@astralrecords.co.uk
www.astralrecords.co.uk
A boutique label that specialises in sourcing, developing, packaging and shopping artists to third party labels and publishers.

Blue Comet Music
St. Peter's College, Oxford, England OX1 2DL
info@bluecometmusic.com
www.bluecometmusic.com
Small label with big promotion opportunities.

CD WOW! 'unsigned...AS YET!'
#2a, Gregories Ct. Gregories Rd. Beaconsfield,
Bucks, HP9 1HQ UK
PH: 44-0-1494-683500
unsigned@cd-wow.com
www.cd-wow.com/unsigned
Sell your music and gain exposure.

cdreeves.co.uk
14 Whitchurch Close, Maidenhead,
Berkshire, SL6 7TZ UK
PH: 01628-674184
Daniel Reeves hello@cdreeves.co.uk
www.cdreeves.co.uk
Albums and e.ps from unsigned bands and independent labels.

Clown Records
PO Box 20432, London, SE17 3WT UK
info@clownrecords.co.uk
www.clownrecords.co.uk
We welcome anyone to send in their music material. We cannot promise anything but consideration will be taken on the music material you send.

Collaborator Records
Paul Corket couk321@yahoo.co.uk
www.collaboratorrecords.com
Specialising in producing limited edition EPs - which feature studio recordings, demos and live versions of songs that will be rerecorded for the artist's first albums.

fierce panda records
PO Box 21441, London, N7 6WZ UK
mrbongopanda@aol.com
www.fiercepanda.co.uk
Send all demos to the above address. The music should be tuneful, handsome and whacked-out. Otherwise we don't give a monkey's cuss what it sounds like or what 'demographic' it fits.

Getmemusic.com
PO Box 4462, Worthing, W. Sussex, BN11 3FY UK
PH: 0871-8725324
www.getmemusic.com
Sell your CD or get one designed, manufactured and released for you!

iMusic Stage
PH: +44 (0)7748-184271
Susan Sarosy Susan@iMusicStage.com
www.iMusicStage.com
We cater to independent artists and bands of all genres, who want to sell CDs, MP3s, DVDs and merchandise online.

Norman Records
#1 Armley Park Court, Stanningley Rd.
Leeds, LS12 2AE UK
PH: 44-0113-2311114
phil@normanrecords.com
www.normanrecords.com
Features Indie CDs from around the world.

Overplay
PO Box 11188, Sutton Coldfield,
England B76 1WX
PH: 0870-112-1382
info@overplay.co.uk
www.overplay.com
Dedicated to the development and exposure of unsigned bands.

The Rocker
Zeitgeist, PO Box 13499, Edinburgh, EH6 8YL UK
PH: 01314671827
S. Hamilton info@the-rocker.co.uk
www.the-rocker.co.uk
Online music distributor and retailer, with associated information site and newsletter.

Rough Trade
130 Talbot Rd. London, England W11 1JA
PH: 020-7229-8541 FX: 020-7221-1146
shop@roughtrade.com
www.roughtrade.com
Send us your music to get on our shelves.

Solarise Records
PO Box 31104, London, England E16 4UE
PH: 44-0-7980-453628
info@solariserecords.com
www.solariserecords.com
Showcases, promotes and sells CDs online from any genre.

Stolenwine Records
PO Box 217, Wilmslow, SK9 2WB UK
info@stolenwine.co.uk
www.stolenwine.co.uk
Indie record label. Sells CDs at a low cost.

Sunrise UK
Silverdene, Scaleby Hill, Carlisle,
Cumbria, CA6 4LU UK
PH: 01228-675822 FX: 01228-675822
Martin Smith info@sunriseuk.co.uk
www.sunriseuk.co.uk
We offer new bands worldwide manufacturing and distribution deals. We are currently seeking new acts.

Supertonic CDs
12 Cavendish Ave. St. Johns Wood,
London, NW8 9JE UK
PH: 07968-199-617
info@supertoniccds.com
supertoniccds.com
Giving musicians the opportunity to sell their music internationally.

Zen Music
Moss Bridge Rd. Rochdale, OL16 5EA UK
FX: 01706-715795
ar@zenmusic.co.uk
www.zenmusic.co.uk
Join to produce your own album.

Australia
Promotional Services

Australian Music Biz
PO Box 30, Chermside South, QLD 4032 Australia
PH: 07-3854-0945 FX: 07-3854-0734
mail@musicbiz.com.au
www.musicbiz.com.au
Promotes local Indie labels on a national level.

NewSouthFolk
POB 328, Moruya, NSW 2537 Australia
PH: 61-2 -4-742736 FX: 61-2-44-742736
Jim MacQuarrie jim@newsouthfolk.com.au
www.newsouthfolk.com.au
A booking agency for Australian and overseas artists.

Vendors and Labels

Automatic Distribution
PO Box 26, S. Melbourne, VIC 3205 Australia
PH: 613-9352-7878 FX: 613-8610-1039
info@automaticdistribution.com
www.automaticdistribution.com
Independent music distribution and online shop.

The CAN
85 Bourke St., Melbourne, VIC 3000 Australia
PH: 03-8662-4223
Jessie Malignaggi jessiem@thecan.com.au
www.thecan.com.au
An online retail and distribution resource for independent artists.

digisounds.com
268B Domain Rd. South Yarra, VIC 3141 Australia
info@digisounds.com
www.digisounds.com
Allows bands to sell music to a global market.

Groovetracks Records
Steve Cole info@groovetracksrecords.com
www.groovetracksrecords.com
Boosts your sales through radio airplay & internet.

Indie-cds.com
85 Oakfords Rd. Wattle Grove, TAS 7109 Australia
PH: 61-3-6295-0735 FX: 61-3-6295-0835
mal@indie-cds.com
www.indie-cds.com
Provides record sales, publicity, and websites for local bands.

Modern World Records
PO Box 422, New Lambton, NSW 2305 Australia
Craig Mitchell modernworld@hunterlink.net.au
www.modernworld.com.au
Online catalogue for Australian Indie CDs.

One World Music
PO Box 396, Camperdown, NSW 1450 Australia
PH: 61-2-9565-4522 FX: 61-2-9565-5677
info@oneworldmusic.com.au
www.oneworldmusic.com.au
Independent record label for Chill-out/World Beat genres.

Pure Pop Records
PO Box 73, Prahran, VIC 3181 Australia
info@purepop.com.au
www.purepop.com.au
Licenses and distributes Indie pop CDs in Australia.

Africa

Merchant Records
44 Ryneveld St., Stellenbosch, South Africa
PH: +27218875705 FX: +27218875705
Helmut Meijer helmut@merchantrecords.com
www.merchantrecords.com
Independent South African Record Label and Publishing House. Produces international standard music in all styles and genres.

Asia

CDJam
2-18-1-501 Kusagae, Chuo-ku,
Fukuoka, 810-0045, Japan
PH/FX: 81-92-716-8848
Jeffrey and Mutsumi Martin jeff@cdjam.jp
www.cdjam.jp
A project to help independent artists located outside Japan promote and sell their music in the Japanese market. We not only will sell your music, we also promote it to local media.

Blues

Alligator Records
New Material, PO Box 60234, Chicago, IL 60660
info@allig.com
www.alligator.com
We will NOT accept inquiries or phone calls regarding the receipt or status of submissions. Also, do not send song files. Send a CD with 4 songs max.

The Blues Loft
PO Box 3454, Bellevue, WA 98009
PH: 425-941-1096
alawrence@jazzloft.com
www.jazzloft.com/bluesloft
Sell your Blues CD, fee free.

Crossroads Blues Agency
PO Box 10168, 7301 GD Apeldoorn,
The Netherlands
PH: 31-55-5214757 FX: 31-55-5787815
www.crossroads.nl
Specializes in European tours of Blues artists.

House of Blues
6255 Sunset Blvd. 16th Fl. Hollywood, CA 90028
PH: 323-769-4600
support@hob.com
www.hob.com
Promotion and distribution of live Blues music.

Silk City Records
PO Box 704, West Paterson, NJ 07424
PH: 973-599-0237 FX: 973-599-0236
Andy Allu silkcity@silkcitycd.com
www.silkcitycd.com
Provides recordings of the finest quality Blues, Folk, Jazz, New Age and Roots artists, both established and emerging.

Stony Plain Records
PO Box 861, Edmonton, AB T5J 2L8
PH: 780-468-6423 FX: 780-465-8941
info@stonyplainrecords.com
www.stonyplainrecords.com
Canada's prominent Roots music label.

Children's

The Children's Group
1400 Bayly St. #7, Pickering, ON L1W 3R2
PH: 905-831-1995 FX: 905-831-1142
moreinfo@childrensgroup.com
childrensgroup.com
Presenting Classical music entertainment for children.

Kids' CDs and Tapes
Old Bank Chambers, 43 Woodlands Rd. Lytham St
Annes, Lancashire, FY8 1DA UK
PH: 01253-731234
info@crs-records.com
www.kidsmusicshop.co.uk
Specialist producers of Children's music.

Kidsmusic
The Fairway, Bush Fair, Harlow, Essex,
England CM18 6LY
PH: 44-01279-444707 FX: 44-01279-445570
www.cypmusic.co.uk
Marketing and distribution of Children's audio.

Music for Little People
PO Box 1460, Redway, CA 95560
PH: 800-346-4445
publicity@mflp.com
www.mflp.com
Producer of Children's music.

Music4Kids Online
220 SW G St., Grants Pass, OR 97526
PH: 541-956-8600
info@music4kids.com
www.music4kidsonline.com
Sells Children's Indie music.

Piano Press
PO Box 85, Del Mar, CA 92014-0085
PH: 619-884-1401 FX: 858-755-1104
Elizabeth C. Axford EAxford@aol.com
www.pianopress.com
Indie record label and producer of Children's music.

Rabbit Ranch Records
PO Box 5020, Champaign, IL 61825
info@rabbitranch.com
www.rabbitranch.com
A Christian Children's music company.

Christian

Promotional Services

Black Gospel Promo
45 E. Cityline Ave. #303, Bala Cynwyd, PA 19004
PH: 410-963-7589
info@blackgospelpromo.com
blackgospelpromo.com
The Gospels source for marketing & publicity.

The BuzzPlant
317 Main St. #205, Franklin, TN 37064
PH: 615-550-2305
susan@buzzplant.com
www.buzzplant.com
Marketing and promotion for Christian music.

Cross Movements
PO Box 5620, Deptford, NJ 08096
PH: 856-845-0984
jd@crossmovement.com
www.crossmovement.com
Accepts demos and sells Gospel CDs.

Crossing Borders
PO Box 1382, Hopkinsville, KY 42240
PH: 270-484-0089
Glenn Pepper gpepper@borderscrossed.com
www.borderscrossed.com
Promoting Christian music of any genre.

First Choice Management & Artist Development
16781 Chagrin #158, Shaker Heights, OH 44137
PH: 216-659-3710 FX: 208-723-3636
Martin Johnson martin@firstchoiceonline.com
www.firstchoiceonline.com
A full service artist management corporation specializing in artist development and promotion of Gospel and Christian artists.

Fruition Artist Agency
PO Box 3721, Brentwood, TN 37024
PH: 615-377-9177 FX: 615-377-9178
Carla Archuletta info@fruitionartistagency.com
www.fruitionartistagency.com
We partner with artists and songwriters that have a unique gift of expression that has the ability to move people with words and melodies.

Gideon Promotions
PO Box 2198, Purley, Surrey, England CR8 2LS
PH: 44-020-8668-3332 FX: 44-020-8660-5822
GideonPro@aol.com
www.gideon-promotions.co.uk
Promoters and agents to Gospel music.

ICM Production Service Center
PO Box 11239, Goldsboro, NC 27532
PH: 919-751-2151
theicmgroup@hotmail.com
www.freewebs.com/icmservice
We are proud of the fact that we have developed a service and system that can bring positive results for your musical goals.

Light It Up! Publicity
452 Pompton Ave. #6, Cedar Grove, NJ 07009
PH: 973-857-3298
Armando Triana armando@sparkpublicity.com
www.LightItUpPublicity.com
A Christian music publicity firm aimed at enhancing the exposure of its artists using all available print and online media outlets.

Prodigal Son Entertainment
115 Penn Warren Dr. Ste. 300, Box 145, Brentwood, TN 37027
PH: 615-377-0057
Scott E. Williams prodigalsonents@aol.com
www.prodigalson-entertainment.com
Artist management & development. Indie & signed mainstream and Christian (no Rap/Urban).

Spark Publicity
452 Pompton Ave. #6 Cedar Grove, NJ 07009
PH: 973-857-3298
Armando Triana armando@sparkpublicity.com
www.SparkPublicity.com
A Christian music publicity firm aimed at enhancing the exposure of its artists using all available print and online media outlets.

Stage Right Talent
2141 Pamela St., Oxnard, CA 93036
PH: 805-604-0030 FX: 805-485-5109
Carlton Batts stagerighttalent@yahoo.com
www.freewebs.com/stageright
A music consultant firm and referral service. Specializing in Gospel, Jazz, R&B, Reggae, Hip Hop, Latin and Pop.

Vendors and Labels

Araunah Music
2 Oxley Square Rd. Gaithersburg, MD 20877
PH: 240-696-6051
Fred Petit contact@araunah.com
www.araunah.com
A Christian label that produces, promotes and distributes the best Christian indies.

Avail Records, Inc.
PO Box 13011, Gainesville, FL 32604
PH: 305-205-0024 FX: 352-372-1634
H. Pierre hpierre@availrecords.com
www.availrecords.com
Specializing in using the gift of music to spread the gospel of Jesus Christ to the world.

Awake Music Group
659 Barking Rd. Plaistow, London, E13 9EX UK
PH: 011-44-8-821-9597
Lucas Langdon info@awakemusicgroup.com
www.awakemusicgroup.com
We provide manufacturing and distribution services for The UK & Europe, to Christian Recording artists from all over the world. The service also includes marketing & promotion.

blackgospelmusic.com
PH: 215-227-5026 FX: 215-893-4321
webminister@blackgospel.com
www.blackgospel.com
Resources for the Black Gospel music community.

Blastbeats.com
PO Box 1018, Little Elm, TX 75068
PH: 972-668-2489 FX: 972-668-2487
staff@blastbeats.com
www.blastbeats.com
Indie/Underground Christian music.

Blue Duck Records
4 Bonnie Dr. Berkley, MA 02779
Jason Ronan blueduckrecords@aol.com
www.blueduckrecords.com
A Christian Indie Label looking for talented Christian bands/Artists to sign. Send a CD with a press kit/bio (must include lyrics) to the above address.

Broken Records
1102 Sam Davis Rd. Smyrna, TN 37167
PH: 615-594-0426 FX: 615-523-1400
brs@brokenrecords.com
www.brokenrecords.com
Connecting artists with fans, consumers and opportunities. Our model is quite simple, artists bring their excellent content, and we bring it to the world. We locate our roster through relationships we forge with artists on our partner site, Indieheaven.com.

By Faith Records
PO Box 431647, Pontiac, MI 48343
PH: 313-531-3808 FX: 313-531-3808
Anthony Frazier contact@byfaithrecords.com
www.byfaithrecords.com
We provide spiritual uplifting through music.

Christian Concert Authority
2234 Ahu Niu Pl. Honolulu, HI 96821
FX: 406-622-3845
Karla@ccauthority.com
www.ccauthority.com
Sells Christian CDs (all genres) online.

Christianbook.com
PO Box 7000, Peabody, MA 01961-7000
PH: 800-247-4784
internet.marketing@christianbook.com
www.christianbook.com
Sells Christian products worldwide.

ChristianDiscs.com
2705 S. Pike Ave. Allentown, PA 18103
service@christiandiscs.com
www.christiandiscs.com
Sells Indie and mainstream Christian CDs.

Con-Trad Music Group
12806 Palm Desert #100, Houston, TX 77099
PH: 832-654-6924
James Sayles jamess@contradrecords.com
www.contradrecords.com
Supports independent and Traditional Gospel music artists.

CPR Music
PO Box 35489, Albuquerque, NM 87176
PH: 505-836-2398 FX: 505-833-1800
Murphy L. Platero cprmusic@prodigy.net
www.nativecprmusic.com
A Native American Christian record label. Provides recording and distribution.

Crossing Music
PO Box 23066, Alexandria, VA 22304
PH: 703-354-5157
customerservice@crossingmusic.com
www.crossingmusic.com
Import and independent Christian music.

Do Love Gospel Records
123 NW 14th Way, #1, Dania, FL 33004
PH: 954-209-5313
D.L. Gilbert
DoLoveGospelRecords@EmailAccount.com
www.DoLoveGospelRecords.com
An independent Gospel label based in South Florida.

FaveStreet
4558-B Capital Blvd. #171, Raleigh, NC 27604
PH: 919-873-1970 FX: 919-873-1972
admin@favestreet.com
www.favestreet.com
Actively promotes Indie Christian music.

Gospel Artist Network
3913 Brainerd Rd. #106, Chattanooga, TN 37411
PH: 423-622-9867 FX: 423-622-9861
info@gospelartistnetwork.com
www.gospelmusicmart.com
A site developed for all Gospel and Christian artists.

Gospel Music Direct
PO Box 522, 226 Preacher Smith Rd.
Silver Creek, GA 30173
PH/FX: 706-378-9184
Richard Tidwell sales@gospelmusicdirect.com
www.gospelmusicdirect.com
We are looking for groups, choirs or any Gospel singers who wish to display their tapes and CDs on our site. We'll advertise and distribute your CDs for you.

HG Records
Humberto Lopez hlopez@hgrecords.com
www.hgrecords.com
A Christian Label that promotes, sells, and plays music.

Holy Hip Hop
PO Box 1023, Pine Lake, GA 30072
globaldistribution@holyhiphop.com
holyhiphop.com
Production, distribution and marketing for Christian Hip Hop music.

independentbands.com
7739 La Verdura Dr. Dallas, TX 75248-3142
FX: 972-980-4023
bandrelations@independentbands.com
www.independentbands.com
Site and service for Christian Indie bands.

Indie Heaven
www.indieheaven.com
Site for all Indie Christian artists.

indievisionmusic.com
PO Box 6305, Laguna Niguel, CA 92607
info@indievisionmusic.com
www.indievisionmusic.com
Source for Indie Christian artists/music.

PasteMusic.com
mail@pastemusic.com
www.pastemusic.com
Promotes lesser-known Indie musicians of all genres.

The PGE Label Group
PO Box 181742, Dallas, TX 75218
PH: 214-324-3118 FX: 214-324-3119
Scott Taylor scott_taylor@pgedist.com
www.pgedist.com
African American Christian distributor.

RAD ROCKERS
PH: 734-439-7029
customer.service@radrockers.com
www.radrockers.com
Mothership of hard to find Christian music.

RGM Records, Inc.
Bruce Ferber bruce@recklessgrace.com
www.recklessgrace.com
Christian record company. Accepts demos.

Rock Solid Music
3779 154 A St., Surrey, BC V3S 0V4
PH: 604-628-2400
info@rocksolidmusic.com
www.rocksolidmusic.com
Contemporary Christian Music of all styles.

The Shepherd's Nook
1794 Marion-Waldo Rd. Marion, OH 43302
PH: 740-389-4000 FX: 740-389-6601
Tom Hypes tom@theshepherdsnook.com
www.theshepherdsnook.com
Carries Christian Indie CDs on consignment.

Spirit Music
Meadow House, Kingcombe Rd. Toller Porcorum, Dorchester, England DT2 0DG
info@spiritmusic.co.uk
www.spiritmusic.co.uk
Worldwide supplier of contemporary Christian music.

vineyardonline.com
5721 E. Virginia St., Evansville, IN 47715
PH: 800-578-7984 FX: 812-479-8805
info@vineyardonline.com
www.vineyardonline.com
Everything Christian.

worshipmusic.com
2432 W. Peoria Ave. #1182, Phoenix, AZ 85029
custcare@worshipmusic.com
www.worshipmusic.com
Promotes Indie Worship music.

Wounded Records
1145 Stierley Rd. N., Wadesville, IN 47638
PH: 812-985-5969 FX: 812-985-5969
Bryant or Tonja woundedr@woundedrecords.com
www.woundedrecords.com
Accepting demos with a positive message. All genres. From recording to production of your project, including distro and promotion, we are here for you.

XPESRX Recording Company
2107 Reserve Dr. Atlanta, GA 30319
PH: 404-816-0914 FX: 419-793-4545
info@xpesrx.com
www.xpesrx.com
Submit any Christian music for review.

Classical

North America

United States

Centaur Records
136 St. Joseph St., Baton Rouge, LA 70802
PH: 225-336-4877 FX: 225-336-9678
info@centaurrecords.com
www.centaurrecords.com
Accepts unsolicited submissions of Classical material.

Cliff's Classics
cliff@cliffsclassics.com
www.cliffsclassics.com
Supports independent Classical musicians.

Composers Recordings, Inc.
16 Penn Plaza #835, New York, NY 10001-1820
PH: 212-290-1680 FX: 212-290-1685
info@newworldrecords.org
www.composersrecordings.com
Sells the CDs of Indie musicians.

Eroica Classical Recordings
4501-D Carpinteria Ave. Carpinteria, CA 93013
PH: 805-684-6140 FX: 805-745-1812
Larry A. Russell cds@eroica.com
www.eroica.com
Sells and distributes Indie Classical music CDs.

Ivory Classics
PO Box 341068, Columbus, OH 43234-1068
PH: 614-761-8709 FX: 614-761-9799
michaeldavis@ivoryclassics.com
www.IvoryClassics.com
Independent Classical record label devoted to pianists.

Jeffrey James Arts Consulting
316 Pacific St., Massapequa Park, NY 11762
PH: 516-797-9166 FX: 516-797-9166
jamesarts@worldnet.att.net
www.jamesarts.com
Management and PR for Classical artists.

KOCH International
22 Harbor Park Dr. Port Washington, NY 11050
classicalmusic@kochent.com
www.kochint.com
Independent music distribution in America.

Music & Arts
PO Box 771, Berkeley, CA 94701
PH: 510-525-4853 FX: 510-524-2111
info@musicandarts.com
www.musicandarts.com
Independent Classical and Jazz label.

New Albion Records
584 Castro St. #525, San Francisco, CA 94114-2594
PH: 415-621-5757 FX: 415-621-4711
ergo@newalbion.com
www.newalbion.com
Develops, records and releases for Indie artists.

Phoenix USA
200 Winston Dr. Cliffside Park, NJ 07010
PH: 201-224-8318 FX: 201-224-7968
sales@Phoenixcd.com
www.phoenixcd.com
A label for recent Classical music.

SibeliusMusic.com
info@sibeliusmusic.com
www.sibeliusmusic.com
Publish your music here for free.

Wildboar Records
2430 Bancroft Way, Berkeley, CA 94704
PH: 510-849-0211 FX: 510-849-9214
wildboar@musicaloffering.com
www.musicaloffering.com
Independent Classical CD store/label.

Telarc
23307 Commerce Park Rd. Cleveland, OH 44122
PH: 216-464-2313
artists@telarc.com
www.telarc.com
Submit your demo to sell music here.

Canada

early-music.com
7753, rue Tellier, Montréal, QC H1L 2Z5
PH: 514-355-1825 FX: 514-355-5628
info@early-music.com
www.early-music.com
Providing an international marketplace for world-class professionals involved in all aspects of Early Music.

Marquis Classics/Marquis Records
30 Kenilworth Ave. Toronto, ON M4L 3S3
PH: 416-690-7662 FX: 416-690-7346
info@marquisclassics.com
www.marquisclassics.com
Accepts submissions from independent musicians in several genres.

Europe

Austria

Vienna Modern Masters
Margaretenstrasse 125/15, A-1050, Vienna, Austria
PH: 431-545-1778 FX: 431-544-0785
Geert de Vos gdv@xs4all.nl
www.xs4all.nl/~gdv/vmm
Produces and internationally distributes CDs of contemporary Classical music.

Denmark

Danacord Records
Norregade 22, DK-1165 Copenhage, Denmark
PH: 45-33-15-17-16 FX: 45-33-12-15-14
daco@danacord.dk
www.danacord.dk
Independent Classical record label.

Germany

FARAO Classics
Schwere-Reiter-Str. 35 Gbd. 20,
80797 Munchen, Germany
PH: 49-89-30777616 FX: 49-89-30777617
info@farao-classics.de
www.farao-classics.de
Founded by professional musicians for musicians!

Pink Tontraeger
Munstertaler Str. 23, D-79219 Stuafen im Breisgau, Germany
PH: 7633-7265 FX: 7633-50441
info@pink-tontraeger.de
www.pink-tontraeger.de
Sells CDs of Classical Indie musicians.

Italy

Stradivarius
stradiva@tin.it
www.stradivarius.it
The leading Italian Classical music label.

United Kingdom

Chandos
Commerce Way, Colchester, Essex, CO2 8HQ UK
PH: 44-1206-225200 FX: 22-1206-225201
enquiries@chandos.net
www.chandos.net
Independent Classical record company.

Divine Art Record Company
8 The Beeches, E. Harlsey,
N. Yorkshire, DL6 2DJ UK
PH: 44-0-1609-882062
Stephen Sutton sales@divine-art.com
www.divine-art.com
We deal in Classical/Experimental/Nostalgia music.

Hyperion
PO Box 25, London, England SE9 1AX
PH: 44-0-20-8318-1234 FX: 44-0-20-8463-1230
info@hyperion-records.co.uk
www.hyperion-records.co.uk
Independent Classical label.

METIER Records
127 Stanford Cottages, Semley,
Dorset, SP7 9AT UK
PH: 44-0-1747-830979 FX: 44-0-1747-830979
info@metierrecords.co.uk
www.metierrecords.co.uk
Independent, full service Classical label.

tutti.co.uk
18 Hillfield Park, London, N10 3QS UK
PH: 44-0-20-8444-8587
help@tutti.co.uk
www.tutti.co.uk
Source for independent Classical labels. Sell your music.

Australia

Move Records
1 Linton Street, Ivanhoe, VIC 3084 Australia
PH: 03-9497-3105 FX: 03-9497-4426
Martin Wright move@move.com.au
www.move.com.au
Classical and Jazz CD label with own studio with grand piano.

Asia

ArtPro Artist Management
PO Box 22044, Tel Aviv, Israel 61220
PH: 972-3-6046690 FX: 972-3-6043016
UriZur@ArtPro.co.il
Margaret@ArtPro.co.il
www.artpro.co.il
All artists are represented exclusively and worldwide.

Naxos.com
Level 11, Cyberport 1, 100 Cyberport Rd.
Hong Kong
PH: 852-2760-7818 FX: 852-2760-1962
Customer.service@naxos.com
www.naxos.com
Selling and distribution of Classical Indie music.

Country

Promotional Services

Honky Tonkin Music
2334 CR 2265, Telephone, TX 75488
PH: 903-664-3741 FX: 903-664-3741
info@honkytonkin.com
www.HonkyTonkin.com
We offer a wide variety of Independent music.

Payne County Line Promotions
3333 E. 68th St., Stillwater, OK 74074
Stan Moffat stan@paynecountyline.com
www.paynecountyline.com
We welcome all genres of music, and accepts gladly your demos, press packets, band news, events etc.

Publicity House/Wildfire Publicity
PO Box 558, Smyrna, TN 37167
PH: 615-825-0019 FX: 760-437-4633
Laura Claffey wildfirepublicity@comcast.net
www.wildfirepublicity.net
We schedule interviews, and coordinate CD reviews with ezines, print magazines, newspapers etc.

Red Haired Girl Publicity
905 N. Tacoma St. #3, Allentown, PA 18109
PH: 484-221-1026
Liz Winchester LizWinchester@earthlink.net
www.RHGPublicity.com
PR firm specializing in publicity for independent musicians and Indie Labels in the Americana & Texas music formats.

Unavoidable Bluegrass Promotions
PH: 317-730-7251
support@bluegrasspro.com
www.bluegrasspro.com
Internet promotion for Bluegrass musicians.

Vendors and Labels

AmericanaMusicplace.com
PO Box 5202, Concord, NC 28027-5202
PH: 704-788-6789
submissions@GoAmericana.com
www.AmericanaMusicplace.com
Featuring Bluegrass, Gospel and Old Time music.

BluegrassAmericana.com
PO Box 5202, Concord, NC 28027-5202
PH: 704-788-6789
submissions@GoAmericana.com
www.bluegrassamericana.com
The sounds and happenings of Bluegrass, Gospel, and Old Time music.

CountySales.com
PH: 540-745-2001 FX: 540-745-2008
info@countysales.com
www.countysales.com
Large selection of Bluegrass music.

Dingo Gold Records
PH: 281-577-0110 FX: 281-577-0175
PO Box 2150, Porter, TX 77365
info@dingogold.com
dingogold.com
The finest in Top Shelf entertainment.

Flat Earth Records
PO Box 30497, Indianapolis, IN 46230
info@flatearthrecords.com
www.flatearthrecords.com
Indie label with a focus on Twang.

Indie World Country Record Report
PO Box 130, Brush Creek, TN 38547
PH: 615-683-8308
www.indieworldcountry.com
Designed to candidly alert the Independent community, the general public and "major" industry about the growth development, aspirations and talents of new singers and songwriters worldwide.

MDH Records
3418 Old Spanish Trail, Seguin, TX 78155
PH: 210-602-4822
Mike Harwell mharwelljr1@netzero.com
www.mikeharwell.4t.com
Country music promotion with class.

Miles of Music
7306 Coldwater Canyon #9,
N. Hollywood, CA 91605
PH: 818-765-8836 FX: 818-759-0336
corrie@milesofmusic.com
www.milesofmusic.com
More music to the gallon!

Old-Time Music Home Page
20 Battery Park Ave. Asheville, NC 28801
PH: 828-285-8850 FX: 828-285-8851
david@lynchgraphics.com
www.oldtimemusic.com
Sells Old-Time (traditional southern string band) music CDs.

Rockabilly Hall of Fame
PO Box 639, Burns, TN 37029
PH: 615-740-7625 FX: 615-740-8181
bob@rockabillyhall.com
www.rockabillyhall.com
Promotes and sells Roots music.

Sound Stop Music
80 Woodwinds Rd. Callaway, VA 24067
PH: 540-483-3373 FX: 540-483-0161
David Cannaday soundstopmusic@aol.com
www.soundstopmusic.com
Independent CD sales for Bluegrass artists, PLUS publishing, BMI for Bluegrass writers.

Dance
Promotional Services

masspool Dj Association
30 Revere Beach Pkwy. Revere, MA 02151
PH: 781-485-1901 FX: 781-485-1902
www.masspool.com
One of the most highly regarded DJ record pools in the US.

Vendors and Labels

BangingTunes.com
F.A.O. Product Dept. 102 Trafalagar St., Brighton, East Sussex, England BN1 4ER
PH: 44-0-1273-622940
info@BangingTunes.com
www.bangingtunes.com
The UK Dance music store.

blackmarket.co.uk
25 D'Arblay St., London, W1F 8EJ UK
PH: 44-2-207-437-0478 FX: 44-0-207-494-1303
mailorder@blackmarket.co.uk
www.blackmarket.co.uk
House, Drum 'n Bass, mix tapes and Underground.

Freestylemusic.com
18565 SW 104th Ave. Miami, FL 33157
PH: 305-234-8033
freestylemusic@mailcity.com
www.freestylemusic.com
Distribution network for independent artists and DJs.

Haywire
Studio A. 21 John Campbell Rd.
London, England N16 8JY
PH: +44 (0) 20-7249 9946
FX: +44 (0) 20-7503 3921
Amanda Burton info@haywire.co.uk
www.haywire.co.uk
We deal with artist management, live bookings & events. We also offer ALL the info on the local music scene.

Knob Records
216 E. 29th St. #3A, New York, NY 10016
PH: 917-449-5250
DJ Style style@knobrecords.com
www.knobrecords.com
Underground Progressive, Tribal house, Trance and Breaks.

Nilaihah Records
Attn: Demo Submission, PO Box 82614,
Columbus, OH 43202
nilaihah@nilaihah.com
www.nilaihah.com
Indie record label for Dance music.

Phuture Sole Recordings
227 Madison Ave. Clifton, NJ 07011
PH: 973-614-0302 FX: 973-614-0302
Sweet Sarah SweetS@PhutureSoleRecordings.com
www.PhutureSoleRecordings.com
We are an independent label specializing in soulful House Dance Music.

Real Estate Records, Elephanthaus Records
2544 W. North Ave. #2B, Chicago, IL 60647
PH: 773-862-9652 FX: 773-862-9662
Veronica Beckman info@elephanthaus.com
www.realestaterecords.com
Indie Electronic label.

Sonic Index Records
1220 N. State St., Bellingham, WA 98225-5016
PH: 360-527-1150
Dave Richards dave@clickpoprecords.com
www.clickpoprecords.com
Specializing in Techno, House, Down Tempo and Alternative music.

Tune Inn Records
2 Wren Ln. Selby, N. Yorkshire, YO8 0PN UK
PH: 44-0-1757-212592 FX: 44-0-1757-212591
pete@tuneinn.com
www.tuneinn.com
Record label or Dance/Techno music.

Tweekin Records
593 Haight St., San Francisco, CA 94117
PH: 415-626-6995 FX: 415-626-5206
Darren Davis darren@tweekin.com
www.tweekin.com
San Francisco's premiere Dance record store.

Waipa Music
10 Raleigh St., Cambridge 2351, Waikato,
New Zealand
PH: 6478276863
Stewart McFarlane stewart@waipamusic.co.nz
www.waipamusic.co.nz
Progressive label actively seeking and promoting Dance/Retro/Electronic/Pop music.

Web-Records.com
Im Vogelsang 15-17, 71101 Schonaich, Germany
PH: 0180-5-555-701 FX: 0180-5-555-702
info@web-records.com
web-records.com
World's biggest Internet shop for Club music.

Experimental

Acids Musicks
PO Box 32552, Santa Fe, NM 87594
Erik Bonner erik@acidsoxx.com
www.acidsoxx.com
Indie label specializing in bedroom-Rockstar Psychopop

Arthropoda Records
1223 Wilshire Blvd., #812,
Santa Monica, CA 90403
PH: 310-930-0990 FX: 310-315-8273
Craig Garner craig@arthropodarecords.com
www.arthropodarecords.com
Record label promoting original thinking.

Artoffact Records
PO Box 81630, Toronto, ON M2R 3X1
demos@artoffact.com
www.artoffact.com
Releasing and promoting Electronic music sounds.

Bad Robot *UK*
Paul Le Hat info@badrobot.co.uk
www.badrobot.co.uk
Serving unsigned and independent music in streaming mp3 audio.

BiP_HOp webzine
BP 64, 13192 Marseille Cedex 20, France
PH: 33-0-491-64-89-15 FX: 33-0-491-64-89-15
ip@bip-hop.com
www.bip-hop.com
Label spreading unconventional sound adventures.

CDeMUSIC
116 N. Lake Ave. Albany, NY 12206
PH: 518-434-4110 FX: 518-434-0308
cde@emf.org
www.cdemusic.org
All genres and styles of non-commercial new music.

Cool Chill Tec Records
42 Cecil Rd. Erdington, Birmingham, B24 8AT UK
PH: 07931-339059
www.cct-records.com
Selling Electronica tunes from around the world.

c367 Records
PO Box 771, Estill Springs, TN 37330
PH: 931-588-3109
Christopher Sisk c367records@gmail.com
www.c367.com
An Electronic music label focusing on Ambient and laid back Experimental music.

eurock.com
Archie Patterson apatters@eurock.com
www.eurock.com
Music retailer that sells Electronic, Progressive and Space music.

Forced Exposure
219 Medford St., Malden, MA 02148
FX: 781-321-0321
mailorder@forcedexposure.com
www.forcedexposure.com
Sells Experimental, Techno, IDM and more.

Frog Peak Music
PO Box 1052, Lebanon, NH 03755
PH: 603-643-9037 FX: 603-643-9037
fp@frogpeak.org
www.frogpeak.org
An artist-run composers' collective dedicated to publishing and producing Experimental and unusual works by its member artists, and is committed to the idea of availability over promotion.

Hello Pussy Records
PO Box 866, Frankfort, IN 46041
ldr_hpr@hotmail.com
www.angelfire.com/super/ldr-hpr
Releases with diverse genres/styles.

Hypnos
PO Box 6868, Portland, OR 97228
mg@hypnos.com
hypnos.com
Source for Aambient, Space and Experimental music.

The Infinite Sector
info@infinitesector.org
www.infinitesector.org
Sharing and promoting Experimental music, Noise and Electronica.

Joyful Noise
PO Box 20109, Indianapolis, IN 46220
Karl info@joyfulnoiserecordings.com
www.joyfulnoiserecordings.com
Spiritually focused Experimental/Noise/Improv label.

The Kitefishing Family
241 E. South Temple #4, Salt Lake City, UT 84111
PH: 801-637-2828
Camden camden@kitefishingfamily.com
www.kitefishingfamily.com
Dedicated to the promotion of all forms of Independent art.

Oddball Musicworks
315 Front St., Upper New York, NY 10960-1407
PH: 845-358-0497 FX: 845-358-0323
David dtp@oddballmusicworks.com
www.oddballmusicworks.com
Signs, produces and promotes artists that fall outside of the mainstream.

ping things *Canada*
rik@pingthings.com
www.pingthings.com
Will sell acceptable submitted CDs.

Plastic By Nature Records
plasticbynature@hotmail.com
morebarn.dnsalias.com/pbnr
A free resource for independent, home recorded musicians.

Postunder Records
19 Haruv St., Alfe Menashe 44851 Israel
PH: 972544346705
Yaron Eshkar postunder@postunder.com
www.postunder.com
An Electronic music label offering both online MP3 releases and CD releases.

Solnze Records
Russiam 129090, Moscow,
per.Vasnezova11/2-9, Russia
PH: +7-095-6845383
Oleg Tarasov info@solnzerecords.com
www.solnzerecords.com
Label/distributor/booking agency for unusual music that's not mainstream.

Sonic Arts Network
Jerwood Space, 171 Union St.,
London, SE1 0LN UK
PH: 44-0-20-7928-7337 FX: 44-0-20-7928-7338
phil@sonicartsnetwork.org
www.sonicartsnetwork.org
Worldwide events, education and information resource.

Squidco
160 Bennett Ave. #6K, New York, NY 10040
PH: 917-535-0265
sales@squidco.com
www.squidco.com
We sell Improvisational, Experimental, Progressive, RIO and otherwise unusual music.

sursumcorda.com
5115 Excelsior Blvd. #235, Minneapolis, MN 55416
FX: 612-677-3272
info@sursumcorda.com
www.sursumcorda.com
Promotes Experimental art and music.

Tract Records
Thomas Heath thomas@tractrecords.com
www.tractrecords.com
Label specializing in Underground Folk, Alt-Country and Experimental. We release compilations on a semi-yearly label. We accept demos.

Tzadik
200 E. 10th St. PMB 126, New York, NY 10003
info@tzadik.com
www.tzadik.com
Avant garde and Experimental music.

Film and TV

Avoid paying a fee to have your music posted. It's important to keep in mind that most Music Supervisors do not shop online for music. The safest deals are those with free services that take a commission from any of your songs that are used.

ALLTVMUSIC
1705 Arrowhead Trail, NE, Atlanta, GA 30345
PH: 404-321-1600
Bill Tullis alltvmusic@aol.com
A free placement service in the USA.

ANOTHER League
5419 Hollywood Blvd. Ste. C PMB 708,
Los Angeles, CA 90099-8112
music@anotherleague.com
www.anotherleague.com
We work hard to place your instrumental songs in television shows and movies. You keep the 'writers share' of the song. We keep the publishing of your song as incentive to push your song. This is an equal split with you - 50/50. Absolutely NO VOCALS!

Auctionsongs.com
PH: 403-348-1062
Chad Gillies Chad@canadianmusicdirect.com
www.auctionsongs.com
You can sell the music or film that you have created to the highest bidder. You do not sell copies of your songs but rather you sell one or both of the copyrights that you own in your music. You do not sell copies of your movie, but rather, complete ownership to the film itself.

Broadjam
313 W. Beltline Hwy. #147, Madison, WI 53713
PH: 608-271-3633
customerservice@broadjam.com
www.broadjam.com
Distribution and promotional services for musicians.

Choicetracks
6855 Petit Ave. Van Nuys, CA 91406
PH: 818-989-3274 FX: 561-892-2356
Ted Lowe info@choicetracks.com
www.choicetracks.com
A one-stop shop for busy music supervisors and creative executives looking for high quality pre-cleared songs.

Cinecall Soundtracks
PO Box 854, Red Bank, NJ 07701
PH: 732-450-8882 FX: 732-450-8884
mail@cinecall.com
www.cinecall.com
Avenue for songwriters to be able to get their songs heard.

Countdown Entertainment
110 W. 26th St. 3rd Fl. New York, NY 10001-6805
PH: 212-645-3068 FX: 212-989-6459
CountdownEnt@netzero.net
www.CountdownEntertainment.com
International artist management & consultant firm.

degyshop.com
6 Industrial Way W. #E, Eatontown, NJ 07724
PH: 732-544-8000 FX: 732-544-5600
info@degyshop.com
www.degyshop.com
Helps music companies find music for their projects.

dittybase
PH: 250-381-8780
sales@dittybase.com
www.dittybase.com
Helps music directors find the perfect track for any project.

Endurance Music
PO Box 841, Dennis, MA 02638
PH: 508-776-2182
Daniel Cartier daniel@endurancemusic.com
www.endurancemusic.com
Making the worrisome task of music supervisors everywhere a little less daunting and a little more fun. Our goal is to supply amazing music to film and television.

Filmtracks
Christian Clemmensen tyderian@filmtracks.com
www.filmtracks.com
Get the score... the true, orchestral magic of film music.

Indie Film Composers
PH: 208-730-8713 FX: 208-730-8713
indifilm@earthlink.net
www.indifilm.com
Subcontracts compositions out to our worldwide affiliates.

Indy Hits
PO Box 4102, Hollywood, CA 90078
PH: 323-276-1000 FX: 323-276-1001
info@bandpromote.com
www.indyhits.com
Working with unsigned bands helping to secure record/publishing deals and film/TV placements.

INgrooves
539 Bryant St. #405, San Francisco, CA 94107
PH: 415-896-2100
info@ingrooves.com
www.ingrooves.com
Works with Indie artists and labels to license your music to the TV & Film industry.

J2R Music
info@j2rmusic.com
j2rmusic.com
Creating and marketing music used in the promotion and release of feature films and as source and underscore for television shows.

LoveCat Music
PO Box 548, Ansonia Stn.
New York, NY 10023-0548
FX: 212-874-2888
info@lovecatmusic.com
www.lovecatmusic.com
We offer film & TV placements, licensing and more.

Luke Hits
615 N. Rossmore Ave. #203,
Los Angeles, CA 90004
PH: 310-236-5853
info@lukehits.com
lukehits.com
Links unsigned bands with high profile Film/TV projects. We love unsolicited demos, and listen to every single one.

The Music Broker Network
Clover Ground, Shepton Mallet, BA4 4AS UK
support@themusicbroker.net
www.themusicbroker.net
Pitches unsigned bands, artists & songwriters to Labels, Publishers and Film/TV studios. Helping unsigned songwriters, bands & composers generate income from their work without giving away their rights or future earnings.

Must Have Music
PO Box 801181, Santa Clarita, CA 91380-1181
PH: 661-645-6948 FX: 661-799-3732
info@musthavemusic.com
musthavemusic.com
Our primary goal is to provide a top quality music library for Film & TV use.

PLAYiNDIES
411-1529 W. 6th Ave. Vancouver, BC V6J 1R1
PH: 604-731-5007 FX: 604-731-5015
Brayden Styles music@playindies.com
www.playindies.com
We bring the building blocks of a strong independent film and music community: opportunities for licensing, distribution and online exposure.

Position Soundtrack Services
PO Box 25907, Los Angeles, CA 90025
PH: 310-442-8170 FX: 310-442-8180
Tyler Bacon tyler@positionmusic.com
www.positionmusic.com
Represents record labels, music publishers and independent artists for the placement of their music in film, television, soundtrack albums, advertising, music premiums and video games. Serves in both roles of finding great music for music supervisors and generating income and promotional opportunities for its clients.

Pump Audio
98 Elizabeth St. #8, Red Hook, NY 12571
PH: 845-758-9187
artists@pumpaudio.com
www.pumpaudio.com
We license your music to TV, Film and Advertising.

Shop For Songs
614 Hampton Dr. Venice, CA 90291
PH: 310-452-4163 FX: 310-452-7403
Jenna Leigh shopforsongs@circleofsongs.com
www.circleofsongs.com/pages/service_sfs.html
Song placement in TV, film, commercials and more. Artists earn 100% writer share and 50% of publisher share. Artists earn 50% of all sync fees.

Song and Film
Josh Zandman staff@songandfilm.com
www.songandfilm.com
Leading music placement company for film and TV.

SongCatalog
401-12 Water St., Vancouver, BC V6B 1A5
PH: 604-642-2888 FX: 604-642-2889
info@songcatalog.com
www.songcatalog.com
Music management, marketing and licensing initiatives.

SongLink
23 Belsize Cr. London, NW3 5QY UK
PH: 44-0-207-794-2540 FX: 44-0-207-794-7393
david@songlink.com
www.songlink.com
Music contacts across the globe.

Soundtrack Express
126 5th Ave. #804, New York, NY 10011
PH: 212-675-6664
content@transmx.com
www.transmediacorp.com
We market music to TV, radio, film and more.

TAXI
PH: 800-458-2111
www.taxi.com
Record and publishing deals, film & TV placement.

Transition Music Corporation
11288 Ventura Blvd. #709, Studio City, CA 91604
PH: 323-860-7074 FX: 323-860-7986
info@transitionmusic.com
www.transitionmusic.com
One of the few publishing companies who currently accepts unsolicited music submissions. We have successfully published more first-time writers (without record deals) than any other publisher. Submissions can include all genres of music. Please visit our website for submission details.

Tunetrader
PO Box 647, Portsmouth, PO1 2ZT UK
PH: +44-845-2262162 (UK)
PH: 727-736-4755 (US)
Nick Hooper enquiries@tunetrader.com
www.tunetrader.com
An online platform for independent and unsigned artists to promote their music towards placement in film, television and advertising. Music listeners welcome to listen and download unsigned and independent music.

WJOY Music Search & Licensing
2675 W. Grand Ave. Ste. 505, Chicago, IL 60612
Attn: Joy Tillis
PH: 773-276-9340
wjoymusic.com
Ad agencies, corporations and independent film makers with the commercial and original music they need. Accepts unsolicited material - please call first!

Folk

Acoustic Music Resource
PO Box 3518, Seal Beach, CA 90740
PH: 562-431-1608 FX: 562-598-5928
amrusa@aol.com
www.acousticmusicresource.com
Because most of the large chain stores only care about the hottest musical fads and fashions of the day, they give short shrift to small independent labels. That's where we come in. For most of the titles we list here, this is the only place you will ever find them!

Camsco Music
28 Powell St., Greenwich, CT 06831
PH: 800-548-3655
dick@camsco.com
www.camsco.com
Your single source for all Folk recordings.

Crow & Wolf Music
911 Central Ave. Albany, NY 12206
PH: 866-544-4129
William Feagin info@crowolfmusic.com
www.crowolfmusic.com
Online Folk and World music shop. Buy and sell your music with us. New and independent artists and old time favorites.

DIG Music
1831 V St., Sacramento, CA 95818
PH: 916-442-5344 FX: 916-442-5382
Holly Holt holly@digmusic.com
www.digmusic.com
Independent record label and artist management company. AAA, Roots/Americana, Singer/Songwriter.

efolk Music
201B N. Greensboro St., Carrboro, NC 27510
PH: 919-968-4810
support@efolkmusic.org
www.efolkmusic.org
Making Indie music available to the world.

FOLK TRAX *Australia*
manager@folktrax.com
www.folktrax.com
If you have Acoustic music related merchandise that you are prepared to consign to us, we will offer it for sale on our site.

Folkadelica Booking Agency
2 Northwood Terr. Haverhill, MA 01830
PH: 978-373-9199 FX: 978-373-9359 Fax
Shawna Torres Shawna@folkadelica.com
folkadelica.com
Representing exceptional contemporary artists from Americana, Bluegrass, Folk, Roots and beyond.

FolkWeb
95 Kidder Ave. Somerville, MA 02144
PH: 617-497-2096 FX: 617-497-2116
robert@folkweb.com
folkweb.com
Selling Indie music to a larger audience.

Green Linnet
PO Box 1905, Danbury, CT 06813
PH: 203-730-0333 FX: 203-778-4443
webmaster@greenlinnet.com
www.greenlinnet.com
Promotes new Celtic music.

Horse Rock Records
PO Box 8656, Palm Springs, CA 92263
PH: 310-497-1326 FX: 760-325-5683
Roger Smith rsmith@horserockrecords.com
www.horserockrecords.com
We specialize in amazing 'Roots' musicians playing a diverse range of musical styles: Lap Steel Guitar, Resophonic Guitar, Americana, Folk, Country and 'Super Picking'!

Independent Music Source Records
PO Box 532, Lumberton, NJ 08048
PH: 215-243-6096 FX: 215-243-6096
demosubmit@imsrecords.com
www.independentmusicsource.org
Specializes in Acoustic, Jazz and Blues.

Trad&Now Music Shop
230 Corrimal St., Wollongong,
NSW 2500 Australia
PH: 02-4225-3792 FX: 02-4229-9368
david@tradandnow.com
www.tradandnow.com
Supporting Independent creativity.

tradmusic.com
2 St Couans Pl. Newton Stewart, Dumfries & Galloway, Scotland, DG8 6LX UK
PH: 01671-403156
enquiries@tradmusic.com
www.tradmusic.com
Promotes traditional music artists throughout the world.

Village Records
PO Box 3216, Shawnee, KS 66203
PH: 913-631-4199 FX: 913-631-6369
sales@villagerecords.com
villagerecords.com
Folk discs, special orders, independent labels and more.

GLBT

Centaur Music
info@centaurmusic.com
PH: 718-852-6777 FX: 718-852-8877
45 Main S. #707, Brooklyn, NY 11201
www.centaurmusic.com
Our products are sold in stores across the U.S and Canada, from independent record stores to gift shops, book stores, pride shops and major chains.

Chainsaw Records
PO Box 11384, Portland, OR 97211
donna@chainsaw.com
www.chainsaw.com
Queer/girl friendly record label.

Gay-MART Music Shop
1148 Davie St., Vancouver, BC V6E 1N1
PH: 604-681-3262 FX: 604-681-9397
suggestions@gaymart.com
www.gaymart.com/shopmusc/shopmusc.html
A wide collection of Music CDs by gay and lesbian artists.

StoneWall Society
info@stonewallsociety.com
www.stonewallsociety.com
Presents a place to sell and buy GLBT art, music, literature, and handcrafted works. Reviews of submitted art in the StoneWall Society monthly E-newsletter.

Woobie Bear Music
woobiebearmusic@adelphia.net
www.woobiebearmusic.com
Features music by bears, music for bears. The latest news, reviews and happenings.

Goth
Promotional Services

Carpe Diem Promotions
Elizabeth Maycox carpediempromo@yahoo.co.uk
www.carpediempromotions.tk
A free international promotion service for underground & unsigned bands/record labels/zines etc.

Darkcell Digital Music
www.darkcelldigitalmusic.net
Contact to promote your label/band.

Vendors and Labels

DSBP *(Ditch Sex Buy Product)*
237 Cagua NE, Albuquerque, NM 87108
PH: 505-266-8274
dsbp@dsbp.cx
www.dsbp.cx
America's Hard Elektro / Harsh Industrial label.

Gore Galore
12 Madison Ave. Evansville, IN 47713
PH: 812-424-5220 FX: 309-410-2893
info@gore-galore.com
www.gore-galore.com
Submit your music for review.

IsoTank
526 S. 5th St., Philadelphia, PA 19147
PH: 215-861-0313 FX: 215-925-9075
isotank@aol.com
www2.mailordercentral.com/isotank
CDs, Videos and Merchandise.

Latex Records
5857 Brookstone Walk, Acworth, GA 30101-8473
E. Minzenmayer latex@latexrecords.com
latexrecords.com
Specializing in Goth/Industrial and related genres.

Metropolis Records
PO Box 54307, Philadelphia, PA 19105
PH: 610-595-9940 FX: 610-595-9944
label@metropolis-records.com
www.metropolis-records.com
Home to Industrial, Gothic and Electronic artists.

MONSTAAR Records
1345 W. North Shore Ave. Chicago, IL 60626
PH: 773-343-9337
control@monstaar.com
monstaar.com
Purveyors of Noise, Experimental, Darkwave, Goth and other cruel & unusual music.

Musicwerks
612 E. Pine St., Seattle, WA 98122
PH: 206-320-8933
musicwerks@musicwerks.org
www.musicwerks.org
Complete selection of Gothic and Industrial CDs.

Planet Mu
PO Box 276, Worcester, WR5 2XJ UK
mike@planet-mu.com
www.planet-mu.com
Exposure for new and already established musicians.

Shocklines
Matt Schwartz help@shocklines.com
www.shocklines.com
If you do horror music, we'd love to sell it.

Van Richter Records
100 S. Sunrise Way #219, Palm Springs, CA 92262
PH: 415-235-3373
manager@vanrichter.net
www.vanrichter.net
Your Aggro-Industrial record label!

Vinema Records
PO Box 12228, Spring, TX 77391-2228
Chris demo@vinema.com
www.vinema.com
We are looking for amazing bands with new sounds that are ready to take it to the next level! We are primarily interested in Industrial Metal/Rock/Goth/Ambient/Darkwave/Synthpop/Electronica etc.

Hip Hop
Promotional Services

215 Execs Entertainment Consulting and Management
G. Mookie McClary gmcclary@215execs.com
www.215execs.com
A one of a kind full scale independent music consulting and management firm. Rap is something you do. Hip Hop is something you live!

Agency Cafe
541 10th St. #274, Atlanta, GA 30318
PH: 678-859-3303
info@agencycafe.com
www.agencycafe.com
One stop shop for booking artists in the genres of Hip Hop, Soul, Reggae and DJ's.

CitiBoyz Music
3311 Shore Pkwy. Ste. Mm, Brooklyn, NY 11235
PH: 917-567-9899 FX: 718-616-0838
Ziggy Gonzalez ziggy@citiboyzmusic.com
www.citiboyzmusic.com
We provide management, music publishing and music production for Hip Hop and Gospel artists.

Crazy Pinoy
PO Box 46999, Seattle, WA 98146
PH: 206-860-4052
Gene Dexter Hiphop206@aol.com
www.CrazyPinoy.com
A promotions resource for Hip Hop record labels, artists and agencies. I can write and implement a national marketing plan, help create an artist's image and consult on their material, look and sound, and get them into situations and rooms that will wholly benefit them.

Heavyweights Record Pool
14731 Manecita Dr. La Mirada, CA 90638
PH: 888-998-2041
Truly OdD heavyweightsent@aol.com
www.heavyweights.org
An outlet for Labels trying to get their records to the most predominant dj's... who actually will play and promote your records.

Q-York Entertainment
1133 Justin Ave. Ste 121, Glendale, CA 91201
PH: 917-567-4622 FX: 718-529-2900
Steven Yassin contact@q-york.com
www.q-york.com
Hip Hop artists, music, videos, online store.

Richh Kiddz Entertainment
1st Ave. at Port Imperial #1202,
West New York, NJ 07093
PH: 404.394.0365 FX: 201.430.3842
Russ Downs russdowns@richhkiddz.com
www.richhkiddz.com
A multifaceted entertainment and marketing company. We help develop, expose and manage independent artists who take the business of music seriously.

shocksoundpromotions.com
3840 E. Robinson Rd. #200, Amherst, NY 14228
PH: 716-578-0097
shocksoundpromo@yahoo.com
www.shocksoundpromotions.com
Promoting urban recording artists, events and products.

Street Work Entertainment
180 Abbey Dr. Mount Wolf, PA 17347
PH: 717-266-4924 FX: 717-266-4924
Fred Walker fred@streetworkent.com
www.streetworkent.com
We help independent artists get noticed in the music business. We help them with mix tapes and by promoting them. We are doing a Barber Shop tour to expose local artists. We are also a production company.

Three 6 Oh Productions
9307 NE 81st Way, Vancouver, WA 98662
PH: 360-576-8603
Paul "Biggz" Hammond Biggz@three6oh.com
www.three6oh.com
A Hip Hop promotions organization spreading the word. We do a lot of national radio, internet and mixtape promotion as well.

Under The Table Distribution
PH: 630-747-3399
utt@underthetablemusic.com
www.underthetablemusic.com
A distribution network for independent Hip Hop labels and artists.

Union Enterprise Recordz
7737 Fair Oaks Blvd. #235, Carmichael, CA 95608
PH: 916-997-2509
uer@unionenterpriserecordz.com
unionenterpriserecordz.com
Independent record company looking for new talent. I have my own radio station and an outlet for independent artists to get their product heard and in stores.

Unsigned Underground
PO Box 2926, Huntington Station, NY 11746
Maximum Pressure Raydiant1@hotmail.com
www.maddmuzik.org
Free unsigned Hip Hop artist promotions.

Vendors and Labels

United States

3A Records
PO Box 29593, Denver, CO 80229
hiphop3a@hiphop3a.com
www.hiphop3a.com
Helping artists produce their full talent.

98 Proof Recordings
PH: 908-433-4639
ninety8pr@yahoo.com
www.98proof.com
A Hip Hop / R&B independent record label.

Addic Records
14 E. Hughes St. PO Box 145, Belfast, NY 14711
PH: 585-365-8021
Scott AddicRecords@hotmail.com
www.addicrecords.com
Hip Hop/R&B Independent Label. Bios, songs, artists, pictures, release dates n' where to purchase artist's Albums!!

Affinity Music
502 Milford St. Brooklyn, NY 11208-4823
PH/FX: 718-649-3212
Baynes ATPENTnet@ATPENT.net
atpent.net/
Label whose goal is to put out good records in any genre. Currently our roster is made up of Hip Hop acts and we are looking to expand with the signing of new artists.

A-N-B Records Inc.
12 Iroqios Dr. Galloway, NJ 08205
PH: 609-673-0277
info@anbrecords.com
www.anbrecords.com
R&B/Hip Hop independent record label.

ATAK Distribution
PO Box 1027, La Canada, CA 91012-1027
PH: 626-398-3229
pminus@atakworldwide.com
www.truehiphop.com
Send a copy of whatever you want ATAK to sell. If it's the dopest thing EVER, it's in the catalog. If it's doo-doo, you might not ever hear from us again.

basically-hiphop
maxjeromeo@basically-hiphop.com
basically-hiphop.com
Playing Underground and mainstream Hip Hop.

Battleaxe Records
deeznuts@battleaxerecords.com
www.battleaxerecords.com
Canadian Indie record company searching for artists.

Block Party Records
320 N. Canon Dr. Beverly Hills, CA 90210
PH: 310 927-9666 FX: 310 492-6111
Tony Hicks tony@blockpartyrecords.com
www.blockpartyrecords.com
Reviews all Hip Hop/Rap music of unsigned artists.

Brick Records
PO Box 281, Boston, MA 02117
PH: 888-513-3998
www.brickrecords.com
An independent Hip Hop record label.

DIYHipHop.com
9 White St. #213, Brooklyn, NY 11206
PH: 718-821-9690
en-L@vinylconnect.com
www.diyhiphop.com
Promotes independent Hip Hop artists.

DJcity.com
PO Box 252175, Los Angeles, CA 90025
PH: 213-232-3273 FX: 801-340-7618
info@djcity.com
www.djcity.com
We specialize in both the party-jammin' major label HipHop and R&B, as well as all the underground label cuts blowin' up round the corner.

Freewill Records
PO Box 39013, Birmingham, AL 35208
PH: 256-457-6350
K.Bibbs freewillrecords@comcast.net
www.freewillrecords.com
Our music is Southern Hip Hop. We offer airplay on our web radio station (Freewill Radio). Booking, forums, mixtapes etc.

FTB Records
Cato Kelly khato@ftbrecords.com
www.ftbrecords.com
Our goal and mission is to promote and give exposure to musicians and models all over the world. To find the best music from unsigned artist, DJ's, producers or independent record labels.

Funk Squad Entertainment
14712 Luna Rd. Victorville, CA 92392
funksquad@funksquadent.com
www.funksquadent.com
An independent Hip Hop label/productions/DJ service.

Get Real Records
3163 Silver Bluff Rd. Aiken, SC 29803
PH: 706-414-3296
Marc Myers getreal@get-real-records.com
www.get-real-records.com
We help Hip Hop artists promote and distribute their music.

HeadBOB
130 Webster St. #105, Oakland, CA 94607
artistsubmissions@headbob.com
www.headbob.com
Provides completely free distribution with artists receiving all of the royalties.

Headquarters Records
PO Box 141, Arlington, VA 22201
PH: 703-912-1720 FX: 703-995-4913
agcee@hotmail.com
www.headquartersrecords.com
About positive vibes that are not offensive.

JaThom Records
PO Box 1579, New York, NY 10025
J.Minor justthemusic@att.net
www.jathomrecords.netfirms.com
Label and distributor that specializes in working with independent artists.

Licorich Record$
PH: 818-687-8990
Jay Plot jayplot@licorichrecords.com
www.licorichrecords.com
Independent Record Label that sells and promotes the hottest Hip Hop.

Mic Fiend Records
PO Box 90173, Long Beach, CA 90809
PH: 206-600-5128 FX: 801-605-4808
gc@micfiend.com
www.micfiend.com
Independent CEO, producer, emcee, web designer & more!

Noc On Wood Records
1809 7th Ave. #1400, Seattle, WA 98101
PH: 800-253-8009
noconwood@noconwood.com
www.noconwood.com
A new breed of record label run by a team of smart, enterprising young executives.

Nomadic Wax
486 Jefferson Ave. Brooklyn, NY 11221
Ben Herson ben@nomadicwax.com
www.nomadicwax.com
African and international Hip Hop production company and label.

ODT Records
655 Ramos St., Odessa, TX 79761
Ph: 432-208-0892
Roy P. odtrecords2k1@hotmail.com
www.odtrecords.com
Hip Hop label offering Rap beats, CD artwork, DVD production and editing, web design, screwed & chopped and more.

Red Brick Records
807 N. Salina, Syracuse, NY 13208
PH: 315-476-8703
mchilds2@twcny.rr.com
www.redbrickrecords.com
Helps all Indie Hip Hop artists.

Rotation Music Entertainment
Attn: A & R, PO Box 93683, Industry, CA 91715
PH: 626-856-7440
Mailbox@rotationmusic.com
www.rotationmusic.com
Send your demos to this Indie Hip Hop label.

Sandbox Automatic
245 West 29th St. 9th Fl. New York, NY 10001
Attn: Submissions
sandbox@pobox.com
www.sandboxautomatic.com
We will check your stuff out and if we are interested, we will contact you back with more instructions. You do not need to follow up on your submission request.

Stones Throw Records
2658 Griffith Park Blvd. #504,
Los Angeles, CA 90039-2520
info@stonesthrow.com
www.stonesthrow.com
Indie record label. Calendar, news, sell CDs etc.

Street Corner Records
PH: 407-595-7569
Dennis Vinegar dmenace@streetcornerrecords.com
www.streetcornerrecords.com
A nationwide retailer and producer of Hip Hop music.

Support Online Hip Hop
www.sohh.com
Hip Hop news, reviews, online sales and more.

UndagroundArtists
PO Box 260435, Queens, NY 11426-0435
Attn: Judge Mental
PH: 877-320-1938
info@undagroundartists.com
www.undagroundartists.com
Showcasing solid Indie Hip Hop talent.

UndergroundHipHop.com
1 Westinghouse Plz. 1st fl. Hyde Park, MA 02136
PH: 617-364-4900
www.undergroundhiphop.com
Do NOT mail us your CD. Read our online submission policy, then send us an E-MAIL with all the information that we request.

Urban Angels Recordings
169 Washington St., Mt. Vernon, NY 10550
PH: 646-217-5392
www.angel4life.com
Our sports and entertainment company's newest label. Dedicated to Urban music on both continents.

Urban Ikon
Box 953, Dept. IB06, Wingdale, NY 12594
David urbanikon@aol.com
www.urbanikon.com
We supply every major chain store and thousands of mom-and-pop stores across the United States directly and through our one-stop distribution partners We're looking for new artists to sign. For consideration, mail a demo CD with a minimum of 4 original songs to the address above.

UrbanMelodies.com
9175 Kiefer Blvd. #249, Sacramento, CA 95828
PH: 916-265-5662 FX: 916-265-5662
Kevin Hellon kevin@urbanmelodies.com
www.urbanmelodies.com
Your online source for emerging Urban Music! We are a normal music store, with the exception that we NEVER close. We focus on six specific genres: Rap/Hip-Hop, R&B, Gospel, Jazz/Blues, Spoken Word and Reggae.

vinylconnect.com
9 White St. #213, Brooklyn, NY 11206
PH: 718-821-9690
Nick nick@vinylconnect.com
www.vinylconnect.com
Submit your demos to get your stuff sold here.

WholeTeam Entertainment
5588 Chamblee Dunwoody Rd. #110,
Dunwoody, GA 30338
PH: 770-300-0175
info@wholeteam.com
www.wholeteam.com
Online distribution, management, production and more.

Zyfex Entertainment
Masta Recka Mastarecka@zyfex.com
www.zyfex.com
Indie label dealing with new artists.

Canada

Camobear Records
21646-1424 Commercial Dr.
Vancouver, BC V5l 3X9
Cass Elliott cass@camobear.ca
www.camobear.ca
An Indie record label distributing Hip Hop music to the people. We also book Hip Hop shows in the Vancouver area.

Germany

Rap.de
Blücherstr. 22, 10961 Berlin, Germany
PH: 030-695-972-10 FX: 030-695-972-40
mischa@rap.de
www.rap.de
Magazine, events calendar, online store & more.

The Netherlands

recordbuddy.com
PH: +31628336304
talents@recordbuddy.com
www.recordbuddy.com
Our aim is to support the upcoming talents by selling CDs / tapes / lp's of Hip Hop talents.

Switzerland

hiphopstore.ch
General Guisan-Str.1 Ch-5000 Aarau, Switzerland
PH: 41-62-834-40-00 FX: 41-62-834-40-09
info@hiphopstore.ch
www.hiphopstore.ch
Online distribution of Indie CDs.

United Kingdom

benzull1972
26 Well St., Great Yarmouth,
Norfolk, NR30 1ER UK
PH: 07833337316
Benny Edgar melbenny@yarco.fsnet.co.uk
www.benzull1972.com
Fast service with cheap prices on new DVDs and UK Hip Hop. We also promote new bands in the UK.

Rap and Soul Mail Order
PO Box 37163, London, E4 7WR UK
PH: 020-8523-9578 FX: 020-8523-9601
info@RapAndSoulMailOrder.com
www.rapandsoulmailorder.com
Will sell your CD online for a low cost.

Jamband

Harmonized Records
6520 Oak Grove Church Rd. Mebane, NC 27302
PH: 919-304-9931
Brian Asplin asplin@homegrownmusic.net
www.harmonizedrecords.com
Our goal is to team up with talented hard-working musicians and help them build their careers through a realistic record label/artist relationship.

Home Grown Music Network
PO Box 340, Mebane, MN 27302
PH: 919-563-4923
feedback@homegrownmusic.net
www.homegrownmusic.net
Promotes the best Indie music being made today.

Sunshine Daydream CDs & Gifts
2027 E. Euclid Ave, Mt. Prospect, IL 60056
PH: 847-299-2622
Mark Paradise sales@sunshinedaydream.biz
www.sunshinedaydream.biz
New & Used CD retail store that specializes in Jam Band music.

Jazz

4 on 6 Media
58 Karee Court, S. Kingstown, RI 02879
FX: 401-633-6376
music4on6@yahoo.com
www.4on6.com
Promotes independent Jazz musicians.

AppleJazz
10825 Wheaton Ct. Orlando, FL 32821
PH: 888-241-2464
info@applejazz.com
www.applejazz.com
Offering online sales of Jazz CDs for Indie artists.

Counterpoint Music
PO Box 25093, Fresno, CA 93729-5093
PH: 559-225-7801 FX: 559-225-7801
info@counterpoint-music.com
www.counterpoint-music.com
Specialists in Jazz CDs!

Funny Valentine Records
72 Ladysmith Rd. Brighton, BN2 4EG UK
PH: 44-1273-677590
Paul Blankley paul@funnyvalentinerecords.co.uk
www.funnyvalentinerecords.co.uk
We are a new label dedicated to making new 'Easy' music featuring strong arrangements and quality songwriting. Porter, Sinatra, Jobim etc. We're currently looking for acts and writers.

InterJazz
9 Ridge Way, Purdys, NY 10578
PH: 914-277-7775
support@interjazz.com
www.interjazz.com
Your online connection to everything Jazz.

Jazz CD Promotional Campaign
8947 Washington Ave. Jacksonville, FL 32208
PH: 904-264-4642 FX: 904-264-4667
Rachelle Bivins mailbox@abyssjazz.com
www.abyssjazz.com
A 12-month marketing tool offering just about everything an independent Jazz artist needs to kick start their promotion for a new CD to over 80,000 readers. Packages submissions to Jazz radio stations and festivals for airplay and booking consideration.

The Jazz Loft
PO Box 3454, Bellevue, WA 98009
PH: 425-646-6406
alawrence@jazzloft.com
www.jazzloft.com
Your online resource for truly Independent Jazz!

Jazz Now Direct
PO Box 19266, Oakland, CA 94619-0266
PH: 510-531-9249
jazznow@sbcglobal.net
www.jazznow.com/jnd
Great independently produced music.

Jazzconnect.com
PH: 800-866-9068
www.jazzconnect.com
Websites, CD store, new releases and artist spotlights.

JAZZCORNER.com
245 W. 25th St., New York, NY 10001
lois@jazzcorner.com
www.jazzcorner.com
News, reviews, interviews, web hosting.

Playscape
64 Belleclaire Ave. Longmeadow, MA 01106
PH: 413-567-7967
info@playscape-recordings.com
www.playscape-recordings.com
Promotes Jazz artists and music.

ropeadope
submit@ropeadope.com
www.ropeadope.com
"Stand Strong". If you'd like to submit artwork, videos, audio mixes, editorial, e-mail them to us.

Utopia Records
PO Box 660-100, Flushing, NY 11366
PH: 718-217-1033 FX: 718-776-0946
Alfonzo Blackwell info@UtopiaRecordings.com
utopiarecordings.com
We believe that with our national distribution and the successful relationships that we have fostered along the way, Utopia Records will continue to release promising Jazz Artists that will bring great music and a legacy that will last a lifetime.

Latin

Barrio Records
PO Box 230801, Boston, MA 02123
info@barriorecords.com
www.barriorecords.com
Source for Latin music. Accepts submissions.

Boogalu Productions
PH: 866-710-6032
www.boogalu.com
Promotes the creative work of artists involved in Cuban culture.

DESCARGA.com
328 Flathbush Ave. #180, Brooklyn, NY 11238
PH: 718-693-2966 FX: 718-693-1316
info@descarga.com
www.descarga.com
The ultimate source for Latin CDs.

Discuba
317 10th St. 3rd y 5th Miramar, Play,
Havana City, Cuba
PH: 537-24-0637 FX: 537-24-2033
ventas@discuba.com
www.discuba.com
Cuban music shop.

Latin Cool Records
PH: 973-571-0848
David Wasserman latincool2@aol.com
www.latincool.com
Supports/sells Latin Indie music.

MaraRecords Brazilian Music Vinyl Record Store
mrec@bigfoot.com
www.mararecords.com
Brazilian Lps, Groove, Bossa, Jazz, Soul, Funk and Rare Records.

Qi Music Distributors
Av. Pedro de Mendoza 1369 30 "10" CP:
C1156ACZ, Argentina
info@holimar.com.ar
www.qiartes.com.ar
Distribution of independent labels and musicians.

Tejanoclassics.com
PH: 281-355-0777
tejanoclassics@worldnet.att.net
www.tejanoclassics.com
An online music vendor for classic and current titles.

Tinku Records
539 Telegraph Canyon Rd. #265,
Chula Vista, CA 91910
PH: 619-397-5120 FX: 619-397-5120
Letty Astudillo info@tinkumusic.com
www.tinkumusic.com
An independent recording label established in 1999 to introduce native Latin rhythms. We currently are focusing on Andean & Latin Folk music.

Tumi
8/9 New Bond St., Pl. Bath, BA1 1BH UK
PH: 44-0-1225-464736 FX: 44-0-1225-444870
info@tumimusic.com
www.tumimusic.com
Website and record label for Latin American and Caribbean music.

Metal

Promotional Services

Represent:Music
734 El Sur Ave. Salinas, CA 93906
PH: 831-794-1614
Jason Hobbs jasonpromos@hotmail.com
www.representmusic.com
Do you have an upcoming Rock CD or DVD release and want to hit hard when it comes out? We can help. We can help you get radio play, internet plays, downloads, chat room discussions...

Risestar Promotion
Palmas de Mallorca #1126, La Reina,
Santiago, Chile
info@risestar.cl
www.risestar.cl
Promotes Hard Rock and Heavy Metal bands worldwide.

Strictly Heavy Management
14807 Empire St., Dale City, VA 22193
Theresa Aldao strichvy@aol.com
strictlyheavymanagement.com
Provides personal musician and band management. We welcome your music submission. Unfortunately, only 1 or 2 bands out of 100 are considered statistically.

V.Q. Promotions
4415 W. Verdugo Ave. Ste. B, Burbank, CA 91505
PH: 818-848-6093 FX: 818-688-3198
Publicity@vqpr.com
www.vqpr.com
Promotions services for Indie Rock bands.

Vendors and Labels

Abaddon Records
151 Stream Rd. Winterport, ME 04496
PH: 207-478-5077
David Davis david@abaddonrecords.com
www.abaddonrecords.com
A Metal and Hardcore independent label.

Beowolf Productions
PO Box 731, Phoenixville, PA 19460
BeowolfCo@aol.com
www.beowolfproductions.com
Covers all styles of Extreme music.

CDSmash
109 Poe Ave. Poteau, OK 74953
Kerry D. Plummer cdsmash@clnk.com
cdsmash.com
Selling the music of Rock and Metal artists. Note that any CD sold thru CD Smash will get played on the station. All Artist are encouraged to send in Station ID's to be added before their music is played.

CYBERTZARA / BlackMetal.Com Records
PO Box 5488, Novato, CA 94948-5488
Attn: A&R
Archon SET-Eblis antinome666@blackmetal.com
www.blackmetal.com
Send promotional copies to the above address. For retail consideration (once the band or label's sample has been approved), our terms preferred are either consignment or trade against our label's own releases.

Emperor Multimedia
126 Martindale Ave. Oakville, ON L6H 4G7
rrca@rrca.diskery.com
anything@rrca.diskery.com
rrca.diskery.com
Promotion, distribution and preservation of Rock music.

FastLane Records
816 Platt Circle, Oklahoma City, OK 73170
PH: 405-703-1676 FX: 405-703-1676
Shawn C. Lane fastlanerecords@cox.net
www.fastlanerecords.com
Our mission is to bring back hard-hitting enjoyable music that hits you right between the eyes and never lets up!

Great White North Records America
PO Box 5705, Ste-Julienne, QC J0K 2T0
PH: 514-525-5995 FX: 514-525-5995
Remi Cote general@gwnrecords.com
www.gwnrecords.com
Production, distribution, manufacturing, licensing for Metal / Hardcore and Grind Releases.

Headbanger's Delight
2497 Plymouth Rock, Holland, MI 49424
PH: 616-399-3456
info@headbangersdelight.com
www.headbangersdelight.com
Promotes Indie Metal bands without major distribution.

Metal Mayhem
32 Lanthorne Rd. Monroe, CT 06468
info@metalmayhem.com
www.metalmayhem.com
Indie Bands, send us your CDs!

Nightmare Records & Distribution
PH: 763-784-9654
Lance King
Lance@nightmare-records.com
www.nightmare-records.com
A label and distributor of Indie based Melodic Hard Rock.

The Pure Rock Shop
403 Pin Oak Dr.
McDonald, PA 15057
music@tprs.com
www.tprs.com
Accepts promotional packages from Metal bands for review and spotlight.

Screaming Ferret Wreckords
PO Box 56, Hillsboro, NH 03244
PH: 603-770-0648
info@screamingferret.com
www.screamingferret.com
Accepts all styles of Metal for review and sales.

Shoutweb.com
3272 Motor Ave. #I, Los Angeles, CA 90034
Jess Redmon jess@shoutweb.com
www.shoutweb.com
Submit your promotional package for review.

StreetTeam.net
124000 Ventura Blvd. #330, Studio City, CA 91604
streetteam.net
Looking for bands who are ready to go to the next level.

Z Records A&R
Mark Alger mark@zrecords.net
www.zrecords.net
Europe's premier Melodic and Classic Hard Rock label.

ZCM Records
Am Kesselhaus 9, 79576 Weil am Rhein, Germany
PH: +41-78-631-75-45
Shelley Slater shelley@zcmrecords.com
www.zcmrecords.com
Independent Metal/Punk/Hardcore label, distro and mail order.

New Age

At Peace Media
1117 E. Putnam Ave. #345, Riverside, CT 06878
PH: 800-575-7715
John Gelb john@atpeacemedia.com
www.esalenmassagevideo.com
We distribute music to the spa and health communities.

Backroads Music
PH: 800-767-4748 FX: 415-924-0648
mail@backroadsmusic.com
www.backroadsmusic.com
6,000 titles of Ambient, New Age, Space, Tribal & Global sounds.

Etherean Music
2525 Arapahoe Ave. #E4-287, Boulder, CO 80302
PH: 303-988-1221 FX: 303-988-1221
www.ethereanmusic.com
Providing the highest quality music since 1985.

Fixion Media represents leading heavy music sites like Blabbermouth.net, Blistering.com, BraveWords.com, HardRadio.com, MetalReview.com, & RockDetector.com. Contact us at 450.689.7106 or view our rates online!

Expose your band to 2 million plus monthly visitors!

Gopher's Underground Music Store
gopher@gopherp.com
www.gopherp.com
Our music store features the best in New Age music.

GROOVE Unlimited
PO Box 2171, 8203 AD Lelystad, The Netherlands
PH: 31-0-320-219496 FX: 31-0-320-218910
info@groove.nl
www.groove.nl
We have a large diversity of New Age, Synth, Spacerock etc.

Hearts of Space
PO Box 5916, Sausalito, CA 94966
PH: 415-331-3200 FX: 415-331-3280
info@hos.com
www.hos.com/radio.html
Submit material for the record label.

LuxMusica Records
5841 Overbrook Ave. Philadelphia, PA 19131
PH: 215-477-9985 FX: 215-879-1457
Jamey Reilly jreilly@virtualux.com
www.luxmusica.com
Peaceful Heart, Quiet Mind. Exceptional Music from around the world that celebrates the light of eternal truth in its many forms.

Magical Blend
PO Box 600, Chico, CA 95927-0600
PH: 530-893-9037 FX: 530-893-9076
info@magicalblend.com
www.magicalblend.com
Home for cultural creativity, spirituality, metaphysics and more.

Music "à la Carte"
1111 Coolamon Scenic Dr. Mullumbimby, NSW 2482 Australia
PH: 61-2-66843143 FX: 61-2-66843144
info@musicalacarte.net
www.musicalacarte.net
International Indie music store for soothing sounds.

Music Design
Attn: New Title Dept. 4650 N. Port Washington Rd.
Milwaukee, WI 53212
PH: 414-961-8380 FX: 414-961-8681
order@musicdesign.com
www.musicdesign.com
The premier wholesaler of music and self-help recordings into non-traditional markets. Specializing in New Age, World, Jazz, and Healing music. Send 1 copy of your CD, Video or DVD along with any label, marketing, pricing and distribution information available to the above address.

New Earth Records
7 Avenida Vista Grande B7-305,
Santa Fe, NM 87508
PH: 505-466-2471 FX: 505-466-2477
info@newearthrecords.com
www.newearthrecords.com
Music that inspires healing, enhances spirit and celebrates life.

NewAgeMusic.com
8033 Sunset Blvd. #472, Hollywood, CA 90046
PH: 323-851-3355 FX: 323-851-7981
info@newagemusic.com
www.newagemusic.com
Production, packaging, marketing and promotion.

Silver Wave Records
2475 Broadway #300, Boulder, CO 80304
PH: 303-443-5617 FX: 303-443-0877
Allen Wollard, Director info@silverwave.com
www.silverwave.com
Independent label producing Native American, New Age and World music. Will consider other genres.

Progressive Rock

The Artist Shop
1337 Forest Glen, Cuyahoga Falls, OH 44221
PH: 330-929-2056
artshop@artist-shop.com
www.artist-shop.com
A cooperative music store for artist owned and independent labels. Our music includes Progressive, Jazz, Fusion, World Music, New Age, Electronic, Ambient and much more.

CD Inzane
PO Box 136, Albertville, MN 55301
www.cdinzane.com
Promotion is what makes a band "become" and we are here to help!!!

Kinesis CDs
1430 Wisp Ct. Hanover, MD 21076-1693
FX: 309-276-9506
info@kinesiscd.com
www.kinesiscd.com
A CD label and mail order specializing in Progressive, Symphonic and Art Rock.

Punk

Promotional Services

Earshot Media
2629 Manhattan Ave. PO Box 301,
Hermosa Beach, CA 90254-2447
info@earshotmedia.com
www.earshotmedia.com
Publicity company for Alternative, Indie, Punk and Metal music.

Thursday Night Scum Publicity
Candace candace@tnspublicity.com
www.tnspublicity.com
We specialize in publicity, artist development, booking & management for Rock/Punk/Metal/Indie bands. Though we like to help the "struggling" musicians, we only accept those whose music we believe in.

Vendors and Labels

Big Beaver Music
218-10A St. NW, Calgary, AB T2N 1W6
Stephen Dyrgas steve@bigbeavermusic.com
www.bigbeavermusic.com
Featuring bands and labels from Canada, USA, Sweden, Australia and Scotland.

Blackened Distribution
PO Box 8722, Minneapolis, MN 55408
PH: 612-722-1134 FX: 612-722-1134
www.profaneexistence.com
Making Punk a threat again!

Double Crown Records
PO Box 4336, Bellingham, WA 98227-4336
Sean Berry records@dblcrown.com
www.dblcrown.com
Surf and Garage Rock label, with an online catalog.

Elevator Music
PO Box 628, Bronxville, NY 10708
PH: 914-509-5870
Viriato fernando@rcn.com
www.elevatormusic.com
Underground fire to light your way.

Eyeball Records
PO Box 1653, Peter Stuyvesant Stn.
New York, NY 10009
info@eyeballrecords.com
www.eyeballrecords.com
Please don't be afraid to send us any questions, but if they are stupid we're going to pass them around the office and make fun of you so choose wisely.

Fall Records
PO Box 20886, Baltimore, MD 21209
info@fallrecords.com
www.fallrecords.com
An Independent record label featuring Indie, Rock, Punk and so on..

FFRUK.com
85-87 Bayham St., London, NW1 0AG UK
PH: 020-7424 7969.
info@fullfrontalrecordings.co.uk
www.ffruk.com
Online Punk record label promoting music, selling CDs and merchandise for Electronic and Punk Rock music. For interviews and reviews contact Steve at steve@ffruk.com

Flying Monkey Records
Dave Baker dave@flyingmonkeyrecords.com
flyingmonkeyrecords.com
We list and sell independently released Punk tunes.

Hi-Fi Disasters
#392-1100 Memorial Ave.
Thunder Bay, ON, P7B4A3
PH: 807-472-9082
Jason Bruce jason@hifidisasters.com
www.hifidisasters.com
Distributor of independent Hardcore, Punk, & Thrash music.

Interpunk
PO Box 651328, Potomac Falls, VA 20165-1328
sales@interpunk.com
www.interpunk.com
Punk bands worldwide. Submit your CDs.

Jello Records
Mountfield, E. Sussex, TN32 5JN UK
PH: 44-1580-881310 FX: 44-1580-882032
Ray ray@jellorecords.com
www.jellorecords.com
An indie music label that has been in existance since the 70's promoting Punk and Rock music. We now have a new studio (Jelly Studios) in Sussex.

Lux.-NOISE Productions
Steinengraben 30, CH-4058 BASEL, Switzerland
PH: 41-61-271-39-05
Michael Hediger info@luxnoise.com
www.luxnoise.com
Record label & promotion company. Alternative/Garage-Rock! NO ELECTRONIC-stuff!

Matchbox Records
198 E. Park Ave. Flushing, MI 48433
PH: 810-423-1711
info@matchboxrecords.com
www.matchboxrecords.com
An independent record label for Rock, Alt, Punk, Metal type genres.

ORG Records
c/o The Old Gramophone Works, 326 Kensal Rd.
London, W10 5BZ UK
Sean organ@organart.demon.co.uk
www.organart.com
If your music is something that excites us then we'll be on the case. We're mostly interested in Punk/Metal/Alternative and Prog.

Paradigm Shift
10 Wheeler St., Montclair, NJ 07042
PH: 973-783-5847
Casey Lee Morgan beardiemalone@aol.com
www.theforeverendeavor.com/paradigmshift.html
A NJ based label that puts out Underground Punk/Rock records. We also organize shows!

Plata Records
Innherredsveien 51A, 7043 Trondheim, Norway
PH: 47-93-02-41-83
Steinar H. Bohn steinar@platarecords.no
www.platarecords.no
Norwegian record company that specializes in Extreme music.

Poppunk.com
PO Box 520, Cranbury, NY 08512
FX: 609-298-6566
steve@poppunk.com
www.poppunk.com
Exposure for Pop/Punk music. Accepts submissions.

punklist.com
303 S. Parsons Ave. Brandon, FL 33511
PH: 813-681-9342
Noi Sawangsri noi@punklist.com
www.punklist.com
Specializing in Hardcore, Punk, Emo and other styles of Underground music.

Radical Records
77 Bleecker St. #C2-21, New York, NY 10012
PH: 212-475-1111 FX: 212-475-3676
keith@radicalrecords.com
www.radicalrecords.com
NYC Indie label seeks Punk, Hardcore bands and the like.

Remembrance Records
13001 Summit School Rd. #1
Woodbridge, VA 22192
PH: 703-499-1720 FX: 703-491-1813
Rana Sobhany remembrancerecords@yahoo.com
www.remembrancerecords.com
Emo, Indie and Hardcore label out of Washington, DC constantly looking for bands who can bring the rock.

RevHQ.com
PO Box 5232, Huntington Beach, CA 92615-5232
PH: 714-842-7584
feedback@revhq.com
www.revhq.com
The best source for Independent music.

Sunday League Records
287 Salem Ave. 2nd Fl. Toronto, ON M6H 3C8
PH: 416-533-0553 FX: 416-533-7793
info@sundayleaguerecords.com
www.sundayleaguerecords.com
Visit our site for submission guidelines. Please do not send MP3s or links to MP3s. CDs only!

truepunk.com
301 E. 34th St. #103, Austin, TX 78705
webmaster@truepunk.com
www.truepunk.com
Unsigned band submit your press kit for exposure.

Unfun Records
PO Box 11886, Berkeley, CA 94712
PH: 408-344-0402 FX: 408-253-1653
Johnny Darko johnny@unfunrecords.com
unfunrecords.com
Label dealing with mainly Rock, Indie, Punk, Hardcore and Electronica genres. We offer distribution for non-label artists as well.

unT3rm dUR(h$chn/tt
PO Box 19 04 71, D-50501 Köln, Germany
PH: +0049 (0) 2234-91-45-95
info@unterm-durchschnitt.de
www.unterm-durchschnitt.de
A DIY Indie Rock, Stoner, Grunge, Garage, Punk label .

Vagrant Records
2118 Wilshire Blvd. #361, Santa Monica, CA 90403
info@vagrant.com
www.vagrant.com
Indie and Punk Rock record label.

Walked in line Records
B.P 04-60840, Breuil le Sec, France
PH: 03-44-50-23-63
thewilteam@wilrecords.com
www.wilrecords.com
The French Underground label.

Wolverine Records
Rochusstr.48, 40479 Düsseldorf, Germany
PH: 0211-719493 FX: 0211-713454
sascha@wolverine-records.de
www.wolverine-records.de
Germany's finest Independent Punk, Ska and Swing label.

Year of the Sun Enterprises
3-304 Stone Rd. W. #520, Guelph, ON N1G 4W4
PH: 519-830-9687
contact@yearofthesun.com
www.yearofthesun.com
Supporting the genres of Punk, Alternative, and Metal. We're always looking to expand our roster with new and exciting bands and artists so feel free to submit your music.

Reggae

CaribbeanMusic.com
www.caribbeanmusic.com
The greatest, largest and fastest growing online resource on the Internet for and about Caribbean music.

Dubroom
www.dubroom.org
MP3s, reviews, forums and much more!

reggaeCD.com
PO Box 100-887, Brooklyn, NY 11210-0887
PH: 718-362-1711 FX: 718-763-6241
info@reggaecd.com
www.reggaecd.com
Online Reggae CD, DVD, video, mp3, t-shirt and merchandise store.

Silverglobe Records
5380 Walkley #4, Montreal, QC H4V 2M7
PH: 514-369-6998
D. Roberts info@silversgloberecords.com
www.silversgloberecords.com
Bringing Reggae music to the public.

Zionway Recordings
2747 Glenwood Ct. #7, Boulder, CO 80304
PH: 720-300-4264 FX: 303-443-8701
Ras Marcus Benjamin jahfamilybenji@aol.com
www.zionway.net
Record label, recording studio and producers of conscious Reggae and Hip Hop music.

Soul/R&B

Promotional Services

4Sight Media Relations
555 Washington Ave. #2F, Brooklyn, NY 11238
PH: 718-789-1818 FX: 718-789-0808
Jackie O. Asare jackieo@4sightmedia.com
www.4sightmedia.com
A diversified public relations firm whose areas of media specialty includes, but is not limited to recording artists, television and motion picture personalities, special events, and other corporate and individual projects that require unique entertainment/music-based experience.

Creativity in Music
PO Box 3481, Bridgeport, CT 06605
PH: 203-331-9982
Gi Dussault npsfunk@optonline.net
www.creativityinmusic.com
Promoting independent musicians - helping them in spreading the word.

The Chittlin Circuit
2403 N. L St., Pensacola, FL 32501
PH: 850-433-1842 FX: 850-454-0014
Taffany Shipp info@chittlincircuit.com
www.chittlincircuit.com
We offer exposure and promotions to independently owned record labels, authors, entertainers, dancers, comedians, movies and actors.

Line Um' Up Entertainment
4771 NW 10th Ct. #106, Plantation, FL 33313
PH: 954-562-9772 FX: 954-731-9978
Kendell Mauzon
lineumupentertainment@hotmail.com
www.lineumupentertainment.4t.com
Artist development, and promotions.

Project For Life Promotion/Artist Management
PO Box 225, Melvin, IL 60952
PH: 217-443-3579
Alicia Grimes
projectforlifemanagement@hotmail.com
www.projectforliferecords.com
Artist management, college/commercial radio promotion and record pool promotion.

Sounds In The Key of Gee
26721 Berg Rd. #219, Southfield, MI 48034
PH: 313-549-7400 FX: 313-371-5689
Gisele Caver geecaver@sbcglobal.net
www.soundsinthekeyofgee.com
Entertainment and event consultants who specialize in the promotion of independent artists.

Us Girlz Entertainment Group
96 Linwood Plaza #234, Fort Lee, NJ 07024
PH: 201-808-6024
Ronnie Robinson veronicagirlz@hotmail.com
www.usgirlz.com
An all female-owned promotions and management company specializing in grassroots promotions and marketing concepts.

Vendors and Labels

United States

Dusty Groove America
Attn: Buyer, 1120 N Ashland Ave.
Chicago, IL 60622
PH: 773-342-5800 FX: 773-342-2180
dga@dustygroove.com
www.dustygroove.com
We tend to only stock music we love, and music that we feel fits into our rather narrow format.

Groove Distribution
1164 N. Milwaukee Ave. Chicago, IL 60622-4019
PH: 773-435-0250 FX: 773-435-0252
www.groovedis.com
The main thing is that you must fit our kind of music (Loungey Dance Music-with a Jazz or Soul influence) AND we have to think we can sell you - which means you have to be REALLY good. Singles are FAR easier to pick up than a full CD (and by single I do mean a 12" VINYL single not a CD single).

It's Soul Time! Records
PO Box 572, Ridgewood, NJ 07451-0572
andy@itssoultime.com
www.itssoultime.com
Focusing on Soul and R&B.

SoMuchSoul Records
2397 Bridge Rd. Oakville, ON L6L 2G9
PH: 905-334-2527
Alex Brans alexbrans@somuchsoul.com
www.somuchsoul.com
Promotes great music from talented artists. Funk, Jazz, Soul Grooves, Rock... we cover it all!

Sound Mindz Entertainment
702 2nd Ave. N., Birmingham, AL 35203
PH: 205-252-5587 FX: 205-397-0320
Tony Gideon tonygideon@hotmail.com
www.soundmindzmusic.com
We are a record company interested in R&B, Blues and Black Gospel.

United Kingdom

Acid Jazz Records
146 Bethnal Green Rd. London, E2 6DG UK
PH: 020-7613-1100
info@acidjazz.co.uk
www.acidjazz.co.uk
Acid jazz is the new Soul, anything with its head and mind in the history and the feet to the dancefloor, eyes to the future. Send demos to the above address.

Crazy Beat Records
87 Corbets Tey Rd. Upminster,
Essex, England RM14 2AH
PH: 01708-228678 FX: 01708-640946
Sales@crazybeat.co.uk
www.crazybeat.co.uk
Are you an artist or a distributor that has something hot that you think we should be promoting, then please get in touch or better still send us a sample. We carry Soul, Jazz, Funk, House, Garage, Dance etc.

Soul Brother Records
1 Keswick Rd. E. Putney, London, SW15 2HL UK
PH: 020-8875-1018 FX: 020-8871-0180
soulbrother@btinternet.com
www.soulbrother.com
We're specialists for new independent Soul and Jazz CDs as well as a good source for rare original vinyl LP's and 12" singles.

Soundmob
PO Box 1137, Liverpool, L69 3ZZ UK
PH: 07766332511
info@soundmob.co.uk
www.soundmob.co.uk
We will build your brand through music, whether we are creating a music policy for your business, supplying you with djs, organising live events or making sure your musical identity is properly promoted through every appropriate media.

Ssoul Limited
Webs House, Woodborough Rd.
Winscombe, BS25 1AD UK
Tony Hickman tony@tonyhickman.co.uk
www.lifeandsoulpromotions.net/webdoc.htm
Our core business is focussed around a web-based radio station that encourages subscriptions. Subscribers benefit from discounts on products, entry fees, webcast broadcasts, downloads and CDs.

Japan

Totown Records
Tamari 30-1, Kakegawa City,
Shizuoka Prefecture, Japan 436-0011
PH/FX: 81-537-23-7585
Malcolm W. Adams info@totown.net
www.totown.net/totownrecords.htm
Originators of the Nu-Jazz-Funk. Dedicated to producing and marketing the highest quality world-class entertainment products in the Asia Pacific region.

Women In Music
Promotional Services

Cat Scratch Productions
PO Box 40891, Denver, CO 80204
PH: 303-775-4723
Kristine Berntsen
catscratch@truenorthmarketing.com
www.catscratchproductions.com
Producing and promoting women's events & women musicians. Please send kit and recent tour info.

Tomboy Entertainment
999 SW 16th Ave. #11 Gainesville, FL 32601
PH: 352-213-0277
Mercy tomboyentertainment@gmail.com
www.tomboyentertainment.com
Promotion and concert events by and for women who want to rock the music industry. A hands on circle of estrogenerated Rock power.

Warrior Girl Music
289 S. Robertson Blvd. #200,
Beverly Hills, CA 90211
PH: 818-442-9294
info@warriorgirlmusic.com
www.warriorgirlmusic.com
Recording, publishing and promotions company that is about developing artists.

Women In the Arts
PO Box 1427, Indianapolis, IN 46206
PH: 317-713-1144
wiaonline.org
Produces and sponsors programs for women in the arts.

Vendors and Labels

chicks on speed records
Rosenthaler Strasse 3, 10119, Berlin, Germany
PH: 0049-30-27-89-05-24 FX: 0049-30-27-89-05-25
promo@chicksonspeed-records.com
www.chicksonspeed.com
Promotes Electronic female musicians.

Daemon Records
PO Box 1207, Decatur, GA 30031 Attn: A&R
hello@daemonrecords.com
www.daemonrecords.com
Indie label covering Southeastern US.

Goldenrod Music
1310 Turner St., Lansing, MI 48906
PH: 517-484-1712 FX: 517-484-1771
music@goldenrod.com
www.goldenrod.com
Full service center for Indie artists, focus on women.

Harmony Ridge Music
123 Bonita, Moss Beach, CA 94018
PH: 650-563-9280 FX: 650-563-9266
hrmusic@hrmusic.com
www.hrmusic.com
Dedicated to female singer/songwriters.

Hippie Chick Twang Records
kim@hippiechicktwangrecords.com
www.hippiechicktwangrecords.com
An all-chick record label of award winning singer/songwriter women..

Kill Rock Stars
PO Box 418, 120 NE State Ave.
Olympia, WA 98501
krs@killrockstars.com
www.killrockstars.com
Send us your demo tapes!!

Ladyslipper.org
PH: 919-383-8773 FX: 919-383-3525
info@ladyslipper.org
www.ladyslipper.org
Our purpose is to further new musical and artistic directions for women musicians.

On the Rag Records
PO Box 251, Norco, CA 92860-0251
PH: 909-273-1402 FX: 909-478-5208
webmistress@ontherag.net
www.ontherag.net
For females in the diy music scene and activist scene.

panx
BP 15058-31033 Toulouse Cedex, France
PH: 33-0-561612145 FX: 33-0-561114895
infos@panx.net
www.panx.net
HardCore, Punk, CyberThrash, Grindcore, TechnoBruit, Crades Mélodies.

SisterRecords
#301, Meijidori Bldg. 2-3-21 Kabukicho,
Shinjuku-ku, Tokyo, Japan 160-0021
PH: 81-3-5292-5550 FX: 81-3-5292-5552
sister@kt.rim.or.jp
www.sister.co.jp/english
Japanese label specializing in female artists of many genres.

Sonic Cathedral
PO Box 8505, Baltimore, MD 21234
rbh@soniccathedral.com
www.soniccathedral.com
Specializing in female vocal Metal.

Womanrock Music Shop
PO Box 1460, New York, NY 10009
PH: 800-610-4867
Brenda Kahn bkahn@womanrock.com
www.womanrock.com/musicshop
Sells your CD, personal artist page and more.

XposeYourself.net
1017 3rd Ave. S., Nashville, TN 37210
PH: 615-313-8633 FX: 615-244-6655
info@xposeyourself.net
xposeyourself.net
A revolutionary new way to introduce YOU to the movers and shakers in the recording industry.

Sign up for
The Indie Contact Newsletter!
Every month you will receive a new list of places to send your music for reviews, radio play etc.

Sennheiser is donating an **E835 microphone** and a pair of **HD280Pro headphones** for our monthly draw.
To sign up visit
www.indiebible.com or send an email to
indiebible@rogers.com
with the word "draw" in the Subject field.

World

African Allstars
4325 Roosevelt Hwy. College Park, GA 30349
PH: 404-684-9955
www.panafricanallstars.com
We feature the best African Music on the web.

Afrodicia
PO Box 19866, Los Angeles, CA 90019
PH: 323-938-0720 FX: 206-279-3020
afrodicia@yahoo.com
www.afrodicia.com
African music, Afrobeat, Afropop and World music.

Atlas Music
Cobian's Plaza 1010, 1607 Ponce de León,
San Juan, Puerto Rico 00909-1838
carlosuriel@atlasmusic.biz
www.atlasmusic.biz
Fosters global musical culture awareness and understanding.

Deep Down Productions
122 Yarmouth Rd. Toronto, ON M6G 1X2
PH: 416-535-0401
info@deepdownproductions.com
www.deepdownproductions.com
Promotes Traditional music from around the world.

Earth Vibe Music
PO Box 5007, Brighton, BN50 9DS UK
PH: 0870-350-9407 FX: 0871-661-5556
contact@earthvibemusic.com
www.earthvibemusic.com
Promoting music from Indie bands and musicians.

Kongoi Productions *Norway*
www.kongoi.com
African music, PR and publishing company.

Muzik Info
Kirti Priyadarshani saptam_music@yahoo.co.in
www.ec21.com/muzikinfo
We promote Indian music and budding talent.

Onzou Records
6630 Sherbrooke St. #2102, Montreal, QC H4B 1N7
PH: 514-489-8859
info@onzou.com
www.onzou.com
Producing traditional West African music.

Putamayo World Music
411 Lafayette St. 4th Fl. New York, NY 10003
info@putumayo.com
www.putumayo.com
Music of other cultures. Submit demos.

Rydem Records
PO Box 1993, Manhattan Beach, CA 90267
PH: 310-704-7503 FX:
Ron Seymour neilmour1@yahoo.com
www.firemusic.net
Getting the music of the Caribbean to the world so that people can hear the voice of the Islands.

Rhyme Records
1 Jackson Dr. N., Poughkeepsie, NY 12603
PH: 845-462-3450 FX: 845-463-7664
Probir K. Ghosh probir@rhymerecords.com
www.rhymerecords.com
Our focus is to promote the rich musical heritage of India.

rock paper scissors
216 W. Allen St. #137, Bloomington, IN 47403
PH: 812-339-1195 FX: 801-729-4911
Dmitri Vietze music@rockpaperscissors.biz
rockpaperscissors.biz
We specialize in publicity and marketing in the U.S. for World Music and Reggae labels, artists, websites etc. We are true World Music enthusiasts.

Six Degrees
1119 Colorado Ave. #21, Santa Monica, CA 90401
FX: 310-576-7434
info@sixdegreesrecords.com
www.sixdegreesrecords.com
Independent music label that produces and markets genre-bending recordings.

World Music Store
56 Browns Mill Rd. Montpelier, VT 05602
PH: 802-223-1294 FX: 802-229-1834
info@worldmusicstore.com
www.worldmusicstore.com
Traditional and Contemporary World music.

Zook Beat
info@zookbeat.com
www.zookbeat.com
Check out up and coming artists and all time favorites!!

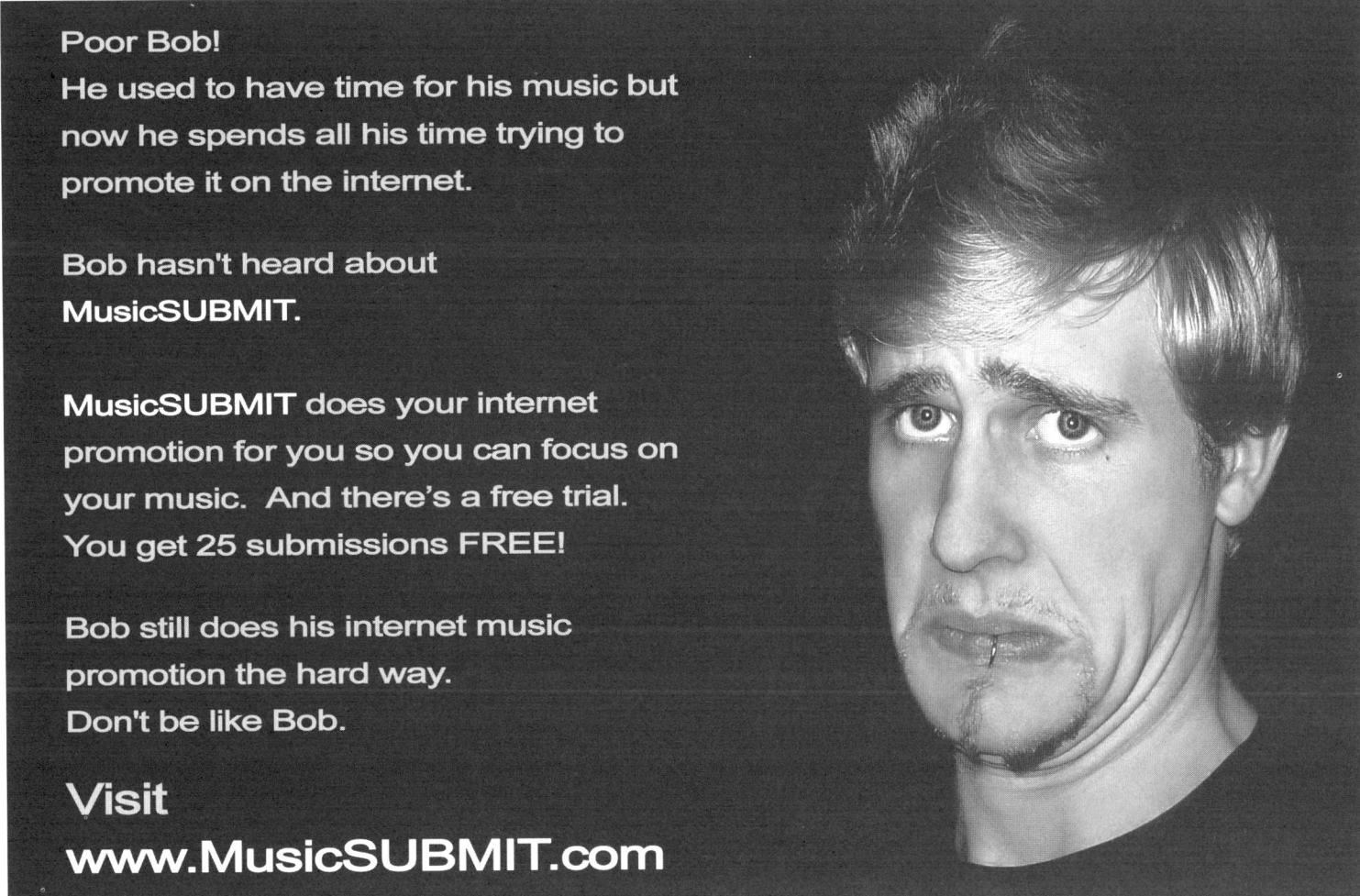

SECTION FIVE: SITES THAT WILL ALLOW YOU TO UPLOAD YOUR MUSIC OR VIDEO FILES

"The Internet is a powerful force, still in its infancy, and shows no sign of letting up. If you want to get your music to where the action is, get online. This is one bus you don't want to miss." - **David Nevue, author of "How to Successfully Promote Your Music on the Internet"**

Digital Music Distributors

1-2-3 Music Store
Alfred Himmelweiss a.himmelweiss@berlin.de
easybe.com
Lets musicians sell their own music downloads independently.

CD Baby Digital Distribution
5925 NE 80 Ave. Portland, OR 97218-2891
PH: 503-595-3000
cdbaby@cdbaby.com
cdbaby.net/dd
You keep all the rights to your music. You just lend us the right to be your digital distributor: to get your music to legitimate music services like Apple iTunes, Rhapsody, Napster, MSN Music, MP3tunes, AOL's MusicNet, Yahoo MusicMatch, and more!

Divine Arts
11501 Dublin Blvd. #200, Dublin, CA 94568
PH: 866-443-8464 FX: 650-618-1816
usa@divine-arts.com
www.divine-arts.com
A leader in digital distribution services for content from the Indian subcontinent.

Indie Pool Digital Distribution Program
PH: 888-884-6343
digidistro@indiepool.net
www.indiepool.com
We're the largest digital retailers for Canada's independent recording artists.

IODA
665 3rd St. #305, San Francisco, CA 94107
PH: 415-777-4632
Vivek info@IODAlliance.com
www.iodalliance.com
We distribute music from independent labels, but typically don't work with individual artists. Artists signed to independent labels should have their labels contact us. IODA is currently partnered with the following digital music services: iTunes, Napster, RHAPSODY, MusicMatch, Audio Lunchbox, MusicNow, MSN Music Service, Downloadpunk.com, Sony Connect, MusicNet, Liquid Audio, Destra, FutureTrax, Downrip, eCast, Wippit, and Musicstream.

The Orchard
100 Park Ave. 17th Fl. New York, NY 10003
PH: 212-201-9280 FX: 212-201-9203
info@theorchard.com
www.theorchard.com
Supplier for North American digital music as well as the leading European DMS providers.

SNOCAP
128 Spear St. 2nd Fl. San Francisco, CA 94105
www.snocap.com
Content registry and clearinghouse that enables record labels, publishers and individual artists to sell their entire catalogs through peer-to-peer networks and online retailers.

Digital Music Sites

Getting your music onto the sites listed in this section varies a great deal cost-wise. Many services will allow you to upload your files for free, while others charge a fee or percentage from each sale that you make. Be wary of large setup fees. Many of the Online Digital Stores deal only with Digital Distribution Services such as CD Baby or The Orchard to get their Indie Music. I have indicated which stores deal only with Distributors throughout this Section.

All Styles

North America
United States

96decibels.com
support@96decibels.com
www.96decibels.com
We provide ICPs, Labels and Artists with value added tools that can easily be incorporated into their current web presence. Educate webmasters to the value of including the Weed Music Directory on their websites.

A and R Online
PO Box 1993, Studio City, CA 91614
Chris info@aandronline.com
www.aandronline.com
A&R source for record companies and music publishers worldwide.

Acid Planet
PH: 608-256-5555 FX: 608-250-1745
www.acidplanet.com
Artist profile for uploading songs and writing reviews.

agent155.com
255 G St. #689, San Diego, CA 92101
info@agent155.com
www.agent155.com
A street-level creative arena, providing an affordable, high-quality online presence for the global artistic and athletic communities.

AGNULA Libre Music
muzik@agnula.org
muzik.agnula.org
Our goal is to create a publicly accessible database of Libre Music, i.e. works which have been put by their authors under a license which allows free redistribution and usage.

amazon.com Digital Music Network
www.amazon.com/exec/obidos/subst/jungle/jungle-gateway.html
Upload your songs, info, lyrics, images and more.

AMPCAST.COM
www.ampcast.com
Dedicated solely to the musical artist.

Apple's iTunes Music
www.apple.com/itunes
Songs must be delivered through a Digital Music Distributor such as www.cdbaby.com or www.theorchard.com

Artist Label
webmaster@artistlabel.com
www.artistlabel.com
Offering free downloads of independent artists.

ArtistNow.com
ArtistNow.com
Members can upload audio, video, images, portfolios, resumes, job postings, e-mail, chat using text, audio and video.

ArtistServer.com
www.artistserver.com
Supporting Independent Music! ARTISTS, get involved, be heard, get feedback - we have the technology!

AT&T Wireless Ringtones
www.attwireless.com/personal/features/fun/music.jhtml
Songs must be delivered through a Digital Music Distributor (www.theorchard.com).

Audio Lunchbox
1021 N. Sepulveda Blvd. #R,
Manhattan Beach, CA 90266
support@audiolunchbox.com
www.audiolunchbox.com
We accept music from labels, distributors and individual unsigned artists.

AudioCandy.com
www.audiocandy.com
Song files are supplied through LiquidAudio.com

AudioLaunch.com
contact@audiolaunch.com
www.audiolaunch.com
Legal MP3 music downloads from independent bands of various genres.

AudioStreet.net
5422 NW 50th Ct. Coconut Creek, FL 33073
audiostreet.net
Offers MP3 hosting, full artist pages with bios, reviews, event listings and much more.

axecity.com
forums@axecity.com
www.axecity.com
Our "Band Profile" area has been made available for you to showcase your band and your music.

GET REAL MONEY FOR YOUR MUSIC!

AUCTIONSONGS.COM

Sell Your Songs For Free!
Set Your Own Price!
No Risk!

Sell/Buy Song Copyrights
Movie and Television Licensing
Buy/Sell guitars, amps equipment
Offer "studio" musician services
Get hired for live gigs!

www.auctionsongs.com

The Band Universe
www.banduniverse.com
A promotion engine for artists. You can enter bio, roster, gigs, recordings and MP3 audio. There is no charge to join!

BandJams.Com
info@freepeers.com
bandjams.com
Showcasing Indie musicians to the industry and fans.

BearShare
info@bearshare.com
www.bearshare.com
Promotes solid independent artists.

beatmaka.com
Marc Hedinger marc@beatmaka.com
www.beatmaka.com
We do everything possible to select only the best music without compromise. Our Review Panel checks each incoming track and assures that only the best ones get online.

The Big Ugly Review
2703 7th St. Box 345, Berkeley, CA 94710
Elizabeth Bernstein music@biguglyreview.com
www.biguglyreview.com
In the music section we have downloadable songs of artists that visitors can listen to. Includes interviews.

Bitmunk
bitmunk.com
You set the amount of money you want to receive for each sale of your music, then different sellers can sell it for whatever price they want on top of that.

bowienet
support@davidbowie.com
www.davidbowie.com
Showcasing members' original music and more.

BuyMusic.com
85 Enterprise #100, Aliso Viejo, CA 92656
www.buymusic.com
Great option for the independent community.

Buzzplay.com
2894 Rowena Ave. Los Angeles, CA 90039
PH: 323-664-2899
LJ Scott info@buzzplay.com
buzzplay.com
We do our best to give bands the chance to have their music and material heard by record labels and professional music reps.

CannibalMusic.com
8900 S. Lake Dasha Dr. Plantation, FL 33324
PH: 954-476-6667 FX: 954-472-5911
Elliot Zimmerman jobu@cannibalmusic.com
www.cannibalmusic.com
Singers can market their MP3 to the world!

CatchMusic.net
contact@catchmusic.net
catchmusic.net
Distribute your music widely without having a major record deal.

Cdigix
3575 S. Fox St., Englewood, CO 80113
PH: 303-783-5444 FX: 303-783-0074
www.cdigix.com
The leading and most comprehensive digital media service provider to colleges and universities today. Songs must be delivered through a Digital Music Distributor (www.theorchard.com).

Clear Channel NEW Music Network
newmusicnetwork@clearchannel.com
clearchannelnewmusicnetwork.com
Share your music with your fans and music industry professionals who want to find new, promising acts.

CollegeMusicRadio.com
management@collegemusicradio.com
CollegeMusicRadio.com
We showcase the best independent artists and bands in the world and visitors decide which songs get played on the our station. We want our listeners to have total control of the music.

cornerband.com
webmaster@cornerband.com
www.cornerband.com
Online musical forum for both independent and record-labeled musicians.

cStream
2 Deer Path, Gladstone, NJ 07934
PH: 617-974-3085
www.cstream.com
We believe that artists should have control over their own music.

culturedeluxe
www.culturedeluxe.com
News, views, reviews, abuse...

CYBERMIDI LIVE
PO Box 120040, Staten Island, NY 10312
cybermidi.com/community
We've got your favorite songs in MIDI the way they were meant to be heard. Feel free to send us some samples of your work and we can talk about including them at Shop CYBERMIDI.

CyberRadio.com
info@CyberRadio.com
cyberradio.com
Featuring not only cutting edge music from up and coming artists, but also bios, pictures, performance schedules, and promotional materials.

DecentXposure.com
411@decentxposure.com
DecentXposure.com
An indie magazine chock full of ringtones, downloads and other ways for fans and bands to get together.

Digibag.com
315 Joliet Ave. Huntington Beach, CA 92648
PH: 714-536-2491 FX: 562-684-4347
info@digibag.com
www.digibag.com
All CD-quality tracks as well as MP3s you can download in seconds, available now!

DigitalSoundboard.net
dave@opcenter.net
www.DigitalSoundboard.net
*Delivers *paid-for* MP3s and FLAC digital music files.*

DiscLogic
2048 Larimer St. #200, Denver, CO 80205
FX: 720-863-2047
info@disclogic.com
www.disclogic.com
Get your content in the DiscLogic download portal.

DMusic
101 Greenwood Ave. #200, Jenkintown, PA 19046
PH: 215-885-3302 FX: 215-885-3303
www.dmusic.com
Get your music played on our broadcasts.

Download Music Store
Joel Erenberg joele55@yahoo.com
www.downloadmusicmart.com
Featuring legal music downloads from independent artists and labels.

Download.com Music
music.download.com
A free artist upload and download site that is part of Download.com.

DOWNLOADSdirect
10900 Wilshire Blvd. #1400,
Los Angeles, CA 90024
listen.artistdirect.com
Showcases downloads from independent bands.

The Dust Stop
70 Watchung Ave. #6, Belleville, NJ 07109
PH: 973-759-1817
Dusty Dave dusty@dustydave.com
www.dustydave.com
We provide FREE sound efx, $5 Instrumental music productions and we also feature talented artists from various parts of the US.

EMusic.com
submissions@emusic.com
www.emusic.com
We work with labels only, NOT with unsigned artists. If you represent a record label and are inquiring about making your catalog, please send an email.

epitonic.com
www.epitonic.com
We aspire to live up to our neologistic moniker, the center from which waves of disruptive purity emit.

FAIRCOPY
info@faircopy.com
www.faircopy.com
Sell your works on P2P networks and on the web.

Free Music Downloads Ezine
www.free-musicdownloads.net
A newsletter packed full of links to free MP3s.

Fresh New Media
Chris info@freshnewmedia.com
www.freshnewmedia.com
A free online exhibit featuring film, video, visual and digital arts, literature for anybody! Join for free and post your work online today!!!

Fresh Tracks Music
1609 N. Wolcott Ste. #305, Chicago, IL 60622
PH: 773-529-6733 FX: 773.529.6737
kip@freshtracksmusic.com
www.freshtracksmusic.com
Revolutionizing how you discover and download today's best new music.

funender.com
www.funender.com
Will review your songs and give you more plays.

Fuse
11 Penn Plaza, 15th Fl. New York, NY 10001
PH: 212-324-3400 FX: 212-324-3445
www.fuse.tv
Submit your music and band info.

Fuseboard
support@fuseboard.com
www.fuseboard.com
Exists to provide a platform for artists, across all genres, to expand their music through collaboration and networking with other artists. Fuseboard provides a toolbox of useful products, services and features.

garageband.com
PH: 415-704-3432 FX: 415-704-3432
artistmanager@garageband.com
www.garageband.com
Rewriting the rules about how the music industry operates.

Groupie Tunes
3100 Main St. #349, Dallas, TX 75226
PH: 214-760-9977 FX: 214-742-1245
customerservice@groupietunes.com
www.GroupieTunes.com
A mobile community dedicated to create a real-time, direct relationship for fans with their favorite artists.

Hightide Music
PH: 612-251-3327
Doug Kasper doug@hightidemusic.com
www.hightidemusic.com
A referral site hosting MP3s of independent bands. Our mission is to bring a greater awareness to independent music.

HipTingle
djspy@spydigital.com
hiptingle.spydigital.com
Helps bands showcase and get feedback on their work and promote upcoming events.

Hollywood Music
admin@hollywoodmusic.tv
www.hollywoodmusic.tv
We're here to help all motivated and talented artists get the visibility they deserve. We offer artists the ability to upload their profile to our website.

HotBands.com
PO Box 27722, Seattle, WA 98125-2722
cd@hotbands.com
www.hotbands.com
We're looking for some quality original bands of all genres.

HouseOfGigs.com
12157 W. Linebaugh #211, Tampa, FL 33626
PH: 888-260-3138 FX: 888-260-3138
info@houseofgigs.com
www.houseofgigs.com
Artists can set up gigs, post songs, buy and sell equipment, check out the latest music news and much more.

How Do We Sound.com
PO Box 865, Lake Dallas, TX 75065
PH: 940-300-3142
Scott scott@netconquer.com
howdoisound.com
A website to upload your media and present it to our audience. For music and comedy, the media is both webcasted through internet radio, as well as listen on demand.

iamusic.com
44 Music Sq. E. #503, Nashville, TN 37203
PH: 615-335-3262 FX: 215-895-9672
add-your-music@iamusic.com
www.iamusic.com/add_your_music.php
For Instrumental music only!

iManifest
Mark McFarland info@imanifest.biz
www.imanifest.biz
Service for musicians to expose their demos to music industry people looking for new artists.

Independent Artists Company
admin@independentartistscompany.com
independentartistscompany.com
We combine the best features from the MP3 era with modern options such as digital singles sales.

Indie Concerts.tv
7095 Hollywood Blvd. #586, Hollywood, CA 90028
PH: 323-822-0474
jay@indie-concerts.tv
www.indie-concerts.tv
Designed to greatly increase your audience, get you more gigs, and increase your revenue.

Direct traffic to your website.

The Indie Link Exchange

A new free and easy way to promote your website

www.indielinkexchange.com/ile

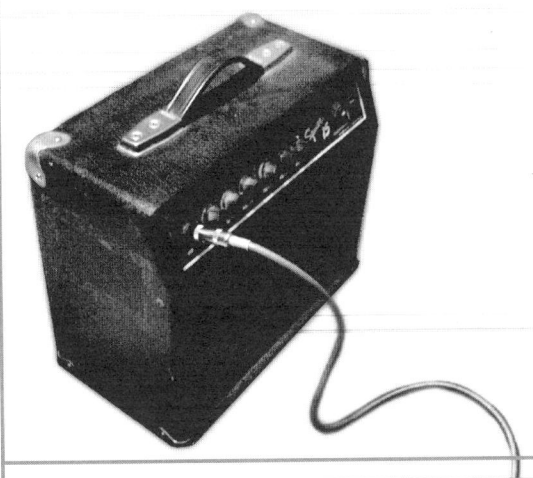

ARE YOU REALLY INTO NEW MUSIC?

real time artist/title info, voting, charting, chat and more

yeah, we're really into this...

www.eoRadio.com | eoRadio))

Indiepad.com
CD Upload, 1894 Hwy. 50 E. #4-207,
Carson City, NV 89701
info-at-indiepad.com
indiepad.com
Sign up and complete our artist registration form and we will convert and upload your CD free of charge!

IndiePodcasting.com
314 Centre St., South Orange, NJ 07079
PH: 973-763-9215
Tony Alexander webmaster@indiepodcasting.com
www.indiepodcasting.com
A new service devoted to promoting unsigned and indie artists using a combination of podcasting technology, syndication, and viral marketing.

Indy
feedback@indy.tv
indy.tv
We make it easy for visitors to find great new independent music. They download our Indy player and double-click. As it plays songs, they rate what they hear.

IndyReview.net
Paul Leclair info@indyreview.net
www.indyreview.net
Our job is to attract visitors to the great variety of music online here! I record a monthly best picks list and promote many of the new artists, I take a personal involvement and have audio interviews with a number of really great bands.

Insound
401 Broadway 26th Fl. New York, NY 10013-3005
PH: 212-777-8056 FX: 212-777-8059
help@insound.com
www.insound.com
Bringing the best underground culture to the surface.

iSOUND.COM
PH: 877-757-6863 FX: 214-965-9007
D.J. Burdick staff@isound.com
www.isound.com
Free place for bands to upload their music and gain exposure to our music community of over 1,000,000 visitors per month!

ItsAboutMusic.com
275A Mill Ln. Phoenixville, PA 19460
Dean Sciarra dean@ItsAboutMusic.com
www.itsaboutmusic.com
Supplying you with the best music we can find from all over the world.

ItsFun.com
info@itsfun.com
www.itsfun.com
Offering you the necessary tools and pricing to control your own destiny.

JukeBoxAlive
311 Montford Ave. Asheville, NC 28801
PH: 828-232-0016
Will Cumberland cumberland@jukeboxalive.com
jukeboxalive.com
Our Advanced Jukebox Player protects your music from being digitally downloaded, yet allows fans to hear your music online. This creates exciting possibilities for you to present yourself to new audiences without being ripped off.

JustEnough TV
PH: 831-624-9100 FX: 831-624-7878
justenoughtv.com
Your source for the latest news, independent videos and music instruction. We are a Microsoft partner and are able to offer indie bands FREE exposure to 7.1 million viewers through our exclusive Indie Channel on MSN Video.

Latest Music Videos
PH: 0802-547-2535
roy@latestmusicvideos.com
www.latestmusicvideos.com
Showcase for many artists and bands of the future.

ListenUp247.com
info@ListenUp247.com
www.listenup247.com
Featuring not only cutting edge music from up and coming artists, but also bios, pictures, performance schedules, and promotional materials.

LocalTracks
info@localtracks.com
www.localtracks.com
You keep complete control of your digital content and set the price for each song.

Lulu.com
3131 RDU Ctr. #210, Morrisville, NC 27560
PH: 919-459-5858
support@lulu.com
www.lulu.com
Upload your music; set your royalty; customize & promote your Lulu storefront.

Magnatune
2070 Allston Way #102, Berkeley, CA 94704
PH: 510-684-4175 FX: 510-217-6374
magnatune.com
Artists get a full 50% of the purchase price.

MediaKinesis.com
media@mediakinesis.com
mediakinesis.com
Get your own pro website, stream MP3 and WMV (video), events calendar, radio station, and more.

Mixposure
management@mixposure.com
www.mixposure.com
Music Promotion, free MP3 downloads, band exposure, music forum. Rate and Review.

The Mod Archive
mods@modarchive.com
www.modarchive.com
Songs on this site are provided for free download by the artists.

MOSIQ.COM
Mosiq.com
Provides musicians with an online presence designed to bring fans and bands together.

MP3 charts.com
www.mp3charts.com
Offers bands the highest possible visibility.

Mp3Allies
donc@mp3allies.com
www.mp3allies.com
The source for the best independant musicians on the Internet!

MP3tunes
www.MP3tunes.com
We use music from CD Baby's digital distribution program. High rev-share to artists, with artists keeping almost $6 of every CD sold and almost $.60 for each song. Even the superstar artists don't command that kind of royalty!

MP3Unsigned.com
admin@mp3unsigned.com
www.mp3unsigned.com
The best MP3s from new and unsigned artists.

MPEG NATION
c/o Digital Silo, 1510 Old Deerfield Rd. #215, Highland Park, IL 60035
PH: 408-850-9658
info@digitalsilo.com
www.mpegnation.com
Our mission is to stream your video content and make it universally accessible and useful.

Mperia
www.mperia.com
You get your music on Mperia by signing up for a free artist account and uploading your songs. It's as simple as that.

MSN Music
music.msn.com
Songs must be delivered through a Digital Music Distributor such as www.cdbaby.com or www.theorchard.com

MSSVision
542 W. University Pkwy. Baltimore, MD 21210
www.mssvision.com
Webcasts your Indie music video.

Music 4 iPods
314 Centre St., South Orange, NJ 07079
PH: 973-763-9215
Tony Alexander webmaster@indiepodcasting.com
www.music4ipods.com
Podcasting is a hot new method of distributing your music to millions of people around the world. Submission guarantees that your music will be sent out to our subscribers in syndicated podcasts.

Music Forte
154 E. Bailey Rd. Unit G, Naperville, IL 60565
PH: 888-659-2867
support@musicforte.com
www.musicforte.com
Musicians - We're ready to start promoting your band and music and it won't cost you a cent!

Music Gorilla
12407 Mopac Expressway N. 100-312,
Austin, TX 78758
PH: 512-918-8978 FX: 212-258-6394
info@musicgorilla.com
www.musicgorilla.com
Exposure to major labels, Indie labels, film studios and publishers.

Music Scene Online
admin@musicsceneonline.com
www.musicsceneonline.com
A community dedicated to the promotion and distribution music from emerging artists.

The Music Tap
postmaster@themusictap.com
www.themusictap.com
Dedicated to helping musicians spread the word about their music.

Music Torch
PO Box 280, Nanuet, NY 10954
PH: 917-232-4624
Kevin Rath kevin@musictorch.com
www.musictorch.com
A digital music store for independent artists who are looking for a place to sell their music.

Musician's Network
305A Old St. Rd. Peterborough, NH 03458
PH: 603-924-1331
www.musiciansnetwork.com
Information and contacts in the world of music.

MusicGiants
926 Incline Way, Incline Village, NV 89451
support@musicgiants.com
musicgiants.com
The only high fidelity solution that combines a music player, a music store, and your music collection.

MUSICMATCH
16935 W. Bernardo Dr. San Diego, CA 92127
support@musicmatch.com
www.musicmatch.com
Send your music submissions for possible review, interview or download offering to us.

MusicNet AOL
www.musicnet.com
Songs must be delivered through a Digital Music Distributor such as www.cdbaby.com or www.theorchard.com

MusicNow
musicnow.fullaudio.com
Songs must be delivered through a Digital Music Distributor such as www.cdbaby.com or www.theorchard.com

MusicRebellion.com
1 N. Meridian St. #220, Indianapolis, IN 46204
PH: 317-638-4154 FX: 317-638-4174
Jeremy Eglen jeremy@musicrebellion.com
www.musicrebellion.com
List your media with MusicRebellion.com.

MusicSpawn.com
35 Village Walk, Covington, GA 30016
PH: 404-202-6344 FX: 770-786-2305
artistsupport@musicspawn.com
www.musicspawn.com
Downloads from new and upcoming artists.

Muzik101.com
220 E. Central Pkwy. #1020,
Altamonte Springs, FL 32714
www.muzik101.com
Add your music to our store.

MyJonesMusic.com
234 9th Ave. N. Seattle, WA 98109
Chris King rvchris@jonessoda.com
www.myjonesmusic.com
Jones Soda Co. has created this free for all Indie music site.

myMPO
PH: 888-841-7224 FX: 310-507-0190
www.mympo.com
For a fee and small percentage of sales myMPO sets up websites their own digital download store. Content for myMPO's main database must be delivered through a Digital Music Distributor (www.theorchard.com).

MyOriginalMusic.com
support@myoriginalmusic.com
www.myoriginalmusic.com
Part of Songwriter Cafe. Sign up for your FREE account, upload your music and share your creations with the world!

MySpace Music
www.myspace.com/index.cfm?fuseaction=music
Upload your music for exposure, reviews and more.

Napster
artistrelations@napster.com
www.napster.com
Contact to get your music featured.

NetMusic
submissions@netmusic.com
www.netmusic.com
Home to the largest collection of independent digital music and movies. Always looking for new and exciting acts to feature.

Netmusician.org
www.netmusician.org
Contact to get your music featured here.

New Music Showcase
Clifford Bowdin bowdin1@cs.com
www.new-music-showcase.com
Upload your music and gain valuable exposure worldwide.

NewViews Music
4200 Park Blvd. #248, Oakland, CA 94602
PH: 510-655-5751 FX: 510-291-8305
Dynell newviews@sbcglobal.net
www.NewViewsMusic.com
Sells music from independent artists, bands, producers, and DJs.

NextRadio Solutions
www.nextradiosolutions.com
Streaming music to hundreds of thousands of users of high-traffic sites. Songs must be delivered through a Digital Music Distributor (www.theorchard.com).

Number One Music
259 W. 30th St. #12FR, New York, NY 10001
reclabels@numberonemusic.com
www.NumberOneMusic.com
We not only host your music - we also promote it by using our targeted exposure method.

Oddio Overplay
www.oddiooverplay.com
Predominantly a catalog of neat-o websites that offer legal and free sharing of music. The primary purpose of this site is to connect artists and audiences.

OneSource e-CD Distribution System
Perry Leopold onesource@pan.com
onesource.pan.com
Sell from your own web site and get paid 100% of the sale.

op easy listening music shop
promos@on-linepromo.com
www.opeasylistening.com
If you are an independent artist or label and would like to sell your music please contact us.

OP Music Shop
promos@on-linepromo.com
www.opmusicshop.com
We have 17 genre specific shops to choose from If you are an independent artist or label and would like to sell your music please contact us.

op pop music shop
promos@on-linepromo.com
www.oppopmusic.com
If you are an independent artist or label and would like to sell your music please contact us.

op rock music shop
promos@on-linepromo.com
www.oprock.com
If you are an independent artist or label and would like to sell your music please contact us.

OSRecords
www.osrecords.com
Providing you with quality music from independent artists, without the usual record industry hype.

PassTheMic.com
4130 Heyward St., Cincinnati, OH 45205
PH: 718-213-4176
www.passthemic.com
Community for independent Hip Hop artists, by choice!

PayLoadz
295 Park Ave. S. #6B, New York, NY 10010
sales@payloadz.com
payloadz.com
It works seamlessly with your PayPal account, enabling you to offer digital music from your web site or online auctions.

phonector USA
90 N.11th St., Brooklyn, NY 11211
contact@phonector.com
www.phonector.com
We can help you sell your music via download distribution and burned audio CD distribution.

Planet-Musician.com
www.planet-musician.com
Upload and promote your music in the artist spotlight forum.

Primetones.com
PO Box 101, Porter, TX 77365
PH: 281-354-7677 FX: 281-354-7677
info@primetones.com
www.primetones.com
Present your music as MP3 tracks and Ringtones.

promosquad
info@promosquad.com
home.promosquad.com
Our website is separated into five main areas: The Promosquad Jukebox (rate new music), Polls/Interactive, Get Famous, the Prize Store, and the Message Boards.

Promotion West
484 Washington St. #106, Monterey, CA 93940
PH: 831 373-6227
John Tallon john@promotionwest.com
www.promotionwest.com
MP3 music download site for unsigned artists.

pureVOLUME
119 Braintree St. #603,
Boston, MA 02134
music@purevolume.com
www.purevolume.com
The place for rising artists to promote their music and shows.

QTRnote.com
PH: 901-763-4186
peter@qtrnote.com
www.qtrnote.com
Can work with accomplished composers.

Radio Radio
553 E. Main St.,
Jackson, TN 38301
PH: 615-986-9271
FX: 866-294-7843
RT Curtis
webmaster@radioradio.us
www.radioradio.us
Create your own store to start selling music. All music that you upload to your own store will automatically be played on our radio station.

RadioSubmit.com
PO Box 1726,
Fredericksburg, VA 22402
PH: 866-432-7965
R.W. Shamy Jr.
radiosubmit@radiosubmit.com
www.radiosubmit.com
An online platform that allows artists and record labels of all genres to submit their music directly to radio stations around the world. Radio stations can now search by artist name, genre, song title or by record label, pre-listen and then download CD-quality music to air on their station. Check our website for submission details.

Radiotakeover
32 Mill St., Mount Holly, NJ 08060
PH: 609-733-1046
info@radiotakeover.com
www.radiotakeover.com
Promotional services for Indie artists.

RedDotNet
2052 Corte Del Nogal, Carlsbad, CA 92009
PH: 973-657-1558 FX: 760-931-8026
www.digitalon-demand.com
Our content is drawn from the All Media Guide.

ResearchMusic
webmaster@researchmusic.com
www.researchmusic.com
We can publish your song or broker your master recording to a record label. ResearchMusic's registered listeners and customers can upload MP3 files for review by our A&R team.

Resort Records
572 Rockrose Ct. Incline Village, NV 89451-8300
PH: 775-832-3766 FX: 775-832-8107
Demos3@resortrecords.com
www.resortrecords.com
Pioneering Internet music delivery retail site.

RHAPSODY
rhapsody-editorial@real.com
www.rhapsody.com
Songs must be delivered through a Digital Music Distributor such as www.cdbaby.com or www.theorchard.com

Ride-On-Music
320 F Business Pkwy. Greer, SC 29651
IronHeartz IronHeartz2004@yahoo.com
IronHeartz.Rideonmusic.com
A service that allows you to get paid for your music downloads. Free for limited service & $5.95 a month for the real deal making money service.

RisingMusic.com
9608 Park Highlands Dr. Dallas, TX 75238
joseph4829@yahoo.com
www.risingmusic.com
Indie bands, get listed to get exposure!

Rock the Web
3633 Lake Kristin Dr. Gretna, LA 70056
PH: 504-957-3906 FX: 425-699-2311
info@mp3collegeradionetwork.com
www.mp3collegeradionetwork.com
Your source for the best MP3 music.

RollingStone.com
rollingstone.com/shop
Owned (and music fulfilled) by Real Networks (Rhapsody). Songs must be delivered through a Digital Music Distributor such as www.cdbaby.com or www.theorchard.com

www.indielinkexchange.com/ile

Ruckus Network
www.ruckusnetwork.com
A subscription download service designed exclusively for colleges and universities. Songs must be delivered through a Digital Music Distributor such as www.cdbaby.com or www.theorchard.com

ShareNewYork.com
PH: 516-967-2795
Ed Bernstein sharenewyork@humanizer.com
sharenewyork.com
Weed storage $1/MB/Year. 60 Days Free. Hear fans tell you what they like about your music.

SignHere Online
contact@signhereonline.net
www.signhereonline.net
Artists upload MP3s. Visitors download and listen to the available selections, and provide feedback via electronic survey. These results are tabulated and made available to interested record labels.

SongCritic.com
J. Atkinson songcritic@comcast.net
www.SongCritic.com
A site where fans can download and listen to your song(s) and then post "reviews" of your tune.

Songfight.org
fightmaster@songfight.org
www.songfight.org
We post a title, people make songs for that title and compete.

SongPlanet.com
feedback@songplanet.com
www.songplanet.com
We offer free artist pages, forums and live chat.

SongScope.com
PO Box 948, Columbus, GA 31902
PH: 770-754-4543
Julie Deese Julie@SongScope.com
SongScope.com
Enables writers to build an online catalog of their songs to pitch to record labels, publishing companies, and producers. In turn we enable Music Industry Professionals to make song requests and search the data base of songs created by the writers building their online catalogs.

songscribbler.com
query@songscribbler.com
www.songscribbler.com
Promote and sell your unpublished music.

Songstuff
songs@songstuff.com
songstuff.net
Post your songs for review, review other's songs, discuss technical, creative and music business issues, chat in our forum.

Sony Connect
www.sonyconnect.com
Songs must be delivered through a Digital Music Distributor such as www.cdbaby.com or www.theorchard.com.

SoundClick
support@soundclick.com
www.soundclick.com
Many free services for Indie bands.

soundhub.com
hello@soundhub.com
soundhub.com
Covers all your digital music needs.

Starbucks Music Download Service
www.starbucks.com
Songs must be delivered through a Digital Music Distributor (www.theorchard.com).

SwayThisWay.com
c/o New Accounts, PO Box 50911,
Los Angeles, CA 90050
PH: 323-254-1934
customersupport@swaythisway.com
www.SwayThisWay.com
We've taken the best Internet technological breakthroughs and combined these to present our audience with a tool to listen, enjoy and purchase music.

Syndicate Entertainment
1016 Morse Ave. #17, Sunnyvale, CA 94089
PH: 408-744-9092
David Mack dmack@se-global.com
www.syndicateentertainment.com
Entertainment company dedicated to the advancement of the independent music community. Sell your music online today!

takeoutpop.com
mori@takeoutpop.com
www.takeoutpop.com
Learn about marketing & promotions, plus much more.

TheTrunk.com
Street 51 W. 3rd St. #101, Tempe, AZ 85281
PH: 480-967-6555
www.TheTrunk.com
We've got 20 tools to offer you including a customizable website, SMS Messaging and MP3 sales.

ToneStac
10755 Scripps Poway Pkwy. #475,
San Diego, CA 92131
FX: 208-279-1564
NewArtistSignup@tonestac.com
www.tonestac.com
The place where dreams come true... because when we do our jobs well, talented people get noticed.

Tower Records Digital Downloads
www.towerrecords.com
Songs must be delivered through a Digital Music Distributor (www.cdbaby.com).

True Independent
393 Oconee St. #35, Athens, GA 30601
Matthew Young mattyoung@trueindependent.com
www.trueindependent.com
The digital music store with a personality. We pay artists 100% of the profits.

TVU Music Television
PO Box 1887, Westerville, OH 43086
PH: 614-890-9977
nikki@tvulive.com
www.tvulive.com
The music video channel that actually plays music videos!

Unsigned Talents
PH: 818-785-2611 FX: 818-785-2611
contact@unsignedtalents.com
www.unsignedtalents.com
Sign up to give talent agents a chance to discover you.

Upto11.net
inform@upto11.net
www.upto11.net
Music lovers visit our site, type a band name into the search box, press "Get Recommendations" and we provide them with a list of recommended bands that they might like.

Virgin Megastore Digital Downloads
www.virgin.com/downloads
VirginDigital.com
Songs must be delivered through a Digital Music Distributor such as www.cdbaby.com or www.theorchard.com

Vitaminic
369 Broadway St., San Francisco, CA 94133
PH: 415-781-7670 FX: 415-781-7682
info@vitaminic.com
www.vitaminic.com
Promotion and distribution of your digital music.

Wal-Mart Music Downloads
www.walmart.com/music
Artists must go through a distributor to get their music online (www.theorchard.com).

Weed
content@weedshare.com
www.weedshare.com
Pays you to share music files.

Weedfiles.com
support@weedfiles.com
www.weedfiles.com/ib
Sell your independent music here.

WorldPhonic
info@worldphonic.com
www.worldphonic.com
An internet music distributor, whose mission is to provide independent musicians an easy way to distribute and profit from music on the internet.

Yahoo Launch
Attn: Media Assets Dept. 2700 Pennsylvania Ave.
Santa Monica, CA 90404
www.launch.com
Submit your videos to get exposed.

ZeBox
no_spam@zebox.com
www.zebox.com
A great efficient music engine for Indie artists.

Canada

Apple iTunes Canada
www.apple.com/ca/itunes
Songs must be delivered through a Digital Music Distributor such as www.cdbaby.com or www.theorchard.com

Decibel.ca
40 Holly St. 7th Fl. Toronto, ON M4S 3C3
PH: 416-322-3121 FX: 416-322-5881
info@decibelgroup.com
www.decibel.ca
CDs and MP3s from Indie labels and unsigned artists. All artists welcome.

Mp3room.com
Suite B - 2306 Bedford Pl.
Abbotsford, BC V2T 4A5
Jayson Lockyer jayson@mp3room.com
www.mp3room.com
Created to promote and showcase the music of independent bands.

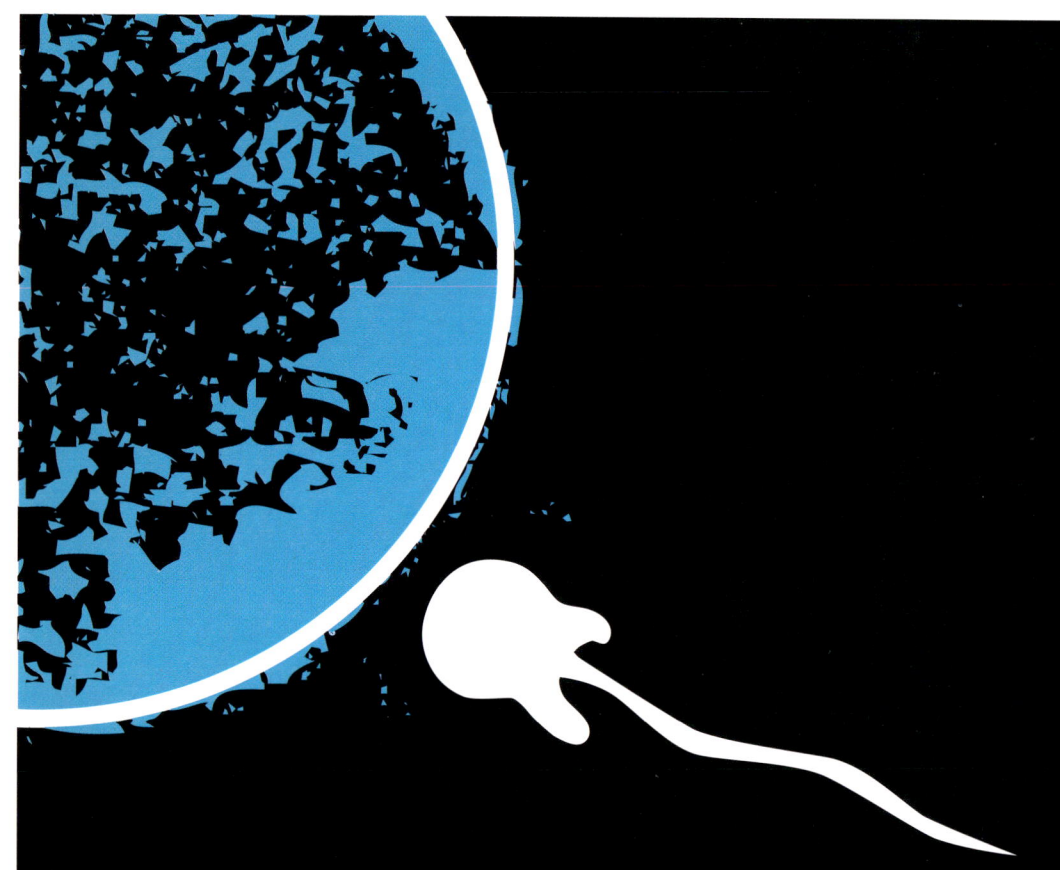

BOOKING IS NOW OPEN IN 139 CITIES ACROSS U.S. CANADA AND EUROPE

GET YOUR BAND READY!

4,551 Live Shows
368 Clubs and venues
24,071 Bands booked

600,000 Dollars in prizes
149 Promo tours produced
12th season of shows

Open Air in Germany
44,161 Attendees
Radio & TV Promotion

Register your band at www.emergenza.net
or call 1-888-923-2263

NoWhere Radio
Box 42065 Southland Crossing PO,
Calgary, AB T2J 7A6
artists@nowhereradio.com
www.nowhereradio.com
Here to help promote independent musicians around the world using new technologies, and bring new music to the barren ears of people from all walks of life!

PureOriginal.com
community@pureoriginal.com
www.pureoriginal.com
A place to share your music and creative ideas.

Puretracks
www.puretracks.com
Songs must be delivered through a Digital Music Distributor such as www.cdbaby.com or www.theorchard.com

zunior.com
283 Danforth Ave. #358, Toronto, ON M4K 1N2
Dave Ullrich dave@zunior.com
www.zunior.com
Artists pay only a 15% administrative fee to use zunior.com. The majority of this goes towards the merchant account, hosting, and bandwidth fees.

South America

Opson-Web
c/ 36 Nª 828, Mercedes, Buenos Aires, Argentina
PH: 02324427265
Hernan Botta hernanbotta@speedy.com.ar
www.opson-web.com.ar
A site based in Argentina where you can upload your music and video files for free!

Search MP3
Av. Das America, 700 Bloco 03 Sala 112,
Rio de Janeiro, Brazil 22640-100
PH: 55-21-2132-7757
www.searchmpthree.com
Register to create your own homepage containing your songs.

Europe

Finland

Mikseri
Arto Aaltonen arto.aaltonen@mikseri.net
www.mikseri.net
Downloads covering all genres.

France

Apple iTunes France
www.apple.com/fr/itunes
Songs must be delivered through a Digital Music Distributor such as www.cdbaby.com or www.theorchard.com

Music75
webmaster@music75.com
www.music75.com
An online site designed to help you create, profile and promote original songs.

Germany

Apple iTunes Germany
www.apple.com/de/itunes
Songs must be delivered through a Digital Music Distributor such as www.cdbaby.com or www.theorchard.com

besonic.com
Hochstadenstr. 15, 50674 Koln, Germany
PH: 49-221-53097-51 FX: 49-221-53097-70
www.besonic.com
Music anytime, anywhere, tailored to the individual likes of users.

ic-musicmedia.com
Stephansplatz 3a, 30171 Hannover, Germany
www.ic-musicmedia.com
We want to give artists worldwide an opportunity to present their music online.

phonector Europe
Gleimstr.60, D-10437 Berlin, Germany
contact@phonector.com
www.phonector.com
We can help you sell your music via download distribution and burned audio CD distribution.

Pooltrax
www.pooltrax.de
Mp3 kostenlos downloaden, Charts, News, Software für Musik & Mp3, uvm. bei POOLTRAX.

Songs Wanted
Willhelm-Dull-Str. 9, 80638, Munich, Germany
PH: 089-157-32-50 FX: 089-157-50-36
ellie@songswanted.com
www.songswanted.com
Helping artists get recognition.

web62.com
www.web62.com
Internet Television. Music coverage.

Weedis
Reinekestr 26 A, 81545 Munich, Germany
PH: 0049-89-452-477-00
Oezlem Guenay admin@weedis.com
www.weedis.com
A progressive platform enabling superdistribution for music and video. The buyer can legally resell and gets a share of up to 35% of the price set by the artist. A highly effective site to use multiple marketing including Peer 2 Peer systems. Very user friendly since the shop is integrated in the file.

Norway

beAudible.com
Vinjesgt 3, 5007 Bergen, Norway
PH: +47-971-49-153
Sigmund Elias Holm beaudible@beaudible.com
www.beaudible.com
We join forces with artists to increase their exposure and availability using Weed technology.

Russia

RealMusic
info@realmusic.ru
realmusic.ru
Covers all genres of music.

Spain

MUSICDLD.COM
Pl. Julio Gonzalez 8, bajos, Barcelona 08005, Spain
PH: +34-932240117 FX: +34-932240118
contacto@musicdld.com
www.musicdld.com
A promotion & digital distribution music portal.

Sweden

MP3Lizard.com
mp3lizard.com
Promote your band for free!

Musicbrigade
Jakob Svanholm
jakob.svanholm@musicbrigade.com
www.musicbrigade.com
We have established ourselves as Europe's leading provider of digital music videos. For a small fee we will take your video, digitize it to our high quality specifications and put it on our site.

Switzerland

MadeinMusic.com
9, rue de Berne, 1201 Geneva, Switzerland
PH: ++41-22-90-690-90 FX: ++41-22-90-690-99
helpmusicians@MadeinMusic.com
www.madeinmusic.com
Boosts the launch of new labels and musicians by remunerating its subscribers for the essential work that they carry out for the distribution of your music!

sounds4all.com
c/o Andreas Stricker, Buemplizstrasse 187, 3018 Bern, Switzerland
PH: 41-079-379-7046
info@sounds4all.com
www.sounds4all.com
You set the prices and receive about 90% of each sale.

United Kingdom

Apple iTunes UK
www.apple.com/uk/itunes
Songs must be delivered through a Digital Music Distributor such as www.cdbaby.com or www.theorchard.com

Arkade
Fetcham Park House, Lower Road, Fetcham, Surrey, KT22 9HD UK
PH: 0118-926-1440
Kevin Harrington
kevin.harrington@bluehorizonmanagement.com
www.arkade.com
Your Music. Your Income. Your Label. Secure sales of MP3s, CDs and merchandise for bands and artists.

Audigist
support@audigist.com
www.audigist.com
Take your music to a wider audience.

Brightskies
PO Box 1683, Ilford, Essex, IG1 4WF UK
PH: +44 (0)20-8518-0428
admin@brightskies.com
www.brightskies.com
We believe we've created a unique, easy to use, fair and completely legal environment from which to sell and discover new music.

contactmusic.com
Gate House, Iron Row, Burley in Wharfdale,
Ilkley, LS29 7DB UK
PH: 44-0-1943-865111 FX: 44-0-1943-865222
hello@contactmusic.com
www.contactmusic.com
If you get a deal through our site, you'll get 100% of the royalties.

CPU Records
c/o Loop Studios, Space 28, North Lotts,
Dublin 1, Ireland
PH: 00353-87-785-8572
Eddie Sheridan info@cpu.ie
www.cpu.ie
Dedicated to unsigned bands around the globe. Has Ireland's first download MP3 chart. Hundreds of artists have made their music available free of charge.

Cube-music
Albany Boathouse, Lower Ham Rd.
Kingston-upon-Thames, KT2 5BB UK
PH: 020-85471543 FX: 020-85471544
info@cube-music.com
www.cube-music.com
Promote your video or audio tracks to UK audiences.

easyMusic.com
www.easyMusic.com
Our "Copyleft" section features music from unsigned artists, including music which can be downloaded for free.

Eat This Music!
PO Box 8479, Prestwick,
Ayrshire, Scotland KA9 2YR
FX: 01292-677918
admin@eatthismusic.com
www.eatthismusic.com
Unsigned bands can get their info out to venues, management companies, promoters etc.

eircom.net Music Club
www.eircom.net/music
Irish download site. Songs must be delivered through a Digital Music Distributor (www.theorchard.com).

IntoMusic
PO Box 41071, London, SW2 1WT UK
PH: 0208-671-6608
info@intomusic.co.uk
www.intomusic.co.uk
Download music featuring independent musicians.

Karma Download
3 Stucley Place, Camden, London, NW1 8NS UK
info@karmadownload.com
www.karmadownload.com
Downloads of the latest talent coming out of their underground scene.

Launch Music on Yahoo UK
uk.launch.yahoo.com
Songs must be delivered through a Digital Music Distributor (www.theorchard.com).

Letstalkmusic.com
Post House, Fitzalan Rd. Arundel,
West Sussex, BN18 9JY UK
PH: 01273-424413
www.letstalkmusic.com
Upload your music for review, enter the showcase CD and more.

Mean Fiddler Music
www.meanfiddler.com
Songs must be delivered through a Digital Music Distributor (www.theorchard.com).

MetroTunes Music Store
www.metrotunes.co.uk
Songs must be delivered through a Digital Music Distributor (www.theorchard.com).

MP3Songs
www.mp3songs.org.uk
Help for unsigned artists.

MTV UK
www.mtv.co.uk
Songs must be delivered through a Digital Music Distributor (www.theorchard.com).

MyCokeMusic
mycokemusic.com
Songs must be delivered through a Digital Music Distributor (www.theorchard.com).

Napster.co.uk
artistrelations@napster.com
www.napster.co.uk
Offers tracks by hundreds of independent and unsigned artists.

Packard Bell Music Station
www.packardbell.co.uk/services/music
Songs must be delivered through a Digital Music Distributor (www.theorchard.com).

peoplesound.com
20 Orange St., London, WC2H 7NN UK
PH: 44-0-207-766-4000 FX: 44-0-207-766-4001
www.peoplesound.com
Get your music heard. by millions of visitors.

poptones.co.uk
dustin@poptones.co.uk
www.poptones.co.uk
New label with streaming webcast.

The Song Site
PO Box 22949, London, N10 3ZH UK
PH: 44-020-8444-0987
simon@thesongsite.com
www.thesongsite.com
Something for everyone, be you artist or label.

Songstuff UK
songs@songstuff.com
www.songstuff.co.uk
Post your songs for review, review other's songs, discuss technical, creative and music business issues, chat in our forum.

SONY Connect Europe
www.connect-europe.com
Songs must be delivered through a Digital Music Distributor such as www.cdbaby.com or www.theorchard.com

Stayaround.com
25 Barnes Wallis Rd. Segensworth East,
Fareham, PO15 5TT UK
PH: +44 (0)1489 889821 FX: +44 (0)1489 889887
info@stayaround.com
stayaround.com
The new word in music. We offer the hottest, freshest and most upfront music around, and let you decide how to listen.

Tesco.com Downloads Store
www.tescodownloads.com
Songs must be delivered through a Digital Music Distributor (www.theorchard.com).

This is Talent
enquiries@thisistalent.co.uk
thisistalent.co.uk
Helping Indie artists get exposure.

Tiscali Music
www.tiscali.co.uk/music
Songs must be delivered through a Digital Music Distributor (www.theorchard.com).

TuneTribe.com
50-52 Paul St., London, EC2A 4LB UK
PH: 020-7613-8200
unsignedartists@tunetribe.com
www.tunetribe.com
You can send us your music on CD along with all the relevant data and we will prepare it for inclusion on the site...for free! You set the price per download.

Vitaminic
info@vitaminic.co.uk
www.vitaminic.co.uk
Promotion and distribution of your digital music.

Wanadoo Music
www.wanadoo.co.uk/music
Songs must be delivered through a Digital Music Distributor (www.theorchard.com).

Australia

Asylum TV
Peter Deske pd54@optusnet.com.au
www.asylumtv.com
TV program focusing on independent artists. Overseas submissions welcome.

ChaosMusic
Locked Bag 12, 45 Collins St., E.
Melbourne, VIC 3000 Australia
PH: 61-3-9654-1144 FX: 61-3-9654-2333
info@chaosmusic.com
www.chaosmusic.com
Indie artists WANTED!!! Sell your CDs/sound files.

eChoonz.net
PO Box 2495, Fitzroy Business Ctr.
Melbourne, VIC 3065 Australia
administration@echoonz.net
www.echoonz.net
We accept tracks from any style of music.

HMV Australia
www.hmv.com.au
Songs must be delivered through a Digital Music Distributor (www.theorchard.com).

MP3Machine.com
PO Box 366, Albion, QLD 4010 Australia
PH: 877-292-1133 FX: 61-7-3862-4832
www.mp3machine.com
Online sales of Indie music.

OrangesAndLime
PO Box 44, Dallas, VIC 3047 Australia
Marquez music@orangesandlime.net
music.orangesandlime.net
We are offering to sign your music into the Weed Distribution System and to convert your songs to weed files for FREE so that you can start making money from your music using the power of the Internet!

sanity.com.au
www.sanity.com.au
Songs must be delivered through a Digital Music Distributor (www.theorchard.com).

Soundbuzz
support@soundbuzz.com
www.Soundbuzz.com
A digital music service provider and the only provider with a regional focus on the Asia-Pacific markets.

Asia

listen.co.jp
www.listen.co.jp
Specializes in Indie/mainstream music.

MCJP
3-19-23 Minamiazabu, Minato-ku,
Tokyo 106-0047, Japan
PH: 81-3-5447-1154 FX: 81-3-5449-0881
info@musiccopyright.jp
www.MusicCopyright.jp
A gateway to the Japanese music market.

Orientaltunes.com
www.orientaltunes.com
Follows the modern trends in Oriental music.

PlanetMG
2 International Business Park, #05-10, Tower 1,
The Strategy, Singapore 609930
FX: 65-6329-8520
admin@planetmg.com
www.planetmg.com
Downloadable music from mainstream & Indie artists.

Blues

op blues music shop
promos@on-linepromo.com
www.opblues.com
If you are an independent artist or label and would like to sell your music please contact us.

Christian

Acaza.Com
Attn: Content Submission,
2220 Green Trails Dr. Antioch, TN 37013
Rick Welke rick@acaza.com
www.acaza.com
Providing upbeat, positive music. Accepts submissions.

CCMPlanet
webmaster@ccmp3s.com
www.ccmp3s.com
Tons of legal Christian MP3 files!

ChristianMp3.com
info@christianmusicentertainmentgroup.com
www.christianmp3.com
We are dedicated to offering Christian Music in modern formats including MP3, CDs and more.

ChristianWeed.com
PO Box 18895, Panama City Beach, FL 32417
FX: 707-549-4436
James Moore info@christianweed.com
christianweed.com
E-mail us (preferably with a link to samples of your material). If we feel your music is marketable, we'll reply with the paperwork you'll need to fill out and fax back to us.

Gospel Swap
info@gospelswap.com
gospelswap.gazellevillage.com
Let us help you to promote and sell your original Gospel music!

Jamsline.com
jamsline@jamsline.com
www.jamsline.com
Get your singles to radio and other industry entities.

op gospel music shop
promos@on-linepromo.com
www.opgospel.com
If you are an independent artist or label and would like to sell your music please contact us.

Triplestrandmp3.com
Dixie Vornbrock ddsj84@yahoo.com
www.triplestrandmp3.com
Supporting the works of emerging & unsigned Christian Music Artists.

Classical

ChoralNet
c/o James Feiszli 4230 Mary Dr.
Rapid City, SD 57702
www.choralnet.org
Extensive resources for Choral artists.

Classic Cat
webmaster@classiccat.net
www.classiccat.net
A directory with links to over 2000 free to download Classical performances on the internet, sorted by composer and work.

The Classical Music Archives
200 Sheridan Ave. #403, Palo Alto, CA 94306
PH: 650-330-8050
www.classicalarchives.com
Submit your music to get exposure.

Classical.com
PO Box 31687, 18 Denbigh Rd.
London, W11 2UX UK
PH: +44-20-8816-8848
info@classical.com
www.classical.com
Online listening, downloads, custom CDs and more.

eClassical.com
Skolgatan 37, SE 413 02 Gothenburg, Sweden
info@eclassical.com
www.eclassical.com
A completely virtual record label.

NetNewMusic
netnewmusic.net
A portal for the world of NON-Pop/Extreme Indie/Avant-whatever music.

OnClassical
Via Ca'Petofi 13 - (36022) Cassola, Vicenza, Italy
PH: +39-0424-533137 FX: +39-0424-533137
Alessandro Simonetto info@onclassical.com
www.OnClassical.com
We are an independent record label. We are starting to sell and distribute high quality Classical music in MP3 or OGG formats. Prices are low, and our featured artists keep 50% of all earnings. We are associated with kunstderfuge.com, the greatest resource of free MIDI files on the net.

op classical music shop
promos@on-linepromo.com
www.opclassical.com
If you are an independent artist or label and would like to sell your music please contact us.

Society of Composers *Composerver*
Ohio State U. School of Music, 1866 College Rd.
Columbus, OH 43210
wells.7@osu.edu
composerver.sss.arts.ohio-state.edu
Submit excerpts, complete pieces and more.

Country

Banjo Newsletter MP3 Soundfiles
bnl@infionline.net
www.banjonews.com
Downloadable MP3 Sound Files of tabs that have appeared in Banjo Newsletter.

CountryWesternBands.com - Country Artist Showcase
PO Box 677, Cave Creek, AZ 85327
PH: 480-595-5057
Cindy info@countrywesternbands.com
www.countrywesternbands.com
The #1 Country Western indie artist showcase. We'll showcase your band to thousands of country music fans.

Mandolin Cafe
www.mandolincafe.com/mp3
www.mandolincafe.com
Introduces new mandolin players.

op country music shop
promos@on-linepromo.com
www.opcountry.com
If you are an independent artist or label and would like to sell your music please contact us.

Dance

7161.com
admin@dancetech.com
www.7161.com
We are a non profit site run by musicians. We have free web space for artists to add their music for streaming. We also offer free homepage creation and other free tools.

Beatport
PH: 800-808-4240
Eloy Lopez eloy@beatport.com
www.beatport.com
Designed to service the evolution of the Digital music culture, redefining how DJs and enthusiasts acquire their music.

BLEEP
info@bleep.com
www.bleep.com
Warp Records selection of downloadable Electronica.

ClubFreestyle.com
www.clubfreestyle.com
Worlds largest Freestyle music community.

Digital Beat Music
Etappitie 3 a 202 95400, Finland
PH: +358-405094034
Kimmo Rinta-Pollari digitalbeat@lycos.com
www.digitalbeatmusic.com
Independent Electronica label and MP3 hosting service for artists.

DJ SETS
6 Iliados Str. PC 54641, Thessaloniki, Greece
PH: +302310-843124
www.djsets.gr
A community where DJs can post their music files and have people rate them.

EDM Digital
8502 Manassas Rd. Tampa, FL 33635
PH: 813-810-0202 FX: 954-337-3338
info@edmdigital.com
www.edmdigital.com
Always looking for new independent labels and artists to submit material for consideration. Please review our How to Submit page located online.

Electromancer *UK*
www.electromancer.com
We are a community of unsigned Electronic musicians and a resource where they can make their music available to visitors and other musicians.

headstrong Dance music
headstrong-hq@zen.co.uk
www.headstrong-hq.com
Put your demos here to get exposure.

InternetDJ.com
www.internetdj.com
Hosts and plays MP3s from Independent musicians.

Magazine X
PO Box 56, Rosepine, LA 70659
PH: 877-571-2357 FX: 877-571-2357
Jazon Dion Fletcher magazinex@xmuzik.com
www.magazinex.org
Free 100 MB MP3 account for Electronic artists seeking to help build an American Electronic network.

MP3ClubTunes.com
sales@MP3ClubTunes.com
www.MP3ClubTunes.com
The best Dance music from around the world. From this site you can download digital recordings or purchase Vinyl and CDs from the Artists.

op dance music shop
promos@on-linepromo.com
www.opdance.com
If you are an independent artist or label and would like to sell your music please contact us.

op electronic music shop
promos@on-linepromo.com
www.opelectronic.com
If you are an independent artist or label and would like to sell your music please contact us.

op trance music shop
promos@on-linepromo.com
www.optrance.com
If you are an independent artist or label and would like to sell your music please contact us.

Pitch Adjust
c/o Patrik Sjeren, Tavastgatan 18, SE-118 24 Stockholm, Sweden
PH: +46-(0) 8-669 6875 FX: +46-(0) 8-669 6875
www.pitchadjust.com
Labels can find new talents, new talents can find a label and promoters can post info.

Play it tonight
#23 - 1917 W. 4th Ave. Vancouver, BC V6J 1M7
FX: 208-246-4676
info@playittonight.com
www.playittonight.com
Downloadable Dance music.

SMART-MUSIC.NET
Vogelsangstr. 30a, 70197 Stuttgart, Germany
PH: +49 (0)179-243-11-40
FX: 49 (0)1212-510-479-968
Bernd Drescher info@smart-music.net
www.smart-music.net
We search the web for the finest free Dance music available. We only feature legal mp3s where the source can be easily identified and we only offer links to full-length, high quality files.

tribal mixes dot com
tribalmixes.com
Website for sharing live DJ mixes and live sets recorded in mp3 format. We love music and share all kinds of stuff including House, Breaks, Techno, Trance, Tribal House and many more.

Virgo Lounge
info@virgolounge.com
www.VirgoLounge.com
An online source for Dance music, industry networking and an event marketplace. Please send us your press release or info about your project or event.

WOMB
350 Lincoln Rd. #318, Miami Beach, FL 33139
PH: 305-673-9488 FX: 305-402-0839
digital@thewomb.com
www.thewomb.com
The first 24/7 worldwide radio & Internet television broadcaster of live mixes & performances. We have launched the first all-in-one download shop for the digital culture.

Xpressbeats
Devonshire House, 223 Upper Richmond Rd. London, SW15 6SQ UK
PH: +44 (0) 20-8780-0612
FX: +44 (0) 20-8789-8668
admin@xpressbeats.com
www.xpressbeats.com
When visitors purchase a download from us you can be sure that, the Artists DJ's, Producers, Songwriters and Independent Labels are being paid for their work.

Experimental

no type
4580, Ave. de Lorimier, Montreal, QC H2H 2B5
PH: 514-526-4096 FX: 514-526-4487
dt@electrocd.com
www.notype.com
New releases of Indie artists.

Parasme Records
42 Milton Rd., Cowes,
Isle Of Wight, PO31 7PX UK
PH: 01983-200416
Parasme ian@parasme.com
www.parasme.com
Ambient, Experimental and Electronic digital distribution record label.

tapegerm
1478 Stetson Cir. Salt Lake City, UT 84104
PH: 801-972-2441 FX: 801-972-2443
feedback@tapegerm.com
www.tapegerm.com
A new and vibrant center for music creativity.

Folk

Cantaria
www.chivalry.com/cantaria
A library of "bardic" Folk songs, mostly from Ireland, Scotland and England.

efolk Music
201B N. Greensboro St., Carrboro, NC 27510
PH: 919-968-4810
artists@efolkMusic.org
www.efolkmusic.org
Independent Folk MP3 and CD source.

Independent Musicians Marketplace
PO Box 497, Mansfield, PA 16933
Debbie Rubin imm@secondfret.com
www.secondfret.com
Independent musicians marketplace.

op folk music shop
promos@on-linepromo.com
www.opfolk.com
If you are an independent artist or label and would like to sell your music please contact us.

GLBT

Dyke TV
PO Box 170-163, Brooklyn, NY 11217
PH: 718-230-4770
Elizabeth Maynard staff@dyketv.org
www.dyketv.org
Lesbian cable access show that airs nation-wide. We do occasionally solicit or welcome music submissions.

Goth

SlagHuis MultiMedia
PO Box 190792, Miami Beach, FL 33119-0792
PH: 305-434-8651 FX: 305-531-5609
Sam Bradford solutions@slaghuismultimedia.com
www.slaghuismultimedia.com
Gothic, Darkwave and Industrial. Get Heard, Get Seen... Online. Today.

Hip Hop

2Man Productions
c-tone@2manproductions.com
www.2manproductions.com
We put your tracks, pictures, info and videos on here for you. You make money when people download your music.

freshsites.com
dolores@freshsites.com
freshsites.com
Promoting independent, Underground Hip Hop culture.

Hip Hop Havoc *Unsigned Heat*
hiphophavoc@gmail.com
www.hiphophavoc.com
Sells mix-tapes of Indie Hip Hop artists. Visit our site for details on how to submit your music for our "Unsigned Heat" section.

Hip Hop Palace.com
PO Box 158, Bowling Green Stn.
New York, NY 10274
hiphoppalaceceo@yahoo.com
www.hiphoppalace.com
Upload your music and be on our radio show.

op hip hop music shop
promos@on-linepromo.com
www.op-hiphop.com
If you are an independent artist or label and would like to sell your music please contact us.

Rapworld
info@rapworld.info
www.rapworld.com
Complete online Hip Hope site/community.

Real-HipHop.com
info2@real-hiphop.com
www.real-hiphop.com
Real MC's, DJ's, fans, music, videos and more.

StreetSoundz.Net
Jeff Farthing advertise@streetsoundz.net
www.streetsoundz.net
A place where listeners can discover and download new and unheard Rap and Hip Hop.

UnderworldHipHop.com
PH: 416-333-2446
Justin Hardy admin@underworldhiphop.com
www.underworldhiphop.com
A free MP3 uploading service for Hip Hop artists. We also do reviews.

Unlimitedtracks.com
922 Hwy. 81 E. Box 315, McDonough, GA 30252
PH: 678-432-1229
Lincoln Parks lparks@Unlimitedtracks.com
www.unlimitedtracks.com
An online store for Urban musicians. Sell your tracks online for .99 cents per track. You can also sell your CD from our site.

Ya Heard
yaheard.bet.com
Unsigned artists upload your original songs and create your own web page.

Jam Band

bt.etree.org / BitTorrent
bt.e@etree.org
bt.etree.org
Provided by the etree.org community for sharing the live concert recordings of trade friendly artists. Please tell your friends and family about new bands that catch your ear, and support these artists by going to see them live and buying their CDs!

etree.org
wiki.etree.org
An online community that uses an independent network of file (FTP) servers that host and distribute Shorten (SHN) audio files.

jambase.com
1 Zoe St., San Francisco, CA 94107
PH: 415-543-7000 FX: 415-543-7775
rhapsody@jambase.com
rhapsody.jambase.com
New, interactive digital music service. Promotes independent artists and bands from around the world.

LIVEDOWNLOADS
www.livedownloads.com
Offering an opportunity to listen to shows from a current tour very soon after they've happened, mastered directly from the soundboard. With some bands, full studio albums are offered as well. Contact us about adding your music.

nugs.net
web1.nugs.net
Artists can harness the demand for their live performances and studio recordings.

Jazz

Any Swing Goes
PO Box 721675, San Diego, CA 92172-1675
PH: 858-484-7716 FX: 801-382-6409
doug@anyswinggoes.com
www.anyswinggoes.com
Focus on the revival of big band and swing music.

Cjazz
8554 122nd Ave. NE #120, Kirkland, WA 98022
PH: 425-827-5441 FX: 425-827-1170
Michele Abrams michele@cjazz.com
www.cjazz.com
Show the world who you are and what you can do.

Jazztronic
contact@jazztronic.com
Jazztronic.com
Our main interest is Electronic Jazz music. We think that Jazz spirit mixed to the new Electronic ways to play music is going to become a great thing.

op jazz music shop
promos@on-linepromo.com
www.opjazz.com
If you are an independent artist or label and would like to sell your music please contact us.

ozzyjazz.com *Australia*
bob@ozzyjazz.com
www.ozzyjazz.com.
Features live Jazz recorded around the world.

Latin

Emepe3.com
407 Lincoln Rd. #12E, Miami Beach, FL 33139
usa@emepe3.com
www.emepe3.com
Sell your music here for free.

FaroLatino.com
Administración, Conesa 960 dpto 1,
Ciudad de Buenos Aires, BA 1426, Argentina
PH: +5411-4551-7527
administracion@farolatino.com
tienda.farolatino.com
"La Cocina del Arte" is a virtual space dedicated to promoting new bands. It offers an online space to bands to promote their products.

Latin Cool Now
David Wasserman latincool2@aol.com
www.latincoolnow.com
Sell your Indie music here.

op latin music shop
promos@on-linepromo.com
www.oplatin.com
If you are an independent artist or label and would like to sell your music please contact us.

Metal

BeatScout
support@beatscout.com
www.beatscout.com
Make money and build an instant fan base.

Ear Assault
Jason admin@earassault.com
www.earassault.com
A place for Metal bands to upload MP3s and gain exposure.

EarAche.com
43 W. 38th St. 2nd Fl. New York, NY 10018
PH: 212-840-9090 FX: 212-840-4033
usamail@earache.com
www.earache.com
Metal MP3s and videos.

The Gauntlet
174 W Foothill Blvd. #235, Monrovia, CA 91016
PH: 310-909-8514 FX: 310-492-5172
moshpit@thegauntlet.com
www.thegauntlet.com
Metal Indie musicians, bi-weekly mailing list, reviews, videos and more.

metalvideo.com
metalvideo@hotmail.com
www.metalvideo.com
Metal videos, MP3s and more.

op metal music shop
promos@on-linepromo.com
www.opmetal.com
If you are an independent artist or label and would like to sell your music please contact us.

Reality Check TV
PH: 415-831-2825
www.realitychecktv.com
Connect to the Metal underground world. We accept submissions!

Vicious Enterprises
Death Priest Admin@ViciousEnterprises.net
www.viciousenterprises.net
Free MP3 downloads from undiscovered talent. You submit we post.

New Age

op new age music shop
promos@on-linepromo.com
www.opnewagemusic.com
If you are an independent artist or label and would like to sell your music please contact us.

Punk

altsounds.com
Chris Maguire chris@altsounds.com
www.altsounds.com
Online community for Alternative music artists to promote their band. Free artist profiles allow you to host MP3s, WMA's or OGG files, upload photos, news, gigs plus much more.

BlankTV
361 Vine St., Glendale, CA 91204
PH: 818-242-3107
Eddie Sunset sunset@blanktv.com
www.BlankTV.com
Free exposure for your videos to a worldwide audience of Indie music lovers.

Doogz.net
Doug doogz@doogz.net
www.doogz.net
Discover and listen to the best in Underground artists.

Download Punk
PH: 818-997-0444 x108
Brian B. content@downloadpunk.com
www.DownloadPunk.com
We do accept submissions directly from unsigned artists, but we do request that they don't send demos, only pressed CDs.

Enough MP3s
PO Box 12 07 50, 68058 Mannheim, Germany
david@enoughfanzine.com
info@enoughfanzine.com
www.enoughfanzine.com
Feel free to upload your band's/label's MP3 files.

Epitaph
2798 Sunset Blvd. Los Angeles, CA 90026
PH: 213-413-7353
publicity@epitaph.com
www.epitaph.com
Post your link. Accepts demos. Keep it Punk!

Kick TV
info@kicktv.org
www.kicktv.org
Streaming music television. Do you play in an Indie/Punk/HC/Metal/Grindcore band and got a video clip? We're the first Italian web TV totally dedicated to Rock music.

punkrockvideos.com
PO Box 143522, Austin, TX 78714-3522
info@punkrockvideos.com
www.punkrockvideos.com
Live video of Punk bands for sale.

Supersphere
jason@supersphere.com
www.supersphere.com
Bringing independently produced media to our contemporaries and peers.

Reggae

Surforeggae
contato@surforeggae.com.br
www.surforeggae.com.br
Reggae MP3s, news, events and more.

Soul / R&B

soulgalore.com
peter@soulgalore.com
www.soulgalore.com
I love promos! Just send me an email and I will send you my address ASAP!

Women In Music

Rawk Girl
Heather Greene rawkgirlbands@yahoo.com
www.rawkgirl.com
A promo service for female musicians to receive profiles and MP3 hosting.

Weedgrrl
PO Box 16940, Sugar Land, TX 77496-6940
info@weedgrrl.com
www.weedgrrl.com
You MUST be a member of GoGirlsMusic.com Elite member roster. More info on GoGirls Elite is at www.gogirlselite.com

World

Calabash Music
211 Pleasant St., Arlington, MA 02476
PH: 781-777-1109 FX: 617-507-7769
info@calabashmusic.com
www.calabashmusic.com
A global marketplace for independent World music.

op world music shop
promos@on-linepromo.com
www.opworldmusic.com
If you are an independent artist or label and would like to sell your music please contact us.

Ouviste.com Music Portal
55 Strathaven Dr #314, Mississauga, ON L5R 4G9
PH: 905-890-1122
Eddy Costa epcosta@sympatico.ca
www.ouviste.com
Your source for Portuguese music! A site for bands and artists, with MP3s, charts, spotlight, news, articles, interviews and a radio show.

SECTION SIX: HELPFUL RESOURCES FOR MUSICIANS AND SONGWRITERS

"If you can achieve one successful thing a day to help your music career then you are on the right track. Pick one thing, just one and do it today!" - **Chris Standring, Founder of A&R Online**

Resources for a Variety of Genres

1340 Media
PO Box 1347, Fairmont, WV 26555-1347
PH: 304-363-5224
Mark Fisher mark1340@verizon.net
www.1340media.com
Provides a low cost bio and press release writing services for independent artists/bands. This address is for independent artists and small PR companies ONLY. We have limited slots available each month for independent artists but all submissions are listened to and considered as equal with label submissions.

14 North Art House
13295 Beckford Ln. Richmond, VA 23238
PH: 804-677-3885
Adam Sledd fourteen_north@yahoo.com
14North.com
A website that helps musicians, artists, writers, and filmmakers promote and sell their work.

335 Design
PO Box 29742, Charlotte, NC 28229
PH: 704-560-2379
contact@335.com
www.335.com
Not selling many CDs through your web site? Let us help! We provide affordable, superior web site design for musicians and music related businesses.

Absolute Indie
PO Box 97, New York, NY 10156
PH: 631-827-3000 FX: 419-831-3032
Andrew Herzman andy@qopelrecords.com
www.absoluteindie.com
A TV show that features indie artists from all over the world. Currently streams on the internet and airs on cable and TV stations in USA, Germany and Australia.

ArtistPromo Hotel Sponsorship
PO Box 685, Shutesbury, MA 01072
PH: 413-259-1227 Mailbox #1
Jaime Campbell Morton artspromo@artspromo.org
www.artspromo.org/hotelsponsor
The hotel donates the room in trade for a stage mention (a thank you - free advertising, essentially) and I get a $35 fee for setting it up ($50 cdn). There is currently a 2-room minimum unless we are taking care of your entire tour.

Artistopia
PO Box 3538, Alexandria, VA 22302
FX: 703-566-7500
Donna Liguria info@artistopia.com
www.artistopia.com
Professional presentation of the music artist to the music industry, with comprehensive profile and press kit building tools, artist development, musician community, and services.

Band Radio Indie News
PO Box 2584, Rocklin, CA 95677
www.bandradio.com/news/indie/submissions
Craft a professional press release for your New CD release, tour etc. and we'll post it.

Band Weblogs
submit@bandweblogs.com
www.bandweblogs.com
This directory gives musicians and creative music writers an opportunity to share opinions, views, daily lives, reviews (and anything else they may write in their blogs) and most importantly, their music, with the world of blog readers!

BandAttack
PH: 315-727-9918
Tom Rock@Bandattack.com
www.bandattack.com
Features hundreds of the best resources available to independent bands and artists from all over the web. Industry news, contests, featured bands, massive directory, articles and more!

Bandit A&R Newsletter
PO Box 22, Newport, PO30 1LZ UK
PH: 44-1983-524110
bandit@banditnewsletter.com
www.banditnewsletter.com
Helping ambitious bands target their demos to labels, publishers etc.

Bandlink CD Intelligence
88 10th Ave. 6th Fl. W., New York, NY 10011
PH: 212-604-9433 FX: 212-604-9964
support@bandlink.com
www.bandlink.com
Internet-powered music CD service.

bandlink.net
webmaster@bandlink.net
www.bandlink.net
Each artist gets their own page with all their info.

bands 411
www.bands411.com
Tools to promote your band on the Internet.

Bands Thriving On Fans
PH: 903-223-7205
ndmuse@gmail.com
bandsthrivingonfans.net
Provides free promotion and support for unsigned bands.

BandsBackStage
205 N. China Lk. Blvd. #138, Ridgecrest, CA 93555
PH: 413-647-3301 FX: 413-647-3301
bandsbackstage@bandsbackstage.com
bandsbackstage.com
Many resources to promote your music.

bandsforlabels.com
PH: 562-627-9251
info@bandsforlabels.com
www.bandsforlabels.com
A free band-label matchmaking site.

Bandwidth Discussion Group
launch.groups.yahoo.com/group/bandwidth
Discussion of web design as it relates to bands, labels, and other music related sites. Everything from adding audio and video; format types, linking strategies, site promotion, search engine placement.

The BardsCrier.com
PO Box 4067, Austin, TX 78765
www.bardscrier.com
A free guerrilla music marketing ezine.

The Buzz Factor
PO Box 43058, St. Louis, MO 63143
PH: 314-963-5296
Bob Baker bob@thebuzzfactor.com
www.thebuzzfactor.com
Low-cost marketing ideas for artists.

CCNow
service@ccnow.com
www.ccnow.com
A low-risk way for small businesses to sell their product online.

CDBaby.net
www.cdbaby.net
Tips on promoting your music, touring the college market, selling more CDs, etc.

cdmusicpage.com
www.cdmusicpage.com
Promoting Independent music with text, images and audio.

Compo-10
compo10.com
Every week we feature 10 artists. They rank each other and the ones who have been ranked best are featured on our main page.

Indieguitarists.com
PO Box 730 Stn. C Toronto, ON M6J 3S1
Monica Yonge info@indieguitarists.com
www.indieguitarists.com
Unsigned bassists & guitarists add your web site for free to the database. Site also contains spotlights, interviews, articles and news.

DigiPie
22647 Ventura Blvd. #145
Woodland Hills, CA 91364
PH: 800-582-0932
Max Davis artists@digipie.com
digipie.com
Offers creators/artists powerful tools to profit from their digital creations from A-Z built into our model and software.

Electric Head
PO Box 7, Howell, NJ 07731
PH: 732-901-8693 FX: 732-364-9598
Allen M. Gottfried electricheadonline@yahoo.com
www.electricheadonline.com
Independent music video, commercial and live concert DVD production. Our services are available to local, regional and national acts. Ask us about other areas served, either at our facilities or on location.

eMusicBlast.com
501 Astor Ct. Franklin Park, NJ 08823
PH: 609-406-0774
Rick Moore rmoore@emusicblast.com
www.emusicblast.com
An online community that brings artists, the industry and fans together.

How to Promote Your Music Successfully on the Internet

Learn the promotion methods one musician uses to bring in over $5000 a month from the Internet!

A message from the Author: The Internet is an *incredible* promotional tool for independent musicians. You can get radio play, grow a fan base, create a distribution channel, manufacture and sell CDs all online. You can use the Internet to create an *amazing* amount of exposure for your music. Wouldn't it be great if literally *thousands* of people heard your music every day? What if you could use your web site to sell 100, 200 or more CDs every month? Guess what? It doesn't take a brain surgeon to make it happen, but it does take a lot of hard work – and you need to *know* what you're doing.

Therein lies the problem. Most musicians just have no idea where to start when it comes to online promotion and distribution. Some get as far as putting up a web site, but stop there. They aren't sure what the next step should be. That's where I can help.

Who am I? I am an independent musician just like you, with one difference: In the last year, I've used the Internet to generate **over $60,000 in income**. Hard to believe, isn't it? But it's true. Today I'm doing the "music business" full-time from my home in Springfield, Oregon. I now invest my time working on my music rather than spending 40-60 hours a week working for someone else. I'm truly an *independent* musician.

My intent with this book is to give you the information you need to begin promoting, selling, and distributing your own music successfully online. I'll give you *proven* ideas you can put to use *immediately*. It doesn't take a ton of money to get started either – that's another great benefit of living in this digital age. Simply put, I'll take you step by step through the same marketing strategies I've used over the last ten years (since 1995) to promote my own music on the Internet and run my music business on my own terms.

I know you're skeptical. I too am a skeptic by nature. Here are just a few of my many testimonials from readers....

"How to Promote Your Music Successfully on the Internet" is an incredible resource! It's not only the hundreds of techniques and tricks, it's how truly inspiring this book is. I sold more than 3000 copies of one of my CDs in 9 months as a result of reading this book." - Mihkel Raud

"I bought your book and I just want to say a big thank you for inspiring me so much. Before downloading the book we were doing well online, but it took a lot of trial and error which in turn took time. After reading your book, things are beginning to skyrocket for us. We have huge interest in our debut album which is released soon and have built up a sizeable fan base which is growing by the day. If I'd have paid 5 times what I did for the book, I would still be absolutely delighted with the results I've got from implementing your methods." - Liam

"I downloaded your book... initially I was skeptical (I am a fellow software type of guy & very analytical about things)... I just wanted to tell you that I LOVE it. Thanks a million - it's worth every penny." - Sheldon Schake

Want to know more? Visit my web site at www.promoteyourmusic.com . There you can read dozens of customer testimonials, get more detailed information, and even ask me questions if you like. LET ME TEACH YOU how to SUCCESSFULLY promote your music from my own life experience! Read all about it at....

www.promoteyourmusic.com

FanList.com
PH: 877-326-5478
info@fanlist.com
www.fanlist.com
We are able to promote your show to a targeted audience, in any city, at any time. We ask for 2 weeks notice before your show, but we've been known to do a rush job or two.

Garygoodstuff
4920 Hwy.9, PMB#326, Alpharetta, GA 30004
PH: 678-938-1670 FX: 678-366-6032
Garygoodstuff Gary@garygoodstuff.com
www.garygoodstuff.com
We are a full service music store that promotes independent music artists on our "Featured Bands", "News" and "Research" pages.

getmpk.com
265 Sunrise Hwy #322, Rockville Centre, NY 11570
PH: 877-570-7471 FX: 877-570-7471
Michael Paternostro info@getmpk.com
getmpk.com
Multimedia press kits on DVD, including all production services - performance/music video, on-camera interviews, audio, photos and DVD programming.

getsigned.com
707 Miamisburg-Centerville Rd. #103,
Dayton, OH 45459
Shawn Fields editor@getsigned.com
www.getsigned.com
EVERYTHING you ever wanted to know about the music biz.

Giglist.com
www.giglist.com
Add and update your gigs online!

GigMasters
PO Box 35, Chappaqua, NY 10514
PH: 800-925-5527
info@gigmasters.com
www.gigmasters.com
A complete entertainment booking agency.

GIGPAGE.com
PO Box 16940, Sugar Land, TX 77496-6940
PH: 281-541-0981
info@gigpage.com
www.gigpage.com
An easy, do-it-yourself calendar for your gigs!

Gold Guitars Music
Box 348, Omar, WV 25638
PH: 304-946-4808
Stephanie gold_guitars@yahoo.com
goldguitars.atspace.com
A music publishing and music supervision company that also offers consultation services. We can also critique your material and give you helpful information to help better your songs.

Goombah
contact@goombah.com
www.goombah.com
Our vision is to develop the world's most meaningful music community by linking like-minded music lovers and the music they play.

GRUUVE Music Search & Syndication
333 Cobalt Way #107, Sunnyvale, CA 94085
PH: 408-678-1000 or 647-722-4181
Daya Baran mail@gruuve.com
www.gruuve.com
We provide artists, DJs, podcasters and content providers a way to build their distribution. GRUUVE offers a free fan club system, track list, photo gallery and event listings.

HearUsPlay.com
webhost@hearusplay.com
www.hearusplay.com
Free utilities that can be utilized by bands that have a strong web presence.

HIP Video Promo
2 Draeger Pl., South River, NJ 08882
PH: 732-613-1779
Andy Gesner hipvideo@aol.com
www.hipvideopromo.com
With a comprehensive database of music video programmers and solid contacts throughout the music video industry, we can get your video to the outlets and viewers most likely to share and appreciate your own musical and visual aesthetic.

Hitsquad.com
PO Box 366, Albion, QLD 4010 Australia
PH: 61-7-3862-3346 FX: 61-7-3862-4832
www.hitsquad.com
Music resource and industry information.

Hostbaby
5925 NE 80th Ave. Portland, OR 97218-2891
PH: 888-448-6369
hostbaby@hostbaby.com
www.hostbaby.com
The best place to host your website/domain!

In Real Time
POB 15371, Boston, MA 02215
PH: 617-233-7426
James McCaffrey info@inrealtime.com
www.inrealtime.com
Provides practical knowledge, educational resources, and services to help independent musicians create and share DIY music and video art with the world through online digital distribution and promotion.

Indie Contact Newsletter
indiecontactnewsletter@rogers.com
www.bigmeteor.com/newsletter
Each month you will receive new listings to contact, as well as several well written articles from industry experts.

Indie Music Central
211 West Verdugo Ave. #103, Burbank, CA 91502
PH: 866-270-0404
Bruce Barr admin@indiemusiccentral.com
www.indiemusiccentral.com
An online meeting place and resource for the independent music community.

IndieBookingAgency.com
PH: 800-708-0907
www.indiebookingagency.com
We specialize in providing live entertainment for special events.

IndieGroup
staff@indiegroup.com
www.indiegroup.com
Full service website for Indie artists.

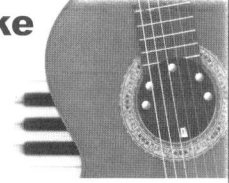

IndieWave
Rob cs@indiewave.net
www.indiewave.net
We offer FREE web hosting for Indie musicians.

Jagermusic.com
20 Cedar St. #203, New Rochelle, NY 10801
bands@jagermusic.com
www.jagermusic.com
Sponsors bands; supplies them with giveaway items.

JamBuddy
www.jambuddy.net
Created by musicians, for musicians, to simply make it easy to hook up, get down, and just JAM.

JMI Publications
PO Box 2405, Bridgeview, IL 60455
comments@jmipub.com
www.jmipub.com
Free music business articles.

photography **MARK PETERMAN**
www.markpeterman.com

480-540-8415

ALBUM PACKAGING

PUBLICITY

PERFORMANCE DOCUMENTATION

SPECIAL RATES FOR INDEPENDENT ARTISTS

BASED IN THE SOUTHWESTERN UNITED STATES, AVAILABLE NATIONALLY

I DON'T NEED A RECORD DEAL!

Daylle Deanna Schwartz,
best-selling author & indie music guru
offers tools to create a successful business around YOUR music in today's climate.

BOOKS:
- **NEW!** *I Don't Need a Record Deal! Your Survival Guide for the Indie Music Revolution*
- *Start & Run Your Own Record Label*
- *The Real Deal: How to Get Signed to a Record Label*

WORKSHOPS: Check Daylle's website for her schedule.

CONSULTING: Daylle does phone consulting for artists and record labels to help them create a strong foundation for success and guide them to reaching the next level.

FREE BI-MONTHLY NEWSLETTER: Subscribe to *Daylle's News & Resources,* which contains articles, helpful resources and interviews with industry pros.

Contact: daylle@daylle.com www.daylle.com

www.idontneedarecorddeal.com

Klipmart
244 5th Ave. 6th Fl. New York, NY 10001
PH: 212-213-9033 FX: 212-725-9090
seth@klipmart.com
www.klipmart.com
Integration and distribution of promotional audio and video content on the Internet.

LagunaTV.com
John Price admin@lagunatv.com
www.LagunaTV.com
We specialize in web video production.

The League of Rockers & The Rolling RocHaus
13318 31st Ave. NE, Seattle, WA 98125-4411
PH: 206-367-3584
James II therollingrochaus@hotmail.com
www.theleagueofrockers.com
Each is a licensed recording, publishing, motion picture & concert promotion company... all wrapped into one!

LiveJournal
www.livejournal.com
A simple-to-use (but extremely powerful and customizable) personal publishing ("blogging") tool, built on open source software.

LocalSound.com
www.localsound.com
Sign up and advertise your songs, check our promoters and more.

Loopwise.com
1404 Ocean #C, Seal Beach, CA 90740
PH: 800-687-2744 FX: 800-687-2744
support@loopwise.com
www.loopwise.com
A virtual internet collaboration system for serious recording artists.

Market Wire
5757 W. Century Blvd. 2nd Fl. Los Angeles, CA 90045
PH: 310-846-3600 FX: 310-846-3700
www.marketwire.com
We post news released by small to large businesses worldwide.

Marketing Your Music
www.marketingyourmusic.com
An array of tips on how to call attention to your music.

MarketingBands.com
PH: 330-807-5236
Dave Jackson cybercooler@hotmail.com
www.marketingbands.com
We promote and share technology so musicians and web site marketers can better spend their marketing dollars, and increase their exposure through cross marketing.

MatchGig.com
support@matchgig.com
www.matchgig.com
Internet presence and tools to expand your audience and visibility online.

Media Kinesis
postmaster@mediakinesis.com
mediakinesis.com
Free 50mb of space for your MP3's. You can even sell your music privately, create a radio station, post images, video, history, messages.

Media Web Source
Dennis Damp mediawebsource@yahoo.com
mediawebsource.com
Articles, songwriter resources, record company submission guidelines, press kit information and more!

The MODE
brew@theMode.com
www.themode.com
Find band mates and network with other musicians.

mojam
www.mojam.com
Promote your upcoming events, add info to your artist page and more.

Muse's Muse Artist Spotlights
jodi@musesmuse.com
www.musesmuse.com/artistspotlights.html
Contact me to have your music featured in this section.

Music Arsenal
12105 W. Center Rd. #280, Omaha, NE 68144
PH: 818-303-3161
Jimmy Winter jimmy@musicarsenal.com
www.musicarsenal.com
A new way for record labels to organize, track and utilize their business information. Our unique application replaces many separate utilities and combines them into one easy to use, time-saving package custom tailored to the music industry.

Music Biz Academy
PO Box 21831, Eugene, OR 97478
musicbiz@rainmusic.com
www.musicbizacademy.com
Helps musicians help themselves.

Music Biz Solutions
PO Box 230266, Boston, MA 02123-0266
PH: 978-887-8041
Peter Spellman success@mbsolutions.com
www.mbsolutions.com
Helps musicians start and grow successful music businesses.

Music Industry News Network *(mi2n)*
18-37 26th Ave. Astoria, NY 11102
PH: 718-932-8242
editor@mi2n.com
www.mi2n.com/submit_top.html
Submit press releases for free.

The Music Pages
www.themusicpages.com
If your band needs a gig or if your club needs a band please visit our Gig Board.

Music Thoughts Discussion Group
musicthoughts-subscribe@egroups.com
launch.groups.yahoo.com/group/musicthoughts
All areas of music are discussed from promotion to tips on playing live.

music2deal.com
1625 Larimer, Ste. 501, Denver, CO 80202
PH: 303-352-0001 FX: 303-352-0000
Sandy Krolick usa@music2deal.com
music2deal.com
An effective and time-efficient alternative to sending demo tapes and material around the world. All tools and services provided by us are designed to suit your needs and save you time and money. Check our website for the contact info for your country.

MusicBrainz
info@musicbrainz.org
www.musicbrainz.org
Collects this information about music and makes it available to the public so that music players can retrieve information about the music that is playing.

MusicCareers.net
guitarnoise_feedback@hotmail.com
www.MusicCareers.net
Articles to help you start or build a career in the music industry with knowledge and confidence.

MusicCrunch
kyle@musiccrunch.com
www.musiccrunch.com
List your site. You can update your profile, add show/gig venues and dates and much more.

Musicians and Injuries
eeshop.unl.edu/music.html
Information to help you avoid repetitive use injuries.

Musician's Cyber Cooler
PH: 330-807-5236
Dave Jackson cybercooler@hotmail.com
www.jammindave.com
Promotional tools and resources for musicians.

Musician's Health
www.musicianshealth.com
Explanation of musician's injuries, along with guidelines regarding injury prevention, optimizing your musical performance, and for achieving an optimum state of health.

Musician's Network
MN@MusiciansNetwork.com
www.musiciansnetwork.com
Where musicians and the music industry meet.

Musician's Network Portal
portal.get-it-all.net
Get career tips, view artist profiles, and sample indie artist music releases. Read articles specifically created for independent musicians.

Musicianzoo.com
16013 S. Desert Foothills Pkwy. #2105,
Phoenix, AZ 85048
musicianzoo@cox.net
www.musicianzoo.com
Promotes local bands, as well as major label artists.

musicNerve.com
Peter Mezensky misspeter@gmail.com
musicNerve.com
Music news site. Submit your information!

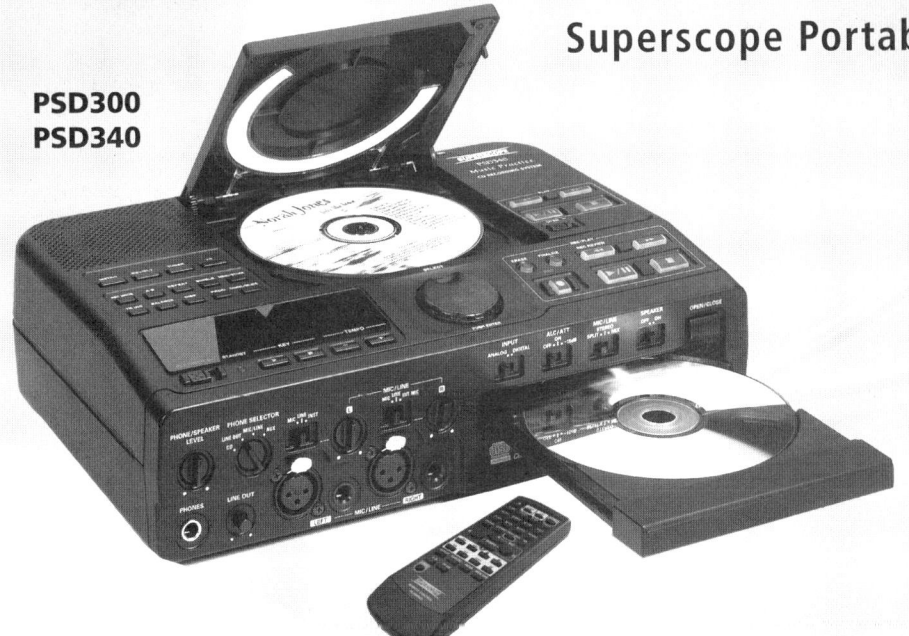

MWS Media
PO Box 402081, Hesperia, CA 92340-2081
Matthew Wayne Selznick mws@mwsmedia.com
www.mwsmedia.com
Provides resources, support, and community for do-it-yourself independent musicians, writers and other creative folks.

MyMusicJob.com
hrexpress@mymusicjob.com
www.mymusicjob.com
Providing assistance to those who make their living in the music industry.

Nimbit Web Services
47 Mellen St., Framingham, MA 01702
PH: 866-864-6248
info@nimbit.com
www.nimbit.com
Host of web services for Indie artists.

Onlinegigs
7040 Lismore Ave. Boynton Beach, FL 33437
PH: 888-595-3122
Jay Flanzbaum support@onlinegigs.com
www.onlinegigs.com
Automates the administration of booking and promoting your band. It is a centralized database of nationwide venues, colleges, festivals and media contacts. It is kept fresh because Onlinegigs members actually help to maintain and contribute to the data simultaneously from different parts of the country.

Online Music Blog
copacetix@gmail.com
www.onlinemusicblog.com
We compile online music news daily. Visit us to submit news.

PayPal
www.paypal.com
The world's largest online payment solution. No start-up fees, no monthly fees.

PowerGig
PO Box 41012, Des Moines, IA 50311
PH: 515-274-8187 FX: 890-775-4701
www.powergig.com
The power tool for finding, booking and promoting gigs.

PR Web
PO Box 333,
Ferndale, WA 98248
PH: 360-312-0892
FX: 360-380-9981
prweb@dataovation.com
www.prweb.com
We have helped over 4,000 companies distribute their press releases.

Press Release Writing Tips
315 Fruitwood Ln.
Knoxville, TN 37922
PH: 865-671-8366
FX: 865-671-8437
info@press-release-writing.com
www.press-release-writing.com
Contains free tips on writing good press releases.

Project Overseer Productions
264 Hereson Rd., Sycamore Grange,
Dumpton Park, CT11 7ET UK
PH: 01843-591672
Chris Bishop projectoverseer@hotmail.com
www.projectoverseer.biz
OMD for music artist's promotion. Community based with industry connections and live reviews system.

Rate Our Band
feedback@digitalwhammy.com
www.rateourband.com
Get the general public's opinion of your band's music and looks.

Rock Web Hosting
PH: 800-381-1063
rockwebwillhelp@hotmail.com
www.rockwebhosting.com
The BEST website deals anywhere!

Savidetup Productions
PO Box 121626, Fort Worth, TX 76121-1626
PH: 817-737-3026
Tim Sisk tim@savidetup.com
www.savidetup.com
Services for the consumer, artist and business communities.

SelfPromotion.com
selfpromotion.com
The net's leading resource for do-it-yourself web promotion.

SongQuarters
sqinfo@hitquarters.com
www.SongQuarters.com
We provide valuable information on the recording status of the world's 500 most successful artists, including which of these are currently looking for songs, and leads for newly signed and developing artists in search of songs.

Sonicbids
580 Harrison Ave. 4th Fl. Boston, MA 02118
PH: 617-275-7222
Panos artists@sonicbids.com
www.sonicbids.com
Our main product is the Electronic Press Kit (EPK™). It's an easy-to-use, web-based graphic interface that contains all the basic information of a musical act such as music, photos or date calendar. The EPK™ can either be e-mailed to anyone with a click of the mouse or submitted in online promoter accounts through a virtual "Drop Box".

spinme.com
Joe Taylor joetaylor@spinme.com
www.spinme.com
Daily news, tools & tips for working musicians.

StagePass News
www.stagepassnews.com
Covering every aspect of the professional life of the musician including career tips. Whether you need to find sponsorship money for your band's tour or how to handle intellectual rights, there is plenty to read here.

starpolish
1 Irving Pl. #P8C, New York, NY 10003
FX: 212-477-5259
info2@starpolish.com
www.starpolish.com
Artists receive a wealth of free resources, including an extensive library of business advice, various self-management tools, a massive contact database and strong exposure opportunities.

Stick'em Up
PO Box 685, Shutesbury, MA 01072
PH: 413-259-1227 Mailbox #1
Jaime Campbell Morton postering@artspromo.org
www.artspromo.org/hotelsponsor
We offer inexpensive, quick solutions to your promotion and postering needs. We assist touring musicians, promoters, speakers,(cultural) artists, small business owners, healing artists and others.

TalentMatch.com
11410 NE 124th St., Kirkland, WA 98034
ms@talentmatch.com
www.talentmatch.com
Designed to help aspiring and accomplished bands, singers, musicians and writers easily gain support, share their talents and gain worldwide exposure.

TheConcertChannel.com
PO Box 32017, Kansas City, MO 64171
greg@theconcertchannel.com
www.theconcertchannel.com
Makes live shows more accessible to the public.

Topica
support@get.topica.com
www.topica.com/channels/music
Browse through hundreds of newsletters on music related subjects.

TOURdatabase.com
Gregg Geil gregg@TOURdatabase.com
www.tourdatabase.com
Our Tour Management System (TMS) is built for musicians, booking agents and record labels. The concept of TMS is to centralize your tour dates which makes your events accessible to any website.

CUSTOM : FULL COLOR • APPAREL & STICKER - PRINTING

We print from your digital files • Order online 24/7 • Browse 100's of prices • Download digital templates • Request custom quotes

Qty	Item	Price
500	POSTCARDS - 4x6, Full Color (4/4) 12pt. Cardstock	$90
	1,000 Qty - $125 / 5,000 Qty - $199	
500	FLIERS - 8.5 x 5.5, (4/4) 100lb. Gloss Text Stock	$98
	1,000 Qty - $118 / 5,000 Qty - $198	
500	BUSINESS CARDS, Full Color (4/4) 12pt. Cardstock	$50
	1,000 Qty - $75 / 5,000 Qty - $99.00	
500	POSTERS - 11x17, Full Color (4/0) 100lb. Gloss Text	$250
	1,000 Qty - $325 / 2,000 Qty - $450	

(4/0 - full color 1 side • 4/4 - full color 2 sides)

FULL COLOR PRINTING

Qty	Item	Price
100	White T-SHIRTS, 1 color print / 1 location	$2.75*ea.
100	Dark / Colored T-SHIRTS, 1 color print / 1 location	$3.75*ea.
100	Dark / Colored HOODIES, 1 color print / 1 location	$10.75*ea.
100	Dark / ZIPPER! HOODIES, 1 color print / 1 location	$13.00*ea.

* Plus one (1) screen charge of $15.00

Many styles are now available in: American Apparel

Apparel Printing

Qty	Item	Price
1000	1 Color STICKERS, 4" Circle or Square	$99
	5,000 Qty. - $399	
1000	2 Color STICKERS, 4" Circle or Square	$150
	5,000 Qty. - $499	
1000	Outdoor Bumper STICKERS, 3.75"x 7.5" vinyl 1 color	$199
1000	Full Color STICKERS, 4" Circle or Square	$499

Choose from (25) ink colors & (6) stocks

Sticker Printing

WWW.JAKPRINTS.COM

Hours: M-F 9-5pm EST • Jakprints, 1300 W. 78th St., Cleveland, OH 44102

JAKPRINTS

Toll Free: 877-246-3132

We accept all major credit cards

---

extraOrdinary life
the new album by gilli moon

An adventurous journey of autobiographical songs and stories, and intimate music conversations about gilli moon's inner truths, emotions and passions, anecdotes about falling in love, and out of it, about living in Hollywood, and about freedom, humour, simplicity and a life long journey of discovery. An ENHANCED CD of 13 songs, a spoken word piece, photo slide show, "making of" video of the studio process, live footage of gilli moon's performances and a music video.

www.gillimoon.com

"...an epic endeavor from an artist already well known for her independent and adventurous spirit. Indeed, this album covers a wide range of styles and emotions that touch every aspect of our lives... a strong sense of self that one gets the impression she's letting us in on her secret life ... an extraordinary one at that ...a beautiful expedition of emotions and stories that comfort, excite and inspire."
- Bernard Baur, Music Connection Magazine

www.gillimoon.com
www.warriorgirlmusic.com
info@warriorgirlmusic.com

THE NEW ENHANCED CD IN STORES AND ONLINE NOW AT GILLIMOON.COM, CDBABY.COM, AMAZON, ITUNES AND MORE!
DOWNLOADS & RINGTONES ALSO AVAILABLE.

The Indie Bible - 7th Edition
www.indiebible.com

TourGiveaways
34 Watts St. #10, New York, NY 10013
PH: 347-623-5523
Mary Crosse mary@tourgiveaways.com
www.tourgiveaways.com
Our free Jampacks service offers select bands the opportunity to receive thousands of free CDs to hand out at their shows–completely paid for by sponsors.

TourVote
info@demandid.com
tourvote.com
Giving YOU a voice in local, live entertainment. Request a live show by any musical artist or group you would like to see locally.

Unsigned Band Web
www.unsignedbandweb.com
Trade reviews, ideas, find answers, get feedback...

USA Musicians Network
PO Box 133, Williamsville, NY 14231-0133
PH: 716-565-1969 FX: 716-565-9779
info@usamusician.com
usamusician.com
Promote your music and local gigs.

Visual Image Marketing
PO Box 120576, Nashville, TN 37212
PH: 615-419-0886
Steve Baker steveb@visualimagemarketing.com
www.visualimagemarketing.com
Promotes & markets music videos to video outlets.

Voyage Beyond Entertainment
PO Box 1284, Hillsville, VA 24343
Michael Anthony fmyshow@gmail.com
www.voyagebeyond.net
Let us translate your words into a powerful message that will hit the mark with your audience! We provide audio for commercials, radio, TV, web sites, pod casts, on hold, telephone services and much more.

Whateverway Productions Inc
1796 NW 22nd St. #415, Boynton Beach, FL 33426
PH: 561-799-4800 FX: 561-630-3591
Greg McLaughlin whateverway@adelphia.net
whateverwayproductions.com
A co-op of like minded artists in the fields of Music, Video and Fine Arts.

Weirdears
Stephen Rose sterose2003@yahoo.com
www.weirdears.com
Online community featuring indie radio, music reviews, discussions and more.

Yahoo! Music Related Groups
launch.dir.groups.yahoo.com/dir/Music
Share photos & files, plan events, send a newsletter and more.

Databases

Abbie's Open Mic Directory
PO Box 472, Stony Point, NY 10980
Abbie Gardner abbie@abbiegardner.com
www.abbiegardner.com/mics.html
A comprehensive list of Open Mics, especially in the North East US.. So if you want to perform... get gigs... meet other musicians...you've come to the right place!! Pick out a club and you could be on stage tonight!

All Media Guide
1168 Oak Valley Dr. Ann Arbor, MI 48108
www.allmusic.com
Massive database of CDs. Add yours!

All Musicians Information
Andy Temple info@allmusicians.info
www.allmusicians.info
A place for artists/musicians/songwriters and music websites to post their information. It is completely FREE but you do have to register to post.

allrecordlabels.com
324 8th St. E. Saskatoon, SK S7H 0P5
scott@lights.com
allrecordlabels.com
A database of record label web site.

ArtistManager.com *UK*
www.artistmanager.co.uk
Matching music industry artists with managers worldwide.

Band Register
PH: 44-0208-940-7518
www.bandreg.com
Database featuring over 330,000 bands.

Celebrity Access
PO Box 429, E. Lyme, CT 06333
PH: 860-691-5000 FX: 860-739-0417
sales@celebrityaccess.com
www.celebrityaccess.com
Contact info on agents, managers, record companies, talent buyers and venues.

Coalition of Independent Music Stores
www.cimsmusic.com
A group of some of the best independent music stores in America. Contact the CIMS office to coordinate their efforts nationwide.

Daily Newspapers around the World
www.refdesk.com/paper.html
Links to hundreds of daily newspapers worldwide.

Discogs.com
PMB # 323, 6663 SW Beaverton-Hillsdale Hwy. Portland, OR 97225-1403
www.discogs.com
A user-built database containing information on artists, labels, and their recordings. Discogs is constantly growing as users submit releases to the database. Refer to our Help section for information on how to submit.

Festival Network Online
festivalnet.com/ib
There's nothing like a live performance! FNO lists more than 7,000 events throughout the U.S. and Canada seeking performers, from local & regional to national & international. Search by 22 different music genres, event attendance, zip code radius & more. Plug in festival dates with club dates.

FestivalFinder
www.festivalfinder.com
Discover the latest details on more than 2,500 music festivals in North America.

Festivals.com
900 4th Ave. #3350, Seattle, WA 98164
PH: 206-621-7723 FX: 206-621-9399
www.festivals.com
Submit your festival photos and join our online communities.

Ground Zero Music Network
Matt Mesnard elwood@extremezone.com
www.GroundZeroMusic.net
Database of bands from around the world.

HitQuarters
PO Box 138, 641 22 Katrineholm, Sweden
PH: 46-150-154-80 FX: 46-150-154-81
info@hitquarters.com
www.hitquarters.com
Presents the world's top record company A&Rs, managers, publishers and producers, including their contact info & track records.

I Need A Musician
PO Box 120534, St., Albans, NY 11412-0534
PH: 718-977-0770 x5 FX: 718-977-0179
info@INeedAMusician.com
www.INeedAMusician.com
Find a Musician, Singer or Producer anywhere at any time!

Indie Link Exchange
indielinkexchange@rogers.com
www.indielinkexchange.com/ile
Free service with listings of over 1000 Indie music sites that wish to exchange links with other music related sites.

International Musicians Trading Post
PO Box 64, Kingston Palms, QLD 4114 Australia
Matt Benbrook free-ads@musicians-classifieds.com
www.Musicians-Classifieds.com
Free on-line classifieds for the music industry and musicians from around the world.

MatchMakerMusic.com
support@matchmakermusic.com
MatchMakerMusic.com
Find live music venues, bands and musicians that match what you need. Book shows, get gigs, plan tours, find record labels, submit electronic press kits and find booking agents.

Music Publishers Directory
mpa.org/agency/publishers.html
A listing of contact information for publishers, both domestic and foreign, and copyright administrating offices.

MusicClassifieds.us
mcwebmaster03@musicclassifieds.us
www.musicclassifieds.us
Features instant posting of ads, over 80 music categories and much more.

MusicContracts.com
631 Woodland St., Nashville, TN 37206
PH: 615-244-9501 FX: 615-244-7178
J. Scott "Skip" Rudsenske skip@jsrlaw.net
www.musiccontracts.com
Sells downloadable copies of the most widely used music business contracts.

MusicianHunter.com
PO Box 272515, Boca Raton, FL 33427
PH: 888-844-8144 FX: 561-243-0058
billingdept@musicianhunter.com
www.musicianhunter.com
Connect with thousands of other artists.

Musician's Contact
PO Box 788, Woodland Hills, CA 91365
PH: 818-888-7879
info@musicianscontact.com
www.musicianscontact.com
Supplying musicians and singers to thousands of employers and band leaders everywhere.

MusiciansRegistry.com
info@MusiciansRegistry.com
www.MusiciansRegistry.com
Introducing up-and-coming musical talents to the general public and those in the music industry. Many of the musicians in this directory have audio and/or video samples available for download.

Newspaper and News Media Guide
www.abyznewslinks.com
Database of HUNDREDS of International newspapers.

OnStageRegister
info@onstageregister.com
www.onstageregister.com
The leading directory of performing artists.

POLLSTAR
tour_dates@pollstar.com
www.pollstar.com
Submit your itineraries to our route book department.

Record Labels & Companies Guide
www.record-labels-companies-guide.com
Info on the majors, independents and everything in between.

record labels on the web
contact2@rlabels.com
www.rlabels.com
Here you'll find 5000+ links to record label web pages.

RecordStoreReview.com
www.recordstorereview.com
Find contact information for record stores worldwide.

SoundRangers.com
PH: 206-352-8818
audioguys@soundrangers.com
www.soundrangers.com
Royalty free music and sound effects download site.

SoundScan
PH: 914-684-5525
ClientServices@soundscan.com
home.soundscan.com
Central clearinghouse for music industry data.

studiofinder.com
PH: 800-468-9353
studio@discmakers.com
www.studiofinder.com
Search for a studio by name, location, equipment, price, and/or area of expertise.

Ultimate Band List
10900 Wilshire Blvd. #1400,
Los Angeles, CA 90024
ubl.artistdirect.com
Music information for ALL bands and ALL kinds. Get listed here.

Virtual-Festivals.com
4 Rowan Court,
56 High St., Wimbledon,
London, England, SW19 5EE UK
FX: +44 (0) 20-8605-2255
editor@virtualfestivals.com
www.virtualfestivals.com
Providing the most comprehensive and frequently updated coverage of the UK and global music festival scene.

Equipment, Merch & Software

ABC Pictures
1867 E. Florida St., Springfield, MO 65803-4583
PH: 888-526-5336
www.abcpictures.com
Quality publicity picture reproduction, posters, 8x10's, headshots & composites for the entertainment industry

ALLPARTS
13027 Brittmoore Park Dr. Houston, TX 77041
PH: 713-466-6414 FX: 713-466-5803
info@allparts.com
www.allparts.com
America's premier guitar and bass parts supplier.

BandHub
PO Box 2000, Boston, MA 02130-0017
PH: 617-648-3838
sales@bandhub.com
www.bandhub.com
A band website, band web applications and band web hosting package.

Bandwear.com
10486 Brockwood Rd. Dallas, TX 75238
PH: 214-342-0715
bandwear.com
A full-service merchandising company.

CafePress.com
1515 Aurora Dr. San Leandro, CA 94577
PH: 510-877-1540 FX: 510-315-3089
Jeff Ridgeway jeff@cafepress.com
www.cafepress.com
Shop, sell or create what's on your mind.

CDstands.com
30 Compton Way, Hamilton Sq., NJ 08690
PH: 609-689-1711
info@cdreview.com
cdstands.com
We manufacture our own line of CD Boxes for artists to sell their music at shows or in stores.

Charlie Cheney's Indie Office
PO Box 496, Jamison, PA 18929
PH: 215-825-6913
Charlie Cheney info@indieoffice.com
www.indieoffice.com
A complete Swiss army knife for your marketing, promotion, sales etc. It prints mailing labels, letters, invoices, contracts, postcards, contact lists, accounts receivable reports, merge letters, you name it... and even sends out personalized mass emails.

Elfenworks Free Website Templates
PO Box 431, Burlingame, CA 94011
info@elfenworks.com www.elfenworks.com
I am giving away free website template zipfiles which musicians can download and use to develop their own websites.Please note that I am NOT taking on new clients. I'm just giving the templates away.

Gracenote CDDB
2000 Powell St. #1380, Emeryville, CA 94608
PH: 510-547-9680 FX: 510-547-9681
licensing@gracenote.com
GracenoteLicensing@gracenote.com
www.gracenote.com/gn_products/cddb.html
The industry standard for music recognition services. Seamless handling of soundtracks and other compilations, expanded album and track fields, credits, genres, ISRC code, web-links and segments provide music fans with access to a huge store of information on their favorite music.

iFanz
322 Culver Blvd. #124, Playa Del Rey, CA 90293
info@ifanz.com
www.ifanz.com
Manages your marketing, image, promotion, merchandizing and career.

Indie Band Manager
PO Box 496, Jamison, PA 18929
PH: 215-825-6913
info@indiebandmanager.com
www.indiebandmanager.com
Database software for independent musicians.

Jakprints
1300 W. 78th St., Cleveland, OH 44102
PH: 216-472-1650 FX: 216-472-6349
www.jakprints.com
We continually strive to help each and every customer big or small, to expand and promote their passion with the highest quality service and merchandise.

LiveWire Contacts
156 Hamilton St., Cambridge, MA 02139
support@LiveWireContacts.com
www.LiveWireContacts.com
A contact manager specifically designed for musicians.

MIDI Classics
Box 311, Weatogue, CT 06089-0311
PH: 800-787-6434 FX: 860-651-4373
Phil Sabatine mcsales@midi-classics.com
www.midi-classics.com
Digital audio hardware and music software. Over 20,000 products listed - sound cards, interfaces, sample CDs, software, cables, keyboards, MIDI controllers and much more!

Musician's Toolkit CD ROM
toolkit@indie-music.com
www.indie-music.com/cgi/affiliates/click.cgi?icn
Toolkit that will help you book gigs and advance your career.

Musician's Friend
PO Box 4370, Medford, OR 97501
PH: 800-391-8762
www.musiciansfriend.com
The largest online music store in the world. Whether you need a guitar pick or a full-blown digital recording system, this is the place to shop online. They offer excellent discounts on all name brand products!

musictoday.com
3305 Lobban Pl. Charlottesville, VA 22903
PH: 434-951-0271 FX: 434-984-6798
feedback@musictoday.com
www.musictoday.com
We possess the qualities necessary to successfully develop a band's career.

Muze
304 Hudson St. 8th Fl. New York, NY 10013
PH: 212-824-0300
info@muze.com
www.muze.com
Our products and services are designed to drive commerce, enhance the consumer experience and increase customer loyalty.

Pickguard FX
18 Valley View Dr. Fisherville, KY 40023
PH: 877-307-6418
Lesa Seibert lesa@pickguardfx.com
www.pickguardfx.com
We are constantly striving to provide our customers with the broadest selection of image-transferred pickguards in the most popular styles.

Rock-n-Roll Web Design and Hosting
PO Box 1922, Salisbury, MD 21802
PH: 410-835-8895
info@rock-n-roll-design.com
www.rock-n-roll-design.com
We offer powerful hosting tools that give you complete control over all content on your site..

Rock Star Promotions
PO Box 5867, Ft. Lauderdale, FL 33310
PH: 954-739-9205
FX: 801-740-6554
Aaron Schimmel
servicedesk@rockstarpromos.com
www.rockstarpromos.com
Dedicated to helping everyone live like a Rock Star, even if you can't play a note!

Seatthole Shirts
PO Box 3137, Bellingham, WA 98227
PH: 360-733-2154
Django Bohren
info@seatthole.com
seatthole.com
High-quality custom t-shirt screen printing and Rock & Roll promotional items for your high-, medium-, low- or no-budget project.

Superscope Technologies
1508 Batavia Ave. Geneva, IL 60134
PH: 630-232-8900
David Pratt dpratt@superscopetechnologies.com
www.superscope.net
Portable dual drive CD recorder for songwriting. Record yourself directly to CD. Play along to CD accompaniment and change key, change tempo, reduce vocals, and set A-B repeat loops. It's easy with the new Superscope PSD340 dual drive CD recorder & CD player. The PSD340 is designed to be as easy to use as a tape recorder. Record ideas, demos, and performances hassle-free.

Vista Prints
www.vistaprint.com
Get 250 free business cards.

Westone Music Products
2235 Executive Circle, Colorado Springs, CO 80906
PH: 719-540-9333 FX: 719-540-9183
Paul Carhart music@westone.com
www.westone.com/music
In-ear musicians monitoring and hearing protection products.

Legal Resources

American Bar Association
www.abanet.org/intelprop
The home page of the ABA Section of Intellectual Property Law.

The Better Business Bureau
bbb.org
Find a local BBB in the US and Canada serving the consumers and businesses in their areas.

Copyright & Fair Use
fairuse.stanford.edu
Stanford U. information on copyright law.

Copyright Kit
www.indie-music.com/free2.php
Free download of Copyright Kit.

Copyright Law in the United States
www.bitlaw.com/copyright
A discussion on the copyright laws.

The Copyright Website
PH: 650-372-9934
info@benedict.com
www.benedict.com
Copyright registration and information resource.

Copyright Your Song
www.loc.gov/copyright/forms/formpai.pdf
The PDF form to file with the U.S. Copyright Office.

Copyright Your Sound Recording
www.loc.gov/copyright/forms/formsri.pdf
The PDF form to file with the U.S. Copyright Office.

Creative Commons
543 Howard St. 5th Fl.
San Francisco, CA 94105-3013
PH: 415-946-3069 FX: 415-946-3001
info@creativecommons.org
creativecommons.org
A nonprofit whose goal is to build a layer of reasonable, flexible copyright in the face of increasingly restrictive default rules.

Findlaw
www.findlaw.com
Provides information and links to resources on all areas of law, including copyright and entertainment law.

GS1 US (Uniform Code Council)
www.gs1us.org
Administers the U.P.C. bar code.

Independent Music Law Advice UK
PH: 07748-593-758
FX: 0207-433-3266
Elliot Chalmers elliot@musiclawadvice.co.uk
www.musiclawadvice.co.uk
Providing accurate and up to date information on all issues related to music law.

Music Law Offices
10008 S. Western Ave.
Chicago, IL 60643
PH: 773-779-9885
FX: 773-779-9190
McCready@music-law.com
www.music-law.com
Free articles on copyright and music publishing.

Song Domain Newsletter Magazine
1225 W. Main St. #237, Mesa, AZ 85201
Jack Kavanagh songdomain@msn.com
Created due to a real need for a new alternative to the "tip sheet" approach for the information and listings writers need for their songs.

SongFile.com
711 3rd Ave. New York, NY 10017
PH: 212-370-5330 FX: 646-487-6779
hfalicensingsupport@songfile.com
www.songfile.com
Get a license to make and distribute a recording.

SongRights.com
PO Box 1441, Austin, TX 78767-1441
PH: 512-304-5275
Rcarter154@aol.com
www.songrights.com
Articles on the basic concepts of law as it pertains to the music industry.

Trademark Search
www.uspto.gov/main/trademarks.htm
Valuable information on trademarks in the US.

United States Copyright Office
101 Independence Ave. SE,
Washington, DC 20559-6000
PH: 202-707-3000
copyinfo@loc.gov
www.loc.gov/copyright
Key publications and the homepages of other copyright-related organizations.

United States Patent and Trademark Office
TrademarkAssistanceCenter@uspto.gov
www.uspto.gov
The official website.

Volunteer Lawyers for the Arts
6128 Delmar, St. Louis, MI 63112
PH: 314-863-6930 FX: 314-863-6932
vlaa@stlrac.org
www.vlaa.org/resources.asp
A variety of programs and services.

Organizations

AFM & AFTRA Intellectual Property Rights Distribution Fund
12001 Ventura Pl. #500, Studio City, CA 91604
PH: 818-755-7780 FX: 818-755-7779
Jo-Anne McGettrick jmcgettrick@mpspf.org
www.raroyalties.org
Recording Artist Royalties Formed for the purpose of distributing royalties from various foreign territories and royalties established by government statute under U.S. Copyright Law.

The Artist Couch Exchange
info@couchexchange.org
couchexchange.org
Network of artists who offer free lodging to other independent touring artists.

American Federation of Musicians of the US and Canada (AFM)
1501 Broadway #600, New York, NY 10036
PH: 212-869-1330 FX: 212-764-6134
www.afm.org
Union representing the interests of the professional musician.

Thousands of shows across North America
Search by 22 music genres & more ~ Free demo
info@festivalnet.com * (800) 200-3737

American Federation of Television & Radio Artists (AFTRA)
5757 Wilshire Blvd. 9th Fl.
Los Angeles, CA 90036-3689
PH: 323-634-8100 FX: 323-634-8194
www.aftra.com
National labor union representing artists.

American Society of Composers, Authors and Publishers (ASCAP)
1 Lincoln Plaza, New York, NY 10023
PH: 212-621-6000 FX: 212-724-9064
info@ascap.com
www.ascap.com
A performing rights society that represents its members.

Association of Music Writers and Photographers
CJ cj@amwp.org
www.AMWP.org
Latest music news and articles. Also lists job openings and contests.

Broadcast Music, Inc (BMI)
320 W. 57th St., New York, NY 10019-3790
PH: 212-586-2000
www.bmi.com
Collects license fees on behalf of those American creators it represents.

Creative Musicians Coalition
PO Box 6205, Peoria, IL 61601-6205
PH: 309-685-4843 FX: 309-685-4879
aimcmc@aol.com
www.aimcmc.com
A fellowship of artists and labels that share and network.

f. Boo Music
PH: 818-846-2312
fboo@pacbell.net
www.fBoo.com
Imagine a community of artists who support each other and combine forces to make each one's unique dream real.

Freelance Musicians' Association
240 Commissioners Rd. W. #G,
London, ON N6J 1Y1
info@freelancemusicians.org
www.freelancemusicians.org
Providing specific services required by musicians.

Future of Music Coalition
1615 L St. NW #520,
Washington, DC 20036
PH: 202-429-8855
FX: 202-429-8857
Michael mbracy@bracytuckerbrown.com
www.futureofmusic.org
A voice for musicians and citizens in Washington.

Guild of International Songwriters and Composers
Sovereign House, 1
2 Trewartha Rd.
Praa Sands, Penzance,
Cornwall, TR20 9ST
England
PH: 01736-762826 FX: 01736-763328
songmag@aol.com
www.songwriters-guild.co.uk
International songwriters organization representing songwriters.

Indie Managers Association (IMA)
554 N. Frederick Ave. #218,
Gaithersburg, MD 20877
PH: 240-638-5060 FX: 240-597-1330
Jeremy Rwakaara jeremy@indiemanagers.com
www.indiemanagers.com
Exists to promote and educate this and the next generation of independent music managers and self-managed artists; and connect managers with artists seeking representation.

International Association of African American Music
PO Box 382, Gladwyne, PA 19035
PH: 610-664-8292 FX: 610-664-5940
iaaam1@aol.com
www.iaaam.com
Promoting, perpetuating and preserving America's indigenous music.

International Songwriters Association
Ireland
jliddane@songwriter.iol.ie
www.songwriter.co.uk
Extensive information service for songwriters, lyric writers and music publishers.

Just Plain Folks
1315 N. Butler Ave. Indianapolis, IN 46219
jpnotes@aol.com
www.jpfolks.com
Organization that networks, promotes and educates musicians.

LIFEbeat
630 9th Ave. #1010, New York, NY 10036
PH: 212-459-2590
info@lifebeat.org
www.lifebeat.org
Mobilizes the music industry to raise awareness and to provide support for the AIDS community.

MadHorns.com
358 N. Summit Ave. #101, Gaithersburg, MD 20877
PH: 240-683-8538
www.madhorns.com
If you've looked around the web, you know there are TONS of resources for rock guitarists, drummers and bass players, oodles of information for Classical instrumentalists and a wealth of Jazz-head sites. Now, horn players that are into Pop, Rock and Funk have a place to call home too!

MusiCares
3402 Pico Blvd. Santa Monica, CA 90405
PH: 310-392-3777 FX: 310-399-3090
Dee Dee deedee@grammy.com
www.grammy.com/musicares
A place to turn in times of financial, medical or personal crisis.

Musicians On Call
216 W. 18th St. #201B, New York, NY 10011
PH: 212-741-2709 FX: 212-741-3465
info@musiciansoncall.org
www.musiciansoncall.org
Using music to complement the healing process for patients in healthcare facilities.

MusicPro Insurance Agency
45 Crossways Park Dr. Woodbury, NY 11797-2002
PH: 800-605-3187 FX: 888-290-0302
insurance@MusicProInsurance.com
www.musicproinsurance.com
Affordable and convenient insurance for musicians, including instruments, equipment, studio, tour, composer's liability, travel accident and health.

Positive Music Association
4593 Maple Ct. Boulder, CO 80301
PH: 303-581-9083
www.positivemusicassociation.com
Established to promote positive music and those who create it, and to establish a new musical genre called "Positive Music." It's about making the world a better place through music.

Recording Industry Association of America (RIAA)
webmaster@riaa.com
www.riaa.org
The trade group that represents the U.S. recording industry. Its mission is to foster a business and legal climate that supports and promotes our members' creative and financial vitality.

SESAC
55 Music Sq. E. Nashville, TN 37203
PH: 615-320-0055 FX: 615-329-9627
www.sesac.com
Performing rights organization in the US.

Society of Singers
6500 Wilshire Blvd. #640, Los Angeles, CA 90048
PH: 323-653-7672 FX: 323-653-7675
sos@singers.org
www.singers.org
Helps professional vocalists, worldwide, in times of crisis.

SoundExchange
1330 Connecticut Ave. NW #330,
Washington, DC 20036
PH: 202-833-0120 FX: 202-833-2141
info@soundexchange.com
www.soundexchange.com
A non profit organization that has been designated by the US Copyright Office to distribute royalties from Internet airplay (ie: XM, Sirius, Live365, AOL, Launch, Spinner etc.) If you have had airplay from any Internet sources, you probably have some royalties waiting for you. Sign up today!

UnitedBands.com
help@unitedbands.com
www.unitedbands.com
A place for bands to trade services, gigs, information and more. United Bands provides networking tools for the bands and artists who realize that through networking, they can improve their position.

Weirdears
www.weirdears.com
Indie and Alternative music forum You'll find great bands featured in our articles section and playing on our radio. There is also an Indie review section.

Songwriting Resources

Circle of Songs
614 Hampton Dr. Venice, CA 90291
PH: 310-452-4163 FX: 310-452-7403
showcase@circleofsongs.com
www.circleofsongs.com
Learn to build a lifetime career in music.

Crazewire
1568 Oliver Ave. #A, San Diego, CA 91209
PH: 858-405-6457
www.crazewire.com
A network for young and aspiring music writers. A community where musicians, journalists, fans, and wannabe-Rock Stars spontaneously connect.

HitWriters.com
Anthony Martin anthony@hitwriters.com
hitwriters.com
Created to promote and give access to the best songwriters in the world—the ones who have made a difference in our culture and attitudes. These are the superstar writers from every genre, whose music forever changed our lives.

Muse's Muse
jodi@musesmuse.com
www.musesmuse.com
Songwriting tips, tools, interactivities and opportunities to connect.

NextHitWriters
Anthony Martin anthony@hitwriters.com
www.hitwriters.com
You will not only get your chance, but the professional attention you deserve - all at a price that won't cut into your string and pick budget.

Singer Song
bandbseek@hotmail.com
www.singersong.com
Find the information you need to start your successful career.

Singer/Songwriter Directory
FX: 561-760-0891
info@singer-songwriter.com
www.singer-songwriter.com
Lists new CD releases, featured CDs and "Site of the Week".

Singer Songwriter Resources
191 Rupert Dr. Bloomsburg, PA 17815
PH: 570-784-3206
Dave Blackledge dave@daveblackledge.com
www.SingerSongwriter.ws
Aiding Indie singer songwriters.

Singers U.K.
singers@singers-uk.org
www.singers-uk.net
Created to help promote professional singers on the internet.

The Singers' Workshop
4804 Laurel Canyon Blvd. #123,
Valley Village, CA 91607
PH: 818-623-6668
www.thesingersworkshop.com
Provides valuable articles that singers need to know.

SingerUniverse
11684 Ventura Blvd. #975, Studio City, CA 91604
Dale info@singeruniverse.com
www.SingerUniverse.com
Features valuable, comprehensive information for pros and newcomers alike. We don't accept unsolicited material. Please contact us before submitting your music.

The Singing Spot
thesingingspot.com
The ultimate resource directory for singers.

Songstuff
John Moxey songs@songstuff.com
www.songstuff.com
Articles, reference material, artist pages, news and forums.

Songwriter101.com
contact@songwriter101.com
songwriter101.com
Everything about the business side of the songwriter's profession.

Songwriters Resource Network
PO Box 135, 6327-C Capitol Hill Hwy.
Portland, OR 97239
info@SongwritersResourceNetwork.com
www.songwritersresourcenetwork.com
A free online news and information resource.

Songwriter's Tip Jar
Robert Cote robert@songwriterstipjar.com
www.songwriterstipjar.com
FREE weekly ezine focused on helping craft a better song.

Songwriting.Org
kent@newsome.org
www.songwriting.org
Post lyrics and audio links for critique and discussion.

Songwriting Contests
jodi@musesmuse.com
www.musesmuse.com/contests.html
Listing of all the best songwriting contests.

Songwriters Directory
201 N. Front St. #515, Wilmington, NC 28401
FX: 910-763-8703
swd@songwritersdirectory.com
www.songwritersdirectory.com
Listings database used by music fans and music industry executives.

Tunesmith
info@tunesmith.net
www.tunesmith.net
Provides info and networking opportunities. Our main goal is to offer our members helpful advice whenever we can, through seminars, message boards etc.

Blues

Blues Bank Collective
PO Box 4076, Portsmouth, NH 03802
PH: 603-436-8596
tjw@bluesbankcollective.org
www.bluesbankcollective.org
Promotes Blues music and its African American heritage.

Blues Festival Guide
PO Box 50635, Reno, NV 89513
PH: 775-337-8626 FX: 775-337-6499
editor@bluesfestivalguide.com
www.bluesfestivalguide.com
An online directory of Blues festivals.

The Blues Foundation
49 Union Ave. Memphis, TN 38103
PH: 901-527-2583 FX: 901-529-4030
bluesinfo@blues.org
www.blues.org
Encourages and recognizes the achievements of Blues artists.

The Blues Highway
thebluehighway.com
Listings of Blues radio shows from all over the world.

Blues Music Association
PO Box 3122, Memphis, TN 38173
PH: 901-572-3843
info@bluesmusicassociation.com
www.BluesMusicAssociation.org
Working together to market the Blues.

BluesFestivals.com
blues@305spin.com
www.bluesfestivals.com
Searchable database for locating Blues festivals around the nation.

Mary4Music.com
PO Box 25922, Baltimore, MD 21224
Mary mary@mary4music.com
www.mary4music.com
Blues, Indie & DIY music links, musician's resources, reviews and band listings.

Children's

Children's Music Network
PO Box 1341, Evanston, IL 60204-1341
PH: 847-733-8003
office@cmnonline.org
www.cmnonline.org
Catalyst for education and community-building through music.

Children's Music Web
pjswift@sbcglobal.net
www.childrensmusic.org
Connecting families with great Children's music.

Children's Music Workshop
newman@childrensmusicworkshop.com
www.childrensmusicworkshop.com
A music education resource for students, parents and teachers.

Kids Music Web
kidsmuze@kidsmusicweb.com
www.kidsmusicweb.com
Contact to join the Kid's music artist listing.

KidScreen
366 Adelaide St. W. #500, Toronto, ON M5V 1R9
PH: 416-408-2300 FX: 416-408-0870
www.kidscreen.com
Serving the information needs of Children entertainers.

Parents' Choice Awards
201 W. Padonia Rd. #203, Timonium, MD 21093
PH: 410-308-3858 FX: 410-308-3877
awards@parents-choice.org
www.parents-choice.org
Details and entry forms are available online.

Christian

Academy of Gospel Music Arts
1205 Division St., Nashville, TN 37203
PH: 615-242-0303 FX: 615-254-9755
www.gospelmusic.org/agma
Supporting growth and development of Gospel artists.

Christian Country Music Association
PO Box 101336, Nashville, TN 37224
PH: 615-742-9210 FX: 615-248-8505
www.ccma.cc
Promoting Christian Country music.

Christian Indies
PH: 877-295-7049
Jeff Henderson jeff@worshiploud.com
www.christianindies.com
Bringing you the best of Christian Indie bands including the most concise databases of band and venue information and resources.

ChristianCoffeehouse.info
PH: 985-781-0830
David Grant info@ChristianCoffeehouse.info
www.hismusic.com
The Internet's most complete, up-to-date list of Christian coffeehouse websites.

ChristianMusicMonthly.com
Mark Weber primopr716@juno.com
ChristianMusicMonthly.com
Covers contemporary Christian and Gospel music in an entertaining and informative way. News, interviews and spotlights.

Creative Soul
PH: 615-400-3910
Eric Copeland ec@CreativeSoulOnline.com
www.CreativeSoulOnline.com
Nashville-based Christian music company designed for artists who need to reach the next level of music ministry.

FindJesusFreaks.com
admin@findjesusfreaks.com
www.findjesusfreaks.com
It's a database/network of free classifieds for Christian musicians.

Gospel Elevations
2710 Barth St., Flint, MI 48504
PH: 810-625-0992
James Robinson jrobin747@yahoo.com
www.gospelelevations.net
A site where people can hear area artist and read their bio and contact them.

Gospel Music Association
1205 Division St., Nashville, TN 37203
PH: 615-242-0303 FX: 615-254-9755
www.gospelmusic.org
Promoting the development of all forms of Gospel music.

Gospel Music Workshop of America
3908 W. Warren Ave. Detroit, MI 48208
PH: 313-898-6900
Manager@gmwa.org
www.gmwa.org
Dedicated to the perpetuation of Gospel music.

Gospel on Demand
1172 Winding Meadows Rd. Rockledge, FL 32955
PH: 321-567-0304 FX: 321-268-1551
www.godmagg.com
Source for Christian culture and music!!!

GospelIndex.com
PO Box 1892, Lowell, MA 01853
PH: 978-590-4609
www.gospelindex.com
Independent and unsigned Gospel music talent.

Heaven's Metal
webmaster@heavensmetal.com
www.heavensmetal.com
Resource for minor-label Christian CD releases.

HeavenSound
gary@heavensound.com
www.heavensound.com
Concert and artist information for supporters of Gospel Music.

Independent Soul
Michael Nicholson staff@independent-soul.com
www.independent-soul.com
A source for locating musical talent for events at a low cost.

Ministry Networks
823 Southdale Rd. East London, ON N6E 1V7
PH: 519-668-2517
ministrynetworks@sympatico.ca
www.ministrynetworks.rockofages.ca
Ask us about a Christian Radio list that suits your style of music to get the air play your music needs. International, Canadian and American Christian radio lists available.

National Association of Christian Rock Radio
nacrr@nacrr.org
www.nacrr.org
Supports those struggling to work in this new and progressive avenue of ministry.

Really Big City Festivals
76 S. LaSalle St. #202, Aurora, IL 60505
PH: 630-803-5060
info@reallybigcity.com
www.reallybigcity.com
Excellent exposure for upcoming Christian bands!

Urban Gospel Alliance
PO Box 5211, Oakland, CA 94605
PH: 510-472-0177
crj_lawn@msn.com
www.urbangospelalliance.com
Broadening Gospel music's reach into the streets.

USA Church
www.usachurch.com
Christian resource that has an entertainment section for most US cities. You can post gigs, music, news etc.

Classical

North America

United States

Afrocentric Voices in Classical Music
Randye Jones rljones@afrovoices.com
www.afrovoices.com
Focusing on African American performers.

American Composers Forum
332 Minnesota St. #145E, St. Paul, MN 55101-1300
PH: 651-228-1407 FX: 651-291-7978
mail@composersforum.org
www.composersforum.org
Supporting composers and developing new markets for their music.

American Guild of Musical Artists
1430 Broadway, 14th Fl. New York, NY 10018
PH: 212-265-3687 FX: 212-262-9088
www.musicalartists.org
Labor organization that represents Operatic, Choral and Dance artists.

American Harp Society
PO Box 38334, Los Angeles, CA 90038-0334
kmoon@UCLAlumni.net
www.harpsociety.org
National society that promotes harpists.

American Music Center
30 W. 26th St. #1001, New York, NY 10010
PH: 212-366-5260 FX: 212-366-5265
center@amc.net
www.amc.net
Encourages the composition of contemporary (American) music.

American Pianists Association
apainfo@americanpianists.org
www.americanpianists.org
Advancing the careers of American Classical and Jazz pianists.

American Viola Society
13140 Coit Rd. #320, LB 120,
Dallas, TX 75240-5737
PH: 972-233-9107
cforbes@uta.edu
www.americanviolasociety.org
Promotion of viola performance and research.

Cadenza Musicians' Directory
PH: 44-20-8840-1564
www.cadenza.org
Directory of performances and artists.

Center for the Promotion of Contemporary Composers
PO Box 631043, Nacogdoches, TX 75963
cpcc@under.org
www.under.org/cpcc
An Internet-based service organization for composers.

Chamber Music America
305 7th Ave. 5th Fl. New York, NY 10001
PH: 212-242-2022 FX: 212-242-7955
www.chamber-music.org
Promotes artistic excellence and economic stability within the profession.

Chorus America
1156 15th St. NW #310, Washington, DC 20005
PH: 202-331-7577
service@chorusamerica.org
www.chorusamerica.org
Strengthens choruses and increases appreciation of Choral music..

Classical Notes
pgutmann@wcsr.com
www.classicalnotes.net
Classical music reviews, articles and commentary.

Classicalist.com
info@classicalist.com
www.classicalist.com
A classical music artists' directory.

classicOL.com
info@classicol.com
www.classicol.com
Get your free website specifically designed for Classical musicians.

ClassiQuest
29 Alscot Ln. Langhorne, PA 19047
PH: 215-891-0560 FX: 215-891-0561
David Osenberg Osenbergdd@aol.com
www.classiquest.com
FREE service for those in the music media.

Composers Concordance
PO Box 36-20548 PABT,
New York, NY 10129
info@composersconcordance.org
www.composersconcordance.org
Soliciting scores via a national search effort.

Copyright and Music
marbeth@marthabeth.com
www.serve.com/marbeth/music_copyright.html
Generalizations about copyright information.

Early Music America
2366 Eastlake Ave. E. #429,
Seattle, WA 98102
PH: 206-720-6270
FX: 206-720-6290
info@earlymusic.org
earlymusic.org
Extensive resources for members.

Early Music Network & News
3 Onslow House, Castle Rd.
Turnbridge Wells,
Kent, TN4 8BY UK
PH: 44-0-1892-11652
FX: 44-0-1892-11652
info@earlymusic.org.uk
www.earlymusic.org.uk
Open for submissions and inclusion on site.

earlyMusic.net
PO Box 854,
Atlanta, GA 30301
PH: 770-638-7554
FX: 770-638-7554
office@earlymusic.net
www.earlymusic.net
Information and services about early music.

hornplayer.net
www.hornplayer.net
Free classifieds and information archive.

International Horn Society
manager@hornsociety.org
www.hornsociety.org
Preservation and promotion of the horn

International Society of Bassists
13140 Coit Rd. #320, LB 120,
Dallas, TX 75240
PH: 972-233-9107
FX: 972-490-4219
info@isbworldoffice.com
www.ISBworldoffice.com
Inspiring public interest in the double bass.

YOUR HANDBOOK FOR THE INDIE REVOLUTION!
Available in both print and .pdf formats

INDIE POWER:

A Business-Building Guide For Record Labels, Music Production Houses, and Merchant Musicians

by Peter Spellman

What they're saying about INDIE POWER:

"INDIE POWER unveils a comprehensive blueprint of creative strategies for music business success in changing times..."
— Dan Kimpel, Music Connection magazine, author, *Networking in the Music Business*

"...offers a comprehensive guide for creating your own 21st century music business from the inside out. Awesome and empowering".
— John Braheny, Songwriting/music industry consultant. Author: *The Craft and Business of Songwriting*

"Spellman's guide opens your eyes and hands to the powerful knowledge you need to create your own world. Read it and soar!"
— Scooter Scudieri, Performing & Recording Artist

"Are you serious about success or just daydreaming? This awesome book is the test."
— Derek Sivers, President, CDBaby

The power's in your corner; now learn how to use it!

Get yours at www.mbsolutions.com

International Trumpet Guild
241 E. Main St. #247, Westfield, MA 01086-1633
FX: 413-568-1913
editor@trumpetguild.org
www.trumpetguild.org
Promotes communication among trumpet players around the world.

International Tuba and Euphonium Association
2253 Downing St., Denver, CO 80205
PH: 303-832-4676 FX: 303-832-0839
ITEA@denverbrass.org
www.iteaonline.org
Promotes performance of the euphonium and tuba.

Internet Bass Clarinet Society
kim@new-music.org
www.new-music.org
Information about bass clarinet performances.

Internet Cello Society
editor@cello.org
www.cello.org
An international cyber-community of cellists.

Meet the Composer
75 9th Ave. 3R #C, New York, NY 10011
PH: 212-645-6949 FX: 212-645-9669
hhitchens@meetthecomposer.org
www.meetthecomposer.org
Increase opportunities for composers..

Musical Chairs
features@musicalchairs.info
www.musicalchairs.info
World-wide orchestral jobs and competitions.

MUSIClassical
c/o SuperSoundStudios, 4063 Higbee St. 2nd Fl. Rear, Philadelphia, PA 19135-4422
RACampbell musiclassical@yahoo.com
www.musiclassical.com
Classical music education and information.

National Association of Composers
503 Tahoe St., Natchitoches, LA 71457-5718
PH: 318-357-0924
nacusa@music-usa.org
www.music-usa.org/nacusa
Promotion and performance of American music.

New Directions Cello Association
501 Linn St., Ithaca, NY 14850
PH: 607-277-1686
ndca@clarityconnect.com
www.newdirectionscello.com
Newsletter, interviews, events and more.

Opera Base
mike.gibb@operabase.org
www.operabase.com
Extensive online resource for opera artists.

Operissimo
opera@operissimo.com
www.operissimo.com
Add your information to our database.

Society of Composers
PO Box 450, New York, NY 10113-0450
secretary@societyofcomposers.org
www.societyofcomposers.org
A professional society promoting new and contemporary music.

Viola Web Site
tasks@viola.com
www.viola.com
Viola events and competitions, articles, resources and publishers.

World Intellectual Property Organization
PH: 41-22-338-91-11
wipo.mail@wipo.int
www.wipo.org
Promoting the use and protection of works of the human spirit, through patents and copyright

Young Artists International
2430 Apollo Dr. Los Angeles, CA 90046-1628
PH: 310-281-3303 FX: 323-969-8742
info@youngartists.org
www.youngartists.org
Develops the careers of exceptionally gifted young musicians.

Young Concert Artists
250 W. 57th St. #1222, New York, NY 10019
PH: 212-307-6655 FX: 212-581-8894
yca@yca.org
www.yca.org
Discovering and launching the careers of extraordinary young musicians.

Europe

France

ConcertoNet.com
67 rue St. Jacques, 75005 Paris, France
concertonet@yahoo.com
www.concertonet.com
Providing information about Classical music worldwide.

La Lettre du Musicien
14 rue Violet, F.75015, Paris, France
PH: 33-01-56-77-04-00 FX: 33-01-56-77-04-09
info@lettre-musicien.fr
www.lettre-musicien.fr
News and information from the Classical music scene in Europe.

United Kingdom

Impulse Classical Music
impulse@impulse-music.co.uk
www.impulse-music.co.uk
Provides personalized pages on performers and composers.

International Assoc. of Music Information Centres
www.iamic.ie
www.iaml.info
Network of organizations promoting new music.

Muso
11th Fl. Portland Tower, Portland St., Manchester, M1 3LF UK
PH: 0161-238-4942 FX: 0161-247-7978
info@muso-online.com
www.muso-online.com
Designed for young professional musicians, students or music enthusiasts wanting to keep up with the latest news and gossip, Muso provides essential advice on courses, careers as well as celebrity interviews and great competitions.

Country

All About Country
5009 Crosswinds Dr. Wilmington, NC 28409
PH: 910-264-6006 FX: 910-3130228
Bill Hennes bhennes105@aol.com
www.allaboutcountry.com
THE website where Country labels & artists can reach radio decision makers. We carry the latest news and information.

Americana Music Association
PO Box 128077, Nashville, TN 37212
info@americanamusic.org
www.americanamusic.org
Promotes awareness of this genre.

Association of North Country Fiddlers
PO Box 100, Norfolk, NY 13667-0100
PH: 315-353-2049
www.fiddlers.org
Get your events listed here free!

Country & Gospel Music Message Board
David W. Kelley
CountryMusicPromoter@webtv.net
community-2.webtv.net/CountryMusicPromoter/CheckoutOurCountry
A site where Country Music DJs from around the world post their playlists.

Country Music Showcase International
PO Box 368, Carlisle, IA 50047
PH: 515-989-3748
haroldl@cmshowcase.org
www.cmshowcase.org
Promotes 14 art forms of Country music.

The Euro Americana Chart
euroamericanachart@hetnet.nl
www.euroamericanachart.nl
Compiled by DJs, journalists, retailers, promoters and other people who are interested in Americana music from all over Europe. Every month they send in their top 6 CDs.

FiddleFork
276 Glenpatrick Dr. Cochrance, AB T4C 1G6
PH: 403-932-6484
info@fiddlefork.com
fiddlefork.com
One stop platform for anything fiddle related.

International Bluegrass Music Association
2 Music Cir. S. #100, Nashville, TN 37203
PH: 615-256-3222 FX: 615-256-0450
ibma@ibma.org
www.ibma.org
Promoting and expanding the success of Bluegrass music.

International Country Music Association
PO Box 292937, Nashville, TN 37229
intlcma@aol.com
www.radiocountry.org
Songwriter and artist pages.

MandoZine
john@mandozine.com
www.mandozine.com
News, spotlights and some reviews.

National Traditional Country Music Association
PO Box 492, Anita, IA 50020
PH: 712-762-4363
bobeverhart@yahoo.com
www.oldtimemusic.bigstep.com
Preserving traditional Country and Bluegrass music.

Society for the Preservation of Bluegrass Music of America
PO Box 271, Kirksville, MO 63501
PH: 660-665-7172 FX: 660-655-7450
Chuck Stearman spbgma@kvmo.net
www.spbgma.com
Preserves traditional Bluegrass music.

Western Music Association
PO Box 35008, Tuscon, AZ 85740
PH: 877-588-3747
Dboots4@aol.com
www.westernmusic.org
Promotes traditional and contemporary music of the Great American West.

Dance

dancetech.com
admin@dancetech.com
www.dancetech.com
Offers 100% independent product reviews, newbie resources, gear listings + FREE on-line music-space & FREE artist/band/DJ homepages for all bands & musicians.

Drum Voice
8993 Mauriac St., Saint-Leonard, QC H1P 2N4
PH: 514-806-4266
Eric Mikhail, Soumya Boussouf
info@drumvoice.com
www.drumvoice.com
Electronic music industry contacts and resources for artists, companies and professionals.

The Electronica Primer
phobos.plato.nl/e-primer
Explains the differences between House, Techno, Breakbeat, Jungle and all other sub-genres from the Electronic Dance and listening music.

Floorelevators.com
www.floorelevators.com/dancedjlinks
Dance music industry directory.

junglescene.com
junglescene.com
Drum 'n Bass community. News, events, audio etc.

littledetroit.net
www.littledetroit.net
Techno and Electro music community.

Pear Music Ltd.
Unit 65a, Eurolink Business Centre, Effra Rd.
London, SW2 1BZ UK
PH: +44 (0) 207-274-2006
FX: +44 (0) 207-274-2552
Esther esther@lovelypear.com
www.lovelypear.com
Releases quality song based tracks with Dance remixes from artists across the globe. Previous releases have been supported by key players in the scene.

quantum lounge
nic info@quantumlounge.net
www.quantumlounge.net
Created as an alternative musical outlet for discerning ears who won't settle for mainstream top 40s or customary Dance culture.

The Record Pool
support@therecordpool.com
www.therecordpool.com
Resource for new and promotional music for today's DJs.

SPRACI
PH: 61-0-402-605-188 FX: 603-691-5915
support@spraci.com
www.spraci.com
A worldwide resource site for parties/clubs/festivals etc.

Experimental

The 8bitpeoples
454 Fort Washington Ave. Apt. 25B,
New York, NY 10033
admin@8bitpeoples.com
www.8bitpeoples.com
A collective of artists sharing a common love for classic videogames and an approach to music which reflected this obsession. Your work should represent some influence, utilization, or extension of the 8bit videogame/home computer aesthetic. Do NOT send MP3s as email attachments.

clan analogue
clananalogue.org
Indie record label that assists with promotional materials.

Electronic Music Foundation
116 N. Lake Ave. Albany, NY 12206
PH: 518-434-4110 FX: 518-434-0308
emf@emf.org
www.emf.org
Increasing the public's understanding of Electronic music.

The Gas Station
15a George St., Bath, BA1 2EN UK
PH: 44-0-125-442546
nick@sonicstate.com
www.the-gas-station.com
The Electronic musicians knowledgebase and number one discussion site.

International Computer Music Association
icma@umich.edu
www.computermusic.org
Serves composers and musicians interested in music and technology.

Other Minds
333 Valencia St. #303,
San Francisco, CA 94103-3552
PH: 415-934-8134 FX: 415-934-8136
otherminds@otherminds.org
www.otherminds.org
A global New Music community where composers, students, and listeners discover and learn about innovative music by composers from all over the world.

Society for Electro-Acoustic Music
1 Washington Sq. San Jose, CA 95192-0095
www.seamusonline.org
Represents every part of the country and virtually every musical style.

YourComputerMusic.com
Timo timo@yourcomputermusic.com
www.yourcomputermusic.com
Our mission is to provide you with information related to computer music making.

Film and TV

Film Music Magazine
11601 Wilshire Blvd. #500, Los Angeles, CA 90025
PH: 310-575-1820
info@filmmusicmag.com
www.filmmusicmag.com
Publication for professionals in the film and television music business.

The Film Music Network
FX: 310-575-1850
info@filmmusic.net
www.filmmusic.net
Facilitates networking among professionals in the film music business.

Film Score Monthly
8503 Washington Blvd. Culver City, CA 90232
PH: 310-253-9595 FX: 310-253-9588
lukas@filmscoremonthly.com
www.filmscoremonthly.com
Magazine about motion picture and television music.

Production Weekly
9669 Santa Monica Blvd. #1177,
Beverly Hills, CA 90210-4303
PH: 800-284-2230 FX: 310-868-2594
info@productionweekly.com
www.productionweekly.com
Provides the entertainment industry with the most comprehensive breakdown of projects in pre-production, preparation and development, for major studio as well as independent films, network and cable television movies, pilots and series, both domestic and international.

Society of Composers & Lyricists
400 S. Beverly Dr. #214, Beverly Hills, CA 90212
PH: 310-281-2812 FX: 310-284-4861
www.thescl.com
Focuses on the creative and business aspects of writing music and lyrics for film and television.

SoundtrackNet
12011 Rochester Ave. #7, Los Angeles, CA 90025
Dan Goldwasser dsg@soundtrack.net
www.soundtrack.net
Articles, news, interviews and resources about Film and Television music. We "personally" don't do anything like music placement, or accept unsolicited demos, etc. It would be like actors sending Entertainment Weekly their demo reels!

Folk

Celtic-Musicians.Net
PO Box 9014, Deakin,
Capital Territory 2600 Australia
postmaster@celtic-world.net
www.celtic-musicians.net
Information about both Traditional and Contemporary Celtic / Folk musicians!

FOLKDJ-L
listserv@lists.psu.edu
www.folkradio.org
An electronic discussion group for DJs and other people interested in folk-based music on the radio.

World Folk Music Association
PO Box 40553, Washington, DC 20016
PH: 202-362-2225
webmaster@wfma.net
wfma.net
Interviews with artists and songwriters, CD and tape reviews and more.

GLBT

Herland Sister Resources
2312 NW 39th, Oklahoma City, OK 73112
PH: 405-521-9696
HerlandSisters@cox.net
members.cox.net/herlandsisters/main.html
Womanist organization with a strong lesbian focus.

Lesbian and Gay Bands of America
PO Box 14874, San Francisco, CA 94114-0874
LGBAinfo@aol.com
www.gaybands.org
Bringing pride and understanding through music.

The Lesbian and Gay Country Music Association
PO Box 190565, San Francisco, CA 94119
PH: 415-773-9482
www.lgcma.com
Created to organize and direct efforts to enlighten the mainstream culture by promoting and supporting openly lesbian and gay country performers.

OutMedia
285 5th Ave. #446, Brooklyn, NY 11215
PH: 718-789-1776 FX: 718-789-8007
Shelly Weiss info@outmedia.org
www.outmedia.org
Our mission is to increase the positive visibility of LGBTQQA people and promote inclusive multiculturalism through the arts.

Outmusic
PO Box 376, Old Chelsea Stn.
New York, NY 10113-0376
PH: 212-330-9197
info@outmusic.com
www.outmusic.com
A network of gay, lesbian, bisexual and transgendered musicians and supporters. Performers, producers, promoters and press/media.

Goth

C8
stevvi@c8.com to
c8.com
Resource which posts articles, interviews, reviews etc.

darksites.com
sire@darksites.com
www.darksites.com
Post information - views, articles, interviews, reviews etc.

HellWire Industrial Music Underground
Syphon syphon@hellwire.com
www.hellwire.com
Music charts offering exposure to artists in the Electronic / Goth / Industrial genres. Includes area to post reviews.

Nocturnal Movements
PO Box 5583, Vancouver, WA 98668
PH: 360-513-9121
Jett Black industrie@sickamongthepure.com
nocturnalmovements.net/cgi-bin/ultimatebb.cgi
Find and post music news, web links, resources, reviews, interviews, media contact info, gig swap info, events, photographers, fetish, graphic designers, comic strip artists, music writers, DJs, and promoters, our collective promotion services, and so much more!!

Hip Hop

HipHop-Network.Com
177 Stillman St., San Francisco, CA 94107
info@hiphop-network.com
www.hiphop-network.com
Represents Hip Hop and everyday life in the Hip Hop community.

HIPHOPDIRECTORY.COM
jamess@hiphopdirectory.com
hiphopdirectory.com
Largest directory of quality Hip Hop and Rap sites.

HipHopHotSpot.Com
PO Box 35534, RPO Strath Barton,
Hamilton, ON L8H 7S6
Remi Blais support@hiphophotspot.com
www.hiphophotspot.com
Supports the growth of Hip Hop artists world wide.

Ill Crew Universal
200 S. McDowell Blvd. Petaluma, CA 94954
PH: 707-778-1314
Steve B. steveb@illcrew.org
www.illcrew.org
A worldwide Hip Hop organization dedicated to the preservation, activism, empowerment, balance and unity of Hip Hop culture expressed in all of its elements.

IndependentHH.com
PH: 262-206-2597
Kevin Muller kevin.muller@independenthh.com
www.independenthh.com
Provides up-and-coming Hip Hop artists with access to resources necessary to network, grow, and reach the next level in their career. We grows by having users submit accurate information about Hip Hop events, stores, open mics, artists etc.

Jackin4Beats.com
pressreleases@jackin4beats.com
jackin4beats.com
Send in your press release!

Listentomydemo.com
931 Monroe Dr. NE, Suite A102 #334,
Atlanta, GA 30308-1795
www.listentomydemo.com
Place your info online for others to see.

The Rap Game 101
therapgame101.com
Breaks down everything from A&R submission to distribution to rotation. Come school or be schooled.

Rappers Resource
PO Box 17223, Indianapolis, IN 46217
PH: 317-782-9948
Sales@rappersresource.com
www.rappersresource.com
Helps everyone associated with the Hip Hop industry.

Spitkicker
331 W. 57th St. #544, New York, NY 10019
www.spitkickers.com
Submit your bio and music to become a featured artist.

TLA-PROnline.com
administrator@tla-pronline.com
www.tla-pronline.com
A place where Independent Rap, Hip Hop and Spoken Word artists are represented. We can help artists get noticed with interviews and press releases.

webjhn.com
6393 Penn Ave. #319, Pittsburgh, PA 15206-4010
PH: 412-216-6790 FX: 412-362-3841
johng@webjhn.com
webjhn.com
Hip Hop and R&B music news and information.

Jam Band

Beginners B&P Instructions
www.mcnichol.com/bnp
Instructions for trading free live music on CD.

BlanksandPostage.com
PO Box 43345, Atlanta, GA 30336
pat@blanksandpostage.com
blanksandpostage.com
Your source for great bands and free music. Dedicated to the spread of free music across the world. We will be selling certain studio releases but all live shows are FREE!!

Coolmusicstuff.com
becky@coolmusicstuff.com
www.coolmusicstuff.com
A listing of hundreds of Jam band tour dates and festivals. If I dig what a band is doing, then I just might put them on the schedule.

Jam Band Meetup
jambands.meetup.com
Post information about your band.

JamBandDirectory.com
PH: 847-255-1946 FX: 847-890-6018
Matthew S. Rosenberg msr@jbdirectory.com
JamBandDirectory.com
Jam Band community featuring a variety of resources.

jamflower.org
info@jamflower.org
www.jamflower.org
We aim to be an important resource for the greater Jam Music scene.

KindWeb
www.kindweb.com
A KindWeb of KindFolk all over the world!

TheJamZone
thejamzone.com
Jam Band resource for new bands, music, band photos and much more.

Live Music Blog
justin@livemusicblog.com
www.livemusicblog.com
A blog featuring a collection of news, articles, discussions, reviews, and links all based around bands that thrive live, with my own special concentration on Jam bands.

Jazz

Creative Music Archive
info@creativemusicarchive.com
creativemusicarchive.com
A place of reference for creative musicians and their music.

Jazz Clubs Worldwide
www.jazz-clubs-worldwide.com
Contact information for hundreds of Jazz Clubs.

The Jazz Vocal Coalition
PO Box 8484, Long Beach, CA 90808
PH: 562-377-0971
Ellen Johnson jzvoc@jzvoc.org
www.jzvoc.org
Helping Jazz Singers by educating, promoting and uniting them.

The Jazzserver
info@jazzserver.org
www.jazzserver.org
Add your group, venue, festival or concerts to earth's coolest Jazz website for free!

JazzWeek
2117 Buffalo Rd. #317, Rochester, NY 14624
PH: 585-235-4685 FX: 775-878-7482
info@jazzweek.com
www.jazzweek.com
The definitive Jazz and Smooth Jazz national radio airplay chart.

The Polish Jazz Network
PO Box 40153, Long Beach, CA 90804
PH: 949-466-3517
info@polishjazz.com
www.polishjazz.com
The doorway to the world of improvised music from Poland. We offer the largest selection of material regarding Polish Jazz on the web.

Sax Talk
www.saxtalk.com
A central spot for sax players to meet, talk, buy and sell saxophones etc. Features an "Artist of the Month".

Latin

AfroCubaWeb
PO Box 1054, Arlington, MA 02474
contact@afrocubaweb.com
www.afrocubaweb.com
Information about current Cuban music events across the country.

AllBrazilianMusic
www.allbrazilianmusic.com
Aimed at providing news, information and critic reviews on Brazilian music.

Salsa Planet
salsaplanet@hotmail.com
www.salsaplanet.net
Covers Salsa events, music, dance workshops and concerts in Europe.

SalsaArtists.com
11271 Ventura Blvd. #151, Studio City, CA 91604
PH: 310-360-5947
info@salsaartists.com
www.salsaartists.com
Connects record companies, up-and-coming stars, unsigned artists and fans.

Metal

Army of Pit Soldiers
armyofpitsoldiers.com
Online community. Post news, bios, gigs etc.

bandpromo.de Germany
www.bandpromo.de
Band promotion, band-shop und band-support.

Hard Radio
feedback@hardradio.com
www.hardradio.com
The Metal site with no Alternative aftertaste.

Heavycore.org
PO Box 4324, Bloomington, IL 61702
poserdisposer@heavycore.org
www.heavycore.org
Promotion for Heavy bands and musicians.

Internet@Metal Germany
Juergen jgarus@nbnet.nb.ca
www.metalius.de
Offers a "free of charge" commercial website for all bands.

Metal HeadQuarters
www.metalheadquarters.com
Keeping Metal music alive.

Metal Map of Europe
metalmap.czweb.org

Metal Underground France
darkbeauty@netcourrier.com
www.metal-underground.com
Si vous désirez figurer parmi la liste des groupes référencés sur mon site, je vous invite à m'envoyer vos informations concernant votre groupe (Biographie, Discographie, Photos, etc. ...)

New Age

The Harp Column
hbrock@harpcolumn.com
www.harpcolumn.com
Interactive discussion groups, a calendar of events and news announcements regarding the harp.

Nuevas Músicas
Priscilla priscilla@yidneth.com
www.yidneth.com/nuevasmusicas
Created to promote the music of New Age artists in Spain and the entire world!

Progressive Rock

Calyx
13 rue du Rif-Tronchard, 38120 St. Egrève, France
PH: 33-4-76-75-11-26.
Aymeric Leroy calyx@club-internet.fr
Working towards being the definitive source of information on the Canterbury Scene.

The Gibraltar Encyclopedia of Progressive Rock
webmaster@gepr.net
www.gepr.net
Designed as a reference for visitors to discover bands that are unfamiliar and to broaden their listening horizons.

Punk

Book Your Own Fucking Life
byofl@byofl.org
www.byofl.org
Guide for the Punk/Hardcore DIY community.

Dirtbag Clothing
1945 E. Francisco #F, San Rafael, CA 94901
PH: 877-347-8224 FX: 415-460-0206
Doug Canning contact@dirtbagclothing.com
dirtbagclothing.com
Killer Sport, Streetwear and Skate clothes. Wear it 'til it stinks!

Geek Stink Breath
Dujo anicegreenday@hotmail.com
www.geekstinkbreath.net
Information about Punk Rock music.

Grunnen Rocks scene
PO Box 6058, 9702 HB, Groningen,
The Netherlands
www.grunnenrocks.nl
News, reviews and more on the worldwide scene.

The idobi Network
1825 New Hampshire Ave. #407,
Washington, DC 20009
PH: 866-441-3088
music@idobi.com
www.idobi.com
Rock/Punk music news, features and interviews.

PunkDates.com
submissions@punkdates.com
www.punkdates.com
We have become "The #1 Source for Show Listings", not only because we list more shows than anyone else, but because of the ethics and values we hold to be true.

PunkRock.org
www.punkrock.org
Artist and label directory.

Reggae

BOOYAKA
www.booyakamagazine.net
The vibes of Reggae, Ska and Dancehall.

IREGGAE
www.ireggae.com
Promoting the sound of Reggae music.

Irielion
PH: 972086519090
Lee lee@irielion.com
www.irielion.com
Irie Dutch/Belgian and Israeli Reggae/Ska concert agenda.

One Love Reggae
PO Box 2026, Sonoma, CA 95476
PH: 707-933-9790 FX: 707-933-9494
Bob Slayton onelove@humboldt.net
www.onelovereggae.com
West coast calendar...clubs by state that do live music.... festivals by month....

Reggae Festival Guide Online
PO Box 50635, Reno, NV 89513
PH: 775-337-8344 FX: 775-337-6499
kaati@reggaefestivalguide.com
www.reggaefestivalguide.com
Find Reggae festivals around the world!

Reggae Sun Television
Inside The Little Pub Complex, 59 Main St.,
Ocho Rios, St. Ann, Jamaica
production@reggaesun.com
www.reggaesun.tv
Our focus is on Jamaica's rich cultural heritage.

Skasummit.com
www.skasummit.com
One of the best places for Ska bands to promote to the Ska scene anywhere in the world.

Special Blend
Liloa Jahfree-I Dunn
liloa@pacificsoundsouternational.com
www.pacificsoundsouternational.com
A Reggae music promotions and sound system collective based in Hawaii.

USABB Reggae
989 Crespi Dr. Pacifica, CA 94044
PH: 650-355-3434 FX: 650-355-3157
info@ReggaeMusic.us
reggaemusic.us
Free service website to all USA based Reggae bands.

Soul / R&B

Amplified
amplified@amplified-online.co.uk
www.amplified-online.co.uk
Our mandate has always been the support and promotion of Black Music not embraced by the mainstream yet loved by millions around the globe.

Goldsoul
www.soulnight.co.uk
Our Northern Soul Night Calendar provides up to the minute information on a selection of top nights throughout the UK. Please submit your events for free!

The Japan African-American Music Society
Tamari 30-1, Kakegawa City, Shizuoka Prefecture,
Japan 436-0011
PH/FX: 81-537-23-7585
Malcolm W. Adams jams@totown.net
www.totown.net/jams.htm
An organization of professional musicians living and working in Japan. Our goal is to improve the economic status, social position and general welfare of our members.

soulportal.dk
Frank Ryle frank@soulportal.dk
www.soulportal.dk
Danish site featuring interviews and music charts. Soul, Jazz, R&B and Hip Hop.

Soulful Kinda Music
daverimmer1@btinternet.com
www.soulfulkindamusic.net
The definitive major reference site for Soul artists discographies. If you have a discography that you would like to see on the site, let me have a copy.

Soulwalking
www.soulwalking.co.uk
General resource with gigs, news, articles and more.

Women in Music

BunnyBass
bunnies@bunnybass.com
www.bunnybass.com
An all-girl bass players picture archive.

Chick Bands that Rock
ju924@hotmail.com
geocities.com/grrlbands
For all the female musicians that Rock.

Chick Singer Night
PO Box 6173, Thousand Oaks, CA 91360
la@chicksingernight.com
www.chicksingernight.com
All singers are welcome to submit demos and perform.

Chicks Rockfest
5857 Childs Ave., Cincinnati, OH 45248
PH: 513-404-0385
Jenny Schmidt chicksrockfest@gmail.com
www.chicksrockfest.com
Annual festival for independent artists who feature at least one girl in their band. We also sponsor fund raising tours throughout the year a.k.a. Chicks on the Road.

DiVAstation.com
yiannis@divastation.com
www.divastation.com
Pictures, bios, news and reviews of some of your favorite female singers.

Donne in Musica *(Women in Music)*
03014 Fiuggi Citta (FR), Italy
PH: 0775-504-480 FX: 0775-504-480
info@donneinmusica.org
www.donneinmusica.org
Holds events promoting women's music in Italy.

Drummergirl
2 E. Broadway, 4th Fl. New York, NY 10038
Happy Mazza dginfo@happymazza.com
www.drummergirl.com
For women who drum.

FEMALE PRESSURE
info@femalepressure.net
www.indigo-inc.at
International database for female DJs and/or producers.

gURLpages
c/o ivillage, 500 7th Ave. 14th Fl.
New York, NY 10018
staff@gURL.com
www.gurl.com
Free web pages service for women.

Heartless Bitches International
supremebitch@heartless-bitches.com
www.heartless-bitches.com
Promoting strong, proud women.

Indiegrrl
4769 Blakely Ave. Bainbridge Island, WA 98110
hsfigueroa@indiegrrl.com
www.indiegrrl.com
For women in the Indie music industry.

IndieMusicCoach.com
PO Box 16940, Sugar Land, TX 77496-6940
PH: 281-541-0981 FX: 281-565-4239
Madalyn Sklar info@indiemusiccoach.com
www.indiemusiccoach.com
One-on-one consulting and coaching for musicians at affordable hourly rates.

International Women in Jazz
PO Box 230015, Hollis, NY 11423
PH: 212-560-7553
www.internationalwomeninjazz.com
Supporting women Jazz artists.

The Kapralova Society
info@kapralova.org
www.kapralova.org
Dedicated to promoting women in the field of Classical Music.

Ladyfest
PO Box 1784, Olympia, WA 98507
info@ladyfest.org
www.ladyfest.org
Worldwide festivals promoting the talents and goals of women. Check our website for a Ladyfest near you.

Lawgirl.com
www.lawgirl.com
A free, interactive legal resource for those in the arts.

The Other Side
Laura Lasley babydoclaz@aol.com
www.guitarnoise.com/otherside.php
Promoting women who play the guitar.

Planet Woman
info@planetwoman.net
www.planetwoman.net
Provides concerts and workshops and particularly aims to perform in areas or to groups, which wouldn't otherwise receive a diverse range of musical live acts.

Professional Women Singers Association
PO Box 884, New York, NY 10024
PH: 212-969-0590 FX: 928-395-2560
info@womensingers.org
www.womensingers.org
Our performing members specialize in a variety of Classical musical genres. Singers are selected by a jury of voice teachers, coaches and directors. The group sponsors concerts, master classes and seminars for both singers and the community at large.

Punk Girl *France*
infos@panx.net
www.panx.net/punkgirl
A cool Punk Rock girl photo gallery.

rockabillygirls.com
609 N. La Fayette Park Pl. Silver Lake, CA 90026
kelly@rockabillygirls.com
www.rockabillygirls.com
Database for Rockabilly, Psychobilly and Swing female-led bands.

Rocket Girl
admin@rocketgirls.net
www.rocketgirls.net
The one stop source for all things grrrl.

SISTA Factory
sistafact@aol.com
www.sistafactory.com
Promotes and showcases diverse performing artists.

Skirt Magazine
info@skirtmag.com
www.skirtmag.com
Features CDs by women each month.

web-goddess.net
web-goddess.net
A portal site for spiffy personal web pages made by chicks.

Women in Jazz
jazzmaster@jazzusa.com
jazzwomen.org
Information about women in Jazz, both past and present.

Women in Music
PO Box 441, Radio City Station,
New York, NY 10101
PH: 212-459-4580
wim@womeninmusic.org
www.womeninmusic.org
Publishes Women in Music Magazine.

Women In Music National Network
31121 Mission Blvd. #300, Haywar, CA 94544
PH: 510-232-2897 FXA: 510-215-2846
admin@womeninmusic.com
www.womeninmusic.com
Supports the activities of women in all areas of music.

Women in Music UK
7 Tavern St., Stowmarket, Suffollk, IP14 1PJ UK
PH: 01449-673990 FX: 01449-673994
info@womeninmusic.org.uk
www.womeninmusic.org.uk
Supports, encourages and enables women to make music.

World Music

Local World Music Guides
info@worldmusiccentral.org
www.worldmusiccentral.org/staticpages/index.php/local_scenes
Offers a series of World music guides for those who want to learn about the local music scenes in specific cities throughout the globe.

www.indiebible.com   301   The Indie Bible – 7th Edition

IndieGate.com
Independent Music Store

create your own online store in seconds!

Sell your CDs, merchandise and digital files directly to your consumers from our site and yours too. Use our exclusive non-branded pages to create a high-powered, full featured storefront within your site in only seconds! No IndieGate logos to distract your visitors. We keep only 20% of each sale, and we provide a FREE GIFT to your customers for each CD they buy. We'll help you set up your storefront, encode your music for sound clips in a Flash powered "IndiePlayer" protecting them from download, and help you market your music. Our powerful database gives you 24/7 access to reports detailing your sales activity, and the ability to edit your store. It's simple, effective and effortless! We also advertise your CDs in our online/offline magazine, the InterMixx Webzine and we offer special marketing programs to help you sell more CDs.

It's only $30.00 to get started so don't wait.

www.IndieGate.com

EXCITING NEW GRAND PRIZE!!!!.....
WIN AN ALL EXPENSES PAID WRITING AND PERFORMING RETREAT TO YOUR CHOICE OF COSTA RICA, IRELAND, NEW ZEALAND, CRETE, SWEDEN, BIG SUR, OR DENMARK !!!

* UNISONG INTERNATIONAL SONG CONTEST *

MORE CATEGORIES!
MORE PRIZES!
MORE OPPORTUNITIES!
SAME PERSONAL ATTENTION!

OVER $60,000 IN CASH & PRIZES

PASSPORT FOR A MUSICAL PLANET

earlyBird entry Deadline December 15 2005

regular entry Deadline March 15 2006

GO WWW.UNISONG.COM

New and Improved Songwriting Competition created by songwriters for songwriters since 1997. We have always prided ourselves on offering creative innovations and the kind of personal attention you can't get with any other contest. That's because we come from the same place as you do. Working songwriters & artists who also happen to do this. So go to the website and see all the cool new stuff we'll be doing this year that others are sure to follow...
— Alan Roy Scott..."Unisong" Founder

SECTION SEVEN: ARTICLES THAT WILL HELP YOU SUCCEED IN THE MUSIC BUSINESS

"Don't forget to applaud the little steps, as well as the big." - **Janet Fisher, Goodnight Kiss Music**

While creating The Indie Bible I have been fortunate enough to have met many of the most knowledgeable people in the Independent Music Industry. Successful authors, publicists, music reviewers, entertainment lawyers etc. I thought it would be a good fit if I presented several of their articles to help you gain insight on how to deal with the many twists and turns of this complicated industry. The articles in this section are sure to be helpful to musicians and songwriters, and especially to those that are just starting out. Every author I asked was kind enough to submit an article that will help you to move forward with your music career. Do yourself a favor, and put their experience to work for you!

o v e r v i e w

STAYING AHEAD OF THE CURVE: MOLDING YOUR MUSIC CAREER FOR MAXIMUM IMPACT

by Peter Spellman, MbSolutions.com
© 2006 All Rights Reserved. Used By Permission

The music biz stands at an historical crossroads – almost every aspect of the way people create, consume and listen to popular music is changing, dwarfing even the seismic shift in the 1880s when music lovers turned from sheet music and player pianos to wax cylinders and later, newfangled 78 rpm phonograph records.

The following highlights some of the most ground-shaking and, (in my opinion), enduring "metatrends" currently shaping the biz. The intent is to give guidelines to both musicians and industry careerists to help set their forward sails on this crazy ocean we call music.

METATREND 1: Empowered Music Consumers

Today may be the very best time to be a music fan, especially one looking for a connection to a favorite artist or guidance and access to the exotic or rare.

Be it the iPod, alluring satellite radio services such as XM, the fan-beloved minutiae posted on Web sites, the availability of live music performances on AOL, the esoteric music videos streaming off Launch.com or the self-tailored satisfaction of burning a homemade mix on CD at home, there is a singular zest to the modern fan experience today.

The public is now driving the market. The challenge to the industry is to respond positively in such a way as to secure the future of music while satisfying customer demand and providing choice.

It's becoming increasingly more difficult for companies to treat us like "mass market" ciphers. The trend is towards "mass customization" where consumers' unique needs are front and center. Some marketing gurus call this trend "The 1-to-1 Future" and the companies that can dance with this trend will prosper.

What You Can Do About It

- Get to know your fans. They are your chief asset going forward and the better you know them, the better you can communicate with them, build loyalty and enlist them in lending their support to you and your music projects.

- Involve them, empower them, mobilize them, let them co-create with you. None of us knows what all of us know. Build a community, a fan club, a subscription service and learn how to pool the wisdom of your following.

- Provide potential customers with as much choice as possible.

- Learn the technologies that will help you customize your communications with customers and fans.

METATREND 2: Music Product to Music as Service

Presenting music as a service, like radio or TV, would seem on the surface to be less profitable than selling millions of CDs, but actually, this change will be positive for the music industry. It will be able to sell more things associated with music. But the actual sale of music as a product will make less sense. It will be a move from transaction-based push to flat-fee pull.

Consumers have clicked, and they demand access to content by any means necessary. Just as AOL has gone from selling you five minutes of access to a take-whatever-you-want model, music too will move to a flat-fee model.

We're not there just yet. But in the next few years, the requisite technology will fall into place. Then most of us will carry a wireless Internet uber-gadget wherever we go – a unified cellphone/MP3 player/ digital assistant/Blackberry/ camera/GPS locater/video recorder/co-pilot for life. This device will receive wireless Internet audio, a loose term I use to describe the various forms of streaming audio starting to appear on the Internet. With streaming audio, you can hear the music you love any time, anywhere.

The future isn't about a change in distribution, it's about the atrophy of distribution itself. Instead of distributing things, we'll get access. It's a critical difference.

The future isn't about downloading songs and burning CDs. It's about just-in-time customized delivery. Music as on-demand service not as industry-dictated product. Just as in the early days of the record industry (c. 1900), music publishing will once again assume the primary role in the biz. Music will become available for diverse uses dictated by consumers and businesses.

How fast will the sun set on the compact disc? Quarter-size CDs that can float among compatible music players, computers, game devices, digital cameras and personal digital assistants are already developed.

Of course, a massive installed base of CD players means that the traditional recording industry markets are not going to disappear or even be impacted by digital distribution in the short term. But rising consumer interest in downloads and an increasingly multi-media business-to-business economy opens new opportunities for composers, editors, sound designers, and all forms of audio producer.

What You Can Do About It

- You should be figuring out how to distribute your work through digital music services now. The Net is your Open Mic to the world. Get yourself onto iTunes, Rhapsody and MusicNet. Learn the virtual ropes.

- As the industry moves away from physical product, it becomes increasingly important for musicians to learn the rules of licensing (read, 'renting') their music.

- Seek out users of music as well as buyers.

- Prepare for a multi-platform approach – value-added packages containing your music, artwork, DVDs, etc AND a container-less presentation using various online showcases, messageboards and portals.

- Develop marketing plans for both your selected singles as well as for your full-length albums. 50% of current online music sales are in the singles format.

METATREND 3: The Next Music Companies

The writing is on the wall for traditional music companies. The record industry grew rapidly, matured, and is now in the throes of transformation. How successful this transformation will be depends on how creatively the musical industrial complex can dance with all the changes spiraling around it.

Unfortunately, so much of the music industry is beholden to corporate owners, itchy for quick profits, and driven by rigid corporate imperatives. This wreaks havoc with artist development; hell, it wreaks havoc with business development, and necessitates high turnover of both artists and employees. Major labels are also saddled with legacy problems regarding production and retail. Thus the geologic tempo of industry change.

But the same forces undoing the larger music companies are empowering individual musicians and micro-businesses.

As with most modern industries, a silent computer on a desk is the wildcard that makes so much tradition redundant. Perhaps the term "record company" itself is becoming outdated – "Music Company" might be more relevant. Many music biz execs echo the words of Steve Becket of Warp Records when he says, "I think we'll mutate into a new type of company – mixture of artist management, publisher, marketing consultant, agent and promoter." "We're a communications company," agrees Marc Jones of Wall of Sound, "and that's what we're becoming more everyday. I don't think the model for a traditional record label will exist in this environment anymore."

But we don't have to solve the dilemma for the mainstream music business about which future to embrace. We're living the side-stream music movement that may inspire the majors but, God willing, will never be completely controlled by them.

Unlike mainstream commercial music, the farther you get out onto the fringes, the more helpful people become. The more participants, the greater the chances that something truly interesting will emerge from the collective rabble.

A new generation of music entrepreneurs is rising with a power in its corner it has never had before. The times are ripe for change and these creators are the spearhead.

What You Can Do About It

- The appetite for music only grows around the globe and you can satisfy it. You'll need to employ your maverick instincts over conventional "business rules", take fuller responsibility for your own success, and beware of "standard industry practices" that can chain your career.

- Concepts like "company", "work", "job" and "career" are morphing. The entire business economy is passing through a transition the likes of which haven't been seen since the industrial revolution. Rather than seeing your "career" as a ladder, think of it as a rouge wave full of rises, dips and switchbacks.

- It's time to think outside the normal channels of business and imagine new kinds of companies. Creative alliances and partnerships are the key. Combining good music, cheap, global distribution and business savvy almost guarantees success in today's music-hungry world.

METATREND 4: Segmenting Music Markets & Niche Music Cultures

I often hear musicians moaning about how consolidation and the monopolization of the media by companies like Clear Channel and Viacom threaten musical diversity, yet I can hear and obtain more interesting music today than I could ever hope to in the 1950s.

The menu of music choices and styles expands daily.

When the Grammys started in 1958 there were 28 categories of awards; last year there were 105! Check out the "Music Styles" page at the allmusic.com and you'll find over forty styles of music, each with a drop-down menu of several "sub-styles."

Even the pop charts, which have made room in recent months for PJ Harvey, Modest Mouse, Diana Krall and Franz Ferdinand, suggests there's an audience starving for something other than junk food.

The music market continues to segment and each segment is a "world", a portal, through which small companies can create value and success.

While good news for niche companies, this is bad news for the musical industrial complex. The major labels cannot justify going after these smaller markets because they are optimized instead for the larger, pop mainstream. These niche music cultures can't generate the sales needed to float the major label boat. While 20,000 unit sales are a cause to celebrate at a micro-label, they hardly register a blip on big company radar screens.

The times call for focus. Mass customization and a segmenting market encourage the development of products and services of a "niche" nature. Since few of us have the time, money or energy to mount national marketing campaigns, it is in our best interest to discover and concentrate on a niche, a segment, that we can explore towards successful enterprise. Whether your specialty is house, trance, bluegrass or neo-soul, learn to work that niche and scope out relationships and opportunities within it.

Micro-media targets the tributaries off the mainstream and if the artist occupies one of these "niche streams", they have an open and ready channel for exposure to their target audience. Each niche stream has its own burgeoning media culture and the smart combination of high-quality music, creative event-making, perseverance and strategic alliances gets people talking.

What You Can Do About It

- What is your niche? Maybe it's arranging music, or the history of rock, or the intricacies of music software. Whatever it is it will lie at the crossroads where your most compelling desires intersect with your background resources and current opportunities in the real world.

- What is your music's niche? If your music can be slotted into an established category, then master that area both musically and business-wise. Know the inlets and outlets for your music, become familiar with the influencers and tastemakers in that realm, and start communicating with them. If your music defies categorization then lead with that.

METATREND 5: The Next 'Big Thing' is Small

The analogy is television. 30 years ago, the three broadcast networks (ABC, CBS, and NBC) had a ninety percent share of the viewing audience. Today it's less than forty. Where's the other 50%? Watching cable channels. Though cable channels have miniscule ratings, they're profitable. Why? Because they've discovered and developed their niche.

And this is what smaller, indie labels do – the Americana sounds of New West Records, Red House Records' focus on singer/songwriters, the creative acid jazz of Instinct Records, and the deep reggae catalog of Trojan insures listeners they can expect quality discs from each company within their respective niche. Indie market share is on the rise!

Lacking vision beyond their own profit lines, major record companies fail to see that the revolution in music delivery occurred in reaction to the industry's mismanagement, not to mention its complicity in force-feeding the public a flavorless diet of sonic pabulum. With the increasingly conservative (read, "risk-averse") stance of the majors today, indie market niches become all the more important to the creative development of music.

The implosion of the musical industrial complex has also resulted in the availability of many formerly-signed artists and talented executives. The past ten years have seen veteran artists like The Pretenders, Rod Stewart, Foreigner, Aimee Mann, Sinead O'Connor, Carole King, Sammy Hagar, Dolly Parton, Hall & Oates, Hanson, Steve Vai, Sophie B. Hawkins and dozens of other either starting their own labels or signing on with smart indies.

What You Can Do About It

- The paternalisms of yesterday have given way to personal responsibility for your own success. The holy grail is NOT a record deal; it's waking up to your own power.

- Signing with a major label today in most cases is a career risk. These divisions-within-corporations are unstable and anti-art environments, and best avoided by aspiring recording artists.

- If you're up for it, start your own company and release your music through it. If you want to delegate the heavy lifting seek out a successful indie label to partner with. But only do so when you've achieved a level of success appealing to a business partner (that is, you're showing net profit for an extended period of time).

Record company bosses think society's top priority today must be restoring record-company revenue and profits. But music lovers and musicians have a different perspective. They want to know how musicians can exploit the extraordinary technology of the Internet to expand the audience and enable more musicians to make a living doing what they love, and improve the quality of life of consumers.

In a sense musicians may be in a better place today than they've ever been before. Taking a cue from the cyber-bard John Perry Barlow, I believe we could be seeing a paradigm shift from the domination of the "music business" to that of the "musician business."

The more things go digital, the more we crave authentic, roots-based music; the more music that's available to us, the more we seek niches that provide meaning and navigation through all the choices; and the more worldwide radio shows through satellite radio, the more we desire shared cultural experience via local djs.

If we had to, all of these trends can be placed under one banner that reads: the larger the world economy the more powerful its smallest players.

Hey, we're talking about you.

Peter Spellman is director of career development at Berklee College of Music, Boston and founder of Music Business Solutions, a training ground for music entrepreneurs. He's the author of The Self-Promoting Musician and Indie Power: A Business-Building Guide for Record Labels, Music Production Houses and Merchant Musicians. Find him at mbsolutions.com

♦

CREATING AN INDIE BUZZ
by Daylle Deanna Schwartz, author of "I Don't Need a Record Deal! Your Survival Guide for the Indie Music Revolution"
© 2006 All Rights Reserved. Used By Permission

People won't buy your music or come to shows if they don't know about it. By working the media, you can create a foundation for your career. Artists ask, "Why would someone write about an unknown artist or play their music?" Lose that mentality if you want to create a buzz around you and your music! If you've got THE GOODS, the potential is there. Once you believe your music is worthy of media exposure, you can work to inform others.

Build your story one press clip and one radio show at a time. Take baby steps up the ladder from teeny publications and local radio stations to larger ones. As your story builds, so will opportunities to increase it even more! According to Dalis Allen, producer of the Kerrville Folk Festival, "Having your record reviewed in [local magazines] may not propel your career to the degree that you want it to end up. But every one of those things adds up. If I see a review of someone's record in Performing Songwriter and then hear their name somewhere else and then see their package, I've seen their name over and over again. It doesn't matter if it's not the most important thing that you're going to do. It's one more step in what you're going to do."

Let people know about you and your music through the media. It may feel useless if your hard work doesn't pay off immediately. Don't lose hope! Every CD that goes out is another chance for progress. Indie artist Jennie DeVoe says, "I give CDs to radio and anyone else who should have it. It's like planting seeds." Plant your own seeds once you have something to pass out. It takes time, but if your music moves people, your career can sprout by means of reviews, radio play and other exposure that builds your foundation.

If you plant enough, you have a better chance for a lovely blooming garden. Indie artist Canjoe John says, "The business of music requires public awareness and major marketing in order to sell. Major labels have major money to market with. Independents must get publicity in order to survive. I send well-written press releases out on a regular basis. I look for every opportunity to get in the news, TV, radio, newspapers, magazines. If I'm in a new town, I call newsrooms to try and get a story. I've been very successful at this and consider getting major free press as much an art as performing major stages." Exposure builds your story!

Start by creating what's known as a one-sheet. It should be a summary of your story on one sheet of paper. Include whatever ammo you have – a short bio, a track listing, tour dates and past venues, radio play, short press quotes and any other notable info. Design the info on your one-sheet in an organized way. Send your one-sheet with a CD to publications for reviews, radio for airplay, venues, potential agents, managers, distributors and almost anyone else you want to get interested in you and your music. Call first to see if they want a full press kit or just a one-sheet with a link to your website.

Check out daily and weekly papers, alternative publications, trade magazines and even papers from schools. Be creative about where you can fit it into publications. If you have a good story or technique relating to your guitar playing, pitch a guitar magazine. If you've made savvy business moves, pitch a business magazine or the biz section of a local paper. Do research at stores with big magazine sections. Find an angle about you or your music and look for music and general publications that might write about it.

Create a good electronic press kit on your website that people can go to for more info and a selection of photos (least 300dpi in quality) that they can download without having to deal with you. Include a private page with full songs and send media people the URL so they can hear your music. Organize a street team of fans who can help you create your buzz. They can make follow-up calls to press and radio stations in their regions. Fanpower combined with your own hard work can create a buzz that will get you to bigger publications and radio stations, which leads to better venues. This can lead to the day you quit your day job because you've created a full time income from your music!

This is a sample from Daylle Deanna Schwartz's newest book, I Don't Need a Record Deal! Your Survival Guide for the Indie Music Revolution (Billboard Books). Daylle is the best-selling author of Start & Run Your Own Record Label and The Real Deal: How to Get Signed to a Record Label. She also presents music industry seminars, does phone consulting for musicians and record labels, and publishes Daylle's News & Resources, a free industry newsletter. She recently launched her new website www.IDontNeedaRecordDeal.com daylle@daylle.com www.daylle.com

radio airplay

GETTING RADIO AIRPLAY
by Lord Litter, host of Lord Litter's Radio Show
© 2006 All Rights Reserved. Used By Permission

It was the late 80's and I was doing freelance work for a commercial radio station. The first thing I discovered was an enormous heap of releases in the hallway. Here are some hints how to approach DJs. An important aspect of a release surely is that it can be used to promote the band/musician. If you don't take care of certain areas, your music *might* be on air, but no one will get to know who you are and where they can buy your music...so the whole promotional effect is lost.

Here are things that give me trouble and that I think may cause other DJs to NOT play the release:

1. Every item you send should have a clearly marked address. Info material will be separated from the CD, so if there is no address on the cover, then you'll get no play listing, your address will be not spread etc...

2. Since the CD became *the* medium of choice, some bands should send magnifying glasses with their releases. Sometimes covers look great but the writing is either much too small, or the use of colors make it impossible to read. Make sure it as *easy as possible* to identity the name of your band, the song order, and a contact address.

3. The more well known a DJ is, the better the promotional effect. It also means that a known DJ gets piles of releases every day. Therefore, the time to care about the individual release shrinks to almost seconds, leaving no time left to care about questions like: What the name of the band is, and what the title of the release is.

4. Give all of your material a professional approach. It is impossible to read ten pages to get the basic info about a band. Send a reduced informative version of your material with the offer to send more if interested. A link to your website is what I appreciate.

5. DJs are human beings - yes they are! Treat them like you want to be treated. No need to send endless letters, but a short "Hey, thanks - airplay really appreciated!" proves that you *care* about your music and about the one that *cares* about your music - the DJ.

6. The best way to get in touch is to check in before you send your music and say something like "We heard about your show from ... would you be interested in our music? If the DJ doesn't answer you can forget him/her anyway. You might not even get playlist later. The basic idea here is to keep it somehow personal. You'll discover that it creates a very positive effect - in some cases you might even find a friend!

7. If you send CDRs (I do broadcast these!) make sure they really work! I have one CD player that doesn't take badly burned CDs. So, if your CD (in the running order of the show) must be played on that player and it doesn't work, it will not be played.

The basic idea is: make it as easy as possible to handle your material. Before you finish your material, take it to the printer, if the required aspects are not clear, change it. I know it's a lot of work, but the alternative would be: become rich, hire a professional promoter and watch how your release will be thrown away with the others. The answer is always "somewhere in the middle" as we say in Germany.

Lord Litter has earned the reputation for producing and delivering what is arguably one of the world's best independent music programs. Since the early 1990s, Lord Litter has known the pulse of independent music, and today, indie musicians from all over the planet know that his program is one of the ultimate destinations for their music. Website: www.LordLitter.de

♦

RADIO AIRPLAY 101 - COMMERCIAL AIRPLAY MYTHS

by Bryan Farrish, Bryan Farrish Radio Promotion
© 2006 All Rights Reserved. Used By Permission

When talking to people who are launching their first couple of projects, invariably the same misunderstood points come up concerning commercial regular-rotation airplay. *Here are some common myths:*

DJ's play the records
This only applies to non-commercial radio, and specialty/mixshow radio. The majority of people in the U.S. listen to commercial regular-rotation radio, and on these stations, the DJs have no say at all in what is going to be played (unless, in the case of a smaller station, the DJ is also the PD). So, the biggest pitfall to avoid is asking a DJ at a commercial station "Can I give you my CD for possible rotation?" The DJ is not allowed to say "No", and he/she is probably not going to explain that only the PD can approve regular rotation. The DJ is just going to say "OK".

Why do they play it?
Good songs do not mystically spread to other stations. Every single song you hear (or every syndicated program you hear) on commercial regular-rotation radio is on that station because of layers of promotion and marketing. The song you hear was the one that made it, it beat out the other 300 songs that were going for adds that week. What you don't hear are the endless phone calls, faxes, trade ads, personal meetings, consultant recommendations, call-out research, and other things which went into getting the station to add the record. The station owners make it a requirement that DJs make it sound like they picked the music themselves.

College or specialty/mix-show will expand to commercial
Just because you do well on non-commercial or specialty/mixshow radio, it does not mean anything will happen on commercial regular-rotation radio. Nothing at all will happen at commercial unless a separate, higher-level campaign is put into place to take the record into regular rotation. The pitfall here is that a listener will hear something on college, and then a month later hear it on commercial, and conclude that the college caused the commercial to happen. The listener did not know that both campaigns were in place simultaneously, and the college simply went for adds a month earlier.

You have to be signed
Untrue, being signed is only a signal to the stations that the basic marketing practices are going to be done right. If you have the budget, you can duplicate the marketing practices of larger labels, provided you know how. The band *Creed* set a good example, of putting their $5 million marketing dollars into the right place.

Request calls will help
They won't hurt but your time is better spent doing other things, like inviting people to your gigs. Stations know which calls are real, and which are bands and their friends. Stations have consultants and seminars which cover this *one* topic.

I can't get airplay without distribution
It depends on the size of radio that you are going after. Smaller commercial regular-rotation stations in smaller markets won't make this too much of a sticking point, especially if you have a powerful radio campaign going, or if you are doing great gigs in their city, or if you have great college or specialty/mixshow results. But the larger stations... which you can't work anyway until you do the smaller ones... won't touch a project that has no distribution.

Airplay without gigs
Again, it depends on the size of radio that you are going after. Not being able to gig is a serious handicap at any station, but you can overcome it in smaller markets with intense radio promo, press, sales, and non-comm results.

Non-monitored stations are of no use
Non-monitored stations are of no use only on the *Billboard*, *R&R*, and the seven *Album Network* mag charts. But *FMQB*, *CMJ* and all specialty/mixshow charts are compiled manually. Since you need to start off on these smaller charts first, this works out just fine.

Bryan Farrish is an independent radio airplay promoter. He can be reached at 818-905-8038 or airplay@radio-media.com. Contact and other articles found @ www.radio-media.com

♦

INDEPENDENT RADIO PROMOTER CHECKLIST

by Bryan Farrish, Bryan Farrish Radio Promotion
© 2006 All Rights Reserved. Used By Permission

If you are hiring a promoter to push your artist to radio, here are a few things you can consider which will help you have the greatest chance of success (and when I say promoter, I mean an airplay promoter, not a club or booking promoter). The big concern with this process is, if you choose the wrong person(s) to promote your artist and end up with bad results, you can't just go back and do it over again. That's it for that CD (at those stations). That CD is now "an old project" at those stations, and you can't go back to them until you have a new release.

Part One: Overview

Using a friend: Non-experienced friends sometimes offer to promote artists to radio for free, or "a few dollars". This is fine as long as you use them for the right tasks, like helping with the mailing. If you are working college radio, in the 20-30 station range, then they could make some calls too. If they try to call *commercial* radio, they will probably stumble after just a couple of weeks. And forget about any capacity of doing reports or trade charts.

Moonlighter: Staff promoters at major labels sometimes offer to "help you out on the side" for a fee. On their days off, or on the weekend, they say they will "make some calls for you". What happens is that their company finds out and disallows it, or the person gets tied up on their days off, and can't do it. Either way, it is a conflict of interest for them.

Publicity: Public relations people sometimes offer to work an artist to radio for airplay. But don't, however, confuse PR with airplay. A real radio campaign has nothing to do with publicity. They are two separate techniques, with different contacts, lead times, terminology, call frequency, and so on. A person who is good at one is usually terrible at the other. This is why they are always separate departments at labels.

Station People: Station employees are sometimes recruited to work an artist, and will tell you that "they know what stations want." This sounds convincing, but in reality, taking the calls (which they do/did at the station), and making the calls, are very different. Until station people are trained (at a label or indie), they make poor promoters.

Big clients: The most-often used sales technique of promoters is to tell you they have worked "some big artist", and that this would benefit you. Ask them what they mean by "worked". Were they solely responsible for charting that artist? Probably not, more than likely, the promoter was probably just partnered with a label or another promoter, or worse, was just an assistant or sidekick. Again, they will NOT tell you they were not the only promoter. You will *have* to ask the artist or the artist's management directly.

Part Two: What to look for in a Promoter

Making contact: Some Indies are always there when you call, others are never there. The ones who never answer that is usually a *bad sign*. If you thought it was difficult reaching them before you hire them, just wait until *after* they get your money. Also be wary, if they say they give clients (and potential clients) a different phone number to call than the one they give the stations. It is more likely you will never get that person on the phone when you do need them.

Reports: Reports are a requirement that well-organized promoters provide to you. Without a report, there is no other way you are going to be able to understand what is going on with your airplay each week... much less someone else such as stores, papers, clubs etc.

Office: If the promoter does not have an office (even a small one), then you will be competing with things like the promoter's sleep, TV, neighbors, dinner, etc.

Assistants: If a promoter handles more than one genre of music at the same time, or if the promoter does college radio at all, then assistants are mandatory. The phone calls have to be made, and no one person can call more than 150 stations a week, do reports, faxes, emails *and* talk to you when you call!

College Radio: College should be considered for every campaign, even if you are doing high-level commercial radio. College radio is relatively inexpensive, and will allow you to create some good looking charts and reports to show retail, press and clubs.

Faxes: Serious promoters use faxes. Faxing is simply the fastest way to get a one-page synopsis of info to the stations... with pictures if needed. They are not cheap, but a good promoter should still include these faxes.

Emails: While you may get excited about email, remember that since email is free, stations get them from every artist on the planet. And all the emails look the same. So, in order to build a solid project, you must use faxes and phone calls, because most artists can't afford them (and that is why you will stand out.)

References: Any promoter worth consideration will have a list of past clients. What you are looking for, is a promoter with projects that are on your (independent) level. A list of "big" clients, doesn't necessarily better, since a promoter used to having massive help from major label staff promoters, national tours, retail promotions, advertising etc., will not have these with your project. You need a promoter who is set up to work with indie projects like yours.

Do your Homework: The "major label" promoter was actually not the promoter that worked the major projects in the first place. They were probably just assistants in the office, or were mail people, or more often than not, they were just outright lying. It happens all the time. Ask the artist directly to find out.

Bryan Farrish is an independent radio airplay promoter. He can be reached at 818-905-8038, or www.radio-media.com. Email for event info: meet@radio-media.com

♦

INTERNET RADIO: THE AFFORDABLE ALTERNATIVE

By Nathan Fisher, live365.com
© 2006 All Rights Reserved. Used By Permission

Many people don't yet think that Internet radio is or could be a viable medium. This is simply not borne out by facts. Internet radio already has millions of listeners per month and is growing stronger by the day. Independent artists who recognize this opportunity have a decided advantage over those who would wait for years to make it on corporate FM radio, often unsuccessfully.

What is Internet radio?
In appearance and feel, Internet radio is similar to regular radio. Instead of turning a dial, you enter a URL. Anyone with a broadband Internet connection can hear CD-quality audio, better sound quality, in fact, than with traditional FM radio. Even dial-up users can get sound quality roughly analogous to AM radio. Another key difference is that under federal law, Internet radio stations are responsible for paying per-performance royalties for each track they play that they do not own the rights to. Regular radio stations are not responsible for per-performance royalties.

Internet radio operates on a different, radically decentralized model: individual DJs decide what music they like and what music to play. And music fans listen; they even pay a premium to listen to ad-free content.

Traditional radio is limited
Traditional radio suffers from play list homogeneity and an astonishing unwillingness to take risks on new artists. FCC regulations, licensing fees and scarce spectrum bandwidth make it virtually impossible for independent stations to exist unless they are run by colleges or are pirated. This is compounded by the deregulation of radio station ownership following the federal Telecommunications Act of 1996, which made it easier than ever for big industry players like Clear Channel and Infinity to own a nationwide empire that can offer a limited range of programming formats. Indeed, in 1996 Clear Channel was a small media company that owned thirty stations. With the benefits of deregulation, Clear Channel now owns over 1,200 stations. Together, Clear Channel and Infinity control forty-five percent of the American radio audience.

What the future holds
Though Internet radio currently gets fewer listener-hours than traditional radio, the number is steadily increasing and has the potential to experience exponential growth in the next few years as broadband connections become increasingly available in portable devices and automobiles. Plus, it's a good bet that the average Internet radio listener is more of a music fan than the average traditional radio listener.

Moreover, Internet radio makes it simple to track listening behavior, accurately gauge total listener-hours and gather demographic data on listeners. You can easily use Live365's Web site to see which stations are playing your music and how many listening-hours they have had over the past month. This is completely unlike traditional radio, whose ratings system is stuck in the proverbial dark ages.

The Live 365 lowdown
Live365 makes it easy for independent artists to get their tracks into broadcasters' hands and listeners' ears. The ever-expanding library (www.live365.com/cgi-bin/library.cgi) is a virtual record pool, (a secure service that lets all Live365 DJs preview and add your tracks directly into their stations' playlists.) You can also allow broadcasters and listeners to download your entire track, if you prefer. Live365 is licensed and pays royalties to ASCAP, BMI and SESAC.

Each week, Live365 reports its DJs' playlists to Radio and Records, College Music Journal, Billboard Online, New Age Reporter, and other web properties. With the help of Radiowave.com, Live365 also compiles and reports a run-of-site weekly airplay chart. As the largest Internet radio network, with thousands of active broadcasters and over 2 million unique listeners a month, Live365 provides independent artists with an unprecedented opportunity for large-scale radio exposure. You can also submit your album or track to Live365's editorial department for consideration to be listed, free of charge (www.live365.com/labelservices.)

Nathan Fisher is the Editor and Music Library Coordinator for Live365. He grew up in idyllic South Minneapolis, where he learned to implicitly mistrust the status quo. After graduating from Pomona College with a degree in Politics, he relocated to Oakland, CA, where he lives a vaguely bohemian lifestyle with several other roommates in their early twenties. For more information about what Live365 has to offer please visit them @ www.live365.com

♦

ALTERNATIVE RADIO TRENDS AND WHAT THEY MEAN TO YOU

By Liz Koch, Notorious Radio
© 2006 All Rights Reserved. Used By Permission

In January 2005, WHFS, a flagship station for the Modern Rock/Alternative format in the Baltimore/DC market, flipped to Spanish programming. Mid-way through 2004 KHRO in El Paso, TX did the same. Even a year ago, two other flagship stations, KNDD "The End" in Seattle and WNNX "99X" in Atlanta, decided to drop the majority of the 'new music' on their playlists, opting instead to play more 'Alternative Gold' (aka Classic Rock for Gen X) with a few 'cool' and 'local' bands thrown in for flavor.

Meanwhile the trends for 2004 show Satellite Radio, which can be heard Nationally, gaining millions of new listeners last year between both XM and Sirius. Web Radio, which can be heard Globally, DOUBLED its listening base in just ONE year and is now listened to by 10% of the ENTIRE U.S. population!!! Whereas it's true technology and digital listening are on the rise, I think there's something much more important going on.

Let's break it down into simple terms: WHFS and KHRO flip, which means they no longer had the listener base to attract advertisers (because sadly that's what Commercial Radio is about: commercials). "The End" and "99X" changed up their formats for two reasons, the first being the above, the second being they saw the writing on the wall before it was too late. But why an 'Alternative Gold' and a 'cool'/local focus? Easy: the risk of losing the displaced Gen X listening community FOREVER, thus losing their base and therefore their advertisers. This group of loyal listeners, who made them what they are, have found themselves less and less able to relate to what was going on the radio. I know because I was one!

These stations also ran the risk of losing local band support, aka the TRUE music heads of the market. Playlists, over the past few years, have become increasingly less open to 'taking a chance'. Less bands got spun more, in the true Pop radio fashion. Also driving the local bands away was the fact that 9 out of 9 of the bands ON that tight playlist were on Major Labels, with Major Label dollars behind them: something most local bands could only dream about competing with, but realizing the reality.

Mix that all together, and what do you have? Disaffected music fans turning off their radios once and for all. The same group of people searching for alternate means to hear something different, something local, something tangible and, sadly, something more interesting.

Enter Web and Satellite radio with no commercials. Enter the displaced DJs and programmers who had either quit traditional radio out of frustration or were forced out for caring too much about the music. In most cases these folks programmed the New Music or 'Specialty' shows, which showcased different sounds from the station playlist, a lot of times playing local and unsigned bands. They did the radio that took the chances that made Radio exciting in the first place. They saw in Web and Satellite radio what had attracted them to Radio in the first place: turning people on to amazing new music. They saw in Web and Satellite radio the exact thing that has led to its rapid growth: the ability to deliver something different with less inane talk and no commercials. They saw the freedom that traditional radio had forgotten about.

So, what does this all mean for you, the indie band who wants to make themselves known? Simple: EVERYTHING!!! If more traditional radio stations embrace the format changes "The End" and "99X" have done, you will have more of a shot of getting heard on your local Commercial Alternative radio station. NOT just on the New Music or Specialty show...in regular rotation! But why only strive for local domination? The numbers show that you can easily gain a National audience by getting on Satellite radio. There is a channel, XM-Unsigned, that plays nothing but bands like yours day in and day out. Billy Zero (the channel's programmer) will even mention your band's website on the air, and link you from the XM website. From there you will see record sales in markets you didn't necessarily think would be into your music. And from THERE you can better focus your touring, marketing and promotional efforts.

But why settle for the US? Web Radio will give you exposure around the globe! It's becoming more and more common for me to hear about independent artists touring Scandinavia or Japan, simply because someone over there heard about the band via the internet and had the means or the contacts to bring the band over. Countries outside of the U.S., Canada, Australia and Britain have a MUCH broader taste in music, and the beauty part is: being "signed to a label" matters a LOT less over there. If your music is available for purchase and your site, etc. come off as legit (even if it's a self-release on your own fake label), you can sell a boatload of records!

Don't you see? It's finally happening! The American music buying public, aka your audience, don't want to be told what to listen to, like, or buy anymore. This mass exodus to new forms of music exposure, coupled with the technology being both more available as well as affordable, is the most important thing to happen in music in YEARS. If a station like Indie 103.1 in Los Angeles (a station who cares about the Music) can go up against the Mothership of the Alternative format, KROQ, and pull enough listeners to make KROQ broaden its playlist, the door is open. Get your foot in there now!

Liz was the Los Angeles/ Orange County Street Marketing Rep for 3 years @ EMI Records. During this period she also worked as Danny Elfman's personal assistant for two & a half years. After her first CMJ (College Music Journal) Convention in 1994, she KNEW that the Music Business was what she wanted to do & that New York City was where she wanted to do it. So, she got her Associates Degree, moved to NYC & began working at Tommy Boy Music in the Underground Rock Dept in 1997. She was at Tommy Boy for almost 5 years before the company folded in March 2002. She now works out of her home in Astoria, Queens, NYC. notorious@notoriousradio.com www.notoriousradio.com

♦

KNOWING THE DIFFERENCE BETWEEN GOOD PR AND BAD PR

by John Foxworthy, Garage Radio
© 2006 All Rights Reserved. Used By Permission

Publicity and networking are the two most important parts of any successful music project. Unless you lack aspirations to venture beyond your local scene, your career risks stagnation without them. This is why it's important to get a handle on how to conduct yourself when interacting with radio, publications, labels or any other facet of the music business ... otherwise you chance snuffing your credibility before you even get out of the gate.

Whether you work PR for your own act or someone else's, your role seems simple ... create and maintain public interest; however, even the most marketable project and the most interesting press releases are hardly enough to achieve these goals. As with anything you do, there are unwritten laws of etiquette you must follow to function effectively as a publicist.

As the Chief Editor of a busy e-zine and Host of a widely listened radio show, bands, labels, publicists and other publications contact me regarding press and airplay on a regular basis. This correspondence is truly the backbone of what I do … it keeps me in the know on many levels and provides me the opportunity to make new contacts. On the other hand, it also aggravates and frustrates me more often than not. I'm learning that better than half of the folks taking responsibility for public relations are most likely shooting themselves in the foot.

Do Your Research

This is a point I just can't stress enough. In fact, I could write this entire article on just that subject. It requires a lot of work, but the rewards will come back ten-fold. There are so many source guides and directories out there that it's virtually impossible to keep up and these are great tools, but used unwisely they can actually work against you. Here's a scenario based on my own experience:

I host a Rock/Punk/Metal radio show that's clearly described as such on my web site, as well as every directory in which it appears. Yet, almost daily I get press releases and requests for airplay from artists who play anything but Rock, Punk or Metal. This probably wouldn't annoy me as much if I didn't also get the same, exact emails to my e-zine inbox.

You may ask me, "What's the problem? Why not just delete the email?"

That's a simple solution and often times I do, but this is the symptom of a behavior that's sure to thwart the efforts of the sender. Think about it … if they're doing it to me, they're doing it to their other contacts as well. It tells me that this is someone who uses the gum-at-the-wall approach and may not be worth looking into … plus they tend to go onto my SPAM list. I also stay in regular contact with my other colleagues in the biz, so they may even end up on a "blacklist" and could even get stonewalled press- wise in the future.

The solution? Take some time to find out to whom your email is going by doing a simple search to check out their site, show, magazine or whatever. It's even acceptable to send a preliminary email to introduce yourself and get a better idea of what they're looking for (or if they even want your correspondence) before you fire off that request. This is also a great way to make first contact, which makes for an appropriate segue into our next topic.

First Contact

I leave my email address publicly accessible to make it easy for people to contact me. This also contributes to the amount of SPAM I receive … a necessary evil in my position … so I spend an average of eleven hours a week sifting through my new messages in an attempt to separate the SPAM from the news. Why? First of all, most people don't know how to effectively title the subject of their message. Secondly, it's first contact … I may not know who sent the email because I've never corresponded with them.

In the last eight years I've trained myself to tell the difference between South African bank scams and artists trying to get exposure for new releases. This doesn't mean I've trained myself to stop deleting messages based on the subject. Titles like, "WE REQUEST YOUR ATTENTION" or "THE NEXT BIG THING" equate to "GET THE LOWDOWN ON THE SMALLEST CAPS" and will quickly prompt most of your potential contacts to hit the delete button.

First contact is the most important contact. The old adage that you never get a second chance to make a first impression holds very true … especially with the sensitive nature with which people have been conditioned regarding SPAM these days. So, the first lesson on the subject is to make sure your email says what it means before it's even opened.

"New Alternative Rock Band From NYC" is a simple, yet operative title for an email to a new contact. They'll get an idea of the message you're trying to get across and you'll notice it wasn't all capitalized, which could be another form of suicide!

Next, you'll want to make sure you tailor the body of your email to fit your expected recipient. Address them by name (if you have it), be cordial, introduce your act (or yourself) and get to the point. Proper grammar and punctuation play a big role here, so if you have no clue what I mean by that, you shouldn't be doing PR in the first place.

Your first email should be more of a request than a release. Remember, you're dealing with people that are busy, so summarizing a description of the music, adding a few stats (including CD sales) and press quotes is quite alright as long as you keep it to a minimum … 3 short paragraphs will suffice. Then, you can include links and contact info for your recipients to explore further if they're interested. DO NOT, and I reiterate, DO NOT email MP3 files or other attachments. This is annoying and will piss your target off in a heartbeat.

After you've made your first contact, it's wise to set a waiting period before following up. Again, these people are busy and prone to a lot of email, so there is a fine line between correspondence and SPAM.

Follow-up

I'm one to appreciate diligence and I'll be the first to admit that some of my attempts to create steady contacts have backfired on me more than once. Now, finding myself on the receiving end, I see what I was doing wrong. A beleaguered ally can quickly become a foe … and it's for this reason I find it essential to define the difference between follow-up and pestilence.

Let's disregard the preceding tips for a moment and imagine you've emailed your press release or a request for coverage to a few addresses. It's possible that a few of the folks you contacted have contacted you back, but there are some that haven't responded. Many of them may be preoccupied with current projects or might even be completely uninterested. You have no way of knowing where they stand, so how do you decide when (or if) to send a second email?

Five business days is a good rule, but hinges on when you sent your initial correspondence. Monday through Wednesday are the best days to get in touch with your potential outlets. Due to the fact that most schedules revolve around the standard workweek, it stands to reason that these are the best days to send your follow-ups. If you still get no responses, you'll be better to write these contacts off and continue your exchange with the responsive set.

Mailing Lists

This falls more closely under the subject of "netiquette" than etiquette. Just because you have contact email addresses, doesn't mean you have contacts. The inventory of rules surrounding mailing lists is another that could be an entire handbook … and could be one of the single most contributors to death in the press/play world, but I'll try to emphasize the biggest no-nos.

Never, never, NEVER add arbitrary email addresses to your list. There's no negotiating this rule … here's why:

Out of hundreds of emails a day, only about 30% apply to my day-to-day dealings. Another 5%-10% are personal and the rest are just garbage. In my capacity, I have to consider every message as a possible contact … even though I have a "strict" policy that defines how I want to communications to be sent.

My standards are such that I never post uninvited news to other sources and with that, I avoid accepting the same. I personally don't have time to sift through everything I get, so a great percentage is deleted out of constraint. What does this mean? I'm flat-out not interested in getting updates from unsolicited suppliers. It also implies that I'd like permission from people to be added to their mailing lists … and I'm pretty sure there are a lot of people out there that feel exactly the same way.

Not separating your contact lists is another hugely horrific move. This is a chapter right out of "BE ORGANIZED!" Sending gig updates to radio shows or publications that specifically do CD reviews is a waste of time. Additionally, sending the next gig on the morning of your next gig is just plain stupid. Your fans may want to know this (even though they probably already do), but it does no good to inform anyone else that you'll be playing CBGB in seven hours. Plan out your itinerary and send a release with your calendar for the next month or so. If your target wants to announce it, they'll have time to get the word out.

It's best to separate the lists of publications, shows, and other entities by type … and tailor your announcements accordingly. You'll never ruin a contact faster than if you send a daily barrage of so-called updates and/or messages containing your personal agenda.

Last, but NOT least is how to send to your lists. Your email program or web-based mail will have the fields "To" "CC," and "BCC." Forget all about the "CC" field when sending to multiple recipients … and I mean FORGET IT! No matter your capacity in the biz, this line is bad MoJo. Every contact in this field can be seen by every other contact that receives the email. Use "BCC" and save yourself a bevy of pissed off contacts!

Is Your News Really News?

I get everything from updates on CD sales figures to reminders that bands will be playing venues ... the same venues ... several times a week. This goes back to a behaviorism, and a destructive one at that. I, and many in my position, are extremely turned off by this and are very likely to disregard further contact.

Constant updates are not a great way to keep your act in the forefront of our minds. We like to stay informed, but it's good form to save up the news. One release with the band's future happenings, or a retrospective of the last month or so will go a lot further than a daily barrage of minor occurrences ... no need to desensitize your awaiting public.

Press Kits

Press kits are arguably the meat and potatoes of exposure for any act. This is a pretty easy subject, as you won't likely get an address which to send them without permission. For those that make their mailing info readily available, it's a good idea to look further and find an email contact. Make your target privy of the impending envelope and allow a week for it to arrive, but DO NOT follow up in a week!

One thing you must understand is that many of these folks get quite a few of these packages every day. I myself get 30 per week, so I really don't have the time I need to properly distribute and/or review them in seven days. In this case a good follow-up rule is probably 2 weeks ... even if you never heard back from your email.

These are the best tips I have without writing an entire book on public relations. My advice is a culmination of my experience and that of the professionals I work with every day. Following it can enhance your effectiveness as a publicist and help create your niche in the music world ... not following it may greatly reduce your chances of success in this fickle world we call the music biz.

In 2002 I co-founded Garage Radio, a site dedicated to the indie community, which has seen great success over the past couple of years. I also hosts a radio show called "The RoadRash Bash," a Rock and Metal extravaganza featuring indie bands and name bands that are on indie labels, but not getting the exposure they deserve. I work with the industry on every level these days and that experience has given me the insight and contacts I need to bring informative commentaries to the people who need them most ... the DIY and independent community.
Contact: www.garageradio.com roadrash@garageradio.com

getting your music reviewed

HOW TO SUBMIT MUSIC FOR REVIEW
by Jodi Krangle, The Muse's Muse
© 2006, Jodi Krangle. All Rights Reserved. Used By Permission.

Getting the attention of music reviewers can be almost as difficult as breaking into a bank - and let's face it - sometimes far less profitable. But a good review is worth its weight in gold. So how does one go about getting reviewers to give your particular package the time of day? I receive quite a few of these packages myself, so while I'm no expert, I do have a few suggestions:

Be polite when making first contact:

1. This may sound like it's too obvious to mention, but trust me - if you contact a potential reviewer by demanding their submissions address because you are simply the best thing that has happened to music since the microphone and the reviewer would be out of their mind to pass you up, you're likely to be disappointed at the response you receive.

2. Your initial contact should be polite and brief. A simple, "Hello, my name is (so and so) and I'm interested in a possible review in your (publication/web site). Would you be able to supply me with the proper contact information so that I can send you my CD?" will be kindly received. Even if it takes the reviewer a little while to get back to you - whether it's by regular mail, e-mail or through the feedback form of a web site - their reply will usually be helpful.

3. One last word on the subject of *first contact*: PLEASE don't send an e-mail with your web site address and only a "Check this out!" line for clarification. You don't want to know how much spam e-mail I receive in a day and messages like that simply make me feel as if I'm being asked to check out the latest in cheesy porn. I delete such messages on sight and I honestly don't know many reviewers who pay them any attention either.

Presentation:

1. The presentation of the CD itself is probably the most important element of your package. It's that CD that will give the reviewer their initial impression of your music. That doesn't mean you have to have spent thousands of dollars on your presentation, a huge CD insert, a gorgeous color cover, etc. That just means that your "look" should be consistent.

Note: if you're not getting a professional printing of anything, a color inkjet printer creating your own letterhead along with a similarly designed CD covering sticker, will work quite nicely.

2. Simplicity is often the best way to go. Above all, avoid sending in a blank recordable CD with black marker written on it. Your contact information should be on the CD and the insert and/or cover. No matter what you do, make sure your contact information is easy to find.

3. The insert certainly doesn't need to be in color but there should be one, if at all possible. The insert is the perfect place to put contact information, credits (the reviewer is often fascinated by who did and wrote what), anecdotal information, etc - the things that make you special and different from the other folks the reviewer will be listening to. If there is a chance the CD might become separated from the rest of your work, you want the reviewer to be able to contact you from that CD alone.

Things to include in your package:

- A brief cover letter addressing the reviewer by name (a MUST)
- A bio (1 page!)
- A CD, with an insert of some kind.
- Up to 3 reviews if you really feel you need them (try to keep this on one or two pages)
- Make sure your contact information is on everything.

Note: Keep in mind that if your CD itself is a nice little package all on its own including inserts, you may not need the bio or the reviews and could probably get away with just sending in the CD and a cover letter. If you have a web site and include the URL to that site in your cover letter, the reviewer can find out tons more information on you should they wish to.

Be patient
Remember to be patient, not that you shouldn't ever re-contact the reviewer. Remind the reviewer you're around! Just don't do it every day. Wait a couple of weeks between contacts. Reviewers have a lot of demands upon their time and are frequently several weeks - or even months behind in their reviews depending on the publication(s) they write for.

Be professional
The way in which you treat people will reflect upon your professionalism even more so than the look of your CD. It takes years to build up a good reputation and only a few minutes to completely destroy it. As with anything in the music business, you never know when someone you were kind to will be in a position to return that kindness. It's all about relationships. Make sure you're the sort of person who fosters good ones and it'll all come back to you.

Be pleasant; don't demand to know why your CD wasn't chosen for a review and/or spotlight if you are told that it wasn't - not unless you actually want to hear what the reviewer has to say. And if that reviewer *does* let you know why, let it be a lesson and move on. Try to keep in contact with the reviewer. It might be that a future release of yours will be better received. I hope these hints have helped. Meanwhile, good luck with your music!

Jodi Krangle is Proprietress of The Muse's Muse Songwriting Resource www.musesmuse.com Visit Judy@www.musesmuse.com/musenews, to find out more about her free monthly e-zine.

♦

INSIDE THE HEAD OF A MUSIC REVIEWER
by Suzanne Glass, CEO Indie-Music.com
© 2006, All Rights Reserved. Used By Permission

What to send? When to follow up? What to say? Should you keep bugging a writer to review your material? What makes writers chose one CD over another to review? And most of all can you increase your chances of getting a published review when you submit a CD? Answer: Absolutely! By understanding a writer's mind, and following a few simple guidelines, you will substantially increase the likelihood your music will be chosen for a review or feature.

Indie-Music.com recently asked our writers; Heidi Drokelman, Jennifer Layton, Les Reynolds, and Erik Deckers, a series of questions designed to let musicians see inside writers' heads, and get a unique look at how the behind-the-scenes process works. After the Q&A, we give a quick checklist for getting your music reviewed successfully.

Q. What impresses you about an artist/musician/band?

A. *Heidi Drokelman:* Number one; the biggest impression is always the music, and the talent (however sometimes hidden it is) of songwriting. The versatility of all the members is important, and having an appreciation for good songwriting, no matter the genre, will always shine through in someone's work. Sure, clean production always sounds nice and makes a big impression when you're only listening to something a few times for review.... but I've been doing this [reviewing] for a long time now, and if the material is there (even in raw form), the first thing I forgive is production quality. When your songs stand out, even if you've recorded on the worst machine you can possibly find, then that's what counts. Even the worst material can't surpass a production snow job.

A. *Jennifer Layton:* There's no one thing. I've been impressed by so many different things. I'm impressed when I hear a musician doing something new that I've never heard before. I'm impressed when I hear a poetic folk song that expresses something so true; I feel it tugging at my heart. No matter what the press kits look like or how fancy the web site is, none of it matters if I'm not touched by the music in some way.

A. *Les Reynolds:* Real talent in at least one area (vocal, instrumental, lyrical) and especially when all those elements come together. Also, if they've got their s*** together —correspond in timely manner, not pushy about reviews, answer questions coherently and communicate well (even if this is through an agent, having the right agent who can do those things is crucial).

Q. What impresses you in a promo pack submission?

A. *Erik Deckers:* "Is the press kit complete? Does it have a bio and headshot or group photo? Are there other articles from other reviewers? If the answer is YES to these questions, then I am impressed. If the press kit contains a three-line bio, or vague and airy generalities discussing the metaphysics of the universe in relation to their music, I am decidedly unimpressed."

A. *Heidi Drokelman:* "Oh, this is a completely relative thing. I look at this part of the packaging after I've already listened to the music. If getting signed by a label is your goal, I'd much rather receive bio materials, a dated letter (it's really hard to separate the volume of mail that some of us receive, so including a dated letter from a band representative is a nice touch), a simple photo that expresses the personality of an artist or band, and on occasion, I enjoy a good piece of gag swag. Taking that extra step, and coming up with a creative piece of swag can push a pack to the top of the pile. However, please refrain from the offensive, even if it's meant in jest."

A. *Jennifer Layton:* "I take a different route with promo packs. I know those materials are expensive, and I have a small office and can't hang on to all the press materials I get each month. Which means that if I don't absolutely love the artist, the promo pack winds up in the trash after I write the review. I feel really guilty about that. So when an artist contacts me about submitting material, I tell them they don't have to bother with headshots or elaborate press kits — just a simple bio sheet that includes the web site address, telling me whatever they want me to know about them. What I'm really interested in is the music."

A. *Les Reynolds:* "It looks like the artist/band took time and care in preparing it and it "fits" with the image and overall music style. Quality photos, if included, also get my attention. While I won't use the pix (except to decorate my pod at work!), it says something about the artist — I can get a "vibe" or feel off that. I am also just impressed with quality photography since I used to be a photographer."

Q. How can bands get your attention?

A. *Erik Deckers:* "Write a personalized note to me, not a generalized form letter."

A. *Heidi Drokelman:* "Bands can get my attention fairly easily, but holding it can be another story altogether. I am all about helping out quality bands and artists, and will take extra steps to make sure that I am doing all I can without showing blatant favoritism (although I AM known for that as well), so some of the ways to do this are: Be courteous: I should clarify because I despise kiss asses just as much as the repeat offender rudeness. I'm not asking for special treatment, just a bit of humanity. Don't be overly pushy. I don't mind the follow-up to check in on the status of a review, but DO NOT expect to get a review every time you send in material. Some pushiness is good, but use common sense to know where the line has been drawn."

A. *Les Reynolds:* "Contact me directly. Keep the lines of communication open, and don't tell me to just go to your mp3 site. I hate that! It's become the universal cop-out (besides —what if the computer is malfunctioning or the internet is down?). Also: if they can describe their music accurately in a sentence— that shows they know who they are and have read my Indie-Music.com bio blurb."

Q. What do bands do which wastes their money, when they send submissions?

A. *Erik Deckers:* "Send crappy press kits. If I don't have much background information on the band, I can't write a good review. If I can't write a good review, then it doesn't help the band much."

A. *Heidi Drokelman:* "If they're unsolicited, it's a huge waste of money in general. Don't just blindly send your discs out to everyone you think has an inkling of interest in your work. Make sure that you contact someone and at least use the proper procedure. I'm sure this may sound lame to you, but the procedure we use is built to enhance our reviews, not to bring you down. On another note, photos, postcards, stickers, bio write-ups, and discs are not a waste of money. Just plan your priorities and work up to the full packet."

A. *Jennifer Layton:* "I hate to see bands spend money by sending me glossy headshots and other expensive materials. While I'm impressed by their professionalism, I'm not a label rep or someone who will have a major influence on their career — I'm just an indie writer. Also, I tell artists not to waste money by sending their submissions by Federal Express. Regular old mail will do fine.

A. *Les Reynolds:* Sending tons of press clippings - one sheet is enough. Sending all sorts of odd-shaped stickers and things that, by themselves — once away from the package — mean nothing. Most

Press kits are guilty of overkill."

Q. How can bands improve their submissions?

A. *Heidi Drokelman:* "Solicit your submissions for review – it will ultimately benefit you more to do some research and look into different publications and specific writers, than it will to blindly send things out. Quality is key - you're looking for someone to thoughtfully review your material, to respect it, and cultivate new contacts for publicity and marketing purposes. Do what you can presently afford, and the rest will fall into place."

A. *Jennifer Layton:* "I think they can tone down their bios a little. I'm aware that most artists write their own bio sheets, so I have to laugh when I read stuff like "This is the most amazing rock band on the music scene today. No one has ever come close to matching their talent and energy." Also, be sure to run your press materials through a spell-checker! One of the funniest bio sheets I ever got was from a folk artist who called himself a great intellectual songwriter, and the word "intellectual" was misspelled."

A. *Les Reynolds:* "Unwrap those CDs - Pleeeze!!! Send quality materials that won't fall apart immediately. Send good quality CDs (occasionally defective ones or discs produced in an odd format is received, and they won't play.)"

Q. How do you deal with your personal music preferences when reviewing? Do you review styles you would not normally listen to/buy?

A. *Erik Deckers:* "It's actually a little harder for an artist to impress me when they're in a genre I already like, because I have some definite ideas about what I enjoy and what I don't. But that means that if an artist CAN impress me, then they've done an excellent job. I do review styles that I normally don't listen to, so if an artist can create something that I enjoy (i.e. country music), then they also get a good review."

A. *Heidi Drokelman:* "Actually, I may be one of the few reviewers that will instantly admit that I use my personal music preference as a barometer for my reviews. I believe that it is almost impossible to take that out of the mix, especially when considering first impressions and different "trends". But this can be a very positive tool, especially when considering things like generational preferences (determining who this music will appeal to), and regional trends."

A. *Jennifer Layton:* "That's been an interesting issue for me. Over the past three years, I've learned not to rule out styles of music I don't normally listen to. I thought I hated all folk music before I started writing for Indie-Music.com, and now I am completely in love with acoustic folk/rock music. The only thing I can't review is rap. I'm a middle-class white girl who still listens to Barry Manilow and the Carpenters occasionally – I have ZERO credibility when it comes to rap and hip-hop."

Q. What do you most enjoy about reviewing indie music?

A. *Erik Deckers:* "It's not the same old schlock I hear on commercial radio. In most cases, it's better.

Heidi Drokelman: I'm still amazed, after all these years, at the quality and talent that's out there. The best thing about reviewing indie music is the sheer unpredictability of it all."

A. *Jennifer Layton:* "I know this sounds dramatic, but writing about indie music for the past three years has changed my life. I'm a lot more open-minded about so many things because I've learned to be more open-minded about the music I listen to. I've met several of the artists I've reviewed and am so happy that I've been able to encourage them by contributing positive reviews to their press kits. I've become such a fan of indie music that I flew up to NYC for my birthday last year to see performances by some of the artists I'd written about."

A. *Les Reynolds:* "The fact that there's an unlimited amount of real talent out there and it keeps coming and won't ever stop. I've heard stuff I would have never heard otherwise, met musicians I'd never even dreamed existed. And the cream is when a real connection is made... that's worth everything."

Q. What most irritates you in writing reviews?

A. *Erik Deckers:* "Getting unsolicited reviews. I'm pretty busy to begin with, and so I have to be selective about whose reviews I undertake. When I get one that I didn't ask for, I don't look favorably upon that artist. If I do manage to get around to doing their review, they've got a bigger hurdle to clear in that I'm already annoyed with them."

A. *Heidi Drokelman:* "The only thing that ever gets me is the volume of the mailings that I get. Making the commitment to give advice, constructive criticism, and deliver it in a way that

Isn't cruel, disconcerting, or rude is never easy. I may have harped a little about bands realizing that the reviewers are human, but remembering how personal the work is to others keeps me in check when delivering my honest opinion about their work."

A. *Jennifer Layton:* "What drives me NUTS is when artists or labels put me on their mailing lists when I didn't ask them to. Some artists have even put me on their lists before they've even sent me the CD for review. The worst was after I wrote a positive review of one band, and then their label put me on the mailing list of every single artist on their roster. That's one of the reasons I don't deal with labels or PR people anymore. If I love an artist's work, I'll ask to be put on the mailing list. And I have done that many times."

A. *Les Reynolds:* "Bad (inaccurate/incomplete) information on liner notes (it happens) or if the info is not legible — that stuff is very helpful and often necessary (in my opinion) in writing reviews. That, and wishing I had nothing to do but write, because most of these artists deserve a timely review."

Review Check List:

1. **Communicate professionally** - Use standard grammar and punctuation, proofread, and use a spell checker. You don't have to write a business letter like you learned in 8th Grade Grammar class, the letter could be creative, but make sure it is identifiable as a business communication and not junk mail. Make sure to directly state you are looking for a review. Don't send mass mailings, it's obvious to the recipient. On the phone, leave useful messages designed to make it easy to call you back (spell your name, and repeat your phone number twice to make copying easy for the listener).

2. **Follow submission guidelines** - Guidelines exist for a reason, which is to help an organization handle a large flow of music submissions in an efficient manner. Each publication does it differently, but if you choose not to follow the guidelines, expect your submission to be late, lost, or worse.

3. **Send a cohesive promo pack** - Writers have differing preferences on what they like to receive as part of a promo pack. Most writers, though, like to read a band biography and a few press clips (it helps in writing a review to know more about an artist), and many also like to see a band photo. If you are unsure what a writer requires, err on the side of sending too MUCH rather than not enough. If you choose not to include photos and graphics, make sure they are easily available on your website, in case the reviewer plans to publish your review with pictures.

4. **Give contact information** - When your review goes up, nothing would be dumber than to make your CD hard to find. Many artists, though, forget to include full contact information including mailing address, phone, email, and website URL.

5. **Identify your genre** - When people read reviews, they want to know, upfront, whether it's their "style" or not. So even if you simply say "a cross of rock, folk, and punk", that is much better than saying "we cannot be categorized". Better to categorize yourself than let a writer do it for you. Many writers are not musicians, and do not know precisely how to describe your genre just by listening. Help them.

6. **Write a meaningful bio** - Drop the lines that say you are "incredible", "changing the face of music", or "talented beyond belief etc.,

7. **Make the writer's job easy** - Since writers are, at the basic level, just people doing their job, it only makes sense that if you can make their job easier, they will like you and try to return the favor. That's just human nature. Include everything the writer needs, be sensitive to their schedule, and provide graphics or answers to any questions promptly.

8. **Follow up courteously** - Writers vary greatly in how they respond to follow-ups. Some people will respond promptly, keeping you up to date at each step of the process. Other writers ignore follow-ups completely. Your best bet is learning each writer personally. As a general rule, follow up about 2-4 weeks after your submission should have arrived with a short note. If you hear nothing, try again in another two weeks. If you again hear nothing, try waiting a month.

Don't threaten or chastise the writers, just ask if a decision has been made about your review yet.

9. **Don't argue with the reviewer** - You can't win. If you don't like the review, you can pass on that reviewer with your next CD. Or you can submit again and see if their opinion has changed. Either way picking a fight about something the reviewer wrote is a waste of your time. If there is a factual error, fine, ask the writer to correct it. But don't argue, "Our choruses are NOT boring! They are complex and emotive". Since the characterization of your choruses as "boring" is only the reviewer's opinion, you are not going to change it. You might, however, piss off the writer for life.

10. **Keep the connection** - You need to cultivate your relationships with writers. Check in with them periodically between CDs, read their other work, let them know if you have news, and send thank-you notes - even if you did not get reviewed. Your goal is to build a relationship. You never know when that relationship may help you out - but you can be sure it will work in your favor if you present yourself as nice, interested, and understanding.

Suzanne Glass is the founder of Indie-Music.com, All the reviewers featured in this piece write for Indie-music. For more information please contact: www.indie-music.com

♦

WHY MOST DEMO RECORDINGS ARE REJECTED
by Christopher Knab author of "Music Is Your Business"
© 2006 All Rights Reserved. Used By Permission

"Getting a deal" has long been the goal of many would-be artists and bands. For mostly naive reasons, most new talent feel that by securing a recording contract with a significant major or independent label, success will be guaranteed. (Talk about naiveté.) To get this 'belief system' up and running, many musicians figure all they have to do is send off their music to a label, and a recording contract will come their way shortly.

How to improve your odds
The following list of 10 Reasons Why Demo Are Rejected was gathered together after years of listening to comments made by Record Label A&R reps at music industry conferences and workshops, as well as from personal interviews with reps, and from many interviews A&R reps have given to the press. The purpose of providing you with this information is to at least improve the odds that your music will get listened to when you submit your demos. This list will look at the most common mistakes musicians make when either shopping for a record deal, or trying to get the attention of A&R Reps with their demo recordings.

10 Reasons Why Demos Are Rejected

1. No Contact Information on CDR and/or CDR container: Put your name, address, email, and phone number on both.
2. Lack of Originality: Just because you *can* record, doesn't mean your music is *worth* recording.
3. The Music Is Good, But The Artist Doesn't Play Live: This applies to all genres of music except electronica and experimental music.
4. Poorly Recorded Material: So you bought Pro-Tools ... so what!
5. Best songs are not identified or highlighted on the CDR: Give the folks a break. For demos-send only 3 or 4 songs and highlight the best ones.
6. Sending Videos In Place Of CDRs: Keep it simple, in the demo mode. All anyone wants is to check out your songwriting and musicianship.
7. Sending Unsolicited Recordings: You sent them, but they never asked for them.
8. Sending The Wrong Music To The Wrong Label: You didn't do your research to find out what labels put out what kind of music.
9. Musicians Can't Play Their Instruments Competently: This is so basic, but you would be astounded at how incompetent most start-up musicians are.
10. The Music Sucks: This criticism is as old as music itself. You may think your music is the greatest thing since frappacinos, but most demo recordings the industry receives are as bad as the first round contestants on American Idol.

Christopher Knab is a music business Consultant, Author and Lecturer. He was recently honored by Seattle's Rocket magazine as "One of the Most Influential People in the Northwest Music Industry." Visit his website at: www.4frontmusic.com or contact him personally at: Chris@Knab.com

tools

WHAT ARE PERFORMANCE RIGHTS ORGANIZATIONS?
by Jer Olsen, CEO MusicBootCamp.com
© 2006 All Rights Reserved. Used By Permission.

Performance rights organizations like BMI, ASCAP and SESAC all perform a similar task but in slightly different ways. Essentially, they all perform the duty of collecting royalties for non-dramatic performances of intellectual property. In simpler terms, they collect the income from radio stations, TV stations, programming companies, Internet marketers and any other entity where music and related intellectual property is used. These royalties are then, in turn, paid to the various publishers and authors associated with a particular recording or performance.

Why do we need them?
The fundamental reason behind the birth of these organizations is the simple fact that individual artists and song writers can't possibly devote the time, attention and research required to collect royalties from the plethora of companies that use their music, even though by law they are entitled to those royalties. Artists depend on these performance rights organizations to do the hunting and collecting for them—a small price to pay for a piece of a much, much bigger pie! There's a saying, "50% of everything is a whole lot better than 100% of nothing!" Well, we don't know exactly how much money these organizations charge for their services, but we can be certain it covers their time and energy (similar to how music publishers earn money for getting music played in movies, TV shows, or recorded by other artists, etc.) The truth is, performance rights organizations are a necessary and helpful tool for musicians and publishers. The toughest decision is choosing which one to align with.

Which one to choose?
Please visit the page of each organization to find on-line information about joining as well as a ton of other terrific resources. Compare and make a decision on which one best suits you. If you don't, you can practically assure yourself of never being paid for airplay.

United States
BMI—Broadcast Music, Inc (www.bmi.com)
ASCAP—The American Society of Composers Authors and Publishers (www.ascap.com),
SESAC (www.sesac.com)
Canada
SOCAN—The Society of Composers Authors and Music Publishers of Canada (www.socan.ca)
The UK
PAMRA—Performing Arts Media Rights Association (www.pamra.org.uk)
PRS—The Performing Right Society (www.prs.co.uk)
MCPS—The British Mechanical Copyright Protection Society Limited (www.mcps.co.uk)
France
SACEM—Societe Des Auteurs Compositeurs Et Editeurs De Musique (www.sacem.fr)
CISAC—Confédération Internationale des Sociétés d'Auteurs et Compositeurs (www.cisac.org)

Germany
GEMA—The German Society For Musical Performing Rights And Mechanical Reproduction Rights (www.gema.de)
Italy
SIAE—Societa Italiana Degli Autori ed Editori (www.siae.it)
Spain
SGAE—Sociedad General de Autores y Editores (www.sgae.es)
Sweden
STIM—Svenska Tonsattares Internationella Musikbyra (www.stim.se)
Australia
APRA-The Australasian Performing Right Association Limited (www.apra.com.au)

Note: If you are looking for information on how to start your own publishing company, inquire on each site or call each company on how to obtain membership as a publisher. Becoming a publisher is not as nearly as difficult as performing the duties of a publishing company since a publisher's main task is exposing compositions and recordings to as many profitable opportunities as possible. Many of the duties of publishing companies can be effectively performed through a membership with the *Harry Fox Agency* (www.harryfox.com).

Jer Olsen is the founder and CEO of MusicBootCamp.com, home of "Dirt-Cheap CD Replication and FREE Music Business Training!" This article is a sample of the many free resources available on the Web site. Jer is also an accomplished musician and producer with several top 20 Billboard hit remixes to his credit. www.MusicBootCamp.com

♦

UPC & BARCODES FOR PENNIES AND SENSE
by Lygia Ferra, LAMusicGuide.com
© 2006 All Rights Reserved. Used By Permission

With all the details that go into making a CD it is easy to put off making certain decisions, especially if there is cost involved or contradictory information.

So what exactly is a barcode?
Bar codes are also called UPC Symbols (generated by the Uniform Code Council (www.uc-council.org.) They are the small black and white lines that correspond to a unique 12 digit number used to track sales of CD's, while Sound scan correlates the information with your barcode in their database. Unless you are planning on starting a record label and putting out a number of releases with several artists, the $750 expense isn't really necessary.

Soundscan
Since Soundscan (www.soundscan.com) has a direct influence on placement in Billboard and CMJ music charts and other forms of recognition, payola has all been obliterated. It is a tracking system that did away with the potentially subjective reports of radio programmers and store managers prior to 1991. Sound Scan's records are not public, so the only way to access their data is open an account at a minimum price of several thousand dollars per year. The only ones checking are the larger labels and bigger companies. If you want to impress, you would need to sell more than 1,000 units to catch their eye.

Why do you need one?
One reason why you may need a barcode at all is that most stores and online retailers require an UPC code on every product they sell. So sparing the $750 expense, you can acquire one through Oasis or Discmakers for "free" when you replicate your discs, or through *CD Baby* for a modest $20 fee.

In the case of CD Baby the agreement does not bind you to the company in any way, other than having them listed as your "Parent Label" in Sound Scan's database. They provide you with the code as an electronic image, and you can include it in any cover art as appropriate.

How do you get credit for sales?
To ensure you are properly credited for all record sales as in the case of Discmakers you fax the necessary forms to Soundscan (914-328-0234), you will need a separate form for each release. Any independent artist or band can have their retail sales tracked through Sound scan, though only a label with two or more acts can take part in their Venue Sales Reporting Procedure. You must also have been in business two years or more, with a $500 fee.

It's never too late
You can always purchase one afterwards and have them printed on stickers. If you do it yourself make sure your printer is at least 720 dpi so they will read correctly. You can easily download a shareware barcode. A simple search for "UPC Barcode" @ shareware.cnet.com, or www.download.com will yield many results.

Alternatives
You can also go through a company (usually with a minimum order of 1,000 stickers) they will print them out for you, saving you the hassle of doing it yourself. If you are only going to sell your product at gigs or through alternative means, you really do not need a barcode at all. But for a mere $20, CD baby will save you all the worry and give you many more possibilities to sell your product.

Sources:
The Uniform Code Council: 1-800-543-8137 www.uc-council.org
Soundscan: (914) 684-5525 www.soundscan.com, clientservices@soundscan.com
Note: If you do decide to bite the bullet and purchase a barcode through the Uniform Code Council the process can take a number of weeks so allow for that extra time.
Independent Records: 1000 stickers Single Format Registration, Price: $55.00
https://www.indierec.com/s-barcodes-register.html
Bar Codes Talk, Inc: 888-728-4009 Florida $30.00 shipping included.

Lygia Ferra is a Singer/Songwriter, Producer and Entrepreneur based in Los Angeles, CA. In addition to helping with the IMB, she is actively involved with developing the La Music Guide site (where this article originally appeared) (www.lamusicguide.com). Please visit www.lygiaferra.com, for more info.

♦

SO, WHAT'S THE SCOOP WITH ELECTRONIC PRESS KITS?
by Panos Panay, CEO Sonic Bids
© 2006 All Rights Reserved. Used By Permission

It seems that the big buzz out there in the music word today is all about Electronic Press Kits (EPK). Should independent musicians use an EPK™ or a traditional press kit when approaching club promoters, festival organizers, radio programmers or record label A&R representatives? Do they work as well as regular press kits or should one stick with the tried and true method of snail mail kits? Are industry insiders even using them?

Electronic Press kit, why is it important?
The answer is simple: like every other major innovation over the years ranging from the Compact Disc to the MP3, the industry was slow to initially accept it but it's fast becoming the ubiquitous standard that everyone from up-and-coming independent artists to word-renown festival directors is using to send and receive information about groups and artists from around the globe.

An EPK™ is like a virtual passport that you can use again and again to gain entry into hundreds of conferences, festivals, clubs, music competitions, colleges, or to even get your songs played on radio or reviewed by record companies or music producers. It contains everything your regular press kit contains and more: music samples, downloadable photos, bio, pres reviews, and even an up-to-date gig calendar (try that with a regular press kit). What's great about an EPK™ is that it takes literally 20 minutes to create one online and you can put it to use and start saving money almost immediately. For the cost of a little more than sending out two regular press kits, you can sign up for an account, create an electronic press kit, and email it out to anyone, anywhere, at anytime. It not only communicates all the information that is found in your average press kit or web site, but it does so more quickly, more efficiently and far more effectively. Think how mind-blowing it is to be able to email someone everything they need to know about you or your band as soon as you get off the phone with them (or better yet, while you are even still talking with them).

Cost effective solution

Think of the implications of this innovation for the average up-and-coming artist. For the first time in history, there is no direct link between how many people you can reach and the cost of reaching them. For example, with a traditional press kit there is a vast cost difference between sending out 10, 100, or 1,000 of them. This means that even though today an independent artist has access to an unprecedented amount of information such as contained in this very book. The ability to take full advantage of this had, until now been limited to all but the richest of us (consider the cost involved in sending a regular press kit to every single possible contact in this guide.)

The Electronic Press Kit has changed all this. Every day there are artists that are sending out their EPK™ to say, 100, or 200 college buyers at practically zero cost and frequently get two or three offers from people that they would normally have to spend way too much money in their attempt to reach them (and often paying way more in reaching them than the actual fee they receive). The cost and effort of emailing an EPK™ to all these buyers is a small fraction of the corresponding investment in regular press kits – not to mention the benefits of the fact that communication is practically immediate (versus waiting for a week or so to get a press kit in the mail).

Conclusion

Does all this mean that you will never have to send another press kit in the mail? What about the promoters who want to listen to a full CD blasting through the speakers of their car stereo? The answer is simple: traditional press kits and CDs still have their place but, save your money and send them to the few people that specifically ask for them after they review your electronic press kit. Then you at least know that these are high prospects that are worth spending an extra $20 in trying to communicate with them.

Panos Panay is the founder and CEO of Sonicbids, the online pioneer of the EPK™ platform Prior to founding Sonicbids, he was VP of the International Division of the Ted Kurland Assoc. Agency, where he was responsible for the international tours of over 50 world-renown artists.

♦

WRITING A BAND BIO
by Suzanne Glass, CEO, Indie-Music.com
© 2006 All Rights Reserved. Used By Permission

Having a little trouble coming up with a decent band bio? Check out these suggestions:

1. Don't worry about writing a book. One page or even a few paragraphs is fine. In fact, most people don't want to read any more than that.

2. Do emphasize your strong points while minimizing areas where you lack. If you have played gigs with well known bands, be sure to list it. If you haven't played many gigs, don't bother mentioning the fact. Go on to your recording, or your other musical experience. Also, while it's OK to "hype" a little bit, never tell any out-and-out lies or make a boast you might not be able to come through on. It will come back to haunt you, and then you will lose all credibility in the reader's eyes. Not to mention these music people talk to each other...and HOW!

3. Do use your band's letterhead to write it on. (You DO have a logo and letterhead, right?) Be consistent in your entire promo package with the image, logo, etc.

4. Don't say your band's music is "not able to be classified". Aside from the fact that a million other bands say the same thing, the music industry contact reading your bio wants and NEEDS to know who you are comparable to. For instance, if someone recommends a movie to you, you probably need to know if it's a horror flick, a romance or whatever before you decide if you want to see it.

5. Do use humor or slight sarcasm if it fits your band's image. But avoid the temptation to go overboard. A bit of humor can make a low budget press kit seem better. Too much is a loser. Also, some types of bands fit into a niche that is more open to humor. Just make sure what you say will not offend anyone.

6. Don't, repeat, DO NOT say you are the coolest, best, or greatest band around, or anything even remotely close to it. Music Industry people want to decide for themselves if you are good or not. Avoid the flowery adjectives.

7. Do list the band's major musical influences. This goes along with trying to give the person an idea of what you sound like. It can work great to come up with a unique description of your music. For instance, Indiana guitarist Michael Kelsey describes his music as "Progressive, aggressive acoustic music".

8. Unless your band has former members of Aerosmith and Van Halen in it, it's probably not a good idea to do one of those story bios. "John was playing in Joe's band until the singer quit. Then John met Steve, who was playing with the Nobodys. They formed a band called The Losers. When the drummer quit, they changed their name to The New Losers", etc. This is irrelevant and, well, boring. Not to mention it shows your lack of ability to keep a band together. It is OK to use an interesting line or two about how the band got started, or how songs are written. It's also OK to add any interesting facts, like maybe your band donates all proceeds from their cassette sales to charity.

9. Of course you want to list all your major accomplishments. Any recordings, awards, education, or whatever.

10. A quick concise listing of each member is good. Sometimes you can do fun things with this like a listing of each members' favorite drink, or other non-relevant stuff. But make sure it works. Nobody really cares what your favorite anything is, so it has to be part of a humorous image. If any members have played in well known bands, it's good to mention it here, but don't make a big deal out of it.

11. You may use a different version of your bio depending on who will be receiving it. For instance, a record label and a club booking agent might need different info to decide if you interest them. A record label wants to know you have it all together: music, business, a fan base, songwriting, etc. A club agent is mostly concerned with whether you have a following that will bring paying business to his club.

12. Do make absolutely sure you have your address and phone number (and your e-mail and website URL, if applicable) listed prominently. This goes for all items in your press kit. Name, address, and number on EVERYTHING. (Demo tape included!)

13. Read other bands' bios. Compare and rewrite. Have other people read and comment on what you write. Make sure it is grammatically correct, with no typos. If you really feel yourself lacking in this area, consider hiring someone to write your bio for you. A good bio is part of the press kit that forms the first impression of your band. Don't mess it up.

Suzanne Glass is the founder of Indie-Music.com, an online magazine that reviews dozens of independent artists each month, includes music charts, audio & internet radio, and how-to-succeed articles for musicians, all at no cost. A paid members option gets your music in rotation with streaming audio, radio, multimedia advertising AND full access to our DIY music industry database with over 7000 venues. www.indie-music.com

♦

WHY MAILING LISTS ARE SO IMPORTANT
by Vivek J. Tiwary, CEO StarPolish.com
© 2006 All Rights Reserved. Used By Permission

The very first piece of business you should attend to is starting and maintaining a mailing list. Your mailing list will be your most direct and personal link to your fans and entertainment industry contacts— in many ways, the mailing list can be considered the "business lifeblood" of a developing artist.

Where to begin
Keep your mailing list on computer, using any good database program. I have found Microsoft Access to be very versatile and easy to use, but any good database software should suffice. Remember to back up your mailing list by keeping identical copies on both your hard drive and a removable disk. You will want to keep the following information about each member of your mailing list: name, snail-mail (i.e. regular postal) address, email address, and perhaps telephone number. Other fields you may want to consider including are company affiliation and job title (if applicable) or school address (if applicable and if your act does/will appeal to a college fan base).

Start your mailing list by personally adding all the folks you think would support your act, and all your entertainment industry contacts you want to keep posted on any new developments. As a test, in addition to your industry contacts, your list should include everyone who would come to a show or would buy/download your music. In other words, if your grandmother who lives in another state would buy a CD, she very much belongs on the mailing list. You will find that apart from industry contacts, these early members are mostly friends and family— that's both normal and acceptable. Don't think that because they're close to you or your band they somehow "don't count." In your early days, where else do you expect to get your support? Remember this important piece of advice; every single name on the mailing list makes a difference.

Building your list
If you are a band, I suggest that one band member maintain the mailing list and that once a week, every band member must submit 10 new names to the mailing list until you exhaust your collective resources of appropriate friends, family, contacts, etc. Be aggressive about your mailing list. Whenever you bump into an old friend or acquaintance on the street and they ask you what's new, tell them about your act and ask them for their information to include on your mailing list. You'll find that as you grow busier with your musical career, your mailing list becomes a good way to keep in touch with people, especially those folks you don't see often.

You must also solicit new names for your mailing list after shows. Prepare one or more clipboards, each loaded with several signup sheets. Each signup sheet should have sections clearly marked for name, address, and email. Space permitting, it may be useful to include a section on "comments" to see what new fans thought of your act. Remember that people may be filling out these sheets in a dark bar or venue and will therefore need to write in big letters, so don't put too many signup boxes on each sheet, and make sure there is plenty of space for each entry— I recommend no more than four new signups per sheet. Make each signup sheet look professional and presentable— have them designed on computer, or if they're hand-made, be extremely neat. Adding artwork or some other creative presentation can never hurt, but remember that the most important thing with the signup sheets is that they are easy to use.

Creative ideas
Provide potential fans with thick, dark-colored pens, again keeping in mind that they may be writing in a dark bar or venue. If possible, go the extra step and bring a penlight with you to make it even easier for them to fill out the form.

At the risk of sounding like a sexist asshole, I'm going to offer the following piece of advice because no one else may tell it to you, and it can quite literally be the difference between 100 and 600 names on your mailing list in the early days of your career. I recommend that an attractive and friendly/personable woman walk around with each clipboard and solicit additions to your mailing list. It is actually a statistically proven fact that audience members— both male and female— are more likely to fill out a mailing list signup form when asked by a friendly/personable woman. I'm not exactly sure why that is, but it's definitely a truth I have observed through years of experience. Try it and see for yourself.

You or any band member can also assist with soliciting names for the mailing list, because potential fans may want to say hello and that can be a good opportunity to solicit signup. You may find it is more ideal to have a friend of the band deal with the mailing list, and have band members selling merchandise behind a table where they can still say hello to their friends while generating and controlling customer traffic.

Mailing list and beyond...
Your mailing list is your lifeline to your fans, supporters, and industry contacts. You should use it regularly to keep in touch with list members and let them know what you've been up to. Even if it has been a fairly inactive period for your act, let the list members know that you're still around but taking some time off from the public eye. One common mistake many developing artists make is using their mailing list only to promote an upcoming show. Your mailing list should be an informational source, like a regular newsletter, informing list members not only about your shows, but new CD releases, new additions to your website, new career developments, funny stories from the road (if you're on tour), etc. On average, you should send a mailing to your list about once a month.

Sending snail-mail or regular postal mailings to a large mailing list can be very expensive— the cost of producing mass flyers and newsletters in addition to the costs of mass postage can add up to depleting your budget. Don't be surprised if in your early days, the money you make from your shows barely covers the cost of mailing announcements about those same shows to your list. Depending on the size of your mailing list, it may be cost-effective to sign up for U.S. Bulk Mail Service, which gives you a per-letter/postcard discount on very large mailings.

Remember that email is free. There is no reason why you can't send at least one email a month to your entire list in newsletter format. But keep these emails on the shorter side, noting the most pertinent details up front— most folks don't like to receive and wade through lengthy emails.

Your information lifeline
If you can afford it, also send monthly postal mailings to bolster your emails (the regular mail pieces can be more lengthy and informative than the emails). But if you can't afford it, focus on the emails and only use the regular post to announce very special events or developments, (An important upcoming show or CD release.) Remember that if you are promoting a concert, you need to mail your postal mailings 10-14 days in advance so they arrive well before the upcoming show date. While mailings/emails are important don't over due it.

Apart from being a lifeline to your fans and contacts, your mailing list is one of your most valuable calling card to the entertainment industry: People who work in the industry— from A & R talent scouts to club owners— are always impressed with large mailing lists. In the same way they are impressed with a large number of CDs sold, your mailing list is a quantifiable way of noting how popular you are. Once you've built a large mailing list, mention its existence and the total number of people on it in appropriate business cover letters.

Every name counts
Lastly never remove a name from your mailing list unless you are confident that each address attached to that name is outdated. While every name may count, if someone asks to be removed from the mailing list, be professional and remove him or her immediately. Never forget that a large mailing list is both an important tool and an impressive asset.

Vivek J. Tiwary is the founder and President/CEO of both StarPolish and The Tiwary Entertainment Group, a multi-faceted entertainment ventures focusing on artist management, marketing consultation, and project production. Contact www.starpolish.com

♦

DESIGNING YOUR CD COVER
by Valerie Michele Hoskins, President of The Pursuit Studio
© 2006 All Rights Reserved. Used By Permission

The images described in this article can be viewed online at:
www.indiebible.com/valh

Visual (graphic and web) design in the music industry is about identity. Who you are, and your product or service must be well represented. What your audience, potential customer or client can expect to hear, feel, experience, or achieve must also be successfully communicated.

The designer and design
A talented visual communications professional understands the power of typography and images, and knows how to use them creatively to meet these expectations. The best creative professional for your project is well-trained, familiar with your industry and your target market, and makes design decisions based on accomplishing specific objectives you have identified. One of the most primary objectives is selling your music to consumers, or music industry professionals (e.g., securing a producer, record label or distributor through a demo.) If you have ever purchased a CD solely based on the cover design, or been attracted to an artist, band, producer or record label based on their logo, poster or web site? If so, the designer has succeeded.

Design plays a part in purchase decisions. When browsing for CDs, choices are made. People usually pick up what visually attracts them and then look at the listed songs, unless they are looking for a specific artist or title. You may get a feel for the CD artist, mood, and messages; and ultimately, hope to be satisfied that the CD delivers what the design and the title suggest.

Examples
Recently, I bought two CDs: *Count Basic* (www.countbasic.com), (see figure 1), and Marilyn Scott, (see figure 2). On the Count Basic cover, what grabbed me was the woman's face bolstered by the low cut dress she wore showcasing her significant cleavage, and a man behind her giving two major thumbs up! I wanted to be that woman. As for Marilyn Scott, she is standing alone on a rocky shore, looking pensively at the ground, barefooted, wearing what looks like a full-length camel hair coat. The image paired with the title created an appealing pensive and serene mood, and I was stirred to buy it.

Let the music take your mind
Music is not defined as visual art, but sound does create mental imagery. One of the reasons I'm not glued to MTV, VH1 or other music video networks, is that I prefer to give my mind complete freedom to conjure its own images in response to music. Music package design (CD, VHS, DVD) is a hors d'oeuvre, an invitation, and a precursor to a total sound experience - perhaps a journey. When you work with a designer, it's important to share the imagery in your mind to help the art direction along. It's also good for the art director and/or designer to listen to the music, so there's a healthy amount of imagery to feed the creative process.

Count the ways
Music professionals use graphic design in specific ways and have definite ideas about what they want the designs to accomplish. Neil Alexander is primarily a performer/composer, but is also active in engineering, production and programming, and has *P-Dog Records* (www.pdogrecords.com), a small independent record label he uses to release his own discs.

Neil has a logo, stationery, CD packaging for his releases, packaging for a CD business card, posters to launch new releases (see figure 3), press releases, and a web site from which people can purchase directly. "I have always found that how CD packaging looks is a big part of its impact, its connection with the listener. Logos and other symbols can become part of the performer's identity. It is in my case. As with any business, consistent graphics help define the company's image and products for the consumer," Neil stated.

Sweet sight of success
When working with a designer, there are definite criteria to use for assessing quality and success. There are well-established design industry factors for every product: logos, posters, CDs, business cards and stationery, advertising, and Web sites. To cover each one specifically in this article would take too long, so these are some of the main criteria to help judge a design's success: 1) It must be unified with the product or service's content or identity. This creates a sense of family, of belonging, and it's immediately apparent; 2) There's an information and visual hierarchy. This means there's a focal point or image that grabs your attention first, and then your eye is led around the design in the order of what's important sequentially; 3) The design has graphic impact and is distinctive and/or memorable. There are many designs competing with yours for attention (lots of demos are sent out to producers, record labels and distributors), so yours must be a major contender; and 4) It must be appropriate for who you want to attract and the environment in which it will be presented. A poster or CD for a country audience will not have the same look and feel presentation as for a heavy metal one.

Who can forget the strong identity between the Stones and that bright, red tongue sticking out logo? It's a very powerful example of a highly successful pictorial visual logo. The logo formats are logotype, initials, pictorial visual, abstract visual, and combination, and a well-trained designer is knowledgeable about them all. The Stones logo has graphic impact, is distinctive and memorable, and is appropriate for its rock audience.

The design process: what you can expect
The designer will meet with you for an initial consultation to answer questions. Some design studios may use a creative brief form. The goal is to crystallize and solidify your identity and vision, so you and the designer are clear about the direction. Usually you will be asked to sign a form approving the concept along with a deposit (or retainer), and then development production begins.

The designer will present thumbnails, (4-10 tiny creative ideas that are sketched out), which you will review, and choose one or two. Once the concept is clear the designer will then create more detailed drawings called rough compositions. Sometimes, if a designer feels very secure about the creative direction of your project, the thumbnail stage will be bypassed, and you'll first see about three roughs. The roughs may be hand-drawn as closely as possible to what a final version would be (see figure 4), or they might be created on the computer.

You review the roughs, and choose one to be developed further (see figure 5). You may receive up to three versions and you choose your favorite: it will be your final design. The designer will work with you to fine-tune it. Once you approve it, it is ready to be printed. If it's a web design, it will be implemented and programmed. You pay the balance due, and the process is complete.

Budget, low budget, no budget
Pricing for different types of projects can range vastly depending upon the business structure and the length of time the business has been operating. The business can be a design studio, freelance or consultant, or a print shop franchise like Kinko's and have years of experience or be newly established in the industry.

If you're interested in reviewing industry standard fees for graphic design, web design, or illustration, take a hike to Barnes and Noble bookstore and glance through the *"Handbook of Pricing and Ethical Guidelines,"* published by The Graphic Artist's Guild of America. It's the creative professional's bible, and includes everything you always wanted to know about fees, contracts, copyright, and other professional issues. The fees quoted are based on nationwide surveys distributed to creative professionals.

Options to consider:
1. Supply your own photos and/or illustrations (see figure 6). Photography and illustration are specialties requiring additional compensation
2. Personally coordinate printing and CD or other types of duplication. Our time is money so coordinating printing for your project and getting your CD duplicated will cost you more
3. Barter for pro bono service. We may reduce the fee or work for free if you'll do some things for us in return
4. Contact your local college or university and request a referral to a recent graduate or current senior student. There are some extremely

talented young people who are eager to get client experience and build their portfolio

5. Explore a business-education partnership project relationship www.portfolios.com/pursuitgallery

Where there is a will, there is a way

Who are you? Whom you want to attract? What do you want to accomplish? A marriage between sight and sound can only have a positive impact on your career. Successful visual design is the key.

Valerie Michele Hoskins is a songwriter, soon-to-be music publisher, educator, and president of The Pursuit Studio, a visual communications creative service for art and entertainment industry professionals and businesses. Contact Valerie at: val.hoskins@thepursuitstudio.biz

♦

THE IMPORTANCE OF MERCHANDISING

by Bronson Herrmuth, author of "100 Miles To A Record Deal"
© 2006 All Rights Reserved. Used By Permission

Whether you have ten fans or a thousand, if you don't have merchandise to sell when you perform, you are losing money, big time. Obviously you want to have a CD to sell at your shows, but T-shirts in the summer, sweatshirts in the fall and ball caps year round are hot selling items that can generate a profit for your small business/band.

Start small think big

Start small and buy more as you sell your inventory. You will find that your fans will buy one or two of everything you have to offer them for sale, given time. Be sure to always buy and sell high quality merchandise so the craftsmanship and durability will be there. You want your shirts or hats to be the one that your fans pull out of their closet to wear often. They actually become "walking billboards" for you, and having a crowd full of people proudly displaying your groups name at all of your shows can be a major plus in building and maintaining a large following. The reality is that most major artists make more money at their live performances from their merchandising then what they actually get compensated to perform. It is a well-established fact.

Your merchandising revenue

It is very important that you treat this as the merchandising division of your small business and maintains a separate book keeping process for your merchandise sales. If you are far enough along with your band to have a business checking account (if not, start one as soon as you can), start a whole separate account for this part of your business. To sell merchandise effectively you have got to keep the money you get for performing separate from the money you make and spend on your merchandising, or it won't work and could turn into a major problem for you down the road. Done properly there is a lot of money to be made selling your bands products.

Don't just give it away

Probably the number one problem you will have to deal with is everyone wanting and expecting you to give them a shirt or cap or CD. It is very important that you do not allow any free ones to anyone, except to the people that provide you income, such as the club owners, club managers, press, radio DJ'S, etc., as promotional giveaways which can't be avoided. Obviously everyone in the band, Family members, close friends are going to expect to get them for free, so what you have to do is figure out exactly how much money you have in each unit of your merchandise, and that will be the specially discounted price for those people-exactly what you have in them. This is essential to the success of your merchandising and the only way that you will ever show a profit when you start out.

Bronson Herrmuth is a music producer, performer, and multi-instrumentalist. He has worked in music publishing for 20 years, and is currently Creative Manager for Al Jolson Black & White Music and Jolie House Music, in addition to being President of Iowa HomeGrown Music, Stepping Stone Prod, and SongRepair.com. Bronson is author of the new book "100 Miles To A Record Deal". For more info visit www.iowahomegrown.com

♦

LEARN THE IMPORTANT SKILLS

by Derek Sivers, CEO CD Baby
© 2006 All Rights Reserved. Used By Permission

Like proper manners, or knowing how to drive, here are some things in the online world you just need to know:

Email:

- Have a good signature file that tells whom you are, how to find you, and entices people to click through to your web address, in 4 lines or less.
- Learn how to make good subject headers, so when your Email is one of 500 in an "IN" box, it will say exactly what is contained inside, from the other person's point of view.
- Learn how to quote someone's email message back to them. Or not.
- Learn how to subscribe to, post messages to, and unsubscribe from to a mailing list.
- Learn Manners. Spelling. Punctuation. How to turn off your caps lock key, and not use 25 exclamation points in a row.
- Learn how to how to communicate personality through these typewriter keys.
- Separate sentences into paragraphs. Reading a computer screen is different from reading a book. There's no paper to waste - leave plenty of space.

Data base skills:

- Know how to work your "address book" program. How to find people, sort, print, add, remove, change, and do bigger find commands (how to find all guitarists in the 818 area code)
- Keep it nice and clean and updated. Keep street address separated from the city, state, zip, country. Don't be sloppy in these early stages.
- Assume you ARE going to get more popular and soon your little address book will need to sort thousands of people.
- If you get really fancy, track each contact you have with someone: each calls, email, and visit. It comes in handy when someone from a year ago calls you up saying, "It's George! Remember?"

Web skills:

- Get comfortable uploading an Mp3 file.
- Sort your bookmarks/favorites into categories/folders so you can find things later.
- The more senses you touch in someone, the more they'll remember you.

Best-case scenario

A live show, with you sweating right on top of someone, the PA system pounding their chest, the smell of the smoky club, the flashing lights and live-in-person performance. WORST: an email, a single web page, or a review in a magazine with no photo. (Let's say that "emotions" are one of the senses.) Whenever possible try to reach as many senses as possible. Have an amazing photo of yourself or your band, and convince every reviewer to put that photo next to the review of your album. Touching their emotions is like touching their body. If you do it, you'll be remembered.

© 2006 Derek Sivers - all rights reserved - if you like this article check out my websites: cdbaby.com | hostbaby.com | agentbaby.com | marketingyourmusic.com | musicthoughts.com | hitmedia.com

♦

WEBSITE BASICS FOR THE SINGER/SONGWRITER

by Valerie DeLaCruz, Recording Artist
© 2006 All Rights Reserved. Used By Permission

You can't market yourself properly anymore without a website. People want instant information, and they like to save time by searching a website when they feel like it. Here are some basics that should be part of a musician's website for maximum value.

Where to begin

First, if you haven't already, you should register your website (domain name.) Even if you don't put anything up on your website, you should register so that you will be guaranteed the name you want once you are ready to add content. Check to see if it's available (www.netsol.com)

Examples of where to register:

www.godaddy.com
www.domainofmyown.com
www.domainsnext.com

What name to choose

It is a good idea to use the name you are best known as for your website name. This is how people search for you. "Free" websites on things like Angelfire, etc. are not that great because the long URL is nearly impossible for someone to remember. Remember, the simpler the better. How would someone who heard about you look you up? I would also not recommend putting a dash between your first and last name because if someone doesn't think of that, they will not find you in a search.

The design

Unless you are great with computers and have hours and hours of time to build your own website, I'd suggest hiring a professional. Finding a "webmaster" should be fairly easy; ask other friends, and check out other websites that you like. The name is usually listed on the homepage with an email link.) I had someone build my site and then teach me how to write simple HTML (or use HTML for Dummies) and an FTP (file transfer program like Fetch.) This way you can update it weekly with gig dates and news, and saves you money.

Note: The opening page is your Home Page and should open up fairly quickly (avoid FLASH and other fancy huge files that will daunt some users' machines). The quickest way to turn someone off is because it was taking too long to download your site.

The basic elements

The Home Page should have a synopsis of what viewers will find on your website. I think it should always include a picture, READABLE typeface (some are so small from trying to cram in so much information, that it's uncomfortable to read. Something I am also a stickler about is having contact information right on the Home Page. I don't make people dig around for it in several layers; again they may give up or be frustrated. I have an email link to me on EACH page of my website. I also have links to my manager, publicist and booking agent, as well as telephone numbers. Buttons should be *very* simple and understandable; ease and convenience should be your first concern.

Buttons you will need:

Bio: This gives background information on you that can be used by a reporter for reviews, concert listings, etc.

News: The most recent stuff that has happened and new stuff about to happen. This keeps people coming back to your site to see what is new.

Music: There must be a place for them to hear clips of songs, either Real Audio or MP3 format. Here is where your albums are shown, track listings, anything to do with your actual music.

Order: This is how people will buy your CDs and merchandise, either by mailorder, or credit card. Paypal is a good way to accept credit cards (www.paypal.com), especially if you don't have a merchant account. Selling your music on sites like CDBaby, CDStreet and Amazon.com, is another viable way.

Schedule: You can use TOUR DATES, or GIGS, anything to indicate that this is where people will find out your schedule.

Reviews: This is where you will place links to sites that have reviews of your music, and you will have actual quotes from media that can be used in a press kit.

Awards: If you have enough, this can warrant its own page; if not, add this information to the Reviews page.

Mailing List: Here is where you will entice people to join your email list so you can send mass emailings when you have something newsworthy (nomination for an award; new CD release) or gig dates.

Links: Some people make a separate links page. I have sprinkled links throughout the text and logos on my site. Hypertext (underlined names or outlined pictures) again creates convenience for the viewer.

Extras: Add as many other buttons that are unique to your situation. I have a button for my music video, a Journal page, and one that I've found really helpful with A&R people and publishers: *Song Pitch*. On this page, I have information for licensing songs and links to hear them. Remember pictures, and caption them to add information, as it reduces the need for a lot of extra text.

Remember, build a great website that will be your calling card. Tell people you meet to check out whatever they want to know on your website. Print your URL on all materials you distribute including press releases, flyers and business cards. Include it on your CDs prominently, not buried in the liner notes, and at the end of your music video.

Valerie DeLaCruz's passionate career pursuit and professionalism has been a model for other grassroots artists. Through hard work and persistence (and talent!) she's continued to make headway in the rough and tumble music industry. Contact: www.valeriedelacruz.com.

♦

BUILDING A MUSIC SITE THAT SELLS: PROMOTE YOUR CD, NOT YOURSELF

by Mihkel Raud, author of "How to Build a Music Website that Sells"
© 2006 All Rights Reserved. Used By Permission.

Marketing your CD on the Internet isn't really that different from marketing any other product on the Net – be it some fancy million dollar mansion in the Hollywood Hills, a how-to-get-divorced-in-less-than-ten-days consulting service, a super-cheap DVD player, or a subscription to some kind of porno website...whatever....it's the same game. To play any game, you have to know the rules.

Break all the rules

When it comes to music, I encourage people to get as crazy as they can. Break all the rules you've ever heard of. Try new! Don't think just of radio! Forget about what anyone else may or may not think of your music! Be yourself! Do what you want to do! And do it now! You have to dare to do!
Still, marketing your music – be it on the Internet or offline – is a totally different ballgame. You need to use some rational sense if you want to see results.

I know that it's pretty uncomfortable to think of your CD as a piece of merchandise. After all, music is supposed to be art, right? It is. Tell the opposite and I'd be the first to protest. Your CD is just as much of a product as a bottle of beer. Your CD is a product that everybody should "need."
This concept of "need" is exactly what sooooooo many musicians fail to understand. Almost every band or singer/songwriter website that I have seen concentrates on the artist.

Basic elements to a site:

- Biography
- Photo gallery
- News
- Gigs
- Sound samples

Think outside the box

There are many possibilities of what to include on your site. Some bands post lyrics, or have discussion boards and chat rooms. The most commonly used concept in the music business is still to build the website around the artist.

So what's wrong with that approach? Nothing really, except that it's so common. And the artist approach will not sell your CDs. You ask… how is that true? Let's look at an example. Let's say you're planning to buy a Mesa Boogie amp. You want to get yourself the best full stack in the world. Visit Mesa (www.mesaboogie.com) and take a close look at what's on that site. Are you being bombarded by raves about just how great a guy Randall Smith is? He's the mastermind behind Mesa amplifiers. Do you see any Smith family snapshots on the front page? Or "better" yet, is there a guest book form asking you to leave Randall an "I love you" message? Nope. None of that "person" stuff is on the Mesa Boogie amp website. Why? Because it's the product you're after, not touchy feely with its inventor. Why on earth should your website be any different?

If you really want to succeed, you need to stand out. In order to beat that competition, you will have to use The Billion Dollar Baby Website Concept, as I have ironically titled the concept (if you know the Alice Cooper song, you know what I mean!) In other words, create a website that is solely focused on your product – the CD.

Your CD as the spotlight

That's right. The only hero of your movie should be your cool-sounding-Grammy-winning-absolutely-fabulous CD. Every other detail of your website has to serve the same master - your CD. Nothing is more important than that music that you want to sell. If you use The Billion Dollar Baby Website Concept, you can turn the whole internet music game upside down. And you will win. It's as simple as that! OK, this may hurt your ego a little bit. I understand perfectly. After all, you wrote the songs. You spent hours singing them in perfect tune. Heck, you may even have produced the CD all by yourself and that's no easy task. But now I'm asking you to spotlight the CD instead of yourself?

Remember this important point. I'm NOT telling you to shut down your existing artist website. On the contrary, it's smart to have one. In fact, you can have a bunch of them…. the more, the merrier. You can have your loyal fans create them for you. However, on your Billion Dollar Baby Concept Website you are going to play a supporting role. Your CD will be the main player.

A separate website?

It is absolutely essential to have a separate website for your CD only. And when the time comes, for your next CD…. plan a separate website for it too. Every time you put out a new CD, you will build a new website designed just for it. My concept demands a lot of time and dedication, and is directly from my own experience. It's loads of work, and is expensive, but is another way to be a success.

I found a medieval music band from Estonia and produced a record of Black Sabbath songs in the 14th Century style of music. "War Pigs" sung in Latin. "The Wizard" played on Gothic harp and a fiddle (www.sabbatum.com.) I sold well over 1000 copies in the first few months. I sold 1000 copies entirely on the Internet with no marketing funds whatsoever. I did it all from my small apartment in Tallinn, Estonia. Now, if I could do it, so will you.

Mihkel Raud is the author of "How To Build A Music Website That Sells". To order your copy, please go to: www.musicpromotiontips.com

♦

MUSIC VIDEOS FOR INDEPENDENT ARTISTS AND LABELS

by Allen M. Gottfried, Owner/Director Electric Head

© 2006 All Rights Reserved. Used By Permission.

With constant advancements in today's video production world, more and more high-end equipment is available at lower costs than ever before. This affords independent artists and labels a way to shoot high-end looking music videos for a budget they can afford, while being able to compete with some of today's top artists and videos that are currently in rotation.

Budgeting, Production Cost, Distribution, Networks

As can be expected, artists are always looking for ways to save money but don't realize that this can compromise the quality of the production. Sure the band's close friend will produce a video with his home camera for a beer and pizza, but what outlets are going to play that video? Probably not many at all. If you feel your band is ready to shoot a professional music video, that you want to promote for national airplay, you need to hire a professional production company to provide the creative talent, crew and cast to deliver a video up to the highest standards.

Budgeting

I speak to many bands and labels on a day-to-day basis and many ask what is a good budget for a video. That is always a rough question to answer because you have to realize the many factors that are involved in producing and distributing a music video. When it comes to developing a budget, I always tell my clients to think logically. You can't shoot on 35mm film, on a big set, with huge explosions, fast cars, and cast, crews and everything in between on a budget of $500…. it's just not going to happen.

Many artists and production companies are opting to shoot on digital tape (Mini-DV, HD) because of the cost savings of equipment, and media, time reductions to set up shots, and increased delivery speeds from camera to editor to label to air.

When you approach a production company and director, you should have some idea of a budget in mind for the video. When you contact the director, you should have the subject song selected, and a rough idea of the creative approach to the video. The director will then write and submit a treatment for the label's and artist's approval along with a budget projection for review and negotiations.

Production Cost

You must remember that the company and production people still have to make a living, even though they are all doing what they love. They all need to make a profit to put food on the table. Here are some things to consider when reviewing a budget projection.

- Crew (Directors, Producers, Cameramen, Art Directors, Grips, PA's) And yes sometimes on a smaller shoot some people will do multiple tasks to save money.

- Cast (Does your shoot require actors and actresses or extras?) (Union, Non-Union?) Many rising stars are willing to work for a much lower amount of money since they are trying to establish their careers, but still expect to be paid a fair amount for their work.

- Locations (Where do you want to shoot your video. In a huge hotel, old house, on city streets?) Depending upon the location of the shoot, certain fees may apply. There are ways to work around or get lower rates or fees, Many private owners typically want to show off what they have, and may charge a lower fee or none for use of their property.

- Insurance / Permits If you have a legit production, you will need insurance and most likely permits to shoot, especially in major cities like NYC and Los Angeles. Minimum required insurance is usually a $1(one) million dollar liability policy for the duration of the shoot. I also recommend adding third party coverage as well. Coverage like this runs from $1000+ depending on how long you are shooting and what insurance requirements there are (i.e. stunts, rentals, pyro). You will also have a better chance of securing a location when you have an insurance policy. The owners feel safer and may cut you more slack.

- Transportation (Is cast, crew or the band flying, driving in from somewhere?)

- Rentals (Rain Machines, Cars, Planes, Limos, Props)

- Food (A fed crew is a happy crew.)

- Duplication and Distribution (How many copies and where to send it?) Duplications usually runs about $30+ for (Beta SP) tapes most stations require. Some of the smaller networks will take Mini-DV, VHS, and DVD, which will save you money and still get you video airplay. Don't forget shipping costs.

Distribution, Networks

Music videos have been around since MTV launched its groundbreaking station in 1981. Ever since, places like MTV, VH1 and BET all helped to promote artists and their videos to the masses. As many may know, such stations as the above adhere to a very strict play list, usually within the top 40 market. What many artists and labels are not aware of is that there are 1000's of other locations nationwide that will potentially get your video major exposure. Everyday, more and more cable TV shows, internet shows and websites are popping up, giving even more exposure options to artists with music videos. Other outlets always looking for new videos include shows produced and developed for nationwide and regional distribution to retail stores, bars, night clubs, bowling alleys, concert venues, etc.

Usually a video will start to be talked up a few months before a CD release, if the track is ready before hand. Just like radio airplay, it is usually best to have your new video added to rotation a few weeks before your CD release date. This will get people familiar with you new track and band, and hopefully they will want to buy that CD as soon as it is out.

Whether you are an unsigned, indie or major label artist, the cost to produce a high quality music video has substantially decreased but the value of having a video to air and compete with other artists is greater than ever and will aid in your musical success.

Electric Head, LLC is an award winning music video and commercial production company based on the East Coast. Our goal is to provide top-notch productions at budget-conscious costs so that bands, corporate and other clients of all sizes promote themselves via media that gets results and competes with the best out there! You can visit Electric Head on the web at www.electricheadonline.com or contact them at (732)901-8693 to discuss your next project.

technical

STREAMING YOUR MP3 FILES
by Luke Sales, GlassWing Media
© 2006 All Rights Reserved. Used By Permission.

So you want to stream your mp3s? No problem! What follows is a brief tutorial about streaming your mp3s online. There are two major parts to play in streaming mp3 files: serving up the files correctly and configuring your computer to receive them. If you are running your own website, you only need to worry about serving the files, but you should know how to receive them too. How else will you be able to test that the streaming works?

Serving up the Mp3s

1. There are several different ways to serve up streaming mp3s. First, you must encode your mp3s at a low bit rate, so that listeners will be able to hear the music without having to stop and download. A good compression setting for most listeners is 32kbps Mono. The audio quality at this setting is fairly low, since we are trying to accommodate listeners with slow Internet connections. You may wish to make two different versions of your music - one at 32kbps mono (for modem users) and another at 128kbps for broadband.

2. Name the mp3 files appropriately (ending with '. mp3') and uploads the files to your web server. Figure out what the address of the files is. For example, yourserver.com/mymusic.mp3, where 'yourserver.com' is the name of your server and 'mymusic.mp3' is the name of the mp3 file.

3. Now create a plain text ".m3u" playlist file containing the address of the mp3 file you wish to stream. This file should be a plain text document that contains only one line. (Use a program like Notepad to create this file). Using the example above, the file would only say yourserver.com/mymusic.mp3

4. Save text file as 'mymusic.m3u', where 'mymusic' is the name of the song. Upload this file to your server. Now just create a link to this file from somewhere on your web site. This sample HTML link would display 'click here to stream' and would link directly to the .m3u file above:

   <a href = "/mymusic.m3u">click here to stream</a>

If the listener's computer is configured correctly, all they need to do is click on this link and their mp3 player should pop up and begin to stream. How does a person set themselves up to hear streaming mp3s?

Receiving and listening to an mp3 stream

If your computer is not set up for mp3 streaming, it will not know what to do with the .m3u playlist file. To solve this problem, install a streaming-capable Mp3 player. Here are some good ones: Windows: Winamp, Kjofol, Sonique, Windows Media Player, or Real Player. Mac: Soundjam, Macamp, or Audion.

Online resources

www.webmonkey.com contains many great tutorials about all aspects of web development (including streaming).

Internet radio? Check out www.shoutcast.com, a free technology that makes it easy to run an Mp3 radio station. If you just want something easy, go to live365.com - you have to pay, but they do all the work.

Create an .m3u play list that contains the address of the mp3 you want to stream. Create a link to this file. That's it - Have fun streaming!

Luke Sales is a trumpet player/programmer/web dude who works for GlassWing Media in Portland. GlassWing will assist no matter how small your projects, assisting with CD-ROMs, DVDs, web sites, and guitar tuning. Contact: www.glasswing.com

♦

PREPARING YOUR DEMO TO MAKE IT BIG
by Garrett Haines, TreeLady.com
© 2006 All Rights Reserved. Used By Permission

Introduction

Having a good demo is probably one of the most important things you can do to help your career. But it might not be for the reasons you think. Understanding the real marketing purposes of a demo can help you get your work to the right people through the most appropriate channels. I'm going to cover three topics: dispelling demo myths, a discussion of how to best use your demo, and finally, some thoughts on the actual completion.

Realities

I don't know where the myth started, but it goes like this: you put together a demo tape, throw it in an envelope, and mail it to a bunch of record labels. It arrives at the "Judging Department" at the record company. Someone there determines that your music is "good enough to deserve a record contract." So, they call you and offer you a contract that includes development money and a five CD deal.

Now, take a deep breath and repeat after me, "It doesn't work that way. It doesn't work that way. It doesn't work that way."

Just about every part of this myth is completely out of synch with how the real world works. First, record companies will not listen to unsolicited tapes. They will either return them to you unopened or pitch them. Why? Because invariably people would claim that a record company stole their demo song for one of their mega-hit starts. By refusing your demo, the record label is protecting itself from exposure to copyright infringement lawsuits.

Second, it's a farce to suggest that people who are "good enough" will get a record contract. This isn't a high school science fair. A demo isn't about being good enough; it's about commercial viability. Never confuse talent with commercial viability; the two are not necessarily related. In fact, the world is overflowing with amazing musical talent, and much of it will go unheard. One west coast producer told me on the condition of anonymity "if the music industry was really about getting the best talent, I would just go down to the local Southern Baptist church on Sunday and grab women out of the front row or the choir. I could find tons of people who are amazing singers, but it's not about that. It's about the whole package."

Third, recent economic trends have affected the way record companies have scouted new talent. "There aren't any development deals any more. They don't exist, a least among the majors," explains Liz Rueger of Independent Artist Representatives. Instead, notes Rueger, record companies are looking for talent that has an established fan base. This would include tour dates, email lists, and even thousands of CD sales.

Making Your Demo Work for You

So, after all of that doom and gloom you might be wondering what's the use in a demo? While a demo might not get you an instant record deal, it is crucial for many aspects of your promotional activities. In short, your demo is your sonic calling card. It will represent you in three main areas: expanding your fan base, improving your industry contacts, and honing your craft.

As noted earlier, having an established fan base is one of the most important things an artist can do. From showing up at gigs, to buying merchandise, to serving as unpaid spokespeople, ardent fans are invaluable. Building a fan base entails getting your music heard.

One of the simplest ways to do this is by playing out at bars and venues. These days, it's almost unheard of for a club manager to book a band that doesn't have a finished demo. Arlene's Grocery is rapidly becoming one of THE places for bands to debut in New York. Sorting through the deluge of applicants is Booking Manager Julia Darling's job. Although the press kit is important, the quality of the demo is ultimately the deciding factor. Darling explains, "I listen to 20 seconds of a song - so instrumentals upfront are annoying. If the song is good of course I listen to more. Fancy paper, artwork, photos, etc; don't matter if the music is not good. I have booked bands whose press kits were literally put together by 5 years olds." Aside from getting gigs, a demo can be something you submit to college and independent radio, a great giveaway at shows, or material you post for download on the Internet.

With respect to improving your industry contacts, your demo can be reviewed by numerous outlets. (Isn't that a great reason to buy the Indie Bible?). Industry pros read reviews, too, as to radio programmers, club managers, and other individuals looking for the "next big thing." A demo is a great calling card for:

- Attracting an agent or manager.
- Expanding your fan base
- Improving industry contacts
- Honing your craft
- Getting gigs
- Selling or giving away at shows
- Starting point for a full-length release
- Submitting to reviewers (like those in the INDIE BIBLE)
- Submissions to local and college radio
- Capturing your songwriting at a point in time.
- Demonstrating that you are serious and can follow through
- Posting songs on your web site
- Completing your press kit
- Providing material to agents and managers

Finally, a demo helps you become a better artist. There are a multitude of reasons it's advantageous to compete a demo. It forces you to write more songs, explore your musical abilities, and make choices about your sonic direction. And even though it may seem trite, completing a demo is proof that you are serious about your craft and can be counted on to deliver. Consider this: of all the bands that ever existed, what percentage were able to complete a demo or full-length recording? Of those who couldn't pull the demo together, how many do you think ever landed recording contracts? I'll bet the number is miniscule. Remember, a record company can't sell CDs if you don't finish recording them.

Completing the Task

There are a few key decisions that must be made in order to get the process started. Which songs will be on the demo? How many? Will you record at home, in a studio, or both? And who will handle the mastering and duplication?

If you've been writing a lot of songs, then you have a portfolio to select from. If you're a new band or songwriter, then you may have an easier time paring down the choices. Solicit the help from a producer, musician, or friend you trust when choosing the material. After working on a song over and over an artist often looses objectivity. A fresh set of ears might be just the thing you need.

The demo needs to be the best songs to sell your music, not necessarily your favorite song. Francisco Pardorla, the Executive Director of San Francisco-based Wraith Records explains, "What people miss is that we're dealing with the music business. Music is the word that modifies business. At the end of the day the ability to sell CDs, tickets, whatever, is the main concern." Make sure you pick the songs that are most compelling from an economic, as well as an artistic standpoint.

A common mistake many bands make is including songs that show their diversity as musicians or singers. Two words: bad idea. Think of your demo as a sandwich. Just because your kitchen has mayonnaise, peanut butter, and vegemite doesn't mean that you should put all three together. Yuck. Three stylistically different songs only serve to confuse the listener. A record executive will think, "Will the real band please stand up." You need to present a clear genre, attitude, and direction. This doesn't mean that you can't have two fast songs and a ballad. But it does mean that your material needs to have a unified sound, style, and feel. If you can't decide which persona you want to assume, then you might need to have more than one demo disc. Just make sure that each one is it's own little consistent sandwich of songs.

Speaking of the number songs on the demo, there are no absolute rules about how many songs you should use. However, most industry veterans agree three is a good standard. Start with your best material first, followed by your second strongest, then the third. Make sure you grab your listener's attention, and keep them listening. If you have a long musical intro or two verses before the main hook, you may be using the wrong tune. Again, solicit the advice of an unbiased listener to gauge the attraction of your chosen songs.

How and where you record has become increasingly important in recent years. There once was a time when the audio quality of your demo was not important. (And for songwriting pitches, there is still some merit to this belief). However recent advances in computer and recording technology have made it possible for to create professional-quality recordings in your garage. Let's face it, even my dog has a copy of ProTools these days. (Although, he still prefers 2" tape). All things being equal, you can assume that your competition will have a demo that could play side-by-side with a commercial release. My advice is to shop around at local recording studios. Some may offer specific demo packages. Others might be willing to work with you on an as needed basis. For example, you could record drums at their place, and take the audio tracks home to work in a project studio. You could return to the professional studio for vocal recording or mixing. If a studio isn't willing to work with you to stretch your budget, I suggest you look elsewhere.

Finally, choosing a mastering a duplication option cannot be overlooked. Rest assured, your competition will invest the effort to have their CD mastered. Mastering is the last chance to correct any errors and put that final professional sheen on your recordings. In addition to dealing with the technical issues of creating the production master for your duplicator, a mastering engineer can tweak your songs in a manner that helps them sound cohesive and provide optimal loudness for your particular genre. Real mastering engineers have tuned rooms, highly accurate full-range speakers, and specialized gear designed for this type of work. Most do not use computer plug-ins. Even if your budget is limited, there are many talented and qualified mastering engineers around.

Duplication is not a good place to skimp, either. After all of the work you put into your demo, what good is it if the CD doesn't play? Be weary of fly-by-night super cheap duplication houses. Even if you pay a little more, go with an established duplicator. In addition to good customer service, a top-flight duplicator doesn't surprise you with hidden fees, unfair shipping rates, or delayed turn around times. After reading the fine print you'll probably find that a reputable duplicator is no more expensive than a bargain shop, when comparing the same exact services. Again, shop around to find the best solution for your situation.

Conclusion

Once a demo leaves your hands, it grows legs. You never know where it will end up. And there are many stories of key people learning about a band via a demo that has changed hands over and over. From building your fan base, to improving your industry position to honing your craft, a demo is one of the most important ingredients to your potential success. This is a tough business, and might only get one chance to make an impression. Make sure your demo is everything you know it can be. After that, cross your fingers, and keep gigging!

Garrett Haines is co-owner of Treelady Studios www.treelady.com His articles have appeared in many music trades including: Tape Op, EQ Magazine, and Rockrgrl. He welcomes your questions or comments at garrett@treelady.com

♦

HOW TO CREATE AND MANUFACTURE YOUR MUSIC

by Hadas, Eric Mueller, Oliver Gos, Recordpressing.com
© 2006 All Rights Reserved. Used By Permission

There are many different variables involved in creating an effective package to market yourself and your music. The artistic element of your release, the cover art and promotional materials, are important as they introduce a new dimension to your aesthetic identity. Flipping through endless racks of CDs and records, it is the artwork that can instantly spark an interest for an otherwise unknown release. The hidden element involved in providing your release this opportunity is a well-developed understanding of the options offered by the printing and media manufacturing industry. The manufacturing process can be extremely frustrating, confusing, and financially straining for musicians and record labels (novices and veterans alike), but with sufficient research and eventually a well-established relationship with the right company, you can make virtually any vision come to life and fit within your budget.

The CD format

It is first essential to determine the medium(s) that will best deliver your message to its intended audience. If you choose to release your music in CD format, the following will assist in the process:

1. **Where to go.** Find an independent operation that offers high quality work at reasonable prices and turnaround times, and most importantly cares about its customers.

2. **Glass mastering.** Confirm that you are getting glass mastered replicated CDs rather than duplicated CD's, to insure the integrity of your product all the way through your entire pressing.

3. **Quality.** Choose a company that offers the best print quality for the booklets, tray card, and CD face. *(The use of offset printing results in the most professional print quality, and usually involves a turnkey filmless process that yields much higher line screen than silk-screening and thus better detail on the print work. This is particularly true on the CD face.)*

4. **Extra charges.** Please make sure to ask about film charges, as some manufacturers won't mention them until after you have committed to the project. In some cases, films can cost as much as $300, so WATCH OUT. Film charges are normal for the CD face, but avoid going with a company that charges for any films beyond that. There are a host of other options available to make your CD release unique.

5. **Enhanced CDs.** Ask if the manufacturer can make your CD an enhanced CD; Adding a video or links to your photos or website only strengthens your release in the eyes of fans or industry people, and a good manufacturer will gladly do this at little or no extra cost.

6. **How to stand out.** Other options to make your CD stand out include making it a dye cut shaped, clear, or even scratch-n-sniff CD. Something utilizing some interesting artwork that takes advantage of the various printed cardboard cases, jackets, and sleeves offered throughout the industry as more hip packaging options for CD's and DVD's. Regardless, find a company who can give you some options to work with, so there is no chance of stifling your potential, or that of your graphic artists'.

What about vinyl?

Many people opt to release their music on vinyl records as well, as this is still a very popular choice for DJ's and collectors of various musical genres. Should you choose to release your music on vinyl, there are some extremely important things to look and listen for.

The finer points are:

- Find a company that can provide you with the highest level of versatility and quality in terms of sound quality and packaging options. There are only a few companies that still press quality vinyl records, and even fewer who also provide in-house printing and packaging. Manufacturing the packaging and vinyl record at the same facility saves shipping charges and hassle.

- Look for a company that uses more modern equipment, like DMM (direct to metal mastering) equipment. DMM processing essentially cuts out one whole generation of the replicating process, reducing the overall cost of making vinyl, while at the same time yielding a wider potential sound range, and significantly reducing the ambient noise, pops, crackles, and hisses that are too often present on cheap vinyl.

- Make sure to get 100% virgin vinyl, not partially recycled compound, as next to mastering this is the most important factor in getting audiophile quality records.

- Ensure that your records are manufactured heavy enough so that you do not receive warped records when they arrive at your door. A good weight for a 12" record pressing is 140g or above, and for a 7" record pressing 40g and above. A few companies will even record pressing much heavier than this.

- Asking the right questions and really comparing apples to apples can be difficult when researching vinyl manufacturing, but it is vital in order to get the most for your money. Vinyl is a great promotional tool, and when designed and manufactured well, can capture the attention of DJ's, collectors, and labels as well, if not better than any other medium.

Make financial sense

It is understood that releasing music independently is financially draining, and many people cut corners left and right because of this. Depending on the stage you're at, a few cut corners might be okay, but there is also a general understanding that professional looking and sounding packages will certainly have a marked advantage at piquing the interest of A&R folks, writers, publishers, booking agents, DJs and club owners. There are ways to cut costs in the manufacturing of your art and music; sacrificing the integrity and quality of your product is not one of these ways. Do the best you can within whatever budget you find yourself working with, and make sure you DO YOUR RESEARCH. Get what you want and pay a reasonable price for it, and if at all possible, keep it independent.

In summary

Definitely find yourself a reputable independent company that can fulfill ALL of your manufacturing needs. Choose a company that is not too small to handle all your needs, and not too big so that you'll find yourself lost in the corporate red tape shuffle. Do your homework as far as pricing goes, and remember cheaper is not necessarily better, and going with a company that promises whistles and bells such as online distribution posters will also increase your bill significantly. Build and maintain a mutually beneficially relationship with a capable company whom you enjoy working with. In the long run it will benefit you much more than the dollar you'd save here and there constantly shopping and bouncing around solely for the cheapest price.

Hadas, Eric Mueller, and Oliver Goss, respectively Marketing Director, General Manager, and President of Recordpressing.com contributed this article. Recordpressing.com is an independent source for high quality CD, DVD, vinyl record, and promotional material manufacturing. If you have questions or comments regarding this article, contact Recordpressing.com at help@recordpressing.com

legal

HOW TO COPYRIGHT YOUR MUSIC
by Nancy Falkow, Ask Nancy
© 2006 All Rights Reserved. Used By Permission

Sometimes musicians think every song written needs to be immediately copywritten, but this isn't always true! Copyrighting, registers your music so that if a situation arises that someone is stealing your music, your registration of copyright is on file, which protects you. So, if you're singing these songs in your living room for your family, you don't need to run to Washington, DC!

What can be copywritten?
Literary works; musical works, including any accompanying words, dramatic works, including any accompanying music, pantomimes and choreographic works, pictorial, graphic, and sculptural works, motion pictures and other audiovisual works, sound recordings and architectural works.

Library of Congress
If you plan on distributing your music through the web you should copyright your songs. Go to the *US Copyright Registration site* and download the forms you need. Each situation is different, read all of the information, and figure out which best applies to you. Put your music and lyrics on tape or cd, fill out the appropriate forms and write the check. It takes up to 6 weeks to receive all the paperwork and registrations.

Internet: www.loc.gov/copyright
Phone: 202/707-3000 (this is NOT a toll-free number)
Write: U.S. Copyright Office, Library of Congress, 101 Independence Avenue, S.E, Washington DC 20559-6000

The forms:
What you need is a properly completed application form, a nonrefundable filing fee ($30)
For each application, and a non returnable deposit of the work being registered (A tape, CD, and/or lyric). You can copyright more than one song on one tape or cd by sending it in as an anthology. In short, you put your songs on one format, give it a name like "Greatest Hits" and send it in. This is the best way to save money. Instead of copyrighting each song for $30, you're copyrighting an entire batch for $30. Remember it's always important to protect yourself and your songs. Good luck!

Nancy Falkow is known throughout the Philadelphia area for writing catchy and melodic pop-folk songs with dynamics and soul. She still finds time to play bass and sing background vocals in an all girl rock band called The Dirty Triplets. Contact: www.nancyfalkow.com

♦

HOW TO TRADEMARK YOUR BAND NAME
by Derek Sivers, CEO CD Baby
© 2006 All Rights Reserved. Used By Permission

Anytime you are promoting, you are also promoting your name - so make sure it's yours!
  I'm giving you some unofficial advice here from my own experience. There are attorneys and specialists that can help you much more. I recommend a book called "*Trademark Legal Care for Your Business & Product Name*" by Stephen Elias (Nolo Press). It covers everything, and even includes the forms you'll need to register. For basic trademark advice, go to my web page of reprints from Nolo Press: (www.hitme.net/useful/c.html)

Research to make sure no one else has your name
Check the PhonoLog at your nearest record store. If you can, check *Billboard's Talent Directory*. (It IS expensive to buy however). If you've got $$, hire a search firm (attorneys) - this is the most reliable, but it will set you back $300-$500. I also heard CompuServe has a trademark research center.

The Library is free
Call the nearest largest Public Library and ask if they have a "*Federal Trademark Register CD-Rom*". (Each state has between 1-3 libraries that will have one). You can go in, and they'll even show you how to do a search. Search for your full band name, then each word individually. *Example*: my band "Hit Me": search "Hit Me" then search "HIT" then search "ME". The reason is there may be a band called "Kick Me" or "Hit Us" that could be a conflict. If you can think of other similar words to search, try those, too. You can also get a printout of all this. If there's nothing even remotely similar, you're doing OK. If someone, even a clothing company, is using your name, then you should consult an attorney.

Trademark & Servicemark:
1. Make sure you search the *Federal* Register, then the *Pending* Register. These are for the names that have been applied for, but not completed yet. Call Washington, DC: (703)308-HELP and ask for the book "*Basic Facts about Registering a Trademark*".

2. Trademark covers a product, while a Servicemark covers a service. As a musical act, we are a *service*. If ALL you do is make CDs and tapes, but never play live, maybe your name only applies to a product. For most of us, it's a service first, then a product second. It's all the same form, just a technicality. Note: You can still use the ® [little (R) in a circle] when you are registered.

3. You can start using "TM" or "SM" after your name now. It means you have *intent* to register, or are claiming legal ownership of that name. You can use the ® *after* and only after the whole registration is complete.

How much does it cost?
Each registration class costs $245. When I called the office help line, they said if you register your Servicemark, that's plenty of protection for now. That is until you start selling loads of T-shirts, hats, action figures! Make sure you get the new forms, since the older forms have $200. A Servicemark for a musical act, you will want to file a "CLASS 41". The description of product/services is: "Entertainment Services in the nature of Musical Performance." Don't forget to do this NOW, or all the work you're doing to promote your act will be wasted.

If you like this article by Derek Sivers please visit his websites@ cdbaby.com | hostbaby.com | agentbaby.com | marketingyourmusic.com | musicthoughts.com | hitmedia.com

TRADEMARKING YOUR LOGO
by Vivek J. Tiwary and Gary L. Kaplan, StarPolish.com
© 2006 All Rights Reserved. Used By Permission

A good logo is an invaluable tool in the imaging and marketing of a developing artist. That is why it's important to design a logo immediately after you have settled on your name. But unlike your name, it's more acceptable to change your logo over the years without losing or confusing fans. *311* and *The Rolling Stones* are great examples of bands that have either changed or modified their logos to adapt with changing times or the themes of certain albums or tours.
  Not every artist has a logo, but a logo can only help. Remember that your name simply and consistently printed in a certain standard font can be a fine logo (e.g. Cheap Trick). I personally like logos that are minimal, easy to remember, tied into the artist's name, and easily reproduced. Like your name, your logo should somehow also be in line with the vibe of your act.

How do you get one?
A band member or friend designing your logo may assure a genuine and intimate connection between the logo and the band. If no one you know is talented in the visual arts, you can seek help from local design companies. Be careful though, as some of these companies can be expensive. Alternately, you can solicit help from local design schools, whose students may be willing to design a logo for free in order to gain working experience and build up their own design portfolios. Try putting

flyers/posters up in the schools or posts on school bulletin boards announcing that you are a local band/songwriter looking for a logo designer.

Be seen

Once you have a logo that you are satisfied with, put it on everything— all over your website, your merchandise, your CD, your letterhead, etc. Make stickers and always keep a small stack of your logo stickers on hand. Stick them on everything and everywhere. Consistency and repetition are critical marketing keys. The more times people see the same logo, the more they will remember it and your act.

Register your logo

Register with the *U.S. Patent and Trademark Office* (or comparable body if you are based in another country). Much like with your name, you acquire rights to your logo when it is publicly used in commerce. This means that when you sell your merchandise, or play a show where your logo is displayed, you automatically obtain some common law rights in that logo. Registering your logo as a trademark, however, will provide you with important additional rights:

Do a search

Assuming that you are the first to use this logo, registering your logo will help secure your right to use it, and prevent others from using the same or a similar logo. Because of the extremely subjective nature of the trademark analysis for logos, it might not be worthwhile to perform a search. It is not with certainty you will discover the same or similar logo being used by another band. If you choose to perform a search, you can try *Thomson & Thomson*, or the folks at (www.tradename.com) A lawyer can take care of the whole thing, since the analysis is so touchy, that only an experienced trademark attorney will be able to offer sound advice.

The good news is it's not quite as disastrous, if you are forced to change your logo. It might not be what you'd ideally like to do, but it pales comparison to having to change your name. If you can afford to hire an attorney to assist you, go ahead and trademark your logo. If your problem is that you're strapped for cash, try to register your trademark yourself by using the website of the U.S. Patent and Trademark Office (www.uspto.gov).

Vivek J. Tiwary is the founder and President/CEO of both StarPolish and The Tiwary Entertainment Group, a multi-faceted entertainment venture focusing on artist management, marketing consultation, and project production. Vivek has 10 years experience in the arts and entertainment industries, Prior to joining StarPolish.com, Gary L. Kaplan spent three years at Skadden, Arps, Slate, Meagher & Flom, one of the world's preeminent law firms. Gary was a member of Skadden's Intellectual Property Department, focusing on patent litigation. Contact: www.starpolish.com

ENTERTAINMENT INDUSTRY LAWYERS: WHO, WHERE AND HOW MUCH?

by Wallace Collins, Entertainment Lawyer
© 2006 All Rights Reserved. Used By Permission

As a creative artist in the entertainment industry you do not need to know everything about the business in order to succeed, but you should hire people who do. When I was a teenage recording artist back in the late 70's, I can remember being intimidated by the "suits". Now that I am on the other side of the desk, I have a broader perspective. I am here to tell you that those "suits" can help you; provided, however, that like any other aspect of your life, you use your instincts in making your selection.

The team: The best place for you to start building your "team" of representatives is with a competent lawyer who specializes in entertainment law, which is a combination of contract, intellectual property (copyright, trademark and patent) and licensing law. Eventually, your team could possibly include a personal manager, a booking agent and a business manager/accountant. Your lawyer can assist you in assembling your team. He may then function as the linchpin in coordinating the activities of your team and insuring that these people are acting in your best interests.

The lawyer: A good lawyer will navigate you safely through the minefield that is the entertainment industry. Record contracts, publishing agreements and licensing arrangements can be extremely complicated. Proper negotiating and drafting requires superior legal skills as well as knowledge of entertainment business and intellectual property practice. Your lawyer can explain the concepts of copyrights, trademark and patents to you and assist you in securing proper protection for your work. In addition to structuring and documenting a deal to maximize the benefits to you, some lawyers also actively solicit deals for their clients.

What to look for: When looking for a lawyer take the time to interview a few before retaining one. Some lawyers are with large firms, but many are solo practitioners. Lawyers have various personalities and legal skills and you should seek out a situation where the "vibe" is right. It is not necessary that your lawyer like or even understand your creation. It is more important that you feel he or she is a trustworthy and competent advisor.

When do I pay?: Keep in mind that a lawyer with other big name clients is not necessarily the best lawyer for you; if it comes down to taking your calls or those of a superstar, which do you think will get preference? A lawyer, much like a doctor, is selling services, so if you go to him for advice you should expect to pay. With the odds of success in this business being what they are, very few lawyers will agree to work for you and wait for payment until you are successful and can pay your bills. You may also find someone who will work on a contingency basis.

The cost:

1. A lawyer specializing in the entertainment field usually charges an hourly fee or a percentage of the money value of your deal. Hourly rates generally run from $200 and up. Percentages are based on the "reasonable value of services rendered" and generally run around 5% of the deal. A few lawyers may charge a set fee, such as $1,000 or $1,500, to review and negotiate certain documents. Check around to see if the fee arrangement proposed is competitive.

2. Most lawyers will require a payment of money in advance or "retainer", which can range anywhere from $1,000 to $10,000. Even those who take a percentage of the deal as a fee may require that you pay a retainer. In addition to the hourly fee or percentage, you are usually required to reimburse your lawyer for his out-of-pocket costs, including long distance telephone calls, photocopies, postage, fax, etc.

3. You should realize that in retaining a lawyer you are making a contract even if your agreement is not written. In return for a fee, the lawyer promises to render legal services on your behalf. However, some lawyers may want a fee arrangement in writing (specifically in connection with a percentage deal) and/or a payment direction letter. A cautious lawyer will advise you that you have the right to seek the advice of another lawyer as to the propriety of a percentage fee arrangement.

As a general rule: You need a lawyer if you are asked to sign anything other than an autograph. Too many aspiring creative artists want to get a deal so badly they will sign almost anything that promises them a chance to do it. Even successful careers have a relatively short life span, especially in the music, movie and television business. Therefore, it is important for you to get maximum returns in the good years and not sign away rights to valuable income.

Never sign anything without having your own lawyer review it first! Do not rely on anyone else (or even their lawyer) to tell you what your contract says. Do not let anyone rush you or pressure you into signing any agreement. There is really no such thing as a standard "form" contract. Any such contract was drafted by that party's attorney to protect that party's interests; your lawyer can help negotiate more favorable terms for you.

Wallace Collins is an entertainment lawyer with the New York law firm of Serling Rooks & Ferrara, LLP. He was a recording artist for Epic Records before attending Fordham Law School. Contact: (212) 245-7300, www.wallacecollins.com

ROYALTIES IN THE MUSIC BUSINESS
by Joyce Sydnee Dollinger, Entertainment Lawyer
© 2006, All Rights Reserved. Used By Permission

What is a royalty? In the real world, the word royalty is synonymous with the power or rank of a king and queen. In the music world, the word royalty is synonymous with *money*. Royalties are the most important entitlements of the musician. These entitlements warrant them to receive money from their craft - the craft of MAKING MUSIC.

Royalties
There are many types of royalties. The list is constantly growing because of the new technology, but here are some to name a few: Artist Royalties, Mechanical (Publishing) Royalties, US Performance Royalties Synchronization Royalties, Grand Rights Royalties, Foreign Royalties for record sells and performances, Lyric Reprint Royalties.

General definition
Artist Royalties, in a nutshell, are monies paid to the recording artist from the record company. They are the share of the proceeds from the sale of the artist's records paid directly to the artist after the artist records material for the record company. This, in turn, gives the record company permission to exploit the musical work in the marketplace.

Recording contracts
In artist recording contracts, artist royalties are usually negotiated in points. When record label business affairs attorneys use that terminology, they are referring to the percentage points the record company will pay an artist on each album sold. For example, if an artist gets 10 points, it usually means that the artist receives 10% of the retail cost of each record sold.

1. **Superstar Deals**
   Royalties usually are:
   - 16%-20% of retail of top-line records plus escalations
   - 18-20% is quite high and the artist must sell a lot of records - usually more than 5 million
   - 100% CD rate and can receive new configuration royalties
   - 12-14% of singles + escalations receive increased royalties when contract options are exercised

2. **Mid-Level Deals**
   Royalties usually are:
   - 14%-16% of retail top-line records plus escalations (escalations usually based on genre)
   - 16% is high and the artist must sell a lot of records
   - 85-90% CD rate and new configurations
   - 12-13% of singles or 3/4 of LP rate receives increased royalties when contract options are exercised

3. **New Artist Deals**
   Royalties usually are:
   - 11%-13% of retail top-line records
   - 75-85% CD rate and new configurations
   - 10-11% of singles

When to renegotiate
If the artist sells a ton of records, the artist can usually re-negotiate with the record label and try to receive increased royalty rates. Here are some topics to try to re-negotiate:

- increased net royalty rates on remaining LPs in the contract
- increased rate for each successive LP
- escalations for attaining sales plateaus
- receiving increased royalty rate on future sales of past LPs
- improvement of the royalty computations
- increase foreign rates, the CD rate, the new technology rate, licensing fees and free goods

Record royalty formula
The record royalty formula is usually based upon a percentage of records that are sold. In using the formula, the record company looks to the retail price of the commercial top-line records and standard deductions that every record company takes from the gross income from the sales of those records. Some of the deductions are: recording costs of the records, packaging, returns and reserves, discounted military sales, video costs, tour support, promotional records and free goods. Please note: records on which royalties are paid are quite different from deductions from gross royalties.

Joyce Sydnee Dollinger is an attorney admitted in New York and Florida. She is also the Vice President of 2 Generations SPA Music Management, Inc., and involved with 2generations.com and SPA Records, Inc. Contact: www.sparecords.com

♦

ARTIST-MANAGEMENT CONTRACTS
by Richard P. Dieguez, Entertainment Lawyer
© 2006 All Rights Reserved. Used By Permission.

Next to a record label deal, the artist management contract is the most exciting agreement an artist will sign. As with any legal document, a contract shouldn't be signed without the advice of a music attorney. Let your lawyer take the blame for "asking too much" or for being such a "tough negotiator". That is what they are being paid to do. Here are the key points to negotiate:

- How long will the agreement be in effect?
- How much will the manager get paid during the agreement?
- How much will the manager get paid after the agreement has ended?

The art of negotiation

1. It is likely you and your manager are will both to have a legitimate difference of opinion as to the amount of time for which the contract will be binding. Whatever the reason, you don't want to get locked in with a loser for the next seven years. On the flipside nothing can be more frustrating for a manager than to have her budding artists go to another manager, where they then make it to the big time.

2. Depending on the particular circumstances of the parties, the negotiation will center on a contract term ranging from as short as six months to as long as several years. What length of time is fair really depends on what you and your manager are each bringing to the relationship you wish to form. For example, let's say that neither of you has too much experience in the music business. In this situation, you're both probably better off with a short-term contract, (6-12months) so that you can check each other out without getting locked in. You can always enter into another agreement if it turns out, at the end of the contract, that you have a future together.

The time and money equation
What happens if you can't agree to a fixed amount of time? Well, to satisfy both parties, the attorneys can always try to hammer out a compromise: a short-term contract with the potential of being converted into a long-term contract. For example, the parties could agree to a one-year contract. Part of the agreement, however, would be that the manager must meet certain conditions during this one-year period — such as getting you a record deal, a publishing deal or even guaranteeing that you earn a minimum amount of income. If the manager fails to meet the conditions, then the contract ends when the year is up. If, however, the manager is successful in meeting the conditions, then he has the right to automatically extend the contract for an additional period of time, say for another year.

Commission
The norm is for the manager to work on a commission. In other words, the manager gets compensated for his efforts by taking a percentage of whatever income you earn as an artist. Obviously, your attorney is going to try to negotiate for as small a percentage as possible. You'll argue that

the manager simply manages, and without your talent, there is nothing to sell to the labels or to the publishers. The manager's attorney is going to negotiate for as high a commission as possible. Their position will be that there is a lot of talent out there — especially in the major music centers like California and New York.

Money talks
So what's the range of the amount of the commission? It can generally be anywhere from 10% to 25% of your gross income. The amount that is settled on may very well depend on the circumstances. Again, the art of compromise may bring new life to a negotiation that is at a deadlock on the issue of the commission amount. Regardless of the particulars, the concept here is that the lower percentage rate should be satisfactory to you, while the manager is also given an incentive to make a bigger percentage if he can get you to earn in excess of a certain amount of gross income. And, of course, getting you over that amount, whether it's $25,000.00 or whatever, will be to your benefit as well.

The manager
Your manager will likely try to apply their commission to every conceivable entertainment-related activity from which you could possibly earn an income. Examples of such money-making activities would be live performances, record sales and the sale of promotional merchandise such as T-shirts, posters, buttons, programs and pictures. If you feel that the commission rate the manager is asking for is too high, you can try to compromise by proposing that you'll accept the commission rate, but only if certain activities are excluded from the commission.

After the contract ends
Another touchy subject is whether the commission on gross income earned by the artist continues after the contract has ended. Your response will probably be "of course not!" After all, once the contract is over, neither party has any further obligation to the other. Once the contract is over, there should be a clean break, but it is not always so clear-cut

You may be fortunate enough to have signed some money-making deals. As agreed, the manager gets his percentage and you keep the rest. But it may be that your money-making contracts will still be in effect for quite some time after your management contract has ended. Since you will continue to profit from a deal he helped you to obtain, the manager may feel that he should also continue to profit even after the artist-manager relationship legally ends.

When you get a new manager
If you enter into a contract with a new manager, that new manager will probably be no different from your former manager on the question of compensation. The new manager's attorney will probably demand that the commission apply to every conceivable entertainment- related activity from which you could possibly earn an income. This would include the money pouring in from deals your former manager obtained! You wouldn't want to be stuck paying two commissions on the same income.

Conclusion
There are many aspects of the artist management contract that will be subject to negotiation. An issue may arise as to who collects the income: the manager, you or possibly a third party like a business manager or accountant. Another traditional sticky point is the extent of the manager's authority to sign contracts on your behalf. There may even be some negotiating points that don't seem crucial to you and the manager but to the attorneys seem to mean everything. The personal circumstances surrounding any given artist management contract can be so unique, that the art of compromise expands the parameters of the so-called "standard" contract.

An NYU Law graduate, Richard P. Dieguez has over 16 years experience in entertainment law. He has represented hundreds of clients across the U.S. and several nations in music, film, television, publishing etc., Mr. Dieguez is also the founder of The Circle, a monthly music industry seminar held in New York City. Contact: www.RPDieguez.com

♦

THE WRITTEN AGREEMENT AMONGST BAND MEMBERS
by John Tormey III, Entertainment Lawyer
© 2006 All Rights Reserved. Used By Permission

AABM
I have seen references to the above-mentioned document as both "Inter-Band Agreement", and "Intra-Band Agreement". Rather than initiate any argument with grammarians as to which term is correct -let's simply call this all-important document the "Agreement Amongst Band Members"; or, "AABM", for short. If one is a musician playing in a multi-member band, is an AABM needed? *Absolutely*, yes!

The agreement
There are some parallels to an agreement amongst band members, and a pre-nuptial agreement between prospective spouses. But I actually find the case for having an *AABM* more compelling than a pre-nup. A marriage should be a function of love. A band formation, on the other hand, is often a commercial exercise.

Written agreements should be required for any collaborative commercial endeavor between 2 or more people. Maybe it seems easier NOT to make it official, but no band member should skip the *AABM*, if the band member takes his or her band or career seriously. It may not be realistic to operate on blind trust, in place of a good written agreement.

If the band formation is not viewed as a commercial exercise, then I suppose the band members can simply agree on a handshake, and then gig for free in the subways. However, the majority of bands that I hear from, are concerned about their financial, as well as their artistic, futures. Many are trying to find a way to become economically self-sufficient on music alone, while preparing to quit their "day jobs". It is best to have an agreement in hand, rather than, to put it off.

When to begin?
No one wants to be required to negotiate and close the AABM once the band is already successful, or once the band has already been furnished with a proposed recording agreement. The optimal time to close the *AABM* is while the band is just being formed or while it is still struggling. A good *AABM* should also be flexible enough to contemplate future changes, such as changes in personnel and,

Artistic direction. It is also likely one of the members may have more of a hand in the writing of the words or the music of the band's original songs, all the more reason for creating the *AABM* as early as possible.

Band members
In the average 4-person band, each member may play a different instrument. Some may have been in the band longer than others, or more experienced in the business of music. Maybe one of you has "connections" to clubs and labels, or more free time to invest in the running of the band's business. Each member can perform a different function in business.

Why a contract?
The real value of a contract - any contract, including the *AABM* - is as a dispute-resolution and dispute-avoidance tool. By dealing with things ahead of time, it may be best to discuss things now; and put the results on paper. Resolve things before having to pay litigators thousands upon thousands of dollars to do it in the courts later.

What happens if…
All of those "what if" questions, may not be the focus at the beginning. Band members may not want to think about, what *may* happen if the bass player departs to raise kids in Maui, or the singer-songwriter front man decides to join the Air Force. If all the other band members all value their investment of time, sweat and money in the band, then they should know and have fully thought through - in advance - the answers to these types of questions. Who owns and administrates the copyrights in the songs? Who is responsible for storing the masters? Who has final say in the hiring and firing of a manager? If the band breaks up, which member or members, if any, may keep using the band's name? And these are just *some* of the questions that should come up.

When to get a lawyer

Every band's situation is different, and the lists of questions to consider will be as different as there are different band personalities and different band members. The band may be better off, if a lawyer prepares the AABM. In a perfect world, all band members would be separately represented by a different attorney, but that is not realistic.

Should all these considerations prevent a band from creating a good AABM? Absolutely not, the band should at least try to resolve amongst its own members, the answers to all of the "what if" questions that will likely come up in the life cycle of any band. The band can try to resolve these questions on paper. Thereafter when affordable, one of the band members may decide to consult with an attorney to review and revise the band's starting-point document - (typically, this turns out in practice to be the band member with the most at stake in the outcome).

Be aware that one attorney may well not be able, or be allowed to represent all band members simultaneously. This is due to concerns about possible conflicts of interest, (especially if different band members have different percentage investments at stake in the band's commercial endeavors.)

It is best to draft some kind of written agreement between band members, since doing so now can save a lot of heartache and expense down the road in the future.

John Tormey III is a New York lawyer who handles general commercial, transactional, and corporate matters. John is also admitted to practice law in California, and in Washington, D.C. John's focus is in the area of entertainment, arts, and media, including endeavors to market artistic material to professional entertainment industry recipients. Please contact: www.tormey.org

marketing and promotion

THE 10 RULES OF SUCCESSFUL INDEPENDENT MUSICIANS

by Nyree Belleville, author of "Booking, Promoting & Marketing Your Music"

© 2006. All Rights Reserved. Used By Permission

Rule One: Be determined and dedicated

On your path you will, inevitably, collide with people who don't understand or like your music. When this happens try to remember that even the most successful musicians have been in your shoes. Every famous artist started out as an unknown musician struggling to get a gig in his or her hometown. Sarah McLachlin and the Counting Crows were playing twenty seat cafes in Canada and Berkeley for tips in their early years. No doubt many bookers told them, "Sorry, we can't fit you in the schedule." Or, "We don't book your kind of music here." Or, "Your band plays too loud for my room." Clearly, they continued with dedication to their plan, determined to keep booking and playing shows.

When you are truly determined to book a show for Friday and your first call doesn't turn up a gig, you will have no problem making another call to a different venue. When you are truly dedicated to "making it" as a musician, you will stay on your planned course of action. You will take the time to figure out, "What do I want to achieve? What is my mission? What are my goals?" True determination and dedication means that you will commit time and energy to your plan and take vigorous action in the pursuit of your dreams.

Rule Two: Believe in yourself

You must believe that every song you write, every recording you make, and every gig you play is the absolute best that you can make it be. However, don't despair if right at this moment you aren't thrilled with every aspect of what you are doing as a musician. Musical development, progress, and pride will come from experience. After ten shows, you will know how to present yourself effectively on stage. After 100 shows, you will find that you are becoming a truly great musician and performer. After 200 shows, fans will approach you saying, "Wow! You're even better than [fill in the blanks with your most revered musical influence]."

Each show that you play will help you to believe in yourself a little more. Each album you make will teach you that you are, indeed, a talented artist. And the more you believe in your talent, the more the audience will believe in you!

Rule Three: Maintain a dual-focus
Be a great musician and a street-smart entrepreneur

First and foremost, to succeed as a musician you must possess great musical talent. You can work towards this by practicing and performing, by working with a great teacher and mentor, and by writing song after song. However, you must also be a wise and wily entrepreneur. Since your ultimate goal is to fund your future artistic exploration (and car and house payments!) through the income you earn from writing and playing music, you must master the full array of entrepreneurial skills. Among them, budgeting (your money and time), marketing (reaching your target audience), setting prices (for CDs, tapes, T-shirts), and selling (your services and your merchandise).

Understand that once you have made the commitment to be a working, professional musician, you have also made the commitment to be a street-smart entrepreneur. You won't sit around waiting to be discovered. Instead, you will put "luck" into your own hands and be responsible for your own lucky breaks. The truth is I've only seen people "be discovered" after working for years with dedication, determination, creativity, and smarts; they are inevitably seen and heard by special people that help advance their career.

Rule Four: Educate yourself. Know your genre inside-out!

It is imperative that you know the ins and outs of your own genre. Fortunately, the information you are looking for can be easily found in books, magazine articles, on the Internet, or in album liner notes. Look closely at the careers of artists whose paths you would like to emulate. Find out, do they release their albums independently or with help from a label? At what point did they start to work with a manager or booking agent? What type of venues do they most often play?

Read magazines in your genre such as "Jazz World" or "Performing Songwriter," which are loaded with useful articles. And watch for newsstand publications such as *"The Musician's Guide to Touring & Promotion"* and the *"Musician's Atlas,"* which are good starting points for venues, contact numbers, and the type of music each venue books. Use the Internet to search for resources, venues, and fellow musicians. You can also search for online chat-groups and discussion lists of musicians, DJs, venue operators, house-concert operators, etc.

Take the time to get to know musicians that are currently performing in and around your area. Join a local songwriter's group and get involved with the local scene. And don't forget to read your local weekly entertainment papers to become familiar with the names of clubs, bands, and concert promoters in your area.

Rule Five: Let go of the "starving artist"

Are you wooed by the vision of the "starving artist?" Don't be! Too many musicians, painters, and writers unthinkingly worship at the altar of the starving artist, believing that selling their art is "selling out." Bah! Think of the thrill you'll get from selling your first CD or depositing a $1,000 check for a one-hour performance.

Utopia, for me, is every musician making enough money from music to play full-time. As artists, we must take full responsibility for making this utopia a reality. We need to accept the responsibility for our own finances. Just as bills are a reality, payment for services rendered is also a reality.

If you need to ease into selling your music, have a friend sell your merchandise for you. But always stand next to your sales table ready to talk to fans, sign CDs, and shake hands. Believe me, your fans are thrilled that you have recorded an album they can listen to over and over again, and they have no regrets about paying you $15 for it.

Rule Six: Create a plan and then follow up on it

One neat thing about making a plan for your career is that it forces you to examine the driving force behind your will to play music for a living. What do you want from a career in music? Do you want to play for 40,000 screaming fans, or will you be perfectly happy playing piano at the local hotel bar for twenty appreciative listeners? Working on a Business and Marketing Plan will help you define your vision and the steps you need to take to succeed. Working on an Artist's Plan will help you set up rituals for preserving and growing yourself as a musician and artist.

You will find that following up on your actions is the difference between attaining and not attaining goals. In fact, the dictionary definition of 'follow up' is "To increase the effectiveness of by further action." Exactly right. Be sure to increase the effectiveness of each package you send out by following up.

Rule Seven: Take action despite your fears

As an independent musician you will wear many different hats each day. Some of the duties and roles you assume may feel natural and easy. If you love to talk on the phone and meeting new people feels like an adventure, then booking shows will be a piece of cake. However, while other roles might not come as easily, don't let fear prevent you from sending out packages or making follow-up calls. In the grand master plan, one person does not have the power to make or break your career. And in order to spread the word about your music, you have to take the steps to let people know about it. Likewise, the more contacts you make, the more often you will be told, "Yes. We would love to book your band. Let's pick a date."

The first ten calls you make might not feel so great. Don't worry; your next ten calls will be easier. By call thirty, you will sound calm, collected, and professional. Learning to deal with people over the phone, in cover letters, and at shows is a learned skill. The more you do it, the better you will be at it.

Rule Eight: Appreciate and respect your fans

Fans of your music are your greatest supporters in the present and they have the greatest power to propel your career forward in the future. *Loreena McKennitt*, a hugely successful independent musician, says that her dedicated fans along with word-of-mouth helped her sell more than four million albums.

Your fans keep you going. They come to hear you play time and time again. They pay you money for your albums. They play your music for friends and word-of-mouth takes off with a life of its own. They bring friends to see you play, making it possible for you to book gigs at bigger venues. They write you letters and send you e-mails that perk you up on down days and inspire you to keep going. They shake your hand and hug you at shows, letting you know in the most personal way how much your music means to them.

So, be sure to respect your fans. After a show, always go stand by your merchandise table. Offer to sign CDs. Be ready and willing to chat with fans. And, make the effort to appreciate your fans. Mail them gig postcards that are easy to read, visually stimulating, and arrive early enough for them to plan an evening around your performance. Take the time and spend some extra money every few months in putting together a newsletter that lets your fans know what your band has been doing and what is planned for the future. Reply to every letter and e-mail that fans send to you with, at least, a thank you and always offer them the highest quality merchandise.

Rule Nine: Build a supportive team

Regardless what stage your career is at, having a great team behind you will make a huge difference. At the beginning, your team might be your best friend who says, "You can do it!" Or, you may team up with another local musician and give each other a helping hand and a shoulder to cry on. At some point, your team may take care of everything from press releases to booking shows.

In building your team, first consider close friends and ardent fans. Thankfully, during the course of your career many fans will offer you help. One fan might know the owner of a club you've been trying to break into and will gladly make the introductions. Another may offer to help put up posters around town for upcoming gigs, or even offer you money to record a new album. Take your fans seriously by, perhaps, meeting the following week for coffee and asking them what they would like to help you with. Find out if they can volunteer their time and expertise until you are making enough money to pay them. Other options are setting up an internship program with the local high school or college for class credit or placing an ad in the local paper.

However you build your team, make sure to surround yourself with people you can trust implicitly. Anyone doing work for you, no matter how insignificant it may seem, is representing you as both an artist and business owner. If you are comfortable with the person and what they want to do, I urge you to give them a try.

Rule Ten: Work harder after every success

Every time you have a great success-a big show or a great review in a major paper-you should get working even harder than you did before. One great review can be transformed into a dozen reviews across the country. A big show with a national act can create relationships with other prominent acts.

Inform the world of your success, using phone, fax, and e-mail after each success. Call several venues that you want to play at and let them know your last show was a sell-out. Call the booking agent you've had your eye on and introduce yourself. Make copies of the great review and include it in your press kit. Mail off five more copies of your album to publications with the new review on top.

Working even harder after good news comes is part of the process of developing momentum. If all goes well, each success will lead to more work and more success. And then eventually you will be so swamped with great opportunities that you will have to hire a team to help out!

Nyree Belleville, the author of "Booking, Promoting & Marketing Your Music" (Hal Leonard/Mix Books) is an independent musician with four independent CD releases. She has taught many musicians how to succeed on their own in the music industry through hew music business seminars and private consultations. For more information about Nyree's seminars, consultations, and music please visit her website at www.nyree.com or call 1-877-42NYREE.

♦

HOW TO BE YOUR OWN PUBLICIST
by Ariel Hyatt, Ariel Publicity
© 2006 All Rights Reserved. Used By Permission

For this article, I interviewed several entertainment writers from across the country. Their comments and advice are included throughout. Writers who will come up throughout are: Mike Roberts (*The Denver Westword*), Jae Kim (*The Chicago Sun Times*), Silke Tudor (*The SF Weekly*).

MYTH: A Big Fat Press Kit Will Impress a Writer.

TRUTH: Writers will only become exasperated by a press kit that is not succinct and to the point. A bio, a photo and 6-8 articles double-sided on white paper is a good sized kit. If a writer wants to read more than that he will contact you for further information. If you don't have any articles, don't worry, this will soon change.

The first step in your journey is to create a press kit, which consists of four parts — the Bio, the Photo, the Articles and the CD.

Jae Kim: "The ultimate press kit is a very basic press kit which includes: a CD, a photo with band members' names labeled on it — not a fuzzy, arty photo — a clear black and white, a bio, and press clips — 10 at most, one or two at least. 40 are way too much."

PART 1: The Bio

Write a one-page band bio that is succinct and interesting to read. I strongly advise avoiding vague clichés such as: melodic, brilliant harmonies, masterful guitar playing, tight rhythm section, etc. These are terms that can be used to describe any type of music. Try to make your description stand out. Create an introduction that sums up your sound, style and attitude in a few brief sentences. This way if a writer is pressed for time, she can simply take a sentence or two from your bio and place it directly in the newspaper. If you try to make a writer dig deeply for the gist, that writer will most likely put your press kit aside and look to one of the other 30 press kits that arrived that week.

TIP: Try to create a bio with the assumption that a vast majority of music writers may never get around to listening to your CD (500 new releases come out in the United States each week). Also, writers are usually under tight deadlines to produce copy — so many CD's fall by the wayside.

Q. **Whose press materials stand out in your memory?**

A. *Jae Kim:* "Action shots of bands. Blur has had a few great photos, and Mariah's are always very pretty. Also, Mary Cutrufello on Mercury has a great photo — enigmatic with a mysterious quality. Her picture was honest and intelligent, just like her music."

A. *Silke Tudor:* "The Slow Poisoners — a local SF band who are very devoted to their presentation. They have a distinct style and everything leads in to something else. Photos are dangerous. If the band looks young and they're mugging you have a pretty safe idea of what they're going to sound like."

PART 2: The Photo

It is very tough to create a great band photo. In the thousands that I have encountered only a few have had creativity and depth. I know it can seem cheesy to arrange a photo shoot but if you take this part seriously you will deeply benefit from it in the long run.

Create a photo that is clear, light, and attention grabbing. Five musicians sitting on a couch is not interesting. If you have a friend who knows how to use PhotoShop, I highly recommend you enroll him or her to help you do some funky editing. Mike Roberts tends to gravitate towards: "Any photos that are not four guys standing against a wall. Also, a jazz musician doesn't always have to be holding a horn."

MYTH: Photos Cost a Fortune to Process in 8 x10 Format.

TRUTH: Photos do not have to be expensive. There a few places to have photos printed for a great price. My personal favorite is ABC Pictures in Springfield, MO. They will print 500 photos (with layout and all shipping) for $80. Click the link to check out their web site or telephone 888.526.5336. Another great resource is a company called 1-800-POSTCARD, (www.1800postcards.com) which will print 5000 full-color, double-sided postcards for $250. Extra postcards not used in press kits can be sent to people on your mailing list, or you can sell them or give them away at gigs

PART 3: The Articles

Getting that first article written about you can be quite a challenge. Two great places to start are your local town papers (barring you don't live in Manhattan or Los Angeles), and any local fanzine, available at your favorite indie record store. Use this book as a resource for CD reviews. Find music that is similar to your band's type of music and then send your CD's to those reviewers. As your touring and effort swell, so will the amount of articles written about your band.

PART 4: The CD

The CD artwork, like the press kit, must be well thought out. You should customize your press kits so that they look in sync with your CD. This way when a writer opens up a package the press kit and the CD look like they go together. Put your phone number and contact info in the CD so if it gets separated from the press kit, the writer knows how to contact you. I asked Eric Rosen, the VP of Radical Records, how he oversees the development of product. He had a few things to say about stickering CD's (placing an extra sticker on the cover to spark the interest of a writer).

"If you are going to sticker your product, be unique in the way you present it — try to be clever about it — plain white stickers are boring." He went on to say that "Recommended Tracks" stickers are great for the press (suggesting no more than two or three selections). Eric does not think that stickers are too advantageous in CD stores, because then "You are just covering up your artwork."

TIP: Don't waste precious CD's! Keep in mind that 500 new CD's come out every week in the United States. Unless you are sure a writer actually writes CD reviews (many are not given the space to run them) don't waste your hard-earned dollars sending that writer a CD. Again, ask the promoter which writers like to receive CD's for review and which ones don't need them.

Q. **What do writers like?**

A. *Silke Tudor:* "When people personalize things and use casual words. If an envelope is hand-addressed, I will notice it right away and I always open things that people put together themselves. Hand-written stuff gets read first . . .The bands that do PR for themselves are the ones that stand out for me"

A. *Mike Roberts:* "Include the name, show date, time, ticket price, place, and who you are playing with. If I don't see the contact number I have 69 other kits to get to."

Q. **What do writers hate?**

A. *Jae Kim:* "I hate those padded envelopes that get gray flaky stuff all over you — I feel like its asbestos." She also dislikes "When I get a package with glitter or confetti in it — it gets all over my desk." "I [also] don't like Q & A sheets" — She prefers to come up with questions herself rather than receive answers pre-fabricated for her and spoon-fed.

A. *Silke Tudor* similarly reports: "I never open anything over my computer."

A. *Mike Roberts:* "I don't have much interest in gimmicks like hard candy. If I tried to eat it, it might kill me. Also you can't expect a writer to shove something in the paper at the last minute. Please give as much lead time as possible."

Q. **What do writers throw in the garbage immediately?**

A. *Mike Roberts:* "Anything past deadline."

A. *Jae Kim:* "Pictures of women's butts or profanity that is degrading to women."

A. *Silke Tudor:* "If I already know the band and I know that I don't like it."

Getting your press materials out there

Once you have a press kit together try to start planning PR for any tour 6-8 weeks before you hit the road. As soon as a gig is booked, ask the promoter for the club's press list (most clubs have one.) Promoters are dependent on this local press to help sell tickets. Have the list faxed or e-mailed to you. Don't be shy — you are working with the promoter to make the show happen and promoters love it when the show is well publicized. Also be sure to ask the promoter who his or her favorite writers are and which ones will like your style of music. When you do call those writers, don't be afraid to say which promoter recommended them and invite them to the show.

If the local promoter has a publicist, let that publicist do his or her job. Pack everything up and mail it to the promoters. Make sure you ask the promoters how many posters they would like and send them along with the press kits. After a few days it's best to call and verify that the material was received. If you can't afford to send kits to everyone, ask the promoters in each area which three or four writers would most likely cover a band that plays your style of music. Also, ask the promoters where the clubs run strip ads (these ads will be in the papers that cover music and inform people in the area about club happenings.)

Publications

If you are servicing press yourself, and the club does not have a press list, pick up The Musician's Atlas, or The Musician's Guide To Touring. Both of these guides are packed with a wealth of information on publicity outlets across the country, as well as venues, record stores, labels, etc. I recommend sending materials 4-6 weeks prior to the gig. Beware of monthly publications — if you are not at least six weeks out, don't bother sending to them.

Call the writers

Most of the time you will be leaving messages on voice mail. Be polite, get right to the point, and be brief!! 9 times out of 10 writers will not call you back.

Persevere

If you are a totally new band and you are worried because a paper did not cover you the first time around, keep sending that paper information every time you play in the area. I have never met a writer that ignores several press kits from the same band sent over and over again. It may take a few passes through in each market, but the more a writer sees over time, the more likely he will be to write about you.

Don't let all that all that voice mail discourage you
I have placed hundreds of articles, mentions, and photos without ever speaking to the writer.

Writers respond more to e-mail
It's free for them and does not take too long to respond to. If you are sending e-mail follow-ups, put a link to your site, or the club's site if you don't have one. You can also send a sound clip if you have the capability. IMPORTANT NOTE: Don't bother sending out materials a few days before the gig. Writers are usually way past their deadlines by then and they won't be able to place your band.

Posters
Posters are a great form of PR and they don't have to cost you a fortune. The most cost-effective way to make posters is to buy 11x17 colored paper from your local paper store (approx. $7 per ream of 500) and run off copies at the copy shop (approx. 7 cents each). Make several white copies and include these with your colored posters — this way the promoter can make extras, if needed. For higher quality posters, I recommend a copy process called docutech. These cost a penny or so more apiece, but they are computer-generated and look better than regular copies. Have whoever designed your poster also design small lay-ups to send out as fliers and ad-mats. Make sure your logo is included on them so the promoter can use them for strip or display advertising.

Have patience
The first few times you play a market, you may not get any press. PR is a slow moving vehicle that can take time to get results. I have worked with some bands that have needed to go through a market 3-4 times before any results started showing up in the press. When sending materials on repeated occasions, include a refresher blurb to remind the writer of your style. Always include the following information: date, show time, ages, ticket price, club name and address, time, and who is on the bill. Don't make writers hunt around for the event info. Make their job as easy as possible by providing as much information. Also keep in mind that some writers will probably not write about you over and over again. If you hit the same markets continually, a great tactic is to change your photo every few months and write "New Band Photo" on the outside of the envelope.

Field staff
Try to enroll a fan to be on your field staff in each market you visit. In exchange for a few tickets to your show, have this person put up posters, hand out fliers, and talk to the college newspaper about writing a feature or the local radio station about spinning your CD. To get a field staff started, include a sign up column on your mailing list and on your web site. If they sign up, they are the people for you! With a bit of planning and focus, you can spin your own publicity wheel. All it takes is foresight and organization. A band that plans well is a band that receives the most PR.

Your website
If you don't already have one — get on it!! Websites can be easy and inexpensive to design — you can buy software that can take you through it step by step. Better yet, have a friend or a fan help you design a site. Your site should include your upcoming tour dates, as most people will visit it to find out when you are coming through town. Another great place to post all of your dates is tourdates.com it's free, and you can also put your bio and photo up as well. More advanced sites include merch as well as CD sales. This is a great idea if you are at the point where you're selling a lot of merchandise. If you're for your own site, at least be sure to link your site to a place where fans can order your CD.

Ariel Hyatt is the President of Ariel Publicity, Artist Relations, and Cyber Promotions, in NYC. For the past five years she has worked closely publicizing a diverse family of touring and developing indie bands including Sally Taylor, Leftover Salmon, K-Floor, and The Stone Coyotes. Contact: www.arielpublicity.com

♦

SELLING YOUR MUSIC ONLINE - A REALITY CHECK
by David Nevue, author of "How to Promote Your Music Successfully on the Internet"
© 2006 All Rights Reserved. Used By Permission

I am often asked how much money a person can really make selling music online. I hear both extremes, both from artists who think they'll use the Internet to make it rich, and others who don't believe anyone can make any money online selling music. The truth is somewhere in between.

What follows is a brief, edited excerpt from the introductory chapter of my book, How to Promote Your Music Successfully on the Internet.

Will you make millions?
Let's get real for a moment. Promoting your music successfully on the Internet is hard work. Don't ever forget that. I've spent years doing this. The Internet is not a shortcut to success — it's simply another tool, one that can be very effective in the hands of someone who knows how to use it. Still, it's important to have realistic expectations before investing your time and money marketing your music online. You're going to face some very heated competition. There literally tens of thousands of musicians out there who already have web pages on the Internet (as of this writing there are over 98,000 artists registered with CDBaby.com alone). How can you compete with all those musicians? They are just the tip of the iceberg, though. Once you embark upon your promotional journey, you are, in a very real sense, competing with every other web page out there. How can you possibly stand out in that crowd? Pretty daunting, isn't it?

According to the Neilsen Netratings web site, there are over 299 million people actively using the Internet. A Georgia Tech survey of actual buyers provided some very interesting statistics: 70% of all buyers searched for the item they bought, 16% searched for a topic related to what they bought, and 4% searched for the name of another product which led them to the final product they purchased. Adding it up, 90% of all buyers used the Internet as a modern-day, digital Yellow Pages. So the question is, what does this tell you about selling your music on the Net?

Quite simply, it means that creating a web page to sell your music is not enough. That's something I discovered very early on. Even if you submit your site to the search engines, you're not likely to see a significant traffic increase. Think about it. If 90% of the buyers out there already know what they are looking for and are searching the Internet for that particular item, how will they find you, someone whose music they have likely never heard of? If they are not looking for you, they won't find you. So, what ARE they looking for? Therein lies the key.

Here's the slap-in-the-face reality: In my experience, the average musician sells between two and five CDs a year from their web site. Sales that low do not justify the expense of putting your music online. Can you do better than five CDs a year? Yes, you can do much, much better, but only if you have a quality product people care about and market it properly. Let me be up front with you. To succeed on the Internet, you must prepare yourself for the long haul and prepare to work hard. Success on the Internet won't come overnight.

As you read on, keep the following questions in the back of your mind. They hold the key to successful online music promotion:

1) What is unique about my music?

2) What general style of music are my fans most interested in?

3) What other artists do my fans compare my music to?

and most importantly...

4) Who is my target customer?

5) What kind of information is my *target* customer searching for on the Internet?

6) How can I use that information to bring that target customer to my web site?

To answer the question I posed at the beginning of this article, no, you are not likely to make millions on the Internet doing just music. But you can bring in a good, steady income. In 2004, I was able to generate an average of about $6,000 per month in total sales just from the Internet (that doesn't include gigs and CD sales at gigs). This income comes not only from CD sales, but sheet music sales (of my own music), book sales, partnerships, advertising revenue, and other sources. But every single thing I do online is related to the music business I love.

It's Not Just About the Money...

There is still the question of using the Internet to advance your music career, and that's something the Internet can help you do also. I've been able to generate a lot of publicity for my music online, and as a result not only do I sell CDs, but I often receive requests to have my music used in independent film and media projects. I've negotiated three distribution deals overseas as a result of someone finding my music online. One company is using my music on an internationally distributed DVD series that raises funds for various charities. Even NBC contacted me to inquire about using my music in a made for TV film. Finally, I'm playing a lot more gigs in a lot more places as a direct result of marketing my music online and as you know, the more you play live, the more doors get opened up for you. You, like me, can use the Internet to create a huge amount of exposure for your music. The more exposure you generate, the more likely you are to gain new fans, sell more music get more gigs and of course, make those contacts you want to make within the music industry.

David Nevue is the founder of The Music Biz Academy, an online resource for musicians at www.musicbizacademy.com. He is also a professional pianist, recording artist, full-time musician, and author of the book, "How to Promote Your Music Successfully on the Internet" which you can read about at www.promoteyourmusic.com

♦

FOUR WAYS TO ATTRACT MORE MUSIC FANS FASTER

By Bob Baker author of "Guerrilla Music Marketing Handbook"
© 2006 All Rights Reserved. Used By Permission

Attracting more fans. Admit it, that's what music marketing is all about — getting more people to come to your shows and buy your CDs. And hopefully, getting a lot more people to do those things.
Why else do you work so hard to travel and play as many places as you can? For what other reason do you meticulously write and record songs? I don't believe the reason is so you can practice and keep up your chops in obscurity. It's not because you want to impress influential managers or A&R people. You work hard because you know you have something of value to offer ... and you want to reach as many people as possible with your music.

How do you promote yourself?

Marketing is the thing that helps you reach that goal. But marketing is also a subject that confuses a lot of musicians. Songwriters and band members the world over knows they need to promote themselves. But many don't know where to start, much less know how to continue effectively. Does this describe you? Do you ever feel like you're spinning your wheels, not sure exactly what you should be doing next to market yourself? If so, this would be a good time to cover some basic marketing concepts for independent musicians.

The VFW hall principle

Let's say you went to an average U.S. city (such as Kansas City or Denver) and you rounded up 1,000 people and gathered them in a giant VFW hall. These 1,000 folks would be randomly chosen and made up of people from all ages, genders and backgrounds. Next, you'd distribute information about your act to these people and play tracks from your new CD for them.

After this direct exposure, what are the chances that one person out of those thousand would be attracted to your music and identity enough to buy your CD or come to your next show? Most musicians, regardless of what style they play, should feel pretty confident about being able to win over at least one new fan from this group of 1,000. That's a one tenth of one percent conversion rate.

Now let's multiply that formula by the entire U.S. population of 285 million people. One tenth of one percent would be 285,000 people. Mind-boggling isn't it? That would be enough fans to make you a bona fide star.

How do the major's do it?

Next, switch gears and consider how major labels market themselves. They select and promote acts that they feel have the potential to appeal to 10 or more of those same 1,000 people. Then the labels spend millions of dollars in what I call shotgun advertising. They spray their marketing message over a targeted chunk of the population (which often amounts to many millions of people), knowing well that only a small percentage will be interested enough to respond and become fans. Sometimes, this widespread tactic works well enough to sell lots of CDs and concert tickets — but it's very expensive.

Where to begin

As an independent artist, you can't afford that type of marketing campaign. But you know those potential fans are out there, and you know that you can be successful by connecting with far fewer people than a major label requires. It's just that your ideal fans haven't found out about you yet — and you're not quite sure how to find them.

Low cost creative ways to go directly to those one-in-a-thousand fans:

1. **Define Your Distinct Musical Identity**

    You must have a firm grasp on what your music is about. And you must be able to define it clearly and quickly. What are your strongest musical traits? What sets you apart from other acts? What attitude or social statement do you make? Being a generic rock, pop or hip hop act won't cut it. Dig deeper and discover your unique identity. When you do finally reach some of those rare potential fans, don't lose them by not being clear about who you are.

2. **Describe Your Ideal Fan**

    Once you have a handle on which you are musically, it's time to paint a clear picture of your ideal fan. Can you articulate how your fans dress, where they work, what TV shows they watch, what they do for fun and who their favorite cultural heroes are? Observe the types of people who come to see you perform and note what they have in common? Knowing precisely who your fans are will dictate what avenues you use to reach them and how you communicate your message once you do reach them.

3. **List Ways of Getting Access to Your Fans**

    Once you know exactly what type of music fan you're going after, start making a list of the various resources these specific people is attracted to. What magazines and newspapers do they read? Where do they hang out? What radio stations do they listen to? What retail outlets do they frequent? What web sites do they surf to? What e-mail newsletters do they subscribe to? For example, if your fans are mostly Harley riders, go to a search engine like Google and start entering keywords related to motorcycles. Evaluate the search results and compile a list of the many good sources you uncover.

4. **Network and Promote Your Music**

    Armed with this targeted list of contacts, get busy! Send e-mail press releases to niche media outlets. Contact the webmasters and editors of appropriate publications. Post messages in specialized forums. Visit and interact via the web sites of similar-sounding bands. Contact organizations and charities related to your musical niche.

In short, go to where your ideal fans are. And market yourself through these outlets relentlessly. Why waste time and money trying to promote to everyone, when you can save money and be far more effective by going directly to those valuable one-in-a-thousand fans?

Bob Baker is the author of "Guerrilla Music Marketing Handbook," "Unleash the Artist Within" and "Branding Yourself Online." He also publishes TheBuzzFactor.com, a web site and e-zine that have been delivering marketing tips and inspirational messages to music people of all kinds since 1995. Get your FREE subscription to Bob's e-zine by visiting www.TheBuzzFactor.com today.

MUSIC MARKETING STRATEGIES

by Derek Sivers, CEO CD Baby
© Copyright, 2006, Derek Sivers. Reprinted with permission.

Call the destination, and ask for directions

Work backwards. Define your goal (your final destination) - then contact someone who's there, and ask how to get there. If you want to be in Rolling Stone magazine, pick up the phone, call their main office in New York City, and when the receptionist answers, say "Editorial, please." Ask someone in the editorial department which publicists they recommend. Then call each publicist, and try to get their attention. (Hint: Don't waste Rolling Stone's time asking for the publicist's phone number. You can find it elsewhere; get off the phone as soon as possible.)

If you want to play at the biggest club in town, bring a nice box of fancy German cookies to the club booker, and ask for just 5 minutes of their advice. Ask them what criteria must be met in order for them to take a chance on an act. Ask what booking agents they recommend, or if they recommend using one at all. Again, keep your meeting as short as possible. Get the crucial info, and then leave them alone. (Until you're back, headlining their club one day!)

I know an artist manager of a small-unsigned act, who over the course of a year, met with the managers of U2, REM, and other top acts. She asked them for their advice, coming from the top, and got great suggestions that she's used with big results.

Put your fans to work

You know those loyal few people who are in the front row every time you perform? You know those people that sat down to write you an Email to say how much they love your music? The guy that said, "Hey if you ever need anything - just ask!" Put them all to work!

Often, people who reach out like that are looking for a connection in this world. Looking for a higher cause. They want to feel they have some other purpose than their stupid accounting job. You may be the best thing in their life. You can break someone out of their drab life as an assistant sales rep for a manufacturing company. You might be the coolest thing that ever happened to a teenager going through an unpopular phase. You can give them a mission!

Gather a few interested fans for pizza, and spend a night doing a mailing to colleges. Anyone wanting to help have them post flyers, or drive a van full of friends to your gig an hour away. Have the guts to ask that "email fan" if she'd be into going through the *Indie Contact Bible* and sending your press kit to 20 magazines a week. Eventually, as you grow, these people can be the head of "street teams" of 20 people in a city that go promote you like mad each time you have a concert or a new CD.

Go where the filters are

Have you been filtered? If not, you should start now. People in the music biz get piles of CDs in the mail everyday from amateurs. Many of them aren't very good. How do you stand out? Filters allow the best of the best pass through. It will also weed out the "bad music", or the music that isn't ready. I worked at Warner Brothers for 3 years. I learned why they never accept unsolicited demos: It helps weed out the people that didn't do enough research to know they have to go meet managers or lawyers or David Geffen's chauffeur *first* in order to get to the "big boys. If you *really* believe in your music, than have the confidence to put yourself into those places where most people get rejected. (Radio, magazines, big venues, agents, managers, record labels, promoters...)

Have someone work on the inside

I prefer to ignore the music industry. Maybe that's why you don't see me on the cover of Rolling Stone. One of my only regrets about my own band was that we toured and got great reviews, toured and got lots of air play, toured and booked some great-paying gigs. BUT... nobody was working the inside of the music business. Nobody was connecting with the "gatekeepers" to bring us to the next level. We just kept doing the same gigs. Maybe you're happy on the outside of the biz. (I know I am.) But if what you want is to tour with major-label artists, be on the cover of *Spin*, heard on the airwaves, or get onto MTV, You're going to have to have someone working the inside of the biz, Someone who loves it. Someone persuasive who gets things done 10 times faster than you ever could, and who's excited enough about it, that they would never be discouraged. Find someone who's passionate about the business side of music, and particularly the business side of YOUR music.

Be a novice marketer not an expert

Get to the point of being a novice marketer/promoter/agent. Then hand it to an expert. Moby, the famous techno artist, says the main reason for his success was that he found experts to do what they're best at, instead of trying to do it himself. (Paraphrased:) "Instead of trying to be a booking agent, publicist, label, and manager, I put my initial energy into finding and impressing the best agent.... I just kept making lots of the best music I could."

If you sense you are becoming an expert, figure out what your real passions in life are and act accordingly. Maybe you're a better publicist than bassist. Maybe you're a better bassist than publicist. Maybe it's time to admit your weakness as a booking agent, and hand it off to someone else. Maybe it's time to admit your genius as a booking agent, and commit to it full-time.

Reach them like you would want to be reached

Reach people like *you* would want to be reached. Would you rather have someone call you up in a dry business monotone, and start speaking a script like a telemarketer? Or would you rather have someone be a cool person, a real person?

When you contact people, no matter how it's done (phone, email, mail, face-to-face) - show a little spunk. If it sounds like they have a moment and aren't in a major rush, entertain them a bit. Ask about their day and expect a real answer. Talk about something non-business for a minute or two. If they sound hectic, skip the long introduction. Know what you want to say ahead of time, just in case.

Every contact with the people around your music (fans and industry) is an extension of your art. If you make depressing, morose, acoustic music, maybe you should send your fans a dark brown-and-black little understated flyer that's depressing just to look at. Set the tone. Pull in those people who love that kind of thing. Proudly alienate those that don't. If you're an in your face, tattooed, country-metal-speedpunk band, have the guts to call a potential booking agent and scream, "Listen you fucking motherfucker. If they like that introduction, you've found a good match. Don't be afraid to be different.

What has worked on you?

Any time you're trying to influence people to do something, think what has worked on YOU in the past. Are you trying to get people to buy your CD? Write down the last 20 CDs you bought, then for each one, write down what made you buy it. Did you ever buy a CD because of a matchbook, postcard, or 30-second web sound clip? What DID work? (Reviews, word-of-mouth, live show?) Write down your top 10 favorite artists of all time, and a list of what made you discover each one and become a fan.

This goes beyond music. Which TV ads made you buy something? What anonymous Emails made you click a link and check out a website? Which flyers or radio ads made you go see a live show by someone you had never heard?

Have the confidence to target

Bad Target Example: Progressive Rocker Targeting Teeny Bopper. On CD Baby, there is a great musician who made an amazing heavy-progressive-metal record. When we had a "search keywords" section, asking for three artists he sounds like, he wrote, "britney spears, ricky martin, jennifer lopez, backstreet boys, mp3, sex, free" What the hell was he thinking? He just wanted to turn up in people's search engines, at any cost. For what, and who? Did he really want a Britney Spears fan to get "tricked" into finding his dark-progressive-metal record? Would that 13-year-old girl actually spend the 25 minutes to download his 10 minute epic, "Confusing Mysteries of Hell"? If she did, would she buy his CD? I suggested he instead have the confidence to target the REAL fans of his music. He put three semi-obscure progressive artists into the search engine, and guess what? He's selling more CDs than ever! He found his true fans.

If you don't say whom you sound like, you won't make any fans

A person asks you, "What kind of music do you do?" Musicians say, "All styles. Everything." That person then asks, "So who do you sound like?" Musicians say, "Nobody. We're totally unique. Like nothing you've ever heard before." What does that person do? Nothing. They might make a vague promise to check you out sometime. Then they walk on, and forget about you! Why??? You didn't arouse their curiosity! You violated a HUGE rule of self-promotion! Bad bad bad!

What if you had said, "It's 70's porno-funk music being played by men from Mars." Or... "This CD is a delicate little kiss on your earlobe from a pink-winged pixie. Or... "We sound like a cross between *AC/DC* and *Tom Jones*." Any one of these, and you've got their interest.

Get yourself a magic key phrase that describes what you sound like. Try out a few different ones, until you see which one always gets the best reaction from strangers. Have it ready at a moment's notice. It doesn't have to narrow what you do at all. Any of those three examples I use above could sound like anything. And that's just the point - if you have a magic phrase that describes your music in curious but vague terms, you can make total strangers start wondering about you.

Touch as many senses of theirs as you can

The more senses you touch in someone, the more they'll remember you. BEST: a live show, with you sweating right on top of someone, the PA system pounding their chest, the smell of the smoky club, the flashing lights and live-in-person performance. WORST: an email, a single web page, or a review in a magazine with no photo.

Whenever it is possible, try to reach as many senses as possible. Have an amazing photo of yourself or your band, and convince every reviewer to put that photo next to the review of your album. Send videos with your press kit. Play live shows often. Understand the power of radio to make people hear your music instead of just hearing about it. Get onto any TV shows you can. Scent your album with patchouli oil. Make your songs and productions truly emotional instead of merely catchy.

Be an extreme version of yourself

Define yourself. Show your weirdness. Bring out all your quirks. Your public persona, the image you show to the world, should be an extreme version of yourself.

A good biz plan wins no matter what happens

In doing this test marketing you should make a plan that will make you a success even if nobody comes along with his or her magic wand. Start now. Don't wait for a "deal". Don't just record a "demo" that is meant only for record companies.

You have all the resources you need to make a finished CD that thousands of people would want to buy. If you need more money, get it from anyone except a record company. And if, as you're following your great business plan, selling hundreds, then thousands of CDs, selling out small, then larger venues, getting on the cover of magazines... you'll be doing so well that you won't need a record deal. If you get an offer you'll be in the position of taking it or leaving it. There's nothing more attractive to an investor than someone who doesn't need his or her money. Make the kind of business plan that will get you to a good sustainable level of success, even without a big record deal.

Don't be afraid to ask for favors

Some people *like* doing favors. It's like asking for directions in New York City. People's egos get stroked when they know the answer to something you're asking. They'll gladly answer to show off their knowledge.

One bold musician I know called me up one day and said, "I'm coming to New York in 2 months. Can you give me a list of all the important contacts you think I should meet?" I ended doing a search in my database, E-mailing him a list of 40 people he should call, and mention my name.

Maybe you need to find something specific: a video director for cheap, a PA system you can borrow for a month, a free rehearsal studio. Call up everyone you know and ask! This network of friends you are creating will have everything you want in life. Some rare and lucky folks (perhaps on your "band mailing list") have time on their hands and would rather help you do something, than sit at home in front of the TV another night. Need help doing flyers, or help getting equipment to a show? Go ahead and ask!

Keep in touch!

Sometimes the difference between success and failure is just a matter of keeping in touch! There are some AMAZING musicians who have sent a CD to CD Baby, and when I heard it, I flipped. In a few cases, I've stopped what I was doing at that moment, picked up the phone and called them wherever they were to tell them I thought they were a total genius. (Believe me - this is rare. Maybe 1 in 500.) Often I get an answering machine, and guess what... they don't call back!! What success-sabotaging kind of thing is that to do? 2 weeks later I've forgotten about their CD as new ones came in.

The lesson: If they would have just called back, and kept in touch, they may have a fan like no other at the head of one of the largest distributors of independent music on the web. A fan that would go out on a limb to help their career in ways others just dream of. But they never kept in touch and now I can't remember their names. Some others whose CDs didn't really catch my attention the first time around, just keep in touch so well that I often find myself helping them more as a friend than a fan.

A short description - 10 seconds or less

Most of the world has never heard your music. Most of the world WON'T hear your music, unless you do a good job describing it. It's like a Hollywood screenplay. You not only have to write a great screenplay, but you have to have a great description of it that you can say in 10 seconds or less, in order to catch people's attention. Find a way to describe your music that would catch anyone's attention, and describe it accurately.

Read about new music

Go get a magazine like CMJ, Magnet, or Alternative Press. You'll read about (and see pictures of) dozens of artists who you've never heard of before. Out of that whole magazine, only one or two will really catch your attention. WHY? I don't have the answer. Only you do. Ask yourself why a certain headline or photo or article caught your attention. What was it exactly that intrigued you? Adapt those techniques to try writing a headline or article about your music.

© 2006 Derek Sivers - all rights reserved. Founder of CD Baby, Derek has been a full-time musician for 8 years, and toured the world as a guitarist sideman with some famous folks. He also ran a recording studio, and worked inside the industry at Warner/Chappell Music for 3 years. Derek cracked the college market and got hired by 400 colleges, and sold a few thousand CD's.

♦

THE BASICS OF BOOKING YOUR OWN TOURS

by Jay Flanzbaum, Onlinegigs.com
© 2006 All Rights Reserved. Used By Permission

To be able to book gigs successfully you'll need a ton of persistence and even better organization. Whether you are booking locally, regionally or nationally you will essentially need the same skills and tools to be effective. Independent bands and agents, by definition, tend to lack the nationwide connections necessary to make the idea of booking an extended tour possible. As a result the ones that are most successful are generally the same ones that understand how to gather, and effectively manage, all of their business related contacts. We've all seen some pretty lousy bands with some damn good gigs, so talent isn't always the main issue.

Data collection

If you haven't already, you are going to have to start collecting contact information for the people that can help you achieve your goals. If your goal is to have a touring career in the music industry then you better find some venues, colleges, festivals, record companies, managers, record stores and media contacts, to do business with. It is never too early to start this process. You should start today even if your CD won't be ready for another 3 years and you don't have a full time drummer yet. Every person you meet and every possible gig that you hear about will need to be recalled at a later date. There are many sources that a beginner, or even a veteran, can turn to for gathering this type of information.

Printed music industry directories like the Indie Contact Bible can have an incredible amount of information to get you started. Alternative news weeklies like the Village Voice or the Boston Phoenix are a great source of local music venues, festivals and college listings. Most major markets in the country have an independent weekly publication; some of them can be found online at www.awn.org. Online music communities like are also an ideal place to find where bands of a similar style are playing.

Data management

Once you start gleaning contact information from printed directories, online communities, newspapers and other bands, you will soon realize that you need a good way to organize and access all of this data. You most likely have pages full of notes, emails with venue referrals and spreadsheets covered with names and numbers. The key now is to be able to effectively organize all of your new found contacts in a way that maximizes your opportunity with each one of them.

Software or web based contact managers like Outlook, Act, Maximizer or Onlinegigs, are all efforts to help you centralize your business related messages, tasks and contact information. It doesn't make sense to dig thru multiple email boxes on different computers to find important messages. Anymore than it would to be unable to find an important phone number because you left your address book in Spokane, WA. Whatever application or method you choose, be sure to get as many of the following features as would apply to your specific needs.

- Complete and total access to all of your important contact and business information in one location
- Multiple, archived backups of your information in case of data loss or equipment failure
- Reminder system for upcoming activities and tasks
- Integrated email & fax messaging with message tracking and searching
- Customizable for your specific industry
- Remotely accessible from any internet connection
- Ability to easily share information with others

Importance of contracts

After a few months of working your task list religiously and following up on every CD in a consistent and professional manner, you should be ready to start booking some gigs. After all the work you have just gone through to find contacts and reach out to each one of them, it would be a shame to lose out on a gig at the last minute. Admittedly, last minute cancellations and double bookings can and will occur. The story usually goes like this:

You sent out your CD in January; to finally book a gig in April for your upcoming August tour. It's just a Tuesday night for 100% of the door, rooms and food; but it's a needed stop-over between Colorado and Nevada. You call a week before the gig from somewhere in Texas and the club has never heard of you. What's worse, there is another band booked on that night and the other band has a confirmed written agreement. In a toss up situation between the band with no proof and the band with a contract, the band with the contract usually wins.

For gigs that are low-dough or no-dough deals, you should still send a written agreement. A written agreement is your only line of defense after all of the work you have gone thru to secure the gig, not to mention the work you will need to do for properly promoting it. Email is the easiest method because you can easily send the same message over and over until you get confirmation. Faxing is also relatively easy, however having to send a snail mail agreement over and over can be a pretty big hassle. Your goal here is to constantly remind the talent buyer of your agreement and put all of the details in front of them. The higher the dollar value on the agreement the more diligent you should be about insisting on a signed, hard-copy version of the agreement.

Getting ready for the road

Putting a group of people on the road for any amount of time comes with responsibilities. There are many people who will need detailed information about your schedule in order for your tour to be effective, safe and organized. Band members and their families, your manager, a publicist and even your fans all need to have access to different information about your trip. At a minimum all of your shows should be listed on your website as soon as they are confirmed. Ideally you would also list set times, the venue's address, phone number, website and any other bands on the bill with you.

The Tour Itinerary however is really the best way to be sure your trip is error free. Everyone on your team should have a chronological listing of each of your tour dates with as much or as little detail as they need. But the master itinerary for you and your band members should list all of the contact info for each venue, set times, payment details, venue capacity, ticket price, age limits and step by step directions from one gig to the next. This is your bible for the trip and the more copies you make the less likely you will be lost in Lincoln, Nebraska without the buyer's phone number or any sense of direction.

The Tour Itinerary is also a crucial tool in satisfying your greatest responsibility as a touring band: Advancing Your Shows. If you want your journey to free of surprises, then you will advance all of your shows. This simply means contacting the venue a week or so before the gig to confirm performance details, get important load in information and find out about any last minute changes. Out of your entire organization of band members, managers, agents, tour managers and interns, there needs to be one person who can assume this role.

Properly promoting your shows

If you have never played before in a particular market, then most likely nobody in that town has any idea who you are. And why would anyone come out to see you play if they have no idea that you are even playing. What you really need is some press or at a minimum just a listing with the local radio and print music calendars.

Your first step is to put together all of the contact names, fax numbers, email addresses etc. for the local media outlets in a 30-60 mile radius of each of your gigs. Then you will have to prepare a professional and concise press release. A good release should be able to convey all of the pertinent information on one page. Radio stations and newspapers get flooded everyday with hundreds of releases, they do not have time to read numerous pages that outline your band's Zen philosophy or each of your bass player's numerous influences. Keep it to the point or they will not read it all. Keep your layout clean; do not use multiple fonts and font sizes or too many colors and graphics.

Make sure your release has a section with the performance details that is easy to pick out and includes: Performance Date, Band Name, Venue Name, Full Address, Phone, Website, Ticket Price, Set Times, Age Limit and any other bands on the bill. Also be sure to include your personal contact information: Contact Name, Phone, Email, and Website. If someone needs to get in touch for a photo or an interview, you will want them to be able to track you down quickly and easily.

Here is where your Contact Management program really comes in handy. You could take the time to create numerous, personalized press releases for each press contact you have found. This would probably take you days depending on the size of the market. If we are talking about New York City, it could take you months. But if you have the proper tools like I mentioned in the section above, you should be able to create one template and send personally addressed releases, by fax or email to hundreds of media contacts all at once.

The dance

You should think of every band outing as a well choreographed dance. All of the administration needs to happen with precision for you to grow each new market. Put a check list in place and follow it like a religion for every gig and pretty soon it will become second nature to you and your band members. Organization alone is not going to make you a success but the sooner you get the basics in place the sooner you can spend time enjoying your music. In today's music marketplace, exposure for independent acts is generally limited to touring. If you want to be heard outside of your local market you are going to have get your band some gigs outside of your local market! Put a solid plan in place and achieve your goals.

Jay Flanzbaum of Onlinegigs got his start as a booking agent putting together national and regional tours for independent bands. Those years running a boutique agency inspired the creation of Onlinegigs, an incredibly powerful booking and promotional tool for independent bands and agents.

distribution

PREPARING FOR DISTRIBUTION
by Daylle Deanna Schwartz, author of "The Real Deal"
© Copyright, 2006, Revenge Productions. Reprinted with permission.

People who want to press up their music in order to sell it are most concerned about getting distribution. Your focus if you want to make money from your music, is to first take yourself seriously as a business. Whether you like it or not, outside of your circle of fans, you and your music are looked upon as products. If you prefer being idealistic, create and perform music for fun. But, if earning a living from your music is an eventual goal, developing a *business attitude* is critical.

What's necessary?
Read books on the biz and attend seminars if you can. Get a good picture of how the music industry operates. Network as much as possible to create a support system of folks you can call on for resources, advice and encouragement. While you shouldn't negotiate your own contracts, you should know enough to discuss the terms of one with your lawyer. Don't be one of those musicians who tell their lawyer, publisher, manager, etc., "Whatever you say." Gather enough knowledge so you can make informed decisions based on input from your representatives. Think of yourself as a professional. Even if you're only pressing up your own music, you're a record label. Act like one! Being responsible will max your chances of others wanting to work with you.

Getting distribution
Getting distribution isn't always a guarantee. You can ship 500 pieces and get them all back if you haven't been able to promote your product to a target audience. Distributors get records into stores. Most don't promote them. Stores tell me that records sell because people know the artist. Before taking in your product, distributors need to see that you have a market already interested in buying it. Creating a demand is what sells records. Distributors want you to have a handle on promotion before they work with your label. Once you have that, they'll want your product.

Do the groundwork
Until you identify your potential market and develop strategies for letting them know about your music, having distribution won't sell CDs. The most important thing you can do first is to target the group who might buy your product and figure out how to reach them. Distributors want product that will sell, and will *want* to work with labels that have artists with a buzz going. They don't care how good the music is if nobody knows about it.

It still amazes me how many folks come to me for consultations and aren't sure who is most likely to buy their music. They tell me since it's good music, everyone will buy. That usually means they have no clue and don't want to bother to figure it out. If you can't target your audience, play your music for people who work in record stores or other music related folks and ask for their honest feedback.

Your audience
Anyone may buy your CD, but promote it to the group more likely to appreciate it. Is it college students? Young adults? Teens? Baby boomers? Once you know that, what kinds of promotion will you do to make them want to buy your record? Figuring this out sounds simple at first but if it was, there would be a lot more records making big money independently. It is more than the music being great, for people to buy your CD. They need to hear your music to be enticed to buy it. How will you reach their ears? What will make them buy it? Figuring out a marketing plan can be the hardest part of putting out your music. Distribution is easy once you get this in place.

Create a demand
The best way to get your product into stores is to develop a story around your act first. Focus your energy on getting reviews, getting radio play (college and public radio are best to start with), selling product on your own, and increasing your fan base by touring. Create a demand, and then put together a one-page synopsis of the artist's story, known as a one-sheet. This has the artist's story - reviews and stories in the media (include quotes), radio play, gigs, direct sales, internet presence, etc, as well as details about the record itself. Include anything that shows the act is marketable, concisely on one sheet of paper. A small photo of the act and/or the album cover should be on the sheet too.

How to get in stores
Send you're one-sheet to potential distributors. Don't send a sample of the music until they request it. The story is more important than the music. Some distributors take calls if you want to try that first. But if their interest is piqued, they'll ask you to fax them a one-sheet. Be prepared. Don't approach distributors until you have a good foundation. Make them take you seriously the first time! Distributors are in the business of selling records. If they think yours will sell, they'll carry it. It's that simple. Start with a local distributor until your buzz gets stronger and you prove you can sell product on a wider scale. Then work your way up to larger ones.

Daylle Deanna Schwartz is the author of Start & Run Your Own Record Label and The Real Deal: How to Get Signed to a Record Label from A to Z, both on Billboard Books. She also teaches full day seminars and does consulting on these topics. Contact: www.outersound.com/revenge

25 THINGS TO REMEMBER ABOUT RECORD DISTRIBUTION
by Christopher Knab, author of "Music Is Your Business".
© 2006 All Rights Reserved. Used By Permission

1. Distributors will usually only work with labels that have been in business for at least 3 years, or have at least 3 previous releases that have sold several thousand copies each.

2. Distributors get records into retail stores, and record labels get customers into retail stores through promotion and marketing tactics.

3. Make sure there is a market for your style of music. Prove it to distributors by showing them how many records you have sold through live sales, internet sales, and any other alternative methods.

4. Be prepared to sign a written contract with your distributor because there are no 'handshake deals' anymore.

5. Distributors want 'exclusive' agreements with the labels they choose to work with. They usually want to represent you exclusively.

6. You will sell your product to a label for close to 50% of the retail list price.

7. When searching for a distributor find out what labels they represent, and talk to some of those labels to find out how well the distributor did getting records into retailers.

8. Investigate the distributor's financial status. Many labels have closed down in recent years, and you cannot afford to get attached to a distributor that may not be able to pay its invoices.

9. Find out if the distributor has a sales staff, and how large it is. Then get to know the sales reps.

10. What commitment will the distributor make to help get your records into stores?

11. Is the distributor truly a national distributor, or only a regional distributor with ambitions to be a national distributor? Many large chain stores will only work with national distributors.

12. Expect the distributor to request that you remove any product you have on consignment in stores so that they can be the one to service retailers.

13. Make sure that your distributor has the ability to help you setup various retail promotions such as: coop advertising (where you must be prepared to pay the costs of media ads for select retailers), in-store artist appearances, in-store listening station programs, and furnishing POP's (point of purchase posters and other graphics).

14. Be aware that as a new label you will have to offer a distributor 100% on returns of your product.

15. You must bear all the costs of any distribution and retail promotions.
16. Furnish the distributor with hundreds of 'Distributor One Sheets' (Attractively designed summary sheets describing your promotion and marketing commitments. Include barcodes, list price, picture of the album cover, and catalog numbers of your product too.
17. Distributors may ask for hundreds of free promotional copies of your release to give to the buyers at the retail stores.
18. Make sure all promotional copies have a hole punched in the barcode, and that they are not shrink-wrapped. This will prevent any unnecessary returns of your product.
19. Don't expect a distributor to pay your invoices in full or on time. You will always be owed something by the distributor because of the delay between orders sent, invoices received, time payment schedules (50-120 days per invoice) and whether or not your product has sold through, or returns are pending.
20. Create a relationship that is a true partnership between your label and the distributor.
21. Keep the distributor updated on any and all promotion and marketing plans and results, as they develop.
22. Be well financed. Trying to work with distributors without a realistic budget to participate in promotional opportunities would be a big mistake.
23. Your distributor will only be as good as your marketing plans to sell the record. Don't expect them to do your work for you, remember all they do is get records into the stores.
24. Read the trades, especially Billboard for weekly news on the health of the industry, and/or the status of your distributor.
25. Work your product relentlessly on as many fronts as possible... commercial and non commercial airplay, internet airplay and sales campaigns, on and offline publicity ideas, and touring...eternally touring!

Christopher Knab is a music business Consultant, Author and Lecturer. He was recently honored by Seattle's Rocket magazine as "One of the Most Influential People in the Northwest Music Industry." Contact: www.4frontmusic.com, Chris@Knab.com

◆

WHY AND WHEN IS CONSIGNMENT BETTER THAN DISTRIBUTION?
by Tim Sweeney, author of "Tim Sweeney's Guide To Releasing Independent Records"
© 2006 All Rights Reserved. Used By Permission

Almost every time I pick up the phone or do a free workshop these days, the inevitable question is, "how do I get national distribution?" My first response is, "why do you need it?"

With that glassy look in their eyes, most artists respond, "Because I want to get my CDs in all the stores across the country." Then I frustrate them by saying, "what if I could do that for you, what are you going to do to make them sell?"

Again inevitably the response is, "I'm going to play shows and tell my mailing list and then probably mail out to college radio across the country." I respond, "so if you are only going to do that, why do you need your CDs in various record stores across the country?" The usual response is, "because once they are in the store, people will buy them."

Why consignment?
Guess what, as much as you would like him to, God doesn't watch over people shopping for CDs and spiritually guide them or smack them on the head, to your CD in the rack out of thousands of choices. People buy CDs they have heard of. Most importantly, they are more likely to buy them on impulse.

What does this have to do with you? It has everything to do with you, especially the fourth quarter of the year. (The quarter when most CDs are sold and the stores have no credit available with distributors.) Why is this important? Because when the stores have little or no credit available, they only want to order what will sell fast. Not CDs that will hopefully sell 2 or 3 copies per month.   So with the stores coming into the time of the year when they ignore independent CDs, what do you do? Consignment!

How it works
The simplest, oldest and fastest way to get paid, form of distribution in our industry. How does it work? Simple. A store takes 5 of your CDs and places them on the shelves. When they sell, they pay you your percentage. If they don't sell, the store doesn't have to pay you. In a distribution relationship, the store has to pay the distributor in 60 days for the CD they have ordered. In most cases, they are paying for the CD before it sells!

With consignment, there's no waiting for 6 months for your distributor to send you a check for 20% of what they owe you. You stop by the store, check how many they have in the bins and most stores will pay you cash right then and there for what you have sold.

Start at home base
You don't need your CDs in all stores across the country. Live shows and the word of mouth generated by the promotion of the shows are 75% of all your sales (and aren't you going to sell your CDs at your shows?). Commercial radio airplay for an independent artist is only 9% and college radio airplay is less than 1% of your sales.

The big question is, are you really going to tour the country every month to play shows for 20 people in clubs 3,000 miles away, just because a college station in a corn field is playing it, for no money?

Use consignment first and become successful in your home market, home state, and the neighboring markets you can reach on a monthly basis. After you have sold 10,000 copies in each market, consider expanding outward.

Learn more about Tim Sweeney, TSA and his International Best Selling books, Tim Sweeney's Guide To Releasing Independent Records, Tim Sweeney's Guide To Successfully Playing Live and Tim Sweeney's Guide To Succeeding At Music Conventions by visiting, www.tsamusic.com

◆

SUCCEEDING WITHOUT A LABEL
by Bernard Baur, Music Connection Magazine
© 2006 All Rights Reserved. Used By Permission

DIY
Music Connection set out to see how realistic the independent route is, and if artists can find success on their own. We found that independent artists are very popular with music fans; and, that acts like *The Dave Matthews Band*, *Godsmack*, *Nickelback* and *The White Stripes* didn't depend on a record company to break them. They did it themselves and sold thousands of records, which naturally attracted hundreds of labels. Moreover, those who enjoyed independent success negotiated deals that were superior to the average deal most artists are offered.

To find out what it takes, MC contacted a variety of artists who took the "Do It Yourself" approach and are making it work. They are self-sufficient artists who found that they didn't need a label to live their dream. They prove that the DIY option is not only viable; it may also be the best course of action. After all, who wouldn't like to call their own shots in a market that's up for grabs?

Choosing the road less traveled
Sitting in a label president's office suite can be surreal, especially when he's explaining what an artist needs to do to get signed. The list is so long (covering a variety of areas) so, you can't help but ask, " If an artist did all of that, why the hell would they need you?"

Well, some artists don't think they need an established label at all. Award winning artist, Aimee Mann, has had three major record deals but now says, "I can't recommend signing a label deal. Why should you give them all the power? Really, it's frustrating. You think labels are supposed to sell records, but they don't always do what they're supposed to so, why deal with them?" In response, Mann formed her own company, *Super Ego Records*, and became a poster girl for DIY success thanks to her Oscar-nominated song from the film *"Magnolia"* and the 200,000 units sold of her *"Bachelor No. 2"* album. Today, she claims to be happier than she ever was at a major. "Now, I have the freedom to do what I want, when I want. And, if any mistakes are made, I get to make them myself rather than have someone make them for me."

The independent mindset
It seems simple. You don't have to be signed to release a record. In fact, if you wait to be signed it could be a very long time according to Tim Sweeney, a consultant who specializes in independent artists. He not only presents workshops on DIY, but has also written books about it. Sweeney maintains, "Less acts are being signed nowadays, and of those that do get a deal only 1-3% will make it beyond a record or two before they get dumped."

DIY avoids that scenario, but artists need to be a special breed to do it right. According to Pat McKeon, former owner of *Dr. Dream Records* and general manager at *Ranell Records*, states, "An independent artist will have to wear more than one hat. When they first start out, they'll probably be doing everything themselves, and not every artist can handle that."

It is also important to understand how much work DIY truly is. K.K. Martin, an indie artist who survived several label deals intimated, "You have to learn about the business and pay attention to it. If you can't do that, find someone you trust, or you'll never progress."

Keeping it real
If you want DIY success, you have to have realistic expectations. Nearly every artist dreams of playing The Forum or appearing on MTV. Unfortunately, that doesn't even happen to major label acts unless they have a hit and are extremely successful. Most independent artists have to set their sights a little lower. That's not to say it could never happen, because it does. But, the fact is you'd have to have fantastic connections or enjoy phenomenal success to reach that level.

"Keeping your goals realistic is essential for all independents," Moon points out. "If you don't do that, you're going to be disappointed." Moon suggests keeping it real and at a level you can achieve. "Set up small goals on a monthly, quarterly and yearly basis. Then, evaluate the results. If you reached your goals, move on – if not, figure out why."

Perhaps the greatest state of mind independent artists need is patience. Angus Richardson, of the band Brother, has known phenomenal success, selling over 150,000 records and playing almost 250 dates a year. Nevertheless, even Brother had to suck it up. " When we didn't get a quick record deal, it would have been easy to get discouraged," Richardson reveals. "But, we believed in our music, our fans and ourselves. And, the fact is," he stresses, "if you get hurt every time you're rejected in this business, you're going to have a lot of scars. Just look around at all the bands that have disappeared"

Touring is key
The most important part of the plan is playing live. Everything, including radio, promotions, distribution and marketing, should revolve around that, it's the way you sell records. Of course, you're going to need a recording, but according to Moon, it need not be up to industry standards. "Even a live recording will do," she says. "Your fans want to hear your songs, not the production."

Most artists have booked themselves before, so this area should be familiar. The difference is that you have to book gigs beyond your backyard. Sweeney suggests that artists should start by looking 2-3 hours in each direction. "That will only cost $30-40 in gas, and you should be able to make that in sales," he says. "If an act is based in Los Angeles, they can look as far as San Diego and Santa Barbara. Eventually, increase the drive time and even look at neighboring states. But, he warns, "don't try to do it all at once."

Naturally, when it comes to touring solo artists have it the easiest. Moon, Malone and Martin only occasionally bring a full band along. "It's a matter of economics as well as personal dynamics," Martin maintains. "Traveling in a van with five other guys can challenge your patience." To cut costs, Malone, who toured eight times across the country in three years, established a network of musicians he hires in each city. "That way," he says, "I only have to pay them for the gig."

Expenses on the road
If you're a real band, expenses become a concern. Tina Broad, Bother's manager, relates that their merchandise table is a critical part of their financial success. "If we didn't have product to sell we couldn't do it. Our merchandise sales (CDs and goods) have a dramatic impact on our ability to tour. Traditionally, we make 2 to 3 times more from our merchandise than we do from tour guarantees or ticket sales." Broad also advises bands to take a serious look at their hospitality riders. "Include things that you need (towels, water, food, backline, etc) so that you have fewer things to deal with, and insist on a 50% deposit so that you're not shouldering all the cash flow until the performance check clears."

Your bank
Touring, recordings, and merchandise obviously require money, and artists should be ready to dip into their own pockets. Sweeney contends that if artists aren't willing to invest in themselves, he questions how serious they are about a career. "However, if resources are severely limited, you just have to start smaller and think smarter," he says. "Find a sponsor to help with costs. Play free shows for them and put their name on your CD. " Moon suggests doing your own artwork or finding a friend who's talented. In fact, every independent artist who is successful uses a network of resources to help them defray costs.

Some, such as *Skywind*, a Minneapolis band who tours over 100 days a year and plays before 1000 or more fans, got their family and friends to loan them seed money. Bill Berry, their manager, indicates, "Everyone got paid back in just over a year. And since then," he relates, "We've been able to pick up sponsorships and lines of credit." Each band member contributes to pay off loans and, by doing this; Skywind has been able buy a van and tour three states.

The bottom line is that you're going to need a budget, so that you know what you can do. Indeed, Brother's manager, Broad advises artists to be realistic about costs. "If you don't know what your real expenses are," she informs, " you're going to be operating in a vacuum."

Art meets commerce
If you want to be an independent artist who's self-sufficient, don't deceive yourself: you are in business, and there are two parts to business – the legal side and the practical side. Legally, you must protect your interests and follow the law. Everyone agrees that you should consult with counsel when setting things up. You may need a band contract, a business license, and an assortment of other things that make you a legal entity.

On the practical side, keep accurate records of all your sales and income. Sweeney informs us that you can simply pay the tax on your sales, to obtain a verifiable record. These figures are all important if you hope to convince anyone – including a label, a distributor or a lender – to work with you. Indeed, Broad says it still makes her guts churn to think that Brother neglected to register the sales from their 2001 Summer Tour. "That was 15,000 unverifiable sales," she sighs. "We've got manufacturing records, but it's not the same."

Marketing & promotions
Mann contends that marketing and promotion is always a challenge, whether you're on a label or not. "It was my biggest cause for concern with every deal I had," she reports. "At least, now, I have the freedom and control to do it the way I want." But, when you're independent, you have to think outside the box. You cannot compete with the majors, so you have to do things differently.

McKeon points out, "All independent promotions must revolve around live gigs. That has to be your focus because it's your moneymaker. After booking gigs, you can contact press, radio and retail." Of all of them, radio is usually the most difficult, but persistence pays off.

Skywind's Berry relates that they maintained a two-year relationship with a local station before their songs were played. "We bought advertising time late at night because it's cheaper and played radio events for free. After they got to know us, they put our songs in rotation." Sweeney suggests attending station concerts and handing out free CDs. "It gets your music to their audience," he says.

Artists should also learn to cooperate with each other. Sweeney advises, "Artists should work towards a common goal, book shows together, share expenses and even buy commercial time on cable TV. Cable companies will sell 30-60 seconds for less than $100 and you can promote your act on MTV. If you run a few commercials a week before your show, you'll see tremendous results."

The distribution monster

Distribution is one of the biggest issues facing all independent artists. You need to stock your CDs wherever you play, but getting distribution isn't easy. For some artists, consignments may be the way to go. Many record stores will accept your CDs on spec and if they sell, will order more. "You might start with only 10-20 in a store, but if they move the orders will increase," Martin explains. "The only problem with consignment is that you have to keep on top of it on a regular basis."

Other artists, like Nashville songwriter, Hal Bynum, have found alternative markets. He reveals, "I've been a songwriter for 50 years, and it's still not easy to get distribution." So, Bynum created a unique package – a book and CD – that Barnes & Noble will carry. "I agreed to make in-store appearances and they agreed to promote me."

Start an organization or join one

Some artists set up their own organization. With the help of her New York manager, Michael Hausman, Aimee Mann founded *"United Musicians,"* a sort of cooperative for artists. Hausman explains, "We found that distributors don't like to work with a single artist. They want product every few months, so we set up *United Musicians* for other artists who may be in the same boat. *R.E.D.* agreed to distribute our records and we're sharing our contacts with artists."

If you're not quite to that stage yet, there are services to meet your needs. The independent network is full of companies that cater to independent artists, and one of the newest and most intriguing *is 101 Distribution*. Damon Evans, 101's executive director, describes his company as an alternative solution to traditional distribution. "We service over 2100 retail stores across the country and into Europe." Essentially, 101 take the work out of consignments. They give stores product on consignment, collect revenue and pay artists every 30 days. Their split with artists is generous (70-80% of wholesale) and they will handle promotions and marketing, unlike other distributors.

The ultimate reward

Of course, for some, whose music may not be mainstream, independence is their only choice; while for others it's by design. But, regardless of whether you're a maverick or an act still seeking a deal, the same rules apply. If you want success, you have to work for it. While DIY may be a lot of work, it can be very rewarding. "It is time consuming and takes a lot of patience but," Gilli Moon concludes, " there's nothing quite like having control over your own destiny. You can be as big or as small as you want and go at your own pace."

Ten steps to success for the independent artist

(All the artists profiled are self-sufficient. They make a living "solely" with their music. This list was compiled from their interviews.)

1. **Believe in yourself**
   You must believe in yourself. Realize that you don't need a label to be a success. Don't be egotistical, but be confident. Be optimistic – believe you are good enough and can get what you want. If you don't have faith in yourself – no one else will.

2. **Be realistic**
   Do research – Get objective opinions - Identify your market. Know that you're going to have to tour. Know when to ask for help. Accept the fact that you probably won't become a star or get on MTV, but that you can make a living playing music.

3. **Make a wish list**
   Create a Wish List – What do you ultimately want and how do you plan to get it? What are the things you need to do and how long will it take? Set reasonable goals and break your Plan into phases: 3 months – 6 months – 1 year – 3 years, etc…

4. **Know your budget**
   If you're serious about a career, you're going to have to invest in yourself. Itemize your expenses and add 20%. Approach Sponsors with a detailed plan. Negotiate deals that take care of the basics: travel, food, lodging, backline, etc… And, don't forget manufacturing and promotional costs.

5. **Take care of business**
   Remember – it is the music "business." Network as much as possible; organize a team, with each person responsible for a specific area. If you're solo, manage your time wisely. Get your own Bar Code. Seek professional advice to set up your business entities. Pay attention to licenses and tax implications. When you tour, get insurance.

6. **Market yourself**
   Think creatively. Make time for "personal appearances" before your gigs. Set up cross-promotions with radio stations, sponsors, venues, and retail stores. Make sure you have enough products to sell – both CDs and merchandise. Offer promotional contests. Play Special Events. Work your mailing list and keep in touch with your fans at least once a month.

7. **Keep records**
   Keep books that reflect income and expenses. Accurately account for sales. Register and report to SoundScan. Maintain tax records. Record your draw – note the venue/locale that draws best. Keep updating your mailing list.

8. **Adapt & adjust**
   Evaluate results: What works – What doesn't? Revise your plan and adjust your approach accordingly. Find ways to increase your fan base and make a profit. What can be done better?

9. **Keep the faith**
   No matter how hard you work, there will be frustrating times. Keep the faith and don't let it deter you. Everyone experiences setbacks. Those that persevere will prevail.

10. **Make it fun**
    If it's not fun anymore – don't do it. Reward yourself (and your team) whenever possible. Acknowledge a job well done. Take a break – enjoy life – then, get back to work.

Bernard Baur is the Review Editor & Feature Writer for Music Connection Magazine. Contact: www.musicconnection.com, Tel: 818-755-0101 Ext.519 EqxManLtd@aol.com

the music business

WHAT IS A BUSINESS PLAN AND WHY DO YOU NEED ONE

by John Stiernberg, Stiernberg Consulting
© 2006 All Rights Reserved. Used By Permission

Frequently, indie music people plunge into the music business with strong musical chops and a lot of ambition, but without a business plan. Too often the results are disappointment and burnout rather than artistic and financial success. Can business problems be anticipated and prevented? Can you learn from the business world and apply lessons without "selling out"? The answer to both questions is yes!

Why have a business plan?

You may have heard the expression "Fail to plan, plan to fail". Most businesses (music or otherwise) do not have written business plans. They may have revenue, checkbooks, and even budgets. By not having a complete business plan, you are also at risk, and may fail as a result.

Six positive reasons to construct a written plan:

1. To have financial and non-financial objectives and measurement criteria so you can track your progress along the way.

2. By describing what business you are in and how you conduct business. This allows you to identify viable business opportunities, and avoid or manage the opportunities that do not make sense for you.

3. You can lower your stress level with a plan, since you spend less time and energy worrying about whether you are doing the right thing. Your plan helps keep you grounded and calm.

4. A business plan is like a song arrangement, set list, or lesson plan. It can even act as a catalyst. It assures that everyone is playing in the same key and performing the material in the right order

5. It may be a competitive tool for success. Relatively few music people have written plans. When you do, you have an automatic edge on your competition. This helps boost your confidence as you build your competitive position in the market.

6. It is essential for securing financing. At some point in your music career, you are likely to need cash for operations or business development and beyond your revenue from your regular business. Your business plan helps you anticipate cash needs. A solid business plan is a requirement of any worthy financial institution

What is in a business plan?
A business plan is a written order of documents that gives your business and its market an outline a purpose over the course of the next several years. It describes what you are going to do, how you are going to do it, and what the consequences are. The main text is 15 to 20 pages long. It includes financial schedules, and extra material included in the reference section or appendix. If it is too long, few people will actually read and use the document. So it's best to keep it brief.

Main sections:

Chapter 1: *Description of your company, business, and industry.* This is where you talk about the music industry and your role in it.

Chapter 2: *Description of products and services.* This is where you describe what you do in detail, plus the features, benefits, and advantages of your product vs. the competition. "Products" are what you get paid for. (Examples of products include: Songwriter: original compositions, songbooks, records. The performer: repertoire, stage show, records, merchandise.)

Chapter 3: *Market overview and marketing strategy.* This is where you describe the size and growth of your target market, your promotional strategy, product distribution channels, types of performance venues, and your team. The marketing section is a "plan within a plan", and is the most important section of the whole document.

Chapter 4: *Management and organizational overview.* This section describes your business experience, history, and personnel needs. This is the place to identify key people, their job functions, and credentials. In addition to yourself, comment here on agents, managers, accountants, lawyers, or other service providers who round out your team. Future needs refers to people who will be added to the business as it grows.

Chapter 5: *Financial summary.* This section includes $ projections for sales revenue, expenses, sources and uses of working capital (cash) over a three year period. These are summarized briefly in the text of the plan, and shown in full detail in the appendix.

Note: Good business plans also include an Executive Summary. This is a one or two page document that includes the essence of the whole business plan. Executive summaries are helpful when seeking financing, especially when many people are reviewing the plan.

What if this all seems a little scary?
You may be a great performer, songwriter, teacher, salesperson, recording engineer, promoter, networker, or fan businessperson. You may find that aspects of running your business are tedious or even scary. That's OK, but it does not take away the need for a business plan.

Key points
A tried-and-true rule of time management: It's easier and less costly to do the planning on paper than to learn by trial and error. Have your business plan early in the game. A big challenge is competing for attention. Is we are continually bombarded with information, and things are unlikely to change. This points to the value of the marketing section of your business plan. *Someone* has to handle the business. If not you, find someone who will balance your strengths and weaknesses as your business grows.

The payoff
Are you (or your friend, spouse, or partner) already in the music business? Are you thinking about "turning pro"? Constructing a business plan is essential for long term success. Your business plan will guide you and help you prevent mistakes and disappointment. Once you are implementing your business plan, you'll find that you are spending more time making great music, bringing entertainment to new audiences, and making a good living doing something you love. From my standpoint, it's worth the effort!

John Stiernberg is principal consultant with Stiernberg Consulting, the Sherman Oaks, and CA-based business development firm. John has over 25 years of music industry experience including eight years as musician and agent, twelve years working for sound equipment manufacturers, and nine years as business analyst and consultant. John's book "Succeeding In Music: A Business Handbook for Performers, Songwriters, Agents, Managers, and Promoters" is published by Backbeat Books. Contact: www.succeedinginmusic.net or e-mail John at askjohn@succeedinginmusic.net

♦

10 KEY BUSINESS PRINCIPLES
by Diane Rapaport, author of "A Music Business Primer"
© Copyright, 2006, Reprinted with Permission.

Given two bands (or two businesses) that have equal talent, the one that incorporates the business principles below will often have a competitive edge.

Business principles to follow:

1. Get to know the people you work with personally. Go out of your way to meet them.

2. Make it easy to for people to associate with your business.
   - Show up for gigs and appointments on time
   - Keep promises you make
   - Phone people back in a timely manner
   - Have a positive attitude
   - Pay your bills on time. If you cannot, call people up and explain your situation.
   - Be nice to secretaries and receptionists. Often the "gatekeepers" for access to their bosses.
   - Develop long-term relationships with service vendors.
   - Key business people have few minutes to listen. State what you want succinctly and politely.
   - Say thank you. Forgive easily. Anyone can make a mistake.

3. Treat your employees courteously, pay them a fair wage, be appreciative of their good work, and when you can afford it, reward them with bonuses and other benefits. They'll repay you with loyalty and good work. Retraining a new employee costs time and money.

4. Listen to the needs of the people and businesses you work with. Find out what is important to them.

5. Do every job and every gig as though it mattered.

6. Provide value added to people you do business with. This can mean everything from playing an extra encore, having special prices for CDs for fans who buy them at gigs; sending out a free newsletter once a month; providing one free CD for every ten a customer buys; and sending favored vendors free goods.

7. Keep track of your money. Negotiate for better rates. Keep business debt to a minimum. Pay your loans on time.

8. Cultivate a good reputation. Be principled in your dealings. Leadership in ethics and good conduct will be rewarded many times over in loyalty, in people speaking well of your business, and, perhaps most importantly, of people you do business with dealing fairly and ethically with you. If you examine the histories of people who are constantly being taken advantage of or stolen from, you will almost invariably find that their business conduct invited it.

9. Good advice is invaluable, and, often freely given. Learn to invite advice. Feedback is important, even when it is negative. Receive criticism with neutrality and graciousness.

10. When you are successful, give something back to the industry that has served you. Share information with other bands. Donate time or profits to a nonprofit organization.

This article is from Diane Rapaport's book, "A Music Business Primer", published by Prentice Hall (Pearson Education). Diane Rapaport is also the author of How to Make and Sell Your Own Recording. Her company, Jerome Headlands Press, designs and produces The Musician's Business and Legal Guide; and The Acoustic Musician's Guide to Sound Reinforcement and Live Recording by Mike Sokol. Contact: jhpress@sedona.net

♦

LOOKING FOR AN AGENT
by Jeri Goldstein, author of "How to Be Your Own Booking Agent and Save Thousands of Dollars"
© 2006 All Rights Reserved. Used By Permission

You have reached that point in your career development when adding an agent to your team would be a logical next step. Before you pick up the phone and start calling around, I suggest you do the following:

Get a clear picture
Take inventory and create an overview of your career position to date. This process and information will help you present a clear picture of your career for yourself and assist you in making a more powerful pitch to any agent you are considering.

Taking inventory includes re-evaluating your past two year's growth. I would include a list of all your past performance venues, the fees you actually received, the capacity of the venue and the number of seats you sold. If you haven't been keeping track of this information, it is not too soon to begin. Along with these details, I would also list the merchandise sales you had for each venue. All of this information helps assess your growth from year to year and venue to venue especially when you play a specific venue a number of times during the year. If your numbers increase each time, there is good indication you are building a following. This is exactly the type of information a booking agent wants to know when determining whether they will invest their time and money to add you to their roster. When you present an organized evaluation of your career development to an agent along with your promotional package, you immediately set yourself above most scouting for an agent.

Define your goals
Create a set of career goals, timelines and projections. Most artists are looking for an agent to relieve them of work they dislike doing for themselves-making calls to book gigs. Look for an agent to help you raise the level of your performance dates and increase the number of dates and the performance fees. Set career goals for the types of venues you would like to play and present this to prospective agents. Determine a specific time line in which you would like to have these goals accomplished. Then based on the kind of concrete information you've gathered from your evaluation (step 1 above), you can make some realistic projections about what percentage of increase you foresee in the next two years. For example, based on last year's information, you are able to determine that your bookings, fees and merchandise will increase by 20% during the next year and 20% the year after. When you present an agent with hard numbers they can more effectively evaluate whether or not it is worth their involvement.

Research
The final step before making phone calls is to do some research. It doesn't matter how well organized you are or how talented you are, if you are calling the wrong type of agent, you are wasting your time. There are many different databases or agency listing one can review. You may need to purchase some of these directories, but it will be well worth the expense when you begin calling appropriate agencies Some resources with agency listings are: Pollstar (www.pollstar.com), The Musician's Atlas (www.MusiciansAtlas.com) and Music Review (www.musreview.com).

Some agents book specific genres music or styles of performance. When researching agencies, determine if the genre of music or the type of performance is compatible with your own. Check their roster of artists to see if you recognize anyone. There may be some acts for which you might open-when finally speaking with someone at the agency, mention that. Create a list of appropriate agencies and make sure you get the names of one or two or the head of the agency if it is a small company. If you know any acts who are working with a specific agent with whom you might be compatible, ask that act if they would mind sharing some information about their agent. You may get some insider information regarding whether or not it is a good time to make your pitch based on whom the agent just signed or if they are looking for new acts to add.

Go to conferences
Another method of researching agents is to attend booking and showcasing conferences. Agents often use these conferences to scout for new talent. Seeing acts in live performance help agents get a sense of audience reaction as well as getting a better picture of what they might potentially be selling. The other great benefit to attending booking conferences is that you can walk around the exhibit hall and meet all the agents who are representing their acts. View their booths to see who is on their roster as well as examining how the agency presents their artists with their booth display. You can get a sense of the agent's organization and creativity by the manner in which they represent the talent. Stand by and listen to the way they pitch their artists to prospective buyers.

With these three tasks under your belt, you can confidently present yourself to appropriate agencies when you feel you are ready to make a pitch. You will present a much more professional overview of your act with a clear evaluation of your past performance and a realistic projection of your future.

Jeri Goldstein is the author of, How To Be Your Own Booking Agent - A Performing Artist's Guide to a Successful Touring Career. She had been an agent and artist's manager for 20 years. Currently she consults with artists, agents, managers through her consultation program Manager-In-A-Box and presents The Performing Biz, seminars and workshops at conferences, universities, arts councils and to organizations. Her book and information about her other programs is available at www.nmtinc.com or phone 1-888-550-6827 toll free.

♦

FINDING A SPONSOR
by Bronson Herrmuth, author of "100 Miles To A Record Deal"
© 2006 All Rights Reserved. Used By Permission

Success in the music business is about separating yourself from the pack. One of the quickest and most effective ways to do this as an artist is to find sponsors. Unless you live in some unpopulated remote region of the world, then you are probably surrounded by plenty of potential sponsors for your music. Basically any individual, company or corporation doing business in your area is a possible sponsor. All it really takes is them wanting to sponsor you, and then you feeling good about promoting whatever the product is that they make, sell, or distribute. In a nutshell that is how a sponsorship works. Your sponsor "supports" you and in return you promote their product.

How does a sponsor support?
A sponsor can support you in many different ways, depending on their product and how active they are in promoting it. To give you a real-life example, my band once had a sponsorship with Budweiser through a regional distributor who we met through a club owner friend after we played his club. We were invited to this distributors warehouse where we were given T-shirts, ball caps, fancy mugs, stickers, etc., all kinds of Budweiser merchandise including several cases of their beer. They paid to have a big banner made with our logo on it, done very professionally and to our satisfaction. We would hang it up behind us whenever we performed. In one corner of the banner it said "Budweiser presents" with their logo and then our logo, much bigger and more prominent. None of this cost us a dime and being sponsored by Budweiser definitely gave us an edge up on our competition when it came time to get gigs in the clubs.

How do you find a sponsor for your music?

1. Target the businesses that actively promote their product on your local radio stations or TV, the ones that are already showing their desire and ability to promote their product effectively in your area, city or town.

2. Call or just stop by their location and meet them. Do your homework first to find out who are in charge, then make an appointment and go meet them. Chances are you may already know them if you live in a small town or city. Maybe someone you know, like a friend or a family member, already has a relationship with him or her. Use any and all connections you have to get started.

3. If they run radio spots and you have original music already professionally recorded, see if they are open to using your music for the background music "bed" in their radio promotions.

4. If you are a songwriter, write them a song. This can be tremendously effective as a starting point to approaching a potential sponsor. Walk in and play them a song you wrote about them and their product.

5. Car dealerships are great places to start looking. Many bands are riding down the road right now in a vehicle that was provided by their sponsor. Good chance that there name or logo is professionally painted on that vehicle too, along with their sponsor's. Car dealerships also do lots of promotions and events where they have live music for their customers. Even if you approach them for a sponsorship and they decline, making them aware of you and your music can turn into some great paying gigs on a consistent, long-term basis.

6. Radio stations can be awesome sponsors. Many radio stations produce and promote concerts and in most cases use local or area talent to open these concerts, not to mention all the free radio exposure you can get if they sponsor you, or even if they just like you. If you have a record out, having a radio station for a sponsor can really help you get exposed in your immediate area quickly. Approach the ones that play your style of music.

Bronson Herrmuth is author of the new book "100 Miles To A Record Deal". For more details please visit him @ www.iowahomegrown.com, or www.songrepair.com

getting music into film and televsion

GETTING YOUR MUSIC INTO FILM
by Scooter Johnson, Musician/Actor
© 2006 All Rights Reserved. Used By Permission.

As more and more music is being made available online for different uses, it is natural for production people to turn to the Internet to find music. Why? Because you can buy anything on the internet! Savvy bands are spending time on film bulletin boards offering up their music for soundtrack use, indie labels are offering licensing options on their websites and composers are banding together and starting their own online write-for-hire agencies. If you or your band mates don't have the time, effort or expertise to find soundtrack opportunities and successfully pitch your music, there are avenues for you.

Who to trust
I'm on movie sets a lot and I can tell you how hard it is to approach the music supervisor or the producer with a CD. They may love it, or I may lose my job. Not wanting to jeopardize my finances I've found a few online companies that specialize in indie music licensing and are non-exclusive (which means you can join as many as you want). Before signing with any company, remember you are entering into a business relationship that involves your work, and payment for the use of that work.

Contracts
The licensing company should have a legal contract that requires the signatures of the owners or the authors/composers of the music sent in. If the company is legit they will want to protect themselves from frauds that will send in other people's music and profit from it. There is also the final license contract with the filmmakers or whomever to peruse - is it for a Master/Sync license, or just a Sync license? (www.ascap.com, www.bmi.com or www.socan.com can define these terms if you are not familiar with the industry jargon).

Fees
The contract should also state very clearly the fees (monthly? yearly? by the byte?) involved and how future-licensing income would be split between you and they, and how often you will be paid.

Pre-cleared or restricted
Ask about whether the tracks are required to be pre-cleared or if you can request restrictions. Some companies have a standard restriction that reads something like 'this track cannot be used on scenes depicting racism, pornography, use of tobacco, alcohol or drugs'. Requesting a restriction will obviously limit the amount of interest your music garners and ultimately the pay-out. Personally I don't care if a European sausage company wants to use my music on a television commercial - I'm an indie musician who can barely pay the rent. Who is going to blame me for taking the money? I'll take that money and invest it in my band's future.

Where to start
Start where you begin all your other research - on your favorite search engine (www.google.com is huge). If you want to go the total DIY personal route based on your location, use your city name and keywords like 'film production', 'indie movies', 'production companies', 'music wanted' etc. Most cities, states and provinces have film associations and unions that keep track of local shoots and list them on their websites with contact information. Be prepared to be your own sales agent - you will have to send each of the interested parties a pitch package (some require two - one for the director and one for the music supervisor). Diligently follow-up, negotiate your terms, and if needed, hire a lawyer to proof your contract.

Licensing agencies
If you are willing to let go of a lot of control, a full-service online licensing agency like *Realia Music Inc.* (www.realiamusic.com) may be worth looking into. One of the larger agencies online, their online catalogue consists of indie music from around the world, and it's pre-cleared and priced by a sliding scale that caps at $5,000/world-wide usage. They have restrictions available but only a special case basis (pre-existing contracts between musicians and other parties - I asked) and provide a one-stop service for people who have limited budgets, tight schedules and credit cards. They have a one-time $5 membership fee and a $1/song submission fee, 50/50 license split and a $2/song shipping fee for songs licensed. Your songs are represented for as long as you wish and if you get an exclusive deal with a publishing company or label, they promise they will remove your songs within 24 hours.

If you have a good idea of what your music is worth and prefer to wrangle your deals yourself try SongCatalog Inc. (www.songcatalog.com). Their system provides a virtual middleman for your negotiations. You submit as many tracks as you wish for placement in their online 'Active List' or in the 'Vault' and pay per track. Fees are billed monthly and start at $4.95 for up to 25 audio files stored in the 'Vault' and $9.95 for up to 25 songs featured on the 'Exchange' (site search engine) and increase by smaller increments every 50/100/200 songs registered. There are different levels of search capabilities that have a separate fee rate but you can check out there website for more details. People who wish to license music register at no cost, are able to browse the catalogue and when a suitable track is located, they send an email, through the website, to the owner who then responds. Dialogue and negotiations ensue. You are ultimately responsible for finalizing your deal.

Smaller Companies
I would advise to check out the smaller companies, they appear to have more staying power than the large online music companies (licensemusic.com - one of the first and definitely the largest - shut down business abruptly months ago and is currently being auctioned off on the

internet through a bankruptcy trustee). Many have forayed into licensing but the complicated traditional licensing system (long protracted negotiations, complicated territorial and usage structures, clearances, exorbitant fees, favored nations, and script/scene approval) has not translated well online. There was no immediacy, no click through satisfaction that everyone has come to expect from the web. Once the costs of software development, technical support, hosting fees and high-priced management were factored in the license fees were unaffordable and potential buyers were back in the nightclubs chatting up bands after their sets.

Be realistic

Online there is a market for indie music, even if the band has broken up, doesn't tour, is brand new or not commercially friendly. It requires very little work to register. You fill in an application, get the appropriate signatures, mail it in and wait for the money to arrive. It is the agency's business to market their catalogue, provide customer service and bring new buyers in.

With record labels setting their standards higher and higher for new signings, showing up with a portfolio of licensed tracks in your package just might be the wedge you need to get in the door. It really doesn't matter where the track was used or for what product. The fact that your music can be sold for hard cash is the attractive quality they are looking for.

Always remember to be realistic with your expectations. Make sure to tell everyone that you have a 'licensing agency' (it does sound impressive and looks even better on your bio). There are hundreds of thousands of bands in the world with at least one album under their belts. As an indie musician with an indie agency, your music will be marketed to projects without a great deal of exposure attached to them. Focus will usually be on the catalogue not the individual bands. There are fees to consider, and it is a relatively new industry - it may take years for it to take off and compete with traditional processes.

Scooter Johnson spent 5 years touring Canada with his Hillbilly band The Hard Rock Miners and has created 5 internationally distributed albums. His search for fame and immortality has almost been concluded and it is time to pass on his knowledge to the next generation of seekers after the flame. Contact: deadcat@shaw.ca

♦

USING INDEPENDENT FILM AS A TECHNIQUE FOR MORE EXPOSURE

By Ryan Vinson, Founder of VersusMedia
© 2006, Ryan Vinson. All Rights Reserved. Used By Permission.

When it comes to independently made films, the first thing to remember is that they will rarely make you rich or famous. The key is to look at these films as career stepping stones, and as a unique chance to gain exposure.

Independent filmmakers are in many ways like independent musicians - they are simply trying to get their craft in front of an audience without completely going broke. Keeping this in mind, don't take it as a slap in the face if a filmmaker does not offer you money to use your song in their film. They may not have the means to pay you. To compensate for the non payment, make sure to ask for a guaranteed credit at the end of the film and for exposure on the film's website.

Film profit percentage points are something else to consider. If the film does end up being purchased, you will then make money on the backend of the deal.

Where to look for opportunities

The most obvious place to look first is your immediate surroundings.

With the explosion of video technology, there are probably just as many individuals making low budget independent films today as there are garage bands. Consider attending any film festivals that take place within a few hours of your home. You are sure to run into a number of fledgling filmmakers who are there looking for ideas. While you're there, pass out flyers, business cards, and CDs if you have them.

Another place to consider is your local college. Get in touch with the instructors of the film department. Post flyers up in that sections of the college. While some smaller community colleges do not have a film program, they should at least have a program in broadcasting and journalism. It would be a good idea to visit this area as well.

Drop by your local television station. They use various forms of music cuts throughout their segments. This can also be held true for Public Access and college shows.

In the modern age, an obvious choice is the Internet. Use search engines to scour for websites of future productions. Join discussion lists dedicated to independent filmmakers. Consider joining amazing organizations like IFP, who strongly support independent films. IFP offers seminars, events and more.

One of the fastest growing online film communities is the much-disputed world of fan films. These are films that are based on copyrighted bodies of work (such as Star Wars, Star Trek, Batman, etc.) and by law can never actually make money. The truly amazing aspect of these films though is that many of them are being made with the same level of care and production as other types of independent films. They are being made by individuals who have learned to make movies through school or on their own. Some fan film communities have grown so large, such as Star Trek New Voyages (www.newvoyages.com), that their website has nearly crashed when a new episode has been made available to download.

Another area quickly gaining steam is the world of videocasting. This is the inevitable next step beyond podcasting, which is limited to just audio casts. Groups of tech savvy people have taken this underground phenomenon, and are quickly making it a mainstream source for news, sitcoms, etc. Videocasting allows filmmakers to make their own short sitcoms, and make them available for download from their website.

Grow with your film collaborator

You may be wondering why you should bother contacting students at universities. The fact is that many of these filmmakers will continue with their passion for film making well after college. Some of the film industry's most notable names used their graduate thesis film to launch their careers. Helping a filmmaker early on can lead to a strong friendship, which can carry far into a both careers.

This applies to filmmakers making fan films too. They may be making low budgeted knock-offs, but they are still honing their production skills as a filmmaker. You never know where a relationship will lead to.

Something else to consider is that if you play live, getting these filmmakers on your side can potentially help your fan base grow through their word of mouth.

Giving them the legal rights to use your music

It is always a good idea to secure your songs with some kind of an agreement. With extremely low budget independent films, such as fan or student films, you can create a simple agreement that merely allows them to use your song for fun. These are usually known as "short form contracts". This contract will simply allow the filmmaker to use your song. If the film starts to generate a lot of interest, you can come back and sign a true agreement.

If you are positive the film will never make any money, such as the case with fan films, you could even just verbally "allow" them to use your song. If they use your song, then there is chance that you'll gain some degree of exposure. Then later, if the film does make money, it's still your property, and you have the right to request a fee and a valid contract.

If you are positive that the film is being made to be sold, then create a valid contract right from the beginning. This lets the filmmaker know that you want to see their film succeed as much as they do. It also creates a unique bond, that will help your chances to get your music into their next project, which will hopefully have a larger budget.

Exposure lasts longer

When it comes to independent films, it's more important to take the risk, than it is to be legally and financially secure. You never know who will see this low budget film. Remember to look at the bigger picture. Focus on the potential exposure and how it may help your career in the long run.

Ryan Vinson is the founder of VersusMedia, a unique entertainment company which connects thousands of filmmakers and musicians worldwide, having assisted over 700 films to date, and offers internationally accepted Digital film contracts that can be signed online. For more info visit VersusMedia at www.versusmedia.com

motivational articles

DEALING WITH REJECTION IN THE MUSIC BUSINESS

By Suzanne Glass, CEO Indie-Music.com
© 2006 All Rights Reserved. Used By Permission

Being a musician, by and large, is a rewarding thing. We get to indulge our muse, spend time with other artistic types, and hear a lot of great sounds. When it comes to jobs, being a musician is great work if you can get it. Unfortunately, it's not all roses. The tremendous amount of competition makes it likely that we will sometimes lose a gig, get fired from a band, or be turned down for a songwriting award. Most of us handle the rejections pretty well most of the time. However, problems can start to occur if you have a run of too many rejections in too short a time. Musicians may begin to doubt their talent, commitment, and even sanity when repeatedly slapped with "no's".

Tips to help you through the hard times:

1. Believe in your music and yourself. People tell you this all the time, and you need to take it seriously. Many mega-hit songs were repeatedly rejected before someone decided to release them to become #1 hits. Believe that your talent is unique, and continue to pursue your own musical path.

2. If you hear the same type of rejection often, ("You need to pick up your choruses" or "Work on your pitch"), you may want to look into the criticism. Having an open mind may help you improve your craft.

3. If you get down on music, take some time out. Go to the beach, the mountains, or your backyard, and do something enjoyable that has nothing to do with music.

4. Give yourself the freedom to quit. This may sound contradictory, though by giving you a mental "out", it can help diffuse the pressure when nothing is going right. Chances are you won't quit, but you will know you have a choice.

5. Go jam with some musician friends who do it just for fun, and forget the business. People who strictly do music as a hobby sometimes have a positive energy that will help your jaded, negative energy slip away, and bring you back to the joy of playing music.

6. If you are in a situation where you can't find a band to jam with, and have excess creative energy, consider another type of art or craft. Doing something creative, even though it's not music, will keep your creative juices flowing. Painting, carving, candle making - activities like these may also open your creative flow and inspire you musically.

7. If the problem is due to a conflict in your band, talk it out honestly with the people involved instead of keeping it to yourself and becoming cynical. Conflicts are common in bands (and every other kind of group), and surviving them means the difference between success and failure, since most bands will break up if the unresolved conflicts are not addressed. It will NOT be a pleasant experience.

8. Write a song about it. Who knows, it might be a masterpiece.

9. Think back on all your successes and good times in music, and focus on that energy. Try to balance the current bad times by realizing it's all part of the flow.

10. If you can't kick the down feelings in a few weeks, don't hesitate to talk to your doctor. Artists are known to have high rates of depression and stress-related illnesses, and today there are many new treatments. Make sure you follow a healthy diet and get some exercise.

Getting through those periods when "music sucks" is an experience all musicians have been through at one time or another. Those that master the down times go on to have productive musical careers. Those that get bogged down in the problems and become bitter are doomed to less happy - and maybe less musical - futures.

Suzanne Glass is the founder of Indie-Music.com, one of the Internet's premier musician websites. The company offers thousands of resources and contacts to achieve success in the music industry, including venues, labels, radio, media, studios, and band listings, plus articles, interviews, and reviews of indie music. Contact: www.indie-music.com

THE PROCESS AND POWER OF PERSISTENCE

by Brian Austin Whitney, Founder of the Just Plain Folks Music Organization
© 2006 All Rights Reserved. Used By Permission

If you speak with successful people in nearly any business, especially those with an artistic bent, one common factor you'll find among nearly all of them is that they were persistent. Whether it was in the face of competition, lack of understanding or acceptance among their peers, or their family asking when they were going to get a day job, those who persist through the ups and downs seem to last the longest and do the best. There is more than just relentlessness to that formula. While being persistent, you need to evolve and develop while staying focused on your goals. To do this you will need a plan in order to progress.

Guide markers to help you along the way:

1. Keep Learning.
One of the things that persistence offers is an ongoing education. You learn by doing and you learn by trial and error. You also learn by reading books and taking advantage of various resources surrounding the music community. But you have to keep doing it. It never stops and you never know everything there is, and even if you did, it changes.

2. Keep making friends.
It really is about whom you know and how well they like you. Sure talent matters, but there is a lot of talent out there. Being friends with the right people is always the tiebreaker, and in a business filled with so many worthy talents, you need the tiebreaker on your side. But that doesn't just mean the well-known stars and the already successful industry figures. In fact, the most important friends you can make are those who are also on their way up or are developing their own network of connections. One of my most important music industry allies is someone I met when I was 22 and he was 15 and we played in a band together in a small town in the middle of nowhere Indiana. Now I run the one of the world's largest music organizations and he is a key player with Virgin's Internet Radio Division. You can never have too many friends and one enemy often turns out to be one too many.

3. Be sincere and honest.
Don't exaggerate your skills. Don't falsely praise other's either. Find your real strengths and emphasize those. Admit those things you need help with and do the same for your peers. It's an old cliché, but if you always tell the truth, you never have to remember your lies. If you are always sincere, people will support you even when you make a mistake or are wrong. And if you DO make a mistake, the quicker you admit it and take full responsibility for it, the quicker others will forgive and forget and in some cases rally to your side to help. Denial of the truth is the biggest downfall of politicians and one of the biggest weaknesses an artist can possess. The best artists are those who are the most honest in both their business and their art.

4. Reinvent yourself.
Few, if any of us get it right the first time. As we mature as artists or performers, we need to take that new knowledge and allow it to adjust the way we write or perform. Being persistent doesn't mean being rigid and unchanging. It means constant motion forward. Traveling to a destination is never a completely straight line. Your style, technique, presentation and approach shouldn't try to be a straight line either.

5. Create your art for yourself, market it for everyone else.
Some artists will insist that your art should only concern yourself, and no one else. This is partially true. But it is also partially deadly to your long-term career. You SHOULD create the art that is true to yourself, true to your vision and true to your heart. But once you bring it to life, you must

shift gears and concern yourself with everyone else. Find out who your audience is, what they want and how you can market your art to them. Are you mainstream? Are you part of a small niche? Learn who you are through the eyes of your potential audience and plan your marketing accordingly. This means lose the attitude about being in a genre or sounding like another artist. Being able to categorize yourself and your music makes it easier for your audience to buy your music, see your show, and become your fan. And that is what it needs to be about. Your job is to remove any barrier between you and the music consuming public at large on their terms, not yours.

6. **Help others along the way.**
Small-minded people think they can succeed by the failures of their peers. Good business people understand that a strong peer makes for a larger and more vigorous market for your work as well. Retailers often build near similar rivals so that customers get used to going to a particular shopping area to buy that product. They use the marketing efforts of their competitors to bring people within their grasp. The same holds true with musicians. If there are bands with similar fan bases and niches as you, it is always in your best interest to work with them and share the limelight and double the spotlight that your combined efforts will bring on the music you all make. Help your fellow bands get gigs. Not only will they return the favor but the music fan base will begin to expect more live music and will start associating all the cooperative bands with the others, and will begin to support all of you instead of just one of you.

7. **Get out of your basement and into your community.**
Even if you are a solo writer who doesn't perform, get out into your community and participate. See other bands. Attend area songwriter and music organization meetings. Spend a few hours at the local music store and get to know the people working there (they are usually the most in touch with who is active in your community musically). Get to know the people at the local recording studios and ask if you can watch some recording sessions now and then. Being out in your community not only networks you with others but it will keep you up on the area industry gossip and goings on. It will also keep you hip to trends and styles and what is working for some and not working for others.

8. **Seize the day.**
Make positive progress every single day. Even if that progress is tiny. If you are performing, *always* give it your best, even if you are performing for 3 people at an open stage at 1 AM. If you are a performer, then treat every performance as if it is *the* pivotal one. Treat every audience member as if THEY hold the key to the rest of your career. If you do that, one day they will. Industry people and those they know come in all shapes and sizes. Never underestimate the impact a great performance by you will have on any audience. Also, never assume that a small opportunity isn't worthy of your best effort. You are creating music because you love it, so give it your all.

9. **Perform every chance you get. Co-Write every chance you get.**
If you are a writer or performer, you probably feel the need and desire to do it at every chance. If you don't feel this desire, it might not be the right career path after all. If you do, it's possible that you can never get your fill of it and struggle to find opportunities, especially if you don't have a band, don't know other writers and so on. Getting out there also means sitting in with others at open stages, singing back up, or playing an instrument for other bands. The same goes for writing. If you hear something interesting by a local writer, suggest co-writing. Challenge yourself to write with folks who write differently or within another genre completely. Stretch your artistic perspective, by performing with different artists doing different types of music. This will only improve your chops, not to mention expose you to a larger audience.

10. **Always remember, the persistent journey IS the thing. Not the destination.**
Your life isn't about the destination. The same is true for your musical life. It is all about your development, your successes and failures, and all the things you do along the way. From the people you will meet, the songs you write and pure joy of the creative effort enjoy it all and learn from it. Succeed on your terms. The journey begins with our first creative step forward and keeps going until we let it.

Sometimes reaching a goal earlier than planned is a great achievement as it shows you have worked hard, pushed ahead and made it happen. However, sometimes reaching a goal far past your original deadline is an even greater achievement. This shows you persisted and never gave up, due to adversity, deficit, criticism and those little life detours that end many dreams and goals. In many ways, this is a reason for even more pride!

Brian Austin Whitney is the Founder of the Just Plain Folks Music Organization, which is one of the largest groups of artists, writers and industry professionals in the world. To become a member, or learn more about all the organization has to offer, visit their website at www.jpfolks.com

♦

BABY STEPS AND THE ROAD TO SUCCESS
By Chris Standring, A&R Online
© 2006 All Rights Reserved. Used By Permission

"If you can achieve one successful thing a day to help your music career on the right path then you are on the right track".

It's very easy to sit at home and get frustrated with the apparent lack of forward movement in your music career. Especially when you know in your heart that you have what it takes to succeed. It's very easy to get discouraged, for the simple reason that it seems "you are only as good as your last event". Musicians and actors are similar in that we like the highs that our performances give us. We thrive on the exhilaration. It's like a drug. When it goes away we want it again.

All about perception
Gearing up to a live event is exciting. We can talk it up to friends and fans, promote it the best way we know how and enjoy the thrill of the performance itself. Then it is over and there may be a lull between events. It can seem like your career is going nowhere. It's very easy to feel that. However, other people's perception may be entirely different and probably is.

The music business is all about perception. It is based on hype and salesmanship ability. I wish it was different but it is not and will never ever be. If your band is perceived to be doing well then people will talk. If your band is perceived to be on the way out then people will also talk. If your band is doing nothing, nobody will talk! It is therefore extremely important that you keep the hype factor up. This is one of the things you need to be focusing on between events. Sit back and think about what you clearly have achieved so far in your career. Think about the things that were absolutely in your control.

Take baby steps
We are constantly bombarded with new creative marketing ideas, most of them excellent, inventive and effective. However, the ideas that you personally will primarily adopt are those ideas that you are totally comfortable with. These are the things that you will make a priority. It's too easy to get overwhelmed with new promotional ideas so we put them off and resort to the things we know we can do. I have two words to give you. BABY STEPS.

How not to get overwhelmed
It's just too damn hard to do every new promotional idea to get your band to the next level at the same time. This is especially true, if you don't have a team of people working with you. Start by doing just one thing today. If you can achieve one successful thing a day to help your music career on the right path then you are on the right track. So the key is to pick one thing, and do it today!

Increase your fan-base
The only way you can get successful as an independent artist is by letting people know you exist. So ask yourself for example, "What can I do today to expand my fan-base?" Well, there are infinite possibilities. Let's say you want to increase your e-mail database. Think about the most effective ways you can do that. The most effective ways to build a database, (but more importantly get those people to be fans and come to

shows), is to personally get to know them. So start with friends, have them refer their friends, and so on. Hand out flyers and sample CD's or tapes to everyone you know. (Make sure you have a good stack in your car.) Grab business cards of all the people you meet and get their e-mail addresses. Send them a very personal e-mail asking them if they would be interested to know about your band.

An overview:

Be creative, DO something that you know you can personally do, to expand other people's awareness of you. It takes a good amount of time but you can help yourself by really being active and productive.

Read everything you can about promoting your own shows and do the things that you are most comfortable doing, the things that you know you can be effective at. Then, step out and try something new.

Do one thing a day to help get to where you want to be, and at the end of each week think about what you have achieved. There is nothing that fuels drive, more than drive itself. There's nothing that fuels lethargy more than sitting at home wishing you were successful and doing little about it!

It can be extremely overwhelming when there seems such a long way to go. So take it one step at a time. That's all truly successful people ever did.

Chris Standring is the CEO and founder of A&R Online www.aandronline.com). He is also a contemporary jazz guitarist presently signed to Mesa/Bluemoon Records. The music is marketed at NAC and Urban AC radio. For more info visit Chris @ www.chrisstandring.com

♦

SO HOW DO WE MAKE OUR DREAM BECOME REALITY?

by Janet Fisher, Director of Goodnight Kiss Music
© 2006, All Rights Reserved. Used By Permission

Define the dream
What is it you are actually trying to do? Be the world's best writer? Become a megastar performer? Lead the church choir? Own a record label that records other acts? You would not believe how many writer/artists come to me, saying they just want to do "something" in the Music Industry. Sorry, you have to specialize a bit more than that!

Sit down with paper and pen. Define EXACTLY what it is in your heart that you dream of. (Hint, the bigger the dream, the harder to achieve... but as long as you are prepared to give what it takes, you'll find a place in the scheme of things.

Research the dream
Let's say you decided that you want to be a great writer, who is successfully cut on the charts, and makes a lot of money. Do you know what the real charts are? Who's on them currently? What labels are consistently charted? What are the styles of the top ten successes been in the last two years?

Do you know what the actual elements of a great standard song are? Can you name the top sellers of all time in your genre, or the top sellers of the current year? How did they attain success? Do you hone your skills and knowledge whenever you have a chance? Can you make the presentation of your art a commercial reality? Not just WILL you, CAN you?

Practice the dream
Go do 150 sit ups without practice. Go write a great song without practice. You have to practice (i.e., actually write) everyday, just like you would with any improvement program. If the newest song you are showing is old, you are not competing as a writer.

Rewrite the dream
If something doesn't go the exact direction you thought it should have, rewrite the situation. If it's the song that has flaws, rewrite it until they are gone. If it's the voice, get some training.

If it's the gig, create one that works for you (when I was playing gigs in KCMO, I went to the Plaza, to nice places that DIDN'T have entertainment. I'd offer the owner a free evening of music, if he liked it, I'd work X amount of weekends for X amount per night. I almost always got the gig, partly because I was prepared, partly because few can resist something for nothing and not sense some obligatory return. (Most wanted entertainment, but had no idea they could afford it. For me, it was a way to go).

If you find that you thought you wanted the big dream, but then you realize that your dream didn't include all the nonsense that goes along with one of those in exchange for your "other dream(s)", (perhaps your family or job?), it is TOTALLY alright to adapt your dreams to accommodate each other. Unfortunately, some dreams require 24 hour dedication to maintain (ask any professional who is a megastar in their field.)

Pursue the dream
Don't give up. That's the first thing anyone successful who is giving advice says, so it MUST be true. Take advantage of all opportunities, work, work, and work at it!

Live the dream
Remember that each time you sing, play, write, perform, discuss, pitch, etc., you are creating a reality that supports your dream. Don't forget to applaud the little steps, as well as the big. You write a birthday song for your sister-in-law, and it makes her cry with your kindness. Your song is used in a campaign for adoption, and though it didn't earn a dime, it was perfect, and said so much to so many. A peer complimented your writing at a recent song pitch. You were the hit of the community musical. It all matters. All these things make us more professional, and give us the reasons for doing the work. They are as important as the royalties, and enrich our life of music. Don't overlook them.

Appreciate your dream
Did you know that most of your little steps are someone else's big dream? Some people would give a great deal to have the opportunity to perform ONE karaoke song in front of an audience, or have anyone use a song for any reason. Appreciate the skills and opportunities you have been blessed with, and that you might even *have* a dream.

Janet Fisher is Managing Director of Goodnight Kiss Music (BMI) www.goodnightkiss.com, along with its sister company, Scene Stealer Music (ASCAP). Both are Music Publishers dedicated to supplying the Entertainment Industries with perfect material for any musical need. Janet is also an author in, and the editor of "Music horror Stories", a collection of gruesome, true tales as told by innocent victims seeking a career in the music business". Contact: janet@goodnightkiss.com

Sign up for
The Indie Contact Newsletter
www.indiebible.com

NOW - reduced pricing... EVEN MORE Radio & XM Satellite exposure, free website and a NO-OBLIGATION FREE CD just for inquiring!

You've probably already heard about the best place to manufacture your disc

So c'mon — give us a call!

You've more than likely already heard—from your fellow musicians, the BBB, and independent reviewers—that Oasis offers the most reliable and innovative CD and DVD manufacturing and marketing services.

So isn't it time for you to give us a call?

We think it is—if you've put your heart and soul into your project. And you want the discs and packaging you send out into the world to truly reflect (or even improve upon) your original vision. And you need help with the crucial task of getting people out there to actually <u>hear</u> your music.

Because if that describes your situation, may we suggest what it calls for?

It calls for Oasis.

:OASIS:
CD MANUFACTURING

web oasisCD.com
tel (888) 296-2747, (540) 987-8810
email info@oasisCD.com

BBB — Oasis is the only national disc manufacturing company certified by both The Better Business Bureau and BBBonline.

Yes, your free disc will be a real CD. It just looks like a classic vinyl record! It uses black polycarbonate and actual grooved surfacing technology!

FREE MONEY-MAKING CD:
"How to Have a Successful CD Release Party...Without Breaking the Bank!"

Just call **(888)296-2747** or visit **oasisCD.com/freeCD** and enter code **IB**
(And if you want a free full-color catalog we'll throw that in too!)

INCLUDED WITH YOUR CD or DVD PROJECT—THE OASIS TOP™ TOOLS OF PROMOTION:

Your Music on an OasisSampler™ Distributed to Radio Nationwide	XM Satellite Radio Airplay	Galaris/Oasis CD-ROM with 14,000+ Music Industry Contacts	Distribution for your CD/DVD: iTunes Music Store amazon.com cdbaby.com TOWER.COM BORDERS.com Waldenbooks.com	A **Full Year** of Electronic Press Kit® Service and Exclusive Live Performance Opportunities: sonicbids	SoundScan®, Music-Career Software, Retail Cases, Barcodes	**FREE** Website with the features musicians need! 6 months free, no obligation!

The Indie Bible – 7th Edition